THE OXFORD

JEWISH DAILY
LIFE IN ROMAN
PALESTINE

In memory of my mother, Frieda Marianne Löbach, née Ackermann,
27.1.1932 – 19.12.2019
May her memory be for a blessing

Catherine Hezser is Professor of Jewish Studies at the School of Oriental and African Studies, University of London.

Since Samuel Krauss's *Talmudische Archäologie* was published in German over one hundred years ago, the study of ancient Jewish daily life has progressed tremendously: critical approaches informed by the social sciences are applied to rabbinic texts and archaeologists have increasingly become interested in investigating the life of ordinary people. Historians of Judaism in the Land of Israel have become aware of the significance of the Graeco-Roman context for properly understanding Jewish culture and practises. *The Oxford Handbook of Jewish Daily Life in Roman Palestine* provides the first comprehensive and up-to-date survey of scholarship on this subject. Written by a team of internationally renowned scholars from different academic disciplines (Jewish Studies, Ancient History, Archaeology, New Testament studies), the chapters introduce the reader to the current state of research on ancient Jewish everyday life. They critically assess the various methodological approaches to daily life and, on that basis, provide guidelines and directions for future scholarship. Ranging from subjects such as clothing and domestic architecture to food and meals, labour and trade, and leisure-time activities, this volume covers the major themes of Jewish daily life in Roman times in an encompassing yet accessible way. The detailed bibliographies allow the readers to further engage with the topics introduced here. The Handbook will prove to be an indispensable reference work and tool for all students and scholars of ancient Judaism, rabbinic literature, Roman provincial history and culture, and ancient Christianity.

THE OXFORD HANDBOOK OF

JEWISH DAILY LIFE IN ROMAN PALESTINE

Edited by

CATHERINE HEZSER

OXFORD

UNIVERSITY PRESS

OXFORD
UNIVERSITY PRESS

Great Clarendon Street, Oxford, OX2 6DP,
United Kingdom

Oxford University Press is a department of the University of Oxford.
It furthers the University's objective of excellence in research, scholarship,
and education by publishing worldwide. Oxford is a registered trade mark of
Oxford University Press in the UK and in certain other countries

© Oxford University Press 2010

The moral rights of the authors have been asserted

First published 2010
First published in paperback 2020

Published in the United States of America by Oxford University Press
198 Madison Avenue, New York, NY 10016, United States of America

British Library Cataloguing in Publication Data
Data available

Library of Congress Cataloging in Publication Data
Data available

ISBN 978–0–19–921643–7 (Hbk.)
ISBN 978–0–19–885602–3 (Pbk.)

PREFACE

·······························

THE idea for this Handbook was born during my conversations with Yaron Eliav and Zeev Weiss during the last five years, when we considered the creation of a new version of Samuel Krauss' multi-volume *Talmudische Archäologie*. Such a new version remains a task of gargantuan proportions that will perhaps be accomplished by scholars in the future. In the meantime, this Handbook is meant to fill the gap, and to provide scholars and students with up-to-date surveys and tools for the study of the various areas of ancient Jewish daily life.

A Handbook is always a joint undertaking, and a collaboration of the contributors, the editor, and the publisher. Since so many different people are involved, the production of such volumes usually takes longer than anticipated, as was also the case with this work. I would like to take this opportunity to especially thank all those who submitted their chapters in time. Yitzhar Hirschfeld, who had agreed to write the chapter on domestic architecture, died shortly after he had signed the contract. May his memory be for a blessing. Special praise is due to those who stepped in at short notice to fill the gaps left by those who could not deliver, or whose submissions did not fit the Handbook's programme.

I would like to express my gratitude to all those colleagues who submitted images and copyright declarations with their texts. I owe special thanks to David Milson who was able to draw a map of Roman Palestine in the shortest of time, and to Uzi Leibner who provided the cover image for this volume from one of his recent excavations.

I am grateful to the Memorial Foundation for Jewish Culture whose grant allowed me to dedicate time to the planning of the Handbook and to do research in Israel. Special thanks are also due to the staff of the Classics and Ancient History Department of Oxford University Press who accompanied this volume.

Catherine Hezser

CONTENTS

List of Figures and Maps   x

List of Abbreviations   xiii

List of Contributors   xiv

Map of Roman Palestine   xvii

Introduction   1

PART I METHODOLOGICAL ISSUES

1. Correlating Literary, Epigraphic, and Archaeological Sources   9
   CATHERINE HEZSER

2. The Graeco-Roman Context of Jewish Daily Life in
   Roman Palestine   28
   CATHERINE HEZSER

3. Gender Issues and Daily Life   48
   TAL ILAN

PART II LIFE IN A ROMAN PROVINCE

4. The Roman Provincial Administration   71
   RUDOLF HAENSCH

5. Courts and the Judicial System   85
   JILL HARRIES

6. Population Structure and Jewish Identity   102
   DAVID GOODBLATT

7. The Languages of Roman Palestine   122
   WILLEM SMELIK

PART III   CITY AND COUNTRYSIDE

8. Infrastructure   145
   BENJAMIN ISAAC

9. Urbanization   165
   JÜRGEN K. ZANGENBERG AND DIANNE VAN DE ZANDE

10. Village and Countryside   189
    ANN E. KILLEBREW

11. Travel and Mobility   210
    CATHERINE HEZSER

PART IV   LABOUR AND TRADE

12. The Household Economy   229
    ALEXEI SIVERTSEV

13. Agriculture and Farming   246
    ZEEV SAFRAI

14. Arts and Crafts, Manufacture and Production   264
    UZI LEIBNER

15. Trade, Commerce, and Consumption   297
    JACK PASTOR

16. Poverty and Charity   308
    GILDAS HAMEL

PART V   FAMILY LIFE

17. The Different Life-Stages: From Childhood to Old Age   327
    JONATHAN SCHOFER

18. Marriage and Divorce   344
    MICHAEL L. SATLOW

19. Clothing   362
    DAFNA SHLEZINGER-KATSMAN

20. Jewellery: The Literary Evidence   382
    TZIONA GROSSMARK

21. Jewellery: The Archaeological Evidence   393
    KATHARINA GALOR

22. Food, Eating, and Meals   403
    DAVID KRAEMER

23. Domestic Architecture   420
    KATHARINA GALOR

24. Death, Burial, and Afterlife   440
    STEVEN FINE

PART VI EDUCATION AND LITERACY

25. Private and Public Education   465
    CATHERINE HEZSER

26. Orality and Writing   482
    CAROL BAKHOS

PART VII RELIGION AND MAGIC

27. The Impact of Paganism and Christianity   503
    GÜNTER STEMBERGER

28. The Synagogue   521
    LEE I. LEVINE

29. Prayer and Liturgy   545
    STEFAN C. REIF

30. Sabbath and Festivals   566
    LUTZ DOERING

31. Magic and Healing   587
    GIUSEPPE VELTRI

PART VIII ENTERTAINMENT AND
LEISURE-TIME ACTIVITIES

32. Bathhouses as Places of Social and Cultural Interaction   605
    YARON Z. ELIAV

33. Theatres, Hippodromes, Amphitheatres, and Performances   623
    ZEEV WEISS

34. Play and Games   641
    JOSHUA SCHWARTZ

Index of Subjects   655
Index of References   670

List of Figures and Maps

	Map of Roman Palestine	xvii
2.1	Relief with theatre masks, Katzrin	34
2.2	Floor mosaic with Dionysiac procession in the triclinium of a villa in Sepphoris	37
2.3	Byzantine pillar with medusa, Caesareu	43
14.1	The so-called 'Gaza Jar' from the Ramat Hanadiv excavations (southern Carmel area)	269
14.2 and 14.3	Byzantine period oil lamps from the Ein Gedi excavations	272
14.4	Stone vessels from the Temple Mount area in Jerusalem, 1st century CE	273
14.5	Glass vessels from a burial cave at Hurfeish, Upper Galilee—an example of the third–fourth century Galilean group	276
14.6	Reconstruction of a warp-weighted loom using weights found in excavations	278
14.7	Reconstruction of lever-and-weight oil press, lever-and-screw oil press, and direct-pressure-screw oil press	283
14.8	Reconstruction of a wine press from Ramat Hanadiv	286
19.1	Notched line pattern	369
19.2	Notched gamma pattern	369
19.3 and 19.4	Ancient Jewish men's clothing	371
19.5 and 19.6	Ancient Jewish women's clothing	372
21.1	Gold assemblage found in a late Roman tomb in Jerusalem drawn by de Ridder	396
21.2	Byzantine period glass pendant with the depiction of a cross and a menorah	398
23.1	Reconstruction of a house at Qatzrin, fourth–fifth centuries CE	421
23.2	Yussuf Qahadi, owner of a house at ed-Dhahiriya, interviewed by Yizhar Hirschfeld, standing in front of his house	422

23.3 Reconstruction of a courtyard house at Capernaum,
      first–second centuries CE   425

23.4 Reconstruction of a house at Horvat Susiya, sixth–eighth
      centuries CE   426

23.5 Reconstruction of the main entrance to the house at
      Horvat Susiya   426

23.6 Plan of Building XII at Mampsis, second–third centuries CE   427

23.7 Plan and sections of Building III at Umm el-Jimal,
      second–third centuries CE   428

23.8 Reconstruction of a house excavated at Horvat Shema',
      fourth–fifth centuries CE   434

24.1 The Tomb of Jason, Jerusalem   444

24.2 The Tomb of Zechariah, Jerusalem   444

24.3 The Tomb of Absalom, Jerusalem   445

24.4 Decorated limestone ossuary of the Nicanor family   449

24.5 Tomb of Nicanor and Menachem Ussishkin, Mt. Scopus,
      Jerusalem   453

24.6 Façade of Bet She'arim, Catacomb 20   454

24.7 Lion sarcophagus, Catacomb 20, Bet She'arim   455

28.1 (a) Galilean-type synagogue, Capernaum; (b) basilical-type
      synagogue, Bet Alpha; (c) transitional-type synagogue,
      Eshtemoa   527

28.2 Panel in Hammat Tiberias synagogue mosaic floor, with
      Temple facade, *menorot*, *shofar*, *lulav*, *etrog*, and incense shovel   530

28.3 Central panel in Hammat Tiberias synagogue mosaic floor,
      with the Zodiac and the sun god Helios   531

28.4 Western wall of Dura Europos synagogue   533

28.5 The three panels of the Hammat Tiberias synagogue
      mosaic floor. Top: Torah shrine and cluster of Jewish
      symbols; middle: zodiac with Helios in the centre;
      bottom: dedicatory inscriptions   535

28.6 Reconstructed drawing of the seven registers of the
      Sepphoris synagogue mosaic floor   537

28.7 Location of mosaic floor in the Bet Alpha synagogue   538

30.1 Oil lamp with attached reservoir (Sabbath lamp?) from
      Hebron, 3rd–4th c. CE   572

30.2 The 'four species' of Sukkot—closed palm frond, myrtle,
      and two willow branches, as well as the *etrog*—on a coin
      from the second year of the Bar Kokhba revolt (133/4 CE)   579

33.1 Sepphoris, the theatre built on the northern slope of
      the acropolis   627

33.2 Gerasa, southern view of the hippodrome   631

33.3 Scythopolis, general view of the amphitheatre   633

LIST OF ABBREVIATIONS

Abbreviations of Qumran texts follow the SBL Handbook of Style
Abbreviations of rabbinic literature follow the list of abbreviations in H. L. Strack/G. Stemberger (1991), *Introduction to the Talmud and Midrash*, Edinburgh: T&T Clark, 401–3.

M. = Mishnah
T. = Tosefta
y. = Talmud Yerushalmi/Palestinian Talmud
b. = Talmud Bavli/Babylonian Talmud
followed by the tractates and chapters.

Josephus' works are abbreviated as follows:

Ant. = Antiquitates
Bell. = Bellum Judaicum
C.Ap. = Contra Apionem

Roman Legal Compendia:

Dig. = Justinian's Digest
C.Th. = Codex Theodosianus

List of Contributors

Carol Bakhos is Professor of Late Antique Judaism at the University of California in Los Angeles.

Lutz Doering is Professor of New Testament and Ancient Judaism at the University of Münster in Germany.

Yaron Z. Eliav is Associate Professor of Rabbinic Literature and Jewish History of Late Antiquity at the University of Michigan in Ann Arbor.

Steven Fine is Professor of Jewish History at Yeshiva University in New York, head of the Department of Jewish History at Yeshiva College, and Director of Yeshiva University's Center for Israel Studies.

Katharina Galor is the Hirschfeld Visiting Assistant Professor at the Program in Judaic Studies at Brown University.

David Goodblatt was Professor in the Department of History and Endowed Chair in Judaic Studies at the University of California, San Diego. He died in September 2019.

Tziona Grossmark is Associate Professor of Galilee Studies at Tel-Hai College in Israel.

Rudolf Haensch is Professor of Ancient History at the Ludwig-Maximilians University in Munich, member of the German Archaeological Institute, and second director of the Kommission für Alte Geschichte und Epigraphik.

Gildas Hamel is Emeritus Senior Lecturer in the History Department of the University of California Santa Cruz.

Jill D. Harries is Emeritus Professor of Classics at the University of St. Andrews.

Catherine Hezser is Professor of Jewish Studies at the School of Oriental and African Studies (SOAS), University of London.

Tal Ilan is Professor of Jewish Studies at the Institut für Judaistik of the Free University Berlin.

Benjamin Isaac is the Fred and Helen Lessing Professor of Ancient History Emeritus at Tel Aviv University.

Ann Killebrew is Associate Professor of the Archaeology of the Levant at the Department of Classics, Ancient Mediterranean Studies, and Jewish Studies at Pennsylvania State University.

David Kraemer is the Joseph J. and Dora Abbell Librarian and Professor of Talmud and Rabbinics at the Jewish Theological Seminary, New York.

Uzi Leibner is Senior Lecturer at the Institute of Archaeology of the Hebrew University in Jerusalem.

Lee I. Levine is Professor in the Department of Jewish History and Archaeology at the Hebrew University in Jerusalem and holds the Rev. Moses Bernard Lauterman Family Chair in Classical Archaeology.

Jack Pastor is Senior Lecturer and Department Chair of History and Land of Israel Studies at Oranim, the Academic College of Education, Israel.

Stefan Reif is Professor Emeritus of Medieval Hebrew Studies, and former Director of the Taylor-Schechter Geniza Research Unit at the University of Cambridge, UK.

Zeev Safrai is Professor of Jewish History in the Department of Land of Israel Studies and Archaeology at Bar-Ilan University, Israel.

Michael Satlow is Professor of Religious Studies and Judaic Studies at Brown University in Providence, Rhode Island.

Jonathan W. Schofer is Associate Professor of Religious Studies at the University of Texas, Austin.

Joshua Schwartz is Professor in the Department of Land of Israel Studies and Archaeology at Bar-Ilan University, Israel.

Dafna Shlezinger-Katsman received her Ph.D in Jewish Studies at Bar-Ilan University, Israel.

Alexei Sivertsev is Professor in the Department of Religious Studies at DePaul University in Chicago.

Willem F. Smelik is Professor of Hebrew and Aramaic Literature in the Department of Hebrew and Jewish Studies at University College London.

Günter Stemberger is Emeritus Professor of Jewish Studies at the Institut für Judaistik of the University of Vienna, Austria.

Giuseppe Veltri is Professor of Jewish Philosophy and Religion and Head of Institute & Director of the Maimonides Centre for Advanced Studies at the University of Hamburg, Germany.

Zeev Weiss is the Eleazar L. Sukenik Professor of Archaeology at the Institute of Archaeology of The Hebrew University of Jerusalem.

Dianne van de Zande is a doctoral candidate at the Faculty of Archaeology at the University of Leiden, Netherlands.

Jürgen K. Zangenberg is Professor of New Testament and Early Christian Literature at the University of Leiden, Netherlands.

MAP OF ROMAN PALESTINE

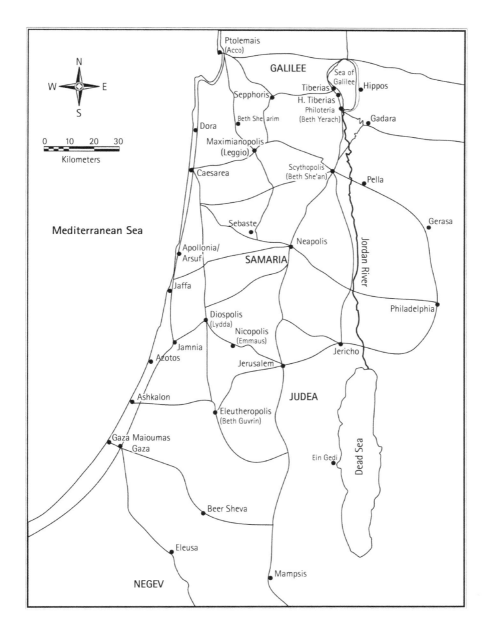

Courtesy of David Milson

INTRODUCTION

CATHERINE HEZSER

A whole a century has passed since the Hungarian Jewish scholar Samuel Krauss published his *Talmudische Archäologie* (three volumes, Leipzig 1910–12), and more than half a century since the German Lutheran theologian and orientalist Gustav Dalman wrote his *Arbeit und Sitte in Palästina* (eight volumes, Gütersloh 1928–42). Ever since, these monumental works have constituted the most essential handbooks on ancient Jewish daily life, and served as essential tools for students and scholars of rabbinic literature and ancient Judaism, as well as for ancient historians, classicists, archaeologists, and scholars of early Christianity. The works provided a detailed survey of Jewish everyday life in Roman Palestine, based mainly on rabbinic texts from the first six centuries CE. The topics addressed in these volumes ranged from housing and household goods to food and food production, clothing and jewellery, work and trade, family and household, schools and education, entertainment and leisure-time activities. Both of these works were written in German and never translated into English, requiring readers whose native language is English to acquire a reading knowledge of German in order to access them.

Today Krauss' and Dalman's works are out-of-date, both with regard to their methodology and the archaeological and epigraphical material they rely on. Since the publication of these works, historical-critical research in rabbinic texts and numerous new and exciting archaeological discoveries have vastly increased our knowledge of the daily life of Jews in Roman Palestine in the first six centuries CE. Therefore the time has come for a new comprehensive volume that provides an overview of the state of scholarship into ancient Jewish everyday life, and offers guidelines for the future study of these topics.

The study of everyday life is a relatively new area of research which historians of ancient Judaism are beginning to discover in the footsteps of historians of Greek and Roman society. Whereas ancient historians had traditionally focused on political history and the history of institutions, more recently the various aspects of the life experience of the ancients are increasingly attracting scholars. As far as Roman society is concerned, a number of scholarly and semi-popular books have been written on the subject (e.g. Carcopino 1941; Dupont 1992; Toner 1995; Adkins/Adkins 1998; Lacon 2000; Aldrete 2004). Special attention has also been paid to particular parts of the Roman Empire, such as Egypt (Lindsay 1963; Casson 2001; Bagnall 2003), and to the public and private life of particular groups, such as ancient Christians (Ermatinger 2007). In addition to these broader surveys, individual monographs have been written on various aspects of the Roman life experience.

The topic of everyday life received most scholarly attention from the 1960s onwards, in the course of a shift of focus from the history of institutions to the history of the ordinary, proposed by the French Annales school (Burke 1990; Schilling 2003), named after the journal *Annales d'Histoire Économique et Sociale*. The articles published in this journal concerned issues of social, economic, and cultural relevance, rather than political and institutional history. The books published by *Annales* historians, such as Fernand Braudel (1902–85), used models developed in the social sciences, and took geographic location into account (cf. Braudel 1949). Their studies mostly dealt with medieval and pre-modern societies, but their approach set a model which was subsequently emulated by historians of (Greek and) Roman antiquity, such as Moses Finley and Keith Hopkins (see, e.g. Finley 1985 and 1992; Hopkins 1978 and 1983).

Krauss and Dalman wrote at a time when methodologically critical reflections on the proper use of the source material and the employment of approaches from related disciplines were not yet prevalent. Nevertheless, at the time when the *Talmudische Archäologie* was written, Krauss' subject matter and approach were unique and innovative. Krauss, who had studied at the Rabbinical Seminary in Budapest and at the *Lehranstalt für die Wissenschaft des Judenthums* in Berlin, stood in the tradition of the *Wissenschaft des Judentums* approach, which developed in Germany at the end of the nineteenth century. In accordance with this approach, he was interested in the historical and philological investigation of rabbinic sources, for which the *realia* of everyday life—neglected in traditional Talmudic scholarship—provided an ideal theme. In Krauss' time, archaeological research in Palestine was taking its first steps, and focused mainly on 'holy' places and buildings rather than on the material remains of ancient everyday life. Therefore Krauss' investigation of the literary sources for everyday life filled a real lacuna within scholarship at the turn of the century.

During the last decades extensive archaeological excavations in the Mediterranean world in general, and in Israel in particular have yielded numerous and variegated finds concerning matters of daily life. The increase of archaeological evidence, combined with a heightened methodological awareness as far as the use of rabbinic literary sources is concerned, have made the creation of a new comprehensive volume mandatory. Although Krauss believed in the historical development of rabbinic sources, he did not distinguish properly between Palestinian and Babylonian, and tannaitic (70 to 200 CE) and amoraic (200 to mid-5th c.) sources. He often used Babylonian Talmudic texts to elucidate practices in Palestine. The identification of different literary forms, parallel versions, redactional revisions, and expansions that is part of any historical-critical study of rabbinic texts today was not yet practised at his time.

Since Jewish domestic architecture and objects of daily life had, for the most part, not been excavated by then, Krauss often relied, when reconstructing ancient practices, on his own observations of 'oriental life' made during his travels to Palestine and Egypt. During the one hundred years which have passed since the publication of his work, archaeological research has made tremendous progress and become more aware of the importance of investigating daily life. In recent decades, historians of ancient Judaism have also shown a great interest in the everyday life of Jews in antiquity, and many books and articles have been published in this regard. Historians of ancient Judaism have recognized the importance of viewing Jewish phenomena in the context of the broader Hellenistic and Roman cultural developments, and a knowledge of these contexts becomes imperative for a proper understanding of Jewish life in Roman Palestine. The essays included in the Handbook will explore how, and to what extent, the specific configuration of everyday practices amongst the Jewish population of the province can be assessed in these wider contexts, and they will suggest ways in which similarities and differences between Jewish and non-Jewish life practices can be investigated.

The study of ancient Jewish daily life must be an interdisciplinary undertaking in which archaeological, epigraphic, and literary sources are evaluated together by archaeologists, ancient historians, and experts of the literary texts. Archaeologists have often limited themselves to a description of material findings, whereas scholars of rabbinic literature do not always take archaeological discoveries into account. A proper understanding of ancient life practices can only be achieved if these two approaches are combined. By taking archaeological, historical, and literary studies into account, and by correlating the different approaches, the authors of these essays will suggest ways in which scholarship on ancient Jewish everyday life can proceed in the future.

Geographically, the essays all focus on one particular Roman province, namely, Roman Palestine. By focusing on one particular geographical area within the larger Graeco-Roman cultural environment, a certain unity can be achieved which would be lacking if the Jewish Diaspora were included. Besides Josephus and the New Testament, the large majority of the literary sources are rabbinic documents which originated in, and were transmitted and edited in, Roman Palestine in late antiquity. The major methodological challenge involved in dealing with everyday life issues is the correlation of these literary sources with the extant archaeological and epigraphic material. The traditional use of the Babylonian Talmud to reconstruct everyday life in Roman Palestine, commonly practised by Krauss, Dalman, and other scholars of their time, is not considered methodologically valid today. Scholars of the Babylonian Talmud have stressed that the daily life of Jews in Babylonia should be seen in the context of ancient Iranian society, a cultural context different from the Graeco-Roman environment which determined Palestinian Jews' life.

Chronologically, the Handbook focuses on the time after the Roman conquest of Palestine by Pompey in the first century BCE, and particularly on the period after the destruction of the Jerusalem Temple in 70 CE, until the end of Byzantine rule and the Islamic conquest of Palestine in the early seventh century CE. With the end of Byzantine rule, the Graeco-Roman epoque came to an end, and Islamic civilization would henceforth dominate the Eastern Mediterranean. The first six centuries CE are particularly significant as the literary and archaeological sources demonstrate. The classical rabbinic documents were edited at that time, and major religious and secular institutions, such as synagogues, theatres, and bathhouses were built in the Land of Israel in late antiquity. At the end of this period, from the late sixth and early seventh century onwards, Babylonian Jewry became dominant, and Palestinian Jewry played a more minor role.

The Handbook contains thirty-four essays which cover the major thematic areas of Jewish everyday life in Roman Palestine. The topics are subdivided thematically into eight sections. The first section addresses the major methodological issues involved in studying ancient Jewish daily life and sets the theoretical parameters for the following chapters. The second and third sections ('Life in a Roman Province'; 'City and Countryside') are devoted to the political, cultural, social, and geographic contexts, and the ways in which they affected Jewish life in Palestine. The fourth and fifth sections ('Labour and Trade'; 'Family Life') deal with the major practical aspects and contexts of daily life, work, and the family, whereas the sixth and seventh sections ('Education and Literacy'; 'Religion and Magic') address educational and religious matters. The eighth and final section discusses the various types of leisure-time activities.

An important aspect of the essays is to provide a basis and direction for the future study of the topics concerned. The essays point out which questions are worth asking and which methodological approaches can be applied. They provide a critical assessment of past and present scholarship, discuss methodological issues, and clarify the state of research on the respective subject matters. They were written for fellow-scholars and post-graduate students in Jewish Studies as well as for colleagues in related disciplines and interested lay-readers. Because of the broad scope of the intended readership, knowledge of ancient Jewish literature and history are not presupposed. Basic issues will be explained in the methodological chapters.

Last but not least it should be noted here that, although the volume attempts to be comprehensive, certain readers will miss particular subject areas which they might consider relevant. For example, there is no chapter on ancient Jewish slavery, since a recent monograph deals with that topic extensively (Hezser 2005), and a mere summary of the book was deemed unnecessary. For other topics, such as Jewish childhood in antiquity, no suitable author could be found. Three chapters were commissioned to authors but never delivered in the end. For that reason, a chapter on the landscape, climate, and geographical characteristics of Roman Palestine is missing here. We point readers to the excellent article by Rehav Rubin (1990) instead. Similarly missing is a chapter on the body and purity. The reader is referred to Fonrobert (2000), to her review essay (2007), and to the literature discussed therein. Finally, a commissioned chapter on ancient Jewish intellectual life seems to have been too challenging to handle, perhaps because our sources mainly reflect the rabbinic perspective. We hope that, despite these lacks, readers will benefit from the topics that *are* covered in this volume and be inspired to conduct their own research to boost the study of ancient Jewish daily life in the future.

BIBLIOGRAPHY

ADKINS, LESLEY/ADKINS, ROY A. (eds) (1998). *Handbook to Life in Ancient Rome*. 2nd ed. Oxford and New York: Oxford University Press.

ALDRETE, GREGORY S. (2004). *Daily Life in the Roman City: Rome, Pompeii and Ostia*. Westport, Conn.: Greenwood Publishing Group.

BAGNALL, ROGER S. (2003). *Later Roman Egypt: Society, Religion, Economy and Administration*. Aldershot/Burlington: Ashgate.

BRAUDEL, FERNAND (1949). *La Mediterranée et le Monde Mediterranéen à l'Epoque de Philippe II*. Paris: A Colin.

BURKE, PETER (1990). *The French Historical Revolution: The French Annales School 1929–89*. Cambridge: Polity Press.

CARCOPINO, JEROME (1941). *Daily Life in Ancient Rome: The People and the City at the Height of the Empire*. London: Routledge (reprinted London: Penguin Press, 1991; New Haven: Yale University Press, 1992).

CASSON, LIONEL (2001). *Everyday Life in Ancient Egypt*. 2nd ed. Baltimore: The Johns Hopkins University Press.

DALMAN, GUSTAV (1928–42). *Arbeit und Sitte in Palästina*. 8 volumes. Gütersloh: Hermann Werner (reprinted Hildesheim: G. Olms, 1964).

DUPONT, FLORENCE (1992). *Daily Life in Ancient Rome*. Oxford: Blackwell Publishers.

ERMATINGER, JAMES W. (2007). *Daily Life of Christians in Ancient Rome*. Westport, Conn.: Greenwood Publishing Group.

FINLEY, MOSES I. (1985). *The Ancient Economy*. 2nd ed. London: Hogarth.

FINLEY, MOSES I. (1992). *Ancient History: Evidence and Models*. New ed. London: Penguin Books.

FONROBERT, CHARLOTTE E. (2000). *Menstrual Purity: Rabbinic and Christian Reconstructions of Biblical Gender*. Stanford, CA: Standford University Press.

FONROBERT, CHARLOTTE E. (2007). 'Purity Studies in Ancient Judaism: An Emerging Subfield?' *The Journal of the Association for Jewish Studies* 31: 161–5.

HEZSER, CATHERINE (2005). *Jewish Slavery in Antiquity*. Oxford: Oxford University Press.

HOPKINS, KEITH (1978). *Conquerors and Slaves*. Cambridge: Cambridge University Press.

HOPKINS, KEITH (1983). *Death and Renewal*. Cambridge: Cambridge University Press.

KRAUSS, SAMUEL (1910–12). *Talmudische Archäologie*. 3 volumes. Leipzig: Gustav Fock (reprinted Hildesheim: G. Olms, 1966).

LANCON, BERTRAND (2000). *Rome in Late Antiquity: Everyday Life and Urban Change, AD 312–609*. New York: Routledge.

LINDSAY, JACK (1963). *Daily Life in Roman Egypt*. London: F. Muller.

RUBIN, REHAV (1990). 'Historical Geography of Eretz-Israel: Survey of the Ancient Period', in *The Land That Became Israel: Studies in Historical Geography*, ed. Ruth Kark. New Haven and London, 23–36.

SCHILLING, DEREK (2003). 'Everyday Life and the Challenge to History in post-War France: Braudel, Lefebvre, Certeau'. *Diacritics* 33: 23–40.

TONER, J. P. (1995). *Leisure and Ancient Rome*. Cambridge: Polity Press.

I

METHODOLOGICAL ISSUES

CORRELATING LITERARY, EPIGRAPHIC, AND ARCHAEOLOGICAL SOURCES

CATHERINE HEZSER

THE premier and most important issue in the investigation of Jewish daily life in antiquity is the question of methodology. The types of sources available for the study of everyday life issues are very diverse with regard to their format, perspective, date, context, and the type of information they provide. Altogether, they comprise literary, epigraphic, and archaeological material. Whether and to what extent all three types of sources are available for one's investigation depends on the specific topic of inquiry. For some topics, especially those concerning social life issues the bulk of the material is literary; for others, especially those concerning buildings and institutions, most of the sources are archaeological. The task of the researcher is to collect and analyse all of the source material and to determine its respective relevance and contribution to the topic at hand. This may sound easier than it actually is, given the complexity of issues relating to the representativeness, dating, and historical trustworthiness of the sources, in addition to problems of interpretation and context. The correlation of literary and material remains has been one of the major methodological problems occupying scholars for at least a century. In the following, we shall first introduce the reader to the various types of source material for the study of Jewish daily life in Roman Palestine. Afterwards, methodological issues concerning the interdisciplinary cultural-historical study of this material will be discussed.

1. THE LITERARY SOURCES

While the works of Josephus and the Gospels of the New Testament relate to Judaism in the Land of Israel at the end of the Second Temple period, that is, the first two centuries of Roman rule, post-70 CE Palestinian rabbinic literature is our major Jewish literary source for Roman Palestine in the first five centuries CE, and especially for late antiquity (3rd to 5th c.). All of these literary sources are written from a particular perspective, and their viewpoint is therefore limited: Josephus was a rebel leader during the first revolt against Rome, and a member of the very Hellenized upper strata of society. He was most interested in presenting the events in Judaea and Galilee, leading to the destruction of the Temple, in a way which allowed him to exculpate himself (Cohen 1979; Schwartz 1990). The New Testament writers were followers of Jesus and members of Christian groups which were in the process of distinguishing themselves from Judaism both theologically and socially. They therefore focus on Jesus' and his followers' activities, and present first-century Judaism from their often polemic Christian point of view (Parkes 1934; Fredriksen/Reinhartz, eds, 2002; Levine 2006). Palestinian rabbinic literature developed over a period of approximately four hundred years and contains traditions of many generations of rabbis who were mostly concerned with matters of halakhah (religious law). Since rabbinic literature is by far the most important literary source for all aspects of Jewish daily life in Roman Palestine, we shall focus on methodological problems concerning this literature here (for introductions see Stemberger 1996; Neusner, ed. 1981; Safrai, ed. 1987; *idem* et al., eds 2006).

The first issue is the problem of dating individual rabbinic traditions. A major chronological distinction exists between so-called tannaitic and amoraic rabbis, traditions, and documents. Tannaitic rabbis lived between 70 and 200 CE, and all traditions attributed to them are called tannaitic traditions. In addition, those rabbinic documents which contain only tannaitic traditions are called tannaitic documents (the Mishnah, Tosefta, and halakhic Midrashim). Amoraic rabbis lived between 200 CE and the early fifth century. Their traditions are called amoraic traditions, and the documents transmitting these traditions, amoraic documents (the Talmud Yerushalmi and amoraic Midrashim). Amoraic documents contain both tannaitic and amoraic traditions as well as an anonymous editorial layer, the so-called *stam*. Although scholars differ over the exact dates at which individual rabbinic documents were edited, it is commonly assumed that the Mishnah is the earliest rabbinic document, edited in the early third century CE, followed by the Tosefta and halakhic Midrashim in the third and early fourth century, and the Yerushalmi and amoraic Midrashim in the fourth and fifth century (see the discussion in the introductions mentioned above).

In the past, scholars believed that rabbinic literature preserved the exact words, opinions, and practices of the rabbis to whom they were ascribed, and they therefore took attributions to particular rabbis literally (e.g. Krauss 1910–12). For example, a statement attributed to, or a story told about, R. Aqiba was considered reliable information about that second-generation tannaitic rabbi. Jacob Neusner and his students have increasingly questioned the historical reliability of attributions (Green 1978). A tradition attributed to a second generation tanna would have been transmitted by his third-generation students at the earliest. It would then have been transmitted orally for many more decades, or even centuries, until it was eventually written down and included in a rabbinic document. It is characteristic for oral traditions to be told in a variety of different versions, and to be changed and adapted to new circumstances during their time of transmission (see Hezser 2001: 190–209 and esp. 203–7; Small 1997; Carol Bakhos' chapter in this volume). It is therefore useless and inappropriate to search for the 'original' version of a particular saying or story. By comparing different textual versions one can merely try to recover the 'earliest' possible version of a tradition, which would have already been subjected to (a number of) editorial revision(s) in addition to the possible changes made during the process of transmission. This shows how complex the historical-critical study of rabbinic literature has become in recent decades.

Another important development of scholarship on rabbinic literature since the 1970s, and especially most recently, is the emphasis on the distinction between Palestinian and Babylonian traditions and documents. Whereas earlier scholarship (e.g. Krauss 1910–12) used Babylonian Talmudic texts to elucidate daily life in Roman Palestine, scholars nowadays stress the difference between Palestinian rabbinic documents within the Graeco-Roman environment and the Babylonian Talmud, which developed in a quite different Persian and Zoroastrian cultural context (Elman 2005). Therefore a study of Jewish daily life in Roman Palestine must always give preference to literary sources transmitted in Palestinian documents. The Babylonian Talmud may occasionally preserve Palestinian traditions which were not included in Palestinian documents, but such traditions may have undergone Babylonian editing. Therefore special caution must be taken in using such traditions, and the Babylonian literary context needs to be examined to identify possible editorial adaptations.

The long period of transmission and redaction of individual traditions should already warn us against taking these traditions literally as reliable historical information about the time of the rabbis they are associated with. Other phenomena which threaten the historical reliability of rabbinic traditions are the literary style, ideological purpose, and limited perspective of the texts (see, e.g. Neusner 1980, 1984, and 1988). Rabbinic texts are usually formulated in a very elliptic style, mentioning the most important halakhic aspects of a particular issue only. For example, rabbinic travel is usually mentioned in the introductory sentence of narratives only, whereas the focus of the stories is on the ensuing halakhic issues and discussions. Case stories are so concise and formulaic that the circumstances of a case are merely alluded to. Scholars wishing to use such texts for investigating daily life must read them 'against the grain', trying to identify reflections of realia and social life beyond the literary stylization and halakhic focus (Goodblatt 1980). This is possible by searching for certain patterns, that is, repeated references to a particular phenomenon in texts of different purposes and literary forms, and by viewing the texts in the broader cultural, historical, political, and economic context in which they were formulated.

Rabbis were Torah scholars for whom Torah study and practice were supremely important in life, and they developed a huge corpus of teachings with which they hoped to regulate almost all aspects of their Jewish contemporaries' daily lives. In contrast to earlier scholarship, rabbis are no longer viewed as institutionalized community leaders who had actual control over their coreligionists (Hezser 1997). They must rather be seen as a decentralized network of like-minded intellectuals with circles of students, whose personal authority was based on charisma and persuasion rather than on institutional enforcement. Therefore we cannot assume that rabbinic rules were actually practised by all Jewish inhabitants of Palestine at that time. Rabbis disagreed amongst themselves with regard to the details of halakhah, and rabbinic literature provides evidence of a pluralism of opinions and approaches (Cohen 1984). A lay person who followed a particular rabbi may have transgressed another rabbi's views on the same issue. Throughout tannaitic and amoraic times there was no commonly agreed-upon rabbinic opinion which people could follow. Therefore the representativeness of rabbinic rules becomes questionable. We cannot automatically assume that a rabbinic rule was followed by any other person than the rabbi himself and his family (Miller 2006: 464: 'The rabbis were largely speaking, studying, and teaching among themselves and their households'). While many Israeli scholars continue to maximize rabbis' influence and authority over their fellow Jews, American and European scholars tend to adopt a more critical and cautious view, considering their impact on ancient Jewish society rather limited and circumscribed (Schwartz 2001: 103–28; see also *idem* 2002).

The developments in the modern study of rabbinic literature and culture referred to above—especially doubts concerning the historical reliability and representativeness of rabbinic traditions—must have a major impact on the study of ancient Jewish daily life. They make the very value of the literary tradition question-able for any type of historical investigation. Often, however, rabbinic sources are our major type of material or at least supplement archaeological material. Therefore careful methodological steps have to be taken when investigating these sources and assessing their contribution to a particular topic.

2. The Epigraphic and Papyrological Sources

Besides the literary sources identified above, two other types of written material are available for the study of Jewish daily life in Roman Palestine: papyrus documents of the early second century CE, which were discovered in Judaean Desert caves (Hezser 2001: 158–60 and 309–27), and synagogue and burial inscriptions, most of them datable to the third century or later (ibid. 364–421).

Amongst the Judaean Desert papyri there are two family 'archives' which contain private documents in Aramaic, Greek, and Nabatean belonging to two women, Babatha and Salome Komaise (Lewis/Yadin/Greenfield, eds 1989; Cotton/Yardeni, eds 1997). While a few of these documents date back to the end of the first century CE, most of them were written shortly before, or at the beginning of the Bar Kokhba revolt. It is assumed that they were hidden in the desert cave for safe keeping during the revolt. The women and their families originally lived in the village of Mahoza, which was part of the Nabatean kingdom until it became the Roman province of Arabia in 106 CE. The families probably sought refuge in the caves when the revolt had broken out in 132 CE. Both women and their families belonged to the upper strata of society, since most of the documents concern property issues (deposits, loans, inheritance disputes, donations, etc.). The rest deal with custody issues, or are marriage contracts which also involve property settlements.

The two main issues to be considered when using these documents in the study of Jewish daily life in Roman Palestine are (a) the representativeness of these documents for Jews in Judaea, or even Palestinian Judaism at large; and (b) the relationship between the legal issues referred to in the documents and (mostly later) rabbinic law. As already mentioned, the families to whom these documents belonged were wealthy property owners. Thus, the documents do not reflect the living conditions of the poor or the middle strata of society. They also lived in a formerly Nabatean area which was turned into the Roman province of Arabia, distinct from the province of Syria-Palestine. This was not an area with which second-century rabbis would maintain regular contact, and legal conditions may well have been different there. Therefore the representativeness of the issues addressed in these documents is questionable, and the particular circumstances in which they were written need to be taken into account. Rabbinic literature was written down and edited later, and rabbinic oral traditions may not have been known at all in this area. Therefore differences between documental marriage contracts and rabbinic regulations concerning the *ketubbah* are not amazing at all. Similarities between rabbinic law and the legal regulations of the contracts do not necessarily indicate rabbinic influence: they may well be based on customary law which rabbis adopted and transformed. The phenomenon that most of the Judaean Desert documents are written in Greek may either suggest a hellenized milieu or concern for their enforcibility in Greek courts (Cotton in Cotton/Yardeni, eds 1997: 206–7 opts for the latter possibility; see also Cotton 1998: 169).

The Jewish epigraphic evidence from Roman Palestine consists of burial inscriptions and synagogue donors' inscriptions. Amongst the burial inscriptions, the earlier Herodian-period ossuary inscriptions can be distinguished from the later sarcophagus inscriptions and inscriptions on plaques in burial caves. Ossuary inscriptions were very brief graffiti inscriptions incised on ossuaries in the vicinity of Jerusalem, used for secondary burial of bone remains (see the collection of Rahmani 1994). By contrast, the later sarcophagi inscriptions were usually incised by stone masons and the texts tend to be more detailed. The catacombs of Bet She'arim in the Jezreel valley, the main burial complex where such inscriptions were found, date from the third to the middle of the fourth century CE.

The large majority of the inscriptions are written in Greek (Schwabe/Lifshitz 1974), and many of the sarcophagi are decorated with pagan (figural) motifs. Although it is traditionally believed that the patriach R. Yehudah ha-Nasi is buried at this place and a number of inscriptions contain forms of the title 'Rabbi', Shaye Cohen has followed E. Goodenough in claiming a distinction between the 'literary rabbis' and the 'epigraphical rabbis' whose Torah scholarship he questioned (Cohen 1981–82). This distinction is based on the assumption that there was a clear boundary between Palestinian 'rabbinism' and pagan art, a boundary which other scholars have questioned (Miller 2004; see also the relevant chapters in this volume). As in the case of the mentioned papyri, the representativeness of these written memorials can be questioned: again, they seem to represent the wealthy, usually quite hellenized strata of society and Diaspora Jews who were buried there. Most Jews would not have been able to afford a burial at Bet She'arim. The so-called epigraphic habit was followed by a small section of the Palestinian Jewish population only (Hezser 2001: 395–97).

Synagogue donors' inscriptions were not set up by the donors themselves or their families but by representatives of the synagogue community in honour of those who supported the building projects. Like the sarcophagi inscriptions, almost all of these inscriptions were set up from the late third century CE onwards only. These dates concur with the dating of most synagogues to the fourth to sixth century CE (see also Levine in this volume). While Hebrew and Aramaic inscriptions were set up for (often anonymous) donors of relatively small amounts of money or minor building parts, the more wealthy donors who financed entire mosaics or synagogue renovations were commemorated in Greek in the central aisles of the buildings (Hezser 2001: 401). This phenomenon indicates again that textual commemoration was a privilege which pertained to certain small circles of late antique Jewish society only.

In the study of ancient Jewish daily life, inscriptions are valuable in a number of regards: for example, burial inscriptions help estimate ancient Jews' age at death (unfortunately, few such inscriptions were set up for women); synagogue inscriptions indicate how synagogues were financed and who obtained leadership roles in synagogue communities. When correlating such information with information gained from rabbinic sources, inconsistencies may occur and questions arise. For example, can the leadership titles mentioned in Greek synagogue inscriptions be identified with those mentioned in Hebrew/Aramaic rabbinic texts, or should we assume different leadership structures for Greek versus Hebrew/Aramaic-speaking synagogues in Roman Palestine? Are rabbinic representations of the life cycle to be understood as idealistic and typological rather than based on actual life experiences? And how does the rabbinic disdain for the Greek language compare with the preponderance of Greek in the papyrological and epigraphic evidence?

3. The Archaeological Sources

Whereas in the past, archaeologists of the Land of Israel in Roman times were mainly interested in synagogues and burial sites, during recent decades archaeologists have increasingly paid attention to domestic architecture and objects of daily life. The positive side of this development is that even smaller objects, such as game pieces and textile fragments, have been preserved and are listed in excavation reports; the negative side is that such objects were usually not considered the most important finds to be publicized in excavations. Therefore a lot of this 'material culture' of ancient Judaism has not been published and studied yet (see, e.g. the chapters by Katzman-Shlezinger and Schwartz in this volume). It takes painstaking research to locate these objects within archaeological reports and to develop more comprehensive studies based on these 'realia'.

One of the main questions facing archaeologists and historians of ancient Judaism is the identification of a building or object as Jewish. How can we separate a 'Jewish' material culture from the broader Graeco-Roman and Christian-Byzantine material culture of the Land of Israel? What lets us assume that a certain building or artefact or incription or image is Jewish rather than Graeco-Roman or Christian? In the past, when 'Jewish' was considered identical with 'rabbinic', such issues were much easier to decide: everything that rabbis rejected was considered foreign or based on foreign influence. Nowadays, since we are much more aware of the varieties of ancient Jewish life and practice, we have to assume that blurred boundaries between Jewish, Christian, and pagan culture existed (Friedheim 2006; Stemberger in this volume). The criteria which are commonly used to identify realia as Jewish obviously provide one type of Jewish culture only: identifiably Jewish symbols and names, and Hebrew as the 'holy language' (see the criteria mentioned by van der Horst to identify Jewish inscriptions in *idem* 1991; see also Lapin 1999). We have to reckon with the possibility that many or even the majority of Jews did not even feel the need to identify themselves, their buildings, clothes, and lifestyles as Jewish, especially if they lived in the Land of Israel, the Jewish homeland, where Graeco-Roman customs and images and architectural styles may not have been considered as much a threat as in the Diaspora, as the lack of pagan images in Diaspora Jewish art versus Jewish art in Palestine suggests.

The archaeological finds themselves are mute, and require identification and interpretation. Their identification and interpretation is possible only if they are seen within a particular context and related to the already known. This contextual knowledge may be based on other similar finds from the same area, analogies from other regions, and ancient literary sources. The study of ancient 'material culture' aims at interpreting ancient objects within the social, economic, political, religious, and cultural context of their time and place. It constitutes a holistic approach to ancient culture, in which objects are viewed and studied as integral elements of ancient life. The identification, cataloguing, and publication of objects can be only the first step in such an endeavour. The next step would be the investigation of those contextual sources which help determine how a certain object was used, and what its significance was within the broader framework of ancient Jewish culture. Only interdisciplinary approaches which correlate archaeological and literary sources are able to study 'material culture' in this broader context of Jewish daily life in Roman Palestine.

4. CORRELATING ARCHAEOLOGICAL, EPIGRAPHIC, AND LITERARY SOURCES

One of the main problems of research on ancient Jewish daily life is the establishment of a proper relationship between rabbinic literary references, documentary material, and archaeological data. How, and to what extent, can the extant literary sources be used to elucidate the excavated material? Or, looked at from the perspective of the student of the text: what is the benefit of archaeological material for the interpretation of a textual passage? Although scholars have been confronted with this problem for a long time already, the question of finding an appropriate approach to the interdisciplinary study of ancient Jewish culture is still unresolved.

In the past, the study of realia was often based on a positivistic approach to rabbinic literature. The goal was to find archaeological evidence of phenomena mentioned in rabbinic sources or, vice versa, to interpret excavated finds on the basis of a simplistic literal reading of rabbinic sources which took the texts at face value as a historical record of ancient Jewish life and practice. Differences between early and late, Palestinian and Babylonian traditions were often not taken into account. Rather, rabbinic literature was seen as a vast treasure trove of bits and pieces of information on almost all aspects of daily life. The resulting studies arranged this information thematically, explained terminology, and tried to harmonize as best as possible the rabbinic references and the 'hard evidence' which excavations provided (see, e.g. Krauss' monumental work, published in 1910–12). For issues on which archaeological material was not available, Krauss used his own experiences in the Near East of the turn of the century as the framework for interpreting the practices of ancient Jewish daily life.

Steven Fine has shown that the 'talmudic archaeology' approach of the early twentieth century, which was also represented by Gustav Dalman, David Kaufman, Ludwig Blau and others, is nowadays called 'Talmudic *realia*' and is practised mostly in the Talmud departments of Israeli universities (2006: 200–1). Shmuel Safrai (Safrai/Stern, eds 1974–76) and Daniel Sperber (1993) can be considered amongst the main representatives of this approach. The focus remains on rabbinic literature, or 'Talmudic literature' as it is often called in an undifferentiated way, with the goal of reconstructing the real-life basis of rabbinic halakhah. This approach may be coupled with the attempt to prove the historical trustworthiness of the literary references, to search for the 'historical kernel' and 'evaluate the historical authenticity of these texts' (Eliav 2002: 239).

On the basis of the more critical and sophisticated approaches to rabbinic texts, which developed during recent decades, new ways of correlating the literary and material evidence have become mandatory. For scholars who distinguish between Roman Palestine and Sasanian Babylonia, study the many different layers of transmission and redaction, and question the historical reliability of the texts, viewing them as literature, legal discourse, and theology rather than as reliable historical evidence, an indiscriminate use of the sources to create a harmonized picture of ancient Jewish daily life is no longer possible. Nowadays, the study of ancient everyday life practices has become much more complex and complicated than was envisioned by scholars a hundred, or even fifty, years ago. If we cannot assume that rabbinic literature provides historically accurate information on the so-called 'realia', how can these texts be used to identify and interpret the excavated material? If rabbinic literature reflects the perspective of the rabbis only, how can these texts be used to make any assumptions about ancient Jewish life in general? Can this literature serve as the proper framework for interpreting aspects of life on which rabbis may not have had any influence? If rabbinic sources lose at least part of their interpretive value, what other contexts and frameworks are available to make sense of the material traces of non- or extra-rabbinic Judaism that survive?

First, it is necessary to move away from the 'treasure-trove' image of rabbinic literature and to engage in detailed and sophisticated analyses of the respective texts instead. Only the knowledge gained on the basis of historical-critical textual studies can be used in the interpretation of the archaeological finds. Thus, it is not very persuasive to claim that a recently excavated basilica-style building in Tiberias served as the 'sanhedrin' or high court of the patriarch (Hirschfeld/Galor 2007: 227–8), when studies based on critical analyses of rabbinic texts have already shown that no such institution is likely to have existed in post-70 times (Goodblatt 1994), and no evidence of the Jewishness or Jewish use of the building has been found. As the excavators have noted themselves, the 'best parallel' to the excavated building is the so-called Governor's Palace in Caesarea, which may even have served as a model for the Tiberias basilica (ibid. 226). While a Caesarean building is immediately identified as a non-Jewish institution, traditional notions about Tiberias as a Jewish town and the seat of the sanhedrin have given rise to this misinterpretation. Archaeologists who are not experts in the study of the literary sources themselves should at least take recent research on rabbinic texts and the history of Roman Palestine into account.

Secondly, since the use of rabbinic texts as historical sources has become problematic, other frameworks of interpretation besides the rabbinic one need to be explored. Such frameworks are provided by Graeco-Roman and early Christian architecture and art, literature, and mythology. For example, for many architectural features of ancient synagogues, church architecture provides the appropriate explanatory base (Fine 2005: 88; see also Levine in this volume). The many theatres excavated in Roman Palestine can be understood properly only in the context of late antique performances and plays (see Weiss in this volume). This approach requires a knowledge and expertise beyond the respective scholar's field of specialization. Scholars of both ancient Judaism and Graeco-Roman culture increasingly realize that Jewish material culture was an integral part of the material culture of the Roman Empire at large.

Altogether then, the study of the material remains of ancient Jews needs to move away from the investigation of mere realia towards a much more integrated, cultural-historical approach which views the excavated objects as traces of the religious, cultural, and everyday life practices of ancient Jews. For example, it is no longer sufficient merely to describe the architectural forms of buildings such as bathhouses, and to provide an analysis of rabbinic references to these institutions: both the material and literary evidence needs to be evaluated in the social and cultural context of the bathing culture of late antiquity (see Eliav in this volume). In this connection, rabbinic and other literary sources may provide important supplementary information to the material finds, providing traces and allusions to ways in which the buildings were used. For such a more comprehensive analysis, methods and models developed by sociologists, anthropologists, and cultural historians may be helpful.

The central focus on rabbinic literature and the view of Jewish daily life through rabbinic lenses has also impacted the study of the epigraphic and papyrological remains. When discussing the question as to what makes a papyrus contract found in Judaean Desert caves Jewish, Hannah Cotton suggests that its eventual 'halachic sanction' can serve as the best criterion (Cotton 1998: 172). She continues: 'Conversely, what is not there [i.e. in later rabbinic documents], or explicitly forbidden [by rabbis], I would designate non-Jewish' (ibid.). This theory is problematic in a number of regards. Clearly, 'Jewish' is identified with rabbinic here and a direct continuation between 'Jewish' practices before the existence of rabbinic documents and the later written halakhic discourse of the rabbis is assumed. Whatever falls outside of the rabbinic spectrum and is not included in later rabbinic works is deemed non-Jewish or based on non-Jewish influences here. Cotton is right in stating that the Judaean Desert documents indicate the limited influence of rabbis over the practices of second century CE Jews. But Jewish practices which differed from the written opinions of rabbis were not necessarily non-Jewish. Ancient Jews used and amalgamated customs and habits from the surrounding cultures, and this very amalgamation was Jewish, even if non-rabbinic.

Greg Woolf has recently pointed out that ancient historians should move away from the strict distinction between Roman and native cultural practices (Woolf 1997). While revisionist studies of Roman imperialism and Romanization viewed these processes in terms of colonialist invasions of 'authentic' native ethnic cultures, recent studies have focused on cultural changes brought about by the interaction itself. Romanization is no longer understood as 'the spread of what was Roman at the expense of what was not' (ibid. 339), or, applied to our example here, the spread of what was non-Jewish at the expense of what was Jewish/rabbinic. Romanization should rather be seen as a process or movement which created new forms and versions of local 'native' cultures, that is, other forms of Judaism besides the rabbinic. Even rabbinic Judaism was not spared from participating in this process, as many recent studies have shown (see the next chapter in this volume).

For the study of the papyrological, epigraphic, and archaeological remains, this means that scholars should be open for encountering Jewish practices which the rabbinic sources did not, or not sufficiently, address, either because rabbis were not interested in them or because they did not wish to highlight them. Rabbis were not the only, and possibly not the most influential, local élite which assumed control over aspects of other Jews' daily life. Wealthy Jewish immigrants from Alexandria and other Diaspora locations, who are frequently mentioned in inscriptions, may have been much more influential than is commonly assumed. The rabbinic world-view of 'us' and 'them', of a rabbinicly defined Judaism and an idolatrous 'other' world, did not reflect actual reality (see also Woolf 1997: 340, who warns ancient historians against tacitly accepting classical Greek and Roman authors' perspective on ancient life). It is more profitable to see ancient Jewish society 'as a structured system of differences that was highly differentiated, by region, class, social locale, age and gender, amongst other dimensions of variability' (ibid.). Therefore the study of ancient Jewish daily life needs to move away from the dichotomy between rabbinic and non-rabbinic, and view Jewish practices in the much broader context of ancient Near Eastern and Mediterranean cultural encounters and transformations that took place during the Roman period.

Based on these more general and theoretical considerations, how then can archaeologists use literary sources and historians and scholars of ancient Jewish literature use the material sources? How can new methodological approaches in the use of these different types of sources be developed? In a recent article on using material and written sources for the study of Roman cultural history, Penelope Allison has pointed to one of the major problems of approaches which require detailed knowledge of more than one discipline: rarely does one scholar acquire critical methodological skills in a field outside of his or her own (2001: 181). With a few exceptions, scholars of rabbinic literature are not trained archaeologists with fieldwork experience who can identify and date excavated finds. Similarly, archaeologists have rarely acquired the critical methodological skills to analyse rabbinic texts on their own. Neither archaeologists nor ancient historians and Talmudists are epigraphers trained in the transcription, translation, and interpretation of epigraphic finds. All of these specialists therefore rely on secondary literature in fields outside of their specialization. In this way, archaeology may easily become 'the handmaiden of history' (cf. ibid.), and ancient Jewish literature a mere minefield of 'historical' information. It is therefore of primary importance that scholars acquire critical analytical skills in the neighbouring disciplines, and comprehend the variety of approaches developed in those fields.

One of the first steps in developing critical methodological approaches to the study of ancient material culture and daily life should be the formulation of appropriate questions for each type of source material available to the scholar (Allison 2001: 181). Archaeological and documentary sources cannot answer the questions one commonly asks of the literary sources and vice versa. With regard to ancient Judaism this means that material remains, when studied on their own, do not tell us anything about rabbinic halakhah. For example, the identification of certain stepped pools, discovered in Galilee and elsewhere, is controversal amongst scholars. While some scholars believe that they served ritual purity purposes (Meyers 2002; Reich 2002), others have questioned this view and suggested several other explanations, such as freshwater reservoirs, storage pits, and bathtubs (Eshel

1997; Miller 2007). Obviously, the material remains themselves do not allow us to determine the relationship of these finds to rabbinic halakhah. Is it therefore appropriate to read them in the light of rabbinic halakhah and to claim an almost universal observance of rabbinic purity laws amongst the Jewish population of Roman Palestine? Or should one rather allow for limits of interpretability and set clear boundaries for the kind of questions material remains can and cannot answer? If such limits are adopted, the alleged *miqvaot* may merely be interpreted as facilities for the storage of water or cleaning purposes, whereas the exact nature of these installations and their relationship to the rabbinic discourse on purity cannot be determined anymore.

Similar restrictions apply to the questions we can ask of the literary sources. Although rabbinic sources do mention synagogues, for example, they do not allow us to reconstruct the appearance of synagogue buildings in antiquity. Rabbis were generally not particularly interested in the material aspects of synagogues but in the religious rituals performed in them. Therefore they tell us a lot about the development of the synagogue liturgy and prayer formulas, but very little about the leadership structure, financing, or building of these institutions (see Reif and Levine in this volume). Rabbinic sources are also of only limited value for the study of theatres in Roman Palestine. Rabbis repeatedly urge their fellow-Jews to attend synagogues and study houses rather than theatres and circuses, but the actual performances in the theatres have left only a few incidental traces in the Jewish literary sources (see also Weiss in this volume). As in the case of the archaeological evidence, the scholar of rabbinic literature needs to formulate appropriate questions and acknowledge that there are many aspects of ancient Jewish daily life for which these texts cannot provide us with answers.

The choice and relevance of the source material depends on the issues examined and the questions asked. In general, literary sources are more suitable for the study of social life and interpersonal relationships, whereas the material sources allow us to envision the physical remains of ancient societies. Some topics may solely, or mostly, rely on the literary evidence (e.g. education; intellectual life, family relationships) while others are mainly concerned with the architecture of buildings (e.g. synagogues, theatres, and stadia). For many topics the interrelationship between the archaeological and literary evidence is of great importance; however, the literary sources may reveal how buildings and artefacts were used, and the buildings and artefacts provide the material context to which the literary sources relate in a variety of ways. The very dependence of one type of evidence on the other should warn us against correlating them in simplistic and methodologically inappropriate ways and show us the need to develop critical analytical approaches to determine the relationship between the two realms.

The need to first study and interpret the different types of sources on their own, with the critical methodology developed for their study, and to accept their respective limitations should warn us against using the literature as the context and framework in which the material evidence is interpreted (Allison 2001: 181). One of the basic mistakes of Krauss' approach was the rabbinic-centredness of his study of ancient Jewish daily life. Only the independent study of each type of evidence allows us to recognize inconsistencies: 'Approaches to material cultural assemblages and contexts need to question the roots of any variability between the interpretation of the diverse sets of data and to be critically self-conscious of the inferences that result from one body of data being used to interpret another' (ibid.). In the harmonized and uniform picture of ancient Jewish daily life created by Krauss (1910–12) the different sets of data are not allowed to challenge and question each other. As the title *Talmudische Archäologie* already suggests, archaeology is used as the handmaiden of rabbinics here. A new approach to ancient Jewish daily life must acknowledge the important and independent role of archaeology, for which the Near Eastern cultural and material context may often be more relevant than rabbinic literature and which may yield results which threaten the centrality of the views and perspective of rabbis.

Local area studies and the contextualization of the archaeological finds within the material culture of the ancient Near East and the Roman Empire at large can reveal what is distinctive (or not) about the various types of material culture discovered in Roman Palestine, in a similar way in which literary comparisons between rabbinic and Graeco-Roman texts help us determine rabbis' participation in the wider discursive practices of the ancient world. Such contextual studies will also provide a broader perspective for correlating archaeological and literary remains. Domestic architecture can serve as an example here. For the types of houses excavated in the Land of Israel and dated to Roman times (cf. Hirschfeld 1995; Galor 2003; see also Galor in this volume) Roman (provincial) domestic architecture seems to provide the most appropriate framework for analysing the building styles. In particular, the Roman *insulae*, multi-unit apartment buildings, are found prominently in both cities (e.g. Sepphoris) and villages (e.g. Korazim) of Roman Palestine. Rabbinic literature contains numerous discussions of domestic legal problems (e.g. damages to shared buildings, disturbance by noise or fumes, trouble with neighbourly trees overreaching one's property), which seem to relate to the circumstances of *insula* dwellers. These texts need to be discussed in conjunction with the archaeological material and in the context of Graeco-Roman archaeological and literary evidence to properly assess ancient Jewish living conditions (see Hezser 1998: 481–577 for a discussion of neighbourly disputes and domestic architecture in the Talmud Yerushalmi).

The interpretation of ancient Jewish art can serve as another example of the need for integrated contextualized studies. Scholarly debate concerning the Zodiac motif on the mosaic floors of late antique synagogues continues (for an introduction to the debate see Hachlili 1977; Levine 2005; see also Levine in this volume). The Zodiac circle representing the twelve months of the year surrounds Helios, whom Greeks and Romans worshipped as Sol Invictus. Helios may be represented by the sun or by a figure driving a chariot. Personifications of the four seasons are usually part of this complex, which is accompanied by biblical salvation scenes such as the Binding of Isaac and Daniel in the Lion's Den. The Jewish depiction differs from the pagan and Christian use of the motif in a number of regards, but the very phenomenon that Jews could represent Helios in the religious context of the synagogue has struck scholars for decades. In the 1950s Erwin R. Goodenough had tried to explain the phenomenon by distinguishing between an 'orthodox' aniconic rabbinic Judaism, which he believed would not have tolerated such images, and a popular syncretistic and mystical Judaism which adopted them from the surrounding culture in a liberal and deliberate way (Goodenough vols 1–3, 1953, abbreviated version by Neusner 1988b; for a collection of Goodenough's articles see Neusner/Frerichs 1986).

Nowadays hardly any scholar would share the view that there was such a harsh opposition between 'the rabbis' and 'the people' in late Roman Palestine. Rabbis are mentioned as donors in synagogue inscriptions (Hezser 2001: 403–6). Shaye Cohen's view that these 'epigraphical rabbis' could not have been Torah scholars and should therefore be distinguished from the 'literary rabbis' is hardly convincing and not accepted by most scholars nowadays (see Cohen 1981–82; Hezser 1997: 119–23; Miller 2004). The so-called 'literary rabbis' did not form a homogeneous group but differed amongst themselves. Rabbinic literature presents ambiguous information on rabbis' relationship to images (see, e.g. the discussions in y. A.Z. ch. 3, 42b–43d). Their relation to (pagan) images needs to be re-examined. Literary references to symbols (e.g. in Midrash and liturgy) have to be studied in relation to the archaeological material (see Neusner 1991; Miller 2004), a task which has not yet been undertaken in a comprehensive and historical-critical way.

The explanations offered range from associating the Zodic-Helios complex with priests, considering it an expression of the Jewish God's power over his creation, and viewing it in the context of the calendar, astrology, and Jewish liturgy (for recent discussions of the issue, see Schwartz 2000; Cohen 2001; Goodman 2003; Levine 2003; Magness 2003; Fine 2005: 199–205). The proper significance of the imagery in the Jewish context can be established only on the basis of a comparison with similar depictions in Graeco-Roman paganism and early Byzantine Christian art. There may have been certain aspects of ancient mythology which were sufficiently open and 'universal' to be shared by Jews, Christians, and pagans, but given different meanings in the respective contexts concerned (see Hezser 2005). The same is true for the biblical motifs and scenes which appear in both synagogues and churches of the fifth and sixth centuries CE, and are sometimes combined with the Zodiac imagery. The issue of Jews and 'pagan' art is a much wider topic—pagan images appear not only in synagogues but also in private houses (e.g. in Sepphoris) and cemeteries (e.g. in Bet She'arim)—which, again, leads us to the necessity of an interdisciplinary approach which integrates the expertise gained by Talmudists, archaeologists, classicists, art historians, and scholars of early Christianity.

SUGGESTED READING

Krauss' *Talmudische Archäologie* (1910–12) can serve as an example of the early approach which used archaeology as the handmaiden of rabbinics. The volume of articles on Roman Caesarea, edited by Raban and Holum (1996), constitutes an example of the new interdisciplinary approach. Goodblatt (1980) examines ways in which rabbinic literature can be used for historical studies. Eliav (2002) and Fine (2006) discuss methodological approaches to correlating archaeological and literary data in the study of ancient Judaism, and Allison (2001) with regard to the study of Roman society.

BIBLIOGRAPHY

ALLISON, P. M. (2001). 'Using the Material and Written Sources: Turn of the Millenium Approaches to Roman Domestic Space'. *American Journal of Archaeology* 105: 181–208.

COHEN, A. (2001). 'The Celestial Host, the Calendar, and Jewish Art', in *Written in the Stars: Art and Symbolism of the Zodiac*. Jerusalem: Israel Museum Publications, 11–18.

COHEN, S. J. D. (1979). *Josephus in Galilee and Rome:. His Vita and Development as a Historian*. Leiden: Brill.

—— (1981–82). 'Epigraphical Rabbis'. *Jewish Quarterly Review* 72: 1–17.

—— (1984). 'The Significance of Yavneh: Pharisees, Rabbis, and the End of Jewish Sectarianism'. *Hebrew Union College Annual* 55: 27–53.

COTTON, H. (1998). 'The Rabbis and the Documents', in *Jews in a Graeco-Roman World*, ed. M. Goodman. Oxford: Clarendon Press, 167–79.

—— and Yardeni, A. (eds) (1997). *Aramaic, Hebrew and Greek Documentary Texts from Nahal Hever and Other Sites*. Documents from the Judean Deserts 27. Oxford: Clarendon Press.

ELIAV, Y. Z. (2002). 'Realia, Daily Life, and the Transmission of Local Stories During the Talmudic Period', in *What Athens Has to Do with Jerusalem: Essays on Classical, Jewish, and Early Christian Art and Archaeology in Honor of Gideon Foerster*, ed. L. V. Rutgers. Leuven: Peeters, 235–265.

ELMAN, Y. (2005). 'The Babylonian Talmud in its Historical Context', in *Printing the Talmud. From Bomberg to Schottenstein*, ed. S. Liberman Mintz and G. M. Goldstein. New York: Yeshiva University Museum.

ESHEL, H. (1997). 'A Note on "Miqvaot" at Sepphoris', in *Archaeology and the Galilee: Texts and Contexts in the Graeco-Roman and Byzantine Periods*, ed. D. R. Edwards and C. T. McCollough. Atlanta: Scholars Press, 131–33.

FINE, S. (2005). *Art and Judaism in the Graeco-Roman World: Towards a New Jewish Archaeology*. Cambridge: Cambridge University Press.

—— (2006). 'Archaeology and the Interpretation of Rabbinic Literature: Some Thoughts', in *How Should Rabbinic Literature Be Read in the Modern World?*, ed. M. Kraus. Piscataway: Gorgias Press, 199–217.

FREDRIKSEN, P./REINHARTZ, A. (eds) (2002). *Jesus, Judaism, and Christian Anti-Judaism: Reading the New Testament Texts After the Holocaust*. Louisville: Westminster John Knox Press.

FRIEDHEIM, E. (2006). *Rabbanisme et paganisme en Palestine romaine*. Leiden: Brill.

GALOR, K. (2003). 'Domestic Architecture in Roman and Byzantine Galilee and Golan'. *Near Eastern Archaeology* 66: 44–57.

GOODBLATT, D. M. (1980). 'Towards the Rehabilitation of Talmudic History', in *History of Judaism: The Next Ten Years*, ed. B. M. Bokser. Chico: Scholars Press, 31–44.

——(1994). The Monarchic Principle: Studies in Jewish Self-Government in *Antiquity*. Tübingen: Mohr-Siebeck.

GOODENOUGH, E. R. (1953). *Jewish Symbols in the Graeco-Roman Period*, vol. 1–3. New York: Pantheon Books.

GOODMAN, M. (2003). 'The Jewish Image of God in Late Antiquity', in *Jewish Culture and Society under the Christian Roman Empire*, ed. R. Kalmin and S. Schwartz. Leuven: Peeters, 133–45.

GREEN, W. S. (1978). 'What's in a Name? The Problematic of Rabbinic "Biography"', in *Approaches to Ancient Judaism: Theory and Practice*, vol. 1, ed. W. S. Green. Missoula: Scholars Press, 77–96.

HACHLILI, R. (1977). 'The Zodiac in Ancient Jewish Art: Representation and Significance'. *Bulletin of the American Society of Oriental Research* 228: 61–77.

HEZSER, C. (1997). *The Social Structure of the Rabbinic Movement in Roman Palestine*. Tübingen: Mohr-Siebeck.

——(1998). '"Privat" und "öffentlich" im Talmud Yerushalmi und in der griechisch-römischen Antike', in *The Talmud Yerushalmi and Graeco-Roman Culture*, vol. 1, ed. P. Schäfer. Tübingen: Mohr-Siebeck, 424–579.

—— (2001). *Jewish Literacy in Roman Palestine*. Tübingen: Mohr-Siebeck.

—— (2005). 'Toward the Study of Jewish Popular Culture in Roman Palestine', in *The Words of a Wise Man's Mouth Are Gracious (Qoh. 10,12): Festschrift for Günter Stemberger on the Occasion of his 65th Birthday*, ed. M. Perani. Berlin and New York: De Gruyter, 267–97.

HIRSCHFELD, Y. (1995). *The Palestinian Dwelling in the Roman-Byzantine Period*. Jerusalem: Franciscan Printing Press.

—— and Galor, K. (2007). 'New Excavations in Roman, Byzantine, and Early Islamic Tiberias', in *Religion, Ethnicity, and Identity in Ancient Galilee: A Region in Transition*, ed. J. Zangenberg et al. Tübingen: Mohr-Siebeck, 207–29.

HORST, P. W. VAN DER (1991). *Ancient Jewish Epitaphs*. Kampen: Kok Pharos Publishing House.

KRAUSS, SAMUEL (1910–12). *Talmudische Archäologie*, 3 vols. Leipzig: G. Fock.

LAPIN, H. (1999). 'Palestinian Inscriptions and Jewish Ethnicity in Late Antiquity', in *Galilee Through the Centuries: Confluence of Cultures*, ed. E. M. Meyers. Winona Lake: Eisenbrauns, 239–68.

LEVINE, A.-J. (2006). *The Misunderstood Jew: The Church and the Scandal of the Jewish Jesus*. San Francisco: Harper.

LEVINE, L. I. (2003). 'Contextualizing Jewish Art: The Synagogues at Hammat Tiberias and Sepphoris', in *Jewish Culture and Society under the Christian Roman Empire*, ed. R. Kalmin and S. Schwartz. Leuven: Peeters, 91–131.

—— (2005). *The Ancient Synagogue: The First Thousand Years*. 2nd ed. New Haven: Yale University Press.

LEWIS, N./YADIN, Y./GREENELD, J. C. (eds) (1989). *The Documents from the Bar Kokhba Period in the Cave of Letters: Greek Papyri.* Jerusalem: Israel Exploration Society.

MAGNESS, J. (2003). 'Helios and the Zodiac Cycle in Ancient Palestinian Synagogues', in *Symbiosis, Symbolism, and the Power of the Past: Canaan, Ancient Israel, and Their Neighbors from the Late Bronze Age through Roman Palaestina,* ed. W. G. Dever and S. Gitin. Winona Lake: Eisenbrauns, 363–89.

MEYERS, E. (2002). 'Aspects of Everyday Life in Roman Palestine With Special Reference to Private Domiciles and Ritual Baths', in *Jews in the Hellenistic and Roman Cities,* ed. J. R. Bartlett. London: Routledge, 193–220.

MILLER, S. S. (2003). 'Some Observations on Stone Vessel Finds and Ritual Purity in Light of Talmudic Sources', in *Zeichen aus Text und Stein, Studien auf dem Weg zu einer Archäologie des Neuen Testaments,* ed. S. Alkier and J. Zangenberg, Tübingen: Mohr-Siebeck, 402–419.

—— (2004). '"Epigraphical" Rabbis, Helios, and Psalm 19: Were the Synagogues of Archaeology and the Synagogues of the Sages One and the Same?' *Jewish Quarterly Review* 94: 27–76.

—— (2006). *Sages and Commoners in Late Antique 'Erez Israel: A Philological Inquiry into Local Traditions in Talmud Yerushalmi.* Tübingen: Mohr-Siebeck.

NEUSNER, J. (1980). 'Story as History in Ancient Judaism. Formulating Fresh Questions', in *History of Judaism: The Next Ten Years,* ed. B. M. Bokser. Chico: Scholars Press, 3–29.

—— (ed.) (1981). *The Study of Ancient Judaism,* 2 vols. New York: Ktav.

—— (1984). 'Introduction: Methodology in Talmudic History', in *Ancient Judais:. Debates and Disputes,* ed. J. Neusner. Chico: Scholars Press, 5–24.

—— (1988a). 'Judaic Uses of History in Talmudic Times'. *History and Theory* 27: 12–39.

—— (ed.) (1988b). *Goodenough's Jewish Symbols: An Abridged Edition.* Princeton: Princeton University Press.

—— (1991). *Symbol and Theology in Early Judaism.* Minneapolis: Fortress Press.

—— and Frerichs, E. S. (eds) (1986). *Goodenough on History of Religion and on Judaism.* Atlanta: Scholars Press.

PARKES, J. (1934). *The Conflict of the Church and the Synagogue: A Study in the Origins of Antisemitism.* London: Soncino Press.

RABAN, A./HOLUM K. G. (eds) (1996). *Caesarea Maritima: A Retrospective After Two Millenia,* Leiden: Brill.

RAHMANI, L. Y. (1994). *A Catalogue of Jewish Ossuaries in the Collections of the State of Israel.* Jerusalem: The Israel Antiquities Authority and the Israel Academy of Sciences and Humanities.

REICH, R. (2002). 'They Are Ritual Baths: Immerse Yourself in the Ongoing Sepphoris Mikveh Debate'. *Biblical Archaeology Review* 28: 50–55.

SAFRAI, S./STERN M. (eds) (1974–76). *The Jewish People in the First Century: Historical Geography, Political History, Social, Cultural and Religious Life and Institutions.* 2 vols. Assen: Van Gorcum.

SAFRAI, S. (ed.) (1987). *The Literature of the Sages. First Part: Oral Torah, Halakhah, Mishna, Tosefta, Talmud, External Tractates.* Assen/Maastricht: Van Gorcum, Philadelphia: Fortress Press.

—— et al. (eds) (2006). *The Literature of the Sages. Second Part: Midrash and Targum, Liturgy, Poetry, Mysticism, Contracts, Inscriptions, Ancient Science and the Languages of Rabbinic Literature.* Assen/Maastricht: Van Gorcum.

Schwabe, M./Lifshitz, B. (1974). *Beth She'arim, vol.2: The Greek Inscriptions*. Jerusalem: Hebrew University.

Schwartz, S. (1990). *Josephus and Judaean Politics*. Leiden: Brill.

—— (2000). 'On the Program and Reception of the Synagogue Mosaics', in *From Dura to Sepphoris. Studies in Jewish Art and Society in Late Antiquity*, ed. L. I. Levine and Z. Weiss. Portsmouth: Journal of Roman Archaeology, 165–81.

—— (2001). *Imperialism and Jewish Society*, 200 BCE to 640 CE Princeton: Princeton University Press.

—— (2002). 'Historiography on the Jews in the "Talmudic Period"', in *The Oxford Handbook of Jewish Studies*, ed. M. Goodman. Oxford: Oxford University Press, 79–114.

Small, J. P. (1997). *Wax Tablets of the Mind: Cognitive Studies of Memory and Literacy in Classical Antiquity*. London and New York: Routledge.

Sperber, D. (1993). *Material Culture in Eretz-Israel during the Talmudic Period* [Hebr.]. Jerusalem: Ben Zvi Institute.

Stemberger, G. (1996). *Introduction to Talmud and Midrash*. Translated and edited by Markus Bockmühl. 2nd ed. Edinburgh: T. & T. Clark.

Woolf, G. (1997). 'Beyond Romans and Natives'. *World Archaeology* 28: 339–50.

CHAPTER 2

THE GRAECO-ROMAN CONTEXT OF JEWISH DAILY LIFE IN ROMAN PALESTINE

CATHERINE HEZSER

FROM the time of Pompey's conquest of Jerusalem in 63 BCE until the Islamic invasion of the Middle East in the early seventh century CE, the Jews of Roman Palestine lived in an environment in which Graeco-Roman, and from the fourth century CE onwards, Roman-Byzantine culture would have been more or less palpable in almost all aspects of daily life. Although the specific form and impact of Graeco-Roman and early Byzantine culture will have varied in accordance with the time periods and geographical locations concerned, one must assume that it nevertheless pervaded Jewish daily life. The encounter will have created variegated fusions and complex alliances between the customs, traditions, and artefacts of the Roman Empire at large and the local Jewish material culture, mores, and practices. Combinations and overlaps between the (probably never really pure, unadulterated, and homogeneous) indigenous culture and the 'foreign' culture of the conquerers had already resulted from the spread of Hellenism in the Land of Israel (see Levine 1998: 3–32), a heritage which Romans—and at least upper-class urban Jews—seem to have happily embraced.

Obviously, Graeco-Roman culture would not have affected all aspects of ancient Jewish life in the same way. We must rather reckon with many different configurations in which Palestinian Jews would have felt the overarching presence of the Roman Empire in their daily pursuits, and in the environment of the villages, towns, and cities in which they lived. Therefore each area and aspect of ancient Jewish everyday life has to be examined separately, and the methods used have to be chosen in accordance with the topic of investigation. Some topics, such as Roman theatres and bathhouses in Palestine and their reflection in rabbinic literature, have already been investigated more than others, such as the Graeco-Roman context of the Palestinian economy and Jewish private life. We have to assume, though, that even the private sphere of the family and Jewish intellectual and religious life will have experienced changes in Roman times.

To argue that Jewish material culture, or even daily life as such, would not have differed significantly from the material culture and daily life in the Roman Empire at large, and therefore does not need investigation, would be a much too simplistic assumption, however. Societies experience changes when confronted with other cultures, especially those of the ruling powers, but they do not succumb entirely to the other way of life; rather they accommodate their own traditional lifestyle to the new circumstances, resulting in various degrees of adaptation, modification, and acceptance of other customs and practices. Therefore a careful historical examination of the different aspects of everyday life of the various provincial populations of the Roman Empire is necessary (see, for example, Lindsay 1963, on daily life in Roman Egypt) to supplement the many already existing studies of daily life in Roman Italy itself (see, for example, Marquardt 1990 [reprint of 2nd ed. 1886]; Carcopino 1941; Cowell 1961; Balsdon 1969; Veyne 1987; Dupont 1992; Adkins 1998; Lancon 2000).

In the following, we shall focus on previous studies of the Graeco-Roman context of Jewish daily life in Roman Palestine. Since the study of ancient Jewish everyday life itself had not received much attention since Samuel Krauss' multi-volume work, *Talmudische Archäologie* (1910–12), until quite recently, the impact of Graeco-Roman culture on Jewish daily life has not been examined much either. The following survey is meant to encourage new studies on the topic. It will point out which areas still need to be investigated. The Graeco-Roman cultural context of Jewish daily life will also be addressed in connection with particular topics in the essays that follow in this volume.

1. THE GRAECO-ROMAN CONTEXT
OF PALESTINIAN JUDAISM

The impact of Graeco-Roman culture on Judaism did not begin with Pompey's conquest of Judaea but in the earlier Hellenistic period. At least from the time of

Alexander the Great onwards, and especially in the second and first centuries BCE, Jews in the Diaspora as well as in the Land of Israel became acquainted with Greek culture and developed their own forms of Hellenism. At the same time, reactionary movements emerged which were opposed to too drastic changes brought about by the encounter with 'foreign' ideas and practices. In his book, *Judaism and Hellenism: Studies in Their Encounter in Palestine during the Early Hellenistic Period* (2nd ed. 1991), Martin Hengel has convincingly argued that Palestinian Judaism differed only gradually from Diaspora Judaism with regard to its openness to Hellenistic culture in the last centuries of the Second Temple period. He has argued that Hellenism was not only a political and economic force, but also had a great influence on Jewish daily and intellectual life. In his book he focuses on the impact of the Greek language, Greek education, Greek literature, and philosophy on Judaism in Palestine. Although the encounter between Palestinian Judaism and Greek culture was not without conflicts and clashes, he concludes that Palestinian Judaism of that time can be called 'Hellenistic Judaism' due to the large degree of cultural 'infiltration' (Hengel 1991: 103).

Hengel identifies a strand in Judaism which was allegedly opposed to Hellenism and its influence. He argues that 'the culmination of this centuries-long development was the Rabbinate in the second century AD' (ibid.). Although he allows for Greek influence on rabbinic education, he assumes that rabbinic Judaism turned inwards and shut itself off from any 'foreign' influences. This view allowed him to distinguish categorically between an open-minded and universalist Hellenistic Judaism which found its continuation and climax in early Christianity, and an allegedly exclusivist Pharisaic-rabbinic Judaism which is, to some extent, seen as an aberration from the Judaism which preceded it (see especially ibid. 309 and 313). Hengel obviously failed to recognize to what extent even rabbinic Judaism had absorbed the ideas and practices of the surrounding Graeco-Roman culture. He also limited his examination of the Hellenistic impact on Judaism to education and intellectual life rather than examining other areas of ancient Jewish life as well.

Saul Liebermann, especially, conducted studies of the Graeco-Roman impact on rabbinic culture. These were published in his books, *Greek in Jewish Palestine,* and *Hellenism in Jewish Palestine* (see *idem* 1994, originally published in 1942 and 1950). Combining a vast knowledge of classical literature and culture with traditional Jewish learning, Lieberman's studies were ground-breaking with regard to viewing rabbinic literature in its larger Graeco-Roman cultural context, and in claiming a variety of interconnections. In contrast to Hengel, Lieberman revealed Palestinian rabbis' participation in, and indebtedness to, Graeco-Roman intellectual life, and some rabbis' familiarity with the Greek language, even if a detailed first-hand knowledge of Graeco-Roman literature and philosophy may be difficult to maintain. Lieberman's methodological approach is mostly philological, focusing on terms, formulations, and motifs with analogies in Graeco-Roman literary sources. In the framework of this philological approach Lieberman suggests that rabbis were well aware of Graeco-Roman ideas, practices, and rhetorical forms. A detailed examination of rabbinic texts within this Graeco-Roman cultural context is therefore necessary to avoid misunderstanding rabbinic argumentation and narrative.

Other earlier studies show a similar focus on rabbis' relationship to 'Greek wisdom', the Greek language, and shared literary forms and motifs (see the bibliographical references in Hezser 2000: 161–87). Based on his observations concerning the rabbinic use of the Hellenistic literary form *chreia*, Henry A. Fischel has argued that the social role of the rabbi resembled that of the 'scholar-believer-bureaucrat' in Graeco-Roman society (Fischel 1973: XII). The sage presented himself as the fulfilment of an educational ideal, an ideal which, in its combination of theory and practice and in the sage's self-distinction from the 'uneducated' masses, was shared by rabbis and Hellenistic 'wise men'. Obviously, both rabbinic and philosophical study were forms of higher education in antiquity, the rabbinic focus on the Torah constituting an alternative to the study of Hellenistic philosophical traditions. The various aspects of these two types of higher education have not yet been properly compared with each other. Exceptions are Shaye J. D. Cohen's and Hayim Lapin's articles on patriarchal and rabbinic academies in the context of Graeco-Roman philosophical schools and early Christian educational institutions, respectively (see Cohen 1981; Lapin 1996). What would be especially interesting and worthy of further exploration is the relationship between the social organization of rabbinic and philosophical teaching and the transmission and eventual codification of the traditions emerging from these settings.

Various aspects of Palestinan Jewish culture were examined in the context of Graeco-Roman society in a project on *The Talmud Yerushalmi and Graeco-Roman Culture*, initiated by Peter Schäfer. The results of these studies are published in three volumes (vols 1 and 3: Schäfer 1998 and 2002; vol. 2: Schäfer/Hezser 2000). As the name of this project indicates, the focus was on the Talmud Yerushalmi, but the topical investigations necessitated the use of other works of rabbinic literature as well. Many of the essays deal with aspects of ancient Jewish daily life (in Schäfer 1998: 203–17: S. Schwartz on the rabbis and urban culture; 219–311: Jacobs on bathhouses; 313–25: J. Schwartz on leisure-time activities; 327–47: Jacobs on theatres and performances; 349–66: Rajak on burial practices; 423–579: Hezser on the distinction between public and private; in Schäfer/Hezser 2000: 51–80: Lapin on rabbis and cities; 189–254: Hezser on friendship; in Schäfer 2002: 73–89: Hayes on illegitimate unions; 91–137: Hezser on slaves; 185–223: Ilan, and 225–43: Satlow on the representation of women).

One of the most important conclusions of this study was the need for methodological plurality: each topic requires its own methodological approach, based on the specific questions asked and the sources available for answering them. Obviously, the investigation of rabbinic reflections on Roman theatres requires a different approach than the much wider issue of rabbis and urban culture does. Although both studies would be based on literary and archaeological material, this material would have to be investigated and presented in different ways. Another important conclusion is the inappropriateness of generalizing statements concerning the impact of Graeco-Roman culture on ancient Jewish daily life. Each aspect of daily life needs to be investigated independently in order to determine similarities and differences between Jewish and Graeco-Roman customs and practices. Furthermore, the traditional search for direct influences of one culture on another has recently been substituted by focusing on the ways in which a culture participates in the broader signifying space provided by its environment. Intertextuality is understood in a much broader sense, then, namely as a text's positioning within its cultural context. Such an investigation allows for a much more variegated comparison between aspects of Jewish and Graeco-Roman daily life without having to claim dependencies (see also Schäfer 1998: 14–16).

One especially important area of research into the Graeco-Roman context of Jewish daily life is the comparison between rabbinic halakhah and Graeco-Roman law. Rabbinic halakhah is concerned with almost all aspects of everyday life, from family relationships to architecture and living conditions. In many of these areas Roman jurists had to deal with very similar problems and came up with partly similar solutions, which are transmitted in similar literary forms. The investigation of similarities and differences between ancient Jewish and Roman law has a long tradition which goes back at least to the 1960s and 70s, when David Daube and Boaz Cohen published their comparative studies (see Daube 1992; Cohen 1966). Nevertheless, many issues concerning family, civil, and economic law are still in need of close investigation. Again, a multidisciplinary approach, which refrains from searching for direct influences but examines analogies, seems to be the most appropriate way of proceeding in this case (see Hezser 2003: 10–13, and the studies published in that volume).

2. WHAT IS JEWISH ABOUT ANCIENT JEWISH DAILY LIFE?

Some scholars have argued that Jews were so well integrated into the empire-wide Graeco-Roman culture that at least some aspects of their daily life experience would have been identical with the daily life of Romans and therefore would not need further investigation. For example, Dale Martin has claimed that 'Jewishness itself has little if any relevance for the structures of slavery amongst Jews.... The relevant factors for slave structures and the existence of slavery itself were geographical and socio-economic and had little if anything to do with ethnicity or religion' (Martin 1993: 113). Even though basic economic structures governing the employment of slaves (e.g. the fact that agricultural slave labour was profitable for large landowners only, at a time when slave prices were low) would have applied to all ancient slave-holding societies, the actual utilization and treatment of slaves would have been determined by other factors which were particular to each society: the specific political circumstances, the socio-economic situation, religious and moral concerns, prejudices, and popular attitudes (see Hezser 2005a: 7–12). Therefore everyday life phenomena such as slavery need to be investigated anew for each society concerned, even if such a study will reveal certain similarities between Jewish and Graeco-Roman society.

Similar considerations apply to other aspects of ancient Jewish daily life. In his study of Jewish marriage in antiquity Michael Satlow has argued: 'With marriage, as with so many other areas, the adjective "Jewish" is fluid and often negotiable' (Satlow 2001: 270). He has suggested that one should distinguish between the civil and religious aspects of marriage and determine 'what it means for a marriage to be "Jewish"'. Does the usage of a particular type of marriage contract make a marriage Jewish? Are there any specifically Jewish courting rituals or roles assumed by the respective members of the family? Or is the rabbinic opposition to intermarriage and the definition of 'illegitimate' unions the Jewish proprium? But then Romans knew of illegitimate unions as well, and guarded the boundaries of the Roman family.

To some extent, the problems involved in defining what is Jewish about ancient Jewish daily life are related to methodological issues. The main body of evidence available for the study of ancient Jewish everyday life are rabbinic literary documents. Obviously, these texts were written from the particular perspective of rabbis, who, after the destruction of the Temple, constituted the Jewish religious elite and were self-declared guardians over Jewish behaviour and identity. We do not know, and cannot determine with any degree of certitude, to what extent their recommendations were followed by the general Jewish population. Scholarly opinions range from viewing rabbis as a small group of intellectuals whose theorizing was out-of-touch with real life, to claiming that their halakhic rules merely reflected common practice, and/or that rabbis were the leaders of local Jewish communities. The truth probably lies somewhere in between these positions.

Archaeological discoveries and the decipherment of papyrological and epigraphic texts have revealed material which allows us to view ancient Jewish daily life from a different, non-rabbinic perspective. In a number of cases a certain discrepancy between the rabbinic presentation and the epigraphic or material evidence emerges. For example, the Elephantine and Judaean Desert papyri contain marriage contracts which have little in common with the rabbinic *ketubbah* (see Satlow 2001: 200–212). Whereas rabbis were opposed to figural depictions, especially if they were related to pagan worship and religion, late antique synagogues show a variety of images adopted from pagan art, such as the zodiac cycle in Hammat Tiberias, Bet Alpha and elsewhere, and David as Orpheus, playing the harp, in the Gaza Synagogue mosaic. Scholars have offered a variety of explanations for the use of pagan art in Jewish contexts. In any case, the very phenomenon suggests that the Jewish populace (including some rabbis) was more open to Graeco-Roman culture than certain rabbinic passages want us to believe.

If one assumes a general Jewish openness to the surrounding culture, the fact that some individuals with variants of the title 'Rabbi' are buried near sarcophagi with figural decorations in the Bet Shearim cemetery should also not surprise us too much (see Cohen 1981–82, who distinguishes, however, between the so-called 'epigraphical' rabbis and the 'literary' rabbis). Not even rabbis seem to have been too bothered by the statues of pagan deities in theatres and bathhouses (see Schwartz 1998), in contrast to Christian leaders, who considered frequenting such locales equal to participating in idolatry (see Hezser 2005b).

Besides distinguishing between the rabbinic perspective and the Jewish population of Roman Palestine at large, one also needs to differentiate between the urban population and the population of the countryside or hinterland, and between the different social strata as far as attachment to the local culture and openness for the empire-wide Graeco-Roman culture is concerned. City dwellers belonging to the upper strata of society would be most likely to have social and business contacts

Fig. 2.1 Relief with theatre masks, Katzrin

Photo: Catherine Hezser

with Gentiles and could therefore hardly evade participation in the Roman cultural environment. They probably considered obtaining a certain amount of Greek education a matter of prestige within the provincial context. Villagers involved in agriculture or crafts may have spent their whole lives in the confined, familial atmosphere of their home village or town. They would stand at the lowest end of the Graeco-Roman cultural barometer. But would their lack of concern for the Roman customs and mores make them more Jewish? Could they entirely avoid being affected by the provincialization of Palestine and the necessary influx of 'foreignness'? Would Graeco-Roman culture have been considered foreign at all in late antiquity, given that centuries of Hellenistic rule had already brought about numerous changes to people's daily lives?

At this point one might insist that a proper definition of 'Jewish' and 'non-Jewish' and 'foreign' / 'alien' with regard to daily life should be suggested. But can such a distinction be made without confusing 'Jewish' with 'rabbinic'? Does rabbinic literature provide the proper standards for defining ancient Jewish identity? Or can all practices and behaviours adopted by Jews be called Jewish, even if they cannot be traced back to Torah or Temple origins (just as many rabbinic halakhic rules cannot)? To claim that the Torah and rabbinic halakhah are the parameters against which Jewishness should be measured would be equal to adopting a modern Orthodox position and retrojecting it onto the ancient world.

Thus, the question of what is Jewish about ancient Jewish daily life may be an altogether wrong question to ask. Rather, one should try to investigate how Jews participated in an empire-wide culture by, at the same time, continuing a variety of local traditions, and how they adopted certain new techniques while also taking advantage of local resources, in the manufacture of goods as well as in areas such as architecture, farm management, and education.

3. MATERIAL CULTURE

The first attempt to examine the ancient Jewish material culture of Roman Palestine in a comprehensive way was undertaken by Samuel Krauss in his already mentioned multi-volume work *Talmudische Archäologie* a hundred years ago (Krauss 1910–12). In this work he also occasionally deals with the Graeco-Roman context of Jewish material culture as far as it was known and studied by scholars at his time. Krauss was not an archaeologist himself, however, and the various aspects of the daily life of Jews in ancient times had not become a major focus of archaeologists excavating in Mandate-period Palestine. Therefore the archaeological material available to him must have been quite limited.

Krauss sometimes tries to compensate for the lack of ancient evidence by referring to his own observations during travels through the Middle East and by using his creative imagination. For example, he draws a colourful picture of road travel in Palestine before the improvements to the road system introduced by the Romans: together with their animals the travellers would have to wade through rivers and streams interrupting the roads; on paths they would be confronted with undergrowth and rubble which could amount to entire hills they had to cross (Krauss 2: 323). This description seems to reflect the situation of the roads in Palestine at the end of the Ottoman period. The assumption that certain features of the Middle East in Krauss' own time can be used as models for the reconstruction of ancient life is also reflected elsewhere in his writing (see, e.g. ibid. 2: 329: bridge building).

Whereas Krauss reckoned with a strong impact of the Greek language and culture on rabbinic literature and terminology (see Krauss 1898–99), he was much more restrained with regard to its influence on the realia of daily life. As far as realia are concerned, he assumed that ancient Jewish life was conducted in an oriental manner, in harmony with traditional Middle Eastern culture as he had experienced it on his travels through Egypt and Palestine. The Orientalism of his age is likely to have influenced his thinking in this regard. Only occasionally, when the Graeco-Roman context is obvious and when explaining loanwords, does he point to Graeco-Roman analogies (e.g. vol. 2: 83–102: discussion of slavery; vol. 3: 38: *afikoman* = dessert; ibid. 43: the practice of reclining).

Research in the material culture of Roman Palestine has greatly advanced since Krauss' time. Numerous new archaeological discoveries have embellished and changed our picture of what ancient Jewish daily life was like. Especially over the last decades some archaeologists have turned their focus away from monumental architecture and public buildings towards the investigation of domestic architecture, pottery, jewelry, and other items of individual and family life. Sometimes the excavated material is investigated within the context of Graeco-Roman material culture, but such an analysis is still not carried out consistently. Much more comparative interdisciplinary research is necessary to determine to what extent Palestinian Jewish material culture followed local Near Eastern models, and to what extent it adhered to patterns and practices encountered in the Roman Empire at large.

One obviously has to distinguish between examples of Graeco-Roman architecture and material culture in Roman Palestine (cf. Weiss 1998), such as temples (see Jacobs 2000), theatres (see Jacobs 1998b), amphitheatres and stadia (see Weiss 1999), bathhouses (see Jacobs 1998a and Eliav 2000), statues (see Eliav 2002), imported amphora, ceramic fineware and other objects, and the local Jewish adoption of Graeco-Roman manufacturing and building styles. Graeco-Roman styles and practices could be imitated, or partly adopted and merged with local traditions and customs, as evident, for example, in the adoption of the basilica style for late antique synagogues, the combination of pagan and biblical motifs in synagogue decoration, the use of locally produced fabrics for the production of Roman-style garments, and the creation of vessels resembling those found elsewhere in the Roman world. Sometimes only a few selected formal, stylistic, and architectural elements may have been adopted and merged with more traditional, local styles. At other times Graeco-Roman items may have been reproduced and imitated locally.

This leads us to the problem of how to identify the Jewish origin and/or use of a particular item of material culture. Obviously, Jewish workshops, artisans, stonemasons, and builders may well have produced or cooperated in the production of buildings, mosaic pavements, pottery vessels, glass items, and jewellery pieces which adhered to Graeco-Roman models entirely. Jews may also have lived in private buildings decorated with pagan images, such as the villa with the Dionysos mosaic in Sepphoris (see Talgam/Weiss 2004; see Fig. 2.2). But the Jewish origin and use cannot be determined in such cases. Therefore our knowledge of the Jewish material culture of Roman Palestine, that is, the material culture produced and used by Jews, will always be limited and one-sided, since it is based on only those realia which can be clearly identified as Jewish.

Such identification can be based on the type of object or building (e.g. late antique synagogues), the context in which they were found (e.g. sarcophagi in Jewish cemeteries), and Jewish symbols or names attached to them. Rabbinic literary sources reckoning with Jewish ownership of Roman-style bathhouses (e.g. y. B.B. 4:6, 14c, discussed in Jacobs 1998a: 239–44), Jewish visits to Roman theatre performances (e.g. y. A.Z. 1:7, 40a, discussed in Jacobs 1998b: 332–38), and Jewish workers' participation in the production of pagan statues and images (cf. m. A.Z. 1:8 and Jacobs 2000: 158; Eliav 2002), indicate, however, that Jewish

Fig. 2.2 Floor mosaic with Dionysiac procession in the triclinium of a villa in Sepphoris

Photo: Catherine Hezser. Publication courtesy of Zeev Weiss

involvement with the material culture of Roman Palestine was not limited to identifiably Jewish items. And we should keep in mind that rabbinic sources provide us with the restricted view of the rabbis only.

4. FAMILY LIFE

One has to assume that the Graeco-Roman context of Palestinian Judaism would also have had an impact on ancient Jews' private lives, on relationships within the family, on gender roles, and on the very constitution of the family itself. Some aspects of ancient Jewish family life in Roman Palestine have already been analysed, others are still in need of investigation and comparison. In the case of social phenomena it is usually much more difficult than in the case of material culture to determine whether we are dealing with the actual influence of one phenomenon on another or with parallel, analogous developments. The possibility of independent developments on the basis of similar circumstances always has to be reckoned with.

It seems that the very structure and constitution of the family changed in Hellenistic and Roman times. The Graeco-Roman *oikos/domus* and the Jewish *bayyit* could comprise the immediate family as well as slaves, clients, and extended kin. In the case of rabbis, their close circles of disciples seem to have been part of the *bayyit* as well (on rabbinic and patriarchal households see Sivertsev 2002 and 2005).

Both Josephus and rabbinic sources suggest that in Roman times the focus was on the nuclear family, consisting of mother, father, and children, rather than on the larger family unit including second- and third-degree relatives (Hezser 2005a: 195). This phenomenon had far-ranging consequences for the ancient Jewish lifestyle. For example, sexual intercourse with slave women was criticized by ancient Jewish leaders, and the children of such unions were considered to be slaves like their mothers. Obviously, in Jewish as in Roman society, a large family with many children was no longer the ideal. Rather, families tried to limit the number of heirs to the family property. The focus on the nuclear family will also have determined domestic architecture and living conditions. One may assume that *insulae* with shared courtyards were not necessarily shared by extended family units, but may have been occupied by a number of unrelated parties. Domestic architecture, family structure, and the composition of the ancient Jewish household need to be studied together in order to properly understand the archaeological remains.

Changed circumstances and concerns will also have had an impact on the respective roles of the householder and his wife, children, and slaves. Would the changed political circumstances of subjugation under the Romans have under-mined the householder's authority within the family, if the family is seen as a smaller prototype of the larger political unit? Would Graeco-Roman status criteria, such as public office, have been substituted by other concerns in Jewish society, such as, for example, domestic control? And if so, what would have been the implications for the situation of women?

Some aspects of the roles of men, women, and children in Palestinian Jewish society have already been examined by scholars such as Tal Ilan, Daniel Boyarin, and Larry Yarbrough (see especially Ilan 1995; Boyarin 1997; Yarbrough 1993). It seems necessary to study the respective gender roles together, and in relation to each other, since changes in the role of men will have had direct repercussions on the role of women. Whether, and to what extent, the role of women in Roman society would have led to changes in the role of women in Jewish society is still uncertain. For example, in Roman *sine manus* marriage, women were often able to maintain their own property, whereas rabbis put emphasis on the wife's dowry, which would have been at the husband's disposal during the time of marriage. Papyrus documents provide evidence of other practices in Jewish society, though, which allowed fathers to transfer property to their daughters by circumventing the husbands. In his study of ancient Jewish marriage practices, Satlow has emphasized that there is nothing particularly Jewish about Jewish marriage (see Satlow 2001), an issue which requires further examination. A particular problem in properly investigating the gender issue obviously lies in the sparcity of Jewish sources outside the rabbinic corpus. Often we are presented with the rabbinic perspective only, which may have been merely theoretical and not representative of Jewish society at large.

Similarities and differences between Graeco-Roman and Jewish society have to be investigated in detail for every aspect of family life. Whereas certain socio-economic structures may have led to similarities between the societies involved, the particular political and social circumstances, religious beliefs, and cultural tradi-tions may have engendered differences. In the case of slavery, for example, both Roman and Jewish sources suggest that in late antiquity slaves were mainly employed in households and as business intermediaries. In many regards, slaves were viewed and treated similarly in Roman and Jewish society, whereas in other respects striking differences are recognizable (see Hezser 2005a for a detailed examination): Jews seem to have viewed manual labour more positively than Romans; they practised debt slavery and self-sale, which were forbidden according to Roman law; they rejected the theory of natural slavery at a time when Greeks and Romans viewed Jews as a slavish nation; and they seem to have refrained from granting masters the right of life and death over their slaves, thereby limiting their authority. It seems that besides the Graeco-Roman context, the biblical heritage and the local Near Eastern tradition were important factors determining Jewish private life.

5. ECONOMIC PRACTICES

For properly understanding the economy of Roman Palestine in late antiquity it is important to view it within the context of the Roman-Byzantine economy at large. To date, Hayim Lapin has presented the first study of the Palestinian provincial economy within the broader Roman context (Lapin 2001). The most important question to be asked is how, and to what extent, Palestinian Jewish economic activity is integrated into the local, regional, and empire-wide economic system. To what extent did Jews collaborate with pagan and Christian farmers and artisans and sell their products to them? Did Jews develop monopolies on certain trades and industries? How was the Palestinian economy interconnected with other economies of the eastern Mediterranean? And finally: What do we know about overland and overseas import and export trade?

These questions can be answered only on the basis of a complex interdisciplinary approach which critically examines Jewish literary and archaeological evidence, and also takes account of recent studies of the economies of other Roman provinces. Zeev Safrai has already argued that the economy of Roman Palestine was an open, rather than a closed, economy (see Safrai 1994). Through various import and export activities, Roman Palestine will have been interlinked with other eastern and western provinces as well as with the Italian heartland. It is necessary to carefully examine these connections, and to determine the nature of the exchange that took place. To determine whether, and to what extent, a certain product was produced for the local market only or exported depends on a number of variables, such as the quantity of local production, the demand for it elsewhere, and possible competition from other locations.

The evidence available for studying this issue does not consist of archaeological data and literary sources pertaining to the Land of Israel only, but includes the study of shipwrecks in the Mediterranean, and the study of remnants of artefacts and vessels from Roman Palestine in other parts of the Roman Empire and beyond (see Kingsley 2004). Kingsley propagates a 'holistic approach' (ibid. 17) to the study of the transport of goods between Roman Palestine and abroad. Local production traditions need to be seen within the context of the economy of the Roman Empire as a whole. Furthermore, the study of travel, communications, and transport should be combined with the study of the economy. Although to date, the import and export network is reflected by a few discovered shipwrecks only, Josephus' generalizing statement that Palestine is 'not a maritime country, neither commerce nor the intercourse which it promotes with the outside world has any attraction on us . . .' (Contra Apionem 1.60) is almost certainly wrong, especially as far as the Herodian period and late antiquity are concerned. For example, with regard to wine amphorae found on shipwrecks, Kingsley writes that 'the volume of deposits recorded suggests that export of these wine jars was a primary economic activity in Byzantine Palestine' (Kingsley 2004: 50–51); 'Palestinian amphorae crop up in almost all excavated Mediterranean sites of late antique date and in varied contexts' (ibid. 94).

The interaction between Jews, Christians, and pagans in the local and inter-regional economy is another related issue that needs to be examined. In all likelihood, economic activities changed considerably when the Roman Empire became Christian, and especially between the late fourth and sixth century CE, on the basis of Christian building activity, travel, and pilgrimage. We do not know whether and to what extent the often re-issued Byzantine law prohibiting Jews from employing non-Jewish slaves would have been effective and have limited Jewish economic activities (see Hezser 2005a: 274). Nevertheless, the development of Christian empire-wide business networks would, at least to some extent, exclude partnerships with Jews. It would be interesting to see whether Jews could nevertheless maintain monopolies on certain specialized types of production and business transactions, and whether Christian competition increased Jewish attempts to build empire-wide business networks as well. Altogether, the question whether and to what extent the economy of Roman Palestine changed from Constantine onwards is still not sufficiently examined. Again, an interdisciplinary approach conducted by historians of ancient Judaism, church historians, and economic historians is destined to yield the best results on these issues.

The study of the ancient Jewish economy should also not shy away from examining certain peripheral issues which are nevertheless significant for a proper understanding of trade relations: the development and handling of the taxation system, the building of roads, ports, and way stations; the shipping industry; the imposition of customs duties; the entire organization of import and export trade. To what extent was Roman Palestine unique in any of these regards, and to what extent was it similar to other Roman provinces, that is, how did provincialization affect the Palestinian Jewish economy?

Michael McCormick has argued that '[t]ransport and communications played a key role in the transformation of the ancient world' (McCormick 2001: 64). These spacial patterns themselves were influenced by 'cultural attitudes . . . , for instance conceptions of pilgrimage, linguistic and cultural familiarity or hostility, and political imperatives' (ibid. 65). He believes that a 'sea change' took place in late antiquity in that 'an unprecedented degree of interregional economic specialization and integration' developed 'which accompanied political and cultural unification' (ibid. 83). It would be necessary to analyse to what extent Jews participated in this 'sea change' and perhaps even profited from it, and to what extent they were marginalized by the development of a 'unified' Christian Byzantine political, cultural—and economic—system which may have appropriated and exploited the resources of Palestine as the Christian 'Holy Land'.

6. Intellectual and Religious Life

Many aspects of Palestinian Jewish intellectual and religious life can likewise be understood properly only against the background of Graeco-Roman culture. The very phenomenon of the sage or wise man surrounded by a set of disciples had an analogy in Hellenistic philosophical circles (see Fischel, above, and Hezser 2000: 162–66). Striving for wisdom—which was defined differently in Jewish and Graeco-Roman culture but always involved familiarity with the literary tradition of the past—was seen as the highest good. Teaching wisdom also involved following a particular life style which set an ideal model for others to follow. In both Jewish and Graeco-Roman society the wise man considered himself the centre of concentric circles which emanated from him to his close disciples and further outwards to the more loosely connected associates and sympathizers in society at large. The sage distinguished himself from the so called 'unlearned' within the populace whom he tried to convert to his own way of life. As such, the sage can be considered part of an empire-wide alternative elite which existed alongside governmental office holders and local grandees. The members of this intellectual elite would compete with each other but also form allegiances. Comparisons between Jewish and non-Jewish sages and their disciples have been initiated by Fischel (1973). Many issues concerning their social organization, lifestyle, ideology, literary traditions, and impact on the population at large still require investigation.

It has also been argued that ancient Jewish educational institutions developed on the basis of Graeco-Roman models. Both Jewish and Graeco-Roman literary sources provide evidence of a distinction between primary and secondary education (see Hezser 2001: 38–109). In both cases, education seems to have been privately funded and informally organized. One may assume that Jewish primary education with its focus on Torah reading, as it was propagated by rabbis and especially prevalent in late antiquity, constituted a deliberate alternative to Greek education, with its focus on the study of Homer. Unlike Graeco-Roman primary schools, the Torah-focused Jewish education seems to have been available to boys only. Obviously, Jewish parents also had the option of sending their children to Greek teachers or of educating them at home. As a member of the upper strata of Jewish society, Josephus claims to have received both a Greek and a Jewish education. We do not know to what extent he was representative in this regard. On the basis of new insights into the forms, contents, and settings of ancient teaching, and the question to what extent written material was used, comparisons between Graeco-Roman and Jewish educational practices are still a necessary task for future scholarship.

Analogies between the architectural styles of late antique synagogues and Roman basilica buildings have already been mentioned above. In addition, certain features of early Byzantine churches, such as the *bema*, an elevated platform, became elements of synagogue buildings. Whether, and to what extent, shared architectural features were used in a similar or different way is still an open question. Liturgical similarities between synagogue and church services are evident from literary sources, and the liturgical developments need to be studied together with the building styles. In particular, the issue of liturgy and performance seems relevant. Even ancient theatre performances were not entirely secular events but served to propagate the Graeco-Roman mythological tradition (see Hezser 2005b). A certain competition between the local Torah-based heritage and the empire-wide pagan mythology may underlie rabbinic contrasts between synagogues and study houses on the one hand, and theatres and circuses on the other.

Besides theatre performances, another way in which Jews would have encountered pagan culture would have been through pagan festivals which were often combined with markets (see Veltri 2000). Rabbinic literature contains many traces of rabbis' knowledge of, and familiarity with, pagan religious customs relating to these holidays. As such, rabbinic sources can serve as evidence, not only of Jewish practices, but of certain aspects of Graeco-Roman provincial culture as well. Rabbinic criticism of the so-called 'ways of the Amorites' resembles criticism of the *paganae consuetudines* by the Church Fathers (see ibid. 94–101). A comparison between Jewish and Christian leaders' attitudes towards the various aspects and expressions of pagan religosity would be a worthwhile scholarly endeavour.

Can we assume that a genuine intellectual exchange took place between Graeco-Roman, Jewish, and Christian intellectuals in Roman Palestine? Recent studies (see, e.g. Stroumsa 1989; Stemberger 2004) have been much more

Fig. 2.3 Byzantine pillar with Medusa, Caesarea

Photo: Catherine Hezser

cautious with regard to assuming direct contacts and interreligious discourse than traditional studies were (see Herr 1971). This is due to a greater awareness of the literary nature of the sources: stories about meetings between rabbis and Roman officials, philosophers, and matrons cannot be taken as historically reliable evidence about actual encounters. On the other hand, rabbinic argumentation, especially in midrashic contexts, sometimes reveals traces of Christian, gnostic, or philosophical ideas (see Visotzky 1995). Altogether, then, generalizations should be avoided. Although few, if any, rabbis may have studied at Graeco-Roman philosophical, rhetorical, or legal schools, or read the writings of philosophers and the Church Fathers, at least some of them would have been familiar with Graeco-Roman and Christian ideas and practices from observation and hearsay, and through encounters on the street or in the marketplace. In all likelihood, we would find a great variety of attitudes towards Graeco-Roman and early Christian culture, both amongst rabbis and amongst the Jews of Roman Palestine at large.

Suggested Reading

Krauss' *Talmudische Archäologie* (Krauss 1910–12), the comprehensive but outdated treatment of the daily life of Jews in Roman Palestine, refers to the Graeco-Roman context sporadically. Saul Lieberman's works *Greek in Jewish Palestine*, and *Hellenism in Jewish Palestine*, which are now published in one volume (Lieberman 1994), constitute the classical statement on the encounter between rabbinic and Graeco-Roman culture. The three volumes of *The Talmud Yerushalmi and Graeco-Roman Culture* (Schäfer 1998–2002) provide a good overview of recent scholarship and approaches.

Bibliography

Adkins, L./Adkins, R. A. (eds) (1998). *Handbook to Life in Ancient Rome*. 2nd ed. Oxford and New York: Oxford University Press.

Balsdon, J. P. V. D. (1969, reprinted in 2002). *Life and Leisure in Ancient Rome*. London: Phoenix Press.

Boyarin, D. (1997). *Unheroic Conduct: The Rise of Heterosexuality and the Invention of the Jewish Man*. Berkeley: University of California Press.

Carcopino, J. (1941, reprinted 1991). *Daily Life in Ancient Rome. The People and the City at the Height of the Empire*. London: Penguin.

COHEN, B. (1966). *Jewish and Roman Law: A Comparative Study*. 2 vols. New York: The Jewish Theological Seminary of America.

COHEN, S. J. D. (1981). 'Patriarchs and Scholarchs'. *Proceedings of the American Academy of Jewish Research* 44: 57–85.

——. (1981–82). 'Epigraphical Rabbis'. *Jewish Quarterly Review* 72: 1–17.

COWELL, F. R. (1961). *Everyday Life in Ancient Rome*. London: B. T. Batsford.

DAUBE, D. (1992). *Collected Works of David Daube. Vol.1: Talmudic Law*, ed. by C. M. Carmichael. Berkeley: Robbins Collection.

DUPONT, F. (1992). *Daily Life in Ancient Rome*. Oxford: Blackwell Publishing.

ELIAV, Y. (2000). 'The Roman Bath as a Jewish Institution: Another Look at the Encounter Between Judaism and the Greco-Roman Culture'. *Journal for the Study of Judaism* 31: 416–454.

—— (2002). 'Viewing the Sculptural Environment: Shaping the Second Commandment', in *The Talmud Yerushalmi and Graeco-Roman Culture*, vol. 3, ed. Peter Schäfer. Tübingen: Mohr-Siebeck, 411–33.

FISCHEL, H. A. (1973). *Rabbinic Literature and Greco-Roman Philosophy: A Study of Epicurea and Rhetorica in Early Midrashic Writings*. Leiden: Brill.

HENGEL, M. (1991). *Judaism and Hellenism: Studies in Their Encounter in Palestine during the Early Hellenistic Period*. 2 vols in one. 2nd ed. Minneapolis: Fortress Press.

HERR, M. D. (1971). 'The Historical Significance of the Dialogues Between Sages and Roman Dignitaries'. *Scripta Hierosolymitana* 22: 123–50.

HEZSER, C. (2000). 'Interfaces Between Rabbinic Literature and Graeco-Roman Philosophy', in *The Talmud Yerushalmi and Graeco-Roman Culture*, vol. 2, ed. P. Schäfer and C. Hezser. Tübingen: Mohr-Siebeck, 161–87.

—— (2001). *Jewish Literacy in Roman Palestine*. Tübingen: Mohr-Siebeck.

—— (2003). *Rabbinic Law in its Roman and Near Eastern Context*. Tübingen: Mohr-Siebeck, 2003.

—— (2005a). *Jewish Slavery in Antiquity*. Oxford: Oxford University Press.

—— (2005b). 'Towards the Study of Jewish Popular Culture in Roman Palestine', in *'The Words of a Wise Man's Mouth Are Gracious' (Qoh 10,12)*. Festschrift for Günter Stemberger on the Occasion of His 65th Birthday, ed. M. Perani. Berlin: De Gruyter, 267–297.

ILAN, T. (1995). *Jewish Women in Greco-Roman Palestine: An Inquiry into Image and Status*. Tübingen: Mohr-Siebeck.

JACOBS, M. (1998a). 'Römische Thermenkultur im Spiegel des Talmud Yerushalmi', in *The Talmud Yerushalmi and Graeco-Roman Culture*, vol. 1, ed. P. Schäfer. Tübingen: Mohr-Siebeck, 219–311.

—— (1998b). 'Theatres and Performances as Reflected in the Talmud Yerushalmi', in *The Talmud Yerushalmi and Graeco-Roman Culture*, vol. 1, ed. P. Schäfer. Tübingen: Mohr-Siebeck, 327–47.

—— (2000). Pagane Tempel in Palästina—rabbinische Aussagen im Vergleich mit archäologischen Funden", in: *The Talmud Yerushalmi and Graeco-Roman Culture*, vol. 2, ed. P. Schäfer and C. Hezser. Tübingen: Mohr-Siebeck, 139–59.

KINGSLEY, S. (2004). *Shipwreck Archaeology of the Holy Land*. London: Duckworth.

KRAUSS, S. (1898–99). *Griechische und lateinische Lehnwörter im Talmud, Midrasch und Targum*. Berlin: S. Calvary.

—— (1910–12). *Talmudische Archäologie*. 3 vols. Leipzig: Gustav Fock (reprinted Hildesheim: G. Olms, 1966).

LANÇON, B. (2000). *Rome in Late Antiquity: Everyday Life and Urban Change, AD. 312–609*. Edinburgh: Edinburgh University Press.

LAPIN, H. (1996). 'Jewish and Christian Academies in Roman Palestine: Some Preliminary Observations', in *Caesarea Maritima: A Retrospective After Two Millennia*, ed. Avner Raban and Kenneth G. Holum. Leiden: E. J. Brill, 496–512.

—— (2001). *Economy, Geography, and Provincial History in Later Roman Palestine*. Tübingen: Mohr-Siebeck.

LEVINE, L. I. (1998). *Judaism and Hellenism in Antiquity: Conflict or Confluence*. Seattle: University of Washington Press.

LIEBERMAN, S. (1994). *Greek in Jewish Palestine/Hellenism in Jewish Palestine*, with a new Introduction by Dov Zlotnick. New York and Jerusalem: The Jewish Theological Seminary of America.

LINDSAY, J. (1963). *Daily Life in Roman Egypt*. London: F. Muller.

MARQUARDT, J. (1990). *Das Privatleben der Römer*. 2 vols. Reprinted 2nd ed. Darmstadt: Wissenschaftliche Buchgesellschaft.

MARTIN, D. B. (1993). 'Slavery and the Ancient Jewish Family', in *The Jewish Family in Antiquity*, ed. S. J. D. Cohen. Atlanta: Scholars Press, 113–29.

McCORMICK, M. (2001). *Origins of the European Economy: Communications and Commerce*. Cambridge: Cambridge University Press.

SAFRAI, Z. (1994). *The Economy of Roman Palestine*. London: Routledge.

SATLOW, M. L. (2001). *Jewish Marriage in Antiquity*. Princeton: Princeton University Press.

SCHÄFER, P. (ed.) (1998). *The Talmud Yerushalmi and Graeco-Roman Culture*, vol. 1. Tübingen: Mohr-Siebeck.

SCHÄFER, P./HEZSER, C. (eds) (2000). *The Talmud Yerushalmi and Graeco-Roman Culture*, vol. 2. Tübingen: Mohr-Siebeck.

SCHÄFER, P. (ed.) (2002). *The Talmud Yerushalmi and Graeco-Roman Culture*, vol. 3. Tübingen: Mohr-Siebeck.

SCHWARTZ, S. (1998). 'Gamaliel in Aphrodite's Bath: Palestinian Judaism and Urban Culture in the Third and Fourth Centuries', in *The Talmud Yerushalmi and Graeco-Roman Culture*, vol. 1, ed. P. Schäfer. Tübingen: Mohr-Siebeck, 203–217.

SIVERTSEV, A. (2002). *Private Households and Public Politics in 3rd–5th Century Jewish Palestine*. Tübingen: Mohr Siebeck.

—— (2005). *Households, Sects, and the Origins of Rabbinic Judaism*. Leiden: Brill.

STEMBERGER, G. (2004). 'Cultural Interaction in Rabbinic Judaism', in *L'interculturalità dell'ebraismo*, ed. M. Peranni. Ravenna: Longo Editore, 59–68.

STROUMSA, G. A. G. (1989). 'Religious Contacts in Byzantine Palestine'. *Numen* 36: 16–42

TALGAM, R. / WEISS, Z. (2004). *The Mosaics of the House of Dionysos at Sepphoris*. Jerusalem: Institute of Archaeology, Hebrew University of Jerusalem.

VELTRI, G. (2000). 'Römische Religion an der Peripherie des Reiches: Ein Kapitel rabbinischer Rhetorik' in *The Talmud Yerushalmi and Graeco-Roman Culture*, vol. 2, ed. P. Schäfer and C. Hezser. Tübingen: Mohr-Siebeck, 81–138.

VEYNE, P. (ed.) (1987). *A History of Private Life*, vol. 1: *From Pagan Rome to Byantium*. Cambridge, Mass.: Harvard University Press.

VISOTZKY, B. L. *Fathers of the World: Essays in Rabbinic and Patristic Literatures*. Tübingen: Mohr-Siebeck.

WEISS, Z. (1998). 'Greco-Roman Influences on the Art and Architecture of the Jewish City in Roman Palestine', in *Religious and Ethnic Communities in Later Roman Palestine*, ed. Hayim Lapin. Bethesda: University Press of Maryland, 219–246.

——— (1999). 'Adopting a Novelty: The Jews and the Roman Games in Palestine', in *The Roman and Byzantine Near East: Some Recent Archaeological Research*, vol. 2, ed. J. H. Humphrey. Portsmouth: Journal of Roman Archaeology, 23–49.

YARBROUGH, O. L. (1993). 'Parents and Children in the Jewish Family of Antiquity', in *The Jewish Family in Antiquity*, ed. S. J. D. Cohen. Atlanta: Scholars Press, 39–59.

CHAPTER 3

···

GENDER ISSUES AND DAILY LIFE

···

TAL ILAN

WOMEN constitute half of humanity, and consequently also half of the Jewish people. Nevertheless, over the last four decades, feminist scholars have shown that the authors of historical studies who use inclusive terminology usually have the male half of the population in mind only (Ilan 2002b). Thus, for example, S. Safrai, in his study on Jewish education in antiquity, wrote: 'During the Second Temple period and even more so after the destruction of Jerusalem and the Temple in 70 CE the entire Jewish community, from its public institutions to the individual families, developed into an education-centered society, which paid particular attention to the education of children' (Safrai, 1976: 946). In this description he failed to notice that 'children' actually excluded half of the child population, and the 'entire Jewish community' actually refers only to its males. This phenomenon is endemic. When reviewing the new updated edition of Emil Schürer's, *The History of the Jewish People in the Age of Jesus Christ* (1973–87), Margarete Schlüter showed how, even as late as the 1970s–1980s (when this new edition was published), the issues of women and gender had not been revised (Schlüter 1999).

Feminist scholars have labelled this approach 'androcentric,' that is, placing the man at the centre of (scholarly) attention. Jewish sources, especially written ones, not least among them the rabbinic corpus, are blatantly androcentric. As I have shown elsewhere, the rabbis only mention women when they discuss an issue specifically concerning women; otherwise, their prime actor is male (Ilan 1997: 54–5). Rabbinic literature views women's role in society as restricted and stereotypical: men operate in public, women in private only. Part of the feminist project is to displace this approach. It maintains that this picture, even when partly true, is heavily tainted by an ideological approach, and that a careful and suspicious reading of the evidence reveals a much more complex picture.

The purpose of this article too is displacement. I therefore propose to describe Jewish women's daily life roughly according to the titles of this book's chapters, so as to demonstrate how and where women's experience can be compared with, and correlated to, that of men. Therefore most of the chapter titles from this book serve as sub-chapter titles in this essay, and under each, one or two examples which describe Jewish women's daily life are presented, showing how it may (or may not) have differed from men's, and how a gendered reading of the text may (or may not) add to the other approaches suggested in this volume.

1. Correlating Literary, Epigraphic, and Archaeological Sources

The major types of sources on Jewish women in Roman Palestine are the same as those on men—rabbinic literature (and a few other literary compositions), inscriptions, and papyri. The differences between these documents are evident—literary sources are edited compositions, intended for posterity and intensely theological and ideological. Papyri and inscriptions are short and formulaic, and they can easily be misunderstood by future generations. Yet almost all of these sources were composed by men, and thus, their worldview is highly androcentric. Interestingly, at least among the papyri from the Judaean Desert, deposited in caves by refugees of the Bar Kokhba revolt, two women's archives were discovered (Lewis 1989; Cotton 1995 and see also Ilan 2000). These include documents that were written by men specifically for women, such as marriage contracts, deeds of gift, and also court minutes of disputes over guardianship and property ownership. Writing such documents forces the author to grapple with uniquely female issues.

These papyri are legal documents. Most of rabbinic literature also consists of legal material. One sixth of the Mishnah (*Seder Nashim*) is clearly devoted to women and their legal status, although even in this case the Mishnah is mostly interested in men when they come into contact with women. The authors and editors envision the best methods to keep women under control (see Neusner 1980). The Mishnah is, therefore, what feminists define as a 'patriarchal' document, imagining a hierarchical society in which a male head of a household has authority over his wife, his children, and in some cases, his household slaves.

In assessing the relationship between the different types of source material at our disposal, it should be remembered that the papyri and the Mishnah do not represent one and the same legal system, and that the papyri are older than the redaction of the Mishnah (traditionally assumed to have taken place around 200 CE). Therefore they should not be studied in the light of the Mishnah, but rather the Mishnah on the basis of the papyri. Thus, if a papyrus was discovered which indicates that Jewish women could divorce their husbands (Ilan 1999: 253–62), and if the Mishnah definitively denies this, we need to understand this contradiction as a development in women's status over time, and not as an error in the reading of the document at hand (see Schremer 1998). In a gendered context it should also be remembered that both the papyri and the Mishnah are prescriptive documents. Although women's daily lives are likely to have been influenced by rabbinic prescriptions to some extent, rabbinic texts do not actually describe the minutiae of these lives in a historiographic way. Thus, when reading these texts for gender issues, one should approach them suspiciously, looking for contradictions, slips of the pen, and references to women in incidental and roundabout ways (see Ilan 2006a for examples).

2. THE GRAECO-ROMAN CONTEXT

Women, at least as much as men, were influenced by the Graeco-Roman environment in which they lived. The issue is sometimes mentioned in passing in the literature but has not merited a full-length study. Yet it is a fruitful field of research. An example demonstrating the greater influence of the surrounding Graeco-Roman culture on women than on men is the use of Graeco-Roman names. Although our record of women's names is much smaller than that of men, it can be shown that the use of Greek and Latin names among women was more common. While 17 per cent of the male population used Greek and Latin names, among women the percentage was 24 per cent (Ilan 2002a: 54–5). This phenomenon seems to have continued throughout Jewish history (Levine-Melamed 1998: 129). It may indicate two things: (a) that there were fewer names for women than for men recorded in the Hebrew Bible or, more likely, (b) that women's Jewishness was less valued and protected against foreign influences. Women were required to preserve their Jewish identity less than men were.

3. PROVINCIAL ADMINISTRATION / COURTS AND THE JUDICIAL SYSTEM

Much has been said about the existence of parallel provincial and Jewish judicial systems, where the former could be approached when the latter (which served more in a capacity of arbitration) failed to satisfy the customer. Although many feminist studies address Jewish women and their status within the halakhah (see primarily Hauptman 1997), to date no comprehensive social-historical discussion of women's roles in the Palestinian rabbinic legal system exists.

Because rabbinic literature associates women with the private domain, their presence in law courts is somewhat unexpected. At least one rabbinic maxim, albeit found in the Babylonian Talmud, states categorically that a man does not wish his wife to disgrace herself in a court of law (b. Ket. 74b). In papyri from the Judaean Desert, which derive from the Roman provincial law courts, Babatha, the owner of one archive, always appears in court accompanied by a guardian. Thus we may suspect that women were not considered by these courts as fully fledged legal entities (Cotton 1996). Yet they did appear before them and did make legal claims. Rabbinic literature, too, is full of stories of Jewish women approaching the Jewish law courts independently of their husbands, sometimes against them or their family, and with no guardian (Valler 2000: 103–49. Note that this study does not distinguish between Palestinian and Babylonian sources).

In most of these stories women are featured, and the issues they contest have to do with specific gender-oriented legislation, but their historicity is doubtful. Nevertheless, the fact that these stories portray women approaching the court indicates that rabbis deemed such actions plausible. One Palestinian rabbinic source even suggests that women could play off the Jewish against the provincial law court. In this source a woman by the name of Tamar, who is displeased with the verdict of the Jewish arbiter, takes her case to the governor's court in Caesarea (y. Meg. 3:2, 74a). The reason this story is told about a woman is because it ends with a pun on her name, but the fact that it is told about a woman suggests that it was considered plausible that women would act in such a way.

4. POPULATION STRUCTURE AND JEWISH IDENTITY

For lack of a statistically valid database, assessing ancient demography is a very risky task. In a conventional demographic study of the population of Roman Palestine one is prone to inquire about its size and about its ethnic make-up. Of no less interest is its gender division. This is an important social factor, because if one assumes empirically that the numbers of males and females born over the centuries have not substantially changed, the question of the sex ratio for every given age group can say something about childcare, health, nutrition, and historical catastrophes such as outbreaks of endemic violence (and war). One may rightfully ask whether daughters received the same childcare as sons. Did they receive the same nutrition? What were the demographic effects of infant marriage, child pregnancies, death at childbirth, etc? Did the Jews of Roman Palestine practise infanticide, and if so, were daughters the objects of this practice more than sons (Schwartz 2004)? It would be of interest to inquire to what extent Jewish society was similar to non-Jewish society with regard to these issues. One particular source for such a demographic study are skeletal remains. Jewish tombs are often easily identifiable, and some of their skeletal remains have been investigated already. My study on the subject marked a beginning (Ilan 1999: 195–214), but more aspects need to be investigated.

5. LANGUAGE DISTRIBUTION

Altogether, Jewish society of Roman Palestine can be considered as trilingual, in which Hebrew, Aramaic, and Greek were used. Since only one of these languages would have been spoken regularly at home, for individuals to acquire a passing knowledge in all three, a special language education would have been necessary. It may be assumed that, since no formal education for women existed, they were less versed in all three, or even two, of these languages. This, however, remains an assumption, because in discussions of these languages, the gender issue is never addressed (see e.g. Schwartz 1995; Hezser 2001: 227–50 for general criteria to be considered). Although the available evidence may be limited, a study devoted to this issue is a desideratum.

Since the documents at our disposal were not written by women, their languages cannot serve as evidence of the languages women knew or used. I confine myself to the few hints strewn here and there on the topic. For example, one source in the Babylonian Talmud describes two Galilean women speaking Aramaic, one to her neighbour and one to a judge, but their speech is so garbled that the first inadvertently insults her friend, and the other is understood as being disrespectful to the judge (b. Er. 53b). This story is intentionally gendered and presents the stereotype of dumb women, who cannot even speak their native tongue properly. Yet it is followed by a story about another woman—Rabbi Judah the Patriarch's slave, whose Aramaic is impeccable and very articulate. Elsewhere, the same woman is presented as being exceptionally well-versed in Hebrew (e.g. y. Meg. 2:2, 73a). The purpose of this last story, however, is to hold this woman as an inimitable example. It gives the impression that in the patriarch's house all spoke Hebrew, even the lowest of his female slaves.

A story told in the Palestinian Talmud relates that Rabbi Abbahu ruled that a man is permitted to teach his daughter Greek because it is considered an ornament for her (y. Shab. 6:1, 7d). He is then accused of ruling leniently on this matter because he desired to teach his own daughter Greek. These stories, rather than constituting evidence of women's language competence, suggest that women can serve as literary tools for the exploration of language proficiency, serving as examples of extreme ignorance as well as high education.

It is therefore of some interest to note the following: the first document from late antiquity that was written by a woman (some time in the Byzantine period: the document is undated and hard to date palaeographcally), a papyrus sent by a certain Harkan, apparently from Palestine, to her brother who migrated to Egypt, is composed in Hebrew with a mixture of Aramaic vocabulary typical of Palestine at the time (Mishor 2000–1).

6. THE HOUSEHOLD

The household is the central context in which women's daily life can be examined. Under this rubric many issues discussed in the present book can be read in relation to gender. One chapter in this book is devoted to urbanization and another to village life. From a gendered perspective, it is vital to inquire whether, and in what regards, the Jewish household was different in these respective surroundings, and how such differences would have influenced women's lives. One chapter in this book is devoted to crafts, manufacture and production, another to trade, commerce and consumption, and yet another to agriculture and animal husbandry. The conventional assumption is that for ancient Jewish women all three types of work were associated with the household economy and practised at home.

Rabbinic literature holds clear views about the household. There are tasks that belong within it and others that belong outside, and while women do the former, men do the latter. The rabbis have a whole range of occupations in mind when they make such assumptions. For example, when the Mishnah describes how a person stands in order to be examined for skin diseases, a man is described as holding a pick and working in the field, while a woman is described as weaving and spinning (M. Neg. 2:4). When a midrash describes the typical utensils a woman would borrow from her neighbour, these include a sieve and a pot, while a parallel story, concerning a man, records him borrowing cereal grain, or simply money (Lev. R. 5:8; 17:2). Numerous texts describe women cooking, baking, cleaning the house, spinning and weaving (e.g. M. Ket. 5:5). While it is clear that some of these labours were conducted for the benefit of the woman's own house, it is also obvious that many could produce surplus which would supply additional income for the family. The rabbis themselves imagine the relationship between husband and wife as an economic one. He provides her with accommodation, clothing, and nourishment, while the surplus she produces belongs to him. The amount she is expected to produce is clearly stated (M. Yeb. 5:9). This gendered division of labour remains constant. It does not differentiate between an urban or village context or between a higher- or lower-class household.

Describing the position of women in Jewish society in the light of these sources is to replicate the rabbinic patriarchal ideology rather than faithfully represent daily life. Yet rabbinic literature itself reveals gender differences occasionally. In an urban context it often places the woman as selling merchandise in the marketplace (M. Hal. 2:7), on her doorstep (T. B.Q. 11:7), or in a shop (M. Ket. 9:4). All of these actions are done in a public context. In a village context, she is represented as participating in grain harvest or olive-picking (M. Yeb. 16:2), as assisting her husband in the field (a *baraita* in b. B.M. 12a) or as raising livestock, mostly poultry (M. B.Q. 10:9; T. B.M. 4:24–25). Miriam Peskowitz's study of women's labour, concentrating on the image of the weaving woman, contains a full catalogue of these labours, together with a number of reading strategies for these texts which overturn the dichotomist division of labour suggested by the dominant rabbinic discourse. She shows that, just as field work was not professionally reserved to men, so, too, weaving was not restricted to women (Peskowitz 1997: 49–76).

7. MOTHERHOOD

Motherhood is the only issue discussed in this chapter which is uniquely female and does not involve comparing women's lot to that of men. It begins with sex, conception, pregnancy (with all its medical complication such as abortion or miscarriage), childbirth (with its attendant dangers), nursing, child-raising, socialization, education, etc. Even with the passage of the child into maturity, motherhood (or parenthood) does not cease.

Many aspects of motherhood need to be explored with relation to Jewish women. Sex is something that men and women do together but results in pregnancy only for women, and its consequences are quite often a woman's problem. Thus, for example, one rabbinic text describes women alone as disposing of the foetus after a miscarriage (*T. Oh* 16:1). Motherhood is often described by rabbis in legal terms. A woman is obligated to raise a man's children, but the children are his. If he divorces her, he keeps the children. Although this is not expressly stated, we learn it from a ruling that states that if she is divorced, she need not nurse his son any more (T. Ket. 5:5) (see Labovitz 2000). Women are also often described as present when children are still very small, tending to their needs (M. Shab. 18:2). However, in texts which refer to older (especially male) children, they are usually rendered invisible. Thus, for example, while women are exempt from residing in the *sukkah* (Lehman 2006), a (probably male) child is required to reside in it once he no longer needs his mother (M. Suk. 8:7). While women are exempt from participating in pilgrimage, a (probably male) child is described as riding on his father's shoulder during such a journey (M. Hag. 1:1). Nevertheless, women are described as mourning their sons much more than fathers (a *baraita* in b. Sanh. 104b). Jewish motherhood in late antiquity still awaits a serious feminist study.

8. POVERTY AND CHARITY

Feminist scholars have often emphasized that women in a patriarchal society are more likely to suffer poverty than men, because a patriarchal environment makes women less educated, less skilled, and strongly dependent on male relatives. Already in the Hebrew Bible widows and orphans are identified as the weakest members of society, most in need of charity. One may assume that this reality did not change in rabbinic times. Sometimes the rabbis incidentally mention the widow and the female orphan (*yetomah*) in the context of poverty (e.g. M. Ket. 6:5), but the issue is not so pervasive. Poverty in rabbinic literature does not appear to be gendered. Much more gendered is the identity of those dispensing charity. Many traditions identify women in this role (e.g. y. Ter. 8:5, 45c; y. Hor. 3:7 48a; b. Shab. 156b; b. Taan 23b). One can speculate on the reasons for this literary presentation, and on its reflection of a daily-life reality, but a serious gender-sensitive analysis of these texts is required before more substantial conclusions can be reached.

9. THE BODY AND PURITY

After the destruction of the Temple most Jewish laws connected with purity were no longer applicable. The one domain on which this event did not make a difference is the issue of menstrual purity. The rabbis viewed women as unclean and able to defile men for as long as two weeks every month, and they took this issue very seriously: an entire Mishnaic tractate (Niddah) is devoted to it. This is the only tractate in Seder Toharot that has generated both a Babylonian and a Palestinian commentary. A sensitive gender reading of the tractate and its commentaries by Charlotte Fonrobert critiqued the male assumptions about gender and the body embedded in these compositions (Fonrobert 2000). She denied the usefulness of these texts for the recovery of women's daily life, however.

Numerous installations which some scholars have identified as *miqvaot*, that is, ritual baths, have been excavated in Israel (Reich 1997: 430–1). The importance of gender for the issue of the *miqvah* seems to elude scholars. Even a gender-sensitive article like that of Eric Meyers on domestic architecture in the town of Sepphoris, fails to deal with the gendered aspects of ritual baths (Meyers 2002: 211–5). Sawicki, who does take note of this issue, sidetracks it by concentrating on levitical and priestly purity and lineage (Sawicki 1997). A gender-sensitive analysis of these finds, in connection with rabbinic texts on women's impurity in the post-70 CE era, is still a desideratum.

10. CLOTHING AND JEWELLERY

Rabbis assumed that women would have produced all the clothes that Jews wore in the Land of Israel in antiquity. As Peskowitz has shown (1997: 77–94), this assumption is based on a gender-biased world view more than on any retrievable historical record. We may assume that Jewish men and women dressed differently, but no feminist reconstruction of these differences exists to date.

Jewellery is another issue that has gender implications. Rabbinic literature assumes that women habitually wore jewellery. M. Shab. chapter 6 is devoted entirely to the question of which articles a person may wear on the Sabbath without being considered as carrying objects. The rabbis clearly distinguish between what they consider feminine adornments—bracelets, earrings, nose-rings and finger-rings (M. Shab. 6:1), and what they consider male adornments—a sword, a bow or a shield (M. Shab. 6:4). They expressly label these weapons as manly jewellery (*takhshit*). Yet, as today, men in the past habitually wore items of jewellery. Rabbinic literature itself bears evidence for this. Thus, signet rings are used for administrative purposes, and in one tradition we learn that (male) members of the patriarchal house wore them (T. A.Z. 5:2). Nevertheless, to date, studies of jewellery in archaeology and rabbinic literature are remarkably gender neutral (e.g. Grossmark 2005).

On the other hand, the oversimplified dichotomous relationship between the jewelled woman and the unadorned man has been accepted by some scholars as the basis of a gender analysis of grave goods and other archaeological finds. In an article on women as archivists among the refugees of the Bar Kokhba rebellion, Peterson suggested that finding documents in the same bag with beads, raw wool and a mirror proves that the archivists were women (Peterson 2000). Also, when a debate erupted over the membership of women in the Dead Sea Sect, based on the skeletal remains found in the cemetery, it was argued that the absence of jewellery on the site was indication enough that the members of the sect were all (or mostly) males (Magness 2002). Exposing these reading strategies is not necessarily meant to contest their results but to reveal the gender assumptions of the writers.

11. Food and Meals

Another area that is conventionally identified as women's domain is the preparation of food. Rabbinic literature imagines women cooking and baking for their husbands (e.g. M. Ket. 5:5), as well as for other men. Thus, for example, women are often described as providing lodging and preparing food for customers, both in aggadic contexts (e.g. Lam. R. 1:1) and in halakhah, where they are designated 'inkeepers' (*pundaqit*: e.g. M. Dem. 2:5). Women as producers of flour and leaven, and as bakers of bread, are repetitive themes in the Mishnah, both with regard to activities and in association with utensils used in the process (M. Zeb. 5:9; M. Toh. 7:4). An unconventional but convincing attempt to reconstruct the reality of these activities was made by Susan Weingarten (2003).

Yet there is little doubt that here, too, the picture was more complex. Thus, for example, the Hebrew word for baker (*nahtom*) has no feminine form, and the preparation of bread was obviously done by persons of both sexes (Weingarten 2005). In a recent study, Meyers attempted to identify a chronological/technological shift during the Roman period, which allowed for the large-scale production of flour but terminated women's monopoly over bread production, hailing the professional baker (Meyers 2006).

12. Domestic Architecture and Living Conditions

Domestic architecture is an important area for gender analysis. If rabbinic literature imagined a segregated environment for women, to what extent does archaeology confirm or deny this assumption, and to what extent does a suspicious reading of the rabbinic texts themselves lend itself to this conclusion? This is exactly the topic explored by Cynthia Baker (2002). She shows that rabbinic literature identifies a wife as a man's house (e.g. M. Yoma 1:1), and imagines her internal organs as architectural components (e.g. M. Nid. 2:5). Baker's sophisticated reading of such rabbinic texts, together with the archaeological evidence, suggests that the issue is complex and surprising.

13. DEATH AND BURIAL

It is interesting to note that rabbis often identify women with death and consider the first woman, Eve, as responsible for bringing death into the world. This has much more to do with concepts and beliefs than with social reality and everyday life, but at least one rabbinic text learns from the association of death with Eve that this is the reason why women lead the funeral procession (Gen. R. 17:8). This statement nicely conflates with others in rabbinic literature suggesting that professional mourners in Jewish society were women (e.g. M. Ket. 4:4; M. M.Q. 3:9). Even the word 'mourner' (meqonenet) is gendered and feminine.

One can speculate on why women were considered ritual experts in a funerary context: perhaps because they were less often required to be ritually pure. One tradition relates that when a person died on Passover eve, women would defile themselves and bury him, so as not to defile their husbands (T. Oh. 3:9). However, a more universal and less specifically Jewish reason can also be suggested. Women were usually considered more emotional than men. Rabbis, too, adhere to this understanding. In one story they relate how a daughter dies and a father refuses to mourn her (b. Shab. 151b).The purpose of the story could be to demonstrate that a daughter's death is less the cause of mourning than a son's, but it could likewise demonstrate that a man is, in general, less emotional than a woman. A parable relates how a father, who has killed his son and has no more energy to mourn him, calls the mourning women to replace him (Lam. R. petihta 2, and Hasan-Rokem 2000: 110–4).

Yet, even as rabbinic sources associate women with death, a careful analysis of the funerary remains from Palestine suggests that women are less conspicuous in death than men. In an analysis of ossuary-burial from the first century, Yifat Peleg has shown how gender ideology is also evident in the domain of burial and death (Peleg 2002). She has demonstrated that women are recorded in epitaphs less frequently than men (see also already Hezser 2001: 407–8); that men are buried individually more often than women; that in inscriptions women are sometimes mentioned as nameless wives only or not at all. Only the investigation of the skeletal remains shows that women are indeed buried in the tomb (Peleg 2002).

14. PRIVATE AND PUBLIC EDUCATION

There is no indication in any source at our disposal that women received a formal, public education (see Hezser 2001: 44 and in this volume). Here rabbinic sources are most decisive. For rabbis, education means Torah scholarship, and more than once it is stated categorically that women are exempt from it. While a minority opinion in the Mishnah states that a father is obligated to teach his daughter Torah (M. Sot. 3:4), one halakhic midrash states explicitly that since a father is required to teach his 'sons' Torah, this excludes daughters (Sifre Deut. 46). The forceful opinion of an important rabbi in the Mishnah (Rabbi Eliezer) maintains that teaching Torah to girls is tantamount to teaching them nonsense (M. Sot. 3:4). It is true that some scholars have attempted to read some rabbinic texts (e.g. M. Ned. 4:3; T. Ber. 2:12) against the grain, suggesting that other rabbinic opinions existed, which encouraged Torah study for women (e.g. Weiss-Halivni 1997). But we have no proof that these reflect social reality. Rabbinic literature, which knows of male rabbis only, can at least be taken as proof of rabbinic exclusion of women from rabbinic scholarship.

The rest is conjecture. Rabbinic literature assumes that when a woman marries she is expected to be trained as a housekeeper—she should know how to clean, bake, cook, launder, spin, and weave (M. Ket. 5:5). One may assume that these skills were taught at home, probably by a mother, or another female member of the family. However, such a view of women's everyday role is somewhat stereotypical and does not represent the entire range of educational options for women. M. Ket. 5:5 itself mentions two groups of women to whom this general rule does not apply. One is the female slave-owner, who need not be proficient in these skills, for she has slaves to do them, and the other is the slave herself, who is probably expected to be proficient in a much larger number of household skills, and whose source of education remains mostly unknown (see further on this Hezser 2005: 142–46). Both the rich woman and the slave may have been Jewish women. In an appendix to this tradition one rabbi argues that all women should learn to work in wool, regardless of their social status. As Peskowitz has nicely shown, however, the association of women with weaving is a social-cultural convention rather than a reflection of reality (Peskowitz 1997: 96–102). We may assume that female slave-owners were women of leisure, who found time to enhance their (intellectual) education, such as the daughters mentioned above, who were encouraged to study Greek, because it was deemed a social ornament for them (y. Shab. 6:1, 7d).

Amongst these, an anomaly such as the female Torah-scholar Beruriah could be located (Ilan 1999: 175–94).

15. ORALITY AND WRITING

Since most studies of literacy in antiquity suggest that the vast majority of the population was illiterate, it should come as no surprise that most women are considered by modern scholars as belonging to this majority (e.g. Hezser 2001: 498). The explicit statement found on a document in Babatha's archive, that the owner of all these documents could not read, much less write them (and perhaps not even sign her name), has only helped to confirm this assumption of a very low female literacy rate. It is therefore necessary to stress that rabbis never state explicitly that men should learn to read but women should not. On the contrary, such statements as 'All are qualified to write a divorce bill ... a woman writes her own divorce bill' (M. Git. 2:5) are taken for granted by rabbis and not contradicted. Therefore, rabbis at least reckon with the possibility that women may be able to write.

One text in the Mishnah has raised special interest. In M. Qid. 4:13 we learn that 'a woman may not teach scribes'. This is obviously a restrictive legal statement, intended to limit the scope of activities a woman is allowed to pursue, but it assumes that women could at least theoretically be professional scribes (Hezser 2001: 124). By stressing such an example I do not mean to suggest that literacy was as widespread among women as amongst men. I only argue that, since literacy was especially associated with professional scribes and with the elite, in such circles gender must not necessarily have been a dividing factor. Thus, in Tosefta Megillah (T. Meg. 3:11–12) we learn that a town may have only one literate person, and that person may be a woman competent to read the Torah (Hezser 2001: 453). The gendered ideology of the Tosefta is voiced by its ruling that the woman should not read to the public, but obviously it recognizes the existence and proficiency of such women, at the same time that it recognizes the illiteracy of many men.

16. SYNAGOGUES AND STUDY HOUSES

As stated above, rabbis barred women from studying Torah. Since study-houses, as we know them from Palestinian rabbinic literature, were rabbinic institutions, it is hardly surprising that this is one location where ideology meets with social reality, and there is no reason to look for women there. The synagogue is another matter. Women's participation in synagogue life and services has interested scholars even in the pre-feminist era. In 1963 Shmuel Safrai published a provocative article in which he claimed that there is no evidence, literary or archaeological, that supports the notion that a woman's section in the ancient synagogue existed (Safrai 1963). Archaeological excavations conducted since then have not substantially altered his conclusions. His reading of the evidence would today have been called a 'suspicious' or 'subversive' reading.

In a subsequent study, consciously indebted to a feminist agenda, Bernadette Brooten investigated other aspects of women's participation in the life of the synagogue, based primarily on archaeological and inscriptional evidence, but supplemented by literary texts (Brooten 1982). For example, Brooten was able to show that women constituted a significant segment amongst synagogue donors. Her study is based on synagogues in both the Land of Israel and the Diaspora. When we focus on Roman Palestine, however, we discover that among the numerous donation inscriptions discovered in forty-five synagogues only three mention women donors—two from Ashkelon (Roth-Gerson 1987:23; 25), two from Naaran, and three from Hamat Gader (Naveh 1978: 54; 60; 95).

Brooten was also interested in women office holders in the synagogue, such as the female archisynagogue, mother of a synagogue, and elder (Brooten 1982). She collected a substantial number of references to such female office holders documented on synagogue and funerary inscriptions. However, not one of these inscriptions originates from Palestine. An interesting study could look into the reasons for these discrepancies between Israel and the Diaspora. One such attempt has already been made (see Kraemer 1999: 50–79), contrasting an allegedly conservative Palestinian Judaism with a more liberal Diaspora community, but other solutions are also possible.

Rabbinic literature does at least imagine women present at synagogue services. One text describes a woman hearing Rabbi Meir preach in a synagogue (y. Sot. 1:4, 16d). Another text imagines a town inhabited solely by priests, who bless a congregation of women present in the synagogue (y. Ber. 5:4, 9d). The Toseftan tradition mentioned above, which imagines women (not) being called to read from the Torah (T. Meg. 3:11) also presupposes a synagogue setting. However, whether and to what extent women actively participated in the synagogue service in the Land of Israel in the Roman period remains unclear. Rabbinic sources are silent on this, and we have no other sources available which could be consulted.

17. SABBATH AND FESTIVALS

Once again, our chief source for assessing the impact of festivals on Jewish everyday life in Roman Palestine is rabbinic literature. Apart from that, the evidence is almost non-existent. Celebrating the Jewish festivals was understood by the rabbis as the highest expression of Jewish identity. One sixth of the Mishnah, the order of Moed (Appointed Times), is devoted to this topic. In order to understand the extent to which festival practices impacted women's lives and were relevant to women, we need to read these texts with extreme caution, since we have no other supporting evidence available.

The chief source for assessing the extent of women's participation in Jewish festivals is M. Qid. 1:7 which states that women are exempt from participating in all positive, time-bound commandments. Translated into practical terms, this ruling would exclude women from all celebrations of the Jewish cultic calendar, that is, the festivals (including the Sabbath and the hours of daily prayer). A rabbinic comment that illustrates this rule by listing examples may support this interpretation: 'What are positive time-bound commandments? Such as building the *sukkah*, taking the *lulav* and putting on phylacteries" (T. Qid. 1:10).

However, we may assume that M. Qid. 1:7 was a mere ideological statement and never reflected actual practice. Palestinian rabbinic literature is full of examples that demonstrate that it was never applied in its entirety. Short episodes are told of women who actively participated in certain festival practices, like Queen Helene who built and resided in a *sukkah* (T. Suk. 1:1), or Michal bat Kushi who put on phylacteries (Mekhilta de-Rabbi Ishmael *pisha* 17). There are also some rulings which clearly contradict the general injunction of M. Qid. 1:7. Thus, M. Ber. 3:3 specifically includes women in the obligation to pray the Eighteen Benedictions (Amidah) and to recite the blessing on food. The lighting of the Sabbath candles at the beginning of the Sabbath was from early on deemed a specifically female commandment (M. Shab. 2:6–7). Interestingly, nowhere in rabbinic literature is this commandment formulated positively. It is only mentioned in the Mishnah, so as to warn women that if they refrained from carrying it out, they would die in childbirth.

A final example is the Passover celebration. M. Pes. 8:1 specifically enjoins women to partake of the Passover sacrifice. Interestingly, this legal ruling contradicts a Qumranic injunction, which excludes women and children from partaking in the mentioned ritual (4Q265). This contradiction between rabbinic and Qumranic halakhah is not surprising. It shows that the desire to exempt women from full participation in Jewish festivals is old and pervasive, even if the communities may have differed on its details. These examples demonstrate that an over-arching patriarchal ideology informs M. Qid. 1:7, a ruling which was only partially applicable in daily life.

Of special interest here is the celebration of Rosh Hodesh (New Moon). A late Midrash (Pirke de R. Eliezer 45) states that women, more than men, observed this festival. From the Palestinian Talmud (y. Taan. 1:6, 64c) it may be inferred that this practice had late antique roots. Similarly, the Mishnah suggests that, at least during Second Temple times, young women celebrated the 15th of Av by dancing in the vineyards in pursuit of husbands (M. Taan. 4:8). Most scholars deny any historical background to this event. However, the unconventional character of this description, which seems to contradict the patriarchal ethos of the Mishnah at least in some regards, militates against dismissing it out of hand. These few and almost marginal texts may lend support to the fact that women had perhaps an alternative ritual time-cycle that they chose to observe, aside from the normative masculine festival cycle, which aimed at limiting their participation and—from medieval times onwards—segregated them off in the ('woman's section') of the synagogue.

That these references are marginal and hardly raise any comments indicates to what extent rabbinic literature is androcentric and requires careful reading against the grain. A large research project is currently being conducted at the Free University Berlin which aims at creating a feminist commentary on the entire order of Moed in the Mishnah and the Babylonian Talmud (Ilan 2007 and 2008 Valler 2009). It is hoped that such a commentary will lead to a more careful reading of this order. Even if it does not increase our understanding of ancient Jewish women's actual lives, it may perhaps serve to deconstruct the usual dichotomist picture of Jewish women and men in Jewish ritual practices.

18. Magic and Healing

As has often been shown, the difference between magic and religion on the one hand, and between magic and medicine on the other is socially constructed. In both cases magic is considered marginal, while its alleged opposite is considered normative. Feminist scholars have shown that while the normative is considered male, magic is often conceived of as female. In rabbinic sources this association of women with magic is particularly prevalent, as scholars have already shown for the Babylonian Talmud (see e.g. Fishbane 1993; Lesses 2001). It is also evident in some Palestinian rabbinic sources. The word for magic (*kishuf*) is often associated with women in these texts. Thus, in M. Abot 2:7 we are informed that whoever increases the number of women in his household increases witchcraft. A *baraita* in the Palestinian Talmud informs us that the best of women practice witchcraft (y. Qid. 4:11, 66b). Another tradition explains the use of the feminine form of the term 'witch' (*mekhashefah*) in the Bible (Ex. 22:17: instructing the Israelites to eliminate them) as resulting from the fact that most women are witches (y. Sanh. 7:13, 25d). A further tradition identifies eighty women, mentioned in the Mishnah as having been executed in one day (M. Sanh. 6:4), as witches (y. Sanh. 6:8, 23c).

The stereotypical world view of women as witches is no indication, of course, that women, more than men, practised what might be identified in modern scholarship as magic. Nevertheless, in many such practices, as evidenced by rabbinic texts and archaeological finds, women were indeed involved. Thus, T. Shab. ch. 6 and part of ch.7 are devoted to the 'ways of the *Emori*', a technical term used by rabbis for ritual actions which they associate with pagan practices and then reject. It includes thirty clauses, of which four (6:14, 15, 17, 18) are formulated in the feminine form, probably indicating that they were more often practised by women. Of the forty-two Jewish amulets I collected (the vast majority emanating from Palestine), twenty-six were written for women (Ilan 2006b: 642).

The reason why women were often identified as witches derives perhaps from the fact that they were often practitioners of folk medicine, which involved recipes that appear similar to magic. Thus, in the Palestinian Talmud, a woman by the name of Timtinis is described as healing Rabbi Yohanan with a recipe that to the modern reader sounds suspiciously magical (y. Shab. 14:4, 14d). Another Jewish woman, Salome, probably from Palestine, is cited by Galan as transmitting a similar sort of medical recipe (Compositio Medicamentorum 2:7). Such recipes are frequently found in medical and magical literature of late antiquity. Jewish women also served as midwives, as many rabbinic sources indicate (e.g. M. Shab. 18:3; M. R.H. 2:5; M. Ḥul. 4:3; M. Kel. 23:4; M. A.Z. 2:1). Perhaps they also performed circumcision, as a critical reading of some texts (e.g. T. Shab. 16:8) may indicate. A comprehensive study of women in these capacities, which would integrate archaeological and literary sources, would be very welcome (for now see Ilan 2006a: 214–58).

19. Bathhouses / Theatres as Locations of Roman Culture

Briefly, Roman culture in Palestine is often identified in rabbinic literature with the institutes of the bathhouse and the theatre. As such, it is perceived as pleasure-seeking, corrupting, and alien. In patriarchal societies, such locations are also perceived as sexually charged and threatening to women. Gender is an important category for analysing entertainment culture in all historical settings, but it is especially important in the Jewish context. To what extent did Jewish women take part in the Roman bathhouse culture? How many mixed bathing establishments existed in Roman Palestine? Would Jewish women have frequented them?

Two rabbinic sources seem to contradict one another on this point. A *baraita* discussing Gentile defilement of a Jewish house, incidentally and with no moral evaluation, mentions a Jewish woman going to a bathhouse on the Sabbath eve (b. A.Z. 38a–b). Another text, however, threatens a woman who attends bathhouses together with men with divorce without compensation (T. Ket. 7:6). The various issues involved in these texts have already been discussed to some extent by Jacobs (1998a: 252–55).

The theatre constitutes a similar problem. Rabbis viewed not just the performances themselves and the topics they raised as immoral, but they also considered the surrounding activities as corrupting. A tradition transmitted in the Palestinian Talmud calls a Jewish man a sinner because he was involved with the institution of the theatre in some capacity. According to the narrative, when he detected a Jewish woman in the vicinity of the theatre, he immediately suspected her to be a prostitute (y. Taan 1:4, 64b; and see also Jacobs 1998a: 256; 1998b: 341–3). In the same vein we should understand the midrash Ruth R. 2:22, where Naomi instructs the new convert Ruth that as a Jewish woman she should not visit the theatre. These sources, as well as others, obviously indicate that there is a gender aspect involved in these institutions, which needs to be further investigated.

SUGGESTED READING

The main studies of women's everyday life, based on rabbinic literature and the archaeological record, are Peskowitz 1997, which discusses women and labour, and Baker 2002, which suggests a connection between space, architecture, rabbinic texts and gender. Hasan-Rokem 2000 suggests folklore as a useful tool for the reconstruction of women's daily life. A general overview of the issue is provided in Ilan 1995.

BIBLIOGRAPHY

BAKER, C. M. (2002). *Rebuilding the House of Israel: Architectures of Gender in Jewish Antiquity*. Stanford: Stanford University Press.

BROOTEN, B. J. *Women Leaders in the Ancient Synagogue: Inscriptional Evidence and Background Issues*. Chico, Calif.: Scholars Press, 1982.

COTTON, H. M. (1995). 'The Archive of Salome Daughter of Levi: Another Archive from the Cave of Letters'. *Zeitschrift für Papyrologie und Epigraphik* 105: 171–208.

COTTON, H. M. (1996). 'The Guardian (epitropos) of a Woman in the Documents from the Judaean Desert'. *Zeitschrift für Papyrologie und Epigraphik* 118: 267–73.

FISHBANE, S. (1993). '"Most Women Engage in Sorcery": An Analysis of Sorceresses in the Babylonian Talmud'. *Jewish History* 7: 27–41.

FONROBERT, C. (2000). *Menstrual Purity: Rabbinic and Christian Reconstructions of Biblical Gender*. Stanford: Stanford University Press.

GROSSMARK, T. (2005). 'Laws Regarding Idolatry in Jewelry as a Mirror Image of Jewish-Gentile Relations in the Land of Israel during Mishnaic and Talmudic Times'. *Jewish Studies Quarterly* 12: 213–26.

HASAN-ROKEM, G. (2000). *Web of Life: Folklore and Midrash in Rabbinic Literature*. Stanford CA: Stanford University Press.

HAUPTMAN, J. (1997). *Rereading the Rabbis: A Woman's Voice*. Boulder, CO: Westview Press.

HEZSER, C. (2001). *Jewish Literacy in Roman Palestine*. Tübingen: Mohr-Siebeck.

—— (2005). *Jewish Slavery in Antiquity*. Oxford: Oxford University Press.

ILAN, T. (1995). *Jewish Women in Greco-Roman Palestine*. Tübingen: Mohr-Siebeck.

—— (1997). *Mine and Yours are Hers: Retrieving Women's History from Rabbinic Literature*. Leiden: Brill.

—— (1999). *Integrating Jewish Women into Second Temple History*. Tübingen: Mohr-Siebeck.

—— (2000). 'Women's Archives in the Judaean Desert', in *The Dead Sea Scrolls: Fifty Years After Their Discovery*, ed. H. Schiffman, E. Tov, J. VanderKam. Jerusalem: Israel Exploration Society, 755–60.

—— (2002a). *Lexicon of Jewish Names in Late Antiquity Part I: Palestine 330 BCE–200 CE*. Tübingen: Mohr-Siebeck.

—— (2002b). 'Jewish Women's Studies', in *The Oxford Handbook of Jewish Studies*, ed. M. Goodman. Oxford: Oxford University Press, 770–96.

—— (2006a). *Silencing the Queen: The Literary Histories of Shelamzion and other Jewish Women*. Tübingen: Mohr-Siebeck.

—— (2006b). 'Women in Jewish Life and Law,' in *The Cambridge History of Judaism*, vol. 4: *The Late Roman-Rabbinic Period*, ed. Steven T. Katz. Cambridge: Cambridge University Press, 627–46.

—— et al. (ed.) (2007). *A Feminist Commentary on the Babylonian Talmud. Introduction and Studies*. Tübingen: Mohr-Siebeck.

—— (2008). *Massekhet Taanit. Text, Translation, and Commentary*. Feminist Commentary to the Babylonian Talmud vol. 11.9. Mohr-Siebeck.

JACOBS, M. (1998a). 'Römische Thermenkultur im Spiegel des Talmud Yerushalmis', in *The Talmud Yerushalmi and Graeco-Roman Culture* vol. 1, ed. P. Schäfer. Tübingen: Mohr Siebeck, 219–311.

—— (1998b). 'Theatres and Performances as Reflected in the Talmud Yerushalmi', in *The Talmud Yerushalmi and Graeco-Roman Culture* vol. 1, ed. P. Schäfer. Tübingen: Mohr-Siebeck, 327–47.

KRAEMER, R. S. (1999). 'Jewish Women and Women's Judaism(s) at the Beginning of Christianity', in *Women and Christian Origins*, ed. R. S. Kraemer and M. R. D'Angelo. New York and Oxford: Oxford University Press, 50–79.

LABOVITZ, G. (2000) '"These are the Labors": Constructions of the Woman Nursing her Child in the Mishnah and Tosefta'. *Nashim: Journal of Jewish Women's Studies and Gender Issues* 3: 15–42.

LEHMAN, M. (2006). 'The Gendered Rhetoric of Sukkah Observance'. *Jewish Quarterly Review* 96: 309–335.

LESSES, R. (2001). 'Exe(o)rcising Power: Women as Sorceresses, Exorcists, and Demonesses in Babylonian Jewish Society of Late Antiquity'. *Journal of the American Academy of Religion* 69: 343–75.

LEVINE-MELAMED, R. (1999). 'Sephardi Women in the Medieval and Early Modern Periods', in *Jewish Women in Historical Perspective*, ed. J. R. Baskin. 2nd ed. Detroit: Wayne State University, 128–49.

LEWIS, N. (1989). *The Documents from the Bar Kokhba Period in the Cave of the Letters: Greek Papyri*. Jerusalem: Israel Exploration Society.

MAGNESS, J. (2002). 'Women and the Cemetery at Qumran', in *The Archaeology of Qumran and the Dead Sea Scrolls*. Grand Rapids: Wiliam B. Eerdmans Publishing Company, 163–87.

MEYERS, C. (2006). 'Harina de otro costal: género y cambios technológicos en la producción de harina en la Galilea romana (Grinding to a Halt: Gender and the Changing Technology of Flour Production in Roman Galilee)', in *Dones i activitats de manteniment en temps de canvi*, eds, P. González Marcén, S. Montón Subías, M. Picazo Gurima. Barcelona: Centre d'Estudis del Patrimoni Arqueològic de la Prehistòria, 25–50.

MEYERS, E. (2002). 'Aspects of Everyday Life in Roman Palestine with Special Reference to Private Domiciles and Ritual Baths', in *Jews in the Hellenistic and Roman Cities*, ed. J. R. Bartlett. London and New York: Routledge, 193–220.

MISHOR, M. (2000–1). 'MS. Oxford Bodleian Library, Pap. Heb. E.120' [Hebr.]. *Lĕšonénu* 63: 53–9.

NAVEH, J. (1978). *On Stone and Mosaic: The Aramaic and Hebrew Inscription from Ancient Synagogues* [Hebr.]. Jerusalem: Israel Exploration Society and Carta.

NEUSNER, J. (1980). *A History of the Mishnaic Law of Women*, vol. 5. Leiden: Brill.

PELEG, Y. (2002). 'Gender and Ossuaries: Ideology and Meaning'. *Bulletin of the American Schools of Oriental Research* 325: 65–73.

PESKOWITZ, M. (1997a). *Spinning Fantasies: Rabbis, Gender, and History*. Berkeley: Berkeley and Los Angeles: University of California Press.

PETERSON, S. (2000). 'Caves, Documents, Women: Archives and Archivists', in *The Dead Sea Scrolls: Fifty Years After Their Discovery*, ed. H. Schiffman, E. Tov, J. VanderKam. Jerusalem: Israel Exploration Society, 761–72.

REICH, R. (1997). 'Ritual Bathes', in *The Oxford Encyclopedia of Archaeology in the Near East*, vol. 4, ed. E. M. Meyers. Oxford: Oxford University Press, 430–1.

ROTH-GERSON, L. (1987). *The Greek Inscriptions from the Synagogues in Eretz Israel* [Hebr.]. Jerusalem: Yad Ben Zvi.

SAFRAI, S. (1963). 'Was There a Women's Gallery in the Synagogue of Antiquity?' [Hebr.]. *Tarbitz* 32: 331–3.

—— (1976). 'Education and the Study of Torah', in *The Jewish People in the First Century*, ed. S. Safrai and M. Stern. Philadelphia: Fortress Press, 945–70.

SAWICKI, M. (1997). 'Spatial Management of Gender and Labor in Greco-Roman Galilee', *Archaeology and the Galilee: Texts and Contexts in the Graeco-Roman and Byzantine Periods*, ed. R. Edwards, C. T. McCollough. Atlanta: Scholars Press, 7–28.

SCHLÜTER, M. (1999). 'Vom Objekt zum Subjekt der Geschichte? (Wie verändert 'Frauenforschung' den Blick auf die jüdische Geschichte?)', in *Jüdische Geschichte in hellenistich-römischer Zeit: Wege der Forschung: Vom alten zum neuen Schürer*, ed. A. Oppenheimer. Munich: R. Oldenbourg, 148–63.

SCHREMER, A. (1998). 'Divorce in Papyrus Se'elim 13: Once Again: A Reply to Tal Ilan'. *Harvard Theological Review* 91: 193–202.

SCHWARTZ, D. (2004). 'Did the Jews Practice Infant Exposure and Infanticide in Antiquity?' *Studia Philonica* 16: 61–95.

SCHWARTZ, S. (1995). 'Language, Power and Identity in Ancient Palestine', *Past and Present* 148: 3–47.

VALLER, S. (2000). *Women in Jewish Society in the Talmudic Period* [Hebr.]. Tel Aviv: Ha-Kibbutz Ha-Meuhad.

—— (2009). *Massekhet Sukkah. Text, Translation, and Commentary.* Feminist Commentary to the Babylonian Talmud vol. 11.6. Tübingen: Mohr-Siebeck.

WEINGARTEN, S. (2003). 'A Feast for the Eye: Women and Baking in the Talmudic Literatures', in *To Be a Jewish Woman* vol. 2, ed. M. Shiloh. Jerusalem: Urim Publication, 45–54.

—— (2005). '"Magiros", "Nahtom", and Women at Home: Cooks in the Talmud'. *Journal of Jewish Studies* 56: 284–97.

WEISS-HALIVNI, D. (1997). 'Talmud Torah for Women' [Hebr.]. *Mayim me-Dalyo*, 15–25.

II

LIFE IN A ROMAN PROVINCE

.

CHAPTER 4

....

THE ROMAN
PROVINCIAL
ADMINISTRATION

....

RUDOLF HAENSCH

1. PRELIMINARY REMARKS

....

Between the first century CE and late antiquity, Judaea seems to have been quite a well-known part of the Roman world based on the great number of literary sources relating to this region: the first-century Jewish historian Flavius Josephus as well as a number of Jewish and Christian texts written and edited between the second and sixth centuries CE. These authors provide a great deal of information concerning the daily life of the inhabitants of Judaea, but they do not deal with all parts of the population; for example, we do not know much about the citizens of the Roman *coloniae* in Judaea (cf. Belayche 2001). What is even more important in this regard is the fact that the Jewish and Christian sources from late antiquity are not very interested in Roman administrators and their daily routine. Rather they are concerned with issues and problems of daily life faced by the Jewish community at the time of the Roman Empire's Christianization, and with the internal quarrels of its Christian groups (for the specific problems of the interpretation of rabbinic sources in our context see e. g. Goodman 1983: 5–14). In his work The Jewish War (*Bellum Iudaicum*), Josephus gives us many pieces of information concerning the first Roman administrators and the Roman army of the middle of the first century CE, but he is mostly concerned with extraordinary events—some misdeeds of the governors and then the first Jewish revolt against Rome—and not with the daily administrative routine.

Thus, despite the large quantity of Jewish and Christian literary sources, in the case of the Roman administration the most important sources are those which are also found in other provinces, that is, inscriptions, especially those on honorific monuments and those concerning building activities. But the number of these sources is not only quite limited, they also illuminate only certain aspects of the Roman provincial administration. They offer the names and titles of the governors (and to a certain extent those of important members of their staff) and tell us about their careers, the army as their most important executive basis, and their building activity. In these inscriptions we hear almost nothing, however, about the most important part of their activity, namely their jurisdiction (but see Haensch 2002: 326), and we do not learn much about the impact of their activities on the daily life of the provincials. Thus we are quite well informed about certain aspects of Roman provincial administration of Judaea but not about others.

This situation has apparently also influenced scholarly research on the topic: to date, no detailed study of the Roman provincial administration of Judaea during the first three centuries CE or the last three centuries of Roman rule has been written. Hannah Cotton and Werner Eck are currently working on a detailed study of the governors of the first three centuries of Roman rule, and both have tackled a number of questions in this context in separate articles (see bibliography). But for an overview in the English language we can refer only to the respective parts of some general studies (see, e.g. Schürer 1973–1987, vol. 1; Millar 1993; Sartre 2001 and 2005; Tsafrir et al. 1994: 9–19).

In this chapter I shall not deal with the administration of the neighbouring *provincia Arabia*, even if a considerable number of Jews lived in its territory (as they did in other provinces), and even though Cotton has argued that the behaviour of the Jews living there towards the Roman government may have been typical of Jews in the eastern parts of the empire (see, e.g. Cotton 1999 and 2002). The governors of Arabia have been dealt with by Sartre (1982; see also Di Segni 1999: 166–178), and the administrative centres by Sartre (1985) and Haensch (1997: 238–244). The Jewish documents were published by Lewis (1989) and Cotton and Yardeni (1997; for the following scholarly debate see, inter alia, Katzoff/Schaps 2005).

2. THE GENERAL CONDITIONS: THE PROVINCES AND THEIR BOUNDARIES

It was only after the expulsion of Archelaus in 6 CE that direct Roman rule was established in Judaea and Samaria. The new part of the empire was administered by a member of the second *ordo* of the Roman society, an equestrian with the title *praefectus Iudaeae* (for this period see especially Lémonon 1981; Schürer 1973–1987, vol. 1). The Roman administration was based in Caesarea, from where the *praefectus* visited Jerusalem and probably also other parts of his province, but only for short periods (Haensch 1997: 227–28, 234–237).

There is an ongoing scholarly controversy on the question of whether Judaea was a province in the full sense of its meaning as, for example, the Baetica was, or if it was only a part of the province of Syria with a separate organization headed by the *praefectus* (see, for example, Cotton 1999: 75–81; Eck 2007b: 24–51; Lémonon 1981: 59–115; Schürer 1973–1987, vol. 1: 357, 360). Our knowledge of the early empire, its large provinces, and the limited beginning of the so-called equestrian administration seems to point to the second possibility.

In any case, the *praefectus* held the most important rights of a provincial governor, namely, the right to condemn people to death and the right to command military units. During this period the army of the province consisted only of the so-called *auxilia* troops, that is, units recruited from non-Romans: five *cohortes* and one *ala*, about 2500 infantry and 500 cavalry men (Josephus, Bell. 3.66; cf. Ant. 20.176; Cotton 2007: 395; Haensch 1997: 237 n. 34). Like other equestrian governors, the *praefectus* was the only authority in his sphere of responsibility, accumulating all relevant powers, that is to say, the jurisdiction, the military command, and the supervision of the financial administration (*pace* Eck 2007b: 42). In provinces with a senatorial governor, on the other hand, these powers were divided between two officials, each one appointed separately by the emperor: the senatorial governor and an equestrian, the so-called financial procurator.

If the *praefectus* of Judaea was subordinated to the governor of Syria, this probably meant only that the *legatus Syriae* could depose him in the case of grave faults and could overrule his decisions in important matters. We know that the *legati Syriae* did do so sometimes, but not often enough, so that some scholars tried to explain these interventions with reference to special permissions by the emperor. In any case, even if Judaea was only part of the province of Syria with a special administration, like the Decapolis (Isaac 1981) and other parts of Syria (Sartre 1999), rather than a separate province, this political situation would not have made much difference to the lives of most of the provincials (concerning the leading strata of society see Eck 2007b: 48). The ethnic and religious differences between the Jewish, Samaritan, and Hellenized pagan sectors of the population, and the social tensions connected with them, would have mattered to them more.

After Herod Agrippa I had for three years (from 41 to 44 CE) united those parts of the Herodian kingdom which had been divided between the sons of Herod in 6 CE, from 44 CE onwards Judaea, Samaria and most parts of the Galilee were administered again by an equestrian, now probably bearing the title *procurator*.

This title had become customary for governors of equestrian rank during the reign of Claudius, as a consequence of certain aspects of his politics.

In order to suppress the first Jewish revolt (66–70 CE) and to prevent another revolt from developing, many more military units were necessary than had been stationed in the province until 66 CE. Such a large number of units, and especially the core formations of the Roman army, the legions, whose soldiers were Roman citizens, could be commanded by a senator only. Thus, Vespasian and the governors of Judaea from the late first until the third centuries came from this leading stratum of Roman society (for a list see Thomasson 1984–1990, vol. 1: 321–326, vol. 3: 41–42; see further Eck 2006). To be more concrete, after the first revolt one legion—the *legio X Fretensis* in Jerusalem—and a number of auxiliary soldiers, corresponding altogether roughly to the number of legionaries (for a probably complete list of their units—two *alae* and seven *cohortes*—see RMD V 332 from the year 90; cf. Cotton 2007: 396) were left in the province.

To command these troops the governor had to be of senatorial rank. Even if all senatorial governors of the so-called 'Imperial' provinces had the same title, namely, *legatus Augusti pro praetore*, there was an important difference between governors of provinces with two or more legions and those with a smaller military presence. While the governors of provinces with two or more legions were senators of the highest rank, originating from the former consuls, the governors of the rest of the provinces were chosen from the former praetors. Judaea was the first province with only one legion—until then Roman provinces had either garrisons of two or more legions, or no legion at all. During the Julio-Claudian period, in provinces with legions as, for example, the Tarraconensis, the governors had always been of consular rank, and their legions had been commanded by senators of praetorian rank, appointed and discharged by the emperor but subordinated to the governor for all matters of daily routine. Now there was one province where the governor was also commander-in-chief of the most important military formation (Thomasson 1973; Eck 2007b: 109–10). Perhaps these praetorian governors of Judaea were subordinated to the governors of Syria in ways similar to the equestrian governors before them. Vespasian had, for example, also subordinated the praetorian governor of Galatia to the consular legate of Cappadocia.

As in the case of all imperial provinces with senatorial governors, the supervision of the financial administration of the province was now dealt with by an equestrian procurator, also appointed and discharged by the emperor and not subordinated to the governor. Apparently there was already one in place at the time of the first Jewish War (Josephus, Bell. 4.238; cf. Cotton 2007: 394).

Both Roman authorities were based at Caesarea. This is understandable in view of the following: Caesarea had supported the Romans during the first revolt and would probably not want to lose its importance; some of the buildings erected by Herod were already used by the Roman administration, especially by the governor (Haensch 1997: 230–31; *idem* 2004a: 315; Patrich 2000; Cotton/Eck 2001; Eck 2007b:

79–82); it was a Roman *colonia*—Caesarea was promoted to this status after the first revolt and perhaps even Roman veterans were settled there (Haensch 1997: 233, n. 17; Eck 2007b: 192, 216–225)—and was therefore most suited to the needs of a Roman governor; the lines of communication to Rome and other centres were shorter in a harbour city; Caesarea was probably already considered the capital of the province by the Romans (Tacitus, Hist. 2.78.4).

On the other hand, the choice of Caesarea is astonishing because Jerusalem had been the traditional centre of the region. There the camp of the legion was established, whose direct commander the governor was. Yet similar conditions can be observed in other provinces with a garrison of one legion commanded directly by a praetorian governor, albeit of a later date, for example, Raetia or Noricum (Haensch 1997, especially 365–66; *idem*, 2004). Once the legion was stationed in Jerusalem, the governor may have spent more time there than before. Furthermore, the roads between Caesarea and Jerusalem (and also between other cities) were apparently ameliorated at that time (Eck 1984: 27–29; *idem* 2007b: 76–77). While the governor occupied the palace built by Herod, for the procurator a new *praetorium* was constructed at Caesarea (Cotton/Eck 2001; Eck 2007b: 94–96; Haensch 1997: 230–31; Patrich 2000).

Apparently, even a number of years before the Bar Kokhba revolt the Romans got the impression that the number of soldiers stationed in Judaea was not sufficient. It was already during the time of Trajan, perhaps as early as 105/6 CE, that a second legion (the *legio II Traiana*?) was stationed—permanently?—in the province (Eck 1984: 27–29, cf. *idem* 2007b: 104–5; on the legion see also Daris 2000: 359; Eck 2007b: 113–14). The number of auxiliary units was probably also increased at that time. Under the *diplomata militaria* from the later second century (for a list see Eck 2006) we find two examples which list three *alae* and twelve *cohortes* (CIL XVI 87 from 139 CE; Eck/Pangerl 2005: 101–3). Thus, even if not all units of a provincial army are necessarily mentioned on a diploma (sometimes there were no soldiers who had served for twenty-five years or more in a specific unit), three *alae* and 12 *cohortes* were probably the whole auxiliary garrison of the province. With the increase in the number of legions, the rank of the governor was lifted. He was now chosen from the former *consules*. Shortly before this reform the boundaries of the province had been extended by including the land of Agrippa II (for a map see Tsafrir et al. 1994: 15).

From the Roman perspective, the necessity of all of these decisions was confirmed by the Bar Kokhba revolt (for the ongoing debate on its significance, see, most recently, Eck 2007a). The province which was now called Syria Palaestina needed a governor with much experience, especially in the military field. Therefore a consular governor was appointed and about 24,000 soldiers stationed there to keep the region in a peaceful state. Further consequences of the second Jewish revolt were the shift of the centre of Judaism to Galilee, because of the high number of Jews who had been killed or sold into slavery in the regions traditionally settled by Jews. The number and significance of the Roman, Hellenized Greek, and Samaritan inhabitants grew to a corresponding degree in the other parts of the province.

These central elements of provincial government persisted until the late third century. It was apparently only after the reign of Probus (276–282 CE) that an equestrian combined both functions, those of the senatorial governor and those of the financial procurator (Eck 2006: 256). A combination of these offices had existed in other provinces for some decades already. From the third century onwards, the governor would use the administrative building of the *procurator,* whereas the former palace of Herod was given up.

Probably some years later and under Diocletian at the latest, another important change took place. The governor lost his military command, which went to the newly created office of the so-called *dux Palaestinae,* who became the commander-in-chief of the units of Palaestina, and especially of the *legio X Fretensis* now stationed at Aila (for examples, see PLRE vol. 1: 144 v. Bacurius, and SEG 31. 1496; cf. ibid. 35. 1537; see also Di Segni 2004, especially 132–33 n. 7). As their principal residence, these *duces* seem to have chosen Beer Sheva (Di Segni 2004: 132–33, in an article dealing with the so-called Beer Sheva Edict). Perhaps at that time, and certainly before 307 (Barnes 1982: 213–215, 223; Kuhoff 2001: 364–65), the boundaries of Palestine were expanded in the south to annex the Negev, southern Transjordan (up to the river Zared/ Wadi Hasa) and the Sinai. Until then, these regions had been part of the *provincia Arabia.*

In 357/8 CE (see Barnes 1982: 214; PLRE vol. 1: 214) this huge province was divided into two provinces, perhaps because it had become too difficult to administer: *Palaestina (Prima ?)* and *Palaestina salutaris,* the annexed southern part of the former *provincia Arabia* with Petra as its capital (for a list of the governors of these provinces in the late third and fourth centuries see PLRE vol. 1: 1108 and Eck 2006: 254–256; for the importance of Petra in late antiquity see Haensch 2004b and especially Frösén et al. 2002, 2007). Around 400 CE the northern part was further divided into two provinces, *Palaestina Prima* and *Palaestina Secunda,* the last one stretching from the area of the Jezreel valley and the Lower Galilee to the regions of Pella and Gadara (for a map see Tsafrir et al. 1994: 17; cf. Dauphin 1998: 66–68). Its capital became Scythopolis (Tsafrir et al. 1994: 16, 223). It seems that this form of Roman organization of the province continued until the Islamic conquest (for a list of the governors of the fifth and sixth centuries see PLRE vol. 2: 1286 and PLRE vol. 3: 2: 1490–91, cf. di Segni 1995: 317–322 and 1999: 166–178; a number of inscriptions, especially from Scythopolis mentioning governors are still unpublished).

While the governors of *Palaestina Secunda* and *Palaestina Tertia* were normally only called governor (*praeses*), those of *Palaestina Prima* could use the title *consularis* up to the 370s, and afterwards the even more prestigious title of *proconsul.* This was because *Palaestina Prima* contained the core of the region of Palestine and, even more important, enclosed many famous Christian monuments. The privileges of the governor of *Palaestina Prima* were enlarged by Justinian (Novella

103). During his reign the governor of *Palaestina Secunda* also obtained the right to the title of *consularis* (Di Segni 1995: 318 n.16). Apart from the titles designating their function, the ranks of the governors were also specified in relation to the ranks of the leading strata of society. Because these titles changed to a considerable degree during the last three centuries of Roman rule, it is not useful to discuss them in detail here.

3. The Personnel of the Roman Governors

The Roman governors were not alone in dealing with the administration of their province (see generally Haensch 1997: 710–726; Rankov 1999; for late antiquity: Palme 1999). The governor had, first, his slaves and freedmen at his disposal (Eusebius of Caesarea, Martyrs of Palestine 11.24), who were not only in charge of certain aspects of his private life but also often served him in confidential matters. Sometimes his family accompanied him. Secondly, important decisions were usually taken only after a council of officers and socially eminent people had convened (Josephus, Ant. 20.117; Acts 25.12). Some of them held a permanent membership in this council. They were paid as so-called *comites praesidis* by the Roman state and came and went with the governor by whom they were appointed. References in the texts of Gregory the Wonderworker (3rd century CE) show that these officials would have been accompanied by their respective family members and servants (Panegyric to Origen 65–72).

The most important part of the personnel of a governor, at least of the senatorial governors of the late first to third centuries CE, came from the units of the provincial army. For a certain period during their time of military duty, a number of soldiers were delegated to the staff of the governor and became so-called *officiales*. The exact number of these *officiales* depended to a certain degree on the strength of the provincial army: on the one hand, the units should not be depleted of too many soldiers; on the other hand, a higher ranking governor with more demanding tasks needed more soldiers to help him. Therefore provinces with two legions would have approximately twice the number of *officiales* than provinces with only one legion.

From the legions the soldiers with the more important tasks, and especially the clerks, were recruited. Among these soldiers we find in Judaea (Syria Palaestina), as in other important provinces, a *centurio* as head of an office, three *cornicularii* as supervisors of the other *officiales*, three *commentarienses*, who were especially responsible for the reports (*commentarii*) of juridical proceedings and the execution of the juridical decisions, ten or twenty *speculatores* as executioners, thirty or sixty *beneficiarii* as all-round officials, often sent out to other places than the capital of the province (AE 2003: 1807), *frumentarii* (AE 2003: 1805), that is, emissaries for special missions (but not agents of a secret service), a few *quaestionarii* as torturers (cf. Pesiqta de Rav Kahana cited by Lieberman 1944: 28–29), an uncertain number of *exceptores* and *librarii* for the real writing work, quite a number of *stratores* under the command of a *centurio strator*, who dealt with the governor's horses, etc. Without doubt the number of functions in such an *officium* would have expanded during the High Empire (and therefore the number of *officiales* in general). For example, the *officium custodiarum* (AE 2003: 1804), the department dealing with imprisonment, seems to have been added only in the later second or third centuries. As already shown implicitly, in the case of Judaea, these officials are mostly documented by inscriptions from Caesarea, published in the last years especially by Eck and Cotton and collected in the annual volumes of Année Epigraphique (AE).

From the auxiliary units came the guards of the governors, the *singulares*, some of whom were mounted on horses. Several hundreds of such soldiers had to accompany and protect the governor during his various duties, some of them also in peaceful times (Eusebius, Martyrs of Palaestine 4. 8; 7.7; on their numbers see Speidel 1978: 11–15; Haensch 1997: 723–24; *idem*, 2004: 315).

The equestrian *procurator* was supported by an imperial freedman with the title *procurator*, who acted as his second, and by an unknown number of the emperor's serfs and freedmen who worked as *tabularii* (clerks and accountants), *dispensatores* and *arcarii* (cashiers) etc. (Boulvert 1970; *idem* 1974; Haensch 1997: 725–26; Weaver 1972). He also had some soldiers delegated to him, probably as a sign of reverence and to protect him. We know of a monument erected to one of the procurators of Syria Palaestina by a *centurio strator*, that is, the commander of his equerries, at Caesarea (Lehmann/Holum 2000, no. 7, cf. AE 1985. 829 = Lehmann/Holum 2000, no. 4).

Late antiquity, and especially the reign of Diocletian, also brought about a number of changes amongst the administrative staff (Palme 1999) working in the three sections of Roman Palestine. The most important ones were the unification of the *officia* of the *legatus* and of the *procurator* to one *officium*, dealing now with jurisdictional and financial matters, and the end of the former practice of recruiting these *officiales* either from the army or the *familia Caesaris*. Even if the *officiales* of late antiquity were nominally part of the Roman army, they no longer had any military background. The governor's palace of that time provides interesting inscriptions from the financial department, which not only name different ranks of *officiales* (Lehmann/Holum 2000, no. 90 = SEG 32. 1498), but also show that one already used phrases from the New Testament to encourage obedience to the provincial administration (Lehmann/Holum 2000, no. 88–89).

4. The Activities of Governors
and Procurators

As already mentioned in the introduction above, we do not know much generally about the daily routine of the governors and procurators of Roman Palestine, except for those activities which are reflected in inscriptions, that is, their building projects and the monuments erected to honour them. Only from the times of Justinian do we have a catalogue of the duties of the *proconsul Palaestinae I* from his Novella 103. From various other sources we get some insight into the activities of earlier governors and procurators (for a general overview see for example Eck 1998: 107–145, 167–185; Demougin 2007; Haensch 2006; for late antiquity, see Slootjes 2006 and Palme 2007).

At different points in his work Eusebius mentions those governors of the late third and early fourth centuries who tried to stop the Christianization of the province by condemning Christians to forced labour or death, as the emperors had ordered them (Eusebius, Historia Ecclesiastica 6. 39. 2: Decius; ibid. 7.12: Valerian; ibid. 7.15: Gallienus. Eusebius, Martyrs of Palestine: Diocletian and the other tetrarchs). Especially illuminating for the limited radius of action of a governor in his province is Eusebius' report about the Christian martyrs under Valerian (Historia Ecclesiastica 7.12): these Christians had to go to Caesarea to provoke the governor; otherwise they would not have been molested, since they were living in the countryside. The report suggests that a huge part of the population lived outside of the perception of a governor unless they tried to call his attention to themselves. This corresponds to what recent studies have shown about the Galilee (Goodman 1983; see generally Millar 1981).

The jurisdiction of a governor did not only deal with the most important crimes (Eck 2007b: 103), but also with a number of minor affairs. Of course, these were often delegated to judges appointed by him, the so-called *iudices delegati* (cf. y. Meg. 3:2, 74b referred to by Goodman 1983: 155–56; see further Cotton/Eck 2005). A recently published inscription from late antique Caesarea offers a full catalogue of fees, not only in the context of criminal trials but also for minor jurisdictional acts (Di Segni/Patrich/Holum 2003 = AE 2003: 1808, cf. BE 2004: 394). These juridical duties were without doubt the most important part of the tasks of a governor. Thus, the typical presentation of a governor, at least during the third and following centuries, was that of a judge sitting on his high tribunal (Eusebius, Martyrs of Palestine 7.7). People are shown waiting for their trials before the *praetorium* (ibid. 7. 1). If one was accused, one could not escape from the *commentarii* (cf. Sifre Num. 180, 1:21, *Pinhas* 134 referred to by Goodman 1983: 166 n. 144; for *commentarii* in general see Haensch 1992: 209–245).

Eusebius also mentions other aspects of the daily routine of a governor, such as offering sacrifices (Martyrs of Palestine 4. 8; see generally Eck 1998: 203–217), and his presence at games (Martyrs of Palestine 3. 3). Papyri offer further insight into the activities of the higher Roman officials during the High Empire. For example, a petition published in *Papiri greci e latine, pubblicazioni della Società Italiana* no. 1026 (= *Corpus papyrorum latinarum* 117, translated in Campbell 1994: 201–2) is one of the thousands of petitions submitted to governors in Roman times (Haensch 1994). In this case, dismissed soldiers asked for confirmation of their dismissal from a legion and not the fleet (where they had begun their military service), because they feared that without such a confirmation they would not get all their privileges as *veterani legionis*. A second papyrus document (*Sammelbuch griechischer Urkunden aus Aegypten* no. 11043, translated in Eck 2007b: 149; for an interpretation see Haensch 1992: 274 n. 186) shows how such a *veteranus* tried to obtain the right to a piece of land which apparently had been part of his pension.

Both of these papyri are typical in a certain way: if one wanted to get the Roman administration involved in one's problems, one had to directly approach the responsible officials. Otherwise, provincials would have had difficulties gaining these officials' attention. The Roman authorities were primarily interested in keeping peace, collecting taxes, and supporting the local administrators if they encountered problems. From a legal point of view, the governor had to decide the most important criminal cases. But if he was not informed of such cases, he would not take any action on his own initiative. While the Greek and Roman sectors of the population would not normally have had any problems in approaching the governor, at least after 136 CE some Jewish provincials may have refrained from doing so (but see Gen. R. 49:9: 'R. Yehudah b. R. Shimon said: [In the case of] a mortal, one can hang up [i.e. announce] against him an appeal, from the commander [*dux*] to the prefect, from the prefect to the commander in chief'; see also ibid. 64:10 and b. Meg. 29a for rabbis' awareness of the possibility of such appeals).

5. DIRECTIONS FOR FUTURE SCHOLARSHIP

Generally speaking, the history of Judaea as a province in late antiquity is a topic which has not yet been well researched. We do possess a number of studies that deal with the specific problems and internal quarrels of Jews and Christians in Judaea during that time. But not much research has been done on the administrative structure of the province and the more 'secular' aspects of its history. For example, one could examine the situation of the governors of late antique Palestine: their social background, their tasks, and especially their role between the different religious groups and leaders living in the province.

The use and interpretation of rabbinic sources for the historical investigation of various aspects of Roman rule in Palestine is a very complex task because of these texts' a-historical nature, that is, the impossibility to date them accurately, and the prevalence of indirect allusions rather than direct references to historical events and personages (see generally Goodman 1983: 5–14). Therefore interdisciplinary approaches, in which classicists, ancient historians, and scholars of rabbinic literature cooperate and share their respective expertise, seem to be the most appropriate way forward.

SUGGESTED READING

The most comprehensive work dealing with the history of Roman Palestine from the first century BCE to the second century CE is the revised English edition of Schürer (1973–87). Cotton and Eck have advanced our knowledge about the Roman administration in Judaea/Syria Palaestina, especially during the second and third centuries CE, in a number of studies, which are partly summarized by Eck (2007b). Jones (1964) remains the most comprehensive survey of late antiquity. Comparatively little research effort has been devoted to the functioning of the Roman state, especially in the provinces, during this period (Slootjes 2006 collected only a part of the relevant material; for a number of studies dealing with specific problems see the journal *Antiquité Tardive* 6, 1998 and 7, 1999).

ABBREVIATIONS

AE = *Année Epigraphique*, Paris: Presses Universitaires de France 1889 ff.

BE = *Bulletin Epigraphique*, annual part of *Revue des Etudes Grecques*, Paris: Les Belles Lettres, 1888 ff.

CIL = *Corpus Inscriptionum Latinarum*.

PLRE = *The Prosopography of the Later Roman Empire*, 3 vols. ed. J.-R. Martindale et al., Cambridge: Cambridge University Press, 1971–1992.

RMD = *Roman Military Diplomas*, ed. M.-M. Roxan and P. Holder, London: Institute of Classical Studies, 1978 ff.

SEG = *Supplementum Epigraphicum Graecum*, Leiden and Boston: Brill, 1923 ff.

BIBLIOGRAPHY

BARNES, T. D. (1982). *The New Empire of Diocletian and Constantine*. Cambridge, Mass. and London: Harvard University Press.

BELAYCHE, N. (2001). *Iudaea-Palaestina: The Pagan Cults in Roman Palestine*. Tübingen: Mohr Siebeck.

BOULVERT, G. (1970). *Esclaves et affranchis impériaux sous le Haut-Empire romain*. Naples: Jovene.

—— (1974). *Domestique et fonctionnaire sous le Haut-Empire romain*. Paris: Les Belles Lettres.

CAMPBELL, B. (1994). *The Roman Army, 31 BC–AD 337*. London and New York: Routledge.

COTTON, H. (1997). 'Die Papyrusdokumente aus der judäischen Wüste und ihr Beitrag zur Erforschung der jüdischen Geschichte des 1. und 2. Jh. n. Chr.'. *Zeitschrift des Deutschen Palästina Vereins* 115: 228–247.

—— (1999). 'Some Aspects of the Roman Administration of Judaea/Syria-Palaestina', in *Lokale Autonomie und römische Ordnungsmacht in den kaiserzeitlichen Provinzen vom 1. bis 3. Jahrhundert*, ed. W. ECK. Munich: Oldenbourg, 75–91.

—— (2002). 'Jewish Jurisdiction under Roman Rule: Prolegomena', in *Zwischen den Reichen: Neues Testament und Römische Herrschaft*, ed. M. Labahn and J. Zangenberg. Tübingen: Mohr-Siebeck, 5–20.

—— (2007). 'The Impact of the Roman Army in the Province of Judaea/Syria Palaestina', in *The Impact of the Roman Army (200 BC–AD 476)*, ed. L. de Blois and E. Lo Cascio. Leiden and Boston: Brill, 393–407.

—— and ECK, W. (2001). 'Governors and their Personnel on Latin Inscriptions from Caesarea Maritima'. *Proceedings of the Israel Academy of Sciences and Humanities* 7: 215–240.

—— and ECK, W. (2005). 'Roman Officials in Judaea and Arabia and Civil Jurisdiction', in *Law in the Documents of the Judaean Desert*, ed. R. Katzoff and D. Schaps. Leiden and Boston: Brill, 23–44.

—— and ECK, W. (2006). 'Governors and their Personnel on Latin Inscriptions from Caesarea Maritima'. *Cathedra* 122: 31–52.

COTTON, H./YARDENI, A. (1997). *Aramaic, Hebrew and Greek Documentary Texts from Nahal Hever and other Sites*. Oxford: Oxford University Press.

COTTON, H./ECK, W./ISAAC, B. (2003). 'A Newly Discovered Governor of Judaea in a Military Diploma from 90 CE'. *Israel Museum Studies in Archaeology* 2: 17–31.

DARIS, S. (2000). 'Legio II Traiana Fortis', in *Les légions de Rome sous le Haut-Empire*, vol. 2, ed. Y. Le Bohec and C. Wolff. Lyon: De Boccard, 359–363.

DAUPHIN, C. (1998). *La Palestine Byzantine: Peuplement et Populations*, 3 vols. Oxford: Archaeopress.

DEMOUGIN, S. (2007). 'L'administration procuratorienne au quotidien: Affaires de chancellerie', in *Herrschen und Verwalten: Der Alltag der römischen Administration in der Hohen Kaiserzeit*, ed. R. Haensch and J. Heinrichs. Cologne, Weimar, and Vienna: Böhlau, 271–287.

DI SEGNI, L. (1995). 'The Involvement of Local, Municipal and Provincial Authorities in Urban Building in Late Antique Palestine and Arabia', in *The Roman and Byzantine Near East: Some Recent Archeological Research*, ed. J. Humphrey, Ann Arbor: Journal of Roman Archaeology, 312–332.

—— (1999). 'Epigraphic Documentation on the Building in the Provinces of Palaestina and Arabia, 4th–7th c.', in: *The Roman and Byzantine Near East: Some Recent Archeological Research*, vol. 2, ed. J. Humphrey. Ann Arbor: Journal of Roman Archaeology, 149–178.

—— (2004). 'The Beersheba Tax Edict Reconsidered in the Light of a Newly Discovered Fragment'. *Scripta Classica Israelica* 23: 131–158.

——/PATRICH, J./HOLUM, K. G. (2003). 'Schedule of Fees (*sportulae*) for Official Services from Caesarea Maritima, Israel'. *Zeitschrift für Papyrologie und Epigraphik* 145: 273–300.

ECK, W. (1984). 'Zum konsularen Status von Judaea im frühen 2. Jh.'. *Bulletin of the American Society of Papyrologists* 21: 55–67.

—— (1998). *Die Verwaltung des Römischen Reiches in der Hohen Kaiserzeit*, vol. 2. Basel and Berlin: Friedrich Reinhardt Verlag.

—— (2006). 'Prosopographische Klärungen zu Statthaltern von Syria Palaestina'. *Zeitschrift für Papyrologie und Epigraphik* 155: 239–252.

—— (2007a). *Rom herausfordern: Bar Kochba im Kampf gegen das Imperium Romanum*, Rome: Unione Internazionale degli Istituti di Archeologia, Storia e Storia dell´Arte in Roma.

—— (2007b). *Rom und Judaea: Fünf Vorträge zur römischen Herrschaft in Palaestina*. Tübingen: Mohr Siebeck.

—— and PANGERL, A. (2005). 'Neue Militärdiplome für die Provinzen Syria und Iudaea/Syria Palaestina'. *Scripta Classica Israelica* 24: 101–118.

—— (2006). 'Eine Konstitution für die Truppen von Syria Palaestina aus dem Jahr 158'. *Zeitschrift für Papyrologie und Epigraphik* 157: 185–191.

FRÖSÉN, J. et al. (2002, 2007). *The Petra Papyri*, vol. I, III. Amman: The American Center of Oriental Research.

GOODMAN, M. (1983). *State and Society in Roman Galilee, A. D. 132–212*. Totowa: Rowman & Allanheld Publishers.

HAENSCH, R. (1992). 'Das Statthalterarchiv'. *Zeitschrift der Savigny-Stiftung für Rechtsgeschichte, Romanistische Abteilung* 109: 209–317.

—— (1994). 'Die Bearbeitungsweisen von Petitionen in der Provinz Aegyptus'. *Zeitschrift für Papyrologie und Epigraphik* 100: 487–546.

—— (1997). *Capita provinciarum: Statthaltersitze und Provinzialverwaltung in der römischen Kaiserzeit*. Mainz: Zabern.

—— (2002). Review of Lehmann/Holum 2000, in *Scripta Classica Israelica* 21: 323–27.

—— (2004a). 'Les capitales des provinces germaniques et de la Rhétie: De vieilles questions et de nouvelles perspectives', in *Simulacra Romae: Roma y las capitals provincials del Occidente Europeo–Estudios Arqueológicos*, ed. J. Ruiz de Arbulo. Tarragona: El Médol, 307–325.

—— (2004b). 'La christianisation de l´armée romaine', in *L´armée romaine de Dioclétien à Valentinien Ier*, Actes du Congrès de Lyon (12–14 septembre 2002), ed. Y. Le Bohec and C. Wolff (ed.), Lyon: De Boccard, 525–531.

—— (2006). 'La gestion financiére d'une province romaine: les procurateurs entre résidences fixes et voyages d'inspection', in *La circulation de l'information dans les états antiques*, ed. L. Capdetrey and J. Nelis-Clément. Bordeaux: Ausonius, 161–176.

—— (2007). 'Types of Provincial Capitals', in *Laudes provinciarum: Retórica y política en la representación del imperio romano*, ed. J. Santos Yanguas and E. Torregaray Pagola. Vitoria: Universidad del Pais Vasco, 265–276.

ISAAC, B. (1981). 'The Decapolis in Syria: A Neglected Inscription'. *Zeitschrift für Papyrologie und Epigraphik* 44: 67–74.

Jones, A. H. M. (1964). *The Later Roman Empire 284–602. A Social, Economic, and Administrative Survey.* Oxford: Basil Blackwell.

Katzoff, R./Schaps, D. (eds) (2005). *Law in the Documents of the Judaean Desert.* Leiden: Brill.

Kennedy, H. (2000). 'Syria, Palestine and Mesopotamia', in *The Cambridge Ancient History. Vol. XIV. Late Antiquity: Empire and Successors, A.D. 425–600*, ed. A. Cameron, B. Ward-Perkins and M. Whitby. Cambridge: Cambridge University Press, 588–611.

Kuhoff, W. (2001). *Diokletian und die Epoche der Tetrarchie.* Frankfurt: Wissenschaftliche Buchgesellschaft.

Lehmann, C. M./Holum, K. G. (2000). *The Greek and Latin Inscriptions of Caesarea Maritima.* Boston: The American School of Oriental Research.

Lémonon, J.-P. (1981). *Pilate et le gouvernement de la Judée.* Paris: J. Gabalda et Cie editeurs.

Lewis, N. (1989). *The Documents from the Bar Kokhba Period in the Cave of Letters, vol. 1: Greek Papyri.* Jerusalem: Israel Exploration Society.

Lieberman, S. (1944). 'Roman Legal Institutions in Early Rabbinics and in the Acta Martyrum'. *Jewish Quarterly Review* 35: 1–57.

Millar, F. (1981). 'The World of the Golden Ass'. *Journal of Roman Studies* 71: 63–75.

—— (1993). *The Roman Near East 31 BC–AD 337.* Cambridge, Mass. and London: Harvard University Press.

Palme, B. (1999). 'Die *officia* der Statthalter in der Spätantike'. *Antiquité Tardive* 7: 85–133.

—— (2007). 'The Imperial Presence: Government and Army', in *Egypt in the Byzantine World, 300-700*, ed. R. Bagnall. Cambridge etc.: Cambridge University Press, 244–270

Patrich, J. (2000). 'A Government Compound in Roman–Byzantine Caesarea', in *Proceedings of the Twelfth World Congress of Jewish Studies. Division B: History of the Jewish People.* Jerusalem: Magnes Press, 35*–44*.

Rankov, B. (1999). 'The Governor's Men: The *officium consularis* in Provincial Administration', in *The Roman Army as a Community*, ed. A. Goldsworthy and I. Haynes. Portsmouth: Journal of Roman Archaeology, 15–34.

Sartre, M. (1982). *Trois études sur l'Arabie romaine et byzantine.* Bruxelles: Latomus.

—— (1985). *Bostra: Des origines à l'Islam.* Paris: Librairie Orientaliste Paul Geuthner.

—— (1999). 'Les metrokomiai de Syrie du Sud'. *Syria* 76: 197–221.

—— (2001). *D'Alexandre à Zenobie.* Paris: Fayard.

—— (2005). *The Middle East under Rome.* Cambridge, Mass. and London: The Belknap Press of Harvard University Press.

Schürer, E. (1973–1987). *The History of the Jewish People in the Age of Jesus Christ (175 B.C.–A.D. 135)*, 3 vols. ed. G. Vermes et al. Edinburgh: T & T Clark Ltd.

Slootjes, D. (2006). *The Governor and his Subjects in the Later Roman Empire*, Leiden and Boston: Brill.

Speidel, M. P. (1978). *Guards of the Roman Armies.* Bonn: Habelt.

Thomasson, B. E. (1973). 'The One-Legion Provinces of the Roman Empire during the Principate'. *Orom* 9: 61–66.

—— (1984–1990). *Laterculi praesidum*, 3 vols. Arlöv: Radius.

Tsafrir, J. et al. (1994). *Tabula Imperii Romani Iudaea–Syria Palaestina. Eretz Israel in the Hellenistic, Roman and Byzantine Periods. Maps and Gazetteer.* Jerusalem: The Israel Academy of Sciences and Humanities.

Weaver, P. R. C. (1972). *Familia Caesaris: A Social Study of the Emperor's Freedmen and Slaves.* Cambridge: Cambridge University Press.

CHAPTER 5

COURTS AND THE JUDICIAL SYSTEM

JILL HARRIES

ROMAN Palestine is unique in the diversity and complexity of its sources for its legal system and the settlement of disputes. Many written sources, as elsewhere in the Roman world, reflect upper-class perspectives. The Roman jurists who commentated on provincial jurisdiction were themselves members of that upper class and wrote within a legal tradition which did not always reflect changing realities 'on the ground'. In Palestine the works of the historian Flavius Josephus are all-important as source material, but he is also in many respects biased. More significant is the extensive rabbinic literature, which represented the rabbis as, in some sense, adjudicators with courts or as informal legal advisors and judges. As we shall see, there is little consensus as to how this literature should be read as evidence for the realities of dispute settlement. In addition, there are increasing numbers of papyri, notably from the so-called Babatha Archive, which provide an alternative perspective to that provided by both the Roman and rabbinic sources.

1. JUDICIAL DIVERSITY

Courts and judges existed for a number of reasons: to punish crimes or offences against the community; to provide remedies for wronged individuals; and to resolve disputes. In Roman Palestine, from about the middle of the first century CE, the highest courts, the decisions of which could be enforced by the ruling power, were those run by the Roman governors (for an overview see Burton 1975; Galsterer 1996). As agents of the Roman state they adjudicated between Roman citizens using Roman law and acted as judges and arbitrators in disputes between non-citizens. They had the power to delegate the hearing of civil cases to carefully chosen deputies (Justinian, Digest 1.21). Evidence from western municipalities shows how lines of demarcation were drawn between gubernatorial and local jurisdictions. In Spain the governor was obliged to post up in public copies of his jurisdictional rules and principles and the magistrates and courts were expected to abide by them (*Lex Irnitana* 85, cf. Galsterer 1988).

Alongside the Roman system were various alternative jurisdictions. Client kings of the Roman state, such as Herod (died 4 BCE) or Herod Agrippa, the friend of the Emperor Claudius, could act as dispute settlers, but could also inflict capital punishment on delinquents: Herod convened a council to act as a court and to judge his wife Mariamne for infidelity (Josephus, Ant. 15.7.5, 217), and later two offenders were condemned for sacrilege and impiety (Josephus, Bell. 1.33.4, 654; Ant. 17.6.3, 161). According to Luke-Acts, Herod Agrippa executed James, the brother of John, with the sword (Acts 12:2). Josephus (Ant. 20.9.1) recorded, however, that a sentence of stoning was passed against James by Ananus the High Priest and his sanhedrin (court). Agrippa also imprisoned Peter with a substantial military guard, pending his appearance in a public trial after the Feast of Passover (Acts 12:4). His use of prison as a place of temporary detention pending trial accords with Roman conventions (Dig. 48.19.8.9). Rabbis are represented in their extensive literature as individual adjudicators, whose legal decisions contributed to a large and unsystematic body of case law. However, they functioned outside the formal operation of the Roman system.

2. ROMAN PROVINCIAL JURISDICTION

An equestrian *praefectus* based at Caesarea represented the Roman government in Palestine from 6 CE until 70 CE. Part of his difficult remit was to deal with the client rulers, descended from Herod, as well as with the Jewish religious establishment and the clashes between different ethnic groups, such as the Jews and Samaritans in c. 52 (Josephus, Bell. 2.12.3–7; Ant. 20.6.1–3), who were referred to Claudius by the governor of Syria, and between Jews and Greeks in Caesarea under Nero, who were also referred to Rome, where they proceeded to lodge complaints against, not only each other, but against the procurator, Felix, as well (Bell. 2.13; 14.4; Ant. 20.8.7; 8.9).

The repeated failures of local prefects or procurators to stand aside from local controversies undermined their standing as impartial adjudicators.

The judicial situation may have improved from the Roman standpoint after the fall of Jerusalem in 70 CE, when Judaea was made a full province under the control of an imperial legate with praetorian powers. In the 130s, following the revolt of Bar Kokhba, the governorship was reclassified as ex-consular, as part of a general re-organization, and the area renamed Syria Palaestina (Millar 1993: 366–74). Although they had many other duties, such as tax collection, the main task of the Roman governors from Hadrian onwards would have been to act as judges, and their preference would have been to operate, as far as possible, under the familiar rules of Roman law.

Sources written by Romans, such as a manual on the Duties of the Proconsul compiled by the Tyrian jurist Ulpian early in the third century CE, provide outlines of the rules that governors were expected as judges to observe. This treatise and comments by other Roman legal experts were preserved in Justinian's Digest, in fragmentary form, in the early sixth century CE. Along with such canonical texts as the exchanges between Trajan and Pliny as governor of Bithynia in the early second century CE, they provide a top-down perspective on how the courts and the judicial system worked or were expected to work throughout the Roman Empire.

More is known about how the courts worked in the city of Rome, where their functioning was influenced by the topography of the city and by legislation passed in the late republic on the criminal courts (*quaestiones*), the procedures of which were tied to the capital (Jones 1972; Bablitz 2007). The criminal statutes and other Rome-based legislation also applied to the provinces in terms of the offences covered and the expected penalties in the event of conviction. Wrongdoing outside the purview of the statutes could be judged and punished *extra ordinem* at the discretion of governors, or cases—such as those involving Jewish religious law—could be rejected as outside a governor's competence (see Lysias' advice to the procurator Felix that accusations against Paul should be rejected on this ground, Acts 23:29).

Under the republic, governors were expected to issue an edict at the outset of their term of office, setting out how they intended to observe the law. This was based on the Praetor's Edict at Rome. Under the empire, governors continued to issue their 'provincial edict': the second-century jurist, Gaius, wrote a commentary on the Provincial Edict, which suggests that it had a fixed form, at least in outline. The provincial process, known as *cognitio*, usually consisted of a single main hearing and was less complex than the procedure expected at Rome. At public criminal trials, the legate or procurator would preside, visible to all on his tribunal. Accessibility was improved by the governor's mobility. He was expected to travel round his province, hearing cases in a number of centres (Burton 1975). He would not have to rely on his own unaided judgement. Governors relied for guidance on a *consilium* or council (Greek *synedrion*, from which is derived sanhedrin), which consisted of appointees of his choice (Crook 1955). These might be personal friends, legal experts or local notables (cf. Acts 25:12: Festus consults his *consilium* on Paul's appeal to Rome). The formation of *consilia* did not in itself confer legitimacy. Josephus notes that when the high priest Ananus convened his sanhedrin to impose a capital sentence, the governor declared his action unlawful (Josephus, Ant. 20.9.1). There is no convincing evidence for the functioning of a Jewish sanhedrin in any sense after 70 CE (Goodblatt 1994). In some provinces, a jury may have been empanelled (for Bithynia see Pliny, Epistles 10.58.1), but this does not appear to have been the case in Roman Palestine.

The governor's role was to act as an investigating magistrate, not merely as president of the court. In public criminal trials of Roman citizens—unlike those of bandits, who could be summarily executed—a named accuser was required, and failure of a criminal charge could result in the bringing of a counter-prosecution for *calumnia* or slander. The governor would hear the speeches of advocates and witnesses and might also interpose questions of his own (for North Africa: Apuleius, Apology 48.7). In serious cases, where there was a conflict in the evidence, torture would be applied. Initially this was confined to slaves (whose evidence required the use of torture), but court practice and imperial indifference allowed the extension of torture to free people of lower status by the fourth century CE (for the rules on interrogations, *quaestiones*, see Digest 48.18). At the end of the trial, the governor would give his verdict and sentence from a written document, which he read out loud.

Appeals (*provocatio*) could be lodged by Roman citizens before the trial began, to have the hearing transferred to the court of the emperor at Rome. After 212 CE, when Roman citizenship became universal, appeal (*appellatio*) to higher authorities could be made against verdict and sentence. For this, an increasing amount of documentation was required, which was to be forwarded by the judge in the lower court within a fixed period of time. Imperial legislation preserved in the Codex Theodosianus (promulgated 438 CE) and the Codex Justinianus (of 529 and 534 CE) shows imperial concern with judicial corruption (Harries 1999: 153–171); in addition, aristocratic correspondence on behalf of litigants reveals active attempts by patrons to influence verdicts in favour of their protégées (on patronage in general, see Wallace-Hadrill, ed. 1989).

3. JURISDICTION IN ROMAN PALESTINE

Separation of the policing from the judicial role of governors could not always be maintained. Factional, ethnic, and social conflict often necessitated drastic intervention. Governors were active in the suppression of 'banditry' (an umbrella term for a variety of unofficial self-help activities). In one example of inter-communal violence, fatalities caused by Jews in a border dispute with Philadelphia provoked the procurator Fadus to punish three Jewish ringleaders out of hand (Josephus, *Ant.* 20.1.1). At other times, non-intervention was the preferred option: when the Christians' 'first martyr', Stephen, was stoned for blasphemy, after being accused by 'Jews of Cyrene and Alexandria as well as the provinces of Cyrene and Asia' (Acts 6:8–7. 59), the Roman authorities apparently stood aside.

Court processes could be inappropriate on other grounds, as public trials could themselves become the focus of public disorder. Magistrates had the power to take executive action without resort to formal legal process. In Acts, Paul and Barnabas, for example, are said to have been expelled from Pisidian Antioch by the local elites (Acts 13:49–50), and at Lystra, Paul was beaten up by the mob and left for dead (Acts 14:19). Crowd demonstrations allegedly also disrupted his visit at Thessalo-nica (Acts 17:5). But another option was conciliation. At Ephesus, where the silversmiths demonstrated in the theatre against the economic implications of Paul's teaching, Paul was successfully dissuaded from addressing the crowd by his friends among the provincial elite of Asia, while another official reminded the demonstrators that they too were liable to be punished (Acts 19:31–8).

Judicial authorities in Palestine might well find themselves dealing with pro-blems that had originated elsewhere. Paul, a Roman citizen from the Greek city of Tarsus in the province of Cilicia, active in the religious politics of Palestine, was no respecter of boundaries. His adventures in Asia had a direct impact on his situation in Judaea, where he found himself denounced for desecration of the Temple by Jews 'from the province of Asia' (Acts 21:27–30). Paul was to spend over two years in prison without trial, and in the end would formally exercise his right of *provocatio* and request a transfer of the hearing to Rome. Yet, at no point did any of the secular authorities involved with his case believe that he had a case to answer (for Herod Agrippa's advice to that effect see Acts 25:32).

The Book of Acts is a literary representation of Roman justice at work and may not be accurate in every detail. However, where it can be compared with what is known independently of Roman legal process, the information is consistent (Sher-win White 1963). Roman officials were required to maintain order in their pro-vinces: the garrison commander at Jerusalem, Claudius Lysias, was doing his job in arresting a man apparently causing a disturbance, and then enquiring into its causes (Acts 21:31–6; 22:24–9). These were policing matters and, where Roman citizens were not involved, summary justice could be meted out to offenders. As a Roman citizen, however, Paul was entitled to the formal legal hearing offered in the governor's *cognitio*. His referral there had the added advantage of removing him from Jerusalem. In procedural terms, both Felix and Festus at Caesarea played by the rules (Acts 24:1–22), but their role as judges was rendered more difficult by their relative lack of knowledge of Jewish religious law (Acts 24:24–6) and its associated disputes (although Felix was married to a Jewish wife and had some understanding of the issues), combined with their fear of religiously inspired riots, and their need to pacify the leaders of that community (Acts 25:9).

4. RABBINIC ARBITRATION

For many provinces, the Roman top-down narrative is the best available. However, in ancient Palestine, as in Egypt, we also have alternative perspectives, emanating from the governed. One highly contentious source of evidence for legal interpretation and for trials is rabbinic literature, specifically the collections of rabbinic sayings known as the Mishnah, which may date from *c.* 200 CE, and the later Palestinian Talmud (or Yerushalmi) and associated midrashic collections. These have generated an extensive literature, in which a lot has been taken for granted as to how traditions work to reflect historical reality. It has been assumed until recently (Hezser 1997: 1–42) that 'rabbinic Judaism' was embedded in institutional structures, including a sanhedrin or high court/council (but see Goodblatt 1994), a patriarch with wide jurisdictional and religious authority (but see Jacobs 1995), and academies based in centres such as Yavneh, where the first such institution was allegedly established after the destruction of the Temple in 70 CE. The rabbis were learned in the Torah and they acted as interpreters of Jewish religious and civil law (the two cannot be clearly distinguished). They developed the halakhah, laws and rules, which were based on the Bible but also included authoritative interpretation based on religious thought and teaching, and acknowledgement of legal custom. The rabbis also, according to many references in rabbinic texts, presided over 'courts'.

Re-assessment of the rabbinic texts in the light of new methodologies, and in terms of comparison with other Near Eastern and Mediterranean societies, is still at an early stage. It is already clear that the texts are problematic if their claims are taken at face value. To start with, rabbis are also present in epigraphic evidence, sometimes mentioned as synagogue donors or buried in sarcophagi in Bet She'arim (Cohen 1981–2). Cohen's view that a distinction should be made between literary and epigraphic rabbis is controversial. Secondly, although some Christian writers refer to Jewish 'sages' in connection with legal matters, for example, acceptance of bigamy or polygamy (Justin Martyr, Dialogue with Trypho 138), there is no independent corroboration for adjudication conducted by purely Jewish rabbinical courts. Thirdly, highly stylized collections like the Mishnah, although transmitting earlier traditions attributed to rabbis, reflect the agenda of the anonymous redactor(s) and their not necessarily accurate perceptions of the past. Thus, while it is possible to analyse a 'rabbinical movement' from the texts, it is far harder to find independent evidence for their activity as judges.

However, the almost complete silence in non-rabbinic sources on the judicial role of rabbis may be explicable. Aside from papyrus and epigraphic finds, the dominant discourse in the sources is that of the Graeco-Roman establishment, which was largely indifferent to the small details of the lives of the relatively poor of the villages, even of the towns. Hezser has argued (1997) that rabbis gained recognition and acceptance through exercise of authority in various ways, including projection of themselves as learned people, membership of a rabbinic family or dynasty, networking, and exploitation, where possible, of social status. She also argues that rabbis were drawn from many walks of life and could be found in both cities and villages, throughout Palestine. Such men, who combined moral reputation with legal knowledge, could be expected to be approached to act as arbitrators in disputes, and would be resorted to by any parties who preferred, for whatever reason, to avoid formal jurisdiction in the Roman or local provincial 'official' system (Goodman 1983: 155–62).

Roman law was fully aware of arbitration as a means of dispute settlement, but the Roman legal writers took notice of it only when their authority was required to enforce the arbitration agreement or *compromissum* (Digest 4.8; Harries 1999: 175–184; 2003: 71–81; Dohrmann 2003: 93). Arbitration outside this framework would operate in terms of what was agreed between the parties (who both had to consent to the process) and the adjudicator, but there was no formal means by which a disputed adjudication by an informal arbitrator could be enforced. It may have been problems with enforcement which prompted an appeal by one 'Judah' to Diocletian (Codex Justinianus 3.13.3): 'agreement by private citizens does not make a (formal) judge (*iudex*) of one who has no (formal) court (*iudicium*) to preside over nor does what he has decided have the authority of a decided case (*res iudicata*)'. What this meant in practice was that the Romans would not recognize the verdict of a judge without a formal court within their own system: consequently, the verdict or the arbitration award could not be enforced by the Roman authorities, nor could it be recognized in any future proceedings before Roman courts.

In Roman terms, therefore, rabbis were 'arbitrators' of small disputes and therefore of no concern to the ruling power (cf. Neusner 1983). The Roman authorities would have had no interest in rabbinic 'cases' as recorded in the literature, which mainly concerned religious lifestyle issues, family disputes, observance of the Sabbath and festivals, and relations with Gentiles. There were also some cases brought concerning property, including damages, and questions concerning tenure or fraud (Hezser 1997: 190–95; for case studies see Hezser 1998; some of the contributions in Hezser, ed., 2003). Where property was at issue, the sums at stake, though significant to the disputants, would not have justified the trouble and expense of a journey to the nearest town to find the governor. Thus, while some of the cases may be theoretical, their content reflects the concerns of Jewish communities, both with religious observance and with the small problems of everyday existence. On occasion, a litigant is found appealing from rabbinic to

Roman jurisdiction. See, for example, the tradition in the Talmud Yerushalmi (y. Meg. 3:2, 74a): 'R. Hiyya, R. Yose, R. Immi were judging [the case of] Tamar. She went and complained against them to [the Roman governor?] Antipita of Caesarea. They sent and wrote to R. Abbahu. R. Abbahu sent and wrote to them: We have already won over three advocates: Tov Yeled, Tov Lamed, and Tarsus–Ebdocus, Eumusus, and Talassios. But Tamar is bitterness and in her bitterness she stands. And we wanted to sweeten her, but "in vain has the smelter smelted" (Jer. 6:29)'.

By contrast with the rabbis, the status of the patriarchs as judges and recipients of special taxes would eventually be of concern to the Roman authorities in late antiquity. Imperial legislation of the period (see Linder 1987 for references) respected Jewish religious traditions, rituals, and laws, as had been imperial policy from the beginning. The origins of the Jewish patriarchate in the third century are uncertain (see Jacobs 1995), but the patriarchs had clearly achieved some status as judges by the later fourth century CE. If the 'leading men and patriarchs', who are consistently associated in the legal texts with synagogues and the excommunication of individuals, a process that is also referred to in rabbinic literature, made a decision, that decision should stand and not be interfered with by Roman governors (Codex Theodosianus 16.8.8, of 392 CE).

Down to the end of the fourth century, privileges for Jewish religious leaders and judges were maintained and the Jewish people were instructed to 'obey their own laws' (C.Th. 16.8.13, of 397). By this, the emperors meant religious law only: a few months later, the position was clarified with the statement that in civil or criminal cases, Jews were subject to Roman law and the Roman courts but that, in civil cases only, and by formal agreement (*compromissum*) between both parties, resort could be made to Jewish judges or patriarchs 'as if before arbitrators' (C.Th. 2.1.10, of 398). A crucial difference between patriarchal jurisdiction in the fourth century, as envisaged in this law, and the rabbinic arbitration model suggested above, was that at that time the patriarchs could summon the Roman authorities to enforce their decisions, 'as if such arbitration had been assigned by the decision of a (Roman) judge'. But this enhanced patriarchal jurisdiction was short-lived: after the patriarch Gamaliel had fallen foul of the Roman authorities in 415 CE, his powers of jurisdiction were removed along with his honorary Roman rank (C.Th. 16.8.22), and by 429 CE the patriarchate was no more (C.Th. 16.8.29).

5. RABBINIC AND ROMAN LAW

Although distinctive in many ways, the evolution of the rabbinic 'legal' tradition had some things in common with cultural features, both locally and in the

Mediterranean world as a whole, a consequence of 'parallel social structures producing similar historical effects' (Alexander 1990: 119; in general: Cohen 1966; Jackson 1975; Hezser 1998 and 2003: 'Introduction'). For example, a bill of divorce could be drawn up in Hebrew and witnessed in Greek or vice versa (M. Git. 9:8, Millar 1993: 378–9), reflecting not only the bilingualism of Palestine, but the wider acceptance by Roman emperors from Septimius Severus onwards that trusts valid in Roman law could be drawn up in languages other than Greek or Latin. There is common ground in debates on aspects of marriage and the questions asked of the status and obligations of slaves (see Hezser 2003). Much exegetical method exhibited in rabbinic writings has parallels in Greek thought (Lieberman 1962 and 1965), and legal terms borrowed from both Greek and Roman law were present in rabbinic legal interpretation (Sperber 1984; in general: Fischel 1973 and 1977; on 'legal fiction' see Moscovitz 2003).

Rabbis may be better understood if their resemblances to the Roman jurists are noted (Alexander 1990: 109–15; Hezser 1998). The functions of both were to give legal advice, interpret the 'unwritten' legal tradition, and pass on their learning to others. Like the Roman legal interpreters, rabbinic literature constructed a line of 'succession', which went back to Moses (M. Abot 1–2; on the Roman legal 'succession' see Pomponius, Enchiridion at Digest 1.2.2.). Both traditions of legal interpretation saw parts of the line of succession in terms of competing 'schools', with an emphasis on the oral transmission of wisdom from teacher to pupil. The differences between the 'schools' cited appear usually to be on points of detail, suggesting, that the 'schools culture' was a manifestation of the loyalty of a succession of pupils to masters. In this respect, both the Jewish and the Roman traditions reflect the intense competitiveness of ancient intellectual activity and the social importance of group affiliation (Malina 1993, 69–70).

Much work remains to be done on both Roman jurists and Jewish rabbis in the context of their legal and social cultures. Although fundamentally different from Jewish law, Roman law itself was founded on early 'sacred law' traditions, established under the kings, sometimes with (alleged) divine guidance. The head of the Roman priestly college of the *pontifices* gave quasi-legal rulings not only on matters of ritual in general but also on religious observances, often preceded by formal investigations relating to the nature and continuance of the *sacra*, or sacred identity, of Roman households. His authority thus extended over 'public law' functions, such as guardianship, certain forms of adoption, and responsibility for funerals. The earliest Roman law code, the Twelve Tables, contained both religious and civil law. Some of the earliest Republican jurists came from the pontifical college, and much difficulty was experienced in the first century BCE by legal thinkers seeking to distinguish pontifical from civil law. The Roman *ius civile*, the citizens' law of a secular state, had well-attested religious origins and, under the empire, its practitioners, the jurists, still laid claim to a superior status as both priests and philosophers (Digest 1.1.1.1).

But the Roman jurist under the early empire also differed from the rabbi in crucial ways. Although his main activity, to interpret and on occasion administer the procedures of the Roman civil law, was in itself low profile, he was often himself a senator or closely connected with the Roman aristocracy. Many jurists of the first century sat on the advisory councils of emperors, and Hadrian may have given legal experts a permanent role on the *consilium*. By the reign of the first Semitic emperor, Septimius Severus, experts in law were established in high posts in the imperial administration as masters of petitions, or even as Prefects of the Praetorian Guard. Most prolific as an author was Domitius Ulpianus of Tyre (a city which rabbis frequented in late antiquity), master of petitions and later Praetorian Prefect to Alexander Severus (for his career, see Honoré 2002: 1–36). The jurists of imperial Rome therefore often had privileged access to the ear of the powerful. Their discipline was not merely academic but practical and political as well.

Some studies already exist on comparisons of Roman with Jewish law. Scholars such as David Daube (Carmichael ed. 1992) have investigated rabbinic, Roman and other contemporary legal cultures on a comparative basis, but direct influence of one legal rule or concept on another from a different tradition is difficult to determine. Similarly, Boaz Cohen (1966) argued for Hellenistic, Roman, and Sassanian influences on rabbinic texts. More importantly, he emphasized the lack of a coherent system to laws and rules in both the Bible and the Talmud. This acceptance of accretion over generations of legal interpretation is a further feature shared with Roman legal culture although, in the case of the latter, the imposition of systems was a matter of persistent concern.

Significant unanswered questions remain, if the intellectual and social worlds of rabbinic and Roman legal interpretation are to be understood both in their own right and in relation to each other. Since Fritz Schulz (1946) there has been no attempt to study all Roman jurists in their particular cultural contexts. Attempts at such studies have been made for the Roman Republic (Frier 1985; Harries 2006), and for provincial jurists (Liebs 1976; on individual jurists see Honoré 1962 and 2002), as well as on their role in imperial law-making (Honoré 1994). As far as the rabbis are concerned, Daube's pupil Bernard Jackson (1975) has highlighted the extent of ignorance as to how far rabbinic law was applied in real life. At this stage it is impossible to assess accurately the extent of Roman legal influence on rabbinic theory and practice.

A number of lines of enquiry, therefore, remain open. The Mishnah, Talmud, and related texts can be studied as a quarry for historical information, but perhaps they should first be assessed as systems of knowledge in their own right. Recent studies of the Theodosian Code have underlined the importance of understanding the precise nature of legal evidence, before seeking to use it to draw wider historical conclusions (analysed by Lee 2002). In what sense were the rabbinic collections, 'codifications' (see Hezser 1998; for codification issues in general see Harries 2007)? Unlike the late Roman law-codes, they were not state sponsored: from what did their authority derive? An important dimension to Roman legal texts was their role as educators in morality as well as law: can we ascribe an educational purpose to the rabbinic collections? While juristic literature consisted of accumulated responses to cases, there existed in parallel a concern with systematization, extending from Cicero's now lost work on reducing the citizen-law to a teachable system down to Justinian's Corpus Iuris Civilis. Are there traces of similar concerns in the rabbinic collections (cf. Moscovitz 2002)?

6. PAPYROLOGICAL EVIDENCE

A second alternative narrative derives from the papyri, which reflect the views of the governed about what the Roman administration was for, and what kinds of law it was appropriate to use (see Cotton/Cockle/Millar 1995). One aspect of this is revealed by the dossier (Yadin/Lewis 1989 and Yadin et al. 2002) of Babatha, a Jewish woman who lived in a village, Maoza, in the Roman province of Arabia (formerly Nabatean territory) in the early second century CE and who may have died during the Bar Kokhba revolt in the early 130s. In her collection, there is little certain evidence of resistance as such to the imposition of the Roman way; rather, this local population may have displayed a willingness to adapt to their rulers' language and usages for practical purposes, and to exploit their legal processes for personal advantage. But the picture is complicated by the hazards of survival and the dangers of generalizing from one region to another (Cotton 1998).

The discovery in the Judaean Desert Cave of Letters of Babatha's archive of legal documents has provided a unique perspective on Roman justice, law, and procedures from the perspective of the governed. Babatha employed a bizarre mix of legal formulae to achieve her ends in property disputes with her extended family, but resort to a Jewish court or even to the principles which would be set out later in the written rabbinic tradition was not amongst them. Documents in her hoard include a number of summons and depositions, census returns, contracts of deposit, the marriage contract of her second husband's daughter by his previous marriage (P. Yadin 18), and his gift to her of half his property and bequest of the rest eleven days later (P. Yadin 19). The last in the collection dates from 132 CE, and it is assumed that the owner died in the Bar Kokhba revolt, aged perhaps little more than 20 years old. The physical form of the legal documents was traditional. Marriage contracts, loans, and many other kinds of legal documents were in the form of double documents, in which the text was written twice, once on the top, which was folded to become the inside, and a second time lower down, so that the document could be identified (Cotton 2003).

Babatha's motive for preserving her collection is unknown. She seems to have been a woman not afraid of initiating or contesting litigation involving members of her family, notably the two guardians of her orphaned son by her first marriage (P. Yadin 12–15, 27) and the other wife of her second husband (P. Yadin 26). Many of the documents are in Greek, and the question of whether or not this reflects some ideological preference for the Roman system has been controversial. Legal documents in Hebrew appear to crop up only in Judaea and only at times of revolt, suggesting that its use was for ideological, nationalist reasons. Conversely Greek, Babatha's preferred language, although she was herself illiterate, could be argued to be a statement of affiliation, a distancing from the mood of revolt gathering in Judaea on the eve of the Bar Kokhba uprising, in which she and hers were to perish (for arguments and references see Hezser 2001: 291–330; Meyer 2007). Various attempts are also made to compare the documents of Babatha and others with rabbinic halakhah recorded later (e.g. Satlow 2001, on marriage). But while there are strong 'Jewish' elements present in Babatha's legal world, and 'Roman' elements were adapted to local preconceptions, the evolution of a mixed legal culture is a complex process. In an area where rabbinic presence and influence seem to have been non-existent, we would not expect too positive an affirmation of their values or legal thought.

The choice of language, therefore, is probably strategic. Trouble was taken, in this area, to make formal documents 'look Roman'. Thus, a minute of the decision of the local council at Petra, the metropolis for Babatha, is described as *acta*, the Latin for minutes, but in Greek letters (P. Yadin 12). The same document refers to the 'tribunal' of the prefect, using the Latin word transliterated into Greek. A practice which may have derived from the Roman *stipulatio*, was the conclusion of an agreement with a formal question and answer. The formula, 'in good faith the question was asked and the answer given that it was rightly done' is found in documents on deposit (P. Yadin 17) and on marriage (P. Yadin 18) and, in a briefer form, in the acknowledgement of ownership of a courtyard (id. 20, lines 16 and 40) and the sale of a date crop (21, lines 27–7; 22, lines 29–30).

The villagers of Maoza were not Roman lawyers. Their adoption of the language of Roman law did not imply understanding or appreciation of its content. Rather, they hoped to impress the men of power with whom they were obliged to deal. Babatha's personal concern with Roman law is most strikingly illustrated in her possession of three copies of a Greek version of the Roman praetor's formula, by which he identified a legal issue and designated a judge to hear the facts of a case. The Greek text refers to actions on guardianship, but its terminology appears to be an adaptation of the formula for deposit, preserved in Gaius' Institutes (4.47), written at Rome a generation later. Where the deposit formula refers to the obligations of the caretaker of a valuable object deposited in his custody, Babatha's formula transfers those obligations to the guardian, and adds a financial cap of 2,500 denarii. Thus in Judaea, (as also in Egypt), the law of deposit served purposes for which it was not originally intended. That is illustrated also by a loan agreement made by Babatha, which she called a deposit: 300 denarii were 'deposited' with her second husband repayable on demand, but, unlike real loans, with no payment date specified (P. Yadin 17).

Litigation among the villagers and Babatha's family had an accepted pattern (Cotton 1993: 106–7). The aggrieved party, or her (usually male) representative, issued a petition to the governor, setting out his or her grievance. This, it was hoped, would generate a subscription from the governor, acknowledging that there was a case to answer. There then followed a summons to the named defendant, issued by the plaintiff, to attend with him or her at a hearing before the governor at Petra or some other location (P. Yadin 26.2–11). Although the subscription stage is not made explicit, Babatha seems to have employed this process against the two guardians of her orphaned son by her first husband, complaining that they had failed to provide adequate maintenance for the child who was resident with her, and arguing that they were holding back part of the returns expected from investing the child's assets. The sum had not been increased eight years later (P. Yadin 27, 19 August 132). Perhaps Babatha was told by the governor that, under Roman law, an action on guardianship could not be brought until the term of the guardianship was over. Perhaps she lost her case, or allowed it to lapse.

No record survived in Babatha's archive of an actual appearance in the governor's court. Whether or not the enforced waits in Petra were worth it, much could be achieved by exploiting the preliminary stages to gain a moral advantage. When Babatha became embroiled with the legal agents of her late husband's offspring, led by the formidable Iulia Crispina, perhaps a Roman citizen, both women hurled summonses at each other, the former citing the governor's subscription, the latter claiming that she had issued her summons, and had it endorsed first (P. Yadin 25, 9 July 131). That these tactics worked is suggested by the concession to Babatha's female relative Shelamzion of a disputed courtyard (P. Yadin 20), although other claims from the same quarter, alleging false entries in the census records continued.

In the governor's court it was not necessarily Roman law that would prevail, if the litigants were *peregrini* (non-citizens). Babatha's now deceased husband Judah had been simultaneously married to Miriam who, on his death, procured a banning order against Babatha, forbidding her to lay hands on his assets (P. Yadin 26). If the case had gone to court, the governor would have been expected to judge on the property of a dead man, who had been accepted as the husband of two women. Bigamy was not much catered for in Roman legal thinking. Roman jurists might have suggested that the contracting of the second marriage showed the husband's intention of ending the first, even if he had not formally done so. Conversely, in 258 CE, the emperor ruled that a bigamist's second wife, who had believed herself to be lawfully married, was innocent of fornication, unlike her husband (Codex Justinianus 9.9.18). Babatha's family would have found the whole issue incomprehensible. On the rightful control of property allegedly mismanaged by the guardians of Babatha's son (P. Yadin 13), the local practice of appointing two guardians, rather than the one expected in Roman legal practice, was followed and accepted (P. Yadin 12–15, 20–5), although Roman law on the responsibilities of guardianship in other respects could in theory still apply.

While, therefore, the governor's decisions had the advantage of coming from an external and neutral authority, resort to them does not imply that litigants were pro-Roman. It suited the convenience of Babatha and others like her to use (or exploit) the outsider rather than local arbiters more liable to be influenced by pressures from the locally powerful (and also, probably, more knowledgeable about her case). As a neutral adjudicator, a hard-working governor might share the plaudits granted by Josephus to the tetrarch Philip Herodes, who toured with his court regularly and would hear cases at a moment's notice (Josephus, Ant. 18. 106–7). But the governor would always be Roman and therefore 'Other', as is perhaps illustrated by the insistence of the council at Petra on referring to the adjudication platform by the transliterated Latin term, *tribunal*, rather than employing a Greek or local term (P. Yadin 14, line 31).

Governors could not judge every dispute and, as we have seen, the rules allowed them to delegate civil, but not criminal, cases to judges appointed by them. Other local adjudicators derived their authority from the Roman establishment, but may not have received formally delegated powers. The jurisdiction exercised by local military commanders in the relatively new Roman province of Arabia in the early second century is illustrated in Babatha's choice to register her date-palm groves for the census in 127 CE with the local cavalry commander (P. Yadin 16). Three years earlier, her second husband had borrowed money from a local centurion at an interest rate of 12 per cent (P. Yadin 11), the agreement being confirmed by the signatures of six witnesses. For these inhabitants of the new Roman Arabia, resort to Rome seems to have been the preferred, and possibly the only, viable option.

The choice of courts and adjudicators, therefore, was a wide one—wider perhaps for those with money who could afford the pressures of possibly long drawn-out litigation in the Roman courts. Babatha's archive shows that even relatively obscure people could hope to use, or manipulate, Roman justice in their interests, and that they were scrupulous in compiling the documents required for them to do so. But they also show that the formal judicial system was only one element in the resolution of disputes.

SUGGESTED READING

On Roman provincial jurisdiction in general, see Burton 1975 and Galsterer 1996. On the Roman Near East Fergus Millar (1993) provides a comprehensive overview.

On the Roman jurists there is no comprehensive work since Schulz (1946). Tony Honoré's entry on 'Lawyers' in the *Oxford Classical Dictionary* (2003) is a useful overview. On the social and legal context of rabbis see Goodman 1983 and Hezser 1997. There is a growing literature on the Babatha archive, see Goodman 1991 and Cotton 1993. For comparisons between Jewish/rabbinic and Graeco-Roman law see Cohen 1966, Jackson 1975, Hezser ed. 2003.

BIBLIOGRAPHY

ALEXANDER, P. S. (1990). 'Quid Athenis et Hierosolymis? Rabbinic Midrash and Hermeneutics in the Graeco-Roman World', in *A Tribute to Geza Vermes: Essays on Jewish and Christian Literature and History*, ed. P. R. Davies and R. T. White. Sheffield: Journal for the Study of the Old Testament Press, 101–24.

BABLITZ, L. (2007). *Actors and Audience in the Roman Courtroom*. London and New York: Routledge.

BURTON, G. P. (1975). 'Proconsuls, Assizes and the Administration of Justice Under the Empire'. *Journal of Roman Studies* 65: 92–106.

CARMICHAEL, C. (ed.) (1992). *The Collected Works of David Daube. Vol. 1: Talmudic Law*. Berkeley: Robbins Collection.

COHEN, B. (1966). *Jewish and Roman Law: A Comparative Study*. 2 vols. New York: Jewish Theological Seminary.

COHEN, S. J. D. (1981–2). 'Epigraphical Rabbis'. *Jewish Quarterly Review* 72: 1–17.

COTTON, H. M. (1993). 'The Guardianship of Jesus, son of Babatha: Roman and Local Law in the Province of Arabia'. *Journal of Roman Studies* 83: 94–108.

—— (1998). 'The Rabbis and the Documents', in *Jews in a Graeco-Roman World*, ed. M. Goodman. Oxford: Clarendon Press, and New York: Oxford University Press, 167–79.

—— (2003). '"Diplomatics" or External Aspects of the Legal Documents from the Judaean Desert: Prologomena', in *Rabbinic Law in its Roman and Near Eastern Context*, ed. C. Hezser. Tübingen: Mohr-Siebeck, 49–61.

——/COCKLE, W. E. H./MILLAR, F. G. B. (1995). 'The Papyrology of the Roman Near East: A Survey'. *Journal of Roman Studies* 85: 214–235.

CROOK, J. A. (1955). *Consilium Principis: Imperial Councils and Councellors from Augustus to Diocletian*. Cambridge: Cambridge University Press.

DOHRMANN, N. B. (2003). 'The Boundaries of the Law and the Problem of Jurisdiction in an Early Palestinian Midrash', in *Rabbinic Law in its Roman and Near Eastern Context*, ed. C. Hezser. Tübingen: Mohr-Siebeck, 83–103.

FISCHEL, H. A. (1973). *Rabbinic Literature and Graeco-Roman Philosophy: A Study of Epicurea and Rhetorica in Early Midrashic Writings*. Leiden: Brill.

—— (1977). *Essays in Greco-Roman and Related Talmudic Literature*. New York: Ktav Publishing House.

FRIER, B. W. (1985). *The Rise of the Roman Jurists: Studies in Cicero's Pro Caecina*. Princeton: Princeton University Press.

GALSTERER, H. (1988). 'Municipiium Flavium Irnitanum: A Latin Town in Spain'. *Journal of Roman Studies* 78: 78–90.

GALSTERER, H. (1996). 'The Adminstration of Justice', in *The Cambridge Ancient History, vol. 10: The Augustan Empire 43 BC to AD 69*. 2nd revised ed. Cambridge: Cambridge University Press, 397–413.

GOODBLATT, D. (1994). *The Monarchic Principle: Studies in Jewish Self-Government in Antiquity*. Tübingen: Mohr-Siebeck.

GOODMAN, M. (1983). *State and Society in Roman Galilee, A.D. 132–212*. Totowa, NJ: Rowman and Allanheld.

—— (1991). 'Babatha's Story'. *Journal of Roman Studies* 81: 169–75.

HARRIES, J. (1999). *Law and Empire in Late Antiquity*. Cambridge: Cambridge University Press.

—— (2003). 'Creating Legal Space: Resolving Disputes in the Roman Empire', in *Rabbinic Law in its Roman and Near Eastern Context*, ed. C. Hezser. Tübingen: Mohr-Siebeck, 63–81.

—— (2006). *Cicero and the Jurists: From Citizen's Law to the Lawful State*. London: Duckworth.

—— (2007). 'Roman Law Codes and the Roman Legal Tradition', in *Beyond Dogmatics. Law and Society in the Roman World*, ed. J. W. Cairns and P. J. du Plessis. Edinburgh: Edinburgh University Press, 85–104.

HEZSER, C. (1997). *The Social Structure of the Rabbinic Movement in Roman Palestine*. Tübingen: Mohr-Siebeck.

—— (1998). 'The Codification of Legal Knowledge in Late Antiquity: The Talmud Yerushalmi and Roman Law Codes', in *The Talmud Yerushalmi and Graeco-Roman Culture*, vol. 1, ed. P. Schäfer. Tübingen: Mohr-Siebeck, 581–641.

—— (2001). *Jewish Literacy in Roman Palestine*. Tübingen: Mohr-Siebeck.

—— (ed.) (2003). *Rabbinic Law in its Roman and Near Eastern Context*. Tübingen Mohr Siebeck.

HONORÉ, T. (1962). *Gaius*. Oxford: Clarendon Press.

—— (1994). *Emperors and Lawyers*. 2nd ed. Oxford: Clarendon Press.

—— (2002). *Ulpian: Pioneer of Human Rights*. 2nd ed. Oxford and New York: Oxford University Press.

—— (2003). 'Lawyers', in *Oxford Classical Dictionary*. 3rd revised edition. Oxford: Oxford University Press, 835–6.

JACKSON, B. (1975). *Essays in Jewish and Comparative Legal History*. Leiden. Brill.

JACOBS, M. (1995). *Die Institution des jüdischen Patriarchen. Eine quellen- und traditionskritische Studie zur Geschichte der Juden in der Spätantike*. Tübingen: Mohr-Siebeck.

JONES, A. H. M. (1972). *The Criminal Courts of the Roman Republic and Principate*. Oxford: Blackwell.

LAPIN, H. (1995). *Early Rabbinic Civil Law and the Social History of Roman Galilee: A Study of Mishnah Tractate Baba Mesia*. Atlanta: Scholars Press.

LEE, A. D. (2002). 'Decoding Late Roman Law'. *Journal of Roman Studies* 92: 185–193.

LIEBERMAN, S. (1962). *Hellenism in Jewish Palestine*. 2nd ed. New York: Jewish Theological Seminary.

—— (1965). *Greek in Jewish Palestine*. 2nd ed. New York: Jewish Theological Seminary.

LIEBS, D. (1976). 'Römische Provinzialjurisprudenz'. *Aufstieg und Niedergang der Römischen Welt* II. 15: 288–362.

LINDER, A. (1987). *The Jews in Roman Imperial Legislation*. Detroit: Wayne State University Press, and Jerusalem: The Israel Academy of Sciences and Humanities.

MALINA, B. J. (1993). *The New Testament World: Insights from Cultural Anthropology.* Louisville: Westminster/John Knox Press.

MEYER, E. (2007). 'Diplomatics, Law and Romanisation in the Documents from the Judaean Desert', in *Beyond Dogmatics: Law and Society in the Roman World,* ed. J. W. Cairns and P. du Plessis. Edinburgh: University of Edinburgh Press, 53–84.

MILLAR, F. (1993). *The Roman Near East, 31 B.C.–A.D. 337.* Cambridge: Harvard University Press.

MOSCOVITZ, L. (2002). *Talmudic Reasoning. From Casuistics to Conceptualization.* Tübingen: Mohr-Siebeck.

—— (2003). 'Legal Fictions in Rabbinic Law and Roman Law: Some Comparative Observations', in *Rabbinic Law in its Roman and Near Eastern Context,* ed. C. Hezser. Tübingen: Mohr-Siebeck, 105–32.

NEUSNER, J. (1983). *Judaism in Society: The Evidence of the Yerushalmi.* Chicago: University of Chicago Press.

SATLOW, M. (2001). *Jewish Marriage in Antiquity.* Princeton. Princeton University Press.

SCHULZ, F. (1946). *A History of Roman Legal Science.* Oxford: Clarendon Press.

SHERWIN WHITE, A. N. (1963). *Roman Society and Roman Law in the New Testament.* Oxford: Clarendon Press.

SPERBER, D. (1984). *A Dictionary of Greek and Latin Legal Terms in Rabbinic Literature.* Ramat Gan: Bar-Ilan University Press.

STEMBERGER, G. (1996). *Introduction to the Talmud and Midrash.* Edinburgh: T.& T. Clark.

WALLACE-HADRILL, A. (ed.) (1989). *Patronage in Ancient Society.* London. Routledge.

YADIN, Y. / LEWIS, N. (1989). *The Documents from the Bar Kokhba Period in the Cave of Letters I: Greek Papyri.* Jerusalem: Israel Exploration Society.

YADIN, Y. et al. (2002). *The Documents from the Bar Kokhba Period in the Cave of Letters II: Hebrew, Aramaic and Nabatean-Aramaic Papyri.* Jerusalem. Israel Exploration Society.

CHAPTER 6

POPULATION STRUCTURE AND JEWISH IDENTITY

DAVID GOODBLATT

1. METHODOLOGICAL CONSIDERATIONS

Population structure normally includes topics such as age distribution, gender distribution, and family size as determined by fertility, mortality, marriage practices, and migration patterns. These variables clearly impact daily life. Unfortunately, Roman-Byzantine Palestine is no exception to the rule that applies to the ancient world in general, namely our lack of 'reliable statistical evidence for general demographic functions' (Frier 2000: 787; compare Parkin 1992: 59; Dauphin 1998: 373; Scheidel 2001: 13; Tropper 2006: 301). The most ambitious effort to study such functions in ancient Palestine, focusing on the last three centuries of our period, emphasizes the limitations of the evidence and concedes that the only method available is to 'faire avec l'inexact, de l'à-peu-près' (Dauphin 1998: 381 and see 349–525 for her treatment). The insufficiency of the data applies even to the most basic of demographic issues: the size of a population in a given place at a given time. Nevertheless, it is precisely this issue that has attracted most attention from historians of antiquity (Scheidel 2001: 49). The present chapter will follow suit and focus on the same topic.

Even the issue of size involves a number of questions. How many Jews lived in Roman-Byzantine Palestine? What percentage were they of the total population of the province? How was the Jewish population distributed among the various regions of the country and among the various types of settlement? Did the percentage of Jews vary over time? Did the Jews live in religiously homogeneous settlements or in mixed ones? The answers to these questions are likely to impact our understanding of daily life. For example, the quotidian experiences of Jews who lived as a minority in a large, multi-ethnic port city like Caesarea presumably differed from those of contemporaries living in an isolated, rural settlement in the hills of what many assume to have been predominantly Jewish Upper Galilee. Or, using chronological rather than geographical distinctions, the daily life of a Jew in Jerusalem during the first century of the period covered here surely differed from that of the Jews who trickled back into Jerusalem during the Byzantine era. Unfortunately, the limitations of our sources make it difficult to ascertain the size, percentage, and fluctuations of the Jewish population. A further complication relates to distinguishing the Jews from the other residents of the country. Of concern here is how people in Roman-Byzantine Palestine understood issues of identity and group affiliation. Postponing till later consideration of this potential complication, we begin with a review of the scholarship on the demography of Palestinian Jews.

2. CENSUS RESULTS

One starting point for demographic research is census results. And the Roman-Byzantine state did carry out censuses. Documentary evidence of provincial censuses survives from Roman Egypt, while literary and epigraphic texts attest earlier counts of Roman citizens. Each set of data has been the subject of demographic research, though their interpretation is by no means free of problems and debate (Bagnall/Frier 1994; Lo Cascio 1994; for censuses from Ptolemaic Egypt see Clarysse/Thompson 2006). Of relevance here is the census of what was to become the first version of the Roman province of Judaea, namely the former territories of Archelaus, comprising Samaria, Judah, Idumea, and the coastal plain from Caesarea to Jaffa. This was conducted in 6/7 CE by Quirinius, legate of Syria, as described by Josephus and by the author of Luke (Josephus, Ant. 18.1–3, 26, Luke 2:1–3; on Luke contrast Fitzmyer 1981: 400–3 with Di Segni 2005: 32–4). Unfortunately, the data collected by Quirinius survives neither in documentary form nor in the literary sources.

The absence of documentary or literary reports on the results of censuses in Judaea-Palaestina continues for the entire Roman-Byzantine period. There is, however, one report of a Roman census that purports to record the number of Jews in the empire as a whole. Some influential historians of the previous century had accepted a statement in the Arabic version of the *Chronography* of the thirteenth-century author Bar Hebraeus. According to this source a census under Claudius in 47 or 48 counted 6.944 million Jews in the Roman Empire (Baron 1971: 871). Were this information reliable, one might try to estimate the percentage of those who resided in Judaea and then calculate their number. However, it seems clear that Bar Hebraeus (or his source) confused a census of Roman citizens with one of Jews (Wasserstein 1996: 309–13; McGing 2002: 92–94; Feldman 2003: 128). A rather different kind of census allegedly conducted less than twenty years later is described by Josephus. He reports (Bell. 6.422–27; compare 2.380) that Cestius Gallus, legate of Syria between 63 and 66 CE, sought to convince Nero of the strength of Jerusalem. To bolster his case, Gallus requested of the chief priests that they 'count the multitude.' The method used was to count the number of paschal lambs offered that year and multiply by ten, which was the average number of persons who shared a lamb at the ritualized Passover eve meal. The lambs numbered 255,600 yielding a population in Jerusalem for the pilgrimage of 2.556 million. Some scholars were tempted to accept the report since the number is not a round or symbolic one, and Josephus was either in Jerusalem at the time or in the city within a year or two of the event he reports (Josephus, Vita 13–17). Most scholars, however, doubt the accuracy of these figures (Jeremias 1969: 77-84; Levine 2002: 250–51; McGing 2002: 97; contrast Feldman 2003: 132–4 who accepts at least the order of magnitude if not the precise number). It is difficult to imagine that a city the size of Jerusalem could host such a large number (equivalent to or in excess of the population of the entire province according to many estimates, see Byatt 1973), or that the world Jewish population could generate such a large number of pilgrims in any given year.

3. POPULATION NUMBERS

With no further records of the results of censuses, those interested in historical demography look at other reports of population numbers in the ancient sources. The consensus today is that these reports are of little value. As Scheidel asserts, 'in general the reporting of numbers in ancient texts can be shown to be heavily controlled by literary conventions.... [T]he large majority of references are no more than symbolic values, at best indicative of a certain order of magnitude and deployed to lend colour or emphasis to the author's exposition' (Scheidel 2001: 49, compare 11; Frier 2000: 787; McGing 2002: 89). These strictures may be illustrated from reports on the population of Jerusalem at the end of the revolt of 66–70. Josephus (Bell. 6.420) claims that 1.1 million died in the siege of that city. Tacitus

(Hist. 5.13.3) reports that the total number of the besieged population, men and women, was 600,000 (compare Josephus, Bell. 5.569 and see Jeremias 1969: 78). Discounting all these numbers as exaggerated, Stern suggests that Josephus' report (Bell. 5.248–50) of 23,400 armed men in Jerusalem at the beginning of the siege, including the contingents from Idumea and Galilee, seems realistic (Stern 1980: 62–3; compare–McGing 2002: 94–95 on the small and so apparently realistic numbers in Josephus' Vita). Assuming a ratio of fighters to population of 1:10 means only about a quarter of a million were trapped in Jerusalem, well under the numbers asserted by both Tacitus and Josephus (see the tables in Lo Cascio 2001: 136–7; ratios as high and higher are suggested for periods of crisis in Rome and approached in Sweden in 1709 and Prussia in 1760). Feldman concludes, 'we need not take Josephus' numbers at face value, but that does not mean that we should disregard the impression that he wishes to convey, namely that the number of Jews was very large' (Feldman 2003: 135). If '600,000' or '1.1 million' are just ways of saying 'a lot of people', however, then these numbers are useless for historical demography.

Given the problematic nature of the numbers reported by ancient authors, historical demographers apply other methods to try and get a sense of the size of ancient populations. The pioneering 1886 study by K. L. Beloch, *Die Bevölkerung der griechisch-römischen Welt*, already used the method of estimating the 'carrying capacity' of a region (Lo Cascio 1994: 26–7). One calculates the amount of food, especially grains that can be produced in the area, and then the number of people this amount could feed. The result will be the maximum population sustainable. Another method, useful for delineated urban areas such as walled towns, develops a density coefficient and then estimates the number of people who could live within a given space. In a series of studies beginning in the 1970s, Magen Broshi applied these methods to Roman-Byzantine Palestine (available with updated bibliographies in Broshi 2001). His conclusion is that the *maximum* population that the country could have sustained in antiquity was about one million, a level not achieved in modern times until 1931. He further suggests that the ancient peak was reached in the late Byzantine era, around 600 (Broshi 2001: 92, 106). Of course these results apply to the overall population, not just to the Jews. Broshi's estimate has won considerable support (for example, Hamel 1990: 137–40; Tsafrir 1994: 18; Schwartz 2001: 13, n. 14; Dauphin 1998: 79 refrains from proposing a number, but on 281 she characterizes Broshi's estimation as 'plus sobrement'). However, there has also been criticism of the methodology employed by Broshi (Scheidel 2001: 50, 59–61; McGing 2002: 99–104). The uncertainties and disagreements about crop yields, minimum dietary requirements and population densities in built-up areas led Safrai to conclude 'it is impossible to determine how many people lived in the Land of Israel during the Mishnah and Talmud periods' (Safrai 1994: 436–7, with quotation on 436). In this, Safrai reflects much of contemporary scholarship as described by Lo Cascio. According to the latter, 'Estimating the size of an ancient population is thought of as an almost impossible exercise, given the uncertainties in the source material' (Lo Cascio 1994: 40; for Byzantine Palestine see Parker 1999: 170–71; for Jews in the ancient world McGing 2002: 106).

4. POPULATION GROWTH

While it is clearly impossible to achieve consensus on an absolute figure, there appears to be broad agreement on relative numbers. That is, most scholars appear to agree that the Roman-Byzantine period witnessed a rise in the population of Palestine, with a peak in the Byzantine era (Tsafrir 1994: 18; Safrai 1994: 437, 440— but see his revised opinion in Safrai 1998: 33—Dauphin 1998: 77–79, 351, 442; McGing 2002: 105; Bar 2004a, 2004b, 2004c). This agreement is based on archaeo-logical evidence both from excavations of urban centres and other sites and from surveys of the region. The assumption behind the methodology is the common sense notion of "a clear correlation between population size and settlement area" (Broshi 2001: 87; compare Dauphin 1998: 79, 281; Wilkinson 1999; McGing 2002: 105). During the past half century intensive archaeological activity has provided evidence for increases both in the areas of cities and also in the number of rural settlements in Roman-Byzantine Palestine. Particularly important are the results so far of the Archaeological Survey of Israel in which units of 10 km by 10 km are intensively examined (on the methodology and limitations of this project see Tsafrir 1996: 271–73 and Dauphin 1998: 45, 49–51; for a broader perspective see Banning 2002 and Collins/Molyneaux 2003). Supplementing this data are surveys conducted under other auspices and excavations of various sites (Tsafrir 1996: 275–77; Parker 1999: 142–49).

Summarizing the results available at the beginning of the current century, Bar estimates that information is available for about 6000 km², or over a third of the total area of Roman-Byzantine Palestine (Bar 2004a: 73; 2004b: 3; 2004c: 308). Even allowing for uncertainties about precise dating of pottery and the inconsistencies in reports of settlement size (see Lapin 2001:40–44), the following picture emerges. In almost every region of the province there is a sharp increase in the number of sites from the Hellenistic to the Roman periods, and in most there is another increase from the Roman to the Byzantine (see the map in Bar 2004c: 309; compare the maps appearing as Figures 3–23, 27–34 in Dauphin 1998 and see Tsafrir 1996: 271, 274; for Palestine east of the Rift Valley see Parker 1999: 143–44). Moreover, according to Tsafrir, the 'great majority of Roman towns in Palestine significantly expanded between the fourth century and the sixth and seventh century...' (Tsafrir 1996: 275; Walmsley 1996). Finally, this period witnessed the expansion of agricultural cultivation into ecologically marginal areas (Dauphin 1998: 119, 520–21;

cf. Bar 2004a; Bar 2004b; Bar 2004c). The evidence from both surveys and excavations appears to support more than just an 'impressionistic portrait of demographic growth' (Parker 1999: 171).

While the view just summarized has wide support, there are some dissenters. Reversing his earlier agreement with the consensus, Z. Safrai argued for a general decline in the population of Palestine in the late fourth and especially in the fifth century (Safrai 1998: 32–36, 83–127; already Adan-Bayewitz 1993: 240–43 suggested this for the Galilee). His case for a demographic downturn, affecting Jews and Christians alike, is based on a sharp decline in the number of fifth century coins across the province, as well as more precise dating of the archaeological evidence, thanks to improved sequencing of Byzantine pottery. The numismatic evidence, however, may not bear the weight Safrai puts on it (Parker 1999: 135–36; Magness 2001: 29–30, n. 76). And it is not clear to me that revisions in dating the material remains suffice to overturn the growth trends detailed by Dauphin and summarized by Bar (Dauphin 1998; Bar 2004c). Another challenge to the consensus comes from Uzi Leibner's research on Eastern Lower Galilee (Leibner 2006 and 2009: 351–76). Leibner uses what he calls a 'high-resolution archaeological survey.' This approach involves visiting sites more than once, 'shovel-testing' selected locations to see if excavated remains match those collected on the surface, and taking advantage of advances in pottery research that allows the identification and dating within a narrow range of a very high percentage of the collected sherds. On the basis of his survey, Leibner claims a 'dramatic decline in settlement and demography' in the area. This was the result of 'a continuous, long-term process, beginning around the mid-third century and continuing well into the late fourth.' He connects the early stages of the process with the alleged third-century crisis of the Roman Empire, and the worsening with historical events in fourth century Palestine (Leibner 2006: 127). It turns out that the peak of settlement and population was reached in what he calls the Mid Roman period, 135 CE to mid-third century CE, and the nadir in the late Byzantine period, mid-sixth to mid-seventh century CE (Leibner 2006: 119–120, though compare 128). Further, though the evidence is less extensive, Leibner suggests a similar decline in the adjacent areas of the Lower Golan and eastern Upper Galilee—both areas of Jewish settlement (Leibner 2006: 120–122 with literature cited; for the Golan see Ben David 2007: 18–26; Leibner 2009: 351–76).

The results and arguments of Leibner are just now beginning to be weighed by the specialists, so it is not yet possible to ascertain whether the current consensus will be overturned. In particular, the dating of the monumental synagogues and their significance for demography will need to be resolved. Even if the theory of population growth in the country as a whole is to be maintained, the place of the Jews in this process is still subject to debate. One possibility is that the Jews did not share in the general trend. Thus Avi-Yonah argued, 'a sharp decline had occurred in the number of Jews in Palestine, both absolutely and in proportion to the rest of the inhabitants' (Avi-Yonah 1984: 241; Safrai 1994: 442; compare Dauphin 1998: 301,

320). He suggests that the Jewish population fell following the revolt of 132–135 CE from 1.3 million to 700,000–800,000. And the decline continued over the remainder of the Roman-Byzantine period. By the early seventh century, he estimates, the number of Jews in the province stood at 150,000–200,000. In percentage terms, the Jewish part of the population of the province fell from a pre-135 CE majority (if a slight one) to less than a third after 135 CE and to a mere 10–15 per cent in the early seventh century (Avi-Yonah 1984: 19–20, 132–33, 240–41). While he admits that the Jews shared in the material prosperity of Byzantine Palestine, Avi-Yonah insists that their numbers declined (Avi-Yonah 1984: 221–22).

Safrai and Leibner allow another option, if we assume a general decline in the population of Palestine that affected Jews and Gentiles alike. The absolute number of Jews might have dropped without a corresponding decline in their percentage of the whole. Neither scholar, however, makes this argument. Leibner does note that surveys of the Upper Golan, with its Christian and 'pagan' population, indicate a 'considerable decline' in settlement—though the process seems to have begun only in the fifth century (Leibner 2006: 124). In any case, we have noted two possibilities: (1) a decline of the Jewish population in both absolute and relative numbers and (2) a decline in absolute numbers while the percentage of Jews and non-Jews remains stable. A third possibility, tentatively suggested by some scholars, is that while the Jews shared in the general population growth in Roman-Byzantine Palestine, other groups did so at a higher rate. As a result, the proportion of Jews in the province declined even as their absolute number increased (see Tsafrir 1996: 279; Isaac 1998: 67; Lapin 1999: 267–8; for the Jews sharing in the demographic growth of Roman-Byzantine Palestine see, for example, Stemberger 2000: 18–21, 314). In order to decide among these possibilities we need some way to isolate the various groups living in the province, so that we can estimate their relative numbers.

5. Jewish Settlements

Avi-Yonah estimated the Jewish population of Palestine over time, both in absolute and relative terms, by counting Jewish settlements. He explains, 'It is very difficult to arrive at a reliable estimate of the numbers of Jews and Gentiles living in Palestine at that period [after 135 CE]. We can only compare the number of places where Jews were known to live with the total number of localities' (Avi-Yonah 1984: 19). The Hebrew original is more precise, speaking of 'the number of Jewish settlements [*hayishuvim hayehudiyyim*] . . . in comparison to the general number of settlements' (Avi-Yonah 1962: 25; compare Alon 1961: 242 who refers to 'the

Hebrew settlements', *hayishuvim ha'ivrim*). The identification of 'places where Jews were known to live' relies on literary notices and archaeological evidence of religious affiliation such as synagogues, inscriptions, and small finds bearing menorahs and the like. This approach seems to assume that outside of the major urban centres, which clearly contained mixed populations, individual settlements had religiously homogeneous populations. Otherwise one could not characterize a settlement as 'Jewish'.

This assumption seemed to be well established. Eusebius, in his Onomasticon, written in the early fourth century, characterizes some villages as either Jewish or Christian. Thus he mentions two places named Anaia, one 'a very large village of the Jews' and the other 'completely Christian' (Eusebius, Onomasticon 26.7, 13–14). Writing around 380 CE concerning events in 351–2 CE, Jerome characterized Diocaesarea (Sepphoris), Tiberias, and Diospolis (Lod) as 'their [that is, the Jews'] cities (*civitates eorum*)' (Chron. ad 282 Olympiad). And a well-known midrashic source lists five pairs of neighbouring and rival towns, one set Jewish and the other Gentile. The text relates to Lam. 1:17, 'the Lord has commanded against Jacob that his neighbours should become his foes' (NRSV translation). The anonymous commentator explains, 'Like Halamish to Naveh, and Susita [= Hippos] to Tiberias and Castra to Haifa and Jericho to Na'aran and Lod to Ono' (Lev. R. 23:5 and parallels, ed. Margulies, 533). In each of the five pairs of rival towns, the first named is Gentile and the second is Jewish. In the absence of named tradents we cannot date the source more precisely than assuming a probable Byzantine era provenance (Isaac 1998: 70 suggests it reflects 'the realty of the fourth to fifth century').

Are the literary sources that describe certain cities, towns and villages as Jewish any more reliable than the ones that report population figures? Recent independent critiques by Dauphin and Isaac cast doubt on some of this evidence. They note that out of the hundreds of villages named by Eusebius, only eighteen are characterized religiously: eleven as Jewish, four as Samaritan, and three as Christian. The best explanation, they argue, is that villages with a homogeneous Jewish or Christian population were the exception rather than the rule (Dauphin 1998: 57, 169–70; Isaac 1998). Isaac, who suggests that the rabbinic source on the five pairs of rival towns may also be remarking on an anomalous situation, concludes that by the time Eusebius wrote, 'the overwhelming majority of villages had a mixed population: pagan, Jewish, Christian, and Samaritan' (Isaac 1998:73). Dauphin draws a different conclusion based on the archaeological evidence. Since only a minority of the total number of sites yield indications of religious affiliation, she suggests that through the end of the fourth century the 'silent majority' of Palestinians were 'pagan' (Dauphin 1998: 170, 185–6). However, it is not clear why absence of indications of religious affiliation should prove not only the absence of Jews or Christians but also the presence of 'pagans'. In fact, she herself is aware of the limitations of the method (Dauphin 1998: 237–38; compare Alon 1961: 243 warning against arguments from silence). Furthermore, evidence of affiliation to one religion need not characterize the entire population of a site.

Despite all these reservations, the method of counting religiously identified sites continues to be used. Since Avi-Yonah wrote, the database has increased greatly. This is the result above all of the archaeological surveys, most of which were not completed until after his death in 1974. The most detailed survey is that of Dauphin (Dauphin 1998: 170–85, 229–32, 237–38). She identifies sites as Jewish, Christian, Samaritan or 'mixed' and then lists the number of each type attested at the end of the fourth century, in the fifth century, in the sixth, and at the beginning of the seventh (Dauphin 1998: 185, 234, 309, 320 with plotting on maps in Figures 42–107 and tabulations in Figures 115–17). The results (combining the certain with the possible) are as follows:

Century	Jewish sites	Christian sites	Samaritan sites	Mixed
End 4th	40	48	5	3
5th	157	168	22	45
6th	93	191	20	42
Early 7th	54	454	18	31

As already mentioned, Dauphin believes the pagans constituted the majority of the population at the end of the fourth century. The Jewish component had apparently declined as a result of the third-century economic crisis (Dauphin 1998: 185–86). However, it is not clear why the Jews should have suffered disproportionately more than other groups, let alone whether Palestine actually felt the brunt of the third-century crisis (Groh 1988; Bar 2002). In any event, in the course of the fifth century, the number of Christians came to roughly equal or slightly surpassed that of the Jews, although the Galilee, Golan, and the Darom (= southern Judah) remained strongly Jewish. In the sixth century the Jews lost ground everywhere (Dauphin 1998: 234, 295, 301–10). By the early seventh century the Jews lost their dominant position even in the Galilee and Golan, as the Christians became the preponderant element in the population of Palestine. Ignoring the Samaritans and localities with mixed population, 89.4 per cent of religiously identifiable Palestinian sites were Christian and only 10.6 per cent were Jewish. Relying on the percentage of Jewish sites out of the total number of sites, she concludes that the Jews constituted as little as 2.35 per cent of the population of the province, even less than the 8 per cent she estimates for the Samaritans (Dauphin 1998: 320). These results, if accurate, would justify Dauphin's assertion of an inexorable 'encirclement' and 'asphyxiation' of the Jewish community of Palestine as the result of a conscious campaign by Church and State over the course of the Byzantine era (see for example Dauphin 1998: 234, 301–02, 307, 309–10, 320).

Several considerations, most noted by Dauphin herself, raise questions about these results. One, as mentioned previously, is the use of arguments from silence. Dauphin emphasizes that early seventh-century sites with religious indicators constitute only 18.35 per cent (= 16 per cent Christian + 2.35 per cent Jewish) of the total of 2,930 for Byzantine Palestine (Dauphin 1998: 320). But then it is not clear to me why Dauphin equates the percentage of Jews with the percentage of sites with Jewish vestiges. She clearly does not limit the Christian population to 16 per cent, the percentage of sites with Christian vestiges in the early seventh century! It seems to me that a better way to evaluate her data is to use the religiously identifiable sites as a representative sample. A sample approaching 20 per cent of the total is a sizeable one and can reasonably be considered representative. Using the total of religiously identifiable sites as representative, the statistics cited above suggest that the Jews constituted almost 12 per cent of the total population in the early seventh century (dividing the mixed settlements among the Christians, Samaritans and Jews we get 64 Jewish sites out of a total of 554 religiously identifiable ones, or 11.6 per cent). This is essentially identical with the range of 10–15 per cent proposed by Avi-Yonah (Avi-Yonah 1984: 240).

A related methodology suggests a significantly higher percentage of Jews in Byzantine Palestine. Instead of *settlements*, it counts the number of religious *buildings* attributable to each community: 'pagan' temples, Jewish synagogues, Samaritan synagogues, and Christian churches. Such buildings are assumed to reflect the existence of a community that supported their construction and maintenance. This approach ignores the problem of the 'silent majority' of sites without such buildings, and obviates the potentially misleading nature of small finds, *spolia*, etc. that might not be in their original locations. Tsafrir counted 390 churches, eighty synagogues, and less than a dozen pagan temples in Western Palestine during the Byzantine era. He concluded, 'the Jewish population comprised no more, and perhaps less, then one quarter of the overall number of inhabitants in Western Palestine' (Tsafrir 1996: 278–79). Interestingly enough, Avi-Yonah had suggested the same percentage of 25 per cent of the overall population of Palestine for the Jews at the end of the third century, and Alon argued for this percentage apparently as late as the Muslim conquest (Avi-Yonah 1984: 133; Alon 1980: 36 with note 10 by the translator, based on Alon 1961: 262). Factoring in the fairly dense Jewish settlement in the Golan (which is east of the Rift Valley) to Tsafrir's data might raise the percentage of Jews he estimates for the Byzantine era even higher.

Variations in the size of settlements limit the reliability of the methods of counting sites and counting (religious) buildings. Along with cities and villages, Dauphin counts monasteries, pilgrimage sites, and farmsteads (details in Dauphin 1998: 621–999). The last three categories mentioned could number only a handful of residents. For example, a dozen farmsteads might not equal a single village in population. Similarly with religious buildings, one urban church could represent a larger population than several village synagogues. Conversely, the existence of a church need not imply a local Christian community. Some marked holy sites that were funded by individuals living elsewhere (compare Dauphin 1998: 80–85, 170–71). Consequently, simply counting buildings or sites can be misleading. Relying on the number of sites may mislead in another way. What really matters is the *area* of settlement. An increase in the number of discrete settlements could coincide with an overall decrease in area settled and a decrease in population (see Portugali 1986: 16–18; areas of sites are given–where available–in the catalogue that appears in Dauphin 1998: 629–999). Conversely, a decline in the number of sites could conceivably coincide with an increase in population. Dauphin notes a sharp decline in the number of Jewish sites along the coastal plain in the sixth century. At the same time she observes that all the major port cities had Jewish populations, including Ptolemais, Shiqmonah, Caesarea, Ashqelon, and Maiumas Gaza (Dauphin 1998: 310). Is it possible that we see here a movement of Jews from countryside to city, something akin to Jewish participation in the 'bourgeois revolution' of the second and third Muslim centuries (Goitein 1964: 7, 100–5)? If so, then their numbers need not have declined. Clearly the procedure of simply tallying sites with religious indicators or counting religious buildings has limitations.

6. REGIONAL CONCENTRATION

A third approach, used by various scholars including Dauphin herself, examines the various regions of the province individually. If the religiously identifiable sites in a region are all, or overwhelmingly, from one community, then the problem of arguments from silence is moderated. The absence of Jewish remains, say, in the presence of rich Christian material across a considerable area is unlikely to be the result of the chance of preservation or discovery. In such a case it seems reasonable to conclude that Christians predominated in the population there and to attribute the sites without religiously identifiable remains to them as well. Using this logic, some scholars have argued that the archaeological evidence indicates religious 'segregation' or homogeneity in several areas of Palestine during the Byzantine period. Indeed many scholars argue, at least in part on the basis of literary sources, that this had been the case in the Roman period (Taylor 1993: 48–85; Safrai 1998: 65–82). Epiphanius, writing around 375, claimed that during the first half of the fourth century the Jews were able to keep Gentiles out of Galilee (Pan. 30.4–12; see however the reading of this account by Jacobs 2004: 48–51). Reinforcing this testimony is the fact that no bishops from the region are reported as attending the Council of Nicaea in 325. The closest sites sending bishops were Zabulon (= Kabul), Maximinopolis and Scythopolis (Tsafrir 1996: 277). The archaeological evidence appears to confirm this picture of regional concentrations of the Jewish population in the Roman period, and demonstrates it for the Byzantine period.

One such body of evidence relates to Upper Galilee, the hilly region lying between the Huleh Valley and the coastal plain. Aviam claims that by the early Roman period we can observe a clear geographical demarcation between Jewish and pagan areas of settlement. A still clearer picture emerges in Byzantine times. In this era there is a sharp division between the eastern part of Upper Galilee, which is overwhelmingly Jewish, and the western part, which is predominantly Christian (Aviam 1999 and 2004: 9–21, 202–3). The exceptions to this picture of geographical religious segregation are few in number and can be explained as involving individuals, not communities. There are only two Galilean settlements where one finds remains of both a church and a synagogue, which might indicate a mixed settlement. However, at Rama the church may come from a later century and so could reflect a change in the population or in its religious affiliation (see Magness/Avni 1999 for a similar argument concerning Jewish and Christian burials in a cemetery at Bet Guvrin in the south). The other case is the famous instance of Capernaum where a synagogue and church sit across the street from each other. Aviam suggests that early Christians built on what was for them a sacred site within a Jewish village. In other words, in this case the church is not evidence for a Christian community of any size. A like interpretation can apply to the evidence from Nazareth (Aviam 1999: 282–83; Aviam 2004: 20, 203; compare Taylor 1993: 293 on Capernaum and 229 on Nazareth and contrast Jacobs 2004: 127–129).

Similar cases for regional segregation by ethnicity or religion have also been made for other parts of Palestine. Gal argues from the remains of synagogues that the Bet Shean and Harod valleys and the surrounding Issachar plateaus were uniformly Jewish. The capital of the region (and eventually of Palaestina Secunda), Scythopolis, was 'a gentile enclave within the heart of the Jewish rural settlement' (Gal 1995). In the Golan Ma'oz suggests a clear regional demarcation between Jewish and Gentile settlements analogous to the Upper Galilee (Ma'oz 1993; contrast Dauphin 1982 and Urman 1995: 607–14, and see the response by Aviam 2004: 20–21 and the discussion of Ben David 2006). Finally, Aviam reports the unpublished survey of Samaria by M. Yiftah that reveals separation between Christian and Samaritan settlements (Aviam 1999: 300). Dauphin concurs that Galilee, Golan, the Bet Shean region, and the *Darom* (= southern Judah) had strong concentrations of Jewish population through the sixth century (Dauphin 1998: 234, 301, 318). However, translating these regional concentrations into percentages and numbers remains to be done (compare Parker 1999: 171).

7. PROBLEMS OF RELIGIOUS DEMARCATION

....

Much of the discussion to this point assumes that it is possible to identify the Jews and distinguish them from the 'pagan', Christian, and Samaritan residents of Roman-Byzantine Palestine. However, some recent scholarship has 'problematized' our ability to make such neat distinctions. This 'problematization' has tended to focus on the late Roman, rather than the Byzantine period. Seth Schwartz argues that the failures of the revolts of 66–70 CE and 132–135 CE resulted in 'the deconstitution of the Jewish "nation"' (Schwartz 2001: 14–15). It was not just the state or polity that ceased to exist. After 135 CE, the religious, cultural, and social system that constituted a 'Jewish corporate identity' 'collapsed', 'disintegrated', and 'shattered' (Schwartz 2001: 1, 15, 103, 114, 159, 175). What had provided—actually or potentially—'the integrating ideology of Jewish society' and 'the ordering principle of the public life of most Jews' disappeared (Schwartz 2001: 98, 179, 199, 240). In its place came the norms of the Graeco-Roman city (Schwartz 2001: 15, 104). This eclipse of Judaism during 'the high imperial' period between 135 and 350 CE was not complete. Judaism survived among the masters whose traditions appear in what we call rabbinic literature. But the rabbis were only a marginal factor during these centuries. In any case, according to Schwartz, it was only after this hiatus of two centuries that Judaism again became 'the integrative ideology of the Jews', as late antique Jews 'began to construct their symbolic world around the Torah, the (memory of the) temple, and related items' (Schwartz 2001: 179, 273). The post-350 CE version of the ideology was significantly altered as it was now 'centered . . . on the synagogue and the local religious community' (Schwartz 2001: 1).

The implication seems to be that we cannot really identify Jews in later Roman Palestine, at least in urban settings, and distinguish them from their 'pagan', Samaritan, or Christian neighbours. If so, then attempting to locate and estimate the size of the Jewish population is fruitless. Only when we get to the Byzantine period, in the second half of the fourth century, can we successfully isolate a Jewish population. In fact, Schwartz' position is rather less extreme than my summary might suggest. He concedes the survival of Judaism as 'a vestigial identity', 'an attenuated sense of a common past, a mild feeling of separation from their neighbors that the latter, who had shared memories of their own, may have conspired to maintain' (Schwartz 2001: 15, 103). The retention by Jews of 'some consciousness of being separate from their Greco-Roman neighbors' is an example of 'the survival of local ethnic identities under the basically uniform surface of high imperial urban culture' (Schwartz 2001: 129). In other words, whatever the state of their ideology or religious notions, it is still possible to isolate the Jews (and others) as ethnic groups. Thus the demographic enterprise is still possible.

Another 'problematization' appears in the work of Daniel Boyarin. Schwartz described a resurrection of Judaism, albeit in altered form, after a hiatus of 200 years. For Boyarin what happened in the fourth century was the first crystallization of Judaism as a distinct religion. In the earlier era the 'religio-cultural histories were inextricably intertwined to the point where the very distinction between syncretism and "authentic" Judaism, Christianity, and "paganism" finally seems irrelevant' (Boyarin 1999: 12). Indeed until the fourth century 'it remained impossible to declare phenomenologically who was a Jew and who was a Christian' (Boyarin 1999: 15). The situation changed only in the Byzantine period. Thus, for Boyarin, distinguishing Jews from their neighbours in the three centuries preceding 350 CE appears to be difficult or even impossible. However, Boyarin subsequently made clear that it was possible in the earlier period to discern 'separate social groups', one of which was 'genealogically Israel' (Boyarin 2004: 21, 62, 71–72). Whether, and to what extent, these Jews met the behavioural standards set by rabbinic masters or shared their ideology is an interesting question. They might have invoked the name of Jesus to heal illness and attended pagan rites in the city square. For the historical demography of the Jews it probably does not matter. Here the categories of Jew, Greek, Phoenician, Syrian, Canaanite, Arab, and Samaritan matter much more. And as Schwartz indicated, these distinctions continued in some form from the early Roman period. In sum, the indistinct religio-cultural borders emphasized by Schwartz and Boyarin could co exist with clear 'ethnic' distinctions.

Schwartz and Boyarin agree that something new emerges in fourth century Palestine, something that differentiates Roman-era Jews from Byzantine ones. For Schwartz, it was the return of pre-135 CE Judaism with its emphasis on Temple and Torah, albeit in a new form centred on the local community and its synagogue. For Boyarin, it is the emergence of rabbinic Judaism as a kind of 'orthodoxy' of Palestinian Jews and, as he subsequently stressed, the 're-ethnicization' of that variety of Judaism (Boyarin 2004: 33, 220). This last point echoes the view of Hayim Lapin, who noted similar developments. Lapin alludes to the 'ethnic resurgence' of the Jews (and also of the Samaritans) in late antique Palestine (Lapin 2001: 193). However, for Lapin this resurgence does not necessarily follow a centuries-long hiatus. Instead it reflects an ongoing process. Lapin stresses the socially constructed nature of ethnic and religious identities. Those constructs are constantly being 'redefined', 'recreated', and 're–articulated'. He writes, 'Communal self re-fashioning is the result over the long term of repeated choices, incorporation, and rejection among the variety of cultural elements that enter the communal horizon in every level of individual or collective life' (Lapin 1998: 8–26, quotation on 23). These processes seem to have resulted in an ethnic resurgence among the Jews in Byzantine Palestine, indicated by the following factors. Beginning in late antiquity 'Jewishness' is explicitly mentioned and perhaps even stressed in epigraphic material from Palestine. Moreover, it is now that the synagogue emerges in that country as 'a distinctive and archaeologically recognizable institution to which communities and individuals committed funds and resources' (Lapin 1999: 267).

Viewing national or ethnic identity as socially constructed is common in contemporary scholarship, including that dealing with Jewish identity in antiquity. Part of this consensus is the realization that the boundaries between groups are often permeable and the cultural criteria for membership in the group may shift over time (Goodblatt 2006: 1–27). One would be hard pressed to identify a contemporary scholar who believes 'that Jewish ethnicity was, in antiquity, a simple, obvious, and unproblematic thing' (Lapin 1999: 242, where he sets up something of a straw man). But permeable boundaries and shifting criteria do not mean that the collective identities did not exist. Common sense suggests otherwise. To cite Lapin, 'Clearly, there were ethnic groups in imperial and late antique Palestine: Jews and Samaritans have continued as self-identified communities down to the present. Clearly, too, there were religious groups including, again, Jews and Samaritans, but also including Christians and the practitioners of a variety of "pagan" cults both native and local and imported' (Lapin 1998: 13). Boyarin might dissent about our ability to distinguish among religious identities in the imperial period, as might Schwartz regarding the ethnic groups. Against such dissenting opinions one might adduce the 'large body of literature produced by Jews and Gentiles over centuries and over a wide geographical area that know precisely who "Jews" are' (Lapin 1999: 242). In the present context I stress the continuity of the kinship element within Jewish identity. This was the 'vestigial' ethnic identity conceded by Schwartz that was the matrix for the re-emergence of Judaism after 350 CE. So, too, this belief in common kinship allowed for Jewishness to survive the religio-cultural re-formulations noted by Lapin and Boyarin in late antiquity. If this explanation is correct, then throughout the Roman-Byzantine era it would have been possible to identify (and count) the Jewish population, allowing for the inevitable marginal cases, 'dual-citizenships', and conflicted identities (see Goodblatt 2006: 17–26).

8. CHANGES IN THE BYZANTINE PERIOD

Whatever the disagreements among them, and whatever our dissent from their arguments, Boyarin, Lapin, and Schwartz all agree that something changed between the Roman and the Byzantine eras, in the course of the fourth century: for Boyarin, the crystallization of Christianity and Judaism as distinct religions in the form of orthodox Christianity and a re-ethnicized rabbinic Judaism; for Schwartz, the return of Judaism after a two-centuries long eclipse in an altered form based on the local community and synagogue; for Lapin, a Jewish identity that stressed ethnicity and focused on the local synagogue building. As suggested above, I would prefer to describe these developments as a shift in the cultural indicators of Jewish national or ethnic identity. However we characterize them, the developments seem amply attested in the literary, epigraphic, and archaeological evidence. And all three scholars agree further that the state favouritism and patronage of Christianity played a major role in causing them. Further examination lies beyond the scope of this essay, focused as it is on demography. However, it may be that demography helps explain these developments.

Lapin already suggested something similar. He observed that the noting of Jewishness in inscriptions, and the emergence of communal synagogues, appeared in the Diaspora well before their attestation in Palestine. Among the factors that led to the new expressions of Jewishness in late antique Palestine, Lapin mentions the demographic decline of the Jews, at least as a percentage of the whole, the official prominence of Christianity, and the conception of Palestine as a Christian Holy Land. The net effect of these factors was to make the Jewish communities of Palestine similar in status to those in the Diaspora, a minority in a land that others claimed as their own. Not surprisingly, then, the Jews of Palestine adapted to the new situation in ways similar to those of their fellow Jews abroad (Lapin 1999: 267–68, compare 261). I am not convinced that the Jews declined in percentage of the total population. Rather their situation changed. Up to the fourth century they were a large minority in a country where no ethnic or religious group held a majority, and where the favouritism of the Roman state was based on socio-economic rather than religious factors. While Rome also had cultural preferences, the various religious and ethnic groups generally found ways to accommodate those preferences. During the Byzantine period, by contrast, a Christian majority gradually emerged and enjoyed clear preferences from the state.

Gradual awareness by the Jews of the deterioration of their status as a result of Christian predominance could well explain the developments noted by Boyarin, Lapin and Schwartz. It could also explain the emergence of clear anti-Christian sentiments in the liturgical poetry of Byzantine Palestine (Yahalom 1999: 67–82), and the identification of 'the nations of the world' as Christians in later Palestinian texts (Boyarin 2004: 220). It might even help explain the building of monumental synagogues. Often taken as a sign of demographic strength, this phenomenon might (also?) reflect a minority group 'trying to express vitality precisely because of their lack of power' (Leibner 2006: 126, n. 66). Again, the deterioration in status need not have been purely demographic in the sense of absolute size of population or even percentage of the whole. Rather, it was a psychological result of the coalescence of most of the rest of the population in one camp, perceived as an 'enemy camp' and favoured by the state.

SUGGESTED READING

On ancient Jewish demography in general see McGing 2002 and Tropper 2006. For Roman-Byzantine Palestine consult Dauphin 1998, Bar 2004b and 2004c, and for a dissenting view see Leibner 2009. On Jewish identity see Goodblatt 2006 (though focused on an earlier period), Cohen 1999 and Lapin 1998 and 1999.

BIBLIOGRAPHY

ADAN-BAYEWITZ, D. (1993). *Common Pottery in Roman Galilee: A Study of Local Trade*. Ramat-Gan: Bar-Ilan University Press.

ALON, G. (1961). *History of the Jews in the Land of Israel in the Time of the Mishnah and the Talmud* [Hebr.], vol. 2. 2nd ed., Tel Aviv: Hakibutz Hameuchad.

—— (1980). *The Jews in their Land in the Talmudic Age (70–640 C.E.)*, vol. I, trans and ed., G. Levi. Jerusalem: Magnes Press.

AVIAM, M. (1999). 'Christian Galilee in the Byzantine Period', in *Galilee through the Centuries: Confluence of Cultures*, ed. E. M. Meyers. Winona Lake, Indiana: Eisenbrauns, 281–300.

—— (2004). *Jews, Pagans and Christians in the Galilee: 25 Years of Archaeological Excavations and Surveys*. Rochester, NY: University of Rochester Press.

AVI-YONAH, M. (1962). *In the Days of Rome and Byzantium* [Hebr.]. 3rd ed., corrected and expanded. Jerusalem: Bialik Institute.

—— (1984). *The Jews under Roman and Byzantine Rule: A Political History of Palestine from the Bar Kokhba War to the Arab Conquest*. Jerusalem: Magnes Press.

BAGNALL, R. S./FRIER, B. W. (1994). *The Demography of Roman Egypt*. Cambridge: Cambridge University Press.

BANNING, E. E. (2002). *Archaeological Survey*. London: Kluwer Academic/Plenum Publishers.

BAR, D. (2002). 'Was There a 3rd-c. Economic Crisis in Palestine?', in *The Roman and Byzantine Near East*, vol. 3, ed. J. H. Humphrey. Portsmouth, Rhode Island: Journal of Roman Archaeology Supplement Series, 43–54.

—— (2004a). 'Frontier and Periphery in Late Antique Palestine'. *Greek, Roman, and Byzantine Studies* 44: 69–92.

—— (2004b). 'Geographical Implications of Population and Settlement Growth in Late Antique Palestine'. *Journal of Historical Geography* 30: 1–10.

—— (2004c). 'Population, Settlement and Economy in Late Roman and Byzantine Palestine (70–641 AD)'. *Bulletin of the School of Oriental and African Studies* 67: 307–20.

BARON, S. W. (1971). 'Population', in *Encyclopaedia Judaica*, vol. 13. Jerusalem: Keter and New York: Macmillan, 866–903.

BEN DAVID, C. (2006). 'Late Antique Gaulanitis Settlement Patterns of Christians and Jews in Rural Landscape', in *Settlements and Demography in the Near East in Late Antiquity*, ed. A. S. Lewin and P. Pellegrini. Pisa/Rome: Istituti Editoriali e Poligrafici Internazionali, 35–50.

—— (2007). 'A Ceramic Survey and the Dating of the Monumental Synagogues in the Golan'. *Cathedra* 124: 13–27.

BOYARIN, D. (1999). *Dying for God: Martyrdom and the Making of Christianity and Judaism.* Stanford: Stanford University Press.

—— (2004). *Border Lines: The Partition of Judaeo-Christianity.* Philadelphia: University of Pennsylvania Press.

BROSHI, M. (2001). *Bread, Wine, Walls and Scrolls.* Sheffield: Sheffield Academic Press.

BYATT, A. (1973). 'Josephus and Population Numbers in First Century Palestine'. *Palestine Exploration Quarterly* 105: 51–60.

CLARYSSE, W./THOMPSON, D. J. (2006). *Counting the People in Hellenistic Egypt,* 2 vols. Cambridge: Cambridge University Press.

COHEN, S. J. D. (1999). *The Beginnings of Jewishness: Boundaries, Varieties, Uncertainties.* Berkeley: University of California Press.

COLLINS J. M./MOLYNEAUX, B. L. (2003). *Archaeological Survey.* Oxford: Altamira Press.

DAUPHIN, C. (1982). 'Jewish and Christian Communities in the Roman and Byzantine Gaulanitis: A Study of Evidence from Archaeological Surveys'. *Palestine Exploration Quarterly* 114: 129–42.

—— (1998). *La Palestine Byzantine: Peuplement et Populations,* 3 vols. Oxford: Archaeopress.

DI SEGNI, L. (2005). 'A Roman Standard in Herod's Kingdom'. *Israel Museum Studies in Archaeology* 4: 23–46.

FELDMAN, L. H. (2003). 'Conversion to Judaism in Classical Antiquity'. *Hebrew Union College Annual* 74: 115–56.

FITZMYER, J. A. (1981). *The Gospel According to Luke (I–IX).* Garden City, New York: Doubleday.

FRIER, B. W. (2000). 'Demography', in *The Cambridge Ancient History,* 2nd ed., vol. 11: *The High Empire A.D. 70–192,* ed. A. K. Bowman, P. Garnsey and D. Rathbone. Cambridge: Cambridge University Press, 787–816.

GAL, Z. (1995). 'Ancient Synagogues in the Eastern Lower Galilee', in *Ancient Synagogues: Historical Analysis and Archaeological Discovery,* vol. 1, ed. D. Urman and P. V. M. Flesher. Leiden: Brill, 166–73.

GOITEIN, S. D. (1964). *Jews and Arabs: Their Contacts Through the Ages.* New York: Schocken Books.

GOODBLATT, D. (2006). *Elements of Ancient Jewish Nationalism.* New York: Cambridge University Press.

GROH, D. E. (1988). 'Jews and Christians in Later Roman Palestine: Towards a New Chronology'. *Biblical Archaeologist* 51: 80–96.

HAMEL, G. (1990). *Poverty and Charity in Roman Palestine: First Three Centuries C.E.* Berkeley: University of California Press.

ISAAC, B. (1998). 'Jews, Christians and Others in Palestine: The Evidence from Eusebius', in *Jews in a Graeco-Roman World,* ed. M. Goodman. Oxford: Clarendon Press, 65–74.

JACOBS, A. S. (2004). *Remains of the Jews: The Holy Land and Christian Empire in Late Antiquity.* Stanford: Stanford University Press.

JEREMIAS, J. (1969). *Jerusalem in the Time of Jesus. An Investigation into the Economic and Social Conditions during the New Testament Period.* Philadelphia: Fortress Press.

LAPIN, H. (1998). 'Introduction: Locating Ethnicity and Religious Community in Later Roman Palestine', in *Religious and Ethnic Communities in Later Roman Palestine,* ed. H. Lapin. Bethesda: University Press of Maryland.

—— (1999). 'Palestinian Inscriptions and Jewish Ethnicity in Late Antiquity', in *Galilee through the Centuries: Confluence of Cultures*, ed. E. M. Meyers. Winona Lake: Eisenbrauns, 239–68.

—— (2001). *Economy, Geography and Provincial History in Later Roman Palestine*. Tübingen: Mohr-Siebeck.

LEIBNER, U. (2006). 'Settlement and Demography in Late Roman and Byzantine Eastern Galilee', in *Settlements and Demography in the Near East in Late Antiquity*, ed. A. S. Lewin and P. Pellegrini. Pisa/Roma: Istituti Editoriali e Poligrafici Internazionali, 105–30.

—— (2009). *Settlement and History in Hellenistic, Roman and Byzantive Galilee*. Tübingen: Mohr-Siebeck.

LEVINE, L. I. (2002). *Jerusalem: Portrait of the City in the Second Temple Period (538 B.C.E.–70 C.E.)*. Philadelphia: Jewish Publication Society of America.

LO CASCIO, E. (1994). 'The Size of the Roman Population: Beloch and the Meaning of the Augustan Census Figures'. *Journal of Roman Studies* 84: 23–40.

—— (2001). 'Recruitment and the Size of the Roman Population from the Third to the First Century BCE', in *Debating Roman Demography*, ed. W. Scheidel. Leiden: Brill, 111–37.

McGING, B. (2002). 'Population and Proselytism: How Many Jews Were There in the Ancient World?' in *Jews in the Hellenistic and Roman Cities*, ed. J. R. Bartlett. London and New York: Routledge, 88–106.

MAGNESS, J. (2001). 'The Question of the Synagogue: The Problem of Typology', in *Judaism in Late Antiquity*, part 3, vol. 4, ed. A. J. Avery-Peck and J. Neusner. Leiden and Boston: Brill, 1–48.

—— and AVNI, A. (1999). 'Jews and Christians in a Late Roman Cemetery at Beth Guvrin', in *Religious and Ethnic Communities in Later Roman Palestine*, ed. H. Lapin. Bethesda: University Press of Maryland, 87–114.

MA'OZ, Z. U. (1993). 'Golan: Hellenistic Period to the Middle Ages', in *The New Encyclopedia of Archaeological Excavations in the Holy Land*, vol. 2, ed. E. Stern. Jerusalem: Israel Exploration Society and Carta, 534–546.

MARGULIES, M. (1956). *Midrash Wayyikra Rabbah. A Critical Edition Based on Manuscripts and Genizah Fragments with Variants and Notes*, part 3. Jerusalem: American Academy for Jewish Research.

PARKER, S. T. (1999). 'An Empire's New Holy Land: The Byzantine Period'. *Near East Archaeology* 62: 134–80.

PARKIN, T. G. (1992). *Demography and Roman Society*. Baltimore: John Hopkins University Press.

PORTUGALI, Y. (1986). 'The Settlement Pattern in the Western Jezreel Valley From the 6th Century B.C.E. to the Arab Conquest' [Hebr.], in *Man and Land in Eretz-Israel in Antiquity*, ed. A. Kasher, A. Oppenheimer and U. Rappaport. Jerusalem: Yad Izhak Ben Zvi, 7–19.

SAFRAI, Z. (1994). *The Economy of Roman Palestine*. London and New York: Routledge.

—— (1998). *The Missing Century. Palestine in the Fifth Century: Growth and Decline*. Leuven: Peeters.

SCHEIDEL, W. (2001). 'Progress and problems in Roman demography', in *Debating Roman Demography*, ed. W. Scheidel. Leiden: Brill, 1–81.

SCHWARTZ, S. (2001). *Imperialism and Jewish Society, 200 B.C.E. to 640 C.E.* Princeton: Princeton University Press.

STEMBERGER, G. (2000). *Jews and Christians in the Holy Land: Palestine in the Fourth Century.* Edinburgh: T&T Clark.

STERN, M. (1980). *Greek and Latin Authors on Jews and Judaism,* vol. 2. Jerusalem: Israel Academy of Sciences and Humanities.

TAYLOR, J. E. (1993). *Christians and the Holy Places: The Myth of Jewish-Christian Origins.* Oxford: Clarendon Press.

TROPPER, A. (2006). 'Children and Childhood in Light of the Demographics of the Jewish Family in Late Antiquity'. *Journal for the Study of Judaism in the Persian, Hellenistic and Roman Period 37:* 299–343.

—— (1994). 'Introduction', in *Tabula Imperii Romani Iudaea Palaestina. Eretz Israel in the Hellenistic, Roman and Byzantine Periods,* ed. Y. Tsafrir, L. Di Segni and J. Green. Jerusalem: Israel Academy of Sciences and Humanities, 7–19.

—— (1996). 'Some Notes on the Settlement and Demography of Palestine in the Byzantine Period: The Archaeological Evidence', in *Retrieving the Past: Essays on Archaeological Research and Methodology in Honor of Gus W. Van Beek,* ed. J. D. Seger. Winona Lake: Cobb Institute of Archaeology and Eisenbrauns, 269–83.

URMAN, D. (1995). 'Public Structures and Jewish Communities in the Golan Heights', in *Ancient Synagogues: Historical Analysis and Archaeological Discovery,* vol. 2, ed. D. Urman and P. V. M. Flesher. Leiden: Brill, 373–617.

WALMSLEY, A. (1996). 'Byzantine Palestine and Arabia: Urban Prosperity in Late Antiquity,' in *Towns in Transition: Urban Evolution in Late Antiquity and the Early Middle Ages,* ed. N. Christie and S. T. Loseby, Aldershot: Ashgate, 126–158.

WASSERSTEIN, A. (1996). 'The Number and Provenance of Jews in Graeco-Roman Antiquity: A Note on Population Statistics', in *Classical Studies in Honor of David Sohlberg,* ed. R. Katzoff. Ramat Gan: Bar-Ilan University Press, 307–317.

WILKINSON, T. (1999). 'Demographic Trends from Archaeological Survey: Case Studies from the Levant and Near East', in *Reconstructing Past Population Trends in Mediterranean Europe (3000 BC–AD 1800),* ed. J. Bintliff and K. Sbonias. Oxford: Oxbow Books, 45–64.

YAHALOM, J. (1999). *Poetry and Society in Jewish Galilee of Late Antiquity.* Tel Aviv: Hakibbutz Hameuchad.

CHAPTER 7

THE LANGUAGES OF ROMAN PALESTINE

WILLEM SMELIK

1. LINGUISTIC VARIETY

Sandwiched between two international languages, Aramaic in the East and Greek in the West, Roman Palestine was a linguistic border area. Long exposed to multiple languages as a result of annexation by successive empires, migration, and pilgrimage, its linguistic history was further enhanced by its status as a transit area for trade through the Fertile Crescent, attracting merchants who spoke foreign languages to an area already populated by various ethnic groups. A poem of Meleager (early first century BCE), who came from the Hellenistic city of Gadara in Transjordan, reflects this regional state of affairs (Hengel 1969: 156): 'If you are Syrian, I say: *Salam*! If you are Phoenician: *Adonis*! But if you are Greek, then: *Chaire*!'

The intersection of administrative and cultural languages with local vernaculars would remain characteristic for Palestine. While the Romans did not impose their own language upon any of their subjects, they published their imperial decrees in the new *lingua franca* of Greek in the eastern part of the empire, although they used Latin for internal official communication. Hardly any province in the Roman Empire was thus monolingual (Eck 2007: 162–63), with Greek being pushed as an official language. In Roman and early Byzantine times the inhabitants of Palestine used Aramaic, Greek, and Hebrew, as well as Latin, Nabataean, Phoenician, proto-Arabic Thamudic, and Safaic as minority languages, and later also Armenian and Georgian.

Dramatic confirmation of the linguistic variety in the region is offered by the Babatha archive, a collection of thirty-six legal documents on papyrus belonging to a Jewish woman called Babatha (Yadin et al. 2002; Hezser 2001: 309–18). These were found tied together in a leather purse in the so-called 'Cave of Letters' in the Judaean Desert, where Jewish survivors of the Bar Kokhba revolt sought refuge and probably found their untimely death at the hand of the Roman oppressors. Babatha was a wealthy Jewish business woman who lived among the Nabataeans in Maoza, where she arranged family matters and property issues. Of these private documents, seventeen are written in Greek, a further nine in Greek with Aramaic/ Nabataean subscriptions and signatures, seven in Nabataean, and three in Aramaic. Aramaic would appear to have been the native tongue of the parties involved, with Greek the chosen language for business and administration, and for those documents drawn up for the Roman legal court in Petra.

In the last century, scholarship on the languages of Roman Palestine revolved around the vernacular status of Hebrew, the discoveries in the Judaean Desert, and sociolinguistics, in particular the issue of diglossia. Archaeological excavations supplied epigraphical data that would play an important part in the evaluation of the three main languages: Hebrew, Aramaic, and Greek. The new texts and methods have raised several questions: was Hebrew replaced entirely by Aramaic and Greek as everyday life languages in the first centuries CE? Modern assessments of the language map of Roman Palestine vary considerably in their answer to this question. Furthermore, did Greek replace Aramaic in certain areas of Jewish life? There is also considerable confusion amongst scholars concerning the respective status of Greek, Aramaic, and Hebrew as 'high' or 'low' languages.

2. THE STATUS OF VERNACULAR HEBREW

Linguistic arguments have always featured in the debate about the languages used in Roman Palestine. In the nineteenth and first half of the twentieth century the majority of scholars considered Mishnaic Hebrew 'Hebraized Aramaic' (Sáenz-Badillos 1993: 162–63). The linguistic peculiarities of Mishnaic Hebrew seemed to be explained adequately by the assumption that this language was either a heavily Aramaized version of Hebrew, or even a Hebraized version of Aramaic. Since Mishnaic Hebrew was deemed an artificial language, Hebrew was thought to have lost its vernacular status to Aramaic at the beginning of the Roman period or even earlier.

The status of Aramaic as the administrative language and *lingua franca* during the rule of the Assyrian and Achaemenid empires resulted in its widespread adoption throughout the Middle East. Therefore it is not surprising that it also gained a firm foothold in Palestine during that period. Scholars have found evidence for the use of Aramaic in the Aramaic portions of the Hebrew Bible, in certain Aramaic terms in the New Testament, and in the Aramaic parts of rabbinic literature. In addition, some legal documents from the Judaean Desert, such as marriage contracts and bills of divorce, were written in Aramaic, and Aramaic appears in personal names and place names. Josephus claims to have originally written The Jewish War in his native tongue, which some identify as Aramaic (Barr 1989: 113; Rajak 1984: 174–84). The ritual use of Jewish Aramaic Bible translations in the synagogue has further been cited as evidence for the vernacular use of the language (Segal 1927: 16), but this argument is no longer as conclusive as it once seemed to be (Smelik 1995: 24–41).

Segal became the most noteworthy proponent of those scholars who argued that Hebrew was still spoken in the first two centuries CE. He claimed that Mishnaic Hebrew had developed naturally from Biblical Hebrew, with distinct colloquial features (Segal 1927; Sáenz-Badillos 1993: 162–64). While he did not entirely deny an Aramaic influence on Mishnaic Hebrew, he highlighted its morphological dissimilarities with Aramaic. By implication, there is no reason to consider Mishnaic Hebrew an artificial language. Yet his analysis did not immediately sway the debate in his favour. The consensus was only set to change upon the discoveries of numerous Hebrew documents from the late Second Temple period in the Judaean Desert. These documents falsified the assumption of a gradual but inevitable decline of Hebrew in the post-exilic period. Moreover, the Hebrew Bar Kokhba letters, the Copper Scroll, and 4QMMT show a clear affinity with Mishnaic Hebrew, suggesting that its usage extended beyond rabbinic circles and preceded the second century CE. Segal's thesis that Mishnaic Hebrew reflects a colloquial dialect of Hebrew has now been widely accepted (Young/Rezetko 2008: 231, 241), but his downplaying of language interference (i.e. Aramaic influence) in rabbinic Hebrew has triggered alternative views of rabbinic Hebrew as a 'mixed language' or 'langue mélangée' (Sáenz-Badillos 1993: 164; Pérez Fernández 1997: 5).

The debate continued, based on the new data from Qumran which scholars began to use. In the Dead Sea Scrolls, Hebrew seems to have been used mostly in a (late) form of Biblical Hebrew, but the Copper Scroll and 4QMMT have been written in a dialect close to Mishnaic Hebrew. That two dialects were in fact used seems confirmed by the observation that colloquial features could be detected in some of the literary scrolls (Rabin 1958: 149, 152; Goshen-Gottstein 1958: 135; Barr 1970: 20–21). The presence of two types of Hebrew has also shed new light on the relationship between biblical and rabbinic Hebrew. Segal's claim that Mishnaic Hebrew developed out of biblical Hebrew has been reexamined in light of the inner-biblical linguistic variety. While the popular linguistic basis of Mishnaic

Hebrew is no longer in doubt, this dialect probably did not descend from biblical Hebrew directly, but rather represents a contemporary dialect which may have its roots in the First Temple period (Rendsburg 1990; Young/Rezetko 2008; Pérez Fernández 1997: 1–15). Consequently, the colloquial character of Mishnaic Hebrew may reflect an earlier vernacular stage of the language. Indeed, most scholars now tend to view Mishnaic Hebrew as the vernacular of the Second Temple period, when biblical Hebrew is deemed to have become restricted to literary usage. Only in the second half of the second century CE, in the aftermath of the two Jewish revolts against Rome, did Mishnaic Hebrew virtually disappear as a vernacular. In the following centuries, Hebrew seems to have been used as a liturgical and academic language only.

The details of the distinct Hebrew dialects remain elusive, though. There is still a debate about the geographical range of Mishnaic Hebrew, which some scholars relate to a northern dialect (see Young/Rezetko 2008: 242). While most scholars maintain that Mishnaic Hebrew was spoken in the first century CE, others challenge this view, although rarely on philological grounds. The question remains whether the colloquial features of Mishnaic Hebrew prove that it was actually *spoken* during the first two centuries CE. Because all available evidence in the form of written sources and literary language may reflect the spoken dialect of earlier periods, inferences about the actual use of Mishnaic Hebrew in daily life during the second century CE are not conclusive. Even if we accept that Hebrew remained a living language amongst certain segments of society, we must address the questions as to how many people still understood Hebrew in the first two centuries CE and, more precisely, to what extent they did so.

According to rabbinic sources, certain provisions were made for those who did not speak Hebrew. Since many people seem to have refrained from the ritual of the first fruits because they did not master Hebrew, the rabbis introduced the practice of prompting so that people could still say the declaration in Hebrew by repeating what they heard the priest say (Sifrei Deut. 301). The rabbinic formulation suggests that this was a long-standing practice until the destruction of the Temple. Another ritual concerning the *sotah*, the wife accused of adultery, required the priest to explain details to her in her own mother tongue (T. Sotah 2:1). A Torah scroll could be written in Greek (M. Meg. 1:8), a ruling which is at odds with other stipulations, most notably the requirement of using the Hebrew square script for the writing of Torah scrolls (M. Yad. 4:5).

These rulings do not identify the vernacular, suggesting that Palestinian rabbis were well aware of the co-existence of different native tongues in Roman Palestine. The increasing rabbinic interest in the exclusivity of Hebrew as evidenced by their emphasis on Hebrew as the 'holy tongue' during the second half of the second century may well indicate the loss of Hebrew as a vernacular (Smelik 2008). This phenomenon would coincide with the still vernacular basis of Mishnaic Hebrew. Had Hebrew not been spoken at all during the first two centuries CE, Mishnaic

Hebrew would have betrayed its merely academic status. Hebrew seems to have undergone some sort of literary revival in the centuries following the redaction of the Mishnah (de Lange 1996), but as a vernacular its use would have been restricted to academic discourse as a secondarily acquired language.

Throughout the period under consideration here, Hebrew retained its place as a religious language, even increasingly so. Whereas works were written in Greek, or at least translated into Greek (e.g. Ben Sira) to gain a wider readership and audience at the end of the Second Temple period, new literary texts were composed in either Hebrew or a mixture of Hebrew and Aramaic in the second to fifth centuries CE. New Bible translations were still produced in Greek well into the third century CE and in the Diaspora even later, but they were now competing with Aramaic translations that initially met rabbinic opposition in Palestine (Smelik 2001: 212–21).

3. Aramaization and Hellenization

Aramaic is widely held to have been the vernacular most commonly used by Jews throughout the Roman period. That Aramaic was widespread in Hellenistic and Roman Palestine seemed obvious to scholars even before the Qumran discoveries because of the Aramaic texts, quotations, loanwords, and names referred to above. In the Temple, Aramaic would have been used by the officials who oversaw the sacrifices and other offerings brought by the people. The Mishnah, admitting that certain administrative seals were written in Aramaic, quotes them in Hebrew (M. Sheq. 5:3). A list of words which were allegedly written on *shofar* chests begins in Aramaic but continues in Hebrew (cf. ibid. 6:5). The obvious translation of these words into Hebrew suggests that other portions in the Mishnah may also not have been formulated in Hebrew originally.

Aramaic is attested in several distinct dialects, some of which are closely related to Jewish literary Aramaic: the dialects of Qumran Aramaic, Targum Onqelos, and Jonathan, and perhaps, if still belonging to the Byzantine period which must be deemed uncertain, the late Jewish literary Aramaic of some Targums to the Writings of the Hebrew Bible. Other texts are written in Jewish Palestinian Aramaic, such as the dialects of the Palestinian Targums and the Palestinian Talmud, the amoraic Midrashim and epigraphic evidence from late Roman Palestine. Non-Jewish dialects are Christian Palestinian Aramaic, Samaritan Aramaic, and Nabataean Aramaic. The variety of Aramaic dialects in Palestine developed after the gradual breakdown of a more or less uniform standard, Achaemenid Aramaic. The literary variety of Jewish Aramaic can be considered its conservative descendant and can be dated to the time from the second century BCE to the second century CE, whereas the dialect of the Palestinian Talmud, Midrashim, and Palestinian Targums (and non-Jewish Palestinian dialects such as Samaritan and Christian Palestinian Aramaic) belong to the third to seventh century CE.

The emergence of several contemporaneous Aramaic dialects in this later period suggests that spoken Aramaic in the first two centuries CE may have differed from the actual literary variants. This possibility attracted the attention of many scholars interested in the vernacular of Jesus and early Christianity and generated a heated discussion (Kahle 1958; Kutscher 1960; cf. Smelik 1995: 10–14). The dialect of the Palestinian Targums might be considered the spoken Western Aramaic dialect which rose to literary expression in the aftermath of the Bar Kokhba revolt (Kutscher 1958: 10, n. 44; Díez Macho 1972: 31–73). Yet it is doubtful whether literary compositions, written by trained traditional scribes, would ever reflect *spoken* language intended for a liturgical context (Kaufman 1985: 122; Ribera Florit 1987: 116–117). The variety of Palestinian Aramaic dialects mainly demonstrates the currency of Aramaic from the third to seventh centuries CE. In this period the Jewish population of Roman Palestine decreased and became a substantial minority. The Roman Empire became Christian, which inevitably increased the presence of Greek in the East. Nevertheless, Aramaic remained the common vernacular amongst Palestinian Jews, with Greek being used as the language of prestige.

How the process of Aramaization unfolded remains unclear (cf. Schwartz 1995). Since Jewish scribes adopted the Aramaic script upon the Jews' return from the Babylonian Exile (cf. Naveh 1971: 29, 122), scribal training will have played some part in this linguistic shift, but even scribal habit and training cannot fully explain the details and mechanisms of this development. There was no established Jewish educational system open to all members of society which might have helped the adoption of a new vernacular. Nor is there geographical or chronological precision in the general observation that Aramaic had become the default mother tongue of all Palestinian and Eastern Jews by the end of the Second Temple period.

It *is* safe to say, though, that Jewish inhabitants of the northern regions, that is, the Galilee, Peraea, and the Golan Heights, would have been inclined to adopt Aramaic at an early stage as a function of both their proximity to the Aramaic-speaking heartland and their late Judaization after Aristobulus' conquest in 104–103 BCE (cf. Josephus, Ant. 13.11.3, 318–19; Bell. 1.3.3, 76; Goodman 1999: 599). But the claim that Aramaic replaced all local vernaculars remains speculative. Aramaic may have become the default regional language, but this observation does not necessarily carry implications for the question of local vernaculars.

Nabataean provides an instructive example. While the Nabataeans did not leave a literary corpus behind, their inscriptions inform us about the use of Nabataean Aramaic for formal purposes. Yet the Nabataeans presumably spoke a form of Arabic, which rarely appeared in written form before the emergence of Islam (Healey 1989: 43; Hoyland 2004: 183–86). A handful of inscriptions containing

Arabic and Arabic loanwords in Nabataean Aramaic are a clue to the true vernacular. As Hoyland remarks, 'this realm was a polyglot entity with different peoples in different regions speaking different languages and dialects, but with Aramaic used by all as the official language irrespective of whether they were Aramaic speakers or not' (Hoyland 2004: 186).

The argument from silence that a local vernacular such as Hebrew had died out is a priori unlikely on the basis of non-Arabic vernaculars still maintained in the Middle East today. On the basis of our current knowledge of modern Aramaic dialects, largely retained in oral traditions with little literary record until the modern Diaspora situation of their native speakers, it is hazardous to assume that all local vernaculars had been abandoned in the Aechemenid and Ptolemaic/Seleucid periods. In ages less mobile than ours, traditional communities which maintained their vernacular but communicated with the wider world in a non-local language, i.e. Aramaic, will have been more widespread than a rigid model of Aramaization allows for.

Even before Aramaic was widely used in Jewish writing, Greek made great headway into the Middle East following Alexander the Great's conquests and the establishment of the Ptolemaic and Seleucid Empires. In the process of Hellenization, Greek replaced Aramaic as the administrative language of choice, and this phenomenon continued during the Roman period. Yet Greek never achieved the same degree of dissemination as Aramaic in the Persian, and Arabic in the Islamic period. The evidence of the Jewish use of Greek is nevertheless impressive in terms of literary production and epigraphy (Hengel 1969: 108–120, 191–195). The use of Greek was not simply confined to the coastal areas of Palestine with its Hellenistic cities, but extended to Lower Galilee, the Jezreel Valley, and Jerusalem as well. Even three of the Bar Kokhba letters are written in Greek, despite their authors' presumed preference for Hebrew or Aramaic. The significance of these letters is highlighted by P. Yadin 52, where the scribe Soumaios (note the Greek name) apologizes for his language choice by indicating that he was unable to communicate in either Aramaic or Hebrew. This seems to imply that Greek had not just become a *lingua franca* but the scribe's native tongue, in which he could write most easily (van der Horst 2001: 160–61).

This leads to the question whether Greek made such headway in Roman Palestine as to replace Aramaic as the common language in certain geographical or social spheres. The preponderance of Greek inscriptions is a case in point. Only in Judaea, the Golan, and small Galilean villages do Hebrew and Aramaic inscriptions equal the number of Greek ones (Lifshitz 1977: 457–459; Barr 1989: 102; van der Horst 1991: 23). Even if the incomplete publication of inscriptions is taken into account, many scholars infer from the available data that Greek was used by native Palestinian Jews (Gundry 1964: 406; van der Horst 1991: 28), and not merely by Diaspora Jews who migrated to Palestine (Sevenster 1968: 147–48; Lifshitz 1977: 458; Mussies 1976: 1057). Lively interest in the Old Greek Bible in the first centuries CE, as evidenced by the revisions of the Septuagint, confirms the importance of Greek in this period (Brock 1972: 26–27; Tov 1992: 143–48; Barthélemy 1963). The famous dictum of Bar Qappara, 'Let the words of the Torah be spoken in the language of Japheth [i.e., Greek] in the tents of Shem' (Gen. R. 36:8) suggests that Greek was spoken in at least some Palestinian synagogues (cf. the discussion of Greek synagogue inscriptions below). The rabbinic discussions about the recitation of the Shema and the Scroll of Esther in Greek (y. Sot. 7:1, 21b; b. Meg. 18a) imply that some Jews understood Greek better than Hebrew.

For the majority of Palestinian Jews Greek was probably not the native language but an acquired vernacular, yet it is difficult to determine the extent of the knowledge and use of Greek among the Jewish population, apart from those who were directly involved with the Roman administration and therefore required to speak Greek. Apart from Greek Bible translations including extra-canonical works such as 4 Ezra and 2 Baruch, the works of Josephus and the no longer extant works of Justus of Tiberias, few extant literary compositions in Greek can be attributed to Palestinian Jews with any degree of certainty.

Provenance is only one of our problems. The Jewish identity of some of the Greek texts is uncertain and they can be either pagan or Jewish. Furthermore, some of these works have been adopted by Christians in the first centuries CE, and their Jewish origins are doubtful. Among the former we can count the work of the historian Thallus (Samaritan, pagan, or Jewish? Schürer 1986, vol. 3: 543–45), as well as magical texts written in Greek: some of them are undoubtedly Jewish, whereas others are pagan borrowings of Jewish magical idiom (Bohak 2008: 194–214).

The distinction between Jewish and non-Jewish magic texts is not straightforward. As Alexander observed, 'it is not yet possible to draw a hard and fast line between Jewish and pagan magic in late antiquity; in fact, given the fundamental syncretism of magic, it may be misguided in principle to do so' (in: Schürer 1986, vol. 3: 346). More recently, Bohak's discussion of ancient Jewish magic has provided a firmer basis. Although borrowings are widely attested in both directions, Bohak argues that Jewish magicians were very selective with regard to the pagan elements they chose to embed in their own tradition. Jewish magic remained distinctively Jewish, and far less syncretistic than has often been taken for granted (Bohak 2008: 350). Unfortunately, the Greek elements in Jewish magic tell us more about their perceived magical usefulness than about the use of Greek among the practitioners. The bilingual amulet published by Kotansky (1991 and 1994) was written by a scribe who had secondarily acquired knowledge of Greek, while Greek phrases in Hebrew transliteration in texts such as the Sword of Moses and Sefer HaRazim testify to familiarity with the Greek language and its magical traditions in the Byzantine period in Roman Palestine (Bohak 2008: 231–47).

Scholars have pointed to the presence of Greek manuscripts at Qumran as an indication of the wide dissemination of Greek by the start of the first century CE (Vanderkam 2001). Yet the language selection of the non-biblical scrolls suggests a remarkable preference for Hebrew over against Aramaic and Greek, with 438 Hebrew scrolls, 104 in Aramaic, and a mere eighteen in Greek, with two written in Nabataean (Puech 1996: 176).

How are we to explain the predominance of Hebrew here? Since the majority of these Hebrew documents are written in a literary dialect that can be derived from late biblical Hebrew, the written evidence does not necessarily mean that Hebrew served as a vernacular. Amongst the biblical scrolls there are also Greek translations and (just) one Aramaic translation, which suggests a primary Greek (or Hebrew) language competence for the audience targeted by the translations.

In a recent essay, Steve Weitzman argues that the indisputable preference for Hebrew is motivated by the sectarians' desire 'to transcend the wayward ways of the multilingual society around them' (Weitzman 1999: 45). If the documents found at Qumran represent a sectarian library, their language selection may indeed reflect a sectarian outlook on life rather than that of Jewish society at large. But even on that premise, this interpretation depends on circular reasoning: Weitzman's thesis is based on evidence culled from non-sectarian sources that together create a tenuous amalgam of references to the esoteric and sacred connotations of Hebrew among the Essenes (cf. Smelik 2008). The documents which formed the library may well have been brought to Qumran from elsewhere. The nature of the library depends on the identity of those who acquired and deposited the manuscripts there. Despite nationalistic and supernatural overtones in some of the texts, the use of Hebrew can be explained in terms of prestige, literary tradition, and a strong connection to the centre of curatorial power: the Temple.

A priori, translations imply that the target language is also the receptor's language. Accordingly, the extent of vernacular Greek amongst ancient Jews becomes prominent in the translations of works into Greek on the assumption that they were not exclusively produced for a Diaspora Jewish audience. That assumption, however, is the catch: how many Palestinian Jews would have understood a Greek Bible translation? The very *raison d'être* of Greek translations like those by Aquila and Symmachus, which were produced in Palestine during the second century CE, either under the auspices of rabbinic authorities (Aquila, following rabbinic traditions) or in close proximity to their circles (Symmachus, cf. Salvesen 1991) suggests that Greek would have been widely understood. Traditionally, the Septuagint had been treated with the same respect accorded to the Hebrew Scriptures, claiming divine inspiration for its very wording, and the high standing of Greek translations among the rabbis (M. Meg. 1.8) signals its traditional importance.

A similarly high status was not extended to the Palestinian Jewish Aramaic Bible translations, at least not by rabbis (Smelik: 2001: 212–21). Rabbis did promote oral Aramaic translations of the Hebrew Bible in synagogues, though. Whatever the origins of the written Targums (academy, liturgy, or private study), their liturgical use is attested by both internal and external evidence. The unique character of these translations has often been understood as a pointer to their *Sitz im Leben* in bilingual communities. In a study of the Septuagint, Rabin perceived the origins of the Targums in monolingual hermeneutics (Rabin 1968: 17; cf. Samely 1992: 158 n. 3): 'A translation of the type of the Targum to the Prophets makes little sense unless the listener also understood the source text without its help, as otherwise all the ingenious allusions would be so much wasted effort'. Perceptive as his comment may be, the argument assumes that all the interpretive intricacies were meant to be understood orally by the illiterate, which is highly questionable. The 'ingenious allusions' Rabin identified were not the purpose of the translation, but the result of the mechanisms of the translation enterprise. We do not know exactly when Aramaic Bible translations became really widespread in Roman Palestine. There is reason to assume that, initially, they did not enjoy the backing of the rabbinic movement which later appropriated them.

4. SOCIOLINGUISTICS

In 1959 Charles Ferguson advanced the linguistic model of diglossia, characterizing a very specific multilingual situation in which two dialects of the same language fulfil distinctive functions within a single society, one termed the high member (H) and the other the low member (L) of the pair (Ferguson 1959, 1964, 1991). The alternation of the languages is governed by their highly specialized functions: H is the prestigious language with a strong literary heritage, thus destined for public and official language situations, while L is the language people acquired first, hence privileged for informal interaction.

Ferguson did not include bilingual patterns in his observations, although he considered the use of distinct languages as analogous to the use of distinct dialects (Ferguson 1959: 325 n.2). Scholars have subsequently suggested modifications to his model. Most notably, Fishman proposed that diglossia could involve bilingualism, and that bilingualism could involve diglossia (Fishman 1967). The debate has led to confusion in the definition of diglossia (Watt 2000; Porter 2000).

Even without the problem of definitions, Ferguson's model is ill-suited to describe the situation of language distribution in Roman Palestine, although a number of scholars have tried to apply it to this area. According to Rabin, Middle Hebrew (L) was the rule in Judaea, with Aramaic as the second (H) language, while in Galilee the reverse was true: Hebrew was H and Aramaic or Greek were L (Rabin 1976: 1036). Lapide argued that Aramaic was L and Hebrew H all over Jewish Palestine (Lapide 1975: 483–501). Cook suggested a diglossia of biblical (H) and mishnaic (L) Hebrew, with Aramaic overlapping with both of these dialects (Cook 1992: 20–21).

All of these models accord too little significance to Greek, however. Spolsky has pointed to the importance of Greek in a model of *triglossia*, and also advocated a differential approach with a different language map according to region and social class (Spolsky 1985: 41). He has suggested that the inhabitants of Judaean villages were monolingual Hebrew speakers, whereas elsewhere Jews were trilingual. Attractive as his model is, he does not offer any justification for the assumed regional use and importance of the languages, nor does he differentiate diachronically, so that his model actually leads to more questions, rather than illuminating the language map of Roman Palestine. Nor are the languages functionally differentiated in his theory. Among the other proposals, Watt's attempt to rescue diglossia should be mentioned here. His refined version of the model allows for varieties of H and L languages, that is, Hebrew and Aramaic (H1, H2, L1 L2), with a tertiary role for Greek (Watt 2000). He excludes Greek from diglossia on the grounds that its inclusion would result in bilingualism, rather than indicate a functionally differentiated use of language.

The pairing of language points to an intrinsic problem in the application of the diglossia model to Roman Palestine. The functional differentiation of languages and dialects cannot be explained on the basis of this limited model. It can also not account for the significance of Greek within the Palestinian language system. To create a (regional and chronological) model that can accommodate colloquial and literary Hebrew, colloquial and literary Aramaic, *and* various Greek dialects is very difficult. Before attempting to map the various dialects and languages, it is necessary to determine the socio-linguistic functions of the languages and dialects involved. The question is not merely: what languages were spoken? Equally important is the question: who spoke what in which context (Fishman 1965)?

Recent studies in bilingualism suggest that language proficiency varied according to various criteria, as Barr has somewhat skeptically pointed out (Barr 1970: 26): one's language competence would have depended on one's social class, occupation, locality, gender, position within the family, socialization and personal history, education, and mobility. In other words, Barr concludes it differed with regard to each individual, and wide generalizations cannot be made.

Nevertheless, attempts to identify those factors which would have stimulated language acquisition may inform our assessment of individual and communal bilingualism and multilingualism. First, the socio-political status of a language would have affected the individual desire to learn that language (Hezser 2001: 237–38). In the Roman Near East, people would have benefited most from speaking Greek, the language of the political and economical elite of the Hellenistic cities, and the language in which the Roman state and the Byzantine church conducted their affairs. Neither the Roman public officials nor the Byzantine church leaders would necessarily have been inclined to learn Aramaic, as visibly demonstrated by the examples of Procopius and Egeria cited above. Conversely, some native Aramaic speakers might feel inclined to acquire at least a rudimentary knowledge of

Greek, whether or not they fostered any objections to the language and the culture it represented (Hezser 2001: 240). Nevertheless, their command of Greek would have depended on several factors and varied by degrees from one person to the next, from a minimal knowledge of the spoken language, to some rudimentary conversational skills and literary ability amongst a few (Wasserstein 1995: 123).

Individuals would also have been aware of the cultural and religious aspects of the language, depending on their local context and level of acculturation. Greek-speaking Jews who immigrated to the Land of Israel from the Diaspora—a small minority—*may* have wished to acquire the language of their native fellow-Jews. The evidence suggests, however, that since language was not part of Jewish identity (Stern 1994:79), the desire and opportunity to learn (Hebrew and) Aramaic will have depended on individual circumstances. Since rabbis emphasized the importance of Hebrew for religious purposes, some Diaspora Jewish immigrants may have acquired some rudimentary knowledge of Hebrew, but their proficiency may have been limited to the ability to recite certain short liturgical texts, such as the *Shema* (or not even that, as rabbinic discussions of the recitation of the *Shema* in Greek suggest for Caesarea).

5. Differentiations

Language choice varies according to social context and geographical environment (Hezser 2001: 243–47). Rural settings are usually less varied in linguistic terms than cities are. The form of an expression (e.g. an inscription), its purpose (e.g. an epitaph, dedication, or announcement), and its location determine the language selection to a considerable extent. Individuals' social sphere and cultural affiliation also influence their attitude towards language use. It is conceivable that rabbis discussed legal and exegetical matters in Aramaic but used Hebrew for (written and/or oral) transmission of traditions (Hezser 2001: 246).

Throughout Roman period Palestine, Hebrew seems to have served as the principal language for the written transmission of religiously relevant information. Beginning with the literary manuscripts found in the Judaean desert, where Hebrew overshadows Greek and Aramaic (Barr 1989: 113), tannaitic literature (Mishnah, Tosefta, tannaitic Midrashim) displays a marked preference for composition in Hebrew, with a partial shift to Aramaic in late antiquity (Talmud Yerushalmi, amoraic Midrashim). Admittedly, the evidence is not as straightforward as it may seem, because we have to allow for selective transmission and editing. Works written in Greek may have been ignored by rabbis of the first centuries CE and/or the editors of the documents. Greek works that came down to us have often been preserved by Christians rather than Jews.

Aramaic may have been chosen as the language of literary composition for specific reasons. The language evidence of the Dead Sea Scrolls suggests that Hebrew was used for legal and liturgical purposes (Levine 1988: 15). Exegetical writings, on the other hand, could be written in Aramaic (Genesis Apocryphon, Qumran Targum of Job). Aramaic was particularly used for narrative portions and for the discourse framing legal discussions in rabbinic literature, as well as for Bible translations. In Midrash Lamentations, the midrashic structure is in Hebrew, while many of its folkloristic elements are written in Aramaic.

Amongst the legal documents from Murabba'at, those written in Aramaic outnumber those written in Hebrew (Milik 1961: 70). Marriage contracts and bills of divorce seem to have been written in Aramaic as known from the Babatha documents and rabbinic literature, although rabbis permitted other languages as well: even a Greek bill with witnesses' signatures in Hebrew is deemed acceptable (M. Gittin: 9.8). Aramaic was a language that was widely understood and therefore convenient. The use of languages in legal documents such as bills and legal records shows an interesting pattern. Just as Demotic disappears from the record in Egypt in the second half of the second century CE, presumably because the Roman administration did not conduct official proceedings and correspondences in Demotic, so Aramaic disappears from the legal documents during the same period (Lewis 1993, 2001).

It is common knowledge that some sages approved of multilingualism in daily life and, to a great extent, in religious matters (cf. y. Sotah 7:2, 21c; y. Meg. 1:11, 71b) and in particular referred to Greek in a positive sense (Veltri 1994). Some rabbis permitted the recitation of the *Shema*, the *Amidah*, and Grace after Meals in any language (M. Sotah 7:1). Many sages seem to have had some knowledge of Greek (Lieberman 1965: 15–26; Sevenster 1968: 38–61), which is also evidenced by their lively interest in Greek versions of the Bible as noted above, despite the fact that they do not seem to have composed works in Greek. At the same time Palestinian rabbis emphasized the significance of Hebrew, though (Sifre Deut. 333; y. Shab. 1:3, 3c; y. Sheq. 3:3, 47c; Midrash Tannaim Deut. 32:43). In contrast to Greek, whose liturgical use some rabbis seem to have permitted, some rabbis discouraged the liturgical and religious use of Aramaic in the early amoraic period (Smelik 2001; b. B.Q. 83a; b. Sotah 49b; ibid. 33a).

The overwhelming use of Greek in Jewish epigraphy of late antiquity, which will be discussed in more detail below, renders the occurrence of Hebrew and Aramaic all the more interesting. Ossuary inscriptions from Jerusalem and its vicinity offer a case in point. The ossuary inscriptions mainly register the name and family of the deceased, with only a few providing additional data such as age, place of origin, profession or title. The vast majority of ossuaries are not inscribed at all (Rahmani 1994: 11, 13). The inscriptions are informal, clumsily written graffiti with spacing and spelling mistakes, which suggests that they were private recordings rather than public announcements. In Rahmani's collection, two-thirds of the inscriptions are written in the Aramaic square script (also termed 'Jewish script', following Naveh 1982: 112), and about a third in Greek script, with about six per cent in both Greek and Aramaic script (Rahmani 1994:12–13). Some of the inscriptions are written in the Greek language but transliterated in Aramaic script. Of the Semitic inscriptions, the majority are in Aramaic. The language distribution is more clearly divided when tomb groups are taken into account: some tombs yield only, or predominantly, Jewish script, while others have inscriptions in Greek only.

6. Epigraphy

Late antique epigraphy is among the most important and frequently cited source of evidence for language use in Roman Palestine. The results are uneven. It is most unfortunate that a comprehensive survey of the available evidence does not exist yet. The available evidence is scattered over many publications, if published at all, and therefore difficult to access by researchers. An eagerly awaited project to publish a comprehensive corpus of Jewish epigraphy in the Hellenistic and Roman period is in preparation (Corpus Inscriptionum Iudaeae/Palaestinae, CIIP). The historical and linguistic evaluation of epigraphy is also rendered difficult by the fact that most inscriptions do not bear a date and cannot be dated securely. For methodological reasons one cannot make direct inferences from epigraphy about the use of languages amongst Jews in Roman Palestine.

Of all Jewish inscriptions from Roman Palestine published to date an estimated 60–70 per cent are written in Greek (Eck 2007: 170; van der Horst 2001). A certain percentage of these are bilingual, written in both Greek and Aramaic/Hebrew (with the latter frequently consisting of the word 'Shalom' only). Of the synagogue inscriptions only approximately one third are written in Greek. This evidence raises a number of questions: does the language distribution of the inscriptions reflect the use of languages amongst Palestinian Jews—with Greek being more significant than most scholars would assume? Are they representative of a cross-section of Jewish society, or merely the middle and upper classes who could afford the cost of epitaphs and tombs?

The epigraphic evidence has often been considered a representation of common language use. Before the discovery of the Qumran scrolls, the relative scarcity of Aramaic texts during the Seleucid period has led scholars to assume that the use of Aramaic was eclipsed by Greek (cf. Fitzmyer 1970). For the Roman period direct conclusions were drawn from the predominance of Greek in inscriptions to the spread of spoken Greek (Lifshitz 1965: 520–38). Even the use of Hebrew in synagogue inscriptions was believed to reflect the continued use of Hebrew well beyond the first centuries CE (Fraade 1992: 277–82).

Such readings of the evidence are problematic. There is no question that Greek enjoyed prestige amongst all strata of Jewish society, but the argument from epigraphy requires serious modification. By default, epigraphic language selection does not reflect the vernacular of those who commissioned or executed the inscription (Harris 1983; cf. Reynolds 2001; Cooley 2002; Millar 1983). The Arabic vernacular of the Nabataeans, whose inscriptions are in Aramaic, is a case in point. Amongst Christians, Aramaic speakers were numerous during the Byzantine period, despite the fact that Christian inscriptions are usually written in Greek, especially in the urban areas, with some Aramaic inscriptions in the countryside (Hoyland 2004: 187–88). Yet even in a Hellenistic town such as Scythopolis at the end of the third century CE, Procopius read the Scriptures in Greek and translated them into Aramaic according to the Syriac version of Eusebius' *De Martyribus Palaestinae* (Mussies 1976: 1059). About a century later, the Gallic pilgrim Egeria (Sivan 1988: 534) reports that the local bishop of Jerusalem 'may know Aramaic, but he never uses it. He always speaks in Greek and has a presbyter beside him who translates his words into Aramaic so that everyone can understand what he means' (Wilkinson 1981: 146), a practice reminiscent of the Jewish bilingual reading of the Tora in Hebrew and Aramaic from the second century CE onwards.

The disparity between the languages used in inscriptions and the common vernacular of the populace also occurs elsewhere in the Roman Empire, for example concerning Greek and Latin at Delos (Adams 2002: 193; 2004: 642–86). The emergence of Hebrew epitaphs in southern Italy from the seventh c. CE onwards does not point to a revival of a Hebrew vernacular, but to the status of Hebrew as an ethnic identity marker, the holy tongue, and the learned language spoken by a small scholarly elite (Leiwo 2002). Whilst the use of Hebrew predominated in southern Italy by the ninth century CE in both epigraphy and literature, the vernacular remained Latin or Greek.

Accordingly, the predominance of Greek in the epigraphy of Roman Palestine may merely express the status of Greek as the most prestigious language, which became the language of Church and State in Byzantine times (Millar 2006: 97). Even the Christian population may have had a significant portion of native Aramaic speakers. Significantly, the proportion of Greek inscriptions rises wherever Roman power is established (Eck 2007: 172). Inscriptions should not be mistaken as an indicator of the vernacular. Epigraphic language selection is rather governed by political factors, social status, and cultural identity. The language with the highest prestige would have been the natural choice for public expression, whereas the selection of other languages must be considered more exceptional and therefore more remarkable (Hoyland 2004: 192 n. 34).

On the basis of faulty Greek in many of the less expensive inscriptions, which might suggest that knowledge of Greek extended to the lower, less educated classes, some scholars have argued for a parity between the vernacular and epigraphic language (Lifshitz 1965: 520–38; Lieberman 1965: 30; van der Horst 2001: 159–62; Cotton/Yardeni

1997: 136–37, 206–208). However, grammatical deficiency does not necessarily point to the lower classes or less educated individuals, since such flaws can be explained as the result of code-switching in bilingual societies (Adams 2004: 305–8). These flaws reflect imperfect language acquisition. Whether they indicate a socio-linguistically low form of language use (see Porter 2000: 60) cannot be determined on the basis of individual documents or texts, but must be established structurally.

Language variation may also reflect socio-cultural distinctions. The Greek synagogue inscriptions seem to fall into one of the following categories: those in Aramaic, Hebrew, or 'Greek with many Semitic features that often utilize similar literary formulae' (Fine 1996: 114); and those composed in *Koine* Greek without Semitic features (ibid.). The first group occurs mainly in those regions where the majority of the inhabitants seem to have been 'Jewish'. The phenomenon may suggest that, at least in this instance, there was a link between epigraphic language choice and the cultural affiliations of those who commissioned the inscriptions. It remains unclear, though, whether and to what extent the epigraphic languages reflect the liturgical use of languages in the local synagogues.

More research into the languages and provenance of the Palestinian Jewish inscriptions is needed. A diachronic and regional differentiation will become more evident when all data is finally available. Regional variation has been suggested in a number of studies. Most of the ossuary inscriptions from the first and early second century found in the Jerusalem area are in Hebrew or Aramaic (Rahmani 1994; Eck 2007: 172). In the later centuries, Greek prevailed in the urban areas, while Aramaic continued to be used in inscriptions found in the countryside (Hezser 2001: 356; Hoyland 2004). It is to be expected that the publication of the CIIP will stimulate further research in this field.

It would be helpful to know whether the respective public or private nature of the inscriptions had any bearing on language selection. Even in private, the use of the most prestigious language would not be surprising, but variation in this regard may reveal the vernacular or cultural distinctions. If the provincial adoption of the epigraphic habit can be interpreted as a sign of Romanization (MacMullen 1982: 238; Millar 1983: 80, 84), the increased use of Semitic languages in synagogue inscriptions of late Roman and Byzantine times may reflect a conscious expression of Jewish identity vis-à-vis the all too visible presence of Christianity (cf. Schwartz 2001).

SUGGESTED READING

A useful overview of the languages used in Roman Palestine is provided by Rabin 1976. A more recent survey which focuses on, but is not confined to, Latin is Eck

2007. For an overview of Jewish literacy and an introduction to socio-linguistics see Hezser 2001. On the status of Mishnaic Hebrew see Young/Rezetko 2008. A helpful survey of Aramaic in the region is presented by Hoyland 2004.

BIBLIOGRAPHY

ADAMS, J. N. (2002). 'Bilingualism at Delos', in *Bilingualism in Ancient Society: Language Contact and the Written Text*, ed. J. N. Adams, M. Janse and S. Swain. Oxford: Oxford University Press, 103–27.

—— (2004). *Bilingualism and the Latin Language.* Cambridge: Cambridge University Press.

BARR, J. (1970). 'Which Language Did Jesus Speak?—Some Remarks of a Semitist'. *Bulletin of the John Rylands Library* 53: 9–29.

—— (1989). 'Hebrew, Aramaic and Greek in the Hellenistic Age', in *The Cambridge History of Judaism*, vol. 2, ed. W. D. Davies and L. Finkelstein. Cambridge: Cambridge University Press, 79–114.

BARTHÉLEMY, D. (1963). *Les Dévanciers d'Aquila.* Leiden: Brill.

BOHAK, G. (2008). *Ancient Jewish Magic: A History.* Cambridge: Cambridge University Press.

BROCK, S. P. (1972). 'The Phenomenon of the Septuagint', in *The Witness of Tradition*, ed. A. S. van der Woude. Leiden: Brill, 11–36.

COOK, E. M. (1992). 'Qumran Aramaic and Aramaic Dialectology', in *Studies in Qumran Aramaic*, ed. T. Muraoka. Leuven: Peeters, 1–21.

COOLEY, A. E. (2002). *Becoming Roman, Writing Latin? Literacy and Epigraphy in the Roman West.* Journal of Roman Archaeology Supplementary Series, 48. Portsmouth, RI: Journal of Roman Archaeology.

COTTON, H. M./YARDENI, A. (1997). *Aramaic, Hebrew, and Greek Texts from Nahal Hever and Other Sites with an Appendix Containing Alleged Qumran Texts.* Discoveries in the Judaean Desert 27. Oxford: Oxford University Press.

DÍEZ MACHO, A. (1972). *El Targum: Introducción à los traducciones aramaicos de la Biblia.* Barcelona: Consejo Superior de Investigaciones Científicas.

ECK, W. (2007). *Rom und Judaea: Fünf Vorträge zur römischen Herrschaft in Palästina.* Tübingen: Mohr-Siebeck, 157–200.

FERGUSON, C. A. (1959). 'Diglossia', in *Word* 15: 325–40.

—— (1964). 'Diglossia', in *Language in Culture and Society: A Reader in Linguistics and Anthropology*, ed. D. H. Hymes. New York: Harper & Row, 429–39.

—— (1991). 'Diglossia Revisited'. *Southwest Journal of Linguistics* 10: 214–32.

FINE, S. (1996). 'Synagogue Inscriptions', in *Oxford Encyclopedia of Archaeology in the Near East*, ed. E. M. Meyers. Oxford: Oxford University Press, 114–18.

FISHMAN, J. (1965). 'Who Speaks What Language to Whom and When?'. *La Linguistique* 2: 67–88.

—— (1967). 'Bilingualism With and Without Diglossia: Diglossia With and Without Bilingualism'. *Journal of Social Issues* 23: 29–38.

FITZMYER, J. (1970). 'The Languages of Palestine in the First Century A.D.'. *Catholic Biblical Quarterly* 32: 501–31.

FRAADE, S. D. (1992). 'Rabbinic Views on the Practice of Targum', in *The Galilee in Late Antiquity*, ed. L. I. Levine. New York: The Jewish Theological Seminary of America, 253–86.

GOODMAN, M. (1999). 'Galilean Judaism and Judaean Judaism', in *The Cambridge History of Judaism*, vol. 3. ed. W. Horbury, W. D. Davies and J. Sturdy. Cambridge, Cambridge University Press, 596–617.

GOSHEN-GOTTSTEIN, M. (1958). 'Linguistic Structure and Tradition in the Qumran Documents'. *Scripta Hierosolymitana* 4: 101–37.

GUNDRY, R. H. (1964). 'The Language Milieu of First-Century Palestine: Its Bearing on the Authenticity of the Gospel Tradition', in *Journal of Biblical Literature* 83: 404–408.

HARRIS, W. V. (1983). 'Literacy and Epigraphy I'. *Zeitschrift für Papyrologie und Epigraphik* 52: 87–111.

HEALEY, J. F. (1989). 'Were the Nabataeans Arabs?'. *Aram* 1: 38–44.

HENGEL, M. (1969). *Judentum und Hellenismus: Studien zu ihrer Begegnung unter besonderer Berücksichtigung Palästinas bis zur Mitte des 2.Jh. v.Chr.* Tübingen: Mohr-Siebeck.

HEZSER, C. (2001). *Jewish Literacy in Roman Palestine*. Tübingen: Mohr-Siebeck.

HORST, P. W. VAN DER (1991). *Ancient Jewish Epitaphs: Contributions to Biblical Exegesis and Theology* 2. Kampen: Kok Pharos Publishing House.

——(2001). 'Greek in Jewish Palestine in Light of Jewish Epigraphy', in *Hellenism in the Land of Israel*, ed. J. J. Collins and G. E. Sterling. Notre Dame: University of Notre Dame Press, 154–74.

HOYLAND, R. (2004). 'Language and Identity: The Twin Histories of Arabic and Aramaic (and: Why did Aramic Succeed where Greek Failed)'. *Scripta Israelica Classica* 23: 183–200.

KAHLE, P. (1958). 'Das palästinische Pentateuchtargum und das zur Zeit Jesu gesprochene Aramäisch'. *Zeitschrift für die Neutestamentliche Wissenschaft* 49: 100–16.

KAUFMAN, S. A. (1985). 'On Methodology in the Study of the Targums and their Chronology'. *Journal for the Study of the New Testament* 23: 117–24.

KOTANSKY, R. (1991). 'An Inscribed Copper Amulet from Evron'. *Atiqot* 20: 81–87.

——(1994). *Greek Magical Amulets: The Inscribed Gold, Silver, Copper, and Bronze Lamellae*, vol. 1: *Published Texts of Known Provenance*. Opladen: Westdeutscher Verlag.

KUTSCHER, E. Y. (1958). 'The Language of the Genesis Apocryphon: A Preliminary Study'. *Scripta Hierosolymitana* 4: 1–35.

——(1960). 'Das zur Zeit Jesu gesprochene Aramäisch'. *Zeitschrift für die Neutestamentliche Wissenschaft* 51: 46–54.

LANGE, N. DE (1996). 'The Revival of the Hebrew Language in the Third Century CE'. *Jewish Studies Quarterly* 3: 342–58.

LAPIDE, P. (1975). 'Insights from Qumran into the Languages of Jesus', in *Revue de Qumran* 8: 483–501.

LEIWO, M. (2002). 'From Contact to Mixture: Bilingual Inscriptions from Italy', in *Bilingualism in Ancient Society: Language Contact and the Written Text*, ed. J. N. Adams, M. Janse and S. Swain. Oxford: Oxford University Press, 168–94.

LEVINE, E. (1988). *The Aramaic Version of the Bible: Contents and Context*. Berlin: De Gruyter.

LEWIS, N. (1993). 'The Demise of the Demotic Document: When and Why'. *The Journal of Egyptian Archaeology* 79: 276–81.

——(2001). 'The Demise of the Aramaic Document in the Dead Sea Region'. *Scripta Classica Israelica* 20: 179–81.

LIEBERMAN, S. (1965). *Greek in Jewish Palestine*. New York: The Jewish Theological Seminary of America.

LIFSHITZ, B. (1965) 'L'hellénisation des juifs de Palestine à propos des inscriptions de Besara (Beth Shearim)'. *Révue Biblique* 72: 520–38.

——(1977). 'Jérusalem sous la domination romaine'. *Aufstieg und Niedergang der Römischen Welt* II.8: 444–89.

MACMULLEN, R. (1982). 'The Epigraphic Habit in the Roman Empire'. *American Journal of Papyrology* 103: 233–46.

MILIK, J. T. (1961). 'Textes Hébreux et Araméens', in *Les Grottes de Murabba'at*, ed. P. Benoit et al. Discoveries in the Judaean Desert 2. Oxford: Oxford University Press, 67–205.

MILLAR, F. (1983). 'Epigraphy', in *Sources for Ancient History*, ed. M. H. Crawford. Cambridge: Cambridge University Press, 80–136.

——(2006). *A Greek Roman Empire: Power and Belief under Theodosius II (408–450)*. Berkeley: University of California Press.

MUSSIES, G. (1976). 'Greek in Palestine and the Diaspora', in *The Jewish People in the First Century: Historical Geography, Political History, Social, Cultural and Religious Life and Institutions*, ed. S. Safrai et al. Compendia Rerum Iudaicarum ad Novum Testamentum I.2; Assen: Van Gorcum, 1040–64.

NAVEH, J. (1971). 'Hebrew Texts in Aramaic Script in the Persian Period?'. *Bulletin of the American School of Oriental Research* 203: 27–32.

——(1982). *Early History of the Alphabet: An Introduction to West Semitic Epigraphy and Palaeography*. Jerusalem: Magnes Press, and Leiden: Brill.

PÉREZ FERNÁNDEZ, M. (1997). *An Introductory Grammar of Rabbinic Hebrew*. Leiden: Brill.

PORTER, S. E. (2000). 'The Functional Distribution of Koine Greek in First-Century Palestine', in *idem, Diglossia and Other Topics in New Testament Linguistics*. Sheffield: Sheffield Academic Press, 53–78.

PUECH, E. (1996). 'Du bilinguisme à Qumran?', in *Mosaïque de langues, mosaïque culturelle: Le bilinguisme dans le Proche-Orient ancient*, ed. F. Briquel-Chatonnet. Paris: Jean Maisonneuve, 171–79.

RABIN, C. (1958). 'The Historical Background of Qumran Hebrew'. *Scripta Hierosolymitana* 4: 144–61.

——(1968). 'The Translation Process and the Character of the Septuagint'. *Textus* 6: 1–26.

——(1976). 'Hebrew and Aramaic in the First Century', in *The Jewish People in the First Century: Historical Geography, Political History, Social, Cultural and Religious Life and Institutions*, ed. S. Safrai et al. Compendia Rerum Iudaicarum ad Novum Testamentum I.2. Assen: Van Gorcum, 1007–39.

RAHMANI, L. Y. (1994). *A Catalogue of Jewish Ossuaries in the Collections of the State of Israel*. Jerusalem: The Israel Antiquities Authority and the Israel Academy of Sciences and Humanities.

RAJAK, T. (1984). *Josephus: The Historian and His Society*. Philadelphia: Fortress Press.

RENDSBURG, G. A. (1990). *Diglossia in Ancient Hebrew*. New Haven: American Oriental Society.

REYNOLDS, J. (2001). 'The Greek of Inscriptions', in *Greek Scripts: An Illustrated Introduction*, ed. P. Easterling and C. Handley. London: Society for Promotion of Hellenic Studies, 11–21.

RIBERA FLORIT, J. (1987). 'De la traducción a la interpretación: el Targum'. *El Olivo* 11: 111–26.

Sáenz-Badillos, A. (1993). *A History of the Hebrew Language*. Cambridge: Cambridge University Press.

Salvesen, A. (1991). *Symmachus in the Pentateuch*. Manchester: University of Manchester.

Samely, A. (1992). *The Interpretation of Speech in the Pentateuch Targums: A Study of Method and Presentation of Targumic Exegesis*. Tübingen: J. C. B. Mohr-Siebeck.

Schürer, E. (1986). *The History of the Jewish People in the Age of Jesus Christ (175 b.c.–a.d. 125)*, vol. 3, ed. G. Vermes et al. Edinburgh: T.&T. Clark.

Schwartz, S. (1995). 'Language, Power and Identity in Ancient Palestine'. *Past & Present* 148: 3–47.

——(2001). *Imperialism and Jewish Society from 200 bce to 640 ce*. Princeton: Princeton University Press.

Segal, M. H. (1927). *A Grammar of Mishnaic Hebrew*. Oxford: Clarendon Press.

Sevenster, J. N. (1968). *Do You Know Greek? How Much Greek Could the First Jewish Christians Have Known?* Leiden: Brill.

Sivan, H. (1988). 'Holy Land Pilgrimage and Western Audiences: Some Reflections on Egeria and Her Circle'. *The Classical Quarterly* 38: 528–35.

Smelik, W. F. (1995). *The Targum of Judges*. Leiden: Brill.

——(2001). 'Language, Locus, and Translation between the Talmudim'. *Journal for the Aramaic Bible* 3: 199–224.

——(2008). 'Language Selection and the Holy Tongue in Early Rabbinic Literature', in *Interpretation, Religion and Culture in Midrash and Beyond: Proceedings of the 2006 and 2007 SBL Midrash Sessions*, ed. L. Teugels and R. Ulmer. Piscataway: Gorgias Press, 91–151.

Spolsky, B. (1985). 'Jewish Multilingualism in the First Century: An Essay in Historical Sociolinguistics', in *Readings in the Sociology of Jewish Languages*, ed. J. A. Fishman. Leiden: Brill, 35–50.

Stern, S. (1994). *Jewish Identity in Early Rabbinic Writings*. Leiden: Brill.

Tov, E. (1992). *Textual Criticism of the Hebrew Bible*. Assen: Van Gorcum, and Minneapolis: Fortress Press.

Vanderkam, J. C. (2001). 'Greek at Qumran', in *Hellenism in the Land of Israel*, ed. J. J. Collins and G. E. Sterling. Notre Dame: University of Notre Dame Press, 175–81.

Veltri, G. (1994). *Eine Tora für den König Talmai: Untersuchungen zum Übersetzungsverständnis in der jüdisch-hellenistischen und rabbinischen Literatur*. Tübingen: Mohr-Siebeck.

Wasserstein, A. (1995). 'Non-Hellenized Jews in the Semi-Hellenized East'. *Scripta Classica Israelica* 14: 111–37.

Watt, J. M. (2000). 'The Current Landscape of Diglossia Studies: The Diglossic Continuum in First-Century Palestine', in *Diglossia and Other Topics in New Testament Linguistics*, ed. S. E. Porter. Sheffield: Sheffield Academic Press, 18–36.

Weitzman, S. (1999). 'Why Did the Qumran Community Write in Hebrew?'. *Journal of the American Oriental Society* 119: 35–45.

Wilkinson, J. (1981). *Egeria's Travels to the Holy Land*. Jerusalem and Warminster: Aris & Phillips.

Yadin, Y. et al. (2002). *The Documents from the Bar Kokhba Period in the Cave of Letters: Hebrew, Aramaic and Nabatean-Aramaic Papyri*. Judean Desert Studies, 3. Jerusalem: Israel Exploration Society.

Young, I./Rezetko, R. (2008). 'Mishnaic Hebrew', in *idem, Linguistic Dating of Biblical Texts*, vol. 1. London: Equinox, 223–49.

III

CITY AND COUNTRYSIDE

CHAPTER 8

INFRASTRUCTURE

BENJAMIN ISAAC

1. PRELIMINARY REMARKS

Merriam-Webster's Collegiate Dictionary provides the following definitions of the modern term 'infrastructure': (1) the underlying foundation or basic framework (of a system or organization); (2) the permanent installations required for military purposes; (3) the system of public works of a country, state, or region; also: the resources (as personnel, buildings, or equipment) required for an activity. The term 'infrastructure' first occurred in French in 1875 and in English in 1927, according to the *Oxford English Dictionary*. It is therefore an anachronistic term when applied to the ancient world. However, this does not necessarily mean it is inapplicable. What it does entail is an obvious need to elucidate what it applies to in a pre-modern world. The second and third definitions cited above are relevant here for, clearly, Roman provinces contained permanent installations required for military purposes and a system of public works. The Roman Empire, as a well-integrated society, had an infrastructure, but at a pre-modern level. We should consider, first, what any Roman province may have had by way of infrastructure and, secondly, what we know about this for the region considered in the present work.

For the Roman period we should therefore distinguish, in so far as possible, between a) military, b) non-military installations, such as aqueducts, and c) civilian structures connected with the provincial government, such as governor's mansions. The governor was commander of the garrison, chief-justice, and head of the provincial administration. It is therefore sometimes difficult to characterize the various structures and forms of organization as either military or non-military. By serving the governor and his staff they could be both.

A) Military installations: These include, first of all, the system of public roads with their bridges, constructed by the military for their own use but maintained by the civilian population, which also used and profited from their existence. Secondly, the permanent military bases housing the provincial garrison fall into this category. Thirdly, the smaller structures such as watchtowers, road-stations and fortified watering holes along the roads were established for the military.

B) Civilian/non-military structures: The only type of infrastructure which fits this category in the period under discussion here are water supply systems (aqueducts). We should exclude public buildings such as theatres, hippodromes, amphitheatres (see Weiss in this volume), temples, and, in the later Roman Empire, churches. In our days one would not normally classify concert halls, churches and cinemas as part of a city's infrastructure.

C) Structures associated with the provincial government, such as governor's palaces, archives, and the organization of the imperial postal system (*cursus vehicularis*, later *cursus publicus*) with its *mansiones* (night quarters) and *mutationes* (staging posts). The term 'postal system' is misleading, for this was a system maintained by, but not for the benefit of, the public. It served the Roman imperial authorities in conveying letters, goods, and persons authorized to use it (Kolb 2000). It is not easy to find material evidence for it. The available evidence is almost exclusively literary and epigraphic. However, in discussing roads and structures along roads, it is necessary to keep in mind that this was an essential function of the imperial government in the provinces. Finally, the ports of Roman Palestine had both a military and a civilian function, in contrast to two ports in Italy which served the military only.

The chronological framework adopted for this chapter starts with the conquest of Judaea by Pompey in 63 BCE. In practice, however, it will be reasonable to treat the period until the war of 66–70 CE as a transitional period, because during part of it Judaea was governed by dependent kings, while the equestrian governors appointed by Rome continued to work on the basis of the existing Hasmonaean-Herodian infrastructure. The survey will end with a description of the situation in the early fourth century CE. Geographically, we shall focus on the territory inhabited by Jews, that is, the province of Judaea-Palaestina in the broad sense, but exclude most of the desert area to the south. The present chapter can, obviously, do no more than provide an inventory with references based on the classification above, while maintaining a chronological framework. This will be based on the available evidence, both literary and archaeological.

2. ROADS IN JUDAEA-PALESTINE

The following section will provide a survey of the system of public roads in the region. Besides the public roads there was a network of secondary roads which partly dated back to the previous periods and partly developed locally in response to urbanization, the construction of public roads, and other social and economic developments (for secondary roads between Lydda and Jerusalem see Fischer/ Isaac/Roll 1996: 98–107). To describe these here would stretch the definition of infrastructure unnecessarily and take more space than is available for this chapter.

The systematic exploration of the Roman road-network in the area under consideration started with the mapping activities of the Palestine Exploration Fund (1871–78), a project which culminated in a series of maps published by the Fund (Conder/Kitchener 1882–88, repr. 1998). The maps indicated Roman roads, based on the presence of milestones and what remained of pavement on the ground. The immense value of this work stems from the fact that it was carried out before the large-scale destruction of the ancient evidence by the development of the modern road-system, which often used the old routes. Exploration went ahead gradually thereafter. The primary evidence for the existence of a Roman public road is the presence of milestones. The literary sources are valuable also as evidence for patterns of movement and the existence of roads between cities and villages. However, recognition of the remains of pavement is an integral part of survey activities. The survey of sites adjacent to the roads, and the comparison of the archaeological material with the sparse evidence from literary sources complete the picture, but to date this research has been done for part of the road network only. The general structure of the road network as a whole is familiar by now, but there remains work to be done. The full collection of known milestones will be published as part of the *Corpus Inscriptionum Iudaeae-Palaestinae* and in the *Corpus Inscriptionum Latinarum* vol. 17. Various reports on the surveys carried out throughout Israel over the past four decades still wait to be published.

Due to the lack of concrete evidence it is impossible to give a description of the road network as it existed before the Roman organization of public roads. The literary sources give us plenty of information about the movements of armies and the routes followed in general, but they provide little detailed information, and there is no archaeological evidence that allows us to describe the actual state of the roads at this time.

Roman roads were constructed for the use of the military organization in the provinces. The economic benefits for the local provincial population, which may have resulted from their existence, were a by-product rather than a primary aim in their construction. As elsewhere in the Roman Empire, the course of the roads was determined by various factors: the topography, the geography of settlement (Möller-Schmitt 1976), itself dependent on natural resources, geo-political factors within the province, and in the larger area, military considerations, the means of transportation, and the level of technology. In the following we shall provide a description of the road-system in its fully developed form, followed by some conclusions regarding its development.

The road-system in the province of Judaea-Palaestina was an integrated system of four north-south arteries and a series of east-west routes. The locations where these roads intersected developed into towns, such as Caesarea Philippi, Diocaesarea, Scythopolis, Caesarea, Neapolis, Antipatris, Diospolis, Nicopolis, Eleutheropolis, Hebron, Jericho, and the legionary base at Legio. Naturally, Jerusalem was one of the nodal centres of the road network before the Roman period for obvious reasons, and continued to function as such after the establishment of the headquarters of the legion X Fretensis there.

2.1. North-South Arteries

1. The coast road from Syrian Antioch to Ptolemais/Acco (Goodchild 1948–49); thence via the coastal towns of Caesarea–Apollonia–Jaffa, to Jamnia–Ascalon–Gaza, and finally to Alexandria in Egypt (Alt 1954; Roll 1996: 552–5).

2. The Caesarea–Antipatris road (Dar/Applebaum 1973), which continued to Diospolis–Eleutheropolis, with branches leading to the Hebron area and to Berosaba.

3. The road along the watershed: Diocaesarea–Legio (Hecker 1961; Isaac/Roll/ Weingarten, work in progress)–Neapolis–Jerusalem–Hebron, with branches making for Berosaba and Mampsis (Dalman 1925).

4. The road through the Jordan valley from Caesarea Philippi, probably along the east bank of the Jordan and the Sea of Galilee to Scythopolis and further to Neapolis or, alternatively, to Jerusalem via Jericho (Beauvery 1957; Wilkinson 1975).

5. Ptolemais–Diocaesarea–Tiberias and thence to Gadara and Bostra in Arabia. It crossed the river Jordan over a bridge with ten arches (Irby/Mangles 1985: 90–91; Isaac/Roll/Weingarten, work in progress).

6. Caesarea–Legio–Scythopolis (Isaac/Roll 1982). The road continued to Pella and Gerasa in Arabia.

7. Caesarea–Sebaste–Neapolis–Coreae (Ilan/Damati 1974–75); from there to Philadelphia on the *Via Nova Traiana*.

8. Jaffa–Neapolis (Roll/Ayalon 1986).

9. Diospolis–Neapolis (Roll/Ayalon 1986).

10. Antipatris–Gophna–Jericho. At Gophna this road crossed the main Neapolis–Jerusalem road.

11. Jaffa–Diospolis–Bet Horon–Jerusalem–Jericho, and from there to Esbus on the *Via Nova Traiana* (for the Bet Horon road see Fischer/Isaac/Roll 1996).

12. Diospolis–Nicopolis–Jerusalem (Fischer/Isaac/Roll 1996).
13. Ascalon–Eleutheropolis–Jerusalem (Alt 1929: 18–23, 124–6; Kallai 1965).
14. Gaza–Eleutheropolis, and further on to the southern Hebron Mountains.

2.2 Roads in the Negev

The road system in the Negev consisted essentially of four roads whose general direction was from the north-west to the south-east, and three other roads which ran from north-east to south-west. The system was linked with the road system in Transjordan to the east. The focus of three of the diagonal roads was the port city of Gaza. The cities of Berosaba, Elusa, Nessana, Oboda, and Mampsis lay at the nodal points of the network in the Negev.

2.2.1 North-West to South-East

15. Gaza–Aila (Arabic: Darb el-Ghaza). It ran southward to Quseima, where it turned to the south-east towards Kuntila. It approached Aila either via Ras en Naqb and the ascent west of Aila or via Ma'aleh Shaharut and Yotvetah (Meshel 1981).
16. Gaza–Elusa–Oboda–Petra (Negev 1966; Meshel/Tsafrir 1974–75). This was originally a Nabataean road which continued to be used in the Roman period (Cohen 1982).
17. Gaza–Moabitis. Passing by Berosaba and Mampsis it reached Charakmoba and Rabbatmoba on the Trajanic road (Negev 1969)
18. The road from Jerusalem to southern Transjordan: Jerusalem–Hebron–Mampsis–Tamara (Hazevah), descending to the Aravah in two stages by elaborate stepped ascents (Ma'aleh Deragot and the Scorpion Pass: Harel 1959). From Tamara the route headed for Aila, with branches towards the copper mines at Phaenon and Petra (Isaac 2006).

2.2.2 North-East to South-West

19. The continuation of the coast road: Ascalon–Gaza–Rhinocorura.
20. The route from Hebron to Sinai: Hebron–Berosaba–Elusa–Nessana.
21. Mampsis–Oboda–Quseima, crossing the southernmost cultivated area of the Negev.

2.3 The Development of the Road System

The chronological development of the road system can be traced to some extent through the dated milestones set up along the roads, and it is important to realize that this is the only criterium we can use with confidence. Sections have been cut through ancient roads in controlled excavations at various sites, but none of these have provided any information that corrects or adds to what is known from the inscribed milestones. The latter data, of course, are also accidental to some extent, as they depend on the survival of the evidence. Many of the later milestone series represent maintenance rather than new construction, and not all of the earliest series have been found. No milestones dated to the time before the reign of Claudius have been found anywhere in the eastern provinces beyond Anatolia, including Judaea-Palestine.

During the reigns of Claudius and Nero, veterans of four legions were settled in a new colony in Ptolemais-Acco in Syria, bordering on Judaea. As part of the same programme, the coastal road from Antioch to Ptolemais was constructed and marked with milestones dated to 56 CE. and inscribed: 'from Antioch to the new Colony of Ptolemais'. This was the first Roman road marked by milestones in Syria. It was a project apparently undertaken for security reasons: under Claudius there were dangerous troubles between Jews and Samaritans which were investigated on the spot by Ummidius Quadratus, governor of Syria (Isaac 1992: 322–23; 1998: 92–94).

In 69 CE M. Ulpius Traianus, commander of the Legio X Fretensis, is mentioned on a milestone of the Scythopolis–Legio road (Isaac/Roll 1976; Isaac 1997: 36–47). At the time of its construction, this road facilitated communications between the legionary winter-quarters at Caesarea and Scythopolis. Eventually, however, this became one of the most important routes crossing Palestine. The road probably continued to Pella and Gerasa, for milestones dated to 112 CE, discovered between these cities, mention the restoration of the road (Thomsen 1917: nos. 215, 216, 218a, 220; Mittmann 1970:157–58).

At the time of Trajan, following the annexation of the new province of Arabia, one legion was stationed at Bostra in the extreme north of the province (Sartre 1985; Kennedy/Riley 1990:124–5; Kermorvant/Leblanc/Lenoir 2003) and a road was constructed from Bostra to the Red Sea. The construction of the road is recorded on milestones of the years 111 and 114 CE (CIL 3:14176.2–3; all milestones known until 1917 are listed in Thomsen 1917, map 1; for the northern section see Bauzou 1998).

Under Hadrian, at least twelve roads were marked by milestones for the first time in Judaea, all dated to years well before the outbreak of the Bar Kokhba revolt, to 120 and 129/130 CE. The series dated to 129/130 CE is contemporary with the emperor's visit to Judaea. This represents a marked increase in Roman activity in the province. The garrison was doubled and the decision was taken to found the Roman colony of Aelia Capitolina at Jerusalem. In Arabia at least one new road was constructed under Hadrian, in 120 C.E: a road from Gerasa via Adra'a to Bostra (Mittmann 1964). This provided the legion in Bostra with organized access into the Decapolis. Under Hadrian a legion was transferred to Legio-Caparcotna and roads were built to provide an organized link with the legion at Bostra. No milestones have been discovered which date to the years of the Bar Kokhba revolt.

The milestones dated to 162 CE are by far the most extensive series attested in Judaea, numbering thirty-one milestones discovered to date. In Arabia, too, milestones were set up with identical texts at this time. It is clear that these milestones were set up in connection with roadwork done for the Parthian campaign of Lucius Verus, which started in the winter of 161/2 CE.

Milestones dated to several years during Septimus Severus's reign have been found in Judaea. There is some evidence that the inscriptions were produced by the citizens of the towns in whose vicinity they were found. A study of the coastal road in Syria has shown that there was a change of organization in 198 CE (Goodchild 1948–9: 91–93). In the province of Arabia there is evidence that the army started moving into the north-eastern desert in the reign of Severus (Kennedy 1980).

As observed in previous publications, the chronology of some of the milestone-texts suggests that they are related to events outside of the province of Judaea. Apart from the series of 162 CE, there are series which coincide with imperial visits to the area (in 129/130 and 198 CE). Other series are mere declarations of loyalty, such as that of Pertinax, or the stones dated to 324–6 CE. There was a short period when milestones were produced as a matter of routine instead of special initiative, from 198 CE until the death of Caracalla. No milestone inscriptions in Judaea are dated later than the reign of Constantine. In Arabia a few inscriptions proclaiming support for Julian the Apostate are the latest in date.

Finally, there are hardly any milestones in the settled area of Judaea dated to the time of the Tetrarchs and their successors. This coincides with the reduction of the garrison in the province in this period. In Syria and Arabia, where troops were not withdrawn but the army reorganized, there are many inscriptions of this period (Isaac 1992: 162–3.). The Roman road-system was originally developed by the army for its own use and later maintained for the army by the local population. It was not substantially restored or expanded until the twentieth century and continued to serve the local population and other armies after the Roman-Byzantine period.

2.4 Roman Roads in Judaea: General Characteristics

In the plain and valleys, roads followed an alignment as straight as possible, familiar from aerial photographs all over the empire. However, if possible, the engineers avoided laying out a road through densely wooded lands or marshlands. In mountainous areas, a route over the watershed or halfway up the slope was preferred to the narrow valleys or river beds, both for security reasons and because the roads are harder to maintain in low-lying terrain which tends to be flooded in winter (examples of sections across roads may be found in Isaac/Roll 1982:

40–41 and 121 with figs. 4 and 5; Roll/Ayalon 1986:125–29; Fischer/Isaac/Roll 1996: 73–75 and 89–92).

Passes or ascents were provided with steps built or cut into the bedrock, notably in the case of roads leading up to Jerusalem. It is uncertain to what extent wheeled traffic was possible along such roads, for it is impossible to date the steps as such.

Where needed, bridges were constructed, but these were not many; in fact, less than ten are known today (their location may be found on the *Barrington Atlas*, sheets 69 and 70). A fully illustrated description and architectural analysis of a bridge west of Scythopolis—Bet Shean is provided by Isaac and Roll (1982: 40–54; pls. 4–9). A good nineteenth-century engraving of the now destroyed bridge near Motza (Qaluniya) exists (Wilson 1880, vol.1: 82 and Fischer/Isaac/Roll 1996: 227–8). A bridge, still partly extant, near Legio (Megiddo, Lejjun) is depicted in another fine engraving (Wilson 1880, vol. 2: 24).

Milestones, which were found along the major roads, were set up for the use of the army and travelling officials (Isaac 1992: 304–9). In principle, they were placed at distances of one Roman mile, that is, at every 1,482 metres, but in practice the distances vary substantially. In Judaea the distances are measured from the main towns, usually, but not always from the centre. It is to be noted that both in Judaea and in Arabia far more milestones have been found in the settled area than in the desert (Isaac 1992: 111–12, 121, 304–5).

2.5 Sources of Information on Roads

Apart from the physical remains of pavements and milestones the following sources provide relevant information:

A. The Peutinger map, for which see: *Tabula Peutingeriana, Codex Vindobonensis 324, Vollständige Faksimile-Ausgabe im Originalformat* (Graz 1976). The information on the map reflects various periods of antiquity from the second century CE onwards.

B. Eusebius's *Onomasticon*, for which see: Erich Klostermann (ed.), *Eusebius, Das Onomastikon der biblischen Ortsnamen* (Leipzig 1904; reprint Hildesheim 1966). Spread over the various *lemmata*, this is the fullest literary source of information on the network of Roman roads in the province.

C. The ancient itineraries:

    (a) The *Itinerarium Antonini Augusti*: ed. G. Parthey and M. Pinder, *Itinerarium Antonini Augusti et Hierosolymitanum* (Berlin 1840); ed. O. Cuntz, *Itineraria Romana I, Itineraria Antonini Augusti et Burdigalense* (Leipzig 1929).

    (b) Theophanes (c. 320 CE), a member of the staff of the *praefectus Aegypti* who travelled to Antioch: Roberts (1952); Rees (1968).

D. The Christian itineraries:
   (a) the traveller from Bordeaux: ed. P. Geyer and O. Cuntz in *Corpus Christia-norum, Series Latina*, Vol. CLXXV (Turnhout), 1–26.
   (b) The obituary of St. Paula: Jerome, *ep.* 108.
   (c) Theodosius, *De Situ Terrae Sanctae* (Topography of the Holy *Land*), ed. P. Geyer, CCSL, Vol. CLXXV, pp. 113–125.

3. ARMY INSTALLATIONS

Our information concerning the Roman army in the region derives, as elsewhere, from a combination of a) literary, b) epigraphic, and c) archaeological sources. Obviously, whatever is available in the literary sources is well known by scholars and does not change over time. The interpretation of the epigraphic material depends on systematic study of what are, in fact, random discoveries, both in Judaea and in other provinces. The archaeological exploration of army sites is far less advanced in the Roman Near East than in the northern and western parts of the empire, for two reasons. The first reason is the particular interests and priorities of archaeologists; the second is the fact that many army units in the Roman Near East were based in an urban environment with a complex earlier and later history. The units based in the steppe and the desert can be considered exceptions in this regard. Those explored in the region under consideration belong to the late Roman and early Byzantine periods (Shatzman 1983; Isaac 1997: 450–469). It should at least be mentioned here that the assumption that there was a Roman system of frontier defence in the desert is highly controversial (denied by Isaac 1992; Whittaker 1994 and 2004; Kennedy 1996; contra: Parker 2006).

The systematic study of the Roman provincial army initially focused on north-western Europe (Britain, the Netherlands, Germany). Scholarly interest in the army in the East developed much later. Scholars were therefore influenced by the earlier concepts and approaches, which were applied—with varying success—to a region with a totally different climate, environment, and social organization. Notably, the eastern provinces were far more urbanized than those in the north-western parts of the empire, and this obviously had consequences for the functions and distribution of the troops. Any attempt to investigate these topics must be based on systematic archaeological study of the material remains, combined with the interpretation of relevant literary sources and epigraphic material. The last few decades have seen a considerable advance in the study of the Roman army in Judaea-Palaestine and in the neighbouring province of Arabia. Even so, there is still much work to do: for instance, no systematic excavation of any large Roman army base in Judaea-Palaestina has been conducted to date.

3.1 The Historical Development of the Roman Army in Judaea-Palestine

In the period between 63 BCE and 67 CE the military organization of Judaea continued the Hellenistic tradition as established by the Hasmonaeans. The available army units acted as a police force for the ruler and as a standing army on campaigns, but also as a local garrison when the army was not on campaigns. In such periods it was based in cities, notably Jerusalem, and at important locations in the countryside (Shatzman 1991).

There were two stages of transformation and reorganization in this period, the first following Pompey's conquest of Judaea (Shatzman 1991, ch. 4), the second following Herod's confirmation as ruler of Judaea in 30 BCE (ibid. ch. 5). The latter stage included the establishment of military settlers in and near Trachonitis (Josephus, Ant. 16.285; Shatzman 1991: 171–3), in Batanaea (Josephus, Ant. 17.24; Shatzman 1991: 175–180; Isaac 1992: 329–30), and of discharged soldiers in Gaba (Josephus, Bell. 3.36, cf. Isaac 1992:328–29) and Samaria-Sebaste (Josephus, Ant. 15.293–6 cf. Isaac 1992: 328). Then there was the standing army, consisting of bodyguards, Jews, and mercenaries from various regions (Josephus, Ant. 17.198–9), and the Sebasteni, local troops from Samaria-Sebaste and its territory (Schürer 1973, vol. 1: 363–64). By 44 CE at the latest there were also troops recruited in Caesarea and its territory.

The army was based in urban and rural sites, some of which had a dual function as both fortification and palace. In Jerusalem there were two fortified army bases: the royal palace and the Antonia. Two other cities are on record as having been garrisoned: Sepphoris (Josephus, Bell. 1.204; 2.56; Ant. 14.414; 17.289) and Caesarea. Several fortifications were erected in the vicinity of the royal palace at Jericho, and further south in the Judaean desert facing Transjordan several such complexes are attested: Hyrcania, Herodium, and Masada, the last two also representing palaces (Shatzman 1991, ch. 6). In Samaritis, overlooking the Jordan valley, Herod restored the large Hasmonaean fort of Alexandrium (Qarn Sartaba; Josephus Bell. 1.308; Ant. 14.419). The largest and best known fortified palace in Transjordan built by Herod is Machaerus (besieged by the Romans in the First Revolt: Josephus, Bell. 7.171–7; Shatzman 1991: 263–5; Kennedy/Bewley 2004: 172–3).

These complexes seem to have fulfilled various functions. Some of them were both army bases and royal palaces: those in cities such as Jerusalem, Sepphoris, and Caesarea, and some in the desert, such as Herodium, Masada, and Machaerus. Others were substantial forts meant to control key sites of the road-system. Then there are the fortified cities themselves: Jerusalem, Caesarea, and Samaria-Sebaste. The latter and a number of smaller towns or villages (Gaba, Heshbon) were populated with discharged veterans. Smaller structures along roads apparently fulfilled police duties; for example, Giv'at Shaul, Kh. ad Daliya, Horvat Mazad, possibly Rujum Abu Hashabe all four of them along the roads to Jerusalem

(Fischer/Isaac/Roll 1996: 124–25, 144–6, 209–216, 244–7). The army units in cities were obviously meant to control the urban population. The palace-forts in the desert may have served as refuge sites in times of trouble. Other establishments controlled movements along the roads, especially those in the desert and along the Jordan valley.

In 70 CE, when Judaea became a regular province governed by a senatorial legate with a legion and units of auxiliary troops, the system was reorganized drastically. The only palaces known for this period are those of the legate and procurator in Caesarea. There were no longer any fortress palaces, and the distribution of the units was concentrated in the settled area of the province. Most of the small military structures along the roads appear to have been abandoned. There is evidence to suggest that the army was mostly based in towns, at least till the reign of Hadrian. During his reign the army was reinforced, and a legionary base established near Megiddo (see below) and possibly elsewhere in the north of the province as well.

3.2 The Geographical Distribution of Roman Army Installations

3.2.1 Jerusalem

In 70 CE the headquarters of the legion X Fretensis were established in Jerusalem to guard the former capital city. This is stated explicitly by Josephus on three occasions (Isaac 1992: 427–8). It also follows from the text of a diploma of 93 CE (ILS 9059), and is clear from inscriptions found in the town. The archaeological material is less easy to interpret. In the areas excavated, no remains of a military base of the second century have been found (Geva 1984; Bar 1998). However, a base must have existed somewhere in town. In the late Roman period there was a unit of horsemen based in the city (Not. Dig. Or. 34.21).

3.2.2 Along the Jerusalem–Jaffa Road

1. Giv'at Ram (Sheikh Bader): 2.5 km from Jerusalem. Brick-ovens and fort (Arubas/Goldfus 2005).
2. Motza (Qulonieh): 5–6 km from Jerusalem, almost certainly to be identified with the veteran settlement established by Vespasian after the Jewish War (at a place named 'Ammaus' according to Josephus), possibly also with the village of Emmaus mentioned in Luke 24:13 (Fischer/Isaac/Roll 1996: 222–229). The site is in a very fertile, well-watered valley. Its spring is mentioned in Byzantine sources and was guarded by a crusading fort. The Roman road passed over a bridge and through a narrow defile.

3. Abu Ghosh: 13.5 km from Jerusalem (Fischer/Isaac/Roll 1996: 113–120). There is a spring with remains of the Roman period and an inscription: 'Vexillatio Leg. X Fret.' (AE 1902. 230). On top of a hill nearby (Kiriath Jearim, Deir el-Azhar) a second inscription was found: 'Vexillatio Leg. X Fret.' and a fragment: '. . . CO . . .' (AE 1926: 136). The site of the spring always remained an important road-station. The hill nearby affords a commanding view of the vicinity.

4. Emmaus-Nicopolis (Imwas): an important city at a major crossroad, 30 km from Jerusalem (Fischer/Isaac/Roll 1996: 151–159). Josephus says that the legion V Macedonica stayed there during the first Jewish War before the siege of Jerusalem, and five inscriptions referring to this legion have been found at the site. At least two of these are epitaphs of serving soldiers who died sometime in the later first century CE. This shows that they stayed there long enough for a stone-mason's workshop to be set up. Another inscription mentions the *coh (ors) VI Ulpi(a) Petr(aeorum)* (AE 1924. 132), a unit attested in the province throughout the second century. A fragmentary inscription mentions an unknown cohort (CIL iii 13588). It is therefore quite likely that army units were permanently based here.

5. The village of Qubab now abandoned (near modern Mishmar 'Ayalon): *c*. 5 km from Emmaus; two inscriptions have been found, one of them certainly military (Fischer/Isaac/Roll 1996: 236–37).

3.2.3 *Four Other Sites*

6. Giv'at Shaul (Kh. al Atrash): 4 km from Jerusalem (Fischer/Isaac/Roll 1996: 124–25). Excavation of a tower (10 x 9.25 m), occupied in the first centuries BCE and CE, that is to say, before the arrival of the legion X Fretensis in Jerusalem following the Jewish revolt. A small fort, measuring 16 x 16 m, was built on the spot in the fourth century CE.

7. A similar small fort of the Byzantine period, excavated but unpublished, was found a little distance to the west.

8. Horvat Mazad/Khirbet el-Qasr, east of Emmaus: excavated by M. Fischer (Fischer/Isaac/Roll 1996: 212–216). Like site no.6, this site was occupied until the end of the first century CE, subsequently deserted and occupied again in the Byzantine period.

9. Rujum Abu Hashabe: on the parallel Bet Horon road a tower was recently excavated east of Upper Bet Horon. It was not occupied after the First Jewish Revolt against Rome (Fischer/Isaac/Roll 1996: 244–246).

3.2.4 *Along the Road to Hebron*

1. Ramat Rahel: 3.5 km south of Jerusalem. This is a site on top of a hill controlling access to the city from the south. Excavated here is a Roman bathhouse with many tiles bearing the stamp of the legion. Furthermore there is a peristyle villa

and various unidentified structures of non-durable material (Aharoni 1962: 24–27; 1964: 38–40, plan I). The military nature of the buildings has not been established beyond doubt.

2. Hebron and Ein Gedi: in or near the city of Hebron itself a *Cohors I Milliaria Thracum* was based (Isaac 1992: 430). Hebron is sited on a crossroads from which roads lead in all directions, one of them to Ein Gedi, where in 124 CE a centurion of the cohort is attested, occupying a *praisidion* flanked by soldiers' housing.

3.2.5 *Along the Road to the North: Samaria and Neapolis*

1. Neapolis, ancient Shekhem (Nablus): controls a crossroads from which roads lead to Jerusalem, to the coastal plain in the west, eastwards to the Jordan Valley and northwards to Scythopolis (Bet Shean). The evidence of military presence at Neapolis is as follows (Isaac 1992: 430–1): (a) a fragmentary inscription mentions a *tribunus* and a *primus pilus* or *praepositus*; (b) countermarks of the legion XII Fulminata on coins struck up to A.D. 86/7 (Howgego 1983: 41–46). The coins were countermarked after 86/7 and probably before 156/7 CE. This almost certainly shows that the legion (or part of it) was based at Neapolis in 115–7 or 132–5 CE; (c) the tombstone of M. Ulpius Magnus, centurion of the legion V Macedonica, presumably from the years of the Bar Kokhba revolt; (d) a city coin: *obv.* Tribonianus Gallus (251–3 CE); *rev.* COL NE[A]POLI and emblems of the legion X Fretensis (Ben Dor 1952: 251–2, Pl. 9, 1); (e) a city coin: *obv.* Volusianus Augustus (251–3 CE); *rev.* COL NEAPOLIS and emblems of the legion III Cyrenaica.

2. Samaria-Sebaste, ancient Shomron: capital of the Kingdom of Israel, military colony established by Herod. It controls the main north-south road. The evidence of military presence at this site is as follows (Isaac 1992: 431): (a) a monumental inscription: 'Vexillatio Leg. VI Ferr.'; (b) a dedication to Jupiter by the 'mil(ites) v(e)xi(lationis) coh(ortium) Pa(nnoniae) Sup(erioris), cives Sisci (ani) (et) Varcian(i) et Latobici'. These inscriptions have been discovered in excavations and their provenance is therefore certain.

3.2.6 *Along the Jerusalem-Jericho Road*

On a site on this road a military stamp has been found (*AE* 1902: 231). This is not conclusive evidence for a military installation, though. The fort at Ma'ale Adumim, attested in late Roman and Byzantine sources, has not been excavated yet. It is not known whether it was occupied in the Roman period (Eusebius, Onomasticon 24.9; Jerome 25.9; Not. Dig. Or. 34.48).

3.2.7 *Along the Jerusalem-Gaza Road*

Eleutheropolis (Bet Govrin: a monumental inscription, 'Vexillatio leg(ionis) VI Ferr(atae)', is said to come from this town (*AE* 1933:158). Near the town, at Erak

Hala on the Roman road, the trunk of a life-size statue, apparently an emperor in military dress, was found (Clermont-Ganneau 1897: 441–42, 464; Vermeule 1959–60: no.288). Bet Govrin, which received city status under Septimius Severus, lies on an important crossroads with other Roman roads leading to Hebron, Ascalon, Lydda, and Emmaus.

3.2.8 Along the Scythopolis-Jericho Road

Tel Shalem, almost 11 km from Scythopolis (near the seventh mile-station, Isaac 1992: 432): an inscription mentions a fort of the legion VI Ferrata. On the site a bronze statue of Hadrian has been found (Foerster 1986; Gergel 1991). Nearby fragments of a very large inscription which mentions Hadrian have been discovered (Eck/Foerster 1999). They probably were part of a triumphal arch. The site lies on the road in the area where the Valley of Bet Shean borders on the arid Jordan Valley.

3.2.9 Caparcotna–Kefar 'Otnay–Legio

The base of the legion VI Ferrata was near the ancient site of Megiddo, a strategic spot where the Caesarea–Scythopolis road reaches the Valley of Jezreel. A branch of the road leads towards the hills of Lower Galilee and Sepphoris, and onwards to Ptolemais-Acco, while another one leads to Ptolemais directly through the plain. Yet another road runs south-east to Samaria (Isaac/Roll 1982, index). The army base was located near a strategic crossroads on a gentle slope which offered no tactical advantage, unlike nearby Megiddo, which lies on an easily defensible mount. An army base certainly existed there before the revolt of Bar Kokhba. This was not an urbanized site.

Kefar 'Otnay was a village with a mixed Jewish and Samaritan population, according to rabbinic sources of the second century CE. Kefar 'Otnay and Antipatris are mentioned as the two stop-over places on the usual route taken by Jews travelling from Galilee to Judaea and vice versa. The legionary base was named after the village: Caparcotna (CIL iii 6814–16), Caporcotani (Tabula Peutingeriana), or Kaparkotnei (Ptolemy). It appears on the Peutinger Table as a road-station on the Caesarea–Scythopolis road. Later the name 'Legio' became common, and this name was retained after the departure of the army at an unknown date in the third century. The civilian settlement, which developed near the base, was important enough to receive city status as Maximianoupolis under the Tetrarchs (Isaac/Roll 1982: 11). This was a rural site chosen as a legionary base because of its proximity to a strategic crossroad. The small town which developed there owed its existence to the base.

3.2.10 Scythopolis?

Scythopolis was a substantial city which lay at an important crossroads. A dedication to Hadrian by the first cohort of the legion X Fretensis was said to come from Scythopolis, although this is not quite certain, but it does derive from that part of the country (Clermont-Ganneau 1897: 168–171). An inscription certainly found in Scythopolis commemorates P. Aelius Capito, a Macedonian who served in the legion XI Claudia (AE 1939: 158). He died at the age of thirty-five after ten years of army service. A unit of this legion participated in the suppression of the Bar Kokhba revolt (CIL iii 14155.2.). It is possible that the unit spent some time in or near the town, but the evidence is not decisive.

3.2.11 *Galilee*

There is surprisingly little evidence of army units in Galilee. Eusebius, in his *Onomasticon*, does not mention garrisons there, but that reflects the late third- to fourth-century military organization. It would be premature to draw conclusions from the absence of evidence. Rabbinic sources associate the army with Sepphoris, one of the two main towns in the region (y. Pes. 4, 31b; T. Shab. 12:9; y. Shab. 16, 15d; y. Yoma 8, 45b; b. Shabbat 125a). In the late Roman period a unit is attested in Galilee (Not. Dig. Or. 34.28), but the literary reference is not supported by archaeological or epigraphic evidence. The Gospels contain a random piece of information: the presence of a centurion at Capernaum (Kefar Nahum, Matthew 8:5–9; Luke 7:2. This text may imply the presence of a unit otherwise unknown. Aurelius Marcellinus, centurion of the legion X Fretensis, was buried at Tiberias by his wife. That certainly does not prove, but may nevertheless suggest, the presence of a unit there. The same may be said of a stamped tile of the legion VI Ferrata, found at Horvat Hazon (Bahat 1974: 160–9). The excavations at Bet Yerah (Khirbet el-Kerak) on the south-western shore of the Sea of Galilee (*Encyclopaedia of Archaeological Excavations in the Holy Land* 1: 253–262) produced the walls of a fort which looks like a fourth-century structure.

3.3 The Roman Army in the Fourth Century

At an uncertain date, presumably in the Tetrarchic period, the army was reorganized, and the major sites in the regions listed above were abandoned or occupied by smaller units (Isaac 1998: 451–469). Most of the army was transferred to the desert then. In the settled area, the attested garrison sites already mentioned above are: Aelia, Sepphoris, Ma'ale Edomim (Adommim), and a unit on the bank of the Jordan. In the southern part of the region (*Palaestina Prima*) the following sites can be mentioned: Birsama (Beer Shema), Menois, Zoar, Chermula (Carmel).

This is not the place to discuss the broader significance of this large-scale change. It should suffice to note that the massive Roman army presence in areas settled by Jews was drastically reduced in the fourth century. Instead of two legions and an approximately equal number of auxiliary soldiers (more than 20.000 troops), we now have evidence of the presence of about eight small units only. It is possible that the number of troops was gradually reduced at an earlier stage through depletion of existing units.

4. Aqueducts

A comprehensive study on aqueducts in the Land of Israel was published recently (Amit/Patrich/Hirschfeld, eds 2002). Aqueducts are also marked on the relevant maps of the *Barrington Atlas* (Talbert 2000).The road system and army bases were all organized and constructed at the initiative and authority of the Roman government or the Hellenistic and Herodian kings before the Roman annexation of Judaea as a province. The aqueducts, on the other hand, were built and maintained at various levels. As listed by Patrich and Amit, there were twenty-eight Graeco-Roman water systems of which eleven were urban. The building and maintenance of most of these aqueducts were the responsibility of the urban authorities. Since they are very well documented and discussed in the above mentioned work edited by Amit, Patrich, and Hirschfeld, it is not necessary to list them here.

However, it is worth noting that one aqueduct of uncertain date, leading water to Jerusalem, and the Hadrianic high-level aqueduct at Caesarea were constructed by Roman army units (di Segni ibid. 48–51). Six or seven water systems were leading to fortresses of Hellenistic (Hasmonaean) and Herodian date, many of them in the desert or at its edge. The respective rulers had probably constructed them for themselves and they were part of the infrastructure of the period (ibid. 306–364, 367–79, 423–6). The aqueduct to the legionary base at Legio was obviously constructed by the legionaries stationed there (Tsuk ibid. 409–411). Note also the system at Ein Boqeq, watering a Herodian *officina* and late Roman fort: (Fischer and Shacham ibid. 403–408). Finally, there are aqueducts constructed on the basis of local initiative: the inhabitants of the site of Qumran (Ilan and Amit, ibid. 381–386), the local inhabitants on and near the south tip of Mt. Carmel at the sites of Ramat Hanadiv and Shuni (Hirschfeld, ibid. 387–400), and those who dwelled at the smaller fortified settlements of Khirbet el-Hammam (Zertal, ibid., 413–416) and Horvat Kefira (Amit and Eshel, ibid. 417–422).

5. Harbours

The eastern Mediterranean coast does not have any good natural harbours: Acco and Joppa were serviceable but had serious shortcomings. Dor (Kingsley/Raveh 1996) and Apollonia-Arsuf must also be mentioned as anchorages. At the latter site, north of Tel Aviv, a small harbour may already have been constructed in the Roman period (Roll/Ayalon 1989: 106–7; Roll/Tal 1999: 6). Caesarea's harbour was the largest of all, an entirely artificial construction undertaken by Herod. It was serviceable throughout the Roman period but may have declined in the Byzantine period, although this is disputed. Its connection with the provincial capital and several main roads enhanced its importance, even though it could never compete with the harbour of Alexandria (Vann, ed. 1992, part 2; Raban 1985; Raban/Holum, eds 1996, parts 1 and 2, and ibid. 628–66; Holum/Raban/ Patrich, eds 1999).

SELECTED READING

Two volumes of a comprehensive road-survey project have been published so far (Isaac/Roll 1982 and Fischer/Isaac/Roll 1996). A basic collection of milestones is available in Thomsen (1917), with further publications by Isaac and Roll (e.g. Isaac/ Roll 1976; Isaac 1978; Roll 2000). Gregory (1995–97) deals with Roman military architecture and Isaac (1992) studies the Roman army in the East. The volume edited by Amit, Patrich and Hirschfeld (2002) provides a survey of aqueducts. Maps of the road system of Judaea-Palestine are available in the *Tabula Imperii Romani* (Tsafrir et al. 1994).

ABBREVIATIONS

AE = L'Année épigraphique
CIL = Corpus Inscriptionum Latinarum
ILS = Inscriptiones Latina Selectae

BIBLIOGRAPHY

AHARONI, Y. (1962). *Excavations at Ramat Rahel: Seasons 1959 and 1960.* Rome: Centro di studi semitici, Istituto di studi del vicino Oriente.
—— (1964). *Excavations at Ramat Rahel: Seasons 1961 and 1962.* Rome Centro di studi semitici, Istituto di studi del vicino Oriente.
ALT, A. (1929). 'Römerstrasse Jerusalem-Eleutheropolis'. *Palästina Jahrbuch* 25: 18–23; 124–26.
—— (1954). 'Stationen der römischen Hauptstrasse von Ägypten nach Syrien.' *Zeitschrift des Deutschen Palästina-Vereins* 70: 154–166.

AMIT, D./PATRICH, J./HIRSCHFELD, Y. (eds) (2002). *The Aqueducts of Israel.* Portsmouth: Journal of Roman Archaeology Supplementary Series.

ARUBAS, B./GOLDFUS, H. (2005). *Excavations on the Site of the Jerusalem International Convention Center (Binyanei Ha'uma): A settlement of the late First to Second Temple period, the tenth legion's kilnworks, and a Byzantine monastic complex* Portsmouth: Journal of Roman Archaeology Supplementary Series.

AVI-YONAH, M. (1950–51). 'The Development of the Roman Road System in Palestine'. *Israel Exploration Journal* 1: 54–60.

BAR, D. (1998). 'Aelia Capitolina and the Location of the Camp of the Tenth Legion'. *Palestine Exploration Quarterly* 130: 8–19.

BAUZOU, T. (1998). 'Le secteur nord de la *via nova* en Arabie de Bostra à Philadelphie', in *Fouilles de Khirbet es-Samra en Jordanie, vol. 1: La voie romaine, le cimetière, les documents épigraphiques*, ed. J. B. Humbert and A. Desreumaux. Turnhout : Brepols, 101–255.

BEAUVERY, R. (1957). 'La route romaine de Jérusalem à Jericho'. *Revue Biblique* 64: 72–101.

BEN DOR, S. (1952). 'Quelques rémarques à propos d'une monnaie de Néapolis'. *Revue Biblique* 59: 251–2.

CLERMONT-GANNEAU, C. S. (1896). *Archaeological Researches in Palestine during the Years 1873–874.* London: Palestine Exploration Fund.

—— (1897). 'Une dédicace de la légion Xe Fretensis à l'empereur Hadrien en Palestine'. *Etudes d'Archéologie Orientale* 2: 168–71.

COHEN, R. (1982). 'New Light on the Petra-Gaza Road'. *Biblical Archaeologist* 45: 240–47.

CONDER, C. R./KITCHENER, H. H. (eds) (1882–1888, repr. 1998). *Survey of Western and Eastern Palestine 1882–1888.* 13 vols. London: Palestine Exploration Fund.

DALMAN, G. (1925). 'Die Nordstrasse Jerusalems'. *Palästina Jahrbuch* 21: 58–89.

DAR, S./APPLEBAUM, S. (1973). 'The Roman Road from Antipatris to Caesarea'. *Palestine Exploration Quarterly* 105: 91–9.

ECK, W./FOERSTER, G. (1999). 'Ein Triumphbogen für Hadrian im Tal von Beth Shean bei Tel Shalem'. *Journal of Roman Archaeology* 12: 294–313.

FISCHER, M./ISAAC, B./ROLL, I. (1996). *Roman Roads in Judaea* II: *The Jaffa-Jerusalem Road.* Oxford: B.A.R.

FOERSTER, G. (1986). 'A Cuirassed Bronze Statue of Hadrian'. *'Atiqot* 17: 139–160.

GERGEL, R. A. (1991). 'The Tel Shalem Hadrian Reconsidered', *American Journal of Archaeology* 95: 231–251.

GEVA, H. (1984). 'The Camp of the Tenth Legion in Jerusalem: An Archaeological Reconsideration'. *Israel Exploration Journal* 24: 239–254.

GOODCHILD, R. G. (1948–49). 'The Coast Road of Phoenicia and its Roman Milestones'. *Berytus* 9: 91–127.

GRAF, D. F. (1989). 'Les routes romaines d'Arabie Pétree'. *Le monde de la Bible* 59: 54–56.

GREGORY, S. (1995–7). *Roman Military Architecture on the Eastern Frontier.* 3 vols. Amsterdam: A. M. Hakkert.

HAREL, M. (1959). 'The Roman Road at Ma'aleh Aqrabim'. *Israel Exploration Journal* 9: 175–9.

HECKER, M. (1961). 'The Roman Road from Legio to Sepphoris' [Hebr.]. *Bulletin of the Jewish Palestine Exploration Society* 25: 175–86.

HOLUM, K. G./RABAN, A./PATRICH, J. (eds) (1999). *Caesarea Papers 2: Herod's Temple, the Provincial Governor's Praetorium and Granaries, the later Harbor, a Gold Coin Hoard and Other Studies.* Portsmouth: Journal of Roman Archaeology Supplementary Series.

Howgego, C. J. (1983). 'The XII Fulminata: Countermarks, Emblems and Movements under Trajan or Hadrian', in *Armies and Frontiers in Roman and Byzantine Anatolia: proceedings of a colloquium held at University College, Swansea, in April 1981*, ed. S. Mitchell. Oxford: B.A.R., 41–46.

Ilan, Z./Damati, E. (1974–75). 'Ancient Roads in the Samarian Desert' [Hebr.]. *Museum Ha'aretz Yearbook* 17–18: 43–52.

Irby, C. L./Mangles, J. (1985). *Travels in Egypt and Nubia, Syria and the Holy Land.* London: Darf Publishers.

Isaac, B. (1978). 'Milestones in Judaea, from Vespasian to Constantine'. *Palestine Exploration Quarterly* 110: 47–60.

—— (1992). *The Limits of Empire: The Roman Army in the East.* 2nd ed. Oxford: Clarendon Press.

—— (1998). *The Near East under Roman Rule: Selected Papers.* Leiden: Brill.

—— (2006). 'Roman Organization in the Arabah in the Fourth Century', in *Crossing the Rift: Resources, Routes, Settlement Patterns and Interaction in the Wadi Arabah*, ed. P. Bienkowski and K. Galor. Oxford: Oxbow Books, 215–221.

—— and Roll, I. (1976). 'A Roman Milestone of A.D. 69 from Judaea: The Elder Trajan and Vespasian'. *Journal of Roman Studies* 66: 15–19.

—— (1982). *Roman Roads in Judaea I, The Scythopolis–Legio Road.* Oxford: B.A.R.

Kallai, Z. (1965). 'Remains of the Roman Road along the Mevo-Beitar Highway'. *Israel Exploration Journal* 15: 195–203.

Kennedy, D. (1980). 'The Frontier Policy of Septimius Severus: New Evidence from Arabia', in *Roman Frontier Studies 1979*, eds. W. Hanson and L. J. F. Keppie. Oxford: Oxbow Books, 879–87.

—— (ed.) (1996). *The Roman Army in the East.* Ann Arbor: Cushing-Malloy.

—— and Riley, D. (1990). *Rome's Desert Frontier from the Air.* London: B. T. Batsford.

Kennedy, D./Bewley, R. (2004). *Ancient Jordan from the Air.* London: B.T. Batsford.

Kermorvant, M./Leblanc, J./Lenoir, M. (2003). 'Le camp de la legion IIIa Cyrenaica et sa zone d'activités'. *Syria* 79: 134–40.

Kingsley, S. A./Raveh, K. (1996). *The Ancient Harbour & Anchorage at Dor, Israel.* Oxford: Tempus Reparatum.

Kolb, A. (2000). *Transport und Nachrichtentransfer im Römischen Reich.* Berlin: Akademie Verlag.

Meshel, Z. (1981). 'The History of the Darb el-Ghaza–the Ancient Road to Eilat and Southern Sinai' [Hebr.]. *Eretz Israel* 15: 358–71.

—— and Tsafrir, Y. (1974–75). 'The Nabataean Road from Avdat to Sha'ar Ramon'. *Palestine Exploration Quarterly* 106: 103–118; 107: 3–21.

Mittmann, S. (1964). 'Die römische Strasse von Gerasa nach Adraa'. *Zeitschrift des Deutschen Palästina-Vereins* 80: 113–136.

—— (1970). *Beiträge zur Siedlungsgeschichte des nördlichen Ostjordanlandes.* Wiesbaden: Harassowitz.

Möller, C./Schmitt, G. (1976). *Die Siedlungen Palästinas nach Flavius Josephus.* Wiesbaden: L. Reichert.

Negev, A. (1966). 'The Date of the Petra-Gaza Road'. *Palestine Exploration Quarterly* 98: 89–98.

—— (1969). 'Seal-Impressions from Tomb 107 at Kurnub (Mampsis)'. *Israel Exploration Journal* 19: 89–106.

PARKER, S. T. (2006). *The Roman Frontier in Central Jordan: Final Report on the Limes Arabicus Project, 1980–1989*. 2 vols. Washington: Dumbarton Oaks.

RABAN, A. (ed.) (1985). *Harbour Archaeology. Proceedings of the First International Workshops on Mediterranean Harbours, Caesarea Maritima*. Oxford: B.A.R.

—— and HOLUM, K. (eds) (1996). *Caesarea Maritima: A Retrospective After Two Millennia*. Leiden: Brill.

REES, B. R. (1968). 'Theophanes of Hermopolis Magna'. *Bull. John Rylands Library* 51: 164–183.

ROBERTS, C. H. (1952). 'The Archive of Theophanes', in *Catalogue of the Greek and Latin Papyri in the John Rylands Library*, vol. 4, ed. C. H. Roberts and E. G. Turner. Manchester: University Press, 104–6.

ROLL, I. (1983). 'The Roman Road System in Judaea'. *The Jerusalem Cathedra* 3: 136–61.

—— (1996). 'Roman Roads to Caesarea Maritima', in *Caesarea Maritima: A Retrospective After Two Millennia*, ed. A. Raban and K. Holum. Leiden: Brill, 549–58.

—— (2000). 'Roman Milestones in the Vicinity of Aphek-Antipatris', in *Aphek-Antipatris I. Excavation of Areas A and B. The 1972–1976 Seasons*, ed. Moshe Kochavi et al. Tel Aviv: Emery and Claire Yass Publications in Archaeology, 39–46.

—— and AYALON, E. (1986). 'Roman Roads in Western Samaria'. *Palestine Exploration Quarterly* 118:113–134.

—— (1989). *Apollonia and Southern Sharon: Model of a Coastal City and its Hinterland* [Hebr]. Tel Aviv: Hakibbutz Hameuchad Publishing House.

ROLL, I./TAL, O. (1999). *Apollonia-Arsuf: Final Report of the Excavations I*. Tel Aviv: Emery and Claire Yass Publications in Archaeology.

SARTRE, M. (1985). *Bostra, des origines à l'Islam*. Paris: Geuthner.

SCHÜRER, E. (1973). *The History of the Jewish People in the Age of Jesus Christ*, vol. 1, ed. G. Vermes and F. Millar. Edinburgh: T.&T. Clark Ltd.

SHATZMAN, I. (1983). 'The Beginning of the Roman Defensive System in Judaea'. *American Journal of Ancient History* 8: 130–160.

—— (1991). *The Armies of the Hasmonaeans and Herod: From Hellenistic to Roman Frameworks*. Tübingen: Mohr-Siebeck.

TALBERT, R. (ed.) (2000). *The Barrington Atlas of the Greek and Roman World*. Princeton: Princeton University Press.

THOMSEN, P. (1917). 'Die römischen Meilensteine der Provinzen Syria, Arabia und Palaestina'. *Zeitschrift des deutschen Palästina-Vereins* 40: 1–103.

TSAFRIR, Y./DI SEGNI, L./GREEN, J. (1994). *Tabula Imperii Romani: Iudaea-Palaestina: Maps and Gazetteer*. Jerusalem: Israel Academy of Sciences and Humanities.

VANN, R. L. (ed.) (1992). *Caesarea Papers 1: Straton's Tower, Herod's Harbour, and Roman and Byzantine Caesarea*. Ann Arbor: University of Michigan.

VERMEULE, C. C. (1959–60). 'Hellenistic and Roman Cuirassed Statues'. *Berytus* 13: 1–82.

WHITTAKER, C. R. (1994). *Frontiers of the Roman Empire: A Social and Economic Study*. Baltimore: Johns Hopkins University Press.

—— (2004). *Rome and its Frontiers: The Dynamics of Empire*. London: Routledge.

WILKINSON, J. (1975). 'The Way from Jerusalem to Jericho'. *Biblical Archaeologist* 38: 10–24.

WILSON, C. W. (1880–84). *Picturesque Palestine, Sinai and Egypt*. 4 vols. London: Virtue & Co.

CHAPTER 9

URBANIZATION

JÜRGEN K. ZANGENBERG
DIANNE VAN DE ZANDE

1. THE BEGINNINGS OF URBANIZATION IN THE LAND OF ISRAEL

For many periods of its history, the Near East, including Palestine, was one of the most densely urbanized regions of the ancient Mediterranean. Urban centres existed especially along the Levantine coast and in the nearby fertile plains. The central hill country, on the other hand, was usually less densely built up. At the end of the Persian period, that is, in the fourth century BCE, important urban centres existed at, for example, Ashqelon, Ashdod, Dor, and Acco on the coast, and at Samaria in the hinterland. In most of these cities, Jews were in the minority. The only predominately Jewish city was Jerusalem; its size, however, did not match that of the coastal centres (Finkelstein 2008).

Phoenicians dominated the coastal strip and controlled trade posts in the hinterland (for instance, Tel Anafa in the Galilee). Through their mobility (maritime trade and colonies), the Phoenicians had introduced Western imports and Western culture since the seventh or sixth century BCE at the latest (Luke 2003; Waldbaum 1997; Wenning 1981). Furthermore, Greek colonies had existed along the coast since the seventh century BCE, and exerted a cultural influence that was picked up by local elites, such as the upper class of Persian-period Samaria, as welcome vehicles to express loyalty and status. As far as our scant evidence allows us to determine, local Jewish elites in Persian-period Jerusalem did not employ

Greek material culture to any large extent. Smaller Palestinian inland settlements mostly continued late Iron Age traditions of urban layout and material culture.

2. THE HELLENISTIC PERIOD: MECHANISMS OF URBANIZATION

From the third century BCE onwards, Palestine was incorporated first into the Ptolemaic and then into the Seleucid Empire: large, trans-regional and multi-ethnic political entities with a centralized government partly based on Greek elites and Greek forms of governance and culture, under rulers who traced their origins and political legitimacy back to the descendants of Alexander the Great. Although the heyday of the classical independent *polis*-state was over with the establishment of these Hellenistic territorial empires, much of its ideological and formal elements were deliberately continued by these rulers and exported into regions which had not had any connection to Greek culture before that time. Land was distributed and settled by colonists such as the *kleruchoi* (military settlers) or citizens from Greek cities.

In Palestine a major phase of urbanization and urban transformation began after the conquests of Alexander the Great (Barghouti 1982; Sartre 2005), a process that was continued by the Romans (Kennedy 1999; Millar 1993). The general settlement pattern shifted profoundly as hilltop *tell* sites, a feature that had dominated the landscape for millennia, were gradually abandoned or reduced to small villages, while large numbers of dispersed settlements started to appear in the plains and in previously unoccupied hilly areas during the late Persian and early Hellenistic periods. Motivations for founding such settlements varied, ranging from the wish to establish a residential centre, to the attempt to integrate recent territorial acquisitions, securing them militarily or transforming them ethnically.

Many features of urban culture remained largely unaltered over many centuries. Urban culture, where it existed, was shaped by Hellenistic architecture, legal structures, and material culture. It was often the indigenous local elites who were the most active recipients and promoters of Hellenism, which, eventually, was to affect all indigenous cultures of the region, including Judaism. At least with regard to Palestine, the number of foreign inhabitants generally remained low and was certainly not sufficient to account for the slow, but steady transformation of Palestinian society towards Hellenism. Hellenism did not level out regional differences, it provided new opportunities of expression on the basis of a new architectural, decorative, and artistic 'language' (on the problem see, e.g. Sartre 2005: 274–96).

2.1 Urban Life

Despite the many differences, there were certain elements common to basically all regions of the Hellenistic world, the most important being the city, the Greek *polis* or Latin *civitas*. To be a 'city' had territorial, architectural, legal, and social implications. Cities functioned as the prime place where non-Greeks came into contact with the correct use of the Greek language, Greek customs, and Greek education, familiarity with which was crucial for anybody who wanted to distinguish himself from a more local background, become a full citizen, and move up the social ladder to be finally accepted as a peer among the 'Greek' cultural elite. At the same time, only the city offered those institutions that helped preserve, cultivate, and refine one's cultural competence and skills: schools, *gymnasia*, and theatres. Common cults, amongst them the ruler cult, the cult of the city founder or the veneration of a particular city deity, as well as local calendars and festivals greatly contributed to the creation of a 'civic identity' and a 'civic consciousness'.

This status was mainly expressed in the city's legal and administrative institutions (Sartre 2005: 156–62). Before the Hellenistic age use of the public sphere was an almost exclusive privilege of the king. Now citizens, notables, officials, artists, and philosophers could express themselves in the public sphere as well. Their ambitions took shape in the form of buildings, inscriptions, and statues. The competition of oligarchic, urban elites for reputation within the city, and of a particular city over against other cities, created an atmosphere of actively donating and sponsoring building projects. Many monumental buildings were financed by citizens who were, in turn, honoured with public recognition and lasting memory through public recommendations and dedicatory inscriptions.

Crucial for any city was a certain degree of internal self-government. Cities entered diplomatic relations with each other and with territorial and foreign rulers. Although the relationship between the territorial government and local institutions was complex and regionally diverse, most Hellenistic rulers were careful not to violate the 'freedom' of a city and, as far as possible, exerted their power indirectly, for example through *euergetism* and treaties with representatives of cities. On the other hand, cities often turned to the king when they felt abused by intermediate officials such as governors, and kings tended to respond swiftly, mostly in favour of the cities. Cities returned such favours by expressing their loyalty to the emperor through dedications and games in honour of the ruler.

Formally, relations between cities and rulers were not based on an equal share of mutual rights and obligations. Any freedom and prosperity that a city enjoyed resulted from the magnanimity of the ruler, who granted concessions on the basis of the city's loyal behaviour towards him, concessions which could be revoked at any time. If burdens imposed by a ruler became too hard, cities could always desert him and side with potential usurpers. Since cities were the centres of economic power within any Hellenistic kingdom, such threats had to be taken seriously.

However, more often than not such a rebellion turned out to be futile, in which case the city had to face the wrath of the ruler it tried to dispose of. Punishment could take many different forms, ranging from the revocation of privileges (for instance taxation, urban status), to the loss of freedom for its citizens or certain groups amongst them, the confiscation of property and, not infrequently, the city's ultimate destruction.

While the newly founded urban centres of the Levant imitated the ideology of the classical Greek *polis*, they were not simple copies of it. By no means does the title *polis* imply that all of the inhabitants of an eastern city, or even the majority, would be ethnic Greeks. Furthermore, not all inhabitants of a *polis* were full citizens and entitled to fully participate in political life. Women, children, slaves, foreign residents, and guests were protected by the city laws, but remained excluded from decision-making processes as well as from many aspects of public life. The Romans later distinguished between two kinds of cities: foreign cities (*peregrini*) in the provinces, which were allowed to maintain their own traditional rights and privileges, and cities that were founded as, or elevated to, the status of *municipium* or *colonia*, whose institutions and legal conditions more or less reflected those of Rome itself (Jacques/Scheid 1998: 240 and 244–50 on cities of peregrine status, *ibid*. 251–66 on communities with Roman legal status; on settlements without the status of a city, such as towns and villages, see below). Until the first *coloniae* were founded in Palestine after the First Jewish Revolt (66–73 CE), cities were governed according to indigenous legal conditions. Before 212 CE, when Caracalla in his *Constitutio Antoniniana* granted all free–born inhabitants of Roman provinces Roman citizenship, very few inhabitants of Palestine had enjoyed that privileged status.

2.2 Religious Life

Religion was part of the daily life of cities. Apart from their general sacred nature, cities were the home of various, often very substantial, temples and sanctuaries, and the stage for all sorts of religious activities (sacrifices, processions, etc.) both in the public and private spheres. Wayside shrines and altars of neighbourhood corporations, guilds, and other cultic associations made the divine present everywhere (Jacobs 2000). Each house in a city was considered sacred space, protected by the ancestral spirits and household gods. Each city usually had a special relationship to a tutelary god or goddess: in the Levant it was often a traditional deity in Hellenized garb (Zeus, Dionysos, Aphrodite). The city's prosperity was personified by its *Tyche* or *Fortuna*. Rulers received cultic honours in various ways. Cities proclaimed themselves on coins or other expressions of official title as, for example, 'holy and inviolable' (Geiger 1990; Sartre 2005: 184f). The religious character of cities was also apparent in numerous local and regional festivals for which the city provided the social context: celebrations connected to the history of the city (founding day), the rulers, the seasons, the army, or certain deities (cf. M. A.Z. 1:3). Despite all religious implications of urban culture, cities provided room for many different cultic activities that did not necessarily need official recognition, including Judaism (see below).

The city's foundation itself was considered a sacred act. Any 'foundation'—regardless of how 'new' it actually was—gave the ruler the opportunity to promote himself as the god-like 'founder hero' (*heros ktistes*), benefactor, and promoter of refined culture. Often a founding myth was added that served as the unifying focus of civic pride and identity. As a result, many cities started to count their years from their 'foundation' and adopted the name of their founder (cf. the numerous cities named after Seleukos, Antiochos, or Ptolemaios, and both the Ptolemaic and Seleucid dynasties' reference to the great hero and model Alexander the Great in Pella).

2.3 Urban Planning and Public Institutions

The foundation of a city did not necessarily imply a totally new creation at a place that was previously uninhabited. Often new cities were founded close to existing settlements that could subsequently be integrated into the new entity (for example, Mabartha and Neapolis). Existing cities could also be enlarged by bringing in new settlers (colonists, veterans), several settlements could be combined into one new city, or the 'foundation' of a city could merely consist in elevating its status.

Urban life and civil consciousness were directly linked to the visible appearance of a city (Ball 2000: 248–306; Sartre 2005: 168–83; Sperber 1998). Urbanization undertaken by Near Eastern Hellenistic rulers featured a widespread use of monumental architecture which included an urban layout with colonnaded streets, temples of different forms and traditions, architectural styles and decoration, baths and *nymphaea*, etc.

In the Hellenistic period, many cities were protected by strong walls (e.g. Dor, Marissa, the acropolis at Samaria, the large temple-city on Mount Gerizim under the Ptolemies, and Jerusalem under the Hasmoneans), and could only be accessed through often impressively decorated gates. In the Roman period, many cities were without defences or existing walls were not enlarged until the political situation called for renewed fortification, for example during the latter third century CE. (Caesarea Maritima, Neapolis, Tiberias, Ashdod, Gaza, Bet Shean in the Roman period; cf. Sperber 1998: 117–27).

Characteristic for Hellenistic city foundations, but rarely fully adopted in the Levant, was the so-called 'Hippodamian' ('checkerboard') system of organizing urban space, streets, and buildings. A regular set-up of broad, parallel axes and perpendicular streets divided the city into rectangular blocks (Sperber 1998: 9–57). Because of topographical restraints, few Palestinian cities fully reflect the

Hippodamian ideal. A good example of this phenomenon is Caesarea Maritima. The main streets are often as regularly built as the local topography and conditions permitted, whereas secondary streets were more irregular (Sperber 1998: 101–16). Backstreets were often used as additional workspace by artisans.

Markets (*agora/forum*) served as commercial spaces and public places of communication and display (Segal 1997: 55–81), and constituted the public heart of a city. Markets could not be opened without official permission. Apart from fresh produce and common goods usually marketed close to their places of origin, markets in larger cities were also ideal places to obtain products from more distant locales (on urban and village markets, see Lapin 2001: 123–52; Rosenfeld/Menirav 2005). Since markets promised high profits through taxes and levies, local authorities supervised permits, quality of produce, and prices. The most important market official was the *agoranomos* or *astynomos*, who is frequently mentioned in rabbinic sources (Sperber 1998: 32–47).

Markets could be organized around large open spaces surrounded by colonnades with buildings containing shops and stalls or booths between the columns (Sperber 1998: 9); or they could be located along streets lined with shops and mixed with residential units (Sperber 1998: 9: Palladius-Street in Scythopolis). The open space was often paved, porches offered traders and passengers some shade, and the colonnaded streets were embellished with statues and/or inscriptions (on colonnaded streets see Segal 1997: 5–53; on the 'sculptural environment' of Roman Palestine and rabbinic reactions towards it, see Eliav 2002; *idem* 2008; Eliav/Friedland/Herbert 2008 in general; Oppenheimer 2008; Pollini 2008; Sartre 2008). Food and meat markets (*macellum*) sometimes formed individual architectural units (e.g. at Gerasa).

A large number of services were available at and around the markets. Donkeydrivers and porters were ready to carry goods home (Sperber 1998: 15). Craftsmen such as potters, basket makers, fullers, wine merchants, or carpenters, often organized in guilds, were concentrated in special quarters (y. M.Q. 2:4, 81b; Sperber 1998: 108). Taverns, food-shops, and pubs were never far from crowded markets and main streets, and many of them also offered the services of prostitutes. Brothels were not far either. Market days often had religious undertones, since they sometimes coincided with pagan festivals or were officially dedicated to a deity (sometimes taxes were even lifted on such days, or the revenue was donated to a charity), making it difficult, but not impossible for Torah observant Jews to participate (Graf 2002: 448–50; Veltri 2000).

Since no city can survive without water, large water storage facilities had to be built within the city walls. The transportation of water to the city was secured through aqueducts, with the earliest post-Iron Age aqueducts from Palestine dating to the Hasmonean period (Amit/Patrich/Hirschfeld, eds. 2002; Sperber 1998: 128–48). Because of the eminent significance of water, its distribution inside the city was supervised by special officials. The main aqueducts usually conducted water to large, lavishly decorated public fountains (*nymphaea*) and to small water fountains further along the road (Segal 1997: 151–68; Sperber 1998: 133–5).

At least in the Roman period, markets, temples, private homes, latrines, and especially public and private baths of larger cities were connected to the freshwater and sewage system. On the basis of bathhouses, often located near the markets, rabbis contemplated whether and to what extent pious Jews should abstain from certain forms of public life (Eliav 2000; Jacobs 1998b: 219–311; Sperber 1998: 58–72; on bathhouses in Palestine see Hoss 2005). Rabbinic sources reflect many aspects of Hellenistic and Roman bathing culture, for example technical details (heating, hot and cold baths), decoration, personnel (vendors, attendants, anointers), available services (massages, exercises), the use of bathing utensils (*strigilis*, soap-oil, unguents), and bathing customs (see also Eliav in this volume). Rabbinic texts on bathing practices are valuable documents showing the participation of rabbinic circles in this common practice and way of life of Hellenistic and Roman society. Rabbinic bathhouse stories even share many literary aspects with similar Roman and Christian narratives (e.g. anecdotes about jokes in baths; fending off demons; sitting in a bath together with heretics; moralizing anecdotes; cf. Jacobs 1998a: 309–11).

Some aspects of ancient bathing culture, however, are rarely or never mentioned in rabbinic texts: only indirect hints can be found on prostitution, and no homo-erotic undertones appear. Especially noteworthy is the silence about medical services that were available in many baths (see Hammat Gader, or a Jewish synagogue in the *palaestra* of the bath-gymnasium complex in Sardis). Just like ordinary Romans, Jews would have visited the bathhouses late in the afternoon. Nowhere do we find the request to set up a special 'Jewish' set of bathing regulations as opposed to the usual pagan ones. As far as baths are concerned, rabbinic standards of decency obviously did not differ much from commonly accepted ones (see the criterion of 'modesty': Derekh Eretz Zuta 7:2; T. Ber. 2:20 on the prohibition on greeting someone in a room where people wander around undressed). Baths were an integral part of the civic life in antiquity, and they were used in that function by rabbis just as by any other ancient person.

Another typical feature of urban life was the theatre (see also the chapter by Weiss in this volume). Ever since Herod first introduced theatres, hippodromes, and *stadia* (for example in Damascus, Sidon, Jerusalem, Caesarea Maritima, and Jericho), they were part of the urban environment of Palestine (Fiensy 1991; Jacobs 1998b; Segal 1995). After the First Jewish Revolt, the number of theatres rose dramatically (Jacobs 1998b: 328). Theatres were used for public performances of various kinds, although not necessarily for bringing complete plays to stage. Hippodromes and *stadia* were used for chariot and horse races and for running and related athletic contests (Weiss 1999; on Caesarea Maritima see Patrich 2002). Amphitheatres, which were present in Palestine from the second century CE only, were used for gladiatorial combats or animal baiting.

Although theatres and similar buildings would have been a familiar sight to any Jew living in a larger town or city, rabbinic attitudes were ambiguous because of the kind of performances that could be viewed in these institutions (y. A.Z. 1:7, 40a; Gen.R. 80:1). Apart from pointing to the waste of time involved in attending a play, rabbis targeted the often indirect or open pagan undertones of many performances. Nevertheless, theatres were important centres of public life and missing a show at the theatre meant missing meeting people or excluding oneself from urban society. Because of their bloody nature, gladiatorial combats were often condemned, a view with which the rabbis agreed not only with Christians, but also with many philosophically inspired pagans (Jacobs 1998b: 333–4 and 346–7). On the other hand, rabbinic literature seems to provide evidence for Jewish gladiators (see, e.g. Weiss 1999: 47–8). We must assume that with or without rabbinical consent, Jewish attendance at these urban forms of entertainment and socializing was frequent (Weiss 1999: 43–9).

2.4 Administrative Organization

The proper functioning of public life and the maintenance of public order were guaranteed by various officials who usually belonged to the local elite (on the characteristics and functions of that elite, see Jacques/Scheid 1998: 275–93). The public administration was housed in various buildings such as the city council, the meeting place of the convention, and the houses of the leading magistrates, high priests, and city officials. Archives for keeping tax or birth records supported the local administration. As local officials were authorized to incarcerate culprits, almost every city had a prison (Sperber 1998: 76f). Both public and private business (lawsuits, negotiations, leisure) was carried out in the *basilica*, a large, often lavishly decorated, multi-purpose hall that functioned as an indoor forum with additional administrative rooms (Schwartz 1998: 158–61; Sperber 1998: 73–7; cf. T. Toh 7:12–14).

Because of the high importance of trade for the city, the surrounding country-side, and the territorial government (levies, customs, and taxes), markets were strictly controlled by special officials (*agoranomoi*; see page 170 above). Temples also often had their own officials who made sure that the specific laws and practices of the cult were followed. The same applies to *gymnasia* or musical *collegia* which played an important role during festivals and processions. City officials were often organized in groups and mostly chosen by lot. Some of their tasks were considered public services, and expenses were expected to be paid by the person who fulfilled the position (*leitourgiai*). The sponsor's compensation was his public recognition. Ordinary citizens contributed to the upkeep of their city by paying fees.

Many cities had kept the right to mint their own coins. Others, such as Sepphoris (66 CE) or Tiberias (around 100 CE) received that right from Rome (Meshorer 1985: 33–5; Sigismund 2007). The right to mint coins always had to be granted by the territorial authorities (the Roman emperors or the Roman Empire as such) and therefore was a special token of loyalty (Chancey 2004). At the end of Emperor Gallienus' reign in the second half of the third century, money in the Roman Empire had lost so much of its value that coinage had to be standardized and city coins disappeared. On the other hand, cities were subjected to a complex and variable system of taxation by the central government (Jacques/Scheid 1998: 245–6; Sartre 2005: 183–8 on 'civic competition'). Apart from these external duties, cities had the right to levy their own taxes, grant privileges, and demand services (Jacques/Scheid 1998: 283–6).

A city's income was mostly spent on public services, such as paying officials, funding public infrastructure and buildings, legislature and jurisdiction, defence, police, public grain supply, or maintaining diplomatic relations with the ruler(s) and other cities. Tax exemption was not an instrument of social policy, but more a reward for distinguished benefactors' extraordinary efforts on behalf of the community. The administration of a city's income and expenses was the responsibility of the treasurers. Temples, which employed their own officials and presented a crucial element of urban life, were also important centres of financial activity. They functioned as banks and owners of large properties, whose revenues were distributed among the cultic personnel or lent out to be invested.

Of course, considerable differences existed between cities with respect to their economic structure. Cities on major trade arteries, that is, those which were located at the sea coast or close to interregional highways, were less dependent on agriculture, and could generate large revenues from the capital flow and the production and transport of goods. Agricultural cities, mostly located in the hinterland, had less opportunity to market their goods and largely depended on income from agriculture, the resources of which were often concentrated in the hands of a few landowners.

In the Hellenistic period, when the Palestinian coastal cities underwent major transformation (Ptolemais, Jaffa, Ascalon, Gaza), a major boost in urbanization took place in the Transjordan region. From the early third century BCE onwards, archaeological evidence shows that a number of cities were founded at, or next to, existing indigenous settlements (e.g. Pella, Dion, Gadara, Gerasa, Philadelphia, as well as Philotheria on the Sea of Galilee under the Ptolemies; Scythopolis under the Seleucids; cf. Ball 2000: 181–97). The purpose of these new foundations was to channel trade and increase income (coastal cities) and, as far as Transjordan is concerned, to secure strategically important territory. The first wave of urbanization therefore affected only the flanks of Jewish Palestine, the coast, and Transjordan, territories that at the beginning were not densely populated by Jews. Only in the following phase of Hasmonean expansion did urbanization take root in Judaea with the successive integration of urban centres into a generally less urbanized central region.

3. Urbanization under Indigenous Jewish Rulers

Ironically, while the Maccabean uprising (second century BCE) was set off to stem the tide of Hellenism, the resulting Hasmonean dynasty more and more turned into the main factor paving the ground for the development of a specific Jewish-Palestinian version of Hellenism. Under the Hasmoneans, urbanization mainly proceeded in the context of territorial expansion, as many Greek and Graeco-Phoenician cities in the coastal plain, the fertile valleys (e.g. Scythopolis), and in Transjordan were incorporated into the Hasmonean territory, and Jewish settlements were established there. The fact that urban centres of Hellenism now existed within territories under Jewish domination had profound effects on Judaism. Increasingly, elements of Graeco-Roman culture appeared in Judaea (architecture and objects), although less frequently than in later periods, for example under Herod. The only 'city' under Hasmonean rule that was entirely Jewish in character was Jerusalem. Although probably not a *polis* in the formal sense, Jerusalem became the main focal point of a 'Palestinian-Jewish' version of urbanism that came to flourish under Herod.

The Hasmonean policy of urbanization through conquest had another effect that should not be underestimated. The now greater proximity of a large number of people of 'foreign' culture triggered the opposition of traditional circles against the rulers and those members of the indigenous elite who embraced the 'new fashions'. While this opposition was not a unified movement, it nevertheless shared some characteristic traits. It was inspired by indigenous, traditional values; it stressed the religiously motivated identity and way of life over against that of the 'foreigners'; and it was often fuelled by xenophobia and the fear of losing out economically. These motivations could easily go hand in hand with internal rivalries among the elite itself, but also with the structural imbalance between city-elites and dependent villagers. In that respect, Jewish anti-Hellenistic and anti-urban opposition is not very different from what we can detect—sometimes with a much smaller textual basis—for example in Egypt (Blasius 2002; Blasius/Schipper, eds. 2002). What remained was an atmosphere of distrust and alienation between some Jewish circles and their Hellenized elites, and a Jewish population that was divided about the blessings and curses of Hellenism and the increasing urbanization of their country.

The arrival of the Roman general Pompey brought an end to Hasmonean expansion and the 'liberation' of many non-Jewish cities, thereby, among other things, creating the Decapolis (Ball 2000: 181–97; Isaac 1990: 152; *idem* 1992: 336–40). These cities expressed their gratitude to the Roman general by beginning their calendar with the year of liberation ('Pompeian year'). Although the governor of the newly created Provincia Syria exerted military control, Palestine remained under self-governance, first under the last Hasmoneans, then—as the chaos of the Roman civil war came to an end—under Herod, King of the Jews and *socius et amicus populi Romani*.

Under the *Pax Augusta*, the long rule of Herod initiated an unprecedented wave of political stability, economic recovery, and of urbanization, stimulated by Herod's own visionary initiative, and a competitive atmosphere among eastern Mediterranean client kings, in which Herod participated (Isaac 1992: 340–2; Richardson 1999). Herod was part of a world that used building projects as prime expressions of one's loyalty toward the emperor and as documents of the ideal ruler's benevolence toward his subjects and the prestige of his royal house. The political circumstances, and Herod's own aspirations, required that he acted as the ruler of both Jews and non-Jews in his territory. He apparently respected the feelings of his Jewish subjects as far as possible and refrained from using human images in his Judaean building projects, thereby contributing to the development of a distinctive Jewish material culture, from the Hasmonean period to the typical 'Herodian' style.

Outside of the predominately Jewish areas, Herod acted like any other Hellenistic king. He founded cities, invested huge amounts of money in their infrastructure (e.g. harbours), and initiated the integration of his territory into the Roman world (see Richardson 1999: 197–202; Sartre 2005: 153–56). The influx of Graeco-Roman culture was especially visible in Herod's new foundation, Caesarea Maritima, which was built with very innovative techniques and constituted the economic centre and pagan capital, as well as the most cosmopolitan place of his realm (Richardson 2002: 104–28; Sartre 2005: 201–2), but also in his other, less researched new cities such as Sebaste and Antipatris (see also Zangenberg 2008: 31–4).

Unfortunately, it is difficult to know how Herod's cities were internally organized. What we do know suggests that the king followed Hellenistic models. Herod's cosmopolitanism also introduced a number of technological innovations to Palestine such as hippodromes, theatres, domed cupolas, and the latest fashion in wall painting. The high degree of integration within the eastern Roman Empire made it also possible to invite foreign architects and artisans to carry out Herod's ideas.

After Herod's death his kingdom was divided amongst his sons, who continued their father's policy of urbanization on a smaller territorial scale and in regions that were until then little affected by urbanism. Antipas transformed the Galilee by founding Tiberias and massively investing in Sepphoris, and Peraea by founding Livias on the spot of an indigenous village (Jensen 2006: 126–86). Philippus followed his father's example by founding Julias on or near today's et-Tell, just east of where the Jordan flows into the Sea of Galilee, and by integrating little urbanized territories in the Hauran and Ituraea.

4. THE ROMAN PERIOD

When the Romans, themselves deeply Hellenized, incorporated the Near East into the Roman Empire, they made extensive use of existing Hellenistic structures, both material and administrative (Richardson 2004: 5). Direct Roman rule, which began in Judaea under governors succeeding Herod's incapable son, Archelaos, who were subordinate to the *legatus Syriae*, was subsequently introduced in regions formerly ruled by Antipas and Philippus, and did not profoundly change this situation. Herod's cities developed and flourished, but antagonism between Jewish and non-Jewish inhabitants grew continuously. Jews and non-Jews increasingly mistrusted each other and quarrelled about religious privileges and political influence. The governors were unable, or unwilling, to remedy the situation and prevented the development of an urban Jewish elite in the Hellenized cities of Palestine, an elite which emerged amongst the urban Jewish communities in the Diaspora under the protective edicts issued by Julius Caesar. For northern Palestine, the transformation of Berytos (between 27 and 14 BCE) and of Ptolemais (in 52/54 CE) into Roman *coloniae* brought about massive territorial changes at the cost of the indigenous—often Jewish—population, and provides a good example of how urbanization could contribute to the alienation of an indigenous rural population (Berlin 2002: 57–73; Berlin/Overman 2002; Isaac 1992: 318–21 and 342–4 on Berytos and 322–23 on Ptolemais; MacMullen 2000: 1–29; Sartre 2005: 155; on colonization in general see Gosden 2004; Jacques/Scheid 1998: 259–63).

The outbreak of the First Jewish Revolt dramatically halted the process of population growth that had characterized the preceding decennia (Leibner 2006). The war devastated the parts of the region populated by Jews, left the Temple destroyed, and Jewish society uprooted. A vast number of Jews were either killed or deported. Many towns and villages, especially in the predominately Jewish hill country, were destroyed, the most famous example being Jerusalem, whereas the more cosmopolitan cities in the coastal plain, such as Caesarea Maritima, Ascalon, and Ptolemais were more or less left unharmed. They were used by the Romans as bridgeheads and supply centres for the invading army. This was also the case with the Hellenized cities of the former Decapolis, now integrated into Syria, and with inland cities if they had remained loyal to Rome. Sepphoris, whose population was acquainted with the role of governmental centre of the Galilee and had not joined the revolt, received the status of *polis* in 67/68 CE. Sepphoris' elevation in status is documented by the issuing of a coin bearing the name *eirenopolis*, 'City of Peace' (Sartre 2005: 154).

A new period of urbanization began after the First Jewish Revolt, but it was now dictated by external goals and funded by foreign resources. Immediately after the war Vespasian established military colonies at strategic locations between Mount Gerizim and Mount Ebal in central Samaria (Flavia Neapolis: Pliny, Natural History 5.14.69; Justinus, 1 Apologia 1.1.1) and between Jerusalem and the coast (Emmaus: Josephus, Bell. 7.217), Joppa received the epithet *Flavia* (Schürer et al. 1979, vol. 2: 113–4; Isaac 1990: 154–5; idem. 1992: 344–9). Whereas the period of massive urbanization under Herod was motivated by internal factors, urbanization after 70 CE followed external reasons: it can be seen as a vigorous attempt by the Roman government to integrate the region of Syria-Palestine into the eastern part of the Roman Empire.

Based on a massive exchange of certain parts of the population (killed and enslaved Jews were replaced by Roman veterans and colonists) and internal population movements (remaining Jews resettled in the Galilee and the south, Jerusalem was taken over by the Tenth Legion), Roman policy after 70 CE was led by strategic considerations to safeguard the vital land connection between Egypt and Mesopotamia, to colonize the region, and to prevent the native population from ever raising their arms again.

Although the new cities were Roman foundations, almost all aspects of urbanization that the Romans used had already been introduced to the region under Herod. Most obvious were the building activities connected with the Roman military presence: roads were built or repaired (the earliest milestones are dated to around 70 CE), camps and posts of army units appear, and the Sixth Legion was stationed at Legio under Trajan (Isaac 1992: 427–35; see also Isaac in this volume). On the other hand, signs of Jewish recovery remain scant for a couple of decades.

The second and third centuries, especially the period of Hadrian (Isaac 1992: 352–9) and the Severans (Isaac 1992: 359–61) constituted the climax of urbanization before the Byzantine period. Cities such as Caesarea Maritima, Bet Shean, and Gerasa were promoted in status (*colonia*) and extensively enlarged and embellished. Jerusalem, too, became a Roman *colonia* with a population of predominately military settlers and the pagan name 'Aelia Capitolina'. The whole process was only briefly interrupted by the Bar Kokhba revolt between 132 and 135, the second and last attempt by Palestinian Jews to regain freedom from Roman occupation and to revert the growing cultural domination by foreigners (Isaac 1992: 323–5 and 352–9; Sartre 2005: 155–6 and 167).

In the second century CE, a new building type, the amphitheatre, was introduced (Neapolis, Scythopolis; see Weiss 1998: 89–91; see also Weiss in this volume). A growing number of Palestinian cities changed their name or added pagan elements to it (Sepphoris, Lydda, Bet Guvrin, Tiberias), and a pagan presence became more and more visible. The quiet years of the second and early third centuries brought enough capital to Palestine to renovate buildings and to refurbish entire cities. Under the Severans, Sebaste and, shortly afterwards, also Neapolis were embellished with new buildings. In Sebaste, for example, the old Herodian forum and other monumental buildings were extensively renovated.

In the third and fourth century recognizably Jewish art and architecture re-emerged, interestingly not as a simple continuation along the sober Herodian lines of aniconic, geometrical, or floral decorations uniquely adapted from late Hellenistic models, but much more Graeco-Roman in character. A good example of the new style is the cemetery of Bet She'arim, where the sarcophagi contained decorations with popularized forms of animals (lions), angels (Nike), and mythological motifs. The openness to iconic art, and the creative and active adaptation of pagan imagery prepared the way for synagogue art of the fourth to sixth centuries.

5. THE RELATIONSHIP BETWEEN CITY AND COUNTRYSIDE

Since much of the Hellenistic and Roman presence was concentrated in the larger towns and cities, and since these urban sites have often been better preserved and documented than the rural areas, the majority of available data comes from urban contexts. Scholarly interest in the character and development of the Roman city in relation to the countryside has been influenced by Marxism, by Weber's *consumer city* model and Finley's adaptation of it (Weber 1966 and 1968; Finley 1999), and by the World Systems approach of Immanuel Wallerstein (Wallerstein 1974–1989, discussed for example by Woolf 1997), who, in turn, drew on the French *Annales School* tradition and notably on Fernand Braudel's work (Braudel 1972–1974). Wallerstein's approach led to an image of the Roman world in accordance with the core and periphery model: a system of economic and cultural cores surrounded by peripheral regions.

Based on sociological models, the economic dependency between town and countryside, as well as the cultural superiority of the urban environment has been a recurring issue of studies of the Roman Empire and its provinces. This scheme has also been utilized for understanding particular regions, for example the agricultural and economic development of the Negev in the Byzantine period, which included an expansion of the settlement area and large agricultural systems with terraced wadis (on this model see in general Lapin 2001).

Through continuous financial support the Roman government encouraged the defence of the border regions by the establishment of agricultural settlements even beyond their natural capacity. Government support could prevent an economic crisis in years of drought, which might otherwise turn the poorer elements of the settled population into nomads in search of work. Such a situation would, in turn, have led to a lesser degree of governmental control (and of defence against Arab raids, an increasing phenomenon in the late Roman period). Municipal activities, government functions, economic affairs, and the cultural and intellectual life of the provinces – all revolved around the city. On the basis of the core-periphery model the city can be considered to have ruled the rural population.

Since the 1970s, and influenced by the social sciences, archaeologists have become increasingly aware of the importance of the landscape. The *longue durée* philosophy developed by Braudel was used by New Archaeology's field survey archaeology, and applied to regional research projects as a theoretical background. In addition to the physical landscape, the conceptual landscape has received growing attention (see, e.g. Horden/Purcell 2000). In the archaeology of the Near East, the development towards a 'landscape archaeology' meant first and foremost a re-direction of focus away from stratified *tells* and the urban, monumental environment to the lesser-known rural areas. This shift has resulted in the excavation of rural sites and studies of villages and small towns (for instance, Ben-Tor et al. 2003; Ben-Tor et al. 2005; Dar 1986; Grossman 1992; Hirschfeld 1997; Maeir/Dar/Safrai 2003; for general overviews see Schwartz 1986). Increasing attention has been paid to agricultural and industrial installations, dwelling houses, and material culture. This shift of focus has led to a much better understanding of the structures, activities, and lifestyles of the ordinary rural and agrarian peasants (Richardson 2004: 6).

Since cities and larger towns have dominated the historiography of the Mediterranean, they are also sometimes assumed to have dominated its landscape (Safrai 1994: 19). Most of the population, however, lived in provincial towns and villages of various sizes. During the first century CE small rural towns and villages increased both in number and in size. Similarly, the number of dwelling houses increased, covering a range of types and sizes (Richardson 2004: 25–6; cf. Hirschfeld 1995). The cultural transformation and Hellenization of smaller towns seems to have been much less influenced by Greek or Roman models. Although these models were gradually adopted, at least initially traditional influences played a larger role.

Town layout was similar to what we can detect in villages, without regular street axes or nifty monumental buildings (Sartre 2005: 167). The difference in size between Hellenistic cities and the larger traditional towns is significant, however: Aelia Capitolina or Scythopolis measured about 120 hectares, Caesarea Maritima 95 hectares and Sebaste approximately 65 hectares, whereas the towns of the Negev only measured between 4 and 17 hectares (Sartre 2005: 167).

In many ways, cities influenced life beyond their own confines. Every *polis* had a subordinate territory of varying size (*chora*), in which villages and farms existed. Graeco-Roman literature refers to three different types of settlement: the independent *polis*, the 'town' or agricultural village (*kome*), and the 'villa' or rural farmstead (*agros*) (Safrai 1994: 17–99; see Mark 6:56). Towns without the legal status of a *polis* were considered to be on the same level as villages whose inhabitants shared an inferior legal status. The city council and its officials usually exerted jurisdiction over the surrounding towns, villages, and farmsteads. In regions where such cities did not exist, smaller units were subsumed under a 'district' (*toparchia*). This district had an administrative centre which did not necessarily have to be a '*polis*' in the stricter, legal sense (cf. Herod's toparchies). Inhabitants of towns and villages could not gain Roman citizenship, since the citizenship of a city usually was an indispensable prerequisite (Jacques/Scheid 1998: 240).

The city and the rural countryside were connected in various ways. Citizens of cities could have property outside the city and have it administered through stewards (cf. Mark 12:1–12 and parallels). Produce from rural territories fed the inhabitants of the cities, was marketed in the city, and was taxed by the city. The city in turn supplied services (such as space, structures, and expertise for all sorts of legal, economic, and social activities) for its rural territory (Freyne 1997: 33).

The rural population was often less Hellenized than their urban counterparts, adding a certain cultural twist to an economic and social imbalance that had the potential to create instability and to spark unrest (discussed by scholars in connection with the conditions in the Galilee before the First Jewish Revolt; see Berlin/ Overman 2002; Freyne 2000: 86–113). The major factor in this asymmetrical relationship was that access to the most important resource, land and its revenue, was unequally distributed. This inequality was reflected in legal regulations and in the obligation to pay contributions and to lend often involuntary services to the urban administration. In that respect, inhabitants of the rural territories were bound to the cities and dependent on them (on the rural population in the Orient, see Jacques/Scheid 1998: 269). The occasional settlement of foreigners in a formerly rural or scantily inhabited territory (e.g. the foundation of Sebaste by Herod, and of Nicopolis and Neapolis under Vespasian) added to the traditional inequality between town and countryside. Despite all of this inequality and dependence, even towns and villages enjoyed a certain level of internal governance, often controlled by the city, but mostly exercised through traditional local elites such as clan heads or elders.

Irrespective of how unbalanced the relationship between city and countryside was at a given moment, it was nevertheless dynamic. Cities were always in danger of losing their status (e.g. Sebaste under Pertinax); important towns were upwardly mobile and could gain *polis*-status in the future. Hellenism spread to the countryside, and with it elements of urban culture that affected entire regions. Although this was a gradual process, people were mobile and distances short, so contact with, and knowledge of, urban culture was unavoidable. It is no wonder that eventually urban features became established in towns as well. In reality, the cultural boundaries between city and town were hardly as clear-cut as mere legal categories might suggest (Schwartz 1998: 204–6; more generally Hingley 2005; Whittaker 1997; Edwards 2007).

6. Rabbis and the City

Traditionally, scholarship assumed that there was an abysmal, everlasting, and fundamental separation between Jews and Hellenism in ancient Palestine (e.g. Feldman 1993). Hellenistic culture was frequently equated with paganism that was believed to have reached its clearest expression in the Greek city (Eliav 2002: 411–12, summarizing Lieberman 1994; Horsley 1996).

In rabbinic texts one can indeed find a whole range of attitudes towards the urban environment: reservation, curiosity, attraction, disgust, and a lot of pragmatism based on a centuries-long coexistence between Judaism and Hellenism in Palestine and the Diaspora (Zangenberg 2009). We may, therefore, ask how 'meaningful' certain fourth-century rabbis' presence in the cities actually was: perhaps late antique rabbis lived in the cities but were not precisely 'of them' (Schwartz 1998: 205). What one can *not* find, however, is a total rejection of urban culture on the assumption that the *polis* as such contradicts the rabbinic lifestyle. Roman and late antique cities provided enough space, both legally and politically, to let Jews practise their religion and maintain their identity (on diversity and toleration in the Mediterranean world, see Goodman 2007, esp. 122–60).

Such coexistence required a lot of compromise from rabbis due to their adherence to the biblical prohibitions of idolatry. Schwartz calls this compromise a spectacular act of (intentional) misinterpretation: rabbis allegedly defined pagan religiosity as consisting of cultic activity only; they affirmed and even extended the biblical prohibitions of idolatry, but in so doing declared the non-cultic religious aspects of urban culture acceptable (Schwartz 1998: 207–8). There may, therefore, have been a fundamental theoretical contradiction between pagan cultic practices and rabbinic observance, but 'on the ground' this *non licet* could hardly be maintained with equal rigour. The fact that rabbis and their co-religionists would constantly be confronted with expressions of paganism in urban environments did not prevent them from inhabiting cities. It could even be argued that this rabbinic pragmatism does not reflect a defensive and protective strategy but allowed them to live in cities, the very places where they could most easily accumulate wealth, social ties, and influence (Schwartz 1998: 208).

When village-based rabbis 'came to town', they did not enter an alien environment. At least from the third century CE onwards many rabbis lived in, or moved to, the cities. Sepphoris, Lydda, Joppa, Caesarea, and Tiberias were centres of Jewish learning. What we can see in the texts is a great amount of mobility of rabbis within Palestine (see also Hezser in this volume), and a familiarity with both the urban and the rural environment. Rabbis who resided and functioned in a rural context would also have been familiar with Hellenism and urban culture. There can be no doubt that rabbis were influenced by their environment and that their environment itself was in constant cultural, political, and social transformation.

Rabbis were probably attracted to cities because they promised a larger audience and constituted the nodal points of networks of trade, communication, patronage, and political power (Schwartz 1998: 205–6; Zangenberg/Attridge/Martin, eds. 2007). Nevertheless, rabbis did not belong to the urban elite of philosophers, officials, and lawyers who governed a *polis*: rather they formed and trained their own (alternative) elite which followed its own traditions and had its own clientele.

In a way, the rabbinic movement presented and promoted an alternative Jewish way of life *in* the city.

In towns and villages, on the other hand, rabbis may have constituted at least part of the local elite and possessed a certain political influence. They also functioned as judges in matters of civil law, as administrators, advisors, and occasionally governors of a town. In a rural context they may have acquired a much broader role and carried out tasks that, in an urban context, they were allowed to fulfil for their own adherents only (Lapin 2001; Levine 1989: 25–33). This situation would have been due to the pragmatic attitude of the Roman authorities, who respected *polis*-constitutions (that placed rabbis in a minority position), but kept traditional local structures outside of *poleis* basically intact (which allowed rabbis to continue fulfilling their role as local, indigenous elites). The second century CE family archives from the Judaean Desert demonstrate that Roman and Jewish courts existed side by side and that Jews could choose which tradition to follow in their legal transactions (Cotton 2004).

Urban culture enabled rabbis to express their views in new ways. Rabbis did not only describe and comment upon many features of Hellenized urban life, they also adopted many terms (loanwords) from the Greek (and Latin) language, and concepts from Graeco-Roman intellectual life, for their own purposes (already Krauss 1898–1899; Lieberman 1994; much more sceptical Feldman 1993: 19–24). At least the urban population of Roman Palestine was probably more or less bilingual (Cotton 1991; Van der Horst 2001; see also Smelik in this volume). Despite the many structural and historical differences between the rabbinic movement and Graeco-Roman rhetorical and philosophical schools, both had functional similarities: reflecting on certain issues, teaching students, and collecting and editing school traditions.

Palestinian cities were also artistic and cultic centres. Public buildings, streets, private houses, and even *necropoleis* outside of the city walls were adorned with images of deities, humans, and animals. Rabbis occasionally refer to these images and were aware of the social and political dynamics associated with erecting statues in the public realm. They also knew the cultural milieu surrounding pagan images, that is, the customs, myths, and emotions revolving around them (Eliav 2002: 415–6). Rabbis were far from expressing general hostility towards statuary on the basis of a strict reading of the second commandment (Ex. 20:4–5; Deut. 5:8), which would have made living in an urban environment quite impossible. They distinguished between a strictly cultic use of images, which was, and remained, forbidden for Jews by the first commandment (Ex. 20:3; Deut. 5:7, 9–10), and a merely decorative function, which could be tolerated (Schwartz 1998). They did not tolerate visits to pagan temples, though (Veltri 2000). We may assume that rabbis' 'pragmatism' helped them to accept the urban space as one of their 'natural habitats' (Veltri 2000). This attitude helped rabbis define their own uniqueness within the environment of the city which was largely defined by Graeco-Roman culture (Eliav 2002:

433; on the heuristic distinction between 'cult' and 'culture' in Jewish literature see Collins 2001; Collins/Sterling, eds. 2001).

SUGGESTED READING

For a historical overview see Sartre (2005). General introductions to the cities of Roman Palestine and their history and culture are provided by Sperber (1998), Richardson (2002), and Meyers (2002). On the issue of urbanization see Woolf (1997) and Lapin (1999 and 2000).

BIBLIOGRAPHY

AMIT, D./PATRICH, J./HIRSCHFELD, Y. (eds) (2002). *The Aqueducts of Israel.* Journal of Roman Archaeology Supplementary Series 46. Portsmouth, RI: Journal of Roman Archaeology.

BALL, W. (2000). *Rome in the East: The Transformation of an Empire.* London and New York: Routledge.

BARGHOUTI, A. N. (1982). 'Urbanization of Palestine and Jordan in the Hellenistic and Roman Times'. *Studies in the History and Archaeology of Jordan* 1:209–29.

BEN-TOR, A./BONFIL, R./ZUCKERMAN, S./BAR-YOSEF, D. E. (eds) (2003). *Tel Qashish: A Village in the Jezreel Valley. Final Report of the Archaeological Excavations (1978–1987).* Jerusalem: The Hebrew University of Jerusalem, Institute of Archaeology.

—— /ZARZECKI-PELEG, A./COHEN-ANIDJAR, S./BEN-AMI, D. (eds) (2005). *Yoqneʿam II: The Iron Age and the Persian Period. Final Report of the Archaeological Excavations (1977–1988).* Qedem Reports 6. Jerusalem: The Hebrew University of Jerusalem, Institute of Archaeology; The Israel Exploration Society.

BERLIN, A. M. (2002). 'Romanization and Anti-Romanization in Pre-Revolt Galilee', in *The First Jewish Revolt: Archaeology, History, and Ideology,* ed. A. M. Berlin, and J. A. Overman. London and New York: Routledge, 57–73.

——/OVERMAN, J. A. (eds) (2002). *The First Jewish Revolt: Archaeology, History, and Ideology.* London and New York: Routledge.

BLASIUS, A. (2002). 'Zur Frage des geistigen Widerstandes im griechisch-römischen Ägypten. Die historische Situation', in *Apokalyptik und Ägypten: Eine kritische Analyse der relevanten Texte aus dem griechisch-römischen Ägypten,* ed. A. Blasius and B. U. Schipper. Orientalia Lovaniensia Analecta 107. Leuven: Peeters, 41–62.

——/SCHIPPER, B. U. (eds) (2002). *Apokalyptik und Ägypten: Eine kritische Analyse der relevanten Texte aus dem griechisch-römischen Ägypten.* Orientalia Lovaniensia Analecta 107. Leuven: Peeters.

BRAUDEL, F. (1972–1974). *The Mediterranean and the Mediterranean World in the Age of Philip II*, 2 vols. London and New York: Harper & Row.

CHANCEY, M. A. (2004). 'City Coins and Roman Power in Palestine. From Pompey to the Great Revolt', in *Religion and Society in Roman Palestine: Old Questions, New Approaches*, ed. D. R. Edwards. New York and London: Routledge, 103–12.

COLLINS, J. J. (2001). 'Cult and Culture. The Limits of Hellenisation in Judaea', in *Hellenism in the Land of Israel*, ed. J. J. Collins and G. E. Sterling. Notre Dame, Ind: University of Notre Dame Press, 38–61.

——/STERLING, G. E. (eds) (2001). *Hellenism in the Land of Israel*. Notre Dame, Ind: University of Notre Dame Press.

COTTON, H. M. (1991). 'Languages of the Legal and Administrative Documents from the Judean Desert'. *Zeitschrift für Papyrologie und Epigraphik* 125: 219–31.

—— (2004). 'The Rabbis and the Documents', in *Jews in a Greco-Roman World*, ed. M. GOODMAN. Oxford: Clarendon Press, 167–79.

DAR, S. (1986). *Landscape and Pattern: An Archaeological Survey of Samaria 800 B.C.E.–636 C.E.* BAR International Series 308. Oxford: British Archaeological Reports.

EDWARDS, D. R. (2004). *Religion and Society in Roman Palestine: Old Questions, New Approaches*. New York and London: Routledge.

—— (2007). 'Identity and Social Location in Roman Galilean Villages', in *Religion, Ethnicity, and Identity in Ancient Galilee: A Region in Transition*, ed. J. Zangenberg et al. Tübingen: Mohr-Siebeck, 357–74.

ELIAV, Y. Z. (2000). 'The Roman Bath as Jewish Institution: Another Look at the Encounter Between Judaism and the Greco-Roman Culture'. *Journal for the Study of Judaism* 31: 416–54.

—— (2002). 'Viewing the Sculptural Environment: Shaping the Second Commandment', in *The Talmud Yerushalmi and Graeco-Roman Culture*, vol. 3, ed. P. Schäfer. Tübingen: Mohr-Siebeck, 411–33.

—— (2008). 'The Desolating Sacrilege: A Jewish-Christian Discourse on Statuary, Space and Sanctity', in *The Sculptural Environment of the Roman Near East: Reflections on Culture, Ideology and Power*, ed. Y. Z. Eliav, E. A. Friedland, and S. Herbert. Leuven: Peeters, 605–27.

——/FRIEDLAND, E. A./HERBERT, S. (eds) (2008). *The Sculptural Environment of the Roman Near East: Reflections on Culture, Ideology and Power*. Leuven: Peeters.

FELDMAN, L. H. (1993). *Jew and Gentile in the Ancient World: Attitudes and Interactions from Alexander to Justinian*. Princeton: Princeton University Press.

FIENSY, D. A. (1991). *The Social History of Palestine in the Herodian Period: The Land is Mine*. Studies in the Bible and Early Christianity 20. Lewiston, NY: The Edwin Mellen Press.

FINKELSTEIN, I. (2008). 'Jerusalem in the Persian (and Early Hellenistic) Period and the Wall of Nehemiah'. *Journal for the Study of the Old Testament* 32: 501–20.

FINLEY, M. I. (1999). *The Ancient Economy*. Sather Classical Lectures 43. Berkeley: University of California Press.

FREYNE, S. (1997). 'Cities of the Hellenistic and Roman Periods'. *Oxford Encyclopedia of Archaeology in the Near East*, vol. 2, ed. E. M. Meyers. New York and Oxford: Oxford University Press, 29–35.

—— (2000). *Galilee and Gospel: Collected Essays*. Tübingen: Mohr-Siebeck.

GEIGER, J. (1990). 'Local Patriotism in the Hellenistic Cities of Palestine', in *Greece and Rome in Eretz Israel: Collected Essays*, eds. A. Kasher, U. Rappaport, and G. Fuks. Jerusalem: The Israel Exploration Society, 141–50.

GOODMAN, M. (ed.) (2004). *Jews in a Greco-Roman World*. Oxford: Clarendon Press.

—— (2007). *Rome and Jerusalem: The Clash of Ancient Civilizations*. London: Allen Lane.

GOSDEN, C. (2004). *Archaeology and Colonialism: Cultural Contact from 5000 BC to the Present*. Cambridge: Cambridge University Press.

GRAF, F. (2002). 'Roman Festivals in Syria Palestina', in *The Talmud Yerushalmi and Graeco-Roman Culture*, vol. 3, ed. P. Schäfer. Tübingen: Mohr Siebeck, 435–51.

GROSSMAN, D. (1992). *Rural Process-Pattern Relationships. Nomadization, Sedentarization, and Settlement Fixation*. New York: Praeger.

HEZSER, C. (1997). *The Social Structure of the Rabbinic Movement in Roman Palestine*. Tübingen: Mohr-Siebeck.

HINGLEY, R. (2005). *Globalizing Roman Culture: Unity, Diversity and Empire*. London and New York: Routledge.

HIRSCHFELD, Y. (1995). *The Palestinian Dwelling in the Roman-Byzantine Period*. Studium Biblicum Franciscanum Collectio Minor 34. Jerusalem: Franciscan Printing Press; Israel Exploration Society.

—— (1997). 'Jewish Rural Settlement in Judaea in the Early Roman Period', in *The Early Roman Empire in the East*, ed. S. E. Alcock. Oxbow Monograph 95. Oxford: Oxbow Books, 72–88.

HORDEN, P./PURCELL, N. (2000). *The Corrupting Sea: A Study of Mediterranean History*. Oxford: Blackwell Publishing.

HORSLEY, R. A. (1996). *Archaeology, History and Society in Galilee. The Social Context of Jesus and the Rabbis*. Valley Forge, PA: Trinity Press International.

HORST, P. W. VAN DER (2001). 'Greek in Jewish Palestine in Light of Jewish Epigraphy', in *Hellenism in the Land of Israel*, eds. J. J. Collins and G. E. Sterling. Notre Dame, Ind: University of Notre Dame Press, 154–74.

HOSS, S. (2005). *Baths and Bathing: The Culture of Bathing and the Baths and Thermae in Palestine from the Hasmoneans to the Moslem Conquest with an Appendix on Jewish Ritual Baths (Miqwa'ot)*. BAR International Series 1346. Oxford: Archaeopress.

ISAAC, B. (1990). 'Roman Administration and Urbanization', in *Greece and Rome in Eretz Israel. Collected Essays*, ed. A. Kasher, U. Rappaport, and G. Fuks. Jerusalem: The Israel Exploration Society, 151–59.

—— (1992). *The Limits of Empire: The Roman Army in the East*, revised edition. Oxford: Clarendon Press.

JACOBS, M. (1998a). 'Römische Thermenkultur im Spiegel des Talmud Yerushalmi', in *The Talmud Yerushalmi and Graeco-Roman Culture*, vol. 1, ed. P. Schäfer. Tübingen: Mohr-Siebeck, 219–311.

—— (1998b). 'Theatres and Performances as Reflected in the Talmud Yerushalmi', in *The Talmud Yerushalmi and Graeco-Roman Culture*, vol. 1, ed. P. Schäfer. Tübingen: Mohr-Siebeck, 327–47.

—— (2000). 'Pagane Tempel in Palästina: Rabbinische Aussagen im Vergleich mit archäologischen Funden', in *The Talmud Jerushalmi and Graeco-Roman Culture*, vol. 2, ed. P. Schäfer and C. Hezser. Tübingen: Mohr-Siebeck, 139–59.

JACQUES, F./SCHEID, J. (1998). *Rom und das Reich in der Hohen Kaiserzeit* 44 v. Chr.–260 n. Chr., vol. 1: Die Struktur des Reiches. Stuttgart and Leipzig: B. G. Teubner.

JENSEN, M. H. (2006). *Herod Antipas in Galilee: The Literary and Archaeological Sources on the Reign of Herod Antipas and Its Socio-Economic Impact on Galilee.* Tübingen: Mohr-Siebeck.

KENNEDY, D. (1999). 'Greek, Roman and Native Cultures in the Roman Near East', in *The Roman and Byzantine Near East*, vol. 2: *Some Recent Archaeological Research*, ed. J. H. Humphrey. Journal of Roman Archaeology Supplementary Series 31. Portsmouth, RI: Journal of Roman Archaeology, 76–106.

KRAUSS, S. (1898–1899). *Griechische und Lateinische Lehnwörter in Talmud, Midrasch und Targum.* 2 vols. Berlin: S. Calvary.

—— (1966). *Talmudische Archäologie*, 3 vols. Hildesheim: G. Olms (reprint of Leipzig: Fock, 1910–12).

LAPIN, H. (1999). 'Rabbis and Cities in Later Roman Palestine: The Literary Evidence'. *Journal of Jewish Studies* 50: 187–207.

—— (2000). 'Rabbis and Cities: Some Aspects of the Rabbinic Movement in its Graeco-Roman Environment', in *The Talmud Jerushalmi and Graeco-Roman Culture*, vol. 2. ed. P. Schäfer and C. Hezser. Tübingen: Mohr-Siebeck, 51–80.

—— (2001). *Economy, Geography and Provincial History in Later Roman Palestine.* Tübingen: Mohr-Siebeck.

LEIBNER, U. (2006). 'Settlement and Demography in Late Roman and Byzantine Eastern Galilee', in *Settlements and Demography in the Near East in Late Antiquity. Proceedings of the Colloquium, Matera 27–29 October 2005*, ed. A. S. Lewin and P. Pellegrini. Biblioteca di Mediterraneo antico 2. Pisa and Rome: Istituti editoriali e poligrafici internazionali, 105–29.

LEVINE, L. I. (1989). *The Rabbinic Class of Roman Palestine in Late Antiquity.* Jerusalem and New York: Yad Izhak Ben-Zvi; Jewish Theological Seminary of America.

LIEBERMAN, S. (1994). *Greek in Jewish Palestine.* New York and Jerusalem: Jewish Theological Seminary of America (reprint of 1941 edition).

LUKE, J. (2003). *Ports of Trade: Al Mina and Geometric Greek Pottery in the Levant.* BAR International Series 1100. Oxford: Archaeopress.

MACMULLEN, R. (2000). *Romanization in the Time of Augustus.* New Haven and London: Yale University Press.

MAEIR, A. M./DAR, S./SAFRAI, Z. (eds) (2003). *The Rural Landscape of Ancient Israel.* BAR International Series 1121. Oxford: Archeopress.

MESHORER, Y. (1985). *City Coins of Eretz Israel and the Decapolis in the Roman Period.* Jerusalem: The Israel Museum.

MEYERS, E. M. (2002). 'Jewish Culture in Greco-Roman Palestine', in *Cultures of the Jews*, ed. D. Biale. New York: Random House and Schocken, 135–80.

MILLAR. F. (1993). *The Roman Near East 31 BC–AD 337.* Cambridge, Mass.: Harvard University Press.

OPPENHEIMER, A. (2008). 'The Jews in the Roman World', in *The Sculptural Environment of the Roman Near East: Reflections on Culture, Ideology and Power*, ed. Y. Z. Eliav, E. A. Friedland, and S. Herbert. Leuven: Peeters, 51–66.

PATRICH, Y. (2002). 'Herod's Hippodrome-Stadium at Caesarea and the Games Conducted Therein', in *What Athens Has to Do with Jerusalem. Essays on Classical, Jewish and Early Christian Art and Archaeology in Honor of Gideon Foerster*, ed. L. V. Rutgers. Leuven: Peeters, 29–68.

POLLINI, J. (2008). 'The Imperial Cult in the East: Images of Power and the Power of Intolerance', in *The Sculptural Environment of the Roman Near East: Reflections on Culture, Ideology and Power*, ed. Y. Z. Eliav, E. A. Friedland, and S. Herbert. Leuven: Peeters, 165–94.

RICHARDSON, P. (1999). *Herod: King of the Jews and Friend of the Romans*. Columbia: University of South Carolina Press.

—— (2002). *City and Sanctuary: Religion and Architecture in the Roman Near East*. London: SCM Press.

—— (2004). *Building Jewish in the Roman East*. Waco: Baylor University Press.

ROSENFELD, B.-Z./MENIRAV, J. (2005). *Markets and Marketing in Roman Palestine*. Supplements to the Journal for the Study of Judaism 99. Leiden: Brill.

SAFRAI, Z. (1994). *The Economy of Roman Palestine*. London and New York: Routledge.

SARTRE, M. (2005). *The Middle East under Rome*. Cambridge, MA and London: The Belknap Press of Harvard University Press.

—— (2008). 'The Nature of Syrian Hellenism in the Late Roman and Early Byzantine Periods', in *The Sculptural Environment of the Roman Near East. Reflections on Culture, Ideology and Power*, ed. Y. Z. Eliav, E. A. Friedland, and S. Herbert. Leuven: Peeters, 25–49.

SCHMITT, H. H./SCHWARZ, H. (2005). 'Stadt, Polis', in *Lexikon des Hellenismus*, eds. H. H. Schmitt and E. Vogt. Wiesbaden: Harrassowitz, 1023–42.

SCHÜRER, E./VERMES,G./MILLAR, F./BLACK, M. (1979). *The History of the Jewish People in the Age of Jesus Christ (175 B.C.–A.D. 135)*, vol. 2. Edinburgh: T&T Clark.

SCHWARTZ, J. (1986). *Jewish Settlement in Judaea. After the Bar-Kochba War until the Arab Conquest 135 C.E.–640 C.E.* [Hebr.]. Jerusalem: Magnes Press.

SCHWARTZ, S. (1998). 'Gamaliel in Aphrodite's Bath: Palestinian Judaism and Urban Culture in the Third and Fourth Centuries', in *The Talmud Yerushalmi and Graeco-Roman Culture*, vol. 1, ed. P. Schäfer. Tübingen: Mohr-Siebeck, 203–17.

SEGAL, A. (1995). *Theatres in Roman Palestine and Provincia Arabia*. Mnemosyne 140. Leiden: Brill.

—— (1997). *From Function to Monument: Urban Landscapes of Roman Palestine, Syria and Arabia*. Oxbow Monograph 66. Oxford: Oxbow Books.

SIGISMUND, M. (2007). 'Small Change? Coins and Weights as a Mirror of Ethnic, Religious and Political Identity in First and Second Century Tiberias', in *Religion, Ethnicity and Identity in Ancient Galilee: A Region in Transition*, ed. J. K. Zangenberg, H. W. Attridge, and D. B. Martin. Tübingen: Mohr-Siebeck, 315–36.

SPERBER, D. (1998). *The City in Roman Palestine*. New York: Oxford University Press.

VELTRI, G. (2000). 'Römische Religion an der Peripherie des Reiches. Ein Kapitel rabbinischer Rhetorik', in *The Talmud Yerushalmi and Graeco-Roman Culture*, vol. 2, ed. P. Schäfer and C. Hezser. Tübingen: Mohr-Siebeck, 81–138.

WALDBAUM, J. C. (1997). 'Greeks *in* the East or Greeks *and* the East? Problems in the Definition and Recognition of Presence'. *Bulletin of the American Society of Oriental Research* 305: 1–17.

WALLERSTEIN, I. (1974–1989). *The Modern World-System*. 3 vols. New York: Academic Press.

WEBER, M. (1966). *The City*. New York and London: Free Press; Collier-MacMillan (reprint of 1921).

—— (1968). *Economy and Society: An Outline of Interpretive Sociology*, 3 vols. Berkeley: University of California Press.

WEISS, Z. (1998). 'Buildings for Entertainment', in *The City in Roman Palestine*, ed. D. Sperber. New York: Oxford University Press, 77–91 and 94–102.

—— (1999). 'Adopting a Novelty: The Jews and the Roman Games in Palestine', in *The Roman and Byzantine Near East*, vol. 2: *Some Recent Archaeological Research*, ed. J. H. Humphrey. Journal of Roman Archaeology Supplementary Series 31. Portsmouth, RI: Journal of Roman Archaeology, 23–49.

WENNING, R. (1981). Griechische Importe aus der Zeit vor Alexander dem Großen'. *Boreas* 4:29–46.

WHITTAKER, C. R. (1997). 'Imperialism and Culture: The Roman Initiative', in *Dialogues in Roman Imperialism: Power, Discourse and Discrepant Experience in the Roman Empire*, ed. D. J. Mattingly. Journal of Roman Archaeology Supplementary Series 23. Portsmouth, RI: Journal of Roman Archaeology, 143–63.

WOOLF, G. (1997). 'The Roman Urbanization of the East', in *The Early Roman Empire in the East*, ed. S. E. Alcock. Oxbow Monograph 95. Oxford: Oxbow Books, 1–13.

ZANGENBERG, J. K. (2008). 'Jesus—Galiläa—Archäologie: Neuere Forschungen in einer Region im Wandel', in *Jesus und die Archäologie Galiläas*, ed. C. Claussen and J. Frey. Biblisch-Theologische Studien 87. Neukirchen-Vluyn: Neukirchener Verlag, 7–38.

—— (2010). 'Archaeology, Papyri, Inscriptions', forthcoming in *The Dictionary of Early Judaism*, ed. J. J. Collins and D. C. Harlow, Grand Rapids: Eerdmans.

——/ATTRIDGE, H. W./MARTIN, D. B. (eds) (2007). *Religion, Ethnicity and Identity in Ancient Galilee: A Region in Transition*. Tübingen: Mohr-Siebeck.

CHAPTER 10

VILLAGE AND COUNTRYSIDE

ANN E. KILLEBREW

ROMAN-period Palestine represents an era of far-reaching religious, cultural, social, and political transformation. From the first century BCE to the mid-seventh century CE, the Jewish village and countryside served as the locale and catalyst for the development of rabbinic Judaism and the birthplace of Christianity. The flourishing of rural Jewish life and its impact on Roman Palestine during this period is part of a larger phenomenon that typified the crucial role of villages in economic prosperity and the development of the empire's eastern provinces. This chapter examines the evidence and its interpretations relevant to reconstructing seven centuries of the daily life of Jewish villages in Roman Palestine. Following a discussion of the key primary sources most significant to this study, I will survey rural Jewish settlement patterns and demography spanning the Roman to Byzantine periods within the larger historical context, explore the physical features of the Jewish village and material culture of everyday life, and examine the impact of these rural Jewish settlements on the economic fabric of Roman Palestine.

1. PRIMARY SOURCES AND MAJOR RESEARCH TRENDS

Contemporary Roman and Jewish texts and the results of archaeological surveys and excavations are the main primary sources for reconstructing daily life in

Roman Palestine. The extensive rabbinic literary compendia (Mishnah, Tosefta, Talmud Yerushalmi, Talmud Bavli, and, to a lesser degree, the biblical commentaries, Midrashim) are our most relevant written sources regarding rural Jewish daily life. Aspects of these ethical teachings and exegetical, homiletical, legal, and narrative texts often relate to everyday matters, particularly in the villages and the countryside. As with all textual evidence, this body of literature should be approached critically and with caution when used as an historical source. Nonetheless these texts are a unique and invaluable tool in reconstructing social, economic, and cultural aspects of the rural areas, and they provide unparalleled insights into daily life in Jewish villages of Roman Palestine (see Z. Safrai 1994: 3–9; for a lively debate regarding the use of rabbinic sources to reconstruct a 'Talmudic history' see Feldman 1999; Kalmin 1999; Kraemer 1999; Neusner 1999; Z. Safrai 1999; and Stemberger 1999). Less useful for our topic are Roman texts, which tend to focus on imperial matters. Josephus' writings, the Dead Sea Scrolls, the New Testament, patristic literature, personal archives or letters, and contemporary inscriptions are also of limited significance due to their narrow chronological range and less frequent mention of matters relating to village daily life.

Archaeological evidence constitutes the paramount primary source for scholarly reconstructions of the realia of Jewish villages and complements the social, economic, cultural, and political aspects revealed in Roman, Christian, and Jewish texts. For well over a hundred years, scholars have integrated material culture remains and written documents, particularly rabbinic texts, with the goal of illustrating rabbinic literature and reconstructing late antique daily life. This fusion of texts, archaeology, and ethnographic studies gave rise to a discipline often referred to as 'Jewish Archaeology' in modern scholarship (for a discussion of the contribution of this multi-disciplinary approach to our understanding of late antique Jewish Palestine see Fine 2005 and 2006; see also the classic works of Applebaum 1987 and S. Safrai 1987). Unlike the corpus of literary texts, archaeology continues to produce new primary materials that have increased exponentially during the last decades.

For much of the twentieth century, most archaeological exploration of the Roman and late antique periods in the Land of Israel focused on urban centres and monumental buildings, especially on the documentation and excavation of synagogues. Often lost in these more art-historical and architecturally oriented studies were aspects of the environmental setting of synagogues, which was usually rural. As a result, the larger archaeological context of these synagogues was ignored, with little effort invested in uncovering the plans of the villages or excavating domestic and other structures at these locations. Beginning with the groundbreaking archaeological work of E. M. Meyers and his team during the 1970s and 1980s at the Galilean villages of Khirbet Shemaʿ (Meyers et al. 1976), Meiron (Meyers et al. 1981a), Gush Halav (Meyers et al. 1990), and Nabratein (Meyers et al. 1981b and 1982), research has increasingly attempted to contextualize these rural

synagogues in their village setting. These investigations, combined with the interpretation of canonical texts and epigraphic materials—an approach that has been
dubbed the 'Meyers' Method' (Peskowitz 2004: 144)—provided the first scientific,
well-documented and published archaeological insights into the daily life of Jewish
villages. Additional excavations of Jewish villages have added substantially to
our understanding of rural Jewish Palestine (these include sites in the Galilee, e.g.
Capernaum: Tzaferis 1989; Meroth: Ilan/Damati 1987; Khirbet Qana: Edwards 2002;
Karm er-Ras: Alexandre 2008; the Golan, e.g. Qatzrin: Maʻoz/Killebrew 1988, Killebrew et al. 2003; Mount Carmel, e.g. Sumaqa: Dar 1999; the coastal plain, e.g.
Shiqmona: Elgavish 1994: 109–147; Samaria, e.g. Um Rihan: Dar et al 1986; Northern
Judaea, e.g. Kiryat Sefer: Magen et al. 2004: 179–242; Modi'in Weksler-Bdolach et al.
2003; Southern Judaea, e.g. Horvat Susiya: Yeivin 1994, Baruch 2005; Judaean Desert,
e.g. Ein Gedi: Hirschfeld 2007). Extensive archaeological surveys conducted during
the past three decades in particular have provided essential information regarding
rural settlement patterns and demography (see Dar 1986; Dauphin/Gibson 1992–93;
Urman 1995; Frankel et al. 2001; for a recent summary of the evidence see Bar 2004a,
2004b, 2004c; 2006).

Ethnography, and the related field of ethno-archaeology, is an auxiliary discipline that aids in our interpretation of both tangible and intangible aspects of past
traditional societies. Ethno-archaeology has been an invaluable tool for our understanding of the function of certain objects of material culture, recovered in
excavations, and the realia of daily life. Although care must be exercised when
drawing analogies between modern and ancient societies, it is well documented
that Roman rural life styles and technologies continued for centuries, and in some
cases, well into nineteenth-century Palestine and later. Thus, ethnographic analogy
assists modern researchers in bridging the vast gap between modern Western
mentalities and lifestyles, and those of more recent traditional societies that often
share common features with the daily life during the Roman period (see the older
approaches of Krauss 1910–1912 and Dalman 1928–1944, and more recently Hirschfeld 1995, which constitutes a successful incorporation of modern ethnographic
studies into the investigation of the Palestinian dwelling in the Roman-Byzantine
periods; see also Killebrew et al. 2003 and Killebrew 2004).

Because of the quantity and diversity of the written sources and the ever-
increasing archaeological evidence, combined with the vast amount of secondary
literature relating to rural Jewish life in Roman Palestine, scholars tend to specialize
in either the late Second Temple or late antique periods, and in more textually based
or archaeologically based studies. As a result, very few fully integrated treatments
exist that include political, social, economic, religious, and material culture aspects
of Jewish village life spanning the first century BCE to the seventh century CE. These
same source materials relating to Jewish village life have been of particular relevance
to two major schools of scholarship—one concerned with questions regarding the
historical Jesus and the emergence of early Christianity (see Horsley 1996; Reed

2000; Crossan/Reed 2001; Chancey 2002; Freyne 2004; Moreland 2004; Richardson 2006) and the second with the development of rabbinic Judaism following the destruction of the Second Temple (see Avi-Yonah 1976; Sperber 1978; J. J. Schwartz 1986; Z. Safrai 1994; Lapin 2001; S. Schwartz 2001; Fine 2005). Both approaches are relevant to the study of rural Palestine and Jewish village life.

2. RURAL JEWISH DEMOGRAPHY AND SETTLEMENT PATTERNS

Roman Palestine was settled by Jews, Samaritans, polytheists, and, during the Byzantine period, increasingly by Christians. A general consensus exists that urban centres included mixed populations. There is less scholarly agreement regarding the religious and ethnic make-up of villages (see Dauphin 1982; Ma'oz 1985; Urman 1995; Isaac 1998). Villages are usually designated as Jewish by the presence of cultural markers such as synagogues, Hebrew or Aramaic inscriptions, elements of material culture that are specifically related to Jewish ritual or religious practices (e.g. *miqvaot* and stone vessels, especially in the early Roman period, Jewish symbols or decorative motifs, etc.), and/or mention of them having Jewish populations in the written sources (see Berlin 2002; Aviam 2007; Moreland 2007). Rarely do synagogues and churches, or pagan temples appear together in non-urban settlements (Capernaum being one notable exception), thus suggesting that village populations tended to be more homogeneous in ethnic and religious affiliation (for a recent summary of the various views see Gregg 2000 who argues against clearly defined religious/ethnic boundaries in the Golan).

Historical events in Roman Palestine played a key role in the demography and Jewish settlement patterns during the late antique period. During the early Roman period, that is, between 63 BCE and 70 CE, the majority of the Jewish population lived in Judaea and Galilee, and to a lesser degree in the Golan, with Jerusalem serving as the Jewish spiritual and cultural centre. In addition to the textual evidence and extensive excavations in late Second Temple period Jerusalem and Jericho that have revealed impressive remains, the discovery in recent years of Jewish villages in the vicinity of Jerusalem confirm that its hinterland served as a major Jewish population centre until the Bar Kokhba Revolt (see, e.g. recent fieldwork in the vicinity of Jerusalem: Amit 2007; at Hurvat Umm el-'Umdan: Weksler-Bdolach et al. 2003; and at Kiryat Sefer: Magen et al. 2004). In the Galilee, both archaeological and textual sources testify to several significant regional centres with large Jewish populations (e.g. Sepphoris and Tiberias), as well as towns (e.g. Jotapath) and villages dominated by Jewish populations (see Edwards 2007 for a summary). While the Jewish population in the Golan apparently declined following the First Jewish Revolt, recovering only during the third or fourth centuries, many early Roman villages and farmsteads in the Galilee continued to be inhabited by Jews, and even expanded in size during the late Roman and Byzantine periods, that is, between 70 CE and the Islamic conquest in the seventh century (see, e.g. Meyers et al. 1978; for a summary of the evidence see Bar 2004a, 2004b, 2004c).

Following the destruction of Jerusalem in 70 CE and the expulsion of Jews from Jerusalem and much of Judaea in the aftermath of the failed Bar Kokhba Revolt in 135 CE, the majority of Jews fled to the Galilee, with smaller numbers settling on the fringes of Judaea (mainly in the south; see J. J. Schwartz 1986), or settling in other areas such as the coastal plain or marginal regions such as the Golan. Archaeological evidence has demonstrated that, contrary to previous interpretations that viewed the late Roman period as a period of decline (see Avi-Yonah 1976: 89–136; Sperber 1978; Schäfer 1995: 170–75), Palestine witnessed a marked increase in settlement intensity and economic prosperity during the late second to fourth centuries CE (see Meyers 1995: 21 and Bar 2002 and 2006 for a summary of the evidence).

A second major debate surrounds demographic fluctuations in Palestine during the fifth century CE. Until recently, scholars postulated that beginning in the mid-fourth century and continuing to the fifth century CE, Palestine experienced a crisis, resulting in a decline in population (Z. Safrai 1998). According to Z. Safrai, this crisis was initially sparked by a rapidly expanding population in the fourth century and over-utilization of the land, coinciding with a general economic decline in the eastern Roman Empire. This is marked by a dearth of fifth-century coins in the archaeological record and the abandonment of some settlements. This view has been challenged by archaeologist J. Magness (2007) and numismatist G. Bijovsky (2000–2002). Magness notes that a significant number of synagogues were constructed during this 'missing century', while Bijovsky posits that the dearth of fifth-century coins can be attributed to the continued circulation of large numbers of the ubiquitous fourth-century coins for well over a century (Bijovsky 2000–2002). A similar phenomenon has been noted by Liebeschuetz (2001: 23) who observed that the shortage of fifth-century coins is 'almost universal' throughout the Roman Empire due to a decrease in the minting of bronze coins. Only after the economic reforms of Anastasius I in the late fifth century were bronze coins once again produced in large quantities, a phenomenon which was accompanied by a similar increase in the number of coins found in the archaeological record.

In summary, caution is advised when attempting to interpret settlement patterns in Roman Palestine based on numismatic evidence and the lack of clearly defined fifth-century CE strata. Some sites, such as Meiron and Khirbet Shema' (Meyers 1982: 115–31), were apparently abandoned during this period. However, the difficulty in identifying the fifth century at Byzantine period sites may not always signify abandonment. Instead, the paucity of clearly defined strata could indicate that at least some settlements experienced uninterrupted occupation, which can be difficult to discern in the archaeological record during periods void of destruction or disaster. Combined with the empire-wide decline in the number of coins minted, the continued use of fourth-century coins, and a very gradual development in ceramic typology, few material culture remains specific to the fifth century would be present at sites that were continuously inhabited.

Less controversial is the archaeological evidence attesting to an increase in population, rural settlement density, and expansion of cultivated land into marginal regions which peaks during the sixth and seventh centuries (see Tsafrir 1996; Bar 2004a, 2004b, 2004c for an overview and summary of the evidence). This phenomenon has been noted throughout the Roman Empire (Barker/Lloyd 1991). Scholars have attributed the dramatic increase in population in Roman Palestine, especially during the Byzantine period, to various factors. The prevailing view proposes that prosperity and economic development were closely tied to the change in Palestine's status to a 'Holy Land' and the influx of Christians. This Christianization of Roman Palestine resulted in the construction of monumental churches and pilgrimage, which in turn led to increased investment in infrastructure and population growth (see Hunt 1982: 83–106). More recently, other scholars have challenged this view arguing that the population increase and accompanying affluence were largely the result of local social and economic developments, encouraged by the relative peace and security provided to the region under Roman *aegis*, and only in part the result of the impact of Christianity (see Bar 2003). Roman imperialism and the resulting relatively stable political conditions, an extensive and secure system of roads, and highly developed trade networks, were no doubt the main factors in the rapid population growth and resulting increase in the number of villages in previously marginal and isolated rural regions in Palestine and throughout the Roman Empire.

3. DEFINITION OF A JEWISH VILLAGE

The majority of Roman Palestine's Jewish population dwelled in the countryside. This is attested by the large number of surveyed and excavated village sites and relative scarcity of large urban centres, especially in the Galilee and Golan. Early Roman and late antique period sources use a variety of terms to classify Jewish settlements. Josephus (Vita 235) mentions two types of Jewish Galilean settlements: cities (*poleis*) or villages (*komai*). As reviewed by S. Krauss (1929) and, more recently, by Z. Safrai (1994: 17–103), there are a variety of terms used in rabbinic literature that

distinguish between different types of Jewish settlements. The most common include: *kerakh* (a large, walled urban settlement, similar to a *polis*, city, in function), *'ir*
(equaling the Aramaic *krt'* and usually translated as a town, pl. *ayarot*, sometimes
with the further designation of *'ayarot gedolot*, large towns, or *benoniyot*, medium-
size towns), and *kfr* (village or *kufarnaya daqiqaya*—small villages; see Hirschfeld
1997: 36–39 for a detailed discussion of terminology, including the equivalent Greek
terms for various rural settlements). Cities included mixed populations of pagans,
Jews, and later Christians. Village populations tended to be more homogeneous in
their social, economic, and religious make-up, usually comprising large extended
families with strong kinship ties. Typically these non-urban settlements lacked the
social stratification found in cities and, with the exception of synagogues, boasted
few impressive monumental civic and public structures that characterize the *polis*.
Few of the external trappings of Hellenization are discernible in the material culture
of these villages and Greek does not appear to have been in common use.

I divide non-urban settlements into three main groups: (1) large village-towns or
medium-sized cities that are usually, but not always, unwalled and greater than
ca. 5 hectares in size; (2) small villages or 'townlets' that are 5 hectares or less, but
average 2–2.5 hectares in size; and (3) farmhouses, usually comprising a few
structures around an open courtyard, often including a tower. Villas, characterized
by large dwellings that belong to the estates of wealthy landowners or aristocrats,
are rare in Roman Palestine (Applebaum 1989; Hirschfeld 1997; Sartre 2005:
225–226). The phenomenon of groups of farmhouses that created a hamlet, or
formed satellite villages in association with a larger village, is attested to in rabbinic
literature and observed in several surveys in Judaea, Samaria, and the coastal plain,
but seldom in the Galilee or Golan (Z. Safrai 1994: 69–74; see also Dar 1988: 31 who
suggests a division into farmsteads, incipient villages and nucleated settlements).
Agricultural installations and terracing systems are also often documented in the
archaeological record of the rural countryside. Most rural populations resided in
either the *'ir* (large village, and its Aramaic equivalent *krt'*) or the *kfr* (small village),
settlement types which are the focus of this chapter.

4. General Layout and Material Culture of Large and Small Villages

4.1 Large Villages

Often termed 'towns' or 'medium-sized cities' (*'ayarot ha-beinoniot*; Yeivin 1987),
large villages can be defined as non-urban settlements that were 5 hectares in size or

more. They usually served as a regional centre of economic activity, but lacked the civic structures and institutions that typify the *polis*. Based on surface surveys or excavations, Chorazim, Khirbet Shemaʻ, and Kfar Einan in the Galilee, Nahef and Naʻaran in the Golan, and Ein Gedi and Horvat Susiya in Judaea fall into the category of large villages. Natural topography, and not a master plan that typified the *polis*, played a key role in the general layout and network of streets of these unfortified 'medium-sized cities' (Yeivin 1987: 74*–75*).

Ein Gedi, specifically described in the fourth century CE by Eusebius as 'a very large village of the Jews' (*Onomasticon* 86. 18), is one of the most extensively excavated large villages in Roman Palestine. Located in the Judaean Desert next to the Dead Sea, this oasis was already famous in the early Roman period for its date palms and the cultivation and production of balsam (Josephus, *Ant.* 9. 1. 2). Excavations at this *c.* 40–hectare site uncovered streets, dwellings, shops, agricultural installations, water-supply systems, and a possible bathhouse. At its peak during the late Roman and Byzantine periods, Ein Gedi boasted a synagogue, erected in the early third century CE at the centre of the village, surrounded by dwellings. The most common house at Ein Gedi included a courtyard surrounded by various rooms. Installations such as stone mortars and baking ovens were common in courtyards. The houses ranged in size from 40 sq. m to 240 sq. m, with a main living room, *c.*18 sq. m, where the family slept, ate, and entertained. Ein Gedi's general village plan comprised the inner core that included the synagogue, surrounded by residential structures, and an outer circle where commercial, small industrial, and storage structures were located. The village was destroyed by a conflagration during the second half of the sixth century and was abandoned (Hirschfeld 2007: 23–104).

4.2 Townlets and Small Villages

Most of the surveyed and excavated Jewish villages are less than 5 hectares in size. These are generally referred to in modern scholarly literature as 'townlets' or 'small villages.' Based on surveys and excavations, hundreds of small villages existed in Roman Palestine, reaching their peak during the Byzantine period. Examples of these small villages have been excavated throughout Roman Palestine and, following the Bar Kokhba Revolt, are especially well represented in the heavily Jewish populated Galilee and Golan. Many of the excavated Jewish villages in the north were occupied from the late Second Temple period through to the late Byzantine or early Islamic periods.

During the past decade, several small Jewish villages dating to the early Roman period, and contemporary with late Second Temple period Jerusalem, have been excavated in the central hill country north of Jerusalem. These settlements have been shown to be Jewish because of the presence of public buildings that have been identified as synagogues. Although usually resettled after the destruction of the Second Temple, many of these Jewish villages ceased to exist or retain their Jewish character following the failure of the Bar Kokhba Revolt. Kiryat Sefer provides a case study of an early Roman village that flourished during the final decades of the Second Temple period. Located north of Jerusalem, the excavated remains include a possible synagogue located in a public square surrounded by several dwellings. The typical house plan comprised several rooms situated around an inner court-yard. The discovery of *miqvaot* associated with these residences attests to the Jewish character of this village. Olive presses indicate that significant quantities of olive oil were produced here. Several coin hoards that included numerous gold coins point to the economic prosperity enjoyed by villagers prior to the First Jewish Revolt (Magen et al. 2004: 179–242).

A feature distinctive to a number of rural settlements in the Judaean Shephelah and Galilee dating to the period of the Bar Kokhba revolt and possibly earlier is the appearance of subterranean hiding complexes. These underground hiding places vividly illustrate the role of villagers in the Bar Kokhba Revolt, and perhaps also the First Jewish Revolt, against the Roman Empire. In addition, the construction of these complexes both in Judaea and the Galilee indicates a more unified front among Jewish rural communities than previously suggested for this period (for recent overviews see Kloner/Zissu 2003 and Shahar 2003).

Sumaqa, situated in the Carmel mountain range, typifies the development of a Jewish village from the early Roman to the Byzantine period. Beginning as a farmstead or villa during the early Roman period, it developed into a small village, or 'townlet', following the Bar Kokhba Revolt. The village increased in size to 3 hectares and boasted a synagogue and residential area with dwelling complexes. On the village periphery, agricultural and industrial installations, including olive and wine presses, and workshops were uncovered. Burial caves were documented in the terraced agricultural lands located outside the village boundaries (Dar 1999).

Unlike Sumaqa, a number of Galilean Jewish villages were already well estab-lished during the early Roman period. Capernaum is representative of Galilean Jewish villages. Due to its role in Jesus' ministry as described in the New Testament, Capernaum is one of the most extensively excavated village sites in Galilee (Corbo 1975; Tzaferis 1989). Estimated at 6 hectares in size, Capernaum, like most villages, grew organically with three to four inter-related household units that developed around shared courtyards. Alleys averaged 2–3 m in width, were usually unpaved, and lacked channels or a sewage system. With the exception of a possible early Roman synagogue, public structures were rare or absent at Capernaum. Household material culture was typical of agricultural villages of the period, comprising undecorated local pottery vessels, many from the Galilean Jewish village of Kfar Hananya, and undecorated lamps referred to as Herodian lamps. Stone vessels, well known from other late Second Temple period sites and indicative of Jewish ethnicity, also appear. This is the typical assemblage of early Roman Jewish villages in Galilee (see Reed 2000: 139–69). During the late Roman and Byzantine periods, Capernaum expanded in size and boasted both a synagogue and octagonal church built on the traditional site of the house of St Peter, indicating the presence of a Jewish population and the importance of Capernaum as a key Christian pilgrimage site. Also typical of Galilean and Golan Jewish villages during the later Roman and Byzantine periods, imported late Roman red tablewares and amphorae, originating from numerous regions in the eastern Roman Empire, were common and indicate an increasingly integrated system of trade and exchange, which included even the smallest of villages.

Based on surveys and excavations of villages, several general patterns can be observed in the components and layout of rural villages. A village typically included a central public area that often prominently included a synagogue which served as the focus of all public and religious life (see Hachlili 1988; Levine 2005 for synthetic studies of synagogues in Roman Palestine, the majority of which have been excavated in villages). In villages, there is little evidence for well-laid out, centrally controlled planning along a specific axis that characterizes cities. Rather, the village grew organically and apparently randomly. As populations increased over time, open areas and alleys were utilized for additions to domestic units for extended families. Workshops and industrial areas were usually, but not always, located at the fringes of villages.

5. Houses and the Material Culture of Households

The domestic house plan is core to understanding the everyday life of the rural Jewish village. It was a simple structure, lacking in the decorative features that signalled status in wealthier urban homes. The architectural layout of the basic household unit in rural Roman Palestine typically comprised a general multi-purpose room (or *traklin*; see, e.g. T. Kelim, T. B.M. 5:3; M. Er. 6:6), storage areas, occasionally an additional room or upper floor sleeping loft, and a court-yard, the latter sometimes shared with another household. Y. Hirschfeld (1995) divides domestic structures into two main groups—houses with an adjoining or side courtyard, which tend to be more common in villages, and houses with an interior courtyard. He further distinguishes four main house types: the simple house, the complex house, the courtyard house, and houses with shops (Hirschfeld 1995: 21–107). In recent years, more elaborate and detailed typologies have been suggested for Roman Palestine (see Guijarro 1997 regarding the possible relation-ship between house style and households, and Richardson 2004 for an analysis and review of the literature; see also J. J. Schwartz 2006: 434–39 for a recent general overview). These basic plans served as the backdrop for daily family activities.

Multiple tasks could take place in the *traklin*, derived, but differing somewhat in function, from the Latin *triclinium*, meaning a dining room with three reclining couches. In its village context, it is doubtful whether peasants dined while reclining on couches. Rather, in this central space the family could receive guests, eat meals, and perform household tasks. At night, it could also be converted into a sleeping area for the family. Seating included chairs or stools, as well as benches, which were common in private houses (see, e.g. M. Kel. 22:2; T. B.Q. 2:9).

All traditional households required considerable storage space because a family's supplies had to be stored for long periods of time. Storage was critical for survival through periods of drought, famine, or crop failure. In the Golan houses, these storage spaces were typically located next to the *traklin*, separated from this larger room by a 'window wall.' Window walls consist of an interior wall with a series of windows and an entrance that allows passage from the larger room to the smaller room. They are common architectural features of this period in basaltic regions such as the Eastern Galilee and Golan. The wall also provided support for the ceiling and second storey above the storage room. A second-storey room is common in many of these houses (see M. Er. 9:4), probably serving as a sleeping loft. In single-storey houses, the bedroom, or *kiton*, was usually located next to the *traklin* (Hirschfeld 1995: 261, 275–76). Villagers slept on beds or sleeping mats and both are mentioned in rabbinic sources (see e.g. M. Nid. 9:4; T. Shab. 16:5; see also J. J. Schwartz 2004).

A third activity space in the traditional village house was the courtyard. This was the location where most of the daily house chores were carried out. Ovens are usually found in the courtyards, indicating their key role in the preparation of meals (T. B.M. 8:29). Occasionally, indoor kitchens have been identified in the archaeological evidence (see e.g. Qasrin: Killebrew/Fine 1991: 51; for a discussion of the *mageireon*, or indoor kitchen, in rabbinic sources see S. Safrai 1987: 733). Certain plants, for example grapevines, pomegranates, melons, and figs (cf. M. Maas. 3:9), chicken coops and dovecotes, large storage containers for water, and toilets are also features of courtyards. Often courtyards were shared by neighbours, and rabbinic literature mentions problems created by the practice (e.g. M. B.B. 1: 5–6; M. Maas. 3:5). Activities similar to those of the courtyard were carried out on the flat rooftops of village houses (see M. Er. 10:3; y. Er. 9, 25c; M. Toh. 9:6). During hot summer nights the roofs of houses could be used for sleeping.

Usually several basic household units shared walls or courtyards, forming large compounds that most likely housed several generations of an extended family. Village household units were added on to the main house according to the needs of the extended families, resulting in houses that underwent constant renovation and expansion, often remaining in use for centuries. After several generations of additions, the result was a large family complex of numerous connected household units, such as those found at most Roman period villages. This is reflected in rabbinic sources that describe the practice of adding a 'wedding house', or new household unit, on to the family complex (see M. B.B. 6:4). These complexes, or what is often referred to in secondary literature as *insulae*, could include fifteen rooms or more (see Killebrew/Fine 1991: 46). Domestic compounds were separated from each other by narrow alleys. These areas were also shared as illustrated by the Tosefta (see T. B.M. 11:16), which deals with the rights of villagers living off the same alley (for more detailed discussions of daily life in a Qasrin village house see Killebrew/Fine 1991; Killebrew et al. 2003; Killebrew 2004).

Most of the artefacts recovered during excavations are ceramic. The majority of vessels found in domestic contexts are related to the very basic activities of cooking, serving, and storage (see Zevulon/Olenik 1978 and Adan-Bayewitz 1993 for recent typologies and detailed discussions). The *kederah* (a rounded cooking pot) and *ilpas* (an open 'casserole') are among the frequently mentioned vessels mentioned in rabbinic sources (for a summary of sources see J. J. Schwartz 2006: 440–41). During the early and late Roman periods, locally produced kitchen and tablewares, most notably from Kfar Hananya and Shikhin, dominated the village pantry. Beginning in the fourth century CE and continuing until the end of the Byzantine period, imported late Roman red tablewares from North Africa, Cyprus, Asia Minor, and other areas of the eastern Roman Empire (Hayes 1972) are increasingly common at even the most modest Jewish villages. Oil lamps and lanterns supplied the limited lighting for interior rooms. These lamps burned a variety of oils, with olive oil being one of the preferred fuels (see M. Shab. 2:1–2).

Household members have been imagined as comprising the typical nuclear family, including a man, a woman, and their children, with assorted third-generation family members (S. Safrai 1987: 748–64). Based largely on rabbinic literature, most contemporary scholars assign traditional gender roles to family members, with males working in the public sphere while women remained secluded in domestic household spaces (see Ilan 1995; Wegner 1988). More recently, new approaches to the textual and archaeological evidence have challenged this view, suggesting that the boundaries between public and private were more fluid, and gender roles less rigidly defined (see Peskowitz 1997; Baker 2004).

6. VILLAGE ECONOMY AND DAILY LIFE

Daily life in rural Roman Palestine revolved around a subsistence-level existence, with production centred in the household. The economy—that is, the production and allocation of goods and services and its organization—of village life was based largely on agriculture, animal husbandry, and household crafts (see Goodman 1983: 21–23; Harland 2002, and especially Z. Safrai 1994: 104–221 for a detailed description and analysis of modes of production). In agrarian Roman Galilee and the Golan, fruit trees, vegetables, legumes, and grains were cultivated for local consumption. Olive production flourished and doubtlessly exceeded the needs of the Galilean and Golan communities, as evidenced by the large number of ancient olive-oil presses found in rural settings (Ben David 1998). Galilean olive oil, in particular, was famous and exported to other regions of the Roman Empire. The faunal evidence from village occupation levels in Roman Palestine as well as textual sources indicate that sheep, goat, and cattle were the most common animal species consumed, with sheep and goat making up the greatest percentage (cf. M. B.Q. 6:1–2). Smaller percentages of chicken, bird, fish, and deer bones are also documented at these sites (see Killebrew et al. 2003: 64).

Although rabbinic traditions mention rich landowners, there is scant archaeological evidence for large farmsteads, villas, or estates (see Z. Safrai 1994: 95–99; Hirschfeld 1997). Based on survey evidence from western Samaria, S. Dar (1986: 86) argues that, in the wake of the First Jewish Revolt, Roman rule resulted in confiscation of lands that were subsequently controlled by a small number of large landowners. According to Dar, this is manifested in the decreased size of extended family courtyard houses, suggesting that the agrarian economy was reorganized around nuclear families forced into tenancy. The extensive archaeological evidence from the Galilee and Golan does not support this interpretation. Rather, the increase in the number of villages, both large and small, indicates that land ownership and its cultivation were largely in the hands of villagers, rather than concentrated in the hands of a small, wealthy elite. Peasants, who made up at least 90 percent of the population, also worked the land as wage labourers or could resort to more marginal activities such as banditry (Harland 2002: 515).

In addition to agricultural and pastoral concerns, villagers engaged in a great variety of crafts (see Applebaum 1987: 680–85). Most of the commercial activities associated with village professions took place in the domestic setting and directly between producer and consumer. Rabbinic texts generally use the term 'householder' to describe these sellers, who often sold their goods in shops or periodic markets (cf. M. Dem. 5:7; M. Shebi. 7:3; M. Hal. 1:6, 2:7; see also Rosenfeld/Menirav 2005: 71).

Shops and workshops have occasionally been identified in the archaeological evidence at several large and small villages. These include two-storied houses where one or more rooms on the ground floor served as a shop (see, e.g. Khirbet Shema': Meyers et al. 1976: 108–110) or single-storey domestic houses where one room served as a shop (e.g. Horvat Susiya: Hirschfeld 1984: 173–74). Less common are shops and workshops which were independent from dwelling houses and served solely for commerce and industry. Such shops/workshops are known from the Ein Gedi village where Y. Hirschfeld (2007: 37–42) discovered a 'Street of the Shops', including a bakery and pottery shop, dating to the Byzantine period. Archaeologists uncovered a similar street with shops to the east of the village square and synagogue at Qasrin (the finds have not yet been published).

In addition to the village shop and workshop, rabbinic sources refer to various types of periodic markets, including those held in villages and towns. The village market, which usually took place on Fridays, served local and nearby inhabitants who gathered in an open area such as a village square (see M. B.Q. 2:2; Dar 1986: 77, 81; Yeivin 1987: 66–70; M. Meg. 3:1–2 suggests a close proximity of these squares to synagogues; a large, open, paved area to the east of the Qasrin synagogue may have also served a similar function). On Mondays and Thursdays large towns and cities hosted regional markets that inhabitants from the surrounding villages also frequented. These markets may have also served other public functions, such as the reading of the Torah (cf. M. Ket. 1:1; M. Meg. 1:1–2). An additional key factor in the economic interaction between village and city is the itinerant peddler, or *rokhel* (M. Shab. 9:7; see Rosenfeld/Menirav 2005: 41–44, 117 for a summary).

Several key research trends relevant to the relationship between village and urban economies have dominated recent secondary literature. Most scholarly attention has focused on the early and late Roman periods in Palestine. Less work has been devoted to Jewish village economies during the later Byzantine period. Topics of debate include redistribution and exchange systems, the role and impact of trade, and the implications regarding the general economic structure of Roman Palestine. Interpretations range from 'primitivist' to 'modernist' approaches, and to viewpoints that expound a barter-based vs. open-market economy, either controlled via a centralized government system, or by localized and decentralized institutions (see Z. Safrai 1994; Horsley 1996; Harland 2002; Edwards 2007 for various views and general discussion of these issues).

The Roman economy in general relied heavily on village households to produce essential foodstuffs. One viewpoint regarding the nature of urban-rural economic interaction holds that villages were self-sustaining and participated in a political economy based on a barter system, rather than on a monetary, or market economy. Based on this model, urban centres exploited and controlled the resources of the rural countryside (see Horsley 1996: 76–85). The majority of scholars have challenged this view, including E. M. Meyers (1995), Z. Safrai (1994) and D. R. Edwards (2007). According to this 'market economy' based approach, villages were more autonomous, and urban elites had less direct involvement in the village economy (see especially Z. Safrai 1994 and Meyers 1995; for an alternative view see Horsley 1995a and b). Edwards and others also point to the great diversity and complexity of economic activity in the villages and farmsteads that goes beyond a 'political economy dominated by elites and imperial interests' (Edwards 2007: 368).

Greater commercialization characterized Byzantine Palestine and the Roman Empire in general. Increased population, prosperity, and diversity were based in part on an integrated and extensive road system and improved security that encouraged trade throughout the empire. In village daily life, this economic integration is illustrated by the appearance of mass-produced and standardized imported late Roman tablewares that characterize ceramic assemblages in even the smallest of settlements.

7. CONCLUSION

This chapter on Jewish village daily life in Roman Palestine builds upon research from a multitude of disciplines, approaches, and viewpoints that span the last 100 years. It presents the main primary and secondary sources most relevant to this topic, and the major debates that have dominated the literature. Although there is an abundance of both primary and secondary literature on the topic, including an ever-increasing archaeological record, much work still needs to be done to integrate the findings from literary, historical, archaeological, economic, sociological, and other approaches to this topic. Research agendas tend to be narrow in their scope and chronological span. Many studies do not cross the early vs. late Roman and Byzantine divide, focus on Roman Palestine from either a Christian or Jewish perspective, or tend to favour either the literary or material culture evidence. With the exception of the presence of synagogues or a few specific artefacts, little in the material culture of daily life in Roman Palestine distinguishes Jewish from Gentile villages. Regardless of ethnic or religious affiliation, these settlements share many features with rural life in other parts of the Roman Empire. Future research that successfully integrates these various disciplines and contextualizes Roman Palestine within its larger eastern Mediterranean setting would contribute significantly to our understanding of the daily life of Jewish villages between the first century BCE and the seventh century CE.

SUGGESTED READING

Bar's very useful publications (2004c and 2006) provide recent summaries and analyses of archaeological surveys and population studies of Roman Palestine, considered in the light of rabbinic sources. Hirschfeld's book on Roman and Byzantine domestic architecture (1995) discusses the archaeological evidence together with ethnographic studies of traditional Palestinian dwellings. Richardson

(2004) builds on the earlier work of Hirschfeld (1995) and others on Roman-period houses. Safrai's essay on the ancient Jewish home and family (1987) remains an indispensible contribution to the study of Jewish domestic life. Safrai 1994 is a good starting point for investigating the rural economy of Roman Palestine.

BIBLIOGRAPHY

ADAN-BAYEWITZ, D. (1993). *Common Pottery in Roman Galilee: A Study in Local Trade.* Bar Ilan Studies in Near Eastern Languages and Culture. Ramat-Gan: Bar Ilan University Press.

ALEXANDRE, Y. (2008). 'The Archaeological Evidence of the Great Revolt at Karm er-Ras (Kfar Kanna) in the Lower Galilee', in *The Great Revolt in the Galilee.* Catalogue No. 28. Haifa: Hecht Museum, University of Haifa, 73–80.

AMIT, D. (2007). 'Remains of Jewish Settlements from the Second Temple Period near Teddy Stadium, Jerusalem' [Hebr.]. *Eretz Israel* 28:152–58.

APPLEBAUM, S. (1987). 'Economic Life in Palestine', in *The Jewish People in the First Century: Historical Geography, Political History, Social, Cultural and Religious Life and Institutions*, ed. S. Safrai and M. Stern. 2nd ed. Philadelphia: Fortress Press, 631–700.

—— (1989). 'The Roman Villa in Judaea: A Problem', in *Judaea in Hellenistic and Roman Times: Historical and Archaeological Essays*, ed. S. Applebaum. Leiden: Brill, 124–31.

AVI-YONAH, M. (1976). *The Jews under Roman and Byzantine Rule: A Political History of Palestine from the Bar Kokhba War to the Arab Conquest.* London: Blackwell.

AVIAM, M. (2007). 'Distribution Maps of Archaeological Data from the Galilee: An Attempt to Establish Zones Indicative of Ethnicity and Religious Affiliation', in *Religion, Ethnicity, and Identity in Ancient Galilee: A Region in Transition*, ed. J. Zangenberg, H. W. Attridge, and D. B. Martin. Tübingen: Mohr-Siebeck, 115–32.

BAKER, C. M. (2004). 'Imagined Households', in *Religion and Society in Roman Palestine: Old Questions, New Approaches*, ed. D. R. Edwards. New York: Routledge, 113–28.

BAR, D. (2002). 'Was There a 3rd-c. Economic Crisis in Palestine?', in *The Roman and Byzantine Near East*, vol. 3, ed. J. H. Humphrey. Journal of Roman Archaeology Supplement 49. Portsmouth, RI: Journal of Roman Archaeology, 43–54.

—— (2003). 'The Christianisation of Rural Palestine during Late Antiquity'. *Journal of Ecclesiastical History* 54: 401–21.

—— (2004a). 'Frontier and Periphery in Late Antique Palestine', *Greek, Roman, and Byzantine Studies* 44: 69–92.

—— (2004b). 'Geographical Implications of Population and Settlement Growth in Late Antique Palestine'. *Journal of Historical Geography* 30: 1–10.

—— (2004c). 'Population, Settlement and Economy in Late Roman and Byzantine Palestine (70–641 AD)'. *Bulletin of the School of Oriental and African Studies* 67: 307–20.

—— (2006). 'Rabbinic Sources for the Study of Settlement Reality in Late Roman Palestine'. *Review of Rabbinic Judaism* 9: 92–113.

BARKER, G. W./LLOYD, J. A. (eds) (1991). *Roman Landscapes: Archaeological Survey in the Mediterranean Region.* Archaeological Monographs of the British School at Rome 2. London: The British School at Rome.

BARUCH, Y. (2005). 'H. Susiya—The Chronology of the Site in Light of Recent Excavations' [Hebr.], in *Judaea and Samaria Research Studies* 14, ed. Y. Eshel. Ariel: The College of Judaea and Samaria, the Center for Judaea and Samaria Studies, 157–67.

BEN DAVID, H. (1998). 'Olive Presses and Oil Production in the Golan in the Mishnaic and Talmudic Periods' [Hebr.]. *'Atiqot* 34: 1–62.

BERLIN, A. M. (2002). 'Romanization and Anti-Romanization in Pre-Revolt Galilee', in *The First Jewish Revolt: Archaeology, History, and Ideology*, ed. A. M. Berlin and J. A. Overman. London: Routledge, 57–73.

BIJOVSKY, G. (2000–2002). 'The Currency of the Fifth Century CE in Palestine—Some Reflections in Light of the Numismatic Evidence'. *Israel Numismatic Journal* 14: 196–210.

CHANCEY, M. A. (2002). *The Myth of a Gentile Galilee.* Society for New Testament Studies Monograph Series 118. Cambridge: Cambridge University Press.

CORBO, V. (1975). *Cafarnao I: Gli edifici della città.* Studium Biblicum Franciscanum 19. Jerusalem: Franciscan Printing Press.

CROSSAN, J. D./REED, J. L. (2001). *Excavating Jesus: Beneath the Stones, Behind the Texts.* New York: Harper San Francisco.

DALMAN, G. (1928–1944). *Arbeit und Sitte in Palästine.* 7 vols. Gütersloh: Bertelsmann.

DAR, S. (1986). *Landscape and Pattern: An Archaeological Survey of Samaria 800 B.C.E.–636 C.E.* British Archaeological Reports International Series 308. Oxford: Archaeopress.

—— (1988). 'The History of the Hermon Settlements'. *Palestine Exploration Quarterly* 120: 26–44.

—— (1999). *Sumaqa: A Roman and Byzantine Jewish Village on Mount Carmel, Israel.* British Archaeological Reports International Series 815. Oxford: Archaeopress.

——/SAFRAI, Z./TEPPER, Y. (1986). *Um Rihan: A Village of the Mishnah* [Hebr.]. Tel Aviv: Hakibbutz Hemeuchad Press.

DAUPHIN, C. (1982). 'Jewish and Christian Communities in the Roman and Byzantine Gaulanitis: A Study of Evidence from Archaeological Surveys'. *Palestine Exploration Quarterly* 114: 129–42.

—— and GIBSON, S. (1992–93). 'Ancient Settlements in their Landscapes: The Results of Ten Years of Survey on the Golan Heights (1978–1988)'. *Bulletin of the Anglo-Israel Archaeological Society* 12: 7–31.

EDWARDS, D. R. (2002). 'Khirbet Qana: From Jewish Village to Christian Pilgrim Site', in *The Roman and Byzantine Near East*, vol. 3, ed. J. D. Humphrey. Journal of Roman Archaeology Supplementary Series 49. Portsmouth, RI: Journal of Roman Archaeology, 101–32.

—— (2007). 'Identity and Social Location in Roman Galilean Villages', in *Religion and Society in Roman Palestine: Old Questions, New Approaches*, ed. D. R. Edwards. New York: Routledge, 357–74.

ELGAVISH, J.(1994). *Shiqmona on the Seacoast of Mount Carmel* [Hebr.]. Tel Aviv: Israel Exploration Society.

FELDMAN, L. H. (1999). 'Rabbinic Sources for Historical Study', in *Judaism in Late Antiquity. Part Three: Where We Stand: Issues and Debates in Ancient Judaism*, vol. 1, ed. J. Neusner and A. J. Avery-Peck. Leiden: Brill, 213–30.

FINE, S. (2005). *Art and Judaism in the Greco-Roman World: Toward a New Jewish Archaeology.* New York: Cambridge University Press.

—— (2006). 'Archaeology and the Interpretation of Rabbinic Literature: Some Thoughts', in *How Should Rabbinic Literature Be Read in the Modern World?* ed. M. Kraus. Piscataway, NJ: Gorgias Press, 199–217.

FRANKEL, R./GETZOV, N./AVIAM, M./ DEGANI, A. (2001). *Settlement Dynamics and Regional Diversity in Ancient Upper Galilee: Archaeological Survey of Upper Galilee*. Israel Antiquities Authority Reports 14. Jerusalem: Israel Antiquities Authority.

FREYNE, S. (2004). *Jesus, A Jewish Galilean: A New Reading of the Jesus Story*. London: T&T Clark International.

GOODMAN, M. (1983). *State and Society in Roman Galilee, A.D. 132–212*. Totowa, NJ: Rowman & Allanheld.

GREGG, R. C. (2000). 'Marking Religious and Ethnic Boundaries: Cases from the Ancient Golan Heights'. *Church History* 69: 519–57.

GUIJARRO, S. (1997). 'The Family in First-Century Galilee', in *Constructing Early Christian Families*, ed. H. Moxnes. London: Routledge, 42–65.

HACHLILI, R. (1988). *Ancient Jewish Art and Archaeology in the Land of Israel*. Leiden: Brill.

HARLAND, P. A. (2002). 'The Economy of First-Century Palestine: State of Scholarly Discussion', in *Handbook of Early Christianity: Social Science Approaches*, ed. A. J. Blasi, J. Duhaime and P.-A. Turcotte. Walnut Creek, CA: Alta Mira Press, 511–72.

HAYES, J. W. (1972). *Late Roman Pottery*. London: British School at Rome.

HIRSCHFELD, Y. (1984). 'Excavations of a Jewish Dwelling at Khirbet Susiya' [Hebr.]. *Eretz Israel* 17: 168–80.

—— (1995). *The Palestinian Dwelling in the Roman-Byzantine Period*. Jerusalem: Franciscan Printing Press.

—— (1997). 'Farms and Villages in Byzantine Palestine'. *Dumbarton Oaks Papers* 51: 33–71.

—— (2007). *En-Gedi Excavations II: Final Report (1996–2002)*. Jerusalem: Israel Exploration Society.

HORSLEY, R. A. (1995a). 'Archaeology and the Villages of Upper Galilee: A Dialogue with Archaeologists'. *Bulletin of the American Schools of Oriental Research* 297: 5–16.

—— (1995b). 'Response: Richard A. Horsley'. *Bulletin of the American Schools of Oriental Research* 297: 27–28.

—— (1996). *Archaeology, History and Society in Galilee: The Social Context of Jesus and the Rabbis*. Valley Forge, PA: Trinity Press International.

HUNT, E. D. (1982). *Holy Land Pilgrimage in the Later Roman Empire AD 312–460*. Oxford: Oxford University Press.

ILAN, T. (1995). *Jewish Women in Greco-Roman Palestine*. Tübingen: Mohr-Siebeck.

ILAN, Z./DAMATI, E. (1987). *Meroth: Ancient Jewish Village: Excavations at the Synagogue and Bet-Midrash* [Hebr.]. Tel Aviv: Society for the Preservation of Nature in Israel.

ISAAC, B. (1998). 'Jews, Christians and Others in Palestine: The Evidence from Eusebius', in: *Jews in a Graeco-Roman World*, ed. M. Goodman. Oxford: Clarendon Press, 65–74.

KALMIN, R. (1999). 'Rabbinic Literature of Late Antiquity as a Source for Historical Study', in *Judaism in Late Antiquity. Part Three: Where We Stand: Issues and Debates in Ancient Judaism*, vol. 1, ed. J. Neusner and A. J. Avery-Peck. Leiden: Brill, 187–99.

KILLEBREW, A. E. (2004). 'Reflections on a Reconstruction of the Ancient Qasrin Synagogue and Village', in *The Reconstructed Past: Reconstructions in the Public Interpretation of Archaeology and History*, ed. J. H. Jameson Jr. New York: Altamira Press, 127–46.

—— and FINE, S. (1991). 'Qatzrin–Reconstructing Village Life in Talmudic Times'. *Biblical Archaeology Review* 17: 44–56.

——/GRANTHAM, B. J./FINE, S. (2003). 'A "Talmudic" House at Qasrin: On the Use of Domestic Space and Daily Life during the Byzantine Period'. *Near Eastern Archaeology* 66: 59–72.

KLONER, A./ZISSU, B. (2003). 'Hiding Complexes in Judaea: An Archaeological and Geographic Update on the Area of the Bar Kokhba Revolt', in *The Bar Kokhba War Reconsidered: New Perspectives on the Second Jewish Revolt*, ed. P. Schäfer. Tübingen: Mohr-Siebeck, 181–216.

KRAEMER, D. (1999). 'Rabbinic Sources for Historical Study', in *Judaism in Late Antiquity. Part Three: Where We Stand: Issues and Debates in Ancient Judaism*, vol. 1, ed. J. Neusner and A. J. Avery-Peck. Leiden: Brill, 201–12.

KRAUSS, S. (1910–1912). *Talmudische Archäologie.* 3 vols. Leipzig: Gustav Fock.

—— (1929). 'The *krach*, the *ir* and the *kfar* in the Talmud' [Hebr.]. *He-'atid* 3:1–50.

LAPIN, H. (2001). *Economy, Geography, and Provincial History in Later Roman Palestine.* Texts and Studies in Ancient Judaism 85. Tübingen: Mohr-Siebeck.

LEVINE, L. I. (2005). *The Ancient Synagogue: The First Thousand Years.* 2nd ed. New Haven CT: Yale University Press.

LIEBESCHUETZ, J. H. W. G. (2001). *Decline and Fall of the Roman City.* Oxford: Oxford University Press.

MAGEN, Y./ZIONIT, Y./SIRKIS, O. (2004). 'Kiryat Sefer—A Jewish Village and Synagogue of the Second Temple Period', in *The Land of Benjamin*, ed. Y. Magen, T. D. Ariel, G. Bijovsky, Y. Zionit, and O. Sirkis. Jerusalem: Israel Antiquities Authority, 179–242.

MAGNESS, J. (2007). 'Did Galilee Decline in the Fifth Century?' in *Religion, Ethnicity, and Identity in Ancient Galilee: A Region in Transition*, ed. J. Zangenberg, H. W. Attridge, and D. B. Martin. Tübingen: Mohr-Siebeck, 259–74.

MA'OZ, Z. (1985). 'Comments on Jewish and Christian Communities in Byzantine Palestine'. *Palestine Exploration Quarterly* 117: 59–68.

—— /KILLEBREW, A. E. (1988). 'Ancient Qasrin—Synagogue and Village'. *Biblical Archaeologist* 51: 5–20.

MEYERS, E. M. (1982). 'Byzantine Towns of the Galilee', in *City, Town and Countryside in the Early Byzantine Era*, ed. R. L. Hohlfelder. New York: Columbia University Press, 115–31.

—— (1995). 'An Archaeological Response to a New Testament Scholar'. *Bulletin of the American Schools of Oriental Research* 297: 17–26.

——/KRAABEL, A. T./STRANGE, J. F. (1976). *Ancient Synagogue Excavations at Khirbet Shema', Israel, 1970–1972.* Annual of the American Schools of Oriental Research 42. Durham, NC: Duke University Press.

——/STRANGE, J. F./GROH, D. E. (1978). 'The Meiron Excavation Project: Archeological Survey in Galilee and Golan, 1976'. *Bulletin of the American Schools of Oriental Research* 230: 1–24.

——/STRANGE, J. F./MEYERS, C. L. (1981a). *Excavations at Ancient Meiron, Upper Galilee Israel 1971–1972, 1974–1975, 1977.* Cambridge, MA: American Schools of Oriental Research.

——/STRANGE, J. F./MEYERS, C. L./RAYNOR, J. (1981b). 'Preliminary Report on the 1980 Excavations at en-Nabratein, Israel'. *Bulletin of the American Schools of Oriental Research* 244: 1–25.

——/STRANGE, J. F./MEYERS, C. L. (1982). 'Second Preliminary Report on the 1981 Excavations at en-Nabratein, Israel'. *Bulletin of the American Schools of Oriental Research* 246: 37–54.

——/MEYERS, C. L./STRANGE, J. F. (1990). *Excavations at the Ancient Synagogue of Gush Halav.* Meiron Excavation Project 5. Winona Lake, IN: Eisenbrauns.

MORELAND, M. (2004). 'The Galilean Response to Earliest Christianity: A Cross-Cultural Study of the Subsistence Ethic', in *Religion and Society in Roman Palestine: Old Questions, New Approaches*, ed. D. R. Edwards. New York: Routledge, 37–48.

—— (2007). 'The Inhabitants of Galilee in the Hellenistic and Early Roman Periods: Probes into the Archaeological and Literary Evidence', in *Religion, Ethnicity, and Identity in Ancient Galilee: A Region in Transition*, ed. J. Zangenberg, H. W. Attridge, and D. B. Martin. Tübingen: Mohr-Siebeck, 133–59.

NEUSNER, J. (1999). 'Rabbinic Sources for Historical Study: A Debate with Ze'ev Safrai', in *Judaism in Late Antiquity. Part Three: Where We Stand: Issues and Debates in Ancient Judaism*, vol. 1, ed. J. Neusner and A. J. Avery-Peck. Leiden: Brill, 123–42.

PESKOWITZ, M. (1997). *Spinning Fantasies: Rabbis, Gender, and History*. Contraversions: Critical Studies in Jewish Literature, Culture, and Society 9. Berkeley, CA: University of California.

—— (2004). 'Gender, Difference, and Everyday Life: The Case of Weaving and its Tools', in *Religion and Society in Roman Palestine: Old Questions, New Approaches*, ed. D. R. Edwards. New York: Routledge, 129–45.

REED, J. L. (2000). *Archaeology and the Galilean Jesus: A Re-examination of the Evidence*. Harrisburg, PA: Trinity Press International.

RICHARDSON, P. (2004). 'Towards a Typology of Levantine/Palestinian Houses'. *Journal for the Study of the New Testament* 27: 47–68.

—— (2006). 'Khirbet Qana (and Other Villages) as a Context for Jesus', in *Jesus and Archaeology*, ed. J. H. Charlesworth. Grand Rapids, MI: Eerdmans, 120–44.

ROSENFELD, B.-Z./MENIRAV, J. (2005). *Markets and Marketing in Roman Palestine*. Supplements to the Journal for the Study of Judaism 99. Leiden: Brill.

SAFRAI, S. (1987). 'Home and Family', in *The Jewish People in the First Century: Historical Geography, Political History, Social, Cultural and Religious Life and Institutions*, ed. S. Safrai and M. Stern. 2nd ed. Philadelphia: Fortress Press, 728–92.

SAFRAI, Z. (1994). *The Economy of Roman Palestine*. London: Routledge.

—— (1998). *The Missing Century. Palestine in the Fifth Century: Growth and Decline*. Leuven: Peeters.

—— (1999). 'Rabbinic Sources as Historical: A Response to Professor Neusner', in *Judaism in Late Antiquity. Part Three: Where We Stand: Issues and Debates in Ancient Judaism*, vol. 1, ed. J. Neusner and A. J. Avery-Peck. Leiden: Brill, 143–67.

SARTRE, M. (2005). *The Middle East Under Rome*. Cambridge, MA: Harvard University Press.

SCHÄFER, P. (1995). *The History of the Jews in Antiquity: Jews of Palestine from Alexander the Great to the Arab Conquest*. Luxembourg: Harwood Academic.

SCHWARTZ, J. J. (1986). *Jewish Settlement in Judea after the Bar-Kochba War until the Arab Conquest 135 C.E.–640 C.E.* [Hebr.]. Jerusalem: Magness Press.

—— (2004). 'Material Culture and Rabbinic Literature in Late Antique Palestine: Beds, Bedclothes, and Sleeping Habits' [Hebr.], in *Continuity and Renewal: Jews and Judaism in Byzantine-Christian Palestine* [Hebr.], ed. L. I. Levine. Jerusalem: Yad Ben Zvi, 191–209.

—— (2006). 'The Material Realities of Jewish Life in the Land of Israel, c. 235–638', in *The Cambridge History of Judaism*. Volume IV: *The Late Roman-Rabbinic Period*, ed. S. T. Katz. Cambridge: Cambridge University Press, 431–56.

Schwartz, S. (2001). *Imperialism and Jewish Society: 200 b.c.e. to 640 c.e.* Princeton: Princeton University Press.

Shahar, Y. (2003). 'The Underground Hideouts in Galilee and their Historical Meaning', in *The Bar Kokhba War Reconsidered: New Perspectives on the Second Jewish Revolt*, ed. P. Schäfer. Tübingen: Mohr-Siebeck, 217–40.

Sperber, D. (1978). *Roman Palestine 200–400: The Land*. Ramat Gan: Bar Ilan University.

Stemberger, G. (1999). 'Rabbinic Sources for Historical Study', in *Judaism in Late Antiquity. Part Three: Where We Stand: Issues and Debates in Ancient Judaism*, vol. 1, ed. J. Neusner and A. J. Avery-Peck. Leiden: Brill, 169–86.

Tsafrir, Y. (1996). 'Some Notes on the Settlement and Demography of Palestine in the Byzantine Period: The Archaeological Evidence', in *Retrieving the Past: Essays on Archaeological Research and Methodology in Honor of Gus W. Van Beek*, ed. J. D. Seger. Winona Lake, IN: Eisenbrauns, 269–83.

Tzaferis, V. (1989). *Excavations at Capernaum*. Winona Lake, IN.: Eisenbrauns.

Urman, D. (1995). 'Public Structures and Jewish Communities in the Golan Heights', in *Ancient Synagogues: Historical Analysis and Archaeological Discovery*, vol. 2, ed. D. Urman and P. V. M. Flesher. Leiden: Brill, 373–617.

Wegner, J. R. (1988). *Chattel or Person? The Status of Women in the Mishnah*. Oxford: Oxford University Press.

Weksler-Bdolach, S./Onn, A./Rapuano, Y. (2003). 'Identifying the Hasmonean Village of Modi'in' [Hebr.]. *Cathedra* 109: 69–86.

Yeivin, Z. (1987). 'On the "Medium-Sized City"' [Hebr.]. *Eretz Israel* 19: 59–71.

—— (1994). 'Sussia—A Jewish Town from the Talmudic Period' [Hebr.], in *Judaea and Samaria Research Studies Proceedings of the 3rd Annual Meeting–1993*, ed. Z. H. Erlich and Y. Eshel. Ariel: The Research Institute, The College of Judaea and Samaria, 191–96.

Zevulun, U./Olenik, Y. (1978). *Function and Design in the Talmudic Period: Exhibition and Catalogue*. Tel Aviv: Museum Haaretz.

....

CHAPTER 11

TRAVEL AND
MOBILITY

....

CATHERINE HEZSER

STUDIES of Graeco-Roman society have shown that opportunities for travel and mobility greatly increased in Roman imperial times, when a comprehensive road network was created which, together with improved seafaring techniques, connected Rome with the various regions of Roman Italy and Roman Italy with the provinces of the eastern Mediterranean (see Casson 1994: 117–27, 163–73; Adams/Laurence 2001: 1–6; Laurence 1999: 39–47; see also Isaac in this volume). One may assume that these developments, which began with the early Roman emperors and continued until late antiquity, had a significant impact on ancient Jewish society. They would not only enable the development of a decentralized Jewish religious leadership in Roman Palestine after the destruction of the Second Temple but also facilitated economic, social, intellectual, and cultural connections and interchanges between the Land of Israel, Babylonia, Egypt, Roman Italy, and the various other regions in which Jews lived.

Unfortunately, issues of Jewish travel and mobility have not been a major topic of research amongst historians of ancient Judaism so far. Besides Samuel Krauss' treatment of the subject of 'Trade and Traffic' in his *Talmudische Archäologie* (Krauss 1911: 316–49) only a few studies which focus on sea travel exist (Sperber 1986; Patai 1998). Krauss as well as the other authors all focus on the material aspects of ancient Jewish travel, and the connection between travel and the economy, while the social and cultural significance of Jewish mobility remains unexamined. In addition, these studies are deficient from the methodological point of view, since they make undifferentiated use of early and late, Palestinian and

Babylonian literary texts as allegedly reliable historical sources. It seems that only in the aftermath of Roman historians' emphasis on the importance of mobility in Graeco-Roman society the relevance of the topic for ancient Judaism has been properly recognized by scholars (see Lightstone 2006: 1–2). The following sections will introduce readers to questions which need to be examined, and to methodo-logical problems and approaches. In examining ancient Jewish mobility, the main questions to be asked are: who travelled where, for what purpose, and what information was exchanged on that occasion? These questions can be answered only on the basis of a critical examination of all available literary, archaeological, epigraphic, and papyrological sources.

1. THE PRACTICALITIES OF TRAVEL

Krauss had already recognized the importance of the road system as the basis of travel in the Middle East, and he acknowledged Roman efforts to create a network of roads which were maintained partly by the state and partly by the local com-munities (Krauss 1911: 323–25). He does not deal with the implications of this phenomenon for Jewish mobility, though, but rather downplays it by stating that in general, the roads of Roman Palestine and Babylonia were bad, a conclusion which he may have reached on the basis of his own travel experiences in the Middle East and by comparing ancient roads with the modern European road system. Accordingly, in Krauss' chapter, the impact of the improved infrastructure on Jewish travel and trade in the Roman period remains unexplored, whereas the terminology used in rabbinic sources is discussed in much detail (though without differentiating the terms according to their Palestinian or Babylonian provenance).

Obviously, archaeological research has yielded many new results with regard to the extent and state of the Roman road system in Palestine and other provinces (see Isaac in this volume). Philip King has described the roads and their relevance for transport and trade in biblical times (King 1999: 94–95), whereas the road system of Roman Palestine has been examined by Moshe Fischer, Benjamin Isaac and Israel Roll (Isaac/Roll 1982; Fischer/Isaac/Roll 1996). What is important here is the convergence of archaeological evidence from both Roman Palestine and the Roman Empire at large: the Romans created a comprehensive road network which would connect the provinces to Roman Italy and enable Roman access and control over distant conquered regions (see Roll 1995: 1166–67). Although the primary purpose of these roads was the movement of Roman administrative and military officials, one may assume that they increased the private mobility of the various population groups of the Roman Empire as well (see section 2 below).

An alternative to overland travel, especially for destinations across the Mediterranean, were sea journeys. A lot has already been written on the advantages and disadvantages of sea versus overland travel (Casson 1994: 149–62; Kolb 2000: 318–19; Salway 2004: 46–50). Depending on the wind and weather conditions, the type of ship, and the destination, sea travel could be faster and less strenuous than road travel. But there were disadvantages as well: one might have to wait for a long time at the harbour until a ship was available; since there were no passenger ships, all provisions for the journey had to be taken on board and the conditions on deck could be quite uncomfortable; and adverse winds, storms, and pirates constituted real dangers one had to reckon with. During the winter months shipping on the Mediterranean would almost come to a standstill. Therefore those who preferred to travel in a more safe and comfortable way would prefer the land route—or at least sail close to the coast, if they did not mind the longer time such a journey would take. Remains of ships and cargoes have been found by underwater archaeologists in the harbour area of Caesarea and other coastal towns (see, e.g. Fitzgerald 1995), but the archaeological evidence has not been evaluated systematically together with the literary evidence so far.

Sperber (1986) and Patai (1998) mainly discuss the (biblical and) rabbinic evidence on Jewish seafaring. Like Krauss, they are mostly concerned with the terminology used in the texts and with the material and practical aspects of sea journeys, such as ships, provisions, and crews. Neither work provides a historical-critical examination of the sources. Early and late, Palestinian and Babylonian texts are quoted and discussed side by side. Literary references are usually considered to provide accurate historical evidence of the various aspects of sea journeys. Nevertheless, these works are useful in collecting relevant literary sources and in sometimes providing references to analogies in Graeco-Roman texts.

What still needs to be done is a critical evaluation of all available sources on the material aspects of Jewish travel. Furthermore, the evidence on Jewish travel has to be studied in the context of travel in Graeco-Roman society: were the practicalities of travel in Roman Palestine the same as in other parts of the Roman Empire? One may assume that this was the case with regard to some aspects, such as the responsibility for road repairs, which would have been administered empire-wide but also involved local communities. Traces of the discussion of such topics can also to be found in rabbinic sources (e.g. M. M.Q. 1:2; T. Sot. 7:23–24). Similarly, Jewish, just like Roman, travellers would have been required to plan their trips carefully to ensure that they carried the necessary provisions (see, e.g. T. B.M. 7:11; Gen. R. 60:11). The chosen means of transport will have depended on the type of journey, the geography, and infrastructure of the area, and the wealth and social status of the person travelling: mules may have been preferable for hilly areas, whereas camels and caravans were best suited for the desert. Those who could afford to do so would have travelled on horseback, in wagons drawn by a number of mules or litters carried by slaves, whereas the poorer strata of society had to walk or ride on asses (which were much cheaper than mules). In all of these regards, Jewish travellers are unlikely to have differed much from non-Jewish travelers, and Jewish sources may provide particular examples and illustrations of phenomena which existed in Graeco-Roman society at large.

Since almost all Graeco-Roman literature is written from the perspective of the upper classes, some of the Jewish literary sources can provide a different perspective. Rabbis seem to have come from a variety of social backgrounds and some rabbis, especially in amoraic times (3rd–5th c. CE) are presented as small farmers, artisans, and merchants: professions which are associated with the middle strata of society. Therefore rabbinic literature contains traditions about travel which derived from, and circulated amongst, ordinary working-class people who did not belong to the social, economic, and political elite. This background may account for the fact that the majority of rabbinic references to overland travel do not specify particular vehicles, and even prominent rabbis are depicted as riding on asses while colleagues and students accompanied them on foot (see, e.g. T. Hag. 2:1; Lev. R. 37:3). In a tannaitic tradition, ownership of one horse is considered a necessary prerequisite of a (non-rabbinic) member of a distinguished family (cf. T. Peah 4:10 par. Sifre Deut. 116:5). By comparison, Graeco-Roman authors considered it self-evident that dignitaries (including famous rhetors and philosophers) would travel in mule- or horse-drawn carriages with a large entourage, or let themselves be carried in litters (see Laurence 1999: 140, with reference to Horace, Satires 1.100–110). Rabbinic sources clearly offer a different perspective on ancient mobility by providing insights into the travel habits and practices of non- and sub-elite social groups.

Both Jewish and Graeco-Roman sources emphasize the dangers involved in travel: bandits and robbers encountered on the road, and stormy seas which could cause shipwrecks. Numerous stories relate precarious travel experiences of rabbis and others (see e.g. T. Yeb. 4:5, 14:7, 10), while legal discussions provide instruction on how to deal with the loss of property or the death or disappearance of a family-member (cf. T. Er. 3:8: one may desecrate the Sabbath when attacked by robbers; T. B.M. 7:13: question of ownership of property saved from robbers; T. Yeb. 4:5 witnessing the death of a man to allow his wife to remarry). A whole series of legal traditions deal with family members who travel overseas. The overseas death of a husband, wife, or son posed a variety of legal problems as far as remarriage, inheritance, and property ownership were concerned. These and other legal aspects of travel need to be compared with similar themes in Graeco-Roman legal sources. Only then can we determine whether and to what extent mobility affected Jewish and/or rabbinic society in a particular way.

Finally, the existence and nature of inns and hostels has been discussed by scholars at some length. Various types of institutions which accommodated travellers existed in the Mediterranean world of the first centuries CE, as Constable has shown (Constable 2003: 1–10). Constable has stressed that these hostels were cross-cultural institutions, in accordance with the name *pandocheion*, 'accepting all comers' (ibid. 11): travellers of different religious, cultural, and social backgrounds would lodge there and necessarily meet each other. They were often held in ill-repute as 'places outside the law, as locales for unruly, criminal, or illicit sexual behavior' (ibid. 15). Unless one had relatives or friends to stay with, however, the only alternative to hostels would have been to spend the night outdoors.

Hostels are frequently mentioned in rabbinic sources (see Rosenfeld 1998; Grossmark 2006). Although rabbinic texts reflect certain reservations against hostels, especially in connection with the danger of idolatry (M. A.Z. 2:1: Gentile inn-keepers suspected of bestiality; Gen. R. 92:6: innkeeper collaborating with bandits), some (especially female) innkeepers are presented in a positive light (cf. M. Yeb. 16:7: care for burial of deceased traveller, T. Yeb. 14:10: the innkeepers' testimony concerning a person's death is deemed trustworthy). It seems that inns were operated by Jews, Samaritans, pagans, and Christians in Roman Palestine (cf. T. A.Z. 2:9: inns may be rented out to Gentiles, 'even though it is certain that the gentile will bring an idol into it'; T. A.Z. 3:1: Samaritan inns), but pagan—and from the fourth century onwards Christian (see Constable 2003: 25-39)—hostels will have been predominant. The Christian hostels were established for the Christian religious traveller, whereas no hostels serving Jewish travellers only, or catering to particularly Jewish needs (e.g. kashrut) are known (except, perhaps as parts of synagogues). Like Roman travelers, rabbis seem to have preferred to stay with colleagues and non-rabbinic sympathizers or clients when away from home, a phenomenon for which the extensive rabbinic network would have been well equipped, but they would also use inns when necessary (see, e.g. Gen. R. 10:8, 92:6).

2. MOBILITY IN ANCIENT JEWISH SOCIETY

While it is impossible to determine the degree of mobility in ancient Jewish society, the sources nevertheless allow us to hypothesize about the social contexts in which travel was undertaken, and the social groups which participated in it. In antiquity, travel was undertaken for various reasons, both voluntary and involuntary, and could be conducted on private or public initiative. One may assume that as a consequence of the first and second revolt against Rome, many Jews were displaced from their farms and estates so that they had to find a living elsewhere. They would move their families from Judaea to Galilee or even leave the Land of Israel for better economic opportunities abroad. In view of the likelihood of migration and dislocation of large numbers of Jews under Roman rule, Lightstone argues that the general Palestine-centred approach to Judaism in late antiquity may be inappropriate (see Lightstone 2006: 2–5). At least some of the expatriates will have continued to maintain contact with their former homeland and probably travelled back and forth for private or business reasons.

Roman military pursuits also uprooted another set of Jews: war captives were enslaved and brought to Roman Italy unless they were sold at Middle Eastern slave markets. The large majority of such slaves will have ended up as strangers in strange lands. While many of them will have remained in Roman Italy and eventually been integrated into their host society, inscriptions suggest that at least some former slaves returned to Roman Palestine after their manumission (see Hezser 2005: 49–54, 227–30).

Besides emigration we also encounter immigration into the Land of Israel during the Roman period. Again, inscriptions as well as literary sources mentioning the place of origin of a person are our evidence for this phenomenon. Both of these bodies of evidence need to be used with caution, though. In the case of inscriptions, most of which appear in a funerary context, it is usually unclear whether a person was merely brought to Palestine for burial, or whether he or she had actually lived there for some time (see the discussion in Gafni 1981). With regard to the burial inscriptions found in the port city of Jaffa which mention relatively close (Alexandria) as well as distant places of origin (Tarsus, Babele, Cappadocia) one may assume that business reasons had brought many Diaspora Jews there (see Hezser 2001: 379).

In the case of literary references to rabbis' places of origin found in rabbinic sources, the question of these texts' historicity becomes crucial. Such references are particularly prevalent in amoraic documents such as Midrash Lev. R. and the Talmud Yerushalmi, where rabbis from various places within the Land of Israel— and sometimes also from the Diaspora—are mentioned. Although the place names may not be historically reliable (and there are manuscript variants and problems associated with the identification of places), those who formulated these traditions assumed that the respective rabbis were active at places away from their hometowns, that is, the references can be considered an indication of general rabbinic mobility, especially in the amoraic period.

Besides relocating on a more permanent basis for political, economic, or private reasons, Jews will also have left their places of residence temporarily in antiquity. Some of the reasons for ancient Jewish mobility have analogies in Graeco-Roman and/or early Christian sources, whereas others do not. Official travel for communal and administrative purposes, and business travel for purposes of local, regional, and international trade relations and the control of one's estates were probably the main causes of mobility in the Roman Empire at large. Accordingly, public officials, businessmen, and landowners will have been the most mobile members of society.

Unfortunately, the local administrative structure of Roman Palestine has not yet been properly investigated. One can only surmise that officers such as tax collectors, as well as various types of intermediaries between the Roman government and the local Jewish communities, would have to travel for professional reasons. Only the higher officials amongst them would have been able to use the *cursus publicus*, the official support network of transport animals, carriages, and road stations (on the *cursus publicus* see Kolb 2000: 49–121). Since bishops were allowed to use the *cursus publicus* for travel to and from official church councils from the fourth century onwards (see ibid. 91–92), perhaps the Jewish patriarchs, during the short period in which they were acknowledged as *viri clarissimi et inlustres* by the Romans (see Codex Theodosianus 16.8.8 from 392 CE), had this service at their disposal as well (according to Kolb 2000: 87, *viri illustres* were occasionally honoured with permission to use the system). Despite the circulation of tales about rabbinic visits to Rome (see section 4 below), rabbinic travel on the *cursus publicus* is highly unlikely. Nevertheless, this lack does not seem to have prevented rabbis from establishing a broad-ranging information network, at least as far as Syria-Palestine and Babylonia are concerned.

The types of travel most often specified in rabbinic sources are visits to teachers and colleagues, visits to bathhouses, travel to attend each other's family events, and travel for professional reasons. Since few rabbis seem to have been large estate owners, travel to supervise their estates is rarely mentioned, in contrast to Graeco-Roman sources which reflect the upper-class perspective, as pointed out above. A type of travel which is also rarely mentioned in rabbinic documents, partly for the same reason, is tourism and holiday travel. Upper-class Romans and even some members of the middle strata of society had holiday homes on the Mediterranean shore and in the mountains where they would spend part of the year (see Casson 1994: 138–48; Perrottet 2002: 65–101). Others would travel to famous sites, especially those known from Homer and mythology, to visit hero memorials, and to receive healing at sites considered holy (see Casson 1994: 230–50). Travel was done for pleasure as well as for cultural and religious reasons (see Elsner/Rubiés 1999: 7). Rabbis' focus on Torah study probably prevented them from 'wasting' time on travel for holiday or sightseeing purposes. Non-rabbinic upper-class Jews such as Josephus, of whom we know so little for the time after 70 CE, may well have resembled Romans in their leisure-time pursuits. Accordingly, one has to reckon with the possibility that villas in the Galilean mountains or on the Mediterranean seashore were the holiday homes of Jewish grandees.

3. Rabbinic Mobility

Palestinian rabbinic documents are our main sources for the time period and area under discussion here. Naturally, these sources are mostly concerned with rabbis and their students. Therefore we know more about rabbinic mobility than about the travel habits of any other members of the Jewish population. This raises the questions whether, and to what extent, rabbinic references to travel are (a) historically trustworthy and (b) representative of travel amongst broader segments of the population. These questions are not easy to answer and have to be examined anew for each aspect of the subject and in relation to every text examined. In relation to point (a) in this context it must suffice to say in a very generalizing way that if a number of texts of different literary forms, appearing in different literary contexts and documents, all refer to the same phenomenon, they may reveal certain patterns and habits of rabbinic society. Concerning point (b), in as far as rabbis were active participants in society at large, following ordinary occupations to make a living and maintaining families, their habits can be seen as representative of other Jews of similar social strata in Roman Palestine. As far as they constituted an intellectual and religious elite, however, their mobility should be compared with that of Graeco-Roman intellectuals and Christian clergy.

Scholars of Graeco-Roman society have studied the mobility patterns of pagan and Christian intellectuals and analysed the ways in which knowledge was exchanged and networks were created (see the articles in Ellis/Kidner 2004; the articles in Menache 1996 are mostly concerned with medieval society). They have argued that increased mobility in late antiquity can not only be assumed for officials, the military, and businessmen, but for academics, ecclesiastics, religious travellers, and other population groups as well (Drinkwater in Ellis/Kidner 2004: XVII). Students left their home towns and countries to travel to centres of philosophical study in search of knowledge (see Watts in Ellis/Kidner 2004: 13). Such travel for educational purposes was quite common in late antiquity and could involve a repeated change of teachers and places. Obviously, the reputation of a teacher and school was important in attracting students. Once they had acquired enough knowledge, students might return to their home towns, or establish their own schools elsewhere, carrying their masters' ideas with them. They would also tend to maintain connections with their former teachers and fellow-students, creating wide-ranging networks of scholars kept alive through occasional contacts, messages, and visits.

Similarly, Christian bishops became part of empire-wide communication networks, their ability to disseminate information in a speedy way increasing their influence in the region (see Sotinel in Ellis/Kidner 2004: 63, see also ibid. 74). Sotinel points to an important phenomenon: 'Due to the period's social, political, and religious developments, the later Roman Empire saw the creation and expansion of large inter-provincial networks of influence that could only be forged and maintained through extensive travel and carefully cultivated lines of communication' (ibid. 74).

Rabbinic mobility within Roman Palestine and between Palestine and Babylonia, as well as the patriarch's maintenance of relationships with the Jewish Diaspora, need to be examined in this context. In the first two centuries CE a decentralized rabbinic network was created in Roman Palestine which was based on personal relationships between scholars located at different places (see Hezser 1997: 171–80).

Contacts were maintained by mutual visits as well as through messages sent through intermediaries. Like the Graeco-Roman philosophical students, rabbinic students would leave their homes to study with a master, and change masters from time to time. By the third century a rabbinic movement existed in Babylonia as well. Throughout late antiquity there was a constant exchange of information and knowledge between these two centres of scholarship. The way such exchange was carried out needs to be studied in the context of, and in comparison with, intellectual exchange amongst Graeco-Roman and early Christian sages. While certain similarities are due to be revealed this way, significant differences need to be taken into account: the rabbinic network was not an empire-wide movement but limited to Palestine and Babylonia, and rabbis were not backed by a centralized church which controlled communication channels.

Numerous rabbinic story traditions tell of rabbis visiting colleagues at other places. Was halakhic exchange the main purpose of such visits? Perhaps social, economic, and intellectual motivations for rabbinic travel were interlinked. To stay with colleagues at distant places provided an alternative to hostels and inns. If so, rabbinic relationships would not be based on scholarship only, but on social and business connections as well. Those rabbis who were most mobile and had most connections may not only have fared well economically but may also have been most prominent within the rabbinic movement.

Patronage ties which linked rabbis to their sympathizers in their local, as well as in other, communities will also have been responsible for a certain amount of mobility amongst rabbis and their clients. Numerous case stories tell of people approaching rabbis and asking them for advice or litigation (see Hezser: 1997: 360–86). Similarly, rabbis are said to have advised entire communities and to have expounded the Torah in synagogues and study houses away from home (see ibid.). Such advice and instruction may have occasionally been given when rabbis passed certain towns and villages en route to other destinations, but it is also imaginable that rabbis travelled to exert their influence outside of their local spheres.

Although our information about the patriarch is subject to the same methodological concerns which govern other aspects of rabbinic culture, scholars agree that at some stage the patriarch established and maintained relations with Diaspora communities (see Menashe 1996: 16). Seth Schwartz has even argued that the Diaspora connection was the patriarch's main basis of authority (see Schwartz 1999). One has to assume that relations between the Land of Israel and the Jewish Diaspora were both financial and religious-ideological. The money which Diaspora Jews had contributed to the Temple before 70 CE. was now collected by the patriarch for other purposes. Diaspora Jews will have continued to view the Land of Israel as their spiritual home and maintained connections through commercial and family channels (see Menashe 1996: 22-25). The interaction between Palestinian Judaism and Diaspora communities outside of Babylonia still needs to be investigated more carefully for the time period under discussion here.

4. Sea Voyages

According to rabbinic stories, rabbis undertook occasional sea voyages, some of them to Rome. The purpose of the journeys is usually not stated in the narratives. The sea journey merely provides the setting for the discussion of a variety of halakhic and religious issues. For example, R. Gamliel and elders are said to have been travelling on a ship when the time for the removal of tithes (one tenth of the harvest) arrived (M. M.Sh. 5:9). In another story, also told about R. Gamliel and elders, the ship had reached the harbour after the onset of the Sabbath and the question arose whether one might disembark on a gangway made by a Gentile (*m. Shabb.* 16:8). Yet another tale relates that some rabbis were on a ship from Brindisi on the Sabbath. How far could they move on the ship, which was obviously located outside the Sabbath limits? 'R. Gamliel and R. Eleazar b. Azariah walked about its entirety. R. Yehoshua and R. Aqiba did not move beyond four cubits, for they wanted to impose strictness upon themselves' (M. Er. 4:1). These stories deal with the problems of observing halakhah while travelling. They provide examples and solutions which would have been relevant to those ancient Jews who tried to participate in the Roman culture of mobility, while at the same time leading a Torah-observant life. They provide examples of the ways in which rabbis acknowledged the importance of travel and moulded halakhic rules so that they would fit a lifestyle in which the necessity of ship voyages (even on the Sabbath) was taken for granted.

A large number of traditions in both the Mishnah and Tosefta address family law issues affecting those who went 'overseas'. For example, rabbis discuss the case of a woman whose husband had gone 'overseas' and allegedly died there, so that she remarried, but the first husband turned out to be still alive and returned home one day (M. Yeb. 10:1). Other traditions address property and inheritance issues. If two people were business and social partners overseas ('their trading and their eating and their drinking was done together'), can the one inherit property from the other once they have returned, although they are not relatives (T. B.B. 8:5)? If a husband wants to move abroad and his wife refuses to come with him, can he force her to do so (T. Ket. 12:5)? The very fact that rabbis discussed these issues in such detail suggests that journeys to places across the Mediterranean were a common feature of ancient Jewish culture and affected many aspects of Jewish life. The rabbinic legal advice for a mobile Jewish society needs to be compared with Graeco-Roman legal sources' treatment of travel-related issues.

The dangers involved in sea journeys are a frequent topic of rabbinic, Roman, and early Christian literary sources. Rabbis who embarked on sea journeys during the wintry season are said to have been scolded and ridiculed by colleagues and relatives (see, e.g. the two stories in Gen. R. 6:5). Shipwrecks will have been a common occurrence and caused many legal problems (cf. T. Er. 3:8: someone travelling on a ship which sinks may violate the prohibitions of the Sabbath to save passengers; T. B.M. 7:14: in case property and lives are lost as a consequence of a shipwreck, the company responsible for the voyage is liable to pay damages for the lost property only, meaning that passengers would always travel at their own risk). The religious problems appear to be particularly Jewish, while the property issues may have analogies in Roman law. Legendary stories tell of prayers and other religious rituals through which rabbis allegedly saved pagan ships from drowning (Patai 1998: 69–70). Similar stories appear in Christian sources of late antiquity and the Middle Ages (see Pryor in Macrides 2002: 38), whereas Graeco-Roman stories mention omens, sacrifices to the gods, and various other rituals meant to ensure divine protection (Casson 1994: 156–61). Such stories are worthy of comparison with regard to their literary forms, motifs, and *Sitz im Leben*. According to Mullett (in Macrides 2002: 282), such saint stories are 'a triumphalist demonstration of the empire-wide operations of the holy'.

Did ancient rabbis travel to Rome? Whereas tannaitic documents contain only a few such stories (e.g. T. A.Z. 6:7: sages meet philosophers; T. Hor. 2:5: R. Yehoshua redeems a Jerusalemite boy), they are more numerous in amoraic documents (e.g. Gen. R. 13:9: R. Eliezer and R. Yehoshua allegedly met with Hadrian; Gen. R. 20:4: R. Gamliel and R. Yehoshua talk with a philosopher; Gen. R. 33:1: R. Yehoshua b. Levi is shocked at the opulence he encounters in Rome; Gen. R. 78:15: R. Yehudah ha-Nasi allegedly met with representatives of the Roman government). Did rabbis' journeys to Rome actually increase from the third century onwards (perhaps as a consequence of the so-called urbanization of rabbis), or were amoraic rabbis more interested in presenting themselves as 'men of the world' who took international travel for granted? Are these stories told about particular rabbis only, to increase their reputation? Are they a feature of particular documents and literary contexts? Stories about encounters between sages and political dignitaries also appear in the philosophical and Christian literary corpora. Again, an examination of the rabbinic narratives in the context of other similar narratives circulating in Graeco-Roman and Christian culture is necessary in order to gain more insights into the character of such tales.

5. RELIGIOUS TRAVEL AND PILGRIMAGE

According to Deut. 16:16, three times a year all male Israelites shall 'appear' before God 'in a place which he shall choose': on Passover (lit.: 'feast of unleavened bread'), Shavuot, and Sukkot. During the Second Temple period the Temple in Jerusalem will have been considered the most holy place, but it is uncertain to what extent the biblical prescription to travel there three times every year was actually followed by Palestinian and Diaspora Jews. Jackie Feldman and Martin Goodman agree that there is no evidence of a mass pilgrimage to the Jerusalem Temple before Herodian times (Feldman 1993: 162; Goodman 1999: 71). Although local Jews from other regions of Palestine may have occasionally made pilgrimages to Jerusalem, for Diaspora Jews such a pilgrimage seems to have been rather unlikely before the Roman period. Improved travel conditions, more frequent commercial exchanges and communications, as well as the Herodian Temple rebuilding programme may have been responsible for the change. Goodman stresses the role of Herod in attracting Diaspora Jews to Jerusalem: he protected pilgrimage routes, entered into diplomacy with Diaspora communities, and appointed high priests with Diaspora origins (Goodman 1999: 73). This promotion of Israel tourism and pilgrimage will have been very beneficial economically for Jerusalem and Judaea. It will also have led to the creation of an infrastructure and facilities, such as hostels and inns, which would serve the visitors. Due to the nature of the sources, the number of Jews who went to Jerusalem on pilgrimage and the frequency of their visits remain uncertain, though.

Did Jerusalem pilgrimage continue after the destruction of the Temple in 70 CE? Even if individual Jews would come to Jerusalem once a year to mourn or say prayers at the ruins of the Temple (as mentioned by the Bordeaux pilgrim in 333 CE), this phenomenon cannot have resembled the mass pilgrimage to Jerusalem in Herodian times, and should probably not be called pilgrimage at all (against Safrai 1980: 376–93). Two factors are important here: First, Jews seem to have been officially prohibited from entering Jerusalem after their defeat by the Romans in the Bar Kokhba revolt. This prohibition was probably never followed and enforced entirely, and later relaxed or annulled, but there will have been little incentive for Jews to go to Jerusalem, which was turned into a pagan, and from the fourth century onwards into a Christian city. Secondly, Palestinian rabbis were not in favour of Jerusalem pilgrimage because they considered the Jerusalem of their days a polluted, destroyed, and unholy city. They had furthermore replaced Temple worship with piety based on Torah scholarship (see the discussion in Hezser 2000: 20–37). Thus, while individual Jews may still have visited Jerusalem in the first centuries, we may assume that, in general, Jewish pilgrimage to Jerusalem came to an end with the destruction of the Temple.

By contrast, Christian religious travel to Jerusalem and the Land of Israel only began in the fourth and fifth centuries CE when the practice was initiated by individual (women) travellers such as Constantine's mother Helena, the Bordeaux pilgrim, Egeria, Melania, and Eudocia, and numerous churches, monasteries, and hostels were built in Jerusalem and elsewhere (see Hunt 1982). Dietz has emphasized that not all types of Christian religious travel should be considered pilgrimage (Dietz 2005: 7). For some itinerant monks, homelessness was a form of asceticism and way of life. Early Christian religious leaders travelled for missionary purposes from city to city in various provinces of the Roman Empire. Even individual Christian travellers did not all come to Jerusalem to visit holy sites. Meetings with holy men in monasteries and desert caves were sometimes bigger attractions than gravesites and buildings. Personal problems at home often initiated temporary—or sometimes permanent displacement. Dietz stresses that these movements should all be seen within the context of the 'overall itinerant character of late antique society' (ibid. 23).

Rabbis' visits to colleagues and Babylonian scholars' travel to the Land of Israel would also fit into this broader scheme of travel for religious purposes in late antiquity. If one does not limit one's understanding of religious travel to a narrowly defined pilgrimage to holy sites, travel for the purpose of Torah study and discussion and students' and laypeople's travel to rabbis for halakhic advice could be seen as particular forms of religious mobility. What we do not seem to find in rabbinic sources, however, is the notion of homelessness and itineracy for its own sake, which is based on the belief that this world is only a temporary home. Amongst some Christian ascetics (allegedly following the model of Jesus), this view led to the idealization of perpetual homelessness until, with death or at the end of time, the soul would eventually find its real home in the heavenly Jerusalem (Dietz 2005).

Much work still needs to be done on the comparison of Jewish, Christian, and pagan mobility in late antiquity. How did certain practices of itineracy and religious/philosophical travel fit into the broader social and economic fabric of Jewish, pagan, and Christian society? How did they affect local communities? What were the ramifications of the creation of new interregional and international networks of relationships? If late antiquity is seen as the foundation period of both Judaism and Christianity, how did mobility help create structures and practices which would endure into the Middle Ages?

6. Mobility and the Transfer
of Knowledge

Since no telephone and internet systems existed in antiquity, mobility and communication were closely interlinked. Oral and written messages could be transmitted through personal contacts and messengers only. Thus the personal connections between the creator of the message, the transmitter, and the recipient were crucial for any communication to be successful. Since common people did not have access to a formal mailing system in antiquity (such a system existed for official governmental communication only, see Riepl 1913), relatives, friends, and business partners would serve as intermediaries, if one could not deliver the message oneself. On this basis one can easily understand that interregional networks for the exchange of knowledge and information could develop only if at least some of their members were mobile. One may also assume that the most mobile individuals had the largest number of contacts. If their mobility was accompanied by other status-marking criteria such as landownership, wealth, family heritage, and scholarship or education—and one may assume that the people with the highest status would tend to score high on a number of these points—it is likely that they were positioned at the nodal points of ancient (Jewish) society. This would mean that they could control and influence the flow of information. They would therefore have had more power and authority than others who scored low as far as these criteria are concerned.

In order to investigate the relationship between mobility and the exchange of knowledge, one would have to determine which sectors of the population would have travelled where, for what purposes, and what kind of information was exchanged, in which ways, on those occasions (I am currently working on a more detailed study on this topic). Obviously our source material is limited and sporadic, so that only certain general patterns can be determined and these should then be analysed within the context of our knowledge of mobility and communication within the larger Graeco-Roman society.

A study of mobility and communication patterns is of the greatest significance for a better understanding of the rabbinic transmission of traditions and the eventual development of rabbinic literary documents. One may assume that rabbinic literature could develop only on the basis of wide-ranging communication networks within Palestine, and between Palestine and Babylonia, which developed from the first century onwards. Since rabbis formed a decentralized movement, with individuals and clusters at many different places, mutual visits amongst colleagues and students' travel to teachers were vital for exchanging and transmitting traditions. By studying rabbis' mobility patterns and determining how they affected the exchange of halakhic information, valuable insights into the emergence, form, and handling of a particularly rabbinic body of traditional knowledge can be gained.

Scholars of ancient society have stressed that close connections existed between the development and use of particular types of media for communication, and the general development of cultures. Christian Frevel has argued that cultural development and media development are intertwined (Frevel 2005: 2). Not only texts and words can serve as media for transferring knowledge in everyday life, but objects, rituals and performances as well. In our text-centered culture it is difficult to understand the significance of other forms of signifying practices in antiquity. In Roman Palestine these signifying practices formed complex nets of information through which cultural identity was formed. Accordingly, the question as to how 'foreign' objects, symbols, and rituals imported into the Land of Israel from abroad would have interacted with local media and participated in the creation of a (complex and variegated) Palestinian Jewish cultural identity needs to be investigated (for consideration into this as far as biblical Israel is concerned see Uehlinger in Frevel 2005: 31–61).

Menashe has pointed out that in the Middle Ages 'the very existence of transportation and transmission channels *per se* did not assure the effectiveness of the communication network' (Menashe 1996: 7). Rather, the behaviour of the individual actors, the 'bearers of communication' within these networks, was decisive for the successful transmission of information. Therefore not only the patterns of behaviour amongst the provenly successful information transmitters (e.g. rabbinic traditions memorialized in written documents for later generations of scholars at more or less distant places) need to be studied, but the gaps and lacunae as well. Where within ancient Jewish society do we find relatively isolated groups whose communication practices were limited to the local level? What was the consequence of such isolation? If rabbis' communication network was basically limited to Palestine and Babylonia, what does this mean with regard to the body of knowledge which they developed? Through which channels did communication between Jews in Roman Palestine and the Diaspora take place, and which channels seem to have been closed or ineffective? One can be certain 'that the elaboration of accurate communication channels played a crucial role in the subsistence of Jewish society' (ibid. 8) and in the formation of Jewish identity. Therefore the study of Jewish mobility and communication within its specific historical, political, social, and economic contexts is of great importance for a better understanding of a variety of aspects of ancient Jewish culture.

SUGGESTED READING

Although Krauss' chapter on trade and traffic is antiquated both with regard to his source material and methodology, it still constitutes the classical treatment of the issues under discussion here (Krauss 1911: 316–49). The same reservations apply to Sperber's and Patai's books on sea voyages (Sperber 1986; Patai 1998), which are the only existing studies on sea travel from the ancient Jewish perspective. Goodman's article (Goodman 1999) discusses Jewish pilgrimage to Jerusalem in the Second Temple period, while Dietz (Dietz 2005) analyses the various forms of Christian religious travel in late antiquity.

BIBLIOGRAPHY

ADAMS, C./LAURENCE, R. (eds) (2001). *Travel and Geography in the Roman Empire*. London: Routledge.

CASSON, L. (1994). *Travel in the Ancient World*. Baltimore: Johns Hopkins University Press (reprint of first ed. 1974).

CONSTABLE, O. R. (2003). *Housing the Stranger in the Mediterranean World: Lodging, Trade, and Travel in Late Antiquity and the Middle Ages*. Cambridge: Cambridge University Press.

DIETZ, M. (2005). *Wandering Monks, Virgins, and Pilgrims: Ascetic Travel in the Mediterranean World*, A.D. 300–800. Pennsylvania: Pennsylvania State University Press.

ELLIS, L./KIDNER, F. L. (eds) (2004). *Travel, Communication and Geography in Late Antiquity. Sacred and Profane*. Aldershot: Ashgate.

ELSNER, J./RUBIÉS, J.-P. (eds) 1999. *Voyages and Visions: Towards a Cultural History of Travel*. London: Reaktion Books.

FELDMAN, J. (1993). 'Les pèlerinages au second Temple', in *La société juive à travers l'histoire*, vol. 4, ed. Sh. Trigano. Paris: Fayard, 161–78.

FISCHER, M./ISSAC, B./ROLL, I. (1996). *Roman Roads in Judaea II: The Jaffa-Jerusalem Roads*. BAR Int. Series 628. Oxford: Tempus Reparatum.

FITZGERALD, M. A. (1995). 'A Roman Wreck at Caesarea Maritima, Israel. A Comparative Study of Its Hull and Equipment'. PhD. thesis, Texas A&M University.

FREVEL, C. (ed.) (2005). *Medien im antiken Palästina*. Forschungen zum Alten Testament, 2. Reihe Bd. 10. Tübingen: Mohr-Siebeck.

GAFNI, I. (1981). 'Reinterment in the Land of Israel: Notes on the Origin and Development of the Custom'. *Jerusalem Cathedra* 1: 96–104.

GOODMAN, M. (1999). 'The Pilgrimage Economy of Jerusalem in the Second Temple Period', in *Jerusalem — Its Sanctity and Centrality to Judaism, Christianity, and Islam*, ed. Lee I. Levine. New York: Continuum, 69–76.

GROSSMARK, T. (2006). 'The Inn As a Place of Violence and Danger in Rabbinic Literature', in *Violence in Late Antiquity: Perceptions and Practices*, ed. H. A. Drake. Aldershot: Ashgate, 55–66.

HEZSER, C. (1997). *The Social Structure of the Rabbinic Movement in Roman Palestine*. Tübingen: Mohr-Siebeck.

—— (2000). 'The (In)Significance of Jerusalem in the Talmud Yerushalmi', in *The Talmud Yerushalmi and Graeco-Roman Culture*, vol. 2, ed. Peter Schäfer and Catherine Hezser. Tübingen: Mohr-Siebeck. 11–49.

—— (2001). *Jewish Literacy in Roman Palestine*. Tübingen: Mohr-Siebeck.

—— (2005). *Jewish Slavery in Antiquity*. Oxford: Oxford University Press.

HUNT, E. D. (1982). *Holy Land Pilgrimage in the Later Roman Empire*, A.D. 312– 460. Oxford: Clarendon Press.

ISAAC, B./ROLL, I. (1982). *Roman Roads in Judaea I: The Legio Skythopolis Road*. BAR International Series 141. Oxford: Tempus Reparatum.

KING, P. J. (1999). 'Travel, Transport, Trade'. *Eretz-Israel* 26: 94–105.

KOLB, A. (2000). *Transport und Nachrichtentransfer im Römischen Reich*. Berlin: Akademie-Verlag.

KRAUSS, S. (1911). *Talmudische Archäologie*, vol. 2. Leipzig: G. Fock.

LAURENCE, R. (1999). *The Roads of Roman Italy: Mobility and Cultural Change*. London: Routledge.

LIGHTSTONE, J. N. (2006). 'Migration (Forced and Voluntary), Communication and the Transformation of Judaism in the Greco-Roman Period: Prolegomena'. Unpublished manuscript, CSBS Conference, May 2006. 1–16.

MACRIDES, R. (ed.) (2002). *Travel in the Byzantine World*. Papers from the Thirty-Fourth Spring Symposium of Byzantine Studies, Birmingham, April 2000. Aldershot: Ashgate.

MENASHE, S. (ed.) (1996). *Communication in the Jewish Diaspora: The Pre-Modern World.* Leiden: Brill.

PATAI, R. (1998). *The Children of Noah: Jewish Seafaring in Ancient Times.* Princeton: Princeton University Press.

PERROTTET, T. (2002). Pagan Holiday. On the Trail of Ancient Roman Tourists. New York: Random House.

RIEPL, W. (1913). *Das Nachrichtenwesen des Altertums, mit besonderer Rücksicht auf die Römer.* Leipzig und Berlin: B.G. Teubner.

ROLL, I. (1995). 'Roads and Transportation in the Holy Land in the Early Christian and Byzantine Times'. *Jahrbuch für Antike und Christentum: Ergänzungsband* 20, 2: 1166–1170.

ROSENFELD, B.-Z. (1998). 'Innkeeping in Jewish Society in Roman Palestine'. *Journal of the Economic and Social History of the Orient* 41: 133–158.

SAFRAI, S. (1980). 'Jerusalem Pilgrimage After the Destruction of the Second Temple' [Hebr.], in *Jerusalem in the Second Temple Period.* Abraham Schalit Memorial Volume, ed. A. Oppenheimer et al. Jerusalem: Yad Yitzhaq Ben Tzvi, 376–93.

SALWAY, B. (2004). 'Sea and River Travel in the Roman Itinerary Literature', in *Space in the Roman World: Its Perception and Presentation*, ed. R. Talbert and K. Brodersen, Antike Kultur und Geschichte 5. Münster: LIT Verlag, 43–96.

SCHWARTZ, S. (1999). 'The Patriarchs and the Diaspora'. *Journal of Jewish Studies* 50: 208–22.

SPERBER, D. (1986). *Nautica Talmudica.* Ramat Gan: Bar-Ilan University Press.

IV

LABOUR AND TRADE

CHAPTER 12

THE HOUSEHOLD ECONOMY

ALEXEI SIVERTSEV

1. Source Material and Approaches

The Jewish household economy in Roman antiquity has become the subject of much scholarly interest and debate over the last few decades. Several trends in scholarship have converged to feed the discussion. On the one hand, there has been a series of attempts to re-evaluate literary sources that deal with the various aspects of Jewish family life, including the household economy. On the other hand, ongoing archaeological excavations in the Middle East have helped us to better understand the physical realities of the Jewish family and its economic activities. A key methodological question that needs to be addressed in this context is to what degree the literary, documentary, and archaeological material can be evaluated together. Can these sources be used to create a harmonious picture of the Jewish household economy in Roman Palestine, or do they reflect a variety of household economies that were chronologically, geographically, and socially distinct? If there is an apparent contradiction between two sources, does it stem from the inaccuracy of one of them, or does it reflect a diversity of socio-economic patterns in Roman Palestine? Reducing available material to a single harmonized picture may be both tempting and misleading. A more prudent approach would be to recognize the diversity of cultural and socio-economic environments in Roman Palestine and to discuss different types of household economy, rather then attempting to fathom a single prevailing pattern.

The Mishnah envisions the householder-dominated Jewish family as the basis of an ideal Israelite society. From the mishnaic point of view, as reconstructed by Neusner, the land-owning Jewish households of relative means constituted the backbone of Jewish economic life in Roman Palestine, and the main units of production and consumption. The ideal mishnaic householder is the *paterfamilias* (the head of a family) who, as a landholder, employed hired labourers to help with work in the fields and managing a small but self-contained farm. Craftsmen, traders, and shopkeepers are occasionally mentioned in connection with the householder's needs, but generally remained on the margins. The mishnaic householder was not a craftsman himself (Neusner 1981: 252, 255). Overall, Neusner identifies the mishnaic householder as 'the undercapitalized and overextended upper-class farmer, who has no appreciation whatsoever for the interests of those with liquid capital and no understanding of the role of trading in commodity futures' (Neusner 1981: 255). A major question remains, however, as to what extent such a portrayal reflects the true state of affairs in Roman Palestine, and to what extent it represents merely the wishful thinking and pious imagination of the compilers of the Mishnah. Neusner himself took a cautious approach and identified the mishnaic description of a household as an 'utter abstraction' that reflected little actual reality (Neusner 1990: 52).

Richard Horsley, however, has suggested that mishnaic households reflected the actual situation of the Jewish household economy of Roman Galilee. This economy was based on self-sufficient and self-supportive units: households produced what they consumed with relatively little access to liquid capital and trade. The money-based exchange of goods, as well as economic specialization and division of labour, is assumed to have been minimal. Each household produced the same basic variety of goods necessary to sustain the existence of its members: agricultural products, clothes, and so on. The trade that existed was fairly basic and usually did not surpass the village level. Wares and other household supplies were produced and traded locally. The integration of a typical Jewish household into regional trade networks was virtually non-existent. According to Horsley, the Galilean household economy represented a non-monetary economic utopia shielded from market interferences and based on cooperation and interaction among neighbours. The economic stratification among neighbours was limited and the use of land relatively uniform. The result was a self-sustaining and self-reproducing egalitarian village society capable of successfully isolating itself from the regional economies and trade networks of the Roman Near East (Horsley 1995: 203–207).

This view of a self-contained household economy contradicts another approach in modern scholarship that emphasizes the significance of trade for the Palestinian village economy, and the integration of the village economy into regional and even international trade networks (Goodman 1983: 54–63; Safrai 1994: 415–31; but cf. Schwartz 2006: 40). Several scholars have further developed Neusner's suggestion that the mishnaic description of economic life is first and foremost an ideological construct that pursues its own goal of imagining a well-ordered and properly functioning Israelite society. To what extent this vision of orderly reality can be projected back onto real history remains questionable (Safrai 1994: 304–15; Baker 2004: 113–28).

Along with this line of argument, Cynthia Baker has suggested a much more diverse and open type of household economy, in which marketplace activities constitute a crucial component of everyday economic life. Rabbinic texts make a concerted attempt to construct a closed-off and self-contained household space by marginalizing the importance of outside contacts and market economy. This mishnaic ideology of household economy, according to Baker, precisely represents a reaction against the much more open economic reality that threatened rabbinic ideas of stability and the controlled environment of the household. For Baker, Jewish households were not just the basic units of production and consumption, but also the basic units of trade in produced goods. The participation in the market economy was just as important for them as other kinds of economic activities (Baker 2002: 77–112).

Seth Schwartz has challenged the theory of a relatively stable and egalitarian agrarian economy empowered by small- and mid-size landowners from a different angle. According to his calculations, the agricultural productivity in Roman Palestine was relatively low, thus creating a highly volatile economic situation in which small and mid-sized landowners always stood in danger of crop failure and financial ruin. The economic life of a typical Jewish household would be very unstable in such conditions. Apparently, there was also a considerable gap between prosperous landholders inhabiting cities such as Tiberias and Sepphoris, and the less wealthy inhabitants of smaller villages and towns. Their lifestyles, exposure to outside influences, and household economies would have varied considerably. Provincial Jewish elites and their families were probably much more Hellenized and Romanized than their less affluent co-religionists (Schwartz 2006: 41–43).

Several proposed reconstructions have specifically emphasized the relative affluence, as well as a significant degree of Hellenization/Romanization, of Jewish households described in rabbinic texts. Shaye J. Cohen characterizes a typical rabbinic sage of the late first to early third centuries CE as someone 'well-to-do, associated with the well-to-do, and interested in questions which were important to the landed classes' (Cohen 1999: 936). Cohen further states that most of the early rabbis resided in the countryside rather than the cities, worked their land and tended their cattle, while trying to observe the prescriptions of the Torah. Even though he acknowledges that 'the economic status of these people will have ranged from the barely comfortable to the very wealthy', Cohen still believes that 'most of them were surely rather well-to-do' and shared economic, social, and cultural interests with the landed elites of the time (Cohen 1999: 930–36).

Unlike Cohen, Hayim Lapin emphasizes the urban setting of a mishnaic household (Lapin 1995: 233). Lapin's householders are affluent absentee landlords residing in cities, selling off the produce for money and, in turn, buying essential goods at the marketplace. They do not engage in production themselves but, rather, use the hired labour of tenants. Lapin's portrayal of the mishnaic household economy brings it closer to the standards of the prosperous landowning Roman elite. The mishnaic householder as constructed by Lapin very much resembles a Roman patrician enjoying the life of luxury in a city, benefiting from the labour of tenant farmers and actively participating in local and regional trade.

Methodologically, one has to recognize that, compared to early rabbinic literature, Josephus' works suggest a significantly more polarized society. This may contribute to the fact that scholars who take Josephus as the starting point of their historical reconstructions often tend to emphasize social extremes, marked by land-owning absentee magnates on the one hand and oppressed peasantry often resorting to rural banditry on the other (Schwartz 1994: 290–306). It remains unclear to what extent a harmonizing account of Josephus' and early rabbinic household economies is possible. It seems that these two sources originated in different social milieus and, as a result, produced two different visions of socio-economic reality.

The rabbinic movement itself was most likely not confined to a particular social class. Its members ranged from the old patrician family of Rabban Gamaliel and his descendants to modest artisans like Yohanan the sandal-maker. Most rabbis probably belonged somewhere in the middle (Hezser 1997: 257–66). In general, one has to avoid the temptation to reduce the entire rabbinic movement to a particular social group. Rabbinic identity was constructed as learning-based, not class-based, and the seeming uniformity of the rabbinic movement may itself be part of the construct. As a result, one should expect that actual rabbis ran a variety of household economies, even though the dominant theme in these texts seems to be that of a reasonably prosperous (but not exceptionally rich) householder managing his estate. To what extent this portrayal reflects the dominant economic pattern within the rabbinic movement itself is not entirely clear. In fact, it still remains far from clear to what extent this portrayal of an 'archetypal' Jewish household reflects any actual socio-economic situation in Roman Palestine, and to what extent it represents the pious fantasy about an ideal Israelite society.

When we turn to textual evidence outside the rabbinic corpus, texts from the Judaean Desert shed additional light on the nature of the Jewish household economy in Roman Palestine. A typical household of the *Damascus Document* (CD) (a collection of rules for the Dead Sea sect) is involved in agriculture, owns cattle, employs male and female servants (or slaves?), but it also participates in a money-based economy, buying and selling goods, and handling liquid capital (CD 10:15–11:20). Sapiential texts from Qumran warn against borrowing or lending money and praise economic self-sufficiency. The addressee of exhortations is repeatedly called 'poor', but what this term implies is not completely clear (4Q416 2 III). Most probably it does not mean destitute, but rather someone of limited means, a small- or mid-size proprietor (4Q418 103 II). There is clear evidence that house-holds that constituted the Dead Sea sect practised a variety of economic occupations, ranging from agriculture to small-scale trade. Having and using liquid capital was a standard part of their lifestyles. These households were not exceptionally rich but had enough income to afford servants or slaves (Sivertsev 2005: 108–10).

A similar picture emerges from the family archives of two Jewish women, Babatha and Salome Komaise, hidden in the caves of the Judaean Desert during the Bar Kokhba revolt of 132–135 CE. The family possessions are calculated in both land holdings and money savings. Land was constantly purchased, mortgaged, and sold. It was a trade commodity. The families in question were not poor. Babatha inherited four date groves from her father (P.Yadin 3). The produce of these groves was sold, providing Babatha with money income. The taxes that Babatha had to pay suggest that her holdings were large and profitable (P.Yadin 7 and 16). Her first husband inherited a family business from his father and left upon his death a substantial inheritance (P.Yadin 5 and 15). Babatha's second husband was less fortunate and had to repeatedly receive loans from either a locally residing Roman soldier or from his second wife, Babatha (P.Yadin 11 and 17). Yet he also owned a courtyard in the village of Ein Gedi that he inherited from his father (and that he used at least once to secure a loan), as well as several date orchards that he bought using Babatha's dowry money (P.Yadin 11, 21, and 22). His other possessions are unknown. Salome Komaise's family was perhaps somewhat less prosperous than that of Babatha, but belonged to the same social class of mid-size Jewish landowners, and probably shared friends and neighbours with Babatha. Once again, the picture of a relatively diverse household economy is confirmed. The families of Babatha and Salome Komaise owned both land and money (Satlow 2001: 97–100). They actively participated in a variety of business transactions: buying and selling both land and its produce, and taking loans and mortgaging land when necessary. Their economic contacts included not only Jews, but also Roman soldiers stationed nearby. Their litigation took place in Roman courts and followed Roman legal procedures. The household economies of these two women were very much part of a larger world and its economy.

Overall, documentary sources from the Judaean Desert display a certain consis-tency in describing household economic patterns in Roman Palestine. This econo-my was shaped by a combination of agrarian economy and trade. Money played an important role, as did a variety of money-related transactions, such as taking loans, mortgaging property, etc. The wealth of such households varied, as did the proportional relationship between different types of occupations: agriculture, crafts, or trade. The exact extent of slave-ownership by Jewish families remains unknown. Yet there are reasons to believe that the ownership of slaves was not uncommon. Households that constituted the Dead Sea sect, as well as some rabbinic households, included slaves, or at least one slave. It appears that slave tasks were by and large limited to the domestic sphere, whereas agricultural work was usually performed by hired labourers. Slaves could be also used as intermediaries in business transactions although the extent of this particular function is unknown (Hezser 2005: 275–84; 298–303).

Early Christian texts provide additional information about Jewish household economy, even though uncertainties about their editorial history may undermine the relevance of these texts for the reconstruction of Jewish life in Palestine. Just like other types of sources, the Gospels reflect the diversity of economic patterns. Mark 1:16–20 and 6:3 refer to family-owned small businesses such as fishing and woodworking as the dominant economic pattern within the Jesus movement. At the same time, Mark 10:29–30 implies that at least some of Jesus' followers came from landowning families. A paradigmatic character of parables in Luke is a relatively affluent proprietor, who owns slaves, fields, and livestock, employs hired labour to work his fields, and occasionally presides at Roman style banquets for his landowning peers (Luke 12:36–38, 42–48; 13:6–9; 14:16–24). He may be an absentee landlord living in the city and using hired labour to cultivate his countryside estates as these parables, along with Mark 12:1–9; 13:34–36 and some passages in Josephus, may indicate (Sherwin-White 1963: 139–43).

On the other hand, in the parable of a lost son in Luke 15:11–32 and the vineyard parables in Matt. 20:1–15 and 21:28–30, the landowner and his male children are actively involved in production activities themselves, while also employing slaves and/or hired labourers. Other passages imply that some of Jesus' listeners could themselves be owners of livestock, land, and slaves, and that the everyday economic routine of their families included selling, buying, and raising crops (Luke 15:4–6 and 17:7–9, 28, 31–37). These parables may be reliable historical witnesses of socioeconomic life in Roman Palestine. The picture they paint resembles the descriptions of household economy in the Judaean Desert documents, as well as in some rabbinic texts. Jewish household economies of Roman Palestine included absentee landlords, small-town artisans and fishermen, and mid-size landowners (Freyne 1980: 165–66). Each of these economies has to be approached and analysed on its own terms.

2. FAMILY MEMBERS AND PRODUCTION ACTIVITIES

Apparently, a nuclear, rather than an extended family constituted the main production unit of the Jewish household economy. There is little evidence that, after marriage, children continued to live with their parents. Social interactions mentioned in the Mishnah are mostly among neighbours, not relatives. The dominant role of a nuclear family significantly increased the role of women and children in the household economy, at the same time blurring the boundaries between private and work-related spheres of family life (Goodman 1983: 36). Skills were often transmitted within families from one generation to the next. Literary and epigraphic sources indicate that several generations of the same family often pursued the same trade. Such a situation would be fully in agreement with practices attested across the Roman Empire. All family members, including wives and children, were actively involved in managing and running family businesses across the Roman world. Jewish households in Palestine were apparently no exception (Goodman 1983: 55–57; Peskowitz 1993: 32–33).

Over the past decade there has been a growing attention among scholars to the problem of private and public space and its possible implications for the question of Jewish household economy in antiquity. M. Ket. 5:5 has often been interpreted as reflecting the Roman-style distinction between public and private economic space within the household (Ilan 1996: 185–86; Cohen 1999: 931). The Mishnah enumerates the tasks that a wife is expected to perform for her husband, such as grinding, baking bread, doing laundry, cooking, feeding her child, making her husband's bed, and working in wool. Most of them can be understood as household tasks performed within the private space of one's house, with minimal exposure to the public sphere of economic activity, such as the marketplace, stores, fields, and gardens. When interpreted in such a way, the Mishnah creates an impression of relatively secluded womenfolk, confined to inner spaces of Jewish houses, and representing the private dimension of household's life, just as their husbands represent the public face of the household. Even though it may remain true for some more Romanized Jewish households, such an interpretation has been challenged recently by a series of works that call into question the very applicability of the distinction between private and public spaces to Jewish life in Roman Palestine.

To begin with, the Mishnah does not rule out the possibility of other, much more public, economic duties by the wife. To be properly understood, the Mishnah has to be read in the context of other mishnaic passages. M. Qid. 4:14 assumes, for example, that a man can be involved in business dealings with women, in which case he cannot remain alone with them. The Tosefta takes it for granted that women sell bread and garments in the market, or that they sell olives because a man may be 'ashamed to be selling at the door of his shop, so he gives to his wife and she sells' (T. B.Q. 11:7). Grinding flour, baking bread, and working in wool become part of economic activities that eventually result in women selling their produce in the market. There is no indication that women were exclusively responsible for the 'indoors' parts of this production cycle. On the contrary, all the evidence points to the fact that they performed the production cycle in its entirety: from grinding, baking, and spinning, to selling the finished product in the marketplace or in the store. The public/private distinction clearly does not work in this connection (Baker 2002: 80–94; Ilan 1996: 184–90).

It appears that the very architecture of Jewish houses in Roman Palestine often undermines any strict distinction between private and public space within the household and the household's economic activities. The excavations at the town of Meiron in Upper Galilee in particular have helped redefine our understanding of living and working spaces in Jewish households during the middle and late Roman periods. The so-called 'insula MI' at Meiron consisted of two adjacent residences and a courtyard. The building had two floors, of which the upper floor most probably constituted residential quarters, and the ground floor housed a workshop and other working areas. Based on the items discovered in some of the rooms of the ground floor, the excavators have suggested that the workshop was used for wood-working activities, such as 'the manufacture of wooden containers of barrels for the thriving Galilean olive and olive oil industry' (Meyers 1981: 37). Other rooms and a courtyard contained remains of needles, stone grinders, and cooking utensils, along with three ovens. Such a distribution of space blurred the boundaries between public/work and the private/residential areas of the house described by the excavators as 'a domestic-industrial complex' (Meyers 1981: 38).

Written texts corroborate such conclusions. Rabbinic sources occasionally portray 'private' houses as areas where production of goods and other economic activities take place. M. B.B. 2:2–3 discusses the rules of setting an oven in a room of one's house or a shop in a shared courtyard. M. Toh. 9:6 implies that olives were dried on rooftops or in the rooms of the house. Such activities as spinning and baking bread probably took place within houses or courtyards as well. At the same time, there is ample archaeological and written evidence that many of the production activities took place outside residential areas. Threshing floors, olive presses, pottery kilns, tanneries, and installations for wine making were often located in specially designated areas of towns and villages, distanced from residential neighbourhoods (Peskowitz 1993: 30–31). Trade activities were usually carried out in the marketplace where stores were set up, although private houses often incorporated shops (Hirschfeld 1995: 98–99). In any case there was continuity between the economic space of one's household and the economic space of publicly owned and publicly used installations. By and large, the Jewish family in its entirety remained a 'working group', to use Miriam Peskowitz's apt definition (Peskowitz 1993: 31).

Only in more affluent Jewish households could there be a clearly articulated distinction between 'public' and 'private' spheres. Such a distinction probably reflected both economic prosperity and cultural Romanization of the household (Hezser 1998: 520–46). In general, one has to acknowledge the social, economic, and cultural diversity of Jewish households. The blanket application of one social pattern to all Jewish households in Roman Palestine seems counterproductive. Affluent and culturally Romanized families of Tiberias, Sepphoris, and other urban centres probably organized their household space differently from families in rural Galilee and Judaea or even from middle- and low-middle-class urban families. Recognition of the social, economic, and cultural diversity of Jewish households will also help us make better sense of archaeological remains. In urban and rural villas, boundaries between public and private space were probably drawn differently from less opulent *insula* houses (Hirschfeld 1995: 57–97; but cf. Meyers 2003: 58–68). Studying the combinations of multiple factors that might have influenced the construction of a household's social, economic, and cultural space remains a major desideratum. Eventually this will help create a typology of Jewish household economies that can better reflect the diversity of social, economic, and cultural life in Roman Palestine than any single pattern applied across the board.

Rabbinic texts routinely envision the family as the economic extension of its *paterfamilias*. The Talmudic dictum that 'the hand of a slave is like the hand of his master' (y. Peah 4:6, 18b) reflects a broader vision of rabbinic intellectuals that embraced, not just slaves, but also minors and, with important qualifications, wives (Hezser 2005: 69–82; 276–80). T. B.Q. 11:2 asserts that any income gained through business activities of either slaves or sons of the head of a household belongs to the latter. The *paterfamilias* possesses the only real economic authority within the household. Other members of the household serve as his agents, projecting the *paterfamilias*' authority outside the family. A further aspect of this principle is reflected in property laws that stipulate that any find made by members of a household ultimately belongs to the *paterfamilias*. According to M. B.M. 1:5, such household members include the householder's minor son or daughter, Canaanite male or female slaves, and his wife. On the other hand, items found by the householder's adult son or daughter, Israelite male or female slaves, and his wife whom he has divorced belong to the finder.

Hezser has convincingly demonstrated the analogy between this law and the Roman law (Hezser 2005: 276–80). The latter stipulated that certain members of a household, who were under the authority of the *paterfamilias* (slaves and children *in potestate*, that is, formally remaining under the authority of their fathers or mastors), 'borrowed' from him capital if they wanted to undertake business dealings on their own. As such, they could not be considered owners of the property that they used in their transactions. The *paterfamilias* remained the sole owner of the property and whatever further income that could be derived from it. Slaves and children *in potestate* could not conduct independent businesses or support themselves by the proceeds from such businesses. The right to independent business ventures could come only as a result of formal emancipation (in the case of a son) or manumission (in the case of a slave). The distinction drawn by the Mishnah between children who are minors and those who are grown up, as well as between Canaanite and Israelite slaves, may reflect a rabbinic version of this concept. Moreover, the Yerushalmi (y. Peah 4:6, 18b) commentary on this passage amplifies it by distinguishing between the two categories of 'adult' children: those who continue to receive support from their fathers (their finds belong to their fathers), and those who support themselves (they keep their finds). Such a distinction comes even closer to the Roman concept of children *in potestate* vs. those emancipated, even though it does not have an equivalent of the Roman notion of emancipation (Hezser, ibid).

The rabbinic concept of the *paterfamilias'* economic authority may very well reflect a provincial adaptation of the Roman law, as well as that of a more general Roman principle of a householder's power over the members of his house. In both cases it is either a free male Israelite or a free male Roman citizen who controls the household and its economic life. Other members of the household lack economic personality and serve as projections and extensions of the dominating figure of *paterfamilias*. T. B.Q. 11:5–7 in particular emphasizes and details their function as sales agents projecting the economic power of the *paterfamilias* through their transactions. The basic assumption behind the Tosefta's regulations is that family members (wives, children, and slaves) who sell in the market, act in the capacity of sales agents for the householder. The Tosefta attempts to protect the interests of the latter by making sure that other members of his household are not perceived as independent participants in business transactions who are free to make income and dispose of it any way they want. All profits that members of a household make ultimately belong to the *paterfamilias*. There are several exceptions, but they tend to confirm the rule: wives are allowed to handle small amounts of 'pocket money' (up to five denars, according to Abba Saul), and all three groups of wives, minors, and slaves can donate small amounts of money to charity collectors. Other than that, however, they act as representatives of the householder, carrying out the duties that he himself is unable or ashamed to fulfil. In this respect, the Tosefta's reference to a wife selling her household's produce at the shop because her husband considers this activity shameful is especially interesting. The wife in this case serves as an economic agent of her husband performing tasks that he is unwilling to perform because of their low social respectability. Slaves and minors may act in this capacity as well, and whatever profit they make is not theirs to keep. Overall, rabbis consistently construct the picture of a *paterfamilias*-dominated household economy in which other members of the household lack any independent capacity and merely reflect the presence and authority of the householder.

3. HOUSEHOLD ECONOMY AND MARRIAGE

This relatively straightforward structure was significantly complicated by Roman and Jewish views on marriage and a wife's role in the household economy. The ambivalence of a wife's economic role is well reflected in a series of mishnaic laws that seek to regulate her involvement in household trade and production activities and which, in the process, pose a key question: whether the wife of a householder is merely his economic agent or represents an independent subject in business activities. In rabbinic texts 'wives are construed as straddling two otherwise (generally) distinct categories—owners and contracted workers' (Baker 2002: 85). The tension between two socio-economic roles of a wife, that of an owner and that of a subject to her husband's authority, shapes the way in which rabbinic tradition addresses the wife's place in the household economy. M. B.Q. 10:9 presents a *locus classicus* of such an ambivalent status by allowing to buy from women 'garments of wool in Judaea or garments of linen in the Galilee or calves in Sharon' as long as the seller is not reputed 'to hide' the income from purchases. The Mishnah acknowledges and accepts the basic notion that women (apparently householders' wives) are actively engaged in trade activities selling the produce of their households. The text also seems to reflect the regional specialization of Jewish household economies: wool garments are associated with Judaea, linen garments with the Galilee, and livestock with the Sharon valley. Spinning is routinely portrayed by the rabbis as the single most important contribution by women to the economic life of the household (Peskowitz 1997: 95–108). Thus we probably see in this Mishnah a reflection of the cycle in which women served as both producers and sellers of goods.

The Mishnah also seeks to ensure that whatever profits the wife makes by selling the results of her work will go to her husband. It is prohibited to buy from someone who is known 'to hide' the profits, in other words, from someone who does not return the full amount of received money to her husband. As Michael Satlow observes, a general distrust of a woman's treatment of her husband's property permeates rabbinic literature. Y. Ket. 6:1, 30c openly states that the reason for the mishnaic requirement that anything found by a wife belongs to her husband is to prevent a wife from selling her husband's property, fraudulently claiming the ownership over it. Ket. 9:1, 32d prohibits a woman from selling her own property in order to ensure that she does not sell her husband's property by claiming it as her own (Satlow 2001: 218–19).

What these passages seem to reflect is the profound uncertainty about a wife's ownership rights. There is evidence that a wife's family continued to exercise at least some degree of authority over her property brought into marriage, even though the Talmud itself usually disapproves of such interferences. According to Satlow Palestinian rabbinic law both 'consistently asserts the rights of the husband over the property of his wife' and 'never completely eliminates the legal instruments that allow wives to evade this overarching control' (Satlow 2001: 218).

Hezser further explains this tension by putting it into the perspective of two legal principles that underlay Roman marriage practices of the time. The most widely spread practice in imperial Roman society was to contract marriage *sine manus*, that is, in a way that allowed the wife to maintain control over her own property brought into marriage. The rabbinic insistence on a husband's control over his wife's property resembles an earlier Roman practice of *manus* marriage, in which the husband acquired complete control and authority over his wife and whatever property she brought into the marriage. The clash of interests between the husband and his wife's family as well as the clash between the two legal principles of Roman family law, are most probably responsible for the ambiguous status of wives and their power of ownership within the rabbinic legislation. Even though the rabbinic ideal lay squarely with what can be described as the rabbinic version of *manus* marriage, the real life in Roman Palestine reflected the tension between the two principles (Hezser 2005: 73–75).

The family archive of Babatha discovered in the caves of the Judaean Desert provides a unique glimpse into how a real-life household economy worked. The archive belonged to a woman named Babatha, the daughter of Shimon and Miriam. Babatha's parents were reasonably well-to-do. When, some time around 120 CE, their daughter married for the first time a local Jewish man, Jesus the son of Jesus, her father gave her four date groves that he had acquired back in 99 CE (P.Yadin 3). After her husband's death, Babatha continued to benefit from the proceeds of the date groves (P.Yadin 7 and 16), even though his own inheritance was now managed by court-appointed guardians for his and Babatha's son Jesus (P.Yadin 12–15).

Babatha's second marriage was to one Judah, the son of Elazar Khtosion from the village of Mahoza. He took Babatha as his second wife some time between 125 and 128 CE. Babatha brought 400 denars as a dowry to this marriage (P.Yadin 10). Judah apparently used them to buy three date orchards in Mahoza (P.Yadin 21–22). Babatha's second husband's financial situation appears to have been quite erratic. Prior to marrying Babatha he went through some hard times, mortgaging his house to secure a short-term loan from a Roman officer that he eventually repaid (P.Yadin 11). In 128 CE he needed money once again, borrowing 300 denars from Babatha (P.Yadin 17). He apparently used 200 of them to provide his daughter from his first wife with a dowry (P.Yadin 18). Judah died two years later, leaving debts to his wives that he was unable to repay. Babatha promptly seized the date orchards that Judah had acquired with her dowry money (P.Yadin 21–25), whereas his other wife, Miriam, seized his house and personal possessions in Mahoza (P.Yadin 26). Babatha later wanted a share of those as well to compensate for the loan that Judah had received from her but failed to repay.

Babatha's story reflects the complexity of economic relationships within a second-century Jewish family. On the one hand, the husband exercises complete authority over the dowry of his wife. Her second husband, Judah, used Babatha's dowry to purchase date orchards. There is no indication that any of their revenues went to Babatha during his lifetime. It also seems likely that all the revenues from the four palm groves that Babatha brought into her first marriage belonged to her first husband, Jesus. Only after his death did she register them as her own property.

At the same time, once the husband tried to reach beyond the limits stipulated by the marriage contract, things could get significantly more complicated. Judah had to borrow from Babatha an additional 300 denars when he found himself in strained circumstances. The loan was meticulously documented and had to be repaid to Babatha. Once Judah's household defaulted on the loan, Babatha took swift action to secure the repayment. Beyond her dowry commitment, Babatha was an independent owner of property, whose relationships with her husband were strictly business-like and reciprocal. There is no indication that Judah had any power over Babatha's possessions other than her dowry. Whatever he borrowed from his wife (or, rather, from his wife's family) had to be documented and repaid. The story of Babatha and Judah resembles the passages from amoraic rabbinic texts in which wives are grudgingly recognized as independent owners of property (Satlow 2001: 218).

At the same time, Babatha's handling of her independent property seems to contradict some basic assumptions that lie behind the tannaitic legislation. As Satlow observes, tannaitic law tends to blur the line between a wife's independent and dotal property. The husband usually has the right to the usufruct of his wife's property, even though there is a clear understanding that this property is different from a dowry. A mishnaic debate attributed to the schools of Hillel and Shammai seeks to distinguish between the wife's property acquired before and after the marriage (M. Ket. 8:1). In the first instance, the wife has full legal right to sell her property; in the second, she has no right to sell it. Generally, however, tannaitic texts are opposed to the wife's right to alienate her property without her husband's consent. Moreover, other tannaitic passages explicitly praise the husband who makes use of his wife's property while intending to divorce her (Satlow 2001: 207–9). As a whole, the rabbinic view of a wife's right to own and make use of independent property is much more restrictive than the real-life practices that emerge from Babatha's archive. It is hard to be certain to what extent this rabbinic approach reflected the actual practices of Jews in Roman Palestine.

The issue of women as independent owners of property is closely related to the practice of marriage payments. Michael Satlow has convincingly demonstrated that as a rule 'Jews made the same kind of marriage payments as their non-Jewish neighbors' (Satlow 2001: 216). As a result, the dominant form of Jewish marriage payments in Roman Palestine was a dowry. The dowry served several purposes: to transmit inheritance to a woman, to compensate the husband for supporting and taking care of his wife, and to provide for a widow/divorcee. All of these purposes are reflected in contemporaneous Jewish documents. Rabbinic texts tend to view dowry precisely as a way of transmitting patrimony to a woman. In parallel to sons who inherit from their fathers, the daughters are maintained and dowered according to both the Mishnah and the Tosefta. This approach is somewhat different from the situation reflected in Babatha's documents. There, dowry serves as a way of passing on the inheritance from the woman's father to her male children. Special clauses guaranteed that the husband would not use the dowry to benefit any other children that he might have. In either case the dowry served as an important inheritance tool within Jewish families (Satlow 2001: 204–09).

Compensation was another way of seeing the purpose of dowry. Tannaitic texts repeatedly uphold the idea of reciprocity in financial relationships between the spouses. The husband's duty to feed, redeem, and bury his wife is directly correlated with his right to the usufruct of her property. T. Ket. 6:4 states that the minimum amount of a woman's dowry should be large enough so that her husband could 'purchase with it for all of her needs.' Several rabbinic texts assert in particular that dowry serves as compensation for the husband's obligation to pay for his wife's medical expenses. Such a perception of dowry, as Satlow observes, appears to be in full agreement with the Graeco-Roman view that dowry serves to maintain one's wife. Once again, economic relationships within a Jewish family seem to reflect larger patterns prevailing in the Roman provincial society of the time (Satlow 2001: 209–12).

Finally, in the case of the husband's death or divorce the dowry allowed the woman financial support. Yet in the case of Babatha the real source of income was not so much the liquid capital of the dowry as the gifts of land provided to Babatha by her father. Sometimes such land endowments could be transferred to the husband in exchange for the guarantees of additional support in case of his death or divorce (Satlow 2001: 212–13). This function of a dowry comes closest to the idea of *ketubba* payment that, according to rabbinic literature, the husband was supposed to pay his wife at the time of divorce. Recently, there has been a growing suspicion that the *ketubba* in this sense represents a rabbinic legal innovation, otherwise virtually unattested in Jewish marriage practices. As Satlow observes, 'The *ketubba* was a tannaitic fantasy, instituted by logical and legal necessity and perhaps also as a response to a sense of crisis' (Satlow 2001: 216). Most probably it was constructed by rabbis on the basis of some early precedents that were 'radically reworked in an ideological way'. It essentially constituted 'a fine for divorce' that served 'to prevent rash divorce, especially of a young woman who had never before been married'. In a way, it served to offset another piece of rabbinic legislation that allowed the husband to unilaterally divorce his wife, thus depriving women of their right to initiate divorce. The *ketubba* payment as envisioned by early rabbis never really caught on in Jewish society of Roman Palestine (Satlow 2001: 213–16). Instead, the practice of Graeco-Roman dowry dominated the scene, even though the dowry payment is occasionally referred to as *ketubba* in our sources. Overall, Jewish financial arrangements associated with marriage closely followed the dominant cultural trends in the Graeco-Roman society of the time.

The relatively straightforward portrayal of economic relationships within the Jewish household that emerges from rabbinic literature is misleading. The reality was more complex. Male Jewish householders dominated the economic life of their families, and yet their power was not as unrestrained as rabbinic texts would like us to believe. Economic relations between the spouses in particular depended on a system of checks and balances that allowed women to own independent property and make use of it. A wife's male relatives were always there to challenge the ambitions of her husband to make unrestricted use of his wife's property. Sometimes the size of a wife's dowry might have exerted indirect influence on her husband's behaviour and ability to divorce her, a fact equally lamented by Graeco-Roman and some Jewish authors (Satlow 2001: 212). In other cases husbands had to borrow money from their wives' independent properties with a legally documented obligation to repay the loan. Overall, the real-life complexity of economic relationships within the Jewish family far surpassed the idealistic picture of the *paterfamilias'* unchallenged supremacy painted in rabbinic sources.

4. CONCLUSIONS

A series of academic studies published in the last few decades has greatly enhanced our knowledge of the Jewish household economy in Roman Palestine. These studies also open venues for future research. It appears that one has to acknowledge economic and social diversity as a key characteristic of Jewish households of the time. We can no longer speak of the household economy in general. Rather, we should always specify what kind of a household we are talking about. Jewish families ranged from very affluent to very poor, and it is quite obvious that their economic and social standing in society was, therefore, diverse. Future discussions of private vs. public spheres of Jewish household space and participation in regional trade and money economy will have to take into account precisely this diversity. An affluent household of Sepphoris would probably be much more involved in the regional economy than a small- or mid-size household of Meiron. Women from affluent families did not have to perform the same amount of work as wives of artisans or small shop keepers, and so on. The recognition of diversity among Jewish households and their economic lives will provide an important methodological perspective in future research.

Other distinctions could also contribute to understanding the diversity of household economies. One of them concerns the regional geography within Roman Palestine. Some scholars have argued that the economies of Upper and Lower Galilee were substantially different because of the geography and natural resources of these two areas, as well as because of the different regional economic systems they belonged to (Meyers 1979: 286–702 and 1985: 115–31). Differences among local economies would naturally contribute to the diversity of household economies throughout the region. Differences between urban and rural economies could also be significant. A prosperous urban householder was often an absentee landlord owning tracts of land in the countryside and using hired labour to cultivate them. His (or his immediate family's) involvement in production activities was naturally quite different from that of even relatively prosperous farmers in Galilean villages.

Another issue that has to be addressed is that of chronological change. What was the relationship between the household economy in Hellenistic and Roman times? What changes (if any) did the Romanization of Palestine bring about? How did the Jewish household economy change in the course of Roman domination of Palestine? Did it stay relatively stable throughout the period? So far, there has been little attention to the historical development of the household economy, especially after the end of the Second Temple period.

Finally, a comparative study of the Jewish household economy and that of other ethnic/religious groups in Roman Palestine is long overdue. Can we indeed speak of a Jewish household economy, or did it reflect the same basic patterns as other household economies across the region? A study of these issues would further our understanding of Jewish families and their economic lives in Roman Palestine.

SUGGESTIONS FOR FURTHER READING

There is no separate comprehensive treatment of the Jewish household economy in antiquity. Two valuable resources on different aspects of the household economy including marriage, slavery, and economic roles of wives and children are Hezser 2005 and Satlow 2001. Baker 2002 and Peskowitz 1993: 24–34 attempt to create an integrated picture of the household economy on the basis of archaeological and rabbinic literary sources. They provide an interesting, albeit somewhat one-sided treatment of the subject, and must be read in the context of Hezser 1998: 423–579. Other publications that deal with the economy of Roman Palestine in general may also have either direct or indirect relevance to our topic.

BIBLIOGRAPHY

BAKER, C. (2002). *Rebuilding the House of Israel: Architectures of Gender in Jewish Antiquity.* Stanford: Stanford University Press.

——(2004). 'Imagined Households', in *Religion and Society in Roman Palestine: Old Questions, New Approaches*, ed. D. Edwards. New York: Routledge.

Cohen, S. J. D. (1999). 'The Rabbi in Second-Century Jewish Society', in *The Cambridge History of Judaism* vol. 3, ed. W. Horbury et al. Cambridge: Cambridge University Press, 922–90.

Freyne, S. (1980). *Galilee from Alexander the Great to Hadrian 323 b.c.e. to 135 c.e.: A Study of Second Temple Judaism*. Wilmington: Michael Glazier.

Goodman, M. (1983). *State and Society in Roman Galilee, a.d. 132–212*. New Jersey: Rowman & Allanheld.

Hezser, C. (1997). *The Social Structure of the Rabbinic Movement in Roman Palestine*. Tübingen: Mohr Siebeck.

—— (1998). '"Privat" und "öffentlich" im Talmud Yerushalmi und in der griechisch-römischen Antike', in *The Talmud Yerushalmi and Graeco-Roman Culture* vol. 1, ed. P. Schäfer. Tübingen: Mohr-Siebeck, 423–579.

—— (2005). *Jewish Slavery in Antiquity*. Oxford: Oxford University Press.

Hirschfeld, Y. (1995). *The Palestinian Dwelling in the Roman-Byzantine Period*. Jerusalem: Fransiscan Printing Press and Israel Exploration Society.

Horsley, R. (1995). *Galilee: History, Politics, People*. Valley Forge, PA: Trinity Press.

Ilan, T. (1996). *Jewish Women in Greco-Roman Palestine*. Peabody, MA: Hendrickson.

Lapin, H. (1995). *Early Rabbinic Civil Law and the Social History of Roman Galilee: A Study of Mishnah Tractate Baba Mesia*. Atlanta: Scholars Press.

Meyers, E. (1979). 'The Cultural Setting of Galilee: The Case of Regionalism and Early Judaism', in *Aujstieg und Niedergary der Römischen Welt* 2.19.1: 286–702.

—— (1985). 'Galilean Regionalism: A Reappraisal', in *Approaches to Ancient Judaism* vol. 5, ed. W. S. Green. Atlanta: Scholars Press, 115–31.

—— (2003). 'The Problems of Gendered Space in Syro-Palestinian Domestic Architecture: The Case of Roman-Period Galilee', in *Early Christian Families in Context: An Interdisciplinary Dialogue*, eds. D. Balch and C. Osiek. Grand Rapids: Eerdmans, 44–69.

——, Strange, J., and Meyers, C. (1981). *Excavations at Ancient Meiron, Upper Galilee, Israel 1971–72, 1974–75, 1977*. Cambridge, MA: American Schools of Oriental Research.

Neusner, J. (1981). *Judaism: The Evidence of the Mishnah*. Chicago: University of Chicago Press.

—— (1990). *The Economics of the Mishnah*. Chicago: University of Chicago Press.

—— (1997). *Spinning Fantasies: Rabbis, Gender, and History*. Berkeley: University of California Press.

Peskowitz, M. (1993). '"Family/ies" in Antiquity: Evidence from Tannaitic Literature and Roman Galilean Architecture', in *The Jewish Family in Antiquity*, ed. S. J. D. Cohen. Atlanta: Scholars Press, 24–34.

Safrai, Z. (1994). *The Economy of Roman Palestine*. London: Routledge.

Satlow, M. (2001). *Jewish Marriage in Antiquity*. Princeton: Princeton University Press.

Schwartz, S. (1994). 'Josephus in Galilee: Rural Patronage and Social Breakdown', in *Josephus and the History of the Greco-Roman Period: Essays in Memory of Morton Smith*, eds. F. Parente and J. Sievers. Leiden: Brill, 290–306.

—— (2006). 'Political, Social, and Economic Life in the Land of Israel, 66–c. 235', in *The Cambridge History of Judaism* vol. 4, ed. S. Katz. Cambridge: Cambridge University Press, 23–52.

Sherwin-White, A. (1963). *Roman Society and Roman Law in the New Testament*. Oxford: Clarendon Press.

Sivertsev, A. (2005). *Households, Sects, and the Origins of Rabbinic Judaism*. Leiden: Brill.

CHAPTER 13

AGRICULTURE AND FARMING

ZEEV SAFRAI

1. INTRODUCTION

The study of agriculture and the rural economy of Roman Palestine has already reached a highly developed stage, although it is carried out by only a small number of scholars. Detailed studies have been published on various topics, such as grains (Feliks 1990), orchards (Felix 1994), spices (Felix 1997), doves (Tepper 1986), the processing of oil and wine (Frankel/Avitsur/Ayalon 1994), rice (Felix 1963), and apiculture (Safrai 1998). There have also been important general surveys of agriculture and the economy of Roman Palestine, such as Felix (1982), Heichelheim (1938), Safrai (1994), and Löw (1967). In the context of this article I intend to provide a survey of research in the areas of agriculture and farming. I shall focus on the following questions:

1) To what extent was the economy open, involving import and export, and how was local agriculture adapted to the structure of the economy?
2) What was the impact of the agrarian structure on agricultural variety?
3) Was the practice of agriculture in Roman Palestine influenced by the Jewish religion of its native inhabitants?
4) To what extent did the agrarian economy of Roman Palestine differ from that of neighbouring provinces?

2. The Available Sources for the Study of Agriculture in Roman Palestine

2.1 Literary Sources

The main type of literary sources for the study of Palestinian agriculture during the first five centuries CE is rabbinic literature. Tannaitic literature was edited between the second and fourth centuries and is mainly legal and ethical in nature. What is particularly important is that this is a literature which was written and edited by people who were mainly occupied with agriculture and the agrarian economy. We learn about various types of crops, packaging, methods of distribution, and other such details. Rabbinic literature differs from Roman agricultural writing in a number of ways: first, it does not contain systematic discussions of the agriculture process; secondly, it was written by the small farmers themselves, who were very familiar with the subject they were writing about. Other types of literary sources of the period under discussion here contribute relatively less information on the subject at hand. The New Testament and Josephus provide incidental information only. For example, some New Testament parables reflect agricultural phenomena such as absentee landlords, *anachoresis* (flight from the land because of tax burdens), the hiring of day labourers, and the payment of wages (see Hezser 1990: 50–94).

The degree of historical reliability of these literary and legal sources has been discussed extensively during the last decades. This debate does not really affect the study of the small details of everyday life reflected in the texts, however. These details, which are usually mentioned in an incidental way or merely constitute the background for a legal ruling or story, may well reflect reality. For example, the Torah prohibits agricultural activities during the Sabbatical Year. It is possible, especially after the destruction of the Temple (70 CE.), that the majority of the population did not observe this law. Nevertheless, the agricultural activities which rabbis listed as permissible and forbidden are logical and pragmatic. Only rarely do we come across a tradition which may be considered 'farmers' folklore'. The interpretation of the sources remains complex and difficult, however. For example, the Jewish sources use a basic volume measure called *se'ah*, whose actual size is disputed amongst scholars (10–13 litres).

In addition to rabbinic sources, scholars of Roman Palestine have at their disposal the texts of Roman historians and agricultural writers (e.g. Pliny, Cato, Varro, and Columella), as well as Egyptian papyri reflecting various aspects of agricultural life.

2.2 Archaeological, Epigraphic, and Papyrological Sources

To date, numerous sites have been excavated in the relatively limited area of Roman Judaea and Syria-Palestine. Amongst them are entire sections of large villages (e.g. Capernaum, Ein Gedi, Sussia), hundreds of work-related installations (e.g. oil presses, wine presses, canals for soaking flax), and isolated structures. Furthermore, dozens of farmhouses (estates) have been excavated and entire villages have been surveyed, such as Rafid (Urman 2006), Umm Rihan (40 dunams), Burak (20 dunams), Hurbet Lebed (5 dunams), and other villages (for the surveys see Hirsch-feld 1997; Safrai 1997). Food caches have been examined (Kislev 1986, 1992, 2003), and many additional localized studies exist.

Unfortunately, the number of inscriptions reflecting an agricultural background is small, and mosaics in public and private buildings rarely show agricultural images, in contrast to mosaics found in North Africa and Syria). The documents from the Judaean Desert (second century CE.) and from Nitzana (seventh century CE.) may be used to shed some additional light on agriculture at the edge of the desert (Lewis 1989; Cotton/Yardeni 1997; Broshi 1992; Kraemer 1958).

2.3 Ethno-Archaeological Information

The traditional Arab village can, to some extent, be used as a model for studying ancient practices and work methods in the region. The history of comparative research in this area is a fascinating subject that reflects the difficult relationship between the Western (Jewish) visitor and the (Arab) residents of the traditional villages. During the 1960s and 70s archaeological research was flourishing in Israel and traditional villages continued to exist, whose lifestyle was only marginally influenced by modern culture. However, the study of traditional agricultural villages encountered many difficulties based on differences in language, culture, and politics, and sometimes researchers met genuine hostility. Scholars continued to be aware of the data emerging from the traditional village, but systematic research was extremely limited. Among the outstanding works in this regard are Dalman (1928–1942); Avitsur (1972, 1976, 1977).

3. THE LAND AND ITS PREPARATION

3.1 Climate and Topography

Since climate issues are discussed in another article in this volume, we shall merely deal with details which directly relate to agriculture. Most areas of the Land of Israel are very suitable for agriculture, with an annual rainfall of over 500 mm. By comparison, 200 mm of annual rainfall is considered in modern Israel the thresh-old for a drought in irrigated agriculture. However, various other problems existed in connection with the preparation of the land. In the coastal plains there were areas of swamps (in the northern and southern Sharon region). These were apparently drained in a large-scale enterprise during the Roman period. On the other hand, the fertile valleys in the Lower Galilee were apparently not drained at that time. In the mountainous regions of the Galilee and the Golan, terraces had to be built and stones had to be removed again and again. The terraces are a dominant feature of the hilly regions of the country. The farmers seem to have considered them the only way to prevent erosion.

The construction of terraces is also familiar to us from other hilly provinces (e.g. Cyprus, Phoenicia, Greece, and Italy, see Price/Nixon 2005). Although no quantitative examination has been carried out, it is clear that the density of the terraces in Palestine is far greater than in the other mentioned provinces and regions. Moreover, it is evident that in Roman Palestine the construction of terraces was a coordinated public enterprise, whereas in the other provinces they were built privately by individual farmers. In those areas of the Land of Israel where almost no terraces were built, such as the Yatir region, the land seems to have been used very little. The building of the terraces seems to have been a multi-generational enterprise which began during the Iron Age, yet most of the terraces that were examined by archaeologists were built during the Roman and Byzantine period. The traditional Arab economy continues this tradition until present times.

3.2 Risks

Although most areas of the Land of Israel receive sufficient rain during the year, rainfall mainly occurs in the winter months (November–March) and may vary from one year to the next. Moreover, not many natural freshwater reservoirs (e.g. springs) exist, and we can estimate that the amount of irrigated land constituted no more than 5 per cent of the entire agricultural potential. Drought years are a quite frequent phenomenon (on average once every three years), and they were a major risk factor for agriculture throughout antiquity. This problem persisted in the entire Roman Empire (Gallant 1991, 113–142), but it was particularly common in the province of Judaea, because of its specific landscape and climate conditions.

The main way of dealing with such agricultural risks in antiquity was to organize agricultural work amongst extended families and nuclear villages. Farmers would offer each other mutual assistance by forming communal and social networks. Rabbis often praise, nurture, and encourage such cooperation. Later in the Roman period the number of estates seems to have increased (see below). The later textual sources offer a different solution to the problem of risk: the burden is transferred from the relatively poor smallholder to the more powerful wealthy landlord. This phenomenon needs to be understood within the context of the patronage system, which was practised throughout the Graeco-Roman world (Wallace-Hadrill 1990).

3.3 Fragmentation of Estates

The property of the ancient farmer, certainly the wealthy farmer, was not always concentrated in a specific place. Often he had a number of plots scattered over a large area or even different regions. Sperber collected evidence of this phenomenon (Sperber 1978: 187–203). Obviously, most of the traditions he mentions concern rich landowners. We can assume that among the masses, ownership of a number of plots was less common.

It seems that in Roman Egypt the splitting of plots of land was practised as a general strategy. Each farmer had several plots, even serfs and poor tenant farmers had a number of small leaseholds (Rowlandson 1996: 124–131). The large number of plots was probably the result of many generations of dividing inheritances, and of buying and selling land. In the Judaean Desert documents (Babatha and Salome Komaise papyri) this phenomenon is also evident. There are both advantages and disadvantages to the system. The main disadvantage is the cost of cultivation: the ploughing and harvesting of one large area is easier than that of many small ones; supervising one field is more cost-effective than supervising many. In addition, the farmer would waste a lot of time travelling to his distant fields.

The Roman agrarian writers discuss the issue of plot fragmentation in much detail (see for example Cato, Agriculture, 1.7.9; Pliny, Letters 3.19 et al). In ancient times the size of a plot seems to have had a much more limited significance than nowadays. Once a plot had reached a certain size, any increase in territory would have lost its advantage. Modern farmers do not consider it worthwhile to bring a heavy and clumsy mechanical device to a small area, but those who depended on ancient agricultural technology would not encounter such a problem.

In the Mishnah, rabbis discuss the issue of minimum plot size in connection with the division of plots. In case a shared property holder demands the dissolution of the partnership, his demand is acceptable if the area is 'large enough to divide'. The measurements mentioned by the rabbis are very modest: '... and [they do] not [divide] a field unless it has nine half-*kabs* for one and nine half-*kabs* for the other ... and not a garden unless it has half a *kab* for one and half a *kab* for the other. R. Akiva says: a quarter [*kab's space for each one*]' (M. B.B. 1:6). This means that the minimum area required for dividing a field is 18 *kabs*, about half a *beit se'ah* (less that 400 sq. m) and in the garden, a square *kab* (slightly over 20 sq. m). Beyond that there is still an advantage to size, but it is not considered critical.

4. THE AGRARIAN SITUATION

Before the Maccabean revolt (167 BCE) agriculture in Judaea was based mainly on small independent farmers, alongside a few large landholders and royal estates. In the eastern Jezreel Valley, for example, there was a large royal estate, and we hear of additional estates from the Zenon papyri. We cannot estimate the size of the royal estates, but there is no reason to assume that they constituted a large percentage of the land. In addition, the Temple would have owned land, but presumably not much, in contrast to pagan temples which sometimes had large landholdings (Pastor 1997: 22–52; Safrai 2003: 114–117).

After the Maccabean revolt, the Hasmonean rulers inherited the lands of the Seleucid kings, and the subsequent conquests created a number of opportunities for confiscating territories. On the other hand, scholars reckon with a demographic growth in Judaea at that time (Tsafrir 1996), which may have caused a shortage of land amongst farmers. Large numbers of landless people streamed into Jerusalem in search of employment. Frequent replacements of the governing elites at the end of the Second Temple period were accompanied by land confiscations. North of Jerusalem a number of abandoned farm buildings from this period have been excavated and may reflect this phenomenon (Magen 2004: 1–28). Some scholars believe that the agrarian tensions and social divisions, together with other factors, led to the First Jewish Revolt against Rome (e.g. Applebaum 1967).

As a consequence of the first (66–70 CE) and second revolt (132–135 CE) the Roman authorities confiscated large areas of land and donated land to their loyalists such as Josephus (Vita 422). A significant change in the agrarian structure ensued. Small farming seems to have declined, a process which had already begun at the end of the Second Temple period and intensified in the third and fourth century CE (Safrai 1998: 40–44). In 380 CE the Colonatus Law was imposed in Palestine, prohibiting tenant farmers from abandoning their fields and leasing land from other owners. It testifies to the expansion of tenant farming in late antiquity and at the same time imposes severe restrictions on it (Clausing 1925; Jones 1958; Goffart 1974).

5. THE DIVISIONS OF AGRICULTURE IN PALESTINE

5.1 The Main Divisions

Agriculture was the main productive industry: it was the source of income and the occupation of most of the inhabitants of the country. Rabbinic literature mentions over 500 crops, of which almost 150 have been identified: amongst them eight types of grain, twenty types of legumes, twenty-four types of vegetables and water-melons, almost thirty fruit trees, about twenty types of herbs, and many non-fruit bearing trees. The three major crops were undoubtedly wheat, olives, and grapes. These three species are mentioned in hundreds of rabbinic sources (Felix 1982: 424–427).

The ancient Jewish diet seems to have mainly consisted of bread made from wheat (less frequently from barley), olives and olive oil, (fresh and dried) fruit and vegetables (Safrai 1994: 112–127; Broshi 1986; Dar 1986: 74: archaeological investigation of two Samaritan villages; see also ibid. 237–244; 147–164). We may assume that drinking wine was less common, at least amongst the poorer strata of society and amongst women (see M. Ket. 5:8; M. Peah 8:5; 8:7; M. Er. 8:2; Broshi 1986). The meal of an ordinary person would have consisted of bread with a vinegar and/or olive oil dip in the morning, and bread with lentil soup and an egg or some other substitute in the evening. At festive meals fish was served, and more rarely, meat. The meals of the wealthy would have been much more diverse than those of the poorer strata of society, as was common throughout the Roman world.

5.2 Wheat

It is clear that wheat was the most important grain crop in Palestine. According to rabbinic sources, grains were grown in a biannual cycle, one year of sowing followed by one fallow year. During the fallow year the land could be used for crops of secondary importance (e.g. lentils). Especially on small farms the harvested grains were probably meant for personal consumption only.

The average crop per dunam is unknown, due to the lack of reliable evidence. Felix has suggested that it was 150–300 kg per dunam (Felix 1990: 140–146), but his calculation is based on a convoluted analysis of a rabbinic text (b. B.M. 105b). Another approach is taken by comparative historical analysis. It has been argued that the average crop in Egypt was about 10 *artaba* (400 litres per 2.7 dunams), in other words, about 15 kg per dunam on a level and irrigated area (Rowlandson 1996: 9–247). Crop estimates from other regions of the empire are not sufficiently proven, since they are based on unreliable literary texts and on later sources (Evans 1981; Spurr 1986: 82–88).

The centres of wheat growing in the Land of Israel were the coastal plain (Lydda, Jamnia), the valleys of the Galilee, the region of Sepphoris, the Yavneel valley, and the Bet Shean valley. There is no evidence of a significant import of wheat to Palestine in ordinary years during the Second Temple and tannaitic periods. On the other hand, Amoraic sources from the third and fourth century CE suggest a large-scale import of wheat (e.g. y. Sheq. 8:1, 51a). During this period local farmers seem to have been unable to provide for the needs of the population, which had to rely on imports whose extent we cannot estimate. A number of other grains are mentioned in the rabbinic sources, such as oats, buckwheat, and rye, but they seem to have been of marginal significance only.

5.3 Olives

The climate of the Middle East was, and still is, particularly suitable for olive growth. Literary sources mention a number of regions that were especially rich in olives (such as the Galilee in general and the Upper Galilee in particular), and large numbers of olive presses have been discovered at archaeological sites (see Leibner in this volume). Apparently in almost every region of the country, with the exception of desert areas, the olive was a very important crop. It was also of great economic importance.

Olives were used mainly for the production of oil, as reflected in rabbinic sources (cf. T. Ter. 3:13). The eating of olives is also mentioned occasionally (M. Ter. 1:9; 2:6; 10:7; T. Ter. 4:3; M. Uq. 2:1 etc.) but seems to have been less significant. Oil was used as a dip for bread and also for cooking purposes. Most people probably had little need of oil for lighting, because they would go to sleep at sundown.

Olive trees were planted at an average interval of 11–12 trees per dunam, and the average yield mentioned in the sources is 12–20 kg per tree (Safrai 1994: 123–125). Cato (ch. 10) reports a lower yield of about 80 kg per dunam. Olive trees produce fruit in alternate years, but they have a stable yield that is less affected by climate changes (Safrai 1994: 118–126). Olives were picked in a variety of ways. Most of the olives were directly transferred to the olive press, where oil was produced from them (Frankel at al. 1994). Others were pickled, scalded, rolled, and salted for eating, or consumed in an unprocessed way.

A number of attempts have been made to estimate the economic significance of the oil industry in Roman Palestine (Safrai 1994: 123–124). Undoubtedly, many communities produced far more oil than they needed (ibid. 127). Literary, papyrological, and archaeological sources suggest that oil, together with wine and other products, was exported to other parts of the Roman Empire, especially during the Byzantine period (Kingsley 1999; Mayerson 1992).

5.4 Grapes

The production of wine out of grapes seems to have been a more profitable ancient industry than the production of olive oil and the harvest of wheat (Safrai 1994: 126–136; Vööbus 1982: 59–60; Bruns/Sachau 1880: 51 and 151; see also Leibner in this volume). In contrast to wheat, however, where the demand remains relatively stable, wine consumption is subject to constant change, depending on price and availability, as well as the respective economic situation. Wine was drunk in a pure state or mixed with hot or cold water. The amounts of water could vary, but a ratio of 2:1—two cups of water to one cup of wine—seems to have been customary (M. Nid. 2:7; b. Shab. 77a; b. Er. 29b; Num. R. 1:2; cf. 2 Macc. 15:38). Wine was a luxury item which enhanced the quality of life (see Midrash Tannaim on Deut. 16:14: 'There is no joy except with wine'; cf. Ben Sira 39:26). It was associated with festive meals and could obtain ritual quality (e.g. in the Passover Seder and the Christian Eucharist). As in the case of olive oil, a large part of the wine production of Roman and Byzantine Palestine seems to have been designated for export, especially to Egypt.

Grapes were mostly grown for wine making. Although fresh grapes were sold at the markets during the harvest season (T. Maas. 2:4; T. Toh. 11:7), and dried grapes were turned into raisins (T. Shebi. 6:29), the production of wine was considered the conclusion of the work with grapes (M. Maas. 1:7; T. Ter. 3:13). Vineyards were probably planted more densely than ordinary trees, but we have no reliable data about the number of plants per dunam and the average yield. The quantitative data given by Cato (11.1) and Columella (3. 3.2) is very high (up to about 3,000 litres of wine per dunam) compared with the traditional Arab economy with a yield of about 600 kg of grapes, that is, 360 litres of wine per dunam (according to my personal investigation). Rabbinic sources associate vineyards and wine-making especially with Judaea, but wine was produced in Galilee as well (cf. y. Meg. 1:12, 72d; y. Git. 3:8, 45b; y. B.B. 6:1, 15c).

5.5 Figs, Dates, and Other Fruit

Although figs were a very important crop (Felix 1994: 83–197), they were used as supplements to the main meal only. There are no rabbinic references to fig orchards, but only to single fig trees receiving special treatment (see also Kislev/Marmorstein 2004). The fig is mentioned as a fruit found in every marketplace, and tithes must be separated from it (M. Dem. 2:1). Figs seem to have grown within the rabbinic boundaries of the Land of Israel as well as in the surrounding regions, such as Transjordan (cf. y. Dem. 2:1, 22b: figs brought from Bosra). Pliny mentions the export of figs to Rome (Plinius, Historia Naturalis 13.51), but the extent of this practice remains unknown. The Mishnah mentions an average yield of 34 kg per tree (M. Shebi. 1:2). Whether this measure is historically reliable is uncertain, since we have no data for comparison from neighbouring countries.

The date orchards of Palestine seem to have been quite famous, since foreign writers who describe the country praise its dates, and those of Jericho in particular (Pliny, Historia Naturalis 13:26–49; Expositio Totius Mundi 31). Dates were grown in the desert regions and in the Jordan Valley (Felix 1994: 113–130). The centres of date cultivation were Ein Gedi, the Bet Shean Valley, the Tiberias region, and mainly Jericho, which in the Bible is called 'the city of dates' (Deut. 34:3). The date palm needs water and a lot of heat and is therefore limited to regions with a tropical climate. The Land of Israel was probably mostly able to supply its own demand for dates, but dates were also imported from Egypt in late antiquity (y. Dem. 2:1, 22b). For the desert monks, dates even served as a bread substitute (Palladius, History 52). Dried dates could be transported long distances and seem to have been exported to Rome (y. M.Sh. 4:1, 54d).

Besides figs and dates, over twenty different kinds of fruit trees are mentioned in rabbinic literature, including pears, peaches, and apples which need a European climate to grow. They were mainly cultivated in the Upper Galilee, but their general significance seems to have been small in comparison with the tropical plants. The carob (e.g. M. Maas. 1:6) seems to have served as food for the poor and for animals (M. Shab. 24:2; M. Maas. 3:4).

5.6 Vegetables and Spices

Although ancient Jewish literary sources mention more than twenty types of vegetables, the ancients do not seem to have known most of the vegetables commonly eaten today. Tomatoes, cucumbers, and peppers were unknown in Roman Palestine and amongst potatoes only sweet potatoes (*bulbusin*) are mentioned. Vegetables were a regular component of the ancient diet and seem to have been eaten at both morning and evening meals. The cultivation of vegetables is very dependent on irrigation. Therefore vegetables were grown in a 'garden' (*gan*) rather than in a field. Rabbis knew that they had a short shelf life and that, except for onions and garlic, they could not easily be stored (T. Peah 1:7). We may assume that vegetables were usually meant for the local market, but occasionally they were transported long distances (e.g. *bulbusin* are said to have been sent to Caesarea from Har Hamelekh in northern Judaea: y. Dem. 2:1, 22c; see also the Rehov inscription, Sussmann 1974: 132; onions from Ashkelon were even sent abroad: Strabo, Geography 16.229).

The most prominent herbs mentioned in rabbinic sources are mustard, coriander, cumin, capers, and above all, pepper. Pepper is a tropical plant, and adapting it to the conditions of Palestine was difficult (Qoh. R. 2:2). It seems to have been of limited regional significance only.

The growth of certain fragrant plants contributed to the reputation of Palestine all over the Roman world. The most outstanding among these plants were persimmon and myrrh. Many Greek writers praise these spices, and especially the balsam, which became a representative crop of the province (Felix 1997: 16–37). Within the boundaries of the Roman Empire itself, balsam and myrrh grew only in the Jordan Valley, and therefore these orchards were of great economic importance, at least until the first century CE.

5.7 Flax and Silk

Flax (*kitna*) was one of the main raw materials for clothing in the Roman Empire (Wild 1970) and is often mentioned in rabbinic sources (Herszberg 1924; Safrai 1994: 155–161). Flax seems to have been a typically Galilean crop, as opposed to wool, which is associated with Judaea (M. B.Q. 10:9; T. Ket. 5:4). The most famous place where flax was grown and processed was the city of Scythopolis/Bet Shean (Diocletian's Edict on Prices, ch. 26; Codex Theodosianus 10. 20. 8). According to rabbinic sources, additional centres of flax production were Tiberias and the Sea of Galilee region (b. M.Q. 18b). In Tiberias there may have been a weaver's union (Schwabe 1967: 181). As late as the seventh century CE we hear of a flax merchant from Neapolis staying in Tiberias (Brock 1973: 314–315). At least some of the facilities for soaking flax discovered in Tel Shosh/Gabea in the Jezreel valley, dated to the third century CE, were abandoned in the course of the sixth century, and olive presses were built over them (Safrai/Linn 1988). This suggests a reduction of flax-growing in favour of olives at that time.

Diocletian's price edict indicates that growing flax was much more profitable than growing wheat. Therefore, the farmer is likely to have exploited the full potential for growing flax, in accordance with the limitations of the sowing cycle (flax is sown once every six years). On average, one sixth or one quarter of the farmland would have been for flax over the long term. Another advantage of flax was that the peak season for flax growing would combine well with a work economy based on growing grains, olives, and grapes. Flax production was a long and complex process which could be accomplished at times when other agricultural work was impossible or limited. Some of the profits would go into the hands of the tax authorities and weaving factories, but we may assume that a large part of the income went to the farmer himself and to the crafts(wo)men.

Although various types of silk are frequently mentioned in rabbinic literature, silk appears to have mainly been imported from abroad (Herszberg 1924: 46–55). Roman Palestine lay at the crossroads of the ancient silk trade and trading in silk would have been common, but the local production of silk seems to have been exceptional.

6. Animal Husbandry

6.1 Shepherding

Goats were primarily raised for milk production, and ewes for shearing off the wool (M. Hul. 11:1). One can distinguish between three types of shepherding practices (cf. M. Betsa 5:7; T. Betsa 5:11; y. Betsa 5:8, 63b; b. Betsa 40a):

- sheep that graze in the desert all year round: these flocks were owned and cared for by nomads;
- sheep that graze in the desert or at the periphery of a settlement in the summer (from Passover until the rainy season in the autumn), and within the confines of the settlement in winter;
- sheep that graze within or close to the settlement itself.

The second type of practice suggests a mixed economy of agriculture and shepherding. The seasonal migration of the sheep required a special type of settlement familiar from Roman Italy (Frayn 1979: 17–46) and other provinces (Isager/Skydgaard 1992: 99–101; Whittaker 1988; Hodkins 1988). In Palestine, a settlement of this type was surveyed in Anab al-Kabir, and around the settlement sheep pens were found, usually consisting of a living room and yards for the sheep (Safrai 1985–6). The third category relates to an economy where shepherding is a secondary practice only. In this case, the land surrounding the settlement was mainly used for agriculture. Many rabbinic sources refer to this latter situation where a farmer has one or two sheep as an auxiliary branch of an agricultural farm. More wealthy farmers would not take their own sheep to the grazing grounds but hire a shepherd for that purpose (M. Betsa 5:3; M. B.Q 6:2, but see M. Shebi. 3:4). There were also regional distinctions: most shepherding took place in Judaea, whereas in the Galilee shepherding was marginal, since most of the land was used for agriculture. We do not know to what extent halakhic rules allowing the raising of small cattle (sheep and goats) at the periphery of settlements or in desert areas only (cf. T. B.Q. 8:10: chicken should not be reared in Jerusalem) played a role in this regard (Gulak 1941).

6.2 Farmstead Farming

The term 'cottage industry' is usually used for a series of agricultural branches which did not require specialization and were practised in the backyards of farmsteads. During the Second Temple period three settlement types were common: single farms (hamlets) where extended families lived in simple but spacious buildings; nuclear villages, in which the individual residential quarters were more restricted; and large estates similar to the Roman *villa rustica*. During the Roman period, the number of nuclear villages seems to have multiplied in Roman Palestine, whereas the number of simple hamlets declined (Safrai 1998: 37–50; Sperber 1978: 119–135). The farm building and estate house could well accommodate cottage industries, whereas the nuclear village with its small and crowed living quarters could not.

By providing many details about chicken farming, rabbinic sources suggest that the raising of chickens was a significant cottage industry in Roman Palestine (e.g. M. Toh. 3:8; M. Ned. 5:1). Chickens produced eggs and constituted meat for private consumption and sale at the local markets. Although they ate any food available, this food had to be provided for them, that is, they had to be properly fed (T. Shab. 24:3). The eggs could either be left for incubation or collected and sold to make an instant profit. The fertility rate of the chicken would have been based on their living conditions and the nutrition offered to them.

The raising of pigeons seems to have been marginal, and had a place of importance only in the Judaean Shefela at the end of the Second Temple period (Tepper 1986; Safrai

1994: 172–179). It is very doubtful whether this occupation was agricultural: the pigeons may have been raised for ritual purposes only. From the first century CE onwards, pigeons are occasionally mentioned as part of the household economy.

We may assume that the average smallholder would have owned a donkey for transportation and a cow for threshing purposes. Occasionally farmers seem to have lent cows to one another, as we learned (T. B.M. 6:14). Not every farmer would have had an ox, which was quite expensive, and we can assume that one ox served to inseminate many cows. The Sharon region is mentioned as a place where calves were raised (M. B.Q. 10:9).

In the Roman Empire the raising of pigs was considered one of the main branches of animal husbandry. Since the eating of pork was already prohibited in the Hebrew Bible and considered a severe transgression of Jewish food laws by rabbis, we may assume that pig farming was not commonly practised by Jews in Roman Palestine (Rosen 1995; Safrai 1994: 172–173). Excavations in the Jewish village of Ein Gedi revealed a small number of pig bones, though (Sadeh 2007: 604–612; Kislev/Marmorstein 2004). The Torah forbids only the eating of pigs, but not the raising and selling of them to non-Jews. Rabbis were more strict when stating that 'pigs should not be raised anywhere' (M. B.Q. 7:7). Not all Jews will have followed this rule and may have occasionally raised pigs to make a profit by selling them to non-Jews. Even rabbis seem to have been very familiar with pigs and knew many details about their nature and form (Felix 1974: 192; Rosen 1996). Nevertheless, there is no doubt that in the Jewish economy the pig was rare, and it is mainly associated with non-Jews (y. A.Z. 2:9, 42a).

Rabbinic sources give the impression that the cottage industry was rather limited in size and mainly the domain of women. By contrast, all the agricultural work outside of the household is connected with men. For people who lived in nuclear villages the fields were rather distant (approximately 1.5–2 km away from the villages on average), and women are mostly associated with the private sphere of the house. Women would probably participate in major agricultural tasks such as the grain or olive harvests, however.

7. The Nature of Agriculture in Roman Palestine

A mixed agriculture seems to have prevailed in Roman Palestine: in most regions of the country a variety of crops were grown. Exceptions were the desert areas which served for grazing only, and the Jericho valley where unique crops (dates, balsam) were grown. In individual villages many different kinds of crops would have been cultivated side by side, and farmers would engage in a variety of occupations.

A Babylonian Talmudic text recommending 'that your assets should be threefold: one third in wheat, one third in olives, and one third in vineyards' (b. B.M. 107a), reflects the economic utopia whereby the household should be autarchic, a situation which could be achieved by dividing the risks and dispersing work over the different seasons.

We do not know to what extent the rabbinic laws of *kilayim*, which prohibited the mixing of certain seeds (Lev. 19:19; Deut. 22:9ff; tractate Kilayim in the Mishnah, Tosefta, and Palestinian Talmud), and would therefore limit the joint cultivation of certain crops, were observed by lay people. Even for those who did observe the rules, there was still a possibility of sowing different types of seeds at reasonable intervals, and of having an orchard inside a sown field. The Palestinian Talmud transmits a dispute as to whether 'it is common' to sow grain among the trees (y. Peah 3:1, 17b). This was a common practice on traditional Arab farms, presumably in order to gain space and have mixed fields. Roman agricultural writers recommend adjacent orchards and adjacent fields of grain instead, even if the estate as a whole had a mixed economy. The agricultural recommendations of rabbis seem to have been based on a combination of both models: mainly adjacent fields, with the possibility of mixed fields as well.

It seems that rabbis' agricultural knowledge was quite advanced, and many rabbis may have actively practised agriculture themselves. We do not have any direct evidence of rabbis' familiarity with Roman agricultural literature, and similarities may have been based on merely observing nature and common practice.

Rabbinic literature indicates that the agricultural economy of Roman Palestine was for the most part very intensive, private, and small-scale, with the goal of self-sufficiency. The smallholder exploited every piece of land, including rocky corners that could be cultivated manually. At the same time there were also large landholders and royal estates. One needs to investigate to what extent gradual changes in this structure took place over the centuries in the direction of an increasing economic class differentiation. It seems that in the Byzantine period most of the agricultural economy consisted of large estates and tenant farmers. This may be the reason for the significant increase in hoards containing gold coins all over the East, as described by Jairos (Banaji 1992: 54–116), mainly for Egypt (Banaji 1999; Hardy 1931), but also evident in Palestine (Waner/Safrai 2001; Safrai 1998: 51–82). As far as agriculture is concerned, the transition from a small farm to a farm with absentee owners has a positive effect on the ability to invest, but a negative effect on the level of expertise and the intensity of the farming.

8. SUMMARY AND CONCLUSIONS

In general, the agriculture of Roman Palestine will probably not have differed much from that of the surrounding Near Eastern provinces, although the exploitation of the land may have been more intensive due to the landscape conditions with mountains, swamps, sand dunes, and desert areas. Agriculture was mainly small scale, aimed at self-sufficiency. Rabbinic literature reflects the prevailing agricultural conditions on which rabbis would rarely have exerted influence. On the basis of the Torah, rabbinic law developed special agricultural rules in the case of *kilayim* (mixed seeds), and in some others areas, for example the prohibition against raising pigs. But in general, there do not seem to have been significant differences between the agricultural practices of the mainly Jewish settlements in Galilee, the Samaritan settlements in Samaria, and Judaea which had become mainly non-Jewish in the second century. The observance of the Sabbatical Year law would have caused certain economic difficulties, but it did not affect the structure of the economy and was probably not strictly observed. There seem to have been certain gender divisions in agriculture as in other domains of daily life. Agricultural field work was mostly considered men's work, whereas women were associated with the auxiliary economy of the household (e.g. chicken farming, weaving, etc.), and with assisting their husbands in major agricultural projects.

SUGGESTED READING

Dar (1986) provides an introduction to the topic from the archaeological point of view, whereas Feliks (1990) is mostly based on rabbinic sources. For a broader perspective on the economy of the province Syria-Palestine, see Heichelheim (1938). Safrai (1994) constitutes the most comprehensive survey of the economy of Roman Palestine to date. Lapin (2001) discusses economic issues in connection with geography, settlement patterns, and regional history.

BIBLIOGRAPHY

APPLEBAUM. S. (1967). 'The Agrarian Question and the Revolt of Bar Kokhba' [Hebr.], *Eretz-Israel* 8: 283–287.

AVITSUR, S. (1972). *Daily Life in Eretz Israel in the XIX Century* [Hebr.]. Tel Aviv: Am Ha-Sefer.

—— (1976). *Man and his Work: Historical Atlas of Tools & Workshops in the Holy Land*. Jerusalem: Carta.

—— (1977). *Changes in the Agriculture of Eretz Israel* [Hebr.]. Tel Aviv: Miloh.

BANAJI, J. (1992). 'Rural Communities in the Late Empire A.D. 300–700, Monetary and Economy Aspects'. PhD. thesis, Oxford University.

—— (1999). 'Agrarian History and the Labor Organization of Byzantine Large Estates', in *Agriculture in Egypt from Pharaonic to Modern Times*, ed. A. K. Bowman and E. Rugan. Oxford: Oxford University Press, 193–216.

BROCK, S. (1973). 'An Early Syriac Document of the Life of Maximus the Confessor'. *Analecta Bodeliana* 91: 314–315.

BROSHI, M. (1986). 'The Diet of Palestine in the Roman Period: Introductory Notes'. *Israel Museum Journal* 5:41–56.

—— (1992). 'Agriculture and Economy in Roman Palestine: Seven Notes on the Babatha Archive'. *Israel Exploration Journal* 42: 230–240.

BRUNS, K. G./SACHAU, E. (1880). *Syrisch-römisches Rechtsbuch aus dem fünften Jahrhundert*. Leipzig: F. A. Brockhaus.

CLAUSING, R. (1925). *The Roman Colonate*. New York: Columbia University Press (repr. Rome: L'Erma di Bretschneider, 1965).

COTTON, H./YARDENI, A. (1997). *Aramaic, Hebrew, and Greek Documentary Texts from Nahal Hever and Other Sites*. Oxford: Clarendon Press.

DALMAN, G. (1928–42). *Arbeit und Sitte in Palästina*. 7 vols. Gütersloh: Bertelsmann.

DAR, S. (1986). *Landscape and Pattern: An Archaeological Survey of Samaria 800 B.C.E.–636 C.E.* Oxford: Archaeopress.

—— et al. (1986). *Um Rihan: A Village of the Mishna* [Hebr.]. Tel Aviv: Hakibbutz Hamuhad.

EVANS, J. K. (1981). 'Wheat Production and its Social Consequences in the Roman World'. *Catholic Quarterly* 31: 428–442.

FELIKS, J. (1963) 'Rice in Rabbinic Literature' [Hebr.]. *Bar-Ilan* 1:177–189.

—— (1982). 'The Jewish Agriculture' [Hebr.], in *Eretz Israel from the Destruction of the Second Temple to the Muslim Conquest*,ed. Z. Baras, et al. Jerusalem: Yad Ben Zvi, 410–441.

—— (1990). *Agriculture in Eretz-Israel in the Period of the Bible and Talmud* [Hebr.]. Jerusalem: Rubin Mass.

—— (1994). *Fruit Trees*. [Hebr.]. Jerusalem: Rubin Mass.

—— (1997). *Trees: Aromatic, Ornamental, and of the Forest* [Hebr.]. Jerusalem: Rubin Mass.

FLACH. D. (1990). *Römische Agrargeschichte*. Munich: C. H. Beck.

FRANKEL, R./AVITSUR, S./AYALON, A. (1994). *History and Technology of Olive Oil in the Holy Land*. Tel Aviv: Eretz Israel Museum.

FRAYN, J. M. (1979). *Subsistence Farming in Roman Italy*. London: Centaur Press.

GALLANT, T. W. (1991). *Risk and Survival in Ancient Greece: Reconstructing the Rural Domestic Economy*. Stanford, Ca: Stanford University Press.

GOFFART, W. (1974). *Caput and Colonate: Towards a History of Late Roman Taxation*. Toronto: University of Toronto Press.

GULAK, A. (1941). 'On the Sheperds and Those Who Raise Small Cattle in the Period of the Destruction of the Temple' [Hebr.]. *Tarbiz* 12: 181–189.

HARDY, E. R. (1931). *The Large Estates of Byzantine Egypt*. New York: AMS Press.

HEICHELHEIM, F. M. (1938). 'Roman Syria', in *An Economic Survey of Ancient Rome*, vol 4, ed. T. Frank. Baltimore: Johns Hopkins University Press, 121–257.

HERSZBERG. A. S. (1924). *The Cultural Life in Israel in the Period of the Mishnah and Talmud* [Hebr.]. Warsaw: Stiebel.

HEZSER, C. (1990). *Lohnmetaphorik und Arbeitswelt in Mt 20,1–16. Das Gleichnis von den Arbeitern im Weinberg im Rahmen rabbinischer Lohngleichnisse*. Freiburg and Göttingen: Vandenhoeck & Ruprecht.

HIRSCHFELD, Y. (1995). *The Palestinian Dwelling in the Roman-Byzantine Period*. Jerusalem: Franciscan Printing Press, Israel Exploration Society.

—— (1997). 'Farms and Villages in Byzantine Palestine'. *Dumbartom Oaks Papers*: 51:33–72.

HODKINS. S. (1988). 'Animal Husbandry in the Greek Polis', in *Pastoral Economics in Classical Antiquity*, ed. C. B. Whittaker. Cambridge: The Cambridge Philological Society, 35–74.

ISAGER, S./SKYDGAARD, J. E. (1992). *Ancient Greek Agriculture*. London: Routledge.

JONES, A. H. M. (1958). 'The Roman Colonate'. *Past and Present* 13: 1–13.

KEHOE, D. P. (1992). *Management and Investment of Estates in Roman Egypt during the Early Empire*. Bonn: Habelt.

KINGSLEY, S. A. (1999). 'Specialized Production and Long-Distance Trade in Byzantine Palestine'. PhD. thesis, Oxford University.

KISLEV M. A. (1986). 'A Barley Store of the Bar-Kochba Rebels (Roman Period)'. *Israel Journal of Botany* 35: 183–196.

—— (1992). 'Vegetal Food of Bar Kokhba Rebels at Abi'or Cave near Jericho'. *Review of Palaeobotany and Palynology* 73: 153–160.

—— (2003). 'Cereals and Fruits from a Collapsed Cave South of Khirbet Qumran'. *Israel Exploration Journal* 53: 74–77.

—— and MARMORSTEIN, M. (2004). 'Seed and Fruit Remains from Hurvat Raqit', in *Raqit: Marinus's Estate on the Carmel, Israel*, ed. S. Dar. Oxford: Archaeopress, 299–302.

KRAEMER, C. L. (1958). *Excavations at Nessana 2–3, part I: Literary Papyri; part 2: Non-Literary Papyri*. Princeton: Princeton University Press.

LAPIN, H. (2001). *Economy, Geography, and Provincial History in Later Roman Palestine*. Tübingen: Mohr-Siebeck.

LAUFFER. S. (1971). *Diokletians Preisedikt.Texte und Kommentar*. Berlin: de Gruyter.

LEWIS, N. et al (eds) (1989). *The Documents from Bar Kokhba Period in the Cave of the Letters. Greek Papyri*. Jerusalem: Israel Exploration Society.

LÖW, I. (1967). *Die Flora der Juden*. 4 vols. Hildesheim: G. Olms.

MAGEN Y. et al. (2004). *The Land of Benjamin*. Jerusalem: Israel Antiquities Authority.

MAYERSON, P. (1992). 'The Gaza "Wine" Jar (Gazition) and the "Lost" Ashkelon Jar (Askalônion)'. *Israel Exploration Journal* 42: 76–80.

PASTOR, J. (1997). *Land and Economy in Ancient Palestine*. London: Routledge.

PRICE, S./NIXON, L. (2005). 'Ancient Agricultural Terraces: Evidence from Texts and Archaeological Survey'. *American Journal of Archaeology* 109: 665–694.

ROSEN, B. (1995). 'Swine Breeding in Eretz Israel After the Roman Period'. *Cathedra* 78: 25–42.

ROUGÉ, J. (ed.) (1966). *Expositio Totius Mundi et Gentium*. Paris: Editions du Cerf.

ROWLANDSON, J. (1996). *Landowners and Tenants in Roman Egypt: The Social Relations of Agriculture in the Oxyrhynchite Nome*. Oxford: Clarendon Press.

SADEH, M. (2007). 'Archaeozoological Finds from En-Gedi', in *En-Gedi Excavations II, Final Report (1996–2002)*, ed. Y. Hirschfeld. Jeruralem: Israel Exploration Society, 604–612.

SAFRAI, Z. (1985–1986). 'Unab e-Kabir—Village Pasture in the Roman-Byzantine Period' [Hebr]. *Israel - People and Land* 2–3: 119–28.

—— (1994). *The Economy of Roman Palestine*. London: Routledge.

—— (1997). 'The Village in Judea' [Hebr.], in *The Village in Ancient Israel*, ed. S. Dar and Z. Safrai. Tel Aviv: Eretz, 11–73.

—— (1998). *The Missing Century: Palestine in the Fifth Century: Growth and Decline*. Leuven: Peeters.

—— (2003). 'The Agrarian Structure in the Time of the Second Temple, Mishnah, and Talmud', in *The Rural Landscape of Ancient Israel*, ed. A. M. Maeir, S. Dar, and Z. Safrai. Oxford: Archaeopress, 105–126.

—— and LINN, M. (1988). 'Excavations and Surveys in the Mishmar Ha'Emeq Area' [Hebr.], in *Geva: Archaeological Discoveries at Tell Abu-Shusham Mishmar Ha-'Emeq*, ed. B. Mazar. Jerusalem: Israel Exploration Society, 167–214.

SCHWABE, M. (1967). 'Tiberias Revealed Through Inscriptions' [Hebr.], in *All the Land of Naftali*, ed. H. Z. Hirschberg. Jerusalem: Israel Exploration Society, 180–191.

SPERBER, D. (1978). *Roman Palestine 200–400: The Land. Crisis and Change in Agrarian Society as Reflected in Rabbinic Sources*. Ramat Gan: Bar Ilan University Press.

SPURR, M. S. (1986). *Arable Cultivation in Roman Italy, C. 200 BC–C. AD 100*. Journal of Roman Studies Monograph 3. London: Society for the Promotion of Roman Studies.

SUSSMANN, Y. (1974). 'A Halakhic Inscription from the Beth-Shean Valley[Hebr.]. *Tarbiz* 43: 88–158.

TEPPER, Y. (1986). 'The Rise and the Fall of Dove-Raising' [Hebr.], in *Man and Land in Eretz-Israel in Antiquity*, ed. A. Kasher et al. Jerusalem: Yad Ben Zvi, 170–196.

TSAFRIR, Y. (1996). 'Some Notes on the Settlement and Demography of Palestine in the Byzantine Period: The Archaeological Evidence', in *Retrieving the Past: Essays on Archaeological Research and Methodology in Honor of G. W. Van Dam*, ed. J. D. Seger. Winona Lake: Eisenbrauns, 269–283.

URMAN, D. (2006). *Rafid on the Golan: A Profile of a Late Roman and Byzantine Village*, ed. S. DAR et al. Oxford: Archaeopress.

VÖÖBUS, A. (ed.) (1982). *The Syro-Roman Lawbook*. Stockholm: Papers of the Estonian Theological Society in Exile.

WALLACE-HADRILL, A. (ed.) (1990). *Patronage in Ancient Society*. London: Routledge.

WANER, M./SAFRAI, Z. (2001). 'Shelf Life of Coins in Palestine Hoards during the Roman and Byzantine Periods'. *Liber Annuus* 51: 305–336.

WHITTAKER, C. R. (ed.) (1988). *Pastoral Economies in Classical Antiquity*. Cambridge: Cambridge Philological Society.

WILD, J. P. (1970). *Textile Manufacture in the Northern Roman Provinces*. Cambridge: Cambridge University Press.

CHAPTER 14

ARTS AND CRAFTS, MANUFACTURE AND PRODUCTION

UZI LEIBNER

1. METHODOLOGICAL INTRODUCTION

Rabbinic literature provides a unique window into the daily life practices and social layers of a particular Roman province that are absent from other contemporary writings. Numerous rabbinic sources deal with craftsmen, products, and manufacturing, and offer valuable details about these aspects of life in Roman Judaea/Palestine.

Using rabbinic literature to examine the above-mentioned issues raises some serious methodological problems, however. Firstly, it is highly debated among scholars whether this literature provides the proper basis for the writing of history, including economic history. Furthermore, rabbinic literature does not discuss crafts or manufacturing as such, but merely mentions various facets of these activities occasionally, if they are related to the halakhic interests of the rabbis. Consequently, our information is in many cases incidental and cannot yield a comprehensive picture. Even if we regard rabbinic traditions as reflecting a specific reality, they rarely satisfy the main concerns of the historian, such as the role of a certain product in the economy, labour, distribution, etc. Since technological and economic practices may have changed and differed in accordance with the respective time periods and geographical regions, a careful historical-critical examination of this literature is required to determine its various layers and to establish the local origin of a tradition, if that is possible at all.

Since the pioneering and monumental work of Krauss (1910–12), which was based primarily on rabbinic sources, and of Dalman (1928–42), our knowledge about daily life in Roman Palestine has increased dramatically. Rabbinic texts have received a lot of scholarly attention with regard to philological and historical criticism. The works of Sperber (1993–2006) on artefacts and devices mentioned in rabbinic literature is a good example of the impact philological and comparative studies have had on the study of material culture. Safrai (1994) has evaluated the role of various products and their trade in the economy of Roman Palestine, and Aberbach (1994) has focused on labour and crafts. The latter two studies are both based mainly on rabbinic sources, including the Babylonian Talmud.

Much more far-reaching for our subject, however, are the archaeological finds in Israel and its environs, especially in the past fifty years. When studied together with the literary sources these allow for a much more detailed and balanced presentation of daily life, and in a sense also offer an opportunity to evaluate the historical reliability of certain rabbinic traditions. Thus, for example, various Palestinian rabbinic traditions mention pottery products from the village of Kefar Hananya, located on the border between Lower and Upper Galilee, praising their quality, and giving the impression that they were common in this region in the Roman period (Adan-Bayewitz 1993: 23–41). Excavations at this site indeed uncovered pottery kilns, and further investigation has established the quality and widespread distribution of these vessels (see below).

This chapter will therefore focus on those productions for which the archaeological data offers new insights and allows new evaluations which go beyond those based on the literary sources. Notwithstanding the immense value of the archaeological data, this evidence has its own share of methodological problems which one needs to be aware of:

A) The uneven preservation of the various types of material creates gaps in our information. Products or installations made of organic materials usually do not survive in the Mediterranean climate characteristic of most of the country, whereas inorganic materials such as metal, pottery, or stone remain relatively intact. Because of the extant remains of the massive stone-made oil presses, for example, our archaeological knowledge of olive oil production far exceeds that of, say, the linen industry.

B) Since the beginning of archaeological research in Israel, attention has been paid primarily to urban planning and monumental buildings, while relatively little focus has been placed on crafts and production, which have primarily been studied only in the past twenty years or so. Archaeological excavation reports usually provide detailed information on a specific site. However, obtaining a regional picture of the role played by the existing industries and products necessitates quantitative studies that synthesize data from many excavations. Few such quantitative studies have been published in Israel to date.

C) Ideally, the dating of the products or installations would enable us to track the scale of changes in a specific industry. However, the dating of the finds is often problematic and impedes quantitative studies. For example, the archaeological data for two of the main products of Roman Palestine, olive oil and wine, comes mainly from surveys in rural areas that document oil or wine presses. The dating of these installations is frequently very broad (e.g. 'Roman-Byzantine', a period of some 700 years) and does not allow for a narrower chronological focus. Nevertheless, there are a few advanced studies of products and installations that offer more accurate dating and more detailed information about the economy of more specific periods and regions (see below).

It is also important to note that integration into the Roman world had a clear impact on the crafts industry in Palestine. This is evident in wood and glass manufacture from the very beginning of our period, as styles and technologies of the Roman *koine* of material culture were quickly adopted in Palestine. Other industries, such as olive-oil production, seem to have been much more traditional and were slower in adopting Roman innovations, sometimes centuries after they were in use elsewhere in the empire.

Generally speaking, production was labour-intensive and technological innovations or labour-saving devices were rare throughout the period. To the best of our knowledge, most of the products were manufactured by small private craftsmen rather than by an organized or centralized 'industry'. Numerous traditions in rabbinic literature deal with the relationships between the producer (*baʿal habayit*) and his employees, while comparatively few mention slaves (see Hezser 2005: 298–303 on the economic functions of slaves). This gives the impression that the work force consisted mainly of free producers who were sometimes assisted by hired help or tenants.

2. Arts and Crafts

2.1 Pottery

Pottery vessels were the most common utensils from everyday life in antiquity. They were found in every household and used for a variety of purposes: transporting and storing goods, cooking and serving food. Indeed, pottery items are the most common artefacts found in excavations. Due to their central place in archaeological research, pottery vessels have merited a great deal of scholarly attention, providing information about their production or distribution that far exceeds any other product in Roman Palestine. Thus, although pottery was a rather insignificant factor in the ancient economy, its durability and ubiquitous presence as well as the state of its research makes it the best tool for trying to track modes of production, distribution, and economic behaviour.

Pottery production requires suitable clay, fuel, water, and, of course, a demand for the finished product. The clay was dug from specific areas and was at times refined by grinding or mixing it with other clays, sand, or crushed rocks, in order to obtain the desired texture. The potter would then shape a lump of clay into a vessel on a potter's wheel, which enabled fast and symmetrical work. The majority of vessels from the Roman period were wheel-made, while few, mainly very large storage jars, were handmade. The latter were probably made close to the consumption site, since it would have been difficult to transport them over longer distances. After drying, the vessels went through the last stage of production of firing in the kiln, usually a round structure with two chambers (e.g. Binyanei Ha'uma, see Arubas/Goldfus 2005: 15). The vessels were stacked upside down in the upper chamber, which was separated from the fire chamber beneath by fired clay bars.

The study of pottery production in Roman Palestine follows the general pattern of research on ancient Jewish daily life: from the literary sources in the past to the remains of material culture over the last few decades. The major study in Hebrew by Brand (1953) lists all references to pottery vessels in rabbinic literature and describes each vessel and its use. The importance of this work lies in its comprehensiveness, but in the 1950s very little archaeological evidence of the common pottery of Roman Palestine was available, so that many of Brand's identifications and examples are based on comparative material from the western parts of the Roman Empire.

The extensive archaeological activity that mainly began from the late 1960s onwards, when numerous Roman and Byzantine sites were excavated, served as the basis for detailed studies of the pottery from these periods. Several production centres were identified throughout Israel, such as Binyanei Ha'uma at the western entrance to modern-day Jerusalem (Berlin 2005a; Magness 2005). The research done on these centres and their products has enabled studies on the scales of production, distribution, and local trade.

Adan-Bayewitz's work (1993) is probably the most advanced study to date on local pottery production and distribution in the Roman eastern Mediterranean. Using chemical and micromorphological analysis, Adan-Bayewitz examined soil samples and pottery collections from various sites throughout the Galilee and Golan. His main achievements here were the identification of production centres and the ability to determine (on the bases of chemical matches) what vessels at various sites came from which production centres. The two main production centres in the Roman Galilee were found to be at Kefar Hananya (KH), on the border between the Lower and Upper Galilee, which produced kitchenware (bowls, casseroles, cooking pots, and jugs); and Shikhin, near Sepphoris, which produced primarily storage vessels (jars, jugs, juglets, kraters, and bowls (Adan-Bayewitz et al. 1995). These were the two predominant production centres in the Galilee in the Roman period, beginning from the late first century BCE until the late fourth to early fifth centuries CE. The production at Kefar Hananya declined in the latter part of the fourth century CE until it totally ceased in the early decades of the fifth. A few additional settlements produced forms that were virtually identical to those of KH or Shikhin, although apparently on a much smaller scale. For example, the chemical analysis of pottery from various Galilean excavations has shown that at sites in the vicinity of KH, such as Meiron, Kh. Shema', and Rama (about 4–8 km from KH), close to 100 per cent of the Roman-dated cooking vessels come from the KH kilns; in Sepphoris (about 25 km from KH), about 75 per cent; and in Jalame (about 45 km from KH), about 55 per cent.

Interestingly, pottery production in the nearby Jewish-settled Lower Golan shows a totally different pattern. The chemical analysis of vessels and the identification of some production locations (largely unpublished) have demonstrated that the demand for this commodity in this region was supplied by many local small manufacturers rather than by dominant centres such as those in the Galilee. The reason for this economic diversity is as yet unclear.

Recent research on different types of local jars and amphorae, their origins and distribution, has contributed much to the study of the economy of the Roman Empire. A few types of these vessels, which apparently originated in Byzantine Palestine, have been found at various sites in the Mediterranean basin (Zemer 1977; Peacock/Williams 1986: 191–9). Indeed, numerous production sites from the Byzantine period which manufactured these types of vessels were identified in the hinterland of the Gaza-Ashkelon area (Yisrael 1995a). They were used, apparently, for the transportation of wine and olive oil (see below), primarily by sea (Johnson/ Stager 1995). Thus, for example, a large estate near Ashkelon with oil presses and enormous wine presses had its own pottery kilns that produced the so-called 'Gaza jars' for transporting the estate's goods (Yisrael 1995b; see Fig. 14.1).

Imported fineware is almost totally absent from Jewish sites dating to the end of the Second Temple period through the first two centuries CE (during the third century imported fineware is absent also in non-Jewish settlements). Besides a few exceptional and wealthy sites, such as the Upper City of Jerusalem, where some imported wares were found (Rosenthal-Heginbottom 2006), the vast majority of the pottery from this period was plain, undecorated, and locally made. This stands in contrast to nearby areas such as Phoenicia, where the *terra sigillata* fineware, for example, was very common. Some scholars have suggested that Jews avoided using imported ware on halakhic or ideological grounds (Adan-Bayewitz/Aviam 1997; Berlin 2005b and 2006). However, from about the mid-fourth century CE imported fineware, known as Late Roman Red Ware (LRRW), became very common at Jewish sites in the Galilee and Golan, even in remote rural settlements. Hence, the

Fig. 14.1 The so-called 'Gaza Jar' from the Ramat Hanadiv excavations (southern Carmel area)

Hirschfeld 2000: 123

existence or absence of imported fineware may be attributed to economic changes (perhaps related to customs duties).

Even after the penetration of fineware into the region, the vast majority of pottery found at Roman and Byzantine sites was made in local production centres that distributed their products to distances ranging from a few to a few dozen kilometres. Some of the pottery was sold in the potter's shop but the majority was apparently distributed through the markets of the larger urban centres. Many traditions in rabbinic literature refer to potters travelling with their wares, probably on their way to the market, for example: 'two potters that were walking ... and the second bumped into the first (and his pots broke)' (M. B.Q. 3:4), or: 'the potter who was passing [a tomb] with his carrying pole [loaded with pottery] upon his shoulder...' (M. Oh. 16:2). Although the pottery was distributed mainly from the urban marketplaces, the production centres were not located in these cities, but rather in the surrounding villages, such as Shikhin near Sepphoris or Binyanei Ha'uma near Jerusalem, mentioned above. Besides the dependence of urban centres on the manufactured products from rural sites, it should be noted that, at least with regard to common pottery, cities such as Sepphoris are indistinguishable from rural sites such as Capernaum, in that the residents of both used virtually the same wares.

Specialized research into local pottery production and distribution, similar to the studies already carried out for the Galilee, is needed for other parts of the Land of Israel. Even for the Galilee our knowledge of these matters remains scanty for the time after the cessation of production at KH and Shikhin around the early fifth century CE. Work is needed to identify the manufacturers and distribution of pottery from the Byzantine period. Analytical study could determine whether the jars from the Byzantine period found at various Mediterranean sites indeed originated in Palestine. A study of this kind can contribute greatly to our knowledge of economic relations in the Byzantine period.

2.2 Oil Lamps

Most of the oil lamps from the Roman period are made of pottery, although bronze and glass lamps were also in use. The lamps consisted of a container for oil with a filling hole at the top, a nozzle (at times more than one) with a hole for the wick, and sometimes a handle at the back. Roman-period lamps are usually of a round form, while those from the Byzantine period are commonly oval. The vast majority of lamps are relatively small in size (diameter of the container: about 5–7 cm), and thus oil had to be added every few hours. This explains why rabbinic sources discuss possible ways to extend the time of lighting on the Sabbath, when the adding of oil to the lamps was forbidden (M. Shab. 2:4; T. Shab. 1.13 and 2:5–7). In the early Roman period, the technique of producing the body of the lamp on a wheel and then attaching the nozzle by hand was still common. From approximately the late first century onwards, however, most lamps were produced using the innovated Roman technique of two-part moulds, which enabled the mass production of popular designs. The two parts would be joined together before they completely dried: the attachment itself would be smoothed over. The wick and filling holes would be pierced or cut out, and a handle, fashioned separately, would then be attached (later on, the handles were integrated into the mould). Lastly, the lamps were fired in the kiln.

The upper surface of the lamp was often decorated with geometric, floral, or figurative scenes. Erotic or mythological scenes were also found in non-Jewish settlements, primarily on imported lamps from the earlier periods. In the late Roman period, religious symbols such as the menorah became popular, as well as the cross in the Byzantine period. The decoration was imprinted on the soft clay, sometimes with a cylindrical stamp rolled on the lamp's surface. In the mould-technique, however, a pattern was often incised into the mould (usually made of limestone), so that the lamps coming off the mould were already decorated.

Oil lamps have merited much scholarly attention in archaeological research, and every published excavation usually contains a chapter or even a monograph, dedicated to this type of find. Elgavish (1962) and Kennedy (1963) provided the first major studies on lamps from Roman Palestine, and Barag published many types in his study of glass vessels (1970). Further research, some represented in catalogues of large collections, was published by Rosenthal-Heginbottom and Sivan (1978), Sussmann (1982), Israeli and Avida (1988), Lapp (1998), Goodnick-Westenholz (2004), and Adler (2004).

The vast majority of lamps found at Roman and Byzantine sites were locally made, whereas imported lamps generally appear in very small quantities. The so-called 'Heredian' lamp was the most common oil lamp in late Second Temple-period Sodaea. A study on the origins of these lamps which were fand in sites in Northern Israel has shown they were produced in various locations. However, while in the predominantly gentile cities of Dor and Bet Shear not of these lamps were locally made, the vast majority of those found in the Sewish sites of Gamla, Yodfat, and Sepphoris were manufactured in Jerusalem and point to the ties of the Jewish population to this city (Adan-Bayewitz et al. 2008). In the early and mid-Roman period the same styles were common throughout the country, but from the late third century onwards distinct styles appear in different regions. Even at sites which were relatively close to each other, such as Bet Shean and Sepphoris (about 35 km apart), the designs and decorations of the lamps in the latter periods are completely different (Hadad 2002; Gärtner 1999), thus pointing to very localized production and distribution. In addition, a distinct group of lamps limited to Samaria and to sites with Samaritan communities is particular to this ethnic community and called 'Samaritan Lamps' (Sussmann 2002).

Evidence of oil lamp production was found at Sepphoris, Bet Shean, Caesarea, Gerasa, Petra, and Beit Nattif (in the lowlands of Judaea). It is noteworthy that all the production centres identified to date, except for the last one, are located in urban areas (Adan-Bayewitz 1995), while pottery manufacturers were located at rural sites, as noted above. This is probably due to the nature of lamp manufacture which necessitated much less clay, fuel, and space than pottery production. In addition, the highest demand for this commodity would be found in cities. Waste material from lamps with both Jewish and pagan symbols (together with clay figurines) found in one workshop at Beit Nattif clearly indicates that a single production centre supplied the needs of various population groups (Baramki 1936). The lamps from the fifth to seventh centuries CE are generally crude, with poor and repetitive decorations, as opposed to the decorative variety of the lamps from the previous period. Undecorated wheel-made lamps also reappear in this period, mainly in southern Israel. See Byzantine period oil lamps in Figs 14.2 and 14.3.

Further research is needed to identify production centres and determine their range of distribution. Such studies should provide a synthesis of finds from entire regions and be based on chemical and micromorphological sampling.

2.3 Stone Vessels

Vessels made of soft limestone and used for storage or tableware are present almost exclusively in the Jewish-settled areas of Roman Palestine, such as Jerusalem, Judaea, and the Galilee. Unlike pottery vessels which, according to rabbinic law, are unusable when they become impure, stone vessels are not susceptible to impurity, thus making them popular among people observing this aspect of Jewish

Figs. 14.2 and 14.3 Byzantine period oil lamps from the Ein Gedi excavations

Hirschfeld 2007: 267, 288

law (see Deines 1993). Many of these vessels seem to imitate commonly known vessels made of pottery, wood, glass, or metal.

Although stone vessels are mentioned in various rabbinic sources, our understanding of their shape, function, manufacturing process, and distribution has been based entirely on archaeological finds, mainly from the past few decades. All these aspects were studied by Magen (2002). Based on the excavation of a large production centre at Hizma, 8 km north-east of Jerusalem, and on the observation of modern-day workshops still producing stone vessels by traditional techniques, Magen was able to reconstruct the methods of their manufacture. All the production sites identified to date are located in caves that also served as quarries, and apparently most of the vessels were produced on location. The most common vessels were mugs (known by archaeologists as 'measuring cups') which were produced by chiselling the outer shape and then removing the interior either by chisel, as practised in Judaea, or on a lathe, as practised in the Galilee. Small lathes were also used for shaping bowls and cups, while large and sophisticated lathes were employed for producing large vessels such as the kraters (identified by some scholars as the *kallal*–M. Parah 3:3), some of which exceeded 80 cm in height and 100 kg in weight.

The largest and most varied assemblages of stone vessels have been found in Second Temple period strata in excavations at Jerusalem, such as in the City of David (Cahill 1992; see Fig. 14.4).

Fig. 14.4 Stone vessels from the Temple Mount area in Jerusalem, 1st century CE

Avigad 1980b:136

Indeed, the concentration of production sites identified in this vicinity indicates that Jerusalem was probably the main centre of production and distribution. Recent surveys and excavations have demonstrated that stone vessels were also very common at Jewish sites distant from Jerusalem. Hundreds of vessels were found, for example, at Gamla in the Golan, and two production centres were identified recently in the Lower Galilee (Magen 2002: 160).

Chronologically, stone vessels seem to have first appeared in the late first century BCE. Their production decreased dramatically after the destruction of Jerusalem in 70 CE, and until recently it was believed that they totally disappeared after the Bar-Kokhba revolt (132–35CE). Recent finds from excavations in the Galilee suggest, however, that stone vessels were in use well into the second century CE, and apparently even in the third and fourth centuries (e.g. Sepphoris: Weiss 2005: 310). Further research is needed to clarify the reasons for the decrease of these vessels, which was apparently related to a general decline in the observance of Jewish ritual purity laws.

Tables and ossuaries were also stone-made vessels that were commonly used, mainly in the early Roman period. Ossuaries were rectangular boxes hewn from single blocks of stone and used for secondary burial. Most of these finds come from Second Temple period Jerusalem, and to date a single workshop has been identified on Mount Scopus, east of the city (Amit et al. 2000). A comprehensive study of ossuaries, including aspects of their classification, ornamentation, technology, chronology, distribution, and inscriptions was published by Rahmani (1994), and further work was done by Hachlili (1988, 2005). Ossuaries first appear in late first century BCE contexts in Jerusalem, but the peak of their distribution was prior to 70 CE. After the destruction of the city, their production decreased, as did the quality and ornamentation of the post-Temple ossuaries. Interestingly, the practice of *ossilegium* was probably introduced into the Galilee only after 70 CE, perhaps by refugees from Jerusalem (Aviam/Syon 2002). The custom of secondary reburial and ossuary production gradually diminished and seems to have totally disappeared by the late third century CE, probably due to social and religious changes.

2.4 Glass

Glass was produced in two stages: the preparation of raw glass and the manufacture of vessels (M. Kel. 8:9), and in two distinct places: the raw glass was produced far away from settlements, at sites with abundant firewood to which suitable raw materials (sand, soda, and lime) could be brought easily. The furnace contained a melting chamber where the raw materials were placed, and an adjacent firing chamber that was heated for some ten to fourteen days to a temperature of up to about 1100° C. After cooling, the large glass slab that was produced was broken into large chunks, which were then marketed to glass-vessel workshops. These contained a furnace with a chamber for melting the glass chunks, a firing chamber, and an annealing chamber where the manufactured vessels cooled slowly.

The technological invention of glassblowing (probably in the Phoenician coastal area) around the mid-first century BCE totally revolutionized the glass industry. This innovation spread rapidly across the Roman world, enabling the production of a much larger variety of vessels at a much faster pace and at significantly lower cost. Glass, which was previously restricted to luxurious or ornamental objects, was now also used to produce daily utensils which were sold in large quantities at relatively low prices (see T. Peah 4:14). Interestingly, the earliest evidence anywhere of glass-blowing consists of the refuse tip of a glass workshop in Jerusalem, dated to the mid-first century BCE (Avigad 1980a: 186–92; Israeli/Katsnelson 2006).

Various glass vessels were common in Roman Palestine, the most prevalent of which were bottles, jugs, juglets, flasks, bowls, cups, and containers for cosmetics and medicines. Vessels were usually decorated with geometric designs, but in the Byzantine period religious motifs began to appear. Despite the widespread production and use of glass in the Byzantine period, the craft seems to have suffered some decline in the quality, variety of shapes, and ornamentation of its products (Israeli 2003: 100).

The pioneering research on Syro-Palestinian ancient glass by Harden (1935, 1949, 1962) was followed by Barag's comprehensive study (1970) on the typology and chronology of Roman-Byzantine glass found at excavations in Israel. The study by Brand (1978), followed by that of Grossmark (1989), focused on glass mentioned in rabbinic sources. A survey for locating production sites, headed by Weinberg, was carried out in the 1960s in northern Israel by the University of Missouri and the Corning Museum. A few sites with evidence of production were studied, and a glass vessel workshop at Jalame in the Western Lower Galilee was excavated, enabling a reconstruction of the manufacturing process (Weinberg 1987, 1988; Brill 1967). Small glass objects (e.g. jewellery) from the Israel Museum were published by Spaer (2001). The large collection of glass vessels from this museum, together with a detailed typology and a summary of production, was published by Israeli (2003).

Chemical analyses of unformed glass chunks and glass vessels found in Israel were undertaken in the past decade by Freestone (Freestone/Gorin-Rosen 1999; Freestone et al. 2000) and have contributed to our knowledge of production and distribution. The main achievement of this research was the ability to compare compositions of raw glass from production centres with raw chunks and glass vessels found at various sites throughout the country and abroad. The chemical composition of glass from Byzantine Palestine is clearly distinguishable from glass found abroad, pointing to an exclusive dependence on local production in the province. The ability to determine that the vast majority of glass vessels used in Roman Palestine was manufactured locally is essential, since the same types are found throughout the Roman world and could have been considered imported.

Indeed, vessels that were undoubtedly imported are extremely rare (e.g. a luxurious first-century jug of Ennion, a famous Sidonian manufacturer, found in the Upper City of Jerusalem; Avigad 1980a: 107–8, 117).

Furthermore, the ever-growing quantities of excavated artefacts, together with fabric- and workmanship-analyses, enable us today to identify distinct local groups of vessels (such as the third–fourth century Galilean group; see Fig. 14.5). This fact points to regionalized production and distribution (Gorin-Rosen/Katsnelson, 2007).

Numerous production sites, both of raw material and of vessels, have been found in recent decades in Israel. A summary of this material was compiled by Yael Gorin-Rosen (2000; 2002). Vessel workshops were identified in both rural settlements and urban industrial areas or marketplaces, where they were located to meet local demands. Rabbinic sources inform us that vessels were sold in workshops, although it is also known that a producer of glass vessels (*zagag*) could peddle his wares (Gen. R. 19:7 and 25:3). The ever-growing archaeological evidence of workshops (e.g. at Sepphoris, Bet She'an, Samaria, Castra, Jalame, etc.) suggests that, at least in the latter part of our period, local workshops were found in most cities of Roman Palestine.

Raw glass industries were identified mainly at sites close to the Mediterranean coast, such as Apollonia/Arsuf and Hadera. Historical sources also point to the coast between Akko and Sidon as both a source of high-quality raw material and a centre of glass vessel production (Strabo, Geographica XVI.758; Josephus, Bell. 2.10.2; Pliny, Historia Naturalis 36.65; Midr. Tannaim to Deut 33:19; Targum Ps.-Jonathan Deut. 30:19).

Fig. 14.5 Glass vessels from a burial cave at Hurfeish, Upper Galilee—an example of the third–fourth century Galilean group

Photo: Tsila Sagiv, courtesy of the Israel Antiquities Authority

Many glass chunks found in shipwrecks along the coast of northern Israel attest that raw glass was, indeed, exported from Roman Palestine (Gorin-Rosen 2000: 54). Interestingly, fragments of an inscription found in Asia Minor containing the edict of prices issued by Diocletian in 301 CE specify prices of Alexandrian and (much cheaper) Judaean raw glass and vessels. Barag believed that these names refer to two kinds of glass, rather than indicating that these items were exported from the two Near Eastern glass-making centres (Alexandrian glass: colourless; Judaean glass: in natural colours of green and blue). Even so, the fact that ordinary glass was generically termed 'Judaean glass' shows that this area served as a primary source for glass in the Roman Empire at large (Barag 1985: 113–6; see also White-house 2004).

2.5 Textiles

Textiles were a major industry in Roman Palestine, consumed by all classes of society and also produced for export. We will focus here on wool and flax, which, according to both historical and archaeological data, were the chief raw materials. The comprehensive studies of Krauss (1910–12, vol.3: 127–75), Herszberg (1924), and Dalman (1928–42, vol. 5) were based primarily on the literary sources; the latter also relied on information extrapolated from contemporary practices. Archaeological finds from the past few decades, originating exclusively from the arid regions of the country, (e.g. Masada: Sheffer/Granger-Taylor 1994) have contributed greatly to our knowledge of the materials, weaving techniques, and dyeing practices, aspects that have been dealt with in some major studies by Shamir (2001, 2005; Shamir/ Baginski 1998).

The manufacture of textiles involved three basic procedures: preparing the fibre, spinning the yarn, and weaving. Wool was sheared and then washed; harvested flax was soaked in water for about two weeks and then pounded to loosen and separate the fibres. These materials were then combed and transformed into a strong, elastic thread by spinning the fibres on a spindle. Wool was generally dyed before spinning, as opposed to flax whose threads were dyed when finished. However, most linen found in Israel was not dyed at all.

The following types of looms for weaving were in use in Roman Palestine: the simple horizontal loom placed on the ground; the warp-weighted vertical loom where loom weights, usually made of pottery or stone, were tied to the bottom of the vertical threads (see Fig. 14.6); and the vertical two-beam loom, to which a bottom beam was affixed instead of loom weights.

The eventual disappearance of loom weights demonstrates that the warp-weighted loom ceased to exist by the late first century CE and was superseded by the two-beam loom, which was both more efficient and produced better cloth.

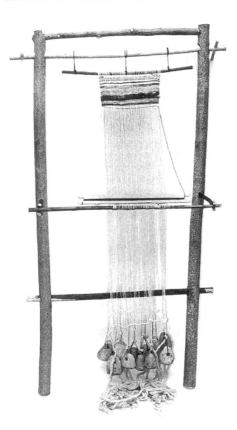

Fig. 14.6 Reconstruction of a warp-weighted loom using weights found in excavations

Shamir/Baginski 1998: 55

Rabbinic sources suggest that wool was more common in Judaea (apparently because raising sheep was more prevalent here), and flax was more common in the Galilee (M. B.Q. 10:9). Flax is not noted in literary sources from the Second Temple period but is frequently mentioned in rabbinic traditions from the second century CE onwards. This has led scholars to believe that the linen industry was not significant in the earlier period and that flax became a main crop only in the second century. However, out of about 1,600 pieces of cloths from Roman Palestine which have been documented to date, the vast majority of which are dated to the early Roman period, some 40 per cent were made of flax and 55 per cent of wool (Shamir 2005: 210). Taking into consideration that almost all of the textile finds were discovered in the Judaean Desert, where wool products would have been expected overwhelmingly, it seems that flax, indeed, already played a significant role in textile manufacture in the early Roman period, if not earlier.

Although the types of garments worn by Jews were similar to those worn by other inhabitants of the Roman Near East, the Jewish sites of Roman Palestine are distinguished by the total absence of textiles of mixed wool and linen (*sha'atnez*), as prescribed by Jewish law (Lev 19:19; Shamir 2005: 207 and 257).

The literary sources dealing with the production of textiles contradict each other to a certain extent, some emphasizing household manufacture and others industrial production. Rabbinic sources often refer to the role of women in the various stages of textile production (e.g. one of the obligations of a woman to her husband is spinning yarn; M. Ket. 5:5 and 5:8; T. Ket. 5:4), indicating that these labours were performed mainly in the local household. Since the profit made on the sale of finished cloth or finished threads was much higher than that made on raw material, it makes sense that private farmers undertook as many stages of production as possible. On the other hand, sources mentioning industrial production (see below), and arguments viewing the sources which associate women with weaving as tendentious rather than realistic (Peskowitz 1997: 77–94), suggest that textile production was mainly industrialized in Roman Palestine. Some of the problems created by the contradictory evidence may be resolved by considering the sources a reflection of different periods, different layers of society, different types of products, or different stages of production. Most of the sources dealing with household production seem to be tannaitic, while those mentioning industrial production come primarily from amoraic and other contemporaneous sources.

Loom weights, the sole archaeological evidence of weaving, seems to support the view that households were extensively engaged in textile production, at least in the early Roman period (when loom weights were still in use). This is corroborated by loom weights found scattered in various domestic spaces (e.g. about 250 early Roman loom weights from various houses and areas in Yodfat, see Aviam 2005: 205–14).

In addition to yarns, which were probably household products, it seems plausible that simple textiles were also domestically made, while complex garments were produced by professionals. Many sources indicate that a person who commissioned the manufacture of a garment furnished the artisan with the necessary raw materials (T. B.M. 7:1, 15–17). Professionals are also mentioned as having been engaged in the stages of processing the raw material (e.g. combers and dyers, M. B. Q. 9:4; M. Qid. 5:14).

Linen exported from Palestine is mentioned in literary sources from the second century CE onwards relating to luxurious textiles. Thus, the second-century CE Greek geographer Pausanias states: 'The fine flax of Elis is as fine as that of the Hebrews' (Graeciae Descriptio, 5.5.2), and Clement of Alexandria (c. 150–211 CE), when accusing women of dressing extravagantly, mentions the purple dyes of Tyre and Sidon and the linens from the land of the Hebrews and Cilicia (Paedagogus 2.11). In Diocletian's price edict from 301 CE, the linen products of Scythopolis were consistently tagged with the highest prices of all the production centres in the Roman East (Ed. Diocl. 26). However, the edict grades three standards of quality for each product, the lowest being for 'the common people and slaves'. This may suggest that, by this time, at least some of the textiles worn by the masses were fabricated on the basis of industrial production rather than household manufacture.

Refined garments from Scythopolis are mentioned in rabbinic traditions attributed to Galilean sages of the late third and fourth centuries (y. Qid. 2:1, 62c; Gen. R. 19:1; 20:21). The discussions reveal the rabbis' close familiarity with such textiles and suggest that some Jews indeed wore such luxurious clothes. Arbel in the Lower Galilee, on the other hand, is mentioned in these texts as being renowned for its coarse and inexpensive linen, suggesting, once again, that by this time the common people also bought textiles from professional producers. The high cost of cloth also resulted in the development of a 'second-hand' textile trade which is attested by both literary sources and archaeological finds. Torn and worn textiles were bought by merchants and either repaired or used for the construction of new textiles (Shamir 2005: 274–75, 288).

Around the mid-fourth century CE, the anonymous author of the *Expositio Totius Mundi et Gentium* states: 'The following are famous for linen clothes: Scythopolis, Laodicaea, Byblos, Tyre, and Berytos, which export linen to the whole world and excel in the richness of all those productions. Likewise Sarepta, Caesarea and Neapolis, as well as Lydda (Lod) export high-quality purple' (Rougé 1966: 163–4; Stern 1974–84: 2, 497). An imperial law dated to 374 CE (Codex Theodosianus 10.20.8), mentions state-owned textile workshops in Scythopolis. These may have been established by Diocletian in order to help fill the needs of the army (Jones 1960: 187). Indeed, the development of Scythopolis as a leading textile production centre in the Roman Empire seems to be related not only to its proximity to high-quality raw flax grown in the Galilee, but probably also to the large number of cash-paid soldiers stationed nearby (the Legio VI Ferrata).

Evidence of imported textiles is almost totally absent and it seems that, perhaps with the exception of wealthy members of the upper strata of society (e.g. the high priest before 70 CE, see M. Yoma 3:7), the needs of the majority of the population were met by local production, which created a whole range of textile qualities.

2.6 Wood

Numerous large- and small-size products such as furniture and coffins, tools and tableware, combs and buttons were made of wood. Archaeological evidence of this organic material has been preserved exclusively in the arid regions of the country. The basic similarities of the assemblages seem to indicate, however, that these finds represent a repertoire that was common elsewhere in the country as well. They are usually published as part of archaeological reports of various sites (e.g. Masada: Liphschitz 1994), or as part of archaeo-botanical studies. Sitry (2006) provides a comprehensive study, which includes aspects of typology, technology, and a timber analysis of about 530 wooden objects from Roman Judaea/Palestine found to date.

At all of the sites the vast majority of products were made of local timber, leading one to assume that transporting raw wood was costly and that the use of foreign material was reserved for specific objects such as combs. Nevertheless, the wooden remains from the various sites reflect the diverse social classes of the consumers. In the village of Ein Gedi, for example, almost all of the burial coffins were made of local wood (Hadas 1994: 49), whereas in the nearby city of Jericho many were made of non-local timber brought from the Judaean hills (Liphschitz/Waisel 1999). Nearly 70 per cent of all the imported wood found in the arid areas of the Land of Israel and dated to the Hellenistic and early Roman period stems from the excavations of Herod's palace at Masada. The timber used at Masada originated from Transjordan, the Judaean hills, and even Lebanon (Liphschitz 1994). Except for this distinctive site, an average of about 22 per cent of the timber found at Hellenistic, Roman, and early Byzantine sites was imported (Liphschitz/Biger 1995).

Both literary sources and archaeological finds indicate that at least one type of tree, the *ficus sycomorus* (Heb. *shiqmah*) was planted and grown intentionally for its wood, used mainly in the construction of buildings (M. Shebi. 4:5; Sitry 2006: 159). An analysis of the craftsmanship of excavated wooden objects, as well as typological studies, have demonstrated that Roman-style products and Roman technological innovations spread to Palestine, and were common even in areas as remote as the Judaean desert.

2.7 Balsam

The balsam of Judaea, which grew only in this province, was renowned throughout the Roman world as the best perfume around. Several authors, mainly from the early Roman period, wrote about this exotic and precious commodity (e.g. Strabo, Geographica 16.2.41; Pliny, Historia Naturalis 12.111–24; Tacitus, Historiae, 5.6.1).

Balsam was cultivated in small-size plots in the Jordan valley only. Jericho, Ein Gedi, and Zoar are mentioned specifically in this regard. The highest-quality balsam was produced by cutting the surface of the tree and extracting the oily liquid. An inferior perfume was produced by extracting the essence from the trimmed foliage and branches.

Balsam was produced mainly for export, and the highest quality seems to have been very expensive (Pliny, Historia Naturalis 12.111–24: 'twice its weight in silver'). Pliny states that the balsam groves in his day belonged to, and were operated by, the Roman *fiscus*, and that the sale of the trimmed branches alone over a five-year period brought the *fiscus* a revenue of 800,000 *sesterces* (200,000 *denarii*). It is not clear to what extent or for how long balsam production was controlled by the Roman *fiscus*. If it was controlled by this body alone, then it probably had only a limited influence on the local economy of the province.

The historical sources and economic implications of balsam production have been discussed by Safrai (1994: 147–55), Patrich (1997), as well as Rosen/Ben-Yehoshua (2007). Our knowledge of balsam production in the late Roman and Byzantine periods is relatively sparse, since it is seldom mentioned by contemporary authors and even then, some obviously relied on earlier sources. No archaeological finds can be associated with any certainty to balsam production. Some scholars suggest, however, that the curse spelled out in the Byzantine-period inscription of the Ein Gedi synagogue, threatening someone who 'reveals the secret of the town to the gentiles', refers to the town's balsam production (Rosen/Ben-Yehoshua 2007).

3. FOOD PROCESSING

In Roman Palestine, as throughout the entire ancient world, agriculture and food processing provided the main employment and source of income for the majority of the population. Rabbinic literature mentions various crops that were grown here, and a few of Jehuda Feliks' major studies on ancient agriculture in Roman Palestine (e.g. 1963, 2005) deal with the sources, identification of these crops, and methods of cultivation. The three most important crops in Roman Palestine were grains (mainly wheat), olives for olive oil, and grapes for wine. In the following we shall focus on olive oil and wine production, for which the archaeological evidence offers new insights.

3.1 Olive Oil

Olive oil was a major component of the people's diet and was also used for other purposes such as lighting fuel, skin ointment, and medication.

After harvesting, the olives were brought to the olive-oil plant (*beit ha-bad*), which was situated in or right near the settlement. The olives were crushed in a mill comprising a circular basin and a threshing wheel turned by animal or manpower. Next, the resultant mash, now in baskets (sg. *eqel*), a wooden frame, a large piece of cloth, or wrapped with a heavy rope, was placed beneath the pressing installation. By exerting pressure on the mash, the extracted liquid consisting of oil and watery lees would flow into a collecting vat. The oil was then separated from the watery lees by skimming or other means. Rabbinic literary sources indicate that the mash was crushed and pressed once or even twice more in order to extract more oil, but this latter oil was considered of inferior quality (M. Men. 8:4; Sifra Emor 13).

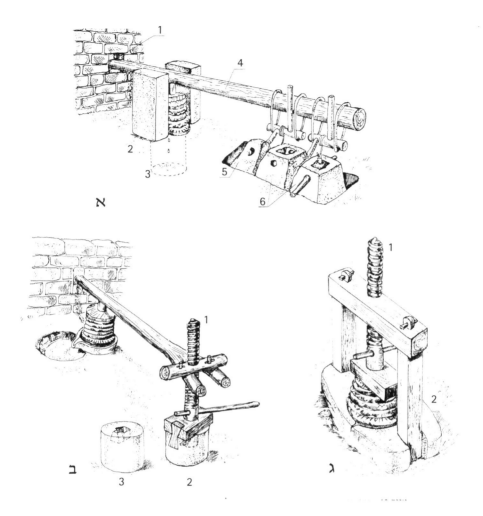

Fig. 14.7 Reconstruction of lever-and-weight oil press (top), lever-and-screw oil press (left) and direct-pressure-screw oil press (right)

Ben David 1998: 55. Reproduction courtesy of Israel Antiquities Authority

While the crushing technique was basically the same in all regions and periods, pressing installations varied from one region to the next, and new techniques were introduced in Roman-Byzantine times. However, even after a new installation was initiated, the old technology continued to be used. This continuity often makes it hard to date installations, and complicates attempts to determine changes in the scale of production. Lever-and-weight presses, common in the Iron Age, continued to be used throughout the Roman period. By this technique, a beam with one end inserted into a niche in the wall would press the olives underneath by hanging stone weights on the free end. The main Roman-period innovation was the introduction of the screw into the press installations. In the lever-and-screw press, the free end of the beam was lowered onto the mash by turning a large perpendicular screw inserted into a nut in the beam. In another type of installation, the direct-pressure screw press, a screw set in a rectangular frame would press down on a board laid on top of the pile of olives (see Fig. 14.7).

The latter two techniques (lever-and-screw press; direct-pressure screw press) were already in use in Italy in the first century CE (Pliny, Historia Naturalis 18.74.317). Although many specimens of these two types of olive presses were discovered in Israel, none of the first, and very few of the second type, can be dated to the Roman period with certainty. Most of these installations definitely belonged to the Byzantine period. The large number of these olive presses datable to that time may indicate that the Byzantine period witnessed a dramatic increase in olive oil production (see below).

General overviews of the role of olive oil in the economy of Roman Palestine can be found in the works of Dalman (1928–42, vol. 4: 153–290) as well as in the collected essays of Amouretti and Brun (1993) and Eitam and Heltzer (1996). Frankel's major archaeological studies (1994, 1999) also contribute greatly to our knowledge of the historical and technical aspects of both olive oil and wine production. One of the main achievements of Frankel's work is the documentation of the distinct contemporaneous technologies utilized in different parts of the country, pointing to diverse regional and perhaps ethnic traditions.

The numerous literary sources mentioning olive oil point to the central role this commodity held in the economy of Roman Palestine. Josephus indicates that Jews avoided Gentile-made oil (Bell. 2.591–3; Vita 74–6), probably due to purity laws. Many rabbinic discussions deal with the production of pure olive oil suitable for ritual offerings and for use by those who observed purity laws meticulously. Indeed, a number of olive oil plants or wineries equipped with miqva'ot (ritual baths) were found in excavations (e.g. at Gamla) and substantiate these practices (Berlin 2006: 104). However, these were found exclusively in Second Temple period contexts, and rabbinic sources also imply the gradual disappearance of stringencies regarding the purity of oil (y. A.Z. 2:8, 41d). It seems, therefore, that at least in the early days, when the observance of purity laws was fairly common, the supply of olive oil in Jewish society depended exclusively on local production.

One tannaitic text prohibits exporting goods 'upon which life depends, such as wine, oil and fine flour' from the Land of Israel and not even from one province to another (T. A.Z. 5:1). Nevertheless, a few sources mention areas or sites known for the high quality and/or large quantity of their olive oil production, which may well have exported their olive oil to other provinces. Both Josephus and rabbinic literature, for example, inform us about olive oil exported from Gush Halav in the Upper Galilee to Syria (Josephus, Bell. 2.591–3; Vita 74–6; Sifre Deut 355). We do not know whether this interregional trade was a regular phenomenon or a unique transaction, nor can we quantify the scale of production in different areas or periods.

Archaeological testimony, on the other hand, enables us to gain insight into these questions. Thus, although oil presses have been found in almost every region of the country (except those with extremely cold or dry climates), the finds in some areas far surpass those from others. In the Lower Golan, for example (Ben David 1998; 2005: 206–9), archaeologists found an average of two to three oil presses per site, and some villages, including relatively small ones, even had five to eight presses. This abundance points to mass olive-oil production that far exceeded the needs of the local population and clearly points to surplus production for marketing purposes. The sixty-eight oil presses documented in this region (of approximately 200 sq. km) stand in sharp contrast to the six oil presses documented in roughly the same size area in the nearby northern Golan.

Furthermore, Ben-David's studies point to a dramatic rise in olive-oil production in the Byzantine period. This is indicated by excavations, technological analyses (a majority of direct-pressure screw presses; see above), and dating of the villages in which the installations were found. While at early and middle Roman period sites, oil presses are rare or totally absent, their number rises remarkably at Byzantine sites. A similar chronological picture, although on a much smaller scale, is documented in my survey of the Eastern Galilee (Leibner 2004: 384–5). The Western Galilee also produced large quantities of olive oil (Frankel 1992; Aviam 2004: 170–79), and here, too, growth in the Byzantine period is indicated. An excavation of some 30 dunams at Kh. Castra (near Haifa), for example, yielded twelve Byzantine olive oil installations, each with two to three presses (Yeivin/ Finkielsztejn 1999: 25). No comparable example is known from the Roman period in Israel.

Thus, in comparison to the Roman period, when olive oil was apparently produced primarily for local consumption, it seems that in the Byzantine period (fourth century CE. onwards) large quantities of surplus were produced for interregional commerce. At the current stage of research, we cannot determine conclusively to what destinations these surpluses were exported, although some clues suggest that, at least from the Galilee and Golan, they were perhaps exported to the Mediterranean coast.

Parallel to the increase in oil production in the Byzantine period, large quantities of fineware (the aforementioned LRRW) from different places in the Mediterranean basin became very common in the Galilee and Golan, even at distant rural sites. As mentioned, pottery vessels were of low economic value and usually did not travel far. Obviously, these LRRW vessels were transported over hundreds of miles of sea and land for a reason. Since these vessels certainly reached the hinterland from the Mediterranean coast, it seems plausible that their appearance in distant regions is connected to the transport system that exported olive oil (and other goods) from the hinterland to the coast. Jars from Byzantine Palestine found at various Mediterranean sites may indeed indicate the destination of the surplus goods produced in that province (Reynolds 1995: 70–83; Kingsley 2004: 50–52). Up to now, however, only the 'Gaza jars', typical of southern Israel, were attested in these Mediterranean sites, and no study has firmly indicated the existence of jars from northern Israel in these destinations. Hence, the suggested model of Golan olive oil marketed to the Mediterranean needs additional proof.

3.2 Wine

Wine, too, was a major component in the ancient diet and also had an important place in religious rituals and social life. The abundant remains of winery installations point to its central place in the land's economy from a very early period onwards. Of the three major crops of Roman and Byzantine Palestine, this was probably the most profitable one (Safrai 1994: 128). After harvesting, the grapes were brought to the wine press (*gat*), which was usually located near the vineyard, since loading and transporting the grapes over a distance would result in their loss of juice.

Wine presses can be divided generally into simple types, comprising a treading platform and a collecting vat, and industrial types, which were usually much larger and included additional devices such as a mechanical press or an intermediate vat for the precipitation of the waste product (see Fig. 14.8).

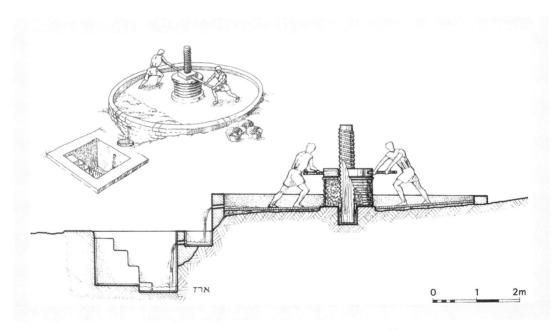

Fig. 14.8 Reconstruction of a wine press from Ramat Hanadiv

Hirschfeld 2000: 123

Some industrial presses had adjacent compartments for storing the grapes until their ripening or processing. The grapes were trodden upon several times on the treading surface. In industrial wineries, the pulp was gathered and pressed by the mechanical press. The juice would flow through an opening into the collecting vat, where it was left to ferment for a few days. Finally, it was transferred into jars, where the fermentation process was completed.

Rabbinic and Graeco-Roman sources indicate that the interior of wine jars was tarred to prevent the wine from seeping through the clay and probably also to preserve its flavour (y. A.Z. 2:4, 41b; ARNA 14; Pliny, Historia Naturalis 14.134). This practice is corroborated by archaeological finds (Kingsley/Raveh 1996: 52). Unlike olive presses, which were costly, resulting in the use of one press by many farmers, the simple wine presses were relatively easy to quarry and construct, allowing many farmers to operate a wine press in their own vineyard.

Dalman (1928–42, vol. 4: 291–413) was the first to widely address the subject of wine production in the Land of Israel. Frankel (1997, 1999) has contributed major studies dealing mainly with ancient wine technology and processing, and Kingsley (1999, 2001, 2004: 86–92) has examined the role of wine production in the economy of Byzantine Palestine.

Rabbis prohibited Gentile-made wine, which they suspected to be used for pagan libations, and whose production was not in accordance with rabbinic purity laws. Although amphorae of imported Italian wines were found at Masada (with inscriptions designating 'wine for King Herod', see Cotton/Geiger 1989), it seems that most Jews did not consume imported wine, since material evidence of imported wine is almost entirely absent from Roman-Byzantine Jewish sites. Jews, however, apparently consumed wine produced by Samaritans, at least up until the third or fourth centuries CE, when it was forbidden by some rabbis (y. A.Z. 5:4, 44b). Numerous rabbinic sources discuss the selling of wine to Gentiles, the employment of Gentiles in Jewish wine production, and the employment of Jews in gentile wineries, indicating that—despite the restrictions—contact between Jews and local non-Jews was probably considerable.

Wine was produced throughout the country, even in arid areas such as the Negev. As in the case of olive presses, some regions (e.g. Judaea) seem to have been richer than others in their possession of wine presses. This impression may partly be due to differences in the intensiveness of archaeological research in a particular region, or in the geological characteristics of an area. For example, wine presses were not hewn in basaltic areas such as the Golan, although wine was most likely produced there, perhaps in wooden presses that have not survived.

Despite the great attention which rabbis devoted to wine production and commerce, rabbinic traditions do not explicitly mention wine for export, and give the impression that wine was merely brought to the local markets or to markets in the nearby urban centres. These sources also give the impression that the transporting to, and trade at, the market were done by the farmer himself rather

than by a professional merchant: 'one who hired a donkey to transport wine...';
'one who left his wine (jars) in the inn and went into the city...' (M. A.Z. 5:1; T. A.Z.
7:6, 12). Various non-Jewish sources from the Byzantine period, on the other
hand, explicitly mention Palestinian wine exported abroad. Around the mid-
fourth century, the anonymous writer of *Expositio Totius Mundi et Gentium* states:
'Ashkelon and Gaza... export the best wine to all Syria and Egypt' (Rougé 1966:
162). Egyptian wine merchants are mentioned in Gaza's port in the fifth century CE
(Grégoire/Kugener 1930: 47) and, indeed, wine from Gaza and Ashkelon is mentioned in a variety of sources from Egypt and from the western empire dating from
the fifth to seventh centuries CE (Dan 1982: 17–18; Mayerson 1985, 1993).

This distinction between the rabbinic and the non-Jewish sources from the
Roman-Byzantine period has traditionally been attributed to the differences in
the nature of the sources. Scholars have viewed the entire Roman-Byzantine period
as basically homogeneous in economic terms. As in the case of olive-oil production, mentioned above, the archaeological evidence of wine production seems to
point to a significant increase in the early Byzantine period, an increase most likely
connected to the creation of surplus intended for interregional trade. The vast
majority of large scale wine presses, for instance, are datable to the Byzantine
period. An enormous wine press discovered in Akhziv, with vats that could hold
59,000 litres when full, is dated to the fourth century (Syon 1998). Likewise, a series
of massive and elaborate wine presses from the Negev (Mazor 1981), Kh. Castra
(Yeivin/Finkielsztejn 1999), the vicinity of Ashkelon (Yisrael 1995b), Rehovot (Roll/
Ayalon 1981), Kh. Zikhrin (Fisher 1985), and many others, are all dated to the
Byzantine period. Some of these large-scale presses are located in small settlements
or estates, indicating that the large quantities of wine produced in them were
intended mostly for trade, and definitely not for local consumption only.

The aforementioned transport jars, which most likely originated from Byzantine Palestine and were found in large quantities at various Mediterranean sites,
form another set of evidence for the significant increase in trade during the
Byzantine period. These jars were found in harbours and as part of cargoes on
shipwrecks off the shores of Cyprus, Greece, and Asia Minor, and as far away as
southern France, indicating that they were involved in maritime commerce
(Kingsley 2004: 50–52). Examples from excavations point to an even further
distribution, reaching Carthage, Britain, and Germany (Frankel 1997: 84; Kingsley
2001: 52–4). Kingsley (ibid.) convincingly argues that these jars were associated
with wine commerce. In light of the above information, olive oil commerce also
seems plausible. The archaeological sites throughout the Mediterranean, where
these Palestinian jars were found, are dated to the fourth to seventh centuries CE,
again demonstrating that the large-scale involvement in international trade was a
phenomenon of Byzantine Palestine.

Conclusions

It seems that considerable economic change occurred in the early Byzantine period from the fourth century onwards: apparently a province which was previously relatively uninvolved in significant interregional trade now begins to take part in such commerce. The reasons for this change are not clear, but may be linked to the establishment of Constantinople in 330 CE, where the empire supplied the masses with wheat and oil brought from the provinces (*annona civica*). It may also partly be due to changes in customs or taxation policies. The question of whether long-distance trade in late antiquity was mainly an outcome of the state's actions, or rather due to market forces and private initiatives has been highly debated of late (Ward-Perkins 2000: 369–70).

As observed for other parts of the Mediterranean (Ward-Perkins 2000: 373–4), the production of large quantities of specialized surplus goods and the involvement in long-distance trade seem to be major factors in the prosperity of some regions in comparison to others that did not engage in such commerce. In the rural Lower Golan, for example, remains of twenty-five monumental synagogues were found, all most probably dating to the fifth and sixth centuries (Ma'oz 1995, vol. 1: 354). As this area specialized in olive-oil production in the Byzantine period, it may suggest that the capital gained by the mass production of trade surplus enabled the construction of these monumental buildings. On the other hand, a much larger area in the Eastern Galilee, having a much higher agricultural potential, yielded only thirteen or fourteen monumental synagogues, not all of which date to the Byzantine period (Leibner 2004: 391–5). Judging by the archaeological remains, this area indeed did not engage in any specialized production. It should be emphasized that the increase in production was not a result of a growth in population but seems to have been connected to changes in economic structure. Indeed, some areas of Palestine, including some of those involved in interregional trade, seem to have suffered from a population decline, primarily in the early Byzantine period (Leibner 2006).

Although signs of decline in settlement are already indicated in some areas in the Byzantine period, the rapid dwindling following the Arab conquest is probably also connected to the disruption of the lucrative long-distance trade, which was a boost for the economy of entire regions. Archaeological investigation indeed indicates that the wine industry waned after the Arab conquest (Ayalon 1997): This was not merely because of the Moslem prohibition of wine (which apparently was not absolute in early Islam). Indeed, the far-reaching effect of being cut off from the Mediterranean trade routes is also reflected in the rapidly declining settlement in the olive-oil producing region of the Lower Golan after the Arab conquest. This negative example also demonstrates the significant impact on Palestine as part of the Roman Empire. The consequences were not restricted to technology only, or to the modes and extent of production patterns, but directly influenced the prosperity of the province.

ACKNOWLEDGMENTS

I would like to thank David Adan-Bayewitz for his valuable comments. Thanks are also due to Orit Shamir, Yael Gorin-Rosen, Judith Gärtner, and Raphael Frankel for their comments on portions of this article.

SUGGESTED READING

Safrai (1994) provides a major study of the economy of Roman Palestine, based mainly on rabbinic sources (including the Babylonian Talmud). Adan-Bayewitz (1993: 201–223, 228–249) presents social and economic conclusions of a comprehensive and meticulous study of local pottery and its trade in northern Palestine. Kingsley (1999: 51–79, 138–85) deals with the role and impact of surplus production and long-distance trade on the economy of Byzantine Palestine, based mainly on archaeological data. Parker (1999) describes the political, religious, settlement and economic changes which transpired in Palestine during the Byzantine period, also based mainly on archaeological evidence.

BIBLIOGRAPHY

ABERBACH, M. (1994). *Labor, Crafts, and Commerce in Ancient Israel*. Jerusalem: Magnes.
ADAN-BAYEWITZ, D. (1993). Common Pottery in Roman Galilee: A Study of Local Trade. Ramat Gan: Bar Ilan University Press.
—— (1995). 'A Lamp Mould from Sepphoris and the Location of Workshops for Lamp and Common Pottery Manufacture in Northern Palestine', in *The Roman and Byzantine Near East: Some Recent Archaeological Research*, ed. J.H. Humphrey. Portsmouth: Journal of Roman Archaeology, 177–182.
—— (2003). 'On the Chronology of the Common Pottery of Northern Roman Judaea/Palestine', in *One Land–Many Cultures: Archaeological Studies in Honor of S. Loffreda*, ed. G. C. Bottini, L. Di Segni and L. D. Chrupcala. Jerusalem: Franciscan Printing Press, 5–32.

——/Asaro, F./Perlman, I./Michel, H. V. (1995). 'Excavations at Sepphoris: The Location and Identification of Shikhin, Part II: The Evidence from Neutron Activation Analysis'. *Israel Exploration Journal*, 45: 180–7.

——/Aviam, M. (1997). 'Iotapata, Josephus, and the Siege of 67: Preliminary Report on the 1992–94 Seasons'. *Journal of Roman Archaeology* 10: 131–165.

—— /Wieder, M./Asaro, F./Giauque, R.D. (2008). 'Preferential Distribution of Lamps from the Jerusalem Area in the Late Second Temple Period (Late First Century B.C.E - 70 C.E)', BASOR 350, 37–85.

Adler, N. (2004). *A Comprehensive Catalog of Oil Lamps of the Holy Land from the Adler Collection*. Jerusalem: Old City.

Amit, D./Seligman, J./Zilberbod, I. (2000). 'Stone Vessel Workshops of the Second Temple Period East of Jerusalem', in *Ancient Jerusalem Revealed*, ed. H. Geva. Jerusalem: Israel Exploration Society, 353–8.

Amouretti, M. C./Brun, J. P. (1993). *La Production du vin et de l'huile en Mediterranée*. Athens: Ecole française d'Athènes.

Arubas, B./Goldfus, H. (eds) (2005). *Excavations on the Site of the Jerusalem International Convention Center (Binyanei Ha'uma)*. JRA Supplementary Series 60. Portsmouth: Journal of Roman Archaeology.

Aviam, M. (2004). *Jews, Pagans and Christians in the Galilee: 25 Years of Archaeological Excavations and Surveys: Hellenistic to Byzantine Periods*. Rochester: University of Rochester Press.

—— (2005). 'Yodefat: A Case Study in the Development of the Jewish Settlement in the Galilee during the Second Temple Period'. [Hebr.]. Ramat Gan: Bar Ilan University Press.

——/Syon, D. (2002). 'Jewish Ossilegium in Galilee', in *What Athens has to do with Jerusalem: Essays on Classical, Jewish and Early Christian Art and Archaeology in Honor of Gideon Foerster*, ed. L. V. Rutgers. Leuven: Peeters, 151–80.

Avigad, N. (1980a). *Discovering Jerusalem*. Nashville, Camden, New York: Thomas Nelson Publishers.

—— (1980b). *The Upper City of Jerusalem* [Hebr.]. Jerusalem: Israel Exploration Society.

Ayalon, E. (1997). 'The End of the Ancient Wine Production in the Central Coastal Plain' [Hebr.], in *Hikrei Eretz: Studies in the History of the Land of Israel Dedicated to Prof. Yehuda Feliks*, ed. Y. Friedman, Z. Safrai, and J. Schwartz. Ramat Gan: Bar Ilan University Press, 149–66.

Barag, D. (1970). 'Glass Vessels of the Roman and Byzantine Periods' [Hebr.]. PhD. thesis, Hebrew University Jerusalem.

—— (1985). 'Recent Important Epigraph Discoveries Related to the History of Glassmaking in the Roman Period'. *Annales Association Internationale pour l'Historie du Verre* 10: 109–116.

Baramki, D. C. (1936). 'Two Roman Cisterns at Beit Nattif'. *Quarterly of the Department of Antiquities in Palestine* 5: 1–10.

Ben David, C. (1998). 'Oil Presses and Oil Production in the Golan in the Mishnaic and Talmudic Periods' [Hebr.]. *'Atiqot* 34: 1–61.

—— (2005). *The Jewish Settlement on the Golan in the Roman and Byzantine Period* [Hebr.]. Qazrin: Golan Research Institute.

Berlin, A. (2005a). 'Pottery and Pottery Production in the Second Temple Period', in *Excavations on the Site of the Jerusalem International Convention Center (Binyanei*

Ha'uma), ed. B. Arubas and H. Goldfus. JRA Supplementary Series 60. Portsmouth: Journal of Roman Archaeology, 29–60.

—— (2005b). 'Jewish Life before the Revolt: The Archaeological Evidence'. *Journal for the Study of Judaism* 36: 417–70.

—— (2006). *Gamla, I: The Pottery of the Second Temple Period: The Shmarya Gutmann Excavations, 1976–1989.* Israel Antiquities Authority Reports 29. Jerusalem: Israel Antiquities Authority.

BRAND, Y. (1953). *Ceramics in Talmudic Literature* [Hebr.]. Jerusalem: Mossad Harav Kook.

—— (1978). *Glass Vessels in Talmudic Literature* [Hebr.]. Jerusalem: Mossad Harav Kook.

BRILL, R. H. (1967). 'A Great Glass Slab from Ancient Galilee'. *Archaeology* 20: 88–95.

CAHILL, J. M. (1992). 'The Chalk Vessel Assemblages of the Persian/Hellenistic and Early Roman Periods', in *Excavations at the City of David 1978–1985 Directed by Yigal Shiloh*, III., ed. A. de Groot and D. T. Ariel. Qedem 33. Jerusalem: Institute of Archaeology, Hebrew University.

COTTON, H. M./GEIGER, J. (1989). 'Wine for Herod' [Hebr.]. *Cathedra* 53: 3–12.

DALMAN, G. (1928–42). *Arbeit und Sitte in Palästina*, 7 vols. Gütersloh: C. Bertelsmann.

DAN, Y. (1982). 'The Foreign Trade of Palestine in the Byzantine Period' [Hebr.]. *Cathedra* 23: 17–24.

DEINES, R. (1993). *Jüdische Steingefässe und pharisäische Frömmigkeit. Ein archäologisch-historischer Beitrag zum Verständnis von Johannes 2,6 und der jüdischen Reinheitshalacha zur Zeit Jesu.* Tübingen: Mohr-Siebeck.

EITAM, D./HELTZER M. (eds) (1996). *Olive Oil in Antiquity: Israel and Neighbouring Countries from the Neolithic to the Early Arab Period.* Padova: Sargon.

ELGAVISH, Y. (1962). 'The Art of the Lamps in Palestine in the Roman and Byzantine Periods' [Hebr.]. PhD. thesis, Hebrew University Jerusalem.

FELIKS, J. (1963). *Agriculture in Palestine in the Period of the Mishna and Talmud.* Jerusalem: Magnes Press.

—— (2005). *The Jerusalem Talmud–Tractate Ma'asrot. Annotated Critical Edition* [Hebr.]. Ramat Gan: Bar Ilan University Press.

FISHER, M. (1985). 'Excavations at Horvat Zikhrin' [Hebr.]. *Qadmoniot* 18: 112–21.

FRANKEL, R. (1992). 'Some Oil Presses from Western Galilee'. *Bulletin of the American Schools of Oriental Research* 286: 39–71.

—— (1994). 'Ancient Oil Mills and Presses in the Land of Israel', in *History and Technology of Olive Oil in the Holy Land*, ed. R. Frankel, S. Avitsur, and E. Ayalon. Arlington and Tel Aviv: Oléarius Editors and Eretz Israel Museum, 19–89.

—— (1997). 'Presses for Oil and Wine in the Southern Levant in the Byzantine Period'. *Dumbarton Oaks Papers* 51: 73–84.

—— (1999). *Wine and Oil Production in Antiquity in Israel and Other Mediterranean Countries.* Sheffield: Sheffield Academic Press.

FREESTONE, I. C./GORIN-ROSEN, Y. (1999). 'The Great Glass Slab at Bet She'arim, Israel: An Early Islamic Glassmaking Experiment?'. *Journal of Glass Studies* 41: 105–16.

——/GORIN-ROSEN, Y./HUGHES M. J. (2000). 'Primary Glass from Israel and the Production of Glass in Late Antiquity and the Early Islamic Period', in *La route du verre: ateliers primaires et secondaires du second millénaire av. J.-C. au moyen âge*, ed. M. D. Nenna. Travaux de la Maison de l'Orient Méditerranéen 33. Lyon: Maison de l'Orient, 65–83.

GÄRTNER, J. (1999). 'Oil-Lamps from Sepphoris from the Hellenistic until the Mameluke Period' [Hebr.]. MA thesis, Hebrew University Jerusalem.

GOODNICK-WESTENHOLZ, J. (2004). *Let There Be Light: Oil-Lamps from the Holy Land.* Jerusalem: Bible Lands Museum.

GORIN-ROSEN, Y. (2000). 'The Ancient Glass Industry in Israel: Summary of the Finds and New Discoveries', in *La route du verre: ateliers primaires et secondaires du second millénaire av. J.-C. au moyen âge*, ed. M. D. Nenna. Travaux de la Maison de l'Orient Méditerranéen 33. Lyon: Maison de l'Orient, 49–63.

—— (2002). 'The Ancient Glass Industry in Eretz-Israel–A Brief Summary'. *Michmanim* 16: 7–18.

——/KATSNELSON, N. (2007). 'Local Glass Production in the Late Roman-Early Byzantine Periods in Light of the Glass Finds from Khirbat Ni'ana, Israel'. *'Atiqot* LVII: 73–154.

GRÉGOIRE, H./KUGENER, M. A. (1930). *Marcus Diaconus: Vie de Porphyre: évêque de Gaza.* Paris: Les Belles Lettres.

GROSSMARK, Z. (1989). 'Jewish Glass-Making in the Land of Israel in the Roman and Byzantine Periods' [Hebr.]. MA thesis, University of Haifa.

HACHLILI, R. (1988). *Jewish Ornamented Ossuaries of the Late Second Temple Period.* The Hecht Museum, Catalogue 4. Haifa: Hecht Museum.

—— (2005). *Jewish Funerary Customs, Practices and Rites in the Second Temple Period.* Leiden: Brill.

HADAD, S. (2002). *The Oil Lamps from the Hebrew University Excavations at Bet Shean.* Qedem Reports 4. Jerusalem: Institute of Archaeology, Hebrew University and Israel Exploration Society.

HADAS, G. (1994). 'Nine Tombs of the Second Temple Period at "En Gedi"'. *Atiqot* 24: 1–62.

HARDEN, D. B. (1935). 'Romano-Syrian Glasses with Mould-Blown Inscriptions'. *Journal of Roman Studies* 25: 163–86.

—— (1949). 'Tomb-Groups of Glass of Roman Date from Syria and Palestine'. *Iraq* 2: 151–9.

—— (1962). 'Glass', in *Excavations at Nessana*, I., ed. H. D. Colt. London: British School of Archaeology in Jerusalem, 76–91.

HERSZBERG, A. S. (1924). *The Cultural Life in Israel in the Period of the Mishnah and Talmud, I: Weaving and the Weaving Industry* [Hebr.]. Warsaw: Stiebel.

HEZSER, C. (2005). *Jewish Slavery in Antiquity.* Oxford: Oxford University Press.

HIRSCHFELD, Y. (2000). *Ramat Hanadiv Excavations: Final Report of the 1984–1998 Seasons.* Jerusalem: Israel Exploration Society.

—— (2007). *En-Gedi Excavations II: Final Report (1996–2002).* Jerusalem: Israel Exploration Society.

ISRAELI, Y. (2003). *Ancient Glass in the Israel Museum: The Eliahu Dobkin Collection and Other Gifts.* Catalogue 486. Jerusalem: Israel Museum.

——/AVIDA, U. (1988). *Oil-Lamps from Eretz-Israel: The Louis and Carmen Warschaw Collection at the Israel Museum Jerusalem.* Jerusalem: Israel Museum.

——/KATSNELSON, N. (2006). 'Refuse of a Glass Workshop of the Second Temple Period from Area J', in *Jewish Quarter Excavations in the Old City of Jerusalem, conducted by Nahman Avigad, 1969–1982, III*, ed. H. Geva. Jerusalem: Israel Exploration Society, 411–60.

JOHNSON, B. L./STAGER, L. E. (1995). 'Ashkelon: Wine Emporium of the Holy Land', in *Recent Excavations in Israel: A View to the West*, ed. S. Gitin. Dubuque, Iowa: Kendall/Hunt Publishing.

JONES, A. H. M. (1960). 'The Cloth Industry under the Roman Empire'. *The Economic History Review* (NS): 183–92.

KENNEDY, C. A. (1963). 'The Development of the Lamp in Palestine'. *Berytus*, 14: 67–115.

KINGSLEY, S. A. (1999). 'Specialized Production and Long-Distance Trade in Byzantine Palestine'. Ph.D. diss. Oxford: University of Oxford.

Kingsley, S. A. (2001). 'The Economic Impact of the Palestinian Wine Trade in Late Antiquity', *Economy and Exchange in the East Mediterranean during Late Antiquity. Proceedings of the Conference at Somerville College, Oxford, 29th May, 1999.* S. Kingsley and M. Decker (eds), Oxford: Oxbow, 44–68.

—— (2004). *Shipwreck Archaeology of the Holy Land: Processes and Parameters.* London: Duckworth.

——/RAVEH, K. (1996). *The Ancient Harbor and Anchorage at Dor, Israel: Results of the Underwater Surveys, 1976–1991.* B.A.R. International Series 626. Oxford: Archaeopress.

KRAUSS, S. (1910–12). *Talmudische Archäologie*, 3 vols. Leipzig: G. Fock.

LAPP, E. C. (1998). *The Archaeology of Light: The Cultural Significance of the Oil Lamp from Roman Palestine.* Ann Arbor, MI: University Microfilms International.

LEIBNER, U. (2004). 'History of Settlement in the Eastern Galilee during the Hellenistic, Roman and Byzantine Periods in Light of an Archaeological Survey' [Hebr.]. PhD. thesis, Bar Ilan University.

—— (2006). 'Settlement and Demography in Late Roman and Byzantine Eastern Galilee', in *Settlements and Demography in the Near East in Late Antiquity*, ed. A. S. Levine and P. Pellegrini. Biblioteca Di Mediterraneo Antico 2. Pisa and Rome: Istituti Editoriali e Poligrafici Internazionali, 105–30.

LIPHSCHITZ, N. (1994). 'Wood Remains from Masada', in *Masada: The Yigael Yadin Excavations 1963–1965 Final Reports*, vol. IV, ed. J. Aviram, G. Foerster, and E. Netzer. Jerusalem: Israel Exploration Society, 321–46.

——/BIGER, G. (1995). 'The Timber Trade in Ancient Palestine'. *Tel Aviv* 22: 121–7.

——/WAISEL, Y. (1999). 'Timber Analysis,' in *Jericho: The Jewish Cemetery of the Second Temple Period*, ed. Y. R. Hachlili and A. E. Killebrew. Israel Antiquities Authority Reports 7. Jerusalem: Israel Antiquities Authority, 88–92.

MAGEN, Y. (2000). 'Jerusalem as the Center of the Stone Vessel Industry', in *Ancient Jerusalem Revealed*, reprinted and expanded edition, ed. H. Geva. Jerusalem: Israel Exploration Society, 244-56.

—— (2002). *The Stone Vessel Industry in the Second Temple Period: Excavations at Hizma and the Jerusalem Temple Mount.* Jerusalem: Israel Exploration Society.

MAGNESS, J. (2005). 'The Roman Legionary Pottery', in *Excavations on the Site of the Jerusalem International Convention Center (Binyanei Ha'uma)*, ed. B. Arubas and H. Goldfus. JRA Supplementary Series 60. Portsmouth: Journal of Roman Archaeology, 69–191.

MA'OZ, Z. U. (1995). *Ancient Synagogues in the Golan–Art and Architecture* [Hebr]. 2 vols. Qazrin: Golan Antiquities Museum.

MAYERSON, P. (1985). 'The Wine and Vineyards of Gaza in the Byzantine Period'. *Bulletin of the American Schools of Oriental Research* 257: 75–80.

—— (1993). 'The Use of Ascalon Wine in the Medical Writers of the Fourth to the Seventh Centuries'. *Israel Exploration Journal* 43: 169–73.

MAZOR, G. (1981). 'The Wine-Presses of the Negev' [Hebr.]. *Qadmoniot* 14: 51–60.

PARKER, S. T. (1999). 'The Byzantine Period: An Empire's New Holy Land'. *Near Eastern Archaeology* 62: 134–80.

PATRICH, J. (1997). 'Agricultural Development in Antiquity: Improvements in the Growing and the Producing of Balsam', in *Hikrei Eretz, Studies in the History of the Land of Israel Dedicated to Prof. Yehuda Feliks* [Hebr.], ed. Y. Friedman, Z. Safrai, and J. Schwartz. Ramat Gan: Bar Ilan University Press. 139–48.

PEACOCK, D. P. S./WILLIAMS, D. F. (1986). *Amphorae and the Roman Economy: An Introductory Guide.* London: Longman.

PESKOWITZ, M. B. (1997). *Spinning Fantasies: Rabbis, Gender, and History.* Berkeley: University of California Press.

RAHMANI, L. Y. (1994). *A Catalogue of Jewish Ossuaries in the Collections of the State of Israel.* Jerusalem: Israel Antiquities Authority and Israel Academy of Sciences and Humanities.

REYNOLDS, P. (1995). *Trade in the Western Mediterranean,* AD *400-700: The ceramic evidence.* Oxford: Tempus Reparatum.

ROLL, I./AYALON, E. (1981). 'Two Large Wine Presses in the Red Soil Regions of Israel'. *Palestine Exploration Quarterly* 113: 111–25.

ROSEN, B./BEN-YEHOSHUA, S. (2007). 'The Agriculture of Roman-Byzantine En-Gedi and the Enigmatic "Secret of the Village"', in *En-Gedi Excavations, II: Final Report (1996–2002)*, ed. Y. Hirschfeld. Jerusalem: Israel Exploration Society and Hebrew University of Jerusalem, 626–40.

ROSENTHAL-HEGINBOTTOM, R. (2006). 'Late Hellenistic and early Roman Lamps and Fine Ware', in *Jewish Quarter Excavations in the Old City of Jerusalem, conducted by Nahman Avigad, 1969–1982, III*, ed. H. Geva. Jerusalem: Israel Exploration Society, 144–67.

——/SIVAN, R. (1978). *Ancient Lamps in the Schloessinger Collection.* Qedem 8. Jerusalem: Institute of Archaeology, Hebrew University.

ROUGÉ, J. (ed.) (1966). *Expositio Totius Mundi et Gentium.* Paris: Editions du Cerf.

SAFRAI, Z. (1994). *The Economy of Roman Palestine.* London: Routledge.

SHAMIR, O. (2001). 'Byzantine and Early Islamic Textiles Excavated in Israel'. *Textile History* 32: 93–105.

—— (2005). 'Textiles in the Land of Israel from the Roman Period until the Early Islamic Period in the Light of the Archaeological Finds' [Hebr]. PhD. thesis, Hebrew University Jerusalem..

——/BAGINSKI, A. (1998). 'Research of Ancient Textiles Discovered in Israel' [Hebr.]. *Qadmoniot*, 31: 53–62.

SHEFFER, A./GRANGER-TAYLOR, H. (1994). 'Textiles from Masada: A Preliminary Selection', in *Masada: The Yigael Yadin Excavations 1963–1965 Final Reports*, vol. IV, ed. J. Aviram, G. Foerster, and E. Netzer. Jerusalem: Israel Exploration Society, 153–256.

SITRY, Y. (2006). 'Wooden Objects from Roman Sites in the Land of Israel: A Typological and Technological Study' [Hebr.]. PhD. thesis, Bar Ilan University.

SPAER, M. (2001). *Ancient Glass in the Israel Museum: Beads and Other Small Objects.* Catalogue 447. Jerusalem: Israel Museum.

SPERBER, D. (1993–2006). *Material Culture in Eretz-Israel during the Talmudic Period.* 2 vols. Jerusalem: Yad Izhak Ben-Zvi and Bar Ilan University.

STERN, M. (1974–84). *Greek and Latin Authors on Jews and Judaism.* 3 vols. Jerusalem: Israel Academy of Sciences and Humanities.

SUSSMANN, V. (1982). *Ornamented Jewish Oil-Lamps from the Destruction of the Second Temple through the Bar-Kokhba Revolt.* Warminster: Aris and Philips.

—— (2002). 'Samaritan Oil Lamps' [Hebr.], in *The Samaritans*, ed. E. Stern and H. Eshel. Jerusalem: Yad Izhak Ben-Zvi. 339–71.

Syon, D. (1998). 'A Wine Press at Akhziv' [Hebr.]. *Atiqot* 34: 85–99.

Ward-Perkins, B. (2000). 'Specialized Production and Exchange', in *The Cambridge Ancient History*, vol. XIV: *Late Antiquity: Empire and Successors* A.D. *425–600*, ed. A. Cameron, B. Ward-Perkins, and M. Whitby. Cambridge: Cambridge University Press. 346–91.

Weinberg, G. D. (1987). 'Specialized Production in a Late Roman Glass Factory'. *Eretz-Israel* 19: 62*–70*.

—— (1988). *Excavations at Jalame: Site of a Glass Factory in Late Roman Palestine*. Columbia, MO: University of Missouri Press.

Weiss, Z. (2005). *The Sepphoris Synagogue: Deciphering an Ancient Message through Its Archaeological and Socio-Historical Contexts*. Jerusalem: Israel Exploration Society and Hebrew University.

Whitehouse, D. (2004). 'Glass in the Price Edict of Diocletian'. *Journal of Glass Studies* 47: 189–91.

Yeivin, Z./Finkielsztejn, G. (1999). 'Horbat Castra–1993–1997' [Hebr.]. *Hadashot Arkheologiyot* 109: 23–27.

Yisrael, Y. (1995a). 'Survey of Pottery Workshops: Nahal Lakhish-Nahal Besor'. *Excavations and Surveys in Israel* 13: 106–107.

—— (1995b). 'The Economy of the Gaza-Ashkelon Region in the Byzantine Period in the Light of the Archaeological Survey and Excavations in the "3rd Mile Estate" near Ashkelon' [Hebr.]. *Michmanim* 8: 119–32.

Zemer, A. (1977). *Storage Jars in Ancient Sea Trade*. Haifa: National Maritime Museum.

CHAPTER 15

TRADE, COMMERCE, AND CONSUMPTION

JACK PASTOR

1. DEFINITIONS

When we refer to commerce, we are referring to the process of buying and selling goods and services, usually for money, from the producers to the consumers. Trade is an activity closely related to commerce, but it can imply an exchange of goods, or be limited to a specific commodity such as the slave trade. Consumption is the use of the goods and products available to the economy.

2. METHODOLOGICAL APPROACHES AND PROBLEMS

Any discussion of trade, commerce, and consumption in Roman Palestine must first deal with the ongoing debate on the character of the ancient economy. Two views have dominated the discussion of the nature of the ancient economy: the 'primitivist' versus the modernist view. The modernists (also called formalists) most notably represented by Rostovtzeff (1957) claim that the ancient economy was in its essence similar to the modern economy; that is, market forces determined prices and economic behaviour such as the movement of commodities in response to price, supply and demand. In their view, the differences between the modern economy and the ancient are differences only of scale and of technological sophistication. In opposition to this view stand the 'primitivists' (also sometimes referred to as substantivists) best exemplified by Finley (1973) who claim that economic thinking as we understand it today did not exist in any significant way in the ancient world, that is, market forces did not determine the direction of the economy.

Publications on the trade and commerce of Roman Palestine eventually end up preferring one or the other of these paradigms to describe the findings of their research. Much of the literature seems to support the so-called modernist view, but there are those who vociferously claim that the modernists have an inflated and unrealistic view of the trade in Roman Palestine, as indeed of the agriculture and the economy in general (Schwartz 2006, Greene 2000). In reply, one might point out that although the critics of the modernists stress the 'embeddedness' of the economy in the social and cultural system of the ancient world (and especially Roman Palestine), indeed, all economies are embedded in the social, cultural, and political institutions and norms of their time. This does not preclude the ancient existence of economic thinking and behaviour that is understandable and can be paralled also in the modern world.

The sources for the understanding of trade and commerce encompass the usual range for the study of ancient history: literature, papyri and parchment documents, inscriptions, archaeological evidence, and numismatics. However, methodological and historiographical problems arise from an unavoidable dependence on a narrow literary base, comprised mostly of a great deal of evidence from rabbinic literature. It has been correctly noted that the nature of this material frees it from the exclusivity of most ancient literary sources which are, on the whole, tied to the world view and class bias of the upper classes (Safrai 1994: 2–3). Nevertheless, there are those who still relegate rabbinic sources to the category of 'elite' literature (Lapin 2001: 5) and ignore Safrai's point that much of the rabbinic evidence on the economy is not dealing with 'economics of the *beit midrash*' but relates 'by the way' to the concrete reality outside the intellectual world of the rabbis (Safrai 1994: 5 and 7).

Moreover, since rabbinic sources were never intended to provide an economic history, some scholars use them in the hope that their specific focus on very particular problems and questions frees them from the agenda and bias one might suspect in more purposeful but wider scale historical writings. At the same time, the anecdotal and sporadic nature of this evidence makes it difficult to construct a continuous and comprehensive view of the economic activities mentioned in these sources. The wide spread of the evidence, while providing insights on specific issues such as markets and peddlars, makes it very difficult to reconstruct a reliable picture of the trade and commerce for all of Roman Palestine, throughout its history, and in all its aspects. The other types of sources, that is, coins, papyri, and archaeological material, provide only a small portion of the evidence, and give an even more scattered view than the rabbinical sources. Supplementing the rabbinic sources, archaeology is used extensively by scholars. Although holding varying points of view and approaches, scholars still rely on the evidence from archaeology to prove their points. This is true for both the 'primitivist' and modernist approaches mentioned above (Lapin 2001, Safrai 1994).

As Lapin (2001: 38–78) has pointed out, a major weakness of the archaeological material as evidence for the economic history of ancient Palestine is that, for the most part, exact dates cannot be obtained for answering specific questions. For example, we do not know when a market reached a certain size, or even exactly when a market was created. Likewise, one cannot accurately date much of the market activity using archaeology. One can know that a vessel was created at a certain time, but not when it was sold, or how many times it changed owners. Vessels are the only product that are relatively well preserved in the archaeological record. They cannot tell us anything about the other products that were traded (Lapin 2001: 84). Finally, the relatively little archaeological work done on village sites makes it almost impossible to get an accurate archaeologically based picture of village markets (on villages see Killebrew in this volume).

To compensate for the problems connected with the literary and archaeological sources that form the basis of the major works on trade, Lapin (2001) uses socioeconomic models (e.g. the 'central-place theory') to flesh out the picture. He argues that models can help us think about trade and markets (and other issues such as settlement) in new and constructive ways. Others such as Safrai, Rosenfeld, and Menirav rely mostly, or even entirely, on rabbinic evidence, as did the 'pioneers' of the economic history of Palestine (Herzfeld 1894, Heichelheim 1959, Avi-Yonah 1964, Klausner 1975).

3. GENERAL CONSIDERATIONS

Markets and commerce are inextricably tied to Palestine's geographic location at the intersection of land and sea routes between the continents. The coastal cities and caravan cities and the land bridge between them created an intersection of trade routes and markets that put Palestine on the trade map well before the Roman conquest. Already prior to that time Palestine served as a conduit for goods between Asia, Africa, and—via the Mediterranean ports—Europe as well. In Hellenistic times its trade activity was directed primarily toward the Ptolemaic kingdom, and was handled for the most part by the Phoenician cities. The major work on Ptolemaic trade with, and through, Palestine is still Tcherikover (1937), who based his historical reconstruction of the Ptolemaic era in Syria-Phoenicia (the Ptolemaic name for the area of Coele-Syria) almost completely on the papyri from the period.

The Roman conquest, by drawing Palestine within the Roman Empire, affected the trade and commerce of Palestine, both by increasing the security and ease of commerce within the limits of the Roman world, and by creating a much larger end-market than ever existed in the Hellenistic period.

At first, because the coastal *poleis* recovered their autonomy and, with it, their traditional economic activity, the Roman conquest did not significantly change the traditional framework of Palestine's trade that had existed prior to the Hasmonean domination of the coast. However, a major spurt in the development of Palestinian trade resulted from the policies of Herod the Great, who advanced the infrastructure of the kingdom by building the great harbour of Caesarea, reconstructing the Temple and its ancillary structures in Jerusalem, and joining far-spread corners of the country such as Gaza and Batanea under one royal administration.

Jerusalem, the major metropolis of Judaea since the time of the Judaean kings, now under Herod's rule, took a great leap forward, making it the pre-eminent consumer centre in Palestine until its destruction in the year 70 CE. Although destroyed as the centre of Jewish worship, the city itself was subsequently developed in two major phases: the building of Aelia Capitolina by Hadrian in the second century and, more extensively, as a Christian centre by Constantine the Great and his successors from the fourth century CE onwards. As a result of the continued activity, Jerusalem remained a major consumer centre, albeit not an emporium until the Muslim conquest of Palestine in the seventh century CE.

The revolt of 66–70 CE, the events surrounding Trajan's war in Mesopotamia, and the Bar Kokhba revolt, all played a part in the development of a Roman road network that certainly contributed to the expansion of trade in Palestine (see Isaac in this volume). It consisted of about 2,500 Roman miles of roads (Roll 2005: 108) in the areas of *Provincia Judaea* and what was later called *Provincia Arabia*, and reached its fullest extent in the third century CE. This network was integrated regionally with the Roman road system of the entire Roman Near East, and tied this area with Egypt, Syria, Asia Minor, and the borders of the Mesopotamian lands. Moreover, this system linked the trade routes of the Arabian peninsula and connected them to points even further east (India, China) that were the source for incense and other highly prized luxury goods (Roll 2005).

Another major contribution of the Romans to the development of the trade of the Palestinian economy might have come about from the presence of two Roman legions in Palestine and their auxiliary units. These seven thousand to twenty-five thousand soldiers would have added considerably to consumer demand (Safrai 1994: 339).

Although Herod's kingdom was divided upon his death, the period from Herod's rule until the Muslim conquest witnessed increasing urbanization, progressing from the urban centres that developed under Herod's sons (eg. Caesarea Philippi, Tiberias, Sepphoris), and the later rule of Roman governors (e.g. Eleuthropolis, Neapolis). This urbanization of Palestine was concomitant with the expansion of the well-developed and maintained road network mentioned above, whose traces are still very much evident today. These factors: the geographic location of Palestine, its continuing existence as a commercial agent, its increasing urbanization, and its well developed road network explain the parallel existence of different types of trade: local, regional, transit, and long-distance. The question of the relative importance of each of the different forms of trade is a complex question which may never be answered.

Generally, one can categorize the main trade activity as local trade, consisting of the sale of local produce in the nearest market, and the purchase there of whatever necessities and luxuries the inhabitants needed. An example of wares that are well attested as locally produced and consumed would be particular types of pottery made in the Galilee and found only there (Lapin 2001: 117–118). Regional trade would best be exemplified by the sale of olive oil from one area to another within the same region, as in the case of John of Gischala who sold the local olive oil product to Jews in southern Syria or Caesarea Philippi (Josephus, Bell. 2.591–591 compare Josephus, Vita 74). Apparently the interregional import of foreign products for sale and consumption in Palestine primarily concerned luxury items such as fine-ware (Lapin 2001: 18), wine, and pickled fish (Safrai 1994: 384, 385). The international trade included export of locally made products to other countries, such as dates and the opobalsam to Italy and asphalt to Egypt (see Lapin 2001: 124; Safrai 1994: 132, 187). The transit trade is perhaps best expressed by the trade in perfumes and spices brought from the Orient by the Nabataeans to the Mediterranean ports of Palestine, and then shipped to Rome (Broshi 1987; Miller 1969; Young 2001).

Very little is definitely known about local trade (Adan-Bayewitz 1985 and 1993). Apparently, it was conducted by two means: local markets, and travelling salesmen called *rochelim* (sg. *rochel*). These latter were independents who purchased products from producers or importers, and travelled the local communities selling cosmetics, small items such as the tools for spinning wool, and sometimes medicines (Adan-Bayewitz 1985; Lapin 2001: 136–137). Rabbinic literature provides many examples of the economic activities of these travelling salesmen. The ubiquity of the *rochel* as a figure in rabbinic literature makes him a recurring subject in the scholarly literature on trade, markets, and life in general in that period (Safrai 1994: 77–80, 231; Rosenfeld/Menirav 2005: 122; Adan-Bayewitz 1985).

The major problem with the historical accuracy of the reconstruction of the *rochel*'s role is that it is based, and can only be based, on rabbinic sources. The *rochel* as an itinerant salesman would not leave an archaeological record. He was not important enough to earn a place in the epigraphic record, and if there were any inscriptions such as rules relating to his work, they have not survived, or have not been found. The contemporary Christian or pagan sources would not have paid any attention to these travelling salesmen, as indeed very little of the Christian literature deals with the daily economic life of later Roman Palestine (Lapin 2001: 125). On the other hand, one should not too easily dismiss the accuracy of the description of the *rochel* in the rabbinic record, since the rabbis had no intrinsic interest in the subject. The very arbitrary incidence of rulings regarding the *rochel* seems to make the rulings a reliable source on this profession.

Although the *rochel* would periodically visit the local villages, the villagers still had to make most of their purchases in the local markets. The vibrancy of this local trade is demonstrated by finds of pottery made in the Galilee but sold in an area that encompassed the Lower and Upper Galilee and the Golan. The local markets would serve a much larger population than one might assume. According to one scholar, the area within one day's travel could include as many as forty villages (Strange 1997: 42). The location of these markets in a hierarchy of markets and settlements is debated by Lapin (2001), based on the lack of archaeological evidence for village markets. Relying heavily on central-place theory, he considers the possibility that a large proportion of the population of the rural countryside lived at sites that did not have any markets at all (Lapin 2001: 118). Moreover, he attempts to use this theory to construct a geographical 'tiering' of the markets that can indicate a hierarchy of settlements. Along with the 'central-place theory' he uses archaeology to 'reconstruct' markets, the products these markets may have sold, and the sellers and buyers who used these markets. In the final analysis, Lapin's conclusions are not very different from those of other scholars such as Safrai (1994), who recognize the existence of geographic models but base their conclusions primarily on the literary evidence.

The local markets are called *shuk* in the Hebrew and Aramaic sources. This word had at least three different meanings, making it difficult to give an all-encompassing definition or to clearly understand the exact intention in each reference. It can mean a permanent purpose-built place for trade, refer to a periodic gathering at a designated place in which wares were sold from displays on the ground or some temporary structure, or indicate any wide spot of ground within the confines of the settlement (Rosenfeld/Menirav 2005: 2–3; Safrai 1994: 238; Lapin 2001: 130).

Purpose-built markets in Palestine are found in almost all urban areas that have been excavated and attested in the archaeological record (Stern 1993–2008; cf. the respective references in the journal of the Israel Antiquities Authority, *Hadashot Arkheologiyot*). On the other hand, there are very few finds of identifiable marketplaces in villages (Safrai 1994: 231). For the most part, the purpose-built markets were constructed on the Greek model of a rectangular open area (*agora*) surrounded by a colonnade (*stoa*), but there were also markets in colonnaded streets (Sperber 1998: 9–11). In cities in which more than one market existed, these markets could be differentiated by their location (upper market, lower market), or by the wares or products that characterized them, such as wool, cheese, pottery, baskets, etc. (Dan 2006b). For example, in rabbinic sources, the term *makolin* usually designated a meat market (Rosenfeld/Menirav 2005: 27), even though the word may be derived from the Roman *macellum*, which was not limited to meat (on archaeological remains of a *macellum* see Segal 1995).

Rabbinic sources suggest that the farmers were often the merchandisers of their own products, as were the craftsmen whose workshops also served as stores. According to one view, craftsmen could not support themselves only by the sales made in their own settlement's market and were forced to bundle their wares at regional markets and fairs. A major product which was marketed at almost all levels, from local to transit trade, was grain. For example, wheat grown in the Susita (Hippos) area was sold in Tiberias (Orman 1985). There seem to have been wholesale dealers in grain (*siton*) called *sidki* (Rosenfeld/Menirav 2005: 45–50) who operated markets dedicated primarily to this product alone, often in major cities, but periodically even in large towns.

The permanent markets of the cities offered their merchandise throughout the work week (Rosenfeld/Menirav 2005: 22). However, small towns and villages had periodic markets that opened in whatever venue seemed suitable, such as a square in the centre of the settlement. Cities also had periodic markets, but these were held on Mondays and Thursdays in order not to contest village markets which were held on Fridays (according to rabbinic sources).

The items of trade were transported by donkey and camel, donkeys being the major form of travel to local and regional markets (Frayn 1996). According to one view, traders would come into the markets bearing their merchandise on donkeys, sell whatever they could, and buy merchandise and products to be sold at the next market they visited (Safrai 1994: 234–237).

The camel provided the land transportation for the long-distance trade between the inland regions of the Middle East and the Mediterranean ports. It made much of the trade in spices, perfumes, and other luxury items possible. Only the camel could have served the Nabataeans in the crossing of the large tracts of desert they had to pass in order to get from the area of modern Yemen to the Mediterranean ports or even the caravan cities of Palestine (Safrai 1994: 272; Millar 2006: 281). In contrast to Egypt, river transport was unavailable to the traders and merchants of Palestine, since the province lacked any seriously navigable rivers. The long coast was well-spotted with anchorages, however, which enabled the sea transport of goods along the north–south axis and served as a link in the trade routes between Asia Minor, Syria, and Egypt.

While the markets usually served the local trade, regional and international trade took place in what might best be described as fairs (Lapin 2001: 141–146). Fairs would last for a few days and were held periodically, not more than once a month, although once a year seems to have been far more common (Safrai 1994: 244). According to Lapin (2001), they did not occur frequently. Whereas the local fairs seem to have served the population of the adjacent areas, the regional and international fairs were dedicated to large-scale trade. Their importance can be judged by the fact that the emperor would grant tax redemptions to merchants who participated in them. These fairs would last from two weeks, in the case of regional fairs, up to eight weeks for the great international fairs (Rosenfeld/Menirav 2005: 53–54).

The most famous of the fairs apparently was the fair at Mamre (Kh. El-Halil, Botnah), although fairs are attested for Gaza, Acco, and Hammat Gader as well. The coin findings at this location indicate a paucity of local coins when compared with the number of coins from other places (Safrai 1994: 256).

Unfortunately, we have no way of knowing the proportion of trade that was international in the sense of export to and from Palestine, in comparison with the amount of trade that was only in transit through Palestine. The archaeological record of ceramic containers only proves that amphorae from different parts of the Mediterranean world passed through the port of Caesarea Maritima (Blakely 1996: 342–344). The remains of amphorae can show us what came in and stayed in the port, not what was imported and then transported to other corners of Palestine, or moved in transit to other areas of the Middle East. Amphorae found in Caesarea do not tell us anything about the type and percentage of vessels and goods that were exported from Palestine (Blakely 1988: 42). Shipwrecks with amphorae, while stimulating the imagination, have not been found in sufficiently large numbers to significantly address the unanswered questions about amounts, and directions, and merchandise, that was exported or imported. This archaeological record can at best support the hit and miss literary record and indicate far-flung trade activity, especially in early Byzantine times (Blakely 1996). Palestinian amphorae have also been found in Roman Italy, giving further proof to the claims for an export trade from Roman Palestine (Arthur 1998).

According to a variety of sources, Palestine's exports included linen clothing, dyed wool, glassware, wine, and oil (Alon 1980–84, vol. 1: 7). In the transit trade, the primary products that moved through the country were the perfumes and spices and other luxury goods (Heichelheim 1959: 200). Apparently, even silk from China passed through the Galilee on its way to the consumers in Rome (Alon 1980–84, vol. 1: 162 and 189; Safrai 1994: 161–162, 389; Neusner 1984: 94–99).

All attempts at quantifying the trade of Roman Palestine—how large a portion it played in the general economy of the empire, or even its importance within Palestine itself—are doomed to failure because of the scattered nature of the evidence. Yet, the accumulated evidence leaves no doubt that trade and commerce were major factors in the economy of the Roman province.

4. Suggestions for Further Research

The following questions have not been sufficiently investigated yet and would warrant further research in the future:

- What is the relationship between economic changes on the one hand, and social and political changes on the other? Are changes in trade behaviour a symptom of social and political changes, or could they have been a cause of such changes?
- How are food consumption and trade related to each other? Would trade opportunities have changed the local diet, or did the diet influence and affect the trade of certain food items? For example, did olive oil become a trade item because it was already part of the Mediterranean diet, or did trade create a desire for (a particular type of) oil?
- How and to what extent did trade change the production of certain goods? If a product was much desired, did the demand for this trade item affect the effort to produce it locally, and lead to changes and development in the production technology?
- Did taxation encourage or discourage trade? Was taxation on trade used consciously to attain fiscal or political ends?

SUGGESTED READING

Safrai (1994) is an indispensible work on all subjects of the economy of Roman Palestine. Rosenfeld/Menirav (2005) is a recent extensive and thorough study of markets, based primarily on the rabbinic sources. Although rabbinic sources are the basis for the discussion, there is recourse to archaeological and numismatic evidence whenever possible. Lapin (2001) takes a different approach by examining the evidence via models drawn from the social sciences. The publications of the Israel Antiquities Authority (*The Archaeological Survey of Israel*, 1964-, and the journal *Hadashot Arkheologiyot: Excavations and Surveys in Israel*) provide information on the material record.

BIBLIOGRAPHY

ADAN-BAYEWITZ, D. (1985). 'The Itinerant Peddler in Roman Palestine' [Hebr.], in *Jews in Economic Life*, ed. N. GROSS. Jerusalem: Zalman Shazar Center, 67–85.

—— (1993). *Common Pottery in Roman Galilee: A Study of Local Trade*. Ramat-Gan: Bar-Ilan University Press.

——/PERLMAN, I. (1990). 'The Local Trade of Sepphoris in the Roman Period'. *Israel Exploration Journal* 40: 152–172.

ALON, G. (1980–1984). *The Jews in Their Land in the Talmudic Age*. 2 vols. Jerusalem: Magnes Press.

ARTHUR, P. (1998). 'Eastern Mediterranean Amphorae between 500 and 700: a view from Italy', in *Ceramica in Italia: VI–VII secolo. Atti del Convegno in onore di John Hayes, Roma, 11–13 Maggio 1995*, vol. 1: Relazioni, ed. Lucia Saguì. Florence: Edizioni All'Insegna del Giglio, 157–183.

AVI-YONAH, M. (1964). 'The Commerce and the Industry in Eretz-Yisrael in the Roman-Byzantine Period' [Hebr], in *idem, Essays and Studies in the Lore of the Holy Land*. Tel Aviv and Jerusalem: Neuman, 125–136.

BAR, D. (2004). 'Population, Settlement and Economy in Late Roman and Byzantine Palestine (70–641 AD)'. *Bulletin of the School of Oriental and African Studies* 67: 307–320.

BEN-DAVID, A. (1975). 'Formation of the Prices on the Free Market at Normal Times, Inflationary Trends and Economic Regression in the Period of the Mishna and the Talmud'. *Proceedings of the Sixth World Congress of Jewish Studies*, vol. 2. Jerusalem: World Union of Jewish Studies, 63–69.

BLAKELY, J. A. (1988). 'Ceramics and Commerce: Amphorae from Caesarea Maritima'. *Bulletin of the American School of Oriental Research* 271: 31–50.

—— (1996). 'Toward the Study of Economics at Caesarea Maritima', in *Caesarea Maritima: A Retrospective After Two Millenia*, ed. A. Raban and K. G. Holum. Leiden: Brill, 327–345.

BROSHI, M. (1987). 'The Role of the Temple in the Herodian Economy'. *Journal of Jewish Studies* 38: 31–37.

—— (1990). 'Commerce in Antiquity: Some Methodological Remarks' [Hebr.], in *Commerce in Palestine Throughout the Ages*, ed. B.Z. Kedar, T. Dothan and S. Safrai Jerusalem: Yad Itzhak ben Zvi, 195–201.

DAN, Y. (1982). 'The Foreign Trade of Palestine in the Byzantine Period' [Hebr.]. *Cathedra* 23: 17–24.

—— (2006a). 'Economic Life in Byzantine Palestine' [Hebr.], in *Studies in the History of Palestine in the Roman-Byzantine Period*. Jerusalem: Yad Izhak ben-Zvi, 58–73.

—— (2006b). 'Internal and External Trade in Palestine of the Second Temple Period' [Hebr.], in *Studies in the History of Palestine in the Roman-Byzantine Period*. Jerusalem: Yad Izhak ben Zvi, 39–57.

DINUR, Y. (1990). 'The Taxes on Foreign and Domestic Trade in the Land of Israel in the Period of the Mishna and the Talmud' [Hebr.], in *Commerce in Palestine Throughout the Ages*, ed. B. Z. Kedar, T. Dothan and S. Safrai. Jerusalem: Yad Itzhak ben Zvi, 140–158.

FINLEY, M. I. (1973). *The Ancient Economy*. Berkeley and Los Angeles: University of California Press.

FRAYN, J. M. (1996). 'Aspects of Trade on the Judaean Coast in the Hellenistic and Roman Periods'. *ARAM Periodical* 8: 101–109.

GREENE, K. (2000). 'Technological Innovation and Economic Progress in the Ancient World: M. I. Finley Re-considered'. *Economic History Review* 53: 25–59.

HEICHELHEIM, F. M. (1959). 'Roman Syria', in *An Economic Survey of Ancient Rome*, vol. 4, ed. T. Frank. Baltimore, reprint Paterson, NJ: Pageant Books, 189–227.

HERZFELD, L. (1894). *Handelsgeschichte der Juden des Alterthums*. 2nd ed. Braunschweig: Joh. Heinrich Meyer.

HOPKINS, K. (1983). 'Introduction', in *Trade in the Ancient Economy*, ed. P. Garnsey, K. Hopkins, and C. R. Whittaker. Berkeley and Los Angeles: University of California Press. ix–xxv.

KLAUSNER, J. (1975). 'The Economy of Judea in the Period of the Second Temple' [Hebr.], in *The World History of the Jewish People, Vol. 7: The Herodian Period*, ed. M. Avi-Yonah. Ramat-Gan: Am Oved, 132–151.

LAPIN H. (2001). *Economy, Geography, and Provincial History in Later Roman Palestine.* Tübingen: Mohr-Siebeck.

MILLAR, F. (2006). 'Caravan Cities: The Roman Near East and Long-Distance Trade by Land', in *Rome, the Greek World, and the East*, vol. 3: *The Greek World, The Jews, and the East*, ed. H. M. Cotton and G. M. Rogers. Chapel Hill: University of North Carolina Press, 275–299.

MILLER, J. I. (1969). *The Spice Trade of the Roman Empire.* Oxford: Clarendon Press.

NEUSNER, J. (1984). *A History of the Jews in Babylonia*, vol. 1. 3rd ed. Chico: Scholars Press.

ORMAN, D. (1985). 'The Economy of Jewish Communities in the Golan in the Period of the Mishnah and Talmud' [Hebr.], in: *Jews in Economic Life*, ed. N. Gross. Jerusalem: Zalman Shazar Center, 35–67.

ROLL, I. (2005). 'Imperial Roads Across and Trade Routes Beyond the Roman Provinces of "Judaea-Palestina" and "Arabia": The State of Research'. *Tel Aviv* 32: 107–118.

ROSENFELD, B.-Z./MENIRAV, J. (2005). *Markets and Marketing in Roman Palestine.* Leiden and Boston: Brill.

ROSTOVTZEFF, M. (1957). *The Social and Economic History of the Roman Empire.* 2nd ed. Oxford: Clarendon Press.

SAFRAI, Z. (1994). *The Economy of Roman Palestine.* London and New York: Routledge.

SCHEIDEL, W./REDEN, S. VON (2002). 'Introduction: Approaching the Ancient Economy', in *The Ancient Economy*, ed. W. Scheidel and S. von Reden. Edinburgh: Edinburgh University Press, 1–8.

SCHWARTZ, SETH (2006). 'Political, Social, and Economic Life in the Land of Israel, 66–c. 235', in *The Cambridge History of Judaism*, vol. 4, ed. S. Katz. Cambridge: Cambridge University Press, 23–52.

SEGAL, A. (1995). *Monumental Architecture in Roman Palestine and Provincia Arabia* [Hebr.]. Haifa: Haifa University Press, 68–73.

SPERBER, D. (1998). *The City in Roman Palestine.* New York and Oxford: Oxford University Press.

STERN, E. (1993–2008). *New Encyclopedia of Archaeological Excavations in the Holy Land.* Jerusalem: Israel Exploration Society & Carta.

STRANGE, J. F. (1997). 'First Century Galilee from Archaeology and from the Texts', in *Archaeology and the Galilee: Texts and Contexts in the Graeco-Roman and Byzantine Periods*, ed. D. R. Edwards and C. T. McCollough. Atlanta, GA: Scholars Press, 39–48.

TCHERIKOVER, V. (1937). 'Palestine Under the Ptolemies'. *Mizraim* 4–5: 9–90.

TEMIN, P. (2001). 'A Market Economy in the Early Roman Empire'. *Massachussetts Institute of Technology, Dept. of Economics Working Paper* No. 01–08 (available at http://ssrn.com/abstract=260995).

YOUNG, G. K. (2001). *Rome's Eastern Trade: International Commerce And Imperial Policy*, 31 BC–AD 305. London: Routledge.

CHAPTER 16

POVERTY AND CHARITY

GILDAS HAMEL

A discussion of poverty and charity in Roman Palestine entails two main problems of method. The first one concerns the bias, time-bound nature, and lack of clarity of our literary sources. One can easily agree that poverty is destitution, when absence of food and shelter means immediate danger to life. But most of the cases discussed in the ancient sources refer to a less threatening lack of goods that is relative to the standard of a given society at a given time. One must be alert to the possibility that people called poor in these sources were defined in such a way that they did not represent the poorest social stratum.

The Hebrew Bible had already raised the issue of poverty, so that it had a determining influence on the authors of the later Jewish and Christian literary sources (the New Testament Gospels, Josephus, rabbinic literature) we use in examining the situation in Roman Palestine. When using these Hebrew-Aramaic and Greek sources, one should be aware of this biblical basis to better understand explicit references to poverty, interpret the silence of the sources on certain aspects of the phenomenon, and evaluate the phenomenon itself. More generally, the historical-critical interpretation of the literary sources needs to be conducted in constant awareness of the partiality and social interests of the authors, whenever they can be identified. The voice of the poor themselves rarely appears in the sources. Fortunately, archaeological research is helping to corroborate the results gained from the literary sources and makes important contributions to our understanding of the demography, land ownership, and social structures of the region.

A second methodological problem in the study of poverty in Roman Palestine concerns the appropriate use of theoretical models. Modern economic and socio-cultural theories are very helpful in conceptualizing poverty. There is a danger, however, in using them exclusively (Harland 2002). A more nuanced social-scientific study of poverty is needed, especially for Judaea of the first century CE (Ling 2006: 99–110).

1. POVERTY AND WEALTH: SOCIAL STRATIFICATION

In an agrarian society where perhaps 90 per cent of the population worked the land, misery and insecurity were primarily linked to hunger. Poverty at its most extreme—destitution—struck many more people in times of famine, when the lack of food security typical of widows, orphans, children, landless and jobless people, away from their family, or without a family, extended to larger segments of the society (Garnsey 1988 and 1999; Garnsey/Scheidel 1998). There were food stores in walled towns and cities as a precautionary method in case of famines, but only a fraction of the population could hope to receive rations. In famines, poor people were reduced to mixing the last remnants of cereals and legumes. Rations of bread and water were progressively diminished. Water became expensive and inaccessible at times. One looked for any available source of food such as wild carobs, vetch, and other plants normally used as fodder.

The reality, however, was that food scarcity, rather than eventual famines, was a permanent feature of this agrarian society (Beaudoin 2007: 17). Except for good harvest years, when there was enough food for everyone, the limitations of food production meant that a substantial part of the population was at subsistence or poverty level and could easily lose the little security it had and fall into destitution. What were the conditions that led to this chronic weakness? What role did economic structures play in causing this susceptibility?

An investigation of structural explanations for the existence of poverty brings up two general questions. The first one is about the physical and demographic constraints on the economy. Was production adequate, assuming a self-sufficient and mostly agrarian economy in Roman Palestine, to satisfy the needs of the population at any given period? The second question has to do with distribution of the production: how constraining were taxation and the distribution of labour, especially the tenancy system, with its rents and debts? On these difficult questions, the sources do not provide quantitative answers, though interpretations of archaeo-logical findings, together with a careful analysis of textual sources, can yield promising results (Reed 2000; Safrai 1994: 436–58). But they do not provide easy solutions, if one attempts to retrace the demographic, economic, and social evolution of Roman and Byzantine Palestine.

2. THE LIMITS OF PRODUCTION

In regard to the first question, whether agrarian production was able to meet the demands of the population of Roman Palestine, one may begin with ancient reports that the country was extraordinarily productive (Josephus, Bellum 3.42–43, 48–50; y. Peah 7:4, 20a–b). Such statements, notwithstanding the tone of exaggeration, have sometimes been accepted as fact in the past. Indeed, there is considerable evidence that farmers used and improved techniques to take advantage of the particular soil and climate conditions. The full use of animal traction, crop rotation, sophisticated distribution of risks, intensification of irrigation—these are some of the aspects of an economy that one should not mistakenly consider 'primitive' because of its agrarian nature. All of the evidence available, however, indicates that seed-to-yield ratios for grain crops were relatively low, perhaps around 5:1 for wheat, one of the staples, irrespective of the degree of intensity of cultivation, with higher yields in some plots and in good years (Broshi 1979; Gabba 1999; Foxhall 1990). Safrai (1994: 110, 364, 436–37) offers a criticism of Broshi's method and argues for higher yields and population numbers because of the intensive nature of cultivation in Roman and Byzantine times. Nevertheless, yields in agriculture were hampered by a number of natural and technical factors, resulting in a weak and very volatile economy.

It has been suggested that a particular weakness, at least in the third and fourth centuries CE, was the fragmentation of Palestinian large estates into small units held by poor tenants. The minute size of plots and units of exploitation would have prevented the use of more efficient techniques available on larger properties, as described by the Latin agricultural writers. The fragmentation of plots would also have prevented self-sufficiency, since small tenants could not afford the diversified means necessary to reach this goal (Sperber 1978: 206).

One possible objection to this reasoning is that large-scale economies of the modern kind were difficult to achieve in antiquity. Furthermore, the scattering of plots and tenants in Roman Palestine, far from being a weakness, could actually help to spread climatic risks as widely as possible, as comparative evidence shows (Halstead 1987 and 1989). The impression given by the Gospels, Josephus, documents from the Judaean Desert, and rabbinic literature is that large, or even average, landowners took a very active interest in their land, directly or through an agent, even if they did not do the work themselves. Tenancies would have been divided up in such a way that tenants and their families could maintain subsistence level. But smallness of scale did not necessarily entail a waste of labour or the impossibility of developing irrigation, or terracing, or the use of large mills or oil presses. All of these could be developed and used cooperatively or under a variety of private arrangements.

If yields were very low, however, a greater proportion of the harvest had to be put aside as seed for the following year, and between one-quarter and one-third had to go on various taxes, tolls, and tithes. Various estimates have been made on the level of taxes, which were considered oppressive, especially during the first century CE. (Gabba 1999: 100). Ben-David (1974: 297–98) estimates at 20.6 per cent the various Jewish taxes and 12.5 per cent the Roman taxes, which would have to be deducted from the amounts needed for subsistence. A large part of the land and of the human and animal workforce would need to be used simply to renew the seed and pay the taxes. Low yields meant that a great amount of time, energy, and soil were devoted to the growing of cereals, legumes, oil, and other foodstuffs necessary for subsistence, and more specifically for the storing and renewal of these resources.

A higher average yield, on the contrary, would allow farmers to decrease the acreage given to grain growing, and feed more people and more animals. This also meant more fertilization and more haulage power. In the case of land under tenancy leases, however, the added benefits were not necessarily transferred to tenants, since the landowners might be able to charge higher rents or reclaim outstanding debts.

In good times, intensive work led to an abundance of cereals, legumes, vegetables, oil, fruits, animals, and other products. It enabled other activities that mostly revolved around agriculture, such as land improvement, building, clothing, pottery, and transportation. Indeed, one basic problem of small-unit farming, namely the surplus of labour at times other than harvests or planting, found an outlet in the production of rural goods for the market (Erdkamp 1999; Lapin 2001). When all is said and done, however, one is forced to admit that all numbers concerning the agricultural production of Roman Palestine and its population remain speculative. Theoretical calculations made on the basis of food production of the land, and density of built-up areas, indicate that the population of Roman Palestine could not number more than one million (Schwartz 2001: 10–11). For the first century CE, more precise calculations of the regional population in villages and cities of Galilee have been made on the basis of the built-up areas and been matched against the possible production of the area (Reed 2000). It is impossible to say whether the local production was (always) sufficient, to what extent grain was imported, and whether there were politically savvy solutions in times of drought or famine.

A high population density usually leads to a scarcity of land. The effects of land scarcity on food production could be compounded by speculative agriculture, not directly geared toward the production of food as a means of subsistence (Gabba 1999, for the early empire). The development of domains devoted primarily to olive and wine cultivation in Roman Palestine seems linked to the issue of urbanization and the easier circulation of money, precisely at a time when the population was expanding and need for food was at its highest.

In sum, the available source material and comparative studies on ancient agriculture indicate that the physical and technical conditions for food production in Roman and Byzantine Palestine were quite limiting, though evolving slowly. The increased development of cities, towns, and villages throughout the period would be an argument for a less negative view. It seems that the question of the theoretical adequacy of food production for a given population must remain open at this stage.

3. SOCIAL STRUCTURE

The second question, concerning the distribution of goods in the economy, requires us to look at the structure and use of labour. In Roman Palestine, as in the Roman Empire at large, the government and landowning elites presiding over religious and civic institutions were supported by a labour force massively employed in agricultural activities and contributing land taxes and ground rents (Jones 1964: 464–5). A major cause of poverty was the pressure put on labour through contractual tenancy arrangements and indebtedness.

The types of labour used in agriculture included rural slavery, day- and seasonal workers, sharecropping, leases on fixed tenancy contracts, and private petty ownership. One may assume that all of these forms of land use co existed at any given time and were dynamic elements of the agrarian system, although our understanding of the various kinds of tenancy in the Roman Empire is still quite limited (Scheidel 1994; Foxhall 1990; Erdkamp 1999: 561). Tenancy on fixed contracts (in kind or in money) seems more abundantly documented, but sharecropping was probably much more common and almost certainly the solution of choice on larger domains. The Gospels and rabbinic literature lead to this assumption, though it is in need of a fully developed argument (Safrai 1994; Lapin 1995). Here, I assume that fixed tenancy arrangements are less important than sharecropping but feature in the sources precisely because they were less common and less clearly covered by regional customs (for which see T. B.M. 9:11; also 9:4, 10, 14). They were more likely to raise questions that required discussion.

Tenancy contracts for a fixed amount of time were usually written, and covered a short period, at least when cereals were concerned, though second-century CE. contracts of five years have been found at Murabba'at (Milik 1961: 124–32). They covered longer periods when fruit trees and vineyards were concerned, which required a longer investment. Fruit-tree plantations were more capital-intensive, but were also more likely to bring in cash to both tenants and owners, especially if they were located near an administrative or military centre or near access roads and sea, since money circulation was attached to cities (cf. T. B.M. 9:19 for wine, olives, and flax to be brought to town; 9:21 for vegetables sold in the market or in the field).

Leases of this kind provided more security to the families that could manage to obtain them, at least in relation to food, since cereals were inter-cultivated. They brought greater freedom than sharecropping to both owner and tenants because less supervision was needed at planting or harvest times. It is also possible that some of these tenants would subcontract to sharecroppers and hire labourers. Even in this seemingly more favourable arrangement, things could go wrong for the tenants. They could lose the animals they brought with them, for instance, or go deep into debt. The fixity of the rent was a problem, though it could be remedied by adjustments (Milik 1961: 125, 128), for example in the event of a drought or other catastrophe (M. B.M. 9:6).

The important point concerning tenancy arrangements, especially sharecropping, is that the independence of the small freeholder was exchanged for more security of access to food. Actual situations may have been quite complicated, with even small landowners sometimes being partly tenants and partly sharecroppers or hired labourers. Members of modest families would be in various situations of dependency, with the social risks normally being spread over many people through complex kinship arrangements. The hope of acquiring land was probably strong, because it was the main path to a secure and virtuous life. Access to land would make it possible to lead a life of food purity, offer sacrifices, pay tithes, be charitable, hire others, make better-suited marriages, and be properly buried.

Did the use of labour evolve over time, for instance with an increase of sharecropping and tenancy arrangements because of Herodian policies in the early Roman period, and again in the second century CE, because of the pressure coming from the expansion of cities, when customary rights would be lost or transformed? Most likely, the evolution of these elements was very complex and involved more than a simple opposition between large landowners and smallholders or tenants. This seems true in Roman Palestine at least, where, except for the Herodian period and possibly the second century as well, it is difficult to detect certain trends in land concentration and exploitation of labour (Safrai 1994). As elsewhere in the Roman Empire, the relative silence of the sources should not be construed as proof of the collapse of an independent peasantry (Garnsey 1987: 76).

Debt was a necessary part of the tenancy and sharecropping system and should not be seen as an aberration or a modern-style incentive to development. One basic reason for indebtedness was that tenants depended on politically powerful elites for access to land, and had little choice in return regarding contractual terms. Another more immediate reason was that harvests were unpredictable in a dry-farming zone such as Roman Palestine, in contrast to better irrigated areas. Knowledge of local conditions was available to priests and later to communal officials who had an interest in the proper accounting of tithes and dues. We may assume that tax records and the precise knowledge of local agricultural conditions were also of great importance to the imperial authorities. The difficulty of predicting a correct rate of return was mitigated by setting rents and taxation (not different in this respect) higher than necessary and modulating indebtedness, in order to get the maximum labour input.

Especially in the case of sharecropping, the factors of production provided by landowners (land, seeds, traction, tools) were set at a very high rate, usually amounting to half of the value of the crop, a circumstance which, together with the smallness of acreage under contract, guaranteed the fall into indebtedness. To avoid this, tenants would commit their entire household's labour to the land, in the hope of having as large a harvest as possible. The greater the amount of grain on the threshing floor, the more security the family would have for the year. They also hoped that landowners, together with the religious and civil institutions they tended to preside over, would offer security in case of failure. In a society driven by notions of honour and shame, indebtedness, and especially the granting of debt relief as generous gift and salvation, ensured for landowners the grateful return of labour.

In a similar manner, Columella coldly reasoned that the landowner walked a fine line between strictly exacting debt payments from tenants—which could be discouraging—and stimulating a better investment of labour in the land, which he himself favoured (De Re Rustica 1.7.1–3). A landowner 'should be more exacting in the matter of work than of payments, as this gives less offence yet is, generally speaking, more profitable'. In Columella's view, or Pliny's (Epistulae 3.19), more work would mean a better yield, making it impossible for tenants (coloni) to ask for reductions in rent or debt. For both Columella and Pliny, the goal was to extract the maximum of labour, which could be accomplished by a dynamic of steep rents, indebtedness, and enlightened benevolence.

Likewise, the larger landowners of Roman and Byzantine Palestine, who were sometimes also religious authorities (e.g. members of the priesthood or rabbis) or closely tied to them, could use the common religious language of debt either in a harsh way, hoping to be paid a bigger proportion of the outstanding debts, or in a more subtle fashion, by showing compassion and expecting more work and faithfulness in return. They were expected to be just and kind to their tenants, especially in matters involving the loan of grain for the sowing season (M. B.M. 5:8). But they could also use the threat of short-term leases, eviction, and physical violence (prison and torture). The threat of a diminution in social status was more immediate, in any case, and with it the possible loss of security in food income.

Finally, another aspect of this debt system was that high revenues were part of the competition for political power among leading families, especially under the pressure of imperial demands. This onerous system of debts and the apparent luxury of rich landowning families in Jerusalem seem to have played an important role in the circumstances leading to the Jewish War and the fall of the Temple (Goodman 1982).

For the time being, one may conclude that a perennial feature of the agrarian society of Roman and Byzantine Palestine was the forced contraction of needs experienced by rural labourers and their families, especially women, children, and anybody physically weak. Consumption was limited by rents and debts set in such a way that they were the ground for a complex playing out by the elites of behaviours that ran the gamut from rigid to compassionate. The religious and political elites themselves had inherited the role of saviours and protectors which they exercised towards the population. Practically speaking, it meant the critical right to collect and store abundant provisions in cities and towns, under the watchful and interested eye of imperial authorities, and the duty to redistribute them in adequate fashion.

4. Perceptions of Poverty and Charity

A primary consideration in regard to the ancient Jewish outlook on poverty and charity is that these phenomena were understood in a religious framework, whereas in Graeco-Roman society, philanthropy, patronage, and state subsidies were seen as civil duties. In Judaism, poverty and charity had already for a long time been the object of an explicit concern. A contextual study of the vocabulary of poverty in the Hebrew Bible indicates that very divergent biblical notions of poverty existed, but the topic was a critical issue, especially in the prophetic and legal traditions (Pleins 1992: 413). In these traditions, a clear difference is made between the poor, defined concretely as dependent and oppressed ('*any*, found eighty times), and the destitute in extreme circumstances ('*evyon*, found sixty times). Both of these words, without losing their social and physical meanings and their focus on dependence and need, had an important religious significance early on.

Common Greek usage recognized the same difference between the poor as destitute (*ptôchos*), and the person making a living in a dependent and menial occupation, at subsistence level, or near subsistence level (*penês*). The working poor remained political and religious participants in their society, whereas the destitute were on the margins of society, having lost all claims on the resources of the group and having become completely dependent on the hospitality of people who could expect nothing in return.

The differentiation made in the Hebrew and the Greek Bible between the two situations seems to have disappeared in Qumran texts, the Gospels, and rabbinic literature. While the use of the biblical term for dependent poor (*'any*) dominates in the Mishnah, Tosefta, and halakhic midrashim, other terms, especially the biblical word for destitute (*'evyon*), are virtually absent. The first term is usually applied to the legal situation of people of small means—with very little land or none at all, but some possessions—regarding the cult, customary rights, and debt (Hamel 1990: 175). In the Targums and the Talmuds, this expression is still used, but a synonym (*misken* or *miskena'*) tends to replace it almost completely. Its similar meaning of dependence and its less obvious religious connotation may explain its use, as the situation of poor people continued to be characterized by the dependence of tenants and labourers on landowners and patrons, at least from the third century CE on.

In Jewish Greek texts, including the Gospels, the difference probably became obscured by the religious connotation attached to both 'dependent poor' and 'destitute', and transferred to their Greek equivalents, usually *ptôchos*. An unusual example of this religious over-determination is found at Bet Shearim in the unique epitaphs of a Jewish family from Palmyra of the second or third century CE that was not without means (Schwabe 1974: nos. 99 and 206). These inscriptions seem to use the epithet *penichros* ('poor') in laudatory fashion similar to the use of *hosios* ('pious'). The transformation was perhaps helped also by the changed social conditions in the Roman period, with a progressively more marked distinction between rich and poor.

Josephus's view of social stratification is more aligned with Graeco-Roman views, where poverty seems concealed in a political language of power. He shows great interest in the elites, the large landowners who are well connected to the royal and priestly families, and who are distinguished by their power, wealth, and social significance, and occasionally virtue, intelligence, and culture. He rarely speaks of poor people directly, and tends to use the political vocabulary of the Greek city, in which the contrast between rich and poor rarely featured in the early Roman Empire. He speaks of the mass of the population as weak, without resources, and needy (*asthenês* especially, *aporos, endeês*). They lack distinction, manners, and education, especially knowledge of the Torah.

Indeed, not only Josephus, but all sources make clear that poverty is not simply a matter of lack of material possessions and social injustice. The lack of physical means also implies an inability to participate fully and honourably in social and religious activities. This lack may be quite relative, as is clear from the tendency indicated above of restricting the use of 'poor' to people within society able to meet religious requirements. Conversely, the more frequent situations of poverty might not be recognized as such, with the consequence that claims to divine protection could not easily be invoked. One wonders, then, if the 'working poor' are not sometimes mentioned in rabbinic literature, similar to Josephus, in ways that make them less clearly identifiable and consequently less deserving of the remedies for poverty specified in the biblical tradition. For instance, the so-called 'people of the land' ('*ammei ha-aretz*), who were reputed to be ignorant of the Torah and failing in such religious duties as tithes and ritual purity, may also have been economically weak. They may not be identified with the poor as a social group, but it is reasonably clear that it is their lack of social and material resources, typical of their situation as workers of the land, that may have prevented them from fulfilling certain religious duties and devoting time to Torah learning.

The social and religious disqualifications or impairments typical of poverty become clear when it comes to two palpable aspects of life: food and clothing. Unsurprisingly, diets varied according to social status. The elites, meaning government officials and important landowners, were the only ones able to hold ceremonial meals frequently, at which they could display more remarkable foods: meat in abundance, white bread and sweets, old wines and fruits. Examples of the ideal appear in the Gospels, Josephus' paraphrase of the biblical stories, and later legal texts. Many people, on the other hand, lived at subsistence levels (Ben-David 1974: 306–10; Hamel 1990: 8–22; compare with Roman Italy: Evans 1980; Frayn 1979). Even in cities, which were better provided with water, bread, and meat (M. Makh. 2:9), people of small means ate inferior foods (M. Ber. 6:3). Poverty meant one had to get by with socially scorned foods: an inferior quality bread, with bran and impurities, baked in common shapes. It also meant that one could not afford meat, or on rare occasions only, nor vegetables, except for certain roots and edible plants grown wild.

One major social disability had to do with the difficulty or impossibility of securing white bread made of pure flour, for which there was a great desire. This bread was ground and sifted from the best grains with much more care than other breads from the best grains, which also meant that it required considerable work by the women who prepared it. It was very different from barley bread or bread made with other dark flour, that is, flour containing varying amounts of bran. Some breads were even made with mixed flours, that is, meal from legumes or from cereals without gluten. This food was not well accepted and denoted low status: eaters of black bread were reputed to be slaves and poor people (M. Makh. 2:8).

The desire to secure whiter bread and meat, fish, or eggs, was especially important for Sabbaths and feast days. Lack of these elements was socially and religiously demeaning. For instance, it was not always possible to follow the religious prescriptions for the Passover meal such as the eating of roast lamb, especially in times of famine or after the destructions wrought by wars. This probably widely shared concern is reflected in the following text from the Tosefta: 'The bitter herbs, and the unleavened bread, and the Passover lamb are a duty on the night of the first day of the feast, but facultative on other days. R. Shimon says: a duty for men, facultative for women' (T. Pes. 2:22, in the Erfurt manuscript: 1:34).

Clothing was an even more visible mark of status than food (Hamel 1990: 73–93). To lack clothing, especially a mantle and shoes, or to have only one set of clothes, was potentially degrading, as were the poor quality of the fabric and the colours used. Complete or relative nakedness indicated very low status and was unacceptable (Jubilees 3:31; Sifre Deut. 32:21). It could even be a sign of madness, as the story about the Gerasene demoniac indicates (Luke 8:27). Worn-out clothes could disqualify from performing certain religious functions (M. Meg. 4:6).

The possession of a mantle, which was also a night cover and a sign of status, marked the main difference between destitution and poverty. Poor people had basic clothing but could not easily renew it, keep it from the reach of creditors (Mekhilta Ex. 22:26), and provide it to all members of the family. The minimum subsistence to be granted to a wife temporarily represented by a guardian gives an idea of what was considered a minimum amount of clothing: 'He must also give her [once a year] a cap for her head and a girdle for her loins. Shoes [he must give her] each major festival, and clothing [of the value] of fifty *zuz* every year.' (M. Ket. 5:8.). The remark about the shoes may indicate a concern for social status and honour. The Mishnah continues: 'About whom are [these] words said? [They apply] to the poor in Israel. But in the case of a distinguished person [i.e., if the husband was a distinguished person], all [is done] in accordance with his honor' (M. Ket. 5:9). The wife in question may not always have received what was her due, and the force of the stipulation may have been theoretical only (Ilan 1996: 88–96).

Certain individuals or groups seem to have deliberately chosen a sort of poverty that was more severe than the poverty experienced by the wife spoken of in the Mishnah. According to Josephus, the Essenes went on the roads very poorly dressed. They changed clothes and shoes only when they fell apart completely or were worn out to the thread (Josephus, Bell. 2.126). But religious wanderers like the Essenes, Jesus's disciples, and the later itinerant monks could rely upon the support of friendly communities, at least to a degree.

The type and abundance of clothes which allowed frequent change was a sure sign of wealth. Poor people, on the contrary, had a single set of cheaper clothing that they would shorten for work, since a long mantle and tunic would have impeded movement. Long tunics and ample mantles, which were normally made of high quality wool, sometimes linen, enhanced the status of elites who didn't need to do physical work to earn their living and who used servants. The contrast is still clear on the floor mosaic from the fifth-century CE Bet Alpha synagogue: Abraham wears a long, striped tunic, whereas his servants have short, undecorated tunics (Fine 1996: 131). The absence of stripes was characteristic of the clothing of slaves and people in menial occupations. Likewise, for an earlier period, the decorated wool clothes found in the Cave of Letters in the Judean Desert were not poor people's clothes (Yadin 1963: 170, 204).

On religious occasions and in daily life, great stress was put on the use of brightly bleached white clothes, which were taken to be evidence of piety and righteousness.

Such clothes were expensive to procure, however, and only available to wealthier people. Not to own them, or to be forced to borrow them for religious festivals could be shameful (M. Taan. 4:8). Another aspect of this stress on white was that rabbinic religious rules of purity and impurity could only be fulfilled completely with such bright clothes, and the expected public approval for a life of apparent piousness and purity then accrued only to those able to afford such items. People wearing darker dress, who could not afford white clothes and would find them unpractical in their work, would be unable to demonstrate that kind of purity and piety, and therefore could not make any claim on the attendant religious and social consideration.

To conclude: in the Hebrew Bible, the Gospels, Mishnah, Tosefta, Talmud, and early Christian texts, poverty is confronted more directly, both as material and social need, than it is in the Graeco-Roman world (Brown 2002). Nevertheless, in Judaism and early Christianity alike, the tendency also existed to interpret poverty in spiritual terms. The material aspects of poverty could be disregarded in various ways, when the poor were not recognized as such.

5. Charity and the Redistribution of Wealth

The Pentateuchal ordinances regarding land redistribution, the sabbatical year, loans, debt cancellation and slavery for debt, tithing, and gleaning by the poor were in part remedies for individual situations, in part attemps at correcting the systemic disequilibriums in land tenure and debt structure. These regulations aimed at maintaining or reestablishing a degree of independence and status for threatened members of a society in which equality was still deemed important (Schwartz 2001: 227–28). In theory at least, there was little room for patronage in that system.

It seems that in the Roman and Byzantine period some of these biblical regulations aimed at alleviating poverty continued to be practised, though it is difficult to determine exactly to what extent this was true. A decree by Caesar on tax reductions, mentioned by Josephus, would indicate that rules concerning the sabbatical year, for instance, were observed in the early Roman period. The tax reduction explicitly mentioned for every seventh year appears to be a matter of principle, on grounds that in that year 'they neither plow nor take fruit from the trees' (Josephus, Ant. 14.206, 202). The sabbatical year and tithe laws were still very important for the community at Rehov in the sixth century (Levine 2000: 204). One presumes that, like every other person, poor Jews would then have had access without restriction to the uncultivated fruit or grain as the law prescribed. Yet there is also evidence from the pre-70 CE period that there were means to elude the laws requiring the remission of debts in the sabbatical year and prohibiting interest on loans (Papyrus Mur. 18; Schwartz 2001: 68–71).

When the Temple in Jerusalem was functioning, it must have had an important role in the alleviation of poverty. The Temple economy, which had developed to a considerable extent under Herod the Great and his successors, was an atypical economy supporting a large personnel. As one of the largest centres of pilgrimage in the ancient Mediterranean world, it had institutions catering for pilgrims and the poor, and it was especially meritorious to give charity during religious festivities. The Temple, not different in this respect from other temples, had a number of contribution boxes (Josephus, Ant. 19.294; Mark 12:41–43; Luke 21:1; M. Sheq. 6:5). Most of the money collected at the Temple, however, went to the personnel and the cult. As to the third tithe or poor tithe added every third year to the second tithe (Josephus, Ant. 4.240), its effect is difficult to determine. Various competing interpretations existed regarding the practice, and it seems that its collection encountered significant difficulties (M. Abot 5:9).

There is considerable evidence, however, that support of the poor occurred at community level and centred on the synagogue. As Levine has shown (2000: 580–602), the synagogue was an institution which developed in the Hellenistic Diaspora, but it was much more extensive in its activities than comparable Graeco-Roman institutions. Its charitable undertakings, especially, seem to have been quite distinctive. First-century CE synagogues seem to have already engaged in charitable activities, for example serving as a hostel for visitors and transients (Levine 2000: 132–3). Late antique synagogues, according to a variety of sources, actually became the centre of a sophisticated communal 'social welfare system' (Levine 2000: 372–3), primarily geared to the provision of food and clothing for the poor.

Charity (*tsedakah*, social justice) was organized as a public concern. Already in the case of the Essenes, the Damascus Rule speaks of a monthly collection administered by an official (*mevakker*) and judges. The collection was meant to be distributed to the 'poor and the needy, the aged sick and the homeless, the captives taken by a foreign people, the virgin with no near kin, and the ma[iden for] whom no man cares' (CD 14:12–16). In every Jewish community, two funds seem to have existed from which the poor and strangers could obtain relief. The weekly money 'basket' (*quppah*) served to support the local poor, who received a weekly allotment. The 'plate' (*tamhui*) was open to any person needing a meal, especially strangers, and functioned therefore like a soup kitchen (Schürer 1979: 437). The donations could be in kind or money. There was continuous need to prevent abuse by claimants and accusations of misuse of funds, especially of favouritism (compare the precautions taken by Paul, 2 Cor. 8:18–24).

The fact that fourteen treasuries of small coins were found in excavations of synagogues in Roman-Byzantine Palestine suggests that the collection of charity funds mentioned in the texts (e.g. T. Peah 4:9) was actually practised. If the participation of the whole community was required, this may have limited to some degree the influence and weight of the Graeco-Roman tradition of urban patronage. Indeed, amongst synagogue inscriptions there is a clear difference between Aramaic inscriptions blessing the community's support anonymously, and Greek inscriptions thanking individually named philanthropists (Levine 2000: 361). Furthermore, the collection of goods and money was separated from their distribution, in such a way that a considerable degree of anonymity could be maintained, and the dignity of recipients preserved. The demand made on the participation of the whole community, no matter how insignificant the contribution, seems to have been a distinctive feature of Jewish charitable practice that would be adopted and spread by Christian communities from the third century CE onwards (Brown 2002: 56).

What was considered to be a standard minimum payment can be reconstructed on the basis of what was to be given to a destitute by the synagogue community fund and to a poor woman by her husband's trustee when the husband was away. It can be calculated that the idealized minimum for an individual was about one and a half pounds of bread per day, which was enough to survive. The total value of food to be granted through a trustee to the temporarily separated wife of a man of humble condition was superior to what was considered the minimum for a poor wanderer: 'Two cabs of wheat or four cabs of barley per week', according to the Mishnah, that is, from one and a half to two pounds of bread per day (M. Ket. 5:8). She was also to receive legumes, a measure of oil, some figs, either dried or pressed in a cake. We don't know whether the woman was considered to be alone or with children in her care. Little children hardly appear in the sources, and fathers had to be reminded of their duty to feed daughters, because daughters had no claim to maintenance, or at least the topic was disputed (M. Ket. 4:6; T. Ket. 4:8).

This level of organization of social aid was so impressive that Julian, in a letter written in 362 CE to Arsacius, the high-priest of Galatia, in which he specifies 'measures to be taken for the relief of the poor', feels compelled to say: 'I order that one-fifth of this be used for the poor who serve the priests, and the remainder distributed by us to strangers and beggars. For it is disgraceful that, when no Jew ever has to beg, and the impious Galilaeans support not only their own poor but ours as well, all men see that our people lack aid from us' (Stern 1980: 549–50, no. 482).

6. Conclusion

Faced with economic and demographic conditions that were hard to change and difficult to predict, the highly stratified Jewish society of Roman and Byzantine

Palestine responded to the critical problem of poverty with communal institutions that continued to reflect and adapt the prophetic and legal traditions of the Bible. These institutions will have limited some of the harmful effects of poverty, though the tendency to frame poverty in religious and social terms meant that a share of the resources went to repair loss of status rather than pure economic lack.

Many questions remain to be investigated. In particular, the evident influence that Jewish care of the poor had on Christian caritative institutions needs to be further examined. It would also be important to study why slaves are completely absent in the Christian preaching and practice of charity (Brown 2002: 61–3, 79), while sporadically mentioned in Stoic-like fashion in rabbinic Midrash (Hezser 2005: 153). Among other things likely to reward additional study, one should mention the structure of land tenure arrangements, the dynamics of labour use, and the demographic evolution. Was there a wider levelling of social differences in the third and fourth centuries CE, for instance, when a lesser differentiation between town and country buildings and an absence of luxury graves seem to have existed, as observed in the Carmel region by H.-P. Kuhnen (1989: 304–23; 330–7)? Did a greater demographic density and intensification of agricultural production lead to more secure rights to land and an increase of landownership, as argued for other periods and places by Boserup and Netting (Netting 1993: 158–61)? The investigation of the role of the elites in redistribution, and the evolution of their religious and civil roles, particularly in regard to tax farming, is an on-going task. Finally, one needs to explore the evolution of social differentiation in the cities of Byzantine Palestine, as they became economically more important and their demographic composition changed.

SUGGESTED READING

Gabba (1999) provides a lucid account of the political and economic situation in the early Roman Empire. For an extended treatment of Jewish society under imperial conditions from the Hellenistic period until the Islamic period, see Schwartz (2001). Patlagean (1977) remains a richly detailed, novel, and methodologically inspiring study of poverty in the early Byzantine period. An excellent account of the range of attitudes and practices of social aid in the Graeco-Roman world at large is Hands (1968). Brown (2002) retraces the evolution of the Christian discourse and practice of redistribution in the late Roman Empire, in changing political circumstances, while often referring to the Jewish and classical background. Hamel (1990) examines poverty and charity in Roman Palestine of the first three centuries CE.

BIBLIOGRAPHY

BEAUDOIN, S. M. (2007). *Poverty in World History*. London: Routledge.

BEN-DAVID, A. (1974). *Talmudische Ökonomie : die Wirtschaft des jüdischen Palästina zur Zeit der Mischna und des Talmud*. Hildesheim: Olms.

BROSHI, M. (1979). 'The Population of Western Palestine in the Roman-Byzantine Period'. *Bulletin of the American Schools of Oriental Research* 236: 1–10.

BROWN P. (2002). *Poverty and Leadership in the Later Roman Empire*. Hanover: University Press of New England.

ERDKAMP, P. (1999). 'Agriculture, Underemployment, and the Cost of Rural Labour in the Roman World'. *The Classical Quarterly* 49: 556–72.

EVANS, J. K. (1980). 'Plebs Rustica. The Peasantry of Classical Italy'. *American Journal of Ancient History* 5: 19–47, 134–73.

FINE, S. (ed.) (1996). *Sacred Realm: The Emergence of the Synagogue in the Ancient World*. New York and Oxford: Oxford University Press and Yeshiva University Museum.

FOXHALL, L. (1990). 'The Dependent Tenant: Land Leasing and Labour in Italy and Greece'. *The Journal of Roman Studies* 80: 97–114.

FRAYN, J. M. (1979). *Subsistence Farming in Roman Italy*. London: Centaur Press.

GABBA, E. (1999). 'The Social, Economic and Political History of Palestine 63 BCE–CE 70', in *The Cambridge History of Judaism*, ed. W. Horbury, W. D. Davies, and J. Sturdy. Cambridge: Cambridge University Press, 94–167.

GARNSEY, P. (1987). *The Roman Empire: Economy, Society, and Culture*. London: Duckworth.

—— (1988). *Famine and Food Supply in the Graeco—Roman World: Responses to Risk and Crisis*. Cambridge: Cambridge University Press.

—— (1999). *Food and Society in Classical Antiquity*. Cambridge: Cambridge University Press.

—— and SCHEIDEL, W. (1998). *Cities, Peasants, and Food in Classical Antiquity: Essays in Social and Economic History*. Cambridge: Cambridge University Press.

GOODMAN, M. (1982). 'The First Jewish Revolt: Social Conflict and the Problem of Debt'. *Journal of Jewish Studies* 33: 417–27.

HALSTEAD, P. (1987). 'Traditional and Ancient Rural Economies in Mediterranean Europe: Plus Ça Change?' *Journal of Hellenic Studies* 107: 77–87.

—— (1989). 'The Economy Has a Normal Surplus: Economic Stability and Social Change Among Early Farming Communities of Thessaly, Greece', in *Bad Year Economics: Cultural Responses to Risk and Uncertainty*, ed. P. Halstead and J. O'Shea. Cambridge: Cambridge University Press, 68–80.

—— and JONES, G. (1989). 'Agrarian Ecology in the Greek Islands: Time Stress, Scale and Risk'. *Journal of Hellenic Studies* 109: 41–55.

HAMEL, G. (1990). *Poverty and Charity in Roman Palestine, First Three Centuries C.E.* Near Eastern Studies 23. Berkeley: University of California Press.

HANDS, A. R. (1968). *Charities and Social Aid in Greece and Rome*. Ithaca: Cornell University Press.

HARLAND, P. A. (2002). 'The Economy of First-Century Palestine: State of the Scholarly Discussion', in *Handbook of Early Christianity: Social Science Approaches*, ed. A. J. Blasi, P.-A. Turcotte, and J. Duhaime. Walnut Creek: AltaMira Press, 511–27.

HEZSER, C. (2005). *Jewish Slavery in Antiquity*. Oxford: Oxford University Press.

ILAN, T. (1996). *Jewish Women in Greco-Roman Palestine*. Peabody: Hendrickson Publishers.

JONES, A. H. M. (1964). *The Later Roman Empire*. Oxford: Blackwell.

KUHNEN, H.-P. (1989). *Studien zur Chronologie und Siedlungsarchäologie des Karmel (Israel) zwischen Hellenismus und Spätantike*. Wiesbaden: Dr. Ludwig Reichert.

LAPIN, H. (1995). *Early Rabbinic Civil Law and the Social History of Roman Galilee*. Atlanta: Scholars Press.

—— (2001). *Economy, Geography, and Provincial History in Later Roman Palestine*. Tübingen: Mohr-Siebeck.

LEVINE, L. (2000). *The Ancient Synagogue; the First Thousand Years*. New Haven: Yale University Press.

LING, T. J. M. (2006). *The Judaean Poor and the Fourth Gospel*. Society for New Testament Studies Monograph Series 136. Cambridge: Cambridge University Press.

MILIK, J. T. (1961). 'Textes Hébreux et Araméens', in *Les grottes de Murabba'ât*, ed. P. Benoit, J. T. Milik, and R. de Vaux. Discoveries in the Judaean Desert 2. Oxford: Clarendon Press, 65–205.

NETTING, R. McC. (1993). *Smallholders, Householders: Farm Families and the Ecology of Intensive, Sustainable Agriculture*. Stanford: Stanford University Press.

PATLAGEAN, E. (1977). *Pauvreté économique et pauvreté sociale à Byzance, 4e–7e siècles*. Paris: Mouton.

PLEINS, J. D. (1992). 'Poor, Poverty—Old Testament', in *The Anchor Bible Dictionary*, vol. 5, ed. D. N. Freedman. New York: Doubleday, 402–414.

REED, J. (2000). *Archaeology and the Galilean Jesus: A Re-Examination of the Evidence*. Harrisburg: Trinity Press International.

SAFRAI, Z. (1994). *The Economy of Roman Palestine*. London and New York: Routledge.

SCHEIDEL, W. (1994). *Grundpacht und Lohnarbeit in der Landwirtschaft des römischen Italien*. Frankfurt: Lang.

SCHÜRER, E. (1979). *The History of the Jewish People in the Age of Jesus Christ (175 B.C.–A.D. 135)*. A new English version revised and edited by G. Vermes et al., vol.2. Edinburgh: T&T Clark.

SCHWABE, M./LIFSCHITZ, B. (1974). *Beth She'arim: The Greek Inscriptions*. Jerusalem: Israel Exploration Society.

SCHWARTZ, S. (2001). *Imperialism and Jewish Society, 200 B.C.E. to 640 C.E.* Princeton: Princeton University Press.

SPERBER, D. (1971). 'Patronage in Amoraic Palestine (c. 220–400): Causes and Effects'. *Journal of the Economic and Social History of the Orient* 14: 227–52.

—— (1978). *Roman Palestine, 200–400. The Land: Crisis and Change in Agrarian Society as Reflected in Rabbinic Sources*. Ramat-Gan: Bar-Ilan University.

STEGEMANN, E. W./STEGEMANN, W. (2002). *The Jesus Movement: A Social History of Its First Century*. Minneapolis: Fortress Press.

STERN, M. (1980). *Greek and Latin Authors on Jews and Judaism: From Tacitus to Simplicius*. Jerusalem: Israel Academy of Sciences and Humanities.

YADIN, Y. (1963). *The Finds from the Bar Kokhba Period in the Cave of Letters*. Jerusalem: Israel Exploration Society.

V

FAMILY LIFE

CHAPTER 17

....

THE DIFFERENT LIFE STAGES: FROM CHILDHOOD TO OLD AGE

....

JONATHAN SCHOFER

SCHOLARS have approached the topic of life cycles among Jews in Roman Palestine from several angles. First, larger works examining Jewish life stages and rites of passage sometimes also include important materials from late antique sources. For example, Ivan Marcus' *The Jewish Life Cycle* (2004) is a recent and thorough treatment that includes a review of earlier work. Secondly, a number of studies have offered detailed treatments of specific life stages and ritual markers in ancient Judaism, including childhood, marriage, family, old age, and funerary practices (Cohen 1993; Kraemer, ed. 1989 and 2000; Rubin 1997; Satlow 2001; Signer 1990; Schremer 2003; Van Henten /Brenner, eds 2000). Thirdly, several articles focus on the significance of particular ages in Judaism, such as the ages of 13, 18, 20, and 40 (Borgen 1961; Gilat 1992; Idel 1980; Schremer 1998). Fourthly, the life stages of women have been examined in broader studies of gender issues (Biale 1984; Wegner 1988; Pantel Zolty 1993; Ilan 1995; Hauptman 1998). In addition, recent years have brought a flurry of new publications on demography, childhood, and old age in Rome and in early Christianity (Bakke 2005; Brandt 2002; Cohen/Rutter, eds 2007; Cokayne 2003; Harlow/Laurence 2002; Parkin 1992 and 2003; Scheidel 2001).

Most of the ancient evidence is textual, and a primary task in the study of Jewish life cycles in Roman Palestine is to gather the respective literary sources, clarify terms, sort out the various traditions in relationship to each other, and situate them in the context of the earlier Jewish tradition (e.g. the Bible and Qumran literature) and evidence from the surrounding cultures (esp. Graeco-Roman society and Christianity). Many relevant rabbinic sources and at least one important passage from Qumran reveal a strong emphasis on the study of sacred texts, setting out an ethos that can be broadly characterized as 'scholastic' (Saldarini 1982; Cabezon 1998). This focus upon education in many respects parallels the broad interest in *paideia* found in Roman society: amongst Jews, the Bible played a similar role as Homer in the Roman context, and the rabbinic study house took the place of the Roman *scholasterion* (Hezser 2001: 70–71, 102–103; on Roman education see Cribiore 2001 and 2007).

Many Greek, Roman, Jewish, and Christian sources set out highly stylized life-cycle accounts, often structured by numerical schemes based on two, three, four, five, six, seven, ten, and twelve. The number could designate either the number of stages or the number of years in each stage. Common in Jewish sources is a focus on ten-year increments, which appears to be a Near Eastern, more than a Greek or Roman conceptualization of age. The pattern appears in an ancient Mesopotamian text, an Egyptian text written in Demotic entitled *The Instruction of Papyrus Insinger*, and the *Rule of the Congregation* of the Dead Sea Scrolls, as well as in several rabbinic passages (Sears 1986; Boll 1913: 22–24; Lichtheim 1980: 198–199; Lichtheim 1983: 152–156, 214–216, Weinfeld 1992, cf. Ben Sira 18: 19).

1. Methodological Issues

The comparison between Jewish and (Graeco-)Roman understandings of life stages involves two specific problems. First, we need to recognize the diversity of views and perspectives in both Jewish and Roman society. In his study of old age in ancient Rome, Tim Parkin emphasizes the wide range of accounts and assessments of old age, warning against generalizations based on single passages (Parkin 2003: 58–59). Secondly, complex comparisons should recognize layers of similarity and difference in any given case. Comparison is then an ongoing process of looking for difference where we first found similarity, and similarity where we recognized difference (Yearley 1990).

The relationship between textual sources and daily life practices is always difficult to determine. This problem is particularly significant in the study of women, for the androcentrism of the literary heritage means that we perceive women only through the eyes of men, who expressed concern with women primarily as daughters, wives, and mothers (see also Ilan in this volume). Many women, especially those beyond the age of child-bearing, are hardly visible in the literary sources. For the study of both women's and men's life expectancy, demography is very important, yet demographic research of Rome in late antiquity has yielded ambiguous results. The average life expectancy is assumed to have been between twenty and thirty years. According to one estimate, less than half of those who reached fifteen (thus discounting childhood mortality) would live to become fifty. The maximum life span, however, was not much shorter than today. In modern societies, more people survive into old age, but those who survive do not necessarily live longer than the elderly in past times (Parkin 1992: 105–106 and notes; Parkin 2003: 22–26, 36–56; Cokayne 2003: 2; Scheidel 2001; Frier 1982).

A more general problem in the study of ancient Jewish life cycles is the overall lack of an analytical framework for evaluating the cultural significance of age and life stages. Past scholarship has already devoted considerable attention to the examination of specific ages, life-cycle events, and the ancient life span, including ritual and exegetical aspects. However, we lack broader conceptualizations concerning the respective cultural markers and the ideology underlying references to age and life stages. The perception of various stages of life emerges from a combination of biological and cultural processes, including the body's growth and decline, gender, reproduction, education, roles, and status within society. Specific stages may or may not be correlated with ages, and the concept of age itself emerges at the intersection of two very different temporalities: bodily changes on the one hand and the movement of the earth around the sun on the other. Notions of age and life cycles combine the descriptive and the prescriptive, partly addressing realms that moderns would call psychology and sociology (Kraemer 1989: 66), and partly reflecting ethical norms. Since a full methodological statement is beyond the scope of this chapter, I would like to draw attention to three approaches, two of which are based on research on Greek and Hellenistic sources.

For the analysis of texts referring to age gradation and life stages, Thomas Falkner's study of the ten stages of life articulated in a poem attributed to Solon in the sixth century BCE can serve as a model (one of the major sources for this poem is Philo's *On the Creation of the Cosmos According to Moses*; see Colson/Whitaker 1929: 72–103, Runia 2001: 70–80, 260–308). Rather than considering Solon's portrait to represent daily life in ancient Greece, Falkner calls attention to the 'differences between the different age structures implicit in Greek literature and the self-conscious and explicitly systematic treatment of age that we find in Solon 27.' He continues, 'Where traditional age-grades are identified without reference to age per se, Solon's are identified quantitatively and chronologically; where traditional age-grades are of unequal duration and proportion, Solon's are equal in length, symmetrical in structure, and conceived in the context of a predetermined sum; and where traditional age structures are integrated into a system of social function and status, Solon's grades are characterized more abstractly and seem devoid of social information.' Falkner summarizes by stating that 'the very premise of the poem entails reconceptualizing age in an untraditional way' (Falkner 1995: 157 and more generally 153–168).

Falkner's approach is a reminder that Jewish texts portraying life stages may be creative and contentious formulations that need to be situated in relation to other, often prosaic, references to age. We cannot presume that the literary sources were normative at the time of their composition and editing. In addition, we should be aware of the fact that discussions of age are relatively sparse in the ancient sources. Age gradation was not a prominent concern of Josephus or the rabbis, a phenomenon which may impinge upon an inquiry into the stages beyond puberty as starting the transition from childhood to adulthood, and beyond age twenty in connection with marriage. These issues are crucial for the analysis of a very important list of life stages transmitted in M. Abot 5:21, which will be discussed at the end of this chapter.

When analysing literary accounts of age and life stages, particularly but not only highly stylized formulations, we should consider that their relation to daily life may be educational rather than representative. The texts may or may not emerge from the actual life experiences of ancient Jews, but they often aim to persuade their readers or listeners to act in certain ways and choose particular paths of living. This pedagogical function may be evident in the phrasing of a given passage or in its larger literary and exegetical context, or both (Fraade 1991; Schofer 2005). In scholastic contexts, such as rabbinic Judaism, this pedagogical concern is often directed towards upholding a particular set of preparatory activities centred on study and learning. Martha Nussbaum discusses Hellenistic philosophers' emphasis on the significance of such activities in the course of life: 'To act justly or courageously, one must undertake creative projects that develop over time; so too for intellectual and creative work; so too for athletic achievement.' Such activities are temporally extended, occurring over long periods, and their significance often emerges only slowly. Preparatory activities are often prominent in descriptions of the early stages of life, therefore premature death is often considered particularly devastating, but they continue throughout a lifetime: 'the elderly, too, have valuable lives; and their activities, too, are interrupted by death' (Nussbaum 1994: 209–210). While Nussbaum focuses on the issues of justice and courage in her discussion, for Jewish scholastic communities the issues of wisdom, understanding, and communal leadership become particularly important.

2. SCHOLASTIC PREPARATION AT QUMRAN

The Qumran *Rule of the Congregation*, which has been dated by scholars as early as 100–75 BCE, sets out a detailed list of ages and corresponding responsibilities as well as privileges for members of the 'congregation' (for the text of 1QSa see Schiffman 1989: 13–26; Charlesworth 1994: 108–17). This list is partial, specifying only the first decades of life. After the age of 30, human life is merely summarized with, 'as the years of a man increase' (1:19; a similar focus on early ages appears in the demotic *Instruction of Papyrus Insinger*, cf. Lichtheim 1980: 198–199; Lichtheim 1983: 152–156, 214–216). Scholars disagree about the relation of this text to actual practice. Schiffman argues that 'the legal materials contained in the Rule of the Congregation were actualized in the everyday life of the sect', whereas Peder Borgen sees the list as 'schematic and tradition-bound', fitting into a 'patterned view' of successive periods of life (Borgen 1961: 271; Schiffman 1989: 9).

The text suggests that a (male) child should start scholastic learning early, in his 'youth' or early childhood, that is, before the age of 10. The prescribed object of study is specified as the 'Book of Hagi/Hagu', whose identity remains uncertain. Schiffman and Fraade argue that this is the Torah (Schiffman 1989: 14–15; Fraade 1993: 56–57), though Charlesworth cites references to 'Hagi/Hagu' in a fragment of a wisdom text from Qumran to argue that the reference is a more esoteric work (4Q417 F2, Charlesworth 1994: 111 n. 14). In any case, the text emphasizes the great significance of this learning for the child's future life: a person's status will be shaped 'according to his understanding along with the perfection of his way' in adulthood (1:17; Fraade 1993: 55–57). According to a scholarly reconstruction, a similar concern with 'understanding' conditions a child's learning (1: 7–8; cf. Schiffman 1989: 15).

The ages of 20 and 25 had a particular meaning for the Qumran sectarians, according to the mentioned text. These were the ages when a male was fully commissioned into the sect. Schiffman writes regarding the age of 20, 'This mustering, however, was not the military conscription that was to begin at age 25. Rather, it was the minimum age for full-fledged membership in the sect and included the rights of testimony, voting in the assembly, and marriage' (1989: 16). Borgen notes that, in this passage, marriage precedes working for a livelihood (1961: 271–272). Unlike other Near Eastern and later rabbinic sources we find an extended discussion here on women 'bearing witness' to a man entering adulthood, though some scholars have suggested emendations so that the passage continues the discussion of a man's role in court proceedings (Davies/Taylor 1996: 223–235; Schiffman 1989: 19).

3. Study and Life Cycle in Rabbinic Sources

Rabbinic texts concerning education and Torah study need to be considered in a context in which literacy—meaning the ability to read documents, letters, and simple literary texts—was probably below 10–15 per cent of the population.

Elementary education in both Jewish and Greco-Roman society was private and informal. Children's education would have centred on the father teaching his sons and perhaps daughters (see Hezser in this volume). Schools are not mentioned in tannaitic sources, though they do appear in amoraic materials. For a Jewish child to engage in primary education focused on reading the Torah in Hebrew, the parents would have to be both economically well off and religious, and only a small proportion of those who received such a primary education would go on to further learning (Hezser 2001: 39, 48–57, 60–69, 95, 496).

In early rabbinic sources fathers are already urged to teach their sons the Hebrew language, prayers, and scriptural texts. Midrash Sifre Deuteronomy comments upon the commandment in Deut. 11:19 to 'teach' God's words 'to your children' with the claim that fathers should speak Hebrew and teach Torah to children from the time that they can speak (Sifre Deuteronomy 46; cf. Tanhuma to Lev. 19:23). In a discussion of religious requirements and exemptions of a minor, the Tosefta states that once a child can talk, the father should teach him the *Shema*, Torah, and Hebrew (T Hag. 1: 2; also b. Suk. 42a–b; Kraemer 1989: 65–80). In addition, several ethical teachings emphasize the necessity to start Torah study in one's youth (*yaldut*) rather than old age (*ziqnut*) (M. Abot 4:20; also ARNA ch. 23, ARNB ch. 35, Deut. R. 8:6). The Babylonian Talmud includes several discussions centred on age 6, or 4 to 6: the point when a child is independent of the mother, the age when the study of Scripture should begin, and the age when a child should enter formal schooling (b. Er. 82a–b, b. Ket. 50a; b. B.B. 21a; Hezser 2001: 40–48, Marcus 1996: 43, contrast b. Ned. 32a).

The life of a rabbi can also have taken a very different course. Several passages describe the lives of great sages, but rather than portraying a figure who began his study at an early age, these men started their Torah study late. A tradition transmitted in a number of Palestinian rabbinic sources sets out a tripartite division of 40-year segments. For example, the amoraic Midrash Genesis Rabbah presents the list as a commentary upon the biblical patriarch Joseph's death at the age of 110 (Gen. R. 100 on Gen. 50:22; cf. Sifre Deut. 357). In rabbinic sources, Moses is often portrayed as a rabbi, and rabbis compared to Moses. In the Hebrew Bible, Moses is said to have died at the age of 120 (Deut. 34:7), which is also the number of years allotted to human beings in the pre-historical account of Genesis 6:3, as well as in Mesopotamian literature as early as Sumerian sources (Klein 1990). Traditions about his long life and his early upbringing at the Egyptian court made Moses a paradigm for later rabbis who came from outside the rabbinic world: Hillel, R. Yohanan ben Zakkai, and R. Akiva. This tradition divides the lives of these sages into three stages, with each stage defined in terms of a particular activity or role. The first forty years are usually said to have been without traditional education, followed by forty years of immersion in learning, and ending with forty years of religious leadership.

In this scheme, no explicit significance is given to the sage's late start in learning (see Azzan Yadin, 'Rabbi Akiva's Youth', forthcoming in the Jewish Quarterly Review). A probably later compilation in Avot de Rabbi Nathan, expands upon this motif by presenting more detailed accounts of two sages' lives: Rabbi Akiva and his teacher, Rabbi Eliezer ben Hyrcanus. Both men are said to have been ignorant of Torah until their adulthood, but eventually they became great sages through their persistence, diligence, and talent. These texts are meant to persuade the reader to study Torah himself, irrespective of his age. An adult man has no valid excuse to refrain from study by citing lack of parental support, poverty, or other commitments, since R. Akiva and R. Eliezer faced those obstacles too, and were able to overcome them (ARNA ch. 6, ARNB ch. 12–13).

4. BEYOND SCHOLASTIC CONCERNS: EARLY AGES IN RABBINIC SOURCES

Although rabbinic sources were developed in scholastic disciple communities, their treatment of early life stages extended beyond study and learning. For example, the Mishnah prescribes the circumcision of male babies at the age of eight to twelve days (M. Shab. 19:5). Puberty seems to have brought with it significant changes in the child's legal status. Earlier rabbinic sources identified the start of puberty through the appearance of 'two [pubic] hairs', while a shift to the more abstract concept of 'thirteen years' emerges during the late antique period (Gilat 1992: 19–31). Schiffman writes that tannaitic law 'assumed that puberty took place somewhere between the age of thirteen (for males) or twelve (for females) and twenty. Along with puberty went the obligation to observe all the commandments. Therefore, while the age of twenty was definitely binding as the maximum, twelve or thirteen served as the minimum age' (1989: 19–20). He notes that (for males) the age of 20 is significant in several respects. A tannaitic source asserts that at age 20 a young man can partake of sacrifices, serve as preceptor, and recite the priestly blessing in the synagogue (T. Hag. 1:3). Amoraic traditions state that judges of capital cases have to be at least 20 years old, and that the heavenly court does not punish anyone below that age (Ezra 3:8; y. Bik. 2:1, 64c; y. Sanh. 4:9, 22b and 11:7, 30b; Gen. R. 58:1, b. Shab. 89b). In addition, some rabbis considered the ages of 18 and 20 ideal times for marriage (Schremer 1998, Schremer 2003: 73–101, Satlow 2001: 104–111; see also Satlow in this volume).

The Mishnah provides extensive discussions about early female life stages, and much of this material is further developed in the Talmuds. There is reference to a father teaching Scripture to his daughter (M. Ned. 4:3; M. Sotah 3:4; Zolty 1993: 55–57,

113–129; Boyarin 1993: 170–180). More generally, Judith Wegner has argued, concerning mishnaic sources, that the salient aspect of rabbinic thinking about young girls is their sexuality and potential for marriage and procreation. The Mishnah distinguishes between betrothal and intercourse with girls before and after the age of 3, stating that if intercourse occurs before that age, the girl does not lose her status as a virgin (M. Nid. 5:4, also M. Ket. 1:2, 1:4, 3:1–2, Wegner 1998: 22–24). The hymen is envisioned as a poked eye, an image which the Babylonian Talmudic commentators understood as a reference to eventual regeneration (b. Nid. 44b-45a; Satlow 1996: 283–284).

For modern readers such discussions are striking, especially the fact that sex with a girl under the age of 3 is not prohibited or presented as abhorrent in rabbinic sources. At the same time, one should note that these texts do not condone such a practice. Rabbinic legislation may rather have been motivated by concern for the future of the girl. If a girl is born into an abusive family or enslaved, but freed before the age of 3, rabbis uphold her status of virginity to enable her later marriage. There are also numerous passages in rabbinic literature that criticize fathers who marry off their daughters when very young (Saldarini 1975: 80–81 n. 31, 298 n. 11, Schremer 2003: 102–125). The onset of female puberty is identified on the basis of 'two pubic hairs' or the age of 12 or 12 and a half. At this age, a father's legal control over his daughter diminishes dramatically, the young woman gains legitimacy concerning vows and the management of property, and her involvement in ritual activities increases (for example, M. Ket 3:8, M. Nid. 5:6–7, 6:11; Wegner 1988: 14–17, 34–37, 115–116). Beyond this stage, rabbinic references to women's ages and life cycles are sparse except for discussions of marriage and menopause (M. Nid. 1:5; Signer 1990: 42).

5. OLD AGE IN RABBINIC SOURCES

In rabbinic texts, and more broadly in Roman society, old age was understood to bring many transformations: changing appearances, fragility, diminished emotional control, and decline of the intellect, but also wisdom and experience that could confer authority (Cokayne 2003: 11–111). The most extensive discussion of old age in rabbinic literature focuses on the negative aspects of ageing, a process of weakening that leads to death. The passage is a midrash on Qohelet 12:1–7, which is transmitted in Leviticus Rabbah 18:1 and a large number of other rabbinic anthologies (Qoh. R. 12:1–7; Targum to Eccles. 12:1–7; y. Sotah 2:2, 18a; b. Shab. 151b–153a; Tanhuma to Gen 25:1; Midrash Zuta to Eccles. 12; Yalkut Shimoni to Qoh. 12; and the Vatican manuscript of Abot de Rabbi Nathan Version A). This text should be treated as a rhetorical statement about the elderly rather than an accurate depiction of everyday life. A number of other passages provide pejorative accounts of an 'old man' (*saba*), which seem to represent popular conceptions of the aged. These depictions link physical with psychological vulnerability: the weakening body brings increased fears of injury and limited mobility. Diminished sensual perception means that sounds can easily be misunderstood, and reduced mental faculties cause an inability to contain internal anxiety.

The longest anecdote thematizing old age transmitted in the mentioned literary unit centres on a rabbi. The account begins with the notion that age makes travel more difficult: an older rabbi can no longer visit a younger one on a regular basis (on rabbis visiting colleagues, see Hezser 1997: 169). The elder teaches the younger about the changes he faces: 'Near things have become far, far things have become near, two have become three, and that which brings peace at home has ceased'. The teaching is then expanded to explain that age brings about a deterioration of perception, for the eyes and ears lose their former capability. Age also limits one's mobility so that one's two legs need the support of a walking stick (a motif that echoes the ancient riddle of the Sphinx). In addition, sexual desire fades. The notion that the elderly lose the vigour of their sexual passions is also frequently mentioned in Greek and Roman sources, with many variations. Often the receding of sexual desire was considered beneficial, a relief that allowed focus on the pleasures of the mind or spiritual purity. Roman sources deprecated sexual activity between the elderly, and even in marriage after the age of procreation. In this context it is striking that the rabbinic narrative maintains that sexual desire is valuable for sustaining a marriage when the couple has reached an advanced age (Cokayne 2003: 115–133; Parkin 2003: 193–202; classical Greek sources include Plato, Republic 328c–329c; Aristotle, Rhetoric 2:13, 1139A, lines 11–14; compare Boyarin 1993: 61–76).

6. THE AGES OF DEATH IN RABBINIC SOURCES

Death can be considered part of life in many respects, and rabbinic sources include extensive discussions on the moment of death, the handling of the dead, funerary rituals, mourning, and the world to come (Rubin 1997, Kraemer 2000). Certain passages which deal with age at the time of death also convey information about the various stages of life. A series of lists, structured largely according to multiples of ten, state the symbolic significance of death at different ages. Even though the age of 50 was not an unusual age of death in antiquity, it appears as the starting point for several lists, and this detail conveys the notion that life has ended too soon. These rabbinic lists have an analogy in an Akkadian account of age (Sultantepe Tablet no. 400, Weinfeld 1992).

The earliest and most developed version of these rabbinic lists appears in the Palestinian Talmud tractate Bikkurim. A discussion of penalties for improper consumption of priestly offerings inspired the discussion of the relationship between death and 'cutting off' from the community or excision (*karet*; for a concise discussion of this concept, see Berkovitz 2006: 58–59). In the Talmudic context this list of deaths at various ages is presented as a received tannaitic tradition. Death at 50 is associated with the punishment of excision, at 52 with Samuel the prophet, at 60 with 'the death named in the Torah', at 70 with love, and at 80 with old age (y. Bik. 2:1, 64c). In the Babylonian Talmud tractate Mo'ed Qatan, a similar list appears as part of the commentary to a mishnaic tradition concerning the handling of a funeral bier (M. M.Q. 3:9). The respective items associated with death at the ages of 50 and 52 are the same as in the Talmud Yerushalmi, but 60 is considered 'death at the hands of heaven', 70 associated with 'gray hair', and 80 with 'might' (b. M.Q. 28a). These typological depictions of age do not seem to have emerged from a systematic reflection on life stages. Rather, they should be considered motifs which were derived from scriptural exegesis. Both Talmuds also cite biblical verses such as Psalm 90:10: 'The years of our life are seventy years, and if with might, eighty years' (y. Bik. 2:1, 64c, b. M.Q. 28a).

Rabbinic reflections on the ages at death are most detailed in the tractate on mourning, Semahot, which is one of the so-called external tractates of the Babylonian Talmud (for a translation see Zlotnick). The text specifies distinct rituals in honour of those who die at specific ages, starting at one day after birth and continuing throughout the entire life-span (Sem. 3:1–8). With regard to the later ages, the items match the Palestinian Talmudic version mentioned above. However, 80 is associated with 'might' as in the Babylonian Talmud (Sem. 3:8).

7. LIFE STAGES OF NON-RABBIS IN RABBINIC SOURCES

Two midrashic collections provide evidence of the ways in which rabbis conceived of a life cycle independent of Torah study. A three-stage model is used to categorize the writings attributed to the biblical king Solomon: he first wrote the Song of Songs, then Proverbs, then Qohelet. Why? According to a statement attributed to Rabbi Yonatan, 'When a man is young, he speaks in song; when he grows up, he speaks in proverbs; and when he become old, he speaks of vanity' (Songs R. 1:10). This tripartite structure has deep roots in Greek sources.

For example, Aristotle divides life into the phases of youth, one's time, and old age, with the prime beginning at age 30 (Rhetoric 2.12–14; Sears 1986, 90–94). In the rabbinic midrash, biblical books are correlated with life stages to portray youth as poetic and erotic, adulthood as wise, and old age as a time of seeing through the absurdities of life. While the subject matter is the Written Torah itself, and speaking in proverbs may reflect scholastic learning, the movement through life makes no direct mention of Torah study, the practice of commandments, or the cultivation of virtue.

Another rabbinic example of envisioning a life independent of Torah study is a list transmitted in the Qohelet Rabbah. This list does not mention study, offers an arguably ironic comparison of humans with animals, and focuses strongly on the psyche and behaviour of the infant (a briefer list of seven stages also appears in the Vatican manuscript of Abot de Rabbi Nathan A). The passage in Qohelet Rabbah is structured according to the number seven, which was a common typology in both classical Greek and biblical sources (Sears 1986: 38–53). Here the number is inspired by the exegesis of Qoh. 1:2, where the word 'vanity' (*hevel*) appears five times, thrice in the singular and twice in the plural. Counting each of the plurals terms as two enables the exegete to generate the number seven.

Four of the items listed in this midrash concern life up to the age of 20, and the focus is on the years one, two/three, ten, and twenty. Afterwards the life stages are envisioned as more general time spans, with the fifth and sixth stages being associated with marriage, and children and their care, followed by the seventh as old age. The list employs vivid metaphors to describe each phase. A child of 1 year is compared to a king, whereas other life stages are compared with animals: at age 2 and 3 humans resemble a pig, at 10 a kid goat, at 20 a horse; a married man is like a donkey, one who bears children is like a dog, and an old man is like an ape. This depiction of life stages shares some similarities with the mentioned text in Song of Songs Rabbah: the notions of dynamic energy and erotic interests at the ages of 10 and 20, and practical concerns in adulthood, resonate with the portrayal of Solomon and his writing of Song of Songs and Proverbs.

The passage in Qohelet Rabbah concludes with the qualification that its course of life is not that of a Torah sage but of an ordinary Jew (*am ha-aretz*): 'This is said about ordinary people, but about the sons of Torah it is said, "King David grew old" (1 Kings 1:1). Even though he grew old, he was a king'. Sages do not lose their dignity with age (cf. honorable references to rabbinic 'elders'). Torah study leads to the preservation of the 'royal' status into which one was born, whereas non-scholars become like animals (Kraemer 1989: 76–77). This final conclusion is transmitted in Aramaic, whereas the rest of the text is almost completely in Hebrew. Perhaps an earlier, generally formulated, family-centred account of childhood, marriage, and child-rearing was later transformed by a final statement encouraging Torah study and elevating sages (the hope that Torah study protects against some of the negative effects of ageing is also expressed in Lev. R. 18:1, b. Shab. 152a).

8. THE LIFE STAGES ACCORDING TO MISHNAH ABOT 5:21

Falkner's considerations concerning the innovation and reformulation of traditions (Falkner 1995, mentioned in section 1 above) are particularly relevant with regard to a rabbinic list of ten life stages transmitted in M. Abot 5:21. This passage has often been the focus of both traditional and modern scholarly treatments of Jewish life cycles. Included in Jewish prayer books, the text was widely read and commented upon, and commentators often used it as a template to which they assimilated and harmonized other rabbinic sources (see for example the commentary on M. Abot by Rabbi Yonah ben Abraham Gerondi, 1200–1263).

The list is presented as a tannaitic tradition, but scholarly analysis has revealed a much more complex development. The passage is not cited in the relevant debates concerning age in the Mishnah and Talmuds (see, for example, b. Ketubot 50a). M. Abot 5:21 is also not referred to in Abot de Rabbi Nathan, nor does Maimonides discuss it in his commentary to M. Abot. Two partial quotations appear in late midrashic collections (Tanhuma Qedoshim 14 to Lev. 19:23, Numbers Rabbah 6:7). Therefore we do not know the date of origin of the passage and to what extent it was already known in Roman Palestine. Ivan Marcus goes so far as to call M. Abot 5:21 a 'pseudo-mishnaic' medieval text (1996: 43–44). Scholars who question the (late) antique date of M. Abot 5:21, nevertheless uphold its significance for the discussion of life cycles (Gilat 1992; Schremer 1998). Should this text be considered relevant in a critical study of life stages among Jews in Roman Palestine, and what is the cultural significance of its formation?

M. Abot 5:21 prescribes a life's path by correlating fourteen ages with particular practices, states, and virtues. The correlation between the respective age and practice or state is unspecified, marked only by the preposition *l-* ('to, for'), which may be followed by a noun or an infinitive. Thus, a certain age may be considered the right time when one can begin a particular activity, when it is appropriate to perform an activity or display a character trait, or when one can obtain the given quality or status. It is not even clear whether the same meaning is carried through the entire list (Marcus 1996: 43–44, Schremer 1998: 458, Weinfeld 1992: 187). Despite these ambiguities, the list prescribes an ideal life of intellectual, emotional, and bodily development for a male immersed in Torah study (Idel 1980: 2). The passage is structured according to ages, with the basic frame consisting of ten-year intervals up to the age of 100.

The first four items focus on the first stages of rabbinic study and practice: Scripture at age 5, Mishnah at age 10, commandments at age 13, and Talmud at age 15 (though these do not necessarily refer to the extant compilations of 'The Mishnah' and 'The Talmud'; see Hezser 2001: 80). The next two items are concerned with social relations, with 18 as the age for marriage and 20 the age for pursuit. This last phrase has been interpreted in various ways: it could refer to a vocation or service, or be linked to marriage. One manuscript directly mentions 'service' at age 20 (Ms. Oxford 407), and another omits the age of 18 and says that age 20 is the right time for acquiring a wife (Ms. Harley 5704; see Sharvit 2004: 217–219, 239, 241). Virtues and social status are attributed to an adult man between the ages of 30 and 50 who has devoted his life to Torah study and observance. Perhaps most notable is that age 40 is linked with 'understanding'. This motif may be associated with a Babylonian tradition that a student needs forty years to attain knowledge from his teacher (b. Avodah Zarah 5a–b), but there are also philosophical texts that link 40 with wisdom or knowledge (such as Marcus Aurelius, Meditations 11.1). For age 60 the term *ziknah* is used, indicating 'old age'. In the Palestinian Talmud it is sometimes associated with frailty, but also conveys a sense of authority through 'being an elder'. This latter sense of honourable age may also underlie M. Abot 5:21 (some witnesses have 'wisdom' instead of 'old age'). The final items on the list concern the ageing of the body, such as hair turning grey, the loss of strength, and ultimate weakening and death.

Parallels to the presentation of the later stages of life in M. Abot can be found in the lists describing ages of death analyzed above, and M. Abot may have drawn at least some of its motifs from a common pool of associations (particularly the Babylonian account in b. M.Q. 28a). At the same time, the lists of ages at death usually configure life in a quite different way. Most notably, they focus on human mortality, emphasizing that people may die at any age. The list in Semahot 3:1–8 focuses on family relations: the life periods starting at the ages of 20, 30, and 40 are associated with a bridegroom, brother, and father, respectively. The overall concern is a man's changing relations within the family, from marriage to fatherhood, rather than the project of learning and cultivation. In M. Abot 5:21 the age of 20 is linked to marriage but the ages of 30 and 40 are associated with 'strength' and 'understanding'. This juxtaposition indicates the scholastic ethos of M. Abot 5:21: after marriage family life is not mentioned any more, and the focus shifts to virtues and public status (Schremer 1998: 60–61).

The rabbinic list conceptualizes age in a way that is not 'untraditional' but still distinctive in the context of Graeco-Roman (especially philosophical) literary sources. A male ideally starts Torah study at an early age, goes through specific stages considered appropriate for his years, attains virtue and status when he becomes older, and eventually experiences bodily decline. M. Abot 5:21 is the only comprehensive account of the ideal life of a rabbinic sage. Other sources may contain elements of this picture but frame them differently or use different imagery altogether. The compilation of M. Abot 5:21 should therefore not be considered a standard account to which other sources can be assimilated, but a (possibly very late) synthesis of the ways in which rabbis conceptualized the male life cycle from birth to death.

9. FUTURE DIRECTIONS

The subject of life stages is very broad, and there are multiple lines of inquiry that can be followed productively in the future. These include more research into specific life stages, particularly old age, especially with regard to women; further research integrating archaeological materials to complement the literary evidence; and comparisons of the Jewish evidence with philosophical and Christian sources. In addition to comparing individual literary motifs and views, scholars should also investigate the question of differing communal problems and concerns. For example, late ancient Christians reflected extensively on the ethical and theological significance of children, and they also employed childhood as a metaphor to talk about adults (Storz 2001; Bakke 2005). These themes are not absent in Jewish sources, but they are much less prominent. In the future we may be able to understand why this phenomenon emerged so much more strongly in one religious tradition than in another, and trace the significance of this difference for the daily life of Jews and Christians in late antiquity.

SUGGESTED READING

Marcus' overview of Jewish life cycles is an indispensable starting point for this topic (2004). Schiffman provides an introduction to the Rule of the Community from Qumran (1989). Valuable collections of essays on the Jewish family and childhood in antiquity are edited by Kraemer 1989 and Cohen 1993. Wegner 1988, Zolty 1992, and Hauptman 1998 provide detailed studies of gender that include reflections on age. For methodological issues, Gilat's treatment of puberty is very helpful (1992).

BIBLIOGRAPHY

BAKKE, O. M. (2005). *When Children Became People: The Birth of Childhood in Early Christianity*. Minneapolis: Fortress Press.

BERKOWITZ, B. A. (2006). *Execution and Invention: Death Penalty Discourse in Early Rabbinic and Christian Cultures*. New York: Oxford University Press.

BIALE, R. (1984). *Women and Jewish Law: The Essential Texts, Their History, and Their Relevance for Today*. New York: Schocken.

BOLL, F. (1913). *Die Lebensalter*. Leipzig and Berlin: B. G. Teubner.

BORGEN, P. (1961). '"At the Age of Twenty" in 1QSa'. *Revue de Qumran*: 267–270.

BOYARIN, D. (1993). *Carnal Israel: Reading Sex in Talmudic Culture*. Berkeley: University of California Press.

BRANDT, H. (2002). *Wird auch silbern mein Haar: Eine Geschichte des Alters in der Antike*. Munich: C. H. Beck.

CABEZÓN, J. I. (1998). *Scholasticism: Cross-Cultural and Comparative Perspectives*, eds. Paul Griffiths and Laurie Patton. Albany, NY: State University of New York Press.

CHARLESWORTH, J. (ed.) (1994). *The Dead Sea Scrolls: Hebrew, Aramaic, and Greek Texts with English Translations. Volume 1: Rule of the Community and Related Documents*. Tübingen: Mohr-Siebeck.

COHEN, A./RUTTER, J. B. (eds) (2007). *Constructions of Childhood in Ancient Greece and Italy*. Hesperia Supplements 41. Princeton: American School of Classical Studies at Athens.

COHEN, S. J. D., ed. (1993). *The Jewish Family in Antiquity*. Atlanta: Scholars Press.

COKAYNE, K. (2003). *Experiencing Old Age in Ancient Rome*. New York: Routledge.

COLSON, F. H./WHITAKER, G. H. (1929). *Philo*, vol. 1. Cambridge, MA: Harvard University Press.

CRIBIORE, R. (2001). *Gymnastics of the Mind: Greek Education in Hellenistic and Roman Egypt*. Princeton: Princeton University Press.

—— (2007). *The School of Libanius in Late Antique Antioch*. Princeton: Princeton University Press.

DAVIES, P. R./TAYLOR, J. R. (1996). 'On the Testimony of Women in 1QSa'. *Dead Sea Discoveries* 3/3: 223–235.

FALKNER, T. M. (1995). *The Poetics of Old Age in Greek Epic, Lyric, and Tragedy*. Norman: University of Oklahoma Press.

FRAADE, S. D. (1991). *From Tradition to Commentary: Torah and its Interpretation in the Midrash Sifre to Deuteronomy*. Albany: State University of New York Press.

—— (1993). 'Interpretive Authority in the Studying Community at Qumran'. *Journal of Jewish Studies* 44: 46–69.

FRIER, B. (1982). 'Roman Life Expectancy: Ulpian's Evidence'. *Harvard Studies in Classical Philology* 86: 213–251.

GILAT, Y. (1992). 'Thirteen Years-Old: The Age of the Commandments?' [Hebr.], in *Studies in the Development of the Halakha*. Ramat-Gan: Bar-Ilan University Press, 19–31.

HARLOW, M./LAURENCE, R. (2002). *Growing Up and Growing Old in Ancient Rome: A Life Course Approach*. New York: Routledge.

HAUPTMAN, J. (1998). *Rereading the Rabbis: A Woman's Voice*. Boulder: Westview Press.

HEZSER, C. (1997). *The Social Structure of the Rabbinic Movement in Roman Palestine*. Tübingen: Mohr-Siebeck.

—— (2001). *Jewish Literacy in Roman Palestine*. Tübingen: Mohr-Siebeck.

IDEL, M. (1980). 'On the History of the Interdiction against the Study of Kabbalah before the Age of Forty' [Hebr.]. *Association for Jewish Studies Review* 5: 1–20.

ILAN, T. (1995). *Jewish Women in Greco-Roman Palestine: An Inquiry into Image and Status*. Tübingen: Mohr-Siebeck.

KLEIN, J. (1990). 'The 'Bane' of Humanity: A Lifespan of One Hundred Twenty Years'. *Acta Sumerologica* 12: 57–70.

KRAEMER, D. (1989). 'Images of Childhood and Adolescence in Talmudic Literature', in *The Jewish Family: Metaphor and Memory*, ed. D. Kramer. New York: Oxford University Press, 65–80.

—— (2000). *The Meanings of Death in Rabbinic Judaism*. New York: Routledge.

LICHTHEIM, M. (1980). *Ancient Egyptian Literature: A Book of Readings*, Volume III: The Late Period. Berkeley: University of California Press.

—— (1983). *Late Egyptian Wisdom Literature in the International Context: A Study of Demotic Inscriptions*. Göttingen: Vandenhoeck and Ruprecht.

MARCUS, I. (1996). *Rituals of Childhood: Jewish Acculturation in Medieval Europe*. New Haven: Yale University Press.

—— (2004). *The Jewish Life Cycle*. Seattle: The University of Washington Press.

NUSSBAUM, M. (1994). *Therapy of Desire: Theory and Practice in Hellenistic Ethics*. Princeton: Princeton University Press.

PARKIN, T. (1992). *Demography and Roman Society*. Baltimore: Johns Hopkins University Press.

—— (2003). *Old Age in the Roman World: A Cultural and Social History*. Baltimore: The Johns Hopkins University Press.

RUBIN, N. (1997). *The End of Life: Rites of Burial and Mourning in the Talmud and Midrash* [Hebr.]. Jerusalem: Hakkibutz Hameuchad.

RUNIA, D. T. (2001). Philo of Alexandria, '*On the Creation of the Cosmos According to Moses Introduction, Translation and Commentary*. Phils of Alexandria Commentary Series'. Leiden: Brill.

SALDARINI, A. (1975). *The Fathers According to Rabbi Nathan (Abot de Rabbi Nathan) Version B*. Leiden: Brill.

—— (1982). *Scholastic Rabbinism: A Literary Study of the Fathers According to Rabbi Nathan*. Chico: Scholars Press.

SATLOW, M. (1996). '"Texts of Terror": Rabbinic Texts, Speech Acts, and the Control of Mores'. *Association for Jewish Studies Review* 21: 283–284.

—— (2001). *Jewish Marriage in Antiquity*. Princeton: Princeton University Press.

SCHEIDEL, W. (2001). 'Roman Age Structure: Evidence and Models.' *Journal of Roman Studies* 91: 1–26.

SCHIFFMAN, L. (1989). *The Eschatological Community of the Dead Sea Scrolls*. Atlanta: Scholars Press.

SCHOFER, J. (2005). *The Making of a Sage: A Study in Rabbinic Ethics*. Madison: University of Wisconsin Press.

SCHREMER, A. (1998). 'Eighteen Years to the Huppah' [Hebr.], in *Sexuality and the Family in History*, ed. I. Bartal and I. Gafni. Jerusalem: The Salman Shazar Center, 43–70.

—— (2003). *Male and Female He Created Them: Jewish Marriages in the Late Second Temple, Mishnah, and Talmud Periods* [Hebr.]. Jerusalem: The Salman Shazar Center.

SEARS, E. (1986). *The Ages of Man: Medieval Interpretations of the Life Cycle*. Princeton: Princeton University Press.

SHARVIT, S. (2004). *Tractate Avoth Through the Ages: A Critical Edition, Prolegomena, and Appendices* [Hebr.]. Jerusalem: The Bialik Institute.

SIGNER, M. A. (1990). 'Honour the Hoary Head: The Aged in the Medieval European Jewish Community', in *Aging and the Aged in Medieval Europe*, ed. M. Sheehan. Toronto: Canada Pontifical Institute of Medieval Studies, 39–48.

STORZ, M. E. (2001). '"Where or When was Your Servant Innocent?": Augustine on Childhood', in *The Child in Christian Thought*, ed. M. J. Bunge. Grand Rapids: Eerdmans, 78–102.

VAN HENTEN, J. W./BRENNER, A. (eds) (2000). *Families and Family Relations as Represented in Early Judaisms and Early Christianities: Texts and Fictions*. Leiden: Deo Publishing.

WEGNER, J. R. (1988). *Chattel or Person? The Status of Women in the Mishnah.* New York: Oxford University Press.

WEINFELD, M. (1992). 'The Phases of Human Life in Mesopotamian and Jewish Sources', in *Priests, Prophets, and Scribes: Essays on the Formation and Heritage of Second Temple Judaism in Honor of Joseph Blenkinsopp.* Sheffield: JSOT Press, 182–189.

WESTBROOK, R. (ed.) (1998). *The Care of the Elderly in the Ancient Near East.* Leiden: Brill.

YEARLEY, L. H. (1990). *Mencius and Aquinas: Theories of Virtue and Conceptions of Courage.* Albany: State University of New York Press.

ZLOTNICK, D. (1966). *The Tractate 'Mourning' (Semahot): Regulations Relating to Death, Burial, and Mourning.* New Haven: Yale University Press.

ZOLTY, S. P. (1993). 'And All Your Children Shall be Learned': *Women and the Study of the Torah in Jewish Law and History.* Northvale and London: Jason Aronson.

CHAPTER 18

....

MARRIAGE AND DIVORCE

....

MICHAEL L. SATLOW

THE modern academic study of Jewish marriage and divorce in antiquity began with the publication in 1860 of Zechariah Fraenkel's study, *Grundlinien des mosaisch-talmudischen Eherechts*. As the title makes clear, for Fraenkel and his contemporaries, the study of Jewish marriage and divorce was first and foremost a study of legal institutions: the laws define the institutions. This legal approach predominated the academic study of Jewish marriage and divorce for slightly over a century, giving way somewhat only in the 1970s to the increasing tendency to see marriage and divorce as social institutions that primarily constitute a subfield of women's studies. It was not until the 1990s that scholars began to study Jewish marriage and divorce as an independent discursive subject, deserving its own systematic and synthetic investigations.

A full survey of the history of scholarship on Jewish marriage and divorce in antiquity is beyond the scope of this essay. The goal of this essay is much more modest: to review the state of scholarship on Jewish marital and divorce practices, primarily the legal institutions governing marriage and divorce (including the *ketubbah*), their demographics, and the customs and rituals associated with them. Nevertheless, a brief review of the history of scholarship will help to highlight and put into context the questions that have informed much of the recent work on Jewish marriage and divorce. Each of the three approaches mentioned above–legal, social, and synthetic–correlates with specific questions that must be kept in mind in order to make sense of, and assess, current scholarly disagreements.

The study of Jewish marriage and divorce in antiquity as legal institutions traditionally focused on the clarification of rabbinic law. This was due in part to its roots in the normative study of Jewish law (halakhah), but also, quite under-standably, to the relative lack of evidence outside of rabbinic sources, a state that lasted until the discovery and publication of the marital documents from the Judaean desert dating from the first and second centuries CE. Aside from describing 'the' rabbinic law of marriage and divorce, though, these studies also tend to focus on two issues, both of which are more generally evident in many areas of study of the Jews in antiquity. The first is the connection between rabbinic law (and non-rabbinic Jewish law to a lesser degree) and reality. Although generally careful, scholars such as Fraenkel (1860), Krauss (1910–12, vol. 2: 24–54), Epstein (1942), and Safrai (1976) have tended to evaluate rabbinic prescriptions as descriptions of popular practice, or at least rabbinic responses to popular practices that can give us a relatively transparent picture of what Jews actually did. While most recent scholars use rabbinic law more cautiously, the questions about *how* this law can best be used still account for differing evaluations of our evidence.

A second focus of the legal approach has been on Jewish difference. Viewing marriage and divorce as bounded *institutions* invites comparison: to what degree were these Jewish institutions distinctive? This has largely been an exercise in comparative law. Boaz Cohen (1948–49) for example, compared some of the rabbinic and Roman legal instruments of betrothal. The general question at the heart of these inquiries—whether and how Jews used marriage and divorce (whether seen as legal or social institutions) as locations of identity formation—remains strong in recent scholarship.

Scholarship on Jewish marital practices began to shift dramatically in the 1970s. In line in the United States with the general turn toward social history, with a particular focus on women, Jewish marriage and divorce began to be studied as social institutions that primarily concern women. Outside of Israel (and in some cases in Israel as well), scholarship on Jewish marriage and divorce was so thoroughly subsumed to women's studies that it became common for scholars to treat marriage and divorce only within the wider context of the situation of Jewish women in antiquity (cf. Ilan 1995: 57–157; Hauptman 1998: 60–76, 102–29). This is not simply an issue of classification. Putting Jewish marriage and divorce—and here again the focus has usually been on rabbinic law—within the context of women's studies has brought with it the question of normative evaluation: did Jews in antiquity treat women well? The question of the 'status' of Jewish women in antiquity can take pernicious forms, as in the invidious (and usually inaccurate) comparison between rabbinic law on women and the stance of Jesus (cf. Kraemer 1999).

Although scholarly interest in the legal status of women has waned (but is still by no means dead), the scholarship produced during this period succeeded in driving a wedge between the law and the study of ancient Jewish marital practices. Interest in women also helped scholars to see the relevance of, and incorporate into their accounts, long-neglected 'non-normative' evidence, primarily inscriptions and pseudepigraphical works. It also fortuitously coincided with the discovery of papyri in the Judaean desert, among which were caches of legal documents from some Jewish women, most famously Babatha. These documents may be dry, legal, and formulaic, but they do provide a rare glimpse of actual marital and divorce practices.

The most recent trend of scholarship on Jewish marriage and divorce takes the next logical step, understanding Jewish marriage and divorce as a discrete field of inquiry, not necessarily connected to women's studies. These synthetic studies (Satlow 2001; Schremer 2003), which to some extent are modelled on developments in classics (e.g. Treggiari 1991; Evans Grubbs 1995), view marriage and divorce as both social *and* legal institutions, embedded in a wide mesh of contexts. This development encourages the application of a wide range of scholarly approaches, especially those drawn from anthropology, sociology, economics, and ritual studies.

This brief survey is not by any means meant to be comprehensive. Even if only seen heuristically, however, it does help to create a map on which most of the present scholarly disagreements can be plotted.

1. LEGAL INSTITUTIONS

The legal aspects of marriage and divorce among Jews in Roman Palestine appear to be fully documented. Although the non-rabbinic literary evidence, such as Philo and Josephus, scarcely mentions these institutions, rabbinic literature devotes several entire, frequently long and complex, tractates to the formation of marital unions (e.g. tractates Qiddushin and Yebamot), the economic relationship between the spouses (Ketubbot), other matters that impinge upon marital life (e.g. Nedarim and Niddah), and divorce (Gittin). Other texts pertinent to marriage and divorce are also scattered liberally throughout both Talmudic and midrashic literature.

The basic legal structure of the rabbinic understanding of marriage and divorce is relatively well known and uncontroversial (cf. Juster 1914, vol. 2: 41–61). For the rabbis, there were two constitutive acts for the formation of a marriage. The first act is 'betrothal' ('erusin; qiddushin). Mishnah Qiddushin 1:1 enumerates three modes by which this might be affected: money, contract, or sexual intercourse. The rabbis preferred the first of these modes, and assumed that in a typical betrothal a man would give an object of modest value to a woman with a statement of intent, and that she would accept it in front of witnesses. From this point they are legally married, and divorce or death of a partner is required to dissolve that marriage. The second stage, *huppah*, generally refers to the sexual consummation of the marriage, which might take place at a time much later than the betrothal. The marriage is accompanied by a contract, the *ketubbah*, which deals with the mainly economic rights and obligations of the partners (although it is supposed to be signed by the groom and his father-in-law or other male guardian, acting on behalf of the wife), and which takes its name from the endowment pledge that the groom promises to his bride upon dissolution of the marriage by either death or divorce. Divorce in rabbinic law is understood as a unilateral action that, except in relatively rare cases, can be instituted only by an unforced husband, and to which the woman's consent is legally irrelevant.

Although most scholars would agree with this basic outline of the rabbinic laws of marriage and divorce, there is wide disagreement on the relationship of this law to lived experience. Does it prescribe, respond to, or even describe actual Jewish behaviour, or is it largely theoretical? Obviously, this relates to wider issues of rabbinic authority and the legal practices of the Jews of Palestine.

The publication of three caches of papyri in the twentieth century has thrown this issue into stark relief. Two of these caches are largely outside the scope of this essay: the documents from the Jewish community in Elephantine, in the Nile Delta (fifth to fourth centuries, BCE) and those from Hellenistic Egypt. The 'documents of wifehood' from Elephantine (cf. Porten 1968: 205–13, 221–25) exhibit nothing that might be labelled as distinctively Jewish. Given the early date and relative isolation of this community, that might not be unexpected. More surprising, however, is the similar absence of distinctively Jewish legal traits among the extant papyri from Jews in Hellenistic Egypt. At least some Jewish communities in Egypt were organized as *politeumata*, semi-autonomous communal organizations that may have had the authority to administer their own civil laws. In one document dated 218 BCE, for example, a woman who apparently married according to the civil law (*politikon*) of the Jews, divorces her husband. This puzzles an editor of the text, Victor Tcherikover, who writes: '[I]t is worth noting that no trace of any mention of Jewish law concerning marriage can be found in the remaining parts of the papyrus. . . . Is it because there existed no fundamental discrepancies between Hellenistic and Jewish law in marriage matters, Jewish law in Egypt being influenced by Hellenistic?' (Tcherikover 1957–64, vol. 1:238, n. 2). Despite the lack of any evidence of a distinctive Jewish marital law within these papyri, Tcherikover was still committed to positing the (theoretical) existence in the third century BCE of such a body of law.

Directly relevant, though, are the trove of legal documents of Jews that date from the first and second centuries CE found in caves in the Judaean desert, among which are those from Nahal Hever (published in Cotton/Yardeni 1997). These documents were written in Aramaic and Greek, and most, like those from Egypt, show few signs of distinctively Jewish legal institutions. While publishing several of these documents, Hannah Cotton came to the conclusion that, 'We should be wrong, though, to assume without compelling proof that the documents reflect the still-to-be-codified halacha' (Cotton 1998: 179). Rather, for Cotton, the varied legal institutions found within these papyri rather provided the material from which the rabbis would later codify a single and distinctive marital law. At the same time, there are isolated features of some of the contracts (e.g. an explicit statement that the marriage contract is 'according to the law/custom of the Jews', perhaps a parallel to the term *politkon* in the divorce document from Egypt) that draw attention to self-conscious distinctiveness, and the Aramaic marriage contract of Babatha ('Babatha's *Ketubba*', as the editors title its first publication; cf. Friedman 1996) bears strong resemblance to the *ketubbah* as described in rabbinic literature. Despite a series of studies by Ranon Katzoff that have argued that particular clauses within these documents can make sense best within the context of rabbinic law (see, for example, Katzoff 1996), the weight of scholarly opinion, especially outside of Israel, appears to me to lean more towards Cotton's position. In any case, this question will best be addressed within the broader context of an understanding of the legal institutions that applied to, and were used by, the Jews of Roman Palestine.

If rabbinic authority is one of the broader background issues against which this scholarly disagreement takes place, women and gender studies is another. From that perspective, the question usually brought to this material is the 'status' (primarily legal status) and rights of women in creating, maintaining, and dissolving unions. This has often, but not uniformly, been accompanied (implicitly or explicitly) by the apologetic/polemical question of whether Jewish/rabbinic law was 'good' or 'bad' for women, especially within the context of their times. There is, again, little disagreement about the relevant stances of rabbinic law itself: men are allowed to betroth their daughters without their consent when they are still minors (cf. Reines 1970); women can be 'acquired' by means of a payment (to the woman herself; M. Qid. 1:1); the *ketubbah* is an agreement made between a groom and his wife's male legal guardian; a husband has the right to annul his wife's vows (and not the reverse; cf. M. Ned. 10–11); women have no statutory inheritance rights under most circumstances (M. B.B. 8:2); only men can institute divorce (M. Yeb. 14:1), to name only a few. Taken by themselves and against today's standards, these laws present a rather bleak assessment of the legal position of Jewish women (or at least those living under rabbinic law) in antiquity. Some scholars, such as Judith Hauptman, have argued that as bleak as it might look to us today, the rabbis were actually somewhat progressive for their time (Hauptman 1998: 244). While the normative question of whether the rabbis were good or bad for women might be relevant within religious communities, formulating the issue thus—with acceptable answers having to fall on a spectrum between two poles—has served to limit a fuller application of gender theory to discussions of marriage and divorce among Jews in Roman Palestine.

Following a suggestion of Naphtali Lewis, Hannah Cotton has argued that one of the Jewish papyri from Nahal Hever is evidence for the institution of 'unwritten marriage', a legally recognized, but undocumented, cohabitation (P. Hev. 65; Cotton/Yardeni 1997: 227–9). Tal Ilan has more provocatively referred to this arrangement as pre-marital cohabitation, suggesting that it was relatively common and represented, in contrast to the patriarchal institution of marriage, a way for women to maintain their autonomy (Ilan 1993; cf. Schremer 1998). Ilan probably presses the evidence too far here, but the issue she raises begins to push the question of legal status beyond judgmental assessments.

The apparent disparity between elements of rabbinic law and the evidence of the papyri might itself be problematized. Why would (largely unenforceable) rabbinic law seem to limit what appears to have been the greater autonomy of women evidenced in the papyri? It is possible that rabbinic law did not serve to limit this autonomy but to square the reality, mentally, with the ideals of an honour and shame culture. Men *should* have more power than they actually did. From this perspective the rabbinic laws can be considered to do cultural work. Whether right or wrong, this model points toward the need for a more sophisticated application of theory to the little evidence we have (Satlow 2001: 109–11).

A full survey of the scholarly debates about specific legal institutions is far beyond the scope of this paper. Rather, I want to briefly survey three larger topics in order to illustrate how the broad issues discussed above play out in modern scholarly treatments. The topics are betrothal, the *ketubbah*, and a woman's right to initiate divorce.

1.1 Betrothal

In rabbinic law, 'betrothal' ('*erusin; qiddushin*) is the legal act that creates a marital union. The institution has parallels in ancient Babylonian law, where scholars have termed the period between betrothal and full cohabitation as 'inchoate marriage'. Such an institution was unknown, however throughout most of the ancient Near East, Greek, and Roman worlds, where betrothal was seen as an engagement agreement between families, violation of which might have had pecuniary penalties, but would not require a formal divorce of the betrothed couple.

There is, in fact, almost no evidence that throughout the period of the Second Temple Jews practised, or even knew of, betrothal as creating an inchoate marriage. The earliest attestation of the institution appears in Matthew 1:18–19, and then in legal dicta ascribed to the schools of Hillel and Shammai. By the latter first and early second century CE rabbis took the institution of *qiddushin* for granted.

Most previous scholarship, to the extent that it discusses betrothal at all, has tended to uncritically accept rabbinic claims for its antiquity and to assume that it was widely practised by the Jews of Roman Palestine. But this is far from clear

(Satlow 2001: 69–82). While the passage in Matthew, in which Mary becomes pregnant between the time of her betrothal to Joseph and marriage to him, suggests that the rabbis did draw from ancient Near Eastern law and limited local practices, rabbinic literature itself suggests that many Jews did not practise it (cf. Gulak 1934; *idem* 1994: 46–71). Indeed, from a social perspective, a binding betrothal accomplishes nothing that a civil agreement with pecuniary penalties does not, while at the same time it creates several serious, potential problems (e.g. the betrothed man disappears, leaving his inchoate bride 'anchored', and unable to remarry). Rabbis might have been interested in it because it solves a technical, legal problem, namely, the legal means for the relinquishing of a right of male control over a woman (Satlow 2001: 77–79). Moreover, the derivation of the word *qiddushin*, often derived from *q-d-sh*, 'holy', is obscure, and is debated in the Talmud itself (b. Qid. 2b).

The scholarly discussion of betrothal frequently has been coloured by apologetics and polemics. Is it an act of sanctification (e.g. Hauptman 1998: 69) or a sale (e.g. Wegner 1988: 42–5)? Is it an ancient or a novel institution? These questions open out into the wider issues of Jewish female autonomy in antiquity and rabbinic legal activity.

1.2 Ketubbah

As used in rabbinic literature, the term *ketubbah* can refer to three separate things: dowry (property that a bride brings into the marriage); a delayed endowment pledge made by the groom, payable to his wife or her heirs on dissolution of the marriage; or the contract that stipulates the legal rights and obligations of each partner. There has been much scholarship on both the *ketubbah* as a marital payment (of whatever kind) and as a written contract.

The point of departure of nearly all discussions of the *ketubbah* as a particular form of marital payment has been a historiographical tradition found in several versions in rabbinic literature (T. Ket. 12:1; y. Ket. 8:11, 32b–c; b. Ket. 82b). The tradition appears in different forms, and attributes to the decree different motivations, but all versions associate the establishment of this payment with a decree (*taqanah*) of Shimon b. Shetach. Thus, according to the conventional scholarly narrative, until the first century BCE, the normative Jewish practice (at least in Judaea) was for women to bring a dowry into their marriages. From the first century on, this norm was modified to include a delayed endowment pledge from the husband (cf. Ilan 1995: 90; Schremer 2003: 233–241).

The extant papyri challenge this narrative (Satlow 1993). Instead, both rabbinic and documentary evidence (i.e. the papyri found in the Judaean Desert) instead point toward a more complex, non-normative mix of marital payments, among which the delayed endowment pledge entered in the late first century CE. Like many rabbinic historiographical traditions, it is possible that the story of Shimon ben

Shetah's *taqanah* was based less upon some kernel of a remembered historical event than it was on a rabbinic attempt to establish, explain, and reinforce their norms.

Contemporary scholars are divided on this issue. Adiel Schremer (2003: 235–7) and Bernard Jackson (2003) have defended the essential historical reliability of the rabbinic narrative of the *taqanah*. The specific points of controversy go beyond the scope of this essay (and would, in any case, undoubtedly reflect my own bias), but it does raise two larger issues. First, this controversy largely reflects the intricate interconnection between (often unstated) theoretical models of how Palestinian society functioned and the place of specifically Jewish law within it, with the interpretation of the evidence. My thesis dovetails well with a larger model of local Jewish communities displaying wide variations of customs and law (cf. Schwartz 2006). 'Jewish law', in the sense of a single actual system of operative norms, is largely an invention of the rabbis, and even then would not receive institutional backing (with coercive power) until the end of late antiquity, if not later. Schremer and Jackson, on the other hand, share an understanding of Jewish law that ascribes to it continuity, development, and—at least in some sense—popular support and adherence. Hence, they (along with Hauptman 1998: 62–8) assert the 'development' of a legal institution from *mohar* (the biblical bride price, paid by a man to his bride's family) to *ketubbah*, and argue that the latter became a standard Jewish marriage payment in late antique Palestine.

The second issue this disagreement raises, however, is a point of agreement. Schremer's argument that the biblical *mohar* was transformed into the *ketubbah* supports his larger argument that the Jewish family in Judaea/Palestine evolved into a more nuclear structure with a supporting, romantic ideology. The development of the *ketubbah* thus serves a sociological function, providing protection to a woman from hasty divorce. Schremer contextualizes this development within a discussion of marital payments generally (Schremer 2003: 261–98) and thus subordinates the technical issue of the development of a legal institution to the importance of understanding the *functional* role of these payments in Jewish society. The extensive use of anthropological and sociological theory and comparison in order to fill out the rather sparse and eclectic data breaks with much of past scholarship.

The scholarship on the development of the *ketubbah* as the Jewish marriage contract is beset by the same tension discussed above: does it make sense to posit the development or evolution of this legal instrument? In his magisterial study *Jewish Marriage in Palestine: A Cairo Geniza Study*, Mordechai A. Friedman provides a subtle response to this tension:

The text of the *ketubba* (plural *ketubbot*), the Jewish marriage contract, is designated in Tannaitic sources as *leshon hedyot*, the language of formulary of laymen. It primarily developed, in the customary law, on the basis of free contract and was given its form by the professional scribes. By the late Second Temple period and the early second century, its formula had begun to crystallize. The Tannaim attached legal significance to its precise wording and formulation and based halakhic decisions on it. They also added to the formulary and emended it (Friedman 1980: 1–2).

Given the variations within Jewish marriage contracts from the second century CE, Friedman's dating of the 'crystallized' form of the contract might be questioned, but the sensitivity to customary law and local customs is well placed. Unfortunately, there is extant only a single *ketubbah* that dates from the mid-second to the eleventh century CE, from Egypt, making it impossible to verify whether ordinary Jews saw the rabbinic descriptions of, and rules regarding, the *ketubbah* as normative. Mark Geller, however, has noted the similarity of the *ketubbah* to some Demotic marital documents (Geller 1978).

Did most Jews, in fact, use any contract to govern their legal obligations to each other? As Catherine Hezser points out (and the relative absence of evidence supports), only families with property might go through the expense and bother of drawing up such a document (Hezser 2001: 301). In fact, as mentioned above, according to one Greek marriage contract from Nahal Hever, Salome Komaise appears to convert her marriage from an 'unwritten' to 'written' type (P. Hev. 65). 'Unwritten marriages' were common throughout the eastern Mediterranean basin, recognized as legitimate and conferring legal rights and responsibilities. There is little reason to suspect that Jews too throughout the region did not employ this institution.

Obviously, the question of enforcement of such marital rights, whether written or not, intersects with the more general question of the legal system(s) used by Judaean and Palestinian Jews in antiquity. Scholars who posit a relatively singular normative trajectory can more easily explain enforcement of such agreements. Presumably, judges would be learned in 'Jewish law' and know how to apply it to legal contracts. Those scholars who see more local variation and widespread use of arbitration, however, still need to explain better how this might function on the ground, especially with contracts that specify a particular custom/law that governs the contract, and in the light of the always available Roman legal apparatus, which in many cases may have consisted of a direct appeal to the provincial governor (cf. Goodman 1991).

1.3 A Woman's Right to Initiate Divorce

Many issues relating to the scholarly study of marriage and divorce of Jews in antiquity have been framed as issues of women's rights: were the laws good or bad for women? Such a framing, even implicitly, further complicates the issue of 'Jewish law' and its enforcement (discussed above) with a normative judgment. The question, of course, to a great extent predetermines the contours of the possible answers, which predictably range across the apologetic–polemical spectrum.

One particularly interesting scholarly discussion often framed as a matter of women's rights is whether Jewish women in antiquity could divorce their husbands. Or did their husbands, following rabbinic law, have the exclusive right to divorce their wives, with or without their consent? Josephus (Ant. 15.259), Mark 10:12, and some documentary evidence point to the possibility that Jewish women could, and did, divorce their husbands (cf. Ilan 1996), although in the same passage Josephus also testifies that this goes against Jewish practice. Bernadette Brooten has argued that Jewish women could indeed divorce their husbands, but the evidence on both sides is more suggestive than conclusive (Brooten 1982). From the third century onwards we have no evidence outside of rabbinic sources on whether a Jewish woman could initiate a divorce.

2. DEMOGRAPHICS OF MARRIAGE AND DIVORCE

Recent scholarship on Jewish marriage and divorce in antiquity has emphasized the importance of understanding the demographic picture (Satlow 2001: 101–32; Schremer 2003: 73–125). Statistics such as the average age of first marriage of men and women, fertility rates, divorce rates, and life expectancy are not only inherently important but also have potentially far ranging implications. Being able to plot ancient Jewish societies demographically also allows for a richer application of social scientific theory.

How one demographically plots Jewish societies, however, is hardly clear. Unlike the situation in Egypt, there is no extensive collection of extant census documents from Judaea/Palestine (cf. Bagnall/Frier 1994). Nor, unlike in Rome, are there statistically significant collections of epitaphs (cf. Saller 1987). Many previous scholarly discussions of the average age of first marriage, for example, were based on a single late addition to Mishnah Abot (5:21), which sets 18 for a man as 'the time for marriage'.

In his far-reaching reassessment of the issue, Schremer (1996) is more sceptical of this and other rabbinic snippets in the face of other contradictory and comparative evidence. Putting more weight on the testimony of Josephus (who married when he was about 30), other apocryphal and pseudepigraphic works compiled in the late Hellenistic or early Roman periods, and a few other rabbinic dicta, Schremer concludes that Jewish men in Palestine (and perhaps also in the western Diaspora), like their Roman counterparts, most typically married when they were around 30.

Presumably, women too would have been somewhat older at marriage than suggested in some rabbinic sources, with an average age at first marriage most likely in their late teens. Schremer buttresses these conclusions with appeals to both modern anthropological approaches, and comparisons with other ancient cultures and the model life tables of modern pre-industrial communities. At the same time, these ages, even if accurate, might apply to the upper classes only.

There are several ramifications of this reassessment. If what appears to be the most relevant model life table for a modern pre-industrial community is applied, we can expect that about half of all women would have fathers living at the time of their marriage. Obviously, given their later age at marriage, few men would have living fathers when they married (Satlow 2001: 109–11). Given these demographic facts, it appears that in contrast to the picture found in rabbinic texts of men arranging marriages for their sons and daughters, in fact most men and women (whose fathers had already died) would probably have taken a more active role in their own mate selection.

This then returns us to the general problem: Why do rabbinic texts seem to prescribe a lower age of marriage than actually occurred? Perhaps these rabbinic dicta create a patriarchal façade of an 'idealized' world in which the male authors can control not only their children, but even their own mortality. This complicates the usual typological distinction of rabbinic literature as offering either 'ideal' or 'accurate' historical portrayals, instead understanding rabbinic literature as ideals that respond to what would have been perceived as an imperfect reality (Satlow 2001: 109–11).

Demographic simulations and the use of cross-cultural comparisons are potentially very powerful tools. On the one hand, they must be used with caution: we must frankly acknowledge that both the quantity and quality of extant data from antiquity are so lacking that there will be some element of speculation involved in the selection and application of any modern theory. But on the other hand, even if they do not yield reliable results, they often raise new questions. Most discussions of marriage in antiquity focus primarily on first marriages. Yet the demographic life tables suggest that anyone, man or woman, who married at 20 years old could expect to be widowed over the next twenty-five years. The two Jewish women (Babatha and Salome Komaise) whose archives dating from the late first and early second century CE were found in the 'Cave of Letters' at Nahal Hever (and thus are arguably the two Jewish women from antiquity about whom we know the most) were both widowed, with one, Babatha, having been widowed twice (Goodman 1991; Satlow 2001: 97–100). We have very little data about the rates of divorce among Jews in antiquity, but it might be reasonable to assume that divorce too would have added a statistically significant number of potential mates for second (or later) marriages. Although ancient texts and modern scholars often hold up first marriage as exemplary, it remains to be determined if they were in the statistical minority.

Polygyny (marriage of a man to more than one woman at a time) is another topic to which demographic and anthropological approaches can fruitfully supplement textual historical analysis. Scholars have long noted both that no biblical or Jewish texts from this period prohibit or even condemn polygyny, and that there is almost no actual historical evidence that Jews of Roman Palestine practised it (Gafni 1989). The discovery of Babatha's archive, though, has reopened this question: her second marriage appears to have been to a man who already had a wife (Lewis 1997, but see Katzoff 1995). Was this phenomenon a statistical blip, or was it actually widespread, although barely visible to modern scholars? Using anthropological studies, Schremer (2001) sensibly draws a contrast between the actual practice of polygyny and the notion of a 'polygynous society.' Jewish society of Roman Palestine, he argues, was polygynous, even if the actual practice of polygyny within it (as within other polygynous societies studied by anthropologists) might have been uncommon.

Anthropological categories can also reframe the discussion of 'intermarriage' as an issue of endogamy vs. exogamy (Satlow 2001: 133–61). Such terms help to highlight the shifting boundaries of who counts as 'in' and who as 'out'. Shaye Cohen has demonstrated a general shift in attitudes toward intermarriage from the biblical to the rabbinic periods (Cohen 1983), while also, in a separate study, pointing to the changing nature of Jewish identity (Cohen 1999). Even though most Jews in antiquity would most likely have valued endogamy and condemned exogamy (as also attested by Roman writers of the first century CE), other Jewish societies within Roman Palestine would have differed with regard to the definition of their boundaries. In the sectarian documents of the Dead Sea Scrolls, for example, priests appear to have been prohibited from marrying Jewish women who were not descended from priests (cf. Himmelfarb 2006: 27–8, against Hayes 2002: 82–9), whereas rabbis were more deeply concerned with prohibiting marriages between Jews and Gentiles, the latter of whom they considered as ritually impure precisely for this reason (Hayes 2002: 145–63).

Levirate marriage was yet another kind of domestic union. According to the Hebrew Bible, if a man died childless, his brother should marry the widow, and any resulting progeny should be ascribed to the deceased brother (Deut. 25: 5–10). As with polygyny, there is little evidence that the Jews in Roman Palestine were at all troubled by this, while at the same time there is equally sparse evidence for its actual practice. Whether the tannaim preferred the performance of levirate marriage or the 'release' (*halitzah*) of the widow (cf. Friedman 1997; Satlow 2001: 186–9; Hezser 2008), it is clear that Jewish writers from Roman Palestine understood the biblical levirate marriage as a Jewish equivalent of the Greek *epiklarate*—that is, the claim that a man has on the property and widow of an heirless male relative—in which the disposition of the family's estate was the primary concern. This might relate to why Palestinian amoraim prefer that a man release the widow from the obligation of levirate marriage. Perhaps as the economic foundations of Roman

Palestine (or at least those of the authors of our extant texts) changed, moving to a more urban economy with smaller or fragmented landholdings, levirate marriage made less sense to them.

Levirate 'marriage' was not the only non-marital domestic arrangement legally recognized and practised by the Jews of Roman Palestine. Rabbinic law does not particularly sanction, but nevertheless recognizes, concubinage as an institution with a distinct standing. Hezser has discussed the rabbinic law relating to marriages among slaves, and the kinds of intimate relationships that might have existed between slaves and masters (Hezser 2005: 179–201).

This brief survey points to both the slipperiness of the extant evidence and potentially new directions for research. Most of the extant data is so incomplete and ambiguous that the only way to make sense of it is to interpret it within some larger model. Previously, the preferred model was that of internal development that assumed that there existed a singular social institution, 'Jewish marriage', that changed through time. The evidence, that is, was interpreted against specifically Jewish evidence from an earlier period. The results of this interpretation could then be compared with Greek, Roman, and Christian marriage, for evidence of similarity and difference.

Some of the scholarly treatments surveyed above use different interpretive frameworks. One such approach is cross-cultural. This approach takes as its hypothesis that Jews live embedded within the wider, hegemonic culture, and that the shreds of evidence about marriage among Jews can be filled out with what we know about these surrounding cultures. Schremer, for example, claims to boost the plausibility of his claim about the average age at first marriage from evidence of Roman practice. Yaakov Elman uses this approach in his study of Babylonian rabbinic positions on marital property (Elman 2003). While there is, in my opinion, much to recommend this approach, it is also somewhat circular: we assume some of what needs to be proved, only to find that the conclusions support the initial assumptions. Another, far less explored kind of comparison, is that between Jews in antiquity and other, non-contiguous ancient societies, such as India, China, or the Maya. Such comparisons would undoubtedly raise fresh questions.

The application of social scientific, especially demographic and anthropological, models might hold more promise. There is a rich collection of scholarly approaches to the family, and they have only just begun to be applied to families in antiquity. Whether the results are compelling or not (the spottiness of our data severely hampers our ability to use some of these models effectively), they at least serve the purpose of raising new questions. Non-marital Jewish unions remain understudied, and might be an especially promising topic to which these social scientific models can be applied.

3. MARRIAGE CUSTOMS AND RITUALS

There is far less scholarship on (and arguably less data about) the Jewish marriage customs and rituals in antiquity than exists on the topics surveyed above (cf. Goldberg 2003: 114–60; Marcus 2004: 124–92). Much previous scholarship read depictions of marriages in ancient Israelite and Jewish texts as normative, or at least representative of wide Jewish practice—the biblical narrative of the marriage of Jacob and Rachel, the description of Tobias's marriage in Tobit, or the more peculiar marriage of Joseph and Aseneth found in the pseudepigrapha, for example, were taken as reflecting widespread marital customs throughout all of antiquity (cf. Krauss 1910–1912, vol. 2: 37–42; Falk 1966: 35–85; Safrai 1976). Today, even those scholars who subscribe to a model that stresses the continuity of Jewish norms would hardly be comfortable with such an approach.

This, however, does not mean that all such previous scholarship is irrelevant. Modern scholars have increasingly recognized the importance of local custom. Different Jewish communities—even down to the level of town and village—in antiquity, undoubtedly followed their own local wedding customs. They most likely shared, with each other and with the non-Jews around them, many of the most important customs: a procession, dancing and rejoicing, a feast, a request for divine blessing, and consummation of the marriage. Given the lack of biblical prescriptions about how a wedding is to be contracted or celebrated, this is hardly surprising. The modern challenge, though, is to try to reconstruct so-called thick descriptions of regional practices. Ancient Jewish literature, primarily rabbinic, testifies to many different wedding practices. These testimonies, however, must be sorted, not only to separate description from wishful thinking, but also to recognize regional distinctions. All texts cannot be assumed to refer to a single proto-typically 'Jewish' wedding.

Related to the issue of description is that of rabbinic ritualization. As with most other life-cycle events, rabbis leave weddings relatively 'unritualized'. That is, despite the enormous body of law that they develop concerning marriage, they rarely script or prescribe what needs to be done or said at a wedding. Rabbis legislated and ritualized matters pertaining to weddings only when they touched upon, or were potentially in conflict with, other rabbinic concerns (Satlow 2001: 162–81). Further work is necessary to plot how and why rabbis ritualized these local customs and, of course, whether they were drawing on, or influencing, wider popular practice.

One area that rabbis do eventually ritualize is the relatively brief wedding liturgy. The scholarship on the remnants of extant Jewish wedding liturgy (found almost exclusively in the Babylonian Talmud) tends to be relatively narrow and technical. These studies usually focus on four areas: origins, especially of the 'seven blessings'; apparent repetitions within the 'seven blessings'; the relationship between these blessings and other contemporary liturgy; and the place of these blessings within the history of liturgy (e.g. Katz 2007). Recently, one scholar has begun to compare some of these texts and marital images found in the Piyyutim (liturgical poems) to Syriac liturgy, a direction that might hold great promise (Münz-Manor 2006).

Another area of potentially fruitful research concerns the meanings or interpretations of wedding and divorce customs and rituals. There is a deep and rich comparative and theoretical literature on ritual generally, much of it by anthropologists and scholars of religious studies (cf. Turner 1967: 93–111; Bell 1992). These models are by no means easily applied to an eclectic set of ancient texts, but they can at least sensitize scholars to the importance of trying to understand the functions performed by ancient Jewish rituals.

4. Conclusions

Nearly all of the scholarship surveyed here treats Jewish marriage and divorce as discrete institutions, whether legal or social. This institutional approach has advantages and disadvantages. On the one hand, it sometimes encourages disembedding marriage and divorce from the larger social and economic contexts that are critical to understanding its practice. Rather than being a fixed system, for example, marital law above all is a set of strategies that families deploy for their specific needs. Even when seen as a social institution, Jewish marital practices can hardly be understood outside of the demographic and economic realities faced by different Jewish communities.

On the other hand, understanding marriage and divorce as an institution allows for comparison and the application of modern methodologies. There are still significant opportunities for this approach, especially as hitherto neglected disciplinary approaches, mainly from the social sciences, are better applied.

Understanding 'marriage' and 'divorce' as discrete and independent institutions, whether social or legal, has to a large measure predetermined the preoccupation of some scholars with questions of distinctiveness. Those questions, though, have now largely been settled. There is now wide (but not unanimous) scholarly agreement that there was little that was substantively and significantly distinctive about Jewish marital and divorce practices in antiquity. This is hardly surprising, and comports with recent scholarly appraisals of Jewish slavery (Hezser 2005), family (Yarbrough 1993), and childhood (Tropper 2006).

I have highlighted the institutional approach to marriage and divorce also in order to problematize it. While there is still much work to be done within its parameters, one might also understand marriage and divorce, not as discrete and reified institutions, but as *dynamic sets of relationships tightly embedded in larger social networks*. It is this direction—considering marriage and divorce as tightly linked to the social, cultural, religious, and economic lives of those who practised them—that to my mind offers the most exciting future scholarly possibilities.

SUGGESTED READING

Two recent synthetic studies are Satlow 2001 and Schremer 2003. The former discusses both the marital ideologies and practices of Jews in antiquity (in both Judaea/Palestine and Babylonia), with a particular focus on Jewish distinctiveness (or its lack). Schremer's study, in Hebrew, concentrates more on the realia of marriage in Roman Palestine. Friedman (1980) remains the classic study of the *ketubbah*. For all of their methodological problems, Epstein (1942) usefully compiles the relevant rabbinic law, and Safrai (1976) provides a wealth of information on marital practices.

BIBLIOGRAPHY

BAGNELL, R. S./FRIER, B.W. (1994). *The Demography of Roman Egypt*. Cambridge Studies in Population, Economy and Society in Past Time. Cambridge: Cambridge University Press.

BELL, C. M. (1992). *Ritual Theory, Ritual Practice*. New York: Oxford University Press.

BROOTEN, B. (1982). 'Konnten die Frauen im alten Judentum sich von ihren Männern scheiden? Überlegungen zu Mk 10:11–12 und 1 Kor 7:10–11'. *Evangelische Theologie* 42: 65–80.

COHEN, B. (1948/49). 'On the Theme of Betrothal in Jewish and Roman Law'. *Proceedings of the American Academy for Jewish Research* 18: 67–135.

COHEN, S. J. D. (1983). 'From the Bible to the Talmud: The Prohibition of Intermarriage'. *Hebrew Annual Review* 7: 27–29.

—— (1999). *The Beginnings of Jewishness: Boundaries, Varieties, Uncertainties*. Berkeley: University of California Press.

COTTON, H. M. (1998). 'The Rabbis and the Documents', in *Jews in a Graeco-Roman World*, ed. M. Goodman. Oxford: Clarendon Press, 167–179.

——/YARDENI, A. (1997). *Aramaic, Hebrew and Greek Documentary Texts from Nahal Hever and Other Sites*. Discoveries in the Judaean Desert XXVII. Oxford: Clarendon Press.

ELMAN, Y. (2003). 'Marriage and Marital Property in Rabbinic and Sasanian Law', in *Rabbinic Law in its Roman and Near Eastern Context*, ed. C. Hezser, Tübingen: Mohr-Siebeck, 227–276.

EPSTEIN, L. (1942). *Marriage Laws in the Bible and the Talmud*. Cambridge, Mass.: Harvard University Press.

EVANS GRUBBS, J. (1995). *Law and Family in Late Antiquity: The Emperor Constantine's Marriage Legislation*. Oxford: Clarendon Press.

FALK, Z. (1966). *Jewish Matrimonial Law in the Middle Ages*. Oxford: Oxford University Press.

FRAENKEL, Z. (1860). *Grundlinien des mosaisch-talmudischen Eherechts*. Jahresbericht des jüdisch-theologischen Seminars Fraenkelscher Stiftung. Breslau Grass, Berth & Co.

FRIEDMAN, M. A. (1980). *Jewish Marriage in Palestine: A Cairo Geniza Study*. 2 vols. New York: Jewish Theological Seminary of America; Tel Aviv: Tel Aviv University.

—— (1996). 'Babatha's *Ketubba*: Some Preliminary Observations'. *Israel Exploration Journal* 46: 55–76.

—— (1997). 'The Commandment of Pulling off the Sandal Takes Precedence over the Commandment of the Levirate' [Hebr.]. *Te'uda* 13: 35–66.

GAFNI, I. (1989). 'The Institution of Marriage in Rabbinic Times', in *The Jewish Family: Metaphor and Memory*, ed. D. Kraemer. New York: Oxford University Press, 13–30.

GELLER, M. (1978). 'New Sources for the Origins of the Rabbinic Ketubah'. *Hebrew Union College Annual* 49: 227–45.

GOLDBERG, H. (2003). *Jewish Passages: Cycles of Jewish Life*. Berkeley: University of California Press.

GOODMAN, M. (1991). 'Babatha's Story'. *Journal of Roman Studies* 81: 169–175.

GULAK, A. (1934). 'A *Simpon* for Betrothal According to the Palestinian Talmud' [Hebr.]. *Tarbiz* 5(3): 126–33.

—— (1994). *Legal Documents in the Talmud* [Hebrew], ed. R. Katzoff. Jerusalem: Magnes.

HAUPTMAN, J. (1998). *Rereading the Rabbis: A Woman's Voice*. Boulder, Colo.: Westview Press.

HAYES, C. E. (2002). *Gentile Impurities and Jewish Identities: Intermarriage and Conversion from the Bible to the Talmud*. New York: Oxford University Press.

HEZSER, C. (2001). *Jewish Literacy in Roman Palestine*. Texts and Studies in Ancient Judaism 81. Tübingen: Mohr-Siebeck.

—— (2005). *Jewish Slavery in Antiquity*. Oxford: Oxford University Press.

—— (2008). 'The Halitza Shoe: Between Female Subjugation and Symbolic Emasculation', in *Jews and Shoes*, ed. Edna Nahshon. Oxford and New York: Berg Publishers, 47–63.

HIMMELFARB, M. (2006). *A Kingdom of Priests: Ancestry and Merit in Ancient Judaism*. Philadelphia: University of Pennsylvania Press.

ILAN, T. (1993). 'Premarital Cohabitation in Ancient Judea: The Evidence of the Babatha Archive and the *Mishnah*'. *Harvard Theological Review* 86: 247–264.

—— (1995). *Jewish Women in Greco-Roman Palestine: An Inquiry into Image and Status*. Tübingen: Mohr-Siebeck.

—— (1996). 'Notes and Observations on a Newly Published Divorce Bill from the Judaean Desert'. *Harvard Theological Review* 89: 195–202.

JACKSON, B. (2003). 'Problems in the Development of the Ketubah Payment: The Shimon ben Shetah Tradition', in *Rabbinic Law in its Roman and Near Eastern Context*, ed. C. Hezser, Tübingen: Mohr-Siebeck, 199–226.

JUSTER, J. (1914). *Les Juifs dans l'empire romain: Leur condition juridique, économique et sociale*, 2 vols. Paris: Paul Geunthner.

KATZ, M. (2007). 'The Blessing of Bridegrooms and the Blessing of Mourners' [Hebr.]. *Kenishta* 3: 155–86.

KATZOFF R. (1991). 'Papyrus Yadin 18 Again: A Rejoinder'. *Jewish Quarterly Review* 82: 171–176.

—— (1995). "Polygamy in P. Yadin?" *Zeitschrift für Papyrologie und Epigraphik* 109: 128-132.

—— (1996). 'Greek and Jewish Marriage Formulas', in *Classical Studies in Honor of David Sohlberg*, ed. R. Katzoff. Ramat Gan: Bar-Ilan University Press, 223–234.

KRAEMER, R. (1999). 'Jewish Women and Christian Origins: Some Caveats', in *Women and Christian Origins*, eds S. Kraemer and M. R. D'Angelo. New York: Oxford University Press, 35–49.

KRAUSS, S. (1910–12). *Talmudische Archäologie*, 3 vols. Leipzig: G. Fock.

LEWIS, N. (1997). 'Judah's Bigamy'. *Zeitschrift für Papyrologie und Epigraphik* 116: 152.

MÜNZ-MANOR, O. (2006). 'All About Sarah: Questions of Gender in Yannai's Poems and Sarah's (and Abraham's) Barrenness'. *Prooftexts* 26: 344–374.

MARCUS, I. (2004). *The Jewish Life Cycle: Rites of Passage from Biblical to Modern Times*. Seattle: University of Washington Press.

PORTEN, B. (1968). *Archives from Elephantine: The Life of an Ancient Jewish Military Colony*. Berkeley: University of California Press.

REINES, H. Z. (1970). 'The Marriage of Minors in the Talmud' [Hebr.], in *Zevi Scharfstein Jubilee Volume*, ed. Zvulun Ravid. Tel Aviv: Scharfstein Jubilee Committee and Hebrew Teachers Union in Israel, 191–200.

SAFRAI, S. (1976). 'Home and Family', in *The Jewish People in the First Century: Historical Geography, Political History, Social, Cultural and Religious Life and Institutions*, vol. 2, ed. S. Safrai and M. Stern. Assen: Van Gorcum, 728–833.

SALLER, R. (1987). 'Men's Age at Marriage and its Consequences in the Roman Family'. *Classical Philology* 82: 21–34.

SATLOW, M. (1993). 'Reconsidering the Rabbinic *ketubah* Payment', in *The Jewish Family in Antiquity*, ed. S. J. D. Cohen. Brown Judaic Studies. Atlanta: Scholars Press, 133–151.

—— (2001). *Jewish Marriage in Antiquity*. Princeton: Princeton University Press.

SCHREMER, A. (1996). 'Men's Age at Marriage in Jewish Palestine of the Hellenistic and Roman Periods' [Hebr.]. *Zion* 61: 45–66.

—— (1998). 'Divorce in Papyrus Se'lim 13 Once Again: A Reply to Tal Ilan'. *Harvard Theological Review* 91: 193–202.

—— (2001). 'How Much Jewish Polygyny in Roman Palestine?' *Proceedings of the American Academy for Jewish Research* 63: 181–223.

—— (2003). *Male and Female He Created Them: Jewish Marriage in the Late Second Temple, Mishnah and Talmud Periods* [Hebr.]. Jerusalem: The Zalman Shazar Center.

SCHWARTZ, S. (2006). 'Political, Social, and Economic Life in the Land of Israel, 66–c. 235', in: *The Cambridge History of Judaism*, vol. 4: *The Late Roman-Rabbinic Period*, ed. S. Katz. Cambridge: Cambridge University Press, 23–52.

TCHERIKOVER, V. (ed.) (1957–1964). *Corpus Papyrorum Judaicarum*. 3 vols. Cambridge, Mass.: Harvard University Press.

TREGGIARI, S. (1991). *Roman Marriage: Iusti Coniuges from the Time of Cicero to the Time of Ulpian*. Oxford: Clarendon Press.

TROPPER, A. (2006). 'Children and Childhood in Light of the Demographics of the Jewish Family in Late Antiquity'. *Journal for the Study of Judaism* 37: 299–343.

TURNER, V. (1967). *Forest of Symbols: Aspects of Ndembu Ritual*. Ithaca: Cornell University Press.

WEGNER, J. (1988). *Chattel or Person? The Status of Women in the Mishnah*. New York: Oxford University Press.

YARBROUGH, O.L. (1993). 'Parents and Children in the Jewish Family of Antiquity', in *The Jewish Family in Antiquity*, ed. S. J. D. Cohen. Brown Judaic Studies, Atlanta: Scholars Press, 39–59.

CHAPTER 19

CLOTHING

DAFNA SHLEZINGER-KATSMAN

THE garment is one of the earliest creations of human culture, and it is also indicative of the culture in which it was worn (Eicher 1995). In the past, scholars regarded clothes as an insignificant and negligible aspect of culture, whereas nowadays the study of clothing is considered vital for a better understanding of ancient societies in general, and Jews in Roman Palestine in particular. In this chapter we shall deal with the garments worn by Jews in the Land of Israel in the Graeco-Roman period on the basis of the available literary and material sources. Did Jews wear different clothes from their Greek and Roman contemporaries, or were they indistinguishable from non-Jews on the basis of their clothing? According to Shaye Cohen, no ancient author ever mentions distinctive Jewish clothing (Cohen 1999: 31, 1993: 4). Did Jews in Palestine perhaps differ from their co-religionists in the Diaspora in this regard?

1. HISTORY OF RESEARCH

The study of Jewish clothing in the Graeco-Roman period is still in its infancy. More detailed and extensive research has been published on Roman clothing habits, however. Two books are especially noteworthy in this regard. The volume by Sebesta and Bonfante (1994) includes detailed articles on various aspects of Roman clothing, and attempts to reconstruct the appearance of ancient garments. Croom (2002) discusses gender-specific Roman attire and traces the historical development of each garment, based on both archaeological finds and Roman literary sources. Unfortunately, such well-researched and detailed scholarly literature is not yet available for the study of Palestinian Jews' clothing in the Graeco-Roman period.

In the past, research on ancient Jewish clothing has focused on two aspects: the study of the weaving process and of the clothing itself. Here we shall deal with the second issue only, as the textile industries are treated elsewhere (see Uzi Leibner's chapter in this book). It should be noted at the outset that the most important archaeological evidence on ancient Jewish clothing is the fabrics discovered in the dry regions of the Judaean desert, but most of this material has not yet been studied and published, a phenomenon which impedes research in this area.

Krauss' chapter on clothing in his multi-volume work *Talmudische Archaeologie* (Krauss 1910: 127–207) can still serve as the basis for the study of this subject. Krauss' study suffers from methodological deficits, however, which are due to the stage of research at his time: rabbinic sources were not yet studied in a historical-critical way, and Israeli archaeology has advanced considerably since then. Krauss does mention many types of clothing, referred to in both Palestinian and Babylonian, early and late rabbinic sources, but he does not provide a comprehensive analysis and discussion of the material.

Since the beginning of the twentieth century, when Krauss' studies were published, not much research on Jewish attire during the Roman period has been carried out. This field of study has actually been neglected for decades. It was only in the 1960s, with the discovery of many new archaeological finds from the Bar Kokhba period (2nd c. CE) in the Judaean Desert, that scholarship on this subject resumed. These finds included many pieces of fabric and tattered garments which once belonged to Jewish refugees who had fled to the desert caves during and after the Bar Kokhba revolt. An important discussion of these clothes remains can be found in Yadin's excavation report (1963: 169–279), an in-depth analysis of the fabrics which also explains various methods of textile production, along with laboratory reports. Yadin compared these pieces of fabric to other fabrics from Palestine and the surrounding areas, especially Syria (Dura Europos and Tadmor) and Egypt, and he weighed this information against rabbinic literary sources. A great advantage of this book is the inclusion of illustrations, drawings, and photos of the fabrics and clothes. A brief discussion of this material can also to be found in Yadin's book on the Bar Kokhba revolt (1971: 66–85).

Whereas Krauss based his research primarily on rabbinic literary sources, Yadin's work is mainly based on archaeological material. These approaches constitute two very different ways of investigating the subject. Krauss discusses a large number of literary references to garments and clothing-related terms, but he does not try to reconstruct the way ancient Jews dressed. Yadin focuses on a relatively small number of material remains, whose names often remain uncertain, but he gives us an impression of the customary daily attire at that time. What makes the archaeological approach problematic is the small number of finds related to Palestinian Jewish clothing. Therefore the study of ancient Jewish clothing often relies on additional sources from the Diaspora, such as the famous murals from the synagogue in Dura Europos.

In his work on Jewish symbols, Goodenough (1964, vol. 9: 124–174) has written about the representation of Jewish clothing in these murals and in ancient art in general. His analysis is primarily based on the artwork, and he places a lot of emphasis (perhaps too much) on the symbolism of costume. For example, in the context of his examination of pagan influences on Judaism and Christianity, he considers white robes to symbolize holiness. Such robes were allegedly worn by Greek philosophers and Jewish sages (for the white clothes worn by the Essenes, see Magness 2002a: 109–122, Tigchelaar 2003, and the discussion below). Goodenough is sometimes inaccurate in his use of rabbinic writings and tends to mention only those literary sources which support his theory about the symbolism of clothes. The advantage of this study is its analysis of the depiction of clothes in the Dura Europos murals, with additional reference to the fabrics found there. Goodenough's study also offers an excellent review of the main garments (*chiton* and *himation*) worn by Diaspora Jews.

Rubens traces Jewish attire throughout the various historical eras including the Graeco-Roman period (1967: 16–28). Like Krauss, Rubens mentions many of the terms used for clothes in rabbinic writings but does not distinguish between Jews who lived in Babylonia and those in the Roman Empire. He also relies too much on written and illustrated Christian sources and makes many unsubstantiated statements which are merely based on Krauss.

Especially important is an article by Roussin (1994) who attempts to create a balance between the material remains of Jewish clothing from the Judaean desert and rabbinic references to clothes. Within the format of an article she is unable to discuss all of the existing archaeological evidence, however, and addresses a wide range of topics in a rather sporadic way. Topical studies include the work of Hamel (1990: 139–195) who discusses the scarcity and poor quality of clothing in connection with economic issues. Schwartz (2004) compares Christian monks and Jewish rabbis' attitudes towards clothes. Magness (2002a) and Tigchelaar (2003) examine the clothing habits of the Qumran Essenes. Brand (1978) focuses on two specific garments, the *epikarsin* and the *haluk,* and Sperber (1993: 126–140) deals with the *unkelai (anakolos)*, the *fiblia (fibula)* and the *pallium.* Elsewhere, he examines several other rabbinic sources that mention clothing (Sperber 2006: 146–161). His discussion is primarily philological and he pays little attention to recent archaeological discoveries. Shlezinger-Katsman (2003) examines the clothes of Jewish women in Roman times on the basis of archaeological material. Additional gender-oriented studies should be carried out for the clothes of particular sections of the population, such as children's clothing, the clothes of the elderly, peasant garments, bridal gowns, and the widow's mantle. There is also a need for the critical study of rabbinic legal and narrative traditions on clothing. Such a study might help us to answer the question whether, and to what extent, rabbinic prescriptions and prohibitions influenced Jewish attire in Roman Palestine.

2. The Available Sources

Two types of source material are available for the study of our topic:

- Jewish literary sources from the Graeco-Roman period: Palestinian rabbinic literature, Jewish Hellenistic writings, Philo and Josephus;
- archaeological discoveries of fabrics and remnants of clothing; depictions of garments on floor mosaics or mural paintings; sculptures.

Rabbinic literature from the first four or five centuries CE contains much relevant information on clothing, such as the names of garments, the way in which they were worn, methods applied in the production of clothes, and various religious laws pertaining to them. However, these issues are usually addressed in a brief and incidental way. Although the focus must be on Palestinian rabbinic sources, at times a cautious use of traditions transmitted in the Babylonian Talmud is necessary. Since rabbinic writings focus on sages and their pupils and present their particular perspective, women and their clothes are rarely mentioned in the literary sources. Examples for the type of evidence available from rabbinic texts are a description of the order in which garments were put on before leaving the bathhouse (Derekh Eretz Rabbah 1) and a detailed list of the 'eighteen garments' one might save from a fire on the Sabbath (y. Shab. 16:5, 15d; b. Shab. 120a).

Most of the fabrics produced in Palestine were made of wool or linen. Both are organic, perishable substances which have survived in very dry regions only, such as the Negev, the Judaean desert and the Arava (Sheffer 1993; Shamir/Baginski 1998; Magness 2002a). Such fabrics were found in the caves of Wadi Murabba'at, in the Cave of Letters at Nahal Hever, in Wadi Dalia, at Masada, and in the Abior Cave near Jericho, and most of them seem to have belonged to the refugees from the Bar Kokhba revolt (132–135 CE). Fabric remains found in the Treasure Cave of Nahal Mishmar, in the Cave of Horror at Nahal Hever, and in the Cave of the Pool at Nahal David have not been studied and published yet.

The fabric finds provide information about clothing materials, methods of spinning, weaving, sewing, and the dyes that were used. They sometimes even allow us to reconstruct the shape of the garment. The identification of the origins of raw materials and dyes is relevant for the history of ancient trade routes and the economy of Roman Palestine.

Interestingly, none of the fabrics found and examined so far are 'mixed' fabrics of wool and linen, in keeping with biblical law (Deut. 22:11), in contrast to fabric finds from other regions of the Middle East (Yadin 1963: 170; Precker 1992: 17; Magness 2002a: 112). References in Josephus and archaeological finds suggest that 'unlike the other Jews of Roman Judaea, who seem to have dressed mainly or entirely in wool, Essene men wore only linen garments' (Magness 2002a: 113; see below).

Relatively few of the fabrics found in the Land of Israel were dyed, and the few that were dyed were woven of wool (Precker 1992: 15, 178). It seems that it was difficult to dye linen in antiquity (Yadin 1963: 252; Sheffer 1993: 66; Shamir/Baginski 1998: 54), but the lack—or choice—of colour could also have had religious, social, or economic reasons. In the Jewish-Hellenistic novel 'Joseph and Aseneth' Joseph is said to have worn 'an exquisite white tunic, and the robe which he had thrown around him was purple, made of linen interwoven with gold' (5:5). A purple robe (although not said to have been made of linen) is mentioned for Jonathan in 1 Macc. 10:64 (see also 2 Macc. 4:38). The colour purple seems to have indicated royalty and authority here.

Unfortunately, the material evidence does not tell us who wore a particular garment, how garments were worn, and how they covered the body. It is not immediately evident whether a garment was worn by a woman or a man. In order to make gender distinctions, additional visual evidence is necessary. In ancient art from the Roman period clothed figures appear in sculptures, stone reliefs, murals, mosaics, and on coins. Ancient 'Jewish' art often lacks figurative images, especially of women, probably because of the biblical prohibition of images (Exod. 20:4). But apart from the fact that figurative images are sometimes found in Jewish contexts, there is also the methodological problem of distinguishing between Jewish and non-Jewish art in Roman Palestine: Does 'Jewish' art use Jewish motifs only? Or should all artwork made by Jews be considered Jewish art (Hachlili 1988: 366–369; 383–395)? Usually the context (e.g. synagogue, Jewish burial ground) allows scholars to identify ancient art as 'Jewish'. In Jewishly defined contexts Jews could also use pagan and figurative motifs.

Figurative depictions of clothing appear in several forms in Jewish art:

A. Stone reliefs: Many such reliefs were carved into the sarcophagi of the late antique Jewish cemetery at Bet Shearim. These depictions seem to have been influenced by ancient Near Eastern art, and portray linear, static figures, which makes the task of identifying articles of clothing difficult.
B. Mosaics: Figures can be found on synagogue mosaic floors in biblical or zodiac scenes. In zodiac scenes, figures may represent the sun god, the various zodiac signs, and the seasons. In biblical scenes, human figures are usually rare. In Bet Alpha, for example, there is one intact scene depicting the biblical story of the 'Binding of Isaac'. In Na'aran there is a fragmented scene of Daniel in the lions' den, and in Meroth and in Gaza there are images of King David.

C. Coins: No human figures were stamped on Jewish coins dating from the Hasmonean period and the first and second revolts against Rome. Some information on Jewish attire can be gained from the so-called 'Iudaea Capta' coins that were minted by the Romans after the destruction of Jerusalem. These coins have images which symbolize Roman victory, among them a Jewish widow and a Jewish prisoner of war.

The limited evidence provided by archaeological finds from the Land of Israel compels scholars to also use comparative information from the Diaspora, such as the murals from the Dura Europos synagogue. These wall paintings depict biblical scenes and incorporate both Eastern and Western artistic styles. Caution must be exercised, though, since Persian and other Eastern influences can often be found there as well.

3. THE TYPES OF JEWISH GARMENTS

On the basis of fabric finds and figural depictions, some scholars have tried to reconstruct the appearance of pieces of clothing worn by Jews in Roman Palestine. It seems that in general the attire of Jewish men and women was quite similar to the clothes worn by non-Jews in the Hellenistic-Roman world (Cohen 1993: 4–8). Amongst the basic types of clothing were the 'tunic' (*haluk*), an undergarment worn directly on the body (called *chiton* by the Greeks and *tunica* by the Romans), and the mantle (*tallit*), an outer garment called *himation* by the Greeks and *pallium/palla* by the Romans. These garments, which were worn by both men and women (Magness 2002a: 111), were usually made of wool or linen, but the tunic was obviously much lighter than the overcoat.

3.1 The Tunic (*haluk*)

The tunic was made of two identical rectangular pieces of fabric which were sewn together. The sides of the fabric were joined together while leaving an opening for the neck and two side openings for the arms. In the woollen pieces, two parallel coloured stripes (called *clavi*) were woven through the threads. When wearing the robe, these two lines were vertical, one at each side of the neck. In Roman society, these bands would symbolize the status of the wearer: the broader the stripes, the higher his rank. According to Yadin, they served as mere decorations in tunics worn by Jews (Yadin 1963: 207–11). Linen tunics seem to have usually lacked these coloured lines, probably because linen was so difficult to dye, and weaving coloured woollen threads into the linen was banned because of the *Shaatnez* prohibition against a garment containing both interwoven wool and linen. However, linen fabric was found with patterns that resembled lines: 'hollow lines' and 'self stripes' (Yadin 1963: 257–62).

Men seem to have worn short tunics, reaching only to their knees, while women wore longer tunics that reached their ankles or their feet. A woman's tunic was often tied at the waist or beneath the bosom with a strip of fabric. It seems that the types of garments worn by adults were also worn by children, only in smaller sizes. A small linen tunic was found in the Cave of Letters (Yadin 1963: 257–58, plate 89; cf. M. Kelim 27:5). It probably belonged to a child and served as an inner garment (ibid. 257). In rabbinic literature, the term *haluk* is used to refer to tunics of both men and women. Particular types of tunics were associated with certain social roles or functions, such as the scholar's tunic (b. B.B. 57b) and the outdoors tunic (M. Kelim. 28:9).

Married Roman women used to wear an additional exterior garment over their *tunica interior*. This exterior garment was called a *stola* (external tunic). This item of clothing could include sleeves. It was usually held together below the breasts and was typically very long, even covering the feet. It is unknown whether Jewish women also wore this outer garment. It is possible that some of the fabric pieces discovered by archaeologists belonged to an outer tunic. Literary sources sometimes mention women wearing several tunics together (T. Nid. 3:5, 7:2; b. Nid. 52b; b. Git. 58a). Obviously, climate conditions would also have determined the type (and number) of garments worn.

3.2 The Mantle (*tallit*)

Mantles worn by both men and women were made from a simple rectangular piece of fabric, which was usually woven of wool. While Romans used different terms for women's (*palla*) and men's mantles (*pallium*), the garments were basically identical (Goldman 1994: 228–229). Roman men wore the *pallium* infrequently, as they considered it an inferior garment with Greek and barbarian connotations. The outer garment of the Roman citizen was the *toga*, which was made from an elliptically shaped piece of fabric. Rabbis seem to have preferred the rectangular mantle, because it had four corners to which the so-called 'show fringes' (*tzitzit*) could be attached. Roman-style clothes worn by Jewish men were not required to have show fringes (Sifre Deut. 234). Therefore Shaye Cohen assumes that 'Romanized Jews - who probably would not have listened to the rabbis anyway - were under no obligation to wear *tzitzit*' (Cohen 1993: 8; cf. y. Dem. 4:6, 24a). According to Cohen, the Yerushalmi text suggests that some Jewish men in Jerusalem were accustomed to wear robes in Roman style. The text can also be interpreted differently, though.

Fig. 19.2 Notched gamma pattern
Drawing: Dafna Shlezinger-Katsman

Fig. 19.1 Notched line pattern
Drawing: Dafna Shlezinger-Katsman

Scholars have pointed to two major differences between male and female overcoats. The first consisted of two decorative patterns in the four corners of the mantle:

- a pattern of a notched line
- a pattern of a notched gamma

Yadin believed that in the first and second centuries CE, the mantles decorated with a notched line were worn by men, and the mantles decorated with a notched gamma by women; from the fourth century CE onwards the notched gamma decoration became prevalent, and was worn by both men and women (Yadin 1963: 227–32; but see Sheffer/Granger-Taylor (1994: 200–1 who think that gammas were worn by both men and women throughout the period under discussion here).

The second major difference between men's and women's coats was that men's coats were usually not dyed at all, or dyed in light colours, whereas women's coats were dyed in more vibrant colours. This colour distinction is mentioned in a rabbinic tradition according to which rabbis prohibited women from wearing 'white' clothing and men from wearing coloured garments (Sifre. Deut. 226; Magness 2002a: 114; Shlezinger-Katsman 2003: 107). Even when women did wear a lightly dyed mantle, they may have taken care to wear a more vibrantly coloured tunic beneath it to give their attire some colour (Shlezinger-Katsman 2003: 107).

It is possible that male and female garments also differed in the way the garment was wrapped around the body, as the Dura Europos synagogue paintings suggest. Men are depicted as wearing their mantles in the Roman manner, with the corners of the garment thrown over the left shoulder and the left arm. Women's way of clothing is depicted in a unique way and may be based on Near Eastern influences:

one corner of the mantle was fastened with a brooch above the left shoulder, whereas the other corner was wrapped around the head like a long scarf. We do not know whether this way of wearing garments was customary amongst all Jewish women in Roman Palestine. Some women might have wrapped their mantles in a manner similar to men, as evidenced by the figure of Virgo in the mosaic of the Hammat Tiberias synagogue, who wears her mantle in the customary Roman way. This way of wrapping the mantle is similar to the way in which the male figures are represented in Dura Europos, with one obvious difference: the mantle of Virgo is wrapped around her head like a long scarf (similar to the female figures in the Dura Europos painting).

We may assume that distinctions between male and female outerwear were not zealously kept, however. Some rabbinic traditions reckon with both wearing the same kind of garment: A statement attributed to R. Judah b. Baba suggests that one should attach showfringes to the mantle of a woman because her husband might wear it too (Sifre Num. 115). According to another tradition, Rabbi Judah Bar Ilai's wife made a thick mantle of wool to serve them both as an outer garment (b. Ned. 49b).

The mantle (*tallit*) was a rectangular garment with four corners. Rabbis required men to wear coats with show fringes attached to them (y. Ber. 9:5, 14d). In several of the Dura Europos murals, straps are attached to all four corners of the mantles worn by men, but according to Cohen, it is uncertain whether these were show fringes or mere tassles (Cohen 1993: 7 n. 20). *Tzitzit* are never mentioned by non-Jewish writers and no show fringes were attached to the mantles found in the Judaean desert Cave of Letters. Yadin believes that fringes were removed from the mantles before the burial (Yadin 1963: 221). A wool bundle dyed pale blue, with a small group of fringes attached to it, was found in the Cave of Letters, which Yadin believed was intended for making *tzitzit* (Yadin 1963: 182–87). We do not know to what extent Jewish men attached show fringes to their garments in antiquity. It may well be the case that show fringes were worn by pietists only, by the Qumran Essenes (Cohen 1993: 7), Pharisees and rabbis (see Hezser 1997: 123–30 on the question whether rabbis could be recognized by the way they wore their garments in antiquity). When discussing the question of who is an 'am haaretz' the sages mention *inter alia* that he has no *tzitzit* on his clothes (b. Ber. 47b).

Rabbinic sources also mention other types of clothing that were wrapped around the body, used by either men or women or both (terms such as *glima, sadin, sudarin, maaforet, radid* are used for them). The term *tallit* is used most frequently to refer to a man's coat rather than a woman's garment. It should be noted, however, that rabbis generally refer to garments worn by both sexes (such as the *tallit*, the *sadin*, and the *sudarin*) as men's clothing. This phenomenon causes methodological difficulties for scholars trying to identify Jewish women's clothing in antiquity (see Figs 19.3 and 19.4, 19.5 and 19.6).

Figs. 19.3 and 19.4 Ancient Jewish men's clothing

Drawings: Dafna Shlezinger-Katsman

3.3 Undergarments

Rabbinic literature mentions an item of clothing called *epikarsin*, which was worn beneath the tunic as an undergarment and is mentioned only in connection with men. It was a rectangular piece of fabric with threads up to ten fingers long attached to its corners (M. Kel. 29:1). These threads were probably used to tie the garment to the body. Another Mishnaic reference states that this garment was tied at the shoulder (M. Miqw. 10:4), probably on the left-hand side (Brand 1978: 177).

3.4 Head Coverings

In the third century CE murals of the Dura Europos synagogue, all male figures are depicted with bare heads except for kings. Women, on the other hand, have their heads covered by their mantles. This is also the way in which the figure of Virgo appears on the synagogue floor of Hammat Tiberias. In 1 Cor. 11:2–16 Paul advises Christian men, who are described as 'an image and glory of God', not to cover their

Figs. 19.5 and 19.6 Ancient Jewish women's clothing

Drawings: Dafna Shlezinger-Katsman

heads during prayer, whereas women are recommended to do so whenever they are in public (see Thompson 1988 on this text). Tertullian, who lived in Cartharge in North Africa at the end of the second century CE, states that Jewish women were wearing veils in public and could thereby be identified as Jews (De Corona 4.2, see Cohen 1993: 5; 1999: 32).

In the New Testament the 'sinful woman' is presented with loose, unbound hair (Luke 7:36–50) and in the rabbinic *sotah* ritual, imposed upon a woman who was suspected of adultery, her hair was exposed (M. Sot. 1:5). Women's hair obviously had an erotic connotation in antiquity (see Tau 1988, Cosgrove 2005: 679, Bronner 1993: 466) and was rarely let loose in public. Thompson notes that 'Greco-Roman women seem to have let down their hair publicly only on special occasions, such as mourning, some Greek wedding ceremonies, or religious rites', such as the worship of Dionysus (Thompson 1988: 112). They had a choice between wearing their long hair braided and in chignons or covered with a veil (see the images from Corinthi-an marble heads and statues ibid. 106–11). Especially in the first centuries CE most western Roman women seem to have preferred the first, unveiled option (on Roman women and veils see also Wilson 1938: 148–149; Sebesta 1994: 48–49; the veil seems to have become more common in late antiquity, see Thompson 1988: 112). Thompson suggests that Paul's recommendations in 1 Cor. 11: 2–16 were meant to distinguish Christian men and women from their pagan counterparts: whereas pagan men would cover their head with their toga during sacrifice, Christian men are recommended to pray with bare heads; whereas pagan women would loosen their hair in religious rites, Christian women are advised to cover their head with a veil (Thompson 1988). A similar self-distinction may also underlie the Jewish practice, but it may also be based on common Near Eastern customs: in the eastern part of the Roman Empire (southern Asia Minor, Syria, Arabia) head coverings seem to have been customary for non-Jewish women as well (see Thompson 1988: 113; Cohen 1993: 5).

The covered head was a sign of both honour and shame, of modesty and subjugation, indicating that the woman belonged to one particular man and was no longer available to other men. Unmarried Greek and Roman girls would wear their hair loose to indicate their freedom (see Cosgrove 2005: 681–82; see also Joseph and Aseneth 15:1, where the heavenly messenger tells Aseneth to remove her veil, 'for you are a chaste virgin today and your head is like that of a young man'). Bronner has suggested that head covering marked the transition from girlhood to womanhood in ancient Jewish society, and that this was a new development of rabbinic times in contrast to the biblical period (Bronner 1993: 466). One of the issues to be examined with regard to rabbinic texts is whether they present women's head covers as a custom or as Torah law, and whether there was a development from early to late and from Palestinian to Babylonian rabbinic sources in this regard.

Several rabbinic texts mention head coverings for Jewish women. The Mishnah states that a woman might lose her *ketubbah* (marriage contract), if she goes outdoors with her head uncovered (M. Ket. 7:6; cf. T. Ket. 7:6; y. Ket. 7:7, 31b; b. Ket. 72a–b). A Palestinian amoraic Midrash asks why men go outdoors with their heads uncovered while women do so with their heads covered (Gen R. 17:8; for an interesting analogy to this question see Plutarch, Moralia 267: 'Why do sons cover their heads when they escort their parents to the grave while daughters go uncovered with their hair unbound?' Plutarch answers that in mourning they do the opposite of what they would usually do). The rabbinic answer provided in the Midrash is that women cover their heads out of shame for sins and the guilt incurred by Eve (Bronner 1993: 470–71; see also ARNB 9:25 and 42:17 for the association with Eve). A man who uncovers a woman's hair in public has to pay 'shame' damages, since he violated her honour (M. B.Q. 8:6, cf. Satlow 1997: 442).

Rabbinic sources also occasionally refer to a woollen hairnet (*svacha*) and a cap (*kipa*) to cover women's hair (M. Kel. 24:16, 28:9–10; T. Kelim B.B. 2:10; M. Ket. 5:8; T. Sot. 3:3; T. B.Q. 11:5). Remnants of woven hairnets were found in the Judaean

Desert Cave of Letters, in the Cave of Horrors, at Masada, and perhaps Wadi Murabba'at (Magness 2002a: 103–6; Ilan 1995: 129–32). An image of a woman with her hair gathered in a net appears in the representation of the month of Tishri in the Zodiac cycle of the Bet Alpha synagogue mosaic. Besides covering their heads with a corner of their mantles or with a cap or hairnet, women could use a scarf made of wool or linen. This scarf was a kind of oversized kerchief that covered the hair and fell to the woman's shoulders and back. Yadin identified five pieces of woollen fabric as remnants of headscarves (Yadin 1963: 246–48). In rabbinic sources the terms *sudarin, sadin,* and *radid* also appear as references to various types of head coverings.

In Babylonia, in contrast to Palestine, Jewish men seem to have sometimes covered their heads as well. According to a Babylonian Talmudic text, men sometimes cover their hair, while women always follow this practice (b. Ned. 30b). Other texts in the Babylonian Talmud mention men covering their heads for certain special occasions, such as: placing a *sudar* or scarf over the head during times of mourning (b. M.Q. 24a), when raising their glass for a blessing (b. Ber. 51a), and when paying their respects to an important person (b. Qid. 8a, 29b). B. Pes. 111b mentions a *sudar* worn by sages. Other Babylonian texts state that Rav Huna never appeared bare headed (b. Qid. 31a; b. Shab. 118b), and that R. Nachman bar Yitzhaq's mother made sure that his head was always covered to show proper humility before God (b. Shab. 156b). These texts have to be studied in the context of clothing habits for males in Persian society at that time. In Babylonia the need to distinguish oneself from Graeco-Roman pagan practices was no longer given, but Zoroastrian customs need to be taken into consideration as well.

3.5 Footwear and Socks

The most common shoe worn by Jews in Roman Palestine was the sandal. Many soles of men's, women's, and children's sandals were found in the Cave of Letters and in other caves of the Judaean Desert. The sandal soles were attached to the feet with leather straps, and these customarily separated the big toe from the other toes, like modern flip-flops. An intact sandal, probably belonging to a woman, was found in a basket in the Cave of Letters (Yadin 1963: 165–68, plate 57). All of the soles that were found were made of several layers of leather fastened together with leather straps, usually without the use of nails. The Mishnah prohibits wearing sandals fastened with nails on the Sabbath only (M. Shab. 6:2; but see y. Shab. 6:2, 8a; b. Shab. 60a). According to Bordowicz, both the literary sources and the archaeological remains point to the Jewish use of nails in sandals, though on a smaller scale than Roman (Bordowicz 2001: 35, 84). He points to rabbinic texts which refer to this type of sandal as a *minal mesumar* (nailed shoe) or *kilgasim* or *golgusim*, a loanword derived from the Latin *caliga*, the most commonly worn nail-bound sandal (Bordowicz 2001: 12 and 77).

Shoes were considered valuable objects in antiquity and not everyone was able to afford them. Slaves and poor people often went barefoot (Baker 1996–97). Sandals would have been cheaper than closed shoes, and they would also suit the warm Mediterranean climate. Whereas rabbinic sources distinguish between closed shoes and sandals only, Roman sources mention a large variety of shoes of different forms, materials, and qualities (Hezser 2008).

The shoe or sandal plays an important role in a Jewish ritual connected with Levirate marriage, the so-called *halitzah* ceremony (Deut. 25:5–10, see Hezser 2008). If the brother-in-law refused to marry his deceased brother's widow, he had to participate in a ritual in which the widow loosens his shoe and spits on the ground in front of him to denigrate him for this behaviour. In rabbinic times, when polygamy became less common, such ceremonies seem to have been customarily performed in the relevant circumstances. Rabbis ruled that only specific types of shoes and sandals could be used in the ceremony (M. Yeb. 12:1), but they were not unanimous in this regard (see Hezser, ibid.).

Among the fabric finds from Roman Palestine, only one item found at Masada could definitively be identified as a child's sock (Sheffer/Granger-Taylor 1994: 221–223). The sock was made of linen and the big toe was separated from the other toes. Several similar remains were found in other areas, mostly in Egypt (Burnham 1972). We may assume that woollen socks were also produced and worn in Palestine. Furthermore, rabbinic sources mention the *anpili/anpilei*, a sock made of fabric or leather (Cohen 1995: 28–29).

The Dura Europos synagogue murals show male figures wearing sandals without socks, whereas women are depicted wearing darkly coloured shoes, and in one case a pair of pale socks. Shoes appear in images of male figures dressed in the Persian-Oriental style (such as in the Dura Europos wall paintings) and in the later Byzantine-Oriental style (such as in the zodiac mosaic of Bet Alpha, or the figure of Cancer in the zodiac at Sepphoris).

3.6 The Clothes of Essenes and Rabbis

Did particular religious sub-sets within the Jewish population of Roman Palestine wear clothes which distinguished them from the rest of the Jewish population? In the case of the Essenes, we do have a group which used clothes as identity markers to set themselves apart from society at large (on Essene clothing see Magness 2002a and 2002b; Tigchelaar 2003). Both Philo (Prob. 85–88; Apol. 12; Hypoth. 11.12) and Josephus (Bell. 2.119–161) mention certain clothing habits which they distinguish from the habits of the rest of the population: clothes are community-owned; they are given to new members as part of their initiation rites; clothes are worn until they are rags; not only the clothes worn at meals but also all ordinary, everyday life clothes are white; nudity is avoided and loincloths are worn by men even when bathing. Most of these aspects fit in well with what we know about the Essenes: that they owned everything in common, rejected riches, were concerned about equality amongst members, and tried to live an ascetic life of purity and strict observances. In that regard, their clothing habits would have supported their lifestyle.

Scholars have particularly studied and commented upon the white clothes associated with Essenes in the literary sources mentioned above. No clothes remains were found at Qumran itself and the requirement for white clothes is not explicitly mentioned in the Qumran Sectarian documents (Tigchellar 2003: 318–19). Nevertheless, Philo's and Josephus' reports seem trustworthy in this regard. Magness assumes that the white clothes were worn by men only rather than by women, and that they were made of non-dyed linen (Magness 2002a: 111). She thinks that this habit was adopted in imitation of Jerusalem Temple priests (ibid. 120–23). The discovery of seventy-seven scraps of linen fabric in Cave I in Qumran would seem to support this view of Magness. These fabrics were used as covers for the scrolls and for the jars which were found in the cave (Crowfoot 1955; Magness 2002a: 115).

According to Tigchelaar, on the other hand, the white, non-dyed nature of the clothes was the distinguishing mark, while they could have been made of linen or wool (Tigchelaar 2003: 311–12, n. 48). Philo mentions thick coats for winter and cheap tunics for summer (Apol. 12), and each man may have possessed and worn only one of these garments at a time. The practice of wearing white garments was similar to that of the Pythagoreans and the Therapeutes mentioned by Philo (Tygchelaar 2003: 304–6). In the Greek Jewish novel *Joseph and Aseneth*, Joseph is said to have been dressed in a white tunic with a purple linen robe thrown around him (5:5; a similar robe is said to have been worn by the heavenly messenger ibid. 14:9). A number of different reasons can be adduced for the choice of white garments: to indicate a life lived in constant purity; as a sign of identification with the Temple priests and/or angels; as a way to easily detect defilement; as a symbol of spirituality; to avoid cross-dressing (since coloured garments were associated with women); to express simplicity and modesty; and as a general criticism of the surrounding (Jewish) society which did not live according to these ideals (see ibid. 310–17).

Unlike the Essenes, post-70 rabbis did not separate themselves from their surroundings, and they do not seem to have worn distinctive clothes to mark their status as sages (see Hezser 1997: 123–30). On the one hand, one tannaitic text suggests that sages were outwardly recognizable by the way they walked, talked, and wrapped themselves in their cloaks (Sifre Deut. 343:11). On the other hand, no special garments of scholars are ever mentioned in Palestinian rabbinic sources (in contrast to the 'haluk and *tallit* of a student of sages' mentioned in b. B.B. 57b). Palestinian rabbis would wear the same type of clothes as other Jews, and the *tallit* (*pallium*) is most often referred to in this regard. Rabbis would have been more observant of the rule of attaching show fringes to their garments, but at least in theory that rule applied to any Jewish male (Hezser 1997: 129–30). Thus, rabbis were not recognizable by the type of their clothing, but perhaps by the way they carried themselves.

3.7 Black Clothing

The Cave of Letters yielded the remains of a woman's black scarf, and in Masada a tattered piece of black fabric was found which may have been part of a tunic. Black clothing was rather unusual and was not worn on an everyday basis by Jews during the Roman period. Like nowadays, this colour symbolized mourning and grief and was worn by both men and women for this purpose (Shlezinger-Katsman 2003: 31–35).

There are references to wearing black at times of mourning in both Jewish Hellenistic (cf. 'Joseph and Aseneth' 14:12, where the angel tells Aseneth to take off her 'black tunic of mourning' and 'dress in a new linen robe') and rabbinic literature (Semahot/Evel Rabbati 4:3, a late or minor tractate of the Babylonian Talmud; Pesiqta Rabbati 26). Black clothing also appears in this context in the Dura Europos synagogue murals: a grieving widow's body is covered by a black mantle, which also covers her head. On this image it seems that beneath the black mantle the widow is not wearing anything at all—her breasts and feet are bare. This representation may be based on customs of mourning practised in ancient Egypt and along the eastern shores of the Mediterranean.

Black is also mentioned as a sign of mourning in connection with the priests disqualified for work in the Temple (M. Mid. 5:4). In addition, black clothing symbolized sin (b. M.Q. 17a) and was worn by those standing trial (y. R.H. 1:3, 57b).

4. SUMMARY

Ancient Jewish men and women seem to have worn the same types of basic clothing, which included a tunic (*haluk*) and mantle (*tallit*). The man's tunic was shorter than the woman's, and women often girdled their garments with a belt or cord at the waist or below the bust. Their mantles often differed in patterns and colours from those of men, and possibly also in the manner they were worn.

The basic wardrobe of Palestinian Jews during the first five centuries CE seems to have been quite similar to that of the Romans. The *tunica* (*haluk*) and the *pallium/palla* (*tallit*) were the common garb of the Roman world. While male Roman citizens eventually changed their overcoat and adopted the elliptically shaped *toga*,

Jews, like other residents of the eastern provinces, continued to wear the rectangular *pallium*. It seems that the main distinction between Jewish and Gentile clothes during the Graeco-Roman period was not the type of garment or shape, but rather the way in which they were produced. Religiously committed Jews would not mix linen and wool into the same fabric. By contrast, many mixed fabrics were found outside of Palestine. This dissimilarity in the type of fabric used would not have been immediately apparent, so that Jews who wore such garments would not have been distinguishable from Gentiles, unless they had show fringes attached to their coats, a rabbinized custom associated with prayer.

5. SUGGESTIONS FOR FUTURE RESEARCH

While there is a large amount of scholarship available on Greek and Roman clothes, very few studies have focused on Jewish clothing during the Hellenistic and Roman periods. The various types of Greek and Roman clothes have been identified on the basis of archaeological and literary sources. More specialized studies deal with particular garments, gender issues, and the symbolism surrounding clothes. The situation is very different for Jewish clothing in antiquity, where even the most basic studies are still missing.

The first and most important step in the study of ancient Jewish clothing would be the collection, identification, and publication of all of the relevant archaeological material. While fabric and clothes remains have been discovered at various archaeological sites, little of this material has been studied and published yet. To cite one example: of the approximately 2,000 cloth fragments found at Masada, only 122 have been published to date (Sheffer/Granger-Taylor 1994: 154).

Additional research must focus on the study of ancient Jewish literary references to garments worn by Jews, both in rabbinic and Greek Jewish literature. Again, little has been done in this regard, particularly from a historical-critical and gender studies point of view (Shlezinger-Katsman 2003). Future studies should differentiate between clothes worn by different sets of people (e.g. children's clothes, bridal clothes, widows' garments, etc.) and different social strata (on the clothes of poor people see Hamel 1990; on slaves' clothes see ibid. 77–78 and Hezser 2005: 261–62). Another interesting area would be the study of the relevance of clothing in rabbinic legal discourse (halakhah). The relevant texts should be collected and analyzed and interpreted within the Graeco-Roman and ancient Near Eastern context. The eventual goal should be a comprehensive survey and cultural-historical study of ancient Jewish clothing, based on both the archaeological and the literary sources, similar to the one prepared by Croom (2002) on Roman clothing.

SUGGESTED READING

Although outdated, the basic study of Jewish clothing in Roman Palestine is still Krauss (1910: 127–207). Yadin (1963: 169–279) provides a basic survey and analysis of the garments and fabric remains found in the Judaean Desert caves. Goodenough (1964, vol. 11: 124–174) discussed (the symbolic significance of) garments represented in Jewish art. Rousin (1994) provides a good synthesis of the archaeological material and rabbinic literary sources. For an additional and more up–to-date study of textiles found in the Land of Israel see Shamir/Baginski (1998).

BIBLIOGRAPHY

BAKER, S. A. (1996–97). 'Loosing a Shoe Latchet: Sandals and Footwear in the First Century'. Brigham Young University Studies 36: 196–206.

BORDOWICZ, I. (2001). 'Hobnailed Sandals–The Archaeological and Historical Evidence' [Hebr.]. Unpublished MA thesis, Bar-Ilan University.

BRAND, Y. (1978). 'Costume in the Talmudic Period' [Hebr.], in *Glassware in the Literature of the Talmud: With Additional Studies and Articles.* Jerusalem: Mossad Harav Kook, 176–185.

BRONNER, L. L. (1993). 'From Veil to Wig: Jewish Women's Hair Covering'. *Judaism* 42 (1993) 465–77.

BURNHAM, D. (1972). 'Coptic Knitting: An Ancient Technique', *Textile History* VI (1972): 116–124.

CLELAND, L./DAVIES, G./LLEWELLYN-JONES, L. (2007). *Greek and Roman Dress From A to Z.* London: Routledge.

COHEN, N. (1995). 'Leather and Leather Products in the Mishnah and Talmud periods' [Hebr.]. Unpublished M.A. thesis, Bar-Ilan University.

COHEN, S. J. D. (1993). '"Those Who Say They Are Jews and Are Not":How Do You Know a Jew in Antiquity When You See One?' in *Diasporas in Antiquity,* ed. S. J. D. Cohen and E. S. Frerichs. Atlanta: Scholars Press, 1–45.

——(1999). *The Beginnings of Jewishness: Boundaries, Varieties, Uncertainties.* Berkeley: University of California Press.

COSGROVE, C. H. (2005). 'A Woman's Unbound Hair in the Greco-Roman World, With Special Reference to the Story of the Sinful Woman in Luke 7:36–50'. *Journal of Biblical Literature* 124 (2005) 675–92.

CROOM, A. T. (2002). *Roman Clothing and Fashion.* 2nd ed. Gloucestershire: Tempus Publishing.

CROWFOOT, G. M./CROWFOOT, E. (1955). 'The Linen Textiles', in *Discoveries in the Judean Desert, vol. 1: Qumran Cave I,* ed. O. P. Barthelemy and J. T. Milik. Oxford: Clarendon Press, 18–38.

——(1961). 'The Textiles and Basketery', in *Discoveries in the Judean Desert, vol. 2: Les Grottes de Murrabba'at,* ed. P. Benoit, J. T. Milik, P. de Vaux. Oxford: Clarendon Press, 51–63.

EDWARDS, D. (1992). 'Dress and Ornamentation'. *Anchor Bible Dictionary* 2: 232–38.

EICHER, J. B. (1995). *Dress and Ethnicity: Change Across Space and Time*. Oxford: Berg Publishers.

GOLDMAN, N. (1994). 'Reconstructing Roman Clothing', in *The World of Roman Costume*, ed. J. L. Sebaste and L. Bonfante. Madison: The University of Wisconsin Press, 213–237.

GOODENOUGH, E. R. (1964). *Jewish Symbols in the Greco-Roman Period*, vols 9–11. New York: Pantheon Books.

HACHLILI, R. (1988). *Ancient Jewish Art and Archaeology in the Land of Israel*. Leiden: Brill.

HAMEL, G. (1990). *Poverty and Charity in Roman Palestine*. Berkeley: University of California Press.

HEZSER, C. (1997). *The Social Structure of the Rabbinic Movement in Roman Palestine*. Tübingen: Mohr-Siebeck.

—— (2005). *Jewish Slavery in Antiquity*. Oxford: Oxford University Press.

—— (2008). 'The Halitzah Shoe: From Female Subjugation to Symbolic Emasculation', in *Jews and Shoes*, ed. E. Nahshon. New York: Berg Publishers, 47–63.

ILAN, T. (1995). *Jewish Women in Greco-Roman Palestine: An Inquiry into Image and Status*. Tübingen: Mohr-Siebeck.

KNOWLES, M. P. (2004). 'What Was the Victim Wearing? Literary, Economic, and Social Contexts for the Parable of the Good Samaritan'. *Biblical Interpretation* 12: 145–74.

KRAUSS, S. (1910). *Talmudische Archäologie*, vol.1. Leipzig: G. Fock.

LLEWELLYN-JONES, L. (ed.) (2002). *Women's Dress in the Ancient Greek World*. London: Duckworth.

MAGNESS, J. (2002a). 'Women at Qumran?', in *What Athens Has to Do With Jerusalem. Essays on Classical, Jewish, and Early Christian Art and Archaeology in Honor of Gideon Foerster*, ed. L. Rutgers. Leuven: Peeters, 89–123.

—— (2002b). *The Archaeology of Qumran and the Dead Sea Scrolls*. Grand Rapids: Eerdmans.

PRECKER, R. (1992). 'Vegetable Dyes and the Dyeing Industry in the Eastern Mediterranean during the Hellenistic, Roman and Byzantine Periods' [Hebr.]. Unpublished MA thesis, Bar-Ilan University.

ROUSSIN, L. A. (1994). 'Costume in Roman Palestine: Archaeological Remains and the Evidence from the Mishna', in *The World of Roman Costume.*, ed. J. L. Sebaste and L. Bonfante. Madison: The University of Wisconsin Press, 182–190.

RUBENS, A. (1967). *A History of Jewish Costume*. London: Vallentine Mitchell.

SATLOW, M. (1997). 'Jewish Constructions of Nakedness in Late Antiquity'. *Journal of Biblical Literature* 116: 429–54.

SCHWARTZ, J. (2004). 'Material Culture in the Land of Israel: Monks and Rabbis on Clothing and Dress in the Byzantine Period', in *Saints and Role Models in Judaism and Christianity*, ed. J. Schwartz, J. and M. Poorthuis. Leiden: Brill, 121–137.

SEBESTA, J. L. (1994). 'Symbolism in the Costume of the Roman Woman', in *The World of Roman Costume.*, ed. J. L. Sebaste and L. Bonfante. Madison: The University of Wisconsin Press 1994: 46–53.

—— and BONFANTE, L. (eds) (1994). *The World of Roman Costume*. Madison: The University of Wisconsin Press.

SHAMIR, O. / BAGINSKI A. (1998). 'Research of Ancient Textiles Discovered in Israel' [Hebr.]. *Qadmoniot* 31: 53–62.

SHEFFER, A. (1993). 'Ancient Textiles Decorated with Color from the Land of Israel' [Hebr.], in *Colors from Nature—Natural Colors in Ancient Times*, ed. C. Sorek, C. and E. Ayalon. Tel Aviv: Eretz Israel Museum, 66–75.

—— (1998). 'Bar Kokhba Period Textiles from Abi'or Cave', in *Refuge Caves of the Bar Kokhba Revolts*, ed. H. Eshel and D. Amir. Tel Aviv: Eretz, 169–75.

—— (2000). 'Textiles', in Encyclopedia of the Dead Sea Scrolls, ed. L. H. Schiffman and J. C. Vanderkam. New York: Oxford University Press, 940–41.

—— and GRANGER-TAYLOR, H. (1994). 'Textiles from Masada: A Preliminary Selection', in *Masada IV: The Yigael Yadin Excavations 1963–65. Final Reports*. Jerusalem: Israel Exploration Society. 153–255.

SHLEZINGER-KATSMAN, D. (2003). 'The Clothing of the Jewish Woman in the Land of Israel during the Roman Period: According to Archaeological Findings' [Hebr.]. Unpublished MA thesis, Bar-Ilan University.

SPERBER, D. (1993). *Material Culture in Eretz-Israel during the Talmudic Period*. [Hebr.], vol.1. Jerusalem: Bar-Ilan University Press and Yad Izhak Ben-Zvi Press.

—— (2006). *Material Culture in Eretz-Israel during the Talmudic Period* [Hebr.] vol. 2. Jerusalem: Bar-Ilan University Press and Yad Izhak Ben-Zvi Press.

TAU, H. (1988). 'Symbolic Significance of Hair in the Biblical Narrative and in the Law'. *Koroth* 9: 173–79.

TIGCHELAAR, E. J. C. (2003). 'The White Dress of the Essenes and the Pythagoreans', in *Jerusalem, Alexandria, Rome: Studies in Ancient Cultural Interaction in Honour of A. Hilhorst*, ed. F. Garcia Martinez and G. Luttikhuizen. Leiden: Brill, 301–21.

THOMPSON, C. L. (1988). 'Hairstyles, Head-Coverings, and St. Paul: Portraits from Roman Corinth'. *The Biblical Archaeologist* 51,99–115.

WILSON, L. M. (1938). *The Clothing of the Ancient Romans*. Baltimore: John Hopkins University Press.

YADIN, Y. (1963). *The Finds from the BarKokhba Period in the Cave of Letters*, vol. 1. Jerusalem: Israel Exploration Society.

—— (1971). *BarKokhba: The Rediscovery of the Legendary Hero of the Last Jewish Revolt against Imperial Rome*. London: Weidenfeld and Nicolson.

YEIVIN, Z. (1971). 'Dress'. Encyclopedia Judaica 6: 212–223.

......

CHAPTER 20

JEWELLERY: THE LITERARY EVIDENCE

......

TZIONA GROSSMARK

1. INTRODUCTION

......

Since the dawn of civilization, people have produced and worn jewellery. Jewellery was worn by women, men and children alike. In earliest times jewellery was made of any substance that was light enough to be hung, tied, threaded or interwoven. Eventually, the creation of jewellery would undergo changes as a result of the adoption and use of more expensive materials that were reshaped by specialized craftspeople.

Jewellery can be defined as objects of personal adornment prized for their beauty, and often for their value as well. But a jewel has more than just decorative and aesthetic value. A jewel is a work of art or fine craftsmanship. It is a token of status which possesses social (sometimes gender-related), political and/or religious traits. A jewel can be considered to possess prophylactic or magical qualities, and may be used as an amulet. Its expensive materials accord it intrinsic economic value.

Jewellery has been created and used by people for many different reasons. Consequently, the study of jewellery can be carried out by a wide range of disciplines, using a variety of approaches. The cultural aspects of jewellery can be studied by applying anthropological and sociological methodology. The study of the material aspects of jewels is conducted by disciplines such as gemology and metallurgy, among others. The detection and examination of jewellery from earlier times is the task of archaeologists, and its aesthetic value or style is studied by art historians. Thus, the study of jewellery is not a discipline in itself, but rather a combination of disciplines and approaches that are roughly divided according to their subject matter into the following categories:

- study of the artefacts, their styles, and their aesthetic values;
- study of manufacturing techniques;
- study of the artisans who created jewellery, their social standing and their professional and social structures;
- study of how jewellery was used, its significance, and its social meanings.

2. Past Scholarship on Ancient (Jewish) Jewellery

Although treasure-hunting and the collecting of antique jewellery led to an amateur archaeological interest in it in the eighteenth to nineteenth centuries, scientific research of jewellery did not predate the end of the nineteenth century, when archaeological digs uncovered large hordes of jewels. The first important publications concerning ancient jewellery were catalogues of major museum collections (Marshall 1907 and 1911), sometimes including comprehensive chapters creating the methodological and theoretical foundations for the study of ancient jewellery. In time, the study of jewellery acquired its recognized place amongst the study of other aspects of daily life in ancient times (Higgins 1961 and 1965; Ogden 1982 and 1992; Tait 1989). A society of 'jewellery historians', aimed at promoting the study of antique jewellery, was founded in 1977 by the Department of Scientific Research at the British Museum. The society publishes a journal entitled *Jewellery Studies*.

The scientific study of jewellery from Hellenistic and Roman Palestine in the Second Temple and rabbinic periods is a new branch of research. Earlier studies, such as the research of S. Krauss (1910: 185–191, 198–207) and of A. S. Hirshberg (1923), dealt with some aspects of jewellery in ancient Jewish society. However, their concern was with the rabbinic literary evidence only. Despite their importance as pioneers in the field, both suffer from methodological problems. They rarely distinguish between earlier (tannaitic) and later (amoraic) literary traditions, nor is there a distinction between Palestinian and Babylonian sources. Moreover, both works antedated the publication of data accumulated by subsequent archaeological research. Dalman (1937: 275–287, 340–353) dedicated two subchapters to jewellery worn by men and women, respectively. Although he provides an impressive amount of literary evidence on jewellery, like Krauss he does not distinguish between the biblical and rabbinic data and between tannaitic and amoraic material. Furthermore, Dalman could not use the archaeological and literary sources discovered since his *Arbeit und Sitte* was published in the first half of the twentieth century. Thus, the three pioneering works, Krauss's *Talmudische Archäologie*, Hirshberg's *Women's Beauty* and Dalman's *Arbeit und Sitte*, despite their undoubted importance for the study of ancient Jewish jewellery, are rather antiquated.

During the twentieth century there has been a steady increase in publications on archaeological finds of jewellery datable to Roman-Byzantine Palestine, but very few papers dealing with the literary evidence of jewellery have been published so far. Some of the publications deal with precious stones (Shalem 1931; Ilani et al. 1991), others with craftsmen (Ayali 1985), and a few discuss a certain type of jewellery, such as the so-called 'Jerusalem of gold' (Paul 1967 and 1977; Hoffman 1969; Grossmark 2009) and the *fibula* (Sperber 1993: 126–131). A doctoral dissertation which examines the rabbinic literary evidence of jewellery has been written by the author (Grossmark 1994a; see also Grossmark 2004 and 2005).

3. The Literary Evidence of Jewellery in Jewish Sources of the Late Second Temple Period

Literary evidence of jewellery from the Hellenistic and early Roman periods can be found in the Apocrypha, in Josephus' writings, and in the New Testament. Data concerning jewellery found in the Apocrypha is usually limited to references to gold and precious stones in allegories. Rarely do we find a jewel referred to by name (Ben Sira 21:21 and 2:5–6), and further descriptions are usually missing. Ben-Sira's poetical description of a metalsmith at work (38:27–28) is an exception.

The Letter of Aristeas, which has been dated by scholars to the time period between 200 BCE and 33 CE (cf. *The Oxford Dictionary of the Christian Church*, s.v. 'Letter of Aristeas', 84), contains a detailed description of the gold items donated by Ptolemy Philadelphus (285–247 BC) to the Temple in Jerusalem with reference to their craftsmanship (Aristeas 52–62). The early date of the text does not raise a methodological problem for our study. The various techniques used by ancient craftsmen would have hardly changed over time due to the apprentice system. Therefore literary texts composed in the Hellenistic period may reflect technological aspects that prevailed in the Roman period as well. The text may, however, reflect the wealth and splendour of the Hellenistic metropolis of Alexandria.

The story is taken up by Josephus in his Antiquities (12.60–84). A comparative philological study of the two versions can provide important information concerning the goldsmith's craft during the first century (for a full account, it is helpful to compare the two texts with Exod. 25:23–40 and 1 Kings 7).

The contribution of Second Temple period historiographical texts to our knowledge of jewellery is quite limited. Golden wreaths that were given as tributes of loyalty or political friendship are mentioned a few times (1 Macc. 13:37; 2 Macc. 14:4; Josephus, Ant. 13.45). Josephus also mentions the expensive jewels that were buried with the dead body of King Herod (Ant. 17.196–197).

The information about jewellery that can be obtained from the New Testament is limited to a very few references to rings (Luke 15:22), golden girdles (Apc. 15:6), and golden crowns (Apc. 3:11; 4:4; 14:14). There is a single reference to women's adornments (1 Peter 3:3). In addition to the sporadic references to jewels, there are a few texts that mention precious stones (1 Cor. 3:12) and, in a parable, there is a single mention of a merchant in search of a pearl of great value (Matt. 13:45–46). The most important text mentioning precious stones is found in chapter 21 of the Apocalypse (21:18–21), with the description of the heavenly Jerusalem. This text has been thoroughly studied and is of some importance, at least for the study of gemological knowledge during the Roman period (Jart 1970; Reader 1981).

To sum up, the evidence of the various aspects of jewellery and its use available from the literature of the late Second Temple period is quite sporadic, but should not be neglected.

4. The Literary Evidence of Jewellery in Rabbinic Literature

4.1. Definition

The Hebrew word *tahshit* is a post-Biblical word meaning adornment or jewel. Talmudic sources clearly distinguished between jewellery and clothing. Different halakhic rules concerning the Sabbath and ritual purity were applied to clothing and to jewellery, and this attests to their being two distinct categories (M. Shab. 6:1; y. Shab. 6:1, 7d; M. Kel. 11: 8–9; 27:1–12). Such a distinction is also well documented in Roman-Byzantine legal texts (Ulpian, Sabinus, 44; cf. Just. Dig. 34.2.25–26; 34.2.37). On the other hand, cosmetics and hairdressing were usually included in the category of women's jewellery (*tahshitei nashim*) throughout the Roman and Byzantine periods (T. B.B. 2:17; cf. b. B.B. 60b; y. M.Q. 1:7, 80d).

4.2 The Nature of the Evidence

Although an amazing quantity of data concerning all aspects of jewellery is found in rabbinic literature, this data is fragmentary. Rabbis were interested in jewellery, jewellery making, and jewellery use only as far as this information served their legal arguments. Therefore, the information supplied by rabbinic sources is limited to the necessary details needed for the respective halakhic or aggadic discussion. Halakhic texts, like other ancient legal texts, sometimes investigate the different aspects of an issue in detail. Details such as the material, form, or decoration of a piece of jewellery may have affected the rabbinic regulations concerning these artefacts, and it is these numerous fragmentary details which need to be investigated. Narrative fictions may contain realistic elements and are no less important as sources of information about ancient Jewish daily life.

4.3 The Repertoire of Jewellery

Our knowledge of the types of jewellery datable to the early Roman period (the latter days of the Second Temple) in the Land of Israel depends solely on archaeological finds. It is only from the later Roman period (i.e. the tannaitic and amoraic periods) that we have some literary evidence as well. However, only a handful of jewels are mentioned by name in rabbinic literature (Krauss 1910: 312–322; Hirshberg 1923: 39–44; Grossmark 1994a: 9–61, ibid. Appendix A, 360–362), usually within a halakhic context.

The most important sources in this regard are the jewellery lists found in rabbinic literature. The earliest ones are those transmitted in Mishnah tractates Kelim and Shabbat and may be dated to the second century CE. One of them lists women's jewellery as susceptible to being contaminated by religious impurity (M. Kel. 11:8). Another one lists jewellery which women were forbidden to wear and go out with into the public domain on the Sabbath (M. Shab. 6:1; T. Shab. 4: 6). A third list, probably also of tannaitic origin, is the prohibition of the use of articles of value decorated with figural motifs (T. A. Z. 5:1).

Nevertheless, it is a Palestinian amoraic list of jewellery based on a biblical text (Isa. 3:18–23; Platt 1979 and 1992) that is the most important text for the study of the kind of jewellery that was used in the Land of Israel at that time (y. Shab. 6:4, 8b). Jews of the late Roman period spoke Aramaic. In order to make the Hebrew terminology of the biblical list understandable to their contemporaries, sages translated, explained, and identified the names of the biblical jewels. The result is a text that contains names of jewels that were in use in the Land of Israel during the amoraic period. It is worth noting that some of the translated names are Greek and Latin loanwords, whereas others are based on Near Eastern Semitic languages. Therefore the text reflects a mixture of eastern and western linguistic influences which prevailed in the Land of Israel during the Roman period.

When discussing legal issues in connection with a certain artefact, sages some-times provide further details. A text from tractate Avodah Zarah of the Tosefta (5:2), dealing with the use of rings, is a good example, showing what kind of information can be gained from a halakhic debate. Signet rings fall into two categories. The first category, described by the Tosefta as a ring 'when it projects', is the signet ring with its seal made by the *cameo* technique (the signet stone is given the form of a relief and the markings which it leaves upon the sealant are embedded). The second category is described as a ring which 'does not project'. The seal of these rings is made by the *intaglio* technique (the seal design is incised and embedded; the *intaglio* seal created design markings that protruded from the sealant). The division into two categories dictated the halakhic attitude to signet rings (Grossmark 2005: 218–20). The implications of the rabbinic legal evidence have only rarely been investigated by scholars involved with jewellery studies.

4.4 The Manufacture of Jewellery

On ancient technologies, such as metallurgy and the treatment of precious stones, a number of studies exist (Singer et al. 1954; Forbes 1964). Research into the tech-nologies used for the manufacture of ancient Jewish jewellery pieces reflected in rabbinic literary sources should be based on these studies.

The work environment and tools used by craftsmen also became the subject of rabbinic legal discussions and narratives. Although the literary sources hardly ever refer to a goldsmith's workshop (Gen. R. 84:1 is quite exceptional in this regard), there are references to tools used by gold- and silversmiths. Details of tools, such as the shape, the material they were made of, and the way a certain tool was used were relevant halakhically (cf. M. Kel. 17:17; T. Kelim B.M. 7:10). Considering the various aspects of the manufacture and trade of jewellery, one needs to take into consider-ation the fact that Roman Palestine was a peripheral area, distant from the great cities of the empire, which were the centres of the manufacture and consumption of luxury goods. Trying to overcome the Nabatean hegemony over the trade routes and caravan traffic from the east to the Mediterranean ports, the Romans directed this traffic southwards via the Sinai Desert to Alexandria. Consequently, the trade of luxuries such as precious stones would bypass the Land of Israel (Warmington 1928: 38–41; Grossmark 2005: 13).

Rabbinic narratives suggest that the trade in precious stones was the domain of Arab merchants (y. B.M. 2:5, 8c; y. Dem. 1:3, 22a). A proper knowledge of precious stones and their origins is therefore difficult to ascertain in Palestinian rabbinic texts (Babylonian rabbinic texts which mention precious stones provide evidence of a good knowledge of the subject matter, however, cf. b. R. H. 23a; b. B.B. 74b). In both tannaitic and amoraic texts, precious stones are usually referred to collective-ly, using the formulaic expression 'precious stones and *margaliot* [pearls]' (cf. M.

Abot 6:9; y. Ber. 8:7, 12c). The use of such formulaic expressions and the lack of detailed references to gems in Palestinian rabbinic sources suggest that the use and knowledge of precious stones was limited amongst Palestinian rabbis.

4.5 Jewellery Makers

The process of differentiation and specialization in jewellery production, which reached its peak in Roman imperial times, did not bypass Roman Palestine. In addition to the biblical *zoref* (goldsmith), who probably worked with different kinds of metals, words such as *zehavi* (goldsmith, from the Hebrew word *zehav*–gold), *kasaf* (silversmith, from the Hebrew word *kesef*–silver) or *mefathei avanim* (workers of precious stones) first appear in tannaitic sources (M. Kel. 29:4, 10; T. Suk. 4:6; M. Kel. 29:5). The word *zehavi* also appears as an attribute attached to the name of some Palestinian rabbis (b. Sanh. 4b; y. Betsa 1:9, 60d). The name 'Bar Chrosana', derived from the Greek word *chrosos* (gold), is also found in Palestinian texts (Gen. R. 18:2). Both names probably attested to the occupation of these individuals or their families.

Some evidence of the social status of jewellery makers and their social organizations can also be gathered from rabbinic literature. Goldsmiths were highly esteemed (cf. Num. R. 2:17). Nevertheless, most of our knowledge about Jewish organizations of goldsmiths derives from funeral inscriptions that were found in the Diaspora, either in Roman Syria (IGRR, III, no. 1031) or in Asia Minor (CIJ, II, 46 no. 793; Grossmark 1994b). The only rabbinic evidence of the possible existence of an organization of gold- and silversmiths locates it in Alexandria (T. Suk. 4:6; y. Suk. 5:9, 55b; b. Suk. 51b). No evidence of the existence of jewellers' organizations in Roman Palestine has been found so far (Grossmark 1994b).

4.6 The Social and Cultural Context of the Use of Jewellery

A study of ancient jewellery must also consider the religious, cultural, and social aspects of the use of jewellery artefacts, either in everyday life (such as amulets) or on special occasions (weddings, burials, etc.).

The general use of amulets during the Roman and Byzantine periods has been thoroughly studied (Budge 1930), as has their use amongst Jews (Schrire 1966; Trachtenberg 1970; Naveh/Shaked 1985). Nevertheless, only a few ancient Jewish texts refer to jewellery pieces that were made and used as amulets. Most of these texts deal with gems considered to possess prophylactic or magical qualities (T. Qid. 5:17). A few texts refer to rings that were used as containers for amulets (T. Shab. 4:9). The literary evidence of the use of amulets needs to be correlated with the archaeological evidence of amulets from Roman Palestinian sites (see Galor in this volume). Also, Jewish amulets should be studied within the context of jewellery and jewellery making in antiquity.

The use of jewels at ancient Jewish weddings is a good example of a cultural context about which our knowledge is entirely based on literary data. Sages paid special attention to the adornment of the bride on her wedding day. A midrashic text enumerates twenty-four jewels to adorn a bride (Gen. R. 18:2; Ex. R. 23:5; 41:5). The list that follows is a citation from a biblical list of precious stones (Ez. 28:13). The specification of twenty-four jewels can be considered a literary motif. Since there are other texts which mention the decoration of brides (M. Sot. 9:14), we can, however, assume that the practice was customary amongst ancient Jews, though.

A further example of the use of jewellery in a specific cultural context is the practice of burying precious artefacts with the dead. Josephus described the precious jewels that were buried with Herod (Ant. 17. 196-197). One may assume that Herod's burial was not representative, because of his status as king of Judaea. Later rabbinic sources, such as a *baraita* in tractate Berakot of the Babylonian Talmud (b. Ber. 18b) or the extra-canonical tractate Ebel Rabbati (also known as Semahot) either ignore the practice of burial gifts or limit it to ordinary inexpensive items. The literary information needs to be compared with archaeological data. When studying Jewish burial gifts and grave goods, one must also take the rabbinic rules of ritual (im)purity into consideration: vessels or jewels found in graves might have been exposed to the dead beforehand and were therefore considered ritually contaminated. These items could not be used by the living and might, therefore, have been buried with the dead.

Another aspect of prime importance is the question whether, and to what extent, ancient Jews used jewellery decorated with figural motifs. The question of the relationship between Judaism and (pagan) figural art has been raised quite often in past scholarship, usually in the context of synagogue art. Nevertheless, the works of Urbach (1999) and Levine (1998) can be considered good points of departure for the study of figural art in Jewish jewellery as well. Rabbinic discussions about the use of a ring decorated with idolatrous motifs in tannaitic and amoraic sources suggest that a pragmatic tendency amongst rabbis and Palestinian sages obviously permitted the use of jewellery decorated with idolatrous images (Grossmark 2005: 216–23).

Many issues concerning the socio-cultural use of jewellery have not been studied properly yet. Such studies will help answer the question to what extent Palestinian Jews differed culturally from their Gentile neighbours. It is already well known that Palestinian Jews were well rooted in many aspects of Graeco-Roman culture. Future studies do not have to question whether Palestinian Jews were influenced by their surroundings, but rather how deep these influences permeated. An assumption, which still needs confirmation, is that the local inhabitants adopted customs and fashions originating in non-Jewish cultures, such as the use of Hellenistic and Roman jewellery, and that rabbis accommodated these practices halakhically (Grossmark 2005: 213–26).

5. CONCLUSIONS AND SUGGESTIONS FOR FURTHER STUDY

Gathering information about jewellery from ancient literature can be a Sisyphean task. Ancient writers were usually not interested in jewellery as such. Therefore, the information they supply is partial, limited to those details which are important for their literary purposes. The scholar of ancient jewellery is confronted with a puzzle consisting of numerous pieces of literary data that have to be carefully sifted, examined, and compared with evidence from other sources and Graeco-Roman culture to reconstruct a larger image. The study of ancient jewellery can be conducted only in an interdisciplinary way.

Our knowledge of the types of ancient jewellery depends almost entirely on archaeological finds (see the following section in this book). The archaeological data needs to be correlated with the literary evidence. The literary evidence suggests that there are hardly any rabbinic restrictions on the shape of jewels manufactured and used by Jews, and that rabbis were pragmatic with regard to accepting the non-Jewish material culture of Rome and Byzantium. Therefore, we have to assume that Palestinian Jews used the same kind of jewellery as their non-Jewish neighbours. Further studies are necessary to determine whether the jewellery used by Jews in Roman Palestine forms an integral part of Roman-Byzantine jewellery of the eastern provinces of the Roman Empire. A comprehensive study might support the assumption that jewellers of Roman Palestine used tools, techniques, and raw materials which were common in the eastern Mediterranean in Roman-Byzantine times.

The various social contexts in which jewellery was used by the Jews of Roman Palestine is another area which would benefit from further study. As a second step, these social contexts need to be compared with similar customs and rituals within the neighbouring non-Jewish communities of the Near East.

6. SUGGESTED READING

One could start with either Higgins (1961) or Ogden (1982): both provide a general overview of ancient jewellery. Although rather antiquated, Krauss (1910 reprinted 1966) discusses a wide range of issues concerning jewellery in rabbinic literature. Grossmark (1994a, available in Hebrew only) is the latest publication on the subject. The English summary attached to this dissertation (399ff.) provides a general picture on the subject.

ABBREVIATIONS

···

IGGR = Inscriptiones Graecae ad Res Romanas Pertinertes
CIJ = Corpus Inscriptionum Judaicarum, ed. J. B. Frey

BIBLIOGRAPHY

AYALI, M. (1985). *A Treasury of Terms for Workers in the Literature of the Talmud and the Midrash* [Hebr.]. Tel Aviv: Hakibbutz Hameuchad.

BUDGE, E. A. W. (1930, reprinted 1978). *Amulets and Superstitions.* London and New York: Oxford University Press.

CROSS F. L./LIVINGSTONE E. A. (eds) (1974, reprinted 1990). *The Oxford Dictionary of the Christian Church.* New York: Oxford University Press.

DALMAN, G. (1937). *Arbeit und Sitte in Palästina,* vol. 5. Guetersloh: Bertelsmann.

FORBES, R. J. (1964). *Studies in Ancient Technology.* Leiden: Brill.

GROSSMARK, T. (1994a). 'Jewelry and Jewelry-Making in the Land of Israel at the Time of the Mishnah and Talmud' [Hebr.]. Ph.D. thesis, Tel Aviv University.

—— (1994b). 'Organizations of Goldsmiths and Silversmiths in Eretz Israel During the Roman and Byzantine Periods' [Hebr.], in: *Proceedings of the Eleventh World Congress of Jewish Studies,* Section B, 1. Jerusalem: The World Union of Jewish Studies, 31–38.

—— (2004). 'A "City of Gold" and "Jerusalem of Gold"' [Hebr.]. *New Studies on Jerusalem* 10: 151–161.

—— (2005). 'Laws Regarding Idolatry in Jewelry as a Mirror Image of Jewish-Gentile Relations in the Land of Israel During Mishnaic and Talmudic Times'. *Jewish Studies Quarterly* 12: 213–226.

—— (2009). '"A City of Gold": In Quest of Talmudic Reality'. *Journal of Jewish Studies* 60: 48–59.

HIGGINS, R. A. (1961). *Greek and Roman Jewellery.* London: Methuen.

—— (1965). *Jewelry from Classical Lands.* London: British Museum Publications.

HIRSHBERG, A. S. (1923). 'Women's Beauty and How They Attained It in the Literature of the Sages' [Hebr.]. *Ha'atid* 4: 1–56.

HOFFMAN, H. A. (1969). '"The 'City of Gold" and the "City of Silver"'. *Israel Exploration Journal* 19: 178–180.

ILANI, Z./GOLDBERG Y./WEINBERGER, J. (1991). *Diamonds and Gemstones in Judaica.* Ramat-Gan: The Harry Oppenheimer Diamond Museum.

JART, U. (1970). 'The Precious Stones in the Revelation of St. John XXI 18–21'. *Studia Theologica* 24: 150–181.

KRAUSS, S. (1910, reprinted 1966). *Talmudische Archäologie,* vol. 1. Leipzig: Fock.

LEVINE, L.I. (1998). *Judaism and Hellenism in Antiquity: Conflict or Confluence?* Seattle: University of Washington Press.

MARSHALL, F. H. (1907, reprinted 1968). *Catalogue of Finger Rings, Greek, Etruscan and Roman, in the Department of Antiquities, British Museum.* London: British Museum Publications.

——— (1911, reprinted 1969). *Catalogue of the Jewellery, Greek, Etruscan and Roman in the Department of Antiquities, British Museum.* London: British Museum Publications.

NAVEH, J./SHAKED, S. (1985). *Amulets and Magic Bowls: Aramaic Incantations of Late Antiquity.* Jerusalem: Magnes Press.

OGDEN, J. (1982). *Jewellery of the Ancient World.* New York: Rizzoli.

——— (1992). *Ancient Jewellery.* London: British Museum Press.

PAUL, S. M. (1967). 'Jerusalem—A City of Gold'. *Israel Exploration Journal* 17: 259–263.

——— (1977). 'Jerusalem of Gold—A Song and an Ancient Crown'. *Biblical Archaeology Review* 3: 33–36.

PLATT, E. E. (1979). 'Jewelry of Bible Times and the Catalog of Isa. 3:18–23'. *Andrews University Seminary Studies* 17: 71–84, 189–201.

——— (1992). 'Ancient Israelite Jewelry', in *The Anchor Bible Dictionary*, vol. 3, ed. D. N. Freedman. New York: Doubleday, 823–834.

READER, W. W. (1981). 'The Twelve Jewels of Revelation 21:19–20. Tradition, History and Modern Interpretations'. *Journal of Biblical Literature* 100: 433–457.

SCHRIRE, T. (1966). *Hebrew Amulets: Their Decipherment and Interpretation.* London: Routledge.

SHALEM, N. (1931). 'The Names of Precious Stones' [Hebr.]. *Leshonenu* 3: 291–299.

SINGER, C. et al. (eds) (1954). *A History of Technology*, vol. 1. Oxford: Clarendon Press.

SPERBER, D. (1993). *Material Culture in Eretz Israel During the Talmudic Period* [Hebr.]. Jerusalem: Yad Izhak Ben Zvi Press; Bar Ilan University Press.

TAIT, H. (ed.)(1989). *Seven Thousand Years of Jewelry.* London: British Museum Publications.

TRACHTENBERG, J. (1970). *Jewish Magic and Superstition: A Study in Folk Religion.* New York: Atheneum.

URBACH, E. E. (1999). 'The Rabbinical Laws of Idolatry in the Second and Third Centuries in the Light of Archaeological and Historical Facts', in *Collected Writings in Jewish Studies.* Jerusalem: Hebrew University, Magnes Press, 151–193.

WARMINGTON, E. H. (1928). *The Commerce Between the Roman Empire and India.* Cambridge: Cambridge University Press.

CHAPTER 21

JEWELLERY: THE ARCHAEOLOGICAL EVIDENCE

KATHARINA GALOR

1. INTRODUCTION

Jewellery tends to be among the best indicators of socio-economic status and its chronological, cultural, and gender-specific nature, and is therefore considered a 'special find' by the archaeologist. In an excavation, jewellery is labelled and packaged separately from the more common finds, such as pottery, glass, and coins. Yet, despite its special status and aesthetic features, and more so than most other categories of finds from Roman Palestine, jewellery has not received the systematic scholarly attention it deserves. The object's inherent value to the reconstruction of daily life and, in particular, of the relations between the Jewish population of Roman and Byzantine Palestine and their Gentile and Christian neighbours, has been largely overlooked.

2. THE STATE OF RESEARCH ON ROMAN JEWELLERY IN PALESTINE

Unlike the literary evidence of jewellery in Roman Palestine, more specifically the rabbinic texts (Grossmark 1994), no complete archaeological and art historical study has been conducted and published. Beyond the region of Palestine, the subject is usually treated as part of a larger geographical area or a broader chronological framework (Hackens/Winkes 1983; Higgins 1961, 1965; Ogden 1982). The relatively large number of museum catalogues devoted to jewellery bespeaks the fact that this special category of ancient objects frequently ends up in collections that do not necessarily emphasize the original context and meaning of the artefact. In excavation reports as well, jewellery finds are often treated marginally, as part of the larger documentation of a site (Coen-Uzzielli 1997: 449–53; Clamer 2003: 171–83; Chernov 2007: 512–15). Few studies deal specifically with Roman-Byzantine jewellery in Palestine. Moreover, the special attention that gold jewellery has received in the context of the ancient 'Jerusalem of Gold' crown is not necessarily unique to Palestine (Paul 1967: 259–63; 1977: 33–36; 2005: 787–94; Hoffner, Jr. 1969: 178–80; Grossmark 2004: 151–61). Studies devoted to Graeco-Roman jewellery in general have often focused primarily, or even exclusively, on gold (Hackens/Winkes 1983; Pfeiler 1970; Bromberg et al. 1997).

3. The Archaeological Context

As most ancient jewellery was, and is, found outside of its original context of use, its value as a source of information on daily life in antiquity is relatively limited. Its most common location within an archaeological site is the burial complex or tomb, reflective of the custom in antiquity of burying the dead with their jewellery. Although mostly found in female tombs, we know men also wore jewellery. Fewer pieces of jewellery are found in Jewish tombs than in pagan and Christian ones. However, this under-representation of jewellery in Jewish burials does not imply that Jews wore less jewellery than their pagan and Christian counterparts. In addition to its discovery in burials, jewellery is sometimes uncovered in vessels hidden under the floor or in walls of houses or caves, most likely deposited there when its owners hastily fled their homes in times of war and peril, with the hope of returning and recovering their valuables. Jewellers collected fragments of jewellery for repair, melting, or reuse and, as a result, jewellery is also sometimes found alongside craftsmen's tools, shedding light on the technical aspects of its production (Gonen 1997: 10). Unfortunately, the provenance of many pieces of ancient jewellery is not known to us. Regardless, however, of the jewellery's history of discovery, the object itself can give us some indication of its original use, and cultural, economic, and chronological context. Contemporary literary evidence and artistic representations of jewellery in the form of statuary, reliefs, mosaics, and paintings should also be taken into consideration when examining ancient jewellery, with an eye toward understanding its use in a given society.

The concern of this overview is to ascertain jewellery's association with Palestine and its contribution to our understanding of daily life during the Roman and Byzantine periods, based on the study of objects discovered in a documented archaeological context. Owing to the difficulty in differentiating between Jewish, pagan, and Christian contexts before the end of the third and the beginning of the fourth centuries CE, it is not always clear to whom the jewellery belonged.

4. JEWELLERY TYPES

The repertoire of jewellery in Roman-Byzantine Palestine, worn primarily but not exclusively by women, seems to correspond exactly to what was worn by contemporaries in other parts of the Roman and Byzantine empires—necklaces, earrings, bracelets, armbands, finger rings, nose rings, diadems, brooches, clothes pins, ornamental chains, and coins. In Talmudic literature, cosmetics and hair accessories were considered an integral part of jewellery (see Grossmark in this volume); we should add to this survey hairpins and hairnets as well as cosmetic paraphernalia. Jewellery boxes and mirrors form a closely associated category of items that should also be considered in this context. Rather than examining jewellery by type or site, we will organize the selected items according to material. For want of a complete catalogue of jewellery in Palestine, the technological and stylistic development of the jewellery for the Roman-Byzantine period in Palestine cannot yet be established. However, even for other regions where typological divisions within the Roman-Byzantine period have been made, scholars were unable to reach common grounds (Gup/Spencer 1983: 118–19). Generally speaking, the chronological trends of jewellery styles and techniques prevalent at the time in the larger region are reflected in the jewellery of Palestine.

4.1 Gold

Gold is probably one of the first-known metals, as it occurs naturally in recognizable quantity and form. Early on, it established its pre-eminence in jewellery production and trade throughout the ancient world (Bromberg et al. 1997: 15–20; Ogden 1982: 10–11). Gold jewellery, perhaps more than any other type of jewellery in Roman-Byzantine Palestine, clearly reveals the characteristic fusion of western and eastern techniques and styles prevalent in other major urban centres of the Roman Near East, such as Antioch and Palmyra (Gup/Spencer 1983: 115–23). Whether most of the jewellery was made locally or was imported is difficult to determine. It is also not clear to what extent the more luxurious items are connected to the privileged status of those who wore them, or if they should be perceived as an indication of social conventions or religious beliefs.

The most elaborate assemblages of gold jewellery from the early Roman period (first century BCE to fourth century CE) come from funerary contexts that are believed to be pagan. Noteworthy are several finds from tombs in Jerusalem dating to the second and third centuries (see Fig. 21.1).

A gold diadem, a disk featuring the impression of the Gorgon's head, and a necklace holding a ring from which five miniature pendants are suspended—a pomegranate, a pointed amphora, a lamp, a basket, and a key—were uncovered in a woman's sarcophagus (Vincent 1900; de Ridder 1920). Another exceptional discovery from a contemporary tomb with a lead coffin contained a brooch with an engraved cameo, an engraved ring, and an earring decorated with a pearl and stones (Kelleher 1986: 236–37 and Gonen 1997: 32). Finally, a bracelet strung with groups of three elongated beads of alternating gold and blue lapis lazuli was

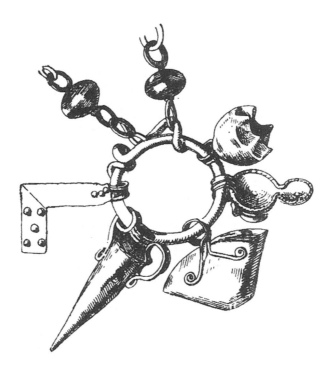

Fig. 21.1 Gold assemblage found in a late Roman tomb in Jerusalem, drawn by de Ridder.

Drawing: de Ridder

found in another Roman period tomb in the city. A third-century CE grave in Kefar Giladi in the Upper Galilee (Kelleher 1986: 32) revealed a gold diadem set with various coloured stones. More common and simpler types of gold jewellery were uncovered in one of the first- to fourth-century Akeldama Tombs in Jerusalem containing an assemblage of twelve earrings (Avni/Greenhut 1996: 7; Winter 1996: 109–10). Those earrings represent a more traditional and less elaborate kind of jewellery that was found in other funerary contexts throughout the country, both at urban and rural sites representing a variety of ethnic and religious populations.

Gold rings, the majority of which were signet rings made by the intaglio technique, were found in pagan, Jewish, and Christian contexts. Representations of biblical figures, saints, and crosses on rings are numerous in the context of fourth- to seventh-century Palestine, as well as in the rest of the Byzantine Empire (Israeli/Mevorah 2006: 161; Biers/Terry 2004: 217). The three-dimensional representation of the Holy Sepulchre on a ring from Jerusalem (Mazar 2000: 63) exemplifies the prominent role of religious cult and belief in Christian society. No equivalent is known in the context of Jewish society at the time.

4.2 Silver and Other Metals

Unlike gold, the use of silver in ancient jewellery is rare (Ogden 1982: 22–23) and only a few examples from Palestine are known (Coen-Uzzielli 1997: 452; Chernov 2007: 515). In contrast, we have numerous testimonies for the use of other metals, such as bronze and iron (Chernov 2007: 514, 115, 534; Coen-Uzzielli 1997: 452). Bracelets and finger rings, usually of simple design, were found in pagan, Jewish, and Christian tombs, similar to the plain annular types known throughout the Roman and Byzantine periods. Iconographic representations on coins and medals, where a specific religious attribution is possible, increase in number during the Byzantine period. However, whereas depictions of crosses on rings are numerous (Biers/Terry 2004: 217; Israeli/Mevorah 2006: 161), no examples of menorahs on Byzantine metal jewellery pieces are known. Several bronze-cast crossbow *fibulae* (Nagy et al. 1996: 231), apparently brought to Palestine by Roman legionaries, were particularly popular between the fourth and fifth centuries CE (Biers/Terry 2004: 182). They were typically worn by men, usually military officers and civil officials. Pins and cosmetic paraphernalia were also frequently made of metals (Dayagi-Mendels 1989: 74).

4.3 Glass

The most common glass jewellery includes bracelets, finger rings, and ear ornaments. Most bracelets and finger rings are made of one piece. In earrings, glass, in the form of beads or pendants, is usually attached to the metal (Spaer 2001: 193). Most of the looped pendants and bracelets, either plain or with a simple tooled decoration, seem to be locally produced. Until the third century CE, beads in Palestine lacked any distinguishing qualities and probably included both imported and locally made examples (Spaer 2001: 30–32). A representative assortment of beads from the Roman and Byzantine periods was found in large multigenerational burial complexes (Winter 1996: 111–15) as well as in individual burials (Clamer 2003: 171–83); these beads were not part of a particular piece of jewellery, but were scattered among other burial items. Three types of looped pendants were common in the Byzantine period—drop- or jar-pendants, juglet pendants, and disk pendants with stamped motifs (Spaer 2001: 170). Representations of saints and crosses on looped circular pendants can be associated with Palestine's Christian population. The Jewish counterparts of these pendants feature a menorah (Spaer 2001: 181; see Fig. 21.2).

Among the more astonishing recent jewellery finds from glass are two rings found in a second-century CE Jewish context on the outskirts of ancient Jerusalem (Bar-Nathan/Sklar-Parnes 2007: 57–64).

4.4 Precious Stones

The popularity of polychromatic combinations of metals with glass, pearls and gemstones increased gradually over the Roman and Byzantine periods. The varieties

(a)   (b)

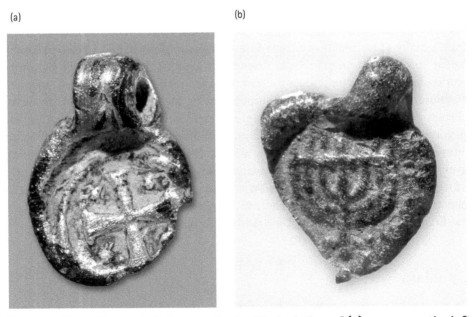

Fig. 21.2 Byzantine period glass pendant with depiction of (a) a cross on the left and (b) a menorah on the right (courtesy of the Israel Antiquities Authority).

of necklace, brooch, and earring designs are almost endless. Although Palestine was not considered a main centre for the production and trade of jewellery, we know that both Gentiles and Jews participated actively (Grossmark 2005: 219). The archaeological evidence appears to suggest that consumers, too, were represented by all religious groups of Roman and Byzantine Palestine. Very elaborate jewellery with colourful embellishments encased in gold is usually considered to be imported rather than locally made, and is often associated with Palestine's pagan or Christian population. Gems and semi-precious stones, such as reddish carnelian, jasper, rock crystal, amethyst, garnet, and malachite were formed, reworked, shaped into beads, or engraved, most frequently to accentuate gold jewellery. Over time, cheaper man-made materials, such as faience, glass, double quartz-based materials, and colourants, replaced coloured stones. The largest number of gems in Palestine can be found on rings that were often used as seals (Bromberg et al. 1997: 109), appearing not only where Roman legionaries were known to have been stationed (Peleg 2003: 52–67), but also in Jewish contexts (Grossmark 2005: 217–19; Hirschfeld/Feinberg Vamosh 2005: 29). A variety of gemstones, such as adamantine, agate, onyx, and sardonyx (Grossmark 2005: 217), were used to produce cameos. The above-mentioned gold brooch found in a second- to third-century grave in Jerusalem features an enclosed onyx cameo of four light and dark layers; the engraving depicts the bust of Minerva in profile.

4.5 Other Materials

Other than bone, sometimes used for hairpins or cosmetic utensils (Avigad 1983: 199; Dayagi-Mendels 1989: 74), objects made of organic materials have rarely survived outside of the Dead Sea region. Most significant are a number of wooden combs and a hairnet from Qumran and Wadi Murraba'at from the first and second centuries (Ariel et.al. 2007: 121; Dayagi-Mendels 1989: 74) and several second-century wooden mirrors with inserted brass disks from the Judaean desert Cave of Letters (Yadin 1971: 118, 157, 158). A cylindrical pyxis and barrel-shaped jewellery box are also to be included in this category of unusual finds. Although these objects were all found in clearly Jewish contexts, nothing suggests that similar objects would not have been also used by other populations of Roman and Byzantine Palestine. Examples of circular clay mirrors from the Byzantine period found in the Jewish village of Ein Gedi (Hirschfeld 2007: 520, 539) are also representative of the region at large.

4.6 Socio-Economic, Cultural, Religious, and Gender-Related Implications of Jewellery Studies

As jewellery is a symbol of social rank and economic status, the lavish and aristocratic tombs tend to include the more luxurious jewellery items. Wealthy urban families buried in large funerary complexes tend to have had more extravagant tastes than the poor, and were often individually interred in rural areas of Palestine. Jewish burials tend to have fewer pieces of jewellery than pagan and Christian ones, as can be seen in burials from the Roman and Byzantine periods (Mazar 1973). Although literary sources clearly state that men and children, besides women, wore jewellery, the frequent presence of jewellery in female burials, and the well-documented representations of adorned women, suggest women were the primary consumers.

The small amount of jewellery from pre-70 CE Palestine probably indicates the region's relatively insulated material culture, which changes gradually with the Roman conquest and its inclusion within the territories of the Roman and Byzantine Empires. It seems that during the Herodian period Jews were relatively strict in their interpretation of the Second Commandment, rendering figural representations almost non-existent. In the course of the late Roman and Byzantine periods, however, this trend was to change dramatically, as is clearly visible in the jewellery that was found and used in Jewish contexts.

As the Christian church gained the upper hand and much of the country's spiritual and economic powers became centralized, so its jewellery reflected the new religion. The most luxurious pieces of jewellery from Byzantine Palestine should not exclusively be associated with individuals and their economic and social status, but with the centralized powers of the Christian faith represented by the Church and its ecclesiastic elite. Whereas the cross of Christianity was mirrored by the menorah of Judaism, the latter's appearance on jewellery from the Byzantine period is far less preponderant.

5. SUGGESTED READING

Gonen (1997) provides a brief and very general survey of jewellery in ancient Israel from pre-historic to modern times. Hirschfeld and Feinberg Vamosh (2005) describe the discovery of a few jewellery pieces that were found in their original domestic context. Grossmark (2005) opens a window into the fascinating world of jewellery and its value as an indicator of religious affiliation.

BIBLIOGRAPHY

ARIEL, D./KATZ, H./SADEH, S./SEGAL, M. (eds) (2007). *The Dead Sea Scrolls by the Israel Antiquities Authority, Jerusalem*. Jerusalem: Israel Antiquities Authority.

AVIGAD, N. (1983). *Discovering Jerusalem.* Nashville, Camden, New York: Thomas Nelson.

AVNI, G./GREENHUT, Z. (1996). *The Akeldama Tombs: Three Burial Caves in the Kidron Valley, Jerusalem.* Israel Antiquities Authority Reports 1. Jerusalem: Israel Antiquities Authority.

BAR-NATHAN, R./SKLAR-PARNES, D. A. (2007). 'A Jewish Settlement in Orine between the Revolts' [Hebr.], in: *New Studies in the Archaeology of Jerusalem in Its Region. Collected Papers,* ed. J. Patrich and D. Amit. Jerusalem: Israel Antiquities Authority, 57–64.

BIERS, J. C./TERRY, J. (eds) (2004). *Testament of Time. Selected Objects from the Collection of Palestinian Antiquities in the Museum of Art and Archaeology, University of Missouri-Columbia.* Madison, NJ: Fairleigh Dickinson University Press.

BROMBERG, A. R./DEPPERT-LIPPITZ, B./DENNIS, J. (1997). *Ancient Gold Jewelry at the Dallas Museum of Art.* Dallas: Dallas Museum of Art.

CHERNOV, E. (2007). 'Metal Objects and Small Finds from En-Gedi', in *En-Gedi Excavations II. Final Report (1996–2002),* ed. Y. Hirschfeld. Jerusalem: Israel Exploration Society, 507–31.

CLAMER, C. (2003). 'Jewellery Finds from the Cemetery, Khirbet Qumran et "Ain Feshkha II", in *Études d'anthropologie, de physique et de chimie,* ed. J.-B. Humbert and J. Gunneweg. Göttingen: Vandenhoeck and Ruprecht, 171–83.

COEN-UZZIELLI, T. (1997). 'Marble Decorations, Wall Mosaics, and Small Finds', in *The Roman Baths of Hammat Gader: Final Report,* ed. Y. Hirschfeld, Jerusalem: Israel Exploration Society, 442–55.

DAYAGI-MENDELS, M. (1989). *Perfumes and Cosmetics in the Ancient World.* Jerusalem: Israel Museum.

GONEN, R. (1997). *Jewelry through the Ages at the Israel Museum.* Jerusalem: Israel Museum.

GROSSMARK, T. (1994). 'Jewelry and Jewelry-Making in the Land of Israel at the Time of the Mishnah and Talmud' [Hebr.]. PhD. thesis, Tel-Aviv University.

—— (2004). 'A "City of Gold" and "Jerusalem of Gold"' [Hebr.]. *New Studies on Jerusalem* 10: 151–61.

—— (2005). 'Laws Regarding Idolatry in Jewelry as a Mirror Image of Jewish-Gentile Relations in the Land of Israel During Mishnaic and Talmudic Times', *Jewish Studies Quarterly* 12: 213–26.

GUP, A. R./SPENCER, E. S. (1983). 'Roman Syria', in: *Gold Jewelry: Craft, Style and Meaning from Mycenae to Constantinopolis,* ed. T. Hackens and R. Winkes. Leuven: Institut superieur d'archéologie et d'histoire de l'art, College Erasme.

HACKENS, T./WINKES, R. (eds) (1983). *Gold Jewelry: Craft, Style and Meaning from Mycenae to Constantinopolis.* Leuven: Institut superieur d'archéologie et d'histoire de l'art, College Erasme.

HIGGINS, R. (1961). *Greek and Roman Jewellery.* 2nd ed. London: Methuen.

—— (1965). *Jewellery from Classical Lands.* London: Trustees of the British Museum.

HIRSCHFELD, Y. (2007). *En-Gedi Excavations II. Final Report (1996–2002).* Jerusalem: Israel Exploration Society.

——/FEINBERG VAMOSH, M. (2005). 'A Country Gentleman's Estate. Unearthing the Splendors of Ramat Hanadiv'. *Biblical Archaeology Review* 31/2: 18–31.

HOFFNER, JR. H. A. (1969). 'The "City of Gold" and the "City of Silver" (Varia)'. *Israel Exploration Journal* 19: 178–80.

ISRAELI, Y./MEVORAH, D. (2006). *Cradle of Christianity: Treasures from the Holy Land,* Jerusalem: Israel Museum.

KELLEHER, B. (1986). *Treasures of the Holy Land*. New York: Metropolitan Museum of Art.

MAZAR, B. (1973). *Beth She'arim: Report on the excavations during 1936–1940*. New Brunswick: Rutgers University Press on behalf of the Israel Exploration Society and the Institute of Archaeology, Hebrew University.

MAZAR, E. (2000). *The Complete Guide to the Temple Mount Excavations* [Hebr.]. Jerusalem: Shoham.

NAGY, R. M./MEYERS, E./MEYERS, C./WEISS, Z. (eds) (1996). *Sepphoris in Galilee. Crosscurrents of Culture*. Winona Lake: North Carolina Museum of Art.

OGDEN, J. (1982). *Jewelry of the Ancient World*. London: Trefoil.

PAUL, S. M. (1967). 'Jerusalem: A City of Gold'. *Israel Exploration Journal* 17: 259–63.

—— (1977). 'Jerusalem of Gold: A Song and an Ancient Crown'. *Biblical Archaeology Review* 3: 38–41.

—— (2005). 'Jerusalem of Gold—Revisited', in *'I Will Speak the Riddles of Ancient Times' (Ps 78:2b): Archaeological and Historical Studies in Honor of Amihai Mazar on the Occasion of his Sixtieth Birthday*, ed. A. M. Maeir and P. de Miroschedji. Winona Lake: Eisenbrauns, 787–94.

PELEG, O. (2003). 'Roman Intaglio Gemstones from Aelia Capitolina'. *Palestine Exploration Quarterly* 135: 52–67.

PFEILER, B. (1970). *Römischer Goldschmuck des ersten und zweiten Jahrhunderts n. Chr. nach datierten Funden*. Mainz: P. von Zabern.

RIDDER, A. DE (1920). 'Parure de Jérusalem au Musée du Louvre'. *Syria* 1: 99–107.

SPAER, M. (2001). *Ancient Glass in the Israel Museum: Beads and Other Small Objects*. Jerusalem: Israel Museum.

VINCENT, L.-H. (1900). 'Une nécropole gréco-romaine à Jérusalem'. *Revue Biblique* 9: 603–607.

WINTER, T. (1996). 'Jewelry and Miscellaneous Objects', in *The Akeldama Tombs: Three Burial Caves in the Kidron Valley, Jerusalem*, eds, G. Avni and Z. Greenhut. Israel Antiquities Authority Reports 1. Jerusalem: Israel Antiquities Authority, 109–16.

YADIN, Y. (1971). *Bar-Kokhba: The Rediscovery of the Legendary Hero of the Second Jewish Revolt against Rome*. London: Weidenfeld & Nicholson, New York: Random House.

CHAPTER 22

FOOD, EATING, AND MEALS

DAVID KRAEMER

1. WHAT DID JEWS IN ROMAN PALESTINE EAT?

Until quite recently, humans have been what is called 'locovores' (eaters of locally grown and produced food) in contemporary parlance: because of limitations in their ability to transport food over longer distances, people had to rely mostly on what was produced in their immediate environment to gain their sustenance. In the absence of effective means of preservation, most foods could not easily be transported over long distances and periods of time, for consumption in faraway locations. Of course, this limitation does not apply to all foods—fruits could be dried, meat and fish salted, and grain and grapes rendered into beer and wine. In fact, evidence for lively trade in foreign delicacies in many periods and places—including the one that concerns us here—is abundant. But transport and preservation added cost, so most people—that is, those who were not wealthy—could not enjoy such delicacies, apart from special occasions. The inescapable reality is, therefore, that Jews in this eastern Mediterranean Roman province must have eaten more or less exactly as did their neighbours.

This recognition allows us to evaluate scholarship pertaining to the Jewish diet in Palestine from the first to the sixth centuries CE. Beginning with Samuel Krauss's groundbreaking *Talmudische Archäologie* (1910, vol. 1: 78–126), scholars who have described the Palestinian Jewish diet in Roman times have relied primarily, though not exclusively (see below), on the evidence of Palestinian rabbinic literature (the Mishnah, Tosefta, Talmud Yerushalmi, and Midrashim). The value of this literature is that it offers a potentially rich testimony relating to Jewish foods and eating (see Safrai 1994: 104–46). The problem is the nature of the source material: this is a literature which speaks for a small segment of the Palestinian Jewish population, motivated by its own particular elitist, polemical, and even sectarian concerns. So the fundamental question, in this as in other matters of historical interest, is: can the rabbinic testimony be believed?

To illustrate the problem, consider a text that has been cited as evidence by virtually everyone who has written on this question. M. Ketubbot 5:8 (lines 1–12 in MS Kaufmann A 50, translated here) enumerates a husband's obligations to his wife in the matter of food:

One who provides his wife through an agent should not provide her with less than two *kabs* of wheat or [and?] four *kabs* of barley [for the six days of the week] . . . He gives her half a *kab* of legumes and half a *log* of [olive] oil and a *kab* of dried figs or a *maneh* of pressed figs, but if he doesn't have these, he assigns her other fruits in their place.
(The next Mishnah suggests that Sabbath food is independent of the measures given here.)

This is a prescriptive, not a descriptive text. Furthermore, it speaks only for the rabbis whose circle produced the Mishnah. On the basis of this text alone, we have no way of evaluating how *what ought to be*, in the opinion of the rabbinic authors, relates to *what is*. Moreover, we have no way of knowing whether the measures given by the rabbis are commonly accepted, generous, or stingy. So does this list offer us a view of the common Palestinian Jewish 'food basket' in the late second century, as some scholars claim? Obviously, the rabbinic text will not, by itself, allow us to answer this question. This illustrates the problem with using rabbinic documents as primary sources for Jewish daily life in this period.

This does not, of course, mean that rabbinic texts are worthless in gleaning information on the Palestinian Jewish diet and related matters during these centuries. It is commonly—and reasonably—assumed by scholars that details or elements that do not directly serve the prescriptive or polemical purposes of rabbinic discourse are more likely to reflect the 'reality on the ground' than details that do. For example, narratives that portray the wicked (Jewish or Gentile) eating pork, or the righteous avoiding it, must be read with suspicion. References to pork-eating can too easily serve as a trope for us to read them as testimonies of historical reality. If, on the other hand, narratives portray residents of second-century Palestine as eating lentils or other legumes, there is little reason to be similarly suspicious of the rabbinic account: no discernible purpose is served by representing either the righteous or the wicked as eating these foods. So the realia represented in rabbinic literature may provide importance evidence on actual practice, as long as the purpose of the texts is evaluated with sufficient suspicion.

If the picture offered in rabbinic literature is supported by evidence preserved in other contemporary literatures—Josephus, the New Testament, Graeco-Roman texts (see Garnsey 1999, Dupont 1999, and Corbier 1999)—then this will strengthen the assumptions based on each. Even more significantly, the careful study of animal and plant remains from the Roman-period Land of Israel will yield results that are in no need of documentary support, though they do, of course, require interpretation (see Dar 1995, Grantham 1996, Hesse/Wapnish 1997, and Lev-Tov 2003). The same is true of archaeological remains pertaining to food production (see, e.g. Dar 1995: 331–2). If the literature of the rabbis is supported by these 'hard facts' (relatively speaking, as they too are in need of interpretation), then we will be able to give greater credence to the picture suggested by their combined testimony.

Based upon the literary and archaeological record, the following can safely be said about the diet in Palestine in the Roman period: Bread was unquestionably the staple of the local diet during these centuries. Claims have been made that it supplied 50 per cent of calories on a regular basis (but see below). In addition, olive oil and legumes (including beans, lentils, chickpeas, and vetch) were common. These were supplemented on the Sabbath (for Jews celebrating the Sabbath; others would have added these supplements on equivalent festive occasions) by fish, other vegetables, and possibly meat (mostly lamb and goat, but also deer, gazelle, chicken, and others). Common fruits included figs, dates, carob, pomegranates, melons, and plums. Water was stored and used for drink, but wine of various qualities, mixed with water, was the most common drink, at least for men (Broshi 2001: 144–56 and 162). Dairy was consumed as cheese and less frequently as milk (Rosenblum 2008: 20–5, following Broshi 2001: 121–43, and Dar 1995: 327–32).

There is little doubt that Jews were actively involved in the production and trade of most, if not all, of these products. Domestic and commercial bakers are frequently mentioned in Palestinian rabbinic literature, and evidence of both kinds of production (grinding stones and ovens in domestic and commercial settings) has been found at many sites. Likewise, the ubiquity of olive presses attests to the involvement of Palestinian Jews in the production of olive oil (Safrai 1994: 188–90). The abundant evidence of markets and a market economy, in Jewish as in non-Jewish settings, supports the same conclusion (Safrai 1994; 222–316; Rosenfeld/Menirav 2005: 133–6).

The claim that bread constituted roughly 50 per cent of the typical daily calorie intake is offered by Broshi (Broshi 2001: 121–4), based upon the measure given in M. Ketubbot 5:8, quoted above. But this assertion must be questioned for reasons already articulated. As we noted, it is impossible to evaluate what the measures given in the Mishnah actually represent. Is the husband asked by the rabbis to be generous with his wife or are they requiring just a minimum? Is the husband, whose support rabbis legislate, assumed to be wealthy or poor? Does their suggested menu apply in years of plenty or years of famine, or both? Is the short list given in the Mishnah (bread, legumes, olive oil, and dried figs) meant to represent all foods consumed in a normal day, or just the portion that must be supplied by the husband? Would some wives, in other words, have other sources available that would lead to a more varied, richer diet? None of these questions can confidently be answered based upon the scant information provided in the Mishnah, so claims for diet based upon this Mishnah must be made extremely carefully. Broshi and those who follow him (see Rosenblum 2008: 20-1) overstep this necessary caution.

At the same time, the abundance of references to bread in the contemporary literature, along with its special place in the table-rituals of Palestinian Jews and Christians, leaves no doubt as to the importance of bread in the Roman-Palestinian diet. Of course, depending upon the social status of the persons in question and natural conditions in any given season, bread—whether from fine or coarse wheat flour or from another grain—might have figured more or less significantly. It does not really matter what percentage of the necessary calorific intake bread supplied. At whatever level, bread was considered the staff of life.

Another question relating to the Palestinian diet in the Roman period concerns meat (and secondarily fish) and its prevalence. Common wisdom, repeated by most who have written on the Palestinian diet of this period (Krauss 1910, vol. 1: 108–110, Broshi 2001: 132), has it that meat was a relatively rare item, consumed only on special, usually festive occasions. References to meat consumption in rabbinic literature generally support this picture (for example, T. Peah 4:10, seeking to illustrate the requirement to support the wealthy who have fallen on hard luck according to their former circumstances, reports a case in which an 'extravagant' amount of meat is supplied; y. Peah 8:8, 21a expresses shock at the suggested quantity. Together, they clearly imply that even the wealthy in Palestine consumed smaller quantities of meat, while the common person consumed just modest amounts). A much repeated economic argument (animals were needed for their labour and for the renewable essential products—such as wool and dairy—of which they were the source) leads to the same conclusion. Even Philo, though admittedly not a Palestinian, supports such an assumption. Though he lived in an Alexandrian setting characterized by great plenty, one in which we might expect meat-eating to be more common, he writes of 'innumerable herds of cattle in every direction' that are milked daily because 'milk is the greatest source of profit to all breeders of stock, being partly used in a liquid state and partly allowed to coagulate and solidify, so as to make cheese' (On the Virtues 144). He does not even mention domestic animals' value as meat.

But the archaeology of Roman and Byzantine sites in Palestine offers what is perhaps a different picture. In a careful collation and analysis of findings from different sites during this period, Justin Lev-Tov summarizes the evidence as follows: 'Taken together, archaeological evidence from animal bones, human bone chemistry, agricultural economics, and even ceramic analysis strongly suggests that the Hellenistic and Roman period populations of Palestine ate meat on a regular basis. As Dar (1995: 332) suggests, it is time to rethink and re-examine the 'meat as luxury food in the ancient world' hypothesis, given the growing amount of archaeological evidence which contradicts this long-held view' (Lev-Tov 2003: 429). It is difficult to evaluate what quantity of bones would allow the conclusion that meat was eaten (by everyone?) 'on a regular basis'. The chronological limits of certain sites seem to make such a conclusion questionable. One would have to ask whether the locations in which the quantities of bones were discovered can be considered representative of Jewish society as a whole, or of particular groups or social classes within it only. In any case, archaeology forces us to re-evaluate long-held assumptions based on literary texts. Indeed, it may well be that meat-eating (in what quantities and forms?) was more than an occasional event.

Though this finding regarding meat is important, even more important, in Lev-Tov's opinion, is the quantity of fish bones discovered at many sites. The bones tend to represent a small number of species: sea bream, tuna, and mackerel, groupers, and mullets (Lev-Tov 2003: 435–6). In Lev-Tov's view, the fact that these are all Mediterranean species, and that they are all found in some abundance at in-land sites, is evidence of a well-organized fishing industry dedicated to catching, preserving, and shipping these specific fish to a dispersed market (437). Summarizing these two bodies of evidence, Lev-Tov writes: 'Rather than the widespread abandonment of the traditional Near Eastern diet which emphasized sheep and goats, we have the situation that dishes featuring Mediterranean fish complemented the pre-existing cuisine' (Lev-Tov 2003: 439). He considers this phenomenon a development of the Roman period (ibid. 440): what is uniquely Roman about the Palestinian diet is the increase of fish in the local diet. To the degree discernible from the remains, other elements of the diet would have remained constant over time.

2. JEWISH AND GENTILE DIETS?

This leads us to another question, namely, whether and to what degree there was a uniquely Jewish diet in antiquity. An answer is complicated by the question that lies at its foundation: what would a uniquely Jewish diet look like? Scholars have already suggested that perhaps the best indicator of a Jewish diet would be the *absence* of species forbidden by the biblical food regulations, particularly the absence of pork. These regulations, elaborated in Leviticus 11 and repeated in Deuteronomy 14, suggest criteria for the 'purity' or 'impurity' of different creatures (with the exception of birds, for which no general criteria are provided), and then offer long lists of forbidden species. Furthermore, though pork has no special status in the biblical context, it is clear that, beginning in the Hellenistic period, whether for religious-political reasons or for culinary-cultural reasons, pork became an especially abhorred food among Jews (see Kraemer 2007: 30–3). Beginning with this recognition, archaeologists have often seen the 'absence' of pork remains, in particular, as evidence of a Jewish settlement or home, and the presence of pork remains as evidence of Gentile residence. But it is difficult to sustain this picture. As Lev-Tov, reports, pig bones (and the bones of other forbidden species) are widespread at Palestinian sites, even if sometimes only relatively low quantities have been found (Lev-Tov 2003: 430). The low quantities, Lev-Tov says, are best explained by the fact that pigs were rare in diets throughout the Near East during these centuries (ibid. 440). Nevertheless, it is also true that pig remains increase in importance later in this period, as the evidence from Byzantine Sepphoris and Tel Hesban shows (ibid. 431).

What does the presence of pig remains, even at Jewish sites, reveal? Some have seen these finds in connection with the appetites of the Gentile population, proposing that Jews may have raised pigs to sell to Gentiles. But Lev-Tov dissents: 'Given that the Carmel and Galilee regions were heavily Jewish in the Roman era it would seem a simpler explanation to suggest that pig bones are present at Jewish settlements because they ate pork' (ibid. 431). This is a reasonable analysis, far more so than the one that seeks to keep pork out of the mouths of Jews. If Seth Schwartz is correct in his conclusion that many Jews in Palestine during this period were effectively common Roman pagans (Schwartz 2001: 129–161), then the presence of pork in the Jewish diet will occasion no surprise. Moreover, the evidence from all periods (even excluding modernity) suggests clearly that some Jews have always transgressed the laws of the Torah, including food laws (Kraemer 2007: 123–137). There is no reason to believe that the period under discussion here was any different.

On the basis of the animal remains alone, it is impossible to judge how many Jews in Roman and Byzantine Palestine 'kept kosher'. Roman writers (Tacitus, Juvenal, others) testify to the Jews' avoidance of pork and sometimes also the meat of other forbidden species, but, again, it is impossible to know the relative proportions of those who constituted an 'exception' and those who followed the 'rule'. What is evident, though, is that the rules known to these Roman writers are those known from the Hebrew Bible. There is no evidence of rabbinic kashrut regulations during this period outside of rabbinic texts. This observation is very important for evaluating Jewish eating habits in Palestine in the first centuries CE.

Rabbinic kashrut (I will use the term 'kashrut' to refer only to rabbinic food regulations), in contrast to biblical food laws, is characterized by new restrictions on the mixture of meat and dairy. Rabbinic regulations with respect to the separation of these categories of food grow increasingly elaborate during the period that concerns us here. But one observation needs to be emphasized: whatever the precise status of the development of these practices at any given stage, laws regulating the mixture of meat and dairy would have been followed only by those Jews who allied themselves with the circles of the rabbis. Ordinary Jews, if they respected Jewish eating regulations at all, would have observed primarily those laws enumerated in the Tanakh (Hebrew Bible), and particularly those in the Torah (Pentateuch). If they were at all familiar with the rabbinic practices, they may well have ignored them.

3. SEPARATING JEW FROM JEW

However much Jewish food practices may have separated Jews from non-Jews (more on this below), they also separated Jew from Jew. Jews who observed rabbinic eating regulations would often have found it impossible to eat in non-rabbinic households, where cheese might easily have been served with meat, and where concerns about drops of milk falling into pots of meat-stew (see M. Hullin 8:3) would have been non-existent. Though rabbinic laws apparently focused on food ingredients, they were also commensality laws. Depending upon the frequency of meat consumption (see above) and the degree of the development of separation practices, the rabbinic and non-rabbinic Jew would have found their mixing greatly restricted whenever the 'table was set'.

The degree of separation is partially a product of how Jews and others in Roman Palestine actually ate. Histories of human eating-technologies commonly assume a picture like the following: the sets of dishes that modern people take for granted were largely unknown before modernity. Except for the wealthy, a cooking pot or two, along with a pan for frying or sautéing, would have sufficed. Soups and stews would have been served in bowls with spoons, but dry foods would have been eaten by hand (hence the attention to what might be stuck on the hand in rabbinic kashrut discussions). Bread (or pita) would have been used for dipping or as a kind of trencher. If this is an accurate picture of eating in Roman Palestine, then for rabbinic Jews, who would have been eating mostly without dishes, the separation of dishes would have been largely irrelevant. Hence, the modern problem of 'kosher dishes', that makes it difficult for a rabbinic Jew to eat with another Jew, would have been minor or non-existent.

But the picture is not so simple. Excavations at Qumran, providing evidence of the practice of at least one community in the late Second Temple period, uncovered a large storage room filled with hundreds of serving and eating vessels. Crucially, vessels for serving and those for eating were stored separately, and there was a far larger quantity of the latter than of the former. Moreover, the eating vessels were simple pottery, clearly manufactured for common use. Together, the quantity and simplicity of these vessels suggest that they were intended for use by individuals during their meals. Included in this large stash were cups, bowls, and flat plates with raised rims. The finds indicate that personal dishes—not only those for communal serving—and plates—not only bowls—characterized the eating habits of the community at Qumran (Haaretz Museum and Ceramics Museum 1979: 14–15).

The discoveries at the Bar Kokhba caves, reflecting early second-century CE practice, similarly show that personal plates were at least sometimes employed for eating in Roman Palestine. Though the number of dishes found at the site is small, their purpose is relatively unambiguous. Four dishes were found in a basket belonging to a woman named Babatha, indicating that they were for personal use. Two are shallow plates, and the other two are bowls. All are of a size appropriate for use by an individual, and all are made of unfinished wood, an inexpensive material. Other plates of a similar nature (either whole or in fragments) were discovered in the same caves, and likewise suggest that Jews and others in Roman Palestine might have used individual dishes for taking their meals (Yadin 1963: 132–5 and plates 39–40).

For those who used plates and other dishes, rabbinic kashrut regulations may well have made sharing a meal with non-rabbinic Jews more difficult (depending upon other principles that defined the application of kashrut laws). But even without these concerns, restrictions would have been in place. Rabbinic Jews distinguished themselves by their different eating practices, and thus maintained their separation from other Jews (for more on rabbinic eating regulations of this period, see Kraemer 2007: 39–86).

The prohibition of mixing dairy and meat was not the only rabbinic regulation which would have separated Jew from Jew. A series of commensality restrictions pertaining to *haverim* ('associates') and *amei ha-aretz* (=common people, literally 'people of the land') were intended—in this case explicitly—to have similar consequences. *Haverim* were individuals who took upon themselves special precautions to (i) maintain the same level of purity for their common foods as would be necessary for cultic foods and (ii) to eat only produce that was definitively tithed (M. Hagigah 2:7, T. Demai 2:2). From the perspective of *haverim*, common Jews were lax in the latter and unconcerned about the former (M. Demai 2:2). If these groups were unable to eat with one another, then eating regulations would have resulted in another significant division between different groups of Jews.

The Palestinian rabbinic sources that speak of these matters do not provide a clear picture, though. Reading the Mishnah and Tosefta (see, for example, M. Demai, ch. 2 and T. Demai, chapters 2, 3 and 5), one gets a sense that the *haverim* represented a very small group, a fraction of Jewish society as a whole. In addition, though many rabbis would have been *haverim*, the two groups seem not to have been identical (Rosenblum 2008: 173–5). Further, when one examines the regulations meant to separate the *haverim* and *amei ha-aretz* carefully, it is evident that they provide means of accommodating the commensality of members of the two groups (Rosenblum 2008: 175–180). As long as the *haver* controls the situation, a friendly meal is easy to arrange. Finally, it is unclear whether the discipline of the *haver*, and therefore the group itself, survived the tannaitic (early rabbinic) period. Unlike other rabbinic kashrut laws, discussion of these laws may, in later generations, have been academic only.

4. SEPARATING JEW FROM GENTILE

Of course, Jewish eating regulations did not only separate different groups of Jews from each other. In fact, it has commonly been assumed (though perhaps wrongly in some measure; see Kraemer 2007: 17–19) that Jewish laws regulating permitted foods have, from the very beginning, been directed at separating Jews from their neighbours. To be sure, observers of Jews through the ages have often testified to this condition. In the period that concerns us here, Tacitus' claims are perhaps the most notorious:

The Jews are extremely loyal to one another, and always ready to show compassion, but toward every other people they feel only hate and enmity. They sit apart at meals and they sleep apart. (Tacitus, Historiae 5.5.1–2; Stern 1980, 2:26).

Philostratus's characterization, penned approximately a century later, is even more extreme:

For the Jews have long been in revolt not only against the Romans but against humanity; and a race that has made its own a life apart and irreconcilable, that cannot share with the rest of mankind in the pleasures of the table nor join in their libations or prayers or sacrifices, are separated from ourselves by a greater gulf than divides us from . . . the more distant Indies (Philostratus, Vita Apollonii 5.33; Stern 1980, vol. 2:341).

In these comments the writers seem to be reflecting the reaction of Gentiles observing Jews who, following restrictions such as those spelled out in M. Avodah Zara chapter 2, refuse to eat the food of non-Jews and hence refuse to eat with them. By the Roman period, such restrictions were arguably traditional in some parts of the Jewish community, having already had a long and respected history. Finding their earliest expression in Daniel 1, such restrictions are expressed (generally in the course of narrative development) in a variety of Palestinian Jewish writings from the Hellenistic and early Roman periods (Freidenreich 2006: 66–76). What is not clear, though, is the status of such assumed restrictions: are they accepted, at least in theory, by a broad swathe of the Jewish community, or do they represent the aspirations of small groups of relatively extreme pietists? The evidence of Tobit 1:10 ('after I was carried away captive to Assyria and came as a captive to Nineveh, everyone of my kindred and my people ate the food of the Gentiles'), in any case, suggests that, in the author's experience, many Jews in the

Hellenistic period—whether in Palestine or the Diaspora cannot be known (Moore 1996: 40–3)—failed to observe this prohibition.

Rabbinic restrictions against partaking of the foods of Gentiles are detailed and obviously intended to apply to all Jews. The text that first enumerates these restrictions is M. A.Z. 2:3–7. According to the Mishnah, there are three categories of such forbidden foods: (1) items where the prohibition includes not only eating but extends to deriving any benefit, (2) items that may not be eaten but from which other benefit (such as the profit from sale) is permitted, and (3) items that may even be eaten. Category 1 includes: Gentile wine, Gentile wine vinegar, Adriatic earthenware (which had been used to store forbidden wine), hides of animals whose hearts were cut out (assumed to be an act of forbidden worship), and meat from an animal that had been offered to an idol. Category 2 includes: milk milked by a Gentile while no Jew was watching, 'their bread and [olive] oil', boiled foods and pickled foods when their custom is to add wine or vinegar to them, minced sardines, brine containing no small fish, *hilaq* (a fish paste), droplets of asafoetida (a gum resin used in condiments), and seasoned salt. Category 3 includes milk milked by a Gentile while a Jew was watching, honey and honeycombs, pickled foods when their custom is not to add wine or vinegar to them, unminced sardines and brine containing small fish, leaves of asafoetida, round olive cakes, and locusts from the storeroom. Depending upon whose opinion is followed, Gentile cheese may fit in category 1 or category 2. Foods in category 1, subject to the most complete prohibition, are those that may have been tainted by association with idol worship. Foods in category 3 are those where there is no such fear, nor is there fear that they contain non-kosher ingredients. Category 2 is somewhat more complicated, and its interpretation is subject to some debate.

Some of the items in category 2 are clearly forbidden because they might contain prohibited substances (the milk might contain un-kosher milk, minced fish might contain forbidden species, etc.). But other items included in this category (bread and olive oil) are somewhat more opaque, seeming to allow for no admixture of un-kosher ingredients, and the meaning of 'boiled foods' is similarly unclear. Post-tannaitic traditions in both Palestine and Babylonia understand the prohibition to apply to all cooked Gentile foods (see y. A.Z. 2:8, 41d; b. A.Z. 37b–38a); if they have cooked it, then the food itself has become 'Gentile' and a Jew may not eat it. Of course, if this is the correct understanding, and if it is put into practice, then Jewish commensality with a Gentile will be almost impossible. But Freidenreich notes that the Tosefta seems to assume that the problem with both pickled and boiled foods is the possibility that forbidden wine or vinegar may have been added to them, and he argues that the Mishnah (not the Tosefta) 'ingredientizes' not only this, but almost all of these food prohibitions (2006: 155–7). If this is the case, then according to the Mishnah, at least, there would be no general prohibition on food cooked by Gentiles.

But even Freidenreich admits that the concern for forbidden ingredients would fail to explain the prohibition on Gentile bread and olive oil (158), and the motivation he proposes for the Mishnaic sages' alleged turn to ingredients—a move that would run contrary to the earlier Hellenistic development—is implausible (he proposes that the sages of the Mishnah are uncomfortable with the fact that the new Jewish prohibitions on Gentile food in the Hellenistic period have no source in the Torah; the Mishnah itself contains a variety of laws that find little or no source in the Torah, and it admits as much explicitly; see Hagigah 1:8). The interpretation that understands these prohibitions to be directed against Gentiles and the taint of their culture and worship (see Rosenblum 2008: 116 and Kraemer 2007: 66–9) seems more likely.

What we witness in the Mishnaic tractate Avodah Zarah, the purpose of which is to delimit and restrict relationships between Jews and others, are rabbinic eating rules that intend to keep these societies apart. At the very least, the three central components of the 'Mediterranean triad'—wine, bread, and olive oil (Garnsey 1999: 13–4)—are subject to these restrictions when they are the product of Gentile culture, and the same may apply to any cooked foods. How many Jews observed these restrictions in Roman Palestine, whether because they followed rabbinic law or because they inherited these practices from pietists in earlier generations, we shall never know. But the non-Jewish testimony quoted above makes it clear that a sufficient number of Jews did heed them to give some Gentile witnesses, however distorted their testimony, the impression that 'Jews' refused to eat with those who were not Jewish.

5. Jewish and Roman Food and Eating Habits

Yet there is an irony embedded in these restrictions. The focus of this legislation on the three culturally preferred foods of Mediterranean (including Roman) civilization constituted a recognition—or, one might say, a construction—of the special status of these foods. By attaching special restrictions to these foods, the rabbis were assimilating Roman preferences. By formulating special, exceptional blessings for recitation before the consumption of at least two of these foods (bread and wine; see M. Berakhot 6:1) they were doing the same. In other words, though rabbis were calling for the separation from Roman pagans by legislating the manner of eating these foods, they were at the same time being Romans by doing the same. In some sense, they were claiming 'We, too, are Romans, only better.'

Indeed, it can hardly be doubted that Palestinian Jews, whether following rabbinic practice or not, were eating the same types of food in basically the same way as other residents of this eastern Mediterranean Roman province. The special place of bread and wine in their meals—and particularly as ritual markers of the onset of festive occasions on the rabbinic-Jewish side, or as ritual symbols of narrative theology on the early Christian side—testified to this reality. So too, according to Lev-Tov, did the increase in fish consumption amongst Jews from the first couple of centuries of the Common Era onwards (Lev-Tov 2003: 440). Both the ritual and substance of Palestinian Jewish meals point to the conclusion that even when they were separate, they were hardly different. From the culinary perspective, Palestinian Jews were provincial Romans.

6. THE PASSOVER SEDER

The one phenomenon that has most often been pointed to as evidence of ancient Jews' Hellenistic and Roman ways of eating is the Passover seder (see M. Pes. 10), a ritual meal that has been seen as a sort of Jewish symposium. Scholars have taken different sides on the question of whether the ancient seder was in fact a Roman symposium. Bokser in his important work (1984) has argued against this equation, whereas many others have argued for it (see, most importantly, Stein 1957). But there are two things upon which virtually everyone would agree: (1) the Passover celebration in the time before the destruction of the Temple in 70 CE differed significantly from the later rabbinic ritual, and was most assuredly not a symposium (Bokser 1984: 14–28), and (2) whether constructing a symposium or an anti-symposium, the rabbis, in formulating their ritual, were employing and/or referencing a uniquely Hellenistic-Roman cultural vocabulary. Both of these points are important for our understanding of the Roman-period Passover meal ritual.

Bokser's survey of the evidence shows that all records of the Passover celebration before the destruction of the Temple in 70 CE portray a meal, organized around the Passover sacrifice, that includes songs of praise, and perhaps wine. There is not yet any hint of an elaborate meal ritual that builds on the manipulation and symbolic meanings of a variety of foodstuffs (outside of the lamb itself, along with matzah and bitter herbs, as required by the Torah (Exod. 12:8)), nor is there any suggestion of narrative recitations of the redemptive event. All evidence points to the fact that the seder, as such, is an invention of the rabbis, the first record of which is found in Mishnah Pesahim chapter 10. One should note that the term 'seder' is not a classical rabbinic term, and has not been used to denote the ritual meal before the medieval period. In fact, the term, meaning 'order', is rather inappropriate to the ritual, since the very point of key steps in the ritual is to do things *out* of their common order so as to surprise the children and provoke questioning. One may assume that in Roman and Byzantine Palestine, Jews who did not identify with the rabbis and their way of life would not have celebrated a seder. What they did in the absence of a sacrificial animal and Temple we do not know, but it is clear that only the relatively few (though perhaps increasing) number of Jews who did subscribe to the rabbinic way would have enacted the rituals, the precise nature of which is in question here (see the later rabbinic discussions in T. Pes. ch. 10 and y. Pes. ch. 10).

Bokser focuses on several elements of the rabbinic ritual that, in his understanding, are specifically intended to differentiate it from the symposium. Among these are the fact that the ritual is explicitly directed at all classes of Jews, unlike the symposium which was a ritual of the 'leisurely wealthy' (to use Bokser's language), and the fact that participants are forbidden to partake of additional wine after the fourth cup, unlike guests at a symposium who would drink excessively, sing and make merry, and then move on to other festivities (Bokser 1984: 62–5). But these very differences also highlight the symposium-like quality of the rabbinic ritual, for they make sense as negations or adaptations only in relationship to the ritual-vocabulary of the symposium, which the seder otherwise resembles in significant ways.

In fact, the similarity between the seder and the symposium emerges from the rabbinic record itself, which employs much the same vocabulary to describe the Passover ritual and the meal ritual (literally: 'the order [seder] of the meal') enacted on other formal occasions. This ritual, described at T. Berakhot 4:8ff. and y. Berakhot 6:6, 10d, commences with the formal seating of guests in relaxed or reclining positions, the washing of hands, and the mixing (= dilution with water) of cups of wine, followed by various hors d'oeuvre. Following this stage, the main meal is served, the quality of which is keyed to the status of the host and the guests. As Lieberman unreservedly comments, this is none other than the symposium; in his language: 'this [Toseftan text] describes the meal customs in antiquity of the upper classes . . . the customs of the Romans in meals, and also of the Greeks' (Lieberman 1955: 62; on the ritual of the symposium, see Vetta 1999). There is no doubt, from the rabbinic record, that the rabbis assumed that they themselves and other Jews would participate in symposia on certain occasions (that is, even apart from the Passover meal), and the seder may reasonably, therefore, be understood as a (non-) symposium—a Roman practice in the fullest sense of the term.

7. MEAL RITUALS

In rabbinic practice (and perhaps in Jewish practice more broadly, despite the absence of a surviving record), special occasions were usually celebrated by meals, and such meals were all marked by special meal rituals. Blessings over wine ('the sanctification of the day') at the beginning of evening meals were instrumental in commencing all Sabbaths and festivals. Special blessings or formulas added to the rabbinic blessing after meals distinguished both wedding celebrations (lasting a week) and mourning practices (see y. Megillah 4:4, 75a and T. Berakhot 3:23–4). On the other hand, special occasions that were not marked by meals and their rituals were distinguished by the negation of meals and eating, that is, by fasting. This included, of course, *Yom ha-Kippurim* (the 'Day of Atonement') and the fasts to commemorate the events associated with the destructions of the Jerusalem Temples (*Tisha be-Av*), but it also included a wide variety of troubles or calamities (or prospective calamities), from droughts to plagues to earthquakes, and even to nightmares (see M. Ta'anit chapters 1, 3 and 4:7, and Diamond 2004: 93–132).

Meal rituals were not restricted to special occasions, nor were they restricted to the rabbis—though it is difficult to know which other groups of Jews observed which meal rituals, and how ancient these rituals may have been. The community whose practice is reflected in Qumran scroll IQS (The Rule of the Community, 6.3–6) prescribed blessings for 'the first fruits of the bread' and new wine to be recited by a priest in the community of no fewer than ten men. Needless to say, several elements of this ritual find an echo in the later rabbinic practice. The Gospels preserve a tradition that describes the practice of hand-washing before eating as a Jewish 'tradition of the elders' (though they seem to associate the practice particularly with the Pharisees); Mark adds that Jews also traditionally wash food from the market before consumption, as well as the vessels with which they eat and prepare food (see Mark 7:1–4, Matt. 15: 1–2, and Luke 11: 37–8). Though not identical with rabbinic practice, the overlap of these rituals is notable. From the anthropological perspective, there can be no doubt that rituals accompanied the meals of Jews as well as of other ancient groups. The specifics of the Palestinian Jewish rituals are, one way or another, reflected in these various traditions.

Rabbis promulgated an elaborate system of blessing rituals to accompany the consumption of food on ordinary days as well. They ruled that the taking of food before reciting a blessing would be equivalent to stealing sacred property (T. Berakhot 4:1). Except for the foodstuffs for which unique blessings existed (i.e. bread and wine), all types of foods were fitted into specific categories. To perform the rabbinic ritual properly, one would have to know which foods belonged to which category as well as the blessing for each category. When several foods were eaten in the same meal, then the privileged food—bread—not only took precedence in blessing, but its blessing covered all of the other foods that accompanied it. When there were different kinds of bread in different conditions, or when only other foods without bread were offered, then the blessings followed cultural and personal priorities. Different rabbinic rulings transmitted in the Mishnah and Tosefta preserve evidence of cultural debates on these issues within the rabbinic community (Kraemer 2007: 73–86). A blessing ritual also marked the end of meals amongst rabbis and their followers. An invitation to bless, the formula of which reflected the size of the meal gathering (M. Berakhot chapter 7), rendered this final blessing more formal by formally inviting the community to enact it. Because such a communal gathering would have been of a public nature, women, slaves, and minors were not included in it (M. Ber. 7:2).

8. The State of the Field and Suggestions for Future Studies

After Samuel Krauss's groundbreaking study (1910, vol. 1: 78–126), research on issues of daily life such as food and eating has, for a long time, been characterized by relative disinterest amongst scholars. Most recently this condition has changed considerably, however, as the doctoral dissertations of Freidenreich (2006) and Rosenblum (2008), and the work of Kraemer (2007), along with the zooarchaeological studies reviewed by Lev-Tov (2003), testify. This recent work has largely been conducted with a more critical eye than earlier studies by Krauss and others, and methodological caution has yielded more balanced results. At present, it is fair to say that we possess a relatively good estimate of the diet and meal-habits of Jews in Palestine in the Roman-Byzantine period. Recent studies are calling for a re-evaluation of the relative place of meat and fish in the ancient (Jewish) diet, and evidence from new excavations may help us gain a better picture of the significance of these foods in the diets of late antiquity. But it is likely that the overall picture will change little. It is hard to imagine what kind of discovery, literary or archaeological, could lead to a major shift.

By contrast, it would be hard, and perhaps even impossible, to gain a more precise grasp of the meal practices of Palestinian Jews during the Roman and early Byzantine period. In this realm, all of the evidence is literary only, and after the first century almost exclusively rabbinic. The rabbis, of course, predominantly transmitted their own desired reality rather than describing what most Jews actually did. So one of the main questions will continue to be the degree to which Palestinian Jews were rabbinized during these centuries, and there is little doubt that this will remain a matter of lively debate.

Nevertheless, given the obvious dependence of humans on food for survival, and the centrality of meals in social relations of all sorts, there is much to be gained by ongoing scholarly attention to the details of the food consumption and eating practices of Jews during this period. Many who have studied these questions have assumed, rightly, that 'you are what you eat'. It is reasonable to expect, therefore, that by examining the eating practices of Jews in Roman and Byzantine Palestine we stand to learn even more about their various identities.

SUGGESTED READING

Rosenblum (2008) provides an excellent review of the findings concerning food production and consumption in Roman Palestine (for a more detailed picture, see Broshi 2001: 121–43), along with a balanced consideration of the eating practices of some Jews and their consequences for commensality with others. Lev-Tov's study (2003) is the most critically prudent consideration of archaeological findings pertaining to animal and fish consumption during the Roman and Byzantine periods. On early rabbinic kashrut and other rabbinic eating practices, see my own work (Kraemer 2007).

BIBLIOGRAPHY

BOKSER, B. M. (1984). *The Origins of the Seder*. Berkeley, Los Angeles, and London: University of California Press.

BROSHI, M. (2001). *Bread, Wine, Walls and Scrolls*. Sheffield: Sheffield Academic Press.

CORBIER, M. (1999). 'The Broad Bean and the Moray: Social Hierarchies and Food in Rome', in *Food: A Culinary History from Antiquity to the Present*, ed. J.-L. Flandrin and M. Montanari. New York: Columbia University Press, 128–40.

DAR, S. (1995). 'Food and Archaeology in Romano-Byzantine Palestine', in *Food in Antiquity*, ed. J. Wilkins, D. Harvey, and M. Dobson. Exeter: University of Exeter Press, 326–35.

DIAMOND, E. (2004). *Holy Men and Hunger Artists: Fasting and Asceticism in Rabbinic Culture*. New York: Oxford University Press.

DUPONT, F. (1999). 'The Grammar of Roman Dining', in *Food: A Culinary History from Antiquity to the Present*, ed. J.-L. Flandrin and M. Montanari. New York: Columbia University Press, 113–27.

FREIDENREICH, D. (2006). 'Foreign Foods: A Comparatively-Enriched Analysis of Jewish, Christian and Islamic Law'. Unpublished PhD. thesis, Columbia University, New York.

GARNSEY, P. (1999). *Food and Society in Classical Antiquity*. Cambridge: Cambridge University Press.

GRANTHAM, B. J. (1996). 'A Zooarchaeological Model for the Study of Ethnic Complexity at Sepphoris'. Unpublished PhD. thesis, Northwestern University.

HAARETZ MUSEUM and CERAMICS MUSEUM (1979). *Vessels from the Period of the Mishnah and the Talmud* [Hebr.]. 2nd ed. Tel-Aviv: Haaretz Museum and Ceramics Museum.

HESSE, B./WAPNISH, P. (1997). 'Can Pig Remains be Used for Ethnic Diagnosis in the Ancient Near East?' in *The Archaeology of Israel: Constructing the Past, Interpreting the Present*, ed. N. A. Silverman and D. Small, 238–70. Journal for the Study of the Old Testament Supplement Series 237. Sheffield: Sheffield Academic Press.

KRAEMER, D. (2007). *Jewish Eating and Identity Through the Ages*. New York and London: Routledge.

KRAUSS, S. (1910). *Talmudische Archäologie*, vol. 1. Leipzig: G. Fock.

Lev-Tov, J. (2003). '"Upon What Meat Doth This Our Caesar Feed...?" A Dietary Perspective on Hellenistic and Roman Influence in Palestine', in *Zeichen aus Text und Stein: Studien auf dem Weg zu einer Archäologie des Neuen Testaments*, ed. S. Alkier and J. K. Zangenberg. Tübingen: Francke, 420–46.

Lieberman, S. (1955). *Tosefta Ki-Fshuta*, vol 1: *Zeraim*. New York: Jewish Theological Seminary of America.

Moore, C. A (1996). *Tobit: A New Translation with Introduction and Commentary*. New York: The Anchor Bible/Doubleday.

Rosenblum, J. D. (2008). '"They Sit Apart at Meals": Early Rabbinic Commensality Regulations and Identity Construction'. Unpublished PhD. thesis, Brown University, Providence.

Rosenfeld, B.-Z./Menirav, J. (2005). *Markets and Marketing in Roman Palestine*. Leiden and Boston: Brill.

Safrai, Z. (1994). *The Economy of Roman Palestine*. New York and London: Routledge.

Schwartz, S. (2001). *Imperialism and Jewish Society, 200 b.c.e. to 640 c.e.* Princeton and Oxford: Princeton University Press.

Stein, S.(1957). 'The Influence of Symposia Literature on the Literary Form of the Pesah Haggadah'. *Journal of Jewish Studies* 7: 13–44.

Stern, M. (1980). *Greek and Latin Authors on Jews and Judaism*, vol. 2. Jerusalem: The Israel Academy of Sciences and Humanities.

Vetta, M. (1999). 'The Culture of the Symposium', in *Food: A Culinary History from Antiquity to the Present*, ed. Jean-Louis Flandrin and Massimo Montanari. New York: Columbia University Press, 96–105.

Wilkins, J. M. Hill, S. (2008). *Food in the Ancient World*. 2nd ed. Oxford: Blackwell.

Yadin, Y. (1963). *Discoveries from the Days of Bar-Kokhba in the Cave of Letters* [Hebr.]. Jerusalem: The Society for the Study of the Land of Israel and its Antiquities.

CHAPTER 23

DOMESTIC ARCHITECTURE

KATHARINA GALOR

1. INTRODUCTION

More than any other architectural space, the dwelling—the hub of most daily activities, including eating, sleeping, and even working—provides us with the greatest insight into daily life in Roman and Byzantine Palestine.

In its early stages, studies of Roman-Byzantine dwellings in Palestine were influenced by similar investigations of Bronze and Iron Age dwellings. This model of studying the archaeological evidence to gain an understanding of daily life in the biblical periods motivated scholars engaged in the study of later periods to recreate the material backdrop for the written documents, primarily the rabbinic texts and the New Testament Gospels.

The earliest archaeological discoveries of domestic architecture in Palestine were primarily the result of random and chance exposure. The relatively late interest in these 'minor' architectural remains was clearly lagging behind much earlier excavations that focused on monumental structures. It would take several generations before large-scale projects and studies of private dwellings, such as those conducted in Pompeii and Herculaneum, would have even a marginal effect on scholars of the eastern Mediterranean and, more specifically, Syria-Palestine. The initial encounter with domestic structures in this part of the ancient world was often a by-product of the more general desire to recreate the physical setting of the written narratives.

2. SCHOLARSHIP ON DOMESTIC ARCHITECTURE

At the beginning of the twentieth century, Samuel Krauss (1910) had already devoted an entire volume to the 'house' in the talmudic era. Nearly half a century later, a similar interest in domestic structures developed among scholars interested in contextualizing the New Testament narratives. H. Keith Beebe's rather textually oriented attempts (1968 and 1975) were only thinly supported by field discoveries. A more restricted chronological and geographical framework imposed itself on the quest for the historical Jesus. The initial inquiry, which was purely literary in nature, has turned more recently to an inclusion of archaeological remains that also document the mundane aspects of rural and urban life in Palestine. Dominique Crossan and Jonathan Reed (2001) have set a good example for attaining a desirable model that integrates literary and archaeological sources for the purpose of recreating first-century Galilee.

Following the 1967 war, excavations conducted in the Old City of Jerusalem—the Jewish Quarter by Nahman Avigad (1983) and the area south of the Temple Mount enclosure wall by Benjamin Mazar (1969)—exposed vast areas of domestic structures in an urban setting. The so-called cities of the Negev were already known in the nineteenth century, but intensive interest in the domestic architecture of the region did not occupy centre-stage until Avraham Negev's explorations (1980, 1988,

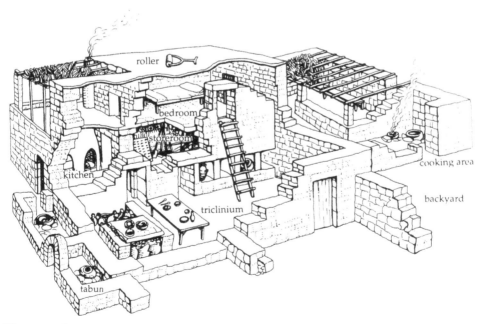

Fig. 23.1 Reconstruction of a house at Qatzrin, fourth–fifth centuries CE

Hirschfeld, *Palestinian Dwelling*, Fig. 190, p. 261.

and 1997) at Mampsis and Oboda and, more recently, of others at sites such as Subeita (Segal 1983).

Among the first archaeological explorations with a clear mandate to uncover domestic structures and recreate daily life in the Roman-Byzantine periods were those by Zvi Ma'oz and Anne Killebrew at Qatzrin in the Golan (see Fig. 23.1; Killebrew/Ma'oz 1988; Killebrew/Fine 1991), Eric Meyers and others (Meyers/ Meyers 1982–83; Meyers/Netzer/Meyers 1986; Hoglund/Meyers 1996) at Sepphoris in the Lower Galilee, and, finally, Yizhar Hirschfeld (2007) at 'Ein Gedi on the western shore of the Dead Sea. Similar efforts were initiated in Jordan by the Australian team at Pella (McNicoll/Smith/Hennessy 1982), the Polish team at Jerash (Gawlikowski 1986), at Umm el-Jimal (de Vries 1998), and at ez-Zantur in Petra (Bignasca et al. 1996).

The only comprehensive study of private dwellings in Roman-Byzantine Palestine was conducted by Yizhar Hirschfeld (1987 and 1995). His innovative work has advanced the field of domestic architecture for Palestine generally and for southern Judaea in particular, and is notable for its comparative use of ethnographic materials (see Fig. 23.2).

Fig. 23.2 Yussuf Qahadi, owner of a house at ed-Dhahiriya, interviewed by Yizhar Hirschfeld, standing in front of his house

Hirschfeld, Palestisian Dwelling, Fig. 136, p. 184.

3. The Literary Evidence

Hirschfeld (1995: 18) has stated that 'rabbinic literature is a gold mine of information on any subject of Palestinian society during the Roman and Byzantine periods, in particular domestic architecture and the household'. These literary sources, however, are only partially relevant and applicable to the study of domestic architecture in Palestine, as they hardly address the chronological and, most importantly, regional variations. Hirschfeld identified two significant methodological problems associated with the use of rabbinic texts for gaining information on Roman-Byzantine dwellings (1995: 18–19). First, the Babylonian Talmud often represents the dwelling culture that existed in Mesopotamia, which is quite different from that of Palestine. Secondly, the main Palestinian sources—the Mishnah, Tosefta, Jerusalem (Palestinian) Talmud, and Midrashim—represent diverse periods and perhaps also different regions. The Jerusalem Talmud, for example, reflects primarily the discussions of the third- and fourth-century CE sages in the Galilee, whereas the Mishnah, which, although completed at the beginning of the third century, reflects ideas and discussions of sages in Judaea and the Galilee from the end of the Second Temple period onward.

As the regional variations of domestic structures are far more significant than those of monumental public buildings, important structural and stylistic differences cannot be fully appreciated on the basis of the literary evidence. The primary value of the rabbinic texts is, therefore, of a theoretical nature and is chiefly relevant to our understanding of spatial, social, and legal interactions between landlords, tenants, and neighbours (see Hezser 1998 for the discussion of neighbourly disputes). An additional source regarding construction and owner-tenant relations is Julian of Ascalon's *Treatise on Urbanism,* a sixth-century private compilation of notes describing the rules and regulations for preventing altercations between neighbours (Saliou 1996 and 2000). Krauss' (1910) systematic treatment of rabbinic texts for reconstructing the houses of late antique Palestine was followed by Hirschfeld (1987 and 1995), Weber (1993), and Galor (1996, 2000, 2003a, and 2003b) in their reconstruction of Roman-Byzantine dwellings in Palestine.

4. Major Sites

To date, a large number of domestic structures dating between the early Roman and late Byzantine periods have been uncovered in Palestine. We will only briefly review here the main sites containing entire neighbourhoods or clusters of private dwellings. Unlike in rural settings, dwellings in urban sites can also be found beside commercial or civic structures (Weiss 2008).

4.1 The Galilee and Golan

More thoroughly surveyed than other regions of Palestine, the north, including the Galilee and Golan, provides us with considerable data that allows us to reconstruct domestic structures within their larger rural or urban contexts (Dauphin/Gibson 1992/93; Yeivin 1971; Meyers/Strange/Groh 1978; Meyers/Meyers 1982–83). In addition to the information culled from traditional excavations, surveys are particularly useful for obtaining population estimates, socio-economic analyses, and urban plans of both private and public structures. Sepphoris in the Lower Galilee, a major city that flourished in the Roman era and in the Byzantine period in particular, has revealed large areas with domestic structures. In addition to a late Roman villa (Talgam/Weiss 2004), numerous dwellings from the Roman-Byzantine period (Hoglund/Meyers 1996; Meyers/Netzer/Meyers 1986) were uncovered on the city's western acropolis. In the Lower City, domestic structures were excavated alongside public ones (Weiss 2008). Excavations at Capernaum, on the northern shore of the Sea of Galilee (Corbo 1975 and 1982; Loffreda 2005), have revealed several blocks of private dwellings dating to approximately the same time period (see Fig. 23.3). Built of local basalt, these structures stand in contrast to the white limestone used for the synagogue at this site. The dwellings at Chorazin (Yeivin 1973, 1982/83 and 1993), Gamla (Ma'oz 1987; Syon/Yavor 2005), and Qatzrin (Killebrew/Fine 1991; Killebrew/Ma'oz 1988) were built to conform with the settlement's main monumental building, the synagogue.

4.2 Judaea

Following the 1967 war, two major projects involving the exposure of private dwellings were undertaken in Jerusalem—the Jewish Quarter excavations directed by Nahman Avigad (1983; Geva 2000 and 2006), including late Hellenistic to early Roman period houses that were occupied up until the destruction of the Upper City in 70 CE, and the southern Temple Mount excavations directed by Benjamin Mazar (1969; E. Mazar 2003), which exposed a densely populated residential area from the Byzantine period. Recent excavations conducted by Rachel Bar-Nathan at Shuafat (Bar-Nathan/Sklar-Parnes 2007) uncovered a suburban quarter of the city that was inhabited in between the two revolts, between 70 and 135 CE The excavation of Herodian palaces and palace fortresses in the Judaean Desert and beyond are also significant for our understanding of domestic architecture (Netzer 1981, 2001, and 2004). Other noteworthy villages with domestic structures built and used

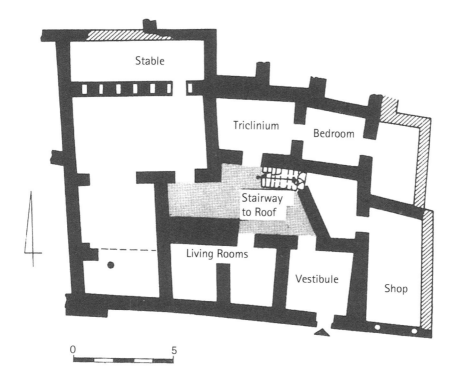

Fig. 23.3 Reconstruction of a courtyard house at Capernaum, first–second centuries CE

Hirschfeld, *Palestinian Dwelling*, Fig. 43, p. 69.

primarily in the Byzantine period are Ein Gedi on the western shore of the Dead Sea (see Figs. 23.4 and 23.5).

4.3 The Negev

Impressive remains of entire desert cities have been exposed in the Negev. The Nabateans' transition from nomadism to sedentism witnessed the transformation of road stations into towns and cities with well-preserved domestic areas from the late Roman and Byzantine periods. Surveys and excavations at two notable sites, Mampsis (see Fig. 6; Negev 1980; 1988; 1997) and Subeita (Segal 1983), have documented architectural features varying slightly in style and building technique from dwellings in the central and northern regions of Palestine.

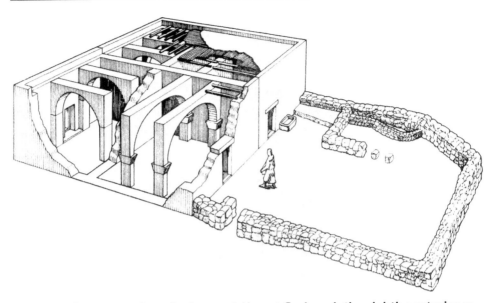

Fig. 23.4 Reconstruction of a house at Horvat Susiya, sixth–eighth centuries CE

Hirschfeld, *Palestinian Dwelling*, Fig. 13, p. 37.

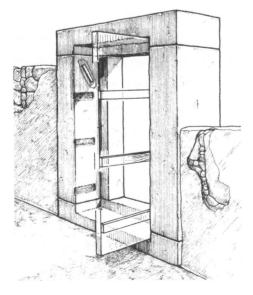

Fig. 23.5 Reconstruction of the main entrance to the house at Horvat Susiya

Hirschfeld, *Palestinian Dwelling*, Fig. 183, p. 30.

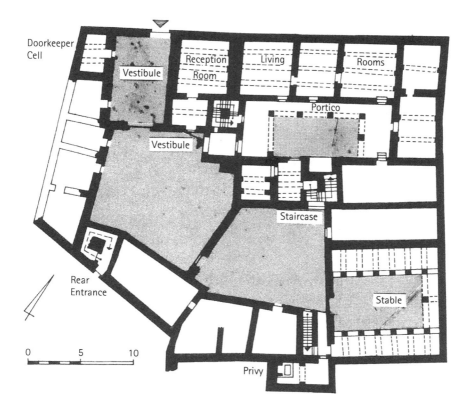

Fig. 23.6 Plan of Building XII at Mampsis, second—third centuries CE

Hirschfeld, *Palestinian Dwelling*, Fig. 51, p. 76

4.4 Transjordan

The exclusive interest in monumental structures in the cities of the Decapolis has more recently shifted to the inclusion of domestic structures, as indicated by excavations conducted at Pella (McNicoll/Smith/Hennessy 1982) and Jerash (Gawlikowski 1986). Our understanding of Petra's role in the Nabataean kingdom and its domestic architecture generally in late antiquity was transformed by the discoveries of the Swiss archaeological team at ez-Zantur (Bignasca et al. 1996). Yet, among the most astonishing and well-preserved examples of multi-storied dwellings are the buildings at Umm el-Jimal (see Fig. 23.7; de Vried 1998).

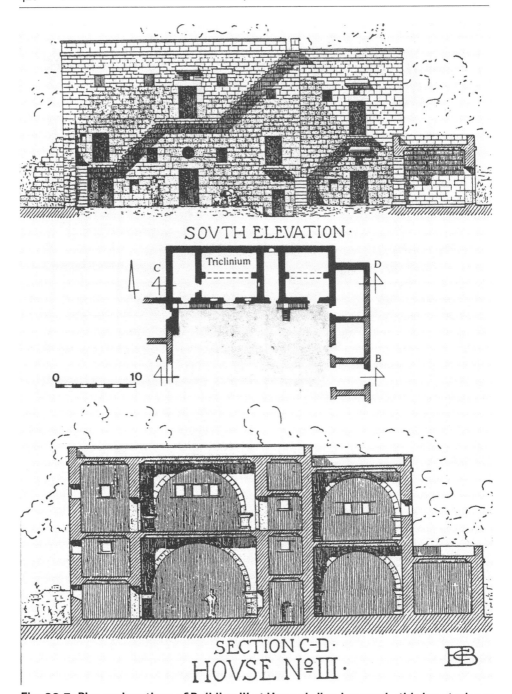

Fig. 23.7 Plan and sections of Building III at Umm el-Jimal, second–third centuries CE

Hirschfeld, *Palestinian Dwelling*, Fig. 24, p. 48

5. A PROPOSED RECONSTRUCTION OF DOMESTIC ARCHITECTURE IN ROMAN-BYZANTINE PALESTINE

The main difficulty in profiling the typical Roman-Byzantine dwelling is the fact that the variety of domestic structures is almost endless. According to the literary sources, the minimal dimensions of a house (*bayit*) were 4 × 6 cubits, or 2 × 3 m (M. Bava Batra 6:4). However, as Hirschfeld correctly pointed out, based on the archaeological evidence, most of the Roman-Byzantine dwellings in Palestine were far larger and more complex (1995: 21–107). Very few examples of freestanding single-room houses exist (Galor 1996: 71); these units seem to be a result of limited available space, especially in densely occupied urban settings and/or of extremely limited economic means. Houses with at least two rooms and a courtyard were more commonly found, although in most cases, three, four, or more rooms were built around one or two courtyards. Despite certain architectural similarities, none of the dwellings excavated in Palestine is identical. It appears that the plan of each building unit was made to conform to the topography of a particular site, to the historical and economical conditions of the period, and to the needs of each specific owner.

The juxtaposition of the courtyard with the rest of the house has formed a foundation for the classification of dwellings. Yeivin (1971: 158–68) distinguishes houses in the Galilee and Golan on the basis of how they were accessed from the street, either directly or through a courtyard. Hirschfeld (1995) differentiates between the 'simple house', consisting of a one-roomed structure built either behind or in front of an open courtyard, and the 'courtyard house', wherein an open space is surrounded on all four sides by the wings of the dwelling. He also notes the limited number of 'peristyle houses' in Palestine (Hirschfeld 1995: 21–107, 290) whose courtyard is surrounded by a colonnade (Ward-Perkins 1974: 38–41).

Although both Yeivin and Hirschfeld assume that each courtyard formed part of one house or family unit, a number of sources indicate that most courtyards were shared by multiple dwelling units or families (M. Arakhin 9:6–7; Weber 1993: 126–27; Galor 1996: 71–74; Hezser 1998). According to Hirschfeld (1995: 24–44), the 'simple house' was characteristic of private rural construction and was used by the vast majority of the country's inhabitants, whereas the relatively spacious 'courtyard house' was to be associated with the wealthy urban families (1995: 57–85). In contrast, Galor suggests (1996: 74–78) that the location of the courtyard and the layout of the associated rooms are determined by the space available for construction and by the topographical conditions. Thus, houses with internal or juxtaposed courtyards could be found in both urban and rural contexts.

5.1 Architectural Features: Plan and Elevation

Both literary sources and excavations indicate that the thickness of the walls varied considerably depending on their function. Walls that were built to delimit the courtyard areas or divide interior spaces were notably thinner than exterior walls supporting a roof, a ceiling, or a second storey (Krauss 1910: 23–25; Hirschfeld 1995: 217–18). Ceilings and roofs were usually placed at a relatively low point, approximately 1.70 m above ground level. The ceiling served either as the roof of the house or, in two-storey dwellings, as support for the upper level. In both cases, the surface was used for daily activities and was therefore completely flat. The New Testament describes a house with a tiled roof (Luke 5:19), however, most roof tiles were found in the context of monumental structures and rarely in association with private dwellings (Hirschfeld 1995: 243). Most roofs were probably surrounded by a parapet or wooden baluster; alternatively, the exterior walls of the house could have extended higher than the level of the roof itself (Killebrew/Fine 1991: 20–21). According to M. Bava Batra: 4:1, the parapet could reach a height of 74 cm and give access to an adjacent building through a passageway (T. Eruvin 6:13). Deut. 22:8 suggests that the construction of a parapet on the roof was an age-old technique.

The Mishnah (Nedarim 7:4; Bava Metzia 10:1; Bava Batra 2:2) distinguishes clearly between the lower (*bayit*) and upper (*aliyah*) levels. Many Roman and Byzantine houses surveyed in ancient Palestine attest to the existence of such an upper storey. In most cases, however, the upper level covered only part of the lower one. The *exedra*, or balcony, is another element of the domestic structure that was sometimes supported by columns (Hirschfeld 1995: 265–66). The upper levels—both the roofs and second storey living areas—could be accessed in different ways. One was by using a ladder. Mishnah Bava Batra: 3:6 mentions the 'Egyptian' ladder, which was light and portable, and the 'Tyrian' ladder, which was a stationary wooden staircase. These ladders were most likely used in the interior spaces of the house. Another way to reach an upper level was via a stone staircase, some built against the exterior wall of the dwelling, others inside the courtyard.

Although the use of arches in roof construction was known in the country from the late first century BCE onward (in the Hauran and the Negev), its structural advantages were barely acknowledged before the Byzantine period. Unlike Roman imperial construction and medieval buildings, the aesthetic aspect of the arch in the domestic architecture of Roman and Byzantine Palestine was never a consideration for its use.

Doorways were rectangular openings usually measuring less than 1 metre in width. In contrast to the usual roughly trimmed stones of the building, thresholds and doorposts could be marked by a more even dressing of the stones. While the interior openings of the house seemed to be simply passageways, most main entrances contained sockets for the insertion of doorposts. In contrast to the archaeological evidence, the literary sources (M. Kelim 11:2; Lev. R. 14:4) suggest that doors had some kind of a cone-shaped hinge that could be introduced into two openings, one in the threshold and one above the entranceway. It seems, however, that this device was used mainly for monumental buildings. Both the archaeological remains (Hirschfeld 1995: 249–55) and literary sources (T. Shab. 1:6) seem to indicate that the door was suspended inside the house, that is, the threshold was located outside when the door was locked. The importance assigned to the main entrance as a strict boundary between a dwelling's interior and exterior, between the public and private domains, also finds expression in T. Gittin 6:1.

Windows in the exterior walls of the first floor must have been rare, as almost none of the houses excavated in Palestine exhibit remains of this feature. Most windows were probably located on the upper levels; however, these only seldomly survive intact. Such a solution ensured the privacy and security of the inhabitants on street level and facilitated the circulation of air and light. In contrast, houses excavated in the Galilee and the Golan frequently had fenestrated interior walls, sometimes referred to as 'window-walls'. Measuring about 70 cm above the floor, the windows were placed at regular intervals along its entire length. This was characteristic of the building style in the Hauran and Bashan regions. 'Window-walls' were usually located in the rooms immediately adjacent to the courtyard, thus allowing air and light to enter the rear rooms.

5.2 Building Materials

Unlike monumental architecture, which frequently used imported materials and adopted construction techniques and styles in vogue outside of Palestine, domestic architecture was usually constrained by the use of local materials and building techniques. Since for many centuries the same materials were used and thus similar techniques applied, the chronological developments of domestic architecture for the Roman and Byzantine periods are rather insignificant and will not be discussed here.

Both the Bible and rabbinic literature mention three basic materials used in the construction of houses—stone, wood, and earth (Lev. 14:45; M. B.M. 10:1; M. Neg. 12:2 and 13:3). Given the fact that these materials are usually mentioned in the same order, it has been suggested that this might be a reflection of the relative degree of their importance (Hirschfeld 1995: 218). The clear preference for stone as a building material in Palestine was primarily due to its abundance. While in the Iron Age the use of stone was confined, for the most part, to the foundations of brick structures, from the Hellenistic period onwards houses built entirely of stone became increasingly common (ibid.). As in the Hauran, most houses in the Galilee and Golan were built of the local black basalt owing to its availability, extreme massiveness, and durability. Another popular type of stone used for private construction in the central and southern parts of Palestine was limestone. In addition to its accessibility, it was easily dressed, yet sturdy under stress. Over and beyond its use for the construction of walls, stone was a basic material for building arches, vaults, ceiling beams, staircases, and pavements, mainly in courtyard areas.

At sites where no evidence of basalt or stone beams and corbels has been found, ceilings were most likely made of wood. Although we have few remains of wooden building components, owing to their decomposition over time, we may assume that there was not a large selection of timber for building (b. B.M. 117b; Weber 1993: 112). Cypress, cedar, and sycamore were freely available, sycamore being the cheapest and most widely used timber. Wood was used primarily for the construction of ceilings and sometimes doors. Mortar, composed of marl mixed with water, was used to bind stones of irregular shape. Some rabbinic sources (e.g. y. Shebi. 9:4, 39a) note that straw was sometimes added. As early as the Iron Age, or perhaps even earlier, lime, generally used in the production of cement, was also used to seal the walls of water cisterns (Reich 1993). Its first systematic use in private construction, however, was in the fifth and fourth centuries BCE (Orlandos 1966–68, vol. 1: 144). Lime-coated or plastered walls are found in numerous cisterns and ritual baths throughout the country.

Flooring materials in ancient Palestine varied greatly. Literary sources inform us that the floors required a certain thickness, in particular for second stories and in surfaces beneath stoves (Weber 1993: 122–23). Generally speaking, courtyards and interior rooms that served as storerooms or livestock shelters were paved, whereas the remaining rooms were covered simply with well-tamped earth. Mosaic pavements, first appearing in the late second century BCE in private dwellings, became increasingly popular in the Roman and Byzantine periods. They were either installed in rooms that had a representational character or in spaces equipped with washing and bathing installations. The flooring was usually a clear reflection of the owner's economic means and the house's standard of construction (Weber 1993: 123). The floors in simple houses were mostly compacted with earth; where built on natural rock, the rock itself was levelled with earth or clay. In wealthier homes, the floors were sometimes made of hewn or polished stone, as in the Jerusalem Temple (M. Tam. 1:1; M. Mid. 1:8), or decorated with mosaics. According to T. Kelim B.M. 11:10, rugs and mats nailed to the floor were used as protection against its rough and cold surface. Most walls and ceilings, and sometimes even floors, were smoothened and coated with a layer of plaster. In addition to the technical advantages of its low cost and quick and easy use in construction, plaster was considered aesthetically desirable in this period.

Very often, well-smoothened plaster provided the base for fresco and stucco wall decorations. From the second century BCE onward, plaster for fresco painting, a technique in which pigments are applied to freshly laid lime plaster, was used to embellish the walls of lavish houses and palaces in Palestine. The exterior walls of houses were typically whitewashed with lime that did not contain any additions. This rather widespread practice also applied to the poorer houses, according to b.

Bava Batra 60b; however, this statement cannot be corroborated by the archaeo-logical evidence (Hirschfeld 1995: 226). Generally speaking, the literary sources conflict with the archaeological evidence that attest to the widespread use of wall decorations. The rabbis permitted a person to plaster the exterior of his house, but he was to leave a small area undone in remembrance of the destruction of the Temple (T. B.B. 2:17).

5.3 Functions of the Various Spaces

The written sources allude to only a few rooms in the house—the *traklin* and the *kiton*—that served multiple functions. The *traklin* (cf. T. Kelim B.M. 5:3; M. Er. 6:6) was the largest and most important room in the private dwelling. It was where the family took its meals and where special celebrations were held. Mishnah Bava Batra 1:6 tells us that the *traklin* could be shared by the joint tenants of a house. The name of this room is derived from the Latin *triclinium*, meaning a dining room with three reclining couches (Richardson 1983). Unlike the *triclinium* of the Roman villa, the *traklin* in Palestine was not used exclusively for dining and representational purposes but also for other daily domestic activities, such as cooking, baking, and washing. The sources mention such rooms that measured at least 10 × 10 cubits, or about 5 × 5 m (y. Ber. 8:6, 12c; 3:5, 6d; Gen. R. 31:11). The other room mentioned in rabbinic literature is the *kiton* (Krauss 1910: 528–29; Jastrow 1903: 1357), derived from the Greek *koiton*, meaning 'bedroom', which was usually located adjacent to the *traklin* (M. Mid. 1:6). Given the fact that it was not unusual for several people to share one bed (M. Nid. 9:4), it was probably uncommon to find more than two bedrooms within one dwelling unit (Galor 2003a).

The exterior spaces of a dwelling, apparently used as frequently as its interior rooms, were the courtyard and the roof, both of which served similar purposes (see Fig. 23.8). Roofs were used for eating and praying, keeping animals, and storing fruit, vegetables, olives, figs, and wine jars (M. Hul. 3:1; M. Toh. 9:6, 9; M. Makh. 6:1–2; T. Pes. 1:3; b. Pes. 85b). The courtyards provided space for wells, drinking troughs and structures for animals, and bathhouses; as well as for activities such as cooking, grinding wheat for flour, washing clothes, and eating (Krauss 1910: 396ff.). The courtyard, like the *traklin*, could have been shared by the tenants of two dwelling units (T. Er. 7:7, 14). Rather than taking up large spaces within the dwelling, store-rooms were most likely either separate buildings in the courtyard or in the cellar areas (Yeivin 1987). In the latter case, they were considered an integral part of the house, although the entrance was usually from the courtyard and not from inside the house.

Water cisterns were dug into the ground and could be filled with rainwater either directly or indirectly, through gutters that conveyed the water to the cisterns. Water supplied via an aqueduct to public facilities such as fountains, bathhouses, and public latrines was found only in large cities. *Miqva'ot* were used by the Jews for

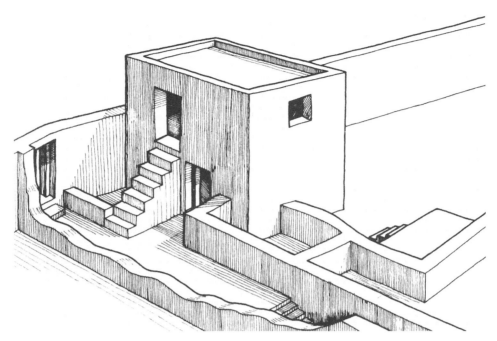

Fig. 23.8 Reconstruction of a house excavated at Horvat Shema', fourth–fifth centuries CE

Hirschfeld, *Palestinian Dwelling*, Fig. 10, p. 33

ritual bathing. In the villages, they usually served an entire community and were frequently found in excavations near olive- or winepresses. In larger towns or cities, almost every individual dwelling unit had its own *miqvah* (Galor 2007: 205–17). Whether this abundance reflects the inhabitants' economic wealth or religious beliefs remains unclear. Sanitary installations, such as bathtubs, latrines, and even bathhouses, were found exclusively in the homes of the very wealthy (cf. b. Shabbat 25b). According to literary sources, members of the lower and middle classes either used chamber pots or relieved themselves in the outdoors (cf. b. Shabbat 8b).

Both literary and archaeological evidence suggests that most domestic spaces could serve a variety of functions. Several solutions for creating internal partitions were implemented to meet this end (Hirschfeld 1995: 267–70). Rabbinic literature makes a clear distinction between permanent partitions and portable dividers. Various objects, such as curtains suspended from ceiling beams (y. Er. 6:6, 23c) and pieces of furniture, for example beds and cupboards (T. Pes. 1:3; y. Pes. 1:1, 27b; y. B.B. 6:2, 15c), could be used as partitions for conducting diverse activities within the household. Sometimes wooden boards or plastered jars (M. Oh. 6:2) were used as internal dividers. Unfortunately, the archaeological remains can attest only to the more permanent solutions, such as continuous or fenestrated walls. Therefore, despite the existence of clear legal and theoretical rules as to space divisions and functions, the physical divisions often remain indiscernible or ambiguous.

6. Socio-Economic, Cultural, Religious, and Gender-Related Implications for the Study of Domestic Architecture

Based on the evidence available from the literary sources and the abundant archaeological material of late, we are able to reconstruct the physical appearance of ancient dwellings in Roman-Byzantine Palestine with a rather high degree of accuracy. This does not imply, however, that all our questions regarding the social aspects of daily life on the domestic scene can be solved: the architectural components alone reveal only a limited amount of information on socio-economic issues, thus compelling the archaeologist to rely more heavily on the presence of small finds such as coins, pottery, and luxury items.

Quality of construction, technological sophistication, as well as the location and size of a dwelling within the larger urban context all seem to be ambiguous indicators of the dwellers in a given space. No single indicator is valid for houses located in either rural or urban contexts, and no narrowly defined characteristics are applicable for dwellings in villages, towns, or cities (Galor 1996: 69–74). Columns, decorative stucco revetments, mosaic floors, and fresco decorations can be found in both large cities (e.g. Jerusalem and Sepphoris) and small towns (e.g. Gamla), in places known to have been exposed to international trade, and those with a remote and rather culturally insulated profile. Attempts to determine religious affiliation have been more successful, particularly for villages and small towns in the late Roman and Byzantine periods, the primary factor being clearly the location of a specific dwelling. Here our ability to differentiate between houses inhabited by Jews or Christians depends almost entirely on the population structure of the village or town and whether its central monumental building was a church or a synagogue (Ma'oz 1985; Frankel et al. 2001: 110–16). Our ability to distinguish between the religious affiliations of the inhabitants of a dwelling in a city is far more difficult as its population was usually mixed (e.g. Tiberias, Sepphoris, and Caesarea). Among the sole indicators for identifying Jewish dwellers are *miqva'ot*, in addition to small finds such as stone vessels, oil lamps with inscriptions or symbols, etc., which may be considered an integral part of the dwelling (Meyers 2000; Galor 2007), as well as *mezuzot*. As the majority of domestic spaces appear to have been multifunctional, attempts to identify gender-specific areas within the Roman-Byzantine household in Palestine remain somewhat tentative (Meyers 2003; Baker 2002).

7. FUTURE RESEARCH

In spite of the increased awareness among scholars that the study of daily life is an important topic of investigation, no standard procedure has been adopted by archaeologists in the field that can help clarify issues such as the diverse functions of domestic areas, gendered space, and the social distribution of private and public spheres. However, the attempt to tackle these issues in theory will, it is hoped, lead to a more unified effort among archaeologists to classify and analyse the relevant material remains, and ultimately provide the scholar with additional data on daily life in the context of domestic space.

SUGGESTED READING

The rabbinic literary sources have been compiled by Krauss (1910). The most comprehensive study of the archaeological remains of Roman-Byzantine dwellings in Palestine is Hirschfeld (1995). For a reconstruction of a dwelling based on both archaeological and literary sources, see Killebrew and Fine (1991). The ongoing efforts of Meyers and others to expose dwellings from this period are best summarized in Hoglund and Meyers (1996), Meyers and Meyers (1982–83), and Meyers, Netzer, and Meyers (1986).

BIBLIOGRAPHY

AVIGAD, N. (1983). *Discovering Jerusalem*. Nashville: T. Nelson.

BAKER, C. M. (2002). *Rebuilding the House of Israel: Architectures of Gender in Jewish Antiquity*. Stanford: Stanford University Press.

BAR-NATHAN, R. /SKLAR-PARNES, D. A. (2007). 'A Jewish Settlement in Orine between the Revolts' [Hebr.], in *New Studies in the Archaeology of Jerusalem in Its Region. Collected Papers*, ed. J. Patrich and D. Amit. Jerusalem: Israel Antiquities Authority, 57–64.

BEEBE, H. K. (1968). 'Ancient Palestinian Dwellings'. *Biblical Archaeologist* 31: 38–58.

—— (1975). 'Domestic Architecture and the New Testament'. *Biblical Archaeologist* 38: 89–104.

BIGNASCA, A. et al. (1996). *Petra. Ez Zantur*, vol. 1: *Ergebnisse der Schweizerisch-Liechtensteinischen Ausgrabungen 1988–1992*. Terra Archaeologica 2. Mainz am Rhein: Phillipp von Zabern, 195–311.

CORBO, V. (1975). *Cafarnao*, vol. 1: *Gli edifici della città*. Jerusalem: Studium Biblicum Franciscanum.

—— (1982). "Ripreso a Cafarnao. Lo Scavo della Città". *Liber Annuus* 32: 427–46.

CROSSAN, J. D./REED, J. L. (2001). *Excavating Jesus: Beneath the Stones: Behind the Texts*. San Francisco: Harper.

DAUPHIN, C. /GIBSON, S. (1992/93). 'Ancient Settlements in their Landscapes: the Results of Ten Years of Survey on the Golan Heights (1978–1988)'. *Bulletin of the Anglo-Israel Archaeological Society* 12: 7–31.

FRANKEL, R. /GETZOV, N. /AVIAM, M. /DEGANI, A. (2001). *Settlement Dynamics and Regional Diversity in Ancient Upper Galilee*. Israel Antiquities Authority Reports 14. Jerusalem: Israel Antiquities Authority.

GALOR, K. (1996). 'Domestic Architecture in the Galilee and the Golan during the Roman and Byzantine Periods'. PhD. thesis, Brown University, RI.

—— (2000). 'The Roman-Byzantine Dwelling in the Galilee and the Golan—"House" or "Apartment?"' *Archaeologia Transatlantica* 18: 17–34.

—— (2003a). 'Wohnkultur im Römisch-Byzantinischen Palästina', in *Zeichen aus Text und Stein. Studien auf dem Weg zu einer Archäologie des Neuen Testaments*, ed. S. Alkier and J. Zangenberg. Tübingen and Basel: Tanz, 183–208.

—— (2003b). 'Domestic Architecture in Roman and Byzantine Galilee and Golan'. *Near Eastern Archaeology* 66: 44–57.

—— (2007). 'The Stepped Water Installations of the Sepphoris Acropolis', in *The Archaeology of Difference: Gender, Ethnicity and the 'Other' in Antiquity: Studies in Honor of Eric M. Meyers*, ed. D. Edwards and C. McCollough. Boston: American Schools of Oriental Research, 205–217.

GAWLIKOWSKI, M. (1986). 'A Residential Area by the South Decumanus', in *Jerash Archaeological Project*, vol. 1, ed. F. Zayadine. Amman: Department of Antiquities, Hashemite Kingdom of Jordan, 107–21.

GEVA, H. (ed.) (2000). *Jewish Quarter Excavations in the Old City of Jerusalem, conducted by Nahman Avigad, 1969–1982*, vol. 1. Jerusalem: Israel Exploration Society and Institute of Archaeology, Hebrew University of Jerusalem.

—— (ed.) (2006). *Jewish Quarter Excavations in the Old City of Jerusalem, conducted by Nahman Avigad, 1969–1982*, vol. 3. Jerusalem: Israel Exploration Society and Institute of Archaeology, Hebrew University of Jerusalem.

HEZSER, C. (1998). '"Privat" und "öffentlich" im Talmud Yerushalmi und in der griechisch-römischen Antike', in *The Talmud Yerushalmi and Graeco-Roman Culture*, vol. 1, ed. Peter Schäfer. Tübingen: Mohr-Siebeck, 423–579.

HIRSCHFELD, Y. (1983). 'Excavations of a Jewish Dwelling at Khirbet Susiya' [Hebr.]. *Eretz Israel* 17: 168–80.

—— (1987). *Dwelling Houses in Roman and Byzantine Palestine* [Hebr.]. Jerusalem: Yad Izhak Ben-Zvi.

—— (1995). *The Palestinian Dwelling in the Roman-Byzantine Period*. Jerusalem: Franciscan Printing Press.

—— (2007). *En-Gedi Excavations*, vol. 2: *Final Report (1996–2002)*. Jerusalem: Israel Exploration Society.

—— (2008). 'A Jewish Dwelling at Horvat Susiya', in *From Antioch to Alexandria: Studies in Domestic Architecture during the Roman and Byzantine Periods*, ed. K. Galor and T. WALISZEWSKI. Polish Archaeology in the Mediterranean, Centre of Mediterranean Archaeology. Warsaw: Warsaw University, 115–25.

HOGLUND, K./ MEYERS, E. (1996). 'The Residential Quarter on the Western Summit', in *Sepphoris in Galilee. Crosscurrents of Culture*, ed. R. M. Nagy, C. Meyers, E. Meyers, and Z. Weiss. Winona Lake, IN: Eisenbrauns, 39–43.

JASTROW, M. (1903). *A Dictionary of the Targumim, the Talmud Babli, Yerushalmi and Midrashic Literature*. New York: Judaic Press.

KILLEBREW, A. / FINE, S. (1991). 'Qatzrin: Reconstructing Village Life in Talmudic Times'. *Biblical Archaeology Review* 17: 44–56.

—— /MA'OZ, Z. (1988). 'Ancient Qasrin. Synagogue and Village'. *Biblical Archaeologist* 51: 5–19.

KRAUSS, S. (1910). *Talmudische Archäologie*, vol. 1. Leipzig: Gustav Fock, 1–77.

LOFFREDA, S. (2005). *Cafarnao*, vol. 5: *Documentazione fotografica degli scavi. 1986–2003*. Jerusalem: Franciscan Printing Press.

MA'OZ, Z. (1985). 'Comments on Jewish and Christian Communities in Byzantine Palestine'. *Palestine Exploration Quarterly* 117: 59–68.

—— (1987). 'The Architecture of Gamla and Its Buildings' [Hebr.], in *Zev Vilnay's Jubilee Volume: Essays on the History, Archaeology and Lore of the Holy Land, presented to Zev Vilnay*, vol. 2, ed. E. Schiller. Jerusalem: Ariel, 147–54.

MAZAR, B. (1969). *The Excavations in the Old City of Jerusalem; Preliminary Report of the First Season, 1968*. Jerusalem: Israel Exploration Society.

MAZAR, E. (2003). *The Temple Mount Excavations in Jerusalem 1968–1978. Directed by Benjamin Mazar. Final Reports*, vol. 2: *The Byzantine and Early Islamic Periods*. Jerusalem: Institute of Archaeology, Hebrew University of Jerusalem.

McNICOLL, A. / SMITH, R. / HENNESSY, B. (1982). *Pella in Jordan*, vol. 1. Canberra: Australian National Gallery.

MEYERS, E. M. (2000). 'Yes, They Are' (Response to H. Eshel, 'The Pools of Sepphoris, Ritual Baths or Bathtubs?—They're Not Ritual Baths'). *Biblical Archaeology Review* 26: 46–49.

—— (2003). 'Roman-Period Houses from the Galilee: Domestic Architecture and Gendered Spaces', in *Symbiosis, Symbolism, and the Power of the Past: Canaan, Ancient Israel, and Their Neighbors from the Late Bronze Age through Roman Palaestina*, ed. W. G. Dever and S. Gitin. Winona Lake, Ind.: Eisenbrauns, 487–99.

—— /MEYERS, C. L. (1982–83). 'Talmudic Village Life in the Galilean Highlands'. *Bulletin of the Anglo-Israel Archaeological Society*: 32–36.

MEYERS, E. M. / NETZER, E. / MEYERS, C. L. (1986). 'Sepphoris: "Ornament of All Galilee"'. *Biblical Archaeologist* 49: 4–19.

MEYERS, E. M. / STRANGE, J. F. / GROH, D. E. (1978). 'The Meiron Excavation Project: Archeological Survey in Galilee and Golan, 1976'. *Bulletin of the American Schools of Oriental Research* 229: 1–24.

NEGEV, A. (1980). 'House and City Planning in the Ancient Negev and the Provincia Arabia', in *Housing in Arid Lands: Design and Planning*, ed. G. Golany. London: Architectural Press, 3–32.

—— (1988). *The Architecture of Mampsis: Final Report*, 2 vols. Qedem 26–27. Jerusalem: Institute of Archaeology, Hebrew University of Jerusalem.

—— (1997). *The Architecture of Oboda: Final Report*. Qedem 36. Jerusalem: Institute of Archaeology, Hebrew University of Jerusalem.

NETZER, E. (1981). *Greater Herodium*. Qedem 13. Jerusalem: Institute of Archaeology, Hebrew University of Jerusalem.

—— (2001). *Hasmonean and Herodian Palaces at Jericho: Final Reports of the 1973–1987 Excavations*, vol. 1. Jerusalem: Israel Exploration Society and Institute of Archaeology, Hebrew University of Jerusalem.

—— (2004). *Hasmonean and Herodian Palaces at Jericho: Final Reports of the 1973–1987 Excavations*, vol. 2. Jerusalem: Israel Exploration Society and Institute of Archaeology, Hebrew University of Jerusalem.

ORLANDOS, A. K. (1966–68). *Les matériaux de construction et la technique architectural des anciens Grecs*, 2 vols. Paris: de Boccard.

REICH, R. (1993). 'The Great Mikveh Debate'. *Biblical Archaeology Review* 19: 52–53.

RICHARDSON, L. R. (1983). 'A Contribution to the Study of Pompeian Dining Rooms'. *Pompeii, Herculaneum, Stabiae: Bolletino dell'associazione internazionle Amici di Pompei* 1: 61–71.

SALIOU, C. (1996). *Le traité d'urbanisme de Julien d'Ascalon (VIe s.). Droit et architecture en Palestine au VIe siècle*. Travaux et mémoires du Centre de recherche d'histoire et civilisation de Byzance, Monographies 8. Paris: de Boccard.

—— (2000). 'Le traité de droit urbain de Julien d'Ascalon. Coutumier et codification', in *La codification des lois dans l'antiquité: actes du Colloque de Strasbourg (Novembre 1997)*, ed. E. Lévy. Strasbourg: Université Marc Bloch, 293–313.

SEGAL, A. (1983). *The Byzantine City of Shivta (Esbeita), Negev Desert, Israel*. B.A.R. International Series 179. Oxford: B.A.R.

SYON, D./YAVOR Z. (2005). 'Gamla 1997–2000'. *Atiqot* 50: 37–71.

TALGAM, R. /WEISS, Z. (2004). *The Mosaics of the House of Dionysos at Sepphoris, excavated by E. Meyers, E. Netzer and C. Meyers*. Qedem 44. Jerusalem: Institute of Archaeology, Hebrew University of Jerusalem, 17–33.

VRIES, B. DE (1998). *Umm el-Jimal: A Frontier Town and Its Landscape in Northern Jordan*, vol. 1: *Fieldwork 1972–1981*. Journal of Roman Archaeology Suppl. Series 26. Portsmouth, RI: Journal of Roman Archaeology.

WARD-PERKINS, J. B. (1974). *Roman Architecture*. Milan: Electa.

WEBER, A. (1993). 'Building Practice and Regulation in the Land of Israel in the Talmudic Age'. PhD. thesis, University College London.

WEISS, Z. (2008). 'Private Architecture in the Public Sphere', in *From Antioch to Alexandria. Studies in Domestic Architecture during the Roman and Byzantine Periods*, ed. K. Galor and T. Waliszewski. Polish Archaeology in the Mediterranean, Centre of Mediterranean Archaeology. Warsaw: Warsaw University, 75–85.

YEIVIN, Z. (1971). 'Survey of Settlements in the Galilee and the Golan from the Period of the Mishnah in the Light of the Sources' [Hebr.]. PhD. thesis, Hebrew University of Jerusalem.

—— (1973). 'Excavations at Khorazin' [Hebr.]. *Eretz Israel* 11: 144–57.

—— (1982/83). 'Korazin: a Mishnaic City'. *Bulletin of the Anglo-Israel Archaeological Society*: 46–48.

—— (1987). 'On the "Medium-sized City"'. *Eretz Israel* 19: 59–71.

—— (1993). 'Chorazin', in *New Encyclopedia of Archaeological Excavations in the Holy Land*, ed. E. Stern. Jerusalem: Carta and Israel Exploration Society, 301–4.

CHAPTER 24

DEATH, BURIAL, AND AFTERLIFE

STEVEN FINE

1. INTRODUCTION

No area of Jewish life in the Graeco-Roman period is better represented in archaeological and literary remains than death. It is no wonder, then, that death, burial, and the afterlife in the history of Roman-period Judaism has interested scholars since the beginning of modern academic research (Bosio 1632, vol. 1: 141–143). An underlying catalyst for this interest in ancient Jewish death, which is far more intensive than the usual antiquarian interest in funerary issues, is the continuing Christian concern with the 'death, burial and afterlife' of the most famous Jew of the first century, Jesus of Nazareth (c. 4 BCE–c. 32 CE). Christian and Jewish scholars have combed ancient Jewish literary sources and scoured the Holy Land for clues to interpret one of history's most significant burials. Often these scholars have been quite successful, leading to significant discoveries and interpretations (e.g. Charlesworth 2006). Fascination with ancient Jewish death as a window into the world of Jesus and the early church goes unabated, as is well illustrated by the recent popular tempest stirred by the supposed 'James ossuary' and the fictitious (and American-media driven) 'Tomb of Jesus' in the Talpiot area of southern Jerusalem (Byme and McNary-Zac 2009).

Modern excavation of Jewish tombs in the Land of Israel began with L. F. De Saucey's exploration of the burial complex of Queen Helena of Adiabene in

Jerusalem in 1863, which De Saucey erroneously identified as the 'Tomb of the (biblical) Kings' (De Saucey 1865: vol 1: 345–410, vol 2: 188–9, 309–11). Working in tandem, scholars in mandatory Palestine, at first motivated by Zionist notions of digging up their 'Old-New Land', were active in the excavation and interpretation of Jewish burial sites—beginning with N. Slouschz's excavation of the 'Tomb of Zechariah' in 1925, and the pioneering work of E. L. Sukenik, his students Max-imillian Kon, Nahman Avigad, and others (Kon 1947: 73–79; Avigad 1954; Mazar et. al. 1973–1976). As with the current case of the so-called 'James ossuary' and the 'Talpiot Jesus Tomb', even legitimate scholars have been overly zealous in supplying popular American Christian piety, and along the way darkened their legacies—the first, and most famous, being E. L. Sukenik himself (Sukenik 1947: 351–365; 1947b esp. 79).

Since the founding of modern Israel in 1948, and especially since the 1967 Six-Day War, Israeli archaeologists have provided important resources for the study of death in Roman Palestine, particularly during the latter Second Temple period. Together with a host of site reports, major studies have recently been produced, at the forefront works by R. Hachlili (2005), A. Kloner and B. Zissu (2008), J. Levison (2002), L. Y. Rahmani (1994), and Z. Weiss (1989). The study of Jewish death during the Roman and Byzantine periods has often been broadened to include the wider issues of 'death, burial and afterlife' in ancient Judaism, in Roman culture and early Christianity, enhancing the academic conversation.

The introduction of death as a historical subject paralleled renewed interest in 'end of life' issues in Europe and North America. The first major study of the history of death was penned by prominent *Annals* scholar Phillippe Arles, with his monumental *L'homme devant la mort* (1977, tr. *The Hour of Our Death*, 1985), though Arles did not deal with Jewish death. His student, Sylvie-Anne Goldberg, began the process of rectifying this lacuna in a case study translated in English as *Crossing the Jabbok: Illness and Death in Ashkenazi Judaism in Sixteenth through Nineteenth Century Prague* (Goldberg 1996). David Kraemer has recently moved toward a history of death in rabbinic literature, with reference to archaeology and broader historical issues (Kraemer 2000).

The history of death in Judaism must be viewed within a still larger frame than Jewish literary and archaeological sources alone. By the Roman period—and even earlier—Jews were an integral part of the ethnic mosaic of the Graeco-Roman world. They had inculturated the mores of the Roman East, of which they were part and parcel. Like all of the nations of the eastern Empire, Jews integrated with the culture of Greece and Rome in ways that were unique to them. This included fealty to laws and traditions associated with their ancestral faith, behaviours that Roman authors often both reviled and respected. Responding to both internal and general stimuli, Jews absorbed, rejected, transformed, and amalgamated with general culture in ways that were both complex and ongoing (Fine 2005a: 53–9). This model of inculturation is well expressed in all areas of culture relating to Jews, and in particular in the area of death, burial, and afterlife. My purpose here is to discuss a few pregnant examples where archaeology and texts can be read together profitably for writing a 'specifically Jewish ethnography of death' in Roman Palestine, to adapt Pierre Nora's solicitous formulation (Goldberg 1996: preface).

Archaeological evidence for the history of burial tends to be monumental. In general, the tombs of the rich, or the near rich, attract attention. The tombs of the poor and unknown are generally preserved in small numbers, if at all. Jewish funerary architecture is preserved from the Hasmonian and Roman period in Jerusalem and environs, roughly from the second century BCE to 70 CE, and again in the third to fifth or sixth century CE Bet She'arim catacombs in the Lower Galilee (Vito 1996: 115–146). In both the earlier and later cases, members of the Jewish elite participated in the general funerary architecture of their times. In fact, one would be hard pressed to distinguish the distinctly Jewish from general late Hellenistic and Roman funerary architecture, and even the specifically Jewish elements may well be seen within the contours of the general practice.

Perhaps most interesting in both first century Judaea and at Bet She'arim are the ways in which Jews chose to express their distinctiveness by adopting and adapting well-known Graeco-Roman models. The same may be said of the far less monumental, though infinitely interesting, Jewish cemetery at Zoar, on the south-eastern shore of the Dead Sea. To date, more than forty tombstones have been found in secondary use in Zoar (Misgav 2006). Uniquely, the Zoar inscriptions are part of a far larger corpus of Byzantine Christian inscriptions from this site, which number more than 420 examples, and stretch over three centuries. Thus, contextualization of the Zoar inscriptions may be deeply focused upon the local context.

In what follows I shall highlight places of interconnectedness and disjunction between archaeological and literary sources, allowing the discussion to be led on the basis of the archaeological and literary sources that exemplify the physical contexts of Jewish death in the Roman period—with an eye toward evidence of belief in the afterlife in each of these contexts.

2. MONUMENTAL TOMBS IN LATE SECOND TEMPLE PERIOD JUDAEA

In his polemical treatise, *Contra Apionem*, Josephus describes Jewish burial customs in ways that well reflect both Jewish and Roman customs: 'The pious rites which it [the Torah] provides for the dead do not consist of costly obsequies or the erection of conspicuous monuments. The funeral ceremony is to be undertaken by the nearest relatives, and all who pass while a burial is proceeding must join the procession and share the mourning of the family. After the funeral the house and its inmates must be purified.' (Josephus, *Contra Apionem*, 2.205; Levison 2002: 247). Josephus' own writings reveal, however, just how commonly Jews created monumental and costly show tombs during the latter Second Temple period. This phenomenon parallels archaeological discoveries over the last two centuries.

The earliest known Jewish burial monument was constructed by Simon the Hasmonaean, who ruled Judaea between 143 and 134 BCE. Simon constructed a magnificent tomb complex for his family in their ancestral home at Modi'in in the Judaean Shephelah (Fine 2005a: 60–81). No longer extant, this tomb is described in great detail in 1 Maccabees 13:27–29: 'And Simon built a monument over the tomb of his father and his brothers; he made it high that it might be seen, with polished stone at the front and back. He also erected seven pyramids, opposite one another, for his father and mother and four brothers. And for the pyramids he devised an elaborate setting, erecting about them great columns, and upon the columns he put suits of armor for a permanent memorial, and beside the suits of armor carved ships, so that they could be seen by all who sail the sea. This is the tomb which he built in Modi'in; it remains to this day.'

This is the earliest example of Jewish monumental funerary architecture of the Graco-Roman period, and clearly served as a model for later monuments. The tomb complex described here is thoroughly Hellenistic in conception. Maximillian Kon suggests a reasonable reconstruction of the Hasmonaean complex: 'It was apparently a very high rectangular structure built from ashlars which served as a base for the upper story of the monument, consisting of seven base structures in the form of towers surrounded by pilasters and crowned by pyramidal or conical tops. The wall-surfaces between the pilasters were decorated with reliefs of weapons and ships' (Kon 1971: 53). The most important precursors include the famous Mausoleum at Halacarnassos in Asia Minor, dating to the fourth century BCE, and the Belevi monument, located close by. Monuments topped with pyramids have been discovered throughout the Levant. Among these are the first century BCE Tomb of Hamrath at Suweida in Syria, where shields and other military implements appear among the decorations of the tomb—just as is described in 1 Maccabees. The monumental tombs at Hermel and Kalat Fakra in Lebanon are also important parallels (Berlin 2002: 141–7; Fedak 1990: 140–50).

Monumental funerary monuments topped with 'pyramids' were a common feature of late Hasmonaean and Roman Jerusalem (Berlin 2005). Two are extant from Hasmonaean Jerusalem: the 'Tomb of Jason' in western Jerusalem (see Fig. 24.1), and the so-called 'Tomb of Zechariah' in the Kidron Valley south-east of the Temple Mount (Rahmani 1967: 61–100; Avigad 1954: 73–132; see Fig. 24.2).

The nearby 'Tomb of Absalom' and the 'Tomb of the Kings' both dating to the Roman period, are crowned with conical 'pyramids', reminiscent of Roman

Fig. 24.1 The Tomb of Jason, Jerusalem

Photo: Steven Fine

Fig. 24.2 The Tomb of Zechariah, Jerusalem

Photo: Steven Fine

monuments at Pompeii and elsewhere (see Fig. 24.3). Like the Hasmonaean tombs, the 'Tomb of the Kings' was crowned with multiple 'pyramids', in this case, three (Kon 1947: 73–79; Fine 2003: 233–41). Josephus described this feature in the context of the internment of Queen Helena of Adiabene some time after 50 CE: 'Monobazus sent her bones and those of his brother to Jerusalem with instructions that they should be buried in the three pyramids that his mother had erected at a distance of three furlongs from the city of Jerusalem'. L. Feldman suggests that the three pyramids were 'presumably for Helena and her two sons, Izates and Monobazus' (Josephus, Ant. 20.95; See also Josephus, Bell. 5. 55, 119, 147, tr. Thackery et al. 1926–1965). Remnants of these conical 'pyramids' were uncovered by Kon (1947: 73–9).

The decorations of the Hasmonaean tombs, described by 1 Maccabees as including armor placed upon columns and 'carved ships', is consistent both with Hellenistic iconography and the art of the Hasmonaean and Herodian periods. The First Maccabees description of the Hasmonaean tombs is quoted with minor variations by Josephus, who, significantly, leaves out the decorations described in 1 Maccabees— perhaps a sign that such imagery was not acceptable to Josephus and some of

Fig. 24.3 The Tomb of Absalom, Jerusalem

Photo: Steven Fine

his contemporaries (Ant. 13. 211–213). Imagery of this sort was all but unknown in Roman Jerusalem, which may contextualize Josephus' decision to elide this imagery—which could well have been removed by his time (Fine 2005a: 73–81).

No archaeological or literary sources provide evidence for rituals that took place in relation to the monumental tombs of Jerusalem. The imposing monumental staircase (9 metres wide) leading down to the so-called 'Tomb of the Kings', significant water installations (for ritual bathing?), and a broad plaza before the well-carved tomb (26 x 27 metres and carved to a depth of 8.5 metres into bedrock), suggest that the tomb of Queen Helena of Adiabene may have witnessed some sort of public ceremonial (Kon 1947). The same may be said of the smaller courtyards before monumental tombs elsewhere in Jerusalem and in the Jericho *necropolis*. Josephus' portrayal of Herod's funerary procession to Herodium expresses the high point of Roman lavishness practised by the ruling class of Judaea in the Roman period (Ant. 17.196–200. See also: Josephus, Bell. 1.670–2:2. On the recently discovered Tomb of Herod at Herodium see Netzer/Kalman/Porat 2008):

They then made preparations for the funeral of the king. Archeleus saw to it that his father's burial should be most splendid, and he brought out all his ornaments to accompany the procession for the deceased. Herod was borne upon a golden bier studded with precious stones of various kinds and with a cover of purple over it. The dead man too was wrapped in purple robes and wore a diadem upon which a gold crown had been placed, and beside his right hand lay his sceptre. Round the bier were his sons and a host of relatives, and after them came the army disposed according to the various nationalities and designations . . . , and they were followed by five hundred servants carrying spices.

John Levison has shown how closely Josephus' descriptions of Jewish funerary practices correspond with Roman practices and ideals. A part from occasional references to specifically Jewish customs, such as seven-day mourning periods in this text, Josephus's descriptions of Jewish customs in the present—as well as in biblical treatments, are fully in line with Roman ideals (Levison 2002: 270–2). Levison astutely notes the lack of *imagines* in this description of Herod's funeral procession. *Imagines*, 'people wearing masks' of the deceased, his ancestors, and other prominent Romans, do not appear in Josephus' rendition, even though these were a common feature of aristocratic Roman funeral processions. Levison attributes this lack of images to specifically Jewish sensibilities against human images, and Josephus does not seem above ignoring art that did not fit his notion of Jewish 'anti-idolism'. In light of Herod's care not to infringe upon this 'anti-idolic' impulse throughout his reign, Levison is probably right (Levison 2002: 273–5; Fine 2005a: 73–81). While reflecting Josephus' apologetic intention, the reality described by Josephus could not have been too far from the truth.

Those at the pinnacle of Jerusalem's social hierarchy were buried in stone sarcophagi, which were rare during this period. Many were decorated with floral patterns. This was the case of Herod's sarcophagus, fragments of which have been identified at Herodium. A large sarcophagus uncovered in the 'Tomb of the Kings', now at the Louvre, is inscribed 'Sadah [or: Sadan] the Queen' in Hebrew and Aramaic, and is generally thought to belong to Helena of Adiabene (Hachlili 2005: 121, 168). A mere seventeen extant stone sarcophagi from Jerusalem are enumerated by R. Hachlili (Hachlili 2005: 115–126). Simple wooden exemplars were preserved in the dry climate of Jericho and elsewhere in the Dead Sea region (Hachlili/Killebrew 1999: 62–62; Hachlili 2005: 75–94).

Images of pyramidal monuments appear as decorations within less-aristocratic Jewish contexts. Monuments similar to the 'Tomb of Zechariah' are incised as decorations on ossuaries from Jerusalem, and images of pyramidal monuments appear as decorations in the necropolis of Jericho (Hachlili 2005: 346–353). The image of a monument crowned by three pyramids is incised on a recently published ossuary (Fine 2003). We cannot know whether, along with the obvious 'drip down' of imagery from the tombs of the upper aristocracy, the pyramidal tomb had some unique ideational significance that made it attractive for Jews. Be that as it may, the ubiquitousness of this imagery is clearly expressed in the archaeological record of first-century Jerusalem, a point noted by Michael Avi-Yonah, who, in constructing his scale model of Herodian Jerusalem at the Holyland Hotel in Jerusalem (now at the Israel Museum), imagined a city where pyramidal monuments punctuated the skyline (see Wharton, 2006: 219–22).

3. Ossuary Burial in Herodian Period Jerusalem and its Environs

A significant transition took place in Jerusalem and its environs sometime during the late first century BCE. The Jerusalem elite moved from burial in charnel pits to secondary burial. An excellent example of this transition is the 'Tomb of Jason', constructed at the beginning of the first century BCE (Rahmani 1967; Avigad 1954: 73–132). At first, bodies were placed in individual loculi (Hebrew: *kokhim*) to decompose, and later the bones were deposited in a charnel pit. In around 20 BCE charnel burial was discontinued, and ossuary burial became the norm. Ossuary burial became a common mode of internment among the elite, according to L. Y. Rahmani, between 20 and 15 BCE (Rahmani 1994: 21–22). Ossuary burial continued in southern Judaea and the Galilee into the third century CE.

Secondary burial was not unique to elite Jews during the Roman period. Significant numbers of ossuaries have been discovered, for example, in western Asia Minor, and date to roughly the same period (Magness 2005: 135–136). Magness notes that 'closer to Judaea, the Nabatean cemetery at Mampsis in the Negev yielded an ossuary containing bones wrapped in linen' (ibid. 135). She elides the fact, noted by A. Negev, that 'the "ossuary-type" tomb contained a coin from year 4 of Rabbel II (74 CE)' (Negev 1993: 892). Ossuary burial does not necessarily reflect Jewish dependence upon Nabataean burial customs. It could also reflect the opposite—or perhaps a parallel development. Further study of ossuary burial in Nabataean contexts is a desideratum.

It seems that for Jews, the advantage of ossuaries was the fact that they allowed for a monumentalized form of burial, in the Roman mode, for a community that was religiously averse to the common Roman custom of cremation. Ossuary burial allowed for increased individualization in burial at a time when individuals of stature were making themselves known for their Graeco-Roman style euergetism in the Jewish public realm—particularly in the Temple—and Jewish authors were increasingly writing in their own names rather than resorting to a pseudepigraphic impulse. Ben Sira is an early example of this practice. For the first century, Philo of Alexandria, Josephus, and the apostle Paul are obvious examples. It is certainly correct that 'the practice of recording name(s) on ossuaries should be understood as reflecting a concern for recording and preserving the memory of the deceased. The preservation of the names of ancestors was of great importance to the upper classes and priestly families, and above all the high priestly families, who based their social standing and claims of legitimacy on their lineage' (Magness 2005: 136). It should nonetheless be noted that just 25 per cent of the 895 ossuaries from the State of Israel collections published by L. I. Rahmani contain inscriptions, and many of these are simple familial identifiers like *imma*, 'mother', and *abba*, 'father' (Rahmani 1994). Significantly, ossuary and sarcophagus inscriptions were generally written in a most non-monumental manner, quickly and often haphazardly. One would have expected more impressive inscriptions if claims of 'legitimacy' were the primary goal.

It is significant that ossuary burial began roughly at the time when Herod the Great began his massive reconstruction of Jerusalem and its Temple. His reconstruction of the Temple, which began *c*. 20–19 BCE, coincides with Rahmani's dating of the origins of ossuary burial in Jerusalem between 20 and 15 BCE. From an economic standpoint, this is the factor that facilitated the transformation. A corollary was the rise of a well-trained community of stone masons. The fabrication of stone ossuaries was predicated upon this industry, just as it was for the fabrication of stone containers, tables, and the like (cf. Magness 2005: 139). In fact, Y. Magen dates the rise of the stone industry to within thirty years of the first ossuaries, about 50 BCE (Magen 2002; Miller 2003).

The relationship between sarcophagi, ossuaries, and the general stone carving industry is confirmed by the high level of decoration of many of the extant sarcophagi and ossuaries, which parallels in its workmanship other utilitarian objects like tables, as well as the geometric plans of mosaic pavements. Mosaics from the northern palace at Masada, with their depictions of the rosette surrounded by frames of geometric design, are an obvious parallel, as are the monumental bas reliefs from the Temple Mount's southern Hulda Gate, and rosette decoration in the synagogue of Gamla (Hachlili 1988: 1–25). Particularly significant are images of funerary monuments and of other monumental buildings on the exteriors of ossuaries, which bring important aspects of the new architectural cityscape of late Hasmonaean/Herodian Jerusalem into the crypts themselves. One group of ossuaries, for example, reproduces in a schematic fashion the borders that are so typical of Herodian masonry in its depiction of an ashlar wall (Hachlili 2005: 370–3; Rahmani 1994: 35). Others present images of colonnades with columns whose capitals bear close resemblance to Herodian capitals, and of building facades of the sorts that were constructed, not only in the necropolis, but along the byways of Herodian Jerusalem as well.

A link between ossuary burial and benefaction to the Temple is expressed archaeologically. An ossuary discovered in a monumental tomb on Mount Scopus (now at the British Museum) is inscribed in Greek: 'The bones of the sons [or: descendants] of Nicanor the Alexandrian, who made the doors', followed by 'Nicanor Alexa' in Aramaic (Hachlili 2005: 172–3; see Fig. 24.4). These gates were remembered and their legend embellished by the rabbis centuries later, who recalled that Nicanor of Alexandria had donated gates of Corinthian bronze to the Temple (M. Yoma 3:9-10; T. Yoma 2:3–4; Jacobson/ Weitzman 1992: 237–248). Together with the ossuary of 'Yehohana daughter of Yehohanan, son of Thophlos, the high priest' and of the family of the high priest Caiaphas, the Nicanor ossuary is

Fig. 24.4 Decorated limestone ossuary of the Nicanor family

Courtesy of the British Museum Image Service

an indicator that the wealthy and well-connected Jews used this form of burial during the first century (Rahmani 1994: no. 881; Greenhut 1994: 219–222; Reich 1994: 223–225. Note also a recently discovered sarcophagus fragment labelled 'son of the high priest', Haaretz 2008). An ossuary belonging to a contractor, builder, or donor to the Temple construction project (we cannot know which), one 'Simeon, builder of the sanctuary' closes the circle (Hachlili 2005: 173; Rahmani 1994: no. 200). Ossuary burial served Jerusalem's elite at least from the time of Herod the Great onward, an elite that was intimately involved with the Temple and Herod's project of rebuilding Jerusalem.

Scholars have debated the religious significance of ossuaries, often asserting that ossuary burial was popular among Jews as a reaction to theological developments. Literary sources from the Second Temple period are not particularly useful for interpreting the ideational context of Jewish burial during this period. It is suggested that Pharisaic notions of bodily resurrection discussed by Josephus, the New Testament, and rabbinic sources sparked the use of ossuaries among Jews. Later rabbinic sources are often marshalled in support of this theory, although no rabbinic tradition actually points toward this explanation. Rather, this modern academic trope is intertwined with the Christian concern with salvation.

The ossuaries of 'Yehohana daughter of Yehohanan, son of Thophlos, the high priest' and of the family of Caiaphas, the high priest of Jesus' trial who, in Acts 5:15, is linked to the party of the Sadducees, reflect a situation in which Jews who were seemingly not Pharisees used ossuaries for secondary burial (Rahmani 1994: no. 881). This is particularly problematic, as the literary sources report that Sadducees did not believe in the resurrection of the dead (Stemberger 1995). There is no reason to suggest, as some have done in order to resuscitate the Pharisee thesis, that non-Pharisees adopted Pharisaic burial customs in a culture in which Pharisaic customs were supposedly the norm (Rahmani 1994: 53–54). In fact, J. Patrick has suggested persuasively that the all-important aqueduct system of first-century Jerusalem was constructed according to Sadducean and not Pharisaic norms (Levine 1997: 114; Patrich 1982: 25–39).

Later rabbinic discussion of ossuary burial does not assume that this mode was particularly Pharisaic or rabbinic, but only that Jews did it, and that the practice required discussion and some minor rabbinic regulation. Secondary burial in ossuaries was an element of what E. P. Sanders calls the 'Common Judaism', that is, the religious *koine* or general Jewish culture of Second Temple period Judaea (Sanders 1992: ix; Fine 1997: 8–9). More than that, Jewish funerary monuments and secondary burial fit well within the contours of general burial practices in the eastern Mediterranean during the Roman period.

Literary sources of the Second Temple period make no mention of ossuary burial, though rabbinic literature provides some contextualization. These rabbinic sources are often cited, particularly by archaeologists, as the *Sitz im Leben* of archaeological discoveries (e.g. Rahmani 1994). Mishnah Baba Batra 6:8 discusses *loculus* burial in a manner that fits well with first-century archaeological remains:

He who sells a piece of property to his fellow to make him a [family] tomb, and similarly, he who receives a piece of property from his fellow to make him a [family] tomb, makes the interior of the cave four by six cubits, and excavates within it eight niches: three on one side, three on the other side, and two opposite them. And the niches will be four cubits long, and their height seven [handbreadths], and their width six [handbreadths]. Rabbi Simeon (ca. 150 C.E.) says: Make the interior of the cave six by eight cubits, and excavate within it thirteen niches: four on one side, four on the other side, three opposite them, and one to the right of the opening, and one at the left. And make a courtyard at the opening of the cave, six by six [cubits] the size of the bier and those entombing it and excavate within it two caves, one on one side and one on the other. Rabbi Shimon says: Four, one on each of its four sides. Rabban Shimon b. Gamaliel says: All depends upon the nature of the stone.

In fact, later rabbinic readers of this and associated texts successfully imagined and drew schematic drawings of this form of burial that parallel the archaeological reality (cf. the commentaries of Rashi and Tosafot on b. Baba Batra 101a). Rabbinic sources provide some inkling of the ritual and ideological experience of ossuary burial. So for example, Mishnah Moed Qatan 1:5 (cf. Kraemer 2000: 343–5; Rahmani 1994: 54): 'Further said Rabbi Meir (*c.* 150 CE): A person collects the bones of his father and mother [during the intermediate days of a festival], because it is gladness to him. R. Jose says a[time of]: It is a time of mourning for him'. The Talmud Yerushalmi expands upon Rabbi Meir's comment, contextualizing the manner of internment that the Mishnah takes for granted: 'Further said Rabbi Meir: A person collects the bones of his father and mother [during the intermediate days of a festival], because it is gladness to him (M. Moed Qatan 1:5); at first they would bury them in mounds [of soil], When the flesh had decayed, they collected the bones and buried them in secret. That day he would mourn, and the following day he was happy, for his fathers rested from judgment' (y. Moed Qatan 1:5, 79d–80a). How much these texts—and other rabbinic comments—reflect the first-century reality cannot be determined. They provide a real glimpse, however, into how a somewhat later literate group of Roman-period Jews, the rabbis, reflected upon, and seemingly experienced, a custom that was uninterrupted—though diminished—from the time of Herod the Great until tannaitic times.

The development of monumentalized burial in Roman Judaea, particularly in the area of Jerusalem, is a function of the Graeco-Romanization of the Jews—I avoid calling this phenomenon 'Hellenization', a neologism dichotomized with 'Judaism' that bears such heavy baggage as to render it almost unusable (see Rajak 2001b). Jews used the same types of monuments as non-Jews during this period, just as their Temple was reconstructed by Herod in the architectural *lingua franca* of the age of Augustus. As with the decoration of the Temple, Jewish funerary art refrained from imagery that could be construed as 'idolatrous', and thus unacceptable from a Jewish standpoint. This had in no way impacted upon Simon Maccabee's general choices in building and decorating the Hasmonaean tombs, nor those of subsequent generations.

Abstaining from possible 'idolatry' was the distinctive element that marked these structures as 'Jewish'. Ossuaries appeared at about the same time as Herod's building projects, as Jerusalemite elites chose to be buried as individuals amongst their family groups rather than being simply 'gathered to their fathers' in charnel pits. The choice of ossuaries—usually stone, but sometimes wood or ceramic—was facilitated by general Graeco-Roman practices. Ossuary burial was an upscale Graeco-Roman way of being interred in the eastern Mediterranean region. At the same time, it allowed wealthy Jews to maintain Jewish family ties intact and support communal religious strictures against idolatrous imagery and, above all, cremation.

4. JEWISH BURIAL PRACTICES IN LATE ANTIQUITY

The mid-second-century patriarch, Shimon b. Gamaliel, is well known for critical attitudes toward ostentation in burial practices. According to y. Sheqalim 2:7, 47a, 'Rabbi Shimon b. Gamaliel says: Monuments (*nefashot*) are not built for the righteous. Their words are their memorial'. The similarity between this statement and Josephus' comments in *Contra Apion* 2: 205 is quite remarkable. Examples of Jewish monumental tombs from the second half of the second century, the lifetime of this sage, are not extant. The same may not be said for later decades—the most prominent example being the apparent tomb of Rabbi Shimon's son, Rabbi Judah the Patriarch, at Bet She'arim.

While numerous Jewish tombs have been uncovered from late antiquity, no monumental Jewish *necropoleis* have yet been uncovered in Palestinian cities with large Jewish populations, including Bet Guvrin, Caesarea, Sepphoris, and Tiberias—nor are necropoleis in these places discussed in rabbinic or non-Jewish sources (Weiss 1989). The *necropolis* of Bet She'arim is the outstanding exception (Mazar, et al. 1973–1976; Stern 1993–2008: 236–248; Levine 2005: 197–225). Its twenty-four excavated burial units stretch to the west and south of the ancient town, near the juncture of major east-west and north-south traffic arteries at the foot of Mt. Carmel and overlooking the western Jezreel Valley (the New Testament's 'Plain of Armageddon). The significance of this massive complex for the local economy cannot be doubted, as dedicatory inscriptions discovered within the large local synagogue commemorate the euergetism of Jews who worked in the funerary industry. Thus we hear of 'Rabbi Samuel who arranges (the limbs of the dead)' and Judah who lays the corpse (Mazar et al. 1973–76, vol. 2: 189–90; Alon 1983: 2: 109–10; Weiss 1992: 363).

Bet She'arim is already mentioned in the Jerusalem Talmud as a burial place for Jews from Caesarea, and elsewhere as the final resting place of Rabbi Judah the Patriarch, the supposed editor of the Mishnah (Safrai 1983: 71–85; Mazar 1985: 293–299; Rajak 2001a: 483). Bet She'arim, identified as such in these literary sources and in a Greek inscription found at the site, perhaps because of the round Roman arches of the facades of catacombs 14 and 20, was a major Jewish necropolis from the third to the fifth centuries CE. Jews with origins as distant as Antioch on the Orontes, Palmyra, Nehardea in Sassanian Babylonia, and Himyar in Arabia were interred at Bet She'arim. Palestinian Jews, together with Jews with origins in nearby Phoenicia (Tyre, Sidon, Beirut, Byblos) predominate. The regional pull of these catacombs is unique in late Roman-period Jewish burial. Scholars have debated the reasons for the prominence of this cemetery as a preferred burial place for Jews of the late Roman and early Byzantine periods. Some have pointed to its significance for Diaspora Jews, both those who immigrated to Palestine themselves (as in the case of members of the 'synagogue of the Babylonians' in Sepphoris (*y. Shab* 6:1, 8a; Roth-Gerson 1987: 107, discusses other Diaspora communities), and those who had their bones transported to the Holy Land for secondary burial. Literary sources preserve discussions of bone transit, even from as far away as Babylonia, and burial in the soil of Palestine was seen by some to ameliorate past sins (Gafni 1999: 73–95).

The current 'master narrative' of Bet She'arim focuses on the presence of rabbinic figures in catacombs 14 and 22, and particularly the apparent burial of

Rabbi Judah the Patriarch and his family in catacomb 14. According to this approach, Jews are thought to have been brought from throughout Palestine and the Diaspora to be interned near the sages and their leader (e.g. Levine 2005). While this may be the case, the obvious projection from the present to the past should occasion caution—as Tessa Rajak has argued forcefully (Rajak 2001a). Bet She'arim has served as a kind of ancient parallel to Arlington National Cemetery, Westminster Abbey, and most importantly, Mt. Herzl in Jerusalem. This approach to Bet She'arim has a long history in Zionist thought and public ritual. A significant parallel to this understanding of Bet She'arim is the first century 'Tomb of Nicanor', which was transformed into a modern Zionist necropolis in 1934, when proto-Zionist thinker Leon Pinsker was buried in what was by then the botanical garden of the Hebrew University, followed in 1941 by Zionist, Menachem Ussishkin (Vilnay 1978a: 5171; see Fig. 24.5)

In a sense, Bet She'arim was treated as a secularized and 'Zionized' parallel to the 'Tombs of the Sanhedrin', a large necropolis in northern Jerusalem that was so designated by medieval Jewish pilgrims, which appeared on Israeli paper money minted from 1958 onwards and was labelled 'Tombs of the Sanhedrin' in Hebrew (Vilnay 1978b: 6475–9) It should be remembered that the excavator, Benjamin Mazar (later president of the Hebrew University, 1953–1961), was a significant member of the Zionist academic elite, the son-in-law of scholar, Zionist leader and future president, Izhak Ben Zvi.

During the last quarter of the twentieth century the question of rabbinic authority, so rife within liberalizing elements of American Judaism, has often focused on the question of rabbinic status at Bet She'arim. Constructing a counter-narrative of rabbinic marginality, some scholars tend to minimize the

Fig. 24.5 Tomb of Nicanor, Mt. Scopus, Jerusalem

Photo: Steven Fine

status of rabbis at Bet She'arim, preferring to see it as an assemblage of wealthy Jews, some associated with a more Hellenized patriarchate that was separating from a distinct 'rabbinic class' and others bearing the title 'Rabbi', but not necessarily identical with those mentioned in rabbinic literature (Cohen 1981: 1–17; Levine 2005: 204–211. On this phenomenon, see also Miller 2004: 27–76; Fine 2005a: 35–46).

My own sense is that the catacombs at Bet She'arim served a broad range of very wealthy Palestinian and eastern Diaspora Jews. 'Rabbis' contiguous with those of rabbinic literature, especially those associated with Rabbi Judah the Patriarch, were buried there in rather tight communities. As Alexei Sivertsev has shown, this would be expected from the household model of organization that seems to have been adopted by the rabbinic community (Sivertsev 2002). While most Jews memorialized their dead in Greek, rabbis did so mostly in Hebrew and Aramaic (see Hezser 2001: 385-86). The wealthy Jews who developed the household and communal catacombs (or just bought graves within larger complexes) at Bet She'arim apparently did so, at least in part, for reasons of status and/or piety. Rabbis were buried there as members of the patriarchal household (see Fig. 24.6).

Fig. 24.6 Façade of Bet She'arim, Catacomb 20   Photo: Steven Fine

Would the presence of rabbis have been a draw to other Jews? One could imagine so, though this is nowhere expressed in the mostly short texts of grave markers. I recall, though, with intentional glibness, that in our own day the presence of Al Jolson, Jack Benny, and other Hollywood luminaries at Hillside Memorial Park in Los Angeles adds lustre to that cemetery, though few would be buried there in order to be close to these culture heroes. More seriously—Jews in later generations made considerable efforts to be buried in close proximity to rabbinic 'holy men', and Christians contemporaneous to Bet She'arim made far more determined efforts to be in proximity to their 'holy men' (Brown 1981; Reiner 1988). One could imagine that the presence of Rabbi Judah the Patriarch and the rabbinic 'household' added to the attractiveness of Bet She'arim as part of the mix that attracted at least some Jews to this hillside in the Lower Galilee (see Fig. 24.7).

Architecturally, there is nothing 'Jewish' about the tombs at Bet She'arim. Were the many menorahs, Aramaic inscriptions and Jewish references removed, this could be mistaken for a general Roman-period necropolis—though the relative conservatism of catacomb art, when compared with non-Jewish tombs, may reflect a Jewish aesthetic similar to the conservatism of Jewish catacomb art in Rome (Fine 2005a: 128–9; Weiss 1996: 360–1). The presence of imagery with no Jewish

Fig. 24.7 Lion sarcophagus, Catacomb 20, Bet She'arim   Photo: Steven Fine

connection whatsoever, like an imported sarcophagus from cave 11 bearing the image of Leda penetrated by Zeus in the guise of a swan, represent the exceptions that prove the rule. This imported sarcophagus, together with other imported sarcophagi decorated with the image of a mounted combatant, human figures with togas, and the head of an Amazon, was procured for burial in this Jewish necropolis. The fact that the Leda sarcophagus was subjected to iconoclastic behaviour and then turned around so that the offending image could not be seen suggests a more conservative response by other Jews—whether contemporaries or later generations (Avi-Yonah 1972: 9–21; Fischer 1998: 206–207).

Bet She'arim provides a few explicit indications of belief in the afterlife. Scholars differ over the question of how significant this theme was in ancient Judaism (Fischer 1978: 236; Nagakubo 1974; Rutgers 2000: 293–310). Jewish funerary inscriptions, particularly in Aramaic, seldom include a gushing forth of expression of such sentiments, though literary sources show that notions of the afterlife were central to Jewish belief and much discussed during this period (Moore 1958, vol. 2: 279–287). An inscription in catacomb 11 invokes a curse against the eternal life of anyone who disturbed the grave: 'I Hesychios, lie here with my wife. May anyone who dares to open [the grave] above us not have a portion [*menos*] in the world to come [{*bion*}*aonio*{*n*}]' (Mazar et al. 1973-76, vol. 2: 112–13). Questionably, Schwabe connects the threat of losing one's 'portion in the world to come' with M. Sanhedrin 10:1: 'All Israel has a portion in the world to come' (ibid. 113). As Schwabe notes: 'The importance of this inscription lies in the fact that it gives expression to the belief in eternal life'.

Some scholars have tried to attach specific meanings to imagery decorating the catacombs—particularly menorahs, images of Torah shrines, conch shells, animals, and ships. Does the fact that amoraic literature imagined the existence of synagogues and study houses in the world to come affect the interpretation of Torah shrines flanked by menorahs on sealing stones of burial *kokhim* (Mazar et al. 1973–76, vol. 1: 110–113; Fine 1997: 120)? While menorahs and Torah shrines were Jewish identity markers, do they represent eschatological beliefs? Does a man with a menorah balancing on his head (cave 3) mean anything special, or is it just an oddity (Goodenough 1953–1967, vol. 1: 92; vol. 2: 93)? We cannot know, just as it is doubtful that any particularly Jewish meaning can be given to the images of (Charon's?) sailing vessel found at Bet She'arim (Goodenough, 1953–67, vol. 1: 97; vol. 3: figs 77–8). This is all very standard, if sparse, Graeco-Roman funerary iconography, with the addition of Jewish ethnic markers. Over-interpretation of this material has been rife during the last half century, particularly among historians of religion who developed 'mystical' and 'non-normative' approaches to these 'symbols' without reference to the very local uses to which this imagery was put by Jews (e.g. Goodenough 1953–67; Smith 1957–8: 473–512; Kraemer 2000: 49–71; Urbach 1958: 189–205).

A second important archaeological resource for the history of Jewish death is a corpus of approximately forty tombstones discovered in secondary use near the village of *Ghor es-Safi* in Jordan, at the south-eastern corner of the Dead Sea. Identified as biblical Zoar (Zoora) in Byzantine times, the Jewish inscriptions discovered represent approximately 1/10th of the more than 420 inscriptions found in secondary use at this site. The Christian corpus of 382 exemplars was recently published by Y. Meimaris and K. Kritikalau-Nikolaropoulou (2005), allowing for broad contextualization of the Jewish epitaphs. Jewish tombstones began to appear during the 1920s, and thirty-one have thus far been published (Naveh 1995, 1999, 2000; Cotton/Price 2001, Misgav 2006: 35–46). Another ten or so unpublished examples are known from private collections in New York and Israel. These date to the time between the mid-fourth and the late sixth century CE. Like many of the Christian tombstones from this site, Jewish epitaphs were painted with ochre pigment, or incised, or both on small limestone slabs that measure approximately 40 x 30 cm, with some a bit larger, others a bit smaller. Some of the incised Christian tombstones were polychrome (Meimaris/Kritikalau-Nikolaro-poulou 2005, no. 150, 246, pl. viii), and I would not be surprised if the same had been true for some inscribed Jewish exemplars. All of the Christian inscriptions were composed in Greek (Meimaris/Kritikalau-Nikolaropoulou 2005), while the Jewish ones were mainly written in Palestinian Aramaic, one being bilingual and one being Greek memorializing an 'archisynagogos', a synagogue leader (Meimaris/Kritikalau-Nikolaropoulou 2005: no. 7, 99–101). The Jewish Aramaic inscriptions present the name of the deceased, the day and month of death according to the Jewish calendar, and the year of death dating from the destruction of the Temple and according to the sabbatical cycle. They often end with the word 'Shalom' and other formulae. The Jewish Greek inscriptions use formulae known from Christian epitaphs.

Jewish Aramaic epitaphs are far more formulaic than Christian exemplars from Zoar, though some development over time is noticeable. A typical example, dating to 438 CE, reads: 'This is the tombstone (*nafsha*) of Hannah daughter of Ha[nie?] the priest, who died on the Sabbath, the first festival day (*yoma tava*) of Passover, the fifth day of the month of Nissan, in the fifth year of the sabbatical [cycle], which is the year three hundred and sixty-nine years since the destruction of the Temple. Peace. May her soul rest. Peace' (tr. Misgav 2006: 37, with minor corrections). Below the inscription is the image of a menorah (seven armed candelabrum), flanked on the right by a *shofar* (horn) and *lulav* (palm branch), and on the left by a Torah shrine. The amount of information on these tombstones is unique for Jewish epitaphs from antiquity, but parallels in length Christian formulae at Zoar. Mention of the sabbatical date and the date of the Temple's destruction is well documented in inscriptions and documents from this period, and the reference to peace, *shalom,* at the end of the inscriptions appears in both burial and synagogue inscriptions elsewhere. Images of menorahs, Torah shrines, *lulavim* (palm, myrtle, and willow bunches) and *etrogim* (citrons), often flanked by birds, appear in the bottom margins of a number of the stones. This is the only imagery used by Jews. Christians had a far wider repertoire in a similar location, and the most common Christian image is that of a cross flanked by birds (Meimaris/ Kritikalau-Nikolaropoulou 2005: 10–13). Three later Jewish epitaphs, dating to 415, 454, and 458 CE conclude with an explicit eschatological longing that draws on Isaiah 52:7, 'He will awaken to the voice of the harbinger of peace' (Naveh 1999: 620–623, nos. 19, 20, 22). Though the Jewish tombstones from Zoar provide Jewish content in a Jewish language, together with Jewish symbols, they are broadly consistent with Christian practice and form a definite sub-category of general burial practice at Zoar during late antiquity.

5. Conclusion

The ethnography of Jewish death in the Graeco-Roman period awaits full exposition. While scholars have focused on archaeological sources, the analysis of literary sources and their comparison from an interdisciplinary perspective and the writing of a synthetic history of Jewish death in antiquity have just begun. In this essay I have sketched some directions that this narrative may take.

Relatively little related to eschatological interests appears in the archaeological record. I am in full agreement with Rutgers in his assertion that references to life after death in Jewish epitaphs dating to the late antique period may very well turn out to be more apparent than real. For that reason, I believe that, in the end, the 'what-we-cannot-prove-we-cannot know-approach: is much less common-sensical than it appears at first blush' (Rutgers 2000: 307). This approach, so widespread in American scholarship of the latter twentieth century, does not convey the depth of how little we truly know—and understand, about ancient Judaism from the limited sources at our disposal. Much work is left to be done, if this fascinating area of Jewish cultural history in the Roman period is to be awakened from its slumber, and death in late antique Judaism is to be understood comprehensively.

Suggested Reading

Kloner and Zissu (2008) provide a general introduction to Jewish burial remains from the Second Temple period. This book provides an excellent introduction to the topic when paired with Hachlili (2005). The collection edited by Byme and McNary-Zak focuses on contemporary Christian interest in ancient Jewish burial through the lens of the so-called 'James ossuary'. Second Temple literary sources on burial practices are best dealt with by Levison (2002), whose main interest is Josephus, and McCane (2003) whose focus is on New Testament studies. For the later Roman period, the final reports of the Bet She'arim excavation (Mazar et al. 1973–1976) are still the best introduction in English, especially when read together with Weiss (1989, 1992), who provides a discussion of significant literary sources relating to burial practice. The Zoar inscriptions are discussed briefly by Misgav (2006), and Kraemer (2000) assembles rabbinic sources on death and the afterlife.

BIBLIOGRAPHY

ALON, G. (1983). 'Burial' [Hebr.], in *Studies in Jewish History*, vol. 1. Tel Aviv: Hakibbutz Hameuchad, 106–10.

ARLES, P. (1985). *The Hour of Our Death*. New York: Vintage Books.

AVIGAD, N. (1954). *Ancient Monuments in the Kidron Valley* [Hebr.]. Jerusalem: Mosad Bialik.

AVI-YONAH, M. (1972). 'The Leda Sarcophagus from Beth She'arim'. *Scripta Hierosolymitana* 24: 9–21.

BERLIN, A. (2002). 'Power and its Afterlife: Tombs in Hellenistic Palestine'. *Near Eastern Archaeology* 65: 141–147.

—— (2005). 'Jewish Life Before the Revolt: The Archaeological Evidence'. *Journal for the Study of Judaism* 36: 453–466.

BYRNE, R./MCNARY-ZAK, B. eds. (2009). *Resurrection of the Brother of Jesus: The James Ossvary Contraversy and the Quest for Relics*. Chapel Hill: University of North Carolina Press.

BOSIO, A. (1632). *Roma Sotterrannea*. 2 vols. Rome: G. Facciotti.

BROWN, P. (1981). *The Cult of the Saints*. Chicago: University of Chicago Press.

CHARLESWORTH, J. H. (2006). *Jesus and Archaeology*. Grand Rapids: Eerdman's Publishing Company.

COHEN, S. J. D. (1981). 'Epigraphical Rabbis'. *Jewish Quarterly Review* 72: 1–17.

COTTON, H. M./PRICE, J. M. (2001). 'A Bilingual Tombstone from Zo'ar (Arabia) (Hecht Museum, Haifa, inv. no. H-3029, Naveh's list no. 18)'. *Zeitschrift für Papyrologie und Epigraphik* 134: 277–283.

DE SAUCEY, L. F. (1865). *Voyage en Terre Sancte*. 2 vols. Paris: Didier et Cie.

FEDAK, J. (1990). *Tombs of the Hellenistic Age: A Study of Selected Tombs from the Pre-Classical to the Early Imperial Era*. Toronto: University of Toronto Press.

FINE, S. (1997). *This Holy Place: On the Sanctity of the Synagogue During the Greco-Roman Period*. Notre Dame, Ind.: University of Notre Dame Press.

—— (2003). 'Another View of Jerusalem's Necropolis During the First Century: A Decorated Ossuary from the Nelson and Helen Glueck Collection of the Cincinnati Art Museum'. *Journal of Jewish Studies* 54: 233–241.

—— (2005a). *Art and Judaism in the Greco-Roman World: Toward a New Jewish Archaeology*. New York and Cambridge: Cambridge University Press.

—— (2005b). 'Between Liturgy and Social History: Priestly Power in Late Antique Palestinian Synagogues?' *Journal of Jewish Studies* 56: 1–9.

FISCHER, M. L. (1998). *Marble Studies: Roman Palestine and the Marble Trade*. Konstanz: Universitätsverlag Konstanz (UVK).

FISCHER, U. (1978). *Eschatologie und Jenseitserwartung im hellenistischen Diasporajudentum*. Berlin and New York: W. de Gruyter.

GAFNI, I. (1999). *Land, Center & Diaspora: Jewish Constructs in Late Antiquity*. Sheffield: Sheffield Academic Press.

GOLDBERG, S. (1996). *Crossing the Jabbok: Illness and Death in Ashkenazi Judaism in Sixteenth through Nineteenth Century Prague*. Berkeley: University of California Press.

GOODENOUGH, E. R. (1953–1967). *Jewish Symbols in the Greco-Roman World*. 13 vols. New York: Pantheon.

GREENHUT, Z. (1994). 'The Caiaphas Tomb in North Talpiot, Jerusalem', in *Ancient Jerusalem Revealed*, ed. H. Geva. Jerusalem: Israel Exploration Society, 219–222.

HAARETZ ARCHIVE (07/10/2008). 'Burial Artifact Inscribed "Son of High Priest" Fund Near West Bank Fence Route', www.haaretz.com.

HACHLILI, R. (1988). *Ancient Jewish Art and Archaeology in the Land of Israel*. Leiden: Brill.

—— (2005). *Jewish Funerary Customs, Practices and Rites in the Second Temple Period*. Leiden: Brill.

——/KILLEBREW, A. (1999). *The Jewish Cemetery of the Second Temple Period*. Israel Antiquities Authority Reports 7. Jerusalem: Israel Antiquities Authority.

HEZSER, C. (2001). *Jewish Literacy in Roman Palestine*. Tübingen: Mohr-Siebeck.

JACOBSON, D. M./WEITZMAN, M. P. (1992). 'What was Corinthian Bronze?' *American Journal of Archaeology* 96: 237–248.

KLONER, A./ZISSU, B. (2008). *The Necropolis of Jerusalem in the Second Temple Period*. Leuven: Peeters.

KON, M. (1947). *The Tombs of the Kings* [Hebr.]. Tel Aviv: Dvir.

—— (1971). 'Jewish Art at the Time of the Second Temple', in *Jewish Art*, ed. C. ROTH. London: Vallentine Mitchell, 51–64.

KRAEMER, D. (2000). *The Meanings of Death in Rabbinic Judaism*. London: Routledge.

LEON, H. J. (1960). *The Jews of Ancient Rome*. Philadelphia: Jewish Publication Society.

LEVINE, L. I. (1997). 'Archaeology and the Religious Ethos of Pre-70 Palestine', in *Hillel and Jesus: Comparative Studies of Two Major Religious Leaders*, ed. J. H. Charlesworth and L. L. Johns. Minneapolis: Fortress, 110–20.

—— (1999). *Judaism and Hellenism in Antiquity: Conflict or Confluence?* Peabody, MA: Hendrickson Publishers.

—— (2005). 'Bet She'arim in Its Patriarchal Context', in *"The Words of a Wise Man's Mouth are Gracious" (QOH 10,12): Festschrift for Günter Stemberger on the Occasion of His 65th Birthday*, ed. M. Perani. Berlin and New York: Walter de Gruyter, 197–225.

LEVISON, J. (2002). 'The Roman Character of Funerals in the Writings of Josephus'. *Journal for the Study of Judaism* 33: 245–277.

MAGEN, Y. (2002). *The Stone Vessel Industry in the Second Temple Period*. Jerusalem: Israel Antiquities Authority.

MAGNESS, J. (2005). 'Ossuaries and the Burials of Jesus and James'. *Journal of Biblical Literature* 124: 121–154.

MAZAR, B. (1985). 'Those who Buried their Dead in Beth Shearim' [Hebr.]. *Eretz Israel* 18: 293–299.

——/Schwabe, M./ Lifshitz, B./ Avigad, N. (1973–1976). *Beth She'arim*, 3 vols New Brunswick: Rutgers University Press.

McCane, B. (2003). *Roll Back the Stone: Death and Burial in the World of Jesus*. Philadelphia: Trinity Press International.

Meimaris Y./ Kritikakou-Nikolaropoulou, K. (2005). *Inscriptions from Palaestina Tertia Ia, The Greek Inscriptions from Ghor es-Safi*. National Hellenic Research Foundation. Paris: Diffusion de Boccard.

Miller, S. S. (2003). 'Some Observations on Stone Vessel Finds and Ritual Purity in Light of Talmudic Sources,' in *Zeichen aus Text und Stein. Studien auf dem Weg zu einer Archäologie des Neuen Testaments*, ed. S. Alkier and J. Zangenberg. Tübingen: Francke Verlag, 402–419.

—— (2004). '"Epigraphical" Rabbis, Helios, and Psalm 19: Were the Synagogues of Archaeology and the Synagogues of the Sages One and the Same?' *Jewish Quarterly Review* 94: 27–76.

Misgav, H. (2006). 'Two Jewish Tombstones from Zoar'. *Israel Museum Studies in Archaeology* 5: 35–46.

Moore, G. F. (1958). *Judaism in the First Centuries of the Christian Era*, vol. 2. New York: Schocken Books.

Nagakubo, S. (1974). 'Investigation into Jewish Concepts of Afterlife in Beth She'arim Greek Inscriptions'. PhD. Dissertation. Durham: Duke University.

Naveh, J. (1995). 'Aramic Tombstones from Zoar' [Hebr.]. *Tarbiz* 64: 477–97.

—— (1999). 'More on the Tombstones of Zoar' [Hebr.]. *Tarbiz* 68: 582–6.

—— (2000). 'Seven New Epitaphs from Zoar' [Hebr.]. *Tarbiz* 69: 916–35.

Negev, A. (1993). 'Kurnub', in *The New Encyclopedia of Archaeological Excavations in the Holy Land*, vol. 3. New York: Simon and Schuster, 882–93.

Netzer, E./Kalman, Y./Porat, R. (2008). 'The Discovery of the Tomb of Herod' [Hebr.] *Ariel:* 182: 6–31.

Patrich, J. (1982). 'A Sadducean Halakha and the Jerusalem Aquaduct'. *The Jerusalem Cathedra* 2: 25–39.

Rahmani, L. Y. (1967). 'Jason's Tomb'. *Israel Exploration Journal* 17: 61–100.

—— (1994). *A Catalogue of Jewish Ossuaries in the Collections of the State of Israel*. Jerusalem: Israel Antiquities Authority.

Rajak, T. (2001a). 'The Rabbinic Dead and the Diaspora Dead at Beth She'arim', in *The Jewish Dialogue with Greece and Rome; Studies in Cultural and Social Interaction*. Leiden: Brill, 479–99.

—— (2001b). 'Judaism and Hellenism Revisited', in *eadem, The Jewish Dialogue with Greece and Rome; Studies in Cultural and Social Interaction*. Leiden: Brill, 3–10.

Reich, R. (1994). 'Ossuary Inscriptions of the Caiaphas Family from Jerusalem', in: *Ancient Jerusalem Revealed*, ed. H. Geva. Jerusalem: Israel Exploration Society, 223–225.

Reiner, E. (1988). *Pilgrims and Pilgrimage to Eretz Yisrael, 1099–1517* [Hebr.]. Jerusalem: Hebrew University.

Roth-Gerson, L. (1987). *Greek Inscriptions in the Synagogues in Eretz-Israel* [Hebr.]. Jerusalem: Ben Zvi Institute.

Rutgers, L. V. (1995). *The Jews of Late Ancient Rome: An Archaeological and Historical Study on the Interaction of Jews and non-Jews in the Roman-Diaspora*. Leiden: Brill.

—— (2000). 'Death and Afterlife: The Inscriptional Evidence', in *Judaism in Late Antiquity*, vol. 4, ed. A. J. Avery-Peck and J. Neusner. Leiden: Brill, 293–310.

Safrai, S. (1983). *Eretz Israel and Its Sages during the Period of the Midrash and the Talmud* [Hebr.]. Israel: Hakibbutz Hameuchad.

SANDERS, E. P. (1992). *Judaism: Practice and Belief 63 BCE–66 CE*. London and Philadelphia: Trinity International.

SIVERTSEV, A. (2002). *Private Households and Public Politics in 3rd–5th Century Jewish Palestine*. Tübingen: Mohr-Siebeck.

SMITH, M. (1957–1958). 'The Image of God: Notes on the Hellenization of Judaism: With Especial Reference to Goodenough's Work on Jewish Symbols'. *Bulletin of the John Rylands Library Manchester* 40: 473–512.

STEMBERGER, G. (1995). *Jewish Contemporaries of Jesus: Pharisees, Sadducees, Essenes*. Minneapolis: Augsburg Fortress.

STERN, E. (1993–2008). *The New Encyclopedia of Archaeological Excavations in the Holy Land*. 5 vols. New York: Simon and Schuster.

SUKENIK, E. L. (1947). 'The Earliest Records of Christianity'. *American Journal of Archaeology* 51: 351–365.

URBACH, E. E. (1958). 'The Rabbinical Laws of Idolatry in the Second and Third Centuries in Light of Archaeological and Historical Facts' [Hebr.]. *Eretz Israel* 5: 189–205.

VILNAY, Z. (1978a). 'Nicanor' [Hebr.], in *Ensyclopedia Ariel*. Tel Aviv: Am Oved, Ministry of Education, 5169–71.

—— (1978b). 'Tombs of the Sanhedrin' [Hebr.], in *Ensyclopedia Ariel*, Tel Aviv: Am Oved, Ministry of Education, 6475–9.

VITO, F. (1996). 'Byzantine Mosaics at Bet She'arim: New Evidence for the History of The Site' [Hebr.]. *Atiqot* 28: 115–146.

WEISS, Z. (1989). 'The Jewish Cemetery in the Galilee in the Period of the Mishnah and the Talmud: An Archaeological Investigation with the Aid of Talmudic Sources' [Hebr.]. Unpublished MA thesis, The Hebrew University, Jerusalem.

—— (1992). 'Social Aspects of Burial in Beth Shearim: Archaeological Finds and Talmudic Sources', in *The Galilee in Late Antiquity*, ed. L. I. Levine. New York and Jerusalem: Jewish Theological Seminary of America, 357–371.

—— (1996). 'Foreign Influences on Jewish Burial in the Galilee in the Period of the Mishnah and the Talmud' [Hebr.]. *Eretz Israel* 25: 360–361.

WHARTON, A. J. (2006). *Selling Jerusalem: Relics, Replicas, Theme Parks*. Chicago: University of Chicago Press.

VI

EDUCATION AND LITERACY

CHAPTER 25

PRIVATE AND PUBLIC EDUCATION

CATHERINE HEZSER

THE traditional assumption of an organized system of Jewish primary education in Hellenistic and Roman times which would have been supplemented by hierarchically organized and centrally controlled rabbinic academies of higher learning after 70 CE has been repudiated by more critical and methodologically sophisticated studies in recent years. In addition, scholars have stressed that Jewish education, just like many other aspects of ancient Jewish culture and society, needs to be examined within the context of Graeco-Roman society. Yet the history of Graeco-Roman education is itself 'in need of a comprehensive revision', as William Harris has pointed out (Harris 1989: 233). Ancient Jews seem to have participated in Graeco-Roman educational practices while at the same time developing specifically Jewish alternatives to Hellenistic learning. With the exception of a lintel inscription mentioning the 'study house of R. Eliezer ha-Qappar', found in the Golan (see Naveh/Shaked 1985: 25), no archaeological remains which could be associated with schools or rabbinic academies have been excavated yet. Therefore literary and legal sources are the only type of evidence available for a study of ancient Jewish education. Many questions still remain open and will hopefully be investigated in the not so distant future.

1. EDUCATION IN GRAECO-ROMAN SOCIETY

One of the most important questions concerning ancient education is whether and to what extent it was publicly organized and financially supported by the state and/ or the local authorities. In his classical study of ancient education, Marrou has pointed out that Roman society merely adapted Hellenistic educational practices for its own purposes, especially as far as the eastern parts of the Roman empire were concerned (Marrou 1965: 152–53). He maintained that already in the Hellenistic period, education was publicly organized. No longer considered the merely private concern of parents, the *polis* or municipality recognized its duty to provide educational services (ibid. 163–64). The Hellenistic rulers did not intervene in the internal and organizational matters of the schools. They would occasionally appear as benefactors, supporting educational institutions with funding. In the Roman Empire the state would sometimes intervene as legislator, reminding the local authorities of their responsibilities, or support teachers indirectly by alleviating their tax burdens (Harris 1989: 235).

It is already obvious from Marrou's account, however, that the offical provisions for public education were limited and that the educational 'system' could not function as smoothly as one might imagine. Firstly, there was no unanimous educational policy amongst the municipal authorities. Secondly and most importantly, primary education was neither organized not funded by the cities nor the state. The political authorities were merely interested in higher education for the ruling strata of society, and in sports and exercise as a precursor of military training (Harris 1989: 236). Therefore, the *ephebeia* and the *gymnasia* were usually the only institutions benefiting from public support (Marrou 1965: 175; Clarke 1971: 8).

Other educational endeavours, and especially primary education, were dependent on private donations and parental initiative. Since the ideal was for Roman children to grow up bilingual, parents of sufficient means would privately hire Greek-speaking teachers for their children or use one of their slaves as tutors (Bonner 1977: 20–46). A number of families could also hire a teacher together and share the costs. Teachers, who were generally despised and had a very low social status, would set themselves up and establish informal 'schools' (according to Cribiore 1996: 6, the term may not even be appropriate for the ancient world) in towns, cities, and some villages, charging a small fee for the instruction of pupils in their private homes, makeshift structures, or public places, in locations which were not specifically designated for that purpose (Marrou 1965: 222, 392; Bonner 1977: 115; Harris 1989: 236). These schools would teach varying levels of literacy and arithmetics to the (probably relatively few) sons and daughters of the middle strata, and in exceptional cases also of the lower strata, of society (e.g. slaves sent to these schools by their masters) who attended them (see Harris 1989: 233; Morgan 1998: 3). Harris stresses that the poor state of these schools 'accurately symbolized the lack of interest in elementary education on the part of both society in general and the authorities in particular' (Harris 1989: 237). The parents', and especially the father's role in securing an education for his children was paramount (Bonner 1977: 11–12). The daughters of the upper classes would be taught by tutors as well (Bonner 1977: 27–28). It is obvious that only those fathers who were educated themselves, or at least valued education and could pay for it, would enable their children to acquire a certain level of cultural knowledge and intellectual skills (cf. Morgan 1998: 33). Only those students who had gained these primary skills and had sufficient leisure time to further their education could move on to study the so-called liberal arts (*artes liberales*): grammar, rhetorics, dialectics (philosophy), arithmetics, geometry, astronomy, and music. As the name indicates, these skills were associated with the free citizen who aquired them for his own sake rather than for economic purposes.

The structure, content, and procedure of education in the Roman period are also debated amongst scholars. There is no evidence of any central institution which would organize or control the content or form of teaching (Morgan 1998: 26–27). Education rather seems to have been 'a self-regulating system' in which 'those who needed it, those who had the resources and those who had the incentive to acquire it were by and large the same group' (ibid. 33). Morgan has stressed the close relationship between education and social status: literate education was 'both a binding and a differentiating force, an indicator and a transformer of cultural status' (ibid. 4). Education in the Greek and Roman cultural tradition was one of the characteristics of the ruling strata of society. Any foreigner who wanted to assimilate to, and be respected within, Graeco-Roman culture had to undergo such training and acquire at least a minimum of Hellenistic cultural knowledge (ibid. 74–75).

The general assumption is that Romans were educated in three stages (but the neat progression of pupils from one level to another has been questioned by Kaster 1983: 325–39): children would proceed from the primary school to the grammar school and from there to higher education in rhetorics, law, philosophy, or a scientific subject. At the primary school level the letters of the alphabet, reading and writing were taught, as well as numbers and elementary arithmetics (Marrou 1965: 229–38; Bonner 1977: 165–88). Writing tablets, exercise books, and abecedaries have been preserved which provide some evidence of the ways in which literacy was taught (Hopkins 1993; Cribiore 1996: 6–7, 27–55; Morgan 1998: 40–48). Although pupils would learn to copy small passages from Homer and sometimes also Virgil, the emphasis was on reading and recitation, since writing was seen as a technical skill acquired in the context of scribal training. Homer was clearly the most important text base of ancient education (Morgan 1998: 78: 'Anyone who learnt anything was likely to read some Homer'). Since the quality and level of the teaching will have varied, depending on the teachers' own qualifications, any generalizations concerning the content of the teaching and a fixed curriculum are problematic (cf. Morgan 1998: 67-71, who opts for a 'core and periphery model' instead).

A wider variety of literary and philosophical texts seem to have been introduced at the secondary, grammar school level, where formal grammar was taught (Marrou 1965: 251–56). Few students will have advanced to this level, however, and even fewer would have proceeded to third-level education, the study at a law school, with a philosopher, or rhetorical training, although law was sometimes seen as a means of social advancement (Rawson 1985: 90; Marrou 1995: 419; Morgan 1998: 57).

Was higher education institutionalized, and if so, which aspects of it were regulated? Philosophical schools developed out of disciple circles. After the death of their founders, some of them continued to exist and were headed by successive lines of teachers in their original location (e.g. the Platonic 'Academy', Aristotle's 'Lyceum', Epicurus' 'Garden'). They emerged through private initiative and the concerted effort of former students rather than being official institutions (Rawson 1985: 38). The Stoics 'had no recognized headquarters and little organization', but the school nevertheless survived its founders and 'had a regular succession of heads' (Clarke 1971: 63). The organizational structure and teaching practice of these and other philosophical schools still needs to be studied in detail: were they exclusive societies or open for discussions with all those who were interested? What was the relationship between the schools' heads and other former disciples? To what extent did their organizational structure reflect—or stand in contradiction to—their philosophical doctrines? How was the succession of heads regulated? Was there a fixed curriculum, examinations, and a graduation ceremony?

Clarke has pointed out that reading, discussing, and commenting on written texts formed an important part of the philosophical teaching practice (Clarke 1971: 87–88). At the same time the teaching was conducted orally: students were supposed to learn by listening to the voice of their teachers, who were considered the physical representations of traditional knowledge, rather than learn from books and notes. Unlike philosophy, legal training was more of a professional education producing experts in law who could function as jurists (to be distinguished from advocates who needed rhetorical skills). Law students would accompany experienced jurists and listen to their case decisions. In Roman imperial times, law schools with a succession of teachers and textbooks in civil law were established in Rome and some places in the East such as Caesarea (Clarke 1971: 115–16; Rawson 1985: 201–14).

Graeco-Roman legal training is an area most suitable for comparision with rabbinic learning, which was also largely legal in nature, whereas rabbinic narrative and Torah interpretation would profit from a comparison with rhetorical education. The forms and contents of Jewish higher education in antiquity should also be compared with Christian higher education, which partly adopted Graeco-Roman models and partly developed its own (theological) disciple circles and schools (see Downey 1958; Clarke 1971: 119–29). Throughout antiquity, Christian theological teaching and scriptural study would have been conducted informally by prominent theologians such as Origen. Only in the sixth century CE did the Western

Church realize the need for a more formalized education of the clergy (Clarke 1971: 128–29). Interestingly, this development seems to have taken place at approximately the same time as rabbinic academies were established in Babylonia (see Rubenstein 2002: 67).

2. JEWISH PRIMARY EDUCATION

Earlier scholars assumed that every Jewish boy in Roman Palestine had access to an elementary school with a fixed curriculum which was part of a well-organized educational system established by the Jewish religious authorities. This view was first expressed in the early studies on the subject conducted at the turn of the twentieth century (Bacher 1903: 50–62; Krauss 1912: 199–203). The apologetic tone of these studies is immediately recognizable. Bacher, for example, alleged that the Jewish focus on education was the 'proprium' of the Jewish religion in contrast to paganism (Bacher 1903: 50). Both he and Krauss assume that Jewish public education was initiated by Ezra the scribe in the fifth century BCE: Ezra's public Torah lectures are presented as 'the birthday of the old Jewish school system' (Bacher 1903: 54, my translation from the German; cf. Krauss 1912: 200). In the following centuries the ideal of educating the masses was allegedly put into practice: all over the country elementary schools were established, an accomplishment which some later rabbinic traditions associate with Joshua b. Gamla and Shimon b. Shetach at the end of the Second Temple period (Bacher 1903: 56–58 and Krauss 1912: 201, with reference to b. B. B. 21a and y. Ket. 8:11, 32c). According to this view, Jewish primary education was well organized and already available to everyone at the beginning of the rabbinic period. Therefore Josephus' remark that all Jews were knowledgeable of Torah law (Contra Apionem 2.18, 178) is considered a proper description of the spread of education amongst ancient Jews.

The notion of the alleged 'universality' of education amongst ancient Jews has been repeated by some later scholars (see, e.g. Arzt 1953: 36; Gerhardssohn 1961: 57–58; Aberbach 1966–67: 90–92; Safrai 1968: 150–51). Nevertheless, certain reservations have also been expressed. For example, Aberbach and Goldin stress that the Talmudic descriptions reflect an ideal rather than reality: even if a school system existed, not every child would have attended a school (Gerhardssohn 1961: 59; Aberbach 1966–67: 164; Goldin 1972: 177). Only a few people would have been able to grant their sons the leisure time to study something which was not economically useful. Furthermore, in contrast to Graeco-Roman society, where boys and girls could be taught together, there is no evidence that Jewish girls attended Jewish elementary schools (Morris 1937: 28–31; Ebner 1956: 35; Aberbach 1966–67: 164;

see also section 5 below). Thus, since 50 per cent of the Jewish population would have been excluded from public education, any claim of universality must be incorrect at the outset. Some scholars stress the father's responsibility in transmitting Torah knowledge (Ebner 1956: 38) and the efforts made by rabbis to provide the Jewish population with teachers and schools. Therefore the higher educational institution of the study house (*bet midrash*) is sometimes considered to have preceded the introduction of the elementary school (*bet sefer*), although both are traced back to the late Second Temple period, to the time of Joshua b. Gamla and Shimon b. Shetach, already mentioned in the earlier model (see Ginzberg 1928: 8–9; Drazin 1940: 27–28).

The greatest methodological problem affecting all of these studies is that they make indiscriminate use of early and late, Palestinian and Babylonian sources. Late Talmudic passages are taken as historical evidence of the organization of Jewish education at the end of the Second Temple period. Although it is sometimes acknowledged that these texts may exaggerate matters (Arzt 1953: 38), they are nevertheless interpreted in order to support the wide-ranging assumptions about Jewish education proposed by the authors (cf. Ebner 1956: 38; Safrai 1968: 150). The traditions concerning Joshua b. Gamla (b. B.B. 21a) and Shimon b. Shetach (y. Ket. 8:11, 32c) are usually harmonized with each other to create the theory of a two- or three-tiered educational scheme (elementary Torah education, secondary Mishnah education, higher education with a rabbi), which was obviously considered parallel to the Graeco-Roman model introduced above.

The methodological deficits of the earlier studies require an entirely new and critical evaluation of all of the evidence of Jewish primary education in antiquity. Morris has already pointed out that neither the Hebrew Bible, nor the New Testament, or any of the Jewish writings of the Second Temple period, including Philo and Josephus, contain any direct references to schools for the primary education of Jewish children (Morris 1937: 3–8, 14–15). This phenomenon suggests that before the rabbinic period, all educational endeavours would have been the outcome of the private initiative of Jewish parents (cf. Perlow 1931: 23–24). Only those parents who valued education themselves and who had the necessary financial means and leisure time to enable their children (mostly sons) to learn would have promoted education. Therefore Morris is right when writing that 'to the mass of the people the concept of education, of teaching and learning as a continuous process unconnected with immediate practical needs, hardly existed in earlier times' (Morris 1937: 8). Josephus' claim that every Jew knew the biblical commandments was obviously apologetic in nature, since only those who knew the regulations could be expected to observe the Torah in their daily lives.

The rabbinic texts put forth by most scholars in support of a widespread school system in Roman Palestine were not only written down many centuries after the 'events' they purport to describe, they were also usually misinterpreted in order to fit the theory. Neither the text about Shimon b. Shetach (y. Ket. 8:11, 32c) nor the one about Joshua b. Gamla (b. B.B. 21a) deals with the founding of schools, or even with the establishment of a school network (Goodblatt 1980: 83–84). The Babylonian text states that 'Joshua b. Gamla came and ordained that children's teachers should be set up in each and every town and district, and that [children] should be entered at [the age of] six or seven [years]' (b. B.B. 21a). These teachers could have been envisioned as private teachers whose teaching was conducted informally, like those present in Graeco-Roman society mentioned above. In addition, the text refers to wishful thinking rather than reality, for how would Joshua b. Gamla, one of the last high priests, have been able to put this ruling into practice so shortly before the outbreak of the first Jewish revolt? The Yerushalmi tradition (y. Ket. 8:11, 32c) mentions that 'Shimon b. Shetach ordained three things: . . . that the children should go to school'. The tradition seems to assume that 'schools' already existed, but no details concerning their nature are provided here (Hezser 2001: 40–42, 46–47). It is possible, and probably quite likely, that the situation of privately established "schools" of later centuries is retrojected into the first century here. There is no supporting evidence from any other sources concerning the organization of a Jewish elementary school system before the destruction of the Temple in 70 CE. In fact, most of the rabbinic sources which mention schools (*batei sefer*) and teachers (*soferim, hazzanim*) stem from the amoraic period, that is, late antiquity (Hezser 2001: 48–51). They refer to schools of a private and informal nature (cf. the Graeco-Roman elementary schools) which supplemented parental education rather than replacing it.

Another way to approach the subject is to ask who would have had an interest in promoting ancient Jewish primary education. An answer to this question depends on another important issue, namely, the curriculum of such schools. Although in reality there may have been a certain diversity, the schools and teachers mentioned in rabbinic sources are all presented as teaching only the reading of the Torah in Hebrew, at a time when the spoken languages were Aramaic and Greek (see the discussion in Hezser 2001: 68–83). More practical skills such as writing and arithmetics are not mentioned at all (on textuality and education in the biblical and the Second Temple period see Carr 2005: 111–276). This would mean that the Jewish elementary schools would have been even more non-vocational than Graeco-Roman schools which focused on Homer, but nevertheless seem to have taught elementary writing and arithmetics as well. The focus on the Torah would have served as a specifically Jewish alternative to the teaching of Homer in Graeco-Roman schools. Like Homer for Greeks and Romans, the Torah was considered the essential body of traditional knowledge which provided a firm basis for Jewish identity (ibid. 70–72). Another more practical aspect is relevant here as well. Every male adult Jew was invited to serve as Torah reader in the synagogue, but only a few individuals will have had the necessary reading skills to carry out this duty. The increased rabbinic support of Jewish primary education in late antiquity seems to coincide with the emergence of synagogues as the religious centers of the Jewish community (ibid. 79–80).

3. JEWISH HIGHER EDUCATION

Study with a rabbi is the only manifestation of a specifically Jewish form of higher education in Roman Palestine known to us. As such, rabbinic study would be comparable with the study of the liberal arts and law in Graeco-Roman society. Both rabbinic study and the study of philosophy and rhetorics required a basic knowledge of the 'classical' tradition, whether the Torah, Homer, or Virgil, as a prerequisite. Those who wanted to study with a rabbi would have to be able to read the Torah, and be familiar with at least some portions of it. Therefore, only those who had already gained an elementary education, whether at home or in one of the informally established schools discussed above, could proceed to rabbinic training.

In the past, scholars had reckoned with the existence of a central academy founded by R. Yochanan b. Zakkai immediately after 70 CE. This academy was allegedly headed by the patriarch until the time of R. Yehudah ha-Nasi (around 200 CE), and by a prominent sage in the amoraic period (3rd to 5th c. CE). It was believed to be a continuous institution with a clear hierarchy and a line of succession in its leadership structure. Rather than being permanently located at one place, however, it would have moved its domicile from place to place, together with the patriarch and the sanhedrin or high court it was associated with. In the amoraic period, when academy and sanhedrin became separate institutions, the central academy would have been located in Tiberias or Sepphoris. Other, local rabbinic academies, which had been subordinated to the patriarchal academy, would become more independent and influential at that time (see Alon 1989: 32–33, 480, 679–80; Safrai 1976: 961–63; Oppenheimer 1978: 80–89).

This hypothesis has been thoroughly dismantled by more critical and methodologically sophisticated studies in recent years. The office of the patriarch does not seem to have existed in the tannaitic period before R. Yehudah ha-Nasi (Jacobs 1995: 115–23, 349) and the existence of a sanhedrin has been disproven entirely on the basis of a detailed analysis of the literary sources (Goodblatt 1994: 232–76). Therefore, neither patriarchal control of the tannaitic academy nor its association with a central high court can be maintained any more. In fact, the existence of a central academy itself, if envisioned as a permanent and hierarchically structured institution with a succession of leaders, has become highly doubtful (Hezser 1997: 195–214).

Rabbinic literature provides two types of evidence of higher level Torah study in Roman Palestine. First, numerous traditions pertain to disciple circles associated with particular rabbis. Individuals who decided to study with a rabbi and were accepted by him would 'serve' that rabbi (*shimush hakhamim*) by living in his household, accompanying him everywhere, and carrying out various mundane and even servile functions (Hezser 1997: 332-35). In turn, they would be able to closely observe the rabbi's practices and to absorb his wisdom. Just as rabbis' halakhic regulations concerned all areas of daily life, no clear-cut distinction was made between Torah study, socializing, and professional work. When the expression 'X sat before R.Y.' is used, it is uncertain whether special study sessions are referred to, or whether instruction took place whenever and wherever the time and occasion were suitable.

Like most philosophical, rhetorical, and legal teaching in Hellenistic and Roman times, Rabbinic instruction was carried out orally rather than in the form of book learning. Although the Torah formed the basis of rabbinic discussion, we may assume that it was mostly quoted and paraphrased from memory rather than through consultation of the scrolls (Hezser 2001: 95–96; 191–209). The memorization of their teachers' opinions and the observation of their practices formed the centre of rabbinic study. A lot of research still needs to be done in the comparison of ancient Jewish and Graeco-Roman modes of learning and teaching. What seems certain, however, is that in both societies, the sage was seen as the foremost representation of traditional knowledge, a phenomenon which directly linked students to individual teachers, and created lines of tradition which spanned many generations until the eventual compiling, writing, and editing of rabbinic documents (Hezser 2000: 162–66). Similarities in the way of teaching, learning, and the transmission of traditions also resulted in the application of similar literary forms (ibid. 167–70), such as the *chreia* or pronouncement story (Hezser 1996).

Secondly, study houses (*batei midrash*) seem to have existed at some places (Hezser 1997: 202–9). These are either associated with a particular rabbi ('the study house of R. X.') or with a particular locale such as Lydda or Sepphoris. Do these expressions refer to two different types of study houses, namely privately owned and public ones? Since the term *bayit* can also mean 'room', the 'study houses' associated with particular rabbis could have been rooms in these rabbis' houses which were customarily used for Torah study. Or they could have been local buildings donated, and/or headed by, these rabbis. Study houses associated with particular places might have been community owned. It is possible that access to these locales and the activities carried out in them differed, depending on whether they were privately owned or public property. Would rabbis be the leaders of local study houses, and if so, what would this office entail? Or should we imagine these locales as communal spaces available to anyone interested in Torah study? They would, then, constitute a separate institution, distinct from rabbis' private disciple circles. Palestinian rabbinic sources provide no evidence of a fixed and continuous leadership structure, and no buildings which could be identified as study houses have been excavated so far, suggesting that any room or building could be used for that purpose (see the discussion in Urman 1995 and Zvi Ilan 1995).

Shaye Cohen has argued that the Palestinian patriarchal academy resembled Graeco-Roman philosophical schools (Cohen 1981: 59–60). His argument is based on the assumption of the patriarchal academy as a 'perpetual institution' with a 'corporate identity', which was allegedly different from the disciple circles of the rabbis. The Babylonian talmudic text quoted in support of this argument

(b. Ket. 103a–b) cannot, however, be taken as historical evidence for an institution-alized patriarchal academy in Roman Palestine. If the patriarch's disciple circle resembled those of the other rabbis, where within Graeco-Roman society would we find the closest analogies to this type of teaching? Cohen already notes that 'the disciple circles of the rabbis were analogous to the disciple circles of the philoso-phers' (60). The philosophical disciple circles as well as the settings in which rhetoric and legal training took place may provide interesting analogies to rabbinic teaching, once they have been examined in detail.

Another worthwhile comparison would be with early Christian teaching. Hayim Lapin has observed that Christian 'schools' in Caesarea, like the one associated with Origen, also consisted of disciple circles (Lapin 1996: 500). He seems to identify at least some rabbinic study circles with the local study houses, though, and assumes that they may have been 'permanent communal institutions' into which some of the study circles may have permutated in amoraic times (ibid.). As already pointed out above, the evidence for disciple circles and *batei midrash* needs to be studied separately in order to avoid harmonizations and confusions. Lapin's other obser-vation, that early Christian teaching is much more based on texts and book learning than the teaching envisioned by rabbis, also needs to be examined in more detail. It seems that early Christian higher learning was more open towards the incorporation of the Graeco-Roman tradition, whereas rabbis focused on the Torah almost exclusively (cf. ibid. 504). Yet the Torah focus did not prevent rabbis from employing Graeco-Roman rhetorical forms and from devising legal rules which resembled those of the Roman legal experts. The Graeco-Roman context of rabbinic teaching will provide many fruitful subjects for future scholarship.

4. JEWISH PARTICIPATION IN GRAECO-ROMAN EDUCATION

Only those Jews who were able to read Greek would have been capable of pursuing a higher Graeco-Roman education, and for the study of law, an additional reading knowledge of Latin would have been necessary. Therefore parents' decision to enable their children (or rather, sons) to acquire a Greek elementary education would determine their later status within the broader Graeco-Roman society in which a certain knowledge of the classical tradition was crucial for advancement. Morgan has noted that as far as the provinces are concerned, the relative acquisi-tion of Graeco-Roman culture within one's own society mattered more than the actual level of Graeco-Roman knowledge achieved: 'a big fish in Panopolis need not, and generally did not, have the education of a big fish in Alexandria' (Morgan

1998: 84). One may assume that the study of philosophy and rhetorics would have been available to a few wealthy Jews of the upper strata only, whereas all those who wanted their children to advance within the Graeco-Roman administrative system would have tried to provide them with an elementary-level Greek education in which Homer was read. Morgan writes: 'The best which those who did not come from cultured Greek backgrounds would be likely to derive from these texts is a number of names and tags, sufficient perhaps to mark them as Greek but hardly enough to integrate them into a cultural elite' (ibid. 118).

The best known example of an upper-class Jew who had obtained a Greek education is Flavius Josephus. The way in which he describes his level of Greek knowledge illustrates Morgan's more general remarks: 'I have also labored strenuously to partake of the realm of Greek prose and poetry, after having gained a knowledge of Greek grammar, although the habitual use of my native tongue has prevented my attaining precision in the pronunciation' (Ant. 20.12.1, 263). Josephus allegedly reached the third level of Greek education, although he is aware of his own limitations in obtaining excellence in the language. For Josephus, a Greek education could be combined with Torah study, and did not interfere with his Jewish identity. He also mentions other prominent Jews who had acquired Greek learning: Justus of Tiberias (Vita 9, 40), members of the Herodian family, and the Jewish aristocracy (C. Ap. 1.9, 51; Bell. 1.31.1, 602). These members of the highest echellons of Jewish society would have been in regular social contact with Greeks and Romans. A Greek education was, therefore, indispensable for them.

Rabbinic literature also gives the impression that Greek learning was the prerogative of the upper strata of Jewish—including rabbinic—society (Hezser 2001: 92–94). As such, a Greek education seems to have been desired for their children by some upwardly mobile rabbis as well. The very fact that the Mishnah transmits a war-time ruling that one should not teach one's children Greek (M. Sot. 9:14) suggests that even in times of conflict with the Romans some Jewish (rabbinic) parents continued to aspire to a Greek education (see also Sevenster 1968: 47). The Tosefta parallel therefore limits the Mishnah's restriction: 'They permitted the household of R. Gamliel to teach their children Greek, because they were close to the government' (T. Sot. 15:8). According to a variant tradition in the Talmud Yerushalmi, this permission was allegedly given to the family of the patriarch R. Yehudah ha-Nasi 'because they were connected with the government' (y. Shab. 6:1, 7d). Thus, rabbis assumed that contacts with the Roman administration would require a Greek education. Schwartz (1999: 220) assumes that the patriarch would have had some Greek rhetorical training. One of the letters of the Roman rhetorician Libanius to the Jewish patriarchs at the end of the fourth century CE suggests that a patriarch might send his son to Antioch to study rhetorics with a pagan rhetorician (see Jacobs 1995: 259–72). Geiger has examined the various institutions of Graeco-Roman higher education in Syria-Palestine in late antiquity and showed that those who wanted to gain philosophical, rhetorical, or legal knowledge did not have to travel far (Geiger 1985, 1992, and 1994; see also Hezser 2001: 104).

While it seems almost self-evident that the upper strata of Jewish society who lived in a cultural environment dominated by Greek culture would strive to acquire a Greek education, the attitudes and practices of the sub-elite and middle strata of society are less obvious. While the rabbinic sources present the view of a religious elite which considered itself the guardian over Jewish identity, epigraphic evidence may reveal the practices of other groups within Jewish society who were more acculturated. Yet even amongst rabbis attitudes towards the teaching of Greek to children were mixed. According to a tradition in y. Shab. 6:1, 7d, R. Abbahu 'wanted to teach his daughter Greek' and quoted a statement of R. Yochanan, that the knowledge of Greek would be an 'ornament' for women. Lieberman has pointed out that rabbis were also not generally opposed to giving sons a Greek education. Their only concern was that time-wise it could interfere with the study of Torah (Lieberman 1962: 100 and 1965: 16).

The rabbinic assumption that in urban environments such as Caesaerea even the most essential Jewish prayers might have been recited in Greek (y. Sot. 7:1, 21b), together with the evidence of Greek burial and synagogue donors' inscriptions (Hezser 2001: 364–421) suggest that the knowledge of Greek was widespread, at least amongst some circles in Roman Palestine. The middle strata of society may have tried to imitate the upper strata in acquiring a Greek education. This education would have been provided by Greek teachers, who would either be employed by wealthy families or offer their services to groups of disciples (Krauss 1912: 203–4; cf. section 1 above). Obviously such teachers would be more available in Greek-speaking urban environments than in the countryside. It seems that neither Josephus, nor some of the rabbis considered a knowledge of the Greek language, literature, and culture incompatible with a strong Jewish identity.

5. WOMEN'S EDUCATION

Scholars almost unanimously agree that girls would not have attended the Jewish elementary schools mentioned in rabbinic sources, especially from the third century CE onwards (see section 2 above). Girls are never associated with these schools which seem to have taught Torah reading only (Perlow 1931: 98; Morris 1937: 31; Tal Ilan 1995: 204). If the goal of these schools was to produce a sufficient number of males who would be able to read the Torah in public in the context of the synagogue service, girls' exclusion from these schools would be understandable, since women were not supposed to read the Torah in public in front of the assembled congregation. But some rabbinic traditions are even more forceful in their exclusion of women from Torah learning, suggesting that, in principle, Torah should not be taught to women (cf. Sifre Deut. 46: '"And you shall teach them to your sons" [Deut. 11:19], your sons and not your daughters'). Rabbis seem to have held different opinions on whether, and to what degree, women should be educated. Some argued that women would need to know the rulings pertaining to them in order to observe them, while others considered Torah knowledge too precious for women (cf. M. Sot. 3:4 and y. Sot. 3:4, 19a). With the exception of one chapter in Tal Ilan's book on Jewish women, the issue of Jewish women's education in antiquity has not yet been sufficiently examined (Tal Ilan 1995: 190–204). This may partly be due to the sparse evidence available, since rabbinic sources are almost exclusively concerned with the education of males.

Jewish parents who wanted their daughters to obtain an education would have to teach them privately and individually, either by instructing them themselves or by having them taught by a private teacher (cf. M. Ned. 4:3: 'he may teach Scripture to his sons and daughters'; cf. T. Ber. 2:12: reference to the possibility of more advanced learning). As already pointed out above (section 4), some rabbis seem to have advocated the teaching of Greek to girls. Others may have wanted their daughters to know at least those biblical and rabbinic regulations which concerned women's practices. Women in rabbinic households would have observed rabbis and listened to their teaching and conversations. They may have obtained a certain amount of knowledge simply by living with rabbis, just as some slaves would have, as suggested by a story about R. Gamliel's slave Tabi who is praised as a 'disciple of sages' (M. Sukkah 2:1). Therefore, occasional rabbinic references to learned women associated with rabbinic households, such as Beruriah, the daughter of R. Hananiah b. Teradion, are not particularly striking (see Tal Ilan 1995: 195–96, 197–200), even if the stories must be seen as 'the product of the imagination of the *amoraim*', as Ilan points out.

Besides female relatives of rabbis, other women may have obtained some elementary Torah knowledge by going to the synagogue and listening to rabbis' expositions. The Talmud Yerushalmi transmits a story about a woman who went to listen to R. Meir against her husband's wish (y. Sot. 1:4, 16d). He was obviously concerned that she might neglect her domestic duties. Listening to rabbis' sermons in the synagogues and to their discussions and teachings in other public spaces would probably have been the only opportunity to gain some Torah knowledge for the large majority of women. What they learned would always be filtered through the perspective of individual rabbis, though, since women would not have had direct access to Torah scrolls, this access being controlled by men.

Unfortunately, we lack information about non-rabbinic Jews' education of their daughters, since all of our literary sources are written from the rabbinic perspective. If even some rabbis are in favour of granting their daughters a Greek education, we may assume that amongst their more assimilated compatriots this view would have been even more prevalent. Therefore it is possible that some Jewish parents, especially in the urban areas, would send their daughters to Greek elementary schools or have them taught by Greek private teachers. This practice would have been especially pominent amongst the upper strata of Jewish society which had most contacts with educated non-Jews.

On the other hand, we have to be careful with regard to assuming too much education, even amongst Jewish women of the upper strata of society. The examples of Babatha and Salome Komaise, property-owning women of the early second century CE who were not even able to write their own names (Hezser 2001: 314–15, 321), should warn us against claiming any higher amounts of literacy amongst Jewish women (ibid. 498–99). Although we have no evidence that ancient Jewish women were able to write, at least some may have learned to read the Torah and/or Homer, depending on their fathers' attitudes towards the education of women.

6. PROFESSIONAL EDUCATION

A literary education would not have been the only type of education available to Jews in Roman Palestine. One may assume that, for various professions, a certain training period was necessary. This could either be accomplished through apprenticeship or through vocational schools which would train people in particular trades, crafts, and techniques. The teaching of arts and crafts (*artes sordidae*) probably took place in workshops, and within families which specialized in the manufacture of particular types of merchandise. Unfortunately, we do not know much about such training, and the sparse sources available for this topic have not yet been properly investigated. Neither has ancient Jewish participation in, and teaching of, the empirical sciences (e.g. medicine and astronomy) been studied sufficiently (see Veltri 1998).

Since writing was a profession in antiquity, special scribal schools must have existed in Roman Palestine (Hezser 2001: 118–26). In Temple times, schools or guilds which taught the writing of scriptural manuscripts may have been associated with the Temple, but other scribes, who had probably learned their craft elsewhere, would have been able to write ordinary letters and documents only (Bar-Ilan 1988: 21; Crenshaw 1998: 111–12). Both types of scribes are frequently mentioned in rabbinic sources which suggests that a wide variety of scribal proficiencies continued to exist after 70 CE. There is no evidence of officially established and funded scribal schools. Most scribal training may have taken place in scribal families and guilds, that is, in a private and informal manner. Some copyists of Torah manuscripts seem to have been knowledgeable in the interpretation of biblical texts and were seen as competitors of rabbis (Hezser 1997: 467–75). Writers of letters and documents will have worked as secretaries in wealthy households, or hired themselves out on the street. There is good reason to assume that, at least in urban areas, many bilingual scribes were needed, and that such scribes would have been employed by the provincial administration.

Legal training was also considered professional training in antiquity (Clarke 1971: 114). Rabbinic sources occasionally mention non-rabbinic Jewish judges as members of local courts (Hezser 1997: 475–80). Such judges, who would not have studied with a rabbi, must have gained their proficiency elsewhere. It remains uncertain where and what types of legal tradition they were experts in. They may have gained their expertise by serving as apprentices of more experienced judges (cf. Clarke 1971: 115). We may assume that, due to the requirement to read Latin, few Jews would have attended the Roman law schools of the ancient Middle East.

SUGGESTED READING

The most important texts, issues, and methodological problems concerning ancient Jewish elementary and higher education are discussed in the context of Jewish literacy by Carr (2005: 111–276) for biblical and Second Temple times, and by Hezser (Hezser 2001: 39–109) for Roman times and late antiquity. Goodblatt provides a critical examination of the talmudic texts usually quoted in support of a school system (Goodblatt 1980, in Hebrew). Of the older studies, Morris and Perlow are the best ones (Morris 1937 and Perlow 1931). Tal Ilan provides the most comprehensive treatment of the education of Jewish women in Roman Palestine (Tal Ilan 1995: 190–204).

BIBLIOGRAPHY

ABERBACH, M. (1966–67). 'The Development of Hebrew Education. From the Times of the Babylonian Exile until the Third Century C.E.' [Hebr.]. *Shvile Hahinukh* 26: 90–94, 157–68; 27: 103–9.

ALON, G. (1989). *The Jews in Their Land in the Talmudic Age (70–640 C.E.).* 3rd ed. Cambridge, Mass.: Harvard University Press.

ARZT, M. (1953). 'The Teacher in Talmud and Midrash', in *Mordechai M. Kaplan Jubilee Volume*, ed. Moshe Davis. English section. New York: Jewish Theological Seminary, 35–47.

BACHER, W. (1903). 'Das altjüdische Schulwesen'. *Jahrbuch für Jüdische Geschichte und Literatur* 6: 48–81.

BAR-ILAN, M. (1988). 'Writing in Ancient Israel and Early Judaism, Part Two: Scribes and Books in the Late Second Commonwealth and Rabbinic Period', in *Mikra. Text Translation, Reading and Interpretation of the Hebrew Bible in Ancient Judaism and Early Christianity*, ed. M. J. Mulder. CRINT II.2. Assen: Van Gorcum, Philadelphia: Fortress Press, 21–38.

BONNER, S. F. (1977). *Education in Ancient Rome: From the Elder Cato to the Younger Pliny*. Berkeley: University of California Press.

CARR, D. M. (2005). *Writing on the Tablet of the Heart: Origins of Scripture and Literature*. Oxford: Oxford University Press.

CLARKE, M. L. (1971). *Higher Education in the Ancient World*. London: Routledge.

COHEN, S. J. D. (1981). 'Patriarchs and Scholarchs'. *Proceedings of the American Academy of Jewish Research* 48: 57–85.

CRENSHAW, J. L. (1998). *Education in Ancient Israel: Across the Deadening Silence*. New York: Doubleday.

CRIBIORE, R. (1996). *Writing, Teachers, and Students in Graeco-Roman Egypt*. American Studies in Papyrology 36. Atlanta: Scholars Press.

DOWNEY, G. (1958). 'The Christian Schools of Palestine: A Chapter in Literary History'. *Harvard Library Bulletin* 12: 297–319.

DRAZIN, N. (1940). *History of Jewish Education from 515 B.C.E. to 220 C.E.* Baltimore: The John Hopkins Press.

EBNER, E. (1956). *Elementary Education in Ancient Israel During the Tannaitic Period (10–220 C.E.)*. New York: Bloch Pub. Co.

GEIGER, J. (1985). 'The Athens of Syria: On Greek Intellectuals in Gadara' [Hebr.]. *Cathedra* 35: 3–16.

—— (1992). 'Greek Rhetoricians in Eretz Israel' [Hebr.]. *Cathedra* 66: 47–56.

—— (1994). 'Latin in Roman Palestine' [Hebr.]. *Cathedra* 74: 3–21.

GERHARDSSOHN, B. (1961). *Memory and Manuscript. Oral Tradition and Written Transmission in Rabbinic Judaism and Early Christianity*. Lund: C. W. K. Gleenep.

GINZBERG, L. (1928). *Students, Scholars and Saints*. New York and Philadelphia: Jewish Publication Society.

GOLDIN, J. (1972). 'Several Sidelights of a Torah Education in Tannaitic and Early Amoraic Times', in: *Ex Orbe Religionum*. Studia Geo Widengren Part 1, ed. C. J. Bleeker et al. Leiden: Brill, 176–91.

GOODBLATT, D. (1980). 'The Talmudic Sources on the Origins of Organized Jewish Education' [Hebr.]. *Studies in the History of the Jewish People and the Land of Israel* 5: 83–103.

—— (1994). *The Monarchic Principle: Studies in Jewish Self-Government in Antiquity*. Tübingen: Mohr-Siebeck.

HARRIS, W. V. (1989). *Ancient Literacy*. Cambridge, Mass.: Harvard University Press.

HEZSER, C. (1996). 'Die Verwendung der hellenistischen Gattung Chrie im frühen Christentum und Judentum'. *Journal for the Study of Judaism* 27: 371–439.

—— (1997). *The Social Structure of the Rabbinic Movement in Roman Palestine*. Tübingen: Mohr-Siebeck.

—— (2000). 'Interfaces Between Rabbinic Literature and Graeco-Roman Philosophy', in *The Talmud Yerushalmi and Graeco-Roman Culture*, vol.2, ed. Peter Schäfer and Catherine Hezser. Tübingen: Mohr-Siebeck.

—— (2001). *Jewish Literacy in Roman Palestine*. Tübingen: Mohr-Siebeck.

HIRSHMAN, M. (2009). *The Stabilization of Rabbinic Culture, 100 C.E.-350 C.E. Texts on Education and Their Late Antique Context*. New York and Oxford: Oxford University Press.

HOPKINS, K. (1993). 'Everyday Life for the Roman Schoolboy'. *History Today* 43: 25–30.

ILAN, T. (1995). *Jewish Women in Greco-Roman Palestine: An Inquiry into Image and Status*. Tübingen: Mohr-Siebeck.

ILAN, Z. (1995). 'The Synagogue and Study House at Meroth', in *Ancient Synagogues: Historical Analysis and Archaeological Discovery*, vol. 1, ed. D. Urman and P. V. M. Flesher. Studia Post-Biblica 47.1. Leiden: Brill, 256–88.

JACOBS, M. (1995). *Die Institution des jüdischen Patriarchen. Eine quellen- und traditionskritische Studie zur Geschichte der Juden in der Spätantike*. Tübingen: Mohr-Siebeck.

KASTER, R. A. (1983). 'Notes On "Primary" and "Secondary" Schools in Late Antiquity'. *Transactions of the American Philological Association* 113: 323–46.

KRAUSS, S. (1912). *Talmudische Archäologie*, vol. 3. Leipzig: G. Fock.

LAPIN, H. (1996). 'Jewish and Christian Academies in Roman Palestine: Some Preliminary Observations', in *Caesarea Maritima: A Retrospective After Two Millenia*, ed. A. Raban and K. G. HOLUM. Leiden: Brill, 496–512.

LIEBERMAN, S. (1962). *Hellenism in Jewish Palestine*. 2nd ed. New York: Jewish Theological Seminary.

—— (1965). *Greek in Jewish Palestine*. 2nd ed. New York: Jewish Theological Seminary.

MARROU, H.-I. (1965). *Histoire de l'éducation dans l'antiquité*. 6th rev. ed. Paris: Èditions du Seuil (English version: *A History of Education in Antiquity*. New York: Sheed and Ward, 1956).

MORGAN, T. (1998). *Literate Education in the Hellenistic and Roman Worlds*. Cambridge: Cambridge University Press.

MORRIS, N. (1937). *The Jewish School: An Introduction to the History of Jewish Education*. London: Eyre and Spottiswoode.

NAVEH, J./SHAKED, S. (1985). *Amulets and Magic Bowls*. Leiden: Brill.

OPPENHEIMER, A. (1978). 'Batei Midrashot in Eretz Israel in the Early Amoraic Period' [Hebr.]. *Cathedra* 8: 80–89.

PERLOW, T. (1931). *L'Éducation et l'enseignement chez les juifs à l'époque talmudique*. Paris: E. Leroux.

RAWSON, E. (1985). *Intellectual Life in the Late Roman Republic*. London: Duckworth.

RUBENSTEIN, J. L. (2002). 'The Rise of the Babylonian Talmudic Academy: A Reexamination of the Talmudic Evidence'. *Jewish Studies. An Internet Journal* 1: 55–68.

SAFRAI, S. (1968). 'Elementary Education: Its Religious and Social Significance in the Talmudic Period'. *Cahiers d'Histoire Mondiale* 11: 148–69.

—— (1976). 'Education and the Study of the Torah', in *The Jewish People in the First Century*, ed. S. Safrai and M. Stern. CRINT I.2. Assen: Van Gorcum. 945–70.

SCHWARTZ, S. (1999). 'The Patriarchs and the Diaspora'. *Journal of Jewish Studies* 50: 208–22.

SEVENSTER, J. N. (1968). *Do You Know Greek? How Much Greek Could the First Jewish Christians Have Known?* Novum Testamentum Suppl. 17. Leiden: Brill.

URMAN, D. (1995). 'The House of Assembly and the House of Study: Are They One and the Same?', in *Ancient Synagogues. Historical Analysis and Archaeological Discovery*, vol. 1, ed. D. Urman and P. V. M. Flesher. Studia Post-Biblica 47.1. Leiden: Brill, 232–55.

VELTRI, G. (1998). 'On the Influence of "Greek Wisdom": Theoretical and Empirical Sciences in Rabbinic Judaism'. *Jewish Studies Quarterly* 5: 300–17.

....

CHAPTER 26

ORALITY AND WRITING

....

CAROL BAKHOS

OUR understanding of the various aspects of orality and writing in Jewish daily life profits from the prolific outpouring of studies in related fields. Not only have works on literacy in the ancient world, the Graeco-Roman world in particular, contributed to our understanding of ancient Jewish literacy, but theoretical and cultural studies of orality in other societies and from other eras provide a sophisticated framework for addressing the roles of writing and orality amongst Jews in Roman Palestine, despite chronological and geographical differences. We will turn our attention to social-anthropological approaches to orality and literacy. To what extent can cultural studies of orality in other societies throw light on ancient Jewish literacy, and how have studies of orality in particular contributed to the scholarly debate on the transmission of the Mishnah? These interrelated matters must be addressed from various perspectives and disciplines. In what follows we will assess previous studies on the broad topic at hand, and consider the best ways in which the available sources should be evaluated. What were the social contexts in which writing and/or oral communication would be used? What was the role of professional scribes in daily life?

1. LITERACY IN GRAECO-ROMAN SOCIETY

The issue of literacy in ancient Graeco-Roman society has received much scholarly consideration and has been widely debated from the social-anthropological and historical perspectives, thus yielding diverging views on the extent of literacy in this era (see the summary in Hezser 2001: 18–26). The broad claim that literacy was the cause of Greek rational thought in particular has provoked a major debate among scholars. The publication of Goody and Watt's article, 'The Consequences of Literacy' (1963), which argues that writing in ancient Greece produced democracy, rational thought, philosophy, and historiography, first incited the controversy. Although the authors made it clear that literacy should not be envisioned as the only cause, their followers overlooked their warning. Moreover, even though Goody himself attempted to refine his own analysis, focusing on the implications of writing, in his later work he returned to the essential argument of the consequences of literacy, namely that writing was one of the major forces behind the development of logical, scientific thought, the establishment of a bureaucracy, law, and the modern state (Thomas 1992: 16–17).

In his major works, *The Literate Revolution in Greece and Its Cultural Consequences* (1982) and *The Muse Learns to Write* (1986), Eric Havelock deals with the effects of the beginning of writing, and the consequences of alphabetic literacy on ancient Greek society. As the title of the first book mentioned above indicates, Havelock maintains that the 'democratized literacy' in ancient Greece was indeed a 'revolution', a view shared by the cultural anthropologist Jack Goody who, in his work *The Logic of Writing and the Organization of Society* (1986), considers the implications of writing on the organization of society and explores the interface between the oral and the written.

Whereas Goody, Havelock and others attempted to demonstrate the extensive, revolutionizing effects of writing, others have railed against their sweeping views. Brian Street's *Literacy in Theory and Practice* (1984) provides a corrective to their claims. Street argues that such analyses of the uses and consequences of literacy more often than not fail to theorize sufficiently for the purposes of cross-cultural comparison. It is frequently assumed that literacy is a neutral technology that can be detached from specific social contexts; the ideological factors bound up with it are ignored (Street 1984: 105). Instead, as Christopher Miller astutely suggests, we should not view literacy 'as a universal phenomenon with predetermined consequences; there are only literacies, each embedded in an ideological context from which it cannot be distinguished' (Goody et al. 1988: 227).

Grand theories such as those espoused by Goody and Havelock are also tempered by the lack of consideration for matters that provide more conjectural grounding, such as the question of the availability of writing materials, the quantity of written sources, and the extent of literacy among the various societal strata.

Moreover, one must ask whether or not Havelock's adherence to a strict differentiation between 'pre-literate' and 'literate' society in ancient Greece withstands scrutiny.

Rosalind Thomas addresses this issue in her works *Oral Tradition and Written Record in Classical Athens* (1989) and *Literacy and Orality in Ancient Greece* (1992), and observes that during the fifth and fourth centuries BCE and later, orality was the primary mode of communication, despite the fact that evidence of a great deal of writing exists. Even in later Roman society, oral performance was greatly valued, alongside the production of written literary texts (Thomas 1992: 159). Finnegan also offers a serious critique of the view that orality and literacy are mutually exclusive. Rather than envisioning a rupture ('Great Divide') between two separate categories, she suggests the relationship of a continuum, or perhaps 'a complex set of continuums' (1992: 272).

These two scholars are certainly not alone in highlighting the complex, synergistic relationship between the written and oral. In discussing literacy in medieval Europe, Brian Stock emphasizes the interpenetration of orality and writing and its effect on thought processes. According to Stock, in the eleventh and twelfth centuries an important transformation took place in Europe: from that time onwards oral discourse functioned within a 'universe of communication governed by texts' (Stock 1983: 3). Together the two modes played a 'decisive role in the organization of experience' (ibid.). In other words, in the mid-twelfth century, when literate norms were established in judicial and governmental arenas, the spoken word continued to play a prominent cultural role (ibid. 9). Both written and oral modes of communication persisted throughout the medieval period. As literacy informed medieval life and thought, and texts were introduced into a largely oral society, modes of reading and writing were affected, and in turn a growing intellectualism emerged. The interplay between written and oral modes of communication was instrumental in enabling new ways of understanding the world as a series of relationships.

Finnegan also emphasizes this connection between oral and written modes of communication in her work. Interaction between oral and written forms is 'extremely common'. In fact, her examination of broadside ballads itself deals a 'death blow' to the idea that the use of writing puts an end to oral literary forms (Finnegan 1992: 160). In early sixteenth-century England, ballads were distributed in large numbers in a special form—the broadside. Ballad singers went around singing samples of their songs in order to sell broadside sheets. Hence, the initial distribution was a mixture of 'print and performance'. The ballads circulated orally even though they started as printed text. Finnegan calls to mind other parallels to this kind of interaction, such as popular Irish songs (ibid. 165). The underlying point in the transmission of oral poetry is the need to disabuse ourselves of romantic theories of the 'nature and purity of "oral transmission"' (160). As we shall see, this mixed and complex mode of textual distribution provides a template of sorts for understanding the transmission of the rabbinic 'Oral Torah' as well.

Whereas the previously mentioned works draw heavily on social-anthropological approaches to literacy, William Harris' monograph on Graeco-Roman literacy is a historical examination that challenges the notion that 'democratizing literacy' in ancient Greece created an unprecedented revolution (1989). Harris provides a less optimistic view of the extent of literacy in antiquity, and demonstrates that it was a relatively rare phenomenon. He directs us to the many important issues to keep in mind when making assertions about such a complicated matter. For example, what do we mean by literacy? Obviously, we have to reckon with many different degrees of this skill in antiquity. Although Harris does not delve deeply into the notion of 'semi-literates', he underscores the need to take them into account. Furthermore, what were the functions and social contexts of writing in the ancient world?

Harris generally distinguishes between two types of literacy: scribal literacy and craftsman's literacy. The former was restricted to a particular social group which used writing for purposes such as record-keeping. This technical writing skill, also referred to by others as 'professional literacy', was predominant in Near Eastern cultures throughout antiquity, and in Europe until the twelfth century. The later term, craftsman's literacy, is used by Harris to refer to 'the condition in which the majority, or a near-majority, of skilled craftsmen are literate', a situation which prevailed in Europe and North America from the sixteenth to the eighteenth century (Harris 1989: 7–8).

Although he admits that attempts to derive a literacy rate are risky, Harris nonetheless sets out to do so. According to his estimate, the literacy rate for Attica in classical times amounted to 5–10 percent (ibid. 114). In Roman imperial times, literacy will have been higher in Rome than elsewhere in Italy (ibid. 259), but altogether below 15 percent, and even lower than that for women (ibid. 266–67). Altogether, on the basis of literary and epigraphic evidence, Harris compellingly argues that literacy did not exceed 10–15 percent of the population (women and slaves included) from the time of the invention of the Greek alphabet shortly before the eighth century BCE to the end of the Roman Empire.

This means that written culture in antiquity was by and large restricted to technical writers on the one hand, and a privileged minority on the other. Written culture by no means replaced oral culture, but rather coexisted with it. Harris acknowledges the profound effects of writing on ancient Greek and Roman societies. For one thing, writing enhanced class differences and served as an 'instrument of class hegemony' (334). Literacy on a large scale is the product of forces that were absent in antiquity. An expansive school system was lacking, as was the demand for a literate workforce. Whatever demand for such workers or secretaries existed at the time was filled for the most part by slaves. Finally, there was no underlying ideology that all citizens should be able to read or write. Under these circumstances, it should be no surprise that mass literacy was absent in antiquity.

Harris' work has not gone unnoticed, prompting scholars to re-evaluate and reformulate their views. Not everyone concurs entirely with his assessment of literacy in antiquity. This is exemplified by the volume of articles discussing Harris' work entitled *Literacy in the Roman World* (Beard, ed. 1991). While the contributors hardly challenge Harris' main point that literacy levels in Graeco-Roman antiquity were very low, they nonetheless examine aspects of his book from various vantage points, calling into question several of his assertions. For example, Mary Beard disagrees with Harris on the functions of writing in Roman pagan religion, for according to her assessment 'there was much more writing associated with the cults, rituals, and sanctuaries of Graeco-Roman paganism than Harris' argument implies' (Beard 1991: 37). Like Harris, she acknowledges that writing played a different role in early Christianity than it did in paganism, yet at the same time she contends that the contrast should not be framed in terms of 'marginality' and 'centrality'. Beard also emphasizes that writing was more than a utilitarian tool; it served 'to define experience, to change perceptions, to display dominance' (ibid. 58).

In 'Conquest by Book' in the same volume, Hopkins finds completely convincing Harris' main hypothesis that only a minority of adult males and a tiny minority of adult females could read and write in all periods of classical antiquity, but draws out the implications of Harris' minimalist case. If adult male literacy was about 10 percent across the Roman Empire, 'there were roughly 2 million adult males who *could* (emphasis in original) read and write to some extent in the empire as a whole. In world history, this was an unprecedented number of literates for a single state' (Hopkins 1991: 135). Hopkins sets out to demonstrate that the sheer mass of people who could read and write, living in Roman towns and in some villages, affected the experience of living in Roman society politically, economically, socially, and culturally. Hopkins does not argue for universal literacy; but despite the fact that a minority of Roman men could read and write, 'the mass of literates, the density of their communications and the volume of their stored knowledge, significantly affected living in the Roman empire. Literacy and writing were active ingredients in promoting cultural and ideological change'. (ibid. 144).

It is important to keep in mind that specific factors—economic, social, and cultural—affect the distribution of writing within a given society. Moreover, their effects vary according to a particular society. One can, however, detect certain pre-conditions that give rise to the spread of literacy. The availability of public teachers and affordable education for everyone, and the accessibility of writing materials and texts, for example, would increase the spread of literacy. Although it is yet to be determined whether the extent of literacy in Graeco-Roman society was as significant as some have surmised, we nonetheless have a good idea of its function in daily life. We know, for example, that in the Roman world there were various forms of textual transmission, and that scribes were employed to perform multiple tasks. One of the biggest challenges scholars face when determining the usage of writing in any pre-modern period is the extent to which the preserved written material accurately reflects that use. Archaeological and geographical factors that determine the survival or absence of evidence must always be taken into account.

2. The Use of Writing Amongst Jews in Roman Palestine

In general, Jews in Roman Palestine engaged in various forms of writing from simple lists, documents, and inscriptions to sophisticated literary works (see the overview in Hezser 2001: 251–444). Sales and loan documents, marriage contracts, labels on jars, donors' and burial inscriptions, magical texts, letters, and literary documents all attest to the varied use of writing. These uses of writing, however, were quite circumscribed and limited to particular strata within society. As in Graeco-Roman society, it was mainly the educated members of the upper strata of society and the intellectual elite who used writing. Given the number of different languages used in Roman Palestine, with Greek being the official administrative language, Aramaic the everyday language of the Jewish population, and Hebrew the language of the Torah and the Temple (Schwartz 1995), the conditions for the spread of literacy must have been quite complicated.

We may assume that, just as amongst Greeks and Romans, writing skills would have been much less common than reading skills among Jews. Since Jewish education seems to have concentrated on Torah reading skills only (Hezser 2001: 68–89; see also Hezser's chapter on education in this volume), families would have had to employ private tutors to teach their children non-professional scribal skills. Indeed, 'education in literacy of any sort outside of professional scribal training remained socially confined to the private household, where it was managed by older family members or hired tutors' (Jaffee 2001: 22). Only the well-to-do were able to afford this luxury.

Writing would have been indispensable for administrative affairs. Those Jews who participated in the provincial administration of Roman Palestine and used writing for that purpose were probably quite assimilated and bilingual (Hezser 2001: 489–90). The upper echelons of society, business people and landowners, would have used written documents and letters, as did some rabbis and editors of rabbinic documents. We may assume, though, that except for occasional informal notes, professional scribes would have been used to actually write these letters, texts, and documents (Hezser 2001: 474–95). In Jewish, as in Graeco-Roman society, writing was not a required skill to manage ordinary everyday life tasks, and it also did not convey a higher status on the person who possessed it. Therefore, even some members of the upper strata of society and religious leaders were able to scribble their own names only (ibid. 169–89).

3. PROFESSIONAL SCRIBES

Ancient scribes' mundane duties consisted of secretarial and administrative tasks. They were record keepers of business and judicial matters, writers of documents, and guardians of archives. As such, they were necessary for the maintenance of a government's administrative activities. Even small city-states of the ancient Near East required the employment of scribes. In addition to government scribes, scribes were needed at the temples, and some scholars assume that a scribal school existed at the Temple in Jerusalem (Crenshaw 1998: 111–12). Scribes also copied manuscripts and literary works (Avrin 1991). Members of the upper strata of society employed scribes as their personal secretaries. Despite the many different functions of scribes, scribal activity was far from extensive in the ancient world. Scribes who were privately employed to copy Greek and Latin texts and who functioned as secretaries in the houses of the wealthy were usually slaves or freedpersons and not held in high esteem (Small 1997: 174 on scribes as 'research assistants').

Throughout the Mediterranean world of the first centuries CE, scribes would perform a range of functions and be found at various socio-economic levels. Yet, as Haines-Eitzen notes (2000: 8), despite their ubiquity, Roman-period scribes seldom received recognition for their work. Even nowadays, scribes are sometimes mentioned in passing only, as in Reynolds and Wilson's book *Scribes and Scholars* (1974). Although scribes are mentioned in the title, nowhere in the book does one come across a sustained discussion of any aspect of who scribes were, what roles they performed, or what their function was in society. Similarly Fantham in a more recent work, *Roman Literary Culture* (1996), treats scribes cursorily, and further demonstrates the difficulty of discussing the social history of ancient scribes extensively given the paucity and nature of our sources. Although almost all ancient texts were written by scribes, little was written about them. The general anonymity of scribes is also evident in Jewish sources, which almost never mention the names of scribes who wrote letters for rabbis (but see y. Sanh. 1:2, 18d, where R. Gamliel and elders' dictation of a letter to Yohanan the scribe is mentioned). Nevertheless, the role of scribes in the biblical period (Bar Ilan 1988; Demsky/Bar Ilan 1988; Schniedewind 2004; Carr 2005; Van der Toorn 2007), and in the first centuries CE (Saldarini 2001; Goodman 1994) is relatively well researched by scholars.

We can with some certainty claim that from the time of the Persian restoration of the Jerusalem Temple in the fifth century BCE until the Second Temple's destruction in 70 CE, the Temple employed various types of scribes (Crenshaw 1998). As the cultic, political, and economic hub of the country, the Temple required the performance of numerous scribal tasks. Beyond the confines of the Temple, even highly literate Jews of the upper strata of society would sometimes employ scribes to write personal memoranda, and wealthy merchants employed (slave) secretaries to write sales documents and to maintain their business accounts.

Scribes were needed for a whole gamut of purposes, ranging from the labelling of items and the writing of sales and loan documents to transcribing complex literary texts. A literary composition was basically an oral endeavour whereby the author would dictate a composition to a scribe. Evidence of the work of professional scribes can be found among the Qumran finds: many different scribal hands worked on the manuscripts which were written in Palaeo-Hebrew, Hebrew square script and Greek (Martin 1958).

Except for the copying of biblical texts, for which the manuscripts found at Qumran provide evidence, no material remains of literary writing exists for the rabbinic period, that is, the first five centuries CE. All surviving manuscripts of rabbinic works can be dated to the post-rabbinic medieval period. We must note the distinction between the scribal ability to copy Torah scrolls and rabbis' creative interpretation and adaptation of Torah knowledge. While some rabbis may have been professional scribes, this was not a skill that pertained to all rabbis. Rabbinic literature attests to the notion that the copying of texts was considered a mere technical skill, from which rabbis distinguished their own more creative intellectual ability (see Hezser 1997: 467–75 on the relationship between rabbis and scribes).

According to Haines-Eitzen, Christian scribes were more involved in the copying of literary texts than was customary for scribes in the Graeco-Roman world (2000: 130–31). Copyists of early Christian texts not only duplicated the texts but also modified, corrected, and interpreted them, because the texts were religiously relevant to them. In other words, the producers of the copies were also the users of the texts. When copying texts in the midst of raging theological debates, they wielded a certain power over their formulation. Haines-Eitzen suggests that this Christian practice may have emerged out of a Jewish scribal context, that is, that Jewish scribes may have been similarly involved in the formulation of the biblical texts they copied, an assumption which requires further study.

4. LETTER WRITING

According to Harris, letters were not a commonplace occurrence in the ancient world: their use was rather limited to certain social circles. They became more common amongst the political elite in the Hellenistic period, but even then they were usually 'inspired by some emergency' (Harris 1989: 127–28). In Roman imperial times, letter writing and the distribution of written decrees allowed the emperor to harness control over distant provinces. Members of the court and influential politicians would increasingly use written communication. Letters were also important for the dissemination of moral and theological instruction among Christians, already at the time of Paul, but especially in the fourth and fifth centuries, when church leaders became prolific letter writers (Stowers 1989; Doty 1973).

We have evidence of ancient Jewish letter-writing practices from papyrus documents and references to letters in the works of Josephus and rabbinic documents (Hezser 2001: 259–90). As in Roman society, letters were primarily used as a means of communication among politicians (the Herodian dynasty), military leaders (Josephus and other rebel leaders of the first revolt against Rome), and religious authorities (rabbis). Especially in amoraic times, rabbis seem to have used letters for the purpose of exchanging halakhic views. Letters were usually dictated to a scribe; the sender merely added his or her signature if he or she was able to do so. On the basis of literary references to letters we do not know whether members of the Herodian family, military leaders, and rabbis wrote their letters themselves or whether they had scribes available to write the letters for them.

5. LATE ANTIQUE DEVELOPMENTS IN THE USE OF WRITING

In amoraic times, that is, from the third century CE onwards, we can detect a general expansion of the Jewish uses of writing, which may be attributed to increased urbanization and to the Roman-Byzantine influence (Hezser 2001: 500–1). Nevertheless, these 'pockets' of writing amongst clearly defined social strata must be understood against the background of the continued and all-pervasive use of orality as the chief means of communication throughout the period under discussion here.

During the first three centuries of Roman rule, writing seems to have been rather limited in Palestinian Jewish society. Some private citizens would have occasionally employed writing for pragmatic purposes—occasional letter-writing, accounts, and notes. Graffiti inscriptions on ossuaries from Herodian-period Jerusalem identified the remains of members of wealthy families, whereas burial inscriptions from the third century onwards were more formal and elaborate, indicating the status of the deceased (Hezser 2001: 364–97). Synagogue dedication inscriptions also belong to that later period (ibid. 397–413). In addition, rabbinic traditions were collected and edited in late antiquity and material evidence of magic writing exists for that time (ibid. 436–44).

As Hezser has observed, there is no evidence that ancient Jews considered illiteracy degrading (2001: 176–89). While upper-class Roman males were expected to possess at least rudimentary reading and writing skills, this seems not to have been the case in Jewish society. But even in Roman society, writing continued to be primarily regarded as a technical skill associated with low-status scribes, 'whereas only the truly educated *litteratus* had a high status' (ibid. 499). In both Jewish and Roman society, parental heritage and land-ownership were the prevailing status criteria, and at least in Roman society public offices as well. Furthermore, what mattered to the rabbis was not the mere skill of writing but the intellectually much more demanding ability to develop Torah creatively and to apply it to new situations. Rabbis' propagation of the value of Torah study may have convinced some of their contemporaries to acquire Hebrew reading skills, but we do not know to what extent rabbis actually succeeded in influencing the Jewish populace in this regard.

6. WOMEN AND LITERACY

Recently, scholars have concerned themselves with the question of women's literacy in antiquity. Harris' study has demonstrated that in societies in which illiteracy is widespread—this is especially the case in traditional societies—a higher proportion of women than men are usually illiterate (Harris 1989: 23). Women who managed their households would also educate their daughters. In wealthy, upper-class Roman households this education may have included instruction in financial affairs, which would have required calculating, and perhaps also some reading and writing skills. A few Greek and Roman women became intellectuals, but this level of higher education must be considered very exceptional. According to Harris, 'Funerary reliefs demonstrate, and some Pompeian portraits of women confirm, that some literary education was thought to be desirable for a woman of good family' (ibid. 252). In general, though, literacy was rather restricted amongst women. As the Babatha and Salome Komaise papyri indicate, even Jewish women from affluent landowning families who managed their own property lacked basic literary skills and were not even able to sign their own names (Hezser 2001: 314–15, 487). This is not surprising since even upper-class males were not necessarily literate, as we have seen.

7. SOCIAL-ANTHROPOLOGICAL APPROACHES TO ORALITY

Milman Parry (1987) and his assistant, Albert Lord (2000) laid the foundational work in orality studies for generations to come. As one of the leading scholars of the Homeric epic tradition, Parry endeavoured to prove the oral character of the *Iliad* and the *Odyssey*. By studying the actual living tradition of epic song-making in Yugoslavia, he set out to trace the development of Homeric poetry and to provide a rational and scientific analysis of the mechanisms and aesthetics of oral poetry. This approach distinguished him from earlier classicists. Occupying his attention was the question of how the poet(s) of the *Iliad* and the *Odyssey* were able to compose these lengthy epic tales. Until then, Homeric scholars were divided into two camps: the 'unitarians' posited a single author, whereas the 'separatists' maintained that the poems were composite constructions of different strata. Parry turned his energy to resolving this issue. It was a daunting dilemma, given that the poems were composed in Greece two and a half millennia ago or even earlier, at a time when most of the population was illiterate.

Parry was struck by the repetitive phrases strewn throughout the 15,000 lines of the *Iliad* and the 12,000 lines of the *Odyssey*, and he came up with an explanation for their appearance. The basic thrust of Parry's thesis is that the epic poems were originally produced orally. According to the Parry-Lord theory, formulaic epithets such as 'glorious Hector' and 'swift-footed Achilles' play a significant role in the poems' composition. The poet seems to have constructed a line of poetry by combining epithets with formulaic phrases in the process of oral performance.

Other scholars had observed the formulaic phrases too, but Parry went a step further by arguing that the poet composed the poems orally. They were songs produced *in* performance. By delving into a vast storehouse of stock phrases and traditional themes, the poet tailored the material to create a personal composition. Unfortunately Parry died in 1935 at the young age of 33, but his assistant Albert Lord made it his life's ambition to complete his mentor's work, which he succeeded in accomplishing. In his work, *The Singer of Tales* (2000), a classic for the general study of oral and written literature and a standard textbook within folklore studies, he elaborated Parry's work. The Parry-Lord theory not only greatly influenced

Homeric Studies, but also textual studies in general from the Hebrew Bible to *Beowulf*, medieval epic poetry, Gaelic poetry and most recently, as we shall see, Mishnaic Studies. Even sceptics of the theory must now contend with it.

What did Parry and Lord learn from the Yugoslav poets? Well, to begin with, these poets crafted their art without knowledge of the written word. They were unable to read or write, which means that there was no fixed text, no cherished archetype, and hence not one correct original version. The performer is the author of the epic poem. That said, he is not creating *ex nihilo*, but rather he is tailoring formulae, patterns, and themes to which authors of the past contributed. They provided the material for the unique performance, and in this sense each epic can be considered the product of several authors. This theory makes it difficult to argue that the only way to explain lengthy oral poems is in terms of memorization, and it puts to rest the search for the one correct and original version of the text.

In her book *Oral Poetry* (1992) Finnegan raises the question whether and to what extent a formulaic style is proof of oral composition. If theorists concede that the use of formulaic expressions is an earmark of both oral and written composition, then how widely can one apply the Parry-Lord theory of oral composition (ibid. 69)? Finnegan also points to another difficulty in the general application of this theory, namely the exact definition of a 'formula' (ibid. 71). Formulae by definition are repetitions, but analysts disagree as to whether the repetitions are metrical, syntactic, or semantic. Scholars differ over the use of the term 'formula' and therefore develop different statistical analyses for the purpose of demonstrating whether or not a style is 'oral-formulaic'. These concerns aside, the Lord-Parry theory and its advocates have yielded important insights into oral literature, and the impact of their work is felt in many areas of study. Given that the Homeric epics provided the textual base for Lord's study, *The Singer of Tales*, it is no surprise that this work has left a lasting imprint on Classical Studies. More recently, orality theories have been applied to the study of the development of the Hebrew Bible (Niditch 1996).

8. THE INTERPLAY BETWEEN ORALITY AND LITERACY IN RABBINIC TRANSMISSION

The question of when and how the rabbinic tradition, which rabbis called the 'Oral Torah' in distinction to the 'Written Torah' of the Hebrew Bible, was put into written form has preoccupied scholars for at least two centuries. The difficulty in part also rests in the fact that rabbinic documents such as the Mishnah do not provide clear evidence of their own genesis or that of other rabbinic works. Furthermore, although the rabbinic sources themselves state that the Oral Law must not be written down, there is evidence that rabbis did possess some traditions in written form. Queries such as the following abound: what was the nature of the material available to the editors of these documents? To what extent did they 'invent' the contents of their discussions, and to what extent were they transmitted to them orally or in written form? Did the editors preserve traditions verbatim or did they shape them according to their needs or desires? Was the editorial process complex and multi-layered, drawn out over a long span of time, or does it reflect the workings of an editor or a circle of editors at a particular period of time? To answer these questions contemporary scholars have steered away from using suspect rabbinic references and have instead focused on the form and content of the rabbinic document itself.

There are two basic camps of thought on the issue of the Mishnah's transmission and development. Scholars such as Lieberman (1950), Gerhardsson (1998), and Zlotnick (1988) argue for an oral transmission of the Mishnah until the production of early medieval manuscripts and others, such as Epstein (1964) and Safrai (1987) assert that from the outset rabbinic compilations were produced as written texts (see Hezser 2002 for a discussion of these theories).

Neusner posits a different approach, one that views the redaction of the Mishnah not as a preservation of tradition, but rather as a creative, purposeful adaptation. He envisions a more singular process of transmission, not based on accurate oral transmission of tradition. The sustained character of transmission is reflected, according to Neusner, in the 'unified and cogent formal character of the Mishnah'. Upon close reading of the 'document', it 'proves systematic and orderly, purposive and well composed' (Neusner 1987: 136). The Mishnah accordingly is the work of tradent-redactors who deliberately formulated traditions.

Modifying and building on Lieberman's work, Hezser suggests that the creation, distribution, and usage of books in Graeco-Roman antiquity is the most suitable context for understanding the development of the Mishnah (Hezser 2002: 167). Jaffee also, cognizant of the need to explore the Graeco-Roman milieu, points to the Graeco-Roman parallels in rhetorical education for the purpose of understanding the ideology of Oral Torah as it developed in the third and fourth century CE within Galilean rabbinic discipleship circles. Moreover, his work unhinges the assumed dichotomy underlying the work of previous scholars, and depicts a process of interpenetration whereby 'traditions were shaped and revised in a continuous circuit of oral performance and written recension—a circuit impossible to break artificially into an "oral substratum" and a "written recension" or vice versa' (Jaffee 2001: 101).

Jaffee's groundbreaking work, *Torah in the Mouth* (2001), provides a corrective to studies of rabbinic literature that erroneously view the transition from oral tradition to written text in evolutionary terms—from oral to written form. His compelling thesis explains the existence of diverse versions of tannaitic teachings, not as mistakes that arise from a purely oral transmission process, but rather as multiple versions that reflect diverse oral performances of a tradition in diverse contexts, especially since in Graeco-Roman rhetorical culture, memorization of a written text led to a variety of versions in various settings. In examining several readings of mishnaic texts, Jaffee highlights how the material as scripted performance is in some ways analogous to a dramatic or musical presentation. Like the broadside ballads which Finnegan examined, the texts are activated, that is, they come to life, in the performance or recitation itself. In point of fact, their existence assumes the act of performance, and in turn the act of performance assumes the existence of the texts.

We also find the notion of the rabbinic oral-literary culture as a circulatory system of performative textuality in Fraade's early work on the tannaitic Midrash Sifre Deuteronomy, where he writes that Oral Torah in written form is 'the literary face of an otherwise oral circulatory system of study and teaching' (1991: 19). He applies this notion not only to the Mishnah but also to the early midrashic literature, which is an appropriate place to examine the 'complex interplay of oral and textual registers of tradition and its transmission' (ibid. 33). After all, it is in midrashic collections that we first encounter expressions of the dual Torah, and moreover, the very structure and rhetoric of midrashic commentary reflects the interplay of orality and writing. Expanding on and refining Lieberman's argument, Fraade presents a 'more "circulatory" understanding of the interrelation of Rabbinic texts and their oral performative enactments: an orality that is grounded in a textuality that remains orally fluid' (ibid. 36).

Drawing on Fraade's, and especially Jaffee's, insights and application of orality studies to rabbinic texts, Alexander illustrates that the transmission of mishnaic traditions involved more than the conveyance of textual material, namely, the 'crafting of their authority' and 'the cultivation of intellectual habits through which to analyze and interpret them' (Alexander 2006: 8). Like Jaffee, she argues that we should steer away from the model of envisioning texts as stable and fixed, whereby variations are deviations from an original. Instead, we should adopt the model that underscores the important role the performer plays in bringing the text to life. She shows how 'traditions could be constructed anew in different performative settings' (ibid. 74). Central to her thesis is the notion that the transmitters of the Mishnah were not passive conveyors of tradition but its very shapers, and the very process of transmission required analytical engagement with the material at hand.

9. FUTURE DIRECTIONS

The study of orality and writing in Roman Palestine is a subject that encompasses many fields of study and disciplines. Not only literary, but also epigraphic, papyrological and numismatic evidence has to be taken into account. Many different factors will have determined the choice of written or oral modes of communication, amongst them geographical location, population distribution, social stratification, and religious values. All studies of ancient literacy and writing must be situated within the appropriate historical, political, social, and economic contexts of the respective societies under investigation. Comparative studies of orality and literacy in Jewish, Graeco-Roman, and early Christian society can reveal both parallels and discrepancies.

In the past, Graeco-Roman culture has served as the proper framework and background for understanding orality and writing amongst Jews in Roman Palestine. If we want to expand our perspective on Jewish orality and writing, we should also take the Islamic period into consideration and examine how early Muslim culture helped to transform a predominantly oral Jewish society into a 'religion of the book' (Beit-Arie 2000). The Cairo Geniza documents can provide the proper basis for a study of Jewish writing practices in medieval daily life (Goitein 1967–93; 1973). On that basis, broader issues can be examined as well: how did early Islamic writing practices influence the Jewish use of writing? What were the effects of the centralization and organization of the Jewish community under Islam on literacy, the distribution of texts, and the control exerted by religious authorities? By taking a chronologically wider view of the development of writing in Judaism, we can avoid transposing phenomena of a later period onto an earlier era.

Finally, if we assume that at least 90 percent of the Jewish population of Roman Palestine was illiterate or barely literate, we must reconsider our understanding of ancient Judaism as a 'book religion' (Hezser 2001: 503–4). Other elements, such as the oral and visual performances of the synagogues and theatres, and the visual imagery of mosaics, wall paintings, statues, and architectural features may have been more significant in ancient Judaism than the philologically oriented scholars of the past have tended to assume.

SUGGESTED READING

Hezser (2001) constitutes the most comprehensive work on the subject of Jewish literacy in Roman Palestine, thoroughly investigating the various types of evidence from a social-historical point of view. Harris' work, *Ancient Literacy* (1989), provides the proper background on literacy in Graeco-Roman society with his claim that the level of literacy was always very low. Jaffee's study, *Torah in the Mouth* (2001), is of fundamental importance for the relationship between orality and literacy in rabbinic culture. Ruth Finnegan's *Oral Poetry* (1992) is an excellent resource for understanding the relationship between written texts and oral performance.

BIBLIOGRAPHY

ALEXANDER, E. S. (2006). *Transmitting Mishnah: The Shaping Influence of Oral Tradition.* New York: Cambridge University Press.

AVRIN, L. (1991). *Scribes, Script and Books: The Book Arts from Antiquity to the Renaissance.* Chicago and London: American Library Association.

BAR-ILAN, M. (1988). 'Writing in Ancient Israel and Early Judaism, Part Two: Scribes and Books in the Late Second Commonwealth and Rabbinic Period', in *Mikra. Text, Translation, Reading and Interpretation of the Hebrew Bible in Ancient Judaism and Early Christianity*, ed. M.J. Mulder. Assen and Maastricht: Van Gorcum, 21–38.

BEARD, M (1991). 'Writing and Religion: Ancient Literacy and the Function of the Written Word in Roman Religion', in *Literacy in the Roman World*, ed. Mary Beard et al. Ann Arbor: University of Michigan Press, 35–58.

—— (ed.) (1991). *Literacy in the Roman World.* Ann Arbor: University of Michigan Press.

BEIT-ARIÉ, M. (2000). 'Publication and Reproduction of Literary Texts in Medieval Jewish Civilization: Jewish Scribality and its Impact on the Texts Transmitted', in *Transmitting Jewish Traditions: Orality, Textuality and Cultural Diffusion*, ed. Y. Elman and I. Gershoni. New Haven: Yale University Press, 225–47.

BOWMAN, A. K./WOOLF, G. (1994). *Literacy and Power in the Ancient World.* Cambridge: Cambridge University Press.

CARR D. M. (2005). *Writing on the Tablet of the Heart: Origins of Scripture and Literature.* New York: Oxford University Press.

CRENSHAW, J. L. (1998). *Education in Ancient Israel: Across the Deadening Silence.* New York: Doubleday.

DEMSKY A./BAR-ILAN, M. (1988). 'Writing in Ancient Israel and Early Judaism, Part One: The Biblical Period', in *Mikra: Text, Translation, Reading and Interpretation of the Hebrew Bible in Ancient Judaism and Early Christianity*, ed. M. J. Mulder. Assen and Maastricht: Van Gorcum, 1–10.

DOTY, W. G. (1973). *Letters in Primitive Christianity.* Philadelphia: Fortress.

EPSTEIN, J. N (1964). *Introduction to the Text of the Mishnah* [Hebr.]. 2 vols. Jerusalem: Magnes Press.

FANTHAM, E. (1996). *Roman Literary Culture: From Cicero to Apuleius.* Baltimore: Johns Hopkins University Press.

FINNEGAN, R. (1988). *Literacy and Orality: Studies in the Technology of Communication.* Oxford: Blackwell.

—— (1992). *Oral Poetry: Its Nature, Significance and Social Context.* Bloomington: Indiana University Press.

FRAADE, S. D (1991). *From Tradition to Commentary: Torah and Its Interpretation in the Midrash Sifre to Deuteronomy.* Albany: State University of New York Press.

—— (1999). 'Literary Composition and Oral Performance in Early Midrashim'. *Oral Tradition* 14: 33–51.

GERHARDSSON, B. (1998). *Memory and Manuscript: Oral Tradition and Written Transmission in Rabbinic Judaism and Early Christianity with Tradition and Transmission in Early Christianity.* Grand Rapids: Eerdmans.

GOITEIN, S. D. (1967–93). *A Mediterranean Society: The Jewish Communities of the Arab World as Portrayed in the Documents of the Cairo Geniza.* 6 vols. Berkeley: University of California Press.

—— (1973). *Letters of Medieval Jewish Traders: Translated from the Arabic with Introductions and Notes.* Princeton: Princeton University Press.

GOODMAN, M. (1994). 'Texts, Scribes and Power in Roman Judaea', in *Literacy and Power in the Ancient World,* ed. A. K. Bowman and G. Woolf. Cambridge: Cambridge University Press, 99–108.

GOODY, J. (ed) (1968). *Literacy in Traditional Societies.* Cambridge: Cambridge University Press.

—— (1986). *The Logic of Writing and the Organization of Society.* Cambridge: Cambridge University Press.

—— (1987). *Interface between the Written and the Oral.* Cambridge: Cambridge University Press.

—— and WATT, I. (1963). 'The Consequences of Literacy'. *Comparative Studies in Society and History* 5: 304–345.

GOODY, J. et al. (1988). 'Selections from the Symposium on "Literacy, Reading, and Power"', Whitney Humanities Center, November 14, 1987. *Yale Journal of Criticism* 2: 193–232.

HAINES-EITZEN, K. (2000). *Guardians of Letters. Literacy, Power, and the Transmitters of Early Christian Literature.* New York: Oxford University Press.

HARRIS, W. V (1989). *Ancient Literacy.* Cambridge: Harvard University Press.

HAVELOCK, E. A. (1982). *The Literate Revolution in Greece and Its Cultural Consequences.* Princeton: Princeton University Press.

—— (1986). *The Muse Learns to Write: Reflections on Orality and Literacy from Antiquity to the Present.* New Haven: Yale University Press.

HEZSER, C. (1997). *The Social Structure of the Rabbinic Movement in Roman Palestine.* Tübingen: Mohr-Siebeck.

—— (2001). *Jewish Literacy in Roman Palestine.* Tübingen: Mohr-Siebeck.

—— (2002). 'The Mishnah and Ancient Book Production', in *The Mishnah in Contemporary Perspective,* ed. A. J. Avery-Peck and J. Neusner. Leiden: Brill.

HOPKINS, K. (1991). 'Conquest by Book', in *Literacy in the Roman World,* ed. M. Beard et al. Ann Arbor: University of Michigan Press, 133–58.

JAFFEE, M. S (2001). *Torah in the Mouth: Writing and Oral Tradition in Palestinian Judaism, 200 BCE–400 CE.* New York: Oxford University Press.

LIEBERMAN, S (1950). *Hellenism in Jewish Palestine.* New York: Jewish Theological Seminary.

LORD, A. B. (2000). *The Singer of Tales.* 2nd ed. Cambridge: Harvard University Press, 2000.

MARTIN, M. (1958). *The Scribal Character of the Dead Sea Scrolls.* 2 vols. Louvain: Publications Universitaires.

NEUSNER, J. (1985). *The Memorized Torah: The Mnemonic System of the Mishnah.* Chico: Scholars Press.

—— (1987). *Oral Tradition in Judaism: The Case of the Mishnah.* New York: Garland.

NIDITCH, S. (1996). *Oral World and Written Word: Ancient Israelite Literature.* Louisville: Westminster John Knox Press.

PARRY, M. (1987). *The Making of Homeric Verse: The Collected Papers of Milman Parry,* ed. A. PARRY. New York: Oxford University Press.

REYNOLDS, L. D./WILSON, N. G (1974). *Scribes and Scholars: A Guide to the Transmission of Greek and Latin Literature.* 2nd ed. Oxford: Oxford University Press.

SAFRAI, S. (ed.) (1987). *The Literature of the Sages. First Part: Oral Torah, Halakhah, Mishna, Tosefta, Talmud, External Tractates.* Assen/Maastricht: Van Gorcum and Philadelphia: Fortress Press.

SALDARINI, A. J. (2001). *Pharisees, Scribes and Sadducees in Palestinian Society: A Sociological Approach.* 2nd ed. Grand Rapids: Eerdmans.

SCHNIEDEWIND, W. M. (2004). *How the Bible Became a Book: The Textualization of Ancient Israel.* Cambridge: Cambridge University Press.

SCHWARTZ, S. (1995). 'Language, Power and Identity in Ancient Palestine'. *Past and Present* 148: 3–47.

SMALL, J. P. (1997). *Wax Tablets of the Mind: Cognitive Studies of Memory and Literacy in Classical Antiquity.* London and New York: Routledge.

STOCK, B. (1983). *The Implications of Literacy: Written Language and Models of Interpretation in the Eleventh and Twelfth Centuries.* Princeton: Princeton University Press.

STOWERS, S. K. (1989). *Letter Writing in Greco-Roman Antiquity.* Philadelphia: Westminster Press.

STREET, B. V. (1984). *Literacy in Theory and Practice.* Cambridge: Cambridge University Press.

THOMAS, R. (1989). *Oral Tradition and Written Record in Classical Athens.* Cambridge: Cambridge University Press.

—— (1992). *Literacy and Orality in Ancient Greece: Key Themes in Ancient History.* Cambridge: Cambridge University Press.

VAN DER TOORN, K. (2007). *Scribal Culture and the Making of the Hebrew Bible.* Cambridge: Harvard University Press.

ZLOTNICK, D. (1988). *The Iron Pillar-Mishnah: Redaction, Form and Intent.* New York: Ktav.

VII

RELIGION AND MAGIC

CHAPTER 27

THE IMPACT OF PAGANISM AND CHRISTIANITY

GÜNTER STEMBERGER

In the Roman period, and also much earlier in Second Temple times, the Jews of the Land of Israel were confronted all the time with non-Jews, first pagans and later Christians also, and this coexistence shaped their daily life. The religious geography changed considerably with the Hasmonean conquests, which led to the inclusion of Idumaea in Jewish territory, forcibly converting non-Jews to Judaism, so that even generations later, Herod could be characterized as a 'half-Jew' (Josephus, Ant. 14. 403) and Galilee was called the 'Galilee of the Gentiles', an expression not actually reflecting the Jewish majority of the region in the first century and later (Chancey 2002: 167–182). The cities on the Mediterranean coast had always been pagan and the same goes for the Decapolis in the north-east, of which only Scythopolis (Bet Shean) belonged to Palestine proper. But even within the central Jewish territory confrontation with paganism could not be avoided and greatly affected Jews' daily life.

1. HELLENISM AND HELLENISATION

The impact of paganism grew considerably with Pompey's conquest of Judaea in 63 BCE and its subjection to the province of Syria. It became even more noticeable under Herod the Great (37–4 BCE), whose building programme affected not only his new cities, Caesarea and Sebaste, with their pagan temples, theatre, hippodrome, and stadium (see Weiss in this volume), but also the Jewish heartland, although Herod made efforts not to transgress Jewish law within Jewish territory. Not only the theatre and hippodrome built in Jerusalem introduced aspects of pagan life, but even the outward appearance of the rebuilt and expanded Temple Mount followed Hellenistic ideals (Netzer 2006).

The development accelerated ten years after Herod's death, when most of the territory was subjected to direct Roman rule. The presence of Roman soldiers was a provocation, in spite of the concession that troops stationed in Jerusalem would usually not carry ensigns adorned with the portrait of the emperor. Bronze coins struck locally in the first century CE did not bear the image of the emperor or of pagan deities, but silver and gold coins which were not locally produced were decorated with portrait heads and pagan motifs. Strangely enough, the Tyrian Shekel, with the head of the god Melkart, was the official coin in the Jerusalem Temple. The date and exact function of the healing sanctuary at the Bethesda pool in Jerusalem is open to discussion. Yet pagans were even allowed to enter the outer courtyards of the Temple, where a balustrade with warning inscriptions in Greek and Latin would try to prevent them from entering the sacred precincts on pain of death. Temple sacrifices were accepted on behalf of non-Jews, mostly for the well-being of the emperor, a practice which seems to have ceased only at the outbreak of the first war against Rome in 66 CE.

It is frequently claimed that the so-called 'eighteen decrees', allegedly decided by rabbis in the upper chamber of Hananyah ben Hizkiyya ben Garon, were meant to mark a radical separation from pagans at the outbreak of the war (thus Hengel 1989b). The first part of the list (transmitted in y. Shab. 1:7, 3c-d) declares 'bread prepared by gentiles, their cheese, their oil, and their daughters, their semen and urine' to be forbidden or impure. The tradition adds as decisions made on this day 'the laws governing one who has suffered a nocturnal emission; the laws covering the uncleanness of gentile territory' (ibid.). In the context of the same discussion, another list includes 'their gifts', most probably sacrifices paid for by Gentiles. The laws transmitted here tend to forbid any contact of Jews with pagans, but the list is a later reconstruction, combining items from different periods, and cannot be dated to one single year.

The question of the impact of the foreign presence in the Land of Israel and of the extent of its influence on Jewish daily life and religion has been discussed for decades under the heading 'Judaism and Hellenism', a discussion shaped above all by Martin Hengel and Louis Feldman. Whereas Hengel insists that even before the Maccabean revolt, Palestinian Judaism was significantly influenced by Hellenism, and that there is no essential difference between Diaspora and Palestinian Judaism in this regard (Hengel 1974; 1989a), Feldman tries to minimize its influence: the few ancient Jewish intellectuals who investigated Greek culture, 'tended, at most, to borrow its style or scholarly techniques and methodology or logic, as perhaps the Pharisees did. They were not interested in theoretical insights, and they discarded the substance of Greek thought as irrelevant' (Feldman 1993: 38). In support of his position, Feldman refers to the subsequent development of the rabbinate, largely denying any Graeco-Roman impact by speaking of the 'alleged Greek influence on the Talmudic Rabbis' (Feldman 1993: 31). It is impossible, however, to think of 'social, political, and economic manifestations as being more open to influence; the kernel to Judaism, its beliefs and practices, as remaining largely unadulterated and unaffected. Taken as an absolute distinction, such a bifurcation is inaccurate and misleading' (Levine 1998: 137).

At the centre of the discussion is the question whether, and to what extent, the adoption of the Greek language and of Graeco-Roman cultural practices can be regarded as something external only, or as affecting Judaism as such, including its religious law, beliefs and rituals. To introduce into this context the notion of syncretism would certainly be misleading, but it would also be naïve to assume that any kind of cultural influence would have touched the 'outside' of Judaism only. The discovery of the legal documents of Babatha and others near the Dead Sea has renewed the discussion about Roman, Hellenistic, and Near Eastern influences on Judaism in general and rabbinic law in particular, especially as far as marriage and financial regulations are concerned. One would have to force the evidence to explain all aspects of these documents on the basis of later rabbinic halakhah and thereby 'prove' the religious unity of Palestinian Judaism after 70 CE. Here, too, the interrelationship with foreign legal conceptions is much more complicated, as recent studies show (Hezser, ed. 2003; Oudshoorn 2007).

2. Paganism in the Early Rabbinic Period

After 70 CE the religious character of the Land of Israel was greatly affected by the loss of the Temple, the increased Roman military presence, and urbanization, with the foundation of a number of Roman *coloniae*. The foundation of Aelia Capitolina with its temple for the Capitolinian *trias* and other pagan sanctuaries in 135 CE must be considered to have been of high symbolic importance. However, since Jews were not admitted to the city, its direct impact on them would have been minimal. More important were the newly founded or re-founded cities, among them the re-foundations of Emmaus as Nicopolis, Lod as Diospolis, and Bet Guvrin as Eleutheropolis. In the north, Scythopolis had always been a Hellenistic city, and Paneas was built at the sanctuary of the god Pan by Herod's son Philip as

Caesarea Philippi, later known as Caesarea Paneas. Sepphoris was renamed Dio-caesarea under Hadrian; Kefar Otnai, camp of a Roman legion, therefore also called Legio, under Diocletian became Maximianopolis. But even Tiberias, founded under Herod's son Antipas between 18 and 20 CE, and since the third century a centre of the rabbinic movement, seems to have had a pagan temple, the Hadria-neum, built under Hadrian and depicted on coins of the year 119, but perhaps never completed (Jacobs 2000: 143–4; Belayche 2001: 93–4, 180). There were only a few regions in the eastern part of Upper Galilee which were not directly affected by this new urbanization. Even there, pagan temples in the north and east of the province would have been in close proximity and had to be passed whenever one wanted to go to Tyre, the most important commercial centre of the region.

Daily life in all urban regions of Palestine was characterized not only by the presence of temples, theatres, circuses, and *stadia*, which could be avoided if one wanted to, but also by regular markets with pagan connotations. Markets were frequently connected with pagan holidays, many of which are mentioned in rabbinic literature (Friedheim 2006: 307–382; Hadas-Lebel 1979: 426–441; Veltri 2000: 104–132). Public baths and fountains were decorated with statues of pagan gods. At road-crossings one might encounter heaps of stones in honour of Mer-curius, or beautiful trees venerated as asheras and the like. One might have as one's neighbour a pagan who venerated his gods on the wall adjoining one's apartment. Coins with pagan motifs were unavoidable and were issued even by cities supposed to have a Jewish administration, such as Sepphoris or Tiberias (Sigismund 2007: 328). Daily goods such as oil-lamps also frequently had pagan decorations. Pagan customs would consciously, or mostly unconsciously, penetrate daily life, and they became part of popular medicine and popular religion, often misnamed as 'super-stition', as, for example, in the case of amulets and apotropaic rites.

Rabbinic regulations in the Mishnah, Tosefta, and Yerushalmi tractate *Avodah Zarah*, vacillate between the strict rejection of everything pagan and interpretations which distinguish between objects of pagan cultic veneration and simple decora-tions, thus making it possible to live in an environment dominated by a non-Jewish culture without losing one's Jewish identity. R. Meir forbids 'all images . . . because they are worshipped once a year', whereas sages prohibit only an image 'which has in its hand a staff, bird, or sphere. Rabban Simeon b. Gamaliel says: Any which has anything at all in its hand' (M. A.Z. 3:1). 'He who finds utensils upon which is the figure of the sun, moon, or dragon, should bring them to the Salt Sea. Rabban Simeon b. Gamaliel says: Those that are found on objects of value are prohibited, but those that are found on objects of no worth are permitted' (ibid. 3:3).

Since they were living in a territory increasingly populated by pagans, Jews could not isolate themselves completely, except perhaps in some far-off villages in north-eastern Galilee. Rather, they had to find a mode of co-existence. There is evidence of Jews and pagans frequenting the same sanctuaries: this phenomenon is best known from Mamre, where Abraham's well attracted pagans and later also

Christians (Sozomen, Historia Ecclesiastica 2.4.4). Rabbis declared the fair of Botna the most debased of all the fairs they prohibited (y. A.Z. 1:4, 39d). Nevertheless, in the fifth century CE, Jews, pagans, and Christians still celebrated together at this place, with separate rites, but still united in the same sanctuary. Votive offerings and other objects found in the local excavations confirm the literary testimonies (Belayche 2001: 96–104).

If Jews no longer observed their religious heritage, rabbis could do little to change their habits. Rather, they tried to give their religiously traditional, though not necessarily rabbinically observant, compatriots guidelines for co-existence and cooperation with non-Jews. While urging them not to join non-Jews in their meals, since practically all food prepared by them was considered impure and forbidden (for exceptions see M. A.Z. 2:8-9), rabbis permitted business dealings with them, the sale and purchase of goods from non-Jews, although with certain limitations. The Mishnah states that 'they do not rent [to gentiles] houses in the Land of Israel, and, it goes without saying, fields' (M. A.Z. 1:9), but the Talmud Yerushalmi, in its comments on this text and its continuation, in many cases regarded this practice as permissible. Jews worked on fields owned by Gentiles and employed Gentile sharecroppers, hired out animals to them, leased fields to and from Gentiles, or jointly owned fields, thus cooperating with non-Jews in many ways (Porton 1988: 173–203). Jews would use Gentile midwives and wet nurses, and also frequent Gentile physicians or barbers, although with certain restrictions. Even more astonishing is the fact that rabbis permitted Jewish workers to cooperate with Gentiles in the construction of public and private bathhouses, with the only restriction that once 'they reach the vaulting on which they set up an idol, it is forbidden [to help build any longer]' (M. A.Z. 1:7). It seems obvious that Jewish goldsmiths are not allowed to 'make ornaments for an idol: necklaces, earrings, or finger rings'. But R. Eliezer adds: 'For a wage it is permitted' (ibid. 1:8). These few examples demonstrate how flexible even rabbis could be as long as no direct Jewish involvement in pagan cults was feared.

The story about Rabban Gamaliel's meeting with the philosopher Proklos b. Philosophos in Aphrodite's bathhouse in Akko is well known (see also Eliav in this volume). The philosopher quotes Deut. 13:18: 'And there shall cleave nothing of the devoted thing to your hand', and asks Gamaliel how he can take a bath in this pagan bathhouse in obvious transgression of the biblical injunction. Gamaliel at first refuses to answer, but once outside, he tells Proklos: 'I never came into her domain. She came into mine. They do not say: "Let's make a bathhouse as an ornament for Aphrodite" But they say: "Let's make Aphrodite as an ornament for the bathhouse"'. The text continues by providing an alternative explanation: 'Another matter: If someone gave you a lot of money, you would never walk into your temple of idolatry naked or suffering of a flux, nor would you urinate in its presence. Yet this thing is standing right at the head of the gutter and everybody urinates right in front of her. It is said only, "... their gods" (Deut. 12: 3)—that which one treats as a god is prohibited, but that which one treats not as a god is permitted' (M. A.Z. 3:4).

The text is frequently understood as evidence for the non-religious character of much religious imagery in Hellenistic cities, a phenomenon which rabbis are believed to have been familiar with. Distinguishing between cultic and non-cultic aspects of paganism, they could live in the city and at the same time remain faithful to their monotheistic religion. Thus, Feldman writes: 'Indeed, the rabbis realized the pagan origins of the baths . . . But such institutions did not bring with them indiscriminate social intermingling and assimilation' and could therefore be regarded as innocuous (Feldman 1993: 42). Later rabbis were no longer satisfied with Gamaliel's answer and explain that it was only meant to put off the philosopher (y. A.Z. 3:4, 42d).

According to Emmanuel Friedheim, one should not use the story as evidence of the decline of paganism in late antiquity. Bathhouses continued to have religious functions and ritual purification retained its place in Roman religion. The statue of Aphrodite in the bathhouse of Acco 'was very probably cultic', and the story documents the vitality of paganism in Palestine of the second and third centuries (Friedheim 2006: 106–107). Seth Schwartz also emphasizes the strength of paganism in Rabbinic Palestine. He argues that the rabbis who could not escape their pagan environment, 'needed to develop a mechanism to allow them to live in the cities and to participate in some of the cities' public activities. This mechanism . . . was a spectacular act of misprision, of misinterpretation, whereby the rabbis defined pagan religiosity as consisting exclusively of cultic activity, affirmed and even extended the biblical prohibitions of it, but in so doing declared the non-cultic, but still religious aspects of urban culture acceptable' (Schwartz 1998: 207–8). They thus developed, consciously or not, an accommodating legislation, rejecting rigorously anything even remotely connected to the pagan cult, but accepting most non-cultic manifestations of Graeco-Roman pagan culture, in order to be able to live in the cities (ibid. 217).

A highly significant example of the Jewish reception of pagan representations and expressions is the necropolis of Bet She'arim, thought to be the burial ground of the patriarchal family, or at least the place where some members of the family and many other rabbis were buried, even if they had no great influence on its use and maintenance. Although there are some Hebrew and Aramaic burial inscriptions and some typically Jewish images, most prominently the menorah and other ritual objects, the great majority of the inscriptions are in Greek. The formula, 'Be of good courage, nobody is immortal', occurs several times. It sounds pagan, but might also be interpreted in Jewish terms. Even more astonishing is the presence of many pagan motifs on Jewish sarcophagi, representations of pagan gods such as Aphrodite, Nike, Eros, and even Zeus, who appears in the form of a swan about to rape Leda.

How can we explain the presence of such scenes in a Jewish cemetery? The position of Erwin R. Goodenough, that these and similar artistic expressions are witness to a heterodox, non-rabbinic, mystical Judaism (Goodenough 1953: 89–102), has been abandoned by scholars nowadays. Others have suggested that these scenes on sarcophagi were not really offensive, since they were hidden away in the catacombs and sometimes placed so that visitors could not see them. Still others regard them as mere decorations: 'Such coffins prove the tolerant attitude of the Jewish leaders of those days with regard to sculpture and figurative art, which by then had lost its original idolatrous connotations' (Avigad/Mazar 1993: 242). None of these interpretations is really satisfactory, however.

The excavations at Sepphoris, long regarded as a mainly or even exclusively Jewish city, brought to light a number of mosaic floors with mainly pagan connotations. The so-called House of the Nile Festival might still be regarded as an ensemble of motifs which have long lost their pagan meanings. The same might be said of the House of Orpheus who could symbolize David or Christ in Jewish and Christian art. The Villa of Dionysos (early third century), named after the mosaic in its *triclinium*, one of the richest Dionysos cycles ever found in the Roman world, cannot be explained so easily. Zeev Weiss suggests that the villa might even have belonged to R. Judah the Patriarch, and that the mosaic was purely decorative. Rina Talgam does 'not rule out the possibility that the House of Orpheus belonged to a Hellenized Jew rather than a pagan citizen. However, this possibility is made most implausible for the House of Dionysos by the depiction of the contemporary Dionysiac cult, which in the proposed reconstruction includes an altar and a cultic statue'; she concludes 'that the house belonged to a pagan citizen who adhered to the Dionysiac religion' (Talgam/Weiss 2004: 130).

Pagan motifs also occur in the decoration of synagogues. The mosaic of Odysseus bound to his ship's mast in order to resist the lure of the sirens, discovered in the House of Leontis at Bet Shean, may not have belonged to the synagogue in the same building complex, but this is not certain. Dionysiac motifs are found in the frieze of the synagogue of Capernaum, a Medusa head in the synagogue of Korazim. But the most discussed motif in this context is the zodiac in its various forms and developments (see also Levine in this volume). Its earliest example appears in the synagogue of Hammat Tiberias with the Sol Invictus in its centre. The later representation in Sepphoris consists of the rays of the sun only, instead of a personal representation of the sun god, but in Bet Alpha we encounter him again, although in a very stylized form.

The zodiac of Hammat Tiberias has been interpreted as a depiction of the calendar, possibly in commemoration of the alleged introduction of a fixed calendar under Hillel II in 358 CE (a tradition which is hardly historically reliable since it is attested for the first time in 1122 CE!), or it is seen as a simple decoration which had become innocuous since paganism had lost its force. But others see in it a clearly pagan symbol which has been accepted in certain Jewish communities, be they on the fringe of official Judaism (as once proposed by Goodenough), or a non-rabbinic Jewish community as suggested by Emmanuel Friedheim. According to

Friedheim, the community behind this synagogue expressed—obviously against the will of rabbis—the supreme power of the unique god with Sol Invictus, an emblem of henotheism, a monotheistic figure in a polytheistic environment (Friedheim 2006: 157–159). He explicitly rejects the position of Ephraim Urbach, who states: 'The consensus of opinion amongst the Sages in the third century was that all idolatrous impulses had been eradicated from amongst the people of Israel as early as the beginning of the Second Temple' (Urbach 1959: 154). Accordingly, rabbis could accept that their fellow-Jews participated in the creation of idols or traded in fragments of idolatrous objects because 'within the Jewish camp the idolatrous impulse was virtually dead, while even in the surrounding gentile world its influence had been greatly weakened. It was a fact that many Gentiles used their idols and images for decorative purposes only, and were ready to desecrate them when necessary' (ibid. 236).

In this context a theory proposed by Seth Schwartz has provoked an intense discussion. Schwartz believes that, in the aftermath of the Jewish revolts against Rome, a large part of the Jewish communities of Palestine accepted a kind of coexistence with their pagan environment, accepting many of their views and practices, and thereby losing much of their own Jewish identity: 'In the second and third centuries, the "Jewish" cities of Palestine and the larger villages in their vicinity were normal participants in the urban culture of the Roman East, a culture that was suffused with pagan religiosity. . . . Whether or not large numbers of Jews regularly worshiped the Greek gods, their ubiquity as symbols is profoundly important as an indication of the postrevolt collapse of any normatively Jewish ideological system' (Schwartz 2001: 158–9). A stronger notion of Jewishness developed only as a consequence of the Christianization of the province after Constantine had become emperor. Only then, Schwartz claims, did the Jewish communities become consciously Jewish, making an effort to visibly express their Jewishness by building a good number of synagogues and introducing evidently Jewish symbols into their decorations as signs of their own religious identity.

During most of the post-Bar Kokhba period and up to Constantine in the early fourth century, Jewish identity remains largely invisible apart from rabbinic texts, which hardly reflect the life of the common people. Earlier research had dated many synagogues to the second and third centuries and thus covered this vacuum, while modern scholarship often opts for a fifth or sixth century date (see also Levine in this volume). Rabbinic texts can offer us only partial evidence of Judaism's reaction to paganism and Jewish-pagan coexistence. How much Jewish identity was compromised in this process is still open to discussion. The diverse opinions brought forth in this discussion are determined by the variant degrees of historical reliability scholars attribute to rabbinic texts and by variant interpretation of the archaeological data. A unanimous interpretation of the historical development is still imperceptible at this stage.

The impact of paganism on Jewish life in Roman Palestine did not reach its sudden end with the Christianization of the province in the fourth century. Paganism survived at least into the fifth century, especially in the south of the province, the region of Gaza. The reign of Julian (361–363 CE) revived old pagan institutions in Palestine. His permission to rebuild the Jerusalem Temple may have lowered Jewish opposition against, or even attracted Jewish sympathies for this pagan revival. Nevertheless, pagans would soon become a suppressed minority, a situation Jews had already experienced for a long time and would continue to endure under the new auspices. From that time onwards the real confrontation was with Christianity, which Jews would often consider to be just another form of paganism.

3. CHRISTIANITY

3.1 The First Three Centuries

Christianity began within Judaism: the Jewish followers of Jesus who associated themselves with Gentile believers soon became a problem for the Jewish authorities in Jerusalem, as is attested in the letters of Paul and the Acts of the Apostles. Jewish Christians did not join their compatriots in the revolt against Rome. Rather, the Jewish-Christian community fled to Pella on the eastern side of the Jordan. The historicity of this report, which first appears in Eusebius, is considered unhistorical by some scholars, but it certainly has some foundation. The question remains, how much the small Jewish Christian community in Palestine would have been noticed by the Jewish majority.

It was once taken for granted that the early rabbis assembled at Yavneh considered the Jewish Christians a threat to the national and religious unity of their people, and therefore enacted certain measures against them. They reputedly tried to keep believers in Christ away from synagogues by introducing the so-called *birkat ha-minim* (benediction, or rather curse of heretics) into the daily Amidah prayer (see Reif in this volume), and closed the biblical canon in order to guard Jews against the influence of Christian books. It is now commonly accepted that the *minim* mentioned in this prayer were not primarily Judaeo-Christians but any Jews deviating from a certain religious consensus, however defined. In modern research there is no agreement on the question whether an earlier form of this benediction may have been directed against the Sadducees or the Romans (Instone-Brewer 2004: 95–119), and when the term *notsrim* was eventually introduced into the text to refer to Christians specifically (Katz 2006: 280–294). Some scholars see evidence of the effects of the *birkat ha-minim* on early Christians in the Gospel of John (John 9:22, 12:42, 16:2) and in Justin Martyr, but the earliest unambiguous testimony comes from Epiphanius of Salamis (fourth century) who states that the Jews curse the Nazoreans three times a day, saying 'May God curse the Nazoreans' (Panarion 29, 9, 2).

How much contemporary Jews and especially the rabbis, knew about Christian doctrine and Christian writings is equally open to discussion. In T. Yad. 2:13 we read that *gilyonim ve-sifre minim* (blank parchments or, alternatively, gospels and books of heretics) do not render the hands unclean, and T. Shab. 13:5 states that they are not saved from fire on the Shabbat. Some authors understand the term *gilyonim* to refer to those parts of a Torah-scroll which are without text, that is, its margins or cover-leaves, or to Torah scrolls written by heretics (Maier 1982: 60); others translate 'gospels and heretical books' and assume that at least some early Christian books were known to the rabbis and other Jews of the period (Katz 2006: 279; Jaffé 2007: 84–101). If we want to understand *gilyonim* as refering to the Gospels, we would have to date this reference to a late stratum of the Tosefta, since even Christian texts do not speak of Gospels in the plural before the late second century CE (Irenaeus of Lyon).

It is probably safer to limit our discussion to the question of how much Jews knew about Jesus and Christian doctrines at that time. The only tannaitic text relevant in this regard is T. Ḥul. 2:22–24, a story about Eleazar ben Damah whom Jacob of Kefar Sama wanted to heal in the name of a certain Jesus ben Pantera. The tradition certainly refers to Jesus of Nazareth (against Maier 1978: 264–267, 273) and ridicules the Christian claim that he is the son of a virgin (*parthenos*), a motif expanded in several later texts. Healing in the name of Jesus is mentioned several times in rabbinic texts. It demonstrates some knowledge of miraculous healings attributed to Jesus and of the claim that his name may still effect healing. People healing in the name of Jesus are mainly mentioned in Galilean contexts. Although rabbinic texts speak of *minim*, not all of them must have been Jewish Christians. Other individual Jews may also have believed in the efficacy of Jesus' name. The passage continues with the story of the arrest of R. Eliezer ben Hyrcanus on account of *minut* (heresy). Freed of the charge, he remembers once to have heard a teaching in the name of Jesus ben Pantiri which pleased him. Listening to a *min* was the fault for which he was arrested. A later version of the story (Qoh. R. 1:24) claims that the teaching he listened to concerned the use of a prostitute's wages for the Temple, that is, it was not a specifically Christian teaching. The story reflects the possibility of encountering Christians in Galilee and rabbinic efforts to keep people away from discussions with them. It does not prove R. Eliezer's Christian leanings, though.

More problematic is the use of *baraitot* ('external' traditions of the tannaitic period but documented only in later writings), which are mostly transmitted in the Babylonian Talmud, for the study of Jewish-Christian relations in the first and second century CE. The story about Gamaliel and his sister Imma Shalom and the corruptible (Jewish-Christian?) judge (b. Shab. 116a–b) contains several motifs which may be understood as allusions to the Sermon on the Mount (Matt. 5:15, 17; Maier 1982: 78–93, however, thinks of Deut 13:1 instead of Matt. 5:17). The story cannot be used as a proof that at least some portions of the Gospel of Matthew were known to Gamaliel in the early second century (against Jaffé 2007: 109–120); rather it shows later Jewish knowledge of Christian texts or at least individual traditions.

The same may be said about rabbinic, mostly Babylonian, texts that evince some knowledge of the life and death of Jesus, of his disciples, and of some Christian doctrines. Johann Maier (1978; 1982) has tried to demonstrate that virtually no rabbinic texts about Jesus originally referred to him. Texts which have been understood as reactions against Christian doctrines can just as well be understood within the larger Jewish biblical tradition. His sceptical and minimalist position must be understood as a wholesome reaction against earlier trends in research, but it certainly went too far. Some scholars still try to find as many allusions as possible to, and reactions against, Christianity, including Pauline doctrines (Jaffe 2007: 153–175), in rabbinic texts. In his recent study, Peter Schäfer (2007) understands most rabbinic texts, which were traditionally considered to refer to Jesus, as really speaking about him and Christian doctrine. But he correctly emphasizes that most of these traditions are transmitted in the Babylonian Talmud, reflecting the Babylonian environment, where Jews would have been much freer to attack Christianity than in Palestine after Constantine's ascension to the throne. Babylonian rabbis were acquainted with a large spectrum of traditions and texts, with a certain preference for the Gospel of John. Palestinian rabbis certainly also knew more about Christianity than is expressed in the classical Palestinian texts. The exact meaning and historical context of many rabbinic traditions is still open to discussion.

A realistic evaluation of the amount and significance of contacts between Palestinian Jews and Christians also depends on the presence and distribution of Christians in the province before Constantine. After the foundation of Aelia Capitolina, Jerusalem was no longer accessible to Jews and Jewish-Christians. Jewish Christians must have moved elsewhere then, some perhaps to the Transjordan region. Some scholars have tried to discover material evidence of Jewish Christians at many different sites (Testa 1992), but the interpretation of these finds is very problematic. We lack clear criteria to identify Jewish Christian material remains. There is possibly some evidence of Jewish Christian communities in the Galilee, mainly in Nazareth and Capernaum (Mimouni 1998: 387–408 against Taylor 1993: 268–294, who is much more sceptical), and perhaps also in the Golan at a later time (Dauphin 1993). A rabbinic story relating that R. Yehoshua ben Levi's grandson was healed by someone in the name of Jesus of Pandera (y. A.Z. 2:2, 40d), may suggest the presence of individual Jewish Christians in Lydda as late as the third century, but it cannot be taken as evidence of a Jewish-Christian community there. In general, Jewish Christians soon became a small minority which was hardly visible. By the fourth century, little concrete knowledge about them was left.

We also do not know much more about Gentile Christians in Roman Palestine in the centuries before Constantine. The major communities were established in Aelia Capitolina and Caesarea. There were smaller communities in the other cities along the Mediterranean coast (but only very late in Gaza), in Judaea, and to some extent in lower Galilee. The almost complete lack of archaeological, epigraphic, and literary documentation, and the small number of Christian martyrs in the persecution under Diocletian, leads to the conclusion that the Christian presence in the Land of Israel up to the early fourth century was very small. One may assume that in many places Jews may have spent their whole life without ever encountering a Christian. Except for Caesarea, where Origen and Eusebius were in contact with Jews and perhaps even with rabbis, in most other locations, Jewish daily life in the first three centuries CE would have hardly been affected by the confrontation with Christianity.

3.2 The Development After Constantine

When Constantine became the sole ruler of the Roman Empire in 324 CE, the Edict of Milan with its recognition of the Christian Church also became effective in the eastern half of the empire, including Palestine. Only a year later it was decided at the Council of Nicaea to build a monumental church on the site of Jesus' tomb in Jerusalem. This was the beginning of an enormous Christian building activity, some of it financed by the state, but also by private initiative. The new Christian buildings in and around Jerusalem did not really affect the Jewish population, since by then they had not been living in the city for a long time already. But the construction of churches and monasteries would gradually transform the physical appearance of the entire province. It was a testimony to the growing Christian population, whose increase was partly due to the conversion of pagans—although one should note that especially in Gaza and other cities of the south pagans resisted the attraction of Christianity well into the fifth century—and partly to Christian immigration. Christian pilgrims soon arrived in ever growing numbers, and at least some of them stayed in Palestine for the rest of their lives. Apart from a few individuals, most notably Joseph of Tiberias, local Jews did not succumb to the attraction of Christianity. Neither Christian nor Jewish sources inform us about conversions of Jews to Christianity.

Christians concentrated mainly in the region of Jerusalem, in the south and along the coast, but also in the Jordan valley south of the Sea of Galilee. They also soon expanded in Lower Galilee, whereas the eastern half of Upper Galilee seems to have remained exclusively Jewish until the end of the Byzantine period. In the Golan, the north was mostly Jewish, the south Christian, but there were mixed zones as well. This geographical distribution meant that, in the rural zones of upper Galilee, Jews could continue to live without necessary contacts with Christians. But in practically all other regions of the province they came into ever closer contact with non-Jews.

Capernaum can serve as an extraordinary example of this contact, since the monumental synagogue is only a block away from the so-called 'House of Peter'. The Christian site was an isolated pilgrims' place in an otherwise Jewish area, but the actual nature of the local coexistence between Jews and Christians is still very controversial (Stemberger 2000: 143–148). Nearby, Tiberias had a Christian bishop in the fifth century, but no church building is archaeologically attested before Justinian, under whom the 'Anchor Church' on the outskirts of the city was built. In Sepphoris, the character of the city became mostly Christian in the fifth century already, although there were also several synagogues. In Bet Shean and its vicinity churches and synagogues were also built in proximity to each other. The same holds true for the region of Gaza from the fifth century. Some of the villages in the Hebron mountains (the Daroma) seem to have remained exclusively Jewish, but they were sometimes located very close to Christian villages or monasteries.

Thus, for most of the Jewish inhabitants of the province, regular contacts with Christians would have been unavoidable, and commercial and cultural exchanges must have been very common at that time. From the writings of the Church Fathers we know that some Christians were attracted to Judaism, attended synagogues, and were accused as 'Judaizers'. One may assume that there were also some discussions on religious issues, since Christian authors such as Eusebius, to some extent also Epiphanius of Salamis (a native of Bet Guvrin/Eleutheropolis in Judaea), and above all Jerome were well acquainted with Jewish traditions. Later rabbinic texts also demonstrate at least some knowledge of Christian doctrines (Visotzky 2003: 161–171).

From the time of Constantine onwards, Christian legislation frequently addressed the legal status of the Jews (collection with commentary: Linder 1987). Some of these laws did not concern Jews only, such as, for example, the frequently repeated laws regarding the duty to participate in the municipal *curia*. In Byzantine Palestine such a law would mainly affect the Jews of Tiberias, Sepphoris, and Lydda, since they formed a substantial part of the inhabitants there. Particularly important for Palestine were laws guaranteeing the status of Jewish self-administration and the patriarch as the official representative of the community (e.g. Codex Theodosianus 16:8:2, 16:8:8 and 16:8.15, issued in the years 330, 390 and 404 CE respectively). The demotion of Patriarch Gamaliel in 415 CE (C.Th. 16:8:22) is important, not only because it foreboded the end of the patriarchate but also because it involved other provisions which were of direct concern for all communities, such as the prohibition on owning Christian slaves. In C.Th. 7:8:2 of the year 373 CE, synagogues were still protected in the same way as other religious buildings. Therefore soldiers were not allowed to take up their quarters in synagogues. Yet the building of new synagogues was officially prohibited, a law which was repeated under Justinian more than a century later. Nevertheless, it seems that this law was only rarely, if ever, enforced, since most synagogues excavated in Byzantine Palestine had been built after this prohibition was decreed (see Levine in this volume).

In other parts of the empire, for example in Illyricum, synagogues were frequently destroyed by Christians, or seized and converted into churches. Initially, the legislator still intervened to protect the Jews and their religious buildings: 'No one shall be destroyed for being a Jew, though innocent of crime.... Their synagogues and habitations shall not be indiscriminately burnt up, nor wrongfully damaged without any reason' (C.Th. 16:8:21 of 420 CE, Linder 1987: 285). For Palestine we have no hard evidence that synagogues were ever destroyed or taken over by Christians although Michael Avi-Yonah claims: 'There is much archaeological evidence that in these times [i.e. under Justinian in the sixth century] one synagogue was destroyed after another.... In Caesarea, Husifah on Mount Carmel and Engedi traces of fire were discovered on the mosaic floors of synagogues; in Caesarea the evidence even included particles of sulphur' (Avi-Yonah 1976: 251). Not all archaeologically attested damage or destruction by fire can be attributed to Christian attacks, however, not even in periods for which the respective official legislation and literary texts suggest increased hostility between Jews and Christians.

With Novella 146 of the year 553 CE, Justinian interfered with internal aspects of the synagogue liturgy, permitting the use of all languages (instead of only Hebrew) for the reading of the Torah: 'What they call *deuterosis*, on the other hand, we prohibit entirely, for it is not included among the Holy Books, nor was it handed down from above by the prophets, but it is an invention of men'. The exact meaning of this clause and its impact on Jewish religious life is disputed amongst scholars. Linder considers this statement a total prohibition of the rabbinic Mishnah, not only in the context of the synagogue, and connects it with post-talmudic references to 'prohibitions imposed by the Byzantine authorities in Palestine on the study of the Torah and on preaching in the synagogue' (Linder 1987: 404). Avi-Yonah suggests that *deuterosis* refers to 'the haggadic commentaries in the Midrashim, used in synagogue services'. He adds: 'There can be no doubt, however, that it remained on paper as regards most of the Jewish communities, and certainly those of the Holy Land' (Avi-Yonah 1976: 250). Whatever the exact meaning of the law, we do not have any evidence of its actual impact on synagogue life in Byzantine Palestine.

Approximately 120 synagogues have been excavated in Byzantine Palestine, and many more are known from surveys. The number of known churches, chapels and monasteries amounts to more than 400. The province was therefore densely covered with religious buildings, a profound transformation in comparison to the time before Constantine. Churches were not only located close to synagogues;

buildings of both religions increasingly followed the same architectural styles and shared a number of internal features (Milson 2006). In many synagogues, the place for the Torah shrine in the apse was separated from the main hall by a chancel screen, as was common in churches for the zone of the altar. Mosaic floors which decorated many of these buildings also shared many motifs, most notably the type of the 'inhabited scrolls'. Frequently only particularly Christian or Jewish symbols, such as the cross or the menorah, help us decide whether a mosaic is Jewish or Christian. We may assume common workshops which worked for both Christians and Jews, and/or pattern-books used by the respective artisans. Despite religious differences, Jews and Christians had much in common in their conception of religious buildings, and probably also in various other areas of religious life. We may assume that they shared a common language of religious culture in Byzantine Palestine.

A situation of peaceful co-existence and contacts in many areas of daily life seems to have predominated most of the time, even if both communities remained separate in the private sphere: mixed marriages were prohibited by law on both sides, and *kashrut* laws would prevent Jews from attending meals prepared by non-Jews. How much or little Jews and Christians knew of each other remains an open question (see Stroumsa 1989).

The apparent peace between the two religious groups must have covered many tensions which would explode and lead to open enmity in times of crisis. The crisis facing the empire since the early seventh century, and ultimately the Persian conquest of Palestine in 614 CE, reveals how much the Jewish population was wary of Christian rule. Contemporary Christian sources not only accuse the Jews of cooperation with the Persians, but also blame them for the killing of many Christians in Jerusalem who were not willing to convert to Judaism. The regime of terror described by these sources may be exaggerated, but Jewish sources—most notably the *Sefer Zerubbavel* and some religious poems—also suggest an atmosphere of violence at a time when Palestinian Jews expected imminent redemption and the re-establishment of a Jewish state and Temple in Jerusalem. Byzantine rule was re-established in 628 CE, but this short time period was only an intermezzo, since Jerusalem surrendered to the Arabs only ten years later. Jews considered the new Muslim rule much preferable to Christianity and less 'pagan'.

Suggested Reading

The best and most up-to-date overall study of paganism in Roman Palestine is the monograph of Nicole Belayche (2001), which covers the archaeological evidence and realia. This work may be read together with Friedheim (2007), who mostly deals with the rabbinic texts relating to the main aspects of paganism. Friedheim's interpretations of the texts are open to discussion on many points. Stemberger (2000) provides a historical overview. A recent collective volume (Limor/Stroumsa 2006) constitutes the most comprehensive treatment of the history of Christianity in Palestine—the ways in which it transformed the province and affected the Jewish population. The rabbinic perspective is analysed by Peter Schäfer (2007) in his stimulating study of traditions dealing with Jesus and Christian doctrines.

BIBLIOGRAPHY

AVIGAD, N./MAZAR, B. (1993). 'Beth She'arim', in *The New Encyclopedia of Archaeological Excavations in the Holy Land*, vol. 1, ed. E. Stern et al. Jerusalem: The Israel Exploration Society, 236–248.

AVI-YONAH, M. (1976). *The Jews under Roman and Byzantine Rule: A Political History of Palestine from the Bar Kokhba War to the Arab Conquest*. Jerusalem: Magnes Press.

BELAYCHE, N. (2001). *Iudaea—Palaestina: The Pagan Cults in Roman Palestine (Second to Fourth Century)*. Tübingen: Mohr-Siebeck.

CHANCEY, M. A. (2002). *The Myth of a Gentile Galilee*. Cambridge: Cambridge University Press.

DAUPHIN, C. (1993). 'Encore des judéo-chrétiens au Golan', in *Early Christianity in Context: Monuments and Documents*, ed. F. Manns and E. Alliata. Jerusalem: Studium Biblicum Franciscanum, 69–84.

FELDMAN, L. H. (1993). *Jew and Gentile in the Ancient World: Attitudes and Interactions from Alexander to Justinian*. Princeton: Princeton University Press.

FRIEDHEIM, E. (2006). *Rabbinisme et Paganisme en Palestine Romaine: Étude historique des realia talmudiques (Ier—IVème siècles)*. Leiden: Brill.

GOODENOUGH, E. R. (1953). *Jewish Symbols in the Greco-Roman Period, vol. I: The Archaeological Evidence from Palestine*. New York: Bollingen Foundation and Pantheon Books.

HADAS-LEBEL, M. (1979). 'Le paganisme à travers les sources rabbiniques des 2e et 3e siècles: Contribution à l'étude du syncrétisme dans l'empire romain', in *Aufstieg und Niedergang der Römischen Welt*, vol. II 19/2, ed. W. Haase. Berlin and New York: Walter de Gruyter, 397–486.

HENGEL, M. (1974). *Judaism and Hellenism: Studies in their Encounter in Palestine during the Early Hellenistic Period*. London: SCM Press.

—— (1989a). *The 'Hellenization' of Judaea in the First Century after Christ*. London: SCM Press.

—— (1989b). *The Zealots: Investigations into the Jewish Freedom Movement in the Period from Herod I until 70 A.D.* Edinburgh: T.&T. Clark.

HEZSER, C. (ed.) (2003). *Rabbinic Law in its Roman and Near Eastern Context*. Tübingen: Mohr-Siebeck.

INSTONE-BREWER, D. (2004). *Traditions of the Rabbis from the Era of the New Testament. Vol. I: Prayer and Agriculture*. Grand Rapids: William B. Eerdmans.

JACOBS, M. (2000). 'Pagane Tempel in Palästina—rabbinische Aussagen im Vergleich mit archäologischen Funden', in *The Talmud Yerushalmi and Graeco-Roman Culture* vol. 2, ed. P. Schäfer and C. Hezser. Tübingen: Mohr-Siebeck, 139–159.

JAFFÉ, D. (2007). *Le Talmud et les origines juives du christianisme. Jésus, Paul et les judéo-chrétiens dans la litterature talmudique*. Paris: Les éditions du Cerf.

KATZ, S. T. (2006). 'The rabbinic response to Christianity', in *The Cambridge History of Judaism vol. 4: The Late Roman-Rabbinic Period*, ed. S. T. Katz. Cambridge: Cambridge University Press, 259–298.

LEVINE, L. I. (1998). *Judaism and Hellenism in Antiquity; Conflict or Confluence?* Seattle and London: University of Washington Press.

LIMOR, O./STROUMSA, G. G. (eds) (2006). *Christians and Christianity in the Holy Land: From the Origins to the Latin Kingdoms*. Turnhout: Brepols Publishers.

LINDER, A. (1987). *The Jews in Roman Imperial Legislation. Edited with Introductions, Translation and Commentary*. Detroit and Jerusalem: Wayne State University Press and The Israel Academy of Sciences and Humanities.

MAIER, J. (1978). *Jesus von Nazareth in der talmudischen Überlieferung*. Darmstadt: Wissenschaftliche Buchgesellschaft.

—— (1982). *Jüdische Auseinandersetzung mit dem Christentum in der Antike*. Darmstadt: Wissenschaftliche Buchgesellschaft.

MILSON, D. (2006). *Art and Architecture of the Synagogue in Late Antique Palestine: In the Shadow of the Church*. Leiden: Brill.

MIMOUNI, S. C. (1998). *Le judéo-christianisme ancien: essais historiques*. Paris: Les Éditions du Cerf.

NETZER, E. (2006). *The Architecture of Herod, the Great Builder*. Tübingen: Mohr-Siebeck.

OUDSHOORN, J. G. (2007). *The Relationship between Roman and Local Law in the Babatha and Salome Komaise Archives: General Analysis and Three Case Studies on Law of Succession, Guardianship and Marriage*. Leiden: Brill.

PORTON, G. G. (1988). *Goyim: Gentiles and Israelites in Mishnah-Tosefta*. Atlanta, Ga.: Scholars Press.

SCHÄFER, P. (2007). *Jesus in the Talmud*. Princeton/Oxford: Princeton University Press.

SCHWARTZ, S. (1998). 'Gamaliel in Aphrodite's Bath: Palestinian Judaism and Urban Culture in the Third and Fourth Centuries', in *The Talmud Yerushalmi and Graeco-Roman Culture* vol. 1, ed. P. Schäfer. Tübingen: Mohr-Siebeck, 203–217.

—— (2001). *Imperialism and Jewish Society: 200 B.C.E. to 640 C.E.* Princeton, N.J.: Princeton Univ. Press.

SIGISMUND, M. (2007). 'Small Change? Coins and Weights as a Mirror of Ethnic, Religious and Political Identity in First and Second Century C.E. Tiberias', in *Religion, Ethnicity, and Identity in Ancient Galilee: A Region in Transition*, ed. Jürgen Zangenberg et al. Tübingen: Mohr-Siebeck, 315–36.

STEMBERGER, G. (2000). *Jews and Christians in the Holy Land: Palestine in the Fourth Century*. Edinburgh: T&T Clark.

STROUMSA, G. A. G. (1989). 'Religious Contacts in Byzantine Palestine'. *Numen* 36: 16–42.

TALGAM, R./WEISS, Z. (2004). *The Mosaics of the House of Dionysos at Sepphoris*. Jerusalem: The Hebrew University.

TAYLOR, J. E. (1993). *Christians and the Holy Places: The Myth of Jewish-Christian Origins*. Oxford: Clarendon Press.

TESTA, E. (1992). *The Faith of the Mother Church: An Essay on the Theology of the Judeo-Christians*. Jerusalem: Studium Biblicum Franciscanum.

URBACH, E. E. (1959). 'The Rabbinical Laws of Idolatry in the Second and Third Centuries in the Light of Archaeological and Historical Facts'. *Israel Exploration Journal* 9: 149–165, 229–245 (reprinted with a new appendix, in *idem*, *Collected Writings in Jewish Studies*, ed. R. BRODY and M. D. HERR. Jerusalem: Magnes Press, 1999, 151–193).

VELTRI, G. (2000). 'Römische Religion an der Peripherie des Reiches. Ein Kapitel rabbinischer Rhetorik', in *The Talmud Yerushalmi and Graeco-Roman Culture*, vol. 2, ed. P. SCHÄFER and C. HEZSER. Tübingen: Mohr-Siebeck, 81–138.

VISOTZKY, B. L. (2003). Golden Bells and Pomegranates: Studies in Midrash Leviticus Rabbah. Tübingen: Mohr Siebeck.

CHAPTER 28

....

THE SYNAGOGUE

....

LEE I. LEVINE

THE synagogue, a unique and innovative institution in antiquity, was central to Judaism and left an indelible mark on Christianity and Islam as well. As the Jewish public space par excellence throughout the Roman world (excluding pre-70 Jerusalem—and perhaps other Jewish cities), the synagogue was always the largest and most monumental building in any given Jewish community, often located in the centre of the town or village.

When the synagogue first appeared in the Hellenistic-Roman era, it was not a quintessentially religious institution, although it did include this dimension. Only in the course of late antiquity (third-fourth centuries CE onward) did its religious component evolve as its most decisive and characteristic feature. Whereas the Jerusalem Temple had served as the main focus of Jewish religious life throughout most of the first millennium BCE, in the centuries following its destruction in 70 CE many of its customs were gradually appropriated by the synagogue.

In addition to its religious role, the synagogue throughout antiquity also functioned as a community centre. No other institution mentioned in our sources might conceivably have competed with the synagogue for communal prominence. The Jewish community not only worshipped in the synagogue, but also studied there, held court, administered punishment, organized sacred meals, collected charitable donations, housed the communal archives and library, and assembled for political and social purposes (Levine 2005: 135–73, 381–411 and bibliography therein).

Over the last generation or two, a series of issues related to the ancient synagogue have arisen and continue to engage scholarly attention. What follows are some of the most salient ones.

1. SECOND TEMPLE SYNAGOGUES

1.1 Origins

Tracing the origin and early development of the synagogue has presented modern scholarship with a seemingly insurmountable task. As often happens with institutions, movements, or ideas of revolutionary proportions, the forces at play in bringing about these new initiatives remain shrouded in mystery. Such new phenomena often germinate unobtrusively, only to emerge later on in a relatively developed form.

Scholars who have addressed the issue of the synagogue's origins have usually attempted to pinpoint a historical context or specific moment that triggered the emergence of this institution. Owing to the lack of any solid evidence, such efforts become exercises in studied guesswork, generating theories ranging over a period of almost 800 years (for discussions of the different views see Levine 2005: 21–44; Runesson 2001: 67–168).

Some date the synagogue's origins to the First Temple period, basing their theories on either specific biblical references (1 Kgs. 8:27–30; 2 Kgs. 4:23) or a dramatic event such as the Josianic reforms of 622 BCE (2 Kgs. 23:1–20). Until recently, most opinions place the synagogue's origins in the post-destruction era, either in the sixth century BCE as a response to the destruction of the First Temple, or the fifth century BCE as part of the reforms of Ezra and Nehemiah, specifically the Torah-reading ceremony (Neh. 8:1–10:40). Others posit the fourth century BCE (the alleged emergence of communal frameworks in Palestine after the return from Babylonian exile), the third century BCE (Ptolemaic Egypt), and even a second or first century BCE date (resulting from developments in Judaea) for the emergence of the synagogue. Scholarly disagreement relates not only to the dating of the synagogue's origins, but also to its original provenance. Some place its first appearance in Babylonia, others in Egypt, and still others in Judaea.

Over the last few decades, much scholarly attention has focused on Ptolemaic Egypt as the locus of the synagogue's origins, fuelled by a number of Hellenistic inscriptions from the third century BCE that constitute the earliest known material evidence for the synagogue. Griffiths (1987) has argued for an Egyptian origin, claiming that the native Egyptian religious institution, the *Per Ankh*, influenced the nature of Egyptian synagogue practice by combining prayer and study.

With rare exception, the above theories share the following common assumptions: (1) dramatically new religious circumstances led to the creation of the synagogue (e.g. the reformation of Josiah in 622 BCE or the destruction of the First Temple and the beginning of the Babylonian exile in 586 BCE); and (2) the religious component of this institution was primary *ab initio*. Nevertheless, this question should be revisited, but from a very different starting point, that is, not from when the synagogue purportedly emerged, but working backwards from a later period for which we have solid evidence about how it functioned. The first-century synagogue served as a centre for a variety of communal and religious functions. We therefore should look for the framework or institution that served the same (or similar) purposes beforehand, and that would be the city-gate.

In biblical and non-biblical literature, the city-gate was the venue for public gatherings and all sorts of communal activity. It served as a marketplace (2 Kgs. 7:1) and as a setting where a ruler would hold court and prophets would speak (1 Kgs. 22:10; Jer. 38:7). Moreover, a variety of communal activities were conducted there, such as the transaction between Abraham and Ephron the Hittite (Gen. 23:10, 18) and the council of city-elders meeting to dispense justice. In the post-exilic period the gate area was utilized by Ezra and Nehemiah: 'The entire people assembled as one man in the square before the Water Gate, and they asked Ezra the scribe to bring the scroll of the Teaching of Moses with which the Lord had charged Israel' (Neh. 8:1).

Assuming that the city-gate was the precursor of the synagogue, we may then conclude that the latter took form as the result of a number of developments—the disappearance of the original setting of the city-gate area in the Hellenistic era, with the changing patterns of urban fortification; and the move to a separate building in place of the previous open-air setting, which was a well-known phenomenon of the Hellenistic age. In this sense, the Jews were reinventing the setting for their communal institution, patterning themselves after Hellenistic models.

1.2 Models for the Second Temple Synagogue

Scholars often sought to classify the synagogue in a Graeco-Roman institutional rubric. Referred to in first-century sources as, inter alia, *collegium, thiasos,* or *synodos* (as well as *proseuche* and *synagoge,* terms likewise borrowed from the larger Graeco-Roman world), the synagogue has been associated in varying degrees with one or another of these Hellenistic frameworks.

Of late, several new approaches have been proposed. On the one hand, Richardson (1996, 2003) has claimed that the synagogue should be defined as a *collegium* based on two considerations: (1) the use of this term in several Roman documents when referring to the Jewish community; and (2) the fact that the synagogue functioned as a social and religious association in much the same way as a *collegium.* On the other hand, Flesher (2001) suggests that the synagogue, having originated in the Diaspora, should be categorized as a type of Graeco-Roman temple, since both institutions seem to have had many activities in common. While Flesher is not the first to notice a connection between synagogue and pagan temple, he has taken the comparison further than others by assuming that the synagogue was viewed as such by Jew and non-Jew alike.

Attempts to find common denominators between the synagogue and Graeco-Roman institutions are certainly legitimate, as there was a great deal of similarity between Graeco-Roman and Jewish practices. Nevertheless, differences ought not to be overlooked. The synagogue's agenda was far more comprehensive than any analogous Graeco-Roman institution, and the legal standing of the Jewish community and its central institution appears to have been quite different from that of other ethnic or religious groups.

1.3 The First-Century Synagogue and the Jerusalem Temple

Scholars have assumed for generations that the Second Temple synagogue competed with the Jerusalem Temple. While the Temple featured sacrifices, the synagogue, in its religious dimension, focused on prayer and the reading of Scriptures; one was led by priests, the other by Pharisees; one was hierarchical, the other participatory; one was restricted to Jerusalem, the other was universal. However, this sharp dichotomy has been rejected in recent decades. For example, most scholars now agree that the Pharisees had nothing to do with the early synagogue, nor did this institution figure into the traditions attributed to them in later rabbinic literature (Cohen 1999). Moreover, the synagogue did not evolve in competition with the Temple, but rather fulfilled other functions and needs of Jewish communities everywhere in the late Second Temple period.

Two contrasting views have been suggested of late. One regards the synagogue as having been heavily influenced by the Jerusalem Temple; the most comprehensive presentation in this vein has been offered by Binder, in his detailed survey of first-century synagogues (1999), wherein he claims that the synagogue was, in fact, an extension of the Temple. Binder asserts that even the latter's functions, officials, liturgy, architecture, sanctity, and art were adopted by the synagogue, thereby declaring that (1) synagogues of the first century were considered sacred institutions; and (2) almost every conceivable aspect of these synagogues was patterned after the Temple.

The evidence for the former view is partial, at best. Synagogue sanctity is indicated for only a handful of Diaspora sites (Goodman 1996) and is never clearly attested for any Palestinian ones. Moreover, Binder's efforts to interpret a number of passages from Josephus (e.g. Bell. 4.7.2, 406–409) that mention *hiera* as referring to Judaean synagogues, and therefore are evidence for the widespread existence of synagogue sanctity, are entirely unconvincing (1999: 123–26, 481).

His second, far more revolutionary, claim, namely, that synagogues everywhere were patterned after the Temple, is indeed difficult to substantiate owing to virtually non-existent supporting evidence. As noted above, these two institutions were very different in nature, function, and organization: One embodied the quintessence of holiness in Judaism, and the other was, at most, a 'diminished sanctuary' (b. Meg. 29a); one focused on sacrifice, the other on Torah reading and prayer, silence in the cultic ritual as against public recitations, priestly leadership in contrast to lay leadership, and a sacral hierarchical framework in contradistinction to a communal one. The fact that the Torah was read in the Temple once a year on Yom Kippur and once every seven years at the *Haqhel* ceremony during the Sukkot festival, or even that sages from diverse sects are reported to have taught on the Temple Mount, has little to do with contemporary synagogue practice and certainly cannot be invoked as a model for the latter. The sanctity universally associated with the Temple was of an entirely different order than the scattered references to the sanctity of some first-century synagogues; synagogue sanctity as such is never noted in contemporary sources.

In contrast to Binder's approach, Flesher (1995) argues that the synagogue and Temple were diametrically opposed religious institutions. He accepts the theory of an Egyptian origin for the synagogue and that it was only later imported to Judaea. However, he claims, synagogues are attested in literary and archaeological sources only for the Galilee, and not for Jerusalem or Judaea owing to the Temple's overwhelming presence in this region. Flesher further posits that the 'Judaisms' of these two types of religious institutions were diametrically opposed. Thus, the only Jerusalem synagogues that we know of by name were those founded by, or catering to, Diaspora communities now residing in the city.

The fact that extant sources associate only Diaspora-related synagogues with Jerusalem (e.g. the Theodotos inscription) is certainly worthy of consideration, but most of the above theory fails in the light of both recent archaeological finds of Second Temple period synagogues in Judaea (e.g. Qiryat Sefer, Modi'in), and because some sources do indeed mention synagogues generally (and not necessarily Diaspora-related ones) in Jerusalem (e.g. Acts 24:12; t. Shab. 16:22). A more basic methodological issue is whether the paucity of sources at hand should caution us against drawing far-reaching conclusions. Flesher's assumption that the Temple and synagogue represented two separate Judaisms is certainly questionable. If they were so different, it is surprising that no source bothered to note this dichotomy. Philo, Jesus, Paul, and Josephus do not seem to have been aware of two Judaisms, thus suggesting that no such incongruities existed in the first century CE.

2. Synagogues of Late Antiquity

The number of synagogues and related literary, epigraphical, and artistic evidence increase geometrically in late antiquity, as do the issues in dispute. The following are the more salient ones.

2. Synagogue Architecture and Its Chronological Implications

One of the most fundamental disputes over the last few decades relates to the chronology and development of the synagogues in late Roman and Byzantine Palestine, which represent the overwhelming majority of ancient synagogues throughout the country. In the course of the mid-twentieth century, archaeologists had accepted as axiomatic a twofold and, later, threefold typological division of buildings based on chronological considerations. Kohl and Watzinger (1916) argued that the monumental and sometimes ornate Galilean synagogue was to be dated to the turn of the third century CE, at the time of the Patriarch R. Judah I. It was assumed that by then the Jewish community had recovered from the traumatic events of the previous century-and-a-half and was now in a position to erect such grandiose structures. R. Judah's political, economic, and religious stature, together with his apparently excellent relations with the Roman authorities, facilitated this development. Kohl and Watzinger's supposition was strengthened by the artistic similarities between the Galilean synagogues and contemporary pagan public buildings of second- and third-century Syria.

With the discovery of Bet Alpha in 1928–29, and other synagogues in the early 1930s, Sukenik took this theory a step further (1934). Given the explicit sixth-century date of the Byzantine synagogue, and noting the striking resemblance between this apsidal synagogue with its mosaic floors and the typical Byzantine basilical church, he posited a second and later basilical-type synagogue. Finally, the discovery of a totally different synagogue model at Eshtemoa in 1934 led to the suggestion of yet another, transitional, phase (the broadhouse type) that linked the two phases defined earlier. Thus, in its fully developed form in the mid-twentieth century, there was universal agreement that the early Galilean synagogue dated to the second-third centuries, the transitional type to the fourth–fifth, and the later basilical-type to the sixth century (see Fig. 28.1a–c ; Avi-Yonah 1961; Tsafrir 1987).

However, this neat compartmentalized reconstruction—coupling typology with chronology—has been undermined by a series of archaeological discoveries during the last third of the twentieth century. The Franciscan excavations at Capernaum

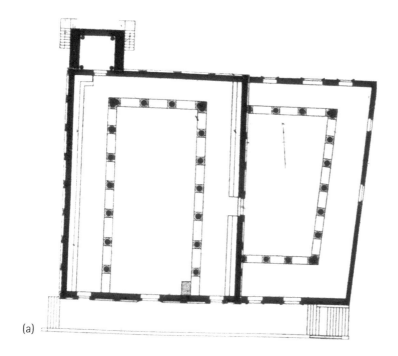

Fig. 28.1a Galilean-type synagogue, Capernaum
Courtesy of Institute of Archaeology, Hebrew University, Jerusalem

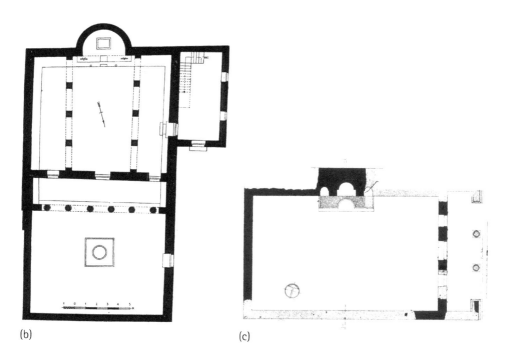

(b)   (c)

Fig. 28.1b Basilical-type synagogue, Bet Alpha
Courtesy of Institute of Archaeology, Hebrew University, Jerusalem

28.1c Transitional-type synagogue, Eshtemoa
Courtesy of Institute of Archaeology, Hebrew University, Jerusalem

dated this Galilean synagogue to the late fourth and fifth centuries and, more recently, a sixth-century setting has even been suggested (Magness 2001: 18–38). Soon thereafter, the finds from excavations at the Khirbet Shema and Meiron synagogues, located some six hundred metres from one another, attested that these structures were probably built in the latter half of the third century. Moreover, each of these buildings represents a dramatically different architectural style according to the old theory: Meiron is a quintessentially Galilean-type structure and Khirbet Shema a broadhouse type, yet they were both built at the same time and in the same locale.

The excavation results from Nevoraya prove that the extant building, known for over a century as one of the Galilean-type structures, was, in fact, the third stage of the synagogue at the site, dating to the sixth century. This is explicitly attested by a lintel inscription found there in the nineteenth century but deciphered by Avigad only in the mid-twentieth (Avigad 1960). The inscription reads as follows: '494 years according to the era (following) the destruction of the Temple (i.e., 564 CE—L. L.), (this synagogue) was built during the tenure of Hanina ben Lizar and Luliana bar Yudan.'

Even after this inscription was deciphered, scholars refused to acknowledge that the synagogue was first built in the sixth century, since such a conclusion would contradict the regnant chronological assumptions of the time. Thus, the term 'built' was interpreted as 'repaired'. However, now that archaeological excavations have determined conclusively that this late stage was built several centuries after the earlier ones, and according to a somewhat different plan, it is clear that the inscription was referring to much more than a mere repair.

Throughout the 1970s and 1980s, several other excavations were conducted at already identified Galilean synagogues—Horvat Ammudim, Gush Halav, Chorazim, and Bar'am. The finds from the first two sites indicate a late third- to early fourth-century date of construction; those from Chorazim indicate a fourth-century date; and those from Bar'am, a fourth- to fifth-century date. Moreover, a number of excavations in the Golan (Qatzrin, Deir Aziz, and Qanatir) place the construction of these synagogues in the fifth and sixth centuries CE. Finally, the discovery of a Galilean-type structure at Merot in the mid-1980s placed another nail in the coffin of the older theory, as the earliest stage of this building was clearly and unequivocally set in the late fourth or early fifth century.

Thus, the linear approach associating each type of building with a specific historical period can be put to rest. Diversity reigned in synagogue art and architecture, as it did in other dimensions of synagogue life. The social implications of this phenomenon are likewise clear. Local tastes and proclivities were the decisive factors in determining what a synagogue looked like and how it functioned.

3. Central Issues in the Study of Jewish Art

Outside the First and Second Jerusalem Temples, there are no traces of a uniquely Jewish art. Only in the first centuries BCE and CE do we first encounter singularly Jewish artistic representations, and even then only sparse remains. The menorah, for example, appears in three instances (not including the famous Arch of Titus replica in Rome), in a Jerusalem context associated with priests as well as in Magdala in the Galilee and Bet Loya in the Shephelah. The coins minted during the First and Second Revolts against Rome (66–74 and 132–135 CE, respectively) seem to bear a series of Temple-related artefacts: the four species used in the Temple on Sukkot; amphorae, musical instruments such as the trumpet, lyre, and harp that were part of the Temple ritual; and in one series of Bar Kokhba coins, a replica of the Temple facade itself. All this changed dramatically in late antiquity, in funerary contexts and especially in the synagogues (Hachlili 1988, 1998).

3.1 Jewish Symbols

One of the most blatant changes with regard to Jewish art in late antiquity is the widespread use of Jewish symbols. While the representation of the menorah is the most ubiquitous motif (Hachlili 2001), symbols such as the Temple facade, *shofar*, *lulav*, and *ethrog*, often found together, are also common (see Fig. 28.2).

The meaning and significance of this last-noted cluster of symbols have long been debated (Levine 2005: 230–36). One popular theory maintains that they were intended primarily to recall the Jerusalem Temple—the facade representing the Temple itself, and the menorah, *shofar, lulav, ethrog*, and incense shovel symbolizing the accoutrements once used there. If this interpretation is to be accepted, then the clear implication is that the memory of the Temple was of paramount importance in many Byzantine Jewish communities. The appearance of this motif in the synagogue might be viewed as triggering a memory of that institution, expressing hopes for its restoration or perhaps reflecting a desire for the synagogue to perpetuate the Temple's sanctity and religious significance.

A second approach regards these religious symbols within the context of the synagogue itself. The facade is thus interpreted as representing the synagogue's Torah shrine, while the other symbols are said to represent the various objects found in the synagogue or used in the synagogue service. By late antiquity, for instance, the *shofar* and *lulav* undoubtedly had become integral parts of synagogue worship during the Sukkot holiday.

Fig. 28.2 Panel in Hammat Tiberias synagogue mosaic floor, with Temple facade,
menorot, shofar, lulav, ethrog, **and incense shovel**

Dothan 1983

A third approach interprets a number of these symbols as referring to the
holiday season during the month of Tishri, when three major Jewish festivals
occur in rapid succession: Rosh Hashanah (the New Year), Yom Kippur (the
Day of Atonement), and Sukkot (the Feast of Booths). Thus, each of the above-
noted symbols can easily be associated with one of these holidays: *shofar*—Rosh
Hashanah; incense shovel—Yom Kippur; *lulav* and *ethrog*—Sukkot.

Another interpretation of this cluster of Jewish symbols views them as representing two basic concepts in Judaism—the Temple and the Torah. Certain
symbols are clearly associated with the Temple setting; others would seem to
indicate the sanctity of the Torah shrine. Since these two dimensions are often
associated with one another, starting with the placing of the two stone tablets
bearing the ten commandments together with Moses' Torah (Deut. 31:9, 26) in
the desert Tabernacle and, later, in the Jerusalem Temple, this combination
may have found expression in the synagogue as well. Finally, it may be assumed
that these symbols were universally acknowledged, but that each community
interpreted them in its own way, either with a Temple or synagogue-Torah-shrine
focus.

3.2 Central Motifs and Scenes

Art historians have invested much effort in trying to explain individual depictions or representations appearing in late antique Jewish art. Such studies have focused on the following topics:

a. *Biblical scenes or figures (excluding those at Dura Europos)*. These include the *Aqedah* (Bet Alpha and Sepphoris), Noah (Gerasa), David (Gaza and perhaps Merot), Daniel (Naʿaran, Susiya, and perhaps Ein Semsem in the Golan), and Aaron with the Tabernacle altar and ritual objects (Sepphoris). Discussions revolve around the meaning of such depictions and whether their selection was arbitrary or intentional (Hachlili 1988: 287–300).

b. *Zodiac and Helios* (see Fig. 28.3). Undoubtedly, this is the most astonishing and enigmatic motif appearing in no less than six Palestinian synagogues, though, interestingly, never in the Diaspora. Was this motif regarded as pagan and, if so, what was it doing in the middle of synagogue floors? If it was not viewed as such, which is probably the case, what, then, was its purpose? The crux of the problem is not so much the zodiac signs themselves (which are frequently mentioned in rabbinic sources and *piyyutim*, synagogue poetry), but in the representation of the sun god Helios, which at least on one occasion (i.e. Hammat Tiberias) appears together with his attributes (halo, sun rays, globe, and sceptre). To date, there has been a wide gamut of theories regarding this motif, ranging from the conservative to the radical—a mere decoration, a

Fig. 28.3 Central panel in Hammat Tiberias synagogue mosaic floor, with the zodiac and the sun god Helios

Dothan 1983

representation of the calendar, God's power as creator or ruler of the world, an archangel (as described in the fourth-century Book of Secrets, *Sepher Harazim*), and, finally, God Himself (Hachlili 2002; Levine 2005: 605–607).

In the process of substantiating one theory or another, a plethora of sources has been invoked—from the Bible, Qumran, Philo, and Josephus to the many and varied rabbinic compositions ranging from the second to twelfth centuries, as well as to the above-noted Book of Secrets, *piyyutim*, mystical literature, and even the thirteenth-century Zohar. While creativity is much in evidence in this regard, certainty remains elusive.

The meanings of other elements appearing in Jewish art have also been the subject of much inquiry, such as the representations of animals (e.g. eagles, lions, birds, and oxen) and inanimate objects (baskets, fruit, bread, grapes, etc.). This approach, most often associated with Goodenough's monumental opus (1953–68) and his conviction that symbolic meaning is to be found everywhere, is quite problematic methodologically. Are we to assume that all such objects bore significance, or could it be that some (many? most?) were chosen only arbitrarily or for aesthetic reasons? Moreover, there is every reason to believe that the above representations were interpreted in various ways by different people and communities at different times. Scholars have been at odds over these issues for generations and undoubtedly will continue to be in the future as well (Levine 2005: 214–24, 382–90, 610–12).

3.3 The Question of Programmatic Compositions

The remains of four relatively well-preserved synagogues (Bet Alpha, Dura Europos, Hammat Tiberias, and Sepphoris) have been the focus of much scholarly attention in the study of Jewish art in antiquity. As such, they present a challenge and offer an opportunity to explain not only a single item or panel, but an entire composition. Do the walls of Dura Europos or the floor of Bet Alpha or Sepphoris represent a well-conceived, overall plan, an all-encompassing programmatic conception intended to convey a specific message (see, e.g. Weiss 2005 and below) or, alternatively, is each panel to be interpreted independently and the sum total to be seen merely as a collection of disparate themes (cf. Schwartz 2001: 257–59)? Even those opting for an overriding idea have reached no consensus; over the years, scholars have presented vastly contrasting interpretations as to the collective meaning of these depictions.

In this respect, the mosaic floor at Hammat Tiberias is different. Its uniqueness lies not in any overall programmatic conception, but rather in the fact that it is the first-known display of several central motifs that were to become basic in the Jewish art of late antiquity, that is, a cluster of Jewish symbols (discussed above) and the representation of the zodiac signs together with Helios, both of which are far and away the most striking depictions of their kind ever to appear in a Jewish setting.

The most significant artistic remains from late antiquity appear in the synagogues at four sites. We will discuss them in the chronological order of their construction.

Dura Europos. The most sensational ancient synagogue has been that of Dura Europos, located on the Euphrates River in Syria, at the eastern extremity of the Roman Empire (see Fig. 28.4). First discovered in 1932, the Dura synagogue was quite modest on its exterior. Its significance lies, however, in the stunning paintings—in as many as sixty different panels—that covered all four walls of its interior. An analysis of these remains is hampered by the fact that only about half of the original number has survived. Thus, any suggestion as to an overall pattern, plan, or message can be regarded as only tenuous, at best. Despite these obstacles, many have tried their hand at their interpretation (Gutmann 1984), including a messianic theme, a mystical one, and an anti-Christian polemic. Some have suggested that different themes are highlighted in each of the three wall registers: historical, liturgical, and moralizing themes, respectively; or the three crowns of Torah, priesthood, and royalty per m. Abot 4:17. Gutmann (1973), focusing on the middle register, claimed that it bears a liturgical message and was intended to reflect the synagogue's Torah-reading ceremony.

As might be expected, a number of scholars have concluded that there is, in fact, no overriding theme or comprehensive programme dictating the selection of the panels at Dura other than the desire to represent important events in the Bible, particularly those reflecting God's protection of Israel, a kind of artistic *Heilsgeschichte*

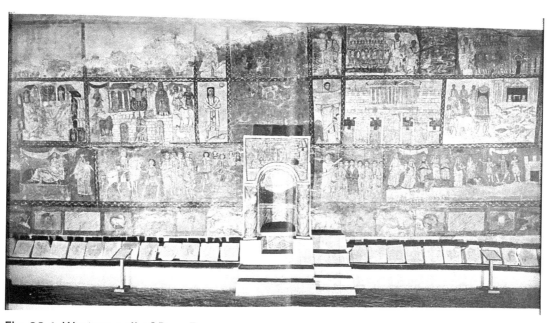

Fig. 28.4 Western wall of Dura Europos synagogue
Courtesy of Institute of Archaeology, Hebrew University, Jerusalem

(salvation history). According to this approach, each individual depiction or set of depictions has its own meaning and significance.

Hammat Tiberias. Excavated in 1961, the building contained a series of strata ranging from the third to eighth centuries, the most impressive one dating to the latter half of the fourth century (Talgam 2000: 100–101). In this stratum, the sanctuary was oriented southward, toward Jerusalem, and featured a nave with one aisle on the west and two on the east. While the mosaic floor in the eastern aisles bore geometric designs and three inscriptions, the central nave boasted three striking panels (see Fig. 28.5).

These included, in the order of one's progression through the hall from the north toward the *bima* in the south: (1) eight dedicatory inscriptions filling nine squares flanked by two lions in a heraldic posture; (2) a striking zodiac with the four seasons in the outer corners and a representation of the sun god Helios in the centre; (3) the cluster of Jewish symbols, including a Torah shrine and a pair each of *menorot, shofarot, lulavim, ethrogim,* and incense shovels.

The benefactors of this building, among the wealthy and acculturated residents of Tiberias, are readily identifiable by the Greek dedicatory inscriptions containing their Greek and Latin names (e.g. Ioullos, Zoilos, Maximos). These benefactors were presumably responsible for financing the synagogue's construction, and several apparently held official positions in the synagogue or community. The dominant role of Greek in this synagogue floor, together with its most impressive mosaic, clearly indicate the cosmopolitan cultural orientation of its donors and probably many, if not most, of its members. Moreover, the heavy involvement of patriarchal circles in financing this mosaic is most evident: one Severos, referred to as 'a *threptos* [disciple or protégé] of the Most Illustrious Patriarchs', is mentioned in two inscriptions, one of which is located at the entrance to the synagogue hall and occupies two squares.

The panel depicting the zodiac and Helios is the centerpiece of this mosaic floor. While its overall design would reappear in other Palestinian synagogues in subsequent centuries, the Tiberias depiction remains not only the earliest such representation, but is undoubtedly the most impressive one artistically, closely approximating the quality of the richly decorated mosaic floors from fourth-century Antioch. The figure of Helios, depicted here in the form of Sol Invictus with his full array of attributes, had become a widely used symbol in the fourth century, both in pagan and Christian circles. Such depictions were unknown in Jewish contexts prior to this time, and Josephus even reports that depicting the zodiac was categorically prohibited in the Jerusalem Temple centuries earlier (Bell. 5.5.4, 213). Even the Mishnah (A.Z. 3:1) looks askance upon the display of several of the symbols appearing here (e.g. the sphere and staff or sceptre). Thus, the first appearance of such a blatantly pagan motif in the centre of an important Tiberian synagogue is as enigmatic as it is fascinating. It has been explained as best reflecting the fourth-century popularity of this design, the relatively cosmopolitan

Fig. 28.5 The three panels of the Hammat Tiberias synagogue mosaic floor: top: Torah shrine and cluster of Jewish symbols; middle: zodiac with Helios in the centre; bottom: dedicatory inscriptions

Dothan 1983

orientation of patriarchal circles, the patriarch's rather close relationship with the emperor Julian, himself a devotee of Helios, and the recent publication of the system of calendrical calculations by the patriarch Hillel II in 358 CE (Levine 2003: 97–115).

Sepphoris. The seven registers of this mosaic floor include representations of the Aqedah (the Binding of Isaac), the zodiac and sun (instead of the image of Helios), an elaborate depiction of the Tabernacle altar, Aaron and a plethora of items related to the Tabernacle-Temple, the familiar cluster of Jewish symbols, and two lions flanking a wreath containing an inscription (see Fig. 28.6).

Weiss has suggested that the overarching theme of this mosaic floor is one of Promise (represented by the Aqedah scene) and Redemption (indicated by the Tabernacle-Temple scenes (Weiss 2005: 225–62). The link between these two foci is the zodiac and the sun, which are thought to represent the power of God as ruler of the cosmos (cosmocrator) who, in this capacity, assures the transition from the one to the other. Kühnel (2000) has advocated a somewhat different interpretation, maintaining that the Tabernacle-Temple motif reflects the continuity of the cult that anticipates redemption, with the Aqedah serving as the historical event pointing in this direction and the zodiac alluding to the natural world order that works in concert with God's plan.

Another explanation offered for this composition is that it corresponds to the themes of many piyyutim that were being introduced in some synagogues in late antiquity. Such an approach assumes a parallel development (or perhaps a direct Christian influence) among Jews that is well documented for churches, namely the illustration of complex themes through pictorial representation (Fine 2005: 186–89). Finally, it has been suggested that the many possible allusions in this poetry to priests and sacrificial themes may reflect priestly influence on the art of this synagogue, suggesting, perhaps, a prominent role that priests may have played in the Sepphoris community of late antiquity (Levine 2003: 115–30).

Bet Alpha. Discovered in the winter of 1928–29 in the Jezreel Valley, Bet Alpha was the first major archaeological discovery of an ancient synagogue (Sukenik 1932). This synagogue is of particular interest owing to the excellent preservation of its plan, inscriptions, and art (see Fig. 28.7). The pièce de résistance is a well-preserved mosaic floor divided into three panels, which include the Aqedah, the zodiac and Helios, and the cluster of religious symbols. Despite the unsophisticated quality of the art itself, a number of suggestions have been offered with regard to the entire composition.

Wischnitzer (1955), for example, viewed the three panels as representing the holiday of Sukkot; Wilkinson (1978) interpreted them as representing the various Temple courtyards and its interior, each panel advancing toward ever-greater holiness; Goodenough (1953–68, vol 8: 167–218) posited that the various panels depict the ascent of the soul from a state of earthly purity to the heavenly and then mystical worlds; Goldman (1966), with a slight variation, understood them as

Fig. 28.6 Reconstructed drawing of the seven registers of the Sepphoris synagogue mosaic floor

Courtesy of the Sepphoris excavations, Hebrew University of Jerusalem

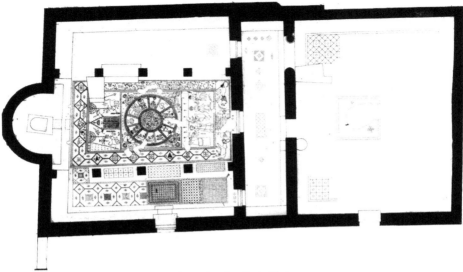

Fig. 28.7 Location of mosaic floor in the Bet Alpha synagogue

Courtesy of Institute of Archaeology, Hebrew University, Jerusalem

conveying movement toward the sacred heavenly portal. Renov (1954) has suggested that the messianic theme is the common thread connecting the various panels.

3.4 The Jewish-Christian Nexus

Numerous studies over the last few decades have claimed that there were many similarities between the synagogue and church in the Byzantine period. This was the case architecturally, as many synagogues were built according to the basilical plan then in vogue in churches (Tsafrir 1987) and many bore similar artistic motifs (Hachlili 1997; Vitto 1995; Talgam 2000). Kessler has suggested that much of Jewish art is, in reality, a polemic against Christian claims, and interprets many of the Dura synagogue panels and Sepphoris mosaics in this vein (Weitzmann/Kessler 1990; Kessler 2000). Other scholars have followed Kessler's lead in this regard (Weiss 2005: 249–56; Kühnel 2000; Revel-Neher 2000).

The Byzantine-Christian nexus is likewise apparent in the widespread use of Jewish symbols in late antiquity. It has already been noted that such symbols were very rare before this time. Only then did they become ubiquitous in cemeteries as well as synagogues both in Palestine and the Diaspora. The fact that the menorah was, in part, a Jewish response to the cross is not simply a speculative assertion: a number of archaeological finds display a menorah precisely where a cross was depicted in Christian contexts. For example, a menorah incised on a chancel screen at Hammat Gader parallels a cross on a chancel screen at Masu'ot Yitzhaq, and lamps hanging from *menorot* in Na'aran resemble those hanging from a cross in North Africa. Crosses decorated late Byzantine oil lamps as well as glass jugs and jars from Byzantine Jerusalem and elsewhere precisely where *menorot* would appear (Levine 2000: 150–52).

The use of symbols as a means of reinforcing group identity seems to have been a hallmark of this period for both Christians and Jews. We are only now beginning to realize the extent of Jewish-Christian interaction in all walks of life during late antiquity, whether hostile or supportive, destructive or fructifying. Within the synagogue context, Byzantine architectural and artistic patterns and motifs were frequently adopted. Thus, even in the case of a uniquely Jewish symbol such as the menorah, the synchronic dimension is clearly a crucial factor in accounting for its widespread appearance in this period as the Jewish symbol par excellence.

4. THE LOCAL FACTOR IN ART AND ARCHITECTURE

The social implications of the diversity of synagogue art and architecture should be obvious. Local tastes and proclivities were decisive factors in determining what a synagogue looked like and how it functioned. This is eminently clear from the material remains, where diversity is the norm. In fact, no two synagogues, even those of the same type and located in geographical proximity, are identical. Differences in architectural plans, artistic representations, and epigraphic evidence are apparent. The latter phenomenon is quite evident when comparing the four synagogues discussed above. Whatever their similarities, differences regarding iconography and the respective selection, representation, and placement of the various panels are no less pronounced.

A striking example of this marked diversity among synagogues is evident in the Bet Shean area. To date, we know of five contemporaneous synagogue buildings that functioned in sixth-century Bet Shean and its vicinity (Levine 2005: 214–24). No other urban setting boasts such a concentration of remains, having not only a geographical but also a chronological propinquity. The synagogues referred to are Bet Shean A, just north of the city wall; Bet Shean B, near the south-west city-gate; Bet Alpha, to the west; Ma'oz Hayyim, to the east; and Rehov, to the south. Despite the fact that all these buildings functioned at one and the same time, they were, in fact, remarkably different from one another in each of the above-mentioned categories.

5. Rabbis and the Synagogue: How Much Influence Did They Have?

Given the fact that the two largest and most important corpora of data regarding the ancient synagogue are rabbinic sources and archaeology, the question naturally arises as to the nature and extent of rabbinic involvement in, and influence on, this institution. The issue is of importance not only for understanding how the synagogue functioned, but also for gaining a perspective on the status of the sages generally in Jewish society of late antiquity (Goodenough 1961; Levine 1992; Cohen 1992; Hezser 1997: 214–24).

In studies of Jewish history in the Graeco-Roman and Byzantine eras, it has traditionally been assumed that the sages were the dominant religious and social force in Jewish society (Alon 1977: 22 n. 11; 1980, vol. 1: 308; Safrai 1982: 27–39). This view continues to engage certain academic circles to this day.

Since the mid-twentieth century, however, there has been a counter-trend advocating a much more circumspect view of rabbinic influence. Two important studies (Goodenough 1953–68, vol. 12: 184–98; Smith 1956: 73–81), coming from entirely different perspectives, have had a powerful influence on the discussion of Pharisaic and rabbinic status in antiquity. The questions raised by these seminal studies are still central to the scholarly agenda, and the perspective suggested by them has been adopted in varying degrees by most scholars.

However, the extent of rabbinic influence is far more complex than any sweeping and facile generalization. First of all, not all rabbis were cut from the same cloth. They differed from each other in personality, socio-economic standing, social context (e.g. urban versus rural), and degree of religious stringency. Some were more involved in political and social issues or in communal life, others less so. Moreover, there were often varied attitudes among them toward the non-rabbinic world (be it Jewish or non-Jewish), and the cataclysmic changes that affected the Jews at large in the first four or five centuries CE may have had major repercussions on the rabbinic class as well (Levine 1989: 23–42; 1992).

There is, therefore, no simple solution regarding rabbinic involvement in, and influence on, if not control of, the ancient synagogue. On the one hand, the rabbis were not all-dominant in Jewish life at the time—politically, socially, culturally, or even religiously. On the other hand, rabbinic influence seems to have been in ascendance in late antiquity, though its pace and degree at any given time is well-nigh impossible to ascertain. Moreover, we should almost certainly distinguish between various areas of synagogue life. In the realm of art, architecture, and institutional life, the answer would probably be more minimalist. A no less significant issue, however, affects the synagogue's religious and liturgical dimensions. Here the picture is not fully clear, although the case for an increasing rabbinic influence as time went on is quite possible. Further refinement in our understanding of this issue remains a primary desideratum.

6. TOWARD THE FUTURE

There is no area of synagogue studies that would not benefit immensely from further research. Whether it is the field of architecture, art, or inscriptions, much remains to be done, and new questions and insights are bound to be forthcoming. Each generation brings its own perspectives, insights, and wisdom to bear on such subjects, and if the past is any indication, sources of stimulation will always be at hand. Likewise regarding the fields of liturgy, synagogue officialdom, or the synagogue's relationship to the rabbis and patriarch, both literary sources and archaeological remains contain rich information that remains to be tapped by future generations of scholars. Finally, the complex and multi-faceted relationship between various aspects of the synagogue and the surrounding Graeco-Roman and Byzantine cultures has always been, and will undoubtedly continue to be, a fertile area of investigation. The more information we are able to cull from the wider Byzantine-Christian context, the more light will be shed on all aspects of the ancient synagogue.

SUGGESTED READING

For a comprehensive history of the ancient synagogues, incorporating all of its various aspects, literary and archaeological, see Levine (2005). The art and archaeological material from both Palestine and the Diaspora have been presented by Goodenough (1953–68), and later Hachlili (1988, 1998, 2001). Important studies on ancient Jewish art include Kraeling (1956), Weiss (2005), and Fine (2005).

BIBLIOGRAPHY

ALON, G. (1977). *Jews, Judaism and the Classical World*. Jerusalem: Magnes.
—— (1980). *The Jews in Their Land in the Talmudic Age*. 2 vols. Jerusalem: Magnes.
AVIGAD, N. (1960). 'A Dated Lintel-Inscription from the Ancient Synagogue of Nabratein', in *Bulletin of the Louis M. Rabinowitz Fund for the Exploration of Ancient Synagogues*, III. Jerusalem: Hebrew University, 49–56.

Avi-Yonah, M. (1961). 'Synagogue Architecture in the Late Classical Period', in *Jewish Art: An Illustrated History*, ed. C. Roth. Greenwich: New York Graphic Society, 157–90.

Binder, D. D. (1999). *Into the Temple Courts: The Place of the Synagogues in the Second Temple Period*. Atlanta: Society of Biblical Literature.

Cohen, S. J. D. (1992). 'The Place of the Rabbi in Jewish Society of the Second Century', in *The Galilee in Late Antiquity*, ed. L. I. Levine. New York and Jerusalem: Jewish Theological Seminary, 157–73.

—— (1999). 'Were Pharisees and Rabbis the Leaders of Communal Prayer and Torah Study in Antiquity? The Evidence of the New Testament, Josephus, and the Church Fathers', in *Evolution of the Synagogue: Problems and Progress*, ed. H. C. Kee and L. H. Cohick. Harrisburg: Trinity International, 89–105.

Dothan, M. (1983). *Hammath Tiberias*, vol. 1: *Early Synagogues and the Hellenistic and Roman Remains*. Jerusalem: Israel Exploration Society.

Fine, S. (2005). *Art and Judaism in the Greco-Roman World: Toward a New Jewish Archaeology*. Cambridge and New York: Cambridge University Press.

Flesher, P. V. M. (1995). 'Palestinian Synagogues before 70 c.e.: A Review of the Evidence', in *Ancient Synagogues: Historical Analysis and Archaeological Discovery*, ed. D. Urman and P. V. M. Flesher. Leiden: Brill, 67–81.

—— (2001). 'Prolegomenon to a Theory of Early Synagogue Development', in *Judaism in Late Antiquity*, Part III: *Where We Stand: Issues and Debates in Ancient Judaism*, vol. 4: *The Special Problem of the Synagogue*, ed. A. J. Avery-Peck and J. Neusner. Leiden: Brill, 121–53.

Goldman, B. M. (1966). *The Sacred Portal: A Primary Symbol in Ancient Judaic Art*. Detroit: Wayne State University Press.

Goodenough, E. (1953–68). *Jewish Symbols in the Greco-Roman Period*, 13 vols. New York: Pantheon.

—— (1961). 'The Rabbis and Jewish Art in the Greco-Roman Period'. *Hebrew Union College Annual* 32: 161–74.

Goodman, M. (1996). 'Sacred Space in Diaspora Judaism Judaism', in *Studies on the Jewish Diaspora in the Hellenistic and Roman Periods*, ed. B. Isaac and A. Oppenheimer. Te'uda 12. Tel Aviv: Ramot, 1–16.

Griffiths, J. G. (1987). 'Egypt and the Rise of the Synagogue'. *Journal of Theological Studies* 38: 1–15.

Gutmann, J. (1973). 'Programmatic Painting in the Dura Synagogue', in *The Dura-Europos Synagogue: A Re-Evaluation (1932–72)*, ed. J. Gutmann. Missoula: American Academy of Religion and Society of Biblical Literature, 137–54.

—— (1984). 'Early Synagogue and Jewish Catacomb Art and Its Relation to Christian Art', in *Aufstieg und Niedergang der römischen Welt*, II, 21.2, ed. H. Temporini and W. Haase. Berlin: de Gruyter, 1313–42.

Hachlili, R. (1988). *Ancient Jewish Art and Archaeology in the Land of Israel*. Leiden: Brill.

—— (1997). 'Aspects of Similarity and Diversity in the Architecture and Art of Ancient Synagogues and Churches in the Land of Israel'. *Zeitschrift des Deutschen Palästina-Vereins* 113: 92–122.

—— (1998). *Ancient Jewish Art and Archaeology in the Diaspora*. Leiden: Brill.

—— (2001). *The Menorah, the Ancient Seven-Armed Candelabrum: Origin, Form, and Significance*. Leiden: Brill.

—— (2002). 'The Zodiac in Ancient Synagogal Art: A Review', *Jewish Studies Quarterly* 9: 219–58.

HEZSER, C. (1997). *The Social Structure of the Rabbinic Movement in Roman Palestine*. Tübingen: Mohr-Siebeck.

KESSLER, H. (2000). 'The Sepphoris Mosaic and Christian Art', in *From Dura to Sepphoris: Studies in Jewish Art and Society in Late Antiquity*, ed. L. I. Levine and Z. Weiss. Ann Arbor: Journal of Roman Archaeology Supplementary Series, 64–72.

KOHL, H./WATZINGER, C. (1916). *Antike Synagogen in Galilaea*. Leipzig: Heinrichs.

KRAELING, C. H. (1956). *The Excavations at Dura-Europos*, vol. 8/1: *The Synagogue*. New Haven: Yale University Press (reprinted 1979, New York: Ktav).

KHNEL, B. (2000). 'The Synagogue Floor Mosaic in Sepphoris: Between Paganism and Christianity', in *From Dura to Sepphoris: Studies in Jewish Art and Society in Late Antiquity*, ed. L. I. Levine and Z. Weiss. Ann Arbor: Journal of Roman Archaeology Supplementary Series, 31–43.

LEVINE, L. I. (1989). *The Rabbinic Class of Roman Palestine in Late Antiquity*. Jerusalem and New York: Yad Izhak Ben-Zvi and Jewish Theological Seminary.

—— (1992). 'The Sages and the Synagogue in Late Antiquity: The Evidence of the Galilee', in *The Galilee in Late Antiquity*, ed. L. I. Levine. New York and Jerusalem: Jewish Theological Seminary, 201–22.

—— (2000). 'The History and Significance of the Menorah in Antiquity', in *From Dura to Sepphoris: Studies in Jewish Art and Society in Late Antiquity*, ed. L. I. Levine and Z. Weiss. Ann Arbor: Journal of Roman Archaeology Supplementary Series, 131–53.

—— (2003). 'Contextualizing Jewish Art: The Synagogues at Hammat Tiberias and Sepphoris', in *Jewish Culture and Society under the Christian Roman Empire*, ed. R. Kalmin and S. Schwartz. Leuven: Peeters, 91–131.

—— (2005). *The Ancient Synagogue: The First Thousand Years*. Revised edition. New Haven: Yale University Press.

MAGNESS, J. (2001). 'The Question of the Synagogue: The Problem of Typology', in *Judaism in Late Antiquity*, Part III: *Where We Stand: Issues and Debates in Ancient Judaism*, vol. 4: *The Special Problem of the Synagogue*, ed. A. J. Avery-Peck and J. Neusner. Leiden: Brill, 1–48.

RENOV, I. (1954). 'The Relation of Helios and the Quadriga to the Rest of the Beth Alpha Mosaic' [Hebr.]. *Bulletin of the Israel Exploration Society* 18: 202–208.

REVEL-NEHER, E. (2000). 'From Dream to Reality: Evolution and Continuity in Jewish Art', in *From Dura to Sepphoris: Studies in Jewish Art and Society in Late Antiquity*, ed. L. I. Levine and Z. Weiss. Ann Arbor: Journal of Roman Archaeology Supplementary Series, 53–63.

RICHARDSON, P. (1996). 'Early Synagogues as Collegia in the Diaspora and Palestine', in *Voluntary Associations in the Graeco-Roman World*, ed. J. S. Kloppenborg and S. G. Wilson. London: Routledge, 90–109.

—— (2003). 'An Architectural Case for Synagogues as Associations', in *The Ancient Synagogue: From Its Origins until 200 C.E*, ed. B. Olsson and M. Zetterholm. Stockholm: Almqvist and Wiksell International, 90–117.

RUNESSON, A. (2001). *The Origins of the Synagogue: A Socio-Historical Study*. Stockholm: Almqvist and Wiksell International.

SAFRAI, S. (1982). 'Recovery of the Jewish Community in the Yavnean Generation' [Hebr.], in *Eretz Israel from the Destruction of the Second Temple to the Muslim Conquest*, vol. 1, ed. Z. Baras et al. Jerusalem: Yad Izhak Ben-Zvi, 18–39.

SCHWARTZ, S. (2001). *Imperialism and Jewish Society, 200 B.C.E. to 640 C.E.* Princeton: Princeton University Press.

SMITH, M. (1956). 'Palestinian Judaism in the First Century', in *Israel: Its Role in Civilization*, ed. M. Davis. New York: Jewish Theological Seminary, 67–81.

SUKENIK, E. L. (1932). *The Ancient Synagogue of Beth Alpha*. Jerusalem: Hebrew University.

—— (1934). *Ancient Synagogues in Palestine and Greece*. London: Milford.

TALGAM, R. (2000). 'Similarities and Differences between Synagogue and Church Mosaics in Palestine during the Byzantine and Umayyad Periods', in *From Dura to Sepphoris: Studies in Jewish Art and Society in Late Antiquity*, ed. L. I. Levine and Z. Weiss. Ann Arbor: Journal of Roman Archaeology Supplementary Series, 93–110.

TSAFRIR, Y. (1987). 'The Byzantine Setting and Its Influence on Ancient Synagogues', in *The Synagogue in Late Antiquity*, ed. L. I. Levine. Philadelphia: Jewish Theological Seminary and American Schools of Oriental Research, 147–57.

VITTO, F. (1995). 'The Interior Decoration of Palestinian Churches and Synagogues', in *Byzantinische Forschungen* 21, ed. A. M. Hakkert and W. E. Kaegi, Jr. Amsterdam: Am M. Hakkert, 284–300.

WEISS, Z. (2005). *The Sepphoris Synagogue: Deciphering an Ancient Message through Its Archaeological and Socio-Historical Contexts*. Jerusalem: Israel Exploration Society.

WEITZMANN, K./KESSLER, H. (1990). *The Frescoes of the Dura Synagogue and Christian Art*. Washington, DC: Dumbarton Oaks.

WILKINSON, J. (1978). 'The Beit Alpha Synagogue Mosaic: Towards an Interpretation'. *Journal of Jewish Art* 5: 16–28.

WISCHNITZER, R. (1955). 'The Beth Alpha Mosaic: A New Interpretation'. *Journal of Social Studies* 17: 133–44.

CHAPTER 29

PRAYER AND LITURGY

STEFAN C. REIF

1. INTRODUCTION: METHODOLOGICAL PITFALLS

Serious but non-specialist students of Judaism approaching the history of the rabbinic prayer-book for the first time might be forgiven for supposing that the matter of its early development is fairly simple. According to this simple theory, texts from the Mishnah, Toseftaj and Talmudim of the early Christian period attest to the central prayers which are created in the Land of Israel, exported to Iraq (Babylonia) and widely accepted by far-flung Jewish communities. The liturgical compositions of the early rabbis, written down and transmitted in Hebrew, are considered novel and fairly exclusive to their own circles, and they are believed to have been recited by Jewish males in the synagogue. Their content allegedly reflects standard rabbinic theology about the status and nature of prayer, and lucid ideas about the precise manner in which it is to be recited. The essential process of compilation, having commenced in the early second century CE, is completed before the end of the time of the compilation of the Palestinian and Babylonian Talmuds, and what comes later represents a mere tinkering with details or, indeed, a slide into literary and theological decadence. Such views, in whole or in part, are not uncommon and may even be found in some of the popular introductions, encouraging the uninitiated to approach the topic with simplistic confidence and optimistic enthusiasm (Mintz 1984: 406, 425). Alas, for those in pursuit of an academic subject that is easily absorbed and swiftly mastered, the situation is vastly more complicated, and notes of caution have to be sounded about how best to proceed with a valid historical analysis.

The authoritative works of early rabbinic literature (for example, the first Mishnah tractate Berakhot) do indeed refer to daily, Sabbath, and festival prayers, as well as to a host of benedictions, but rarely give more than a brief title for any of them, manifestly eschewing the opportunity of providing a detailed text. It may not therefore be valid to assume that what is known to the early rabbis as, for example (b. Pes. 118a, b. Taan. 28b and b. Shab. 118b), *Hallel* (collection of Psalm chapters) or *pesuqei de-zimra* (verses of praise), is wholly identical with what is contained in the later prayer-books, or cited by the post-talmudic authorities, under such nomenclature. The preparation of critical texts of rabbinic works is in many senses no more than in its infancy, but what is already clear, especially with regard to liturgical matters, is that what was personally familiar to scribes was just as likely, or perhaps even more likely, to be copied down by them as the text that they had been asked to transmit, in whatever format it existed.

And what indeed was the medium for the transmission of both the authoritative works themselves and the liturgical compositions to which they make regular reference? The fact is that the educational system of the rabbis until about the eighth or ninth century CE was predominantly oral. The teachers took pride in mastering subjects and arguments by heart and encouraging their pupils to do likewise, and there was more than a degree of hesitancy about committing to text what was essentially the 'Oral Tradition' (*Torah Shebe'al Peh*), and perhaps thereby risking a confusion with the 'Written Tradition', that is, Scripture (*Torah Shebikhtav*). The earliest forms of *midrashim* (biblical exegesis), *targumim* (biblical translations) and what later evolved into masoretic prescriptions (notes on the textual tradition of the Hebrew Bible) also appear to have been oral, leaving the distinct impression that rabbinic theory and practice permitted no more than the occasional written note (Elman/Gershoni 2000; Hezser 2001; Jaffee 2001).

2. MANUSCRIPT EVIDENCE

What the researcher is then faced with are liturgical prescriptions laid down by the tannaitic and amoraic rabbis (rabbis who lived between 70 and 200 CE, and from the early third to the mid-fifth century CE, respectively), followed later by halakhic explanations and decisions made by the geonic teachers from the seventh to the eleventh centuries, and the manuscript versions of authorized prayer-books compiled for the first time in the ninth and tenth centuries (Brody 2006). If the problems and methods of transmission make it difficult for us to presuppose that what is known from the post-talmudic periods is precisely what was inherited from their earlier counterparts, an additional complication is added to any possible historical reconstruction by the rich evidence of the tenth to thirteenth centuries available from the Cairo Genizah (Reif 2000). If liturgical texts from that source do not tally with those that are presupposed and sanctioned by the geonic leadership in Iraq, are we to conclude that the former are older versions that had been forgotten or suppressed in the Mesopotamian *yeshivot* (talmudic academies)? Alternatively, is it more likely that they represent formulations that were freshly coined in the post-talmudic period under the influence of the poets and cantors who had composed the whole new genre of liturgical poems (*piyyutim*) that had made such inroads into the liturgy?

The most general point to be made about the Genizah evidence is that it reconstructs for us not only the rite of the Land of Israel in the period leading up to the invasion by the Crusaders, but also provides the prayer versions preferred by the Babylonian Jewish community. There was clearly a constant exchange of information and communication between Jews in the Land of Israel and Babylonia, attesting to a considerable degree of elasticity, rather than of monolithic authority, with regard to the prayers. More specifically, lost benedictions have come to light; variations in the form and content of the *Shema* (commencing with Deut 6:4), the *Amidah* ('Standing Prayer'), the *Birkat ha-Mazon* (Grace after Meals), the *Qiddush* (a blessing over wine on the Sabbath), and the Passover *Haggadah* (the ritual 'guidebook' of the Passover evening meal) have been discovered; and the terminology used to refer to the Sabbaths and festivals has been shown to have been much broader than previously thought. In addition, hundreds of fragments have pointed to the variety of customs relating to the pentateuchal and prophetic lectionaries used in the synagogue, and to the use of the Hebrew Bible in the rabbinic liturgy (Fleischer 1988, 1990, 1991; Wieder 1998; Reif 1991 and 1999).

Whichever of these views (or their variations) one adopts, the Genizah data remain central to the historical understanding of Jewish liturgy. If they constitute a breakaway from, or an adaptation of, what was authorized by the tannaitic and amoraic rabbis of the first four centuries CE, then that thread of tradition was clearly not as strong in the late talmudic period as some have led us to believe. On the other hand, if they represent alternative versions that had existed from talmudic, or even tannaitic times, they testify to a greater degree of variety than is often supposed. Either way, the existence of one sanctioned form for each prayer and benediction, that would not tolerate variation, seems highly unlikely. It should be added that while the manuscripts of the prayer-books of Natronai Gaon and Sa'adya Gaon (9th–10th c. CE) appear to be reliable witnesses to what these leading rabbis codified for those who addressed questions to them, the texts that we have inherited of Amram Gaon's liturgy date from a few centuries later, and have been subjected to alterations that reflect the liturgical practices of each of those who participated in the transmission (Brody 2006: 63–66).

3. Prayer in the Second Temple Period

Returning now to the two centuries leading up to the destruction of the Second Temple and the loss of Jewish independence in 70 CE, the point has immediately to be made that there was no one exclusive area of Jewish liturgical expression. The Temple in Jerusalem obviously stood at the centre of worship in and around that city. Although there were a few formulas to be recited on special occasions, the cultic rituals performed there were generally conducted in silence, and the liturgy was essentially the performance of the sacrificial system (Knohl 1995). Some of the later literature of the Hebrew Bible, as well as items in the Apocrypha and Pseudepigrapha, indicate that people did, on appropriate occasions, congregate on the Temple site and take the opportunity of expressing praise and thanks to God, perhaps by way of Psalm selections (Reif 1993: 47). In the final years of the Temple's existence such praise may also have included the recitation of such biblical passages, as the Decalogue (Exod. 20:1–14) and the *Shema*. The study of such and other passages was another activity which was taking on liturgical aspects (Weinfeld 2001 and M Tamid 5:1).

During those final years before the destruction of the Second Temple, the Land of Israel and the Jewish Diaspora had seen the emergence of an institution that ultimately evolved into what came to be known as the synagogue. It is not clear whether it represented a communal centre which could compete with the Temple, but what is beyond doubt is that its original functions were social, educational, and even recreational, rather than purely liturgical (Levine 2000). Intriguingly, an inscription from Jerusalem commonly dated to the first century CE, spells this out. It records the generosity of Theodotos and his family in building, and perhaps also leading, a synagogue meant for the reading of the Torah, the observance of religious precepts, and as a hostel for visitors. No mention whatsoever is made of prayer here (Roth-Gerson 1987: 76–86). There are tannaitic traditions about the existence of another communal practice known as the *ma'amadot* (local groups or divisions). Those male Israelites who could not accompany the priests and Levites from their local area when it was their turn to function in the Jerusalem Temple would gather in their home towns to fast, recite scriptural passages, and perhaps also to pray (M. Taan. 4:2). Since such an activity is not one that is in any way central to the rabbinic tradition, it seems reasonable to suppose that the tannaitic traditions are referring to something with a historical reality rather than a figment of their imagination.

The reason why prayer was not central to these pre-70 CE Jewish institutions is that it had originally been an expression of personal rather than communal religiosity, not part of Temple activities, and even perhaps in some ways competing with them. Its style had more in common with oaths, curses, blessings, and prophecy, and it was a democratic rather than elitist function, open to all individuals, rather than controlled by a special class of intermediaries (Greenberg 1983). The recitation of blessings was an important aspect of such personal prayers and had already taken on a formal introduction along the lines of 'You are blessed, Lord' (*barukh atah adonay*), as in 1 Chr. 29:10. Gradually during the Second Temple period, the two opposing expressions, represented by the formal Jerusalem cult and the personal prayers of individuals, moved towards each other, and began a process of integration that ultimately took different forms in later rabbinic Judaism and early Christianity. This process of formalizing communal prayer and using it on special occasions was already in existence in the period leading up to the origins of Christianity. Certain groups, among them those with close attachment to mystical and apocalyptic ideas, recited regular prayers at specific times, but there is no obvious consistency of text and context. The clearest evidence is found in the liturgical customs recorded among the documents found at Qumran, and it will be useful to compare the liturgical content of these documents with that of the apocryphal book of Ben Sira and the later rabbinic customs (Reif 2006a: 51–69).

All three types of post-biblical sources (Qumran texts, Ben Sira, rabbinic traditions) have hymns, prayers, and benedictions, and utilize biblical vocabulary to which they attach their own linguistic and religious significance. They also enjoy common themes, such as the election of Israel, the status of Zion, the holiness of Jerusalem, the return of the Davidic dynasty, and the manifestation of God's great power now and in the future. Although Ben Sira's greatest affection in the liturgical sphere is reserved for the Temple, he also acknowledges the possibility of worshipping God by intellectual and educational means. He does not provide timetables for prayers, and angels, apocalypse, and eschatology are not among his special interests. The Qumran texts, for their part, refer to the regular recitation at stipulated times or occasions of communal prayers, even if there is no overall consistency of formulation or context. They demonstrate a greater liturgical intensity than other contemporary works, but do not appear to have opted for an overall consistency in the manner in which they formulated prayer or incorporated it in their devotions. Some elements of rabbinic formulations are reminiscent of what is to be found in the Qumranic prayers but the format, the vocabulary and the usage have all taken on a distinctive character that reflects the ideology of early rabbinic Judaism (Nitzan 1994; Schuller 2004; Chazon 1998; Falk 1998; Alexander 2006).

4. RABBINIC INNOVATIONS

Although the early rabbis inherited various aspects of theory and practice from earlier contexts of worship, they undoubtedly shaped their own liturgical response to what were for them the calamitous events of the first two centuries CE. But there was no unanimous view about the place of prayer in their religious outlook. For some rabbis, it replaced the Temple and took on the role of formal and central liturgy ('avodah). In that case it was at least of equal importance to devotional study of the Torah and correct ethical behaviour (gemillut ḥesed). For others, it was study or ethical behaviour that had taken over from the Temple, so that prayer amounted to no more than one of the 613 religious requirements demanded of the practising Jew. There was also a conviction on the part of certain circles that nothing could ever replace the Temple, and that what it had achieved for the religion of Israel would simply have to remain in abeyance until, in the messianic age, its buildings and rituals were fully restored.

There was also considerable ambivalence about the role of the mystic in prayer. Was the efficacy of prayer dependent on the remarkable piety of special individuals, with all the attendant preparations for achieving high degrees of spirituality, and on a mysterious and even magical aspect that only the most saintly possessed? Did prayer always have to be an intense religious experience? The alternative view was a more pragmatic one, admitting the frailties of humanity and the inability of ordinary individuals to become ascetics at will, and proposing that their recitation of fixed formulas three times a day, together with the use of the *tallit* (prayer shawl) and *tefillin* (phylacteries), would meet the religious requirement. The early rabbinic works also include debates about the language, length, locality, and direction of prayer. The discussions centred on whether Greek and Aramaic could match Hebrew, whether prayers should be recited antiphonally, and whether brevity was the soul of liturgical piety. Also included in the debates were whether the synagogue was always a better place for prayer than the home, and whether it was always necessary to face Jerusalem during one's recitations. Here, too, there is often no clear indication of only one right and proper practice (y. Ber. 1:8, 3c; 4:1, 7a; 4:5, 8c and 5:1, 8d–9a; y. R.H. 1:3, 57b; y. Taan. 3:4, 66c; see the discussion in Reif 1993: 88–121).

Faced with a variety of liturgical customs emanating from different contexts and circles, leading tannaitic rabbis of the first two centuries after the Temple's destruction set about creating some standards and consistency. Efforts were made (as already recorded in tractate Berakhot of the Mishnah and Tosefta) to lay down authoritative rulings with regard to the prayers that were already of central significance, such as the *Shema, Amidah,* and *Birkat ha-Mazon*. The fact that each of these prayers already had its own characteristics, which were not necessarily mutually consistent, indicates the significance they had already achieved by this time. But it was by no means too late to give them a wholly rabbinic flavour. The basic texts were surrounded by benedictions that reflected central points of rabbinic theology, and attempts were made to create a degree of consistency between and within them. The precise nature of the obligation was defined and discussions centred on precisely what had to be recited by whom and when. A central plank of this new liturgical ideology was the drive to link up all the prayers and customs so as to reduce the tendency to opt for one or the other, as earlier groups may have done. For instance, the ideal was to demand (by promises of great reward) a continuity between the use of the *tallit* and *tefillin* on the one hand, and the recitation of the benedictions, the *Shema*, and the *Amidah* on the other (b. Ber. 14b–15a and 60b; y. Ber. 2:2, 4a; Zahavy 1989: 242–54).

The synagogue was of importance to many, but not all, of these rabbis, and had not yet attracted to itself all the liturgical rituals. The study house (*bet midrash*) and the home were still alternative loci for such rituals. Some early teachers positively preferred not to move out of the study context for any purpose, including individual or communal prayer (b. Ber 8a; y. Ber. 1:5, 3b and 4:6, 8c). Some prayers and benedictions seem to have had their origin in the academic setting, particularly those centring on Torah study, although their incorporation into the daily liturgy was not completed until a later date (b. Sotah 49a and b. Ber. 11b; y. Ber. 7:1–2, 11a–b; Heinemann 1977: 251–75).

Perhaps the best example of a Torah-based liturgy is the Passover *Haggadah*. Its earliest form in Mishnah Pesaḥim ch. 10 takes for granted the existence of the Temple, and constituted an exposition of the Israelite Exodus from Egypt and the obligation to eat the paschal lamb which accompanied the family meal on the first eve of Passover, together with a selection of biblical praises of God (*hallel*). What the early rabbis set out to do was to utilize the liturgical and pedagogical elements in this domestic ceremony to stress their own religious outlook, and to give the proceedings a formalized and authorized structure which might prevent other groups (such as the Jewish Christians) imposing their interpretations upon it. In an age which had seen the loss of Jewish political freedom, they sought to console their followers by stressing at the Passover meal that true Jewish freedom, which originated with the Exodus from Egypt, was a religiously eternal privilege that had been divinely granted and could therefore never be removed (Goldschmidt 1969; Bokser 1984).

The rituals for announcing the arrival and departure of the Sabbath, the *Qiddush* and the *Havdalah*, were also domestic in origin and appear to have predated the tannaitic period. Such a conclusion is supported by the fact that the early rabbis chose to mark the beginning and end of the Sabbath within their own evening prayers (t. Ber. 3.7; b. Ber. 33a–b and b. Pes. 100b–101a; y. Ber. 1:8, 3d and 5:2, 9b–c). The *Qiddush* and *Havdalah* were therefore left with a residual domestic significance, but were still given a more rabbinic form and content (Reif 2004: 443).

Progress was also made within the rabbinic circles of the first two or three centuries CE in the matter of transforming what had been an earlier interest in scriptural reading and study into a more formal liturgical exercise. The religious education of the people through the lessons of the Hebrew Bible had been a long-established practice and, taken together with the scribal traditions and the development of biblical and post-biblical wisdom literature, testify to a Jewish interest in the relationship between the intellect and the soul. Greek and Aramaic translations of the Hebrew Bible, the *pesher* system of biblical exegesis that permeates the Qumranic writings, the allegorical teachings of Philo of Alexandria, the use of *tefillin* and *mezuzot* (pentateuchal texts fixed to door posts) as ritual objects with scriptural content, as well as the interpretation of Scripture championed by both early Christianity and rabbinic Judaism—all these trends made it virtually impossible for rabbis to ignore the liturgical claims of the Hebrew Bible. Use was made of pentateuchal, prophetical, and hagiographical readings, but the precise details of the lectionaries, if they were already established as such, are known only from later periods. It is even controversial whether the triennial cycle that was used in the Land of Israel in the post-talmudic period was always the rite used in the homeland, or whether it had once shared its liturgical role with the annual cycle that became standard in Babylonia. Again, the rabbis attached their own liturgical trappings to such readings, hauling them into the colourful wardrobe of precepts and customs by which they chose to identify their religious affiliations (Perrot 1988, Alexander 2006, Fishbane 1988, and Kasher 1988).

5. Questions of Detail

Were rabbis legislating for their own small circles only? Was the Hebrew language the chosen medium for prayer? Did all communities of the Jewish world of that time subscribe to similar liturgical principles and practices? Should we suppose that the liturgical contexts were exclusively male? Did mystics play an important role in the liturgical inspiration of the rabbis and their followers? These are among the most difficult questions to answer, especially with regard to the period before the synagogue rites and customs became more formalized, centralized, and authorized, from about the fourth century CE onwards. Since it is generally the victors in any religious controversy who write the history, it is inevitably not an easy task to uncover the alternative and opposing viewpoints. But the fact that the rabbinic sources consistently promise rewards in this and the next world for adhering to their views, and forms of damnation to those who decline to do so, indicates that they were engaged in a battle to spread their religious message. The epigraphic and archaeological evidence, as well as the literary material from non-Jewish sources, seem to support the notion that rabbinic Judaism was a major factor in Jewish life in Roman Palestine. But it also testifies to the existence of Jews who were more attracted to the Greek and Roman lifestyle and culture than rabbis liked, and even rabbinic texts themselves record many examples of surprising degrees of tolerance of such acculturation (see the contributions of S. Schwartz, J. Schwartz, Levine, and Linder in the *Cambridge History of Judaism* vol. 4, 2006).

The Jewish attraction to Greek was sufficiently strong for the language to be specially recognized by rabbis as one of the great languages of the world. According to a tradition transmitted in the Palestinian Talmud, Hebrew was the language of revelation, Greek was best for lyrical use, Latin for military purposes, and Aramaic for funerals (y. Meg. 1:11(9), 71b). In spite of rabbinic reservations about the study of Greek wisdom, they even permitted the use of Greek for major parts of the Jewish liturgy (y. Sotah 7:1, 21b; Lieberman 1965). The liturgical use of Greek must have been even more common in the major centres of Hellenistic culture such as Egypt. The Jewish people of the first three centuries CE were therefore liturgically trilingual, and Aramaic, as the vernacular of many Jews in Roman Palestine, would have been the natural language to use for private prayers. In Babylonia too, Aramaic, in its eastern rather than western form, was widely employed by the Jews but, interestingly enough, it seems to have been Hebrew that predominated in the local liturgy. Once Hebrew was established as the main liturgical language, there could later be a relaxation in this matter, and Aramaic could once again find a respected place in prayers (Breuer 2006).

When rabbis from the Land of Israel visited Diaspora communities in the third century CE, they were probably sometimes surprised by the liturgical variation that they found there (b. Meg. 22a). If that was the case within close-knit rabbinic communities, one may justifiably speculate that there were other Jewish communities within the Hellenistic world which perhaps had even greater variety in their prayers. There is evidence of Jewish prayers in Greek, sometimes with contents that parallel the *Amidah*, that were undoubtedly in circulation in the third and fourth centuries CE and may also have been used in earlier and later times (van der Horst 2002).

It is among such Greek-speaking communities that one finds evidence of a more central role for women in the synagogue. According to early rabbinic literature, it was only because of the fear of inappropriate behaviour that women and men were separated at one of the Temple ceremonies (m. Suk. 5:2 and m. Mid. 2:5). There is also no categorical evidence from archaeological discoveries that there were women's sections or galleries in the earliest synagogues. It seems that the rabbinic position about the role of women in Jewish liturgy is somewhat more lax than the approach taken by the geonic authorities in Islamic Mesopotamia.

Epigraphic evidence from Diaspora synagogues suggests that some communities would allow women to obtain certain honourable roles and titles in the synagogue (Levine 2000: 471–90). Titles referring to them as 'heads' or 'mothers' of synagogues are attached to the names of some women in inscriptions, and it has been suggested that such titles might betray functional and not merely honorific status (Brooten 1982 and Horbury 1999).

The matter of the role of mysticism in early Jewish prayer is also more complicated than some historians might assume. Jewish interest in the end of times, in angels, in the divine chariot (*merkavah*), in cosmology, and in apocalyptic visions is attested in the later books of the Hebrew Bible as well as in the Apocrypha and Pseudepigrapha and in numerous texts found at Qumran. During the first few centuries CE such mystical themes, as well as detailed speculation about the divine palaces (*hekhalot*), and the nature of the Godhead, became a major preoccupation of groups of Jewish mystics, who were possibly influenced by the Gnostic teachings then being disseminated among the intellectuals of the Christian and pagan worlds. It was among such groups that *hekhalot* hymns were composed. Most of the leading rabbinic teachers were at first ambivalent at best, and maybe even somewhat sceptical about the religious value and theological safety of such material (and of the use of magic in amulets), so that it is no surprise to find mystical traces absent from the prayer forms that were regarded as central in the first three centuries CE. Gradually, however, the evolving prayer book absorbed elements of such hymnology into its standard content, choosing only those parts that seemed less esoteric (and grotesque?), and to a degree sanitizing the content by placing it in fairly mundane contexts (Goetschel 1987; Schäfer 1992; Swartz 1992; Elior 2006; Alexander 2006).

One also has to take into consideration that the liturgy of the rabbinic period was hardly concerned about historical and chronological matters. A limited interest in such matters may have existed in the Land of Israel rather than in Babylonia, but it did not manifest itself to any significant degree in any of the rabbinic circles until the post-talmudic era. The biblical patriarchs receive only cursory note in the daily *Amidah* of the rabbinic period, Moses hardly appears at all in the Passover Haggadah, and the mention of David in the Babylonian version of the *Amidah* has more to do with eschatology than history. Similarly, historical events such as the Exodus from Egypt are included only as theological ciphers. But this situation changes in the later talmudic and early geonic periods, say, between the sixth and eighth centuries. By way of illustration, the later *Ge'ulah* ('Redemption') benediction lays a little more stress on God's rescue of the Israelites from Egypt and their praise of Him after the crossing of the Red Sea; the Hanukkah story becomes a little less concerned with a miracle involving oil and somewhat more with the victory of a few, weak but pious Jews over the numerous and strong but wicked Gentiles (Reif 2006b; Henshke 2007).

6. Late Antiquity

Other changes that occurred in the late talmudic and early geonic periods signify the onward evolution of Jewish liturgy, and not what Elbogen regarded as its medieval decadence (Elbogen 1993: 213). As talmudic authority grew and became more centralized from its Babylonian base, there was a growing tendency to lay down stricter liturgical guidelines, even in matters that had once been regarded as more peripheral. Prayer came to be centred more and more in the synagogue to the extent that rituals once performed in other places were transferred there. Prayers earlier regarded as individual and optional were added to the daily routine, so that it became the community that dictated to the congregant rather than important worshippers adding their personal contributions to the overall liturgy. The cycles of scriptural readings acquired a more formal structure, and the process of reciting them moved away from the didactic towards the ceremonial. Even targumic renderings and midrashic expositions which had once been educational in essence, acquired a more ritualized character (Reif 2006a: 181–84).

The basic framework of prayer, consisting of the *Shema* and the *Amidah*, was prefixed and suffixed by what began as introductory or concluding material, but ended up by being regarded almost as central as the framework itself. Among such appended items were collections of chapters from the Psalms and sets of supplicatory prayers and hymns, as well as verses and sayings praising the Torah and its study (Elbogen 1993: 66–76). One of the most important newcomers to the liturgy was the *Qedushah*. Although forms of joint human-angelic praise from earlier times are already attested at Qumran and the genre was apparently adopted and expanded among mystical circles in the Land of Israel, there is no doubt that by the period of late antiquity it had, perhaps not without considerable controversy, found more earnest champions for its adoption and broader use within the Babylonian centres. But the precise manner of its adoption within the rabbinic liturgy is unclear.

The same may be said for the *Qaddish*. This prayer, destined to become so famous for its later, medieval use in connection with the death of close relatives, has similarities in language to phrases found in Jewish and Christian sources that long predate the time of the redaction of the Talmuds. There is, however, no mention of it as a whole prayer in any rabbinic text, but merely of the one, albeit central, phrase *yehe sheme rabba mevorakh* ('May His great name be blessed': Sifre Deut 32:3, §306). Its language is also similar to that of targumic texts (Lehnardt 2002: 46–48). These factors indicate that its use in rabbinic liturgy is unlikely to have commenced before the completion of the Talmuds. It may have been meant to support the rabbinic view that both the present material world and the future world, destined to be introduced by the coming of the messiah, are relevant to Jewish religious thought and practice (Weitzman 2001).

6.1 Piyyutim

There was another Jewish liturgical development in late antiquity that made an even greater impact on the content and structure of rabbinic prayer. Whether or not inspired by the same cultural and religious factors that spawned the hymnography of the early Eastern churches, or indeed more directly influenced by it, the creation of liturgical poems (*piyyutim*) was a revolutionary development in Jewish worship. There are of course examples of earlier Jewish poetry in the Hebrew Bible, at Qumran, among the *hekhalot* mystics and, in fragmentary form, scattered in the Talmud and in some epigraphic material. It has even been suggested that the *selihot* and *hosha'not* (lyrical requests for forgiveness and salvation) mentioned in the Mishnah may have originated in Temple times (Heinemann 1977: 139–55). *Piyyut*, however, as composed in pre-Islamic Palestine by such figures as Yose ben Yose, Yannai and Eleazar Qallir, was undoubtedly a unique genre. Attached as it was to the synagogal reading of the Sabbath and festivals—much as were the targumim and midrashim—the poetry of these cantor-composers wove together biblical motifs, religious notions, historical personages and events, as well as rabbinic law and lore, and was inserted into various parts of the statutory liturgy (Shinan 2006). By way of an exalted style, alphabetic acrostics, metonymy, rhythm (and later rhyme), and the expansion of biblical Hebrew through a liberal coinage of novel linguistic forms, these poets provided fresh challenges for themselves as composers and for the worshippers in the synagogue.

Later explanations of the origins of the genre (such as by the eighth-century Jewish polemicist Pirqoi ben Baboi) refer to the banning of Jewish prayer in time of persecution and its replacement by *piyyutim*, but an inner literary dynamic seems historically more likely. Perhaps the tendency of the late talmudic period towards liturgical consistency and codification was robbing the Jewish worshipper of a capacity for innovation and creativity and the *piyyutim* provided an opportunity of rectifying this state of affairs. These poets and cantors were so successful that their work threatened to overshadow the central rabbinic prayers, and this led to opposition to *piyyutim* on the part of Babylonian rabbinic luminaries such as Yehudai Gaon of Sura in the mid-eighth century. Ultimately, compromises were made on both sides and, as so often in the history of Jewish liturgy, what had set out as an aggressive reaction or innovation subsequently became a part of the established prayer book. There is no doubt that the variations in the content and structure of the statutory prayers that occurred in the geonic period were at least partly motivated by the freshness brought to liturgical expression by the composers of *piyyutim* (Fleischer 1975: 7–113; Carmi 1981: 13–18; Weinberger 1998: 19–28; Levine 2000: 552–60).

6.2 The *Shema*

Although the *Shema* as it came to be used in the rabbinic period effectively constituted a rabbinic composition preceded and followed by rabbinic benedictions and utilizing three pentateuchal passages (Deut. 6:4–9 and 11:13–21, Num. 15:37–41), the background to that development is broader in context and somewhat more complicated. It consequently sheds general light on how the early rabbinic liturgy emerged and evolved. It also demonstrates some of the theological issues that drove that emergence and evolution. The first passage of the *Shema* stresses pure monotheism, devotion to God, education as a religious exercise and, like other parts of Deuteronomy, the framework is intense, didactic, and homiletic. The second passage includes similar items but is theologically more wide-ranging. It refers to serving as well as loving God, and promises reward for correct behaviour, and punishment for the opposite. The Talmud Yerushalmi records a difference of opinion between the rabbis Ḥanina and Ilai as to whether there is any essential difference between the two passages of the *Shema* (y. Ber. 2:1, 4a). The third passage deals with the "show" fringes and the reminder they provide of the need for observance and sanctity. It notes God's rescue of Israel from Egypt and the special relationship between Israel and God. Aspects of the content of these three passages are similar to parts of the Decalogue, but the latter has literary unity and a different style, lacking mention of a devoted relationship with God as well as the didactic aspect (Weinfeld 2001).

There are verses in the later books of the Hebrew Bible indicating that both the *Shema* and the Decalogue were regarded as having special religious significance (2 Kgs 23:25, Isa. 51:1–3, Jer. 32:39–41, Prov. 3:1–12; Jer. 7:9, Hos. 4:2, Ps. 50:7, 18–19, Ps. 81:10–11). They are also found together in the Nash Papyrus from about 200 BCE, and there are *tefillin* from Qumran that contain parts of the *Shema* and the Decalogue (XQ Phyl 1–4). Josephus, and perhaps Philo, refer to regular biblical readings that may well have been a form of the *Shema* (Reif 2006a: 112–17). The theological discussions recorded in Mark 12:28–34, 10:17–19 and Matthew 22:34–40 also testify to the special theological significance of both the *Shema* and the Decalogue. An early mishnaic text (m. Tamid 5.1) mentions both items in its reconstruction of the prayers once recited on the Temple Mount.

From other early tannaitic traditions it becomes clear that there was no unanimity amongst rabbis on the question as to whether the liturgical *Shema* originally consisted of one, two, or three passages, or perhaps even only the opening part of the first passage. It also emerges that early rabbis saw the recitation of the *Shema* as a declaration of their acceptance of the yoke of the kingdom of heaven that might in certain circumstances even demand martyrdom (Reif 2006a: 118–22). It is tempting to see this as a confident, religious response to a depressing, political situation. Rabbis also argued forcefully that the *Shema* was superior in religious content to the Decalogue and that there were good theological reasons for this preference.

In terms of liturgical development, it may be concluded that the *Shema* became almost the equivalent of a catechism for the rabbis. It was expanded and contextualized and a special way of reciting it, perhaps in a form of antiphony, together with the prayer leader, was adopted (Mekhilta de R. Ishmael on Exod. 15:1) Hence its growing centrality in the rabbinic liturgy. Perhaps even more dramatically, rabbinic liturgy took a phrase that may originally have read *barukh shem kevodo le-'olam va'ed* ('Blessed be His glorious name for ever') and, adding the word *malkhut* ('kingship'), inserted it between verses 4 and 5 in the first *Shema* passage. This constituted not only a categorical affirmation of the central theological significance of the *Shema* for recognizing God's kingship, but also a recognition that biblical texts could be treated as adjustable rabbinic liturgy rather than pure Scripture (Kimelman 2001; Reif 2006a: 118–24). An aggadic passage put it more colourfully, claiming that the angelic choir on high does not begin its praise of God until Israel has recited the *Shema* here below (Sifre Deut. 32:3, §306).

6.3 The *Amidah*

The *Amidah* ('standing [prayer]', also called *Ha-Tefillah*, 'The Prayer' par excellence, and *Shemoneh Esreh*, because of its eighteen daily benedictions) was recited in the morning and afternoon, but there was disagreement about its obligatory nature in the evening, and about the addition of a nineteenth benediction in early rabbinic times. This prayer is of an altogether different character from the *Shema*, and it is more likely to have originated in popular circles, where the benediction, both laudatory and imprecatory, was more a characteristic aspect of ordinary life than it was of the more intellectual circles of scribes or priests. Such benedictions (*berakhot*) were formalized in early rabbinic Judaism for the general praise of God, and were also recited before performing a religious obligation, in appreciation of physical enjoyment, and as an act of gratitude.

The rules in the Mishnah (m. Ber. 1–5) concerning when and how the *Shema* and the *Amidah* are to be recited also differ, again indicating their different origins, and there are talmudic discussions that contrast their religious status (y. Ber. 1:1, 2a–b). They were linked by the second-century CE rabbis, not because they had much in common, but because of the need to establish a more comprehensive framework for the daily prayers. The form and structure of each of the *Amidah's* benedictions are not consistent, and although the phraseology is close to Biblical Hebrew it also has elements of rabbinic language. The linguistic impression is that there has been some reworking of original formats, but not at any one time nor with any unified intent. The earliest parallels to the theology, phraseology and vocabulary, apart from those found in the Hebrew Bible, occur in Ben Sira 36 and 51, permitting the conclusion that such language and ideology was already circulating in Judaea in the second century BCE, without suggesting that there existed a proto-*Amidah* at that time (Heinemann 1977: 218–27 and Luger 2001).

The topics covered by the *Amidah* include reference to the biblical patriarchs, resurrection, sanctity, knowledge, repentance, pardon, redemption, healing, plentiful produce, end of exile and persecution, restoration of autonomy, removal of apostasy (possibly once aimed at Jewish Christians, cf. Horbury 1982), blessing of the righteous and of converts, Jerusalem and Davidic dynasty (either one or two benedictions), successful prayer, cultic restoration, thanksgiving, and peace (including the priestly benediction for peace). The first and last three benedictions were also part of the Sabbath and festival *Amidot*, which had day-specific central benedictions that were fewer in number. The available evidence has not yet allowed scholars to clarify whether the daily *Amidah*, with its mundane content, is older or younger than the Sabbath and festival *Amidot*, which avoid such content and restrict themselves to praising God, noting his special gift to Israel of the holy days.

The introductory and concluding benedictions obviously reflect specific rabbinic theology, the first three stressing the special link with the patriarchs, the belief in an after-life and the requirement to acknowledge the holiness of God, while the last three pray for the restoration of the Temple, make the theological point that everything that God does is good and has to be gratefully received, and long for a divinely inspired peace (Elbogen 1993: 24–54; Fleischer 1993). The rabbis' need to justify the centrality of the *Amidah* becomes evident by their anxiety to link it with the patriarchs, the prophets, the legendary leaders of the Jewish people in early Second Temple times ('Men of the Great Assembly'), and with the Temple service, thus according it a respectable pedigree (y. Ber. 2:4, 4d; y. Ber. 4:5, 8c; b. Ber. 26b; b. Ber. 33a). A tradition attributed to the late third century CE rabbi Samuel ben Naḥman regards its recitation at the beginning, middle, and end of the day as a simple reflection of the natural cycle (y. Ber. 4:1, 7a).

7. HISTORICAL ANALYSIS

The historical analysis of Jewish liturgical developments in Roman Palestine begins with the proponents of the scientific and critical study of Judaism (*Wissenschaft des Judentums*) who flourished mainly in central Europe in the nineteenth century. Leopold Zunz (1859) set the tone with his studies of liturgical poetry and the use of the homily, while Moritz Steinschneider (1857) dealt with the literary and bibliographical history, and Seligmann Baer (1868) and Ze'ev Jawitz (1910, 1922) offered important philological insights into the textual history of the prayers.

Detailed analysis of the developments of prayers over time and the examination of their respective historical contexts were not, however, undertaken until Ismar Elbogen produced his comprehensive study of the whole topic early in the twentieth century (republished 1993). He paid attention to non-rabbinic sources, pointed to the distinctions between Palestine and Babylonia, and was among the first to make use of the liturgical material from the Cairo Genizah, most of which had been brought to Cambridge and first studied by Solomon Schechter (1898). Elbogen was sympathetic to contemporary liturgical reform, had an antipathy towards mysticism, and an unwillingness to recognize medieval liturgical achievements.

In the period between the two world wars, Louis Finkelstein (1925, 1928–29) attempted, not altogether convincingly, to date the early forms of the *Amidah* and the Grace After Meals well before the Christian period, and Jacob Mann (1925) pioneered research into the earliest known Palestinian rites by way of the Genizah discoveries. A useful, if popular, contribution was made by Abraham Zvi Idelsohn (1932) with his summary of what scholars had demonstrates until his time, and the attention he paid to the Jewish liturgical connections with Christianity, Karaism, Kabbalah, and poetry.

From the middle of the twentieth century onwards, one can distinguish two main trends in the study of Jewish prayer and liturgy: one was to publish the various manuscript readings that shed light on the earliest liturgical rites of the post-talmudic period, as was done by Ernst Daniel Goldschmidt (1969) and Naphtali Wieder (1998); the other was to concentrate on the overall historical and literary development of the prayers, as championed by Joseph Heinemann (1977). Heinemann argued that the variety of texts found in the Genizah demonstrate that there was never one standard text, even in the early rabbinic period. Ezra Fleischer (1975, 1988), who also published and analysed many early manuscripts especially from the Genizah (and led the field in the study of *piyyutim*), challenged this view and argued that the early tannaitic Rabban Gamaliel had already established a formalized liturgy, that the annual lectionary cycle was followed in the Land of Israel in the first centuries CE, and that the Genizah evidence points to the revolutionary changes made by cantor-poets rather than to earlier variations. Of importance for the topic in recent decades have been the historical and textual surveys by Stefan Reif (1991, 1993, 2006a), the close analysis of the Qumran tests by Moshe Weinfeld (2004), Esther Chazon (1998), and Daniel Falk (1998), the extensive series of publications relating to the connections between early Christianity and rabbinic Judaism by Paul Bradshaw and Larry Hoffman (1991–98), and the historical and textual reconstructions of Tzvee Zahavy (1987, 1989). Fresh insights have been provided by Peter Schäfer (1992) and Rachel Elior (2006) into mystical ideas and compositions; important data about the role of women has been collected by Bernadette Brooten (1982), Avraham Weiss (1990), Judith Baskin

(1991), Susan Grossman and Rivka Haut (1992), and William Horbury (1999); the study of the early history of the synagogue has received an impressive boost from Lee Levine (2000) and Uri Ehrlich (2004) has completed an innovative study of physical movement in early rabbinic prayer. Robert Brody (1998) has illuminated various aspects of geonic activity, and Joseph Tabory (1992–93) has compiled indispensable bibliographies, while Ruth Langer and Steve Fine (2005) have promoted the subject in numerous other ways.

The developments of recent decades indicate a more intensive interest in the topic of early rabbinic prayer than ever before, and point the direction to be taken in future work. Perhaps the most significant element in the liturgical research of the early twenty-first century is the recognition that it has to be a multi-disciplinary effort. Among the future aims of such an effort will be the better understanding of the *Amidah's* textual history, describing and classifying all the liturgical fragments from the Cairo Genizah, tracing the changes of linguistic and literary styles from the late talmudic age to the early medieval period, and assessing the degree of influence exercised by liturgical poetry on the statutory prayers.

Suggested Reading

Students wishing to acquaint themselves with the overall situation by way of volumes in English should consult the works of Elbogen (1993), Heinemann (1977), Reif (1993, 2006a), Chazon (1998), and Bradshaw/Hoffman (1991–98) as listed in the bibliography.

Bibliography

ALEXANDER, P. S. (1988). 'Jewish Aramaic Translations of Hebrew Scriptures', in *Mikra. Text, Translation, Reading and Interpretation of the Hebrew Bible in Ancient Judaism and Early Christianity*, ed. M. J. Mulder. Assen and Philadelphia: Van Gorcum and Fortress, 217–53.

—— (2006). *The Mystical Texts: Songs of the Sabbath Sacrifice and Related Manuscripts*. London: T&T Clark.

BAER, S. (ed.) (1868). *Seder Avodat Yisrael* [Hebr.]. Rödelheim. Lehrberger.

BASKIN, J. R. (ed.) (1991). *Jewish Women in Historical Perspective*. Detroit: Wayne State University Press.

BOKSER, B. M. (1984). *The Origins of the Seder: The Passover Rite and Early Rabbinic Judaism*. Berkeley: University of California Press.

BRADSHAW, P. F./HOFFMAN, L. A. (eds) (1991–98). *Two Liturgical Traditions*, 6 vols. Notre Dame: Notre Dame University Press.

BREUER, Y. (2006). 'Aramaic in Late Antiquity', in *The Cambridge History of Judaism*, vol. 4, ed. S. T. Katz. Cambridge: Cambridge University Press, 457–91.

BRODY, R. (1998). *The Geonim of Babylonia and the Shaping of Medieval Jewish Culture*. New Haven: Yale University Press.

—— (2006). 'Liturgical Uses of the Book of Psalms in the Geonic Period', in *Prayers That Cite Scripture*, ed. J. L. Kugel. Cambridge: Harvard University Press, 61–81.

BROOTEN, B. J. (1982). *Women Leaders in the Ancient Synagogue*. Chico: Scholars Press.

CARMI, T. (ed.) (1981). *The Penguin Book of Hebrew Verse*. Harmondsworth: Penguin.

CHAZON, E. G. (1998). 'Hymns and Prayers in the Dead Sea Scrolls', in *The Dead Sea Scrolls after Fifty Years: A Comprehensive Assessment*, vol. 1, eds P. W. Flint and J. C. VanderKam. Leiden: Brill, 244–70.

EHRLICH, U. (2004). *The Nonverbal Language of Prayer: A New Approach to Jewish Liturgy*. Tübingen: Mohr-Siebeck.

ELBOGEN, I. (1993). *Jewish Liturgy: A Comprehensive History*. Philadelphia, New York and Jerusalem: Jewish Publication Society and Jewish Theological Seminary of America.

ELIOR, R. (2006). 'Early Forms of Jewish Mysticism', in *The Cambridge History of Judaism*, vol. 4, ed. S. T. Katz. Cambridge: Cambridge University Press, 749–91.

ELMAN Y./GERSHONI, I. (2000). *Transmitting Jewish Traditions: Orality, Textuality and Cultural Diffusion*. New Haven: Yale University Press.

FALK, D. (1998). *Daily, Sabbath and Festival Prayers in the Dead Sea Scrolls*. Leiden: Brill.

FINKELSTEIN, L. (1925). 'The Development of the Amidah'. *Jewish Quarterly Review* N.S. 16: 1–43, 127–70.

—— (1928–29). 'The Birkat Ha-Mazon'. *Jewish Quarterly Review* N.S. 19: 211–62.

FISHBANE, M. (1988). 'Use, Authority and Interpretation of Mikra at Qumran', in *Mikra: Text, Translation, Reading and Interpretation of the Hebrew Bible in Ancient Judaism and Early Christianity*, ed. M. J. Mulder. Assen and Philadelphia: Van Gorcum and Fortress, 339–77.

FLEISCHER, E. (1975). *Hebrew Liturgical Poetry in the Middle Ages* [Hebr.]. Jerusalem: Keter.

—— (1988). *Eretz Israel Prayer and Prayer Rituals as Portrayed in the Geniza Documents* [Hebr.]. Jerusalem: Magnes.

—— (1990). 'On the Beginnings of Obligatory Jewish Prayer' [Hebr.]. *Tarbiz* 59: 397–441.

—— (1991). 'Rejoinder to Dr Reif's Remarks' [Hebr.]. *Tarbiz* 60: 683–88.

—— (1993). 'The *Shemone Esre*—Its Character, Internal Order, Content and Goals' [Hebr.]. *Tarbiz* 62: 179–223.

GOETSCHEL R. (ed.) (1987). *Prière, Mystique et Judaïsme: Colloque de Strasbourg (10–12 Septembre 1984)*. Paris: Presses Universitaires de France.

GOLDSCHMIDT, E. D. (1969). *The Passover Haggadah: Its Sources and History* [Hebr.]. Jerusalem: Bialik.

GREENBERG, M. (1983). *Biblical Prose Prayer as a Window to the Popular Religion of Ancient Israel*. Berkeley: Univerity of California Press.

GROSSMAN, S./HAUT, R. (eds) (1992). *Daughters of the King: Women and the Synagogue* Philadelphia: Jewish Publication Society.

HEINEMANN, J. (1977). *Prayer in the Talmud: Forms and Patterns*. Berlin: de Gruyter.

HENSHKE, D. (2007). '"The Lord Brought Us Forth from Egypt": On the Absence of Moses in the Passover Haggadah'. *Association of Jewish Studies Review* 31: 61–73.

HEZSER, C. (2001). *Jewish Literacy in Roman Palestine*. Tübingen: Mohr Siebeck.

HOFFMAN, L. A. (1979). *The Canonization of the Synagogue Service*. Notre Dame. University of Notre Dame Press.

HORBURY, W. (1982). 'The Benediction of the Minim and Early Jewish-Christian Controversy'. *Journal of Theological Studies* 33: 19–61.

—— (1999). 'Women in the Synagogue', in *The Cambridge History of Judaism*, vol. 3, eds W. Horbury, W. D. Davies and J. Sturdy. Cambridge: Cambridge University Press, 358–401.

HORST, P. VAN DER (2002). *Japheth in the Tents of Shem: Studies on Jewish Hellenism in Antiquity*. Leuven: Peeters.

IDELSOHN, A. Z. (1932). *Jewish Liturgy and Its Development*. New York: Holt, Reinhart and Winston.

JAFFEE, M. S. (2001). *Torah in the Mouth: Writing and Oral Tradition in Palestinian Judaism, 200 BCE–400 CE*. Oxford: Oxford University Press.

JAWITZ, Z. W. (1910). *Die Liturgie des Siddur und ihre Entwicklung nach den Urquellen untersucht und systematisch geordnet*. Berlin: Itzkowski.

—— (1922). *Siddur: Service of the Heart* [Hebr.]. Berlin: Itzkowski.

KASHER, R. (1988). 'The Interpretation of Scripture in Rabbinic Literature', in *Mikra: Text, Translation, Reading and Interpretation of the Hebrew Bible in Ancient Judaism and Early Christianity*, ed. M. J. Mulder. Assen and Philadelphia: Van Gorcum and Fortress, 547–94.

KIMELMAN, R. (2001). 'The *Shema* Liturgy: From Covenant Ceremony to Coronation', in *Knishta: Studies of the Synagogue World*, vol. 1, ed. J. Tabory. Ramat-Gan: Bar-Ilan University Press, 9–105.

KNOHL, I. (1995). *The Sanctuary of Silence: The Priestly Torah and the Holiness School*. Minneapolis: Fortress.

LANGER, R./FINE, S. (eds) (2005). *Liturgy in the Life of the Synagogue: Studies in the History of Jewish Prayer*. Winona Lake: Eisenbrauns.

LEHNARDT., A. (2002). *Qaddish: Untersuchungen zur Enstehung und Rezeption eines rabbinischen Gebetes*. Tübingen: Mohr-Siebeck.

LEVINE, L. I. (2000). *The Ancient Synagogue: The First Thousand Years*. New Haven: Yale University Press.

—— (2006). 'Jewish Archaeology in Late Antiquity: Art, Architecture, and Inscriptions', in *The Cambridge History of Judaism*, vol. 4, ed. S. T. Katz. Cambridge: Cambridge University Press, 519–555.

LIEBERMAN, S. (1965). *Greek In Jewish Palestine. Studies in the Life and Manners of Jewish Palestine in the II-IV Centuries C.E.* 2nd edition. New York: Feldheim.

LINDER, A. (2006). 'The Legal Status of the Jews in the Roman Empire', in *The Cambridge History of Judaism*, vol. 4, ed. S. T. Katz. Cambridge: Cambridge University Press, 128–73.

LUGER, Y. (2001). *The Weekday Amidah in the Cairo Genizah* [Hebr.]. Jerusalem: Orhot.

MANN. J. (1925). 'Genizah Fragments of the Palestinian Order of Service'. *Hebrew Union College Annual* 2: 269–338.

MINTZ, A. (1984). 'Prayer and the Prayerbook', in *Back to the Sources: Reading the Classic Jewish Texts*, ed. B. W. Holtz. New York: Summit Books, 403–29.

NITZAN, B. (1994). *Qumran Prayer and Religious Poetry*. Leiden: Brill.

PERROT, C. (1988). 'The Reading of the Bible in the Ancient Synagogue', in *Mikra: Text, Translation, Reading and Interpretation of the Hebrew Bible in Ancient Judaism and Early Christianity*, ed. M. J. Mulder. Assen and Philadelphia: Van Gorcum and Fortress, 137–59.

REIF, S. C. (1991). 'On the Earliest Development of Jewish Prayer' [Hebr.]. *Tarbiz* 60: 677–81.

—— (1993). *Judaism and Hebrew Prayer: New Perspectives on Jewish Liturgical History.* Cambridge: Cambridge University Press.

—— (1999). 'The Genizah and Jewish Liturgy: Past Achievements and a Current Project'. *Medieval Encounters* 5: 29–45.

—— (2000). *A Jewish Archive from Old Cairo: The History of Cambridge University's Genizah Collection.* Richmond: Curzon.

—— (2004). 'Prayer in Early Judaism', in *Deuterocanonical and Cognate Literature. Yearbook 2004: Prayer from Tobit to Qumran*, eds R. Egger-Wenzel and J. Corley. Berlin: de Gruyter, 439–64.

—— (2006a). *Problems with Prayers: Studies in the Textual History of Early Rabbinic Liturgy.* Berlin: de Gruyter.

—— (2006b). 'The Function of History in Early Rabbinic Liturgy', in *Deuterocanonical and Cognate Literature. Yearbook 2006: How Israel's Later Authors Viewed its Earlier History*, eds N. Calduch-Benages and J. Liesen. Berlin: de Gruyter, 321–39.

ROTH-GERSON, L. (1987). *The Greek Inscriptions from the Synagogues in Eretz-Israel.* Jerusalem: Ben-Zvi.

SCHÄFER, P. (1992). *The Hidden and the Manifest God: Some Major Themes in Early Jewish Mysticism.* Albany: State University of New York Press.

SCHECHTER, S. (1898). 'Genizah Specimens: Liturgy'. *Jewish Quarterly Review* 10: 654–59.

SCHULLER, E. (2004). 'Prayer at Qumran', in *Deuterocanonical and Cognate Literature. Yearbook 2004: Prayer from Tobit to Qumran*, eds R. Egger-Wenzel and J. Corley. Berlin: de Gruyter, 411–28.

SCHWARTZ, J. (2006). 'The Material Realities of Jewish Life in the Land of Israel, c. 235–638', in *The Cambridge History of Judaism*, vol. 4, ed. S. T. Katz. Cambridge: Cambridge University Press, 431–56.

SCHWARTZ, S. (2006). 'Political, Social and Economic Life in the Land of Israel, c. 66–235', in *The Cambridge History of Judaism*, vol. 4, ed. S. T. Katz. Cambridge: Cambridge University Press, 23–52.

SHINAN, A. (2006). 'The Late Midrashic, Paytanic, and Targumic Literature', in *The Cambridge History of Judaism*, vol. 4, ed. S. T. Katz. Cambridge: Cambridge University Press, 678–98.

STEINSCHNEIDER, M. (1857). *Jewish Literature from the Eighth to the Eighteenth Century.* London: Longman, Brown, Green, Longmans and Roberts.

SWARTZ, M. D. (1992). *Mystical Prayer in Ancient Judaism: An Analysis of* Ma 'aseh Merkavah. Tübingen: Mohr-Siebeck.

TABORY, J. (1992–93). *Jewish Prayer and the Yearly Cycle: A List of Articles.* Supplement to *Kiryat Sefer* 64. Jerusalem: Jewish National and University Library.

WEINBERGER, L. J. (1998). *Jewish Hymnography: A Literary History.* London: Littman.

WEINFELD, M. (2001). *The Decalogue and the Recitation of the Shema: The Development of the Confessions* [Hebr.]. Tel Aviv: Hakibbutz Hameuchad.

—— (2004). *Early Jewish Liturgy: From Psalms to the Prayers in Qumran and Rabbinic Literature* [Hebr.]. Jerusalem: Magnes.

WEISS, A. (1990). *Women at Prayer: A Halakhic Analysis of Women's Prayer Groups.* Hoboken: Ktav.

WEITZMAN, M. (2001). 'The Origin of the *Qaddish*', in *Hebrew Scholarship and the Medieval World*, ed. N. de Lange. Cambridge: Cambridge University Press, 131–37.

WIEDER, N. (1998). *The Formation of Jewish Liturgy in the East and the West* [Hebr.], 2 vols. Jerusalem: Ben-Zvi.

ZAHAVY, T. (1987). *The Mishnaic Law of Blessings and Prayers*. Atlanta: Scholars Press.

—— (1989). 'Three Stages in the Development of Early Rabbinic Prayer', in *From Ancient Israel to Modern Judaism: Intellect in Quest of Understanding. Essays in Honor of Marvin Fox*, vol. 1, eds J. Neusner, E. S. Frerichs and N. M. Sarna. Atlanta: Scholars Press, 233–65.

ZUNZ, L. (1859). *Der Ritus des synagogalen Gottesdienstes geschichtlich entwickelt*. Berlin: Springer.

CHAPTER 30

SABBATH AND FESTIVALS

LUTZ DOERING

1. INTRODUCTION

The observance of the Sabbath and the festivals involves recurring Jewish ritual praxis which relates to 'time' as structured by the annual calendar and the seven-day week. Due to their religious significance, these days and seasons enable a communal, holistic experience of covenantal identity. On each of these holidays ritual practice can take place in two or more of the following realms: the Temple, the home, the synagogue, and the open space. The specific religious rites and customs which Jewish tradition associated with these locales, as well as the actors involved, vary according to the nature of the holiday, and bestow it with a distinctive character. After the destruction of the Temple in 70 CE, some elements of the holiday rituals were modified and transferred to the synagogue (Stökl 2007).

In terms of methodology, ritual theory developed by social anthropologists is a very useful approach for researching Sabbath and festivals (Bell 1992), since it allows scholars to analyse religious consciousness and (public) behaviour culminating on these days (Stökl 2003: 1–2, 6–7; cf. Bell 1997: 120–8). At the same time, the specific character of the sources requires us to take the intrinsic logic and rhetoric of rabbinic halakhah and other ancient Jewish texts into account. More recently, the gendered rhetoric of rabbinic discourse on festivals has been examined in the light of ritual theory (Lehman 2006; cf. Ilan 2008, the first volume of a feminist commentary on the Order of Festivals of the Babylonian Talmud).

Attention must be paid to the literary-historical development of the rabbinic material (for the Mishnah cf. Neusner 1983) and to differences between rabbinic documents. An approach which is exclusively, or mainly, based on literary sources should be replaced by a cautious and critical use of all relevant types of evidence, including papyri, inscriptions, and occasionally artefacts.

2. THE SABBATH

The Sabbath may be considered a festival day *sui generis* due to its weekly recurrence. In this form it is attested from around the time of the Babylonian Exile onwards. In biblical texts dated to that time, 'Sabbath' and 'seventh day' are identified (e.g. in the Decalogue: Exod. 20:8–11; Deut. 5:12–15). Although its prehistory is debated, the weekly Sabbath is Israel's unique contribution to the structuring of time. The priestly strata of the Pentateuch present this holiday as the culmination of the week of creation (Gen. 2:2–3; Exod. 20:11; 31:17). The biblical association of the Sabbath with creation lent later Sabbath observance an element of *imitatio dei* (*et angelorum*), as witnessed, for example, in Jubilees 2:17–24 (Doering 1997: 185–8), the Songs of the Sabbath Sacrifice found at Qumran and Masada, and the rabbinic *Qedushah* (Newsom 1985: 20–1).

The Sabbath enjoys special prominence in the 364-day calendar as attested by several ancient Jewish sources, such as 1 Enoch 72–82, the Qumran Temple Scroll, calendar texts from Qumran, and Jubilees (Albani 1997: 119). The structure of this calendar is 'sabbatical', the year consisting of fifty-two complete weeks, with virtually no overlap of any of the annual festivals with the Sabbath. Matters are different with the lunisolar calendar which was adopted by most Jews in late Hellenistic and Roman Palestine. In this calendar, festival dates may coincide with the Sabbath and collide with its observance, so that it is difficult to determine whether certain festival activities override the Sabbath.

2.1 Abstention from Work

One of the hallmarks of Sabbath observance is abstention from work. The biblical Sabbath commandment prohibits 'labour' (*melakhah*, cf. Exod. 20:10; Deut 5:14), but the Bible does not define this term, and only a few actions are specifically mentioned as forbidden, such as ploughing and harvesting (Exod. 34:21), lighting fires (35:3), gathering wood (Num. 15:32–6), carrying burdens (Jer. 17:19–27; Neh. 13:15), or doing business (Isa. 58:13; Neh. 10:32; 13:15–22). Some of these biblical references are highly enigmatic and invite interpretation, such as the expression 'speaking a word' (Isa. 58:13) or the instruction, 'each of you stay where you are; no one may leave his place on the seventh day' (Exod. 19:29).

For the study of post- and extra-biblical Sabbath law, legal-historical comparison has been the dominant research approach (Schiffman 1975; Doering 1999; assessment in Doering 2006). One of the results of these studies is the appreciation of variegation in practices. While most ancient Jews probably observed the Sabbath commandment in one way or another, there was no uniform way of doing so. Practices seem to have differed in connection with marital sex, the saving of human life, warfare, fasting, and the distance one was allowed to walk on the Sabbath. Strict legislation, such as that represented by the Book of Jubilees (mid-2nd c. BCE), inflicts punishment on certain activities without differentiation or exception (Jubilees 2:24–33; 50:6–13; Doering 1997), including those which later rabbinic halakhah considers merely derivative (such as drawing water) or not prohibited at all (such as sex or [defensive] warfare).

In Jubilees the default punishment for such transgressions is death, but we do not know whether this reflects legal reality or is merely rhetorical. The Sabbath law of the Damascus Document (CD 10:14–11:18) and other fragments from Qumran (4Q251, 4Q265, 4Q264a, 4Q421, ed. Baumgarten et al. 1999, for the latter two cf. Noam/Qimron 2009, with extensive reconstructions) shows a similar approach, albeit with traces of differentiation. In CD 12:3–6 the limited punishment of a seven-year custody is imposed on transgressors of the Sabbath laws, and in CD 10:21 and 11:5–6 the Sabbath limit is set at 1,000 cubits (500–550 yards) for humans and 2,000 cubits for grazing cattle. Although the use of any tools is forbidden on the Sabbath, one may employ one's garment in rescuing a person from a water-hole, thereby showing concern for human life in danger whilst avoiding a breach of the Sabbath (CD 11:16–17; 4Q265 6 6–7; Doering 1999: 201–4, 232–5). Nevertheless, this is a far cry from the later rabbinic rule that saving a human life *overrides* the Sabbath. Any act of carrying objects into or out of a house is forbidden in the Qumran texts (CD 11:7–11; 4Q251 1–2 4–5; 4Q265 6 4–5) as it is in the later Mishnah, but the Mishnah makes interesting concessions to those who perform the act together and thereby incur no liability (M. Shab. 1:1). Some of the Qumran references to the Sabbath are concerned with issues of ritual purity (e.g. purification before the Sabbath; no voluntary 'intermingling', which may—also—refer to sexual activities; cf. Doering 2000).

In their Palestinian narrative setting, the New Testament Gospels suggest that plucking grain (Mark 2:23–4) and curing diseases that are not life-threatening on the Sabbath (ibid. 3:2) were considered impermissible by 'the Pharisees' (cf. Doering 2010). Fleeing on the Sabbath would have been considered undesirable by some (Matt. 24:20, apparently reflecting concerns of at least some of the implied readers), carrying burdens was clearly deemed forbidden by others (John 5:10). The Passion and Resurrection narratives show awareness that burials, and the purchase of cloth and spices, should not happen on the Sabbath (Mark 15:42–46; 16:1; Luke 23:56).

Jesus' arguments to justify his healing of the man with the withered hand on the Sabbath affirm that the Temple service (Matt. 12:5) and circumcision (John 7:22–23) may override the Sabbath. Animals may be removed from a pit (Matt. 12:11–12; Luke 14:5; cf. the Roman ruling for *feriae*, Macrobius, Saturnalia 1.16.11; contrast CD 11:13–14; 4Q265 6 5–6; T. Shab. 14 [15]:3) and 'released' from the manger (M. Shab. 7:2 later prohibits untying knots). It should be noted, however, that it is unclear whether all of these statements actually originated in Palestine. Some of them may have been added in the process of redaction.

While Jesus and his early Christians followers apparently argued about the nature and observance of the Sabbath, other Jews in first-century Palestine seem to have been more straightforwardly pragmatic. On a series of ostraca (ed. Yardeni 1990, still under-researched), the despatching of goods such as fig-cakes or bread is recorded for certain days, of which the Sabbath is most frequently mentioned. This would apparently contradict the prohibition of carrying burdens on the Sabbath mentioned in some Jewish literary sources (see above; cf. Philo, De Migratione Abrahami 91). The script of the ostraca is the Hebrew square script typically used by Jews, and the language is close to the Jewish-Palestinian Aramaic of the Targumim, probably suggesting a Jewish writer and deliverer. These ostraca may provide evidence of Jews who gave precedence to economic concerns on the Sabbath (Doering 1999: 387–397; cf. the alleged practice of the Alexandrian 'extreme allegorists', Philo, De Migratione Abrahami 89–93).

We know surprisingly little about Pharisaic Sabbath halakhah. To be sure, Pharisees may have shared much of what writers such as Josephus or Philo report about Sabbath law, and they may even have championed some of these regulations in the first place. But our sources do not permit us to go much further than that. We know even less about the Sabbath law of the Sadducees (cf. Regev 2005: 59–90). According to the Gospels, the Pharisees considered the plucking of corn and the curing of non-life threatening diseases inadmissible on the Sabbath (see above). In the tannaitic controversies between the 'Boethusians' (related to, but perhaps not identical with, the 'Sadducees') and their counterparts (sometimes labelled 'Pharisees', sometimes not), the former oppose the cutting of the *'omer* in the night following the first day of Passover, which may coincide with the onset of the Sabbath, as well as the willow ceremony on the seventh day of Sukkot, if this is a Sabbath, because they did not consider these to 'override' the Sabbath (M. Men. 10:3; T. Suk. 3:1). Perhaps the opposite view was that of the Pharisees, although they are not mentioned in this connection. According to M. Er. 6:1–2, the (Pharisaic) family of R. Gamaliel participated in the *'eruv* (linking courtyards to allow carrying, see below), while Sadducees are portrayed as not accepting this legal fiction. The Houses of Hillel and Shammai, who may have been Pharisees (Ottenheijm 2004: 54–64), are portrayed in rabbinic sources as having engaged in a number of debates about the Sabbath. The most important of these debates allegedly dealt with work processes, such as soaking dye or drying flax in the oven, which were started on Fridays before the onset of the Sabbath. The Shammaites are said to have required all of these processes to be completed before the Sabbath started (M. Shab. 1:5–9; cf. Mekhilta Sh. Yitro, on Exod. 20:8; y. Shab. 1:8, 4a), although they apparently did not object to kindling Sabbath lamps, which continue to burn after the onset of the Sabbath (see below).

The changes brought about by the destruction of the Temple in 70 CE were not particularly radical for Sabbath observance: apart from the Sabbath burnt offering (Num. 28:9–10), which was discontinued at that time, the main realms in which Sabbath observance took place continued to be the house and the synagogue. Two letters of Bar Kokhba from the time of the Second Jewish Revolt against Rome seem to show awareness of Sabbath observance (P. Yadin 50, ed. Yadin et al. 2002: 287–92, concerning travel; Mur. 44, ed. Benoit et al. 1961: 161–3, apparently concerning transport of grain; cf. Oppenheimer 2005). Second-century CE documentary papyri from the border region between Judaea and Arabia never seem to be dated on a Sabbath, which some consider sufficient evidence of Sabbath observance amongst those who composed and/or wrote these documents (Katzoff/Schreiber 1998).

Although the Mishnah also continues earlier notions and traditions relating to the Sabbath (Gilat 1992: 32–108), it is innovative in offering relevant definitions and systematizations of what should be considered forbidden work (Cohen 2007: 134–8). M. Shab. 7:2 provides a list of thirty-nine prohibited 'principal categories of labour' ('avot melakhah), allegedly derived from the Torah, that are elsewhere further subdivided into different categories of 'labour'. This list focuses on the sphere of the household, farm, and workshop: The first eleven 'principal labours' are related to the production of bread, starting with ploughing and sowing, harvesting and binding sheaves, etc., and ending with baking; the next group is concerned with the production of clothing; a third one deals with the production of leather, beginning with hunting and slaughtering deer; this is followed by other 'principal labours', such as writing, building activities, lighting and extinguishing fires as well as carrying objects from one domain to the other.

In connection with carrying objects on the Sabbath, the concept of different 'domains' was invented by the rabbis, principally distinguishing between the 'private' and the 'public domain' (cf. the specifications in T. Shab. 1:1–2; Hezser 1998: 438–51). However, in order to be punishable, the act of carrying objects from one domain to another has to fulfil certain criteria: the entire action has to be performed by *one* individual (M. Shab. 1:1; 10:5), in a single act (10:2), in a regular way (10:3), and exceeding certain minimum quantities (ch. 8; 9:5–7). Punishment of offences against Sabbath laws of the Torah is clearly defined: a sin offering if the act was inadvertent (M. Sanh. 7:8; M. Shab. 7:1), and either 'eradication' by God (i.e. early childless death; Mekhilta Shabbta Ki tissa 1, on Exod. 31:14; M. Sanh. 7:8), or death by stoning if it was deliberate (M. Sanh. 7:4; T. Shab. 1:3), but the latter only if the act was witnessed and the culprit had been admonished, which reflects the rather theoretical nature of the rabbis' death penalty discourse here as elsewhere (cf. Shemesh 2003: 101–26; Berkowitz 2006).

The concept of domains was flexible enough to allow for the combination of shared urban areas such as courtyards—which had an ambiguous status, being neither 'private' nor 'public domain'—through the legal fiction of *'eruv hatserot*: by the deposit of a common meal, several courtyards are linked to form one 'private domain' within which carrying is allowed (Mishnah tractate Eruvin; T. Shab. 1:5; Fonrobert 2004: 71 calls the *'eruv* 'a concerted effort to formulate a theory of neighborhood'). A similar concept (*'eruv tehumin*) was applied to the general Sabbath limit (2,000 cubits; cf. M. Sot. 5:3), which could be doubled by designating a Sabbath abode at its end (cf. M. Er. 4:7–9).

Other prohibitions, which are sometimes already recorded indiscriminately in earlier Jewish sources, have been labelled by the rabbis *shevut*, often deemed a type of 'rabbinic' injunctions, and are not punishable at all. M. Betsa 5:2, though fraught with terminological problems, lists an array of activities such as climbing trees, riding, sitting in court, and betrothing. Even the prohibition of commerce on the Sabbath, which could be based on passages from the biblical Prophets and Writings (see above), is elsewhere treated as *shevut* (cf. Gilat 1992: 87–108). Generally, the handling of objects (in the private domain) on the Sabbath is governed by the complementary concepts of *mukhan* and *muqtseh* (the latter term is amoraic). Food to be handled and used on the Sabbath has to be 'prepared' beforehand (*mukhan*; cf. Exod. 16:5), but, in contrast to Second Temple sources anticipating this concept (Jubilees 2:29; 50:8; CD 10:22; cf. Josephus, Bell. 2.147), rabbinic texts allow human intention to play a major role in designating objects for use on the Sabbath (and festivals). The rabbinic concepts of *mukhan* and *muqtseh* are not limited to food; 'set aside' from use (*muqtseh*) is any object that 'has no permitted use on the Sabbath (e.g. a saw, a hammer)', or that has not been intended for use by its owner beforehand, or that 'did not yet exist or was not yet in one's possession on the eve of the Sabbath' (Cohen 2007: 136). The influence of early rabbinic Sabbath legislation on the Jewish public remains unclear. Most provisions 'can be understood as reflecting the private rules of a circle of masters with their disciples' (Goldenberg 1978: 260).

The use of Sabbath lights is attested for the Jewish Diaspora as early as the first century CE (Seneca, Ep. 95.47). In Palestine, Sabbath lamps were allowed to be kindled before the onset of the Sabbath and to continue burning throughout the holiday. Since oil was not allowed to be supplied on the Sabbath proper, sages debated about the types of oil reservoirs that could be used to allow the lamps to burn for a sufficiently long period (M. Shab. 2:4; y. Shab. 2:4, 5a). Archaeologists have claimed that some oil lamps and lampstands found in Palestine reflect a

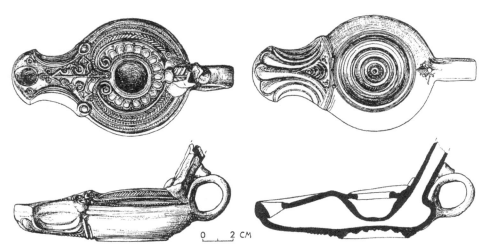

Fig. 30.1 Oil lamp with attached reservoir (Sabbath lamp?) from Hebron, 3rd–4th c. CE

Sussman 1970: 80. Courtesy of Israel Antiquities Authority

practice governed by such halakhic concerns (Hebron, 3rd–4th c.; Sussman 1970, see Fig. 30.1; Horvat ʿUzah, 4th c. CE; Eshel/Avshalom-Gorni 1996).

2.2 Sabbath Joy

The Sabbath is not only a day of abstention from work but also of joy (ʿoneg; cf. Isa. 58:13). Thus, according to a number of sources, fasting was forbidden (Jubilees 50:12; Judith 8:6; M. Ned. 9:6; y. Ned. 8:1, 40d; y. Taan. 3:13, 67a), and rabbis assume that usually three meals would have been eaten on that day (cf. M. Shab. 16:2; the exact number was debated: b. Shab. 117b). However, there is some evidence that in the western Diaspora Jews fasted on the Sabbath (as reported by Roman authors; cf. Williams 2004; Horbury 2004 on cena pura, eaten whilst it was still Friday). R. Eliezer, a Palestinian rabbi in the late first/early second c. CE, allegedly advocated fasting on the Sabbath, but pointed out that this was for the sake of Torah study only (b. Betsa 15b; b. Pes. 68b; cf. Gilat 1992: 109–22). Another feature of Sabbath joy, as promulgated by the rabbis, is engagement in marital sex (see the euphemistic reference to 'eating garlic', cf. M. Ned. 8:6; y. Meg. 4:1, 75a) during Sabbath night, a practice which Jewish pietists (Jubilees 50:8; b. Nid. 38a-b: 'early hassidim') and Samaritans (M. Ned. 3:10, emendation; cf. Safrai 1965: 23–4) allegedly prohibited. Rabbinic discourse on this topic may be viewed as 'covert polemic' against such pietists (Broshi 1992: 596). The beneficial nature of the Sabbath has also given rise to various eschatological hopes connected with its symbolic significance (Weiss 2003: 169–70 and *passim*).

2.3 The Sabbath as a Day of Study and Worship

In various ancient Jewish sources, the Sabbath is also portrayed as a day of study. Already in the Second Temple period we hear of Jews both in the Diaspora and in various Palestinian settings who assemble for teaching and study on the Sabbath, usually in the synagogue (for Palestine cf. Philo, Prob. 81–2: Essenes; Josephus, Bell. 2.289: Caesarea; Ant. 16.43; C. Ap. 2.175; further Mark 1:21; 3:1; 6:2; Luke 4:16–17; 13:10 etc.: Galilee). Most of these texts refer to the reading and interpretation of biblical books, particularly the Torah, although there is no clear evidence of a fixed reading cycle in pre-rabbinic sources. Whether fragments from Qumran (4Q251, 4Q264a, 4Q421) attest similar gatherings depends on one's respective reading and interpretation of these texts (Doering 1999: 246–8; Noam/Qimron 2009: 80–88 reconstruct *prohibitions* against private reading of certain books on the Sabbath, cf. M. Shab. 16:1; T. Shab. 13 [14]:1, but do not deny that the second reference in 4Q264a and 4Q421 seems to allow public reading and learning on the Sabbath).

Rabbinic texts provide further differentiations. Certain rabbis allegedly held special teaching sessions. We hear, for example, that R. Meir used to teach in the synagogue of Hammat Tiberias every Sabbath night (y. Sotah 1:4, 16d; Goldenberg 1978: 262 states that this was probably 'as a private holy man, not a public functionary'). The blessings for the sanctification of the Sabbath (*kiddush*), recited at its onset over a cup of wine, and the prayers for the distinction between the holy day and ordinary weekdays (*havdalah*) remained largely tied to domestic meals (which sometimes *preceded* the *kiddush:* T. Ber. 5:2), and occasionally also corporate dinners of associations (*havurot*; cf. M. Er. 6:6), although these seem to have been more frequent in the Diaspora (cf. Horbury 2004: 238–40; Klinghardt 1996: 258–67 speculates on common meals at the end of Sabbath services). The formulation of these prayers was already disputed amongst the houses of Hillel and Shammai (M. Ber. 8:1, 5).

Whereas some tannaitic sources are ambiguous about visits to the synagogue once the Sabbath has started (T. Ber. 5:3), prayer in the synagogue later became customary at the beginning and end of the holiday. Synagogue services on Sabbath mornings comprised the reading of the Torah and a series of blessings. Luke 4: 16–19 mentions a reading from the Prophets (later called *haftarah*). A triennial Torah reading cycle was adopted in the amoraic period. In earlier times there may have been an annual cycle, as in Babylonia (thus Fleischer 2003; others disagree). Furthermore, a series of seven blessings was recited during Sabbath and festival services. Of the seven blessings, the first three 'were praises of God; the fourth referred to the particular day, whether Sabbath or holiday; the fifth referred to the

Temple ritual; the sixth was a final blessing which expressed thanks to God; and the seventh was an appendix which included the priestly blessing of Israel' (Tabory 2006: 561). Notable is the doxological and non-petitionary character of the Sabbath prayers (y. Shab. 15:3, 15b; Lev. R. 34:16), a feature already attested by liturgical texts from Qumran (Chazon 1992–93; Falk 1998: 125–54), not all of them products of the sect. Although the issue is disputed amongst scholars (McKay 1994), it seems that already in Second Temple times the sabbatical gatherings of non-priestly Jews had the character of 'worship' (cf. Ps.-Philo, Liber Ant. Bibl. 11:8), not least because the Torah readings and interpretations had ceremonial implications (van der Horst 1999).

3. The Festivals

The term 'festival' (*moed*, also the name of the second order of the Mishnah and Talmud) is a general category comprising various days of different origin and character. While each festival has its own liturgical tradition, different types of festivals may also be distinguished from each other by the 'labour' prohibited on them. Before the destruction of the Temple some festivals were associated with pilgrimages to Jerusalem. The Pentateuch mentions the three pilgrimage festivals (*haggim*: Passover/Matsot, Shavuot, and Sukkot), as well as the first day of the seventh month ('Day of Sounding [the *shofar*]', later to become the New Year: Rosh Hashanah) and the tenth day of this month (Day of Atonement: Yom Kippur). The first and last day of Passover and Sukkot, as well as the other (one-day) festivals mentioned, are called 'holy convocation' (*miqra' qodesh*). They required additional offerings (*musaf*; cf. Num. 28–29) and carried a prohibition of labour (Lev. 23:8, 21, 25, 27–28, 35–36). Rabbis extended the permission to prepare food, which originally applied to Passover only (Exod. 12:16), to almost all other festivals (cf. M. Meg. 1:5), which should be celebrated with 'food and drink and clean garments' (Sifre Num. 147). The Day of Atonement was a fast day, however, which was preceded and followed by festive meals. Most of the other rabbinic provisions for the Sabbath applied to the festivals as well (M. Betsa 5:1–2).

Related to these festivals (cf. Num. 10:10) was the day of the new moon (*rosh hodesh*) which, within the framework of a lunisolar calendar, was originally proclaimed on the basis of the testimony of reliable witnesses (M. R.H. 2:5–7). Since the introduction of a permanent calendar in the fourth c. CE, this day has come to be merely announced in the synagogue on the preceding Sabbath. Labour was permitted, although women used to abstain from it (y. Taan. 1:6, 64c). On the intermediate days of Passover and Sukkot (*holo shel moed*, 'the profane [days] of the festival'), certain restrictions for work were imposed (see the Mishnah and Talmud tractate Moed Qatan). The tendency to use these days for leisurely activities rather than Torah study is criticized by rabbis (y. M.Q. 2:3, 81b). There were no binding labour restrictions for festivals of the Second Temple period such as Hanukkah or Purim, although some people apparently refrained from work on the latter (Tabory 2006: 568).

3.1 The Biblical Pilgrimage Festivals

3.1.1 *Passover*

Already in the biblical tradition the two originally independent festivals of Passover (cf. Exod. 12) and Matsot (cf. Exod. 23:15) were merged to form a unity (cf. Deut. 16:1–8; Lev. 23:5–8). Passover used to centre on the Temple, where animals (either lamb or kid: Exod. 12:5) were slaughtered on Passover eve (the 14th of Nisan), and on the domestic realm (in Jerusalem), where they were roasted and eaten during the night. In addition, on the seven days of the festival no leavened grain (*hamets*) might be used. In Temple times the function of the Passover sacrifice seems to have been apotropaic and community-enhancing rather than expiatory (Schlund 2005). According to Exod. 12:6, the slaughtering was scheduled to the 'twilight' hour. In the first century CE it seems to have taken place in the afternoon, 'between the ninth and the eleventh hour'; the slaughtering proper was performed by the leaders of parties between ten and twenty people in size sharing a sacrificial animal (Josephus, Bell. 6.423). The Mishnah states that the slaughtering was organized in three batches, and priests assisted with pouring the blood at the base of the altar (M. Pes. 5:5–7). In a famous debate, Hillel allegedly argued that, when the 14th of Nisan coincides with the Sabbath, the slaughtering of the Passover animal overrides the Sabbath commandment (T. Pes. 4:13–14; y. Pes. 6:1, 33a; b. Pes. 66a). The focus of Passover on the community is also indicated by the exclusion of any uncircumcised man from the meal (Exod. 12:43–49). In Temple times, the pilgrims who travelled to Jerusalem for the Passover festival had to purify themselves before they could deliver the sacrifice. They would therefore usually arrive in Jerusalem a week before the festival (Josephus, Bell. 6.290; cf. John 11:55; 12:1). Those who remained impure were deferred to the Second Passover a month later (Num 9; cf. M. Pes. 7:6; T. Pes. 8:10). The exclusion of women and minors from partaking of the animal in several texts from Qumran (11QT^a 17:8–9; 4Q265 3:3; cf. Jubilees 49:17) is a stringency, not shared by Josephus (Bell. 6.426) or rabbis (cf. M. Pes. 8:1), that is motivated by purity concerns. These texts also insist that the animal should be eaten in the Temple courtyards rather than at home (11QT^a ibid.; Jubilees 49:16–20; cf. Deut. 16:7).

Not much is known about domestic Passover practices and prayers in Temple times. The narrative of Jesus' last supper, presented as a Passover meal in the Synoptic Gospels, famously features food and drink typical of common meals, not Passover in particular. The evidence for domestic Passover celebrations in the Diaspora before 70 CE remains inconclusive, and it does not seem likely that any domestic liturgy existed which was modelled after Exod. 12 (Leonhard 2006: 15–72). Apparently, in Temple times, the Passover meal involved the eating of the lamb ('roasted over fire', Exod. 12:9; in clay ovens, according to M. Pes. 7:1–2), *maror* ('bitter herbs') and *matsah* (unleavened bread), as well as reciting the *Hallel* (Ps. 113–118; cf. Friedman 2002: 421–58).

After 70 CE the focus on sacrifice may have continued at first, as suggested by T. Pes. 10:12, a discussion of sacrificial laws, and M. Pes. 10:4, a reference to *roasted* meat resembling the sacrificial animal (*gedi mequlas*, 'roasted kid/lamb' [?], was banned later, cf. T. Betsa 2:15, probably for this very reason). The *seder* ('order') of the meal during Passover night in M. Pesahim chapter 10 re-invents Passover as a domestic festival independent of the Temple (Bokser 1984), adding the side dish of *haroset* (a fruit condiment), and requiring each participant to drink four cups of wine and to dip twice (Friedman 2002: 421–58).

Does the *Haggadah*, the 'narrative' recalling of the Exodus experience (evidenced by manuscripts from the early Middle Ages onwards), have any place in the early *seder*? Scholars are divided over this issue. While some scholars think that this element of remembrance was already part of the Passover ritual in some form before 70 CE (with the meal *preceding* the commemoration: Tabory 1999), others think that the *Haggadah* developed only after 70 CE, in dialogue and debate with the early Christians (Yuval 1999), or that it did not even receive a fixed form during the entire rabbinic period. According to the latter view, the famous question about the character of the holiday asked by the son ('Why is this night different from all [other] nights?', with the paternal answers referring to the specific elements of the meal: eating *matsah, maror*, roasted meat, and dipping twice, M. Pes. 10:4) served as a mere template in case the father and son were unable to engage in the commemorative 'table talk' appropriate for this night (Leonhard 2006: 88–9). In any case, the Mishnah assumes that the remembrance of the life and salvation of the Israelite ancestors in Egypt should start with Deut. 26:5 and close with the first part of the *Hallel* psalms, with the ritual meal and the rest of the *Hallel* following this commemoration (M. Pes. ibid.).

Connected to Passover is the *'omer* ceremony, which concerns the first sheaf of the new barley crop. According to Lev. 23:11, the *'omer* is to be waved 'on the day after the Sabbath'. While the adherents of the 364-day calendar thought that this text referred to the weekly Sabbath, the later rabbis and their precursors took 'Sabbath' to mean 'festival' here (Sifra Emor pereq 12:1, 100b). Thus, the sheaves were reaped after the first day of Passover had ended with nightfall, even on a Sabbath (see under 2.1 above). After the destruction of Temple the *'omer* day remained relevant for the permission of new grain and for determining the date of Shavuot.

3.1.2 *Shavuot*

This festival, which is called 'Weeks' (perhaps understood as *shevuot*, 'oaths', in Jubilees 6:10–11 and 29:7; cf. Eiss 1997: 165–6), follows seven weeks after the reaping and waving of the '*omer* (Lev. 23:15–16), that is, on the 50th day thereafter (cf. its Greek name *pentekoste*: Tobit 2:1; Josephus, Bell. 6.299; Acts 2:1), in the third month (Sivan). According to the calendar used by the rabbis, the date of this festival could coincide with any day of the week, whereas in the calendars of the Boethusians and the Qumran sectarians the festival always fell on a Sunday, like the '*omer* day. Marking the beginning of the wheat harvest, the festival concluded the period beginning with Passover, hence its alternative (Palestinian) name, 'Atseret, 'Conclusion' (of Passover) (M. Hal. 4:10; M. R.H. 1:2, etc.; cf. Josephus, Ant. 3.262). According to rabbinic opinion, new grain (*hadash*) of any kind was permitted 'in the country' after the '*omer* had been offered, but in the Temple wheat for meal offerings was permitted only from Shavuot onwards (M. Men. 10:6). The relevant ritual was the offering of the 'two loaves' of wheat bread, together with accompanying sacrifices (Lev. 23:16–20; Sifra Emor pereq 13, 101a–b).

   More generally, during Temple times, Shavuot was the festival of first fruits (*hag ha-bikkurim*, cf. Num. 28:26): people were allowed to bring their first fruits, from among the 'seven species' (Deut. 8:8: vine, fig tree, pomegranate, olive tree, honey, in addition to wheat and barley), to a priest in the Temple any time between then and Sukkot (M. Bik. 1:3; cf. Philo, Spec. Leg. 2.220). However, texts from Qumran preserve a more staggered sequence of seven-week periods, with individual first fruit festivals for barley (the day of the '*omer*), wheat (Shavuot), wine, and oil (11QT[a] 18–23; 4Q251 frg. 9, *olim* 5; cf. Baumgarten 1976). For the first two items, this schedule is corroborated by Philo, Spec. Leg. 2.179–80. This suggests different approaches to first fruits and their respective festivals in late Second Temple times.

   Further aspects of the Festival of Weeks are the commemoration of the covenant (cf. Ps.-Philo, Liber Ant. Bibl. 23:2) and of the giving of the Torah. Already in Jubilees 6:1–22, the context of Shavuot is God's covenant with Noah. Scholars have suggested that 1QS 1:16–2:25a refers to a ceremony of covenant renewal, celebrated by the Qumran *yahad* annually at the Festival of Weeks (Delcor 1976: 288–93). A fragment of the Damascus Document (4Q266 11 16–18; ed. Baumgarten 1996: 76–78) mentions within the concluding section of the document an assembly of 'the camps' 'in the third month', but does not give an exact date. One could further argue that Jubilees already suggests a link between the festival and the giving of the Torah (disputed by Eiss 1997: 175–6): The book is presented as a revelation to Moses, called onto the mountain on the 16th of the third month (Jubilees 1:1), the day *after* Shavuot in the calendar used by the authors of Jubilees, perhaps *following* the giving of the Torah, called 'the book of the *first* law' (Jubilees 6:22). However, it is only in rabbinic texts that Shavuot is *explicitly* called 'festival of Torah giving' (b. Pes. 68b; cf. Seder Olam Rabbah 5: ten commandments; on this day, Exod. 19 is supposed to be read: T. Meg. 4 [3]:5; y. Meg. 3:7, 74b), perhaps in an attempt to strengthen its significance, because the festival lacked a specific domestic ritual.

3.1.3 Sukkot

This festival, due to its importance, has attracted wide scholarly interest, with respect to both its history (Rubenstein 1995) and ideological implications (Ulfgard 1998). It starts on the 15th of the seventh month (Tishri) and lasts for seven days, on which an eighth day with its own character (Shemini 'Atseret) follows. The ancient importance of Sukkot is reflected in the fact that it became 'the Festival' par excellence (cf. Josephus, Ant. 8.100; 13.372; M. R.H. 1:2; Ulfgard 1998: 231–51). Its public character may have been partly responsible for this phenomenon, as well as the integration of popular rituals, originally focusing on the Temple. Apart from dwelling in booths (see below) and the prescription of a high number of sacrificial animals (Num. 29:12–38), we note the following rituals:

(1) The procession with the 'four species' (Lev. 23:40): a bundle consisting of a palm branch (*lulav*, also denoting the whole set), myrtle (*hadas*), and willow (*'aravah*) as well as citron (*'etrog*; cf. Josephus, Ant. 3.245; see Fig. 30.2). The branches were supposed to be 'shaken' in several directions during the recitation of Ps. 118 as part of the *Hallel* (M. Suk. 3:9), although other sources merely report the 'holding' of the *lulav* (Rubenstein 1995: 154–6).

(2) The willow ceremony: willow branches were erected at the sides of the altar, and while a simple circumambulation of the altar with the recitation of Ps. 118 took place on the first six days (not on Sabbaths), there was a sevenfold circuit on the seventh day, accompanied by the beating of branches (M. Suk. 4:5–6; Rubenstein 1995: 109 suggests that 'the normal prohibition banning non-priests from the inner temple precincts was suspended' at that time). The latter ceremony overrode the Sabbath (M. Suk. 4:3; but see above on the Boethusians' objection against this).

(3) The water libation: celebrating the beginning of the rainy season, the (high?) priest on all days of the festival (with modifications on the Sabbath) poured out water at the altar, which was drawn from the Siloam pool (M. Suk. 4:9–10; cf. John 7:37–8);

(4) A night-long joyous celebration in the Temple courtyards in preparation of the drawing of water on the next morning, with illuminations, music, and dance (*simhat bet ha-shoevah*: M. Suk. 5:1–5; T. Suk. 4:1–9).

Fig. 30.2 The 'four species' of Sukkot—closed palm frond, myrtle, and two willow branches, as well as the *'etrog*—on a coin from the second year of the Bar Kokhba revolt (133/4 CE)

Courtesy of Classical Numismatic Group, Inc.

Of these holiday rituals, the taking of the *lulav* and the recitation of the *Hallel* were transferred to the synagogue after 70 CE (M. Suk. 3:12: 'a memory of the Temple'), although a *procession* with the *lulav* is unattested before the geonic period (cf. Stökl 2007: 242–247, 254). A text from the Tosefta (T. Ber. 6:10) mentions that a blessing was recited when the *lulav* was taken, and according to a text from the Talmud Yerushalmi (y. Suk. 3:10, 53d) the *lulav* should be shaken thrice. An Aramaic letter by Bar Kokhba requests a sizable supply of the four species, and a related Greek letter orders 'wands and citrons' (P. Yadin 57 and 52; new ed.: Yadin et al. 2002: 322–8, 351–62). It has been suggested that Sukkot symbolism on coins from the Bar Kokhba period has eschatological overtones (Lapin 1993: 130–5).

Another feature of Sukkot which continued after 70 CE is the requirement of dwelling in booths (cf. Lev. 23:42). The booth (*sukkah*) is conceptually an impermanent home temporarily functioning as one's regular abode (cf. M. Suk. 2:9). Rabbinic texts discuss at length what constitutes a proper *sukkah* (M. Suk. 1:1–2:3) and which daily practices should be conducted in it (Sifra Emor pereq 17:5, 103a: eating, drinking, rejoicing, and bringing one's utensils there. For Palestinian rabbis and Babylonian ones before Rava, lack of resemblance with a permanent home was *not* decisive: Rubenstein 1993). Women, slaves, and minors were exempt from the duty of dwelling in the *sukkah* (M. Suk. 2:8), since they are exempt from all positive commandments governed by time (cf. M. Qid. 1:7). Because this rule is ignored in many other cases, such as observance of the Sabbath, which is binding on women as well, it has been suggested that the *sukkah* symbolizes 'a (potentially) ideal masculinized home, whose domestic activities and objects are maintained while its most commonplace element, the wife, is imagined to be absent' (Lehman 2006: 328; there is no explicit discourse on this issue in Palestinian sources, though).

3.2 Further Biblical Festivals

3.2.1 *New Year (Rosh Hashanah)*

Originally, the first day of the seventh month (Tishri) had been a day of rest and 'holy convocation', its only distinctive rite being the sounding of the *shofar* (Lev. 23:24; Num. 29:1). By the time of the Mishnah, however, it had acquired the role of New Year, and the notion of judgment was attached to it (M. R.H. 1:1–2; cf. already Ps.-Philo, Liber Ant. Bibl. 13:6). Additional benedictions, *zikhronot* (references to God as the one who remembers), *malkhuyyot* (references to God's kingship), and *shofarot* (references to the *shofar*), were introduced into the liturgy, and the *shofar* was sounded (M. R.H. 4:5–6). In antiquity, before the introduction of a calendar whose dates could be calculated, New Year depended on the testimony of reliable witnesses (of the new moon). The notion of a coherent ten-day period beginning with the New Year and ending with the Day of Atonement, known as the 'Days of Awe', developed in medieval times only.

3.2.2 *Day of Atonement (Yom Kippur)*

This festival, which takes place on the tenth day of the seventh month of the Jewish calendar (for its various names cf. Stökl 2003: 15–17) is characterized by atonement, fasting, and affliction. In Temple times, the high priest would administer a complex ritual outlined in Lev. 16. More details are provided in the Mishnah tractate Yoma, which contains a number of later rabbinic embellishments (Stökl 2003: 19–28). The priestly ritual for the Day of Atonement required a week-long preparation for the high priest (including his isolation, purification, and instruction). On the day itself he would bathe and put on white linen garments after the morning *tamid*; sacrifice a bull as a sin offering as well as a goat; enter the holy of holies three or four times, mentioning the ineffable Divine name and sprinkling the blood of these animals on the *kapporet* ('mercy seat'); send another goat as the symbolic 'scapegoat' for the community's sins into the desert after having laid hands on its head and delivered a collective confession; bathe again and change garments, then slaughter concluding sacrifices and the evening *tamid*. The Temple ritual and its various details had an enormous impact on theological imagination, both Jewish (cf. tractate Yoma in the Mishnah and Talmud) and Christian (cf. the Letter to the Hebrews in the New Testament).

Alongside this ritual, which was increasingly transformed 'from a one-man performance to one-man *show* with participation of the people' (Stökl 2003: 60), Jews would abstain from work and 'afflict themselves' (Lev. 16:29–31; 23:27–32; Num. 29:7). In M. Yoma 8:1 this biblically prescribed 'affliction' is interpreted as abstention from food, drink, sex, wearing of sandals, washing, and anointing. Elsewhere there is evidence of stricter self-punishments, but also of the notion of joy (cf. Stökl 2003: 34–5). These practices were continued after the destruction of the Temple. There were also specific prayers for the day, as already attested in Qumran texts (1Q34, 4Q508, 4Q509: all part of 'Festival Prayers'; Falk 1998: 156–61, 165–9 suggests non-sectarian provenance). During the course of the rabbinic period, the liturgy for the Day of Atonement was expanded: a special concluding prayer (*ne'ilah*), confessions, Torah readings concerned with the Day of Atonement and particularly the *seder 'avodah*, synagogal re-enactments of the atonement ritual and the high priest's 'three confessions with the responses of the people and the two countings that accompanied his sprinkling of the blood' (Stökl 2003: 59–60) were added.

3.3 Festivals Introduced in Second Temple Times

3.3.1 *Purim*

The festival of Purim originated in the (eastern) Diaspora and was introduced in the Land of Israel in the Hellenistic period. The Book of Esther relates how the Jews of Persia were saved from destruction on the basis of Esther and her uncle Mordecai's intervention and promulgates the festival of Purim as a commemoration of these events (Esther 9:20–32; cf. 2 Macc. 15:36: 'Mordecai's Day'). The absence of the Book of Esther from the Qumran texts may indicate resistance against the festival amongst those responsible for the writing and/or collection of the manuscripts (the book or similar traditions may nevertheless have been *known* at Qumran). As a possible reason for this resistance it has been suggested that the festival's usual date, the 14th of Adar, would always fall on a Sabbath in the 364-day calendar (VanderKam 1998: 384–5). Other Palestinian Jews would have adopted the festival, however. The colophon of the Septuagint version of Esther (Addition F 11) labels the book a 'Purim letter' and claims that it was translated by a member of the Jerusalem community and communicated to Egyptian Jews in the late second or first century BCE. Since the Jews of Susa (Shushan) celebrated the original feast on the 15th of Adar (Esth. 9:18), it has become customary to assign the annual festival to this date in 'cities walled since the days of Joshua' (M. Meg. 1:1; see y. Meg. 1:1, 70a for a reference to such places; note the unavailability of Jerusalem after 135 CE, cf. Hezser 2000).

In antiquity the main feature of Purim was the public reading of the Esther scroll (*megillah*), initially only during daylight hours (M. Meg. 2:4; T. Meg. 2:4), later also at night (y. Meg. 2:3, 73b). While the Mishnah (M. Meg. 2:4) seems to include women among those eligible to read from the *megillah*, the Tosefta (T. Meg. 2:7) explicitly exempts women from reading, and the Talmud Yerushalmi (y. Meg. 2:4, 73b) requires the text to be read out *to* women. Gifts are traditionally sent to the poor on this day (M. Meg. 1:3–4; cf. Esther 9:22). In a leap year, Purim is celebrated during the *second*, intercalated month of Adar (M. Meg. 1:4).

3.3.2 *Hanukkah*

This festival, commencing on the 25th of Kislev and commemorating the rededication of the Temple under Judah Maccabee in 164 BCE is first mentioned in 1–2 Maccabees, albeit with differences in detail. 1 Macc. (4:36–59) recounts how, after the cleansing of the Temple, Judah and his brothers resumed sacrifice on the 25th of Kislev, and celebrated the festival for eight days, while 2 Macc. (1:9, 18; 2:16; 10:5–6) has the cleansing happen on the 25th of Kislev and models Hanukkah as an eight-day festival after Sukkot (see 3.1.3 above).

The kindling of a set of eight candles would eventually become the major domestic ritual. According to Josephus, the festival's name was 'Lights', but he was not quite sure about the reason for this designation (Ant. 12.325). It has been suggested that Hanukkah became a festival of lights only in the time of Herod, when he combined the commemoration of his ascension to power (*Herodis... dies*: Persius, Satires 5.179–84? cf. Horbury 2003) with his rededication of the Temple (Benowitz 2003).

In rabbinic literature this holiday is only sparsely attested (see below, 3.3.3). A later passage in the Babylonian Talmud (b. Shab. 21b) mentions a debate between the Hillelites and Shammaites on the question whether to start with lighting one candle and increase the number daily or, conversely, reduce the number, starting with eight. In this connection the Talmud also tells the famous story of the small flacon of oil which was left untouched and miraculously burnt for eight days.

3.3.3 *The Festivals Mentioned in the Fast Scroll*

The Fast Scroll (Megillat Taanit; ed. Noam 2003), whose rabbinic name (M. Taan. 2:8) is somewhat misleading, is 'a list of about thirty-five dates drawn in Aramaic and arranged in calendar order. Its goal, as stated in its opening sentence, is to keep the Jews from fasting on "days on which miracles had been performed for Israel". On days commemorating especially important events [. . .] it was forbidden not only to fast, but even to eulogize the deceased' (Noam 2006: 339, quoting y. Taan. 2:13, 66a). Most of these dates relate to military victories (such as Nicanor's Day) and other favourable events (e.g. Hanukkah) in the Hasmonean period. Two are based on events mentioned in the Bible (e.g. Purim), and a few relate to the Roman era. It has been argued that 'the Scroll was written during the three decades preceding the fall of the Temple' (Noam 2006: 350), with possible references to the reigns of Trajan and Hadrian (ibid. 347) added later.

The Fast Scroll's authority was somewhat weakened in early rabbinic times. The dominant view was that communal fasts of several days should not be discontinued on Hanukkah and Purim (M. Taan. 2:10; T. Taan. 2:5). In the amoraic period the Scroll's halakhic validity was further challenged, although the prohibition to decree fasts on Hanukkah and Purim *proper* remained in force (y. Meg. 1:6, 70d). Nevertheless, the Scroll enjoyed further interest in the medieval period (see the scholion), and an external tractate of the Babylonian Talmud (Soferim 17:4) relates that in

Palestine the Fast of Esther was postponed until after Purim 'on account of Nicanor and his associates', suggesting that Nicanor's Day was still celebrated on the 13th of Adar (cf. 2 Macc. 15:36) in the geonic period.

3.4 Public Fasts

The last rubric to be discussed here are fast days (cf. Levine 2001). Apart from public fasts held on an irregular basis at times of enduring droughts (M. Taan. 1), Palestinian Jews observed a number of regular memorial fasts. Some of these fasts commemorated stages in the capture of Jerusalem and destruction of the First Temple by the Babylonians which were remembered after the destruction of the Second Temple: the 17th of Tammuz (breach of the city wall), the 9th of Av (destruction of the Temple), the 3rd of Tishri (murder of Gedaliah, Jer. 41:2), and the 10th of Tevet (beginning of the siege). In addition, the Fast of Esther was commemorated (see above). On Passover eve some Jews seem to have fasted because they were firstborn sons, others in order to save their appetite for the nightly meal (y. Pes. 10:1, 37b).

Suggested Reading
···

On Sabbath law and practice in ancient Judaism up to the early rabbinic period see Doering (1999); for Sabbath law in the Damascus Document as compared with other ancient Jewish sources see also Schiffman (1975). Neusner (1983) provides a discussion of mishnaic Sabbath and festival law, taking account of the development of subjects and organized chronologically according to periods of tannaitic activity. There are a number of good studies on individual festivals: Bokser (1984) and Leonhard (2006) on Passover, Rubenstein (1995) and Ulfgard (1998) on Sukkot, and Stökl (2003) on Yom Kippur.

Bibliography

ALBANI, M. (1997). 'Zur Rekonstruktion eines verdrängten Konzepts: Der 364-Tage-Kalender in der gegenwärtigen Forschung, in *Studies in the Book of Jubilees*, ed. M. Albani, J. Frey and A. Lange. Tübingen: Mohr-Siebeck, 79–125.

BAUMGARTEN, J. M. (1976). '4Q Halakah[a] 5, the Law of *Hadash*, and the Pentecontad Calendar'. *Journal of Jewish Studies* 27: 36–46.

—— (1996). *Qumran Cave 4: XIII. The Damascus Document (4Q266–273)*. Discoveries in the Judean Desert 18. Oxford: Clarendon Press.

—— et al. (1999). *Qumran Cave 4: XXV. Halakhic Texts*. DJD 35. Oxford: Clarendon Press.

BELL, C. (1992). *Ritual Theory, Ritual Practice*. New York and Oxford: Oxford University Press.

BELL, C. M. (1997). *Ritual: Perspectives and Dimensions*. New York and Oxford: Oxford University Press.

BENOIT, P. ET AL. (1961). *Les grottes de Murabba'ât*. Discoveries in the Judean Desert 2. Oxford: Clarendon Press.

BENOWITZ, M. (2003). 'Herod and Hanukkah' [Hebr.]. *Zion* 68: 5–40.

BERKOWITZ, B. (2006). *Execution and Invention: Death Penalty Discourse in Early Christian and Rabbinic Cultures*. Oxford: Oxford University Press.

BOKSER, B. M. (1984). *The Origins of the Seder: The Passover Rite and Early Rabbinic Judaism*. Berkeley: University of California Press.

BROSHI, M. (1992). 'Anti-Qumranic Polemics in the Talmud', in *The Madrid Qumran Congress: Proceedings of the International Congress on the Dead Sea Scrolls Madrid 18–21 March, 1991*, vol. 2, ed. J. Trebolle Barrera and L. Vegas Montaner. 2 vols. Leiden: Brill, Madrid: Editorial Complutense, 589–600.

CHAZON, E. G. (1992–93). 'On the Special Character of Sabbath Prayer: New Data from Qumran'. *Journal of Jewish Music and Liturgy* 15: 1–21.

COHEN, S. J. D. (2007). 'The Judean Legal Tradition and the *Halakhah* of the Mishnah', in *The Cambridge Companion to the Talmud and Rabbinic Literature*, ed. C. E. Fonrobert and M. S. Jaffee. Cambridge: Cambridge University Press, 121–143.

DELCOR, M. (1976). 'Das Bundesfest in Qumran und das Pfingstfest', in *idem, Religion d'Israël et Proche Orient ancien: Des Phéniciens aux Esséniens*. Leiden: Brill, 281–297.

DOERING, L. (1997). 'The Concept of the Sabbath in the Book of Jubilees', in *Studies in the Book of Jubilees*, ed. M. Albani, J. Frey and A. Lange. Tübingen: Mohr-Siebeck, 179–205.

—— (1999). *Schabbat: Sabbathalacha und -praxis im antiken Judentum und Urchristentum*. Tübingen: Mohr-Siebeck.

—— (2000). 'Purity Regulations Concerning the Sabbath in the Dead Sea Scrolls and Related Literature', in *The Dead Sea Scrolls: Fifty Years after their Discovery 1947–1997. Proceedings of the Jerusalem Congress, July 20–25, 1997*, ed. L. H. Schiffman, E. Tov and J. C. VanderKam. Jerusalem: Israel Exploration Society and The Shrine of the Book, Israel Museum, 600–609.

—— (2006). 'Parallels without "Parallelomania": Methodological Reflections on Comparative Analysis of Halakhah in the Dead Sea Scrolls', in *Rabbinic Perspectives: Proceedings of the 8th International Symposium of the Orion Center for the Study of the Dead Sea Scrolls and Associated Literature, January 2003*, ed. S. Fraade, A. Shemesh and R. A. Clements. Leiden: Brill, 13–42.

—— (2010). 'Sabbath Laws in the New Testament Gospels', in *The New Testament and Rabbinic Literature*, ed. R. Bieringer, F. García Martínez, D. Pollefeyt and P. J. Tomson. Leiden: Brill, 207–253.

EISS, W. (1997). 'Das Wochenfest im Jubiläenbuch und im antiken Judentum', in *Studies in the Book of Jubilees*, ed. M. Albani, J. Frey and A. Lange. Tübingen: Mohr-Siebeck, 165–178.

ESHEL, H./AVSHALOM-GORNI, D. (1996). 'A Sabbath Lampstand from H. Uza' [Hebr.]. *Atiqot* 29: 57*–61*.

FALK, D. K. (1998). *Daily, Sabbath, and Festival Prayers in the Dead Sea Scrolls*. Leiden: Brill.

FLEISCHER, E. (2003). 'Remarks Concerning the Triennial Cycle of the Torah Reading in Eretz Israel" [Hebr.]. *Tarbiz* 73: 83–124.

FONROBERT, C. E. (2004). '"From Separatism to Urbanism: The Dead Sea Scrolls and the Origins of the Rabbinic "Eruv"'. *Dead Sea Discoveries* 11: 43–71.

FRIEDMAN, S. (2002). *Tosefta Atiqta: Pesah Rishon. Synoptic Parallels of Mishna and Tosefta Analyzed with a Methodological Introduction* [Hebr.]. Ramat Gan: Bar Ilan University Press.

GILAT, Y. D. (1992). *Studies in the Development of the Halakha* [Hebr.]. Ramat Gan: Bar Ilan University Press.

GOLDENBERG, R. (1978). *The Sabbath-Law of Rabbi Meir.* Atlanta: Scholars Press.

HEZSER, C. (1998). '"Privat" und "öffentlich" im Talmud Yerushalmi und in der griechisch-römischen Antike', in *The Talmud Yerushalmi and Graeco-Roman Culture*, vol. 1, ed. P. Schäfer. Tübingen: Mohr-Siebeck, 423–579.

—— (2000). 'The (In)Significance of Jerusalem in the Talmud Yerushalmi', in *The Talmud Yerushalmi and Graeco-Roman Culture*, vol. 2, ed. P. Schäfer and C. Hezser. Tübingen: Mohr-Siebeck, 11–49.

HORBURY, W. (2003). 'Herod's Temple and "Herod's Days"', in *Messianism among Jews and Christians: Twelve Biblical and Historical Studies.* London and New York: T&T Clark, 83–122.

—— (2004). '*Cena pura* and Lord's Supper', in *The Beginnings of Christianity: A Collection of Articles*, ed. J. Pastor and M. Mor. Jerusalem: Yad Ben-Zvi, 219–265.

HORST, P. W. VAN DER (1999). 'Was the Synagogue a Place of Sabbath Worship Before 70 CE?', in: *Jews, Christians, and Polytheists in the Ancient Synagogue: Cultural Interaction During the Greco-Roman Period*, ed. S. Fine. London: Routledge. 18–43.

ILAN, T. (2008). *Massekhet Ta'anit: Text, Translation, and Commentary.* A Feminist Commentary on the Babylonian Talmud 11/9 Tübingen: Mohr-Siebeck.

KATZOFF, R./SCHREIBER, B.M. (1998). 'Week and Sabbath in Judaean Desert Documents'. *Scripta Classica Israelica* 17: 102–114.

KLINGHARDT, M. (1996). *Gemeinschaftsmahl und Mahlgemeinschaft: Soziologie und Liturgie frühchristlicher Mahlfeiern.* Tübingen and Basle: Francke.

LAPIN, H. (1993). 'Palm Fronds and Citrons: Notes on Two Letters from Bar Kosiba's Administration'. *Hebrew Union College Annual* 64: 111–135.

LEHMAN, M. (2006). 'The Gendered Rhetoric of Sukkah Observance'. *Jewish Quarterly Review* 96: 309–335.

LEONHARD, C. (2006). *The Jewish Pesach and the Origins of the Christian Easter: Open Questions in Current Research.* Berlin: De Gruyter.

LEVINE, D. (2001). *Communal Fasts and Rabbinic Sermons: Theory and Practice in the Talmudic Period* [Hebr.]. Tel Aviv: Hakibbutz Hameuchad.

MCKAY, H. A. (1994). *Sabbath and Synagogue: The Question of Sabbath Worship in Ancient Judaism.* Leiden: Brill.

NEUSNER, J. (1983). *A History of the Mishnaic Law of Appointed Times*, vol. 5. Leiden: Brill.

NEWSOM, C. (1985). *Songs of the Sabbath Sacrifice: A Critical Edition.* Atlanta: Scholars Press.

NOAM, V. (2003). *Megillat Ta'anit: Versions, Interpretation, History. With a Critical Edition* [Hebr.]. Jerusalem: Yad Ben-Zvi.

—— (2006). 'Megillat Taanit—The Scroll of Fasting', in *The Literature of the Sages, Second Part: Midrash and Targum, Liturgy, Poetry, Mysticism, Contracts, Inscriptions, Ancient Science and the Languages of Rabbinic Literature*, ed. S. Safrai et al. Assen: Royal Van Gorcum, Minneapolis: Fortress, 339–362.

——/QIMRON, E. (2009). 'A Qumran Composition of Sabbath Laws and Its Contribution to the Study of Early Holakah 'Hebr. *Dead Sea Discoveries* 16: 55–96.

OPPENHEIMER, A. (2005). 'Sabbatheiligung im Bar-Kochba-Aufstand', in *Between Rome and Babylon*, ed. N. Oppenheimer. Tübingen: Mohr-Siebeck, 292–302.

OTTENHEIJM, E. (2004). *The Role and Significance of Intention in the Controversies about Sabbath and Purity between the Houses of Shammai and Hillel [Dutch]*. Amsterdam: Amphora Books.

PARK, S. (2008). *Pentecost and Sinai: The Festival of Weeks as a Celebration of the Sinai Event*. London: T & T Clark.

REGEV, E. (2005). *The Sadducees and Their Halakhah: Religion and Society in the Second Temple Period* [Hebr.]. Jerusalem: Yad Ben-Zvi.

RUBENSTEIN, J. L. (1993). 'The *Sukka* as Temporary or Permanent Dwelling: A Study in the Development of Talmudic Thought'. *Hebrew Union College Annual* 64: 137–166.

—— (1995). *The History of Sukkot in the Second Temple and Rabbinic Periods*. Atlanta: Scholars Press.

SAFRAI, S. (1965). 'Teaching of Pietists in Mishnaic Literature'. *Journal of Jewish Studies* 16: 15–33.

SCHIFFMAN, L. H. (1975). *The Halakhah at Qumran*. Leiden: Brill.

SCHLUND, C. (2005). *'Kein Knochen soll gebrochen werden': Studien zu Bedeutung und Funktion des Pesachfests in Texten des frühen Judentums und im Johannesevangelium*. Neukirchen-Vluyn: Neukirchener Verlag.

SHEMESH, A. (2003). *Punishments and Sins: From Scripture to the Rabbis* [Hebr.]. Jerusalem: Magnes Press.

STÖKL BEN EZRA, D. (2003). *The Impact of Yom Kippur on Early Christianity: The Day of Atonement from Second Temple Judaism to the Fifth Century*. Tübingen: Mohr-Siebeck.

—— (2007). 'Templisierung: Die Rückkehr des Tempels in die jüdische und christliche Liturgie der Spätantike', in *Rites et croyances dans les religions du monde romain*, ed. J. Scheid. Vandœuvre and Geneva: Fondation Hardt, 231–287.

SUSSMAN, V. (1970). 'A Shabbat Lamp' [Hebr.]. *Atiqot* (Hebrew series) 6: 80–81.

TABORY, J. (1999). 'Towards a History of the Paschal Meal', in: *Passover and Easter: Origin and History to Modern Times*, ed. P. F. Bradshaw and L. A. Hoffman. Notre Dame: University of Notre Dame Press, 62–80.

—— (2006). 'Jewish Festivals in Late Antiquity', in *The Cambridge History of Judaism*, vol. 4: *The Late Roman—Rabbinic Period*, ed. S. T. Katz. Cambridge: Cambridge University Press, 556–572.

ULFGARD, H. (1998). *The Story of Sukkot: The Setting, Shaping, and Sequel of the Biblical Feast of Tabernacles*. Tübingen: Mohr-Siebeck.

VANDERKAM, J. C. (1998). 'Authoritative Literature in the Dead Sea Scrolls'. *Dead Sea Discoveries* 5: 382–402.

WEISS, H. (2003). *A Day of Gladness: The Sabbath Among Jews and Christians in Antiquity*. Columbia: University of South Carolina Press.

WILLIAMS, M. H. (2004). 'Being a Jew in Rome: Sabbath Fasting as an Expression of Romano-Jewish Identity', in *Negotiating Diaspora: Jewish Strategies in the Roman Empire*, ed. J. M. G. Barclay. London: T&T Clark, 8–18.

—— (2005). 'Jewish Festal Names in Antiquity—A Neglected Area of Onomastic Research'. *Journal for the Study of Judaism* 36: 21–40.

YADIN, Y. et al. (2002). *The Documents from the Bar Kokhba Period in the Cave of Letters: Hebrew, Aramaic and Nabatean-Aramaic Papyri*. Jerusalem: Israel Exploration Society.

YARDENI, A. (1990). 'New Jewish Aramaic Ostraca'. *Israel Exploration Journal* 40: 132–152.

YUVAL, I. J. (1999). 'Easter and Passover as Early Jewish-Christian Dialogue', in *Passover and Easter: Origin and History to Modern Times*, ed. P. F. Bradshaw and L. A. Hoffman. Notre Dame: University of Notre Dame Press, 98–124.

···

CHAPTER 31

MAGIC AND HEALING

···

GIUSEPPE VELTRI

A large number of studies already exist on topics related to magic, superstition, healing, and sciences in Graeco-Roman Palestine and its vicinity, especially as far as the political and cultural environment of rabbinic Judaism is concerned. It is impossible to provide a comprehensive account of the various aspects of practical and theoretical magic in ancient Judaism here. This chapter will therefore restrict itself to offering an outline of the major research questions and scholarship on magic and science, assisting the reader in his or her future study of these topics.

1. MAGIC

···

1.1 Magic in Past and Present Scholarship

Modern studies on the magical tradition in Judaism go back to the German *Wissenschaft des Judentums* ('science of Judaism') in the nineteenth century. Initially, only sporadic studies were conducted on the subject, but eventually scholarly interest in these issues increased, and a new discipline was created which investigated the extent and nature of Jewish magic and healing in antiquity and the Middle Ages. Interest in magic developed especially out of the incipient folklore studies of the early nineteenth century, and was based on a re-evaluation of the phenomenon of Jewish mysticism. After almost two centuries of scholarship and research we can now distinguish between the following trends in the literary, cultural and anthropological study of magic: 1) the polemic-apologetic approach of the last century; 2) studies based on new discoveries in the archaeological and philological realms; 3) folklore and folk life studies; 4) the impact of the study of Jewish mysticism on magic; and finally 5) the halakhic-theological approach.

1.1.1 *The Polemic-Apologetic Approach*

The study of rabbinic texts on magic, superstition, and healing was not the primarily interest of the 'science of Judaism' scholars. On the contrary, these scholars, most of whom wrote in German, avoided approaching the subject, largely because of the enlightened vision of Judaism as a rational religion. They feared that if they focused on magic, the entire Jewish tradition might be viewed as an extension of the medieval mystical movement of Kabbalah. Nevertheless, from the second half of the nineteenth century onwards, the study of the topic evolved quite naturally as an expression of these rationalists' polemic against the 'obscure' earlier centuries, and as an apology for the Jewish adoption of non-Jewish traditions and customs, including magic and superstition.

The first modern treatise on Jewish magic was written by Gideon Brecher (1850), a physician in Prossnitz (Prostějon, Moravia), who considered magic an incidental phenomenon in Judaism, adopted from the non-Jewish environment in the biblical and rabbinic periods. A similar approach was adopted by Rabbi David Heymann Joël (1883), who collected rabbinic legal and narrative sources on the topic. His book was aimed at proving that biblical and tannaitic sources (rabbinic sources of the first two centuries CE) were free of magical beliefs and practices, an erroneous view also shared by Israel Finkelscherer in his brief book on Maimonides (Finkelscherer 1894). In addition to these publications, some detailed studies on particular aspects of rabbinic folklore appeared at that time. Amongst others, mention should be made of the works of Max Grünbaum (1877) and Israel Lévi (1878), who pointed to parallels to Jewish magic in the Graeco-Roman world.

The scholars who wrote these early studies of ancient Jewish magic and superstition were primarily concerned with upholding a rationalist image of Judaism in the post-Enlightenment period rather than with actually analysing ancient rabbinic discourse. Nevertheless, their work is important in mapping out magic in ancient Jewish literature and tradition, an indispensable foundation stone in the modern scientific study of the topic.

1.1.2 *Archaeological and Philological Research*

At the end of the nineteenth century the publication of philological commentaries on Aramaic texts from Babylonia, and the interest in Greek magical papyri opened a new era of research, offering a deeper insight into the world of magic from Babylonia to the Mediterranean coast. For the study of Jewish magic, the discovery of Greek and Aramaic parallels constituted a decisive step forward in research, which culminated with the handbook of Jewish magic created by Joseph Blau (1898). This short work has remained a classic work of Jewish ethnological studies until today. The Babylonian Aramaic incantation bowls, first published by Thomas Ellis in 1853 (in Layard 1853: 434–445), opened a new epoch of philological research. Nearly half a century later, James A. Montgomery (1913) presented a collection of the Aramaic incantation texts. Indeed, since the early 1900s, research on the magic bowls has continued almost without interruption. Important here are Edwin Yamauchi's publication of Mandaic texts (1967; see also McCullough 1967), Victor P. Hamilton's work on Syriac incantation bowls (1971), and Charles D. Isbell's study on Aramaic texts (1975). Recently, the interest in Aramaic texts has been revived by the publication of new archaeological discoveries (see Naveh/Shaked 1985; 1993; Levene 2003; see also Shaked, ed. 2005), which shed new light on the Aramaic literary production of both Palestinian and Babylonian Judaism in late antiquity.

Another very important branch of scholarship is the publication of new literary texts, fragments, papyri, and other documents relating to Graeco-Roman magic (a bibliography until 1994 is available in Brashear 1995). It would go beyond the scope of this chapter to list only a fraction of the huge scholarly output in this area. It should suffice to mention the well-known collection of Karl Preisendanz (1928). New texts have recently been published by Merkelbach and Totti (1990–1992) and by Daniel and Maltomini (1990–92). Hans-Dieter Betz (1992) published an English translation. Furthermore, the very important studies on the 'defixiones' (curse tablets), amulets, gems, and other magic devices by August Audollent (1904), John G. Gager (1999) and Roy Kotansky (ed. 1994–99) need to be mentioned.

When analysing Jewish magic and superstition in Roman Palestine, the comparison with Graeco-Roman texts and traditions is of course obligatory. Yet students of Jewish magic should be very careful when comparing Jewish and Graeco-Roman magical texts. The newly developed scholarly interest in Jewish and Greek magic reintroduces the old question of the relationship between Greek magical papyri and amulets, and biblical and post-biblical Jewish tradition. As Morton Smith has emphasized (Smith 1986: 455, see also Sperber 1985), the very difficulty in determining what is Jewish in Greek papyri and amulets is based on the notorious problem of defining Judaism in the first centuries CE. Since magic was an eclectic phenomenon, it is almost impossible to distinguish between Jewish and Greek elements in magic (for instance, with regard to angelology and *nomina barbara*, 'unheard of words', 'foreign words', 'mysterious words'). A naïve and hastily claimed interest in purported 'parallels' is best avoided when investigating the origin and context of certain themes and motifs. The main question is whether it is correct to assume that one particular motif in a Greek amulet or papyrus (e.g. Solomonic power over demons) qualifies the text as 'Jewish'.

The definition of what constituted Jewish identity in antiquity is also important for the choice of the relevant texts for comparative studies (see now Bohak 2008). The literary creativity of Judaism in the first centuries CE was mainly conducted orally, and only in a relatively late period was it put down in writing. For that reason, students of ancient religion and folklore should not merely focus on biblical and post-biblical Greek Jewish literature, but also take the later rabbinic literature into account.

1.1.3 Folklore and Folk Life Studies

Motivated by the general interest in anthropology and ethnography at the beginning of the twentieth century, scholars began to focus their research on Jewish folklore. A famous forerunner in this field was the Romanian Rabbi Moses Gaster, *Hakham* of the Spanish and Portuguese congregation in London, who was a member of the executive councils of various societies of folklore studies. He published widely on Jewish magical texts, superstitions, and amulets (see Gaster 1925–28). Although the quality of his philological work is often not of a high calibre and his theories are sometimes questionable, Gaster distinguished himself as a polymath with a substantial interest in folklore and ancient and medieval literature. The Ashkenazic (German Jewish) Rabbi Max Grunwald can also be considered amongst the scholarly progenitors of Jewish folklore studies. He edited a journal and year book, was one of the principal founders of the Hamburg Jewish Museum, and published a huge number of essays mostly based on his collection of texts, manuscripts, and amulets (see the summary in Grunwald 1944–45). Equally indispensable for the study of ancient Jewish folklore is the monograph by Joshua Trachtenberg (1939), based almost entirely on Ashkenazic tradition. His book has been republished several times and still constitutes the most often consulted and quoted handbook on Jewish magic in the Middle Ages. Trachtenberg's monograph should be read together with Hirsch J. Zimmels' work on the work of the magician. This work represents the first attempt to describe Jewish magic on the basis of the medieval rabbinic *Responsa* literature (Zimmels 1952).

Modern approaches to magic and folklore have been developed by many scholars in Israel, Europe, and the US. A survey of the state of research can be found in Veltri (1997) and most recently in Harari (2006; see also Bohak 2008), who is concerned with the definition of magic, the occult, demons, divinations and astrology in rabbinic literature.

1.1.4 Mysticism, Kabbalah, and Jewish Magic

A peculiar chapter in the history of scholarship on magic is the investigation of the relationship between Jewish magic and mysticism (Kabbalah). In the nineteenth and early twentieth century, the prevailing attitude to Jewish mysticism was

extremely negative, since mysticism was deemed a product of irrational and irreli-
gious thought, comparable to superstition. Until recently, scholars who studied early
Jewish mystical texts (Hekhalot literature) distinguished between what they considered 'high mysticism' and elements which are regarded as a product of magical beliefs
(see Schäfer 1993: 73). The famous bibliographer Moritz Steinschneider and the
historian Heinrich Graetz (see Veltri 1997: 12–13) avoided dealing with the subject
altogether, except for some negative comments belittling its significance.

Only with the work of Gershom Scholem did Jewish mysticism become a *bona
fide* field of scholarly inquiry, developing into an academic sub-discipline. Scholem's interest in Jewish mysticism was profoundly influenced by the romantic and
idealistic intellectual milieu of his German cultural environment. His inclination
for the mystical and the mysterious, the fragmentary and the imperfect, in which he
believed to have recognized the essential motive of (Jewish) existence, is reminiscent of the cosmological and linguistic ideas of Neoplatonist and Hermetic provenance (e.g. the conception of mystical language, Scholem 1972). Exploring the
development of the concept of micro-and macrocosm, and the rise of mystical
and magical trends that culminated in early Jewish mysticism and Kabbalah,
Scholem's interest extended to every imaginable genre of Jewish esoteric literature
(Veltri 1997: 12–16. By being traced back to Hermeticism and Neoplatonism, the
mystical and magical elements in Judaism that were rejected by such rationalists
as Maimonides regained their philosophical respectability.

Although Scholem published physiognomic texts and conjuration formulae (see
Scholem 1941 and 1965; Veltri 1997), he was not interested in the practical, pragmatic use and misuse of divine power, names, conjurations, recipes, etc. Rather, his
concern was with the theurgic interpretation as the core of Jewish mysticism and
magic. Despite modern criticism of Scholem, it is undeniable that the study of
Jewish mysticism, magic, and superstition owe much to his sustained scholarship
which helped create a new sub-discipline that is still a powerful magnet for a new
generation of students and scholars today.

A further decisive impulse to the study of magic and superstition (demonology,
chiromancy, physiognomic, astrology, etc.) was given in the last decade of the
twentieth century by new research on mysticism and magic, and the publication of
magical texts and fragments from the Cairo Genizah. This new research was
initiated and carried out by Schäfer and Shaked (1994–99), Naveh and Shaked
(1985 and 1993), and Schiffman and Swartz (1992). The newly published texts raised
fresh questions about the relationship between magic and liturgy, mysticism,
rabbinic Judaism and the Graeco-Roman environment, and the significance
of magic in Palestinian Judaism. Ancient and medieval texts such as the *Sword
of Moses* (Harari, ed. 1997), *Havdalah de Rabbi Aqiva, Sefer Ha-Malbush, Sefer
ha-Yashar* (Wandrey 2004), *Inyan Sota* (Veltri 1993), *Sefer Ha-Razim,* (see Rebiger
et al. 2008–9; see also Veltri 1997: 262–264) have been newly discovered and edited,
initiating new studies and debates.

1.1.5 *The Halakhic-Theological Approach*

A halakhic-theological debate on the value of magic can already be found in rabbinic texts, as outlined below. The modern (largely Orthodox) discussion of Jewish magic was deeply influenced by the view that Jewish mysticism was a culture of the common people (*am ha-aretz*), a conclusion based on the sociological approach (for Hekhalot literature see Halperin 1980). As far back as the 1960s, Lieberman (1965: 91–114) suggested that magic belonged to the culture of the so-called masses. Accordingly, it was assumed that ancient rabbis looked at the phenomenon with a sense of resignation, being unable to stamp out superstitious practices and beliefs which originated in a Graeco-Roman environment. Even Orthodox scholars conceded that rabbis may have adopted some magic practices. But they stressed that the elite strata of society were enlightened. A slightly different view was adopted in Reform Jewish circles, as Louis Jacobs (1984) claims: in his view, rabbinic Judaism applied the category of *huqqot ha-goy* (laws of the Gentiles) to magic. Magic is seen as the adoption of Graeco-Roman customs which gradually penetrated Judaism.

This ideologically inspired approach does not take into consideration the fact that we possess evidence only of the rabbinic perspective on magic. The world beyond rabbinic literature cannot be conceived as a simple struggle between the common people and the elite. We lack literary evidence of ancient Jewish popular culture, which rabbis present from the viewpoint of the intellectual elite.

1.2 Some Thoughts on Magic and Methods in Studying Magic

1.2.1 *Magic and Its Tradition*

The nature of magic can be found in the process which leads from the hidden to the revealed, and vice versa. Neither the starting point nor the goal of this process is magical, but rather the path and procedure themselves. The magician is less interested in the theory than in the practical effects, bringing about cures with magical formulas: magic as applied *praxis*. A certain energy is unleashed when particular conditions are fulfilled. However, even if a practice is crowned by success, rules cannot necessarily be derived from it. Magic is the empirical science par excellence, most evident in its affinity to medicine. Both magic and medicine are sciences applied to human beings in particular locations and times, and both lay claim to the empirical totality of their achievements. Their knowledge is empirically bound by the parameters of their respective historical time period, but their claims are empirically absolute, beyond any temporal framework.

Empirical totality means that the magician considers something absolutely important for a particular individual, but not necessarily for everyone. Contrary to certain speculations which may claim otherwise, the centre of every magical concept is the person him- or herself. It is not *super-stitio* that inspires this world view and value system, but that which is perceived anthropologically as the 'I' or ego. Everything else serves this ego, just as colours and internally envisioned images serve a painter. Equipped with this awareness, the magician sets out to study the possible and the impossible, things that can be used as *materia magica*. The magician is neither monotheist nor polytheist, only a pragmatist interested in achieving certain effects.

We are not always able to decipher the structure of the interwoven magical texts, to disentangle the substructures of the often seemingly innumerable criss-crossing 'beams of light', simply because we lack an overview of all the necessary strands. The reason for this difficulty is not the concealment of magical techniques by the ancient practitioners, but rather our own ignorance of how these practices were handed down. Rarely do we have at our disposal detailed texts explaining the origins and development of certain practices and beliefs. Even in the case of the few known examples, such as the writings of the Roman Apuleius (Veltri 1997: 53 ff.), the Neoplatonist Iamblichus, or the Church Father Origen (Janowitz 1991), it is always advisable to ask whether their explanations really do fit the facts at hand. As a rule, we know only of isolated traditions and customs which are generically classified in handbooks, anthologies, and *excerpta*, treated as deviations in legal texts (law codices), or described and prosecuted in case files (notably in the files of the Inquisition) as capital crimes.

1.2.2 *Definition of Magic and the Rabbis*

The primary issue in studying magic concerns the meaning of the term. This aspect involves the scholar in the complex and much-discussed problem of religion's relationship to science, and the question of whether it is appropriate to use the label 'magic' for certain ancient phenomena. The term 'magic' has been burdened with ideological connotations since the Enlightenment, not to mention its religious and legal implications since the dawn of the written tradition. Yet there is no semantic substitute for describing this phenomenon, and for distinguishing it from religion and science. Therefore, one should continue to use the term because of its practical and heuristic value.

Evans-Pritchard (1965: 111) states: 'To try to understand magic as an idea in itself, what is the essence of it, as it were, is a hopeless task. It becomes more intelligible when it is viewed not only in relation to empirical activities but also in relation to other beliefs, as part of a system of thought.' I suggest that we put the question differently, for I do not think that one can speak of magic as (part of) a 'system of thought'. The term 'system' implies the organization of ideas—a typical philosophical objectification. When speaking of magic, it is preferable to see its semantic and historical environment as the 'holistic world', the world in which human beings live and operate. Yet Evans-Pritchard is correct in stressing that magic is understandable only in relation to many different aspects of human life.

The category of magic itself is an empty concept for defining a historical and existential relationship between subjects and their respective environments. The magician as practitioner illustrates how his or her (real or illusive) power can only be understood in terms of a relationship. Like an actor, the magician cannot exist or act without an audience. In almost every historical period the magician was the most consulted, but also the most despised member of his or her community, because he claimed and was attributed a special power over things, people, and coming events. He or she was supposed to be an especially skilled master, able to control not only supernatural forces and energies required for healing and the prediction of the future, but also for injuring or even killing people. To understand the power of the magician in ancient society, it is necessary to stress that a magician's authority was based on true or illusionary success in doing things that others could not do. From this point of view, it is clear why ancient scholarship was so eager to determine the nature of magic and to identify the real, authentic magician. If magic is to be defined as a hermeneutic effort to interpret and change reality, the achievements of ancient scholarship in understanding the power of its hermeneutics (by critique, avoidance, or acceptance) were considerable.

The implications of this understanding of magic for its relationship to rabbinic Judaism are obvious. Rabbis were a scholarly elite, for whom the hermeneutical method was virtually the only key to gaining knowledge and, consequently, to defending rabbinic power against undesirable competitors, such as magicians, physicians, and astrologers. It was not fear of the power of magic that compelled rabbis to analyse, oppose, or accept magic, but rather the magician's claim to be able to change reality, contrary to common experience and the 'natural' rules governing human existence.

In the ancient and early medieval period, rabbis were confronted with many hermeneutic, scientific, philosophical, and theological questions which originated from the debate about magic and its efficiency: were magicians' and physicians' successes merely due to illusions and tricks, or to the genuine application of supernatural or unknown natural powers? If the magician really utilized supernatural powers, how was his handling of such energy possible and theoretically justifiable? As a direct consequence of monotheistic beliefs, a theological dilemma arose: if magic comes from the one and only God—and it must come from him—might it be used against his will? Or is God's power independent of his will? The assumption of the existence of a second, perhaps evil, but supreme and autonomous, power in heaven would undermine every monotheistic concept (Segal 1977).

In rabbinic discussions of magic and magicians, two very important aspects of rabbis' mentality are revealed: (1) the readiness to accept sources of knowledge other than the biblical text and the oral tradition, since rabbis absorbed the achievements and practices of medicine and astrology; (2) the perseverance in criticizing magic by trying to unveil the innumerable tricks and strategies of the magician. Rabbis' pragmatic attitudes to the *scientiae et artes* were almost always coupled with a belief in the magic and theurgic power of the word, substantially a Neoplatonic and Hermetic idea.

The challenge to define magic, healing, and science, and to circumscribe their respective spheres of influence is very old. The question of how to distinguish between magic and medicine had important legal implications. For example, the preparation and use of *pharmaka* ('potions') was already considered a capital offence in a law code dating back to 479 BCE. Hippocrates, the founder of the Greek medical school, advised physicians and midwives not only to refrain from believing in demons and evil forces, but to be non-superstitious (*adeisidaímones*). Plato discussed the consequences of injuring or killing someone by poison in his Laws (chapter 11, 933d–e).

The decisive criterion in this legal discussion is not the action itself which might cause a serious injury, but the practitioner's degree of professional competence. As a physician he must be conscious of the danger of poisoning; as a prophet or diviner he has to be concerned about the effects of his treatment. Consequently, his professional qualification distinguishes the physician from the private person. The professional is aware of the effects of his ministrations. The necessity of providing proof of being a proficient magus or doctor, prophet or diviner is the main aspect of rabbinic discussions of the *subjecta agentia*, the professional qualification for such practice.

1.2.3 On Methodology

Ancient Judaism engaged in lively discussions about magic (Veltri 1997; Harari 2006; Boak 2008). In the rabbinic circles of the first centuries CE a very intensive discourse took place about the identification of forbidden customs, professions, and beliefs. The starting point of this halakhic debate was the biblical text. This biblical premise also constitutes the first methodological difficulty for modern research, for it is not easy to identify the boundaries between scriptural exegesis and historical reality, empirical facts and legal precedents (*ma'aseh*), purely derivative hermeneutics and actual experience. Rabbinic halakhah oscillated between Bible and history, rhetoric and experience. What we gain from the rabbinic texts has perhaps nothing to do with the real conditions of that period, but it can also not be assumed that it was only an academic exercise.

A second, complementary aspect should be taken into consideration and borne in mind when we deal with magic. Because rabbis lacked executive power, the verdicts of their courts, if any, were potentially ineffective. In both Graeco-Roman and rabbinic legislation, magic was chiefly dealt with in criminal law, and its punishment comparable to that of premeditated murder. We must perforce wonder how rabbis could reconcile their impotence to execute such a sentence with the 'artificial' halo of legal freedom they communicate by ignoring the empirical legal situation.

The tendency to stress the intellectual aspects of rabbinic Judaism is indirectly based on the tacit premise that rabbis represented the intelligentsia of Judaism in late antiquity, an enlightened class aware of their own authority in developing halakhah and conscious of the practical difficulties in uprooting popular customs and 'foreign' ideas. Rabbis obviously maintained contacts with their Gentile neighbours, whose 'idolatrous' practices they rejected, and whose philosophical ideas they accepted only in part, as many modern scholars claim (Urbach 1975: 97 ff; Lieberman 1965: 91 ff). The biblical and rabbinic emphasis on monotheism (see Hayman 1991: 1–15), as well as an idealistic nineteenth-century vision of history led modern scholars to the questionable distinction between the rabbinic elite and the 'others', that is, the common people.

There were some noteworthy differences in legal competence between the Roman rulers and the rabbis. The Roman emperors tried to suppress the occult sciences, such as magic practices and astrology, because they allegedly attempted to undermine the imperial claim to be the sole authority and interpreter of history (Fögen 1993). By incriminating these 'alternative' sciences, the emperors tried to stem the erosion of their political power. Rabbis also tried to impose their will upon others, but they could do so only by means of argumentation, by persuading their followers and the common people. Rabbis had no power to impose capital punishment upon those who practised magic.

To describe rabbinic attitudes toward magic and science in terms of an enlightened minority's confrontation with the 'pleasures and fears' of the common people, as Saul Lieberman did (1965: 91–114), must be considered inappropriate, if not dangerous. The mutual flow of ideas between rabbis and their environment can be encountered in the confrontation with, and tacit acceptance of, widespread patterns of behaviour, as I try to explain below.

2. HEALING

2.1 Greek Wisdom and the Sciences

When studying ancient Jewish attitudes to healing and medicine, one of the most important questions concerns the impact of Graeco-Roman medicine on rabbinic Judaism. Some authors deny any contact between these two entities (Kagan 1952), arguing that Jews were not allowed to have any contact with the so-called 'Greek wisdom.' If we look at the empirical and natural sciences (botany, zoology, medicine, agronomy, etc.), however, it is astonishing how similar Graeco-Roman knowledge and methods were to those of Palestinian rabbis. Immanuel Löw's *Flora der Juden* (1881; see also 1924–34, 1969), Lewysohn's *Die Zoologie des Talmuds* (1858), Julius Preuss's *Biblisch-talmudische Medizin* (1911), as well as the material mentioned cursorily in Saul Lieberman's multi-volume commentary on the Tosefta (1955–1988), and Daniel Sperber's work (1990–95), clearly demonstrate how close rabbis were to their Graeco-Roman colleagues in this regard.

We have to ask whether such similarities can be interpreted as a tacit reception of the common sciences by rabbis. Did rabbis apply an eclectic pragmatic approach to Graeco-Roman medicine and healing? Should we reckon with a process of conscious acceptance of certain scientific findings? Only if we assume that rabbis consciously adapted the healing knowledge of their environment is it worthwhile to investigate rabbinic 'attitudes' to theoretical and practical sciences. The mere evidence of individual parallels cannot be considered proof of an influence of medical sciences on the rabbis, however. The question of this relationship is still open and much debated amongst scholars.

Modern scholarship on healing in rabbinic literature is sparse. An important classic in the field is Preuss' already mentioned *Biblisch-talmudische Medizin* (1911), a handbook which is still useful today, a century after its composition. Mention should also be made of Samuel Kottek's studies on ancient medicine (Kottek 1994 and 1996; Kottek/Horstmanshoff, eds 2000). A new comprehensive study of Jewish medical knowledge and practice in Palestine and Babylonia is still a desideratum.

2.2 Rabbinic Approaches to the Sciences: A Critical Note

The history of the ancient and modern sciences is neither linear nor consistent. The optimistic approach of the nineteenth century, which tried to interpret classical Greek attitudes to the sciences as being rationally and scientifically proven, is no longer credible. There is also hardly any proof and no real evidence that the Babylonian and the Egyptian healing methods provided the seed of the theories of Hippocrates and Galen. The main difference between the Babylonian and Egyptian sciences on the one hand, and Greek science on the other, is the latter's speculative reflections about human health. We have a huge number of lists of medical remedies, parts of the human body, *materia medica ac magica*, plant names, and symptoms in Akkadian, as well as in Egyptian texts. However, they offered no theory of how the human body works and functions, or what constitutes health and disease.

Modern conceptions of science and the ancient approach to the sciences differ profoundly. Modern natural scientists, such as the scholars of botany or zoology for instance, aim to find rules which can explain one or many phenomena. If an old rule cannot explain a new phenomenon, scientists attempt to find a new rule capable of accounting for the old and new phenomena. Neither the old Babylonian nor the later Jewish sciences followed this approach. A (magical) recipe, a remedy, or a plant could be used as a *possible* cure. Palestinian as well as Babylonian sources provide many discussions about remedies, herbal concoctions, or medical-magical procedures. It is not only the traditional exegetical premise of rabbinic hermeneutics to discuss everything at length, but also the method of the ancient empirical sciences. A look at Pliny's encyclopedic work (ed. 1938–1962), Columella's work on agriculture, Dioscurides' *Materia medica* (ed. 1906–1914) as well as Marcellus Empiricus, *De Medicamentis* (ed. 1968) reveals a method of presenting medical-magical findings and beliefs which is quite similar to rabbinic discourse on the Bible.

As is well known, science is based on the observation of phenomena and their subsequent evaluation through the lens of theory. Most modern scholars do not unhesitatingly endorse Edgar Zilsel's (1942) thesis that the beginnings of modern science lie in the experiments of the plebeian classes of artists, engineers, and surgeons, whose empirical findings were not re-evaluated, even theoretically, before Roger Bacon, Galileo Galilei and William Gilbert. Nevertheless, one cannot deny that empirical experimentation is singularly useful for confirming and contrasting theories.

This could be the reason why rabbis insisted on empirical and pragmatic criteria to judge customs, medical procedures, and remedies. On the basis of this attitude, some texts and traditions, transmitted in early rabbinic writings, are fully intelligible: take, for example, the halakhic examination of foreign customs, and the so-called 'ways of the Amorite' (Veltri 1997). According to biblical sources, the Amorites were among the former inhabitants of Canaan (cf. Genesis 10:16 and Exodus 8:17), whose 'abominable' practices the Israelites were not allowed to adopt (cf. Deuteronomy 20:17–18 and Ezekiel 21:29ff.). In rabbinic discussions, the 'ways of the Amorite' became a halakhic category which included most kinds of forbidden foreign customs. The whole list of the 'customs of the Amorite' is a conglomeration of different magical genres, superstitions, and medical-magical recipes, which can be compared with Greek and Roman magic literature, as for instance the *Papyri Graecae Magicae*, but also with the works of Pliny and Columella. The customs forbidden by rabbis and labelled 'ways of the Amorite' encompass all aspects of everyday life, and show the variety of procedures and beliefs which rabbis took into consideration in this regard. The contextualization of the customs of the Amorites points to two characteristics of the category: it is synonymous with alien pagan 'foreign customs' and, at the same time, it is an anti-category, calling attention to what rabbis considered 'healing' versus 'quackery' or even dangerous cures.

In conclusion, it is necessary to stress that the cultural settings in which the Jewish attitude to science developed were not the academic institutions and the philosophical schools of their age, but the practices of everyday life. Not rabbis' preoccupation with the Torah was the determining factor in accepting foreign knowledge, but the actual demands of their day: whatever is to be considered healing should not be avoided. In this respect, rabbis were innovative: since the Written Torah is against medicine, the only true physician can be God.

SUGGESTED READING

Although Blau's book is antiquated, both with regard to his source material and his methodology, it still constitutes the classical treatment on magic (Blau 1898). New perspectives on the research on ancient Jewish magic can be found in Veltri (1997: 1–25) and Harari (2006) and now in the detailed book by Bohak (2008). For the *status questionis* of the history of healing and medicine Geller (2000) and Kottek (2000) can be recommended. Kottek's volume provides an impressive survey of the various aspects of ancient Jewish medicine and offers an outline and guideposts for future inquiries.

BIBLIOGRAPHY

AUDOLLENT, A. (1904). *Defixionum tabellae quotquot innotuerunt tam in Graecis Orientes quam in totius Occidentis partibus praeter Atticas in corpore inscriptionum Atticarum editas.* Paris: Fontemoing.

BETZ, H. D. (ed.) (1992). *The Greek Magical Papyri in Translation: Including the Demotic Spells.* 2nd ed. Chicago: University of Chicago Press.

BLAU, L. (1898). *Das altjüdische Zauberwesen.* Strassburg: K. J. Trübner.

BOHAK, G. (2008). *Ancient Jewish Magic. A History.* Cambridge, UK and New York: Cambridge University Press.

BRASHEAR, W. M. (1995). 'The Greek Magical Papyri: An Introduction and Survey; Annotated Bibliography (1928–94)'. *Aufstieg und Niedergang der Römischen Welt* II.18.5: 3381–3684.

BRECHER, G. (1850). *Das Transcendentale: Magie und magische Heilarten im Talmud.* Vienna: Klopf and Eurich.

DANIEL, R. W. MALTOMINI, F. (eds) (1990–1992). *Supplementum Magicum.* Opladen: Westdeutscher Verlag.

DIOSCURIDES, (1906–14). *Pedanii Dioscuridis Anazarbei De Materia Medica Libri quinque.* 3. vols, ed. Max Wellmann. Berlin: Weidmann.

EVANS-PRITCHARD, E. P. (1965). *Theories of Primitive Religion*. Oxford: Clarendon Press.

FINKELSCHERER, I. (1894). *Moses Maimunis Stellung zum Aberglauben und zur Mystik*. Breslau: Schottländer.

FÖGEN, M.-T. (1993). *Die Enteignung der Wahrsager. Studien zum kaiserlichen Wissensmonopol in der Spätantike*. Frankfurt: Suhrkamp.

GAGER, J. G. (1999). *Curse Tablets and Binding Spells from the Ancient World*. New York: Oxford University Press.

GASTER, M. (1925–28). *Studies and Texts in Folklore, Magic, Medieval Romance, Hebrew Apocrypha and Samaritan Archaeology*, 3. vols. London: Maggs.

GELLER, M. J. (2000). 'An Akkadian Vademecum in the Babylonian Talmud', in *From Athens to Jerusalem: Medicine in Hellenized and Jewish Lore and Early Christian Literature*, ed. S. Kottek and M. Horstmanshoff. Rotterdam: Erasmus Publishing, 3–32.

GRÜNBAUM, M. (1877). 'Beiträge zur vergleichenden Mythologie aus der Hagada'. *Zeitschrift der deutschen Morgenländischen Gesellschaft* 31: 183–359.

GRUNWALD, M. (1944–45). 'Folklore and Myself' [Hebr.]. *Edoth* 2: 1–22.

HALPERIN, D. J. (1980). *The Merkabah in Rabbinic Literature*. New Haven: American Oriental Society.

HAMILTON, V. P. (1971). 'Syriac Incantation Bowls'. PhD. thesis, Brandeis University.

HARARI, Y. (ed.) (1997). *The Sword of Moses: A Critical Edition and Study* [Hebr.]. Jerusalem: Academon Press.

—— (2006). 'The Sages and the Occult', in *The Literature of the Sages, Part 2: Midrash and Targum, Liturgy, Poetry, Mysticism, Contracts, Inscriptions, Ancient Science and the Languages of Rabbinic Literature*, ed. S. Safrai et al. Assen and Maastricht: Van Gorcum and Fortress Press, 521–64.

HAYMAN, P. (1991). 'Monotheism—A Misused Word in Jewish Studies?' *Journal of Jewish Studies* 42: 1–15.

ISBELL, C. D. (1975). *Corpus of the Aramaic Incantation Bowls*. Missoula: Society of Biblical Literature and Scholar Press.

JACOBS, L. 1984. *A Tree of Life: Diversity, Flexibility and Creativity in Jewish Law*. Oxford: The Littman Library and Oxford University Press.

JANOWITZ, N. (1991). 'Theories of Divine Names in Origen and Pseudo-Dionysus.' *History of Religions* 30: 359–371.

JOËL, D. H. (1883). *Aberglaube und die Stellung des Judenthums zu demselben*, 2 vols. Breslau: Jungfer.

KAGAN, S. R. (1952). *Jewish Medicine*. Boston: Medico-Historical Press.

KOTANSKY, R. (ed.) (1994–1999). *Greek Magical Amulets: The Inscribed Gold, Silver, Copper, and Bronze Lamellae*, 2. vols. Opladen: Westdeutscher Verlag.

KOTTEK, S. (1994). *Medicine and Hygiene in the Works of Flavius Josephus*. Leiden: Brill.

—— (1996). 'Hygiene and Healing among the Jews in the Post-Biblical Period: A Partial Reconstruction'. *Aufstieg und Niedergang der Römischen Welt* II, 37.3, 2843–65.

—— and Horstmanshoff, M. (eds) (2000). *From Athens to Jerusalem: Medicine in Hellenized and Jewish Lore and Early Christian Literature*. Rotterdam: Erasmus Publishing.

LAYARD, A. (1853). *Discoveries among the Ruins of Nineveh and Babylon*. New York: Harper.

LEVENE, D. (2003). *A Corpus of Magic Bowls: Incantation Texts in Jewish Aramaic from Late Antiquity*. London: Kegan Paul.

LÉVI, I. (1878). 'Über die Spuren des griechischen und römischen Alterthums im talmu-dischen Schriftthum', in *Verhandlungen der Versammlung Deutscher Philologen und Schulmänner.* Leipzig: Teubner, 77–88.

LEWYSOHN, L. (1858). *Die Zoologie des Talmuds. Eine umfassende Darstellung der rabbi-nischen Zoologie, unter steter Vergleichung der Forschungen älterer und neuerer Schriftstel-ler.* Frankfurt.: J. Baer:

LIEBERMAN, S. (ed.) (1955–1988). *Tosefta Ki-Fshutah: A Comprehensive Commentary on the Tosefta* [Hebr.], 10 vols. New York: Jewish Theological Seminary.

—— (1965). *Greek in Jewish Palestine.* New York: Jewish Theological Seminary.

LÖW, I. (1881). *Aramäische Pflanzennamen.* Leipzig: Engelmann (repr. Hildesheim: Olms 1973).

—— (1924–34). *Die Flora der Juden,* 4 vols. Vienna and Leipzig: Löwit (repr. Hildesheim: Olms 1967).

—— (1969). *Fauna und Mineralien der Juden,* ed. Alexander Scheiber. Hildesheim: Olms.

MARCELLUS EMPIRICUS (1968). *Marcellus Burdigalensis. De medicamentis,* ed. M. Nieder-mann and E. Liechtenhan. 2nd edn. Berlin: Akademie Verlag.

McCULLOUGH, W. S. (1967). *Jewish and Mandean Incantation Bowls in the Royal Ontario Museum.* Toronto: University of Toronto Press.

MERKELBACH, R./TOTTI, M. (1990–1992). *Abrasax: Ausgewählte Papyri religiösen und ma-gischen Inhalts,* 3. vols. Opladen: Westdeutscher Verlag.

MONTGOMERY, J. A. (1913). *Aramaic Incantation Texts from Nippur.* Philadelphia: University Museum.

NAVEH, J./SHAKED, S. (1985). *Aramaic Incantations of Late Antiquity.* Jerusalem: Magnes.

—— (1993). *Magic Spells and Formulae: Aramaic Incantations of Late Antiquity.* Jerusalem: Magnes.

PREISENDANZ, K. (1928). *Papyri Graecae Magicae: Die griechischen Zauberpapyri,* 3 vols. Stuttgart. Teubner (repr. 1973–1974).

PREUSS, J. (1911). *Biblisch-talmudische Medizin.* Berlin: Karger (repr. Wiesbaden: Fourier, 1992. English translation by F. Rosner, *Biblical and Talmudic Medicine,* New York: Sanhedrin, 1978).

Rebiger, B. et al. (2008–9). *Sefer ha-Razim I und II. Das Buch des Geheimnisse I und II.* Tübingen: Mohr-Siebeck.

SCHÄFER, P. (1993). 'Merkavah Mysticism and Magic', in *Gerschom Scholem's Major Trends in Jewish Mysticism,* ed. P. Schäfer and J. Dan. Tübingen: Mohr-Siebeck, 59–78.

—— and Shaked, S. (eds) (1994–99). *Magische Texte aus der Kairoer Geniza,* 3 vols. Tübingen: Mohr-Siebeck.

SCHIFFMAN, L. H./SWARTZ, M. D. (eds) (1992). *Hebrew and Aramaic Incantation Texts from the Cairo Geniza.* Sheffield: JSOT Press.

SCHOLEM, G. (1941). *Major Trends in Jewish Mysticism.* Jerusalem: Schocken.

—— (1965). *Jewish Gnosticism, Merkabah Mysticism and Talmudic Tradition.* 2nd ed. New York: Jewish Theological Seminary.

—— (1972). 'Der Name Gottes und die Sprachtheorie der Kabbala'. *Neue Rundschau* 83: 470–95.

SHAKED, S. (ed.) (2005). *Officina Magica: Essays on the Practice of Magic in Antiquity.* Leiden: Brill.

SEGAL, A. F. (1977). *Two Powers in Heaven: Early Rabbinic Reports about Christianity and Gnosticism.* Leiden: Brill.

SMITH, M. (1986). 'The Jewish Elements in the Magical Papyri'. *Society of Biblical Literature Seminar Papers* 25: 455–462.

SPERBER, D. (1985). 'Some Rabbinic Themes in Magical Papyri'. *Journal for the Study of Judaism* 16 (1985): 93–103.

—— (1990–1995). *Customs of Israel: Sources and History* [Hebr.], 5 vols. Jerusalem: Mossad Harav Kook.

TRACHTENBERG, J. (1939). *Jewish Magic and Superstition: A Study in Folk Religion*. New York: Behrman's Jewish Book House (repr. Philadelphia: University of Pennsylvania Press, 2004).

URBACH, E. E. (1975). *The Sages: Their Concepts and Beliefs*. Cambridge, Mass. and London: Harvard University Press.

VELTRI, G. (1993). 'Inyan Sota: Halakhische Voraussetzungen für einen magischen Akt nach einer theoretischen Abhandlung aus der Kairoer Geniza'. *Frankfurter Judaistische Beiträge* 20: 23–48.

—— (1997). *Magie und Halakhah*. Tübingen: Mohr-Siebeck.

—— (2002). 'The Figure of the Magician in Rabbinical Judaism: From Empirical Science to Theology'. *Jerusalem Studies in Arabic and Islam* 26: 187–204.

WANDREY, I. (2004). *Das Buch des Gewandes und Das Buch des Aufrechten*. Tübingen: Mohr-Siebeck.

YAMAUCHI, E. (1967). *Mandaic Incantation Texts*. New Haven: American Oriental Society.

ZILSEL E. (1942). 'The Sociological Roots of Science'. *American Journal of Sociology* 57: 245–279.

ZIMMELS, H. J. (1952). *Magicians, Theologians, and Doctors: Studies in Folk Medicine and Folklore as Reflected in the Rabbinical Responsa*. London: E. Goldston.

VIII

ENTERTAINMENT AND LEISURE-TIME ACTIVITIES

CHAPTER 32

<h1>BATHHOUSES AS PLACES OF SOCIAL AND CULTURAL INTERACTION</h1>

YARON Z. ELIAV

1. INTRODUCTION: HISTORY, TECHNOLOGY, AND CULTURE

The Roman public bathhouse was an impressive architectural complex, featuring both hot and cold water installations as well as a wide range of other services—a sauna and massage parlours, swimming pools, gardens, meeting rooms, food and oil stands, open courts for recreation and sports, and at times even libraries and brothels (Nielsen 1990; Yegül 1992; Fagan 1999; Dix/Houston 2006). The forerunner of this institution may be seen in the bathing facilities of the Greeks, mainly those incorporated into the *gymnasium* (Ginouvès 1962; DeLaine 1988: 14–17). But washing the body in the *gymnasium* was a secondary undertaking, inferior to athletic and intellectual activities, and limited to the privileged few who attended this place. Early Greek public baths also existed in the Hellenistic period, but on a much smaller scale and with limited attendance compared with the later Roman establishments. The Roman baths emerged almost concurrently in Asia Minor and southern Italy in the second century BCE, spread throughout the empire by the end of the first century BCE, and reached their peak in the first few centuries of the common era.

In ancient times, maintaining a regular supply of water required remarkable effort and resources. Throughout the Mediterranean world, people accumulated rain in cisterns, dug wells, and drew on natural springs and rivers, but water was generally used sparingly, for essential practices like drinking. Washing and keeping clean were neither a top priority nor a frequent undertaking. Therefore, in the centuries before Roman arrival, it would have been unimaginable that practically everyone in the known world would attend a public bath on nearly a daily basis and immerse one's body in warm water. Such was the enormity of the Roman transformation.

Roman engineers and architects refined and disseminated various technological advances over the centuries, including the development of cement and concrete as cohesive substances and the growing employment of the arch. These facilitated a crucial, and relatively easy-to-build, system for water transportation—the aqueduct (from the Latin *aqua*, water, and the verb *ducere*, to lead or to bring forward; Adam 1994: 73–87, 158–95, 235–63; Hodge 1992). Large and small, implemented in multiple variations, the aqueducts made possible the growing popularity of the baths by providing an abundant water supply to cities, towns, and military camps. By the second century CE, thousands of bathhouses dotted the Mediterranean world, in cities, towns, and even small villages. In the fourth century CE, the city of Rome alone offered over 800 baths (856 is the number cited in the *Curiosum urbis regionum XIV* and the *Notitia Regionum urbis XIV*, ed. Jordan, 573; but cf. Fagan 1999: 357). Using taxes and contributions from the upper strata of society, municipal authorities erected bathhouses for public use, usually free of charge. Other privately owned baths charged the masses entrance fees; groups and associations built semi-public baths and limited their access to members only; the military added their own, as did the rich who wished to bathe in the private confines of their villas and mansions. Attending the baths, usually in the late hours of the afternoon before dinner, became a standard component of everyday life (Fagan 1999: 22, and the sources listed in n. 28).

In addition to bathing, the bathhouse embodied many cultural facets of the Roman realm. Its space was suffused with sculpture and mosaics, representing local and imperial power as well as the mythological ethos of the time (Manderscheid 1981; *idem* 2004: 23–24; more below). Magic and medicine were frequently carried out there (see below), along with an array of hedonistic experiences that cherished the human body—from athletics to nudity, and from sex to massages and the anointment with oils and perfumes (e.g. Ovid, Ars 3.638–640; CIL 4.10677–8). As it catered to people from all walks of life, the bathhouse became a social arena, a unique environment where social hierarchy was both determined and blurred, and where the governing class and the elite blended with the lower strata of society, including the poor, women, and slaves (Fagan 1999: 189–219; more below). Over time, the emergence of the Roman bath would significantly alter daily habits and would foster far-reaching cultural consequences. Ultimately, it came to encapsulate *Romanitas*: the Roman experience of life.

2. ARCHITECTURE AND FUNCTION

A typical bathhouse may have included a changing variety of facilities, but ultimately it consisted of water and heat (on the following see Lucian, *Hippias*; Nielsen 1990; Yegül 1992). Warming the water became relatively easy with another technological innovation, ingenious in its simplicity—the hypocaust system (from the Greek *hypokauston*, 'heating from underneath'). Builders would suspend the bathhouse floor (thus named *suspensura*) on numerous small pillars (*pilae*) made of layered tiles. A furnace in a side chamber (*praefurnium*) channelled hot air into the void under the raised floors, heating them and the water above—before flowing outside through vertical canals at the sides of the room (see Vitruvius, *De Architectura* 5.10). This hot chamber (known as the *caldarium*) usually included a communal pool (*alveus*), a basin (*labrum*) for cold water, and at times benches around the walls. In addition to the heated nucleus, two other rooms offered engagement with varying temperatures—the *frigidarium*, a valuated room with cold water pools (known as *piscinae*), and the *tepidarium*, a mediating room between the cold and the warm. Other standard bathhouse chambers included the changing room (*apodyterium*), which provided niches and shelves for the storage of clothing, a sauna for both dry and wet sweat (*laconicum* and *sudatorium*, respectively), and a latrine. Outside the main building an open court (*palaestra*)—often surrounded by porticos—accommodated sports and exercise and frequently included an open-air swimming pool (*natatio*).

These basic components of the baths were designed in numerous shapes and sizes. Some were built on a circular plan where you walked in a specific direction from room to room, others were more linear in their contours, and many others maintained their own unique look. The huge, imperial baths of Rome (usually called *thermae*) could house thousands of attendants at once. The large urban facilities all over the empire (normally called *balaneia*) could host hundreds of bathers, and numerous others were smaller. Over time, bathing routines evolved, and people typically attended the bathhouse during the afternoon, before dinner. A standard procedure involved working out in the *palaestra*, followed by alternating between hot and cold baths, attending the sauna, and if they had the means, ending (or beginning) with a massage, and by applying oil and then scrapping it off with a strigil.

3. JEWS IN THE BATHS: SCHOLARLY DEBATES

Some modern scholars suggest that Jews in the ancient world were hostile toward the baths, arguing that many avoided this institution and renounced its pagan connotations. Ronny Reich, for example, substantiates such a claim for Jews of the early Roman era by citing the lack of archaeological findings of baths in Jewish settlements from the Second Temple period, as well as with numerous halakhic 'problems' that early rabbinic sources associate with this institution (Reich 1988; for others who adhere, although without elaboration, to such a model, see Eliav 2000: 422, n. 10). Other scholars simply characterize the baths as an 'idolatrous venue' (Friedheim 2002), which by its very definition entails resentment and repudiation. In fact, the opposite is true (Eliav 1995a, 2000, 2003). Jews—just like their fellow residents of the Roman Mediterranean—were quite enthusiastic about the benefits of the baths and frequented this establishment with almost no reservations. Reservations that they did voice were not unique to them as Jews, but rather part of the broad cultural discourse about the baths that were shared by their fellow citizens of the Roman world. As a result, the baths became a remarkable intersection of culture, a locus of disagreements, contests, and evolving social traditions.

The divergent views among scholars emanate from general methodological and conceptual disagreements regarding the position of the Jews within the cultural milieu of their time. Until recently, modern scholars have tended to examine the relationship between Judaism and Graeco-Roman culture in terms of the conflicts and tensions that purportedly divided them. Most textbooks portrayed Judaism throughout its ancient history as a coherent (if not homogeneous) unity, a culture that, despite internal conflicts, disputes, and differences over both minor and major issues, arraigned itself steadfastly against the outside world in its Greek, and then Roman, guise. This contrast prevailed in all areas of life, from daily behaviour to language and literature, and legal and governing institutions. Consequently, by making Roman culture and Judaism two distinct, separate, and to a large extent hostile categories, these modern writers went on to define the connection between them in terms of 'influence', a category usually carrying a negative connotation of assimilation. Some Jews willingly and consciously 'Hellenized'— that is, they adopted some aspects of the 'bad' Graeco-Roman culture, whether language or personal name, or, even worse, they abandoned their original way of life entirely and went to graze in foreign fields.

Only in the last generation have these scholarly assumptions come under question, as new models of the cultural dynamics that defined Jewish life have emerged. The understanding of the Jewish engagement with bathhouses—an institution that seems to exemplify the essence of Graeco-Roman culture—has evolved within the contours of this scholarly debate. Unlike the traditional view espoused and applied to the study of the baths by Reich, Friedheim, and others,

Eliav has argued that the traditional 'cultural strife' model cannot inclusively define the essence of the encounter between Judaism and the Graeco-Roman way of life (Eliav 2000). He suggested an alternative model, which can be termed 'filtered absorption' or 'controlled incorporation.' The argument at the foundation of this thesis is that many foreign elements—components of the pagan-Gentile civilization adjacent to the Jewish domain in Palestine—were gradually absorbed by the Jewish population in a controlled manner, omitting or neutralizing those aspects which offended their traditional practices. This process was not uniform, and there was no authoritative power enforcing it. Such a never-ending meeting of cultures resulted in a diverse and porous Jewish society, embedded in the cultural textures of its surroundings and carving its identity and ways of life from inside this broader sphere. The establishment of the Roman bathhouse in Jewish society, and its role(s) therein, provides a good example of this process.

4. DISSEMINATION, ACQUAINTANCE, AND ADAPTATION

The wide dissemination of the Roman baths in the East did not occur until the first century CE. But already in the early Roman and Hellenistic periods, archaeological data indicates that wealthy Jews were fast to incorporate Roman-style bathing into their dwellings, as can be seen in the Hasmonean palaces in Jericho (Small 1987; Netzer 2001: 100–14), or the estate in south Judaea called 'the palace of Hilkiyah' (Damati 1972). In the early Roman period, Josephus records the existence of bathhouses in Herod's fortified palaces at Jerusalem (Josephus, Bell. 5.168, 241). Similarly, archaeological excavations add evidence for baths in Herod's strongholds at Jericho, Cyprus (on the hilltop west of Jericho), Herodium, Masada, and Machaerus (Netzer 2006). The excavations in Ein Zur at Ramat ha-Nadiv, northeast of Caesarea, have uncovered a semi-public bathhouse in a large Jewish estate, dating to before the destruction of the Second Temple (Hirschfeld 2000: 311–29).

All of the above are private baths built by the affluent in their estates. But even regular Jewish towns from the late Second Temple period seem to include this establishment. One of the attempts to assassinate Herod took place while the king was entering the inner rooms of a public bath at Isana, a Jewish village some twenty kilometres north of Jerusalem (Josephus, Bell. 1.340–341; Ant. 14.462–464). Remnants of another bath were unearthed in the Jewish village of Artas, not far from 'Solomon's pools', south of Jerusalem (Amit 1994: 12–15 and n. 38). From the era subsequent to the destruction of the Second Temple, bathhouses were found in Jewish towns such as Ein Gedi on the shores of the Dead Sea (although scholars have misidentified this as a military bath; Stern 1993: 404–405), and in Rama in the Upper Galilee (Tzaferis 1980). From the end of the second century CE onwards, bathhouses became a regular fixture in every city and town of Roman Palestine, the prime examples of which can be seen in Bet Shean/Scythopolis (Mazor 1999), Tiberias, Sephoris, and Caesarea Maritima (see the relevant entries in Stern 1993).

Hardly surprisingly, Jews were quite aware of the bathhouse and its various facilities. In a statement attributed to second century CE rabbinic scholars, the construction of bathhouses is listed among the 'fine [or: corrupt, according to another view] works' of the Roman nation (b. Shab. 33b). Other rabbinic sources show an intimate and detailed acquaintance with the architectural structure of the bathhouse. The building's interior, consisting of a series of rooms, each designed for a different function in the bathing cycle, is the setting for the halakhic three-fold division of the bath into 'a place where people stand dressed', 'a place where people stand naked', and 'a place where people stand both naked and dressed' (T. Ber. 2:20). Another source designates the various parts of the bath as the 'inner rooms', 'outer rooms', 'the furnaces room', 'the cloakroom' (or perhaps the massage room, depending on the interpretation of the transliterated Graeco-Latin term 'olyarin), the 'storage room for the woods' and the 'pools' (T. B.B. 3:3). The heating technique of the hypocaust system, and its various architectural elements—the pillars, the raised floor, and the perils associated with them—provided a talmudic author with the raw material for the legendary anecdote concerning the miraculous adventures of the fourth century CE R. Abbahu in the bathhouse of Tiberias (y. Betsa 1:6, 60c ; b. Ket. 62a). The scene in which the bathhouse floor collapses and a random pillar happens to be in the path of R. Abbahu's fall, although fantastic in its very nature, is modelled on a common hazard of the bathhouse heating system, namely the crumpling floors of the hypocaust (Eliav 2002a: 235–252).

Early rabbinic legal traditions refer to the bathhouse in the most neutral terms, testifying to the flawless integration of this institution into Jewish life. One such discussion revolves around the usage of a bath on the Sabbath (M. Makh. 2:5; T. Shab. 17:18). The need to continuously preserve the bath's furnace seems to conflict with the rabbinic halakhah that prohibits maintaining a fire on the Sabbath. And indeed, rabbinic law eventually ruled that one may not use the bath on the Sabbath. But in a good example of the faulty presumptions of scholarship, Reich concluded that such dilemmas meant that rabbis and Jews avoided the baths altogether (Reich 1988).

Such an understanding is problematic on a few levels. First, in the case of baths on the Sabbath, early legal traditions provide ways to deal with the problem of burning wood, and thus allowing Jews to attend even on the Sabbath (y. Shab. 3:1, 6a; Eliav 1995b). Further, the rabbinic discussions of the halakhic practicalities associated with the baths, such as how to comply with the laws of the Sabbath, can only occur because they accept the legitimacy of this establishment, and perceive it as a habitual tenet of Jewish life. In contrast, rabbis refuse to devote their intellectual energy to technical questions related to pagan temples (beyond simply prohibiting them), since in their minds it is inconceivable that a Jew would enter such a place. Admittedly, many rabbinic traditions present ideal institutions that do not exist in reality (such as the Jewish high court known as the Sanhedrin, or the many traditions about the long-gone Temple in Jerusalem), or focus on theoretical legal problems that are not grounded in actuality. But the Roman bathhouse, unlike the Sanhedrin or the Jerusalem Temple, occupies no prestigious status in Jewish memory that would justify heightened attention, and thus detailed legal discussions about it must emerge from the experiences of daily life.

Similar conclusions regarding the neutral, uncontested status of public bath-houses emerge from the halakhic traditions relating to ritual purity. A halakhah in the Tosefta relating the procedures of a *niddah* (menstruating woman)—the most common form of impurity in post-Second Temple Jewish society—refers to 'women's [public] baths' (T. Nid. 6:15), and the same passage in the Mishnah applies the term 'house of the impure women', thus at least hinting at the existence of separate facilities for menstruating women (M. Nid. 7:4, according to the reading of the better manuscripts). Similar to documented practices in the *miqvah* (a purifying immersion pool), it may be possible that in the bathhouse, too, Jews took measures to separate the impure and the pure (Eliav 1995a: 21 n. 82). Other rabbinic sources refer to *miqva'ot* that function in public bathhouses, and such were also found in archaeological excavations (Grossberg 2001). If certain halakhic prescriptions were met, the rabbis seem to even approve the performance of ritual purification in the cold water pools of the baths (e.g. T. Miqv. 6:4). Sources that voice uneasiness with this practice have nothing to do with negative attitudes toward the baths but rather with stipulations regarding the usage of *miqva'ot* outside the borders of the Land of Israel (T. Miqv. 6:3; clearly understood by Grossberg 2001:179; *pace* Oppenheimer 2008: 55).

Moving from legal formulations to more explicit views about the bathhouse, rabbinic sources by and large voice a very positive tone. In one of many such examples, a rabbinic statement equates the biblical description of the 'luxuries of common people' (Qoh. 2:8) with the contemporary bathhouse (Qoh. R. 2:8). Rabbis seem infatuated, like everyone else, with the effortless opportunity to immerse one's body in warm water (Lam. R. 3:18 [based on Geniza fragment Taylor Schechter Collection 6.62]; b. Shab. 25b). All in all, the Jews, as far as we can tell, had no objections to the bathhouse as an institution, not even in the early stages of its absorption in the region. This conclusion goes beyond the physical evidence that bathhouses existed. A priori, there could have been bathhouses that Jews strongly resented. But despite the interpretations of some scholars, close examination reveals that the sources do not voice such objections, neither during the last century of the Second Temple period nor in the centuries thereafter. On the contrary, exhaustive examination of rabbinic texts shows that the bathhouse was an integral and legitimate component of Jewish life in those times.

5. STATUARY OF THE BATHS

Statues adorned Roman public bathhouses, constituting an indispensable part of every visitor's encounter (Manderscheid 1981; *idem* 2004: 23–24; see also DeLaine 1988: 25–27). Chiselled on the pediment, or standing full size on its tip (*acroterion*), or placed on the cornice, figurative art welcomed the bather at the building's facade. Inside, sculptured pieces populated almost every possible spot—reliefs engraved on friezes, busts (*protomai*) carved out of the *abaci* (the square slabs at the top of the column's capital), life-sized three-dimensional images arranged on beams spanning the columns, in special niches in the wall or scattered around on pedestals. The subject repertoire offered a diverse mix: emperors, benefactors, gods, mythological scenes, and important personalities memorialized for various reasons.

As elsewhere in the Roman urban landscape, the function of these artefacts extended beyond their decorative value. Public sculptures were the 'mass media' of the Roman world. They occupied urban centres throughout the empire, serving what art historians call a 'plastic language' that communicated political, religious, and social messages. Sculptural displays evoked a complex spectrum of emotions— from fear and loathing to aesthetic admiration—and of ideas, from reflections on the nature of the divine to the implications of social hierarchy, patronage, and power (Eliav et al. 2008). How then, could Jews partake in a scene seemingly full of precisely the kind of idolatry that was forbidden to them?

This profusion of images in the baths has led Friedheim to characterize the place as 'idolatrous' (Friedheim 2002). But such a claim does not capture the complex nature of the bathhouse or its statues. On the one hand, in the minds of the people who used it, as testified by numerous literary and epigraphic references, the place registered as totally secular, a non-consecrated establishment (*locus profanus*). On the other hand, this designation can be quite misleading when applied to the ancient world, in which one's entire reality was perceived through what we today would call 'religious lenses' (Eliav 2003). In a cultural environment saturated with religion, it is reasonable to assume that a statue of a god, even if not within the religious context of a temple, was still perceived as a religious figure. The many inscriptions unearthed in bathhouses throughout the empire demonstrate the abundant spirituality that was intrinsic to the baths. First, the steps of the bathhouse were personified as gods and goddesses; nymphs were housed there as well. Rooms and sometimes entire bath complexes were named after gods (Dunbabin 1989). Some bathhouses, admittedly only relatively few, operated in the sanctuary compounds of various gods, and this is probably the meaning behind the mishnaic idiom 'A bathhouse of idolatry' (M. A.Z. 4:3). Secondly, the 'Emperor's cult', which commingled religion with *Realpolitik*, was practised at the baths (DeLaine 1997: 77–84). Thirdly, ceremonial aspects of religion were unquestionably practised at the thermal baths, which, like other medicinal establishments (such as the Asclepieion), were patronized by the curative gods, and the healing process included a ceremonial thanksgiving offer to the god in charge, as well as other rituals.

Jewish sources too express this complex, multifaceted situation. One rabbinic view considers the statues at the bath to be idols (*avodah zarah*), and consequently it even prohibits construction of the 'vault' (*kipah*; niche?) where they stand (M. A.Z. 1:7). This position coincides with the rabbinic view that negates the entire sculptural environment of the Roman world under the pretence that 'all statues are [to be perceived as] being worshipped [whether they actually are or not]' (M. A.Z. 3:1; Eliav 2002b). Such perceptions of bathhouse statues also inform the question that the rabbinic author places in the mouth of Proklos who, according to a famous anecdote, challenged Rabban Gamaliel when the latter attended the bath of Aphrodite in Acco (M. A.Z. 3:4, see also Schwartz 1998 and Yadin 2006 on this story; Stemberger in this volume). Rabban Gamaliel's response to Proklos introduces the other side of the coin. In his opinion, the presence of Aphrodite in the context of the bath is not considered idolatry. Many rabbis shared this view.

Adjacent to the above-mentioned halakhah that prohibits all statues in the Roman world, the Mishnah presents an opposing view—'[a statue] is not forbidden except one that has a stick or a bird or a ball' (M. A.Z. 3:1). This perspective should be understood in the light of remarks such as Cicero's (in De Natura Deorum 1.29.81), about the ability of people to identify divine sculpture and to differentiate it from the many statues that surrounded it. The ancients were able to do this by 'reading' the widely known attributes and iconography that the artists assigned to the figures. Here we see the shared 'plastic language' that informed the interaction of ancient people with sculptured artefacts, and allowed them to distinguish between a divine statue—one infused with the divine spirit (the *pneuma*) and considered a sacred object (*res sacra*)—and a statue that was not. The items listed by the rabbis in the Mishnah—the stick, the bird, and the ball—were, at least in their eyes, such identifying signs of a deity. In the Tosefta other elements are added to the list, such as a sword, a crown, a ring, and a snake (T. A.Z. 5:1). In other words, we can see the rabbis utilizing the common 'plastic language' in order to create their own differentiation between worshipped, sacred statues (*res sacra*) and not worshipped, profane (*profanus*) objects.

Rabban Gamaliel's position takes the distinction of the rabbis a step further, adding the practical function—what may be called the 'identifying context' of a statue—to the plastic language criterion of the previous rabbis. Aphrodite was surely a 'worshipped deity' (in the sense defined by the rabbis above) along with other sculptured pieces of her kind that received rituals, were worshipped at temples, and so on. Nevertheless, Rabban Gamaliel maintains that a statue in a given location is forbidden only if that particular one is used in ritual worship, and therefore Aphrodite in the baths is permitted.

Another tradition in the Palestinian Talmud can be explained along similar lines. In this passage, the third-century R. Simeon b. Lakish encountered a group of people sprinkling liquids in honour of an Aphrodite statue in the bathhouse of Bostra (y. Shebi. 8:11, 38b). According to the talmudic account, after relating this incident to his colleague and teacher R. Yohanan, the latter permitted it retro-actively (i.e. he ruled that the act did not turn the statue into an idol and consequently the bath into a prohibited location), and asserted, 'A thing of the public is not forbidden' (ibid.).

This anecdote further elaborates the halakhic principle developed in the Rabban Gamaliel story above. According to the position presented by the Talmud, not only is a statue of a deity standing outside of a ritual context not considered a forbidden idol (R. Gamaliel's position), but even the actual performance of an informal ritual deed in its honour (known in Roman terminology as *dedicatio*) does not revoke its previous non-idolatrous status. The explanation provided for this ruling—'A thing of the public is not forbidden'—conveys the reasoning behind R. Yohanan's interdiction. According to his view, if a statue of a god stands in a public, non-cultic context and is considered non-idolatrous (*profanus*), the unofficial devotion of individuals cannot change its unsanctioned status.

To conclude this discussion, it seems that rabbinic differentiation between various statues, based on whether they were worshipped or not, is anchored in the conceptual framework of the Roman world. These are not some peculiar classifications of the rabbis that would have sounded ridiculous to the people of the time, whether Jewish or not, rather they are halakhic formulations of accepted, widespread conceptions stemming from the common ways of 'viewing' statuary in the Roman world. When applied to the bathhouse, these rabbinic rulings allowed those Jews who wished to follow them to engage this space peacefully, and with the comfort that they were not violating their religious principles. Others, of course, may have followed stricter views, recorded, for example, in a tradition about the shattering of bathhouse statues (y. A.Z. 4:4, 43d). Finally, bathhouses lacking three-dimensional ornamentation were not unheard of (e.g. Sidonius, Epistulae 2.2.4–7). Although the record from Palestine does not provide evidence for such, one may not rule out the possibility that some may have existed in Jewish towns as well.

6. SOCIAL ENCOUNTERS

By their very nature, public bathing facilities in the Roman world attracted people from all walks of life. These establishments relied on a spatial layout in which hierarchal, communal, and cultural boundaries were—if only for a short while—blurred, and even erased. Similar to the situation that anthropologists describe in the cafés of nineteenth-century Paris, bathhouses drew people together and eliminated the various and more obvious status marks that differentiated them in the outside world: in the baths a person was separated from his clothes and jewellery, without the identifying signs of career or home, stripped of most symbols of his social status. Many sources illustrate the colourful social tapestry of the baths, as the higher echelons of society rubbed shoulders with people of the lowest strata. Such mixings obscured certain designations of the social order. Unlike theatres and stadiums, where reserved seats and segregated sections delineated social rank and stature, in the bath (despite some notable exceptions) people shared the space quite evenly. At the same time, the close proximity with 'others' provided an ideal venue to demarcate and reaffirm social lines, whether communal, political, or religious (Fagan 1999: 206–219).

Rabbinic stories and anecdotes associated with the public baths, both real and fictional, if analysed in a historical-critical way, may provide illuminating snap-shots of the social dynamics that took shape in this institution, in the provincial setting of Palestine (for a discussion of bathhouse stories in the Talmud Yerushalmi see Jacobs 1998). Many of the elements featured in these texts resemble typical bathhouse life throughout the empire. Such are the beggars and thieves who crowd the place in some rabbinic stories (e.g. y. Ber. 2:8, 5c; y. Peah 8:9, 21b), and are known to have been a constant annoyance to bathers all over the Mediterranean (Fagan 1999: 36–38). In another example, when R. Abbahu, a fourth-century rabbinic scholar and a local dignitary in Caesarea, visits the bathhouse of Tiberias, the Talmudic story assigns Gothic slaves to accompany him, accentuating his (perhaps imagined) political distinction (y. Betsa 1:6, 60c). Here too, many non-Jewish sources speak of the role of slaves in the shared social environment of the public baths—keeping the populace away from their masters, thus carving an elevated arena within the shared space, guarding the clothes from thieves, and providing extra services such as drying their owners with towels or anointing and massaging them with oil (many of these references are collected in Fagan 1999). Rabbinic sources operate in the same social milieu and depict the slaves in the baths in similar ways (e.g. Sifre Num. 115; T. Qid. 1:5).

Other bath stories depict rabbinic figures coming into contact and conversing with a variety of characters who normally would be outside their circles. The famous mishnaic tradition mentioned above portrays a pagan philosopher chal-lenging Rabban Gamaliel's attendance in an Acco bathhouse due to the presence of a nude statue of Aphrodite (M. A. Z. 3:4). Another source narrates a clash between rabbinic sages and a Christian 'heretic', who met them at the baths, defied them with his magic skills, and eventually challenged the biblical tradition about God's violent miracles against the Egyptians at the Red Sea with the 'new' Jesus narrative of a pacifistic walk on the Sea of Galilee (y. Sanh. 7:19, 25d). Needless to say, the rabbinic authors normally depict their own as emerging with the upper hand. But for the social historian the very fact that these authors chose the bathhouse as the backdrop for their tales illustrates the social mechanisms that evolved in this establishment. How did Jews react to this relatively borderless social setting? Did some rabbis worry about mixing with women, heretics, socially inferior people in the baths, while others thought it normal, or even beneficial? Our sources do not provide a clear answer; all we have, as discussed above, is a general lack of reservation about the bathhouse in rabbinic references. It seems that rabbis, and other Jews for that matter, were quite enthusiatic about attending this institution.

7. NUDITY

Men and women throughout the Roman world normally bathed together, usually with their bodies fully exposed (Ward 1992). Questions about this habit's exclusivity (did everyone bathe in the nude?), chronological scope (did people always bathe in the nude? and if not, when did this phenomenon begin or end?), and geography (was nude bathing practised everywhere?), are a more complicated matter, which has not always received sufficient attention. Centuries of Christian and Jewish piety since the Middle Ages, typically endorsing a suppression of the body, have distorted our vision of Roman times. It was a much more revealing landscape, in the physical sense of the word, than ours. People urinated into buckets in the middle of the street (and the urine was then used as detergent), men and women shared open toilets at the public latrines. Overall, in this pre-underwear age, body parts that we today tend to conceal were much more on display.

Although some bathing establishments implemented partial segregation between the sexes (the Stabian baths in Pompeii are the most documented example), and some emperors legislated against the sexual licentiousness that transpired at the baths (e.g. Scriptores Historiae Augustae. Vita Hadriani 18.10), only a few of the numerous structures that archaeologists have uncovered throughout the Mediterranean basin contain a double bathing arrangement that could accommodate the separate and simultaneous usage by men and women (Nielsen 1990: 146–8; Ward 1992: 128–39). Here and there we hear of different hours for men and women (the best known source is CIL 2, suppl. 5181), but on the whole people engaged in this institution together, and even if some (perhaps members of the upper strata of society) utilized certain bathing garments (see in detail Eliav 2000: 444–8), many, if not most, did not.

References to nude people in the baths resonate in several rabbinic passages. For example, a previously cited tradition specifically mentions 'a place where people stand naked' in the bath (T. Ber. 2.20), although it does not speak of the presence of women at the same place. A later source which cites this tradition labelled the bath as a 'house [room?] of the nude' (Teffilin 17, ed. Higger, 47–8). People engaging in nude bathing are in the background of the mentioned tale about R. Gamaliel visiting the bathhouse of Aphrodite (M. A.Z. 3:4). Their bare flesh led to R. Gamaliel's refusal to respond to Proklos' question inside the bath, since rabbinic law prohibits 'holy' activity—such as prayer or discussing halakhah—in the presence of undressed bodies (e.g. M. Ber. 3:5). Mixed bathing also figures in the proscription dealing with a woman who 'washes and bathes in the public bath with just anyone' (T. Ket. 7:6). A story preserved by the fourth-century Church Father Epiphanius tells of the misconduct of a Jewish patriarch's son with a beautiful woman he met at the hot room of the thermal baths in Gadara (Adversus Haereses [Panarion] 30.7.5–6, ed. Holl, 342).

Some Jews may have had reservations about the nudity and licentious atmosphere that pervaded the mixed baths (Testament Reuven 3:11; T. Ber. 2:14, 20–21; Epiphanius, Adversus Haereses [Panarion] 30.7.5–6), just as others, including the Romans themselves (chief among them more than a few emperors) and the Church Fathers (Zellinger 1928; Berger 1982), voiced similar disdain. Indeed, some sources allude to separated bathing in Jewish and Christian circles. In the course of warning against mixed bathing, a Syriac Christian guidebook instructs that, 'When there is a bath of women (*baln'a denasha'*) in the town or in the village, a believing woman shall not bathe in a bath with a man' (Didascalia Apostolorum 3). An identical designation appears in a rabbinic tradition regarding a *niddah*, that is, a menstruating woman (T. Nid. 6:15), and a parallel passage calls the same place 'a house of impure women' (M. Nid. 7:4; Eliav 2000: 444). In a similar vein, a Christian story relates that Symeon 'the fool' thoughtlessly rushed into the women's baths in the Syrian city of Emesa (modern Homs), describing it as 'two baths next to each other, one for men and one for women' (Leontius Neapolitanus, Vita Symeonis Sali 35, PG 93.1713). A rabbinic tradition dealing with the disclosure of a woman's physical defects before marriage also indirectly proves at least the theoretical possibility of sexual segregation at the baths. Among the various possibilities, the Mishnah states: 'And if there was a bathhouse in that town he may not make complaints even of secret defects, since he can inquire about her from his women kinsfolk' (M. Ket. 7:8). The vague mention of 'a bath' apparently means that there may have been only one bathhouse, and segregation between men and women could have been based on different hours of bathing.

It is clear that mixed, nude bathing existed and was well known among the Jews of Roman Palestine. But there were also ways to avoid such an experience, either by arranging separate hours for men and women or by creating different facilities altogether. The scarcity of the sources does not allow firm conclusions as to the extent of these alternatives.

8. MAGIC AND THE PERILS OF THE BATHS

One important aspect of public bathhouses has gone relatively unnoticed in recent scholarship—the notion of the bathhouse as what anthropologists label a 'scary place' (Low/Lawrence-Zúñiga 2003: 225–7; Eliav 2009). On the most rudimentary, sensual level, the enclosed, dim space of the bathhouse may have intimidated some attendants, who were more accustomed to stroll the open, urban landscape of Mediterranean cities. The bathhouse also featured many hazards that endangered its clientele—water and humidity resulted in slippery floors; the hot steam in the ceramic and copper pipes that ran the walls could scorch the bare flesh that piled into the crowded halls, and so could the boiling water in the tubs and pools. Even more daunting were the frequent collapses of the floors. As mentioned before, the heart of the ingenious, water-warming hypocaust system were the raised floors of the hot rooms, which allowed for hot air to be channelled underneath. Its one weakness lay in its vulnerability: the combination of water and humidity with the weight of the bathers, together with inefficient building practices, resulted in the frequent disintegration of these suspended floors. It was not uncommon that a person would come to relax in the baths and find himself or herself falling into the searing vacuums underneath the floors. As in much of the ancient world, danger—and the unease and anxiety that accompanied it—were present even in places of leisure.

On a psychological level, the intermingling of the sexes in an environment that did not preclude physical exposure may have contributed to a different kind of unrest. The spectrum of reactions that nudity provoked in the mind of the ancients could contain anything from agitation to a sense of exigency. The uncontrolled reactions of the body—from sweating to the intense pulsing of the blood, and from bodily odours to involuntary erections—all could result in uneasiness, tension, and trepidation. Finally, the mixing of cultures and classes in the public baths, as discussed above, took away the security mechanisms that social boundaries provide. People exposed not only their hidden body parts but also their beliefs and cultural assumptions. This situation could have many effects, but on its most basic level it could be quite daunting. All in all, the bathhouse—with its huge, dark, sweaty and slippery halls, a place of possible physical danger and infused with sexual intimidation, as well as its boundary-transgressing cultural mixture—seems to fit quite well the anthropological model of a 'scary place'.

Various rabbinic sources refer to the perils of the baths. The collapsing floors of the hypocaust were discussed previously in the story about R. Abbahu. The Talmud relates that another rabbi, R. Mana, used to deposit his will prior to attending a heated bath (y. Ber. 4:4, 8b). A later (medieval) rabbinic collection enumerates numerous safety measures that developed over the years, geared to cope with the risks of the baths: for example, one should not bring one's oil in a glass vessel because it 'endangers life' (if someone slips and the glass shatters), spit on the floors, or greet one's fellow (probably a superstitious precaution). Also mentioned is the life-threatening danger of jumping into a shallow pool (Derekh Eretz Rabbah 10:2–3, ed. Higger, 301–303; Kallah Rabbah 9.15–17, ed. Higger, 338–339).

As an existential tool in the world of the ancients, magic pervaded every corner of life and acquired numerous manifestations. In one of its most popular expressions, magical techniques supplied remedy for anxiety (analogous to what some drugs offer today), a means of coping with the realm of fear. This aspect of magic applied to the Roman bathhouse as well, as testified by the many magical sources, as well as references to spirits and demons that relate to this place (e.g. Preisendanz, Papyri Graecae Magicae 2.50, 36.69–77, 127.3–4; Bonner 1932; Dunbabin 1989).

Rabbinic material, largely unnoticed by scholars dealing with this topic, adds significant information to the study of magic in the public bathhouse. Illustrating the richness of the sources is a Palestinian story about the encounter between the Jewish patriarch, R. Yudan Nesia, his companion Shmuel bar Nahman, and the emperor Diocletian (y. Ter. 8:10, 46b–c; Gen. R. 63). The plot evolves around the space of two bathhouses, a safe one in Tiberias and a hostile one in Paneas. The protagonist in charge of mediating between the rabbis and the various dangers they need to overcome is a miraculous creature named *Angitaris* (and in some versions *Antigras/Agentin*). The rabbinic narrator's efforts to 'convert' the *Angitaris* by placing the right views in his mouth ('bathe yourself and your creator will perform miracles') does not detract from his true nature—he is the demon of the baths, in charge of neutralizing the hazards of the fire (thus his name, which apparently stems from the Latin *ignis*–fire) and the consequential steaming waters.

Similar spirits are well known from Graeco–Roman sources and so are the many ways to appease them, the most popular of which was tossing a magical bowl into the furnace of the baths prior to entering (Bonner 1932: 208). In *Sefer ha-Razim*, a Jewish magical recipe book from late antiquity that was found in the Cairo Genizah, we find: 'if you wish to extinguish a bath so its blaze does not grow and burn . . .' (ed. Margalioth, 93), followed by a page-long list of magical devices that one can apply in order to overcome this risk. Two of the angels mentioned in that same passage of *Sefer ha-Razim* (although their role is admittedly unclear) are *Agra* and *Gentes*, and the similar phonetics with the rabbinic *Angitaris* is self-evident. Similarly, the rabbis formulated a special prayer, a sort of magical enchantment, for entering the baths, meant to guard Jews from its various hazards—everything from slipping to getting scorched, and from an unwanted erection to being harmed by a collapsing hypocaust (and not the roofs or the walls, as medieval commentaries, as well as nineteenth-century scholars, both unfamiliar with the mechanisms of Roman baths, wrongly thought; T. Ber. 6:17; y. Ber. 9:6, 14b; Derekh Eretz Rabbah 10:1, ed. Higger, 295–6).

Magic also helped bathers to confront the social difficulties experienced in the 'wild' world of the baths. Another rabbinic story discussed above (y. Sanh. 7:19,

25d) locates in the bathhouse a confrontation between a Christian heretic and three leading rabbis, R. Eliezer, R. Yehoshua, and R. Aqiva. Here it is worth highlighting the magical practices that both sides implement in the debate. The heretic, upon recognizing the three sages, declares ('*amar ma demar*' 'he said what he said')—a typical talmudic phrase to indicate the use of a magic formula. He is then able to use the cavity under the dome of the bathhouse—a known region of spirits and demons—to capture the rabbis; they in turn must apply their own magical strengths to strike back. In short, magic functions here as a tool that copes with the socially threatening aspects of the baths.

Altogether then, the rabbis do not appear to have been mere outside observers of the magical landscape that transpired in Roman bathhouses. Rather, they are presented as regular practitioners of magic, part and parcel of the cultural landscape in the Graeco-Roman milieu, and habitual participants in its daily mechanisms. They attended the bathhouses as frequently as any other inhabitant of Roman towns and cities, and they coped with its challenges using the same means available to all, namely magical techniques and formulas. Like so many others, rabbis tried to put a Jewish spin on these magical practices, especially by relating the source of its power to the God of Israel. By doing so, they were no different from other ethnic and religious groups in the Roman Mediterranean. Each group—from the Egyptians and the many other adherers of Serapis to the Persians and the numerous other believers in Mithras (who had a very prominent presence in the baths), and from Christians to Syrians, from Phoenicians to Arabs—all ascribed their magical abilities in the baths to the power of their particular deity. The Jews of the ancient world proved no exception to this rule. Like so many of their far-flung brethren in the Roman world, they were captivated and unnerved, intrigued and dubious, and ultimately unable to resist the bathhouse.

LIST OF ABBREVIATIONS

CIL = Corpus Inscriptionum Latinarum.

SUGGESTED READING

The study of Roman bathhouses has flourished in the last two decades, with a series of detailed monographs providing easy access to various aspects of the subject, from material evidence, both physical remains and inscriptions, to the vast amount of information about this establishment embedded in Graeco-Roman literature (most notably Nielsen 1990; Yegül 1992; Fagan 1999). A good updated bibliography is Manderscheid 2004. Unfortunately, these general studies do not pay much attention to the ancient Jewish aspects of this topic, and when they refer to it they present idiosyncratic views on the interaction of Jews with the Roman culture and way of life. Recent work by Judaic studies scholars strives to amend this situation (Jacobs 1998; Eliav 2000), but a comprehensive study of the engagement of Jews with the Roman public bath, exhausting the numerous references scattered in rabbinic literature and applying updated methodology, remains a desideratum.

BIBLIOGRAPHY

ADAM, J.-P. (1994). *Roman Building: Materials and Techniques.* Bloomington: Indiana University Press.

AMIT, D. (1994). 'What Was the Source of Herodion's Water?' [Hebr.]. *Cathedra* 71: 3–20.

BERGER, A. (1982). *Das Bad in der byzantinischen Zeit. Miscellanea Byzantina Monacensia* 27. Munich: Institut für Byzantinistik und neugriechische Philologie.

BONNER, C. (1932). 'Demons of the Bath', in *Studies Presented to F. L.I. Griffith*, ed. S. R. K. GLANVILLE. London: Egypt Exploration Society and Oxford University Press, 203–8.

DAMATI, E. (1972). 'Khirbet el-Mûraq'. *Israel Exploration Journal* 22: 173.

DELAINE, J. (1988). 'Recent Research on Roman Baths'. *Journal of Roman Archaeology* 1: 11–31.

—— (1997). *The Baths of Caracalla.* Journal of Roman Archaeology Supplementary Series 25. Portsmouth: Journal of Roman Archaeology.

DIX, T. K./HOUSTON, G. W. (2006). 'Public Libraries in the City of Rome from the Augustan Age to the Time of Diocletian'. *Mélanges d'Archéologie et d'Histoire de l'École Française de Rome: Antiquité* 118: 671–717, 730.

DUNBABIN, K. M. D. (1989). '*Baiarum grata voluptas*–Pleasures and Dangers of the Baths'. *Papers of the British School at Rome* 57: 6–46.

ELIAV, Y. Z. (1995a). 'Did the Jews at First Abstain from Using the Roman Bath-House?' [Hebr.]. *Cathedra* 75: 3–35.

—— (1995b). 'Pylè–Puma–Sfat Medinah and a Halacha Concerning Bath-houses' [Hebr.]. *Sidra* 11: 5–19.

—— (2000). 'The Roman Bath as a Jewish Institution: Another Look at the Encounter between Judaism and the Greco-Roman Culture'. *Journal for the Study of Judaism* 31: 416–54.

—— (2002a). 'Realia, Daily Life, and the Transmission of Local Stories During the Talmudic Period', in *What Athens Has to do with Jerusalem: Essays on Classical, Jewish and Early Christian Archaeology In Honor of Gideon Foerster*, ed. L. V. Rutgers. Leuven: Peeters, 235–65.

—— (2002b). 'Viewing the Sculptural Environment; Shaping the Second Commandment', in *The Talmud Yerushalmi and Graeco-Roman Culture*, vol. 3, ed. P. Schäfer. Tübingen: Mohr-Siebeck, 411–33.

—— (2003). 'On Idolatry in the Roman Bath House–Two Comments' [Hebr.]. *Cathedra* 110: 173–80.

—— et al. (eds) (2008). *The Sculptural Environment of the Roman Near East: Reflections on Culture, Ideology, and Power.* Leuven: Peeters.

—— (2009). 'A Scary Place: Jewish Magic in the Roman Boathouse', in *Man Near a Roman Arch: Studies Presented to Prof. Yoram Tsafrir*, eds. L. Di Segni et al. Jerusalem: Israel Exploration Society, 88–97.

FAGAN, G. G. (1999). *Bathing in Public in the Roman World*. Ann Arbor: University of Michigan Press.

FRIEDHEIM, E. (2002). 'Rabban Gamaliel and the Bathhouse of Aphrodite in Akko: A Study of the Realia of Eretz-Israel in the 2nd and 3rd Centuries C.E.' [Hebr.]. *Cathedra* 105: 7–32.

GINOUVÈS R. (1962). *Balaneutiké: Recherches sur le bain dans l'antiquité grecque*. Paris: Boccard.

GROSSBERG, A. (2001). 'A Mikveh in the Bathhouse' [Hebr.]. *Cathedra* 99: 171–184.

HIRSCHFELD, Y. (2000). *Ramat Hanadiv Excavations: Final Report of the 1984–1998 Seasons*. Jerusalem: The Israel Exploration Society.

HODGE, A. T. (1992). *Roman Aqueducts and Water Supply*. London: Duckworth.

JACOBS, M. (1998). 'Römische Thermenkultur im Spiegel des Talmud Yerushalmi', in *The Talmud Yerushalmi and Graeco-Roman Culture* vol. 1, ed. P. Schäfer. Tübingen: Mohr Siebeck, 219–311.

LOW, S. M./LAWRENCE-ZÚÑIGA, D. (eds) (2003). *The Anthropology of Space and Place: Locating Culture*. Malden: Blackwell.

MANDERSCHEID, H. (1981). *Die Skulpturenausstattung der kaiserzeitlichen Thermenanlagen*. Berlin: Gebr. Mann.

—— (2004). *Ancient Bath and Bathing: A Bibliography for the Years 1988–2001*. Portsmouth: Journal of Roman Archaeology.

MAZOR, G. (1999). 'Public Baths in Roman and Byzantine Nysa-Scythopolis (Bet She'an)', in *Roman Baths and Bathing*, vol. 2, eds. J. DeLaine and D. E. Johnson. Portsmouth: Journal of Roman Archaeology, 292–302.

NETZER, E. (2001). *Hasmonean and Herodian Palaces at Jericho: Final Reports of the 1973–1987 Excavations*, vol. 1. Jerusalem: Israel Exploration Society.

—— (2006). *The Architecture of Herod, the Great Builder*. Tübingen: Mohr-Siebeck.

NIELSEN, I. (1990). *Thermae et Balnea: The Architecture and Cultural History of Roman Public Baths*, 2 vols. Aarhus: Aarhus University Press.

OPPENHEIMER, A. (2008). 'The Jews in the Roman World', in *The Sculptural Environment of the Roman Near East: Reflections on Culture, Ideology, and Power*, eds. Y. Z. Eliav et al. Leuven: Peeters, 51–68.

REICH, R. (1988). 'The Hot-Bath House (*balneum*), the Miqweh and the Jewish Community in the Second Temple Period'. *Journal of Jewish Studies* 39: 102–7.

SMALL, D. B. (1987). 'Late Hellenistic Baths in Palestine'. *Bulletin of the American Society of Oriental Research* 266: 59–74.

SCHWARTZ, S. (1998). 'Gamaliel in Aphrodite's Bath: Palestinian Judaism and Urban Culture in the Third and Fourth Centuries', in *The Talmud Yerushalmi and Graeco-Roman Culture*, vol.1, ed. P. Schäfer. Tübingen: Mohr-Siebeck, 203–17.

STERN, E. (1993). *The New Encyclopedia of Archaeological Excavations in the Holy Land*, 4 vols. Jerusalem: The Israel Exploration Society and Carta.

TZAFERIS, Y. (1980). 'A Roman Bath at Rama'. *Atiqot* 14: 66–75.

WARD, R. B. (1992). 'Women in Roman Baths'. *Harvard Theological Review* 85: 125–47.

YADIN, A. (2006). 'Rabban Gamliel, Aphrodite's Bath and the Question of Pagan Monotheism'. *Jewish Quarterly Review* 96: 149–79.

YEGÜL, F. (1992). *Baths and Bathing in Classical Antiquity*. New York: The Architecture History Foundation, Cambridge/Mass. and London: MIT Press.

ZELLINGER, J. (1928). *Bad und Bäder in der altchristlichen Kirche: Eine Studie über Christentum und Antike*. Munich: Max Hueber.

CHAPTER 33

THEATRES, HIPPODROMES, AMPHITHEATRES, AND PERFORMANCES

ZEEV WEISS

PUBLIC spectacles in theatres, hippodromes (or circuses), and amphitheatres held an important place in Roman life throughout the empire. The increased number of festival days in the Roman period, and especially the massive construction of theatres, hippodromes, and amphitheatres throughout the empire during the first three centuries of the Common Era, provide abundant evidence for their popularity. Wishing to maintain a positive rapport with Rome and to integrate Roman cultural patterns into his realm, Herod the Great was the first to introduce games and spectacles in the Roman East, thereby revolutionizing the leisure habits of the indigenous populations. Very few cities had theatres, hippodromes, or amphitheatres at the time of Herod the Great and his successors, but by the end of the first century CE, and especially during the second and third centuries CE, many buildings were constructed in Roman Palestine for the primary purpose of housing entertainment for the local populace. Holding games in some of these buildings continued into the early Byzantine period (late fourth to fifth centuries CE), and in some cases even beyond. However, in the course of the sixth century these institutions declined and eventually disappeared.

1. THE CURRENT STATE OF RESEARCH AND OBJECTIVES FOR FUTURE STUDY

Many studies have examined the buildings for public spectacles and competitions in their wider context, the most salient being M. Bieber's renowned investigation of Greek and Roman theatres (1961), and other, more recent, inquiries on the same topic (Beacham 1991; Sear 2006). Some examine the Roman circuses (Humphrey 1986), while others take a close look at the amphitheatres (Golvin 1988; Bomgardner 2000). Each focuses on one type of structure, scrutinizing it from a variety of perspectives and occasionally referring to the archaeological finds emerging from ancient Palestine. Almost none provides a comprehensive inventory, description, and analysis of these finds.

The vast amount of material evidence from ancient Palestine associated with these buildings has yielded several publications, each devoted to the study of a single structure from a specific site while comparing its archaeological and architectural features to similar known edifices in the region (Ostrasz 1991; Kloner/ Hübsch 1996; Sear/Huston 2000). Rarely do they discuss the nature of these institutions in their wider context. Studies dealing more extensively with theatres, hippodromes, and amphitheatres in ancient Palestine indeed exist but are flawed by the narrow scope noted above (Frézouls 1959, 1961; Segal 1995; Porath 2003); they also neglect to relate to the types of performances held therein or to the socio-cultural aspects of these buildings and their influence on the local populace.

Other studies examine the subject in the light of rabbinic literary sources (Jacobs 1998; Levinson 1998), yet such publications make little attempt at delving into the broader context of a tradition, or at understanding it within its contemporary socio-cultural setting. Moreover, relevant archaeological material that could illustrate this information is scantily enlisted. Several philological studies explain and interpret words, terms, and ideas connected to institutions of leisure activities against the reality of Hellenistic-Roman culture (Herr 1994; Penkower 2000), but these are interspersed throughout larger works and deal with only isolated occurrences. They do not presume to encompass the entire phenomenon and its socio-cultural implications, or its place in Roman urban life and in the Jewish settlements of ancient Palestine.

The current state of research in most cases provides a comprehensive examination pertaining to each and every building constructed for pubic performances or competitions in our region. This information is essential for any broad analysis associated with the subject. However, future study should take an interdisciplinary approach and focus on *all* building types in the region designated for public spectacles and competitions. Although the performances held in theatres, hippodromes, and amphitheatres each had its own fabric and character, and presumably attracted a mixture of segments within Roman society, their combined study within the confines of one region will lend to the understanding that these institutions were the product of specific social and cultural circumstances. The wealth and variety of the available archaeological, epigraphic, and literary evidence, including valuable information gleaned from the rabbinic and early Christian corpora, together with the modern scholarly works dealing with relevant facets of this diverse subject, will not only provide further information about each and every structure or performance, but, in addition, will provide insight into the role of Roman public spectacles and competitions in ancient Palestine, their cultural impact upon the region, and the attitudes of Jewish society toward this realm of life.

2. DISTRIBUTION, LOCATION, AND FINANCE

Theatres were found in twenty-three cities in western Palestine, Transjordan, and the southern Hauran (hereafter 'ancient Palestine'). Each city had at least one theatre, and some had two or even three, for example, Gadara, Amman, and Gerasa. Literary sources mention theatres in Jerusalem, Gaza, and Ashkelon; however, these have not yet been exposed. Hellenized cities like Ptolemais, Eleutheropolis, Jaffa, and others, probably had at least one theatre, giving us a total of over thirty theatres in our region. While hippodromes have been exposed in eight cities of ancient Palestine, literary sources mention that other urban centres, such as Jerusalem, Gaza, and Ashkelon also had this type of building. Amphitheatres were found in only five (or possibly six) cities in our region, and we lack any other evidence for the existence of these structures, apart from Josephus' problematic reference to the amphitheatres built by Herod the Great in Jerusalem, Caesarea, and Jericho (Humphrey 1996; Porath 2004).

In ancient Palestine, theatres were more popular than other types of buildings for public spectacles and competitions. However, it seems unlikely that an unfavourable attitude in the cities toward other building types, especially the hippodrome, used for chariot-racing and athletic contests, was responsible for this disproportion. Rather, it appears that outlays for the construction and long-term maintenance of these buildings and the holding of shows in them, as well as the costs of constructing other public buildings, were beyond the financial means of most cities in Roman Palestine.

The theatre in ancient Palestine was usually located in the urban layout, while the hippodrome and amphitheatre, added at a later stage of urban development, were always constructed outside the city limits, in most cases near one of the roads leading to or from it (Weiss 1999: 23–25). As elsewhere in the Roman world, various factors affected the location of the building in ancient Palestine, for example, a restricted budget to cover the expenses of erecting all these structures at once, a lack of space in the city's centre, controlling the mob in the larger structures, or the existence of suitable topographical conditions on the outskirts of the city.

These buildings and the performances held in them were financed by the city (Weiss 1999: 25–26). Taxes, revenues from municipal properties, and *summae honorariae* (i.e. payment made by civic magistrates for the privelage of holding public office) often served as the source for funding such projects, but, as is evident from several dedicatory inscriptions found in the region, it was mainly private donations of the wealthy residents that enabled the construction and operation of the buildings for public spectacles and competitions. Rabbinic sources also suggest that such buildings in Roman Palestine were backed by contributions from the cities' affluent inhabitants (see, for instance, the anonymous parable in Exodus Rabbah 51: 8). The sources not only mention the actual payment for building such structures, but also make reference to the financing of games, for example, in the case of gladiatorial and animal-baiting contests held in the amphitheatres (Exodus Rabbah 30:24).

3. THE THEATRE: ITS ARCHITECTURE AND PERFORMANCES

The first theatres in ancient Palestine were built by Herod in Jerusalem, Caesarea, and Jericho. Additional theatres were constructed at a later date, from the end of the first century CE on, but mainly in the second and third centuries.

The theatre in ancient Palestine was usually constructed in conformity with the urban layout, near or along one of the main streets and close to the other public buildings (Segal 1994: 105–111; Weiss 1995: 48–52), in order to provide easy access to it. The theatre's lower *cavea* was usually constructed partially on a natural slope in the city, although the Roman construction method of consecutive vaults allowed for the building of such a structure anywhere, even on a plateau. This is probably the reason why, in certain localities, the theatre did not run exactly parallel to the streets; in others it deviated slightly from the alignment of the city's infrastructure and was sometimes even built outside the civic centre (Sepphoris, see Fig. 33.1), or on the outskirts of a city, adjoining the city-wall (Neapolis).

Fig. 33.1 Sepphoris, the theatre built on the northern slope of the acropolis

Photo: G. Laron

The theatres in Palestine can be divided into three groups (Weiss 1995: 52–59). Large theatres, with an outer diameter of 90–100 m and a capacity of approximately 6,000–8,000 seats, were built in the large cities such as Bostra, Caesarea, and Scythopolis. Medium-sized ones, with a diameter of 60–80 m and a capacity of 2,000–4,000 seats, were built in smaller cities that served as the centres of their regions, for example, Sepphoris, Sebaste/Samaria, and Gadara. The small theatres had a diameter of 20–50 m and could seat 1,000–1,500 people. Such small structures were built in the suburbs (for example, Shuni and Hammat Gader), or in addition to the main theatre in large cities (e.g. Scythopolis, Philadelphia, and Gerasa). The large population and wide variety of performances in some cities may have necessitated the construction of two structures, a theatre and an *odeon*.

The above data indicates the direct relationship between the size of a theatre and the city in which it was located. Large theatres existed in the metropolitan cities of ancient Palestine boasting sizeable populations. Construction on such a scale was not related to the administrative rank of the city (whether a governor's seat or a district capital), but was related to the size of the city, the number of its inhabitants, and its financial resources. In cities which were of no lesser significance financially, culturally, and socially, but had fewer inhabitants than the metropolitan centres, only medium-sized theatres were built. The building of a small theatre does not necessarily indicate a lesser inclination toward theatrical performances, but was in line with the city's needs and financial capability to undertake grandiose projects.

The theatres in ancient Palestine were designed according to the contemporary Roman model and resembled those structures known elsewhere in the empire (Weiss 1995: 59–105): the upper *cavea* was built on arches and vaults that also served as passageways (*vomitoria*) to enter and exit the theatre; there was a horizontal (*ima*, *media*, and *summa cavea*) and vertical (*cunei*) division of the seats in the auditorium into sections and tiers of seats; special wooden or stone seats for dignitaries were installed in the stone-paved *orchestra*, which was partially separated from the other parts of the theatre; and the stage (*pulpitum*) and stage building (*scaena*), whose façade (*scaena frons*) faced the spectators, was richly decorated with varied architectural elements.

Nevertheless, these theatres also exhibited typically local features. The creation of a desirable incline for the *cavea* by utilizing a natural slope together with vaults is the most significant one. Certain elements distinguish the theatres of Transjordan from those in Western Palestine, for instance, the separation of the *cavea*, where the common people sat, from the *orchestra*, which was reserved for dignitaries. To maintain this division, a stone barrier was built between the *orchestra* and the *cavea* in the theatres of Western Palestine, whereas a podium about 1.5 m high at the bottom of the *cavea* served the same purpose in the theatres of Transjordan.

The seating arrangement in Roman theatres, and in ancient Palestine as well, was dictated by social standing. Thus, the architecture ensured not only easy traffic in and out of the theatre, but also separated the audience by class (Kolendo [Varsovie] 1981; Zanker 1990: 147–53). Whereas the masses entered the *cavea* through the various *vomitoria*, the side entrance (*parodoi*) led distinguished guests directly to their seats in the *orchestra*. The division of the seating in the buildings for public spectacles, including theatres, is echoed in words attributed to Resh Lakish, a third-century Palestinian sage. The exegesis of a verse in Ecclesiastes is based on a reality with which he and his audience were familiar (Qohelet Rabbah 12:5; Weiss 1995: 92–98). According to this statement, all Roman officials in the provinces who attended local contests entered the building via the same gate, but each was then seated in a row commensurate with his rank.

Classical comedies, tragedies, and satires were rarely presented in the Roman theatre. Mimes and pantomimes of a merrier and lighter bent were very popular in imperial Rome and performed widely in ancient Palestine as well. The mime, as a secular art form, took a critical and derisive stance toward religion (Beacham 1991: 129–140): parodies of the gods were often presented, Jews and Judaism were mocked on stage, and in the course of time Christianity also became a rich source for mimes. The bulk of information regarding these performances in ancient Palestine comes from literary sources (Weiss 1999: 31–32).

For example, a statement attributed to Rabbi Abbahu, who lived at the end of the third century in Caesarea, refers to a short mime performance that originally consisted of a few acts and may have been viewed by the inhabitants of Roman Caesarea who would make fun of the Jews and their custom of keeping the Sabbath and the sabbatical year (Lamentations Rabbah, Proem 17). The tradition mentions several actors participating in the mime, their roles and dialogues, their words of criticism and ridicule, and the presentation of live animals on the stage—all familiar features of mime performances in the first centuries of the Common Era. We may assume that mimes conveying an anti-Jewish message were often presented in theatres throughout the Roman world, and the mentioned midrashic tradition seems to confirm this reality.

Pantomimes featured a single actor wearing a simple garment and a mask who played all the roles (Beacham 1991: 140–53; Jory 1996). Dancing without words and accompanied by a chorus and music were the main elements of such performances. Several inscriptions and literary sources indicate that such pantomimes were staged in the theatres of ancient Palestine (Weiss 1999: 32–33). One passage in the Talmud Yerushalmi refers to a leading pantomime artist who performed in the Caesarea theatre. His real name is unknown but he is called *Pantokakos* in the Talmud because of his evil deeds (y. Taan. 1:4, 64a; Ginzberg 1928: 403–4). His alleged conversation with Rabbi Abbahu affords a detailed description of his activities in the theatre of Roman Caesarea. A performance could consist of a dance accompanied by the clapping of hands or involving the clashing of cymbals. His responsibilities as a leading pantomime included engaging actors for the theatre and teaching them how to perform. In this tradition he relates to Rabbi Abbahu that a Jewish lady was seeking work in the theatre. Lurking behind the columns of the *scaena frons* while *Pantokakos* was working there, she asked him to hire her in order to earn enough money to save her husband (Jacobs 1998: 341–44). Although participation of Jewish women in the theatre cannot be fully deduced from this story, it nevertheless provides some information about how actors found employment in the theatre as well as demonstrating the active participation of women in the public shows (Webb 2002).

4. HIPPODROME AND STADIUM: A MULTIPURPOSE STRUCTURE FOR CHARIOT RACES AND ATHLETIC CONTESTS

Both chariot races and athletic contests were held in the hippodrome of ancient Palestine, unlike the practice in other parts of the Roman Empire, where each activity was housed in its own structure (Humphrey 1986: 535–39). The hippo-drome in ancient Palestine, sometimes called a stadium or even an amphitheatre in the literary sources, was adapted to meet these needs. Its length was made suitable to both types of contests and its width enabled chariot-racing within the structure.

The first hippodromes in our region were built by King Herod in Jerusalem, Jericho, and Caesarea (Patrich 2002; Netzer 2006: 277–81). Additional buildings were constructed in Tiberias and Taricheae, presumably by Herod's son Antipas, who ruled over the Galilee after his father's death (Weiss 2007: 390–91). A compar-ative analysis of the buildings constructed in the Herodian period indicates that there was no fixed plan for hippodromes. Some were designed according to the Roman model (Caesarea and possibly Tiberias), while others combined diverse architectural elements in one structure, essentially creating a new plan (e.g. Jericho and Samaria). Herodian hippodromes were actually multipurpose structures in which chariot races, athletic contests, gladiatorial combats, and animal-baiting were held (Humphrey 1996: 125–27).

The hippodrome in ancient Palestine has several common features, following the imperial edifice inspired by the Circus Maximus in Rome and rebuilt by Trajan (Weiss 1995: 143–53). It was a rectangular structure with one of its short sides ending in a semicircle (*sphendone*), and the chariots' starting gates (*carceres*) located on the opposite side. A low barrier (*euripus*) decorated with basins (pools containing water), statues, columns, and obelisks ran down the middle of the hippodrome, separating the tracks that the charioteers rounded several times. A tiered seating area (*cavea*) encompassed the perimeter of the track, except for the side on which the starting gates were located. Various entrances or exits (*vomitoria*) interspersed around the structure afforded the spectators access to and from their seats in the *cavea*. This basic plan, with certain additional changes to meet local needs, was characteristic of the Palestinian hippodromes built in the second and third centuries CE.

Most of the known hippodromes in ancient Palestine were constructed in the second to third centuries CE beyond the city limits, usually adjacent to one of the main roads leading into the city (Weiss 2002). These were monumental structures that were greatly influenced by the architecture then prevalent throughout the empire, and can be classified into two groups according to their dimensions and the size of the city's population (Weiss 1995: 143). Large hippodromes (approxi-mately 120 × 450 m) were located in the largest cities (Caesarea and Bostra), whereas smaller ones (approximately 70 × 261 m) were found in other cities (Neapolis, Gerasa; see Fig. 33.2). It is estimated that the large hippodromes could seat about 16,000 spectators, and the small ones only about 10,000.

Competitions and games were held periodically in Roman Palestine (Schwartz 1992; Weiss 1999: 36–37; 2004: 32–35). In the second and third centuries CE, cities organized games in honour of the Caesars and local deities, and provided the necessary facilities and prizes for the winners (Pleket 1975). The various games

Fig. 33.2 Gerasa, southern view of the hippodrome

Courtesy of Prof. Yoram Tsafrir

throughout the empire attracted the best athletes from the cities of the eastern provinces. Winners of the chariot races and athletic contests held in the region were crowned with a garland and were awarded a cash prize and a palm branch as a sign of victory. This is reflected, for example, in a sermon cited by Rabbi Avin, a fourth-century Palestinian sage who compared the victory of a charioteer in the hippodrome and his acceptance of a palm branch to the waving of the *lulav* (palm branch) on the Feast of Tabernacles, which served as a sign of victory in one's judgment before God on the Day of Atonement, a metaphor for the race itself (Midrash on Psalms 17:5).

Chariot-racing was particularly popular in this period and was first held in Palestine in Herod's day (Patrich 2002: 41–46). In the ensuing centuries these races were financed by private patrons and followed the prevalent tradition in the Roman East, whereby the number of contestants in each race varied and participation in them was not restricted to certain groups. The number of stalls found in the *carceres* of the local hippodromes implies that this was the number of competitors participating in the race—ten in the smaller buildings and twelve in the larger ones. Each race started when a clear signal was given and the gates in the *carceres* were opened all at once (Weiss 1995: 170–74). The charioteers charged forward onto the race course and encircled the central barrier (*euripus*) seven times. The race in most cases was either in a *quadriga* (a chariot harnessed to four horses) or a *biga* (a chariot harnessed to two horses) driven by a single charioteer or a team of two to three riders. Only later, in the fourth century, were factions introduced in Roman Palestine, greatly changing the character and organization of competitions in the region (Dan 1981; Saradi 2006: 295–306).

The games and contests known to have taken place in our region include combat sports—wrestling, boxing, and *pankration*—which was a combination of the two (Weiss 1995: 163–70; 1999: 38–39). Wrestling was tame compared with boxing and *pankration*, in which the combatants fought with pieces of metal in their gloves (Poliakoff 1987: 75–79). In this respect, boxing and *pankration* did not differ much from gladiatorial fights. Of all the athletic contests that took place in Roman Palestine, combat sports matches are mentioned most extensively in rabbinic literature. The sources do not distinguish between the above-listed types of combat sports, but they do present a clear picture of a variety of contests held in Roman Palestine. In some cases, they seem to describe scenes taken from gladiatorial combats, spectacles no less cruel than the Roman combat sports. A statement attributed to the third-century Resh Laqish mentions that the winner was awarded a garland (Exodus Rabbah 21:11). The sages not only mention the actual contests (Tanhuma Genesis, Vayigash, 3) but also the shouting and cheering of the spectators (Genesis Rabbah 87:4).

Races over various distances, usually multiples of the stadium, were key events in the games held in this period (Weiss 1999: 39). Other competitions involved jumping as well as discus- and javelin-throwing. In the pentathlon, for instance, athletes competed in a number of sports—a one-stadium race, jumping, discus- and javelin-throwing, as well as wrestling. Such athletic contests were also held in Roman Palestine, but we have only scanty evidence for their existence.

5. Gazing at Death in the Arena: The Amphitheatre and Its Shows

Gladiatorial combats and animal-baiting in the amphitheatre were particularly popular in the Roman period (Hopkins 1983: 1–30; Barton 1993: 11–81). Josephus tells us that Herod built the first amphitheatres in our region, but a study of the historical and archaeological data from the Herodian period indicates that he built hippodromes and not Roman-style amphitheatres (Humphrey 1996; Porath 2004). Only in the second and third centuries CE were elliptical Roman amphitheatres

Fig. 33.3 Scythopolis, general view of the amphitheatre

Photo: G. Laron. Publication courtesy of Prof. Yoram Tsafrir

erected in our region (Weiss 1999: 39–41). One can assume that these structures were initially built to satisfy the growing desire for Roman culture by the population that settled in the central administrative cities of Palestine at the end of the first century CE, and especially after the Bar Kokhba revolt. It seems that once gladiatorial games and animal-baiting were firmly established in the main cities, the local populace, including the Jews, also began to enjoy these spectacles, despite their original disapproval.

The Palestinian amphitheatre, like the hippodrome, was built outside the city, adjacent to one of the roads leading to or from it. Its architectural plan was based on the well-known Roman model, but a distinction should be made between two types of structures—one planned from the outset as an amphitheatre (Caesarea and Eleuthropolis: Roller 1982; Kloner/Hübsch 1996), and the other built at the semicircular end of the hippodrome that was no longer in use (Neapolis and Scythopolis: Magen 2005: 179–212; Tsafrir/Foerster 1997: 133–35; see Fig. 33.3). Both held the same kinds of performances, although the shape of the arena and its measurements varied from building to building. Certain recurrent elements in several of these structures, such as the *podium* at the bottom of the *cavea*, the main entrances on the axis of the building, the animal cages scattered around the building and the platform for dignitaries (*pulvinar*) with a shrine (*sacellum*) beneath it, allow us to conclude that these were prevalent features in the amphitheatres of Roman Palestine.

Gladiatorial combats and animal-baiting were performed in the arenas of Roman Palestine (Weiss 1999: 41–43) and are referred to in rabbinic literature by their Greek names, *monomachia* (Genesis Rabbah 96), and *kunegesia* (Pesikta de Rav Kahana 28:3). The gladiatorial games (*munera gladiatorum*) involved two combatants. The *retiarius*, half-naked and armed with a net and a trident, fought against the *myrmillones*, who was armed with a shield and sword and wore a helmet on his head. The battle continued until one of them was defeated or killed. We may assume that the fighting techniques and weapons used in the spectacles staged in the amphitheatres of our region were in accordance with the custom throughout the Roman world. Aside from the simple exhibition of the animals, two kinds of animal-baiting took place in the amphitheatre. Wild animals were either baited and killed by men (*bestiarii*) or preyed upon by other animals (*venationes*). The long list of animals participating in such games in Roman Palestine includes bulls, lions, bears and rams.

Slaves, prisoners of war, condemned criminals, and sometimes even hirelings participated in these contests (Wiedemann 1992: 68–92). In the mid-third century CE the Roman Empire, including Palestine, experienced an economic crisis that often led people to take part in gladiatorial shows because of the handsome monetary rewards they were offered. The search for sources of income during this crisis, as well as the desire to gain glory not related directly to legal or social status, led certain people, including Jews, to offer their services as gladiators or animal baiters. One such case allegedly came to the attention of R. Abbahu in Caesarea (y. Gittin 4:9, 46b; cf. b. Gittin 46b–47a). The gladiators were trained in a special school headed by *lanistae*, who took charge of, and supplied combatants for, the games. In a tradition transmitted in the Babylonian Talmud Resh Lakish (who himself is said to have been a gladiator prior to his entry into the world of rabbinic Torah study) mentions that on the eve of a show, the gladiators were given a festive meal, in which their requests were fulfilled (b. Gittin 47a; Brettler/Poliakoff 1990). The next day, the events opened with a spectacular procession accompanied by music, during which the gladiators displayed their arms. Immediately thereafter, the animal-baiting contest began, followed by the gladiatorial games. The variety of spectacles and their sequence were intended to hold the attention of the audience for the entire show.

6. THE JEWS OF LATE ANTIQUE PALESTINE AND ROMAN PUBLIC SPECTACLES

The Jews, as an important demographic component in the local population of late antique Palestine, were undoubtedly familiar with the Roman public spectacles and competitions, which flourished, for the most part, during the first centuries of the Common Era. It has traditionally been assumed that most Jews condemned the Roman public spectacles following the advice of the rabbis, who viewed these games as idolatry and steered as far away from them as possible (Krauss 1948: 220; Goodman 1983: 81–83). The theatre, hippodrome, and amphitheatre were considered essentially pagan buildings and, therefore, attending the events held in them was strictly forbidden. Thus, scholars believed that Jews refrained from going to these places of entertainment, which were considered 'a seat of scoffers' (T. Avodah Zarah 2:5).

A re-examination of the attitudes of Jewish society toward Roman public spectacles in ancient Palestine, mainly through the valuable information culled from rabbinic literature, leads us to quite a different conclusion (Weiss 2001: 433–39). Based on the limited historical sources at our disposal, it is difficult to determine whether Jews actually attended Roman public spectacles in the Hero- dian period. It becomes clear from rabbinic literature and elsewhere that Jews did, in fact, frequent these spectacles from the second century onwards. The rabbinic injunctions against such attendance confirm the reality in which they lived. Jews residing in both the Jewish and non-Jewish cities of Roman Palestine watched and participated in the games and spectacles despite the rabbis' injunction to avoid them. Both *tannaim* (first and second centuries CE) and *amoraim* (third to early fifth centuries CE) based their objections to the Roman public spectacles on moral and religious grounds, although a careful reading of the sources, as we shall demonstrate below, indicates a shift in their position over the course of time.

Expressing their unequivocal disdain for Roman public spectacles, the *tannaim* seem to have prohibited any association with them whatsoever. Their staunch attitude is conveyed by words such as 'forbidden', 'not', and 'no'—which leave no room for doubt regarding their intention. Rabbi Meir and other rabbis, for instance, seem to have agreed that the Roman buildings for public spectacles should not be attended. Even if each rabbi had provided a different reason, their position was clear: 'He who goes into the theatres of non-Jews, it is prohibited because of idolatry, says Rabbi Meir. And sages say: [If one goes into the theatre] when they offer sacrifices, it is forbidden because of idolatry. But if not, it is forbidden merely because one would sit in the seat of scoffers' (T. Avodah Zarah 2:2). Thus, rabbis forbade attending the theatres and circuses not only because of idolatry, but also because the activities taking place in both venues were considered immoral. The theatrical performances, they believed, were arenas of rowdiness, vulgarity, lewdness, and pornography, and therefore not a proper setting for Jews (Herr 1989: 89–92; Jacobs 1998: 336–37).

In principle, the *amoraim* seem to have held a similar view as the *tannaim*, although they used a different tone. Unlike their predecessors, they refrained from harsh condemnation and never used explicit terms. Rather, they tried to persuade their communities in a non-confrontational manner. For example, a tradition attributes the following words to the third-century *amora* Rabbi Shimon ben

Pazi: 'Happy is the man that has not gone to theatres and circuses of idolaters and has not stood in the way of sinners, [happy is] he who does not attend contests of wild beasts' (b. Avodah Zarah 18b). In this statement, Rabbi Shimon ben Pazi does not explicitly prohibit going to the spectacles, and he does not even condemn one who attends them; he simply praises him who does not set foot in such places. At the same time, however, he is sending a clear message to others—that it would be better if they would also conduct themselves in a like manner. A similar tone is expressed in amoraic traditions transmitted in Palestinian rabbinic documents (e.g. Genesis Rabbah 67:3; Pesiqta de Rav Kahana 15:2).

These and similar statements clearly demonstrate rabbis' objections to attending Roman public spectacles, while offering reasons to justify their attitudes, such as religious and moral restraints against pagan behaviour. At the same time, however, they reflect a real phenomenon, wherein members of the Jewish population frequented these institutions on a regular basis, just like their non-Jewish neighbours. One cannot assume that the various halakhic teachings and sermons mentioned earlier were merely rabbinic rhetoric regarding the Roman public spectacles in general, and not a reaction to the prevalent social reality in which Jews were actively engaged, for if the Jewish population had no contact whatsoever with these places of entertainment, why would the rabbis feel compelled to belabour an irrelevant issue? It is well known that expressions of opposition among the rabbis often reflected unacceptable social realities. They often scolded and were very critical while stressing what they believed to be the desirable behaviour. This is clearly the case here. Jews attended the Roman public spectacles despite rabbinic objections. The shift in the strategy of the *amoraim*, as opposed to the *tannaim*, seems to reflect the reality they faced. As Jews now increasingly frequented the various performances, both as spectators and participants, the rabbis realized that if they did not change their tactics, their admonition would fall on deaf ears.

A few rabbinic sources indicate that Jews were not only spectators at these public performances, but some were actual participants (Weiss 2001: 439–43). Very few sources refer to actors performing in the theatre like *Pantokakos* mentioned earlier, who allegedly met with Rabbi Abbahu in Caesarea and described to him his work as a leading pantomime. Other traditions may suggest Jewish participation in chariot races or athletic competitions held in the hippodrome, while a relatively large number of sources connect individual members of Jewish society to the amphitheatre. For instance, in some of his academic discourses, Resh Laqish, one of the most prominent rabbis in third-century Palestine, alludes to his previous experience as a gladiator before entering the world of Torah study (y. Terumot 8:5, 45d). Although the historical reality and actual extent of this phenomenon cannot be determined, we may assume, based on the available material, that active participation of the Jewish population in these performances existed but was limited.

The familiarity of the Jews with the Roman public spectacles, both as viewers and participants, had ramifications on the content of rabbis' sermons (Grossmark

2000; Weiss 2001: 443–48). Many *amoraim* used parables and terminology taken from the world of public spectacles to explain a difficult word in the Bible, a verse, or a special point to be learned from a biblical story (Pesiqta de Rav Kahana 28:3). Some sources allude to the physical appearance of these buildings (Exodus Rabbah 15:22), whereas most of them deal with the performances and their terminology (Midrash on Psalms 17:5), as well as the portrayal of the participants or the audience (Genesis Rabbah 77:3). The assortment of sermons and halakhic discourses embedded in rabbinic literature testifies to the fact that rabbis intentionally used the prevalent language of the entertainment world in their sermons, thereby displaying a certain familiarity with the social and cultural environment of their listeners. An increased use of phrases borrowed from the Roman public spectacles is an indication of the active involvement and familiarity of the Jewish community, rabbis included, with these public events.

7. CONCLUSIONS

Public spectacles and competitions in the Roman Near East of Herod's day were a revolutionary innovation. Not only were the physical appearance and monumental character of the buildings new features, but the various performances held in them introduced the local population to a new cultural behaviour that was, until then, completely foreign to Jewish tradition and culture. Herod's dream of integrating Palestine culturally within the rest of the Roman Empire became a reality far beyond his reign and the boundaries of his realm. It has become evident that the Jews as well as the Gentiles of Roman Palestine frequented the buildings that housed public spectacles and competitions, both in cities with a mixed population and in the Jewish cities of the Galilee. The Jewish community's attitude to the Roman spectacles and competitions attests to the profound influence of Graeco-Roman culture on their daily life in late antiquity. This was not the adoption of a custom that fitted the Jewish way of life but, rather, a conscious choice to embrace one of the most conspicuous symbols of Roman urban culture.

SUGGESTED READING

Several studies devoted to specific types of buildings present overviews of the archaeological finds of theatres, hippodromes, and amphitheatres in ancient

Palestine (Segal 1995; Humphrey 1986), while others focus on one city and discuss the buildings found in that locale or the performances held there (Kloner and Hübsch 1996; Sear and Huston 2000; Porath 2003; Weiss 2004). The articles by Jacobs (1998), Levinson (1998), and Grossmark (2000) analyse the rabbinic evidence, although none provides an overall picture of the archaeological remains. Weiss (1995; 1999; 2001) takes an interdisciplinary approach, examining the role of Roman public spectacles and competitions in ancient Palestine, and the buildings in which they took place, their cultural impact on the region, and the attitudes of Jews toward this aspect of their daily life.

BIBLIOGRAPHY

BARTON, C. A. (1993). *The Sorrows of the Ancient Romans: The Gladiator and the Monster.* Princeton: Princeton University Press.

BEACHAM, R. C. (1991). *The Roman Theatre and Its Audience.* London and New York: Routledge.

BIEBER, M. (1961). *The History of the Greek and Roman Theatre.* Princeton: Princeton University Press.

BOMGARDNER, D. L. (2000). *The Story of the Roman Amphitheatre.* London and New York: Routledge.

BRETTLER M. Z./POLIAKOFF, M. (1990), 'Rabbi Simeon ben Lakish at the Gladiators' Banquet: Rabbinic Observations on the Roman Arena'. *Harvard Theological Review* 83: 93–98.

DAN, Y. (1981). 'Circus Factions (Blues and Greens) in Byzantine Palestine', in *The Jerusalem Cathedra* I, ed. L. I. Levine. Jerusalem: Yad Izhak Ben-Zvi, 105–19.

FRÉZOULS, E. (1959). 'Recherches sur les théâtres de l'Orient Syrien, I'. *Syria* 36: 203–27.

—— (1961). 'Recherches sur les théâtres de L'Orient Syrien, II'. *Syria* 38: 54–86.

GINZBERG, L. (1928). *Geniza Studies.* New York: Jewish Theological Seminary.

GOLVIN, J. C. (1988). *L'amphithéâtre romain,* 2 vols. Paris: E. de Boccard.

GOODMAN, M. (1983). *State and Society in Roman Galilee, A.D. 132–212.* Totowa: Rowman and Allenheld.

GROSSMARK, Z. (2000). 'Images of God in Rabbinical Literature Borrowed from the Sphere of the Roman Spectacles' [Hebr.], in *Proceedings of the Twelfth World Congress of Jewish Studies, Jerusalem, July 29–August 5, 1997–History of the Jewish People, Division B.* Jerusalem: Hebrew University, 75–84.

HERR, M. D. (1989). 'External Influences in the World of the Sages of Palestine—Acceptance and Rejection' [Hebr.], in *Acculturation and Assimilation, Continuity and Change in the Culture of Israel and the Nations,* ed. Y. Kaplan and M. Stern. Jerusalem: Zalman Shazar Center, 83–106.

—— (1994). 'Synagogues and Theatres (Sermons and Satiric Plays)' [Hebr.], in *Knesset Ezra: Literature and Life in the Synagogue, Studies Presented to Ezra Fleischer,* ed. S. Elizur et al. Jerusalem: Yad Izhak Ben-Zvi, 105–19.

HOPKINS, K. (1983). *Death and Renewal.* Cambridge and New York: Cambridge University Press.

HUMPHREY, J. H. (1986). *Roman Circuses—Arenas for Chariot Racing*. London: B. T. Batsford.

—— (1996). '"Amphitheatrical" Hippo-Stadia', in *Caesarea Maritima—Retrospective after Two Millennia*, ed. A. Raban and K. G. Holum. Leiden: Brill, 121–29.

JACOBS, M. (1998). 'Theatres and Performances as Reflected in the Talmud Yerushalmi', in *The Talmud Yerushalmi and Graeco-Roman Culture*, vol. 1, ed. P. Schäfer. Tübingen: Mohr-Siebeck, 327–47.

JORY, E. J. (1996). 'The Drama of the Dance: Prolegomena to an Iconography of Imperial Pantomime', in *Roman Theatre and Society*, ed. W. J. Slater. Ann Arbor: University of Michigan Press, 1–27.

KLONER A./HÜBSCH, A. (1996). 'The Roman Amphitheatre of Bet Guvrin: A Preliminary Report on the 1992, 1993 and 1994 Seasons'. *Atiqot* 30: 85–106.

KOLENDO (VARSOVIE), J. (1981). 'La répartition des places aux spectacles et la stratification sociale dans l'Empire Romain'. *Ktema*, 6: 301–15.

KRAUSS, S. (1948). *Persia and Rome in the Talmud and Midrashim* [Hebr.]. Jerusalem: Mossad Ha-Rav Kook.

LEVINSON, J. (1998). 'Fatal Fictions' [Hebr.]. *Tarbiz*, 68: 61–86.

MAGEN, Y. (2005). *Flavia Neapolis: Shechem in the Roman Period* [Hebr.]. Jerusalem: Israel Antiquities Authority.

NETZER, E. (2006). *The Architecture of Herod, the Great Builder*. Tübingen: Mohr-Siebeck.

OSTRASZ, A. A. (1991). 'The Excavation and Restoration of the Hippodrome at Jerash: A Synopsis'. *Annual of the Department of Antiquities of Jordan* 35: 237–50.

PATRICH, J. (2002). 'Herod's Hippodrome-Stadium at Caesarea and the Games Conducted Therein', in *What Athens Has to Do with Jerusalem*, ed. L. V. Rutgers. Leuven: Peeters, 29–68.

PENKOWER, J. S. (2000). 'The Textual Transmission of Rashi's Commentary, Kimhi's Commentary, and Targum Jonathan on Ezekiel 27:6' [Hebr.], in: *Studies in Bible and Exegesis*, vol.5, ed. M. Graciel. Ramat Gan: Bar-Ilan University, 315–39.

PLEKET, H. W. (1975). 'Games, Prizes, Athletes and Ideology'. *Arena* 1: 49–89.

POLIAKOFF, M. (1987). *Combat Sports in the Ancient World: Competition, Violence and Culture*. New Haven: Yale University Press.

PORATH, Y. (2003). 'Theatre, Racing and Athletic Installations in Caesarea' [Hebr.]. *Qadmoniot* 36: 25–42.

—— (2004). 'Why Did Josephus Name the Chariot-Racing Facility at Caesarea "Amphitheatre"?' *Scripta Classica Israelica* 24: 63–67.

ROLLER, D. (1982). 'The Wilfrid Laurier University Survey of Northeastern Caesarea Maritima'. *Levant*, 14: 90–103.

SARADI, H. (2006). *The Byzantine City in the Sixth Century: Literary, Images and Historical Reality*. Athens: Society of Messenian Archaeological Studies.

SCHWARTZ, D. R. (1992). '"Caesarea" and Its "Isactium": Epigraphy, Numismatics and Herodian Chronology', in *Studies in the Jewish Background of Christianity*, ed. D. R. Schwartz. Tübingen: Mohr-Siebeck, 167–81.

SEAR, F. (2006). *Roman Theatres: An Architectural Study*. Oxford and New York: Oxford University Press.

—— and HUSTON, A. (2000). 'Reconstructing the South Theatre at Jerash'. *Ancient Near Eastern Studies* 37: 3–25.

SEGAL, A. (1994). 'The Location of the Theatre in the City Landscape of Roman Palestine and Provincia Arabia', in *Aspects of Theatre and Culture in the Graeco-Roman World*, ed. A. Segal. Haifa: Haifa University, 103–24.

—— (1995). *Theatres in Roman Palestine and Provincia Arabia*. Leiden: Brill.

TSAFRIR, Y./FOERSTER, G. (1997). 'Urbanism at Scythopolis-Beth Shean in the Fourth to Seventh Centuries'. *Dumbarton Oaks Papers* 51: 85–146.

WEBB, R. (2002). 'Female Entertainment in Late Antiquity', in *Greek and Roman Actors: Aspects of an Ancient Profession*, ed. P. Easterling and E. Hall. Cambridge and New York: Cambridge University Press, 282–303.

WEISS, Z. (1995). 'Games and Spectacles in Roman Palestine and their Reflection in Talmudic Literature' [Hebr.]. PhD. thesis, Hebrew University Jerusalem.

—— (1999). 'Adopting a Novelty: The Jews and the Roman Games in Palestine', in *The Roman and Byzantine Near East: Recent Archaeological Research*, vol. 2, ed. J. H. Humphrey. Journal of Roman Archaeology Suppl. 31. Portsmouth: Journal of Roman Archaeology, 23–49.

—— (2001). 'The Jews of Ancient Palestine and the Roman Games: Rabbinic Dicta vs. Communal Practice' [Hebr.]. *Zion* 66: 427–59.

—— (2002). 'New Light on the Rehov Inscription: Identifying 'The Gate of Campon' at Bet Shean', in *What Athens Has to Do with Jerusalem*, ed. L. V. Rutgers. Leuven: Peeters, 211–33.

—— (2004). 'Games and Spectacles in Ancient Gaza: Performances for the Masses Held in Buildings Now Lost', in *Christian Gaza in Late Antiquity*, ed. B. Bitton-Ashkelony and A. Kofsky. Leiden: Brill, 22–39.

—— (2007). 'Josephus and Archaeology on the Cities of the Galilee', in *Making History: Josephus and Historical Method*, ed. Z. Rodgers. Leiden: Brill, 387–414.

WIEDEMANN, T. (1992). *Emperors and Gladiators*. London and New York: Routledge.

ZANKER, P. (1990). *The Power of Images in the Age of Augustus*. Ann Arbor: University of Michigan Press.

CHAPTER 34

PLAY AND GAMES

JOSHUA SCHWARTZ

1. INTRODUCTION

Leisure-time activities are of cultural importance in every society. Every society has its own pastimes, and Jewish society is not exceptional in this regard (Schwartz 2003: 132–141; Schwartz 2004b: 128–140). Play and games are among the most important leisure-time activities (Avedon/Sutton-Smith 1971). Participation in them is one of the most significant characteristics of a society, both in terms of the relationship between an individual and society and from a national, ethnic standpoint. Some scholars maintain that play is so significant sociologically that a culture or society can be examined on its basis. Games always have a greater significance than mere diversion and entertainment. They can be seen as microcosms of entire social systems (Huizinga 1955; Caillois 1962).

There are many views as to why people play. Some scholars examine children's games (e.g. Schwartzman 1976; Chanan/Francis 1984), others those of both adults and children (Ellis 1973; Avedon/Sutton-Smith 1971). Some scholars think that one of the purposes of playing games is to burn up excessive energy and to divert destructive tendencies into harmless pursuits. Others stress the pure enjoyment of play, or present it as a means of learning in the process of passing through society's 'evolutionary stages'. Besides sociological, psychoanalytical, and developmental theories of play one can find ecological approaches which examine the influence of the environment on play and game behaviour (Ellis 1973).

Play is a universal pastime: it can be found amongst people of different cultures, religions, and ethnicities, and amongst different age groups. Although play may be conducted as a solitary pursuit, it is usually practised together with others, in groups based on social ties. The composition of the circle of players depends upon a variety of factors. Play enables social contact and proximity outside of the ordinary course of social relations. Play, especially that of children, may be sensitive to external (e.g. political) messages directed at the players during their play time, messages which may be based on current events.

Just like everyone else, Jews of all time periods and ages engaged in play and games. One can distinguish between certain games and aspects of play which seem to have been universal, that is, which can be found in all societies, and others which were particular to Jewish society. It is therefore impossible to divorce the study of play and games in ancient Jewish society from the larger context of ancient leisure-time activities, and from the sociological and anthropological study of play. Interestingly, many modern games are just variant versions of ancient games common in many societies.

In the following we shall examine the games and toys of Jews in Roman Palestine within the historical framework of play, games, and toys within Graeco-Roman society. Sports and athletics, particularly those undertaken in some sort of 'official' capacity, will not be discussed in this chapter (see the chapter on 'Theatres, Hippodromes, Amphitheatres, and Performances' in this volume). While the 'official' games conducted in amphitheatres are outside of the purview of our discussion, we shall deal with 'informal' games involving athletic activity.

2. Early Studies of Games in Ancient Jewish Society

Since play and games are universal activities, one would assume that there would be a good deal of discussion on these activities in Jewish society throughout the ages. One has to be aware of the fact, however, that most ancient and medieval Jewish literary works were composed by rabbis. While rabbis are not opposed to these pastimes and occasionally even foster and appreciate them, their literature cannot be considered 'popular' literature, and does not reflect popular culture. Rabbis did not consider play and games an issue requiring much discussion unless related to certain halakhic or moral issues. In rabbinic sources the extent of the discussion of the topic is therefore very limited, in contrast to Roman literary sources. Roman writers were enthusiastic about certain leisure pastimes, such as gambling and ball play, and therefore produced a copious literature on these matters, such as *De parvae pilae exercitio* ('On Exercise with a Small Ball') by the second-century CE physician Galen (Kühn 1821). However, while most of the ancient Graeco-Roman 'books' on these pastimes have apparently not survived, references to these activities, as well as to other play pastimes are found in many extant works, and particularly in the *Onomasticon* of the second-century CE rhetorician Iulius Pollux (Becker 1846; Väterlein 1976; Ziegler 2004). Rabbis, on the other hand, saw popular leisure-time activities as a necessary evil, distracting from Torah study. This rabbinic view seems to have been dominant in Jewish society for a long time.

Most of the early scholarly interest in these matters is found in works on 'Talmudic Archaeology' and ancient Jewish daily life (Löw 1875: 279–317; Krauss 1912: 102–119). While these studies serve as the basis for any modern study of Jewish play and games in antiquity, they are limited in scope, dealing with the topic in one chapter only within the context of works of a much larger scope. These early scholars basically collected relevant rabbinic sources from tannaitic and amoraic, Palestinian and Babylonian documents, 'analysed' them in accordance with the limited methodological tools of their times, and sometimes compared them with similar phenomena in the ancient world. While still a good starting point for any study, they remain just that.

3. RABBINIC LITERATURE AND ARCHAEOLOGY

The most serious methodological problem in the study of play and games also concerns other areas of research into the material culture of Jews in Roman Palestine, namely, the use of rabbinic literary sources (Schwartz 2006: 431–433). As already mentioned in a number of other chapters in this volume, rabbinic traditions appear in an edited form in the extant documents. The editors integrated them into larger thematic contexts. Therefore the exact date and place of origin of individual traditions cannot be determined any more.

Furthermore, there is only sparse evidence concerning play and games, so that traditions from different time periods and locations may have to be investigated together. This leads to the following methodological questions: are traditions from the tannaitic period still relevant in amoraic times? Are traditions transmitted in the Babylonian Talmud applicable to Palestine and vice versa? One might argue that the universal nature of many aspects of play, games, and toys, and the fact that they change very slowly over time, make it possible to cross chronological and/or geographical boundaries, a procedure which is not considered legitimate for other areas of ancient Jewish history (Schwartz 1995b; 1998c).

There are instances, however, in which local and chronological differences can be determined. For example, the literature of the Palestinian sages often reflects a more guarded attitude toward play and games. Perhaps Palestinian rabbis were more familiar with the games of the surrounding Graeco-Roman world and with the 'dangers' inherent in some of them, while the Babylonian Talmud seems to reflect a more open attitude (Schwartz 1998b). These differences make it necessary to use caution in trying to use Babylonian literature for the study of play in Roman Palestine. One also has to keep in mind that the relatively little amount of rabbinic evidence on play and games is not a reliable indicator of the actual amount of play activity in Palestinian Jewish society.

It is also difficult to determine whether, and to what extent, rabbinic literature reflects practices in Jewish society at large. As mentioned above, there is no ancient Jewish literature resembling the lost Graeco-Roman treatises on play or the extant works and references mentioned above. It is hard to imagine a body of literature more inappropriate for the investigation of games, play, and toys than rabbinic literature. Although rabbis were not opposed to these matters, they hardly considered them important components of ancient Jewish religion and life. Rabbis were an intellectual elite and treated all subjects from their particular perspective. Despite these limitations, rabbinic literature remains our major literary source for the study of ancient Jewish popular culture, including the topic under discussion here.

The second major type of evidence consists of archaeological remains. Difficulties arise with regard to identifying particular items as toys and game pieces. Is a small item just an implement, or is it a miniature which might have been used as a toy? Even items that look like toys and have the right size for toys might, in the end, be classified as votive offerings or cult objects, archaeologists' catch phrases for objects whose purpose is unclear. One also has to be aware of the possibility that any object, even one not intended as a play object, might be used as a toy. People of different ages and genders may relate to objects in different ways vis-à-vis their potential as toys. Therefore determining when and whether a specific object was used as a toy is a very difficult and sometimes impossible task faced by the ancient historian (Lillehammer 1989; Wilkie 2000; Baxter 2005; Wileman 2005).

4. General Scholarship on Play

Because of the universal nature of play and the fact that games often change very little over time, any study of play and games focusing on a particular period and location has to be aware of the state of general research on the topic (Murray 1952; Opie/Opie 1969; Bell 1979; Laser 1987; Dawson 1994). In addition, there are works dealing with toys and games in the ancient world, including the Near East (Becq de Fouquieres 1869; Falkener 1892; White 1971; Fitta 1998; Finkel 2007), and those which deal with Graeco-Roman society specifically (Marquardt/Mommsen 1882; Richter 1891; Wentworth Thompson 1933; Austin 1934, 1935, and 1940; Väterlein 1976; Schmidt 1977; Toner 1995; Purcell 1995). Much relevant material can be found in studies of children and childhood in antiquity (Aries 1962; Rawson 2003). Since certain types of plays and games occupied adults as well, books on Roman leisure culture may provide important information (Balsdon 1969; Toner 1995). Studies of play in medieval times may also be helpful (Orme 2002). Although most of these works rarely make reference to Jewish society, they can provide background material or even missing links to understand the respective Jewish literary traditions.

5. ANCIENT JEWS AT PLAY

As already mentioned above, the first studies of play, games, and toys in Jewish society were written in the late nineteenth and early twentieth century as parts of larger works on various aspects of daily life (Löw 1875: 279–317; Krauss 1912: 102–119). They were based on the methodology and state of research on rabbinic literature and archaeology at that time. Since then a number of more specialized works have appeared.

The unpublished doctoral dissertation of R. D. Crabtree entitled 'Leisure in Ancient Israel (before 70 A. D.)' (Crabtree 1982) focuses on leisure and recreation, but also deals with play and games to some extent. This work contains little analysis of the relevant Jewish literary sources, and shows methodological deficiencies. Despite these shortcomings, it provides an important theoretical background to the study of leisure and recreation in Jewish society in general and to play and games in particular. The same is true for the 1976 study of Y. Sorek on *Physical Culture in the Land of Israel in the Mishnah and Talmud Period* (Sorek 1976), which does contain rabbinic references to play and games, but mostly from the perspective of physical education. It is weak, however, in its analysis of the relevant source material and its social historical significance.

In 1992 Ulrich Hübner's monograph *Spiele und Spielzeug im antiken Palästina* was published (Hübner 1992). Like Crabtree, Hübner's work mainly deals with the biblical period and the Second Temple period. His study is mainly based on archaeological material with less attention paid to literary sources. The work has a catalogue-like nature and there is very little analysis of either the archaeological or literary sources. Hübner has continued to publish on this topic (Hübner 2000). In addition to these studies, Meir Bar-Ilan lectured at the World Congress of Jewish Studies on 'Children's Games in Antiquity', with an emphasis on family and childhood as reflected in rabbinic sources (Bar-Ilan 1994).

In the past, scholars have shown little interest in the study of play and games in Jewish society, with the exception of the study of gambling (see below). Jews seem to have had a certain affinity to this pastime, a phenomenon which created many halakhic problems. Most of the discussion revolved around the understanding of M. R.H. 1:8 and M. Sanh. 3:3 which state that the testimony of someone who plays with dice (*ha-mesaheq be-kubiya*) is not acceptable. According to a statement attributed to Rabbi Yehudah, this rule applies only in the case of a professional gambler, whereas the testimony of the occasional gambler is not disqualified.

Rabbinic traditions seem to equate gambling with dicing and related board games (M. R.H. 1:8; M. Sanh. 3:3; T. Sanh. 5:2: *ha-mesaheq be-kubiya*, 'he who plays with *psephasim*'), and sometimes also with pigeon flying (M. Ed. 2:7; T. Ed. 1:10–11; M. R.H. 1:8; M. Sanh. 3:3; M. Shebu. 7: 1). The rabbis never pronounced a clear-cut prohibition against gambling, however, and we may assume that many Jews took advantage of this situation in terms of their own leisure-time activities. It is not surprising then that most of the studies dealing with gambling in rabbinic literature are critical of the practice (Bamberger 1917; Rifkind 1926; 1934; 1935; 1946; Bazak 1960; 1961). Leo Landman's articles constitute the most detailed study of the halahkic history of gambling and were considered the most definitive statement on this issue for a long time (Landman 1966–1967; 1967–1968). A few years later the halakhah of gambling was reexamined by Wahrhaftig (1972). While these studies were more interested in the development of halakhah or Jewish law than in social history of any kind, and while some of them extend chronologically far beyond the Roman period, through the Middle Ages and even up to modern times, they are invaluable for the understanding of the Jewish attitude to gambling. Moreover, since in general the basic structure or format of games remains the same through-out the ages, a later reference might help understand the earlier workings of a game. Clearly though, none of these studies analysed Jewish gambling within the particular framework of the Roman period. They also made little reference to the relevant archaeological remains, whether Jewish or Graeco-Roman.

Schwartz has recently re-analysed the relevant literary sources on gambling, and evaluated them together with archaeological findings. He has also tried to locate the phenomenon of gambling within the social realties of the Graeco-Roman world (Schwartz 1998a), which was often quite attracted to, and occupied with, gambling activities. The most popular forms of gambling activities were those related to dice, astragals and board games. These games required little equipment and were relatively easy to play. Many such dice and/or board games of the Graeco-Roman world, for example, *petteia*, referring to games played with *pessoi* or 'pieces', *poleis* or 'cities', *latrunculi* (*ludus latrunculorum*), *ludus duodecim scriptorium*, *alea* or *tabula*, are mentioned in Graeco-Roman literature. While they could be played alone, they were usually played at social gatherings and were most popular in taverns or brothels. Because of their connection to these institutions, negative social behaviour was associated with them. While one could win large sums of money in these games, the opposite was true as well. Needless to say, such practices would have been problematic for halakhically observant Jews (Schwartz 1998a; Rieche 2007; Purcell 2007; Bell 2007).

Schwartz' analysis of Jewish literary and archaeological sources suggests that Jews were not very much involved in gambling, whether in Hellenistic and Roman Palestine or in the Graeco-Roman world at large. This would explain rabbis' somewhat lenient attitude towards the 'casual' gambler (see above). There is no material evidence for Jewish women's or children's participation in gambling activities. Rabbis were concerned about children being tempted by games which could be turned into gambling. They forbade the eating of nuts at the table on the eve of the Rosh Hashanah holiday because nut games, popular with children, would often be turned into gambling games in Roman society (Schwartz 1997c).

While it is hard to determine the reasons for the relative lack of Jewish participation in gambling, one may assume that the middle and/or lower strata of Jewish society simply lacked the necessary money to engage in this activity. Perhaps rabbinic prohibition and people's adherence to Jewish 'family values' made this pastime less attractive to Jews. In the Middle Ages, however, Jewish society would become infected with gambling, just like the surrounding non-Jewish culture (Schwartz 1998a).

A number of studies on individual aspects of play, games, and toys in Jewish society during the Roman period were published during the last couple of years. Schwartz 1993 and 1998c sought to determine the nature of the 'child's cart' mentioned in M. Betsa 2:10 in relation to the laws of the Sabbath. This toy was studied in the context of the different types of children's carts in Graeco-Roman antiquity. The study showed that rabbinic literature actually provides much relevant information on this toy which was used in both Jewish and non-Jewish society.

Similar case studies examined ball games in ancient Jewish society, particularly during the Roman period (Schwartz 1994; 1995b; 1997b). Ball games can be considered to be amongst the most common games played in many different societies from ancient to modern times. Boys and girls, adults and children participate(d) in this activity (Mendner 1956; cf. Herzog 2002), as did Jews during the Hellenistic, Roman and Byzantine periods. While various aspects of Jewish ball games have been studied in the past (Krauss 1912: 109–11; Mendner 1956: 47; Simri 1969; Hübner 1992: 38–42), no thorough treatment of the topic and detailed analyses of the relevant rabbinic passages existed.

In Schwartz' studies, mentioned above, Jewish traditions relating to ball games were examined within the framework of play in Graeco-Roman society. On the basis of Jewish and non-Jewish sources it was possible to determine some physical characteristics and properties of the balls used for play in Jewish society, and to identify various ball games prevalent in that society. As in Graeco-Roman society, the little round ball and the activities surrounding it encapsulated an entire world of values and norms far beyond the limited parameters of casual tossing and catching, much as is the case today regarding many formal and informal ball games. Jewish society was clearly influenced by the play and game traditions of the surrounding culture, as becomes evident, especially in the case of ball games.

There was, however, not a small amount of cultural 'baggage' attached to many of these games in the ancient world. In the Graeco-Roman world, simple ball games were often considered cultural and ethnic signifiers. Ball playing was widespread throughout all social strata, and it is related that even Zeus played with a ball (Apollonius Rhodius, *Argonautica* 3.135–139; Gardiner 1930: 231). Roman army commanders, kings and emperors excelled in ball playing and were proud of their skills. The second-century CE physician Galen dedicated an entire work to the health benefits of exercising with a small ball (*De parvae pilae exercitio*; cf. Robinson 1981: 185–190).

Jewish society was not inimical to adopting the games with their 'baggage', unless they trespassed upon Jewish national, religious, or moral values, such as in the tradition of the destruction of Tur Shimon during the Bar Kokhba period (y. Taanit 5:4, 69a). This tradition relates that the settlement of Tur Shimon was destroyed because of licentiousness and because of ball playing. While ball play would, under normal circumstances, have been considered innocent, during the Second Jewish Revolt against Rome a game considered so Roman would have been deemed unacceptable by Jewish leaders. Moreover, while rabbis might normally have ignored the potential dangers of 'mixed' ball games—a popular way for a young girl to snare a boy, according to the Roman poet Ovid (*Ars Amatoria* 3.361–368)— they could hardly have sanctioned such practice during a war against Rome.

Obviously, the development of play and games in ancient Jewish society was based on a combination of Jewish versions of 'universal' games and play, unique Jewish game tradition, such as playing 'rabbi' (y. Meg. 1:11, 71d; Gen. R. 1:11; cf. b. Shab. 104a), and the adaptation of practices common in the surrounding Graeco-Roman culture. In a few exceptional cases this adaptation could be problematic, if the attached cultural signifiers stood at variance with Jewish cultural norms (Schwartz 1995a; 2003; 2004b). For example, rabbinic traditions which present Ishmael as playing games involving or possibly leading to idolatry, sex, and murder (T. Sot. 6:6) mark him as an outsider, since these games were considered non-Jewish by rabbis. Ishmael was guilty of play-acting in a non-Jewish manner. His play was seen as an expression of his alleged preference for non-Jewish society. Accordingly, rabbis considered Sarah right in demanding that he be sent away. Abraham, however, was not free of guilt in this matter (Ex. R. 1:1). Play was intrinsically connected to education and family. Letting a child play with the wrong toys or allowing his play to get out of hand without sufficient parental discipline or supervision could have disastrous consequences. Needless to say, rabbis often considered play a waste of time (Num. R. 2:15), or even as a malicious and vicious act directed against the authority of adults (Midr. Ps. 34:1).

Nevertheless, rabbis considered it normal, and indeed even acceptable, for youngsters to be playing indoors or outside in the residential courtyard, street, market, or fields. Nuts (Cant. R. 6:7), dates (M. Maas. 4:2; b. Betsa 34b), pottery pieces (M. Kel. 24:1), toy carts and wagons were commonly used as toys in ancient Jewish society. Children could also play with animals, especially on farms. A rabbinic tradition suggests that Jewish children, like their non-Jewish counterparts, also played with locusts (M. Shab. 9:7). Some children seem to have kept dogs and cats as pets (Schwartz 2000; 2001; 2004a). Jewish boys engaged in war games similar to those that were common in the non-Jewish world: they may have worn 'toy helmets' or played with small 'toy' shields (Schwartz 2004b: 135–136. cf. Grossman 1994). Rabbinic literature also recognized the importance of parents playing with their children, and it was not inappropriate for a father to be involved in such games, even if he was a famous sage (Mid. Ps. 92:13; b. Shab. 154b). Obviously, for rabbis the best type of play was play-acting in imitation of sages (y. Meg. 1:11, 71d).

6. Suggestions for Further Study

In spite of the fact that play and games are such an important aspect of the daily life of just about everyone, not only Jews, it is surprising that so little work has been devoted to such an important topic. As already mentioned, there are many difficulties facing the student of play with regard to identifying relevant sources and applying an appropriate methodology. A proper study of the topic requires interdisciplinary cooperation and expertise in many fields, including the social sciences, Graeco-Roman culture, rabbinic literature, and archaeology. It is possible to devote article-length studies to almost each and every game and toy mentioned in rabbinic sources, especially since the number of relevant finds discovered in archaeological excavations is constantly increasing. There is hardly any archaeological excavation of importance in Israel which does not produce game pieces of some kind, even if they are not always recognized as such by the archaeologists and do not always appear in the official publications (Schwartz 1998a: 158–162).

Future research should focus on studying additional types of games and toys. Samuel Krauss' pioneering study of games comprised fewer than twenty pages (Krauss 1912: 102–121), only three of them being devoted to children's games (ibid. 107–110). In most of the general studies on play and games in Jewish society, individual games, toys and pastimes were not examined in detail. More recently, Schwartz' work has shown that it is possible to devote full-length studies and articles to individual games and toys. The relatively few rabbinic literary sources referring to Jewish play and games have proven to be quite revealing when examined and analysed in detail.

The challenge for the scholar of Jewish daily life in Hellenistic and Roman-Byzantine Palestine is the timelessness of ancient games (and of the rabbinic sources which refer to them). It is hardly possible to make chronological distinctions and to trace the development of games in ancient Judaism. While the comparative study of Jewish and Graeco-Roman literary sources and the evaluation of the relevant archaeological material is important, toys and games have proven to be long-lasting—that is, a Roman-period Jewish game may be identified on the basis of earlier or later material—and universal. Therefore, even amongst some of the games played by children and adults today, we may detect certain similarities with the games played by Jews in Roman Palestine.

It is necessary to continue detailed studies of individual games and toys, in their particular setting of ancient Palestine, but also in the more general context of universal play activity transcending chronological and geographical boundaries. The eventual goal of such individual studies should be a comprehensive book-length synthesis of the topic in the context of the social history and material culture of the Jews of Roman Palestine. The more comprehensive works on games published to date (e.g. Hübner 1992) resemble Krauss 'catalogue' model rather than dealing with the complex issues outlined above. As the saying goes, 'You are what you play'. The games and toys that occupied a child or adult in antiquity can serve as a mirror of or window into that society. Play is serious and deserves serious study.

SUGGESTED READING

The best general introduction to play is still that of Huizinga (1955). On the Roman world, and particularly the play world of children, Väterlein (1976) remains a classic. Hübner (1992) is the best general introduction and catalogue of ancient Jewish play and games and Schwartz (1997b and 1998c) serve as good examples of 'topical' studies on toys and games in Jewish society of the Roman period.

BIBLIOGRAPHY

ARIES, P. (1962). *Centuries of Childhood: A Social History of Family Life*. New York: Vintage Books.

AUSTIN, R. G. (1934). 'Roman Board Games I'. *Greece and Rome* 10: 24–34.

—— (1935). 'Roman Board Games II'. *Greece and Rome* 11: 76–82.

—— (1940). 'Greek Board Games'. *Antiquity* 14: 257–271.

AVEDON, E. M./SUTTON-SMITH, B. (1971). *The Study of Games*. New York and London: John Wiley & Sons.

BALSDON, J. P. V. D (1969). *Life and Leisure in Ancient Rome*. London, Sydney, and Toronto: The Bodley Head.

BAMBERGER, M. L. (1917). 'Spielverbote in talmudischer und nachtalmudischer Zeit'. *Jeschurun* 4: 516–521.

BAR-ILAN, M. (1994). 'Children's Games in Antiquity' [Hebr.]. *Proceedings of the Eleventh World Congress of Jewish Studies (Division B)*, 1: 23–30.

BAXTER, J. E. (2005). *The Archaeology of Childhood: Children, Gender, and Material Culture*. Walnut Creek: Altmira Press.

BAZAK, Y. (1960). 'Dice Games in Jewish and in Local Law' [Hebr.]. *Hapraklit* 16: 47–60.

—— (1961). 'Dice Games as a Problem of Mental Health in Halakhah' [Hebr.]. *Sinai* 48: 111–122.

BECKER, I. (1846). *Iulii Pollucis Onomasticon*. Berlin: F. Nicolai.

BECQ DE FOUQUIERES, L. (1869). *Les Jeux des Anciens: leurs descriptions, leur origine, leurs rapports avec la religion, l'histoire, les arts et les moeurs*. Paris: C. Reinwald.

BELL, R. C. (1979). *Board-Games from Many Civilizations*. New York: Dover Publications.

—— (2007). 'Notes on Pavement Games of Greece and Rome', in *Ancient Board Games in Perspective*, ed. I. L. Finkel. London: British Museum Press, 98–99.

CAILLOIS, R. (1962). *Man, Play and Games*. London: Thames and Hudson.

CHANAN, G./FRANCIS, G. (1984). *Toys and Games of Children of the World*. Barcelona and Paris: Unesco.

CRABTREE, R. D. (1982). 'Leisure in Ancient Israel (before 70 A. D.)'. PhD. Thesis, Texas A&M University.

DAWSON, L. (1994). *The Complete Hoyle's Games*, revised and updated by L. H. Dawson. Ware, Hertfordshire: Wordsworth.

ELLIS, M. J. (1973). *Why People Play*. Englewood Cliffs, NJ: Prentice Hall.

FALKENER, E. (1892). *Games Ancient and Oriental and How to Play Them*. London: Longmans, Green and Co.

FINKEL, I. L. (ed.) (2007). *Ancient Board Games in Perspective*. London: British Museum Press.

FITTA, M (1998). *Spiele und Spielzeug der Antike*. Stuttgart: Theiss.

GARDINER, E. N. (1930). *Athletics of the Ancient World*. Oxford: Clarendon Press.

GROSSMAN, H. (1994). 'War as Child's Play: Patriotic Games in the British Mandate and Israel'. *Israel Studies* 9: 1–30.

HABAS, L. (2002). 'Games in the Ancient World', in *Play: A View from Psychoanalysis and from another Place*, ed. E. Perroni. Tel-Aviv: Yediot Ahronot, 23–48.

HERZOG, M. (2002). *Fussball als Kulturphaenomomen: Kunst–Kult–Kommerz*. Stuttgart: W. Kohlhammer.

HÜBNER, U. (1992). *Spiele und Spielzug im antiken Palästina*. Göttingen: Vandenhoeck und Ruprecht.

—— (2000). 'Les Jeux d'Enfants et les Jouets dans la Palestine Antique'. *Revue Biblique* 107: 163–174.

HUIZINGA, J. (1955). *Homo Ludens: A Study of the Play Element of Culture*. Boston: Beacon Press.

KRAUSS, S. (1912). *Talmudische Archäologie*, vol. 3. Leipzig: Fock.

KÜHN, C. G. (ed.) (1821). *Galenus, Claudius: De parvae pilae exercitio. Claudii Galeni opera Omnia*, vol. 5: *Medicorum graecorum opera quae exstant*. Leipzig: Knobloch.

LANDMAN, L. (1966–1967; 1967–1968). 'Jewish Attitudes Toward Gambling'. *Jewish Quarterly Review* 57: 298–319 and 58: 34–62.

LASER, S. (1987). *Sport und Spiel*. Göttingen: Vandenhoeck and Ruprecht.

LILLEHAMMER, G. (1989). 'A Child is Born: The Child's World in an Archaeological Perspective'. *Norwegian Archaeological Review* 22: 89–105.

LÖW, L. (1875). *Die Lebensalter in der Jüdischen Literatur*. Szegedin: S. Burger.

MARQUARDT, J./MOMMSEN, T. (1882). *Handbuch der Römischen Alterthümer*, vol. 7.2: *Das Privatleben der Römer*. Leipzig: S. Hirzel.

MENDNER, S. (1956). *Das Ballspiel im Leben der Völker*. Münster: Aschendorff.

MURRAY, H. J. R. (1952). *A History of Board Games Other than Chess*. Oxford: Clarendon Press.

OPIE, I./OPIE, P. (1969). *Children's Games in Street and Playground*. Oxford: Clarendon Press.

ORME, N. (2002). *Medieval Children*. New Haven and London: Yale University Press.

PURCELL, N. (1995). 'Literate Games: Roman Urban Society and the Game of Alea'. *Past and Present* 147: 3–37.

—— (2007). 'Inscribed Imperial Roman Gaming-Boards', in *Ancient Board Games in Perspective*, ed. I. L. Finkel. London: British Museum Press, 90–97.

RAWSON, B. (2003). *Children and Childhood in Roman Italy*. Oxford: Oxford University Press.

RICHTER, W. (1891). *Jeux des Grecs et des Romains*. Paris: Le Promeneur.

RIECHE, A. (2007). 'Board Games and their Symbols from Roman Times to early Christianity', in *Ancient Board Games in Perspective*, ed. I. L. Finkel. London: British Museum Press, 87–89.

RIFKIND, I. (1926). 'The Reproach of Gaming' [Hebr.] *HaDoar* 5: 101–102.

—— (1934). 'On the History of Gaming in Israel' [Hebr.]. *Horev* 1: 82–91.

—— (1935). 'The Games of Dicers' [Hebr.]. *Horev* 2: 60–66.

—— (1946). *The Fight Against Gambling Among Jews: A Study of Five Centuries of Jewish Poetry and Cultural History* [Yiddish]. New York: YIVO Institute for Jewish Research.

ROBINSON, R. S. (1981). *Sources for the History of Greek Athletics*. Chicago: Ares.

SCHMIDT, R. (1977). *Die Darstellung von Kinderspielzeug und Kinderspiel in der griechischen Kunst*. Vienna: Selbstverlag des Österreichischen Museums für Volkskunde.

SCHWARTZ, J. (1993). 'A Child's Wagon' [Hebr.]. *Tarbiz* 63: 375–392.

—— (1994). 'Ball-Playing in Ancient Jewish Society'. *Proceedings of the Eleventh World Congress of Jewish Studies (Divson B)*, 1: 17–24.

—— (1995a). 'Ishmael at Play: On Exegesis and Jewish Society'. *Hebrew Union College Annual* 66: 203–221.

—— (1995b). 'Ball Play in Jewish Society in the Second Temple and Mishnah Periods' [Hebr.]. *Zion* 60: 247–276.

—— (1997a). 'Pigeon Flyers in Ancient Jewish Society'. *Journal of Jewish Studies* 48: 105–119.

—— (1997b). 'Ball Playing in Ancient Jewish Society: The Hellenistic, Roman and Byzantine Periods'. *Ludica, annali di storia e civilta del gioco* 3: 139–61.

—— (1997c). 'On the Prohibition against Eating Nuts on the Eve of Rosh ha-Shanah' [Hebr]. *Talilei Orot* 7: 112–115.

—— (1998a). 'Gambling in Ancient Jewish Society', in *Jews in the Graeco-Roman World*, ed. M. Goodman. Oxford: Clarendon Press, 145–165.

—— (1998b). 'Aspects of Leisure-Time Activities in Roman Period Palestine', in *The Talmud Yerushalmi in Graeco-Roman Culture*, vol. 1, ed. P. Schäfer. Tübingen: Mohr-Siebeck, 313–325.

—— (1998c). 'A Child's Cart'. *Ludica, annali di storia e civilta del gioco* 4: 7–19.

—— (2000). 'Dogs and Cats in Jewish Society in the Second Temple, Mishnah and Talmud Periods'. *Proceedings of the Twelfth World Jewish Congress, Division B, History of the Jewish People*, 25*–34*.

—— (2001). 'Cats in Ancient Jewish Society'. *Journal of Jewish Studies* 52: 211–234.

—— (2003). 'The Relationship Between Jews and Non-Jews in the Mishnah and Talmud Period in Light of Their Attitudes to Play and Leisure Time Activities' [Hebr.], in *Jews and Gentiles in the Holy Land in the Days of the Second Temple, the Mishnah and the Talmud: A Collection of Articles*, ed. A. Oppenheimer *et al.* Jerusalem: Yad Ben-Zvi Press, 132–141.

—— (2004a). 'Dogs in Jewish Society in the Second Temple Period and in the Time of the Mishnah and Talmud'. *Journal of Jewish Studies* 55: 246–277.

—— (2004b). 'Jew and Non-Jew in the Roman Period in Light of Their Play, Games, and Leisure-Time Activities,' in *God's Word for Our World, Theological and Cultural Studies in Honor of Simon John De Vries*, ed. J. Harold Ellens et al. London and New York: Clark International and Continuum, 128–140.

—— (2006). 'The Material Realities of Jewish Life in the Land of Israel, c. 235–638', in: *The Cambridge History of Judaism*, vol. 4: *The Late Roman-Rabbinic Period*, ed. S. T. Katz. Cambridge: Cambridge University Press, 431–456.

Schwartzman, H. B. (1976). 'The Anthropological Study of Children's Play'. *Annual Review of Anthropology* 5: 289–328.

Simri, U. (1969). 'The Religious and Magical Function of Ball Games in Various Cultures', in *Proceedings of the First International Seminar on the History of Physical Education and Sport*, ed. U. Simri. Netanya: Wingate Institute, 2–17.

Sorek, Y. (1976). *Physical Culture in the Land of Israel in the Mishnah and Talmud Period* [Hebr.]. Netanya: Wingate Institute.

Toner, J. P. (1995). *Leisure and Ancient Rome*. Cambridge: Polity Press.

Väterlein, J. (1976). *Roma Ludens: Kinder und Erwachsene beim Spiel im antiken Rom*. Amsterdam: Gruner.

Wahrhaftig, S. (1972). '*Hozeh*, Lotteries and Gambling According to the Halakhah' [Hebr.]. *Sinai* 71: 229–240.

Wentworth Thompson, D. (1933). 'Games and Playthings'. *Greece and Rome* 2: 71–79.

White, G. (1971). *Antique Toys and Their Background*. New York: Arco.

Wileman, J. (2005). *Hide and Seek: The Archaeology of Childhood*. Stroud, Gloucestershire: Tempus.

Wilkie, L. (2000). 'Not Merely Child's Play: Creating a Historical Archaeology of Children and Childhood', in *Children and Material Culture*, ed. Joanna Sofaer Derevenski. London and New York: Routledge, 100–113.

Ziegler, D. (2004). 'Spiele und Spielzug in der Antike', at http://www.klassischearchaeologie. phil.uni-erlangen.de/realia/spiele/spiele.html

Index of Subjects, Names, and Places

A

Aaron 531, 536
Abba Saul 238
Abior Cave 365
Abraham 318, 506, 523
Abu Gosh 156
academies 465, 469, 472
Acco 148, 150, 158, 160, 165, 276, 304, 507, 508, 615; *see also* Ptolemais
Achaemenid Empire 124, 128
Achilles 492
Adar (month) 581, 583
Aelia Capitolina 150, 159, 177, 179, 300, 505, 513, 514; *see also* Jerusalem
Africa 299
    North 88, 200, 248, 372, 539
afterlife 440–62; *see also* death
Agrippa II 75
Aila 76, 149
Akeldama Tombs (Jerusalem) 397
Akhziv 288
Akko, *see* Acco
Alexander the Great 30, 128, 166, 169
Alexander Severus 94
Alexandria 19, 89, 148, 161, 215, 384, 387, 388, 474
Alexandrium 154
Amazon 456
Amidah 134, 511–12, 547, 550, 551, 553, 554, 555, 558–9, 560, 561
    Eighteen Benedictions 62, 558
Amman 625
Ammaus 155
amoraic period 386, 471, 474, 490, 582, 643
amoraim 635, 636, 637
Amorites 598

amphitheatre 623–40; *see also* theatre
Amram Gaon 547
Anab al-Kabir 257
Anaia 109
Ananus 86, 88
Anastasius I 193
Anatolia 150
'Anchor Church' 515
androcentrism 48, 49, 328
animal husbandry 256–8
Antioch 148, 150, 152, 396, 452, 475, 534
Antioch, Pisidian 89
Antiochos 169
Antipas 175, 176, 506, 630
Antipatris 148, 158, 175
Antipita of Caesarea 92
Antonia 154
Aphrodite 168, 507, 613, 614, 615
Aphrodite's bathhouse (Acco) 507, 508, 613, 615, 617
Apollonia 148, 160, 276
Apuleius 593
Aqedah 531, 536
Aquila 130
Arab conquest 178, 289
Arabia 13, 72, 76, 95, 98, 148, 150, 151, 152, 153, 300, 373, 452, 570
Arabic language 127–8, 136
Arabic period 128
Arabs 115, 387, 517, 620
Aramaic language 52, 53, 122, 123, 124, 126–31, 132, 133–4, 135, 136, 137, 138, 321, 337, 347, 386, 446, 448, 454, 456, 457, 471, 487, 508, 550, 553, 569, 582
Aramaization 126–31

Aravah 149, 365
Arbel 280
Arch of Titus replica (Rome) 529
Archelaus 72, 103, 176, 445
Archeological Survey of Israel 106
Aristobulus 127
aristocracy 94, 446, 475
Aristotle 468
Armageddon (Plain of) 452
Armenian language 123
army:
    in Judaea-Palestine 154–5
    Roman 71, 73, 74, 77, 78, 153–61, 648
Arsacius 321
Arsuf, see Apollonia
art 16, 22, 177, 178, 366, 379, 529–39, 541
Artas 609
Asclepieion 613
Aseneth 357, 373, 376, 377
Ashdod 165, 169
Ashkelon 61, 112, 148, 149, 158, 165, 173, 176,
    255, 268, 288, 625
Asia 89, 299
Asia Minor 200, 277, 288, 300, 303, 373, 388,
    443, 447, 605
Assyria 411
Assyrian empire 124
athletic contests 630–3
Attica 485
Augustus 451
Aurelius Marcellinus 159
Av (month) 583

B
Babatha 13, 51, 95–8, 123, 233, 240–1, 242,
    348, 354, 410, 478
    archive and letters 60, 85, 95, 97, 99, 123,
    134, 240, 241, 250, 318, 346, 354, 355, 370,
    374, 491, 505
Babele 215
Babylonia 4, 210, 211, 216, 217, 218, 223,
    224, 358, 364, 374, 412, 452, 469,
    522, 545, 547, 552, 553, 554, 560, 573,
    588, 589, 597

Sassanian 17, 452
Babylonian Aramaic incantation bowls
    589
Babylonian Exile 127, 522, 567
Babylonian Jewry 4
Babylonian law 349
Bacon, R. 598
Baetica 73
balsam 281–2
Bar'am 528
Bar Hebraeus 104
Bar Kokhba caves 410
Bar Kokhba letters 124, 128, 570, 579
Bar Kokhba period 363, 510, 579, 648
Bar Kokhba revolt 13, 49, 57, 75, 87, 95, 96,
    123, 127, 150, 151, 157, 158, 159, 177, 192,
    193, 196, 197, 221, 233, 274, 300, 363, 365,
    633
Bar Qappara 129
Barnabas 89
Bashan region 431
Batanaea 154, 300
bathhouses 64–5, 171, 216,
    433–4, 507–8
    and the Jews 608–14; see also rabbis, 'and
        bathhouses'
    and magic 618–20
    and nudity 616–17, 618
    as places of social and cultural interac-
        tion 605–22
    statuary in 612–14
bayyit 38
Beer Sheva 76
Beirut 452
Beit Nattif 271
Ben Sira 447
Beowulf 493
Berosaba 148, 149
Beruriah (Torah scholar) 60, 477
Berytos 176, 280
bestiality 214
Bet Alpha 33, 318, 366, 374, 375, 509, 526, 531,
    532, 536–8, 539
Bet Govrin 113, 157–8, 177, 452, 505, 515

Bet Horon 148, 156
bet midrash 470, 551; *see also* study house
Bet She'arim 14, 23, 34, 90, 177, 316, 366,
    442, 452–6, 459, 508–9
Bet Shean 152, 157, 169, 177, 271, 276, 509,
    515, 539, 610
  synagogue 539
  valley 113, 158, 252, 254, 256 *see also*
    Scythopolis
Bet Yerah (Khirbet el-Kerak) 159
Bethesda pool (Jerusalem) 504
betrothal 349–50; *see also* marriage
bigamy 97
Binding of Isaac 23, 366; *see also* Aqedah
Birkat ha-Mazon 547, 550
Birsama (Beer Shema) 159
Bithynia 87, 88
body 55–6
Boethusians 569, 577, 578
Book of Hagi/ Hagu 331
Book of Secrets 532
Bordeaux pilgrim (333 CE) 221
Bostra 148, 150, 151, 254, 614, 627, 631
Botna, fair of 507
bread 317, 405, 406, 409, 412, 413, 414, 416,
    504, 570, 576, 577
Brindisi 219
Bronze Age 420
Burak 248
burial 15, 58–9, 197, 214, 215, 394, 396–8, 400,
    440–62, 568; *see also* inscriptions, 'burial'
Byblos 280, 452
Byzantine churches 42
Byzantine culture 28, 541; *see also*
    Christian-Byzantine culture
Byzantine empire 395, 397, 400
Byzantine law 41
Byzantine rule 4, 517
Byzantium 390

C

Caesar 319
Caesarea 24, 51, 73, 74, 75, 78, 79, 86, 89, 103,
    112, 133, 148, 150, 154, 155, 158, 160, 169,
    170, 171, 175, 176, 177, 179, 181, 212, 255,
    271, 280, 300, 304, 435, 452, 468, 474,
    476, 504, 514, 516, 573, 609, 610, 615,
    625, 626, 627, 629, 630, 631, 633, 634,
    636
Caesarea Philippi 148, 300, 301, 506
Caiaphas 449
Cairo Geniza documents 496, 547, 560, 561,
    591, 619
calendar 566, 567, 574, 576, 577, 580
Canaan 598
Canaanites 115, 237
Cancer 375
Caparcotna 158
Capernaum 113, 159, 191, 192, 197, 198, 248,
    269, 424, 513, 515, 526
  synagogue 509
Cappadocia 74, 215
Caracalla 151, 168
Carmel 159, 160, 191, 197, 322, 408, 452
Carthage 288, 372
Castra 109, 276
Cato 247, 253
Cave of the Pool (Nahal David) 365
Cestius Gallus 104
Charakmoba 149
chariot races 630–3
charity 55, 308–24
  and the redistribution of wealth 319–21
Charon 456
childhood 327–43, 358; *see also* education
China 300, 304, 356
Christ, *see* Jesus
Christian-Byzantine culture 15, 16, 23, 41
Christian church 400, 514
Christian art and culture 220, 509
Christianity 1, 2, 18, 30, 44, 111, 112, 113, 115,
    116, 117, 127, 137, 189, 191, 222, 301, 319,
    322, 327, 328, 364, 400, 440, 441, 449,
    457–8, 468, 474, 486, 503–20, 521, 549,
    552, 560, 629
Christianization 71, 79, 194, 510, 511
Christians 116, 129, 133, 136, 172, 192, 194,
    195, 214, 217, 218, 221, 373, 393, 394, 399,
    406, 435, 490, 569, 576, 617, 620;
    see also Christianity

church fathers 43, 44, 515, 593, 617
Cicero 95
Cilicia 89, 279
circumcision 64, 569
Circus Maximus (Rome) 630
circus 506, 623, 624; *see also* amphitheatres
citizenship 179
City of David 273
civil war 174
class (strata) 434, 466–7, 475, 476, 478, 483,
    487, 488, 489, 490, 492, 592, 606, 615,
    616, 618, 629, 647, 648
Claudius 74, 86, 104, 150
climate 5, 153, 248–9, 253, 254, 255, 265, 285,
    310, 368, 375, 446
clothing 56–7, 317, 318, 362–81, 570
    black 377
    footwear and socks 374–5
    and gender 368–77
    Greek 378
    head coverings 371–4
    mantle (tallit) 367, 368–70, 377, 378,
        550, 551
    Roman 362, 378, 379
    tunic (*haluk*) 367–8, 377, 378
    undergarments 371
coins 193–4, 259, 299, 304, 367, 393, 397, 435,
    504, 506, 529
    Bar Kokhba 529, 579
    Iudaea Capta 367
    see also money
Colonatus law 251
coloniae, Roman 71, 75, 176, 177, 505
colonization 176
Columella 247, 314, 598
concubinage 356
conquest 300, 400
Constantine 41, 151, 221, 300, 510, 513, 514,
    515, 516
Constantinople 289
Corinthian marble heads 373
corruption 88
Council of Nicaea 113, 514
courts, *see* judicial system
cremation 447; *see also* burial

Crusaders 547
Cyprus 200, 249, 288, 609
Cyrene 89

D

Damascus 171
Damascus Document 568, 577, 583
Damascus Rule 320
Daniel 531
Daniel in the Lion's Den (biblical scene)
    23, 366
Darb el-Ghaza 149
Darom (southern Judah) 110, 113
dates (fruit) 254–5
David 33, 366, 509, 531, 554
Davidic dynasty 549, 559
Dead Sea 196, 399, 422, 425, 442, 446, 457,
    505, 506, 609 Salt Sea
Dead Sea sect 57, 232, 233
death 58–9, 334, 335–6, 339, 440–62
    at the arena 633–4
    as punishment 568, 570–1
Decalogue 548, 557, 558
Decapolis 73, 150, 174, 176, 427, 503
Decius 79
Delos 136
democracy 483
Demotic language 134
Diaspora 3, 14, 16, 30, 61, 117, 126, 128, 130,
    133, 176, 181, 215, 217, 218, 220, 221, 224,
    234, 320, 362, 364, 367, 388, 412, 452,
    453, 454, 504, 523, 524, 525, 531, 538, 541,
    548, 553, 554, 571, 572, 573, 576, 581
diglossia 131
Diocaesarea 109, 148, 506
Diocletian 76, 78, 79, 91, 277, 280, 506, 514,
    619
Dion 173
Dionysiac cult 509
Dionysos 168, 373
Dionysos mosaic (Sepphoris) 37, 509
Diospolis (Lod, Lydda) 109, 148, 149, 505;
    see also Lydda
divorce 55, 65, 93, 134, 241, 242, 344–61
    women's right to 352–3

Domitius Ulpianus of Tyre 94
Dor 160, 165, 169
Dura Europos 363
  synagogue (murals) 364, 367, 369,
    370, 371–2, 375, 377, 531, 532,
    533–4, 538

E

Eastern churches, early 556
economy 202, 229–45, 260, 297–307
  central-place theory of 299, 302
  primitivist *vs* modernist view of 297–9
education 42, 48, 52, 59–60, 127, 132, 167,
    217, 223, 329, 331, 332, 486, 557
  private and public 465–81, 487
  universality of 469–70
  and women 48, 52–4, 476–8
Egeria 132, 136, 221
Egypt 2, 3, 29, 36, 53, 90, 96, 103, 134, 148,
    174, 177, 210, 252, 254, 259, 288, 300, 301,
    303, 348, 352, 353, 363, 375, 377, 551, 553,
    554, 557, 576
  Hellenistic 347
  Ptolemaic 522
  Roman 250
Ein Boqeq 160
Ein Gedi 157, 191, 196, 201, 233, 248, 254, 258,
    281, 282, 399, 422, 425, 516, 609
Ein Zur (at Ramat ha-Nadiv) 609
Elephantine 347
Elephantine papyri 33, 347
Eleutheropolis 148, 149, 157, 300, 505, 515,
    625, 633
Elusa 149
Emesa 617
Emmaus 155, 156, 158, 176, 505
Enchiridion 93
endogamy *vs* exogamy 355
Enlightenment 593
Ennion (Sidonian manufacturer) 276
Ephesus 89
Ephron the Hittite 523
Epicurus' Garden 468
epigraphy 135–7
Epiphanius of Salamis 112, 515

epitaphs, Jewish 58, 135, 136, 156, 316, 353,
    457–8
Eros 508
Eshtemoa 526
Essenes 130, 318, 320, 364, 366, 573
  clothes of 375–7
  Qumran 364, 370
Esther 581
Eucharist 254
Eudocia 221
euergetism 447, 452
Euphrates 533
Eusebius 79, 80, 109, 159, 511, 514, 515
Eve 58, 374
Exodus 551, 554, 557
Ezra 469, 522, 523

F

Fadus 89
family life 38–9, 229, 230
Fast of Esther 583
Fast Scroll (Megillat Taanit) 582–3
fasting 582, 583
Feast of Tabernacles 632
Felix 86, 87, 89, 90
festivals 566–86
Festus 88, 89
figs 254–5
fish 201, 252, 301, 317, 403, 405, 406, 407, 412,
    414, 417, 418, 474
fishing industry 407
Flavia Neapolis 176
flax 255–6, 277, 278, 279, 280, 313, 569
food and meals 57, 317, 403–19, 571, 574, 575,
    576, 577, 579, 580
food processing 282–8
France, southern 288
French Annales school 2, 178

G

Gaba 154
Gadara 76, 122, 148, 173, 617, 625, 627
Gaius 87
Galatia 74, 321
Galen 597

Galilee, Sea of 148
Galileo Galilei 598
Gallienus, emperor 79, 173
gambling 646, 647; *see also* games, 'and
    play'
games 623, 632
    and play 641–53
Gamla 274, 284, 435
    synagogue 448
geonic period 546, 547, 553, 554, 555, 556,
    561, 579, 583
Gaza 148, 149, 157–8, 173, 288, 300, 304, 366,
    511, 514, 515, 531, 625
    jars 268, 286
    synagogue 33
gender 38, 39, 48–68, 102, 132, 200, 238–43,
    258, 260, 279, 327, 328–9, 333–4, 340,
    345–6, 348, 349, 368, 369, 370, 372–3,
    382, 393, 399–400, 435–6, 476, 553–4,
    560, 566, 574, 575, 579, 581, 607, 611, 630,
    647
    and bathhouses 616–7
    and education 476–8
    and literacy 491–2
    see also clothing, 'and gender'; divorce;
        jewellery; marriage; wives
Gentiles 35, 65, 91, 108, 109, 112, 113, 116, 203,
    214, 219, 282, 284, 287, 355, 378, 389, 393,
    399, 404, 407–9, 412, 413, 503, 504, 507,
    510, 511, 514, 554, 592, 596, 609, 637
Georgian language 123
Gerasa 148, 150, 170, 173, 177, 271, 531, 625,
    627, 631
gladiatorial combats 171, 172, 633, 634
glass 275–7, 304, 393, 397–8
Gnostic teachings 554
gold 394, 395–7
Gophna 148
Gorgon's head 396
grapes 253–4, 403; *see also* wine
Greece 2, 249, 288, 329, 349, 441, 483, 484,
    485, 492
    courts 14
    gymnasium 605
    public baths 605

Greek culture and literature 30, 166, 329,
    378, 476, 504, 553; *see also* Homer
Greek language 15, 30, 36, 52, 53, 93, 96, 122,
    123, 126, 127, 128–9, 130, 131–7, 167, 182,
    195, 315, 316, 321, 347, 386, 448, 454, 457,
    471, 474, 475, 476, 477, 487, 489, 504,
    505, 508, 534, 550, 553
Greek magical papyri 588, 589, 598
Greek wisdom 596–7
Greeks 115, 122, 415, 487, 491, 605
Gregory the Wonderworker 77
Gush Halav 190, 284, 528

H
Hadera 276
Hadrian 87, 94, 150, 155, 158, 177, 220, 300,
    506, 582
Hadrianeum 506
Haifa 109, 285
Halamish 109
Halicarnassus, mausoleum at 443
halitzah ceremony 375
Hammat Gader 61, 171, 304, 539, 627
Hammat Tiberias 33
    synagogue 370, 372, 509–10, 531, 532–3,
        534–6, 573
Hanukkah 554, 575, 582
Har Hamelekh 255
Harkan 53
Harod valley 113
Hasmonaean period 170, 173, 174, 175, 251,
    300, 367, 442, 444, 451, 503, 582
Hasmonaeans 154, 169
Hauran 175, 430, 431, 625
heaven 336
Hebrew language 52, 53, 122, 123, 130, 132,
    133–4, 135, 137, 332, 337, 446, 454, 471,
    487, 489, 508, 545, 550, 552, 553
    Biblical 124, 125, 130, 556, 558
    Middle 131
    Mishnaic 123–6, 138
    rabbinic 124
    vernacular 123–6, 128
Hebron 148, 156–7, 158
    mountains 149, 515

Hector 492
Hekhalot literature 591, 592
Helena (Constantine's mother) 221
Helena (queen of Adiabene) 62, 440–1, 444, 445, 446
Helios 22–3, 531, 532, 534, 536
Hellenism 28, 30–1, 35, 38, 42, 154, 166, 174, 175, 177, 178, 180–1, 442, 444, 503–5, 524; see also Hellenistic period; Hellenization
Hellenistic period 166–73, 299, 300, 322, 353, 378, 384, 406, 407, 411, 412, 413, 424, 431, 465, 473, 490, 521, 523, 581, 605, 609, 647
Hellenization 126–31, 179, 180, 195, 231, 451, 454, 503–5, 509, 608
henotheism 510
Herculaneum 420
heresy 512
Hermeticism 591, 595
Herod Agrippa I 73, 74, 75, 76, 86, 89
Herod the Great 86, 154, 157, 161, 171, 174–5, 176, 177, 179, 180, 221, 281, 287, 300, 320, 385, 445, 446, 448, 449, 451, 503, 504, 505, 582, 609, 623, 625, 626, 630, 632, 633, 637
  burial of 389, 445–6
Herodian dynasty 490
Herodian kingdom 73
Herodian period 313, 400, 444, 447–51, 491, 630, 633, 635
Herodium 154, 445, 446, 609
Heshbon 154
Hilkiyah, palace of 609
Hillel:
  Hillelites 582
  house of 569, 573
  school of 241, 349
Hillel II 509, 536
Hippocrates 595, 597
hippodrome 504, 623–40; see also stadia
Holy Land 440, 452, 516
Holy Sepulchre 397
homosexuality 171
Homer 42, 216, 328, 467, 471, 472, 475, 478

Horvat 'Ammudim 528
Horvat Susiya 191, 196, 201
hostels 213–14, 221
household 1, 12, 38–9, 53–4, 93, 168, 197–202, 204, 229–44, 258–60, 266, 279–80, 314, 409, 423, 434–6, 454–5, 570
House of Dionysos 509
House of Leontis (Bet Shean) 509
House of the Nile Festival 509
House of Orpheus 509
House of Peter 515
Huleh Valley 113
Husifah (on Mount Carmel) 516

I

Iamblichus 593
identity 32–3, 35, 50, 51–2, 102–21, 133, 137, 223, 224, 355, 456, 471, 476, 506, 510, 590
idolatry 34, 181, 451, 507, 509, 510, 596, 608, 612, 613, 614, 635, 648
Idumaea 103, 105, 503
Iliad 492
Illyricum 516
Imma Shalom 513
India 300, 356
infanticide 52
inscriptions 72, 78, 79, 109, 117, 128, 133, 136, 151, 156, 157, 158, 167, 190, 192, 215, 316, 435, 442, 465, 548, 567, 612, 629
  burial 13, 14, 15, 215, 442, 447–8, 455, 456, 457, 476, 487, 508
  ossuary 14, 134–5, 491
  synagogue 13, 14, 15, 23, 61, 135, 137, 321, 452, 457, 476, 491, 522, 528, 534, 536, 541, 554
insulae, Roman 22, 38
intertextuality 32
Ioullos 534
Iranian society 4
Iraq 545, 547
Irenaeus of Lyon 512
Iron Age 166, 170, 249, 283, 420, 431, 432
Islam 127, 289, 521
Islamic civilization 4
Islamic (Muslim) conquest 76, 111, 193, 300

Islamic period 128, 196, 322, 496
Italy 249, 284, 301, 485
    Roman 29, 40, 210, 211, 215, 257, 304, 317
    southern 136, 606
Ituraea 175
Iulia Crispina 97
Izates 444

J

Jacob 109, 357
Jaffa 103, 148, 155–6, 173, 215, 625; see also
    Joppa
James 86
James ossuary 440, 441
Jerash 422, 427
Jericho 109, 148, 154, 157, 158, 171, 192, 254,
    281, 365, 446, 609, 625, 626, 630
    valley 258
Jerome 109
Jerusalem 14, 28, 48, 73, 74, 75, 87, 89, 103,
    104, 105, 128, 134, 136, 137, 147, 148, 149,
    150, 152, 154, 155–9, 160, 165, 169, 171,
    174, 176, 177, 192, 193, 196, 197, 221, 222,
    224, 251, 257, 267, 269, 271, 273, 274, 275,
    300, 315, 320, 367, 368, 385, 396, 397, 398,
    424, 435, 441, 443, 445, 446, 450, 451,
    453, 491, 504, 511, 514, 517, 521, 524, 525,
    529, 534, 539, 548, 549, 550, 559, 574, 575,
    581, 583, 609, 625, 626, 630
    Jewish Quarter 421, 424
    Kidron Valley 443
    Old City of 421
    ossuary burial in 447–51
    Talpiot 440
    Temple 220, 221, 376, 384, 416, 432, 448,
        488, 489, 504, 511, 517, 521, 524–5, 530,
        534, 548, 550, 551, 553, 559, 611
    Temple Mount 421, 424, 443, 448, 504,
        525, 557
    Upper city 268, 276, 424
'Jerusalem of Gold' 394
Jesus 10, 127, 191, 197, 222, 234, 318, 345, 421,
    440, 509, 511, 512, 513, 514, 518, 525, 568,
    569, 615
    Last Supper 576

    Tomb 440, 441
Jesus of Pandera/Pantera/Pantiri 512–3
jewellery 56–7
    archaeological evidence for 393–402
    literary evidence for 382–92
    Roman 393–4
Jewish revolt 156, 168, 171, 176, 180, 193, 197,
    201, 214, 251; see also Jewish war
Jewish war 74, 155, 156, 315, 471; see also
    Jewish revolt
Jezreel Valley 76, 128, 158, 250, 256, 452, 536
John 86
John of Gischala 301
Jonathan 366
Joppa 160, 176, 181; see also Jaffa
Jordan 148, 159, 175, 422, 511
Jordan Valley 148, 154, 155, 157, 158, 254, 255,
    281
Joseph (patriarch) 357
Joseph (Mary's husband) 350
Joseph of Tiberias 514
Josephus 3, 10, 38, 40, 42, 71, 85, 86, 88, 98,
    103, 104, 105, 124, 129, 155, 156, 190, 216,
    232, 234, 247, 284, 308, 310, 316, 317, 318,
    319, 330, 346, 353, 365, 366, 376, 384, 405,
    442–3, 444–5, 446, 447, 449, 459, 469,
    470, 475, 476, 490, 525, 532, 557, 569,
    582, 625, 633
Joshua 581
Joshua b. Gamla 469, 470, 471
Josianic reforms (622 BCE) 522
Jotapatah 192
Judaean Desert 123, 124, 133, 154, 182, 191,
    196, 232, 233, 234, 240, 248, 250, 281, 310,
    345, 363, 364, 365, 374, 399, 424
    caves 13, 19, 347, 379
    papyri 13, 14, 19, 33, 49, 51, 346, 350
Judaean hills 281
Judah ha-Nasi 52, 423, 452, 453, 454,
    455, 509, 526; see also patriarch
    (patriarchate)
Judah (Babatha's husband) 97, 240, 241
Judah Maccabee 582
judges 79, 85–7, 89, 90, 92, 98, 182, 320, 333,
    352, 479; see also judicial system

judicial system 51, 85–101, 182, 233
Julian the Apostate 151, 321, 511, 536
Julias 175
Julio-Claudian period 74
Julius Caesar 176
Jupiter 157
justice, *see* judicial system
Justin Martyr 512
Justinian 76, 79, 515, 516
Justus of Tiberias 129, 475
Juvenal 408

K

Kabbalah 560, 588, 590–1
kallal 273
Karaism 560
kashrut (food laws) 408–9, 410, 411, 418, 517
Kefar ʿOtnay 158, 506
ketubbah 14, 33, 242, 344, 347, 348, 350–2, 359, 373
Kfar Hananya (KH) 197, 200, 265, 267, 268, 270
Khirbet Shemaʿ 190, 193, 196, 268, 528
kilayim 259, 260
Kislev (month) 582
knowledge, transfer of 222–4
Korazim 22, 196, 424, 509, 528

L

landscape archaeology 179
Laodicaea 280
Late Roman Red Ware (LRRW) 268, 285
Latin 122, 136, 137, 182, 386, 474, 479, 504, 534, 553
law:
   Greek 14, 32, 93, 99, 168, 441, 595
   Hellenistic 347, 348, 413
   Jewish 351, 352, 504
   Roman law 32, 39, 86, 87, 91, 92–5, 96, 97, 98, 99, 220, 237, 238, 240, 479
Lebanon 281, 443
Leda (and the swan) 456, 508
Legio 148, 150, 152, 160, 177, 506
legions:
   III Cyrenaica 157

V Macedonica 156, 157
VI Ferrata 158, 159, 280
X Fretensis 148, 150, 155, 157, 158, 159
XI Claudia 159
XII Fulminata 157
Levant, the 168, 169, 443
Levantine coast 165
Libanius 475
life expectancy 329, 353
literacy 60, 138, 331, 466, 478, 479, 482–99
liturgy 545–65; *see also* prayer
Livias 175
Lod 109; *see also* Lydda; Diocaesarea
love 336
Lucius Verus, Parthian campaign of 151
Lyceum 468
Lydda 147, 158, 177, 181, 252, 280, 473, 513, 515; *see also* Diocaesarea; Lod
Lysias 87, 89
Lystra 89

M

M. Ulpius Magnus 157
M. Ulpius Traianus 150
Mabartha 169
Maccabaean uprising (revolt) 174, 250, 251, 504
Machaerus 154, 609
magic 63–4, 129, 554, 618–20
   and healing 587–602
   and medicine 595, 606
Mahoza 13, 95, 96, 123, 240
Maimonides 338, 588, 591
Maiumas 112
Mampsis 148, 149, 422, 425
   Nabataean cemetery 447
Mamre (Kh. El-Halil, Botnah) 304, 506
Mandaic texts 589
Mandatory Palestine 441
Mariamne (Herod's wife) 86
Marissa 169
marital law 347, 348; *see also* divorce; marriage
market, markets 40, 43, 44, 54, 170–1, 172, 173, 201, 202, 230, 231, 232, 235–6, 238,

254, 255, 257, 269, 276, 287, 289, 298, 299, 300, 301, 302–3, 305, 311, 313, 405, 407, 416, 506, 523, 649
marriage 93, 97, 102, 134, 213, 313, 327, 331, 617
  Christian 356
  Greek 356
  and household economy 238–43, 244
  Jewish 33, 39, 52, 95, 96, 234, 241, 333, 334, 337, 339, 344–61
  Levirate 355–6, 375
  Roman 239–40, 335, 356, 359
martyrdom 557
marxism 178
Mary (mother of Jesus) 350
Masada 154, 278, 280, 287, 265, 374, 375, 377, 378, 448, 567, 609
material culture 16, 35–8, 166, 189, 190, 192, 195–200, 203, 266, 267, 390
Matsot festival 574, 575
Maximinopolis 113, 158, 506
Maximos 534
meat 406–9, 410, 412; see also food and meals
Medusa 509
Megiddo 155, 158
Meiron 190, 193, 236, 243, 268
  synagogue 528
Melania 221
Meleager 122
Melkart 504
menorah 456, 457, 508, 517, 529, 538–9
Mercurius 506
Merot 191, 366, 528, 531
Mesopotamia 177, 300, 423, 547
  Islamic 553
Mesopotamian literature 332
Michal bat Kushi 62
Middle Ages 220, 222, 224, 576, 587, 590, 594, 616, 646, 647
Milan, Edict of 514
Minerva 399
Miqvah/miqvaot (ritual bath) 21, 56, 192, 197, 284, 433–4, 435, 611

Miriam 97, 240
Mithras 620
Moabitis 149
mobility 214–16; see also travel
Modi'in 443, 525
mohar 351
money 173, 232, 233, 238, 243, 346, 630, 647
Monobazus 444
monotheism 557, 593, 596
morality 95
Mordecai 581
mosaics 366, 448, 496, 509, 517, 534, 536, 606; see also Jewish art
Moses 93, 332, 530, 554, 577
motherhood 54–5
Mount Ebal 176
Mount Gerizim 169, 176
Mount Scopus 274, 448
mourning 377, 451; see also death
Murabba'at 134, 312
mysticism 554, 588, 590–2

N

Na'aran 61, 109, 196, 366, 531, 539
Nabataean kingdom 13, 149, 387, 427
Nabataens 123, 127, 136, 301, 303, 425, 447
  language 122, 123, 127, 130
Nabratein 190
Nahal Hever 347, 349, 352, 354
  Cave of Horror 365, 374
  Cave of Letters 365, 368, 374, 377, 399
Naomi 65
Nash Papyrus 557
Natronai Gaon 547
Nazareth 113, 513
Nazoreans 512
Neapolis 148, 157, 169, 177, 180, 256, 280, 300, 626, 631, 633
Negev 76, 149, 178, 179, 287, 288, 365, 421, 425, 430, 447
Nehardea 452
Nehemiah 522, 523
Neoplatonism 591, 595
Nero 86, 104, 150
Nessana 149

Nicanor 583
  the Alexandrian 448
  Day 582, 583
  ossuary 449
Nicopolis 148, 149, 180, 505
Nike 177, 508
Nile Delta 347
Nineveh 411
Nissan (month) 457, 575
Nitzana 248
Noah 531, 577
Noricum 75

O

Oboda 149, 422
Odysseus, mosaic of 509
Odyssey 492
oikos/domus 38; *see also* household
oil lamps 270–1, 435, 506, 539, 571
old age 327–43
olive oil 282–6, 301, 405, 412, 413
olives 253, 311, 313
Oral Law 494
Oral *vs* Written Tradition 546
orality 392–3, 482–99, 546, 590, 595
Orient 180, 301
Orientalism 36
Origen 468, 474, 514, 593
Orontes 452
Orpheus 33
ossilegium 275
ossuaries 274, 275, 442, 446, 447–51, 491;
  see also inscriptions, 'ossuary'
ostraca 569
Ottoman period 36

P

pagan (art and culture) 14, 23, 33, 43, 178,
  389, 531
paganism 23, 115, 180, 181, 301, 364, 374, 486,
  503–20, 524, 598, 609, 611
pagans 195, 214, 217, 222, 373, 394, 399,
  408, 413
Palaestina Prima 76, 159
Palaestina Secunda 76, 77, 113

Palaestina Tertia 76
Palaestina Salutaris 76
Palmyra 316, 396, 452
Pan (god) 505
Panias 505, 506
Passion (of Jesus) 568
Passover 62, 86, 104, 220, 256, 317, 457, 547,
  569
  Haggadah 547, 551, 554, 576
  Matsot festival 574, 575–7, 583
  Seder 254, 414–15
paterfamilias 237–8, 243
patriarch, patriarchate 18, 31, 38, 49, 52, 53,
  54, 55, 56, 62, 63, 64, 90, 92, 216, 217,
  218, 332, 349, 354, 451, 452, 453, 454, 455,
  472, 473, 474, 475, 508, 509, 515, 526,
  534, 536, 541, 554, 559, 617, 619
Paul (apostle) 87, 88, 89, 372, 447, 490,
  511, 525
Paula 153
Pax Augusta 175
peddler 202, 298; *see also* rochel
Pella 76, 148, 150, 169, 173, 422, 427, 511
Per Ankh 522
Peraea 127, 175
Persia 11, 374, 581
  conquest of Palestine (614 CE) 517
Persian period 128, 165
Persians 620
Pertinax 151, 180
Peter (apostle) 86, 198
Petra 76, 96, 97, 98, 123, 149, 271, 422, 427
Pharisees 370, 416, 449–50, 505, 524,
  568, 569
Philadelphia 89, 148, 173, 627
Philip (Herod's son) 505
Philippus 175, 176
Philo (of Alexandria) 346, 365, 376, 406,
  447, 470, 525, 532, 552, 557, 569
Philotheria 173
Phoenicia 249, 268, 299, 452
Phoenician language 122
Phoenicians 115, 165, 620
pilgrimage 220–2, 224
Pirqoi ben Baboi 556

piyyutim 358, 531, 532, 536, 547, 556, 560

Plato 595

Platonic Academy 468

Pliny 87, 247, 254, 281, 314, 598

Plutarch 373

poetry:
   epic 492–3
   Gaelic 493
   Homeric 492

polygamy 375

polygyny 355

polytheism 192, 510, 593

Pompeii 420, 444
   Stabian baths 616

Pompey 4, 28, 29, 146, 154, 174, 503

Pomponius 93

population 102–17, 127, 129, 216, 375, 452,
   470, 487, 496, 514, 517, 518, 636

pottery 266–70, 290, 301, 302, 311, 393,
   435, 649

poverty 55, 308–24
   and wealth 309–10

prayer 522, 525, 617, 619
   role of mysticism in 554
   in the Second Temple period 548–9

prayer book 338, 545, 546, 547, 556

Probus, reign of (276–282 CE) 76

Procopius 132, 136

Proklos b. Philosophos 507, 613, 617

prostitution 171

Ptolemaic empire 128, 166, 169, 299
   period 128, 300

Ptolemaios 169

Ptolemais 112, 150, 158, 173, 176, 625;
   see also Acco

Ptolemy 158

Ptolemy Philadelphus 384

Purim 575, 581, 582, 583

purity 55–6

Pythagoreans 376

Q

Qallir 556

Qanatir 528

Qatzrin 191, 199, 200, 202, 422, 424, 528

Quirinius 103

Qumran 129, 130, 160, 232, 330–1, 376, 399,
   409, 410, 489, 555, 556, 557, 567
   Aramaic (dialect) 126
   Temple Scroll 567
   texts (literature) 316, 328, 549, 552, 554,
      560, 567, 574, 575, 577, 581

R

Rabban Gamaliel 219, 220, 232, 475, 477,
   488, 507, 508, 560, 569, 613, 614,
   615, 617

Rabban Shimon b. Gamaliel 450, 451, 452,
   506

Rachel 357

Ramat Hanadiv 160

Ramat Rahel 156–7

Rashi 450

Red Sea 150, 554, 615

Rehov 319, 539

resurrection 568

Rhinocorura 149

Rift Valley 106, 111

road, roads 36, 41, 75, 146, 147–58, 159, 160,
   161, 171, 177, 194, 202, 210–13, 216, 300–1,
   313, 318, 425, 506, 626, 631, 633

rochel 301–2; *see also* peddler

Romanitas 607

Romanization 19, 137, 231, 244, 451

Rome (city of) 75, 87, 88, 89, 94, 96, 105,
   172, 210, 216, 219, 220, 254, 301, 304, 328,
   329, 353, 390, 441, 455, 468, 485, 606,
   607, 629

Rosh Hashanah 530, 574, 580, 647

Rosh Hodesh 63

Ruth 65

S

Sa'adya Gaon 547

Sabbath 56, 62–3, 65, 91, 213, 219, 270, 317,
   365, 375, 385, 386, 404, 405, 416, 457,
   546, 547, 551, 556, 559, 566–86, 610,
   629, 647
   day of study and worship 573–4
   joy 572–4

laws 568, 569, 570, 583
Sabbatical Year 247, 260, 319, 320
Sadducees 449–50, 511
    Sabbath law of 569
Safaic (language) 123
Salome 64
Salome Komaise 13, 233, 352, 354, 478
    papyri 250, 491
Samaria 72, 73, 103, 157, 158, 165, 169, 176,
        191, 195, 201, 252, 260, 271, 276, 630
Samaritans 115, 116, 150, 192, 214, 287, 572
Samuel the Prophet 336
sanhedrin 18, 86, 87, 88, 90, 611
Sapiential texts 232
Sarah 648
Sardis 171
Sarepta 280
schools 332, 466, 470, 471, 473, 478, 479;
    see also education
science 596–9
scribes 478, 482, 486, 487, 546, 558
    professional 488–9
Scythopolis 76, 113, 136, 148, 150, 152, 157,
        158–9, 170, 173, 174, 177, 179, 256, 271,
        279, 280, 503, 505, 610, 627, 633; see also
        Bet Shean
Sea of Galilee 159, 173, 175, 256, 424, 514, 615
seafaring 212, 219–20
Sebaste 148, 154, 157, 175, 177, 180, 504, 627
Second Commandment 400
Seleucid:
    kings 251
    period 128, 135
Seleucid empire 128, 166, 169, 173
Seleukos 169
Semitic languages 386
Sepphoris 22, 23, 37, 56, 109, 154, 158, 159,
        172, 175, 176, 181, 192, 231, 236, 243, 252,
        268, 269, 271, 274, 276, 300, 375, 408,
        422, 424, 435, 452, 472, 473, 506, 509,
        515, 531, 532, 536, 538, 610, 626, 627
Septimius Severus 93, 94, 151, 158
Septuagint 129, 130, 131
Serapis 620
settlements 108–12, 192–5, 260, 408, 624

Severans 177
Severos 534
sex 54, 214, 334, 335, 346, 347, 568, 572, 580,
        606, 616, 648
    sexual desire 335
    sexuality 334
Shammai:
    house of 569, 573
    school of 241, 349
        Shammaites 570, 582
Sharon region 239, 249, 258
Shavuot 220, 574, 577–8
Shekhem (Nablus) 157
Shelamzion 97
Shema (prayer) 129, 133, 134, 332, 547, 548,
        550, 551, 555, 557–8
Shephelah 197, 257, 443
Shikhin 200, 268, 269, 270
Shimon (Babatha's father) 240
Shimon b. Shetach 350–1, 469, 470, 471
Shiqmonah 112, 191
Shmuel bar Nahman 619
Sidon 171, 276, 279, 452
Siddur see also prayer hook
silk 255–6, 304
silver 397
Simon the Hasmonian 443
Simon Maccabee 451
Sinai 76, 149
Sinai Desert 387
Sivan (month) 577
slavery 32–3, 38, 39, 41, 59, 77, 88, 93, 168,
        212, 215, 233–4, 237, 238, 244, 266, 279,
        297, 319, 356, 358, 375, 417, 466, 477, 489,
        515, 579, 607, 615, 634
Sol Invictus 22, 509, 510, 534
Solomon, King 336, 337
Solomon's Pools 609
Solon 329
Songs of the Sabbath Sacrifice 567
Soumaios 128
Spain 86
Sphinx 335
spices 255, 304
stadia 506, 615, 630–3; see also hippodrome

Stephen (apostle) 89
Stoics 468
stone vessels 271–5, 435
stones, precious 398–9
study house 470, 473, 474, 551; see also bet
    midrash
Subeita 422, 425
Sukkot 220, 525, 529, 530, 536, 569, 574, 577,
    578–9, 582, 583
Sumaqa 191, 197
Sun god 509
Susa (Shushan) 581
Susita (Hippos) 109, 303
Susiya 531
Sword of Moses 129
Symeon 'the fool' 617
Symmachus 130
synagogue 15, 18, 21, 22, 23, 33, 37, 43, 92,
    107, 109, 111, 112, 113, 114, 115, 116–17, 124,
    129, 130, 137, 171, 178, 190, 191, 192, 193,
    196, 197, 198, 202, 203, 218, 282, 289,
    320, 333, 366, 389, 424, 435, 471, 477,
    496, 509, 510, 511, 515–17, 521–44, 545,
    547, 548, 550, 551, 553, 554, 556, 561, 566,
    570, 573, 574, 579
  Galilean 526–8
  and gender 553–4
  of late antiquity 526–8, 536, 540
  in Second Temple period 522–5
  and study houses 60–1, 456, 551
    see also inscriptions, 'synagogue'
syncretism 505
Syria 13, 73, 74, 75, 77, 78, 81, 86, 87, 103, 104,
    150, 151, 174, 176, 177, 216, 247, 248, 260,
    284, 288, 300, 301, 303, 363, 373, 388,
    420, 443, 475, 503, 526, 533
Syriac (language) 136
  incantation bowls 589
  liturgy 358
Syrians 115, 122, 620

T

Tabernacle 530, 531, 536
Tabi (R. Gamliel's slave) 477

Tacitus 104, 105, 408, 411
Tamar 51, 92
Tammuz 583
taqanah 351
Targum 126–7, 130–1, 134, 316, 546, 555,
    556, 569
  Jonathan 126
  Onqelos 126, 130–1
Taricheae 630
Tarraconensis 74
Tarsus 89, 215
taxation 173, 233, 247, 289, 305, 311, 314, 319,
    322, 606, 626
Temple 220, 221, 376, 384, 416, 432, 448, 488,
    489, 504, 511, 517, 521, 524–5, 530, 534,
    548, 550, 551, 553, 559, 611
  destruction of 4, 10, 11, 33, 48, 55, 89, 90,
    125, 176, 197, 210, 221, 247, 315, 414, 457,
    471, 489, 505, 521, 522, 548, 550, 566, 570,
    574, 576, 580, 583, 609
Ten Commandments 530
Tertullian 372
Tetrarchs 151, 158
Tevet (month) 583
textiles 277–80
Thallus 129
Thamudic (language) 123
theatre 64–5, 171–2, 175, 496, 504, 506, 615,
    623–40; see also amphitheatre
Theodotos inscription 548
Theophanes 152
Therapeutes 376
Thessalonica 89
Thophlos 448, 449
Tiberias 18, 109, 148, 159, 169, 172, 175, 177,
    181, 192, 231, 236, 254, 256, 300, 303, 435,
    452, 472, 506, 515, 534, 610, 615, 619, 630
Tishri (month) 530, 578, 580, 583
Tobias 357
Tomb:
  of Absalom 443
  of Hamrath 443
  of Jason 443, 447
  of the Kings 443, 444, 445, 446

of Nicanor 453
of Zechariah 441, 443, 446
of Sanhedrin 453
topography 87, 147, 153, 170, 196, 248–9, 429
Torah shrine 456, 457, 517, 530, 534
torture 88
Tosafot 450
Trachonitis 154
Trajan 75, 87, 150, 177, 300, 582, 630
Transjordan 76, 122, 149, 154, 173, 174, 281,
     427, 513, 625, 628
travel 220–2, 224; *see also* mobility
Tribonianus Gallus 157
triglossia 132; *see also* diglossia
Twelve Tables (Roman law code) 93
Tyre 279, 280, 452, 506
Tyrian Shekel 504

U
Ulpian 87
Ummidius Quadratus 150
urbanization 53, 147, 165–88, 220, 300–1,
     312, 490, 505, 506

V
Valerian 79
Varro 247
vegetables 255, 311, 313, 405; *see also* food
     and meals
Vespasian 74, 155, 176, 180
Via Nova Traiana 148
villa 156, 179, 195, 197, 201, 216, 237, 257, 424,
     433, 606
   of Dionysos 37, 509
Virgil 467, 472
virginity 334, 373
Virgo 370, 372

W
Wadi Dalia (Masada) 365
Wadi Murabba'at caves 365, 374, 399
wedding 357, 358, 373, 388, 389, 416;
     see also marriage
wheat 252
wine 286–8, 304, 312, 313, 317, 403, 412, 413,
     414, 415, 416, 576, 577
wisdom 42, 93, 334
women, 13–15, 31–9, 48–65, 97, 105, 168, 200,
     221, 233–43, 252, 258, 260, 279, 315–17,
     327–40, 344–55, 364–77, 382–6, 395,
     400, 417, 476–8, 485–92, 553–60, 574–5,
     579–82, 607–17, 629, 647
wood 280–1

X
xenophobia 174

Y
Yannai 556
Yavneh 90, 148, 252, 511
Yehudai (Gaon of Sura) 556
Yemen 303
Yodfat 279
Yom Kippur 416, 525, 530, 574, 580–1,
     583, 632
Yose ben Yose 556

Z
Zenon papyri 251
Zeus 168, 456, 508, 648
Zoar 159, 281, 442, 457, 458, 459
Zodiac 22, 33, 366, 374, 509, 531, 532, 534, 536
Zohar 532
Zoroastrians 11, 374

Index of References

1. Hebrew Bible

Genesis

2:2–3 567
6:3 332
10:16 598
23:10 523
23:18 523

Exodus

8:17 598
12 575, 576
12:5 575
12:6 575
12:8 414
12:9 576
12:16 574
12:43–49 575
15:1 558
16:5 571
19 578
19:29 568
20:1–14 548
20:3 182
20:4 366
20:8–11 567
20:8 570
20:10 567
20:11 567
22:17 63
23:15 575
25:23–40 385
31:14 570
31:17 567
34:21 567
35:3 567

Leviticus

11 407

14:45 431
16 580
16:29–31 580
19:19 259, 278
23:5–8 575
23:8 574
23:11 576
23:15–16 577
23:16–20 577
23:21 574
23:24 580
23:25 574
23:27–32 580
23:27–28 574
23:35–6 574
23:40 578
23:42 579

Numbers

9 575
10:10 574
10:32 567
13:15–22 567
13:15 567
15:32–6 567
15:37–41 557
28:9–10 570
28:26 577
28–9 574
29:1 580
29:7 580
29:12–38 578

Deuteronomy

5:7.9–10 182
5:12–15 567
5:14 567
6:4–9 557

6:4 547
8:8 577
11:13–21 557
11:19 477
12:3 507
13:1 513
13:18 507
14 407
16:1–8 575
16:7 575
16:16 220
20:17–18 598
22:8 430
22:9ff 259
22:11 366
25:5–10 355, 375
26:5 576
31:9, 26 530
34:3 254
34:7 332

1 Kings
1:1 337
7 385
8:27 522
22:10 523

2 Kings
4:23 522
7:1 523
23:1–20 522
23:25 557

Isaiah
3:18–23 386
51:1–3 557
52:7 458
58:13 567, 568, 572

Jeremiah
6:29 92
7:9 557
17:19–27 567
32:39–41 557
38:7 523
41:2 583

Ezekiel
21:29ff 598

Hosea
4:2 557

Psalms
17:5 632, 637
34:1 648
50:7, 18–19 557
81:10–11 557
92:13 649
113–18 576
118 578

Proverbs
3:1–12 557

Lamentations
1:17 109

Ecclesiastes (Qohelet)
1:2 337

Esther
9:18 581
9:20–32 581
9:22 581

Daniel
1 411

Ezra
3:8 333
4 129
23:13 389

Nehemiah
8:1–10:40 522
8:1 523

2. Apocrypha and Pseudepigrapha

Ben Sira
2:5–6 384
21:21 384
36 559
38:27–8 384
39:26 254
51 559

1 Enoch
72–82 567

Joseph and Aseneth
5:5 366, 376
14:9 376

Joseph and Aseneth (*cont.*)

14:12 377

15:1 373

Jubilees

1:1 577

2:17–24 567

2:24–33 568

2:29 571

3:31 318

6:1–22 577

6:10–11 577

6:22 577

29:7 577

49:16–20 575

49:17 575

50:6–13 568

50:8 571, 572

50:12 572

Judith

8:6 572

Letter of Aristeas

1:52–62 384

84 384

1 Maccabees

4:36–59 582

10:64 366

13:27–9 443

13:37 385

2 Maccabees

1:9, 18 582

2:16 582

4:38 366

10:5–6 582

14:4 385

15:36 581, 583

15:38 253

Ps.-Philo, Liber Ant. Bibl.

11:8 574

13:6 580

23:2 577

Test. Reuven

3:11 617

Tobit

1:10 411

2:1 577

3. Qumran Texts

1Q34 581

1QS 6:3–6 416

1QS 1:16–2:25a 577

1QSa 331

4Q251 568, 573

4Q251 1–2, 4–5 568

4Q251 frg. 9 577

4Q264a 568, 573

4Q265 62, 568

4Q265 3:3 575

4Q265 6:4–5 568

4Q265 6:5–6 569

4Q265 6:6–7 568

4Q266 11:16–18 577

4Q417 F2 331

4Q418 103 II 233

4Q421 568, 573

4Q508 581

4Q509 581

4QMMT 124

11QT^a 575

11QT^a 17:8–9 575

11QT^a 18–23 577

Damascus Document (CD)

10:14–11:18 568

10:21 568

10:22 571

11:5–6 568

11:7–11 568

11:13–14 569

11:16–17 568

12:3–6 568

14:12–16 320

4. Targumim

Ps.-Jonathan

Deut. 30:19 276

Targum of Job 134

Targum to Eccles.

12:1–7 334

5. Philo and Josephus

Philo

Apol.

  12 376

Hypoth.

  11:12 376

Migr. Abr.

  89–93 569

  91 569

On the Virtues

  144 406

Prob.

  81–2 573

  85–8 376

Spec. Leg.

  2.179–80 577

  2.220 577

Josephus

Antiquitates

  3.245 578

  3.262 577

  4.240 320

  8.100 578

  9.1.2 196

  12.60–84 385

  12.325 582

  13.11.3, 318–19 127

  13.45 385

  13.211–13 445

  13.372 578

  14.202 319

  14.206 319

  14.403 503

  14.414 154

  14.419 154

  14.462–4 609

  15.7.5, 217 86

  15.259 353

  15.293–6 154

  16.43 573

  16.285 154

  17.6.3, 161 86

  17.24 154

17.196–200 445

17.196–7 385, 389

17.198–9 154

17.289 154

18.1–3, 26 103

18.106–7 98

19.294 320

20.1.1 89

20.6.1–3 86

20.8.7 86

20.8.9 86

20.9.1 86, 88

20.12.1, 263 475

20.95 444

20.117 77

20.176 73

Bellum Judaicum

  1.204 154

  1.3.3, 76 127

  1.31.1, 602 475

  1.33.4, 654 86

  1.308 154

  1.340–1 609

  1.670–2:2 445

  2.10.2 276

  2.12.3–7 86

  2.13 86

  2.56 154

  2.119–161 376

  2. 126 318

  2. 147 571

  2. 289 573

  2. 380 104

  2. 591–3 284

  2. 591–1 301

  3.36 154

  3.42–3 310

  3.48–50 310

  3.66 73

  4.238 74

  4.7.2, 406–9 524

  5.5.4, 213 534

  5.55 444

  5.119 444

Bellum Judaicum (*cont.*)

5.147 444
5.168, 241 609
5.248–50 105
5.569 105
6.290 575
6.299 577
6.420 104
6.422–7 104
6.423 575
6.426 575
7.171–7 154
7.217 176
14.4 86

Contra Apionem

1.9, 51 475
1.60 40
2.18, 178 469
2.175 573
2.205 442–3

Vita

9 475
13–17 104
40 475
74–6 284
74 301
235 194
422 251

6. New Testament

Matthew

1:18–19 349, 350
5:15 513
5:17 513
8:5–9 159
12:5 569
12:11–12 569
13:45–6 385
15:1–2 416
20:1–15 234
21:28–30 234
22:34–40 557
24:20 568

Mark

1:16–20 234
1:21 573
2:23–4 568
3:1 573
3:2 568
6:2 573
6:3 234
6:56 179
7:1–4 416
10:12 353
10:17–19 557
10:29–30 234
12:1–12 180
12:1–9 234
12:28–34 557
12:41–3 320
13:34–6 234
15:42–6 568
16:1 568

Luke

2:1–3 103
4:16–17 573
5:19 430
7:2 159
7:36–50 372
8:27 318
11:37–8 416
12:36–8 234
12:42–8 234
13:6–9 234
13:10 573
14:5 569
14:16–24 234
15:4–6 234
15:11–32 234
15:22 385
17:7–9 234
17:28 234
17:31–7 234
21:1 320
23:56 568
24:13 155

John

 5:10 568
 7:22–3 569
 7:37–8 578
 9:22 512
 11:55 575
 12:1 575
 12:42 512
 16:2 512

Acts

 2:1 577
 5:15 449
 6:8–7.59 89
 12:2 86
 12:4 86
 13:49–50 89
 14:19 89
 17:5 89
 19:31–8 89
 21:27–30 89
 21:31–6 89
 22:24–9 89
 23:29 87
 24:1–22 89
 24:12 525
 24:24–6 89
 25:2 77
 25:9 90
 25:12 88
 25:32 89

1 Corinthians

 3:12 385
 11:2–16 372, 373
 29:10 549

2 Corinthians

 8:18–24 320

James

 2:2 385

1 Peter

 3:3 385

Apocalypse of John (Revelation)

 3:11 385

 4:4 385
 14:14 385
 15:6 385
 21:18–21 385

7. Early Christian Writings

Clement of Alexandria

Paedagogus 2.11 279

Didascalia Apostolorum

 3 617

Epiphanius of Salamis

Panarion/Adversus
    Haereses

 29.9.2 512
 30.4–12 112
 30.7.5–6 617

Eusebius of Caesarea

Historia Ecclesiastica

 6.39.2 79
 7.12 79
 7.15 79

Martyrs of Palestine

 3.3 80
 4.8 78, 80
 7.1 79
 7.7 78, 79
 11.24 77

Onomasticon

 24.9 157
 26.7, 13–14 109
 86.18 196

Gregory Thaumaturgos

Panegyric to Origen

 65–72 77

Jerome

Chronicle

ad 282 Olympiad 109

Epistles

 108 153

Justin Martyr

Dialogue with Trypho

 138 90

Dialogue with Trypho (*cont.*)

Justinus

Apologia

   1.1.1 76

Leontius Neapolitanus

Vita Symeonis Sali

   35 (PG 93.1713) 617

Palladius

History 52 254

Sozomen

Historia Ecclesiae

   2.4.4 507

Tertullian

De Corona

   4.2 372

8. Rabbinic Literature

Mishnah

Berakhot

   3:3 62

   3:5 617

   6:1 413

   6:3 317

   7 416

   7:2 417

   8:1, 5 573

Peah

   8:5 252

   8:7 252

Demai

   2 410

   2:1 254

   2:2 410

   2:5 57

   5:7 201

Shebiit

   1:2 254

   3:4 257

   4:5 281

   7:3 201

Maaserot

   1:6 255

   1:7 254

   3:4 255

   3:5 199

   3:9 199

   4:2 649

Maaser Sheni

   5:9 219

Hallah

   1:6 201

   2:7 54, 201

   4:10 577

Bikkurim

   1:3 577

Shabbat

   1:1 568, 570

   1:5–9 570

   2:1–2 200

   2:4 270, 571

   2:6–7 62

   6 56

   6:1 56, 385

   6:2 375

   6:4 56

   7.1 570

   7:2 569, 570

   8 570

   9:5–7 570

   9:7 202, 649

   10:2 570

   10:3 570

   10:5 570

   11:8 386

   16:1 573

   16:2 572

   16:8 219

   18:2 55

   19:5 333

   24:2 255

   18:3 64

Erubin

   4:1 219

   4:7–9 571

   6:1–2 569

   6:6 198, 433, 573

8:2 252
9:4 199
10:3 199

Pesahim
5:5–7 575
7:1–2 576
7:6 575
8:1 62, 575
10 414, 551
10:4 576

Sheqalim
5:3 126
6:5 320

Yoma
1:1 58
3:7 280
3:9–10 448
8:1 580

Sukkah
1:1–2:3 579
2:1 477
2:8 579
2:9 579
3:9 578
3:12 579
4:3 578
4:5–6 578
4:9–10 578
5:1–5 578
5:2 553
8:7 55

Betsa
2:10 647
5:1–2 574
5:2 571
5:3 257
5:7 256

Rosh Hashanah
1:1–2 580
1:2 577, 578
1:8 646
2:5–7 574
2:5 64
4:5–6 580

Taanit
1 416, 583
2:8 582
2:10 582
3 416
4:2 548
4:7 416
4:8 63, 319

Megillah
1:1–2 202
1:1 581
1:3–4 581
1:4 581
1:5 574
1:8 125, 130
2:4 581
3:1–2 202
4:6 318

Moed Qatan
1:2 212
1:5 450–1
3:9 58, 336

Hagigah
1:1 55
1:8 413
2:7 410

Yebamot
5:9 54
10:1 219
12:1 375
14:1 348
14:10 214
16:2 54
16:7 214

Ketubbot
1:1 202
3:8 334
4:4 58
4:6 321
5:5 54, 57, 59, 235, 279
5:8 252, 279, 318, 321, 374, 404, 405
5:9 318
6:5 55
7:6 373

Ketubbot (*cont.*)

    7:8 617

    8:1 241

    9:4 54

Nedarim

    3:10 572

    4:3 59, 333, 477

    5:1 257

    7:4 430

    8:6 572

    9:6 572

    10–11 348

Sotah

    1:5 372

    3:4 59, 333, 477

    5:3 571

    9:14 389, 475

    7:1 134

Gittin

    2:5 60

    9:8 93, 134

Qiddushin

    1:1 346, 348

    1:7 62, 579

    1:10 62

    4:13 60

    4:14 235

    5:14 279

Baba Qamma

    2:2 202

    3:4 269

    6:1–2 201

    6:2 257

    7:7 258

    8:6 374

    9:4 279

    10:9 54, 239, 255, 258, 278

Baba Metsia

    1:5 237

    5:8 314

    9:6 313

    10:1 430, 431

Baba Batra

    1:5–6 199

    1:6 250, 433

2:2–3 236

2:2 430

3:6 430

4:1 430

6:4 200, 429

6:8 450

8:2 348

Sanhedrin

    3:3 646

    6:4 64

    7:4 570

    7:8 570

    10:1 456

Shebuot

    7:1 646

Eduyot

    2:7 646

Avodah Zarah

    1:7 507, 613

    1:8 37, 507

    1:9 507

    2 411

    2:1 64, 214

    2:3–7 412

    2:8–9 507

    3:1 506, 534, 613

    3:3 506

    3:4 508, 613, 615, 617

    4:3 612

    5:1 288

Abot

    1–2 93

    2:7 63

    4:17 533

    4:20 332

    5:21 330, 338–9, 353

    6:9 387–8

    5:9 320

Zebahim

    5:9 57

Menahot

    8:4 282

    10:3 569

    10:6 577

Hullin
  3:1 433
  4:3 64
  8:3 409
Arakhin
  9:6–7 429
Tamid
  1:1 432
  5:1 548, 557
Middot
  1:6 433
  1:8 432
  2:5 553
  5:4 377
Kelim
  8:9 275
  11:2 430
  11:8–9 385
  11:8 386
  17:17 387
  22:2 199
  23:4 64
  24:1 649
  24:16 374
  27:1–12 385
  27:5 368
  28:9–10 374
  28:9 368
  29:1 371
  29:4, 10 388
  29:5 388
Ohalot
  6:2 434
  16:2 269
Negaim
  2:4 53
  12:2 431
  13:3 431
Parah
  3:3 273
Toharot
  3:8 257
  7:4 57
  9:6 199, 236

  9:6, 9 433
  17:17 388
Miqvaot
  10:4 371
Niddah
  1:5 334
  2:5 58
  5:6–7 334
  6:11 334
  7:4 611, 617
  9:4 199, 433
Makhshirin
  2:5 610
  2:8 317
  2:9 317
  6:1–2 433
Yadayim
  4:5 125
Uqsin
  2:1 253
Tosefta
Berakhot
  2:12 59, 477
  2:14, 20–21 617
  2:20 171, 610, 616
  3:7 551
  3:23–4 416
  4:1 416
  4:8ff 415
  5:2 573
  5:3 573
  6:10 579
  6:17 619
Peah
  1:7 255
  4:9 321
  4:10 213, 406
  4:14 275
Demai
  2 410
  2:2 410
  3 410
  5. 410

Demai (*cont.*)
  Shebiit
    6:29 254
  Terumot
    1:9 253
    2:6 253
    3:13 253, 254
    4:3 253
    10:7 253
  Maaserot
    2:4 254
  Shabbat
    1:1–2 570
    1:3 570
    1:5 571
    1:6 431
    1:13 270
    2:5–7 270
    4:6 386
    4:9 388
    6 64
    6:14 64
    6:15 64
    6:17 64
    6:18 64
    7 64
    12:9 159
    13[14]:1 573
    13:5 512
    14[15]:3 569
    16:5 199
    16:8 64
    16:22 525
    17:18 610
    24:3 257
  Erubin
    3:8 213, 219
    6:13 430
    7:7, 14 433
  Pesahim
    1:3 433, 434
    2:22 317
    4:13–14 575
    8:10 575

  10 415
  10:12 576
Yoma
    2:3–4 448
Sukkah
    1:1 62
    3:1 569
    4:1–9 578
    4:6 388
Betsa
    2:15 576
    5:11 256
Taanit
    2:5 582
Megillah
    2:4 581
    2:7 581
    3:11–12 60
    3:11 61
    4[3]:5 578
Hagigah
    1:2 332
    1:3 333
    2:1 213
Yebamot
    4:5 213
    14:7.10 213
Ketubbot
    4:8 321
    5:4 255, 279
    5:5 55
    6:4 242
    7:6 65, 373, 617
    12:1 350
    12:5 219
Sotah
    2:1 125
    3:3 374
    6:6 648
    15:8 475
Gittin
    6:1 431

Qiddushin
  1:5 615
  5:17 388

Baba Qamma
  2:9 199
  8:10 257
  11:2 237
  11:5–7 238
  11:5 374
  11:7 54, 235

Baba Metsia
  4:24–5 54
  5:3 198
  6:14 258
  7:1, 15–17 279
  7:11 212
  7:13 213
  7:14 220
  8:29 199
  9:4 312
  9:11 312
  9:19 313
  9:21 313
  10 312
  11:16 200
  14 312

Baba Batra
  2:17 385, 433
  3:3 610
  8:5 219

Sanhedrin
  5:2 646

Avodah Zarah
  1:3 169
  2:5 635
  2:9 214
  3:1 214
  5:1 284, 386, 613
  5:2 56, 387
  6:7 220
  7:6, 12 288

Horayot
  2:5 220

Hullin
  2:22–24 512

Kelim Baba Metsia
  5:3 433
  7:10 387
  11:10 432

Ohalot
  3:9 58
  16:1 54

Toharot
  11:7 254

Miqvaot
  6:3 611
  6:4 611

Niddah
  6:15 611, 617

Yadayim
  2:13 512

Talmud Yerushalmi (Palestinian
    Talmud)
Berakhot
  1:1, 2a–b 558
  1:8, 3c 550
  1:8, 3d 551
  2:1, 4a 557
  2:2, 4a 551
  2:4, 4d 559
  2:8, 5c 615
  3:5, 6d 433
  4:1, 7a 550, 559
  4:4, 8b 618
  4:5, 8c 550, 559
  5:1, 8d–9a 550
  5:2, 9b–c 551
  6:6, 10d 415
  7:1–2, 11a–b 551
  8:6, 12c 433
  8:7, 12c 388
  9:5, 14d 370
  9:6, 14b 619

Peah
  3:1, 17b 259
  4:6, 18b 237

Peah (*cont.*)
    7:4, 20a–b 310
    8:8, 21a 406
    8:9, 21b 615

Demai
    1:3, 22a 387
    2:1, 22b 254
    2:1, 22c 255
    4:6, 24a 368

Shebiit
    8:11, 38b 614
    9:4, 39a 432

Terumot
    8:5, 45c 55
    8:5, 45d 636
    8:10, 46b–c 619

Bikkurim
    2:1, 64c 333, 336

Shabbat
    1:3, 3c 134
    1:7, 3c–d 504
    1:8, 4a 570
    2:4, 5a 571
    3:1, 6a 610
    6:1, 7d 53, 59, 385, 475, 476
    6:1, 8a 452
    6:2, 8a 375
    6:4, 8b 386
    14:4, 14d 64
    15:3, 15b 574
    16, 15d 159
    16:5, 15d 365

Erubin
    6:6, 23c 434
    9, 25c 199

Pesahim
    1:1, 27b 434
    4, 31b 159
    6:1, 33a 575
    10 415
    10:1, 37b 583

Sheqalim
    2:7, 47a 451

3:3, 47c 134
8:1, 51a 252

Yoma
    8, 45b 159

Sukkah
    3:10, 53d 579
    5:9, 55b 388

Betsa
    1:6, 60c 610, 615
    1:9, 60d 388
    5:8, 63b 256

Rosh Hashanah
    1:3, 57b 377, 550

Taanit
    1:4, 64a 629
    1:4, 64b 65
    1:6, 64c 63
    1:6, 64c 574
    2:13, 66a 582
    3:4, 66c 550
    3:13, 67a 572
    5:4, 69a 648

Megillah
    1:1, 70a 581
    1:6, 70d 582
    1:11[9], 71b 134, 553
    1:11, 71d 648, 649
    1:12, 72d 254
    2:2, 73a 52
    2:3, 73b 581
    2:4, 73b 581
    3:2, 74a 51, 92
    3:2, 74b 79
    3:7, 74b 578
    4:1, 75a 572
    4:4, 75a 416

Moed Qatan
    1:5, 79d–80a 451
    1:7, 80d 385
    2:3, 81b 575
    2:4, 81b 170

Sotah
    1:4, 16d 61, 477, 573

2:2, 18a 334

3:4, 19a 477

7:1, 21b 129, 476, 553

7:2, 21c 134

Ketubbot

6:1, 30c 239

7:7, 31b 373

8:11, 32c 469, 470, 471

9:1, 32d 239

Nedarim

8:1, 40d 572

Gittin

3:8, 45b 254

4:9, 46b 634

Qiddushin

2:1, 62c 280

4:11, 66b 63

Baba Metsia

2:5, 8c 387

Baba Batra

4:6, 14c 37

6:1, 15c 254

6:2, 15c 434

Sanhedrin

1:2, 18d 488

4:9, 22b 333

6:8, 23c 64

7:13, 25d 64

7:19, 25d 615, 619–20

11:7, 30b 333

Avodah Zara

1:4, 39d 507

1:7, 40a 37, 172

2:2, 40d 513

2:4, 41b 287

2:8, 41d 284, 412

2:9, 42a 258

3, 42b–43d 23

3:4, 42d 508

4:4, 43d 614

5:4, 44b 287

Horayot

3:7, 48a 55

Talmud Bavli (Babylonian Talmud)

Berakhot

8b 389

11b 551

14b–15a 551

26b 559

33a–b 551

33a 559

47b 370

51a 374

60b 551

Shabbat

8b 434

21b 582

25b 434, 611

33b 610

60a 375

77a 253

89b 333

104a 648

116a–b 513

117b 572

118b 374, 546

120a 365

125a 159

151b–153a 334

151b 58

152a 337

154b 649

156b 55, 374

Erubin

29b 253

53b 52

82a–b 332

Pesahim

66a 575

68b 572, 578

85b 433

100b–101a 551

111b 374

118a 546

Sukkah

42a–b 332

51b 388

Sukkah (*cont.*)

Betsa
  15b 572
  34b 649
  40a 256

Rosh Hashanah
  23a 387

Taanit
  23b 55
  28b 546

Megillah
  18a 129
  22a 553
  29a 80, 525

Moed Qatan
  17a 377
  18b 256
  24a 374
  28a 336, 339

Ketubbot
  50a 332, 338
  62a 610
  72a–b 373
  82b 350
  103a–b 474

Nedarim
  30b 374
  32a 332
  49b 370

Sotah
  33a 134
  49a 551
  49b 134

Gittin
  46b–47a 634
  47a 634
  58a 368

Qiddushin
  2b 350
  8a 374
  29b 374
  31a 374

Baba Qamma
  83a 134

Baba Metsia
  12a 54
  105b 252
  107a 259
  117b 432

Baba Batra
  21a 332, 469, 470, 471
  57b 368, 377
  60b 385, 432–3
  74b 387
  101a 450

Sanhedrin
  74b 388
  104b 55

Avodah Zarah
  5a–b 339
  18b 636
  37b–38a 412
  38a–b 65

*External tractates of the Babylonian
   Talmud*
Semahot
  3:1–8 336, 339
  3:8 336
  4:3 377

Soferim
  17:4 582

Midrashim
Mekhilta
  on Exod. 15:1 558
  on Ex. 22:26 318
  on Exod. 20:8 570
  on Exod. 31:14 570

Sifra
  Emor 12:1 576
  13 282, 577
  17:5 579

Sifre Numbers
  115 370, 615
  147 574
  180 134; 79

Sifre Deuteronomy
　11:19　332
　32:3　555
　32:21　318
　46　59, 477
　226　369
　234　368
　333　134
　343:11　377
　355　284
　357　332
　301　125

Midrash Tannaim (Deut.)
　16.14　253–4
　32:43　134
　33:19　276

Genesis Rabbah
　6:5　219
　10:8　214
　13:9　220
　17:8　58, 373
　18:2　388, 389
　19:1　280
　20:4　220
　20:21　280
　31:11　433
　33:1　220
　36:8　129
　49:9　80
　58:1　333
　60:11　212
　63　619
　64:10　80
　67:3　636
　77:3　637
　78:15　220
　80:1　172
　84:4　387
　87:4　633
　92:6　214
　96　634
　100　332

Exodus Rabbah
　1:1　648

15:22　637
21:11　632
23:5　389
30:24　626
41:5　389

Leviticus Rabbah
　14:4　430
　18:1　334, 337
　23:5　109
　34:16　574
　37:3　213

Cant. Rabbah
　6:7　649

Lam. Rabbah
Proem 17　629

Pesiqta de Rav Kahana
　15:2　636
　28:3　634, 637

Pesiqta Rabbati
　26　377

Tanhuma
　on Gen. 25:1　334
　on Lev. 19:23　338
　Vayigash 3　633

Other rabbinic works
Avot de Rabbi Nathan Version A
　6　333
　14　287
　23　332

Avot de Rabbi Nathan Version B
　9:25　374
　12–13　333
　35　332
　42:117　374

Derekh Eretz Rabbah
　1　365
　10:1　619
　10:2–3　619

Derekh Eretz Zuta
　7:2　171

Kallah Rabbah
　9.15–17　619

Kallah Rabbah (*cont.*)
Seder Olam Rabbah
5 578

Yalkut Shimoni
to Qoh. 12 334

9. Graeco-Roman Writers
Apollonius Rhodius
Argonautica
3.135–39 648

Apuleius
Apology
48.7 88

Aristotle
Rhetoric
2:12–14 337
2:13 335

Cato
Agriculture
1.7.9 250
11.1 254

Cicero
De Natura Deorum
1.29.81 613

Columella
De Re Rustica
1.7.1–3 314
3.3.2 254

Expositio Totius Mundi
31 254

Horace
Satires
1.100–110 213

Macrobius
Saturnalia
1.16.11 569

Marcus Aurelius
Meditations
11.1 339

Ovid
Ars Amatoria
3.638–40 606
3.361–8 648

Pausanias
Graeciae Descriptio
5.5.2 279

Persius
Satires
5.179–84 582

Plato
Laws
11, 933d–e 595
Republic
328c–329c 335

Pliny
Epistles
3.19 250, 314
10.58.1 88
Natural History
5.14.69 176
12:111–24 281
13:26–49 254
13:51 254
14.134 287
18.74.317 284
36:65 276

Plutarch
Moralia
267 373

Scriptores Historiae Augustae
Hadrian
18.10 616

Seneca
Epistles
95.47 571

Sidonius
Epistles
2.2.4–7 614

Strabo
Geography
16.229 255
16.2.41 281
16.758 276

Tacitus
History
2.78.4 75

5.5.1–2 411
5.6.1 281
5.13.3 105

Vitruvius
De Architectura
5.10 607

10. Legal Texts
Diocletian
Edict on Prices
26 256, 279

Gaius
Institutes
4.47 96

Justinian
Codex
3.13.3 91
9.9.18 97

Digest
1.1.1.1 93
1.2.2 93
1.21 86
4.8 91
34.2.25–26 385
34.2.37 385
48.18 88
48.19.8.9 86

Novella
103 76–77, 79
146 516

Lex Irnitana
85 86

Theodosius
Codex
2.1.10 92
7.8.2 515
10.20.8 256, 280
16.8.2 515
16.8.8 92, 216, 515
16.8.13 92
16.8.15 515

16.8.21 516
16.8.22 92, 515
16.8.29 92

Ulpian
Sabinus
44 385

11. Papyri
P. Hev.
65 349, 352

P. Yadin
3 233, 240
5 233
7 233, 240
10 240
11 98, 233, 240
12–15 96, 98, 240
12 96
13 98
14 98
15 233
16 98, 233, 240
17 96, 97, 233, 240
18 95, 96, 240
19 95
20–5 98
20 96, 97
21–25 240
21–22 240
21 96, 233
22 96, 233
25 97
26 96, 97, 240
26.2–11 97
27 96, 97
50 570
52 128, 579
57 579

Papyri Graecae Magicae
2.50 619
36.69–77 619
127.3–4 619

9 780198 856023